The 2010 Pulitzer Prize for Editorial Cartooning was awarded to Mark Fiore, self-syndicated, for his animated cartoons appearing on SFGate.com, the *San Francisco Chronicle* website. The first online-only journalist to win a Pulitzer Prize, he was cited because "his biting wit, extensive research and ability to distill complex issues set a high standard for an emerging form of commentary." The figures below show only selected frames from his animated cartoons, which also ran with audio. See http://www.markfiore.com.

★ Chapter 1, "Freedom, Order, or Equality?" contends that conservatives and communitarians defend the social order, which includes the traditional unions of men and women, while libertarians and liberals support the freedom of same-sex people to marry. Here, Fiore criticizes members of Congress who espoused traditional values but practiced homosexuality.
(Mark Fiore)

★ Chapter 19, "Domestic Policy," opens with a vignette about the health-care debate. This cartoon by Mark Fiore plays on the contention that the legislation that ultimately became law would create government "death panels" that would decide the fate of senior citizens.
(Mark Fiore)

The Challenge of Democracy 11th Edition with California Politics and Government

California Edition

Kenneth Janda | Jeffrey M. Berry | Jerry Goldman

CENGAGE
Learning™

Australia • Brazil • Japan • Korea • Mexico • Singapore • Spain • United Kingdom • United States

CENGAGE
Learning™

The Challenge of Democracy 11th Edition
with California Politics and Government
California Edition

THE CHALLENGE OF DEMOCRACY, AMERICAN GOVERNMENT IN
GLOBAL POLITICS, ELEVENTH EDITION
Janda | Berry | Goldman

© 2012, 2009, 2008 Wadsworth, Cengage Learning. All rights reserved.

Executive Editors:
 Maureen Staudt
 Michael Stranz

Senior Project Development Manager:
 Linda deStefano

Marketing Specialist:
 Courtney Sheldon

Senior Production/Manufacturing Manager:
 Donna M. Brown

PreMedia Manager:
 Joel Brennecke

Sr. Rights Acquisition Account Manager:
 Todd Osborne

Cover Image:
Getty Images*

*Unless otherwise noted, all cover images used by Custom
Solutions, a part of Cengage Learning, have been supplied
courtesy of Getty Images with the exception of the Earthview
cover image, which has been supplied by the National
Aeronautics and Space Administration (NASA).

For product information and technology assistance, contact us at
Cengage Learning Customer & Sales Support, 1-800-354-9706

For permission to use material from this text or product,
submit all requests online at **cengage.com/permissions**
Further permissions questions can be emailed to
permissionrequest@cengage.com

This book contains select works from existing Cengage Learning resources and
was produced by Cengage Learning Custom Solutions for collegiate use. As such,
those adopting and/or contributing to this work are responsible for editorial
content accuracy, continuity and completeness.

Compilation © 2011 Cengage Learning

ISBN-13: 978-0-495-98854-0

ISBN-10: 0-495-98854-5

Cengage Learning
5191 Natorp Boulevard
Mason, Ohio 45040
USA
Cengage Learning is a leading provider of customized learning solutions with
office locations around the globe, including Singapore, the United Kingdom,
Australia, Mexico, Brazil, and Japan. Locate your local office at:
international.cengage.com/region.

Cengage Learning products are represented in Canada by Nelson Education, Ltd.
For your lifelong learning solutions, visit **www.cengage.com/custom.**
Visit our corporate website at **www.cengage.com.**

Printed in the United States of America

Brief Contents

Contents

Boxed Features

Features

Preface

As we prepared the preface to the previous edition of *The Challenge of Democracy* in the early fall of 2008, it was both an anxious time and a hopeful time. It was an anxious time for America as our economic system had suffered a severe shock with the collapse of the mortgage market, which in turn destabilized the banking industry and many major Wall Street firms. The real estate industry had built too many homes and then sold too many of those homes to individuals and speculators who could not really afford what they had purchased. Rising real estate prices hid the problem for a time, but then the bubble burst. When the large investment bank Lehman Brothers failed in September 2008, it became clear that the nation's banks were carrying dangerously large loads of bad mortgages and that the economy was in for some tough times.

Still, it was a hopeful time as well. The election of Barack Obama just a few months later generated enormous optimism. Obama's iconic election poster simply said, "Hope." And Americans were hopeful. As we write these words two years later, hope has diminished. The terrible economic problems that began before Obama took office continue to plague the United States. Although the recession is over and economic growth has returned, persistent high unemployment casts a pall over the nation. Public opinion has turned sour, and President Obama's popularity has fallen to low levels.

Throughout the chapters of the book, we pay particular attention to the past two years and many of the policy changes put into place by President Obama and the Democratic Congress. If nothing else, this has been a consequential administration. The Troubled Asset Relief Program (TARP), together with actions taken by the Federal Reserve Board, stabilized the teetering banking industry. Yet critics, including the newly emergent tea party movement, claimed TARP was a taxpayer "bailout" for badly run financial institutions. The administration's $787 billion economic stimulus package and other smaller stimulus-related measures helped the nation turn from a declining growth rate to a positive one. Conservatives, though, have lambasted these initiatives as too expensive and emphasized the resulting long-term debt that future generations will have to pay off. The Obama health-care reform plan will bring health insurance to virtually all Americans and institute many other significant changes. Health reform was surely the most controversial new policy enacted by Congress, and it generated a firestorm of debate. Conservatives believe that it will severely damage our health-care system and overload the country with debt. Defenders point to a disturbing inequality where many Americans lack access to health care because they have no insurance.

As we proceed through the chapters, we will lay out in some detail the policies and problems faced by the Obama administration during its first two years in office. We'll leave it to you, our readers, to decide yourself whether you believe the administration is moving in the right direction or has taken a flawed approach to solving the nation's ills.

Yet *The Challenge of Democracy* is not a book centered on current events. Rather, we use the recent past to illustrate enduring features of American government. As with the previous ten editions of this book, we build our text around two primary themes that remain as relevant today as when we first conceived of this project. The first is the clash among the values of freedom, order, and equality; the second focuses on the tensions between pluralist and majoritarian visions of democracy. Knowledge of these conflicts enables citizens to recognize and analyze the difficult choices they face in politics.

Over time we also recognized the growing impact of world politics on our governmental process. Our seventh edition (summer, 2001) added a third theme, globalization. The subsequent events of September 11, the war in Iraq, and the ongoing struggle in Afghanistan made the importance of globalization evident to all Americans. But globalization involves much more than the problems of conflict and terrorism. More than ever before, Americans are becoming citizens of the world. We cannot escape the deepening interrelationships with the rest of the world, even if it were desirable to do so. Each day, trade, travel, immigration, and the Internet make the world a more interdependent place. In spite of all the forces that should bring different countries and cultures to a better understanding of one another, the world is far from a peaceful place. Thus, *The Challenge of Democracy* examines some of the ramifications of a smaller world on the large landscape of American politics.

Underlying both the updating of world events and the enduring relevance of our themes is our continuing effort to bring the best recent political science research into *The Challenge of Democracy*. Despite being a little gray around the temples—okay, a lot of gray around the temples—the three of us are students, too. We continually look for recent books and journal articles by our colleagues in the discipline that tell us something new, something important, and something that the readers of *The Challenge of Democracy* should know about. One of the tasks of authors of introductory texts is to synthesize original research, interpret sophisticated scholarly work, and convey what we know as political scientists to students just starting out in their exploration of the discipline. We invite our readers to look closely at our footnotes, the evidence that supports what we say in the text. If you feel that we missed a source that is particularly important, please let us know.

Thematic Framework

Through all eleven editions, we have striven to write a book that students will actually read, so we have sought to discuss politics—a complex subject—in a captivating and understandable way. American politics isn't dull, and its textbooks needn't be either. Equally important, we have sought to produce a book that students would credit for stimulating their thinking about politics. While offering all of the essential information about American government and politics, we feel that it is important to give students a framework for analyzing politics that they can use long after their studies have ended.

To accomplish these goals, we built *The Challenge of Democracy* around three dynamic themes that are relevant to today's world: the clash among the values of freedom, order, and equality; the tensions between pluralist and majoritarian visions of democracy; and the fundamental ways that globalization is changing American politics.

Freedom, Order, and Equality

The first theme is introduced in Chapter 1 ("Freedom, Order, or Equality?"), where we suggest that American politics often reflects conflicts between the values of freedom and order and between the values of freedom and equality. These value conflicts are prominent in contemporary American society, and they help to explain political controversy and consensus in earlier eras. For instance, in Chapter 3 ("The Constitution") we argue that the Constitution was designed to promote order and that it virtually ignored issues of political and social equality. Equality was later served, however, by several amendments to the Constitution. In Chapter 15 ("Order and Civil Liberties") and Chapter 16 ("Equality and Civil Rights"), we demonstrate that many of this nation's most controversial issues represent conflicts among individuals or groups who hold differing views on the values of freedom, order, and equality. Views on issues such as abortion are not just isolated opinions; they also reflect choices about the philosophy citizens want government to follow. Yet choosing among these values is difficult, sometimes excruciatingly so.

Pluralist and Majoritarian Visions of Democracy

The second theme, introduced in Chapter 2 ("Majoritarian or Pluralist Democracy?"), asks students to consider two competing models of democratic government. One way that government can make decisions is by means of *majoritarian* principles—that is, by taking the actions desired by a majority of citizens. A contrasting model of government, *pluralism,* is built around the interaction of decision makers in government with groups concerned about issues that affect them.

These models are not mere abstractions; we use them to illustrate the dynamics of the American political system. In Chapter 11 ("Congress"), we discuss rising partisanship in Congress. As parties have become more ideologically homogeneous, they have been demonstrating greater unity in their votes on the floor. Yet majoritarian tensions with pluralism remain in Congress. In Chapter 10 ("Interest Groups"), we also see the forces of pluralism at work. Interest groups of all types populate Washington, and these organizations represent the diverse array of interests that define our society. At the same time, the chapter explores ways in which pluralism favors wealthier, better organized interests.

Globalization's Impact on American Politics

The third theme, the impact of globalization on American politics, is introduced in Chapter 1 and then discussed throughout the text. The traditional notion of national sovereignty holds that each government is free to govern in the manner it feels best. As the world becomes a smaller place, however, national sovereignty is tested in many ways. When a country is committing human rights violations—putting people in jail for merely disagreeing with the government in power—should other countries try to pressure it to comply with common norms of justice? Do the democracies of the world have a responsibility to use their influence to try to limit the abuses of the powerless in societies where they are abused?

Another facet of globalization is the growth of international trade. In many ways the world has become a single marketplace, and industries in one country often face competitors from many other countries around the world. Must a country just stand by and let jobs "emigrate" from within its borders to other countries where companies can produce the same quality goods at cheaper prices? How will the United States cope with the rising demand for oil worldwide as economies like those of China and India expand? These are just some of the issues that the Eleventh Edition explores.

Throughout the book we stress that students must make their own choices among the competing values and models of government. Although the three of us hold diverse and strong opinions about which choices are best, we do not believe it is our role to tell students our own answers to the broad questions we pose. Instead, we want our readers to learn firsthand that a democracy requires thoughtful choices. That is why we titled our book *The Challenge of Democracy*.

Our framework travels well over time. The civil rights struggles of the 1960s exemplified the utility of our theme emphasizing equality, as do more contemporary controversies surrounding gay rights, the rights of persons with disabilities, and affirmative action. We're just beginning to understand the privacy and personal freedom issues involving the Internet. Our theme of pluralism versus majoritarianism remains compelling as well. Pluralist images of America predate the adoption of the Constitution. In his defense of the proposed Constitution, James Madison defended the pursuit of self-interested goals by various groups in society, each looking out for its own good. A contrary view of democracy—majoritarian government—emphasizes control of government by majorities of voters through our party system. But the party system sometimes has a hard time channeling a majority of voters into majority rule. Prior to the Civil War, fissures in the party system made it difficult to understand exactly where the majority stood. More recently, in the 2000 election, Democrat Al Gore won more popular votes than Republican George Bush, but Bush won a majority of the electoral college, and—because a presidential election is a federal election—that's the majority that counts. Since the mid-1950s, more often than not, we've had divided government where one party controls the White House but the other controls at least one of the two houses of Congress. Which majority should be followed in such instances?

Our framework also travels well over space—to other countries with very different political heritages. One of the most important aspects of globalization is the number of countries that have recently made a transition to democracy or are currently trying to make that change. The challenge of democratization, however, is illustrated by recent developments in Iraq. Elections have been held, but democracy has been hindered by the lack of order. The relevance of our other major theme is illustrated as well. One of the most difficult problems faced by those who wrote the country's new constitution was the dispute between the majority Shiites, who, not surprisingly, wanted a government that facilitates majority rule, and the minority Sunnis and Kurds, who wanted a more pluralistic system with firm protections against majority dominance.

One of our greatest satisfactions as authors of a book on American democracy is that it has been used in a number of countries where democracy has at least a foothold, if it hasn't yet fully flowered. Our publisher has donated copies of earlier editions of our book to English-speaking faculty and students in Bulgaria, Croatia, the Czech Republic, Georgia, Ghana, Hungary, Kenya, Poland, Romania, Russia, Slovakia, and South Africa. Moreover, the brief edition of our text has been translated into Russian, Hungarian, Georgian, Czech, and Korean. We are pleased that *The Challenge of Democracy* is now available to many more students in these countries—students who have been confronting the challenge of democracy in times of political transition.

Substantive Features of the Eleventh Edition

Chapter-Opening Vignettes

As in previous editions, each chapter begins with a vignette to draw students into the chapter's substance while exploring the book's themes. Chapter 1 ("Freedom, Order, or Equality?") opens with a comparison of the Great Depression during the 1930s and the Great Recession that we've experienced these past few years. Bad as our unemployment is today, it was considerably worse during the Depression. In Chapter 6 ("The Media), we contemplate the future of journalism, noting the decline of newspaper circulation and production and the rise of Internet news aggregation. Democratic accountability requires a vibrant free press and an informed citizenry, but the challenges facing the newspaper industry might pose a significant threat to both. In Chapter 15 ("Order and Civil Liberties"), we examine a student's opposition to saluting the flag and reciting the Pledge of Allegiance. Many teachers will recognize that this matter was resolved by the Supreme Court in the midst of

World War II, but it came back to life in 2010. A relatively new problem, driving while texting, is the topic at the opening of Chapter 17 ("Policymaking"). It's a terribly dangerous practice, but only some states restrict it to preserve safety (or what we might call order).

"Politics of Global Change"

In light of the growing emphasis in our book on globalization, we initiated a set of boxed features on global change in the Seventh Edition. In these boxes, which are now called "Politics of Global Change," we examine various elements of political change—some troubling, some hopeful. In Chapter 2 ("Majoritarian or Pluralist Democracy?"), our feature examines the emerging environmental movement in the Czech Republic. A legacy of its Communist past is a reliance on heavy industry, which in turn means a high level of air pollution. In the new Czech democracy, interest groups are now free to form and demands for clean air have grown. Yet the country still needs the jobs that its aging industries provide. In Chapter 11 ("Congress"), the feature examines the new Iraqi parliament, created with the help of the United States. It notes the grave challenges that new legislatures face in satisfying the competing demands of pluralism and majoritarianism, of freedom and order, and of freedom and equality. In Chapter 18 ("Economic Policy"), the feature contemplates the sharply rising proportion of government debt held by foreign investors. In simple banking terms, the United States owes the rest of the world (and increasingly, China) a whole lot of money.

"Compared with What?"

We firmly believe that students can better evaluate how our political system works when they compare it with politics in other countries. Thus, each chapter has at least one boxed feature called "Compared with What?" that treats its topic in a comparative perspective. In Chapter 4 ("Federalism") we examine public sector employment in the United States and other federal systems. The government may be everywhere as long as you know where to look. The "Compared with What?" feature in Chapter 12 ("The Presidency") focuses on Japan where, like the United States, a newly elected head of state saw his popularity plummet in the wake of a bad economy. Yet Prime Minister Hatoyama was forced out of office by his own party after less than a year. Again turning to the "Policymaking" chapter, we consider the rates of smoking in fourteen different countries. The percentages vary widely, and government policies can influence the decision to smoke or not smoke through the level of taxes imposed and the degree to which they educate the public about the dangers of tobacco.

"In Our Own Words"

We have enriched the close connection that we initiated in previous editions between the words in our text and technology. Each chapter opens with information on "In Our Own Words," downloadable audio summaries that speak of the major objectives of each chapter. In this edition, we've also dramatically increased the number of marginal callouts that tie in chapter content to the self-test at the award-winning IDEAlog website. (See "For the Student: Effective Learning Aids" later in the preface for more information on "In Our Own Words" and IDEAlog.)

Additional Resources for Students

Each chapter concludes with a brief summary. At the end of the book, we have included the Declaration of Independence, an annotated copy of the Constitution, and a glossary of key terms.

Versions of the Text

The Challenge of Democracy is now available in four versions.

Challenge of Democracy, 11e
Janda • Berry • Goldman
Hardcover version: ISBN-10: 0495906182 ISBN-13: 9780495906186
Paperback version: ISBN-10: 049591293X ISBN-13: 9780495912934
848 Pages • 20 Chapters • ©2012
Challenge of Democracy, 11e, No Separate Policy Chapters Version
Janda • Berry • Goldman
ISBN-10: 1111724814 ISBN-13: 9781111724818
Paperback • 704 pages • 16 Chapters • © 2012
Challenge of Democracy, Essentials, 8e
Janda • Berry • Goldman • Hula
ISBN-10: 1111341915 ISBN-13: 9781111341916
Paperback • 624 Pages • 14 Chapters • ©2012

For the Instructor: Innovative Teaching Tools

Our job as authors did not end with writing this text. From the beginning, we have been centrally involved with producing a tightly integrated set of instructional materials to accompany the text. With help from other political scientists and educational specialists at Cengage Learning, these ancillary materials have grown and improved over time.

Multimedia and Online Teaching Resources

Cengage Learning now offers these exciting resources for instructors:
PowerLecture DVD with JoinIn™ and ExamView®
ISBN-10: 0840035217 | ISBN-13: 9780840035219
This DVD includes two sets of PowerPoint slides, a book-specific and a media-enhanced set; a Test Bank in both Microsoft Word and Exam View

formats; an Instructor Manual; JoinIn clicker questions; and a Resource Integration Guide.

- **Interactive, book-specific PowerPoint® lectures** make it easy for you to assemble, edit, publish, and present book-specific lectures for your course. You will have access to outlines specific to each chapter of the text as well as photos, figures, and tables found in the text.
- **Media-enhanced PowerPoints slides** can be used on their own or easily integrated with the book-specific PowerPoint outlines. Look for audio and video clips depicting both historic and current events; animated learning modules illustrating key concepts; tables, statistical charts, and graphs; and photos from the book as well as outside sources at the appropriate places in the chapter.
- **Test bank in Microsoft® Word and ExamView® computerized testing** offers a large array of well-crafted multiple-choice and essay questions along with their answers and page references.
- **Instructor's Manual** includes learning objectives, chapter outlines, discussion questions, suggestions for stimulating class activities and projects, tips on integrating media into your class (including step-by-step instructions on how to create your own podcasts), suggested readings and Web resources, and a section specially designed to help teaching assistants and adjunct instructors.
- **JoinIn™ "clicker" questions** test and track student comprehension of key concepts.
- **The Resource Integration Guide** outlines the rich collection of resources available to instructors and students within the chapter-by-chapter framework of the book, suggesting how and when each supplement can be used to optimize learning.

CourseMate

Printed text plus CourseMate Printed Access Card

ISBN-10: 1111706743 ISBN-13: 9781111706746

This media-rich website offers a variety of online learning resources designed to enhance the student learning experience. These resources include video activities, "In Our Own Words" audio summaries, critical-thinking exercises, simulations, animated learning modules, interactive timelines, primary source quizzes, flashcards, learning objectives, glossaries, and crossword puzzles. Chapter resources are correlated to key chapter learning concepts, and users can browse or search for content in a variety of ways.

NewsNow is a new asset available in CourseMate. It is a combination of weekly news stories from the Associated Press and videos and images that bring current events to life for the student. For instructors, NewsNow includes an additional set of multimedia-rich PowerPoint slides posted each week to the password-protected area of the text's instructor companion website. Instructors may use these slides to take a class poll or trigger a lively debate about the events that are shaping the world right now.

The **Engagement Tracker** assesses student preparation and engagement. Use the tracking tools to see progress for the class as a whole or for individual students. Identify students at risk early in the course. Uncover which concepts are most difficult for your class. Monitor time on task. Keep your students engaged.

CourseMate also features an **interactive eBook** that has highlighting and search capabilities along with links to simulations, animated PowerPoints that illustrate concepts, Interactive Timelines, Video Activities, Primary Source Quizzes and Flashcards. Go to cengagebrain.com/shop/ISBN/0495906182 to access your **Political Science CourseMate** resources.

Aplia

Available for Spring 2011 classes!

Text plus Aplia Printed Access Card

ISBN-10: 1111488266| ISBN-13: 9781111488260

Aplia is dedicated to improving students' learning by increasing their engagement with your American Government course through premium, automatically graded assignments. Aplia saves instructors valuable time they'd otherwise spend on routine grading while giving students an easy way to stay on top of course work with regularly scheduled assignments.

Organized by specific chapters of their textbook, students receive immediate, detailed explanations for every answer they input. Grades are automatically recorded in the instructor's Aplia grade book.

American Government CourseReader

Text plus CourseReader Printed Access Card

ISBN-10: 1111653682 | ISBN-13: 9781111653682

The CourseReader allows instructors to create a customized reader using a database of hundreds of documents, readings, and videos. Instructors can search by various criteria or browse the collection to preview and then select a customized collection to assign their students. The sources are edited to an appropriate length and include pedagogical support—a headnote describing the document and critical-thinking and multiple-choice questions to verify that the student has read and understood the selection. Students are able to take notes, highlight, and print content. The CourseReader allows the instructor to select exactly what students will be assigned with an easy-to-use interface and also provides an easily used assessment tool. The sources can be delivered online or in print format.

Instructor Companion Website

The instructor companion site includes the Instructor's Manual; text-specific PowerPoints containing lecture outlines, photos, and figures; and NewsNow PowerPoints.

WebTutor on WebCT or Blackboard

Printed Text plus WebCT Printed Access Card
ISBN-10: 1111648808 | ISBN-13: 9781111648800
Printed Text plus Blackboard Printed Access Card
ISBN-10: 1111648816 | ISBN-13: 9781111648817

Rich with content for your American government course, this Web-based teaching and learning tool includes course management, study/mastery, and communication tools. Use WebTutor™ to provide virtual office hours, post your syllabus, and track student progress with WebTutor's quizzing material.

CourseCare

Available exclusively to Cengage Learning, CourseCare is a revolutionary program designed to provide you and your students with an unparalleled user experience with your Cengage Learning digital solution.

CourseCare connects you with a team of training, service, and support experts to help you implement your Cengage Learning Digital Solution. Real people dedicated to you, your students, and your course from the first day of class through final exams.

Political Theatre 2.0
ISBN-10: 0495793604 | ISBN-13: 9780495793601

Bring politics home to students with Political Theatre 2.0, up to date through the 2008 election season. This is the second edition of this three-DVD series and includes real video clips that show American political thought throughout the public sector. Clips include both classic and contemporary political advertisements, speeches, interviews, and more.

JoinIn™ on Turning Point® for Political Theatre
ISBN-10: 0495095508 | ISBN-13: 9780495095507

For even more interaction, combine Political Theatre with the innovative teaching tool of a classroom response system through JoinIn™. Poll your students with questions created for you, or create your own questions.

The Wadsworth News Videos for American Government 2012 DVD
ISBN-10: 0495573094 | ISBN-13: 9780495573098

This collection of three- to six-minute video clips on relevant political issues serves as a great lecture or discussion launcher.

Great Speeches Collection

Throughout the ages, great orators have stepped up to the podium and used their communication skills to persuade, inform, and inspire their audiences. Studying these speeches can provide tremendous insight into historical, political, and cultural events. The Great Speeches Collection includes the full text of over sixty memorable orations for you to incorporate into your course. Speeches can be collated in a printed reader to supplement your existing course materials or bound into a core textbook.

ABC Video: Speeches by President Barack Obama
ISBN-10: 1439082472 | ISBN-13: 9781439082478

DVD of nine famous speeches by President Barack Obama, from 2004 through his inauguration, including his speech at the 2004 Democratic National Convention; his 2008 speech on race, "A More Perfect Union"; and his 2009 inaugural address. Speeches are divided into short video segments for easy, time-efficient viewing. This instructor supplement also features critical-thinking questions and answers for each speech, designed to spark classroom discussion.

Election 2010: An American Government Supplement
ISBN-10: 1111341788 | ISBN-13: 9781111341787

Written by John Clark and Brian Schaffner, this booklet addresses the 2010 congressional and gubernatorial races, with both real-time analysis and references.

The Obama Presidency – Year One Supplement

Kenneth Janda – Northwestern University
Jeffrey M. Berry – Tufts University
Jerry Goldman – Northwestern University
ISBN-10:0495908371 | ISBN-13:9780495908371

Much happens in the first year of a presidency, especially a historic one like that of Barack Obama. This full-color sixteen-page supplement by Kenneth Janda, Jeffrey Berry, and Jerry Goldman analyzes such issues as health care, the economy and the stimulus package, changes in the U.S. Supreme Court, and the effect Obama's policies have had on global affairs.

Instructor's Guide to YouTube for Political Science

Instructors have access to the Instructor's Guide to YouTube, which shows American government instructors where on the Internet to find videos that can be used as learning tools in class. Organized by fifteen topics, the guide follows the sequence of an American government course and includes a preface with tips on how to use Internet videos in class.

USPolitics.org

The Eleventh Edition continues to be supported by **uspolitics.org**, Kenneth Janda's personal website for *The Challenge of Democracy*. His site offers a variety of teaching aids to instructors who adopt any version of *The Challenge of Democracy* for courses in American politics. It is divided into two sides: the student side is open to all users, but the instructor side is limited to teachers who register online at **uspolitics.org** as *Challenge* adopters. The site offers some material not contained on Cengage Learning's own website, yet it also provides convenient links to the publisher's site.

For more information on the teaching tools that accompany *The Challenge of Democracy,* please contact your Cengage Learning sales representative.

For the Student: Effective Learning Aids

- **CourseMate.** CourseMate, accessible at **www.cengagebrain.com/shop/ISBN/0495906182**, offers students a variety of rich online learning resources designed to enhance the student experience. These resources include video activities, audio summaries, critical thinking activities, simulations, animated learning modules, interactive timelines, primary source quizzes, flashcards, learning objectives, glossaries, and crossword puzzles. All resources are correlated with key chapter learning concepts, and students can browse or search for content in a variety of ways.

- **IDEAlog.** IDEAlog, which won the 2005 Instructional Software Award from the American Political Science Association, is closely tied to the text's "value conflicts" theme. It is directly accessible at http://IDEAlog.org and is also available on the student website. IDEAlog first asks students to rate themselves on the two-dimensional trade-off of freedom versus order and freedom versus equality. It then presents them with twenty questions, ten dealing with the conflict of freedom versus order and ten pertaining to freedom versus equality. Students' responses to these questions are classified according to libertarian, conservative, liberal, or communitarian ideological tendencies.

We invite your questions, suggestions, and criticisms of the teaching/learning package and *The Challenge of Democracy.* You may contact us at our respective institutions or through our collective e-mail address **cod@northwestern.edu.**

Acknowledgments

All authors are indebted to others for inspiration and assistance in various forms; textbook authors are notoriously so. For this edition we were fortunate enough to have Professor Deborah Schildkraut of Tufts University revise Chapters 6, 11, and 19. She contributed greatly to the quality of this new version of *The Challenge of Democracy.* We want to again thank Patricia Conley, a Visiting Professor at the University of Chicago, for her work on earlier editions of the book.

We again want to single out Professor Paul Manna of the College of William and Mary, who has assisted us in many different ways. Lukasz Hankus of nonstopworkshop.com provided invaluable support for the new and improved version of IDEAlog; Kimball Brace, President of Election Data Services, supplied us with updated election data; Robert Coen, Northwestern University Professor Emeritus of Economics, gave us a careful review of Chapter 18, "Economic Policy"; Axel Dreher, at KOF, the Swiss Economic Institute, contributed data on globalization; and Simon Winchester helped us understand the history of the 1883 Krakatoa volcanic eruption. Timely

Authors Jerry Goldman, Kenneth Janda, and Jeffrey Berry at Boston's Fenway Park

information technology suggestions and assistance came from Jeff Parsons of The Oyez Project, Professor James Ferolo of Bradley University, and Dr. Francesco Stagno d'Alcontres of Centro Linguistico d'Ateneo Messinese. We also wish to express our gratitude to Julieta Suarez-Cao of Northwestern University, Hope Lozano-Bielat of Boston University, and Andrew Gruen of Cambridge University for their helpful research assistance. We extend thanks as well to Joseph B. Maher, Esq., Deputy General Counsel, DHS; Brad Kieserman, Esq., Chief Counsel, FEMA; and Professor Timothy R. Johnson, University of Minnesota.

We have been fortunate to obtain the help of many outstanding political scientists across the country who provided us with critical reviews of our work as it has progressed through eleven separate editions. We found their comments enormously helpful, and we thank them for taking valuable time away from their own teaching and research to write their detailed reports. More specifically, our thanks go to the following:

David Ahern, *University of Dayton*

Philip C. Aka, *Chicago State University*

James Anderson, *Texas A&M University*

Greg Andranovich, *California State University, Los Angeles*

Theodore Arrington, *University of North Carolina, Charlotte*

Denise Baer, *Northeastern University*

Richard Barke, *Georgia Institute of Technology*

Brian Bearry, *University of Texas at Dallas*

Linda L. M. Bennett, *Wittenberg University*

Stephen Earl Bennett, *University of Cincinnati*

Elizabeth Bergman, *California State Polytechnic University, Pomona*

Thad Beyle, *University of North Carolina, Chapel Hill*

Bruce Bimber, *University of California, Santa Barbara*

Michael Binford, *Georgia State University*

Bonnie Browne, *Texas A&M University*

Jeffrey L. Brudney, *Cleveland State University*

Jane Bryant, *John A. Logan College*

J. Vincent Buck, *California State University, Fullerton*

Gregory A. Caldeira, *Ohio State University*

David E. Camacho, *Northern Arizona University*

Robert Casier, *Santa Barbara City College*

James Chalmers, *Wayne State University*

John Chubb, *Stanford University*

Allan Cigler, *University of Kansas*

Stanley Clark, *California State University, Bakersfield*

Ronald Claunch, *Stephen F. Austin State University*

Guy C. Clifford, *Bridgewater State College*

Gary Copeland, *University of Oklahoma*

Ruth A. Corbett, *Chabot College*

W. Douglas Costain, *University of Colorado at Boulder*

Cornelius P. Cotter, *University of Wisconsin, Milwaukee*

James L. Danielson, *Minnesota State University, Moorhead*

Christine L. Day, *University of New Orleans*

David A. Deese, *Boston College*

Victor D'Lugin, *University of Florida*

Douglas C. Dow, *University of Texas at Dallas*

Art English, *University of Arkansas*

Matthew Eshbaugh-Soha, *University of North Texas*

Tim Fackler, *University of Texas, Austin*

Dennis Falcon, *Cerritos Community College*

Henry Fearnley, *College of Marin*

Elizabeth Flores, *Del Mar College*

Patricia S. Florestano, *University of Maryland*

Richard Foglesong, *Rollins College*

Steve Frank, *St. Cloud State University*

Mitchel Gerber, *Hofstra University*

Dana K. Glencross, *Oklahoma City Community College*

Dorith Grant-Wisdom, *Howard University*

Paul Gronke, *Duke University*

Sara A. Grove, *Shippensburg University*

David J. Hadley, *Wabash College*

Willie Hamilton, *Mt. San Jacinto College*

Kenneth Hayes, *University of Maine*

Ronald Hedlund, *University of Wisconsin–Milwaukee*

Richard Heil, *Fort Hays State University*

Beth Henschen, *The Institute for Community and Regional Development, Eastern Michigan University*

Marjorie Randon Hershey, *Indiana University*

Roberta Herzberg, *Indiana University*

Jack E. Holmes, *Hope College*

Peter Howse, *American River College*

Ronald J. Hrebenar, *University of Utah*

James B. Johnson, *University of Nebraska at Omaha*

William R. Keech, *Carnegie Mellon University*

Scott Keeter, *Pew Center*

Sarah W. Keidan, *Oakland Community College (Michigan)*

Linda Camp Keith, *Collin County Community College*

Beat Kernen, *Southwest Missouri State University*

Haroon Khan, *Henderson State University*

Dwight Kiel, *Central Florida University*

Nancy Pearson Kinney, *Washtenaw Community College*

Vance Krites, *Indiana University of Pennsylvania*

Clyde Kuhn, *California State University, Sacramento*

Jack Lampe, *Southwest Texas Junior College*

William Lester, *Jacksonville State University*

Brad Lockerbie, *University of Georgia*

Joseph Losco, *Ball State University*

Philip Loy, *Taylor University*

Stan Luger, *University of Northern Colorado*

David Madlock, *University of Memphis*

Michael Maggiotto, *University of South Carolina*

Edward S. Malecki, *California State University, Los Angeles*

Michael Margolis, *University of Cincinnati–McMicken College of Arts and Sciences*

Thomas R. Marshall, *University of Texas at Arlington*

Janet Martin, *Bowdoin College*

Steve J. Mazurana, *University of Northern Colorado*

Michael McConachie, *Collin College*

Wayne McIntosh, *University of Maryland*

David McLaughlin, *Northwest Missouri State University*

Don Melton, *Arapahoe Community College*

Melissa Michelson, *California State University, East Bay*

Dana Morales, *Montgomery College*

Jim Morrow, *Tulsa Junior College*

David Moskowitz, *The University of North Carolina, Charlotte*

William Mugleston, *Mountain View College*

William Murin, *University of Wisconsin–Parkside*

David Nice, *Washington State University*

David A. Nordquest, *Pennsylvania State University, Erie*

Bruce Odom, *Trinity Valley Community College*

Laura Katz Olson, *Lehigh University*

Bruce Oppenheimer, *Vanderbilt University*

Richard Pacelle, *Indiana University*

William J. Parente, *University of Scranton*

Tony Payan, *University of Texas, El Paso*

Robert Pecorella, *St. John's University*

James Perkins, *San Antonio College*

Denny E. Pilant, *Southwest Missouri State University*

Marc Pufong, *Valdosta State University*

Curtis Reithel, *University of Wisconsin–La Crosse*

Russell Renka, *Southeast Missouri State University*

Chester D. Rhoan, *Chabot College*

Michael J. Rich, *Emory University*

Richard S. Rich, *Virginia Tech*

Ronald I. Rubin, *Borough of Manhattan Community College, CUNY*

Gilbert K. St. Clair, *University of New Mexico*

Barbara Salmore, *Drew University*

Todd M. Schaefer, *Central Washington University*

Denise Scheberle, *University of Wisconsin–Green Bay*

Paul R. Schulman, *Mills College*

William A. Schultze, *San Diego State University*

Thomas Sevener, *Santa Rosa Junior College*

Kenneth S. Sherrill, *Hunter College*

Sanford R. Silverburg, *Catawba College*

Mark Silverstein, *Boston University*

Charles Sohner, *El Camino College*

Robert J. Spitzer, *SUNY Cortland*

Terry Spurlock, *Trinity Valley Community College*

Candy Stevens Smith, *Texarkana College*

Dale Story, *University of Texas at Arlington*

Nicholas Strinkowski, *Clark College*

Neal Tate, *University of North Texas*

James A. Thurber, *The American University*

Ronnie Tucker, *Shippensburg University*

John Tuman, *University of Nevada, Las Vegas*

Bedford Umez, *Lee College*

David Uranga, *Pasadena City College*

Eric M. Uslaner, *University of Maryland*

Lawson Veasey, *Jacksonville State University*

Charles E. Walcott, *Virginia Tech*

Richard J. Waldman, *University of Maryland*

Thomas G. Walker, *Emory University*

Benjamin Walter, *Vanderbilt University*

Shirley Ann Warshaw, *Gettysburg College*

Gary D. Wekkin, *University of Central Arkansas*

Jonathan West, *University of Miami*

Zaphon Wilson, *Armstrong Atlantic State University*

John Winkle, *University of Mississippi*

Clifford Wirth, *University of New Hampshire*

Wayne Wolf, *South Suburban College*

Mikel Wyckoff, *Northern Illinois University*

Ann Wynia, *North Hennepin Community College*

Jerry L. Yeric, *University of North Texas*

Finally, we want to thank the many people at Wadsworth/Cengage Learning who helped make this edition a reality. There's not enough room here to list all the individuals who helped us with the previous editions, so we say a collective thank-you for the superb work you did on *The Challenge of Democracy*. Political Science Editor Edwin Hill could not have been more supportive, and we especially appreciate how tolerant he is of the constant stream of kvetching and moaning e-mails that we send his way. Betty Slack, our developmental editor, was a delight to work with. She had a light touch editing and shaping the changes we made in the manuscript. Matt DiGangi at Cengage was a model of organization as he served as the nerve center of this whole operation. There's lots of moving parts in the production of a textbook, and Matt kept everything moving in the right direction. Our direct production contacts were extraordinarily efficient and helpful. A million thanks to Alison Eigel Zade, Carly Bergey, and Matt Baker, all of whom seemed to create order out of the chaos we created. Finally, thanks, too, to the sales representatives who do such a terrific job of bringing each new edition of *The Challenge of Democracy* to the attention of those who might use it.

K. J.   J. B.   J. G.

DEDICATED TO THESE PEOPLE WHO TAUGHT US:

Robert S. Feldman, encouraging K. J. during graduate study at Indiana University

Robert Peabody, inspiring J. B. during graduate study at Johns Hopkins

Richard B. Meltzer, for 50+ years of friendship with J. G.

The Challenge
of Democracy

Freedom, Order, or Equality?

Jupiterimages

The Great Depression of the 1930s was sparked by the collapse of the stock market in October 1929. Soon afterward, the nation's banks began to fail—more than 1,000 each year and an estimated 4,000 in 1933 alone.[1] Unemployment rose from 3 percent of the labor force before the collapse to almost 25 percent in 1933 and remained high for years, averaging nearly 18 percent from 1930 to 1940.[2] Unemployment was still almost 10 percent in 1941, until World War II put people to work at national defense.

The Great Recession of our era technically began in December 2007 when employers' payroll employment declined.[3] But the home mortgage market began to collapse months earlier. By the summer of 2008, the nation's financial institutions neared widespread failure, the stock market plunged, and the entire economy was in crisis. The term Great Recession was in use by December.[4] Unemployment approached levels of the 1930s.[5] The official unemployment rate, which counts only people looking for work, rose from 4.8 percent in December 2007 to 10.2 percent in October 2009. Adding in those who gave up looking, 17.3 percent of the population was unemployed in December 2009.[6]

National rates don't reveal that unemployment for couples with children under age 18 had doubled from 2007 to 2009 or that married parents with both working dropped from 67 to 60 percent in two years.[7] They don't show that from 1999 to 2009 the number of manufacturing jobs declined by 33 percent, by 12 percent in construction, and by 50 percent in motor vehicles and parts.[8] They don't tell that more than half of all unemployed workers borrowed money from friends or relatives after losing their jobs or that 60 percent drew down their savings accounts to make ends meet.[9] Despite the hardships suffered by millions of Americans in the Great Recession, the Great Depression was worse: Eighteen percent of the people were out of work for a decade, industrial production declined 32 percent (versus 17 percent in 2009), and about 9,000 banks failed (versus fewer than 175 through 2009).[10] What can government do to end such intense economic downturns? Should it do anything at all?

On March 5, 1933, the day after his inauguration, President Franklin Delano Roosevelt proclaimed a four-day bank holiday, suspending "all transactions in the Federal Reserve and other banks, trust companies, credit unions, and building and loan associations."[11] On March 9, Congress overwhelmingly passed the Emergency Banking Relief Act, which gave the president control over financial transactions in currency, credit, silver, and gold; permitted the Treasury Department to decide which banks could reopen; and effectively placed the government in control of the banking industry. Most economists credit Roosevelt's unprecedented use of government power with stopping the run on banks, thus preventing citizens from withdrawing even more of their deposits and preventing further collapse of financial institutions.

President George W. Bush's administration used government power to forestall a collapse of the home mortgage market in 2008. On Sunday, September 7, Treasury Secretary Henry Paulson announced the takeover of Fannie Mae and Freddie Mac, two private companies responsible for most of the nation's new home mortgages.[12] Two weeks later, Secretary Paulson along with Federal Reserve

Chair Ben Bernanke announced a $700 billion Troubled Asset Relief Program (TARP) to buy out failing banks and automobile companies. Some described their actions as socialism, not capitalism. Nevertheless, the nation avoided a financial collapse akin to that of the 1930s.

President Barack Obama inherited Bush's $700 billion TARP program and embarked on his own $787 billion economic stimulus program to improve the economy. (See the opening pages of Chapter 2 for more on Obama's decision.) It funded tax cuts; benefits for unemployment, education, and health care; and job creation through contracts, grants, and loans.[13] Unemployment continued to rise in the months after its passage, but the economy actually grew by the end of 2009, and economists credited the stimulus program.[14] Still, a poll in mid-January 2010 found more people disapproved than approved of Obama's handing of the economy.[15] People worried about federal spending, the growing deficit, and government's role in the economy in general. Clobbered by imports of foreign glass (particularly from China), one West Virginia glassmaker said, "I need some relief from government to stay in business, but I'm not sure it is the government's role to keep me in business."[16] What do you think? Should government spend billions to stabilize the financial system and to combat unemployment when taxpayers must bear the burden?

Our main interest in this text is the purpose, value, and operation of government as practiced in the United States. As the worried West Virginia glassmaker indicates, however, we live in an era of **globalization**—a term for the increasing interdependence of citizens and nations across the world.[17] So we must consider how politics at home and abroad interrelate, which is increasingly important to understanding our government.[18]

We probe the relationship between individual freedoms and personal security in the United States. We also examine the relationship between individual freedom and social equality as reflected in government policies, which often confront underlying dilemmas such as these:

Which is better: to live under a government that fiercely protects individual freedom or under one that infringes on freedom while fiercely guarding against threats to physical and economic security? *Which is better:* to let all citizens keep the same share of their income or to tax wealthier people at a higher rate to fund programs for poorer people? These questions pose dilemmas tied to opposing political philosophies that place different values on freedom, order, and equality.

This book explains American government and politics in the light of these dilemmas. It does more than explain the workings of our government; it encourages you to think about what government should—and should not—do. And it judges the American government against democratic ideals, encouraging you to think about how government should make its decisions. As the title of this book implies, *The Challenge of Democracy* argues that good government often poses difficult choices.

College students often say that American government and politics are hard to understand. In fact, many other people voice the same complaint. About 70 percent of people interviewed in 2008 agreed with the statement, "Politics and government seem so complicated that a person like me can't understand what's going on."[19] We hope to improve your understanding of "what's going on" by analyzing the norms, or values, that people use to

globalization
The increasing interdependence of citizens and nations across the world.

judge political events. Our purpose is not to preach what people ought to favor in making policy decisions; it is to teach what values are at stake.

Teaching without preaching is not easy; no one can completely exclude personal values from political analysis. But our approach minimizes the problem by concentrating on the dilemmas that confront governments when they are forced to choose between important policies that threaten equally cherished values, such as freedom of speech and personal security.

A prominent scholar defined *politics* as "the authoritative allocation of values for a society."[20] Every government policy reflects a choice between conflicting values. All government policies reinforce certain values (norms) at the expense of others. We want you to interpret policy issues (for example, Should assisted suicide go unpunished?) with an understanding of the fundamental values in question (freedom of action versus order and protection of life) and the broader political context (liberal or conservative politics).

By looking beyond the specifics to the underlying normative principles, you should be able to make more sense out of politics. Our framework for analysis does not encompass all the complexities of American government, but it should help your knowledge grow by improving your comprehension of political information. We begin by considering the basic purposes of government. In short, why do we need it?

The Globalization of American Government

Most people do not like being told what to do. Fewer still like being coerced into acting a certain way. Yet billions of people in countries across the world willingly submit to the coercive power of government. They accept laws that state on which side of the road to drive, how many wives (or husbands) they can have, what constitutes a contract, how to dispose of human waste—and how much they must pay to support the government that makes these coercive laws. In the first half of the twentieth century, people thought of government mainly in territorial terms. Indeed, a standard definition of **government** is the legitimate use of force—including firearms, imprisonment, and execution—within specified geographical boundaries to control human behavior. Since the Peace of Westphalia in 1648 ended the Thirty Years' War in Europe, international relations and diplomacy have been based on the principle of national sovereignty, defined as "a political entity's externally recognized right to exercise final authority over its affairs."[21] Simply put, **national sovereignty** means that each national government has the right to govern its people as it wishes, without interference from other nations.

Some scholars argued strongly early in the twentieth century that a body of international law controlled the actions of supposedly sovereign nations, but their argument was essentially theoretical.[22] In the practice of international relations, there was no sovereign power over nations. Each enjoyed complete independence to govern its territory without interference from other nations. Although the League of Nations and later the United Nations were supposed to

government
The legitimate use of force to control human behavior; also, the organization or agency authorized to exercise that force.

national sovereignty
A political entity's externally recognized right to exercise final authority over its affairs.

introduce supranational order into the world, even these international organizations explicitly respected national sovereignty as the guiding principle of international relations. The U.N. Charter, Article 2.1, states: "The Organization is based on the principle of the sovereign equality of all its Members."

National sovereignty, however, is threatened under globalization. Consider the international community's concern with starving refugees in the Darfur region of Sudan. The U.N. Security Council resolved to send troops to end the ethnic conflict, which cost some four hundred thousand lives. The Sudanese government, suspected of causing the conflict, opposed the U.N. action as violating its sovereignty.[23] Nevertheless, the humanitarian crisis in Sudan became closely monitored by the U.N., which deployed troops there in early 2008 and had over 15,000 there in 2010.

Global forces also generate pressures for international law. Consider the 1982 Law of the Sea Treaty, which governs maritime law from mineral rights

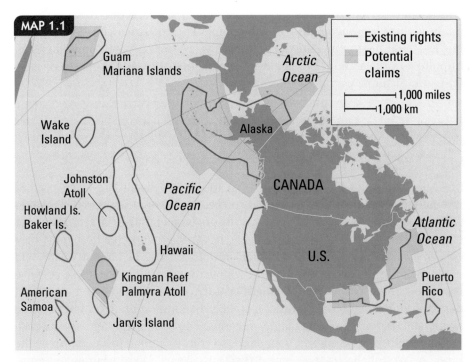

Sea Change

This map shows how much seabed would be open to the United States for oil, gas, and mineral mining under the Law of the Sea Treaty. The additional territory amounts to 291,000 square miles, most of that in waters opened by ice melting because of global warming. Although 155 nations had entered the treaty by the end of 2007, the United States had not. The treaty had been blocked in the Senate by opponents who feared it would undermine U.S. sovereignty by delegating authority to an International Seabed Authority. Commercial interests and the U.S. Navy, however, favored the treaty. President Bush recommended its passage, and so did President Obama.

Source: Nick Timiraos, "Arctic Thaw Defrosts a Sea Treaty," in Wall Street Journal (Eastern Edition), 11/3/2007. Copyright 2007 by Dow Jones & Company, Inc. Reproduced with permission of Dow Jones & Company, Inc., in the format textbook via Copyright Clearance Center.

to shipping lanes under an International Seabed Authority (see Map 1.1). Although President Ronald Reagan did not sign it, the treaty came into force in 1994 when ratified by sixty nations. President Clinton signed the treaty then, but conservative senators kept it from being ratified, fearing loss of U.S. sovereignty. After global warming began to melt the Arctic ice, the U.S. Navy backed the treaty for guaranteeing free passage through international straits, and oil and mining companies favored its 350-mile grant of mineral rights around Alaska. It was reported out for ratification in 2007 with President George W. Bush's support.[24] However, opponents argued against getting LOST (Law of Sea Treaty), and it remained unratified during Obama's first year.[25]

Our government, you might be surprised to learn, is worried about this trend of holding nations accountable to international law. In fact, in 2002, the United States "annulled" its signature to the 1998 treaty (no country had ever unsigned a treaty) to create an International Criminal Court that would define and try crimes against humanity.[26] Why would the United States oppose such an international court? One reason is its concern that U.S. soldiers stationed abroad might be arrested and tried in that court.[27] Another reason is the death penalty, practiced in the United States but abolished by more than half the countries in the world and all countries in the European Union. Indeed, in 1996, the International Commission of Jurists condemned the U.S. death penalty as "arbitrarily and racially discriminatory," and there is a concerted campaign across Europe to force the sovereign United States to terminate capital punishment.[28]

The United States is the world's most powerful nation, but as proved by the events of September 11, 2001, it is not invulnerable to foreign attack. Although the United States is not the most "globalized" nation (see "Politics of Global Change: The Globalization of Nations"), it is nevertheless vulnerable to erosion of its sovereignty. As the world's superpower, should the United States be above international law (like the Law of the Sea Treaty) if its sovereignty is compromised?

Although this text is about American national government, it recognizes the growing impact of international politics and world opinion on U.S. politics. The Cold War era, of course, had a profound effect on domestic politics because the nation spent heavily on the military and restricted trading with communist countries. Now we are closely tied through trade to former enemies (we import more goods from China—still communist—than from France and Britain combined), and we are thoroughly embedded in a worldwide economic, social, and political network. (See Chapter 20, "Global Policy," for an extended treatment of the economic and social dimensions of globalization.) More than ever before, we must discuss American politics while casting an eye abroad to see how foreign affairs affect our government and how American politics affects government in other nations.

IDEALOG.ORG

Our IDEAlog.org self-test poses twenty questions about the political values seen in Figure 1.2. One of the questions in the IDEAlog self-test is about the death penalty. Take the quiz, and see how you respond.

The Purposes of Government

Governments at any level require citizens to surrender some freedom as part of being governed. Although some governments minimize their infringements

Politics of Global Change

The Globalization of Nations

This text presents a working definition of *globalization* as "the increasing interdependence of citizens and nations across the world." But citizens and nations differ in their degree of global interdependence, and their interdependence can change over time. Axel Dreher at KOF, the Swiss Economic Institute, generated an annual Index of Globalization (scaled from 1 to 100) using *economic* data on investment flows and restrictions; *social* data on personal contact, information flows, and cultural factors; and *political* data on embassies and international obligations—24 variables in all. The KOF index scored 181 countries annually for 1970 to 2007. Here are 8 of the 181 countries; their 2007 rankings are in parentheses. Belgium and Myanmar anchored the top and bottom in 2007. Canada ranked considerably higher than the United States, which was 27th. The report states: "All in all, globalization in the USA has stagnated since the end of the 1990s. Similar to most other industrialised countries, social globalization in the USA has remained unchanged for several years now. This is also true for political globalization which was rising until 1993 and has stagnated since." In contrast, note the impressive increases by Russia (not scored prior to 1990), China, and India, which are playing ever larger roles in the world.

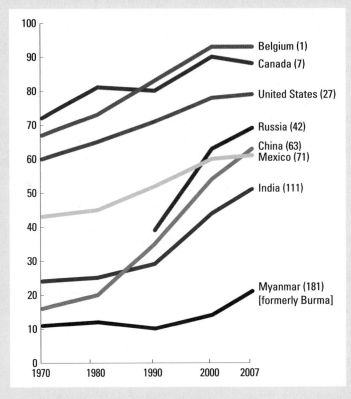

Source: KOF Swiss Economic Institute, KOF Index of Globalization 2010 Press Release; Axel Dreher, "Does Globalization Affect Growth? Evidence from a New Index of Globalization," *Applied Economics* 38 (2006): 1091–1110, updated 22 January 2010, both available at http://globalization. kof.ethz.ch.

on personal freedom, no government has as a goal the maximization of personal freedom. Governments exist to control; *to govern* means "to control." Why do people surrender their freedom to this control? To obtain the benefits of government. Throughout history, government has served two major purposes: maintaining order (preserving life and protecting property) and providing public goods. More recently, some governments have pursued a third purpose, promoting equality, which is more controversial.

Maintaining Order

Maintaining order is the oldest objective of government. **Order** in this context is rich with meaning. Let's start with "law and order." Maintaining order in this sense means establishing the rule of law to preserve life and protect property. To the seventeenth-century English philosopher Thomas Hobbes (1588–1679), preserving life was the most important function of government. In his classic philosophical treatise, *Leviathan* (1651), Hobbes described life without government as life in a "state of nature." Without rules, people would live as predators do, stealing and killing for their personal benefit. In Hobbes's classic phrase, life in a state of nature would be "solitary, poor, nasty, brutish, and short." He believed that a single ruler, or sovereign, must possess unquestioned authority to guarantee the safety of the weak and protect them from the attacks of the strong. Hobbes named his all-powerful government "Leviathan," after a biblical sea monster. He believed that complete obedience to Leviathan's strict laws was a small price to pay for the security of living in a civil society.

Most of us can only imagine what a state of nature would be like. But in some parts of the world, whole nations have experienced lawlessness. That has been the situation in Somalia since 1991, when the government was toppled and warlords feuded over territory. Today, the government controls only a portion of the capital, Mogadishu, and Somali pirates seize ships off its shore with impunity.[29] Throughout history, authoritarian rulers have used people's fear of civil disorder to justify taking power. Ironically, the ruling group itself—whether monarchy, aristocracy, or political party—then became known as the *established order.*

Hobbes's conception of life in the cruel state of nature led him to view government primarily as a means of guaranteeing people's survival. Other theorists, taking survival for granted, believed that government protects order by preserving private property (goods and land owned by individuals). Foremost among them was John Locke (1632–1704), an English philosopher. In *Two Treatises on Government* (1690), he wrote that the protection of life, liberty, and property was the basic objective of government. His thinking strongly influenced the Declaration of Independence; it is reflected in the Declaration's famous phrase identifying "Life, Liberty, and the Pursuit of Happiness" as "unalienable Rights" of citizens under government. Locke's defense of property rights became linked with safeguards for individual liberties in the doctrine of **liberalism**, which holds that the state should leave citizens free to further their individual pursuits.[30]

order
Established ways of social behavior. Maintaining order is the oldest purpose of government.

liberalism
The belief that states should leave individuals free to follow their individual pursuits. Note that this differs from the definition of *liberal* later in this chapter.

Not everyone believes that the protection of private property is a valid objective of government. The German philosopher Karl Marx (1818–1883) rejected the private ownership of property used in the production of goods or services. Marx's ideas form the basis of **communism**, a complex theory that gives ownership of all land and productive facilities to the people—in effect, to the government. In line with communist theory, the 1977 constitution of the former Soviet Union declared that the nation's land, minerals, waters, and forests "are the exclusive property of the state." Years after the Soviet Union collapsed, Russia remains deeply split over abandoning the old communist-era policies to permit the private ownership of land. Even today's market-oriented China still clings to the principle that all land belongs to the state, and not until 2007 did it pass a law that protected private homes and businesses.[31]

communism
A political system in which, in theory, ownership of all land and productive facilities is in the hands of the people, and all goods are equally shared. The production and distribution of goods are controlled by an authoritarian government.

public goods
Benefits and services, such as parks and sanitation, that benefit all citizens but are not likely to be produced voluntarily by individuals.

Providing Public Goods

After governments have established basic order, they can pursue other ends. Using their coercive powers, they can tax citizens to raise money to spend on **public goods**, which are benefits and services available to everyone, such as education, sanitation, and parks. Public goods benefit all citizens but are not likely to be produced by the voluntary acts of individuals. The government of ancient Rome, for example, built aqueducts to carry fresh water from the mountains to the city. Road building was another public good provided by the Roman government, which also used the roads to move its legions and protect the established order.

Government action to provide public goods can be controversial. During President James Monroe's administration (1817–1825), many people thought that building the Cumberland Road (between Cumberland, Maryland, and Wheeling, West Virginia) was not a proper function of the national government, the Romans notwithstanding. Over time, the scope of government functions in the United States has expanded. During President Dwight Eisenhower's administration in the 1950s, the federal government outdid the Romans' noble road building. Although a Republican opposed to big government, Eisenhower launched the massive interstate highway system, at a cost of $27 billion (in 1950s dollars). Yet some government enterprises that have been common in other countries—running railroads, operating coal mines, generating electric power—are politically controversial or even unacceptable in the United States. Hence, many people objected when the Bush administration took over General Motors and Chrysler in 2008 to facilitate an orderly bankruptcy. People disagree about how far the government ought to go in using its power to tax to provide public goods and services and how much of that realm should be handled by private business for profit.

Promoting Equality

The promotion of equality has not always been a major objective of government. It gained prominence only in the twentieth century, in the aftermath of industrialization and urbanization. Confronted by the paradox of poverty amid plenty, some political leaders in European nations pioneered extensive government programs to improve life for the poor. Under the emerging concept of the welfare state, government's role expanded to provide individuals with medical care, education, and a guaranteed income "from cradle to grave." Sweden, Britain, and other nations adopted welfare programs aimed at reducing social inequalities. This relatively new purpose of government has been by far the most controversial. People often oppose taxation for public goods (building roads and schools, for example) because of cost alone. They oppose more strongly taxation for government programs to promote economic and social equality on principle.

The key issue here is government's role in redistributing income, that is, taking from the wealthy to give to the poor. Charity (voluntary giving to the poor) has a strong basis in Western religious traditions; using the power of the state to support the poor does not. (In his 1838 novel, *Oliver Twist,* Charles Dickens dramatized how government power was used to imprison the poor, not to support them.) Using the state to redistribute income was originally a radical idea, set forth by Karl Marx as the ultimate principle of developed

Rosa Parks: She Sat for Equality

Rosa Parks had just finished a day's work as a seamstress and was sitting in the front of a bus in Montgomery, Alabama, going home. A white man claimed her seat, which he could do according to the law in December 1955. When she refused to move and was arrested, outraged blacks, led by Dr. Martin Luther King, Jr., began a boycott of the Montgomery bus company. Rosa Parks died in 2005 at age ninety-two and was accorded the honor of lying in state in the Capitol rotunda, the first woman to receive that tribute.

(Gene Herrick/AP Photo)

IDEALOG.ORG

How do you feel about government programs that reduce income differences between rich and poor? Take IDEAlog's self-test.

communism: "from each according to his ability, to each according to his needs."[32] This extreme has never been realized in any government, not even in communist states. But over time, taking from the rich to help the needy has become a legitimate function of most governments.

That function is not without controversy. Especially since the Great Depression of the 1930s, the government's role in redistributing income to promote economic equality has been a major source of policy debate in the United States. In 2007, for example, Congress increased the minimum wage for workers paid on an hourly basis from $5.15 per hour (set in 1997) to $7.25. Despite inflation, the minimum wage had been frozen for ten years, and the increase passed only because Democrats included it in a deal on funding the Iraq war.

Government can also promote social equality through policies that do not redistribute income. For example, in 2000, Vermont passed a law allowing persons of the same sex to enter a "civil union" granting access to similar benefits enjoyed by persons of different sexes through marriage. By 2010, the legislatures or courts in Connecticut, Iowa, Massachusetts, and New Hampshire put similar laws into effect. In this instance, laws advancing social equality may clash with different social values held by other citizens. Indeed, 31 states blocked same-sex marriages through public referenda.[33]

A Conceptual Framework for Analyzing Government

Citizens have very different views of how vigorously they want government to maintain order, provide public goods, and promote equality. Of the three objectives, providing for public goods usually is less controversial than maintaining order or promoting equality. After all, government spending for highways, schools, and parks carries benefits for nearly every citizen. Moreover, services merely cost money. The cost of maintaining order and promoting equality is greater than money; it usually means a trade-off in basic values.

To understand government and the political process, you must be able to recognize these trade-offs and identify the basic values they entail. Just as people sit back from a wide-screen motion picture to gain perspective, to understand American government you need to take a broad view—a view much broader than that offered by examining specific political events. You need to use political concepts.

A concept is a generalized idea of a set of items or thoughts. It groups various events, objects, or qualities under a common classification or label. The framework that guides this book consists of five concepts that figure prominently in political analysis. We regard the five concepts as especially important to a broad understanding of American politics, and we use them repeatedly throughout this book. This framework will help you evaluate political events long after you have read this text.

The five concepts that we emphasize deal with the fundamental issues of what government tries to do and how it decides to do it. The concepts that relate to what government tries to do are *order, freedom,* and *equality.* All governments by definition value order; maintaining order is part of the meaning of government. Most governments at least claim to preserve individual freedom while they maintain order, although they vary widely in the extent to which they succeed. Few governments even profess to guarantee equality, and governments differ greatly in policies that pit equality against freedom. Our conceptual framework should help you evaluate the extent to which the United States pursues all three values through its government.

How government chooses the proper mix of order, freedom, and equality in its policymaking has to do with the process of choice. We evaluate the American governmental process using two models of democratic government: *majoritarian* and *pluralist.* Many governments profess to be democracies. Whether they are or are not depends on their (and our) meaning of the term. Even countries that Americans agree are democracies—for example, the United States and Britain—differ substantially in the type of democracy they practice. We can use our conceptual models of democratic government both to classify the type of democracy practiced in the United States and to evaluate the government's success in fulfilling that model.

The five concepts can be organized into two groups:

- Concepts that identify the values pursued by government:
  Freedom
  Order
  Equality
- Concepts that describe models of democratic government:
  Majoritarian democracy
  Pluralist democracy

The rest of this chapter examines freedom, order, and equality as conflicting values pursued by government. Chapter 2 discusses majoritarian democracy and pluralist democracy as alternative institutional models for implementing democratic government.

The Concepts of Freedom, Order, and Equality

These three terms—*freedom, order,* and *equality*—have a range of connotations in American politics. Both *freedom* and *equality* are positive terms that politicians have learned to use to their own advantage. Consequently, freedom and equality mean different things to different people at different times, depending on the political context in which they are used. *Order,* in contrast, has negative connotations for many people because it symbolizes government intrusion into private lives. Except during periods of social strife or external threat (for example, after September 11), few politicians in Western democracies openly call for more order. Because all governments infringe on freedom, we examine that concept first.

Freedom

Freedom can be used in two major senses: freedom of and freedom from. President Franklin Delano Roosevelt used the word in both senses in a speech he made shortly before the United States entered World War II. He described four freedoms: freedom of religion, freedom of speech, freedom from fear, and freedom from want. The noted illustrator Norman Rockwell gave Americans a vision of these freedoms in a classic set of paintings published in the *Saturday Evening Post* and subsequently issued as posters to sell war bonds (see the feature "The Four Freedoms").

freedom of
An absence of constraints on behavior, as in *freedom of speech* or *freedom of religion.*

Freedom of is the absence of constraints on behavior; it means freedom *to* do something. In this sense, *freedom* is synonymous with *liberty.*[34] Two of Rockwell's paintings, *Freedom of Worship* and *Freedom of Speech,* exemplify this type of freedom. Freedom of religion, speech, press, and assembly (collectively called "civil liberties") are discussed in Chapter 15.

freedom from
Immunity, as in *freedom from want.*

Freedom from is the message of the other paintings, *Freedom from Fear* and *Freedom from Want.*[35] Here freedom suggests immunity from fear and want. In the modern political context, *freedom from* often symbolizes the fight against exploitation and oppression. The cry of the civil rights movement in the 1960s—"Freedom Now!"—conveyed this meaning. This sense of freedom corresponds to the "civil rights" discussed in Chapter 16. If you recognize that freedom in this sense means immunity from discrimination, you can see that it comes close to the concept of equality.[36] In this book, we avoid using *freedom* to mean "freedom from"; for this sense, we simply use *equality*. When we use *freedom,* we mean "freedom of."

Order

When *order* is viewed in the narrow sense of preserving life and protecting property, most citizens concede the importance of maintaining order and thereby grant the need for government. For example, "domestic Tranquility" (order) is cited in the preamble to the Constitution. However, when *order* is viewed in the broader sense of preserving the social order, some people argue that maintaining order is not a legitimate function of government (see "Compared with What? The Importance of Order and Freedom in Other Nations"). *Social order* refers to established patterns of authority in society and traditional modes of behavior. It is the accepted way of doing things. The prevailing social order prescribes behavior in many different areas: how students should dress in school (neatly, no purple hair) and behave toward their teachers (respectfully); who is allowed to marry (single adults of opposite sexes); what the press should not publish (sexually explicit photographs); and what the proper attitude toward religion and country should be (reverential). It is important to remember that the social order can change. Today, perfectly respectable men and women wear bathing suits that would have caused a scandal a century ago.

A government can protect the established order by using its **police power**—its authority to safeguard residents' safety, health, welfare, and morals. The extent to which government should use this authority is a topic of ongoing debate in the United States and is constantly being redefined by the courts. In the 1980s, many states used their police powers to pass legislation that banned smoking in public places. In the 1990s, a hot issue was whether government should control the dissemination of pornography on the Internet. After September 11, 2001, new laws were passed increasing government's power to investigate suspicious activities by foreign nationals in order to deter terrorism. After the underwear bomber was thwarted from blowing up an airliner on Christmas Day 2009, airports began using full-body scanners to probe through clothing. Despite their desire to be safe from further attacks, some citizens feared the erosion of their civil liberties. Living in a police state—a government that uses its power to regulate nearly all aspects of behavior—might maximize safety, but at a considerable loss of personal freedom.

Most governments are inherently conservative; they tend to resist social change. But some governments aim to restructure the social order. Social change is most dramatic when a government is overthrown through force and replaced. This can occur through an internal revolution or a "regime

police power
The authority of a government to maintain order and safeguard citizens' health, morals, safety, and welfare.

Feature Story

The Four Freedoms

Norman Rockwell became famous in the 1940s for the humorous, homespun covers he painted for the *Saturday Evening Post*, a weekly magazine. Inspired by an address to Congress in which President Roosevelt outlined his goals for world civilization, Rockwell painted *The Four Freedoms*, which were reproduced in the *Post* during February and March 1943. Their immense popularity led the government to print posters of the illustrations for the Treasury Department's war bond drive.

The Office of War Information also reproduced *The Four Freedoms* and circulated the posters in schools, clubhouses, railroad stations, post offices, and other public buildings. Officials even had copies circulated on the European front to remind soldiers of the liberties for which they were fighting. It is said that no other paintings in the world have ever been reproduced or circulated in such vast numbers as *The Four Freedoms*.

(Norman Rockwell/CORBIS)

(Norman Rockwell/CORBIS)

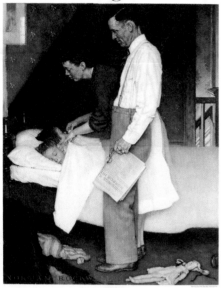

(Norman Rockwell/CORBIS)

(Norman Rockwell/CORBIS)

change" effected externally. Societies can also work to change social patterns more gradually through the legal process. Our use of the term *order* in this book encompasses all three aspects: preserving life, protecting property, and maintaining traditional patterns of social relationships.

Equality

As with *freedom* and *order, equality* is used in different senses to support different causes. **Political equality** in elections is easy to define: each citizen has one and only one vote. This basic concept is central democratic theory, a subject explored at length in Chapter 2. But when some people advocate political equality, they mean more than one person, one vote. These people contend that an urban ghetto dweller and the chairman of the board of Microsoft are not politically equal despite the fact that each has one vote. Through occupation or wealth, some citizens are more able than others to influence political decisions. For example, wealthy citizens can exert influence by advertising in the mass media or by contacting friends in high places. Lacking great wealth and political connections, most citizens do not have such influence. Thus, some analysts argue that equality in wealth, education, and status—that is, **social equality**—is necessary for true political equality.

political equality
Equality in political decision making: one vote per person, with all votes counted equally.

social equality
Equality in wealth, education, and status.

Compared with What?

The Importance of Order and Freedom in Other Nations

Compared with citizens in twenty-nine other nations, Americans do not value order very much. The World Values Survey asked respondents to select which of four national goals was "very important":

- Maintaining order in the nation
- Giving people more say in important government decisions
- Fighting rising prices
- Protecting freedom of speech

The United States ranked twenty-eighth in the list of those selecting "maintaining order" as very important. While American citizens do not value government control of social behavior as much as others, they do value freedom of speech more highly. Citizens in only three countries favor protecting freedom of speech more than citizens in the United States.

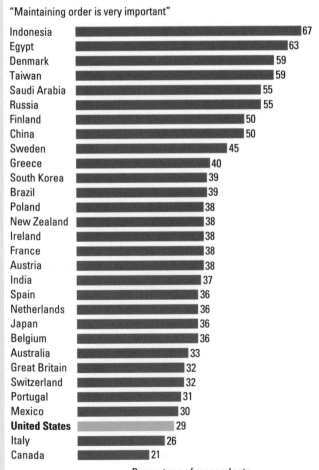

"Maintaining order is very important"

Country	Value
Indonesia	67
Egypt	63
Denmark	59
Taiwan	59
Saudi Arabia	55
Russia	55
Finland	50
China	50
Sweden	45
Greece	40
South Korea	39
Brazil	39
Poland	38
New Zealand	38
Ireland	38
France	38
Austria	38
India	37
Spain	36
Netherlands	36
Japan	36
Belgium	36
Australia	33
Great Britain	32
Switzerland	32
Portugal	31
Mexico	30
United States	29
Italy	26
Canada	21

Percentage of respondents who value "order"

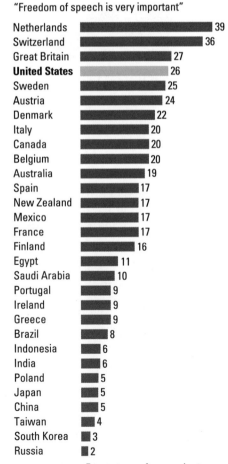

"Freedom of speech is very important"

Country	Value
Netherlands	39
Switzerland	36
Great Britain	27
United States	26
Sweden	25
Austria	24
Denmark	22
Italy	20
Canada	20
Belgium	20
Australia	19
Spain	17
New Zealand	17
Mexico	17
France	17
Finland	16
Egypt	11
Saudi Arabia	10
Portugal	9
Ireland	9
Greece	9
Brazil	8
Indonesia	6
India	6
Poland	5
Japan	5
China	5
Taiwan	4
South Korea	3
Russia	2

Percentage of respondents who value "freedom"

Source: These are combined data from the 1999–2001 and 2005–2007 waves of the World Values Survey. See Ronald Inglehart, "Materialist/Postmaterialist Priorities Among Publics Around the World" (discussion paper presented at the Institute of Social Research (ISR), University of Michigan, 14 February 2008).

Equality in the Military

While they still have a long way to go, women are being treated more equally in the military. Although they are not allowed in units engaged in direct combat, women nevertheless often find themselves in other combat situations and consequently risk being killed. As of February 2009, 102 women in the U.S. military had been killed by hostile fire in Iraq. That's more than twice as many women killed in the military from the end of World War II to the start of the Iraq war.

Source: Hannah Fischer, "United States Military Casualty Statistics: Operation Iraqi Freedom and Operation Enduring Freedom," Congressional Research Service, 7-5700, RS22452, March 25, 2009. *Photo*: Scott Olson/Getty Images News/Getty Images.

There are two routes to promoting social equality: providing equal opportunities and ensuring equal outcomes. **Equality of opportunity** means that each person has the same chance to succeed in life. This idea is deeply ingrained in American culture. The U.S. Constitution prohibits titles of nobility and does not make owning property a requirement for holding public office. Public schools and libraries are open to all. For many people, the concept of social equality is satisfied by offering equal opportunities for advancement; it is not essential that people actually end up being equal. For others, true social equality means nothing less than **equality of outcome**.[37] President Lyndon B. Johnson expressed this view in 1965: "It is not enough just to open the gates of opportunity.... We seek ... not just equality as a right and a theory but equality as a fact and equality as a result."[38] According to this outlook, it is not enough that governments provide people with equal opportunities; they must also design policies that redistribute wealth and status so that economic and social equality are actually achieved. In education, equality of outcome has led to federal laws that require comparable funding for men's and women's college sports. In business, equality of outcome has led to certain affirmative action programs to increase minority hiring and to the active recruitment of women, blacks, and Latinos to fill jobs. Equality of outcome has also produced federal laws that require employers to pay men and women equally for equal work. In recent years, the very concept of affirmative action has come under scrutiny. In 2003, however, the U.S. Supreme Court supported affirmative action in the form of preferential treatment to minorities in college admissions.

equality of opportunity
The idea that each person is guaranteed the same chance to succeed in life.

equality of outcome
The concept that society must ensure that people are equal, and governments must design policies to redistribute wealth and status so that economic and social equality is actually achieved.

Some link equality of outcome with the concept of government-supported **rights**—the idea that every citizen is entitled to certain benefits of government—that government should guarantee its citizens adequate (if not equal) housing, employment, medical care, and income as a matter of right. If citizens are entitled to government benefits as a matter of right, government efforts to promote equality of outcome become legitimized.

Clearly, the concept of equality of outcome is quite different from that of equality of opportunity, and it requires a much greater degree of government activity. It also clashes more directly with the concept of freedom. By taking from one to give to another, which is necessary for the redistribution of income and status, the government clearly creates winners and losers. The winners may believe that justice has been served by the redistribution. The losers often feel strongly that their freedom to enjoy their income and status has suffered.

Two Dilemmas of Government

The two major dilemmas facing American government early in the twenty-first century stem from the oldest and the newest objectives of government: maintaining order and promoting equality. Both order and equality are important social values, but government cannot pursue either without sacrificing a third important value: individual freedom. The clash between freedom and order forms the original dilemma of government; the clash between freedom and equality forms the modern dilemma of government. Although the dilemmas are different, each involves trading some amount of freedom for another value.

The Original Dilemma: Freedom Versus Order

The conflict between freedom and order originates in the very meaning of government as the legitimate use of force to control human behavior. How much freedom must a citizen surrender to government? The dilemma has occupied philosophers for hundreds of years. In the eighteenth century, the French philosopher Jean Jacques Rousseau (1712–1778) wrote that the problem of devising a proper government "is to find a form of association which will defend and protect with the whole common force the person and goods of each associate, and in which each, while uniting himself with all, may still obey himself alone, and remain free as before."[39]

The original purpose of government was to protect life and property, to make citizens safe from violence. How well is the American government doing today in providing law and order to its citizens? More than 66 percent of the respondents in a 2009 national survey said that they were "afraid to walk alone at night" in areas within a mile of their home.[40] Simply put, Americans view violent crime (which actually has decreased in recent years[41]) as a critical issue and do not believe that their government adequately protects them.

Contrast the fear of crime in urban America with the sense of personal safety while walking in Moscow, Warsaw, or Prague when the old communist

rights
The benefits of government to which every citizen is entitled.

governments still ruled in Eastern Europe. It was common to see old and young strolling late at night along the streets and in the parks of these cities. The old communist regimes gave their police great powers to control guns, monitor citizens' movements, and arrest and imprison suspicious people, which enabled them to do a better job of maintaining order. Police and party agents routinely kept their citizens under surveillance—eavesdropping on phone conversations, opening mail from abroad—to ensure that they were not communicating privately with the capitalist world outside official channels. Communist governments deliberately chose order over freedom. With the collapse of communism came the end of strict social order. Respondents in a 2009 survey in nine former communist countries in Eastern Europe said that crime and illegal drugs were among their top national problems.[42]

The crisis over acquired immune deficiency syndrome (AIDS) adds a new twist to the dilemma of freedom versus order. Some health officials believe that AIDS, for which there is no known cure, is the greatest medical threat in the history of the United States. By 2007, more than 1.1 million cases of AIDS had been reported to the Centers for Disease Control, and more than 550,000 of these people died.[43]

To combat the spread of the disease in the military, the Department of Defense began testing all applicants for the AIDS virus in the mid-1980s. Other government agencies have begun testing current employees, and some officials are calling for widespread mandatory testing within the private sector as well. Such programs are strongly opposed by those who believe they violate individual freedom. But those who are more afraid of the spread of AIDS than of an infringement on individual rights support aggressive government action to combat the disease.

The conflict between the values of freedom and order represents the original dilemma of government. In the abstract, people value both freedom and order; in real life, the two values inherently conflict. By definition, any policy that strengthens one value takes away from the other. The balance of freedom and order is an issue in enduring debates (whether to allow capital punishment) and contemporary challenges (whether to prohibit links to controversial YouTube videos on MySpace sites). And in a democracy, policy choices hinge on how much citizens value freedom and how much they value order.

The Modern Dilemma: Freedom Versus Equality

Popular opinion has it that freedom and equality go hand in hand. In reality, the two values usually clash when governments enact policies to promote social equality. Because social equality is a relatively recent government objective, deciding between policies that promote equality at the expense of freedom, and vice versa, is the modern dilemma of politics. Consider these examples:

During the 1960s, Congress (through the Equal Pay Act) required employers to pay women and men the same rate for equal work. This legislation means that some employers are forced to pay women more than they would if their compensation policies were based on their free choice.

During the 1970s, the courts ordered the busing of schoolchildren to achieve a fair distribution of blacks and whites in public schools. This action was motivated by concern for educational equality, but it also impaired freedom of choice.

During the 1980s, some states passed legislation that went beyond the idea of equal pay for equal work to the more radical notion of pay equity—that is, equal pay for comparable work. Women had to be paid at a rate equal to men's even if they had different jobs, providing the women's jobs were of "comparable worth." For example, if the skills and responsibilities of a female nurse were found to be comparable to those of a male laboratory technician in the same hospital, the woman's salary and the man's salary would have to be the same.

During the 1990s, Congress prohibited discrimination in employment, public services, and public accommodations on the basis of physical or mental disabilities. Under the 1990 Americans with Disabilities Act, businesses with twenty-five or more employees cannot pass over an otherwise qualified disabled person in employment or promotion, and new buses and trains have to be made accessible to them.

During the first decade of the 2000s, Congress passed the Genetic Information Nondiscrimination Act (GINA). Signed by President Bush in 2008, it prohibited companies from discriminating in hiring based on an individual's genetic tests, genetic tests of a family member, and family medical history.

These examples illustrate the challenge of using government power to promote equality. The clash between freedom and order is obvious, but the clash between freedom and equality is more subtle. Americans, who think of freedom and equality as complementary rather than conflicting values, often do not notice the clash. When forced to choose between the two, however, Americans are far more likely to choose freedom over equality than are people in other countries.

The conflicts among freedom, order, and equality explain a great deal of the political conflict in the United States. These conflicts also underlie the ideologies that people use to structure their understanding of politics.

Ideology and the Scope of Government

People hold different opinions about the merits of government policies. Sometimes their views are based on self-interest. For example, senior citizens favor discounts when riding public transportation. Policies also are judged according to individual values and beliefs. Some people hold assorted values and beliefs that produce contradictory opinions on government policies. Others organize their opinions into a **political ideology**—a consistent set of values and beliefs about the proper purpose and scope of government.

How far should government go to maintain order, provide public goods, and promote equality? In the United States (as in every other nation), citizens, scholars, and politicians have different answers. We can analyze their

political ideology
A consistent set of values and beliefs about the proper purpose and scope of government.

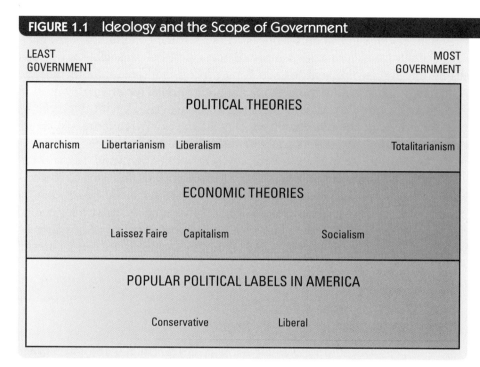

FIGURE 1.1   Ideology and the Scope of Government

LEAST
GOVERNMENT

MOST
GOVERNMENT

POLITICAL THEORIES

Anarchism   Libertarianism   Liberalism   Totalitarianism

ECONOMIC THEORIES

Laissez Faire   Capitalism   Socialism

POPULAR POLITICAL LABELS IN AMERICA

Conservative   Liberal

We can classify political ideologies according to the scope of action that people are willing to allow government in dealing with social and economic problems. In this chart, the three rows map out various philosophical positions along an underlying continuum ranging from least to most government. Notice that conventional politics in the United States spans only a narrow portion of the theoretical possibilities for government action. In popular usage, liberals favor a greater scope of government, and conservatives want a narrower scope. But over time, the traditional distinction has eroded and now oversimplifies the differences between liberals and conservatives. Figure 1.2 offers a more discriminating classification of liberals and conservatives.

positions by referring to philosophies about the proper scope of government—that is, the range of its permissible activities. Imagine a continuum. At one end is the belief that government should do everything; at the other is the belief that government should not exist. These extreme ideologies, from the most government to the least government, and those that fall in between are shown in Figure 1.1.

Totalitarianism

Totalitarianism is the belief that government should have unlimited power. A totalitarian government controls all sectors of society: business, labor, education, religion, sports, the arts. A true totalitarian favors a network of laws, rules, and regulations that guides every aspect of individual behavior. The object is to produce a perfect society serving some master plan for "the common good." Totalitarianism has reached its terrifying full potential only in literature and films (for example, in George Orwell's *1984,* a novel about "Big Brother" watching everyone), but several societies have come perilously close to "perfection." Think of Germany under Hitler and the Soviet Union under Stalin. Not many people openly profess totalitarianism today, but the concept is useful because it anchors one side of our continuum.

Socialism

Whereas totalitarianism refers to government in general, **socialism** pertains to government's role in the economy. Like communism, socialism is an economic system based on Marxist theory. Under socialism (and communism),

totalitarianism
A political philosophy that advocates unlimited power for the government to enable it to control all sectors of society.

socialism
A form of rule in which the central government plays a strong role in regulating existing private industry and directing the economy, although it does allow some private ownership of productive capacity.

the scope of government extends to ownership or control of the basic industries that produce goods and services. These include communications, mining, heavy industry, transportation, and energy. Although socialism favors a strong role for government in regulating private industry and directing the economy, it allows more room than communism does for private ownership of productive capacity. Many Americans equate socialism with the communism practiced in the old closed societies of the Soviet Union and Eastern Europe. But there is a difference. Although communism in theory was supposed to result in what Marx referred to as a "withering away" of the state, communist governments in practice tended toward totalitarianism, controlling not just economic life but also both political and social life through a dominant party organization. Some socialist governments, however, practice **democratic socialism.** They guarantee civil liberties (such as freedom of speech and freedom of religion) and allow their citizens to determine the extent of the government's activity through free elections and competitive political parties. Outside the United States, socialism is not universally viewed as inherently bad. In fact, the governments of Britain, Sweden, Germany, and France, among other democracies, have at times since World War II been avowedly socialist. More recently, the formerly communist regimes of Eastern Europe have abandoned the controlling role of government in their economies for strong doses of capitalism.

Capitalism

Capitalism also relates to the government's role in the economy. In contrast to both socialism and communism, **capitalism** supports free enterprise—private businesses operating without government regulation. Some theorists, most notably the late Nobel Prize–winning economist Milton Friedman, argue that free enterprise is necessary for free politics.[44] This argument, that the economic system of capitalism is essential to democracy, contradicts the tenets of democratic socialism. Whether it is valid depends in part on our understanding of democracy, a subject discussed in Chapter 2. The United States is decidedly a capitalist country, more so than Britain or most other Western nations. Despite the U.S. government's enormous budget, it owns or operates relatively few public enterprises. For example, railroads, airlines, and television stations, which are frequently owned by the government in other countries, are privately owned in the United States. But our government does extend its authority into the economic sphere, regulating private businesses and directing the overall economy. Both American liberals and conservatives embrace capitalism, but they differ on the nature and amount of government intervention in the economy they deem necessary or desirable.

Libertarianism

Libertarianism opposes all government action except what is necessary to protect life and property. **Libertarians** grudgingly recognize the necessity of government but believe that it should be as limited as possible and should

democratic socialism
A socialist form of government that guarantees civil liberties such as freedom of speech and religion. Citizens determine the extent of government activity through free elections and competitive political parties.

capitalism
The system of government that favors free enterprise (privately owned businesses operating without government regulation).

libertarianism
A political ideology that is opposed to all government action except as necessary to protect life and property.

libertarians
Those who are opposed to using government to promote either order or equality.

not promote either order or equality. For example, libertarians grant the need for traffic laws to ensure safe and efficient automobile travel. But they oppose laws requiring motorcycle riders to wear helmets, and the libertarian ethos in New Hampshire keeps it the only state not requiring seat belts. Libertarians believe that social programs that provide food, clothing, and shelter are outside the proper scope of government. Helping the needy, they insist, should be a matter of individual choice. Libertarians also oppose government ownership of basic industries; in fact, they oppose any government intervention in the economy. This kind of economic policy is called **laissez faire**, a French phrase that means "let (people) do (as they please)." Such an extreme policy extends beyond the free enterprise that most capitalists advocate.

Libertarians are vocal advocates of hands-off government in both the social and the economic spheres. Whereas Americans who favor a broad scope of government action shun the description *socialist,* libertarians make no secret of their identity. The Libertarian Party ran candidates in every presidential election from 1972 through 2008. However, not one of these candidates won more than 1 million votes.

Do not confuse libertarians with liberals—or with liberalism, the John Locke–inspired doctrine mentioned earlier. The words are similar, but their meanings are quite different. *Libertarianism* draws on *liberty* as its root (following Locke) and means "absence of governmental constraint." While both liberalism and libertarianism leave citizens free to pursue their private goals, libertarianism treats freedom as a pure goal; it's liberalism on steroids. In American political usage, *liberalism* evolved from the root word *liberal* in the sense of "freely," like a liberal serving of butter. Liberals see a positive role for government in helping the disadvantaged. Over time, *liberal* has come to mean something closer to *generous,* in the sense that liberals (but not libertarians) support government spending on social programs. Libertarians find little benefit in any government social program.

Anarchism

Anarchism stands opposite totalitarianism on the political continuum. Anarchists oppose all government in any form. As a political philosophy, anarchism values absolute freedom. Because all government involves some restriction on personal freedom (for example, forcing people to drive on one side of the road), a pure anarchist would object even to traffic laws. Like totalitarianism, anarchism is not a popular philosophy, but it does have adherents on the political fringes.

Anarchists sparked street fights that disrupted meetings of the World Trade Organization (WTO) from Seattle (1999) to Geneva (2009). Labor unions protested meetings of the WTO, which writes rules that govern international trade, for failing to include labor rights on its agenda; environmental groups protested its promotion of economic development at the expense of the environment. But anarchists were against the WTO on *principle*—for concentrating

laissez faire
An economic doctrine that opposes any form of government intervention in business.

anarchism
A political philosophy that opposes government in any form.

Anarchists in Pittsburgh

Anarchism as a philosophy views government as an unnecessary evil used by the wealthy to exploit everyone else. When the G-20 countries met in Pittsburgh during September 2009 to discuss the global financial crisis, self-described anarchists marched in protest but were kept miles from the summit meeting.

(Chris Hondros/Getty Images News/Getty Images)

the power of multinational corporations in a shadowy "world government." Discussing old and new forms of anarchy, journalist Joseph Kahn said, "Nothing has revived anarchism like globalization."[45] Although anarchism is not a popular philosophy, it is not merely a theoretical category.

Liberals and Conservatives: The Narrow Middle

As shown in Figure 1.1, practical politics in the United States ranges over only the central portion of the continuum. The extreme positions—totalitarianism and anarchism—are rarely argued in public debates. And in this era of distrust of "big government," few American politicians would openly advocate socialism. However, almost 130 people ran for Congress in 2008 as candidates of the Libertarian Party. Although none won, American libertarians are sufficiently vocal to be heard in the debate over the role of government.

Still, most of that debate is limited to a narrow range of political thought. On one side are people commonly called *liberals;* on the other are *conservatives.* In popular usage, liberals favor more government, conservatives less. This distinction is clear when the issue is government spending to provide public goods. Liberals favor generous government support for education, wildlife protection, public transportation, and a whole range of social programs. Conservatives want smaller government budgets and fewer government programs. They support free enterprise and argue against government job programs, regulation of business, and legislation of working conditions and wage rates.

But on other topics, liberals and conservatives reverse their positions. In theory, liberals favor government activism, yet they oppose government regulation of abortion. In theory, conservatives oppose government activism, yet they support government surveillance of telephone conversations to fight terrorism. What's going on? Are American political attitudes hopelessly contradictory, or is something missing in our analysis of these ideologies today? Actually something *is* missing. To understand the liberal and conservative stances on political issues, we must look not only at the scope of government action but also at the purpose of government action. That is, to understand a political ideology, it is necessary to understand how it incorporates the values of freedom, order, and equality.

American Political Ideologies and the Purpose of Government

Much of American politics revolves around the two dilemmas just described: freedom versus order and freedom versus equality. The two dilemmas do not account for all political conflict, but they help us gain insight into the workings of politics and organize the seemingly chaotic world of political events, actors, and issues.

Liberals Versus Conservatives: The New Differences

Liberals and conservatives *are* different, but their differences no longer hinge on the narrow question of the government's role in providing public goods. Liberals do favor more spending for public goods and conservatives less, but this is no longer the critical difference between them. Today that difference stems from their attitudes toward the purpose of government. **Conservatives** support the original purpose of government: maintaining social order. They are willing to use the coercive power of the state to force citizens to be orderly. They favor firm police action, swift and severe punishment for criminals, and more laws regulating behavior. Conservatives would not stop with defining, preventing, and punishing crime, however. They tend to want to preserve traditional patterns of social relations—the domestic role of women and business owners' authority to hire whom they wish, for example. For this reason, they do not think government should impose equality.

Liberals are less likely than conservatives to want to use government power to maintain order. In general, liberals are more tolerant of alternative lifestyles—for example, homosexual behavior. Liberals do not shy away from using government coercion, but they use it for a different purpose: to promote equality. They support laws that ensure equal treatment of homosexuals in employment, housing, and education; laws that force private businesses to hire and promote women and members of minority groups; laws that require

conservatives
Those who are willing to use government to promote order but not equality.

liberals
Those who are willing to use government to promote equality but not order.

public transportation to provide equal access to people with disabilities; and laws that order cities and states to reapportion election districts so that minority voters can elect minority candidates to public office. Conservatives do not oppose equality, but they do not value it to the extent of using the government's power to enforce equality. For liberals, the use of that power to promote equality is both valid and necessary.

A Two-Dimensional Classification of Ideologies

To classify liberal and conservative ideologies more accurately, we have to incorporate the values of freedom, order, and equality into the classification.[46] We can do this using the model in Figure 1.2. It depicts the conflicting

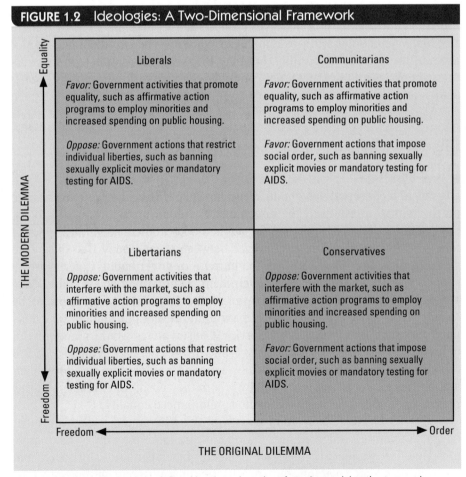

FIGURE 1.2   Ideologies: A Two-Dimensional Framework

Liberals

Favor: Government activities that promote equality, such as affirmative action programs to employ minorities and increased spending on public housing.

Oppose: Government actions that restrict individual liberties, such as banning sexually explicit movies or mandatory testing for AIDS.

Communitarians

Favor: Government activities that promote equality, such as affirmative action programs to employ minorities and increased spending on public housing.

Favor: Government actions that impose social order, such as banning sexually explicit movies or mandatory testing for AIDS.

Libertarians

Oppose: Government activities that interfere with the market, such as affirmative action programs to employ minorities and increased spending on public housing.

Oppose: Government actions that restrict individual liberties, such as banning sexually explicit movies or mandatory testing for AIDS.

Conservatives

Oppose: Government activities that interfere with the market, such as affirmative action programs to employ minorities and increased spending on public housing.

Favor: Government actions that impose social order, such as banning sexually explicit movies or mandatory testing for AIDS.

Equality — Freedom (THE MODERN DILEMMA)

Freedom ◄——————► Order

THE ORIGINAL DILEMMA

The four ideological types are defined by the values they favor in resolving the two major dilemmas of government: how much freedom should be sacrificed in pursuit of order and equality, respectively. Test yourself by thinking about the values that are most important to you. Which box in the figure best represents your combination of values?

values along two separate dimensions, each anchored in maximum freedom at the lower left. One dimension extends horizontally from maximum freedom on the left to maximum order on the right. The other extends vertically from maximum freedom at the bottom to maximum equality at the top. Each box represents a different ideological type: libertarians, liberals, conservatives, and communitarians.[47]

Libertarians value freedom more than order or equality. (We will use *libertarians* for people who have libertarian tendencies but may not accept the whole philosophy.) In practical terms, libertarians want minimal government intervention in both the economic and the social spheres. For example, they oppose affirmative action and laws that restrict transmission of sexually explicit material.

Liberals value freedom more than order but not more than equality. They oppose laws that ban sexually explicit publications but support affirmative action. Conservatives value freedom more than equality but would restrict freedom to preserve social order. Conservatives oppose affirmative action but favor laws that restrict pornography.

Finally, we arrive at the ideological type positioned at the upper right in Figure 1.2. This group values both equality and order more than freedom. Its members support both affirmative action and laws that restrict pornography. We will call this new group **communitarians**.[48] The term is used narrowly in contemporary politics to reflect the philosophy of the Communitarian Network, a political movement founded by sociologist Amitai Etzioni.[49] This movement rejects both the liberal–conservative classification and the libertarian argument that "individuals should be left on their own to pursue their choices, rights, and self-interests."[50] Like liberals, Etzioni's communitarians believe that there is a role for government in helping the disadvantaged. Like conservatives, they believe that government should be used to promote moral values—preserving the family through more stringent divorce laws, protecting against AIDS through testing programs, and limiting the dissemination of pornography, for example.[51]

The Communitarian Network is not dedicated to big government, however. According to its platform, "The government should step in only to the extent that other social subsystems fail rather than seek to replace them."[52] Nevertheless, in recognizing the collective nature of society, the network's platform clearly distinguishes its philosophy from that of libertarianism:

> It has been argued by libertarians that responsibilities are a personal matter, that individuals are to judge which responsibilities they accept as theirs. As we see it, responsibilities are anchored in community. Reflecting the diverse moral voices of their citizens, responsive communities define what is expected of people; they educate their members to accept these values; and they praise them when they do and frown upon them when they do not.[53]

Although it clearly embraces the Communitarian Network's philosophy, our definition of communitarian (small *c*) is broader and more in keeping with the dictionary definition. Thus, communitarians favor government

communitarians
Those who are willing to use government to promote both order and equality.

programs that promote both order and equality, somewhat in keeping with socialist theory.[54]

By analyzing political ideologies on two dimensions rather than one, we can explain why people can seem to be liberal on one issue (favoring a broader scope of government action) and conservative on another (favoring less government action). The answer hinges on the purpose of a given government action: Which value does it promote: order or equality?[55] According to our typology, only libertarians and communitarians are consistent in their attitude toward the scope of government activity, whatever its purpose. Libertarians value freedom so highly that they oppose most government efforts to enforce either order or equality. Communitarians (in our usage) are inclined to trade freedom for both order and equality. Liberals and conservatives, on the other hand, favor or oppose government activity depending on its purpose. As you will learn in Chapter 5, large groups of Americans fall into each of the four ideological categories. Because Americans increasingly choose four different resolutions to the original and modern dilemmas of government, the simple labels of *liberal* and *conservative* no longer describe contemporary political ideologies as well as they did in the 1930s, 1940s, and 1950s.

Summary

The challenge of democracy lies in making difficult choices—choices that inevitably bring important values into conflict. This chapter has outlined a normative framework for analyzing the policy choices that arise in the pursuit of the purposes of government.

The three major purposes of government are maintaining order, providing public goods, and promoting equality. In pursuing these objectives, every government infringes on individual freedom. But the degree of that infringement depends on the government's (and, by extension, its citizens') commitment to order and equality. What we have, then, are two dilemmas. The first—the original dilemma—centers on the conflict between freedom and order. The second—the modern dilemma—focuses on the conflict between freedom and equality.

Some people use political ideologies to help them resolve the conflicts that arise in political decision making. These ideologies define the scope and purpose of government. At opposite extremes of the continuum are totalitarianism, which supports government intervention in every aspect of society, and anarchism, which rejects government entirely. An important step back from totalitarianism is socialism. Democratic socialism, an economic system, favors government ownership of basic industries but preserves civil liberties. Capitalism, another economic system, promotes free enterprise. A significant step short of anarchism is libertarianism, which allows government to protect life and property but little else.

In the United States, the terms *liberal* and *conservative* are used to describe a narrow range toward the center of the political continuum. The usage is probably accurate when the scope of government action is being discussed. That is, liberals support a broader role for government than do conservatives.

But when both the scope and the purpose of government are considered, a different, sharper distinction emerges. Conservatives may want less government, but not at the price of less order. In other words, they are willing to use the coercive power of government to impose social order. Liberals too are willing to use the coercive power of government, but for a different purpose: promoting equality.

It is easier to understand the differences among libertarians, liberals, conservatives, and communitarians and their views on the scope of government if the values of freedom, order, and equality are incorporated into the description of their political ideologies. Libertarians choose freedom over both order and equality. Communitarians are willing to sacrifice freedom for both order and equality. Liberals value freedom more than order and equality more than freedom. Conservatives value order more than freedom and freedom more than equality.

The concepts of government objectives, values, and political ideologies appear repeatedly in this book as we determine who favors what government action and why. So far, we have said little about how government should make its decisions. In Chapter 2, we complete our normative framework for evaluating American politics by examining the nature of democratic theory. There, we introduce two key concepts for analyzing how democratic governments make decisions.

 CourseMate Visit www.cengagebrain.com/shop/ ISBN/0495906182 for flashcards, web quizzes, videos and more!

CHAPTER

2

Majoritarian or Pluralist Democracy?

AP Photo/Manuel Balce Ceneta

"I won."

That is what President Barack Obama said to congressional leaders gathered at the White House just three days after he was sworn into office.[1] The topics at hand were competing philosophies for repairing the American economy, which was in the throes of a deep recession marked by historically high unemployment: A total of 2.6 million jobs had been lost in 2008. Not only had the collapse of the real estate market and the broad economic downturn led to Obama's decisive victory over Republican John McCain a few months earlier, but also the Democrats made strong gains in the congressional elections and were in firm control of both the House and Senate. Republicans and Democrats were united on only one thing: something should be done to stimulate the economy and to prevent it from declining further.

The Republican leaders stood fast for their party's philosophy of small government and low taxes, recommending that the stimulus package emphasize tax cuts and tax incentives. As Republican House leader John Boehner put it, "Government can't solve this problem."[2] The Democrats had a different view. In their mind tax cuts would have to be massive to work, and that would require cutting government programs or adding commensurate tax increases back after the economy recovered (and tax increases are never popular). The Democrats supported direct government spending on public works like roads and bridges, thus putting some unemployed immediately to work. Along with infrastructure support, the plan included large payments to the states to help them avoid laying off employees since

state tax revenues cratered in the wake of the recession. A small tax cut for low- and middle-income workers was also part of the package.

Which philosophy is better? There is no conclusive answer among economists, but in a sense, that underlying question is academic; as Obama pointed out, he and the congressional Democrats won the election. Their philosophy would carry the day. When the House of Representatives voted on the stimulus plan, not a single Republican supported it while almost all the Democrats voted in favor. The Senate vote followed along party lines as well, with just three Republican senators crossing over to back the plan.[3]

On the surface it seemed like democracy had worked its will as the majority had spoken. Yet beneath the surface of the Democratic plan, another dynamic was at work. The overall package appropriated $787 billion to be spent to try to reverse the downward spiral of the recession. But as Congress was formulating the specifics of the spending plan, there was a vast array of choices as to exactly what the money would be spent on. Interest groups (organizations that advocate before government) lobbied Congress furiously for their own priorities. Business was especially active as different industries pushed legislators to support spending or create tax breaks that would help that particular industry. During the time Congress was developing the stimulus plan, a vice president of the National Association of Manufacturers said, "We see opportunity at every junction."[4] Interest groups went into high feeding-frenzy mode. Some got what they wanted; others were disappointed. Representatives and senators listened to the many voices from different parts of the American economy and then made their choices. The vote in 2008 faded into the background as legislators negotiated among themselves with an eye on which types of businesses and nonprofits in their districts or states would gain under alternative proposals.

These actions illustrate very different models of government. Should Congress follow the president, who won a majority of the vote, in interpreting his stimulus package as what the people want? Or is majority opinion a blunt and imprecise instrument, and should closer consideration be given to the rich and diverse constituencies that form our body politic? These questions bring us to the broader question: What is democratic government?

The Theory of Democratic Government

The origins of democratic theory lie in ancient Greek political thought. Greek philosophers classified governments according to the number of citizens involved in the process. Imagine a continuum running from rule by one person, through rule by a few, to rule by many.

At one extreme is an **autocracy,** in which one individual has the power to make all important decisions. The concentration of power in the hands of one person (usually a monarch) was a more common form of government in earlier historical periods, although some countries are still ruled autocratically. North Korea under Kim Jong-il is an example.

Oligarchy puts government power in the hands of an elite. At one time, the nobility or the major landowners commonly ruled as an aristocracy. Today, military leaders are often the rulers in countries governed by an oligarchy.

At the other extreme of the continuum is **democracy,** which means "rule by the people." Most scholars believe that the United States, Britain, France, and other countries in Western Europe are genuine democracies. Critics contend that these countries only appear to be democracies: although they hold free elections, they are actually run by wealthy business elites, out for their own benefit. Nevertheless, most people today agree that governments should be democratic.

The Meaning and Symbolism of Democracy

Americans have a simple answer to the question, "Who should govern?" It is "The people." Unfortunately, this answer is too simple. It fails to define who *the people* are. Should we include young children? Recent immigrants? Illegal aliens? This answer also fails to tell us how the people should do the governing. Should they be assembled in a stadium? Vote by mail? Choose others to govern for them? We need to take a closer look at what "government by the people" really means.

The word *democracy* originated in Greek writings around the fifth century B.C. *Demos* referred to the common people, the masses; *kratos* meant "power."

autocracy
A system of government in which the power to govern is concentrated in the hands of one individual.

oligarchy
A system of government in which power is concentrated in the hands of a few people.

democracy
A system of government in which, in theory, the people rule, either directly or indirectly.

The ancient Greeks were afraid of democracy—rule by rank-and-file citizens. That fear is evident in the term *demagogue*. We use that term today to refer to a politician who appeals to and often deceives the masses by manipulating their emotions and prejudices.

Many centuries after the Greeks defined democracy, the idea still carried the connotation of mob rule. When George Washington was president, opponents of a new political party disparagingly called it a *democratic* party. No one would do that in politics today. In fact, the term has become so popular that the names of more than 20 percent of the world's political parties contain some variation of the word *democracy*.[5] But although nearly all Americans in a 2004 survey (94 percent) regarded democracy as "the best form of government," less than 30 percent wanted the United States to promote democracy to other countries as a foreign policy goal (see Figure 2.1).[6] Americans reflexively support democracy as the best form of government but are less certain of what democracy entails or of alternative models of democracy.

There are two major schools of thought about what constitutes democracy. The first believes democracy is a form of government. It emphasizes the procedures that enable the people to govern: meeting to discuss issues, voting in elections, running for public office. The second sees democracy in the substance of government policies, in freedom of religion and the provision for human needs.[7] The procedural approach focuses on how decisions are made; the substantive approach is concerned with what government does.

FIGURE 2.1   Public Support for U.S. Policy of Promoting Democracy Abroad

Some presidents, such as Woodrow Wilson and George W. Bush, have made promoting democracy abroad a major foreign policy objective of their administrations. Americans, however, show some caution in this regard, with only about a quarter of respondents in a poll saying they believe it is "very important" for this country to help "bring a democracy form of government to other nations."

Source: PIPA/Knowledge Networks and Chicago Council on Foreign Relations Poll, "Americans on Democratization and U.S. Foreign Policy," 15–21 September 2005. Copyright © 2005 PIPA. Reproduced by permission.

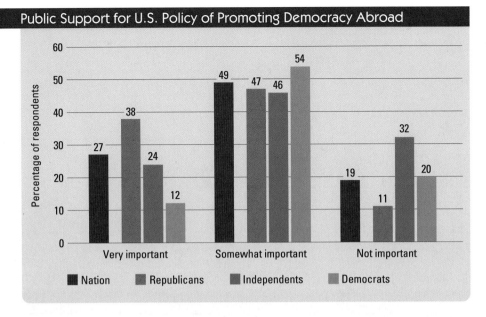

The Procedural View of Democracy

Procedural democratic theory sets forth principles that describe how government should make decisions. The principles address three distinct questions:

1. *Who* should participate in decision making?
2. *How much* should each participant's vote count?
3. *How many* votes are needed to reach a decision?

According to procedural democratic theory, all adults should participate in government decision making; everyone within the boundaries of the political community should be allowed to vote. If some people, such as recent immigrants, are prohibited from participating, they are excluded only for practical or political reasons. The theory of democracy itself does not exclude any adults from participation. We refer to this principle as **universal participation**.

How much should each participant's vote count? According to procedural theory, all votes should be counted *equally*. This is the principle of **political equality**.

Note that universal participation and political equality are two distinct principles. It is not enough for everyone to participate in a decision; all votes must carry equal weight. President Abraham Lincoln reportedly once took a vote among his cabinet members and found that they all opposed his position on an issue. He summarized the vote and the decision this way: "Seven noes, one aye—the ayes have it."[8] Everyone participated, but Lincoln's vote counted more than all the others combined. (No one ever said that presidents have to run their cabinets democratically.)

procedural democratic theory
A view of democracy as being embodied in a decision-making process that involves universal participation, political equality, majority rule, and responsiveness.

universal participation
The concept that everyone in a democracy should participate in governmental decision making.

political equality
Equality in political decision making: one vote per person, with all votes counted equally.

(© Jack Spratt/The Image Works)

Mopeds and Democracy

Some years ago on picturesque Block Island, off the state of Rhode Island, citizens were buzzed by summer vacationers riding rented mopeds. Denied by their state legislature the right to regulate moped rentals, the citizens voted in a town meeting to secede and join the neighboring state of Connecticut. The Rhode Island legislature grudgingly gave in to the rebellion and granted Block Island the right to restore peace, quiet, and public order.

Finally, how many votes are needed to reach a decision? Procedural theory prescribes that a group should decide to do what the majority of its participants (50 percent plus one person) wants to do. This principle is called **majority rule**. (If participants divide over more than two alternatives and none receives a simple majority, the principle usually defaults to *plurality rule*, under which the group does what most participants want.)

A Complication: Direct Versus Indirect Democracy

The three principles of universal participation, political equality, and majority rule are widely recognized as necessary for democratic decision making. Small, simple societies can meet these principles with a direct or **participatory democracy**, in which all members of the group, rather than representatives they elect to govern on their behalf, meet to make decisions, observing political equality and majority rule.[9] The origins of participatory democracy go back to the Greek city-state, where the important decisions of government were made by the adult citizens meeting in an assembly. The people ruled themselves rather than having a small number of notables rule on their behalf. (In Athens, the people who were permitted to attend the assemblies did not include women, slaves, and those whose families had not lived there for generations. Thus, participation was not

majority rule
The principle—basic to procedural democratic theory—that the decision of a group must reflect the preference of more than half of those participating; a simple majority.

participatory democracy
A system of government where rank-and-file citizens rule themselves rather than electing representatives to govern on their behalf.

universal. Still, the Greek city-state represented a dramatic transformation in the theory of government.)[10]

Something close to participatory democracy is practiced in some New England towns, where rank-and-file citizens gather in a town meeting, often just once a year, to make key community decisions together. A town meeting is impractical in large cities, although some cities have incorporated participatory democracy in their decision-making processes by instituting forms of neighborhood government. For example, in Birmingham, Alabama; Dayton, Ohio; Portland, Oregon; and St. Paul, Minnesota, each area of the city is governed by a neighborhood council. The neighborhood councils have authority over zoning and land use questions, and they usually control some funds for the development of projects within their boundaries. All adult residents of a neighborhood may participate in the neighborhood council meetings, and the larger city government respects their decisions.[11] In Chicago, the school system uses participatory democracy. Each school is primarily governed by a parents' council, not by the citywide school board.[12]

Citizens warmly embrace the concept of participatory democracy.[13] Yet in the United States and virtually all other democracies, participatory democracy is rare. Few cities have decentralized their governments and turned power over to their neighborhoods. Participatory democracy is commonly rejected on the grounds that in large, complex societies, we need professional, full-time government officials to study problems, formulate solutions, and administer programs. Also, the assumption is that relatively few people will take part in participatory government. This, in fact, turns out to be the case. In a study of neighborhood councils in the cities mentioned above, only 16.6 percent of residents took part in at least one meeting during a two-year period.[14] In other respects, participatory democracy works rather well on the neighborhood level. Yet even if participatory democracy is appropriate for neighborhoods or small towns, how could it work for the national government? We cannot all gather at the Capitol in Washington to decide defense policy.

New technologies have raised hopes that e-government might facilitate greater public involvement. **E-government** refers to the online communications channels that enable rank-and-file citizens to acquire information and documents as well as to register opinions and complaints to government officials.[15] E-government has made it much easier for citizens to find out about various government programs and services. For example, documents explaining government services in languages other than English can sometimes be found at a city hall website. Some states even permit a person to file a criminal complaint online. In Missouri, for example, the website for the state attorney general includes a form residents can fill out to inform the attorney general that some land site or property owner is violating environmental laws.[16]

E-government is a long way from e-democracy. So far it has not facilitated greater public deliberation and has expanded public involvement in only marginal ways. Still, it does make it easier to write your congressman

E-government
Online communication channels that enable citizens to easily obtain information from government and facilitate the expression of opinions to government officials.

(or state representative, or mayor, or whomever), so it does offer people a quick and convenient way to voice their opinions. Governments at all levels are experimenting with new forms of e-government in the hope that, over time, it will engage citizens more directly in the governmental process.

The framers of the U.S. Constitution had their own conception of democracy. They instituted **representative democracy**, a system in which citizens participate in government by electing public officials to make decisions on their behalf. Elected officials are expected to represent the voters' views and interests—that is, to serve as the agents of the citizenry and act for them.

Within the context of representative democracy, we adhere to the principles of universal participation, political equality, and majority rule to guarantee that elections are democratic. But what happens after the election? The elected representatives might not make the decisions the people would have made had they gathered for the same purpose. To account for this possibility in representative government, procedural theory provides a fourth decision-making principle: **responsiveness**. Elected representatives should respond to public opinion—what the majority of people wants. This does not mean that legislators simply cast their ballots on the basis of whether the people back home want alternative A or alternative B. Issues are not usually so straightforward. Rather, responsiveness means following the general contours of public opinion in formulating complex pieces of legislation.[17] By adding responsiveness to deal with the case of indirect democracy, we have four principles of procedural democracy:

- Universal participation
- Political equality
- Majority rule
- Government responsiveness to public opinion

The Substantive View of Democracy

According to procedural theory, the principle of responsiveness is absolute. The government should do what the majority wants, regardless of what that is. At first, this seems to be a reasonable way to protect the rights of citizens in a representative democracy. But think for a minute. Christians are the vast majority of the U.S. population. Suppose that the Christian majority backs a constitutional amendment to require Bible reading in public schools, that the amendment is passed by Congress, and that it is ratified by the states. From a strictly procedural view, the action would be democratic. But what about freedom of religion? What about the rights of minorities? To limit the government's responsiveness to public opinion, we must look outside procedural democratic theory to substantive democratic theory.

Substantive democratic theory focuses on the *substance* of government policies, not on the procedures followed in making those policies. It argues that in a democratic government, certain principles must be incorporated into government policies. Substantive theorists would reject a law that

representative democracy
A system of government where citizens elect public officials to govern on their behalf.

responsiveness
A decision-making principle, necessitated by representative government, that implies that elected representatives should do what the majority of people wants.

substantive democratic theory
The view that democracy is embodied in the substance of government policies rather than in the policymaking procedure.

requires Bible reading in schools because it would violate a substantive principle, freedom of religion. The core of our substantive principles of democracy is embedded in the Bill of Rights and other amendments to the Constitution.

In defining the principles that underlie democratic government—and the policies of that government—most substantive theorists agree on a basic criterion: government policies should guarantee civil liberties (freedom of behavior, such as freedom of religion and freedom of expression) and civil rights (powers or privileges that government may not arbitrarily deny to individuals, such as protection against discrimination in employment and housing). According to this standard, the claim that the United States is a democracy rests on its record of ensuring its citizens these liberties and rights. (We look at how good this record is in Chapters 15 and 16.)

Agreement among substantive theorists breaks down when the discussion moves from civil rights to social rights (adequate health care, quality education, decent housing) and economic rights (private property, steady employment). Ordinary citizens divide on these matters too (see Figure 2.2). Theorists disagree most sharply on whether a government must promote social equality to qualify as a democracy. For example, must a state guarantee unemployment benefits and adequate public housing to be called democratic? Some insist that policies that promote social equality are essential to democratic government. Others restrict the requirements of substantive democracy to policies that safeguard civil liberties and civil rights. Americans differ considerably from the citizens of most other Western democracies in their view of the government's responsibility to provide social policies. In most other Western democracies, there is much more support for the view that jobs and incomes for the unemployed are a right.[18]

IDEALOG.ORG

Should the government try to improve the standard of living for all poor Americans? Take IDEAlog's self-test.

FIGURE 2.2   Health Care: Government's Responsibility?

Is health care a right in a democracy like ours? Opinions change over time and, interestingly, support for the position that health care is government's responsibility began to drop before Barack Obama took office. There's a sharp partisan split, with Republicans more antagonistic toward a government role in health care and Democrats more supportive.

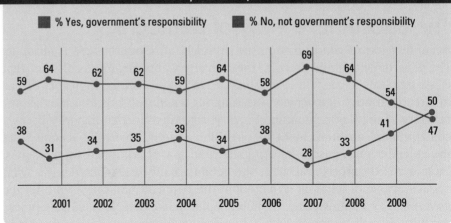

■ % Yes, government's responsibility   ■ % No, not government's responsibility

59 64 62 62 59 64 58 69 64 54 50
38 31 34 35 39 34 38 28 33 41 47

2001 2002 2003 2004 2005 2006 2007 2008 2009

A theorist's political ideology tends to explain his or her position on what democracy really requires in substantive policies. Conservative theorists have a narrow view of the scope of democratic government and a narrow view of the social and economic rights guaranteed by that government. Liberal theorists believe that a democratic government should guarantee its citizens a much broader spectrum of social and economic rights. In later chapters, we review important social and economic policies that our government has followed over time. Keep in mind, however, that what the government has done in the past is not necessarily a correct guide to what a democratic government should do.

Procedural Democracy Versus Substantive Democracy

The problem with the substantive view of democracy is that it does not provide clear, precise criteria that allow us to determine whether a government is democratic. It is, in fact, open to unending arguments over which government policies are truly democratic. Substantive theorists are free to promote their pet values—separation of church and state, guaranteed employment, equal rights for women—under the guise of substantive democracy. When Americans are asked to define democracy in their own terms, roughly two-thirds mention freedoms, rights, or liberties. Relatively few describe democracy in terms of the political process or social benefits.[19]

The procedural viewpoint also has a problem. Although it presents specific criteria for democratic government, those criteria can produce undesirable social policies, such as those that prey on minorities. This clashes with **minority rights**, the idea that all citizens are entitled to certain things that cannot be denied by the majority. Opinions proliferate on what those "certain things" are, but nearly everyone in the United States would agree, for example, on freedom of religion. One way to protect minority rights is to limit the principle of majority rule—by requiring a two-thirds majority or some other extraordinary majority for decisions on certain subjects, for example. Another way is to put the issue in the Constitution, beyond the reach of majority rule.

The issue of prayer in school is a good example of the limits on majority rule. No matter how large, majorities in Congress cannot pass a law to permit organized prayer in public schools because the U.S. Supreme Court has determined that the Constitution forbids such a law. The Constitution could be changed so that it would no longer protect religious minorities, but amending the Constitution is a cumbersome process that involves extraordinary majorities. When limits such as these are put on the principle of majority rule, the minority often rules instead.

Clearly, then, procedural democracy and substantive democracy are not always compatible. In choosing one instead of the other, we are also choosing to focus on either procedures or policies. As authors of this text, we favor a compromise. On the whole, we favor the procedural conception of

minority rights
The benefits of government that cannot be denied to any citizen by majority decisions.

democracy because it more closely approaches the classical definition of democracy: "government by the people." And procedural democracy is founded on clear, well-established rules for decision making. But the theory has a serious drawback: it allows a democratic government to enact policies that can violate the substantive principles of democracy. Thus, pure procedural democracy should be diluted so that minority rights and civil liberties are guaranteed as part of the structure of government. If the compromise seems familiar, it is: the approach has been used in the course of American history to balance legitimate minority and majority interests.

Institutional Models of Democracy

A small group can agree to make democratic decisions directly by using the principles of universal participation, political equality, and majority rule. But even the smallest nations have too many citizens to permit participatory democracy at the national level. If nations want democracy, they must achieve it through some form of representative government, electing officials to make decisions.[20] Even then, democratic government is not guaranteed. Governments must have a way to determine what the people want, as well as some way to translate those wants into decisions. In other words, democratic government requires institutional mechanisms—established procedures and organizations—to translate public opinion into government policy (and thus be responsive). Elections, political parties, legislatures, and interest groups (which we discuss in later chapters) are all examples of institutional mechanisms in politics.

Some democratic theorists favor institutions that closely tie government decisions to the desires of the majority of citizens. If most citizens want laws banning the sale of pornography, the government should outlaw pornography. If citizens want more money spent on defense and less on social welfare (or vice versa), the government should act accordingly. For these theorists, the essence of democratic government is majority rule and responsiveness.

Other theorists place less importance on the principles of majority rule and responsiveness. They do not believe in relying heavily on mass opinion; instead, they favor institutions that allow groups of citizens to defend their interests in the public policymaking process. Global warming is a good example. Everyone cares about it, but it is a complex problem with many competing issues at stake. What is critical here is to allow differing interests to participate so that all sides have the opportunity to influence policies as they are developed.

Both schools hold a procedural view of democracy, but they differ in how they interpret "government by the people." We can summarize the theoretical positions by using two alternative models of democracy. As a model, each is a hypothetical plan, a blueprint for achieving democratic government through institutional mechanisms. The majoritarian model values

participation by the people in general; the pluralist model values participation by the people in groups.

The Majoritarian Model of Democracy

The **majoritarian model of democracy** relies on our intuitive, elemental notion of what is fair. It interprets "government by the people" to mean government by the *majority* of the people. The majoritarian model tries to approximate the people's role in a direct democracy within the limitations of representative government. To force the government to respond to public opinion, the majoritarian model depends on several mechanisms that allow the people to participate directly.

The popular election of government officials is the primary mechanism for democratic government in the majoritarian model. Citizens are expected to control their representatives' behavior by choosing wisely in the first place and by reelecting or voting out public officials according to their performance. Elections fulfill the first three principles of procedural democratic theory: universal participation, political equality, and majority rule. The prospect of reelection and the threat of defeat at the polls are expected to motivate public officials to meet the fourth criterion: responsiveness.

Usually we think of elections only as mechanisms for choosing among candidates for public office. Majoritarian theorists also see them as a means for deciding government policies. An election on a policy issue is called a

majoritarian model of democracy
The classical theory of democracy in which government by the people is interpreted as government by the majority of the people.

referendum. When citizens circulate petitions and gather a required minimum number of signatures to put a policy question on a ballot, it is called an *initiative.* Twenty-one states allow their legislatures to put referenda before the voters and give their citizens the right to place initiatives on the ballot. Five other states provide for one mechanism or the other. Eighteen states also allow the *recall* of state officials, a means of forcing a special election for an up or down vote on a sitting governor or state judge. Like initiatives, a specified percentage of registered voters must sign a petition asking that a vote be held. If a recall election is held, a majority vote is necessary to remove the officeholder. Recalls, which are relatively uncommon, were put into state constitutions as a safety valve to enable voters to remove an incumbent who proved to be dishonest or truly incompetent.[21]

Statewide initiatives and referenda have been used to decide a wide variety of important questions, many with national implications. Although they are instruments of majoritarian democracy, initiatives are often sponsored by interest groups trying to mobilize broad-based support for a particular policy. Voters in both California and Maine recently reversed their state legislatures, which had approved same-sex marriage. The referenda returned marriage in those states to heterosexual couples only.

In the United States, no provisions exist for referenda at the federal level. Some other countries do allow policy questions to be put before the public. In a national referendum in 2009, a clear majority of voters in Switzerland voted to ban construction of minarets on any of the country's mosques. (Minarets are the thin spires atop a mosque.) This vote was clearly hostile to the country's small (5 percent) Muslim population. One of the dangers of referenda is the power of the majority to treat a minority in a harsh or intimidating way.[22]

The majoritarian model contends that citizens can control their government if they have adequate mechanisms for popular participation. It also assumes that citizens are knowledgeable about government and politics, that they want to participate in the political process, and that they make rational decisions in voting for their elected representatives.

Critics contend that Americans are not knowledgeable enough for majoritarian democracy to work. They point to research that shows that only 36 percent of a national sample of voters said that they follow news about politics "very closely."[23] Two scholars who have studied citizens' interest in politics conclude that most Americans favor "stealth" democracy, noting, "The kind of government people want is one in which ordinary people do not have to get involved."[24] If most citizens feel that way, then majoritarian democracy is not viable, even with the wonders of modern information technology.

Defenders of majoritarian democracy respond that although individual Americans may have only limited knowledge of or interest in government, the American public as a whole still has coherent and stable opinions on major policy questions. Public opinion does not fluctuate sharply or erratically, and change in the nation's views usually emerges incrementally. People can hold broad if imprecise values that are manifested in the way they vote and in the opinions they express on particular issues.

My Moms Got Married!

After the California Supreme Court ruled that gay marriage was to be allowed in that state, 18,000 same sex couples wed. This included Tori (left) and Kate Kendall, who brought their five-month-old, Zadie, to the ceremony. Five months after the court decision, however, voters passed an initiative (Proposition 8) that banned gay marriage in California. Same sex marriage supporters then took the case to federal court and in August of 2010, a judge overturned the initiative because he believed that it instituted a discriminatory framework that had no "rational basis." Opponents of gay marriage were incensed and argued that the will of the people should be paramount. The case is now on appeal.

(David McNew/Getty Images)

An Alternative Model: Pluralist Democracy

For years, political scientists struggled valiantly to reconcile the majoritarian model of democracy with polls that showed widespread ignorance of politics among the American people. When 40 to 50 percent of the adult population doesn't even bother to vote in presidential elections, our form of democracy seems to be "government by *some* of the people."

The 1950s saw the evolution of an alternative interpretation of democracy, one tailored to the limited knowledge and participation of the real electorate, not an ideal one. It was based on the concept of *pluralism*—that modern society consists of innumerable groups that share economic, religious, ethnic, or cultural interests. Often people with similar interests organize formal groups—the Future Farmers of America, chambers of commerce, and the Rotary Club are examples. Many social groups have little contact with government, but occasionally they find themselves backing or opposing government policies. An organized group that seeks to influence government policy is called an **interest group**. Many

interest group
An organized group of individuals that seeks to influence public policy; also called a *lobby*.

interest groups regularly spend much time and money trying to influence government policy (see Chapter 10). Among them are the International Electrical Workers Union, the American Hospital Association, the Associated Milk Producers, the National Education Association, the National Association of Manufacturers, and the National Organization for Women.

The **pluralist model of democracy** interprets "government by the people" to mean government by people operating through competing interest groups. According to this model, democracy exists when many (plural) organizations operate separately from the government, press their interests on the government, and even challenge the government. Compared with majoritarian thinking, pluralist theory shifts the focus of democratic government from the mass electorate to organized groups. The criterion for democratic government changes from responsiveness to mass public opinion to responsiveness to organized groups of citizens.

The two major mechanisms in a pluralist democracy are interest groups and a decentralized structure of government that provides ready access to public officials and is open to hearing the groups' arguments for or against government policies. In a centralized structure, decisions are made at one point: the top of the hierarchy. The few decision makers at the top are too busy to hear the claims of competing interest groups or consider those claims in making their decisions. But a decentralized, complex government structure offers the access and openness necessary for pluralist democracy. For pluralists, the ideal system is one that divides government authority among numerous institutions with overlapping authority. Under such a system, competing interest groups have alternative points of access for presenting and arguing their claims.

Our Constitution approaches the pluralist ideal in the way it divides authority among the branches of government. When the National Association for the Advancement of Colored People (NAACP) could not get Congress to outlaw segregated schools in the South in the 1950s, it turned to the federal court system, which did what Congress would not. According to the ideal of pluralist democracy, if all opposing interests are allowed to organize and if the system can be kept open so that all substantial claims are heard, the decision will serve the diverse needs of a pluralist society. Countries going through the process of democratization can find the emergence of pluralism a challenge as new groups mean new demands upon government (see "Politics of Global Change: Green Shoots Sprout in the Czech Republic").

Although many scholars have contributed to the model, pluralist democracy is most closely identified with political scientist Robert Dahl. According to Dahl, the fundamental axiom of pluralist democracy is that "instead of a single center of sovereign power there must be multiple centers of power, none of which is or can be wholly sovereign."[25] Some watchwords of pluralist democracy, therefore, are *divided authority, decentralization*, and *open access*.

On one level, pluralism is alive and well. As will be demonstrated in Chapter 10, interest groups in Washington are thriving, and the rise of many citizen groups has broadened representation beyond traditional business, labor, and professional groups. But on another level, the involvement of

pluralist model of democracy
An interpretation of democracy in which government by the people is taken to mean government by people operating through competing interest groups.

Americans in their groups is a cause for concern. Political scientist Robert Putnam has documented declining participation in a wide variety of organizations. Americans are less inclined to be active members of civic groups like parent–teacher associations, the League of Women Voters, and the Lions Club. Civic participation is a fundamental part of American democracy because it generates the bonding, or social glue, that helps to generate trust and cooperation in the political system.[26] In short, pluralism is working well in terms of promoting representative democracy because Americans are happy to have their interest groups act on their behalf in Washington or at the state level. At the same time, declining civic participation makes it difficult to enhance instruments of direct democracy at the local level.[27]

The Majoritarian Model Versus the Pluralist Model

In majoritarian democracy, the mass public—not interest groups—controls government actions. The citizenry must therefore have some understanding of government and be willing to participate in the electoral process. Majoritarian democracy relies on electoral mechanisms that harness the power of the majority to make decisions. Conclusive elections and a centralized structure of government are mechanisms that aid majority rule. Cohesive political parties with well-defined programs also contribute to majoritarian democracy because they offer voters a clear way to distinguish alternative sets of policies. In terms of Congress, American parties are becoming more majoritarian as there is more unity among both Republicans and Democrats (see Figure 2.3).

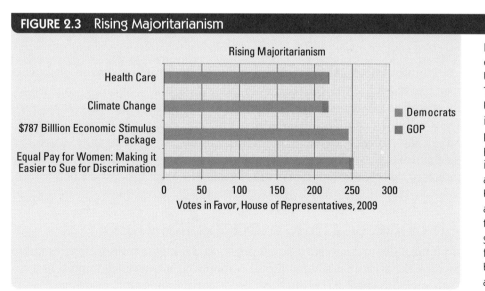

FIGURE 2.3   Rising Majoritarianism

For some years now, our two congressional parties have been increasingly polarized. There is less in the way of bipartisanship—parties working together to fashion compromise legislation. Some people believe that this trend is a good thing as voters have a clear choice. Others believe that we do better as a country when our two parties moderate their ideologies and come together to fashion solutions that can bridge the gap between left and right.

Source: Susan Milligan, "Obama Domestic Agenda Largely a One-Party Effort," *Boston Globe,* 17 November 2009.

Politics of Global Change

Green Shoots Sprout in the Czech Republic

These days, the air is a lot cleaner in the Czech Republic. Local environmental groups can surely take some of the credit as they have pushed hard to persuade the government to adopt strict pollution control requirements.

The Czech Republic was born out of the collapse of communism in Eastern Europe during the late 1980s. It used to be part of Czechoslovakia, a country that was formed in 1918 at the end of World War I. Czechoslovakia was a parliamentary democracy until the Nazis invaded the country; then, when the Germans were defeated in World War II, the Soviet Union put a communist regime in power. This authoritarian government directed the economy and placed a heavy emphasis on industrial production, which resulted in an increasing number of factories spewing forth an unhealthy mix of pollutants.

The "Velvet Revolution" toppled the communist regime at the end of 1989, and on January 1, 1993, the separate Czech and Slovak Republics came into being as independent states. The Czech Republic is the western half of the former Czechoslovakia; its current population is roughly 10.5 million citizens.

As democracy emerged in the former communist Eastern European countries, leaders quickly formed political parties and citizens took great pride in exercising their new-found freedom to vote in open, democratic elections. Freedom also meant that for the first time since before the Nazi invasion, Czechs could form real interest groups. As pluralism began to take hold, environmental groups were quickly established, a couple of hundred in just the first year of freedom. Over the years, groups such as Hnutí DUHA (Rainbow Movement), Jihočeské matky (South Bohemian Mothers), and the Czech chapter of Greenpeace have gained notice.

Still, environmentalism has yet to develop as a mass movement in the Czech Republic. Memberships in these organizations are small and environmental protection has not become nearly the priority among citizens that it is in many democracies, including the United States. Various reasons have been offered as explanation for the middling success of the Czech groups. One is that after so many years of deprivation under

Pluralism does not demand much knowledge from citizens in general. It requires specialized knowledge only from groups of citizens, in particular, their leaders. In contrast to majoritarian democracy, pluralist democracy seeks to limit majority action so that interest groups can be heard. It relies on strong interest groups and a decentralized government structure—mechanisms that interfere with majority rule, thereby protecting minority interests. We could even say that pluralism allows minorities to rule.

An Undemocratic Model: Elite Theory

elite theory
The view that a small group of people actually makes most of the important government decisions.

If pluralist democracy allows minorities to rule, how does it differ from **elite theory**—the view that a small group (a minority) makes most important government decisions? According to elite theory, important government decisions are made by an identifiable and stable minority that shares certain characteristics, particularly vast wealth and business connections.[28]

communism, the Czechs are more interested in economic prosperity and the acquisition of consumer goods than in preserving the environment. Another line of thought is that the long rule of the communists, when citizens had virtually no involvement in government, weakened a sense of civic obligation. In crude terms, people had become used to the government handling all problems of society, and it was quite a change to be expected to take responsibility and to pay dues to advocacy groups working on behalf of the environment or other causes.

Nevertheless, the environmental movement has had some success. Perversely, perhaps, respect grew for these groups in the wake of their failure to stop the building of the Temelín nuclear plant. Although the government eventually approved the plant, the environmental groups put energy corporations very much on the defensive. The environmentalists proved to be surprisingly resourceful and demonstrated a high level of expertise in this complicated area of public policy. Increasingly, the government began to treat the groups as collaborators, and these organizations have had significant access to the government's Ministry of Environment. The ministry, in turn, has directed grants to some of these groups, and other funding has come from foundations and from the European Union.

The environmental movement has put down firm roots in the Czech Republic and seems destined to grow as citizens become increasingly concerned about preserving their quality of life and protecting the natural heritage of their country.

Sources: Steven M. Davis, "Building a Movement from Scratch: Environmental Groups in the Czech Republic," *Social Science Journal* 41 (June 2004): 375–392; Thomas E. Shriver and Chris Messer, "Ideological Cleavages and Schism in the Czech Environmental Movement," *Human Ecology Review* 16 (Winter 2009): 161–171; Andreas Beckmann, "A Quiet Revolution," *Central Europe Review* 1, no. 12 (September 13, 1999); Martin Horak, "Environmental Policy Reform in the Post-Communist Czech Republic," *Europe-Asia Studies* 53 (March 2001): 313–327. *Photo*: Pavel Šeplavý/Alamy.

Elite theory argues that these few individuals wield power in America because they control its key financial, communications, industrial, and government institutions. Their power derives from the vast wealth of America's largest corporations and the perceived importance of the continuing success of those corporations to the growth of the economy. An inner circle of top corporate leaders not only provides effective advocates for individual companies and for the interests of capitalism in general but also supplies people for top government jobs, from which they can continue to promote their interests. Elitists might point, for example, to former vice president Dick Cheney. He went from previous work as secretary of defense for President George H. W. Bush to becoming head of Halliburton, a large oil services company, and then back to government, where, as George W. Bush's vice president, he acted as an outspoken proponent of more energy exploration.

According to elite theory, the United States is not a democracy but an oligarchy.[29] Although the voters appear to control the government through elections, elite theorists argue that the powerful few in society manage to define the issues and constrain the outcomes of government decision making to suit their own interests. Clearly, elite theory describes a government that operates in an undemocratic fashion.

Elite theory appeals to many people, especially those who believe that wealth dominates politics. The theory also provides plausible explanations for specific political decisions. Why, over the years, has the tax code included so many loopholes that favor the wealthy? The answer, claim adherents of elite theory, is that the policymakers never really change; they are all cut from the same cloth. Even when a liberal Democrat like Barack Obama is in the White House, many of the president's top economic policymakers are typically drawn from Wall Street or other financial institutions.

Political scientists have conducted numerous studies designed to test the validity of elite theory, but it has proven to be an exceptionally difficult idea to prove in any conclusive manner. Our government and society are enormous and enormously complex. If there were an elite that controlled American politics, it would have to be rather large as there are many wealthy and well-connected notables. What would be the coordinating mechanism that facilitated control by such an elite? And if such an elite exerted such influence, why wouldn't it be clearly evident?[30] Although not all studies come to the same conclusion, the preponderance of available evidence documenting concrete government decisions on many different issues does not generally support elite theory—at least in the sense that an identifiable ruling elite usually gets its way. Not surprisingly, elite theorists reject this view. They argue that studies of decisions made on individual issues do not adequately test the influence of the power elite. Rather, they contend that much of the elite's power comes from its ability to keep issues off the political agenda. That is, its power derives from its ability to keep people from questioning fundamental assumptions about American capitalism.[31]

Consequently, elite theory remains part of the debate about the nature of American government and is forcefully argued by some severe critics of our political system. Although we do not believe that the scholarly evidence supports elite theory, we do recognize that contemporary American pluralism favors some segments of society over others. On one hand, the poor are chronically unorganized and are not well represented by interest groups. On the other hand, business is very well represented in the political system. As many interest group scholars who reject elite theory have documented, business is better represented than any other sector of the public. Thus, one can endorse pluralist democracy as a more accurate description than elitism in American politics without believing that all groups are equally well represented.

Elite Theory Versus Pluralist Theory

The key difference between elite and pluralist theory lies in the durability of the ruling minority. In contrast to elite theory, pluralist theory does not define government conflict in terms of a minority versus the majority; instead, it sees many different interests vying with one another in each policy area. In the management of national forests, for example, many interest groups—logging companies, recreational campers, and environmentalists, for example—have joined the political competition. They press their various viewpoints on government through representatives who are well informed about how relevant issues affect group members. According to elite theory, the financial resources of big logging companies ought to win out over the arguments of campers and environmentalists, but this does not always happen.

Pluralist democracy makes a virtue of the struggle between competing interests. It argues for government that accommodates the struggle and channels the result into government action. According to pluralist democracy, the public is best served if the government structure provides access for different groups to press their claims in competition with one another. Note that pluralist democracy does not insist that all groups have equal influence on government decisions. In the political struggle, wealthy, well-organized groups have an inherent advantage over poorer, inadequately organized groups. In fact, unorganized segments of the population may not even get their concerns placed on the agenda for government consideration, which means that what government does not discuss (its "nondecisions") may be as significant as what it does discuss and decide. Indeed, studies of the congressional agenda demonstrate that it is characterized by little in the way of legislation concerned with poor or low-income Americans, while business-related bills are plentiful.[32] This is a critical weakness of pluralism, and critics relentlessly attack the theory because it appears to justify great disparities in levels of political organization and resources among different segments of society.[33] Pluralists contend that as long as all groups are able to participate vigorously in the decision-making process, the process is democratic.

On Tonight's Menu, Lots of Green

Elitist critics of American government point to the advantages that the wealthy have in our political system. The campaign finance system contributes to this belief. This Washington fundraiser gives lobbyists and wealthy donors a chance to mingle with policymakers and remind them who supports them financially.

(Rob Crandall/The Image Works)

The Global Trend Toward Democracy

We have proposed two models of democratic government. The majoritarian model conforms with classical democratic theory for a representative government. According to this model, democracy should be a form of government that features responsiveness to majority opinion. According to the pluralist model, a government is democratic if it allows minority interests to organize and press their claims on government freely.

No government actually achieves the high degree of responsiveness demanded by the majoritarian model. No government offers complete and equal access to the claims of all competing groups, as is required by an optimally democratic pluralist model. Still, some nations approach these ideals closely enough to be considered practicing democracies.

Establishing Democracies

Whether a political system is "democratic" is not a simple yes-or-no question. Governments can meet some criteria for a procedural democracy (universal participation, political equality, majority rule, and government responsiveness to public opinion) and fail to meet others. They can also differ in the extent to which they support freedom of speech and freedom of association, which create the necessary conditions for the practice of democracy. Various scholars and organizations have developed complicated databases that rate countries on a long list of indicators, providing a means of comparing countries along all criteria.[34] One research institution has found a global trend toward freedom every decade since 1975, though in the past few years there has been a slight drop in the number of democracies.[35] **Democratization** is a difficult process, and many countries fail completely or succeed only in the short run and lapse into a form of authoritarianism (see Compared with What? Democratization in Africa). One recent comparison of thirty collapsed democracies with thirty-two stable democracies concluded that social cleavages are more likely to cause collapse than the nature of governmental institutions.[36]

One reason that democratization can be so difficult is that ethnic and religious conflict is epidemic. Such conflict complicates efforts to democratize because antagonisms can run so deep that opposing groups do not want to grant political legitimacy to each other. Kenya had been one of Africa's most stable democracies, but widespread rioting ensued there in 2007 after a disputed election. The incumbent party may have engaged in fraud to keep itself in power. The primary cleavage between the incumbent and opposition parties was largely ethnic and tribal in nature, and this added fuel to the fire in the wake of the election. The ongoing protests along with international pressure forced the disputed winner to agree to a coalition government with the main opposition party. The country has continued to struggle, as bitter antagonisms remain.[37]

Ethnic and religious rivals are often more interested in achieving a form of government that oppresses their opponents (or, in their minds, maintains order) than in establishing a real democracy. After the United States went to war against the Taliban regime of Afghanistan because of its support of Osama bin Laden, it was faced with rebuilding a country with an enduring history of ethnic and tribal warfare. Even within the largest ethnic group, the Pashtuns (about 50 percent of the population), there was little unity.

democratization
A process of transition as a country attempts to move from an authoritarian form of government to a democratic one.

Compared with What?

Democratization in Africa

Democratization is an extremely difficult process because a country trying to move toward such a form of government is vulnerable to those who were advantaged in the previous regime or to those who would like to grab power. The governments of democratizing countries may be fragile, with little support from a population that does not appreciate the challenges and trade-offs that lie before its legislature and bureaucracies. In Africa some countries have successfully achieved significant levels of democracy, but many others have been unable to escape the grips of authoritarianism. Some have become democratic for a period, only to be replaced, often violently, by an authoritarian regime.

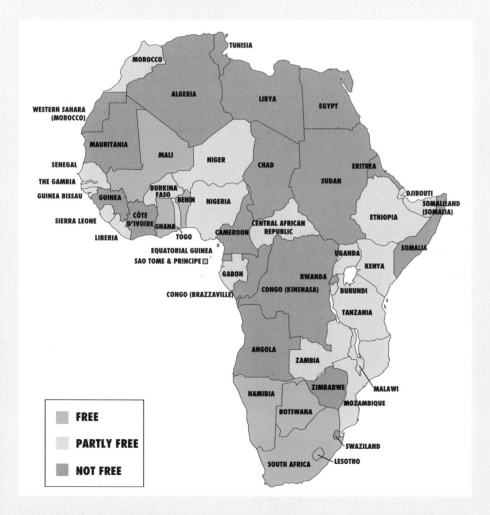

Source: Freedom House, "Map of Freedom, 2009," available at http://www.freedomhouse.org/template .cfm?page=363&year=2009.

Tribal and subtribal rivalries divided Pashtuns, and enmity between Pashtuns and other ethnic and linguistic groups such as Tajiks, Uzbeks, and Turkmen presented the United States and its allies with a mosaic of ethnic antagonisms. This ethnic and tribal rivalry has made it especially difficult for a centralized, national government to extend its reach across the country and elicit the support of the population.[38]

The political and economic instability that typically accompanies transitions to democracy makes new democratic governments vulnerable to attack by their opponents. The military will often revolt and take over the government on the ground that progress cannot occur until order is restored. As we noted in Chapter 1, all societies wrestle with the dilemma of choosing between freedom and order. The open political conflict that emerges in a new democracy may not be easily harnessed into a well-functioning government that tolerates opposition.[39] Despite such difficulties, strong forces are pushing authoritarian governments toward democratization. Nations find it difficult to succeed economically in today's world without establishing a market economy, and market economies (that is, capitalism) give people substantial freedoms. There is a strong relationship between economic prosperity and democracy; countries that have free markets tend to protect political freedoms as well.[40] Thus, authoritarian rulers may see economic reforms as a threat to their regime.

The United States has always faced a difficult foreign policy problem determining the degree to which it wants to invest in promoting democracy abroad. It is a noble goal, to be sure, but it may be difficult to impose democracy on a population that does not want it. After many years of violence between insurgents and American troops as well as considerable terrorism inflicted by Iraqis on each other, Iraq has become more stable and has taken important steps toward democracy through elections. Yet this progress came at a terrible cost in lives and in astronomical sums to pay for the American soldiers who have occupied the country since 2003. Americans soured on the war in Iraq and punished the Republicans in the elections of 2006 and 2008. Democrat Barack Obama has found limited support for U.S. military intervention in Afghanistan. Prior to announcing a surge of 30,000 more troops in late 2009, approval of Obama's handling of the war in Afghanistan had fallen to just 35 percent in the polls.[41]

Established democracies are also not free of the destabilizing effects of religious and ethnic conflict. Such countries usually try to cope with such pressures with some form of pluralism so that different groups feel they are being treated fairly by their government. Indeed, majoritarian democracy can be risky where ethnic and religious rivalries endure because a majority faction can use its votes to suppress minorities. Even in stable democracies where ethnic conflict is muted, disillusionment can grow and undermine confidence in the actions of government.[42] India, the world's largest democracy and a burgeoning economic power, is still plagued by periodic religious violence. In 2008 there was a terrible spate of violence directed at the tiny Christian minority in the state of Orissa. Mobs destroyed 1,400 homes, leaving thousands homeless, and 80 churches and prayer houses were set on fire.[43] More broadly, the tension between the Hindu majority and the significant Muslim minority in India is always palpable and violence occasionally erupts.[44]

American Democracy: More Pluralist Than Majoritarian

It is not idle speculation to ask what kind of democracy is practiced in the United States. The answer can help us understand why our government can be called democratic despite a low level of citizen participation in politics and despite government actions that sometimes run contrary to public opinion.

Throughout this book, we probe to determine how well the United States fits the two alternative models of democracy: majoritarian and pluralist. If our answer is not already apparent, it soon will be. We argue that the political system in the United States rates relatively low according to the majoritarian model of democracy but that it fulfills the pluralist model quite well. Yet the pluralist model is far from a perfect representation of democracy. Its principal drawback is that it favors the well organized, and the poor are the least likely to be members of interest groups. As one advocate of majoritarian democracy once wrote, "The flaw in the pluralist heaven is that the heavenly chorus sings with a strong upper-class accent."[45]

In recent years the parties have become more sharply divided along conservative and liberal dimensions, thus making our system a bit more majoritarian than has traditionally been the case. In particular, the two parties in Congress have become more ideologically homogeneous, thus giving voters a clearer opportunity to select a party more cohesive in its programmatic intent.[46] Yet this step toward majoritarianism has led to widespread criticism that our system of government is becoming too bitterly partisan. That is, as the members of Congress have become more ideological, they seem to have become less inclined to work together to achieve moderate, compromise solutions to the nation's problems. Some critics have also charged that ideological activists, who have mobilized more than moderates, have hijacked the parties and pulled them more sharply toward conservative and liberal extremes.[47] For those uncomfortable with more ideological parties, the continuing strong counterbalance of pluralism is welcome.

Given the survey data that show that the people's trust in American government has fallen over the years, it may seem that pluralist democracy is not serving us very well. Indeed, many Americans describe government and politicians in the harshest terms. Radio talk show hosts like Rush Limbaugh and politicians themselves pile invective on top of insult when they talk about what's wrong with Washington.[48] Compared with citizens in other developed nations, Americans fall in the middle concerning their satisfaction with democracy in the United States. But it's not at all clear that Americans would be more satisfied with another type of democracy.

This evaluation of the pluralist nature of American democracy may not mean much to you now. But you will learn that the pluralist model makes the United States look far more democratic than the majoritarian model would. Eventually, you will have to decide the answers to three questions:

1. Is the pluralist model truly an adequate expression of democracy, or is it a perversion of classical ideals, designed to portray America as democratic when it is not?
2. Does the majoritarian model result in a "better" type of democracy?
3. If it does, could new mechanisms of government be devised to produce a desirable mix of majority rule and minority rights?

Let these questions play in the back of your mind as you read more about the workings of American government in meeting the challenge of democracy.

Summary

Is the United States a democracy? Most scholars believe that it is. But what kind of democracy is it? The answer depends on the definition of *democracy*. Some believe democracy is procedural; they define *democracy* as a form of government in which the people govern through certain institutional mechanisms. Others hold to substantive theory, claiming that a government is democratic if its policies promote civil liberties and rights.

In this book, we emphasize the procedural concept of democracy, distinguishing between direct (participatory) and indirect (representative) democracy. In a participatory democracy, all citizens gather to govern themselves according to the principles of universal participation, political equality, and majority rule. In an indirect democracy, the citizens elect representatives to govern for them. If a representative government is elected mostly in accordance with the three principles just listed and also is usually responsive to public opinion, it qualifies as a democracy.

Procedural democratic theory has produced rival institutional models of democratic government. The classic majoritarian model, which depends on majority votes in elections, assumes that people are knowledgeable about government, want to participate in the polit-

ical process, and carefully and rationally choose among candidates. But surveys of public opinion and behavior and voter turnout show that this is not the case for most Americans. The pluralist model of democracy, which depends on interest group interaction with government, was devised to accommodate these findings. It argues that democracy in a complex society requires only that government allow private interests to organize and to press their competing claims openly in the political arena. It differs from elite theory—the belief that America is run by a small group of powerful individuals—by arguing that different minorities win on different issues.

In Chapter 1, we discussed three political values: freedom, order, and equality. Here we have described two models of democracy: majoritarian and pluralist. The five concepts are critical to an understanding of American government. The values discussed in this chapter underlie the two questions with which the text began:

• Which is better: to live under a government that allows individuals complete freedom to do whatever they please, or to live under one that enforces strict law and order?

- Which is better: to let all citizens keep the same share of their income, or to tax wealthier people at a higher rate to fund programs for poorer people?

The models of democracy described in this chapter lead to another question:

- Which is better: a government that is highly responsive to public opinion on all matters, or one that responds deliberately to organized groups that argue their cases effectively?

These are enduring questions, and the framers of the Constitution dealt with them too. Their struggle is the appropriate place to begin our analysis of how these competing models of democracy have animated the debate about the nature of our political process.

 CourseMate   Visit www.cengagebrain.com/shop/ISBN/0495906182 for flashcards, web quizzes, videos and more!

Hisham Ibrahim/Getty Images

"You are the 'conventionists' of Europe. You therefore have the power vested in any political body: to succeed or to fail," claimed Chairman Valéry Giscard d'Estaing in his introductory speech on February 26, 2002, to the members of the Convention on the Future of Europe. The purpose of the convention, according to Giscard d'Estaing, was for the members to "agree to propose a concept of the European Union which matches our continental dimension and the requirements of the 21st century, a concept which can bring unity to our continent and respect for its diversity." If the members succeeded, he reassured them, no doubt they would in essence write "a new chapter in the history of Europe."[1] Integrating and governing twenty-seven nation-states with a total population of 500 million is, to say the least, a daunting task, especially considering that many of those nation-states at one time or another were bitter enemies.

Over two centuries earlier, on March 31, 1787, from his home at Mount Vernon, George Washington penned a letter to James Madison. "I am glad to find," Washington wrote, "that Congress have recommended to the States to appear in the Convention proposed to be holden in Philadelphia in May. I think the reasons in favor, have the preponderancy of those against the measure."[2] Roughly two months later, in May, Washington would be selected by a unanimous vote to preside over the Constitutional Convention, known then as the Federal Convention, which was charged with revising the Articles of Confederation. Acting beyond its mandate, the body produced instead a new document altogether, which remains the oldest operating constitution in the world.

The path to a European constitution was strewn with pitfalls. Many substantial hurdles stood in the path of a final version. Would nations forgo their own tax, foreign, and defense policies in favor of a single European voice? Would the current unanimity voting principle be replaced with a less restrictive rule, which would have to be adopted unanimously? In a single week in 2005, France and the Netherlands, two of the European Union's founding nations, rejected the scheme by large majorities. The opponents, who ranged across the ideological spectrum, rallied young and old to attack the constitution.[3] The French version weighed in at nearly two hundred pages and contained more details than voters could grasp. These factors, combined with current economic and political issues, probably made the constitution an easy target. The setbacks in France and the Netherlands encouraged seven nations to postpone their own ratification processes, despite the fact that eighteen nations had already ratified the constitutional text (three by referendum: Spain, Luxembourg, and Romania).

Although the process in 1787 on one side of the Atlantic may have differed from that on the other side in 2002, the political passions that these efforts spawned were equally intense and highlight the fragility inherent in designing a constitution. And no wonder. The questions that challenged America's founders and that confronted the women and men charged with setting a future course for Europe do not have easy or obvious answers. A thoughtful European observer asked the same kinds of questions that confronted the delegates at Philadelphia: "How can a balance be achieved in the representation of large and small states? How much power should be conferred upon the federal level and what should be the jurisdiction of the EU today? What fundamental set of values underpins political unity? Is there a European equivalent to 'life, liberty and the pursuit of happiness'?"[4]

The solution took a new form of agreement known as the "Treaty of Lisbon," also referred to as the Reform Treaty, which was signed on December 13, 2007, during a European summit. Except for Ireland, all member nations submitted the treaty to their respective legislatures. The treaty's approval required unanimity. Since voters were notoriously uneasy about EU policies, it seemed prudent to keep them at bay while the elected representatives debated the treaty's advantages and disadvantages. The Reform Treaty presented a still-longer version of the previous constitutional text but dropped nearly all the state-like symbols and terminology (the European flag and anthem, among others). It planned for an EU president, created a diplomatic service under a single foreign-affairs head, and smoothed the ability to make decisions by reducing the number of areas that called for unanimity among member nations.

Approval would prove uneasy. Ireland rejected the treaty in 2008, halting once more the effort toward European integration. But the sobering effects of economic toil soon gave Ireland a chance to reconsider. In October 2009, Irish voters agreed to the treaty by a substantial margin, hoping that the new EU would stave off economic catastrophe caused by the worldwide collapse in the financial sector.[5] Finally, on December 1, 2009, the treaty went into effect, bringing the EU one step closer to unity.

Economic forces continued to pound the EU through 2010 as creditors questioned whether the debt-ridden nations of Greece, Ireland, Italy, Portugal, and Spain would be able to pay or refinance their bonds. While political unity might be a step closer to reality, economic unity may yet come asunder.

The American experience is sure to shed light on the future of a single Europe. In fact, the American experience parallels the European story, since Americans' first step toward unity resulted in failure and then an effort at redesign that ultimately proved successful. This chapter poses questions about the U.S. Constitution. How did it evolve? What form did it take? What values does it reflect? How can it be altered? Which model of democracy—majoritarian or pluralist—does it fit better? In these answers may lie hints of the formidable tasks facing the EU as it moves toward political unity.

The Revolutionary Roots of the Constitution

The U.S. Constitution contains just 4,300 words. But those 4,300 words define the basic structure of our national government. (In contrast, the failed European constitution was more than 60,000 words long. The Reform Treaty is still longer at 68,500 words.) A comprehensive document, the Constitution divides the national government into three branches, describes the powers of those branches and their connections, outlines the interaction between the government and the governed, and describes the relationship between the national government and the states. The Constitution makes itself the supreme law of the land and binds every government official to support it.

Most Americans revere the Constitution as political scripture. To charge that a political action is unconstitutional is akin to claiming that it is unholy. So the Constitution has taken on symbolic value that strengthens its authority as the basis of American government. Strong belief in the Constitution has led many politicians to abandon party for principle when constitutional issues are at stake. The power and symbolic value of the Constitution were forcefully demonstrated in the Watergate affair (see the feature "Remembering Watergate and the Constitution").

The U.S. Constitution, written in 1787 for an agricultural society huddled along the coast of a wild new land, now guides the political life of a massive urban society in the postnuclear age. The stability of the Constitution—and of the political system it created—is all the more remarkable because the Constitution itself was rooted in revolution. What is the evidence regarding the life expectancy of constitutions generally? (See "Compared with What? The Longevity of Constitutions.")

The U.S. Constitution was designed to prevent anarchy by forging a union of states. To understand the values embedded in the Constitution, we must understand its historical roots. They lie in colonial America, the revolt against British rule, and the failure of the Articles of Confederation that governed the new nation after the Revolution.

Harmony.eu?

In November 2009, leaders of the 27 countries of the EU chose Herman Von Rompuy as the EU's first president and Catherine Ashton as the High Representative for foreign policy. The choice of these respected but little-known figures may augur a less united and forceful political union. Mr. Rompuy, an economist by training, enjoys writing haiku. One recent effort may prefigure his new role: "A fly zooms, buzzes; Spins and is lost in the room; He does no one harm."

(© European Union, 2010)

Freedom in Colonial America

Although they were British subjects, American colonists in the eighteenth century enjoyed a degree of freedom denied most other people in the world. In Europe, ancient customs and the relics of feudalism restricted private property, compelled support for established religions, and limited access to trades and professions. In America, landowners could control and transfer their property at will. In America, there were no compulsory payments to support an established church. In America, there was no ceiling on wages, as there was in most European countries, and no guilds of exclusive professional associations. In America, colonists enjoyed almost complete freedom of speech, press, and assembly.[6]

By 1763, Britain and the colonies had reached a compromise between imperial control and colonial self-government. America's foreign affairs and overseas trade were controlled by the king and Parliament, the British legislature; the rest was left to colonial rule. But the cost of administering the colonies was substantial. The colonists needed protection from the French

Compared with What?

The Longevity of Constitutions

Compared with other constitutions across the world, the U.S. Constitution is an antique. Ratified in 1788, it is the world's second oldest constitution. (The tiny land-locked microstate of San Marino boasts the oldest constitution, dating to 1600.) But few 220-year-old antiques still work more or less as their designers intended. Other countries have constitutions, but they tend to come and go.

A national constitution is the fundamental law of a land. It must give voice to a set of inviolable principles that limit the powers of government by setting up governmental institutions and defining their relationships and patterns of authority. Even dictatorships require institutions through which to govern.

Some stable democracies lack a single document as a written constitution. Perhaps the most notable example is Britain, whose fundamental law inheres in other documents, such as the Magna Carta. Other democracies, like Brazil, have gone in the opposite direction by adopting "hyperconstitutions." Brazil tries to pack into its 1988 charter just about every facet of public life, making it one of the longest constitutions ever drafted, nearly six times the length of the U.S. Constitution.

How long do constitutions last? Constitutions have lasted only about seventeen years on average worldwide since 1789. The figure here illustrates many short life spans compared to long life spans, which vary by region and time. African constitutions survive on average ten years. Latin American constitutions last little more than twelve years. For example, the Dominican Republic and Haiti have changed their constitutions every three years. Constitutions in Western Europe last thirty-two years, while constitutions in Asia survive about nineteen years. From 1789 through World War I, the

and their American Indian allies during the Seven Years' War (1756–1763), an expensive undertaking. Because Americans benefited the most from that protection, their English countrymen argued, Americans should bear the cost.

The Road to Revolution

The British believed that taxing the colonies was the obvious way to meet the costs of administering the colonies. The colonists did not agree. They especially did not want to be taxed by a distant government in which they had no representation. Nevertheless, a series of taxes (including a tax on all printed matter) was imposed on the colonies by the Crown. In each instance, public opposition was widespread and immediate.

A group of citizens—merchants, lawyers, and prosperous traders—created an intercolonial association called the Sons of Liberty. This group destroyed taxed items (identified by special stamps) and forced the official stamp distributors

average life span of a constitution was twenty-one years. It has dropped to twelve years since the end of World War I. And whereas the life expectancy of individuals worldwide is increasing, the life expectancy of constitutions is not.

Three reasons may explain constitutional durability: (1) they tend to derive from an open, participatory process; (2) they tend to be specific; and (3) they tend to be flexible through amendment and interpretation.

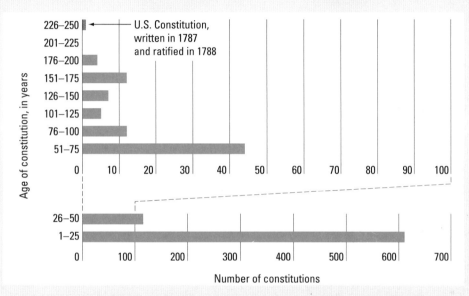

Source: Tom Ginsburg, Zack Elkins, and James Melton, "The Lifespan of Written Constitutions" (Paper No. 3, Law and Economics Workshop, University of California at Berkeley, 21 January 2008, available at http://repositories.cdlib.org/cgi/viewcontent.cgi?article=1212&context=berkeley_law_econ and http://www.loc.gov/law/help/guide/nations/sanmarino.html, accessed 12 February 2008). Thanks to Prof. Tom Ginsburg, codirector of the Comparative Constitutions Project at the University of Illinois, who graciously shared his data for the figure.

to resign. In October 1765, residents of Charleston, South Carolina, celebrated the forced resignation of the colony's stamp distributor by displaying a British flag with the word *Liberty* sewn across it. (They were horrified when a few months later local slaves paraded through the streets calling for "Liberty!")[7]

Women resisted the hated taxes by joining together in symbolic and practical displays of patriotism. A group of young women calling themselves the Daughters of Liberty met in public to spin homespun cloth and encourage the elimination of British cloth from colonial markets. They consumed American food and drank local herbal tea as symbols of their opposition.[8]

On the night of December 16, 1773, a group of colonists in Massachusetts reacted to a British duty on tea by organizing the Boston Tea Party. A mob boarded three ships and emptied 342 chests of that valuable substance into Boston Harbor. The act of defiance and destruction could not be ignored. "The die is now cast," wrote George III. "The Colonies must either submit or triumph."[9] In an attempt to reassert British control over its

Uniquely American Protest

Americans protested the Tea Act (1773) by holding the Boston Tea Party (*background, left*) and by using a unique form of painful punishment, tarring and feathering, on the tax collector (*see* "STAMP ACT" upside-down on the Liberty Tree). An early treatise on the subject offered the following instructions: "First, strip a person naked, then heat the tar until it is thin, and pour upon the naked flesh, or rub it over with a tar brush. After which, sprinkle decently upon the tar, whilst it is yet warm, as many feathers as will stick to it."

(Courtesy of the John Carter Brown Library at Brown University)

recalcitrant colonists, Parliament in 1774 passed the Coercive (or "Intolerable") Acts. One act imposed a blockade on Boston until the tea was paid for; another gave royal governors the power to quarter British soldiers in private American homes. The taxation issue became secondary; more important was the conflict between British demands for order and American demands for liberty. The Virginia and Massachusetts assemblies summoned a continental congress, an assembly that would speak and act for the people of all the colonies.

All the colonies except Georgia sent representatives to the First Continental Congress, which met in Philadelphia in September 1774. The objective was to restore harmony between Great Britain and the American colonies. In an effort at unity, all colonies were given the same voting power—one vote each. A leader, called the president, was elected. (The terms *president* and *congress* in American government trace their origins to the First Continental Congress.) In October, the delegates adopted a statement of rights and principles; many of these later found their way into the Declaration of Independence and the Constitution. For example, the congress claimed a right "to life, liberty, and property" and a right "peaceably to assemble, consider of their grievances, and petition the king." Then the congress adjourned, planning to reconvene in May 1775.

Revolutionary Action

By early 1775, however, a movement that the colonists themselves were calling a revolution had already begun. Colonists in Massachusetts were fighting the British at Concord and Lexington. Delegates to the Second Continental Congress, meeting in May, faced a dilemma: Should they prepare for war, or should they try to reconcile with Britain? As conditions deteriorated, the Second Continental Congress remained in session to serve as the government of the colony-states.

On June 7, 1776, owing in large part to the powerful advocacy of John Adams of Massachusetts, a strong supporter of independence, the Virginia delegation called on the Continental Congress to resolve "that these United Colonies are, and of right ought to be, free and Independent States, that they are absolved from all allegiance to the British Crown, and that all political connection between them and the State of Great Britain is, and ought to be, totally dissolved." This was a difficult decision. Independence meant disloyalty to Britain and war, death, and devastation. The congress debated but did not immediately adopt the resolution. A committee of five men was appointed to prepare a proclamation expressing the colonies' reasons for declaring independence.

The Declaration of Independence

Thomas Jefferson, a young farmer and lawyer from Virginia who was a member of the committee, became the "pen" to John Adams's "voice."[10] Because Jefferson was erudite, a Virginian, and an extremely skilled writer, he drafted the proclamation. Jefferson's document, the **Declaration of Independence**, was modestly revised by the committee and then further edited by the congress. It remains a cherished statement of our heritage, expressing simply, clearly, and rationally the many arguments for separation from Great Britain.

The principles underlying the Declaration were rooted in the writings of the English philosopher John Locke and had been expressed many times by speakers in the congress and the colonial assemblies. Locke argued that people have God-given, or natural, rights that are inalienable—that is, they cannot be taken away by any government. According to Locke, all legitimate political authority exists to preserve these natural rights and is based on the consent of those who are governed. The idea of consent is derived from **social contract theory**, which states that the people agree to establish rulers for certain purposes, but they have the right to resist or remove rulers who violate those purposes.[11]

Jefferson used similar arguments in the Declaration of Independence. (See the appendix.) Taking his cue from a draft of the Virginia Declaration of Rights,[12] Jefferson wrote,

> We hold these truths to be self-evident, that all men are created equal, that they are endowed by their Creator with certain unalienable rights, that among these are life, liberty, and the pursuit of happiness. That to secure these rights, governments are instituted among men, deriving their just powers from the consent of the governed. That whenever any form of government becomes destructive of these ends, it is the right of the people to alter or to abolish it, and to institute new government, laying its foundation on such principles, and organizing its power in such form, as to them shall seem most likely to effect their safety and happiness.

Historian Jack Rakove maintains that Jefferson was not proposing equality for individuals. Rather, he was asserting the equality of peoples to enjoy the

Declaration of Independence
Drafted by Thomas Jefferson, the document that proclaimed the right of the colonies to separate from Great Britain.

social contract theory
The belief that the people agree to set up rulers for certain purposes and thus have the right to resist or remove rulers who act against those purposes.

Feature Story

Remembering Watergate and the Constitution

The Watergate affair remains the most serious constitutional crisis since the Civil War. Yet today, two-thirds of Americans admit they don't know the basic facts.[1] It began when midnight burglars made a small mistake: they left a piece of tape over the latch they had tripped to enter the Watergate office and apartment complex in Washington, D.C. A security guard found their tampering and called the police, who surprised the burglars in the offices of the Democratic National Committee at 2:30 A.M. The arrests of the five men—four Cuban exiles and a former CIA agent—in the early hours of June 17, 1972, triggered a constitutional struggle that eventually involved the president of the United States, Congress, and the Supreme Court.

The arrests took place a month before the 1972 Democratic National Convention. Investigative reporting by Carl Bernstein and Bob Woodward of the *Washington Post,* and a simultaneous criminal investigation by Assistant U.S. Attorney Earl J. Silbert and his staff, uncovered a link between the Watergate burglary and the forthcoming election.[2] The burglars were carrying the telephone number of another former CIA agent, who was working in the White House. At a news conference on June 22, President Richard Nixon said, "The White House has had no involvement whatsoever in this particular incident."[3]

At its national convention in July, the Democratic Party nominated Senator George McGovern of South Dakota to oppose Nixon in the presidential election. McGovern tried to make the break-in at the Democratic headquarters a campaign issue, but the voters either did not understand or did not care. In November 1972, Richard Nixon was reelected president of the United States, winning forty-nine of fifty states in one of the largest electoral landslides in American history. Only then did the Watergate story unfold completely.

Two months later, seven men answered in court for the break-in. They included the five burglars and two men closely connected with the president: E. Howard Hunt (a former CIA agent and White House consultant) and G. Gordon Liddy (counsel to the Committee to Re-Elect the President, or CREEP). Five, including Hunt, entered guilty pleas. Liddy and James McCord (one of the burglars) were convicted by a jury. The Senate launched its own investigation of the matter. It set up the Select Committee on Presidential Campaign Activities, chaired by a self-styled constitutional authority, Democratic senator Sam Ervin of North Carolina.

A stunned nation watched the televised proceedings and learned that the president had secretly tape-recorded all of his conversations in the White House. (Although presidents dating to Franklin Roosevelt had tape-recorded conversations in the White House, Nixon's system for recording was by far the most comprehensive.)[4] The Ervin committee asked for the tapes. Nixon refused to produce them, citing the separation of powers between the legislative and the executive branches and claiming that "executive privilege" allowed him to withhold information from Congress.

Nixon also resisted criminal subpoenas demanding the White House tapes. Ordered by a federal court to deliver specific tapes, Nixon proposed a compromise: he would release written summaries of the taped conversations. Archibald Cox, the special prosecutor appointed by the attorney general to investigate Watergate and offenses arising from the 1972 presidential election, rejected the compromise. Nixon retaliated with the

same rights of self-government that other peoples enjoyed. "It was the collective right of revolution and self-government that the Declaration was written to justify—not a visionary or even utopian notion of equality within American society itself."[13]

"Saturday night massacre," in which Attorney General Elliot L. Richardson and his deputy resigned, Cox was fired, and the special prosecutor's office was abolished.

The ensuing furor forced Nixon to appoint another special prosecutor, Leon Jaworski, who eventually brought indictments against Nixon's closest aides. Nixon himself was named as an unindicted co-conspirator. Both the special prosecutor and the defendants wanted the White House tapes, but Nixon continued to resist. Finally, on July 24, 1974, the Supreme Court ruled that the president had to hand over the tapes. At almost the same time, the House Judiciary Committee voted to recommend to the full House that Nixon be impeached for, or charged with, three offenses: violating his oath of office to faithfully uphold the laws, misusing and abusing executive authority and the resources of executive agencies, and defying congressional subpoenas.

The Judiciary Committee vote was decisive but far from unanimous. On August 5, however, the committee and the country finally learned the contents of the tapes released under the Supreme Court order. They revealed that Nixon had been aware of a cover-up on June 23, 1972, just six days after the break-in. He ordered the FBI, "Don't go any further in this case, period!"[5] Now even the eleven Republican members of the House Judiciary Committee, who had opposed impeachment on the first vote, were ready to vote against Nixon.

Faced with the collapse of his support and likely impeachment by the full House, Nixon resigned the presidency on August 9, 1974, and Vice President Gerald Ford became president. Ford had become the nation's first unelected vice president in 1973 when Nixon's original vice president, Spiro Agnew, resigned amid his own personal scandal. Ford then became the first unelected president of the United States. A month later, acting within his constitutional powers, Ford granted private citizen Richard Nixon an unconditional pardon for all crimes that he may have committed. Others were not so fortunate. Three members of the Nixon cabinet (two attorneys general and a secretary of commerce) were convicted and sentenced for their crimes in the Watergate affair. Nixon's White House chief of staff, H. R. Haldeman, and his domestic affairs adviser, John Ehrlichman, were convicted of conspiracy, obstruction of justice, and perjury. Other officials were tried, and most were convicted, on related charges.[6]

The Watergate affair posed one of the most serious challenges to the constitutional order of modern American government. The incident ultimately developed into a struggle over the rule of law between the president, on the one hand, and Congress and the courts, on the other. In the end, the constitutional principle separating power among the executive, legislative, and judicial branches prevented the president from controlling the Watergate investigation. The principle of checks and balances allowed Congress to threaten Nixon with impeachment. The belief that Nixon had violated the Constitution finally prompted members of his own party to support impeachment, leading the president to resign. In 1992, 70 percent of Americans still viewed Nixon's actions as having warranted his resignation.[7] In some countries, an irregular change in government leadership provides an opportunity for a palace coup, an armed revolution, or a military dictatorship. But here, significantly, no political violence erupted after Nixon's resignation; in fact, none was expected. Constitutional order in the United States had been put to a test, and it passed with high honors.

---

[1]ABC News Poll, 17 June 2002 (telephone interview of 1,004 participants).

[2]Carl Bernstein and Bob Woodward, *All the President's Men* (New York: Warner, 1975); Stanley I. Kutler, *The Wars of Watergate* (New York: Knopf, 1990).

[3]Bernstein and Woodward, *All the President's Men*, p. 30.

[4]William Doyle, *Inside the Oval Office: The White House Tapes from FDR to Clinton* (New York: Kodansha International, 1999), p. 169.

[5]*The Encyclopedia of American Facts and Dates* (New York: Crowell, 1979), p. 946.

[6]Richard B. Morris (ed.), *Encyclopedia of American History* (New York: Harper & Row, 1976), p. 544.

[7]Gallup Organization, *Gallup Poll Monthly* (June 1992): 2–3.

He went on to list the many deliberate acts of the king that had exceeded the legitimate role of government. The last and lengthiest item on Jefferson's original draft of the Declaration was the king's support of the slave trade. Although Jefferson did not condemn slavery, he denounced the king for

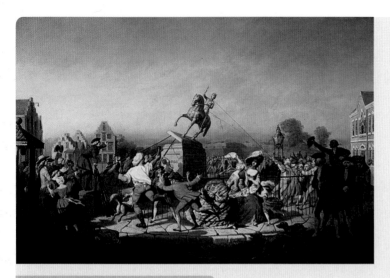

Toppling Tyrants: Then and Now

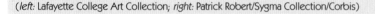

A gilded equestrian statue of George III (*left*) once stood at the tip of
Manhattan. On July 9, 1776, citizens responded to the news of the
Declaration of Independence by toppling the statue. It was melted down
and converted into musket balls. In 2003—with a little help from American
soldiers—Iraqi citizens (*right*) toppled a statue of their deposed leader,
Saddam Hussein.

(*left*: Lafayette College Art Collection; *right*: Patrick Robert/Sygma Collection/Corbis)

enslaving a people, engaging in the slave trade, and proposing that if the
slaves were freed, they would attack their masters. When South Carolina and
Georgia, two states with an interest in continuing the wretched practice,
objected, Jefferson and the committee dropped the offending paragraph.
Finally, Jefferson declared that the colonies were "Free and Independent
States," with no political connection to Great Britain.

The major premise of the Declaration of Independence is that the people
have a right to revolt if they determine that their government is denying them
their legitimate rights. The long list of the king's actions was evidence of such
denial. So the people had the right to rebel, to form a new government.

On July 2, 1776, the Second Continental Congress finally voted for independence. The vote was by state, and the motion carried 11–0. (Rhode Island
was not present, and the New York delegation, lacking instructions, did not
cast its yea vote until July 15.) Two days later, on July 4, the Declaration of
Independence was approved, with few changes. Several representatives
insisted on removing language they thought would incite the colonists. In
the end, even though Jefferson's compelling words were left almost exactly
as he had written them, the adjustments tugged at the Virginian's personal
insecurities. According to historian Joseph Ellis, while the congress debated
various changes to the document, "Jefferson sat silently and sullenly,
regarding each proposed revision as another defacement."[14]

By August, fifty-five revolutionaries had signed the Declaration of Independence, pledging "our lives, our fortunes and our sacred honor" in support of their rebellion against the world's most powerful nation. This was no empty pledge: an act of rebellion was treason. Had they lost the Revolutionary War, the signers would have faced a gruesome fate. The punishment for treason was hanging and drawing and quartering—the victim was hanged until half-dead from strangulation, then disemboweled, and finally cut into four pieces while still alive. We celebrate the Fourth of July with fireworks and flag waving, parades, and picnics. We sometimes forget that the Revolution was a matter of life and death.

The war imposed an agonizing choice on colonial Catholics, who were treated with intolerance by the overwhelmingly Protestant population. No other religious group found the choice so difficult. Catholics could either join the revolutionaries, who were opposed to Catholicism, or remain loyal to England and risk new hostility and persecution. But Catholics were few in number, perhaps twenty-five thousand at the time of independence (or 1 percent of the population). Anti-Catholic revolutionaries recognized that if Catholics opposed independence in Maryland and Pennsylvania, where their numbers were greatest, victory might be jeopardized. Furthermore, enlisting the support of Catholic France for the cause of independence would be difficult in the face of strong opposition from colonial Catholics. So the revolutionaries wooed Catholics to their cause.[15]

The War of Independence lasted far longer than anyone expected. It began in a moment of confusion, when a shot rang out as British soldiers approached the town of Lexington, Massachusetts, on April 19, 1775. The end came six and a half years later with Lord Cornwallis's surrender of his army of six thousand at Yorktown, Virginia, on October 19, 1781. It was a costly war: a greater percentage of the population died or was wounded during the Revolution than in any other U.S. conflict except the Civil War.[16]

Still, one in five colonists remained loyal to the British Crown. In New York, several hundred signed their own declaration of dependence. Prominent family names were easy to spot. But most signers were ordinary people: carpenters and blacksmiths, farmers, bakers, and perfumers. The document lacked Jefferson's rhetorical force, however. After the war, the loyalists were stripped of their rights, property, and dignity. As many as 80,000 abandoned the new United States for other parts of the British Empire. About half headed north to Canada, including 3,000 blacks, former slaves who secured their freedom by fighting for the British. In another migration, 1,200 of these former slaves relocated in 1792 to Sierra Leone, where they formed an experimental free black colony.[17]

With hindsight, of course, we can see that the British were engaged in an arduous and perhaps hopeless conflict. America was simply too vast to subdue without imposing total military rule. Britain also had to transport men and supplies over the enormous distance of the Atlantic Ocean. Also, the Americans' courtship of Britain's rivals, owing in large part to the indefatigable advocacy and diplomacy of John Adams,[18] resulted in support from the French navy and several million dollars in Dutch loans that helped to bolster General Washington's revolutionary forces. Finally, although the

Americans had neither paid troops nor professional soldiers, they were fighting for a cause: the defense of their liberty. The British never understood the power of this fighting faith or, given the international support for the American cause, the totality of the forces arrayed against them.

From Revolution to Confederation

By declaring their independence from England, the colonists left themselves without any real central government. So the revolutionaries proclaimed the creation of a **republic**. Strictly speaking, a republic is a government without a monarch, but the term had come to mean a government based on the consent of the governed, whose power is exercised by representatives who are responsible to them. A republic need not be a democracy, and this was fine with the founders; at that time, democracy was associated with mob rule and instability (see Chapter 2). The revolutionaries were less concerned with determining who would control their new government than with limiting its powers. They had revolted in the name of liberty, and now they wanted a government with strictly defined powers. To make sure they got one, they meant to define its structure and powers in writing.

The Articles of Confederation

Barely a week after the Declaration of Independence was signed, the Second Continental Congress received a committee report entitled "Articles of Confederation and Perpetual Union." A **confederation** is a loose association of independent states that agree to cooperate on specified matters. In a confederation, the states retain their sovereignty, which means that each has supreme power within its borders. The central government is weak; it can only coordinate, not control, the actions of its sovereign states. Consequently, the individual states are strong.

The congress debated the **Articles of Confederation**, the compact among the thirteen original colonies that established the first government of the United States, for more than a year. The Articles were adopted by the Continental Congress on November 15, 1777, and finally took effect on March 1, 1781, following approval by all thirteen states. For more than three years, then, Americans had fought a revolution without an effective government. Raising money, troops, and supplies for the war had daunted and exhausted the leadership.

The Articles jealously guarded state sovereignty; their provisions clearly reflected the delegates' fears that a strong central government would resemble British rule. Article II, for example, stated, "Each state retains its sovereignty, freedom, and independence, and every power, jurisdiction, and right, which is not by this Confederation expressly delegated to the United States, in Congress assembled."

Under the Articles, each state, regardless of its size, had one vote in the congress. Votes on financing the war and other important issues required the consent of at least nine of the thirteen states. The common danger,

republic
A government without a monarch; a government rooted in the consent of the governed, whose power is exercised by elected representatives responsible to the governed.

confederation
A loose association of independent states that agree to cooperate on specified matters.

Articles of Confederation
The compact among the thirteen original states that established the first government of the United States.

Britain, had forced the young republic to function under the Articles, but this first effort at government was inadequate to the task. The delegates had succeeded in crafting a national government that was largely powerless.

The Articles failed for at least four reasons. First, they did not give the national government the power to tax. As a result, the congress had to plead for money from the states to pay for the war and carry on the affairs of the new nation. A government that cannot reliably raise revenue cannot expect to govern effectively. Second, the Articles made no provision for an independent leadership position to direct the government (the president was merely the presiding officer of the congress). The omission was deliberate—the colonists feared the reestablishment of a monarchy—but it left the nation without a leader. Third, the Articles did not allow the national government to regulate interstate and foreign commerce. (When John Adams proposed that the confederation enter into a commercial treaty with Britain after the war, he was asked, "Would you like one treaty or thirteen, Mr. Adams?")[19] Finally, the Articles could not be amended without the unanimous agreement of the congress and the assent of all the state legislatures; thus, each state had the power to veto any changes to the confederation.

The goal of the delegates who drew up the Articles of Confederation was to retain power in the states. This was consistent with republicanism, which viewed the remote power of a national government as a danger to liberty. In this sense alone, the Articles were a grand success. They completely hobbled the infant government.

Disorder Under the Confederation

Once the Revolution had ended and independence was a reality, it became clear that the national government had neither the economic nor the military power to function effectively. Freed from wartime austerity, Americans rushed to purchase goods from abroad. The national government's efforts to restrict foreign imports were blocked by exporting states, which feared retaliation from their foreign customers. Debt mounted and, for many, bankruptcy followed.

The problem was particularly severe in Massachusetts, where high interest rates and high state taxes were forcing farmers into bankruptcy. In 1786, Daniel Shays, a Revolutionary War veteran, marched on a western Massachusetts courthouse with fifteen hundred supporters armed with barrel staves and pitchforks: they were protesting against high taxes levied by the state to retire its wartime debt.[20] Later, they attacked an arsenal. Called Shays's Rebellion, the revolt against the established order continued into 1787. Massachusetts appealed to the confederation for help. Horrified by the threat of domestic upheaval, the congress approved a $530,000 requisition for the establishment of a national army. But the plan failed: every state except Virginia rejected the request for money. Finally, the governor of Massachusetts called out the militia and restored order.[21]

The rebellion demonstrated the impotence of the confederation and the urgent need to suppress insurrections and maintain domestic order. Proof to skeptics that Americans could not govern themselves, the rebellion alarmed

Voting for Independence

The Second Continental Congress voted for independence on July 2, 1776. John Adams of Massachusetts viewed the day "as the most memorable epocha [significant event] in the history of America." In this painting by John Trumbull, the drafting committee presents the Declaration of Independence to the patriots who would later sign it. The committee, grouped in front of the desk, consisted of (*from left to right*) Adams, Roger Sherman (Connecticut), Robert Livingston (New York), Thomas Jefferson (Virginia), and Benjamin Franklin (Pennsylvania).

Trumbull painted the scene years after the event. Relying on Jefferson's faulty memory and his own artistic license, Trumbull created a scene that bears little resemblance to reality. First, there was no ceremonial moment when the committee presented its draft to the congress. Second, the room's elegance belied its actual appearance. Third, the doors are in the wrong place. Fourth, the heavy drapes substitute for actual venetian blinds. And, fifth, the mahogany armchairs replaced the plain Windsor design used by the delegates. Nevertheless, the painting remains an icon of American political history.

(© Francis G. Mayer/Corbis)

all American leaders, with the exception of Jefferson. From Paris, where he was serving as American ambassador, he remarked, "A little rebellion now and then is a good thing; the tree of liberty must be refreshed from time to time with the blood of patriots and tyrants."[22]

From Confederation to Constitution

Order, the original purpose of government, was breaking down under the Articles of Confederation. The "league of friendship" envisioned in the Articles was not enough to hold the nation together in peacetime.

Some states had taken halting steps toward encouraging a change in the national government. In 1785, Massachusetts asked the congress to revise the Articles of Confederation, but the congress took no action. In 1786, Virginia invited the states to attend a convention at Annapolis, Maryland, to explore revisions aimed at improving commercial regulation. The meeting was both a failure and a success. Only five states sent delegates, but they seized the opportunity to call for another meeting—with a far broader mission—in Philadelphia the next year. That convention would be charged with devising "such further provisions as shall appear ... necessary to render the constitution of the Federal Government adequate to the exigencies of the Union." The congress later agreed to the convention but limited its mission to "the sole and express purpose of revising the Articles of Confederation."[23]

Shays's Rebellion lent a sense of urgency to the task before the Philadelphia convention. The congress's inability to confront the rebellion was evidence that a stronger national government was necessary to preserve order and property—to protect the states from internal as well as external dangers. "While the Declaration was directed against an excess of authority," observed Supreme Court Justice Robert H. Jackson some one hundred fifty years later, "the Constitution [that followed the Articles of Confederation] was directed against anarchy."[24]

Twelve of the thirteen states named seventy-four delegates to convene in Philadelphia, the most important city in America, in May 1787. (Rhode Island, derisively renamed "Rogue Island" by a Boston newspaper, was the one exception. The state legislature sulkily rejected participating because it feared a strong national government.) Fifty-five delegates eventually showed up at the statehouse in Philadelphia, but no more than thirty were present at any one time during that sweltering spring and summer. The framers were not demigods, but many historians believe that such an assembly will not be seen again. Highly educated, they typically were fluent in Latin and Greek. Products of the Enlightenment, they relied on classical liberalism for the Constitution's philosophical underpinnings.

They were also veterans of the political intrigues of their states, and so were highly practical politicians who knew how to maneuver. Although well versed in ideas, they subscribed to the view expressed by one delegate that "experience must be our only guide, reason may mislead us."[25] Fearing for their fragile union, the delegates resolved to keep their proceedings secret.

The Constitutional Convention, at the time called the Federal Convention, officially opened on May 25. Within the first week, Edmund Randolph of Virginia had presented a long list of changes, suggested by fellow Virginian James Madison, that would replace the weak confederation of states with a powerful national government rather than revise it within its original framework. The delegates unanimously agreed to debate Randolph's proposal, called the **Virginia Plan**. Almost immediately, then, they rejected the idea of amending the Articles of Confederation, working instead to create an entirely new constitution.

Virginia Plan
A set of proposals for a new government, submitted to the Constitutional Convention of 1787; included separation of the government into three branches, division of the legislature into two houses, and proportional representation in the legislature.

James Madison, Father of the Constitution

Although he dismissed the accolade "Father of the Constitution," Madison deserved it more than anyone else. As do most fathers, he exercised a powerful influence in debates (and was on the losing side of more than half of them).

(© Bettmann/Corbis)

The Virginia Plan

The Virginia Plan dominated the convention's deliberations for the rest of the summer, making several important proposals for a strong central government:

- That the powers of the government be divided among three separate branches: a **legislative branch**, for making laws; an **executive branch**, for enforcing laws; and a **judicial branch**, for interpreting laws.
- That the legislature consist of two houses. The first would be chosen by the people, the second by the members of the first house from among candidates nominated by the state legislatures.
- That each state's representation in the legislature be in proportion to the taxes it paid to the national government or in proportion to its free population.
- That an executive, consisting of an unspecified number of people, be selected by the legislature and serve for a single term.
- That the national judiciary include one or more supreme courts and other, lower courts, with judges appointed for life by the legislature.
- That the executive and a number of national judges serve as a council of revision, to approve or veto (disapprove) legislative acts. Their veto could be overridden by a vote of both houses of the legislature.
- That the scope of powers of all three branches be far greater than that assigned the national government by the Articles of Confederation and that the legislature be empowered to override state laws.

By proposing a powerful national legislature that could override state laws, the Virginia Plan clearly advocated a new form of government. It was to have a mixed structure, with more authority over the states and new authority over the people.

Madison was a monumental force in the ensuing debate on the proposals. He kept records of the proceedings that reveal his frequent and brilliant participation and give us insight into his thinking about freedom, order, and equality.

For example, his proposal that senators serve a nine-year term reveals his thinking about equality. Madison foresaw an increase "of those who will labor under all the hardships of life, and secretly sigh for a more equal distribution of its blessings. These may in time outnumber those who are placed above the feelings of indigence."[26] Power, then, could flow into the hands of the numerous poor. The stability of the senate, however, with its nine-year terms and election by the state legislatures, would provide a barrier against the "sighs of the poor" for more equality. Although most delegates shared Madison's apprehension about equality, the nine-year term was voted down.

The Constitution that emerged from the convention bore only a partial resemblance to the document Madison wanted to create. He endorsed seventy-one specific proposals, but he ended up on the losing side on forty of them.[27] And the parts of the Virginia Plan that were ultimately included in

legislative branch
The law-making branch of government.

executive branch
The law-enforcing branch of government.

judicial branch
The law-interpreting branch of government.

the Constitution were not adopted without challenge. Conflicts revolved primarily around the basis for representation in the legislature, the method of choosing legislators, and the structure of the executive branch.

The New Jersey Plan

When in 1787 it appeared that much of the Virginia Plan would be approved by the big states, the small states united in opposition. They feared that if each state's representation in the new legislature was based only on the size of its population, the states with large populations would be able to dominate the new government and the needs and wishes of the small states would be ignored. William Paterson of New Jersey introduced an alternative set of resolutions, written to preserve the spirit of the Articles of Confederation by amending rather than replacing them. The **New Jersey Plan** included the following proposals:

- That a single-chamber legislature have the power to raise revenue and regulate commerce.
- That the states have equal representation in the legislature and choose its members.
- That a multiperson executive be elected by the legislature, with powers similar to those proposed under the Virginia Plan but without the right to veto legislation.
- That a supreme tribunal be created, with a limited jurisdiction. (There was no provision for a system of national courts.)
- That the acts of the legislature be binding on the states—that is, that they be regarded as "the supreme law of the respective states," with the option of force to compel obedience.

After only three days of deliberation, the New Jersey Plan was defeated in the first major convention vote, 7–3. However, the small states had enough support to force a compromise on the issue of representation in the legislature. Table 3.1 compares the New Jersey Plan with the Virginia Plan.

New Jersey Plan
Submitted by the head of the New Jersey delegation to the Constitutional Convention of 1787, a set of nine resolutions that would have, in effect, preserved the Articles of Confederation by amending rather than replacing them.

TABLE 3.1	Major Differences Between the Virginia Plan and the New Jersey Plan	
Characteristic	**Virginia Plan**	**New Jersey Plan**
Legislature	Two chambers	One chamber
Legislative power	Derived from the people	Derived from the states
Executive	Unspecified size	More than one person
Decision rule	Majority	Extraordinary majority
State laws	Legislature can override	National law is supreme
Executive removal	By Congress	By a majority of the states
Courts	National judiciary	No provision for national judiciary
Ratification	By the people	By the states

The Great Compromise

The Virginia Plan provided for a two-chamber legislature, with representation in both chambers based on population. The idea of two chambers was never seriously challenged, but the idea of representation according to population stirred up heated and prolonged debate. The small states demanded equal representation for all states, but another vote rejected that concept for the House of Representatives. The debate continued. Finally, the Connecticut delegation moved that each state have an equal vote in the Senate. Still another poll showed that the delegations were equally divided on this proposal.

A committee was created to resolve the deadlock. It consisted of one delegate from each state, chosen by secret ballot. After working straight through the Independence Day recess, the committee reported reaching the **Great Compromise** (sometimes called the Connecticut Compromise). Representation in the House of Representatives would be apportioned according to the population of each state. Initially, there would be fifty-six members. Revenue-raising acts would originate in the House. Most important, the states would be represented equally in the Senate, with two senators each. Senators would be selected by their state legislatures, not directly by the people.

The deadlock broke when the Massachusetts delegation divided evenly, allowing the equal state vote to pass by the narrowest of margins, 5 states to 4.[28] The small states got their equal representation, the big states their proportional representation. The small states might dominate the Senate and the big states might control the House, but because all legislation had to be approved by both chambers, neither group would be able to dominate the other. To be perpetually assured of state equality, no amendment to the Constitution could violate the equal state representation principle.[29]

Compromise on the Presidency

Conflict replaced compromise when the delegates turned to the executive branch. They did agree on a one-person executive, a president, but they disagreed on how the executive would be selected and what the term of office would be. The delegates distrusted the people's judgment; some feared that popular election of the president would arouse public passions. Consequently, the delegates rejected the idea. At the same time, representatives of the small states feared that election by the legislature would allow the big states to control the executive.

Once again, a committee composed of one member from each participating state was chosen to find a compromise. That committee fashioned the cumbersome presidential election system we still use today, the **electoral college**. (The Constitution does not use the expression *electoral college*.) Under this system, a group of electors would be chosen for the sole purpose of selecting the president and vice president. Each state legislature would choose a number of electors equal to the number of its representatives in Congress. Each elector would then vote for two people. The candidate with the most votes would become president, provided that the number of votes constituted a majority; the

Great Compromise
Submitted by the Connecticut delegation to the Constitutional Convention of 1787, and thus also known as the Connecticut Compromise, a plan calling for a bicameral legislature in which the House of Representatives would be apportioned according to population and the states would be represented equally in the Senate.

electoral college
A body of electors chosen by voters to cast ballots for president and vice president.

person with the next-greatest number of votes would become vice president. (The procedure was changed in 1804 by the Twelfth Amendment, which mandates separate votes for each office.) If no candidate won a majority, the House of Representatives would choose a president, with each state casting one vote.

The electoral college compromise eliminated the fear of a popular vote for president. At the same time, it satisfied the small states. If the electoral college failed to elect a president, which the delegates expected would happen, election by the House would give every state the same voice in the selection process. Finally, the delegates agreed that the president's term of office should be four years and that presidents should be eligible for reelection with no limit on the number of terms any individual president could serve. (The Twenty-second Amendment, ratified in 1951, now limits the presidency to two terms.)

The delegates also realized that removing a president from office would be a serious political matter. For that reason, they involved both of the other two branches of government in the process. The House alone was empowered to charge a president with "Treason, Bribery, or other high Crimes and Misdemeanors" (Article II, Section 4), by a majority vote. The Senate was given the sole power to try the president on the House's charges. It could convict, and thus remove, a president only by a two-thirds vote (an **extraordinary majority**, a majority greater than the minimum of 50 percent plus one). And the chief justice of the United States was required to preside over the Senate trial. Only two presidents have been impeached by the House: Andrew Johnson and Bill Clinton; neither was convicted.

The Final Product

Once the delegates had resolved their major disagreements, they dispatched the remaining issues relatively quickly. A committee was then appointed to organize and write up the results of the proceedings. Twenty-three resolutions had been debated and approved by the convention; these were reorganized under seven articles in the draft constitution. The preamble, which was the last section to be drafted, begins with a phrase that would have been impossible to write when the convention opened. This single sentence contains four elements that form the foundation of the American political tradition:[30]

- *It creates a people:* "We the people of the United States" was a dramatic departure from a loose confederation of states.
- *It explains the reason for the Constitution:* "in order to form a more perfect Union" was an indirect way of saying that the first effort, the Articles of Confederation, had been inadequate.
- *It articulates goals:* "[to] establish Justice, insure domestic Tranquility, provide for the common defence, promote the general Welfare, and secure the Blessings of Liberty to ourselves and our Posterity"—in other words, the government exists to promote order and freedom.
- *It fashions a government:* "do ordain and establish this Constitution for the United States of America."

extraordinary majority
A majority greater than the minimum of 50 percent plus one.

The Basic Principles

In creating the Constitution, the founders relied on four political principles—republicanism, federalism, separation of powers, and checks and balances—that together established a revolutionary new political order.

Republicanism is a form of government in which power resides in the people and is exercised by their elected representatives. The idea of republicanism may be traced to the Greek philosopher Aristotle (384–322 B.C.), who advocated a constitution that combined principles of both democratic and oligarchic government. The framers were determined to avoid aristocracy (rule by a hereditary class), monarchy (rule by one person), and direct democracy (rule by the people). A republic was both new and daring: no people had ever been governed by a republic on so vast a scale.

The framers themselves were far from sure that their government could be sustained. They had no model of republican government to follow; moreover, republican government was thought to be suitable only for small territories, where the interests of the public would be obvious and the government would be within the reach of every citizen. After the convention ended, Benjamin Franklin was asked what sort of government the new nation would have. "A republic," the old man replied, "if you can keep it."

Federalism is the division of power between a central government and regional governments. Citizens are thus subject to two different bodies of law. Federalism can be seen as standing between two competing government schemes. On the one side is unitary government, in which all power is vested in a central authority. On the other side stands confederation, a loose union of powerful states. In a confederation, the states surrender some power to a central government but retain the rest. The Articles of Confederation, as we have seen, divided power between loosely knit states and a weak central government. The Constitution also divides power between the states and a central government, but it confers substantial powers on a national government at the expense of the states.

According to the Constitution, the powers vested in the national and state governments are derived from the people, who remain the ultimate sovereigns. National and state governments can exercise their power over people and property within their spheres of authority. But at the same time, by participating in the electoral process or by amending their governing charters, the people can restrain both the national and the state governments if necessary to preserve liberty.

The Constitution lists the powers of the national government and the powers denied to the states. All other powers remain with the states. Generally, the states are required to give up only the powers necessary to create an effective national government; the national government is limited in turn to the powers specified in the Constitution. Despite the specific lists, the Constitution does not clearly describe the spheres of authority within which the powers can be exercised. As we will discuss in Chapter 4, limits on the exercise of power by the national government and the states have evolved as a result of political and military conflicts; moreover, the limits have proved changeable.

republicanism
A form of government in which power resides in the people and is exercised by their elected representatives.

federalism
The division of power between a central government and regional governments.

FIGURE 3.1   The Constitution and the Electoral Process

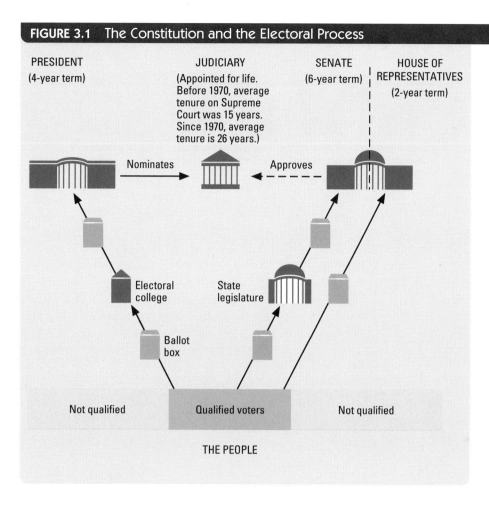

PRESIDENT
(4-year term)

JUDICIARY
(Appointed for life.
Before 1970, average
tenure on Supreme
Court was 15 years.
Since 1970, average
tenure is 26 years.)

SENATE
(6-year term)

HOUSE OF
REPRESENTATIVES
(2-year term)

Nominates

Approves

Electoral
college

State
legislature

Ballot
box

Not qualified

Qualified voters

Not qualified

THE PEOPLE

The framers were afraid of majority rule, and that fear is reflected in the electoral process for national office described in the Constitution. The people, speaking through the voters, participated directly only in the choice of their representatives in the House. The president and senators were elected indirectly, through the electoral college and state legislatures. (Direct election of senators did not become law until 1913, when the Seventeenth Amendment was ratified.) Judicial appointments are, and always have been, far removed from representative links to the people. Judges are nominated by the president and approved by the Senate.

Separation of powers and checks and balances are two distinct principles, but both are necessary to ensure that one branch does not dominate the government. **Separation of powers** is the assignment of the lawmaking, law-enforcing, and law-interpreting functions of government to independent legislative, executive, and judicial branches, respectively. Separation of powers safeguards liberty by ensuring that all government power does not fall into the hands of a single person or group of people. However, the Constitution constrained majority rule by limiting the people's direct influence on the electoral process (see Figure 3.1). In theory, separation of powers means that one branch cannot exercise the powers of the other branches. In practice, however, the separation is far from complete. One scholar has suggested that what we have instead is "separate institutions sharing powers."[31]

Checks and balances is a means of giving each branch of government some scrutiny of and control over the other branches. The aim is to prevent the exclusive exercise of certain powers by any one of the three branches. For example, only Congress can enact laws. But the president (through the veto power) can cancel them, and the courts (by finding that a law violates the Constitution) can strike them down. The process goes on as Congress

separation of powers
The assignment of lawmaking, law-enforcing, and law-interpreting functions to separate branches of government.

checks and balances
A government structure that gives each branch some scrutiny of and control over the other branches.

FIGURE 3.2   Separation of Powers and Checks and Balances

Separation of powers is the assignment of lawmaking, law-enforcing, and law-interpreting functions to the legislative, executive, and judicial branches, respectively. The phenomenon is illustrated by the diagonal from upper left to lower right in the figure. Checks and balances give each branch some power over the other branches. For example, the executive branch possesses some legislative power, and the legislative branch possesses some executive power. These checks and balances are listed outside the diagonal.

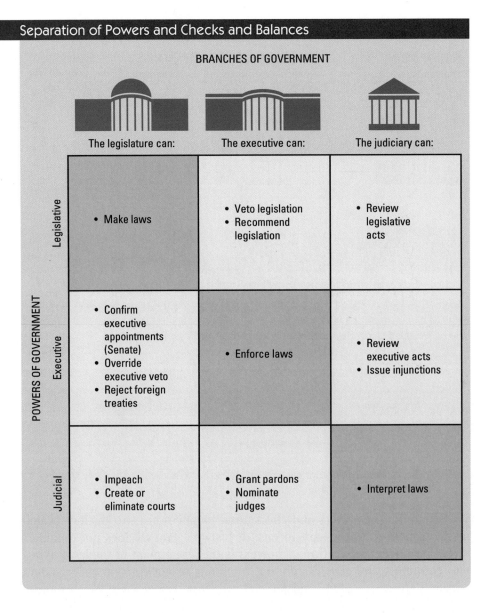

BRANCHES OF GOVERNMENT

POWERS OF GOVERNMENT	The legislature can:	The executive can:	The judiciary can:
Legislative	• Make laws	• Veto legislation • Recommend legislation	• Review legislative acts
Executive	• Confirm executive appointments (Senate) • Override executive veto • Reject foreign treaties	• Enforce laws	• Review executive acts • Issue injunctions
Judicial	• Impeach • Create or eliminate courts	• Grant pardons • Nominate judges	• Interpret laws

and the president sometimes begin the legislative process anew, attempting to reformulate laws to address the flaws identified by the Supreme Court in its decisions. In a "check on a check," Congress can override a president's veto by an extraordinary (two-thirds) majority in each chamber. Congress is also empowered to propose amendments to the Constitution, counteracting the courts' power to invalidate. Figure 3.2 depicts the relationship between separation of powers and checks and balances.

The Articles of the Constitution

In addition to the preamble, the Constitution contains seven articles. The first three establish the separate branches of government and specify their internal operations and powers. The remaining four define the relationships among the states, explain the process of amendment, declare the supremacy of national law, and explain the procedure for ratifying the Constitution.

Article I: The Legislative Article. In structuring their new government, the framers began with the legislative branch because they considered lawmaking the most important function of a republican government. Article I is the most detailed, and therefore the longest, of the articles. It grants substantial but limited legislative power to Congress (Article I begins: "All legislative Power herein granted...."). It defines the bicameral (two-chamber) character of Congress and describes the internal operating procedures of the House of Representatives and the Senate. Section 8 of Article I articulates the principle of **enumerated powers**, which means that Congress can exercise only the powers that the Constitution assigns to it. Eighteen powers are enumerated; the first seventeen are specific powers. For example, the third clause of Section 8 gives Congress the power to regulate interstate commerce. (One of the chief shortcomings of the Articles of Confederation was the lack of a means to cope with trade wars between the states. The solution was to vest control of interstate commerce in the national government.)

The last clause in Section 8, known as the **necessary and proper clause** (or the elastic clause), gives Congress the means to execute the enumerated powers (see the appendix). This clause is the basis of Congress's **implied powers**—those powers that Congress needs to execute its enumerated powers. For example, the power to levy and collect taxes (clause 1) and the power to coin money and regulate its value (clause 5), when joined with the necessary and proper clause (clause 18), imply that Congress has the power to charter a bank. Otherwise, the national government would have no means of managing the money it collects through its power to tax. Implied powers clearly expand the enumerated powers conferred on Congress by the Constitution.

Article II: The Executive Article. Article II grants executive power to a president. The article establishes the president's term of office, the procedure for electing the president by means of electors, the qualifications for becoming president, and the president's duties and powers. The last include acting as commander in chief of the military; making treaties (which must be ratified by a two-thirds vote in the Senate); and appointing government officers, diplomats, and judges (again, with the advice and consent of the Senate).

The president also has legislative powers—part of the constitutional system of checks and balances. For example, the Constitution requires that the president periodically inform Congress of "the State of the Union" and of the policies and programs that the executive branch intends to advocate in the coming year. Today, this is done annually in the president's State of the Union address. Under special circumstances, the president can also convene or adjourn Congress.

The duty to "take Care that the Laws be faithfully executed" in Section 3 has provided presidents with a reservoir of power. President Nixon tried to use this power when he refused to turn over the Watergate tapes despite a

enumerated powers
The powers explicitly granted to Congress by the Constitution.

necessary and proper clause
The last clause in Section 8 of Article I of the Constitution, which gives Congress the means to execute its enumerated powers. This clause is the basis for Congress's implied powers. Also called the *elastic clause*.

implied powers
Those powers that Congress needs to execute its enumerated powers.

How Many Pens Does It Take to Sign a Bill into Law?

Answer: It depends on the number of people a president wants to thank. The president gives his approval to legislation by signing it into law. Beginning in the 1960s, the bill-signing ceremony became an art form, garnering much press attention. The president would typically employ many pens in small strokes for his signature and then distribute the pens as souvenirs to the people instrumental in the bill's passage. Here President Barack Obama picks up the first pen (*left*), signs a portion of his signature (*middle*), then jokes about the multiple pens he will use to complete his signature on the American Recovery and Reinvestment Act, Tuesday, February 17, 2009, during a ceremony at the Denver Museum of Nature and Science (*right*). We wonder whether the pens were manufactured in the United States.

(AP Photo/David Zalubowski)

judicial subpoena in a criminal trial. He claimed broad executive privilege, an extension of the executive power implied in Article II. But the Supreme Court rejected his claim, arguing that it violated the separation of powers, because the decision to release or withhold information in a criminal trial is a judicial, not an executive, function.

Article III: The Judicial Article. The third article was left purposely vague. The Constitution established the Supreme Court as the highest court in the land. But beyond that, the framers were unable to agree on the need for a national judiciary or on its size, its composition, or the procedures it should follow. They left these issues to Congress, which resolved them by creating a system of federal (that is, national) courts, separate from the state courts.

Unless they are impeached, federal judges serve for life. They are appointed to indefinite terms "during good Behaviour," and their salaries cannot be reduced while they hold office. These stipulations reinforce the separation of powers; they see to it that judges are independent of the other branches and that they do not have to fear retribution for their exercise of judicial power.

Congress exercises a potential check on the judicial branch through its power to create (and eliminate) lower federal courts. Congress can also restrict the power of the federal courts to decide cases. And, as we have noted, the president appoints, with the advice and consent of the Senate, the justices of the Supreme Court and the judges of the lower federal courts. Since the 1980s, especially, the judicial appointment process has become highly politicized, with both Democrats and Republicans accusing each other of obstructionism or extremism in several high-profile confirmation debates.

Article III does not explicitly give the courts the power of **judicial review**, that is, the authority to invalidate congressional or presidential actions because they violate the Constitution. That power has been inferred from the logic, structure, and theory of the Constitution and from important court rulings, some of which we discuss in subsequent chapters.

The Remaining Articles. The remaining four articles of the Constitution cover a lot of ground. Article IV requires that the judicial acts and criminal warrants of each state be honored in all other states, and it forbids discrimination against citizens of one state by another state. This provision promotes equality; it keeps the states from treating outsiders differently from their own citizens. For example, suppose Smith and Jones both reside in Illinois, and an Illinois court awards Smith a judgment of $100,000 against Jones. Jones moves to Alaska, hoping to avoid payment. Rather than force Smith to bring a new lawsuit against Jones in Alaska, the Alaska courts give full faith and credit to the Illinois judgment, enforcing it as their own. The origin of Article IV can be traced to the Articles of Confederation.

Article IV also allows the addition of new states and stipulates that the national government will protect the states against foreign invasion and domestic violence.

Article V specifies the methods for amending (changing) the Constitution and guarantees equal state representation in the Senate. We will have more to say about this amendment process shortly.

An important component of Article VI is the **supremacy clause**, which asserts that when the Constitution, national laws, and treaties conflict with state or local laws, the first three take precedence over the last two. The stipulation is vital to the operation of federalism. In keeping with the supremacy clause, Article VI requires that all national and state officials, elected or appointed, take an oath to support the Constitution. The article also mandates that religious affiliation or belief cannot be a prerequisite for holding government office.

Finally, Article VII describes the ratification process, stipulating that approval by conventions in nine states would be necessary for the Constitution to take effect.

judicial review
The power to declare congressional (and presidential) acts invalid because they violate the Constitution.

supremacy clause
The clause in Article VI of the Constitution that asserts that national laws take precedence over state and local laws when they conflict.

The Framers' Motives

Some argue that the Constitution is essentially a conservative document written by wealthy men to advance their own interests. One distinguished historian who wrote in the early 1900s, Charles A. Beard, maintained that the delegates had much to gain from a strong national government.[32] Many held government securities dating from the Revolutionary War that had become practically worthless under the Articles of Confederation. A strong national government would protect their property and pay off the nation's debts.

Beard's argument, that the Constitution was crafted to protect the economic interests of this small group of creditors, provoked a generation of historians to examine the existing financial records of the convention delegates. Their scholarship has largely discredited his once-popular view.[33] For example, it turns out that seven of the delegates who left the convention or refused to sign the Constitution held public securities worth more than twice the total of the holdings of the thirty-nine delegates who did sign. Moreover, the most influential delegates owned no securities. And only a few delegates appear to have directly benefited economically from the new government.[34] Still, there is little doubt about the general homogeneity of the delegates or about their concern for producing a stable economic order that would preserve and promote the interests of some more than others.

What did motivate the framers? Surely economic considerations were important, but they were not the major issues. The single most important factor leading to the Constitutional Convention was the inability of the national or state governments to maintain order under the loose structure of the Articles of Confederation. Certainly, order involved the protection of property, but the framers had a broader view of property than their portfolios of government securities. They wanted to protect their homes, their families, and their means of livelihood from impending anarchy.

Although they disagreed bitterly on the structure and mechanics of the national government, the framers agreed on the most vital issues. For example, three of the most crucial features of the Constitution—the power to tax, the necessary and proper clause, and the supremacy clause—were approved unanimously without debate; experience had taught the delegates that a strong national government was essential if the United States were to survive. The motivation to create order was so strong, in fact, that the framers were willing to draft clauses that protected the most undemocratic of all institutions: slavery.

The Slavery Issue

The institution of slavery was well ingrained in American life at the time of the Constitutional Convention, and slavery helped shape the Constitution, although it is mentioned nowhere by name in it. (According to the first national census in 1790, nearly 18 percent of the population—697,000 people—lived in slavery.) It is doubtful, in fact, that there would have been a Constitution if the delegates had had to resolve the slavery issue, for the southern states would have opposed a constitution that prohibited slavery. Opponents of slavery were in the minority, and they were willing to tolerate its continuation in the interest of forging a union, perhaps believing that the issue could be resolved another day.

The question of representation in the House of Representatives brought the slavery issue close to the surface of the debate at the Constitutional Convention, and it led to the Great Compromise. Representation in the House was to be based on population. But who counted in the population? States with large slave populations wanted all their inhabitants, slave and free, counted equally; states with few slaves wanted only the free population counted. The delegates agreed unanimously that in apportioning representation in the House and in assessing direct taxes, the population of each state was to be determined by adding "the whole Number of free Persons" and "three fifths of all other Persons" (Article I, Section 2). The phrase "all other Persons" is, of course, a substitute for "slaves."

The three-fifths formula had been used by the 1783 congress under the Articles of Confederation to allocate government costs among the states. The rule reflected the view that slaves were less efficient producers of wealth than free people, not that slaves were three-fifths human and two-fifths personal property.[35]

The three-fifths clause gave states with large slave populations (the South) greater representation in Congress than states with small slave populations (the North). If all slaves had been included in the count, the slave states would have had 50 percent of the seats in the House, an outcome that would have been unacceptable to the North. Had none of the slaves been counted, the slave states would have had 41 percent of House seats, which would have been unacceptable to the South. The three-fifths compromise left the South with 47 percent of the House seats, a sizable minority, but in all likelihood a losing one on slavery issues.[36] The overrepresentation resulting from the South's large slave populations translated into greater influence in selecting the president as well, because the electoral college was based on the size of the states' congressional delegations. The three-fifths clause also undertaxed states with large slave populations.

Another issue centered on the slave trade. Several southern delegates were uncompromising in their defense of the slave trade; other delegates favored prohibition. The delegates compromised, agreeing that the slave trade would not be ended before twenty years had elapsed (Article I, Section 9). Finally, the delegates agreed, without serious challenge, that fugitive slaves would be returned to their masters (Article IV, Section 2).

In addressing these points, the framers in essence condoned slavery. Tens of thousands of Africans were forcibly taken from their homes and sold into bondage. Many died on the journey to this distant land, and those who survived were brutalized and treated as less than human. Clearly, slavery existed in stark opposition to the idea that all men are created equal. Although many slaveholders, including Jefferson and Madison, agonized over it, few made serious efforts to free their own slaves. Most Americans seemed indifferent to slavery and felt no embarrassment at the apparent contradiction between the Declaration of Independence and slavery. Do the framers deserve contempt for their toleration and perpetuation of slavery? The most prominent founders—George Washington, John Adams, and Thomas Jefferson—expected slavery to wither away. A leading scholar of colonial history has offered a defense of their inaction: the framers were simply unable to transcend the limitations of the age in which they lived.[37]

Nonetheless, the eradication of slavery proceeded gradually in certain states. Opposition to slavery on moral or religious grounds was one reason.

Economic forces, such as a shift in the North to agricultural production that was less labor intensive, were a contributing factor too. By 1787, Connecticut, Massachusetts, New Jersey, New York, Pennsylvania, Rhode Island, and Vermont had abolished slavery or provided for gradual emancipation. No southern states followed suit, although several enacted laws making it easier for masters to free their slaves. The slow but perceptible shift on the slavery issue in many states masked a volcanic force capable of destroying the Constitutional Convention and the Union.

Selling the Constitution

Nearly four months after the Constitutional Convention opened, the delegates convened for the last time, on September 17, 1787, to sign the final version of their handiwork. Because several delegates were unwilling to sign the document, the last paragraph was craftily worded to give the impression of unanimity: "Done in Convention by the Unanimous Consent of the States present." Before it could take effect, the Constitution had to be ratified by a minimum of nine state conventions. The support of key states was crucial. In Pennsylvania, however, the legislature was slow to convene a ratifying convention. Pro-Constitution forces became so frustrated at this dawdling that they broke into a local boardinghouse and hauled two errant legislators through the streets to the statehouse so the assembly could schedule the convention.

The proponents of the new charter, who wanted a strong national government, called themselves Federalists. The opponents of the Constitution were quickly dubbed Antifederalists. They claimed, however, to be the true federalists because they wanted to protect the states from the tyranny of a strong national government. Elbridge Gerry, a vocal Antifederalist, called his opponents "rats" (because they favored ratification) and maintained that he was an "antirat."[38] Such is the Alice-in-Wonderland character of political discourse. Whatever they were called, the viewpoints of these two groups formed the bases of the first American political parties, as well as several enduring debates that politicians have wrestled with as they have attempted to balance the tradeoffs between freedom, order, and equality.

The *Federalist* Papers

The press of the day became a battlefield of words, filled with extravagant praise or vituperative condemnation of the proposed constitution. Beginning in October 1787, an exceptional series of eighty-five newspaper articles defending the Constitution appeared under the title *The Federalist: A Commentary on the Constitution of the United States*. The essays bore the pen name Publius (for a Roman consul and defender of the Republic, Publius Valerius, who was later known as Publicola); they were written primarily by James Madison and Alexander Hamilton, with some assistance from John Jay. Reprinted extensively during the ratification battle, the *Federalist* papers remain the best single commentary we have on the meaning of the Constitution and the political theory it embodies.

Not to be outdone, the Antifederalists offered their own intellectual basis for rejecting the Constitution. In several essays, the most influential published under the pseudonyms Brutus and Federal Farmer, the Antifederalists attacked the centralization of power in a strong national government, claiming it would obliterate the states, violate the social contract of the Declaration of Independence, and destroy liberty in the process. They defended the status quo, maintaining that the Articles of Confederation established true federal principles.[39]

Of all the *Federalist* papers, the most magnificent and most frequently cited is *Federalist* No. 10, written by James Madison. He argued that the proposed constitution was designed "to break and control the violence of faction." "By a faction," Madison wrote, "I understand a number of citizens, whether amounting to a majority or minority of the whole, who are united and actuated by some common impulse of passion, or of interest, adverse to the rights of other citizens, or to the permanent and aggregate interests of the community." No one has improved upon Madison's lucid and compelling argument, and it remains the touchstone on the problem of factions to this day.

What Madison called factions are today called interest groups or even political parties. According to Madison, "The most common and durable source of factions has been the various and unequal distribution of property." Madison was concerned not with reducing inequalities of wealth (which he took for granted) but with controlling the seemingly inevitable conflict that stems from them. The Constitution, he argued, was well constructed for this purpose.

Federalist No. 10 is available at www.cengagebrain.com/shop/ISBN/0495906182.

Through the mechanism of representation, wrote Madison, the Constitution would prevent a "tyranny of the majority" (mob rule). The people would control the government not directly but indirectly through their elected representatives. And those representatives would have the intelligence and the understanding to serve the larger interests of the nation. Moreover, the federal system would require that majorities form first within each state and then organize for effective action at the national level. This and the vastness of the country would make it unlikely that a majority would form that would "invade the rights of other citizens."

The purpose of *Federalist* No. 10 was to demonstrate that the proposed government was not likely to be dominated by any faction. Contrary to conventional wisdom, Madison argued, the key to mending the evils of factions is to have a large republic—the larger, the better. The more diverse the society, the less likely it is that an unjust majority can form. Madison certainly had no intention of creating a majoritarian democracy; his view of popular government was much more consistent with the model of pluralist democracy discussed in Chapter 2.

Madison pressed his argument from a different angle in *Federalist* No. 51. Asserting that "ambition must be made to counteract ambition," he argued that the separation of powers and checks and balances would control efforts at tyranny from any source. If power is distributed equally among the three branches, he argued, each branch will have the capacity to counteract the others. In Madison's words, "usurpations are guarded against by a division of the government into distinct and separate departments." Because legislative power tends to predominate in republican governments, legislative authority is divided between the Senate and the House of Representatives, which have different methods of election and terms of office. Additional protection arises from federalism, which divides power "between two distinct governments"—national and state—and subdivides "the portion allotted to each ... among distinct and separate departments." Madison called this arrangement of power, divided as it was across and within levels of government, a "compound republic."

Federalist No. 51 is available at www.cengagebrain.com/shop/ISBN/0495906182.

The Antifederalists wanted additional separation of powers and additional checks and balances, which they maintained would eliminate the threat of tyranny entirely. The Federalists believed that such protections would make decisive national action virtually impossible. But to ensure ratification, they agreed to a compromise.

A Concession: The Bill of Rights

Despite the eloquence of the *Federalist* papers, many prominent citizens, including Thomas Jefferson, were unhappy that the Constitution did not list basic civil liberties—the individual freedoms guaranteed to citizens. The omission of a bill of rights was the chief obstacle to the adoption of the Constitution by the states. (Seven of the eleven state constitutions that were written in the first five years of independence included such a list.) The colonists had just rebelled against the British government to preserve their basic freedoms. Why did the proposed Constitution not spell out those freedoms?

The answer was rooted in logic, not politics. Because the national government was limited to those powers that were granted to it and because no power was granted to abridge the people's liberties, a list of guaranteed freedoms was not necessary. In *Federalist* No. 84, Hamilton went even further, arguing that the addition of a bill of rights would be dangerous. To deny the exercise of a nonexistent power might lead to the exercise of a power that is not specifically denied. For example, to declare that the national government shall make no law abridging free speech might suggest that the national government could prohibit activities in unspecified areas (such as divorce), which are the states' domain. Because it is not possible to list all prohibited powers, wrote Hamilton, any attempt to provide a partial list would make the unlisted areas vulnerable to government abuse.

Bill of Rights
The first ten amendments to the Constitution. They prevent the national government from tampering with fundamental rights and civil liberties, and emphasize the limited character of national power.

But logic was no match for fear. Many states agreed to ratify the Constitution only after George Washington suggested adding a list of guarantees through the amendment process. Well in excess of one hundred amendments were proposed by the states. These were eventually narrowed to twelve, which were approved by Congress and sent to the states. Ten became part of the Constitution in 1791, after securing the approval of the required three-fourths of the states. Collectively, the ten amendments are known as the **Bill of Rights**. They restrain the national government from tampering with fundamental rights and civil liberties and emphasize the limited character of the national government's power (see Table 3.2).

TABLE 3.2	The Bill of Rights

The first ten amendments to the Constitution are known as the Bill of Rights. The following is a list of those amendments, grouped conceptually. For the actual order and wording of the Bill of Rights, see the appendix.

Guarantees	Amendment
Guarantees for Participation in the Political Process	
No government abridgement of speech or press; no government abridgement of peaceable assembly; no government abridgement of petitioning government for redress.	1
Guarantees Respecting Personal Beliefs	
No government establishment of religion; no government prohibition of free religious exercise.	1
Guarantees of Personal Privacy	
Owner's consent necessary to quarter troops in private homes in peacetime; quartering during war must be lawful.	3
Government cannot engage in unreasonable searches and seizures; warrants to search and seize require probable cause.	4
No compulsion to testify against oneself in criminal cases.	5
Guarantees Against Government's Overreaching	
Serious crimes require a grand jury indictment; no repeated prosecution for the same offense; no loss of life, liberty, or property without due process; no taking of property for public use without just compensation.	5
Criminal defendants will have a speedy public trial by impartial local jury; defendants are informed of accusation; defendants may confront witnesses against them; defendants may use judicial process to obtain favorable witnesses; defendants may have legal assistance for their defense.	6
Civil lawsuits can be tried by juries if controversy exceeds $20; in jury trials, fact finding is a jury function.	7
No excessive bail; no excessive fines; no cruel and unusual punishment.	8
Other Guarantees	
The people have the right to bear arms.	2
No government trespass on unspecified fundamental rights.	9
The states or the people retain all powers not delegated to the national government or denied to the states.	10

Ratification

The Constitution officially took effect upon its ratification by the ninth state, New Hampshire, on June 21, 1788. However, the success of the new government was not ensured until July 1788, by which time the Constitution had been ratified by the key states of Virginia and New York after lengthy debate.

IDEALOG.ORG

Are you for or against government regulation of basic cable programming (like MTV or E)? Take IDEAlog's self-test.

The reflection and deliberation that attended the creation and ratification of the Constitution signaled to the world that a new government could be launched peacefully. The French observer Alexis de Tocqueville (1805–1859) later wrote:

> That which is new in the history of societies is to see a great people, warned by its lawgivers that the wheels of government are stopping, turn its attention on itself without haste or fear, sound the depth of the ill, and then wait for two years to find the remedy at leisure, and then finally, when the remedy has been indicated, submit to it voluntarily without its costing humanity a single tear or drop of blood.[40]

Constitutional Change

The founders realized that the Constitution would have to be changed from time to time. To this end, they specified a formal amendment process, and one that was used almost immediately to add the Bill of Rights. With the passage of time, the Constitution has also been altered through judicial interpretation and changes in political practice.

The Formal Amendment Process

The amendment process has two stages, proposal and ratification; both are necessary for an amendment to become part of the Constitution. The Constitution provides two alternatives for completing each stage (see Figure 3.3). Amendments can be proposed by a two-thirds vote in both the House of Representatives and the Senate or by a national convention, summoned by Congress at the request of two-thirds of the state legislatures. All constitutional amendments to date have been proposed by the first method; the second has never been used.

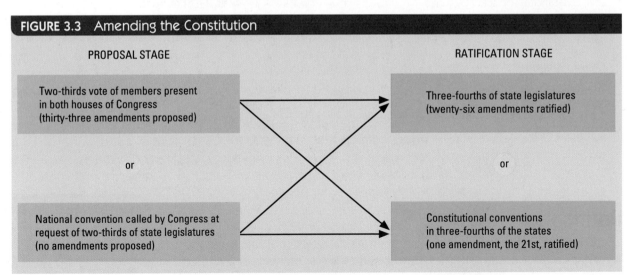

FIGURE 3.3 Amending the Constitution

PROPOSAL STAGE

Two-thirds vote of members present in both houses of Congress (thirty-three amendments proposed)

or

National convention called by Congress at request of two-thirds of state legislatures (no amendments proposed)

RATIFICATION STAGE

Three-fourths of state legislatures (twenty-six amendments ratified)

or

Constitutional conventions in three-fourths of the states (one amendment, the 21st, ratified)

Amending the Constitution requires two stages: proposal and ratification. Both Congress and the states can play a role in the proposal stage, but ratification is a process that must be fought in the states themselves. Once a state has ratified an amendment, it cannot retract its action. However, a state may reject an amendment and then reconsider its decision.

A proposed amendment can be ratified by a vote of the legislatures of three-fourths of the states or by a vote of constitutional conventions held in three-fourths of the states. Congress chooses the method of ratification. It has used the state convention method only once, for the Twenty-first Amendment, which repealed the Eighteenth Amendment (prohibition of intoxicating liquors). Congress may, in proposing an amendment, set a time limit for its ratification. Beginning with the Eighteenth Amendment, but skipping the Nineteenth, Congress has set seven years as the limit for ratification.

Note that the amendment process requires the exercise of extraordinary majorities (two-thirds and three-fourths). The framers purposely made it difficult to propose and ratify amendments (although nowhere near as difficult as under the Articles of Confederation). They wanted only the most significant issues to lead to constitutional change. Note, too, that the president plays no formal role in the process. Presidential approval is not required to amend the Constitution, although the president's political influence affects the success or failure of any amendment effort.

Calling a national convention to propose an amendment has never been tried, and the method raises several thorny questions. For example, the Constitution does not specify the number of delegates who should attend, the method by which they should be chosen, or the rules for debating and voting on a proposed amendment. Confusion surrounding the convention process has precluded its use, leaving the amendment process in congressional hands.[41] The major issue is the limits, if any, on the business of the convention. Remember that the convention in Philadelphia in 1787, charged with revising the Articles of Confederation, drafted an entirely new charter. Would a national convention called to consider a particular amendment be within its bounds to rewrite the Constitution? No one really knows.

Most of the Constitution's twenty-seven amendments were adopted to reflect changes in political thinking. The first ten amendments (the Bill of Rights) were the price of ratification, but they have been fundamental to our system of government. The last seventeen amendments fall into three main categories: they make public policy, they correct deficiencies in the government's structure, or they promote equality (see Table 3.3). One attempt to make public policy through a constitutional amendment was disastrous. The Eighteenth Amendment (1919) prohibited the manufacture or sale of intoxicating beverages, extinguishing the fifth largest industry in the nation. This amendment and the Thirteenth, barring the ownership of slaves, were the only provisions to limit the activities of citizens.[42] Prohibition lasted fourteen years and was an utter failure. Gangsters began bootlegging liquor, people died from drinking homemade spirits, and millions regularly broke the law by drinking anyway. Congress had to propose another amendment in 1933 to repeal the Eighteenth. The states ratified this amendment, the Twenty-first, in less than ten months, less time than it took to ratify the Fourteenth Amendment, guaranteeing citizenship, due process, and equal protection of the laws.

Since 1787, about ten thousand constitutional amendments have been introduced; only a fraction has survived the proposal stage. Once Congress has approved an amendment, its chances for ratification are high. The Twenty-seventh Amendment, which prevents members of Congress from

TABLE 3.3		Constitutional Amendments: 11 Through 27		
No.	**Proposed**	**Ratified**	**Intent***	**Subject**
11	1794	1795	G	Prohibits an individual from suing a state in federal court without the state's consent.
12	1803	1804	G	Requires the electoral college to vote separately for president and vice president.
13	1865	1865	E	Prohibits slavery.
14	1866	1868	E	Gives citizenship to all persons born or naturalized in the United States (including former slaves); prevents states from depriving any person of "life, liberty, or property, without due process of law," and declares that no state shall deprive any person of "the equal protection of the laws."
15	1869	1870	E	Guarantees that citizens' right to vote cannot be denied "on account of race, color, or previous condition of servitude."
16	1909	1913	E	Gives Congress the power to collect an income tax.
17	1912	1913	E	Provides for popular election of senators, who were formerly elected by state legislatures.
18	1917	1919	P	Prohibits the making and selling of intoxicating liquors.
19	1919	1920	E	Guarantees that citizens' right to vote cannot be denied "on account of sex."
20	1932	1933	G	Changes the presidential inauguration from March 4 to January 20 and sets January 3 for the opening date of Congress.
21	1933	1933	P	Repeals the Eighteenth Amendment.
22	1947	1951	G	Limits a president to two terms.
23	1960	1961	E	Gives citizens of Washington, D.C., the right to vote for president.
24	1962	1964	E	Prohibits charging citizens a poll tax to vote in presidential or congressional elections.
25	1965	1967	G	Provides for succession in event of death, removal from office, incapacity, or resignation of the president or vice president.
26	1971	1971	E	Lowers the voting age to eighteen.
27	1789	1992	G	Bars immediate pay increases to members of Congress.

*P: amendments legislating public policy; G: amendments correcting perceived deficiencies in government structure; E: amendments advancing equality.

voting themselves immediate pay increases, was ratified in 1992. It had been submitted to the states in 1789 without a time limit for ratification, but it languished in a political netherworld until 1982, when a University of Texas student, Gregory D. Watson, stumbled upon the proposed amendment while researching a paper. At that time, only eight states had ratified the amendment. Watson earned a C for the paper; his professor remained unconvinced

that the amendment was still pending.[43] Watson took up the cause, prompting renewed interest in the amendment. In May 1992, ratification by the Michigan legislature provided the decisive vote, 203 years after congressional approval of the proposed amendment.[44] Only six amendments submitted to the states have failed to be ratified.

Interpretation by the Courts

In *Marbury* v. *Madison* (1803), the Supreme Court declared that the courts have the power to nullify government acts that conflict with the Constitution. This is the power of judicial review. (We will elaborate on judicial review in Chapter 14.) The exercise of judicial review forces the courts to interpret the Constitution. In a way, this makes a lot of sense. The judiciary is the law-interpreting branch of the government; as the supreme law of the land, the Constitution is fair game for judicial interpretation. It is problematic, in theory at least, that the Constitution does not expressly authorize courts to exercise this power. Judicial review is the courts' main check on the other branches of government. But in interpreting the Constitution, the courts cannot help but give new meaning to its provisions. This is why judicial interpretation is a principal form of constitutional change.

What guidelines should judges use in interpreting the Constitution? For one thing, they must realize that the usage and meaning of many words have changed during the past two hundred years. Judges must be careful to think about what the words meant at the time the Constitution was written. Some insist that they must also consider the original intent of the framers— not an easy task. Of course, there are records of the Constitutional Convention and of the debates surrounding ratification. But there are also many questions about the completeness and accuracy of those records, even Madison's detailed notes. And at times, the framers were deliberately vague in writing the document. This may reflect lack of agreement on, or universal understanding of, certain provisions in the Constitution. Some scholars and judges maintain that the search for original meaning is hopeless and that contemporary notions of constitutional provisions must hold sway. Critics say that this approach comes perilously close to amending the Constitution as judges see fit, transforming law interpreters into lawmakers. Still other scholars and judges maintain that judges face the unavoidable challenge of balancing two-hundred-year-old constitutional principles against the demands of modern society.[45] Whatever the approach, unelected judges with effective life tenure run the risk of usurping policies established by the people's representatives.

Political Practice

The Constitution is silent on many issues. It says nothing about political parties or the president's cabinet, for example, yet both have exercised considerable influence in American politics. Some constitutional provisions have fallen out of use. The electors in the electoral college, for example, were supposed to exercise their own judgment in voting for the president and vice president. Today, the electors function simply as a rubber stamp, validating the outcome of election contests in their states.

Meanwhile, political practice has altered the distribution of power without changes in the Constitution. The framers intended Congress to be the strongest branch of government. But the president has come to overshadow Congress. Presidents such as Abraham Lincoln and Franklin Roosevelt used their formal and informal powers imaginatively to respond to national crises. And their actions paved the way for future presidents, most recently George W. Bush, to enlarge further the powers of the office.

The framers could scarcely have imagined an urbanized nation of 300 million people stretching across a landmass some three thousand miles wide, reaching halfway over the Pacific Ocean, and stretching past the Arctic Circle. Never in their wildest nightmares could they have foreseen the destructiveness of nuclear weaponry or envisioned its effect on the power to declare war. The Constitution empowers Congress to consider and debate this momentous step. But with nuclear annihilation perhaps only minutes away and terrorist threats a real if unpredictable prospect since September 11, 2001, the legislative power to declare war is likely to give way to the president's power to wage war as the nation's commander in chief. Strict adherence to the Constitution in such circumstances could destroy the nation's ability to protect itself.

An Evaluation of the Constitution

The U.S. Constitution is one of the world's most praised political documents. It is the oldest written national constitution and one of the most widely copied, sometimes word for word. It is also one of the shortest, consisting of about 4,300 words (not counting the amendments, which add 3,100 words). The brevity of the Constitution may be one of its greatest strengths. As we noted earlier, the framers simply laid out a structural framework for government; they did not describe relationships and powers in detail. For example, the Constitution gives Congress the power to regulate "Commerce ... among the several States" but does not define interstate commerce. Such general wording allows interpretation in keeping with contemporary political, social, and technological developments. Air travel, for instance, unknown in 1787, now falls easily within Congress's power to regulate interstate commerce.

The generality of the U.S. Constitution stands in stark contrast to the specificity of most state constitutions and the constitutions of many emerging democracies. The California Constitution, for example, provides that "fruit and nut-bearing trees under the age of four years from the time of planting in orchard form and grapevines under the age of three years from the time of planting in vineyard form ... shall be exempt from taxation" (Article XIII, Section 12). Because they are so specific, most state constitutions are much longer than the U.S. Constitution. The longest by far is the Alabama constitution, which is more than 300,000 words. That's longer than *Moby Dick* or the *Bible*.

The constitution of the Republic of Slovenia, adopted in December 1991, prevents citizens from being "compelled to undergo medical treatment except in such cases as are determined by statute." In the Republic of Lithuania, the national constitution, adopted in October 1992, spells out in significant detail some of the free-speech rights of its citizens, including the protection that "citizens who belong to ethnic communities shall have the right to foster their language, culture, and customs."[46] The U.S. Constitution remains a beacon for others to follow (see "Politics of Global Change: A New Birth of Freedom: Exporting American Constitutionalism").

Freedom, Order, and Equality in the Constitution

The revolutionaries' first try at government was embodied in the Articles of Confederation. The result was a weak national government that leaned too much toward freedom at the expense of order. Deciding that the confederation was beyond correcting, the revolutionaries chose a new form of government—a compound or *federal* government—that was strong enough to maintain order but not so strong that it could dominate the states or infringe on individual freedoms. In short, the Constitution provided a judicious balance between order and freedom. It paid virtually no attention to equality. (Recall that the equality premise in the Declaration of Independence was meant for the colonists as a people, not as individuals.)

Consider social equality. The Constitution never mentioned the word *slavery*, a controversial issue even then. In fact, as we have seen, the Constitution

Politics of Global Change

A New Birth of Freedom: Exporting American Constitutionalism

When the founders drafted the U.S. Constitution in 1787, they hardly started from scratch. Leaders like James Madison and John Adams drew on the failed experiences of the Articles of Confederation to chart a new course for our national government. They also leaned heavily on the ideas of great democratic thinkers of the past. Today, given the 220-year track record of the United States, it is no wonder that many other nations have looked to the American experience as they embark on their own democratic experiments.

In the past ten years especially, democratizing countries on nearly every continent have developed new governing institutions by drawing at least in part on important principles from the U.S. Constitution and Bill of Rights. This is certainly the case in the former communist countries of Eastern Europe, most of which are just beginning their third decade of newly established democratic rule. Enshrining democratic ideals in a written constitution corresponds to the ascendancy of freedom worldwide (see the accompanying figure). Free and partially free countries are in ascendance; not-free countries are in decline.

Echoing the U.S. Declaration of Independence and the Constitution's preamble, for example, Article 1 of the Estonian constitution declares unequivocally that "the supreme power of the state is vested in the people." Specific guarantees protecting individual rights and liberties are also written in great detail in the constitutions of these new democracies. The Latvian constitution, for example, takes a strong stand on the defense of privacy, stating that "everyone has the right to inviolability of his or her private life, home and correspondence." Interestingly enough, the constitution of Slovakia explicitly protects in its Article 12 the right to self-select a nationality without any external imposition by claiming that "every person has the right to freely decide which national group he or she is a member of" and that all "manner of influence or coercion that may affect or lead to a denial of a person's original nationality shall be prohibited." In these countries formerly compounded by different nationalities, nationalism entails a more complicated issue than in America, probably closer to our race-related issues.

Some of these newly democratic nations, however, have opted for a constitutional design with a separation of powers less rigid than one established by the American model. A parliamentary system poses fewer constraints on executive authority as long as it is sustained by a legislative majority. In this sense, prime ministers do not face fixed mandates or term limits. As long as they are backed by the popular vote expressed in a

implicitly condones slavery in the wording of several articles. Not until the ratification of the Thirteenth Amendment in 1865 was slavery prohibited.

The Constitution was designed long before social equality was ever even thought of as an objective of government. In fact, in *Federalist* No. 10, Madison held that protection of the "diversities in the faculties of men from which the rights of property originate" is "the first object of government." More than a century later, the Constitution was changed to incorporate a key device for the promotion of social equality—a national income tax. The Sixteenth Amendment (1913) gave Congress the power to collect an income tax; it was proposed and ratified to replace a law that had been declared unconstitutional in an 1895 Supreme Court case. The income tax had long been seen as a means of putting into effect the concept of progressive taxation, in which the tax rate increases with income. The Sixteenth Amendment

parliamentary majority, they can remain in office indefinitely. However, they can be removed from office as soon as they lose their popular support by means of a parliamentary nonconfidence vote. For instance, if a midterm election changes the composition of the chamber, the new majority can select a new government. Under the same scenario, the American president, who can be removed from office only by the extraordinary recourse of impeachment, is forced to govern facing a divided government and the possibility of gridlock. In sum, different institutional designs have been devised to tackle some of the weaknesses associated with the American Constitution.

Because there is no ready-made formula for building a successful democracy, only time will tell whether these young constitutions will perform well in practice. Experience has taught us that constitutions can be quite fragile, lasting on average just a generation. Longevity depends on a few key factors plus a measure of luck. (See also "Compared with What? The Longevity of Constitutions.")

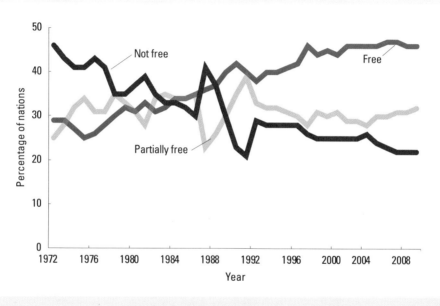

Source: International Institute for Democracy, *The Rebirth of Democracy: Twelve Constitutions of Central and Eastern Europe,* 2nd ed. (Amsterdam: Council of Europe, 1996); A. E. Dick Howard, "Liberty's Text: Ten Amendments That Changed the World," *Washington Post,* 15 December 1991, p. C3; Freedom House, "Freedom in the World 2009," available at http://www.freedomhouse.org/uploads/fiw09/tablesandcharts/Table of Independent Countries FIW 2009.pdf and http://www.freedomhouse.org/uploads/Chart116File163.pdf (accessed 22 December 2009).

gave progressive taxation a constitutional basis.[47] Progressive taxation later helped promote social equality through the redistribution of income; that is, higher-income people are taxed at higher rates to help fund social programs that benefit low-income people.

Social equality itself has never been, and is not now, a prime constitutional value. The Constitution has been much more effective in securing order and freedom. Nor did the Constitution take a stand on political equality. It left voting qualifications to the states, specifying only that people who could vote for "the most numerous Branch of the State Legislature" could also vote for representatives to Congress (Article I, Section 2). Most states at that time allowed only taxpaying or property-owning white males to vote. With few exceptions, blacks and women were universally excluded from voting. These inequalities have been rectified by several amendments (see Table 3.3).

Political equality expanded after the Civil War. The Fourteenth Amendment (adopted in 1868) guaranteed all persons, including blacks, citizenship. The Fifteenth Amendment (ratified in 1870) declared that "race, color, or previous condition of servitude" could not be used to deny citizens the right to vote. This did not automatically give blacks the vote; some states used other mechanisms to limit black enfranchisement. The Nineteenth Amendment (adopted in 1920) opened the way for women to vote by declaring that sex could not be used to deny citizens the right to vote. The Twenty-fourth Amendment (adopted in 1964) prohibited the poll tax (a tax that people had to pay to vote and that tended to disenfranchise poor blacks) in presidential and congressional elections. The Twenty-sixth Amendment (adopted in 1971) declared that age could not be used to deny citizens eighteen years or older the right to vote. One other amendment expanded the Constitution's grant of political equality. The Twenty-third Amendment (adopted in 1961) allowed residents of Washington, D.C., who are not citizens of any state, to vote for president.

The Constitution and Models of Democracy

Think back to our discussion of the models of democracy in Chapter 2. Which model does the Constitution fit: pluralist or majoritarian? Actually, it is hard to imagine a government framework better suited to the pluralist model of democracy than the Constitution of the United States. It is also hard to imagine a document more at odds with the majoritarian model. Consider Madison's claim, in *Federalist* No. 10, that government inevitably involves conflicting factions. This concept coincides perfectly with pluralist theory (see Chapter 2). Then recall his description in *Federalist* No. 51 of the Constitution's ability to guard against concentration of power in the majority through separation of powers and checks and balances. This concept—avoiding a single center of government power that might fall under majority control—also fits perfectly with pluralist democracy.

The delegates to the Constitutional Convention intended to create a republic, a government based on majority consent; they did not intend to create a democracy, which rests on majority rule. They succeeded admirably in creating that republic. In doing so, they also produced a government that developed into a democracy—but a particular type of democracy. The framers neither wanted nor got a democracy that fit the majoritarian model. They may have wanted, and they certainly did create, a government that conforms to the pluralist model.

Summary

The U.S. Constitution is more than an antique curiosity. Although more than two hundred years old, it governs the politics of a strong modern nation. It still has the power to force from office a president who won reelection by a landslide. It still has the power to see the country through government crises.

The Constitution was the end product of a revolutionary movement aimed at preserving existing liberties. That movement began with the Declaration of Independence, which proclaimed that everyone is entitled to certain rights (among them, life, liberty, and the pursuit of happiness) and that government exists for the good of its citizens. When government denies those rights, the people have the right to rebel. The Declaration also invoked the principle of equality, but it aimed to assure equality of peoples rather than equality of individuals.

War with Britain was only part of the process of independence. A government was needed to replace the British monarchy. The Americans chose a republic and defined the structure of that republic in the Articles of Confederation. Although the Articles guaranteed the states the independence they coveted, they were a failure: they left the central government too weak to deal with disorder and insurrection.

The Constitution was the second attempt at limited government. It replaced a loose union of powerful states with a strong but still limited national government, incorporating four political principles: republicanism, federalism, separation of powers, and checks and balances. Republicanism is a form of government in which power resides in the people and is exercised by their elected representatives. Federalism is a division of power between the national government and the states. The federalism of the Constitution conferred substantial powers on the national government at the expense of the states. Separation of powers is a further division of the power of the national government into legislative (lawmaking), executive (law-enforcing), and judicial (law-interpreting) branches. Finally, the Constitution established a system of checks and balances, giving each branch some scrutiny of and control over the others.

American experience teaches that agreeing to a workable constitution is no easy task. The EU failed in its recent attempt to adopt a constitution. Voters in France and the Netherlands were wary of central authority and the necessary loss of their sovereignty. Not to be outdone, proponents of European integration sought ratification from member states of a treaty that aimed to accomplish much of the same objectives of the failed constitution. Although first derailed by Irish voters, the treaty sprang back to life in 2008 as the worldwide financial crisis prompted Irish voters to rethink and reverse their previous judgment. The EU has taken an important step toward unity, but full political integration has yet to be achieved as economic storms of the Great Recession rock member states.

When work began on ratification of the U.S. Constitution, a major stumbling block proved to be the failure of the Constitution to list the individual liberties the Americans had fought to protect against the potential tyranny of a stronger central government. With the promise to add a bill of rights, the Constitution was ratified. The ten amendments that make up the Bill of Rights guaranteed participation in the political process, respect for personal beliefs, and personal privacy. They also contained guarantees against government overreaching in criminal prosecutions. Over the years, the Constitution has evolved through the formal amendment process, the exercise of judicial review, and political practice.

The Constitution was designed to strike a balance between order and freedom. It was not designed to promote social equality; in fact, it had to be amended to redress inequality. The framers compromised on many issues, including slavery, to ensure the creation of a new and workable government. They did not set out to create a democracy. Faith in government by the people was virtually nonexistent two centuries ago. Nevertheless, the framers produced a democratic form of government. That government, with its separation of powers and checks and balances, is remarkably well suited to the pluralist model of democracy. Simple majority rule, which lies at the heart of the majoritarian model, was precisely what the framers wanted to avoid.

The framers also wanted a balance between the powers of the national government and those of the states. The exact balance was a touchy issue, skirted by the delegates at the Constitutional Convention. Some seventy years later, a civil war was fought over that balance of power. That war and countless political battles before and since have demonstrated that the national government dominates the state governments in our political system. In Chapter 4, we will look at how a loose confederation of states has evolved into a "more perfect Union."

CourseMate   Visit www.cengagebrain.com/shop/ ISBN/0495906182 for flashcards, web quizzes, videos and more!

Federalism

AP Photo/Ross D. Franklin

"The problem is all these illegals," said Luis, a legal Mexican immigrant who has lived and worked in Arizona for 16 years. "They come here expecting to find paradise, and it isn't. You have to work hard for everything. But at least there is work."[1] These are difficult times, especially in Arizona. The Great Recession; the ensuing trail of high, long-term unemployment; and, the housing market collapse wreaked devastation on the state. Illegal immigration surged along with increased drug smuggling, human trafficking, and associated gang violence across Arizona's 362-mile border with Mexico.

For years, Arizonans—including Luis and his fellow legal immigrants—have borne the burden of illegals who have sought work and opportunity in the United States. President George W. Bush was determined to reform immigration laws, staunching the illegal tide, but he failed. Immigration reform was political kryptonite, weakening even the most powerful politicians who tried to address the issue. The public seethed at the prospect of illegals taking jobs from American citizens; of illegals using the social safety net to secure heath care, education, and housing; and, of pregnant illegals crossing the border for the sole purpose of delivering their babies on American soil, thus qualifying their children immediately for American citizenship.[2] All of this and more proved too much for conservative Arizonans and their politicians.

In 2010, under Governor Jan Brewer, the state legislature adopted a law—SB1070—taking immigration matters into its own hands. The law is both broad and strict; it goes far beyond efforts in other states to address the problem of illegal immigration. More significantly, it goes further than the United States government has chosen to go.

U.S. law requires foreigners who are not citizens living in the United States—called *aliens*—to register with the government and carry their registration papers.[3] SB1070 took this requirement a step further by criminalizing the failure to carry the necessary papers. The new law obligates the police to determine a person's immigration status, when practicable during a "lawful stop, detention or arrest," if there is reasonable suspicion that the person is an illegal alien. The law also cracked down on those who hire, transport, or shelter illegal aliens.[4] Critics argued that citizens or legal aliens with brown skin would be caught up in such sweeps. Defenders of the law maintained that racial profiling was prohibited.

David Salgado, a Phoenix police officer, challenged SB1070 in federal court on the ground that the provisions forced him into an untenable dilemma. On the one hand, if he enforced the law, he would be engaged in racial profiling by stopping only members of a given racial class to check for proper immigration status. On the other hand, if he failed to enforce the law, he would be subject to sanctions from his superiors, including the prospect of losing his job.[5]

The federal government intervened in the lawsuit, sending one of its highest-ranking officials from the Justice Department to argue its position. The argument did not focus on racial profiling, the issue that animated the press and the public. Rather, the United States rested its case on federalism grounds: the Constitution and laws of the United States place the matter of immigration solely in the hands of the national government, and the states remain duty-bound under the Constitution's supremacy clause (Article VI) to bow to national authority.

On July 28, just one day before the law was to go into effect, federal judge Susan Bolton blocked the main provisions of the law, including the requirement that police check the immigration status of those arrested or stopped. Her reasoning adopted the position of the United States: principles of federalism give exclusive power over immigration matters to the national government, trumping state efforts at regulating or enforcing national immigration laws as in Arizona.[6]

Two elements of federalism are at work here. The first element is the respective **sovereignty**, or quality of being supreme in power or authority, of national and state governments. In the case of Arizona's efforts to confront illegal immigration, this distinction between different sovereignties was clear to Judge Bolton: authority rests principally with the national government. She did not invalidate the entire law, but only those portions that intrude on the national government's delegated or implied powers. The states cannot simply act on their own when the Constitution (Article I, Section 8, Clause 4) and laws of the United States assign responsibility for immigration and naturalization to the national government. A second element of federalism is the power of national (i.e., federal) courts to assure the supremacy of the U.S. Constitution and national laws. Such power was necessary, though not sufficient, to yoke separate states into one nation, or as the motto goes, "E pluribus unum."

Sovereignty also affects political leadership. A governor may not be a president's political equal, but governors have their own sovereignty apart from the national government. In this chapter, we examine American federalism in theory and in practice. Is the division of power between the nation and states a matter of constitutional principle or practical politics? How does the balance of power between the nation and states relate to the conflicts between freedom and order and between freedom and equality? Does the growth of federalism abroad affect us here at home? Does federalism reflect the pluralist or the majoritarian model of democracy?

IN OUR OWN WORDS

Listen to Jerry Goldman discuss the main points and themes of this chapter.

www.cengagebrain.com/ shop/ISBN/0495906182

Theories and Metaphors

The delegates who met in Philadelphia in 1787 were supposed to repair weaknesses in the Articles of Confederation. Instead, they tackled the problem of making one nation out of thirteen independent states by doing something much more radical: they wrote a new constitution and invented a new political form—federal government—that combined features of a confederacy with features of unitary government (see Chapter 3). Under the principle of **federalism**, two or more governments exercise power and authority over the same people and the same territory.

Still, this new national government did not intrude explicitly into the states' domain. The new constitution granted Congress express authority for only one service within the states, the creation of a postal system. Powers were meant to be exclusive or shared. For example, the governments of the United States and Pennsylvania share certain powers (the power to tax, for instance), but other powers belong exclusively to one or the other. As James Madison wrote in *Federalist* No. 10, "The federal Constitution forms a happy

sovereignty
The quality of being supreme in power or authority.

federalism
The division of power between a central government and regional governments.

combination ... [of] the great and aggregate interests being referred to the national, and the local and particular to state governments." So the power to coin money belongs to the national government, but the power to grant divorces remains a state prerogative. By contrast, authority over state militias may sometimes belong to the national government and sometimes to the states. The history of American federalism reveals that it has not always been easy to draw a line between what is "great and aggregate" and what is "local and particular."*

Nevertheless, federalism offered a solution to the problem of diversity in America. Citizens feared that without a federal system of government, majorities with different interests and values from different regions would rule them. Federalism also provided a new political model.

The history of American federalism is full of attempts to capture its true meaning in an adjective or metaphor. By one reckoning, scholars have generated nearly five hundred ways to describe federalism.[7] Perhaps this is not surprising given one scholar's view that the American federal system "is a highly protean form, subject to constant reinterpretation. It is long on change and confusion and very low on fixed, generally accepted principles."[8] Still, before complicating the picture too much, it will be useful to focus on two common representations of the system: dual federalism and cooperative federalism.

Federalist No. 10 is available at www.cengagebrain.com/shop/ISBN/0495906182.

Dual Federalism

The term **dual federalism** sums up a theory about the proper relationship between the national government and the states. The theory has four essential parts. First, the national government rules by enumerated powers only. Second, the national government has a limited set of constitutional purposes. Third, each government unit—nation and state—is sovereign within its sphere. And fourth, the relationship between nation and states is best characterized by tension rather than cooperation.[9]

Dual federalism portrays the states as powerful components of the federal system—in some ways, the equals of the national government. Under dual federalism, the functions and responsibilities of the national and state governments are theoretically different and practically separate from each other. Of primary importance in dual federalism are **states' rights**, which reserve to the states all rights not specifically conferred on the national government by the Constitution. According to the theory of dual federalism, a rigid wall separates the nation and the states. After all, if the states created the nation, by implication they can set limits on the activities of the national government. Proponents of states' rights believe that the powers of the national government should be interpreted narrowly.

dual federalism
A view holding that the Constitution is a compact among sovereign states, so that the powers of the national government and the states are clearly differentiated.

states' rights
The idea that all rights not specifically conferred on the national government by the U.S. Constitution are reserved to the states.

---

*The phrase Americans commonly use to refer to their central government—*federal government*—muddies the waters even more. Technically, we have a federal system of government, which encompasses both the national and state governments. To avoid confusion from here on, we use the term *national government* rather than *federal government* when we are talking about the central government.

FIGURE 4.1   Metaphors for Federalism

The two views of federalism
can be represented
graphically.

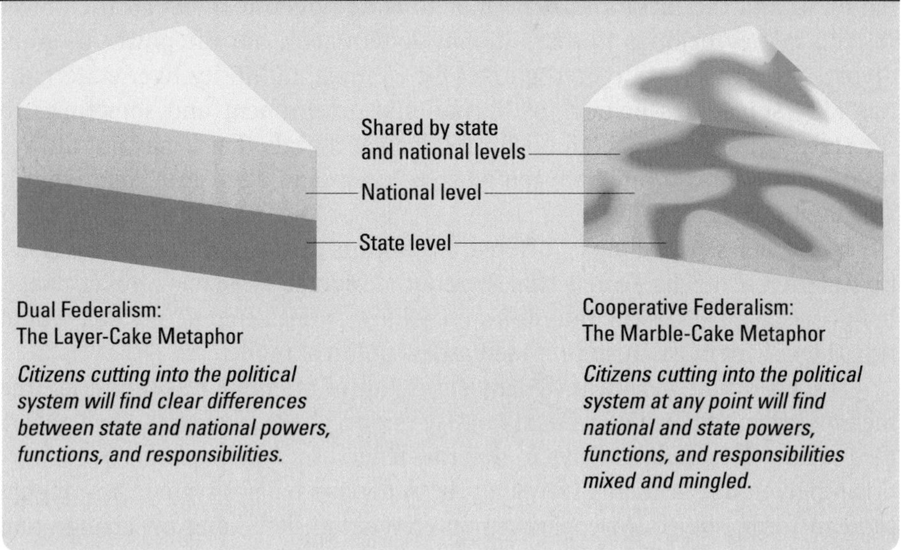

Shared by state
and national levels

National level

State level

Dual Federalism:
The Layer-Cake Metaphor

*Citizens cutting into the political
system will find clear differences
between state and national powers,
functions, and responsibilities.*

Cooperative Federalism:
The Marble-Cake Metaphor

*Citizens cutting into the political
system at any point will find
national and state powers,
functions, and responsibilities
mixed and mingled.*

Debates over states' rights often emerge over differing interpretations of a given national government policy or proposed policy. Whether the Constitution has delegated to the national government the power to make such policy or whether it remains with the states or the people is often an open and difficult question to answer. States' rights supporters insist that the activities of Congress should be confined to the enumerated powers. They support their view by quoting the Tenth Amendment: "The powers not delegated to the United States by the Constitution, nor prohibited by it to the States, are reserved to the States respectively, or to the people." Conversely, those people favoring national action frequently point to the Constitution's elastic clause, which gives Congress the **implied powers** needed to execute its enumerated powers.

Regardless of whether one favors national action or states' rights, political scientists use a metaphor to describe the idea of dual federalism. They call it *layer-cake federalism* (see Figure 4.1), in which the powers and functions of the national and state governments are as separate as the layers of a cake. Each government is supreme in its own layer, its own sphere of action. The two layers are distinct, and the dimensions of each layer are fixed by the Constitution.

Dual federalism has been challenged on historical grounds. Some critics argue that if the national government is really a creation of the states, it is a creation of only thirteen states–those that ratified the Constitution. The other thirty-seven states were admitted after the national government came into being and were created by that government out of land it had acquired. Another challenge has to do with the ratification process. Remember that special conventions in the original thirteen states, not the states' legislatures, ratified the Constitution. Ratification, then, was an act of the people, not the states. Moreover, the preamble to the Constitution begins, "We the People of

implied powers
Those powers that Congress
needs to execute its enumerated powers.

the United States," not "We the States." The question of just where the people fit into the federal system is not handled well by dual federalism.

Cooperative Federalism

Cooperative federalism, a phrase coined in the 1930s, is a different theory of the relationship between the national and state governments. It acknowledges the increasing overlap between state and national functions and rejects the idea of separate spheres, or layers, for the states and the national government. Cooperative federalism has three elements. First, national and state agencies typically undertake government functions jointly rather than exclusively. Second, the nation and states routinely share power. And third, power is not concentrated at any government level or in any agency; the fragmentation of responsibilities gives people and groups access to many venues of influence.

The bakery metaphor used to describe this type of federalism is a *marble cake* (see Figure 4.1).* The national and state governments do not act in separate spheres; they are intermingled in vertical and diagonal strands and swirls. In short, their functions are mixed in the American federal system. Critical to cooperative federalism is an expansive view of the Constitution's supremacy clause (Article VI), which specifically subordinates state law to national law and charges every government official with disregarding state laws that are inconsistent with the Constitution, national laws, or treaties.

Some scholars argue that the layer-cake metaphor has never accurately described the American political structure.[10] The national and state governments have many common objectives and have often cooperated to achieve them. In the nineteenth century, for example, cooperation, not separation, made it possible to develop transportation systems, such as canals, and to establish state land-grant colleges. Overall, then, the layer cake might be a good model of what dual federalists think the relationship between national and state governments *should* be, but several examples reveal how it does not square all that well with recent or even distant American history. Critics also take issue with the adequacy of cooperative federalism to explain the modern interaction between states and nation. We examine this new theory later in this chapter.

A critical difference between the theories of dual and cooperative federalism is the way they interpret two sections of the Constitution that define the relationship between the national and state governments. Article I, Section 8, lists the enumerated powers of Congress and then concludes with the **elastic clause,** which gives Congress the power to "make all Laws which shall be necessary and proper for carrying into Execution the foregoing Powers" (see Chapter 3). The Tenth Amendment reserves for the states or the people powers not assigned to the national government or denied to the

cooperative federalism
A view holding that the Constitution is an agreement among people who are citizens of both state and nation, so there is much overlap between state powers and national powers.

elastic clause
The last clause in Article I, Section 8, of the Constitution, which gives Congress the means to execute its enumerated powers. This clause is the basis for Congress's implied powers. Also called the *necessary and proper clause.*

---

*A marble cake is a rough mixture of yellow and chocolate cake batter resembling marble stone. If you've never seen or eaten a slice of marble cake, imagine mixing a swirl of vanilla and chocolate soft freeze ice cream.

states by the Constitution. Dual federalism postulates an inflexible elastic clause and a capacious Tenth Amendment. Cooperative federalism postulates suppleness in the elastic clause and confines the Tenth Amendment to a self-evident, obvious truth.

Federalism's Dynamics

Although the Constitution establishes a kind of federalism, the actual and proper balance of power between the nation and states has always been more a matter of debate than of formal theory. Three broad principles help to underscore why. First, rather than operating in a mechanical fashion, American federalism is a flexible and dynamic system. The Constitution's inherent ambiguities about federalism, some of which we have discussed already, generate constraints but also opportunities for politicians, citizens, and interest groups to push ideas that they care about. Second, because of this flexibility, both elected and appointed officials across levels of government often make policy decisions based on pragmatic considerations without regard to theories of what American federalism should look like. In sum, politics and policy goals rather than pure theoretical or ideological commitments about federalism tend to dominate decision making. Third, there is a growing recognition among public officials and citizens that public problems (such as questions involving tradeoffs of freedom, order, and equality) cut across governmental boundaries. This section develops the first claim, and we explore the other two in later sections of this chapter.

The overall point these three claims illustrate is that to understand American federalism, one must know more than simply the powers that the Constitution assigns the different levels of government. Real understanding stems from recognizing the forces that can prompt changes in relationships between the national government and the states. In this section, we focus on four specific forces: national crises and demands, judicial interpretations, the expansion of grants-in-aid, and the professionalization of state governments.

National Crises and Demands

The elastic clause of the Constitution gives Congress the power to make all laws that are "necessary and proper" to carry out its responsibilities. By using this power in combination with its enumerated powers, Congress has been able to increase the scope of the national government tremendously during the previous two centuries. The greatest change has come about in times of crisis and national emergencies, such as the Civil War; the world wars; the Great Depression; the aftermath of September 11, 2001; and the Great Recession of 2009. As an example, consider the Great Depression.

The Great Depression placed dual federalism in repose. The problems of the Depression proved too extensive for either state governments or private businesses to handle, so the national government assumed a heavy share of responsibility for providing relief and pursuing economic recovery. Under the New Deal, President Franklin D. Roosevelt's response to the Depression, Congress enacted various emergency relief programs designed to stimulate economic activity and help the unemployed. Many measures required the cooperation of the national and state governments. For example, the national government offered money to support state relief efforts; however, to receive these funds, states were usually required to provide administrative supervision or contribute some money of their own. Relief efforts were thus wrested from the hands of local bodies and centralized. Through the regulations it attached to funds, the national government extended its power and control over the states.[11]

Some call the New Deal era revolutionary. There is no doubt that the period was critical in reshaping federalism in the United States. The national and state governments had cooperated before, but the extent of their interactions during President Franklin Roosevelt's administration clearly made the marble-cake metaphor the more accurate description of American federalism. In addition, the size of the national government and its budget increased tremendously. But perhaps the most significant change was in the way Americans thought about their problems and the role of the national government in solving them. Difficulties that at one time had been considered personal or local were now viewed as national problems requiring national solutions. The general welfare, broadly defined, became a legitimate concern of the national government.

In other respects, however, the New Deal was not so revolutionary. For example, Congress did not claim any new powers to address the nation's economic problems. Rather, the national legislature simply used its constitutional powers to suit the circumstances. Arguably those actions were consistent with the overall purpose of the U.S. Constitution, which, as the preamble states, was designed in part to "insure domestic Tranquility ... [and] promote the general welfare."

Concerns over terrorist attacks on U.S. soil have expanded national power. In the month after the events of September 11, 2001, Congress swiftly passed and the president signed into law the USA-PATRIOT Act. (USA-PATRIOT is an acronym for Uniting and Strengthening America by Providing Appropriate Tools Required to Intercept and Obstruct Terrorism.) Among other provisions, the law expanded significantly the surveillance and investigative powers of the Department of Justice. After some disagreement about its structure and organization, federal policymakers created the Department of Homeland Security in 2002, a new department that united over twenty previously separate federal agencies under a common administrative structure. In a move to further expand domestic surveillance activities, President George W. Bush gave approval to wiretaps without warrants of American citizens suspected of terrorist ties. Congress had established a process for obtaining judicial warrants before or after such surveillance, but the president maintained that he had inherent power as commander in chief to act without regard to the congressional act.[12]

The role of the national government has also grown as it has responded to needs and demands that state and local governments were unwilling or

An Environmental Catastrophe

On April 20, 2010, an oil rig explosion in the Gulf of Mexico, 41 miles from the coast of Louisiana, caused a sea floor oil gusher of unprecedented proportions. Nearly 5 million barrels of oil leaked into the Gulf before the well was capped on July 15. The well owner, British Petroleum, bore full responsibility for the damage and will pay billions of dollars in claims for the cleanup and loss of jobs throughout the Gulf states. The disaster occurred in waters under the jurisdiction of the national government. State and local officials played a subordinate role. President Barack Obama (*left*), LaFourche Parish (Louisiana) president Charlotte Randolph (*center*), and U.S. Coast Guard Admiral Thad Allen (*right*) look at booms set out to collect oil during a tour of areas affected by the oil spill.

(AP Photo/Evan Vucci)

unable to meet. To address the severe economic downturn saddling the nation, President Obama proposed and Congress quickly passed a $787 billion economic stimulus package in February 2009. No Republicans in the House of Representatives and only 3 Republicans in the Senate voted for the legislation, a clear signal of the charged partisan atmosphere in Washington. The American Recovery and Reinvestment Act offered substantial direct aid to states beleaguered by the recession in the form of Medicaid payments, extended unemployment benefits, school and infrastructure spending, and other grants. Several Republican governors rejected the money, arguing that the strings attached would mandate the states to more spending in the future. But the bluster receded as furious state legislators in both parties demanded the much-needed funds. When the deadline arrived, all governors signed on.[13]

Judicial Interpretation

How federal courts have interpreted the Constitution and federal law is another factor that has influenced the relationship between the national government

Brother, Can You Spare a Billion?

Congress passed, and President Obama signed, the American Recovery and Reinvestment Act in February 2009. This $787 billion package of federal spending includes direct aid to the states battered by the collapse of the economy in 2008. The aim is to create jobs and spur investment. Road repair and infrastructure projects are key components. You can track spending by zip code and much more at www.recovery.gov.

(AP Photo/Jim Prisching)

and the states. The U.S. Supreme Court, the umpire of the federal system, settles disagreements over the powers of the national and state governments by deciding whether the actions of either are unconstitutional (see Chapter 14). In the nineteenth and early twentieth centuries, the Supreme Court often decided in favor of the states. Then, for nearly sixty years, from 1937 to 1995, the Court almost always supported the national government in contests involving the balance of power between nation and states. After 1995, a conservative U.S. Supreme Court tended to favor states' rights, but not without some notable and important exceptions. Exploring the Court's federalism jurisprudence provides a useful window on changes to the system that have transpired since the nation's founding.

Ends and Means. Early in the nineteenth century, the nationalist interpretation of federalism prevailed over states' rights. In 1819, under Chief Justice John Marshall (1801–1835), the Supreme Court expanded the role of the national government in the landmark case of *McCulloch* v. *Maryland*. The Court was asked to decide whether Congress had the power to establish a national bank and, if so, whether states had the power to tax that bank. In a unanimous opinion that Marshall authored, the Court conceded that Congress had only the powers conferred on it by the Constitution, which nowhere mentioned banks.

However, Article I granted Congress the authority to enact all laws "necessary and proper" to the execution of Congress's enumerated powers. Marshall adopted a broad interpretation of this elastic clause: "Let the end be legitimate, let it be within the scope of the constitution, and all means which are appropriate, which are plainly adapted to that end, which are not prohibited, but consist with the letter and spirit of the constitution, are constitutional."

The Court clearly agreed that Congress had the power to charter a bank. But did the states (in this case, Maryland) have the power to tax the bank? Arguing that "the power to tax involves the power to destroy," Marshall insisted that a state could not tax the national government because the bank represents the interests of the whole nation; a state may not tax those it does not represent. Therefore, a state tax that interferes with the power of Congress to make law is void.[14] Marshall was embracing cooperative federalism, which sees a direct relationship between the people and the national government, with no need for the states to act as intermediaries. The framers of the Constitution did not intend to create a meaningless document, he reasoned. Therefore, they must have meant to give the national government all the powers necessary to carry out its assigned functions, even if those powers are only implied.

Especially from the late 1930s to the mid-1990s, the Supreme Court's interpretation of the Constitution's **commerce clause** was a major factor that increased the national government's power. The third clause of Article I, Section 8, states that "Congress shall have Power ... To regulate Commerce ... among the several States." In early Court decisions, beginning with *Gibbons* v. *Ogden* in 1824, Chief Justice Marshall interpreted the word *commerce* broadly to include virtually every form of commercial activity. But later courts would take a narrower view of that power.

Roger B. Taney became chief justice in 1836, and during his tenure (1836–1864), the Court's federalism decisions began to favor the states. The Taney Court took a more restrictive view of commerce and imposed firm limits on the powers of the national government. As Taney saw it, the Constitution spoke "not only in the same words, but with the same meaning and intent with which it spoke when it came from the hands of its framers and was voted on and adopted by the people of the United States."[15] In the infamous *Dred Scott* decision (1857), for example, the Court decided that Congress had no power to prohibit slavery in the territories.

The judicial winds shifted again during the Great Depression. After originally disagreeing with FDR's and the Congress's position that the economic crisis was a national problem that demanded national action, the Court, with no change in personnel, began to alter its course in 1937 and upheld several major New Deal measures. Perhaps the Court was responding to the 1936 election returns (Roosevelt had been reelected in a landslide, and the Democrats commanded a substantial majority in Congress), which signified the voters' endorsement of the use of national policies to address national problems. Or perhaps the Court sought to defuse the president's threat to enlarge the Court with justices sympathetic to his views. ("The switch in time that saved nine," rhymed one observer.) In any event, the Court abandoned its effort to maintain a rigid boundary between national and state power.[16]

commerce clause
The third clause of Article I, Section 8, of the Constitution, which gives Congress the power to regulate commerce among the states.

The Umpire Strikes Back. One scholar has gone so far as to charge that the justices have treated the commerce clause like a shuttlecock volleyed back and forth by changing majorities.[17] Looking at the period from the New Deal through the 1980s, the evidence to support that claim appears rather unconvincing. However, in the 1990s, a series of important U.S. Supreme Court rulings involving the commerce clause suggested that the states' rights position was gaining ground. The Court's 5–4 ruling in *United States* v. *Lopez* (1995) held that Congress exceeded its authority under the commerce clause when it enacted a law in 1990 banning the possession of a gun in or near a school. A conservative majority, headed by Chief Justice William H. Rehnquist, concluded that having a gun in a school zone "has nothing to do with 'commerce' or any sort of economic enterprise, however broadly one might define those terms." Justices Sandra Day O'Connor, Antonin Scalia, Anthony Kennedy, and Clarence Thomas—all appointed by Republicans—joined in Rehnquist's opinion, putting the brakes on congressional power.[18]

Another piece of gun-control legislation, known as the Brady bill, produced similar eventual results. Congress enacted this law in 1993. It mandated the creation by November 1998 of a national system to check the background of prospective gun buyers in order to weed out, among others, convicted felons and those with mental illness. In the meantime, the law created a temporary system that called for local law enforcement officials to perform background checks and report their findings to gun dealers in their community. Several sheriffs challenged the law.

The Supreme Court agreed with the sheriffs, delivering a double-barreled blow to the local-enforcement provision in June 1997. In *Printz* v. *United States* (1997), the Court concluded that Congress could not require local officials to implement a regulatory scheme imposed by the national government. In language that seemingly invoked layer-cake federalism, Justice Antonin Scalia, writing for the five-member conservative majority, argued that locally enforced background checks violated the principle of dual sovereignty by allowing the national government "to impress into its service—and at no cost to itself—the police officers of the 50 States." In addition, he wrote, the scheme violated the principle of separation of powers by congressional transfer of the president's responsibility to faithfully execute national laws to local law enforcement officials.[19]

Federalism's Shifting Scales. In what appeared to signal the continuation of a pro–states' rights trajectory, in 2000 the justices struck down congressional legislation that had allowed federal court lawsuits for money damages for victims of crimes "motivated by gender." The Court held that the Violence Against Women Act violated both the commerce clause and Section 5 of the Fourteenth Amendment. Chief Justice Rehnquist, speaking for the five-person majority, declared that "the Constitution requires a distinction between what is truly national and what is truly local."[20]

But just as an umpire's strike zone can be ambiguous—is it knees to belt or knees to letters?—the Court more recently has veered from its states' rights direction on federalism. Perhaps the best-known decision in this vein is

Bush v. *Gore,* the controversial Supreme Court decision resolving the 2000 presidential election. That tight election did not result in an immediate winner because the race in Florida was too close to call. Florida courts, interpreting Florida election law, had ordered ballot recounts, but a divided Supreme Court ordered a halt to the process and gave George W. Bush the victory. In an unrelated case from 2003, the Court also ruled against the states when it declared unconstitutional, by a 6–3 vote, a Texas law that had outlawed homosexual conduct between consenting homosexual adults. In the process, the decision also overturned a prior Court decision from the 1980s that had upheld Georgia's right to maintain a similar law.[21]

In three recent death penalty cases, the Court reflected the ambiguity and dynamic nature that frequently characterize the American federal system. In 2002, the Court denied state power to execute a defendant who was mentally disabled, reasoning that because many states had deemed such a practice inappropriate, "evolving standards of decency" in the nation suggested it was time to halt the practice.[22] In 2005, the Court again relied on evolving standards of decency to strike down a state death penalty for seventeen-year-olds.[23] In both cases, the Court acted against the policy of individual states by asserting national power to declare that the death penalty in such circumstances amounted to cruel and unusual punishment and thus violated the Constitution. But in 2008, the Court rejected a challenge to the state's use of lethal injection in administering the death penalty. Opponents of the procedure had argued that it posed a risk that the prisoner would suffer acute but undetectable pain in violation of the Eighth Amendment's stricture against cruel and unusual punishments.[24]

IDEALOG.ORG

Should people convicted of murder get the death penalty or life in prison? Take IDEAlog's self-test.

Grants-in-Aid

Since the 1960s, the national government's use of financial incentives has rivaled its use of legislation and court decisions as a means of influencing its relationship with state governments. Simultaneously, state and local governments have increasingly looked to Washington for money. Leaders at these lower levels of government have attempted to push their own initiatives by getting leverage from new national interest in a variety of policy areas. Thus, if governors can somehow convince national policymakers to adopt laws that buttress state priorities, then these state officials can advance their own priorities even as Washington's power appears to grow. Through a sort of back-and-forth process of negotiation and debate, the dynamics of the American federal system are revealed yet again. The principal arena where many of these interactions take place is in debates over federal grants-in-aid.

A **grant-in-aid** is money paid by one level of government to another level of government to be spent for a given purpose. Most grants-in-aid come with standards or requirements prescribed by Congress. Many are awarded on a matching basis; that is, a recipient government must make some contribution of its own, which the national government then matches. For example, the

grant-in-aid
Money provided by one level of government to another to be spent for a given purpose.

nation's primary health-care program for low-income people, Medicaid, works on this sort of matching basis. Grants-in-aid take two general forms: categorical grants and block grants.

Categorical grants target specific purposes, and restrictions on their use typically leave the recipient government relatively little formal discretion. Recipients today include state governments, local governments, and public and private nonprofit organizations. There are two kinds of categorical grants: formula grants and project grants. As their name implies, **formula grants** are distributed according to specific rules that define who is eligible for the grant and how much each eligible applicant will receive. The formulas may weigh factors such as state per capita income, number of school-age children, urban population, and number of families below the poverty line. Most grants, however, are **project grants**, which are awarded through a competitive application process. Such project grants have focused on health (substance abuse and HIV-AIDS programs); natural resources and the environment (radon, asbestos, and toxic pollution); and education, training, and employment (for disabled, homeless, and elderly persons).

In contrast to categorical grants, Congress awards **block grants** for broad, general purposes. They allow recipient governments considerable freedom to decide how to spend the money. Whereas a categorical grant promotes a specific activity—say, developing an ethnic heritage studies curriculum in public schools—a block grant might be earmarked only for elementary, secondary, and vocational education more generally. The state or local government receiving the block grant then chooses the specific educational programs to fund with it. The recipient might use some money to support ethnic heritage studies and some to fund consumer education programs. Or the recipient might choose to put all the money into consumer education programs and spend nothing on ethnic heritage studies.

Grants-in-aid are a method of redistributing income. Money is collected by the national government from the taxpayers of all fifty states. The money is then funneled back to state and local governments. Many grants have worked to reduce gross inequalities among states and their residents. But the formulas used to redistribute income are not impartial; they are highly political, established through a process of congressional horse-trading.

Although grants-in-aid have been part of the national government arsenal since the early twentieth century, they grew at an astonishing pace in the 1960s, when grant spending doubled every five years. Presidents Nixon and Reagan were strong advocates for redistributing money back to the states, and political support for such redistribution has remained strong. Controlling for inflation, in 1990 the national government returned $172 billion to the states. By 2006, the amount had increased to $363 billion.[25] The main trend, as illustrated in Figure 4.2, is an enormous growth in health-care spending, which now approaches 50 percent of all national grant funds to the states.

Whatever its form or purpose, grant money comes with strings attached. Some strings are there to ensure that recipients spend the money as the law specifies; other regulations are designed to evaluate how well the grant is

categorical grants
Grants-in-aid targeted for a specific purpose by either formula or project.

formula grants
Categorical grants distributed according to a particular set of rules, called a formula, that specify who is eligible for the grants and how much each eligible applicant will receive.

project grants
Categorical grants awarded on the basis of competitive applications submitted by prospective recipients to perform a specific task or function.

block grants
Grants-in-aid awarded for general purposes, allowing the recipient great discretion in spending the grant money.

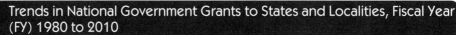

FIGURE 4.2   Trends in National Government Grants to States and Localities, Fiscal Year (FY) 1980 to 2010

National government grants to states and localities vary substantially. In 1980, education programs accounted for the biggest slice of the national government pie. In 1990, grants for health programs, reflecting the expanding costs of Medicaid, took the biggest slice, reaching more than 30 percent of all national government grants to state and local governments. In 2000, health grants exceeded 43 percent of all such national government spending. By 2010, health grants consumed nearly 50 percent of national government grants to the states, yet another indicator of the nation's health-care crisis.

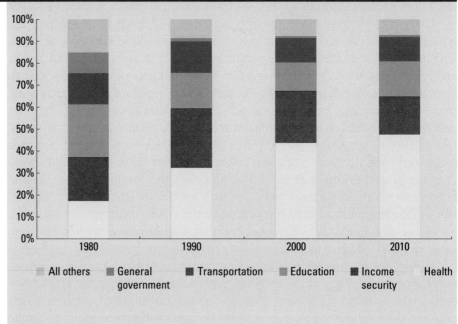

Source: Historical Tables, *Budget of the United States Government,* FY2010, Table 12.3, http://www.gpoaccess.gov/usbudget/fy10/hist.html. Dollar amounts are in billions of constant FY1996 dollars.

working. To these ends, the national government may stipulate that recipients follow certain procedures. The national government may also attach restrictions designed to achieve some broad national goal not always closely related to the specific purpose of the grant. Consider the issue of drunk driving, for example.

The use of highway construction funds has proved an effective means to induce states to accept national standards. Congress threatened to reduce millions of dollars in these funds if states did not agree to prohibit the purchase or consumption of alcoholic beverages by persons under the age of twenty-one. Some states objected, claiming that the Tenth and Twenty-first amendments assigned them responsibility for matters such as alcoholic beverage consumption. In *South Dakota* v. *Dole* (1987), the Supreme Court conceded that direct congressional control of the drinking age in the states would be unconstitutional. Nevertheless, the Constitution does not bar the indirect achievement of such objectives. The seven-member majority argued that, far from being an infringement on states' rights, the law was a "relatively mild encouragement to the States to enact higher minimum drinking ages than they would otherwise choose." After all, Chief Justice William H. Rehnquist wrote, the goal of reducing drunk driving was "directly related to one of the main purposes for which highway funds are expended—safe interstate travel."[26] By 1988, every state in the nation had approved legislation setting twenty-one as the minimum drinking age.

In October 2000, following a three-year battle in Congress, President Bill Clinton signed new legislation establishing a tough national standard of .08

percent blood-alcohol level for drunk driving. Thirty-one states define drunk driving at the .10 percent standard or do not set a specific standard. States that now refuse to impose the lower standard stand to lose millions in government highway construction money.[27] The restaurant industry was not cheering the result. It characterized the law as an attack on social drinkers, who are not the source of the drunk-driving problem. The lure of financial aid has proved a powerful incentive for states to accept standards set by the national government, especially when those standards are aligned with priorities that the states and their citizens generally accept (here, reducing the incidence of drunk driving).

Professionalization of State Governments

A final important factor that has produced dynamic changes in the American federal system has been the emergence of state governments as more capable policy actors than they were in the past. While political scientists generally agree that the rise of competitive party politics in the South (see Chapter 8), the expansion of the interest group system (Chapter 10), and the growth of money in elections (Chapter 9) have all produced significant changes in American politics, nevertheless, many scholars and students rarely consider the expanded capabilities of state governments in the same light. That oversight is important, especially when one considers how far the states have come during the past four decades and how their progress has influenced the shape of American federalism.

It was not long ago that states were described as the weak links in the American policy system. Despite the crucial role that they played in the nation's founding and the legacy of dual federalism, observers both inside and outside the government were skeptical of their ability to contribute actively and effectively to national progress in the post–World War II era. In an oft-quoted book, former North Carolina governor Terry Sanford leveled heavy criticisms at the states, calling them ineffective, indecisive, and inattentive organizations that may have lost their relevance in an increasingly complicated nation and world.[28] Writing nearly twenty years earlier, in 1949, journalist Robert Allen was even less kind; he called the states "the tawdriest, most incompetent, most stultifying unit in the nation's political structure."[29]

But since the 1960s especially, states have become more capable and forceful policy actors. These changes have created better policy outcomes that have benefited citizens across the United States while simultaneously contributing to dynamic changes in the American federal system. If the situation was so bleak less than five decades ago, what happened to bring about the change? Several factors account for the change in perspective.[30]

First, the states have made many internal changes that have fostered their capabilities. Both governors and state legislators now employ more capably trained and experienced policy staff rather than part-time assistants with responsibilities across a wide range of policy areas. Second, legislatures now meet more days during the year, and elected officials in states receive

Compared with What?

Working for the Public

The national government in the United States employs about 2 million people. But if we factor in individuals employed through federal grants and contracts, the number of federal government employees balloons to around 15 million. When we factor in all public employees at the national, state, and local levels, we get a greater sense of the presence of government in our lives.

Figure A compares the number of public sector workers at all levels controlling for population across several countries. In this comparison, public sector employment is about 71 workers for every 1,000 Americans. This is about average across all the countries compared. Public sector employment in the United States is about half of that in Norway and Sweden, much smaller countries with substantial public welfare programs. Public sector employment in the United States is greater than that in the economically powerful countries of Germany and Japan.

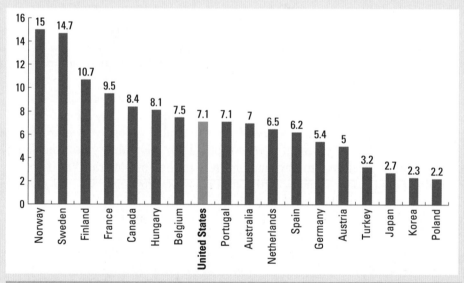

Figure A: Public Sector Employment as a Percentage of Total Population (2005)

higher salaries. Third, the appeal of higher salaries, in particular, has helped to attract more highly qualified people to run for state office. Fourth, the increasing ability of states to raise revenue, as a result of state tax and budgetary reforms that have transpired since the 1960s, has also given states greater leverage in designing and directing policy, rather than previous generations, where local property taxes played a more significant role in relation to state budget and tax policy. And, fifth, the unelected officials who work in state departments and administer state programs in areas such as

The distribution of public sector employment between the national level on the one hand and the state and local levels on the other produces a different picture. (See Figure B.) By far, most public sector workers in the United States are found at the state and local levels. Higher state and local employment is also characteristic of other federal systems, such as those of Australia, Germany, and Canada.

So if you ponder the question "Where is my government?" a postal worker would satisfy the federal part of the answer. Local government employees are far more numerous, working at the firehouse, the police station, or at your local public school.

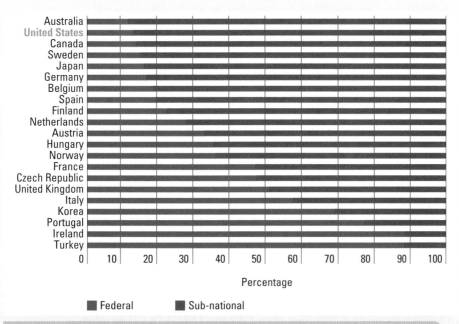

Figure B: Distribution of Employment between the Federal and Subnational Levels of Government (2005)

Source: Adam Sheingate, "Why Can't Americans See the State?" *The Forum* 7, no. 4 (2010): 1–14; Paul C. Light, "The New True Size of Government," *Organizational Performance Initiative: Research Brief, Number 2* (Robert F. Wagner Graduate School of Public Service, New York University, August 2006), p. 11.

transportation, social services, and law enforcement have become better educated. For instance, professional and service occupations account for more than half of all jobs at the state and local levels. In 2010, professional workers represented one-fifth of all state and local government employees. Most of these professional jobs require a college degree.[31]

As evidence of the dynamic relationships between the national government and the states, changes in national policy have also helped the states develop. Many federal grants-in-aid include components designed explicitly to foster capacity-building measures in state governments. Because the national government recognizes—often for political or practical reasons—that several of its domestic initiatives depend on capable implementation from state actors, members of Congress and presidents often design national laws with these capacity-building elements in mind.

One example is the Elementary and Secondary Education Act (ESEA), which became law in 1965. This act, passed as part of President Lyndon Johnson's Great Society effort, was designed to provide federal assistance to the nation's disadvantaged students. Though it is often overlooked, Title V of the law contained several provisions designed to strengthen state departments of education, the agencies that would be responsible for administering the bulk of other programs contained in the ESEA. Thus, although the law was often portrayed as an assertion of national power (which it was), it also helped set in motion changes that would allow state governments to improve their capabilities to make and administer K–12 education policy. Those new capabilities, which subsequent federal laws and internal state efforts have fostered, continued to influence the shape of both federal and state education policy, especially during the most recent revision of the ESEA as the No Child Left Behind Act of 2001.[32]

All of this is not to say that the states are without problems of their own. In some ways, they have been victims of their own success. Now that state capitals have become more viable venues where citizens and interest groups can agitate for their causes, the states have begun to face ever-increasing demands. Those requests can strain state administrators and legislative or gubernatorial staffs, who, while better educated and equipped than their predecessors, still struggle to set priorities and please their constituents.

Ideology, Policymaking, and American Federalism

As the previous section illustrated, American federalism appears to be in constant motion. This is due in large part to what some political scientists call **policy entrepreneurs**: citizens, interest groups, and officials inside government who attempt to persuade others to accept a particular view of the proper balance of freedom, order, and equality. The American federal system provides myriad opportunities for interested parties to push their ideas.

In essence, the existence of national and state governments—specifically, their executive, legislative, and judicial branches and their bureaucratic agencies—offers these entrepreneurs venues where they can attempt to influence policy and politics. Sometimes when doors are closed in one place, opportunities may be available elsewhere. The most creative of these entrepreneurs can work at multiple levels of government simultaneously, sometimes coordinating with one another to score political and policy victories.

In this section, we explore how views about American federalism can influence the shape of the nation's politics and policy. We also relate these

policy entrepreneurs
Citizens, members of interest groups, or public officials who champion particular policy ideas.

issues to our ongoing discussion of political ideology, which we introduced in Chapter 1 (see Figure 1.2).

Ideology, Policymaking, and Federalism in Theory

To begin our discussion in this section, it will be helpful to return to the cake metaphors that describe dual and cooperative federalism. Looking at those models of the nation's federal system helps capture some of what could be considered conventional wisdom about political ideology and federalism—in particular, the views of conservatives and liberals. In their efforts to limit the scope of the national government, conservatives are often associated with the layer-cake metaphor. In contrast, it is often said that liberals, believing that one function of the national government is to bring about equality, are more likely to support the marble-cake approach and more activism from Washington. Let's explore each of these general claims in a bit more detail.

Conservatives are frequently portrayed as believing that different states have different problems and resources and that returning control to state governments would promote diversity. States would be free to experiment with alternative ways to confront their problems. States would compete with one another. And people would be free to choose the state government they preferred by simply voting with their feet and moving to another state. An additional claim frequently attributed to the conservative approach to federalism is that the national government is too remote, too tied to special interests, and not responsive to the public at large. The national government overregulates and tries to promote too much uniformity. States are closer to the people and better able to respond to specific local needs.

In contrast, pundits and scholars often argue that what conservatives hope for, liberals fear. Liberals remember, so the argument goes, that the states' rights model allowed extreme political and social inequalities and that it supported racism. Blacks and city dwellers were often left virtually unrepresented by white state legislators who disproportionately served rural interests. The conclusion is that liberals believe the states remain unwilling or unable to protect the rights or provide for the needs of their citizens, whether those citizens are consumers seeking protection from business interests, defendants requiring guarantees of due process of law, or poor people seeking a minimum standard of living.

Looking in general terms at how presidents since the 1960s have approached federalism issues seems to provide some support for these descriptions of liberals and conservatives.

President Lyndon Johnson's efforts to forge a Great Society are often characterized as the high-water mark of national government activism. With the range of programs in housing, education, and urban renewal developed during Johnson's tenure and his extensions of FDR's New Deal, it was clear to many observers that the marble cake seemed to dominate LBJ's thinking about federalism. In 1969, Richard Nixon advocated giving more power to state and local governments. Nixon wanted to decentralize national policies through an

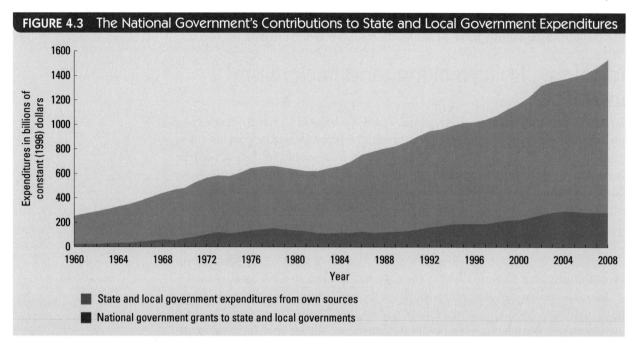

FIGURE 4.3 The National Government's Contributions to State and Local Government Expenditures

In 1960, the national government contributed roughly 11 percent of total state and local spending. After rising in the 1960s and 1970s, that total stood at almost 25 percent by 1980. The national share declined during the 1980s, and by 1990 it was barely 15 percent. By 2005, the national government's share had moved up to 21 percent, and by 2008, it dropped back to 18 percent.

Source: Calculations from Historical Tables, *Budget of the United States Government,* FY2009, Table 15.2 (adjusted to 1996 dollars). Available at http://www.gpoaccess.gov/usbudget/fy10/hist.html.

effort dubbed New Federalism. The president's New Federalism called for combining and reformulating categorical grants into block grants. The shift had dramatic implications for federalism. Block grants were seen as a way to redress the imbalance of power between Washington and the states and localities. Conservatives in Washington wanted to return freedom to the states. New Federalism was nothing more than dual federalism in modern dress.

Charging that the federal system had been bent out of shape, President Ronald Reagan promised what to some could be called "new New Federalism" to restore a proper constitutional relationship among the national, state, and local governments. The national government, he said, treated "elected state and local officials as if they were nothing more than administrative agents for federal authority."[33]

Reagan's commitment to reducing federal taxes and spending meant that the states would have to foot an increasing share of the bill for government services (see Figure 4.3). In the late 1970s, the national government funded 25 percent of all state and local government spending. By 1990, its contribution had declined to roughly 17 percent. By the end of 2000, that figure had increased again, inching up to about 23 percent, where it remains today.

While it would be inaccurate to describe Bill Clinton and Lyndon Johnson as liberals cut from the same cloth, President Clinton, unlike Nixon and Reagan, saw much more potential for the national government to produce policy successes, especially in areas such as education and environmental protection. Clinton's approach might be described as seeing the national government as a policy guru, guiding and encouraging states to experiment with vexing problems.

When George W. Bush took the White House in 2000, there appeared to develop yet another bend in the nation's federalism road. Generally, Bush, who described himself as a "compassionate conservative," was "notably inattentive to federalism considerations in office," expanding federal authority in areas where Republicans were loathe to tread such as education, prescription drug coverage, and driver's licenses.[34] Bush's approach was a move away from the Republican effort in 1994 to scale back the national government while ignoring the potential costs—in human and social terms, for example—of their proposals.

The Obama administration has traversed a careful path in disputes with the states. The Arizona example that opened this chapter is a case in point. Recall that conservative Arizonans sought strict enforcement against illegals to stem perceived disorder in their state. Liberal Arizonans maintained that individual freedom would suffer with strict enforcement against illegals. Avoiding either prong of this dilemma, the Obama administration argued successfully that federalism principles resolved the dispute in favor of the national government, putting an end to Arizona's efforts at immigration enforcement.

Ideology, Policymaking, and Federalism in Practice

Despite the correlation between presidential preferences regarding federalism and refrains such as "liberals love the national government" and "conservatives favor states' rights," these simplifications are only sometimes correct and, in fact, are often misleading. Recall our admonition from Chapter 1 that to grasp the differences between conservatives and liberals, one needs to understand not only these general labels but also the purposes of government under discussion. One illustration emerges from debates over the federal preemption of state power.

National Intervention in State Functions. **Preemption** is the power of Congress to enact laws by which the national government assumes complete or partial responsibility for a state government function. When the national government shoulders a new government function, it restricts the discretionary power of the states. Congressional prohibition of state or local taxation of the Internet is an example of complete preemption.[35] It represents a loss of billions of dollars to state and local governments. Partial preemption occurs with the enactment of minimum national standards that states must meet if they wish to regulate the field. The Do Not Call Implementation Act of 2003 is an example of partial preemption. States retained authority to regulate telemarketing provided they met the minimum standards spelled out by the act.[36]

Preemption is a modern power. Congress passed only twenty-nine preemptive acts before 1900. In the ensuing sixty years, Congress preempted the

preemption
The power of Congress to enact laws by which the national government assumes total or partial responsibility for a state government function.

power of states to legislate in certain areas an additional 153 times. The pace of preemption has accelerated. By 2000, or in just forty years, Congress enacted an additional 329 preemption statutes.[37] From 2001 to 2005, 64 new laws preempted state authority.[38] The vast majority of these recent preemption efforts were partial preemptions dealing with terrorism or environmental protection. For example, states are now forbidden to issue licenses to carriers of hazardous materials without a determination by the secretary of transportation that the person is not a security risk. This is a provision in the USA-PATRIOT Act.

Congressional preemption statutes infringe on state powers in two ways: through mandates and restraints. A **mandate** is a requirement that a state undertake an activity or provide a service, in keeping with minimum national standards. A mandate might require that states remove specified pollutants from public drinking water supplies, for example.

In contrast, a **restraint** forbids state governments from exercising a certain power. A restraint might prohibit states from dumping sewage into the ocean.

The increased use of preemption has given birth to a new theory of federalism. The pressure to expand national power inherent in cooperative federalism has reduced the national government's reliance on fiscal tools such as grants-in-aid. Instead, the national government has come to rely on regulatory tools such as mandates and restraints to ensure the supremacy of federal policy. According to this view, cooperative federalism has morphed into **coercive federalism**.[39]

Constraining Unfunded Mandates. State and local government officials have long objected to the national government's practice of imposing requirements without providing the financial support needed to satisfy them. For example, the provisions in the Americans with Disabilities Act require nearly all American business owners to make their business premises available to disabled customers, without providing any funds for the cost of reconstruction or additional interior space. By 1992, more than 170 congressional acts had established partially or wholly unfunded mandates.[40]

One of the early results of the Republican-led 104th Congress (1995–1997) was the Unfunded Mandates Relief Act of 1995. The legislation requires the Congressional Budget Office to prepare cost estimates of any newly proposed national legislation that would impose more than $50 million a year in costs on state and local governments or more than $100 million a year in costs on private business. It also requires a cost analysis of the impact of new agency regulations on governments and private businesses. Congress can still pass along to the states the costs of the programs it mandates, but only after holding a separate vote specifically imposing a requirement on other governments without providing the money to carry it out. Some observers expected that a Republican-controlled Congress and a Republican president would turn back the tide of unfunded mandates. However, that was not to be. Many mandates have fallen outside the precise contours of the Relief Act. While it is likely that the cost estimates have served to temper or withdraw some

mandate
A requirement that a state undertake an activity or provide a service, in keeping with minimum national standards.

restraint
A requirement laid down by act of Congress, prohibiting a state or local government from exercising a certain power.

coercive federalism
A view holding that the national government may impose its policy preferences on the states through regulations in the form of mandates and restraints.

mandates, the Relief Act has acted merely as a speed bump, slowing down others rather than deterring new efforts at regulation.[41] (It is important to note that the law does not apply to legislation protecting constitutional rights and civil rights or to antidiscrimination laws.)

The act's critics argue that large proportions of state appropriation budgets still must cover the costs of programs imposed by the national government. The National Conference of State Legislatures estimated, for example, that Real ID, a federally mandated program that imposes security, authentication, and issuance standards for states to issue driver's licenses and identification cards, will cost $11 billion through 2012.[42] To pay for the program, states may be forced to raise fees or taxes. In tough economic times, state legislators are loathe to ask constituents to pay higher taxes. Since 2001, the federal government has passed along more than $100 billion worth of unfunded mandates to the states.[43]

If Republicans were expecting a return of powers to the states during the presidency of George W. Bush, then they were likely disappointed. On his watch, the national government increased its power over the states. Through coercive federalism, the national government now calls the tune for still more activities that were once the sole province of individual states.

Federalism and Electoral Politics

In addition to affecting the shape of American public policy, federalism plays a significant role in electoral politics. We have much more to say about elections in Chapter 9. For now, we focus on the ways that federalism is related to the outcome of both state and national elections.

National Capital–State Capital Links

State capitals often serve as proving grounds for politicians who aspire to national office. After gaining experience in a state legislature or serving in a statewide elected position (governor or attorney general, for example), elected officials frequently draw on that experience in making a pitch for service in the U.S. House, the Senate, or even the White House. The role that state political experience can play in making a run for the presidency seems to have become increasingly important in recent decades. Consider that four of the previous six candidates to be elected to the highest office in the land, a period dating back to 1976, had formerly served as governors: Jimmy Carter (Georgia), Ronald Reagan

Nutrition Facts

Serving Size ¾ cup (31g)
Servings Per Container about 11

Amount Per Serving	Cinnamon Toast Crunch	with ½ cup skim milk
Calories	130	170
Calories from Fat	30	30
	% Daily Value[**]	
Total Fat 3g*	5%	5%
Saturated Fat 0.5g	2%	2%
Trans Fat 0g		
Polyunsaturated Fat 0.5g		
Monounsaturated Fat 2g		
Cholesterol 0mg	0%	1%
Sodium 220mg	9%	12%
Potassium 45mg	1%	7%
Total Carbohydrate 25g	8%	10%
Dietary Fiber 1g	4%	4%
Sugars 10g		
Other Carbohydrate 14g		
Protein 1g		
Vitamin A	10%	15%
Vitamin C	10%	10%
Calcium	10%	25%
Iron	25%	25%
Vitamin D	10%	25%
Thiamin	25%	30%
Riboflavin	25%	35%
Niacin	25%	25%
Vitamin B$_6$	25%	25%
Folic Acid	25%	25%
Vitamin B$_{12}$	25%	35%
Phosphorus	4%	15%
Magnesium	2%	6%
Zinc	25%	30%
Copper	2%	2%

* Amount in cereal. A serving of cereal plus skim milk provides 3g total fat, less than 5mg cholesterol, 280mg sodium, 250mg potassium, 30g total carbohydrate (16g sugars) and 5g protein.

** Percent Daily Values are based on a 2,000 calorie diet. Your daily values may be higher or lower depending on your calorie needs:

		Calories	2,000	2,500
Total Fat	Less than		65g	80g
Sat Fat	Less than		20g	25g
Cholesterol	Less than		300mg	300mg
Sodium	Less than		2,400mg	2,400mg
Potassium			3,500mg	3,500mg
Total Carbohydrate			300g	375g
Dietary Fiber			25g	30g

Label Me

Food labeling follows a single national standard today as a result of the Nutrition Labeling and Education Act of 1990. The act preempted states from imposing different labeling requirements.

(© Sarah-Maria Vischer/The Image Works)

Wave This Senate Seat Good-Bye

Presidents routinely come to the aid of fellow office seekers, hoping to increase their party's fortunes in local and statewide races. Hoping to hold a 60-vote majority in the U.S. Senate, President Obama took to the hustings on behalf of Democrat Martha Coakley. She was running to fill the vacancy created by the death of Edward Kennedy, Massachusetts' long-serving liberal senator. But it was too little, too late. Coakley lost to Republican Scott Brown, who came from behind to win, campaigning across the state in his 2005 GMC Canyon pick-up.

(AP Photo/Michael Dwyer)

(California), Bill Clinton (Arkansas), and George W. Bush (Texas). George H. W. Bush and Barack Obama are the exceptions. Today, several prominent members of Congress also have past experience in statewide offices. Examples are Senator Judd Gregg (Rep.), former governor of New Hampshire; Senator Mark Warner (Dem.), former governor of Virginia; and Senator Claire McCaskill (Dem.), former state auditor of Missouri.

It is hard to underestimate the value of previous political experience in attempting to mount a campaign for national office. In addition to learning the craft of being a politician, experience in state politics can be critically important for helping a candidate to build up a network of contacts, die-hard constituents, and potential fundraisers. Past governors also have the benefit of being plugged into organizations such as the National Governors' Association and the Republican and Democratic governors' groups, which can help to cultivate national name recognition, friendships, and a reputation in Washington. Finally, considering that presidential elections are really a series of fifty different state-level contests, given the structure of the electoral college, a candidate for the White House can benefit tremendously from a friendly governor who can call into action his or her own political network on the candidate's behalf.

If state-level experience and friends can sometimes catapult an individual to national office, once secure in the Congress or the White House, national-level politicians frequently return to the states to stump for local favorites. In the 2002 election cycle, with a closely divided House and Senate, President George W. Bush and his key political strategist, Karl Rove, adopted an aggressive approach to the midterm election campaign. The president traveled across the country speaking on behalf of Republican candidates, increasing the party's majority by eight seats in the House and four in the Senate. But the same strategy proved disastrous for Bush and fellow Republicans in the 2006 elections. Republicans lost thirty seats and their majority in the House and six seats and their majority in the Senate. And Democrats claimed a majority of gubernatorial elections. Presidential popularity (and unpopularity) cuts both ways.[44]

Congressional Redistricting

Perhaps even more important than activities on the campaign trail is the decennial process of congressional redistricting, which reveals crucial connections between federalism and the nation's electoral politics. Most generally, **redistricting** refers to the process of redrawing boundaries for electoral jurisdictions. This process, which occurs at all levels of government, becomes an extremely high-stakes game in the two years after each decennial national census in the United States. During that window of time, the U.S. Census Bureau produces and releases updated population counts for the nation. Those numbers are used to determine the number of seats that each state will have in the U.S. House, which are apportioned based on population.

While it is relatively straightforward to determine how many seats each state will have, where the new district lines will be drawn is a hugely complicated and political process. Even in states that may not have lost or gained seats but have had population shifts—some areas grow at a rapid rate while others lose population, for example—the task of redistricting carries huge stakes. In large part, this is because state legislatures typically have the task of drawing the lines that define the congressional districts in their states. Given that this process happens only once every ten years and that the careers of U.S. House members and their party's relatively long-term fortunes in Congress can turn on decisions made in these state-level political debates, it is no wonder that the redistricting process commands significant national attention.

A final way that federalism can influence redistricting is through a process called *preclearance*. Under Section 5 of the Voting Rights Act, several states are required to submit their redistricting plans to the U.S. Department of Justice for approval. The process is quite complicated, but in essence it requires that states show how their proposed plans will not be "retrogressive in purpose or effect," meaning they will not dilute minority voting strength. Passing the test of preclearance, however, does not mean that a state's redistricting plans cannot be challenged for civil rights purposes or other grounds as defined in federal law and court decisions, such as rulings affirming the one person–one vote principle.

In short, both the politics of drawing congressional boundaries and the interactions between Justice Department officials and state legislators responsible for preclearance reveal the intimate connections between federalism and the redistricting process.[45]

Federalism and the American Intergovernmental System

We have concentrated in this chapter on the links between the national and state governments in the federal system. Although the Constitution explicitly recognizes only national and state governments, the American federal system has spawned a multitude of local governments as well. It is worth considering these units because they help to illustrate the third main principle that we

redistricting
The process of redrawing political boundaries to reflect changes in population.

outlined near the beginning of this chapter: a growing recognition among public officials and citizens that public problems cut across governmental boundaries. Finding the right mix of national, state, and local involvement is a perennial challenge that dogs even the most savvy and experienced public officials.

Thousands of Governments

Based on data from 2007, the most recent year available, the U.S. Census Bureau estimates that in addition to the one national government and fifty state governments, the United States is home to over 89,000 local governments of different sorts.[46] These governments are mainly the product of the previous century of American history, with nearly all coming into existence during the 1900s.

Americans are citizens of both a nation and a state, and they also come under the jurisdiction of these various local government units. These units include **municipal governments**, the governments of cities and towns. Municipalities, in turn, are located in (or may contain or share boundaries with) counties, which are administered by **county governments**. (Sixteen states further subdivide counties into *townships* as units of government.) Most Americans also live in a **school district**, which is responsible for administering local elementary and secondary educational programs. They may also be served by one or more **special districts**, government units created to perform particular functions, typically when those functions, such as fire protection and water purification and distribution, spill across ordinary jurisdictional boundaries. Examples of special districts are the Port Authority of New York and New Jersey, the Chicago Sanitation District, and the Southeast Pennsylvania Transit Authority. Together, school districts and special districts add more than 50,000 units of government to the mix.

Local governments are created by state governments, either in their constitutions or through legislation. This means that their organization, powers, responsibilities, and effectiveness vary considerably from state to state. About forty states endow their cities with various forms of **home rule**—the right to enact and enforce legislation in certain administrative areas. Home rule gives cities a measure of self-government and freedom of action. In contrast, county governments, which are the main units of local government in rural areas, tend to have little or no legislative power. Instead, they ordinarily serve as administrative units, performing the specific duties assigned to them under state law, such as maintaining roads and administering health programs.

How can the ordinary citizen be expected to make sense of this maze of governments? And do these governments really benefit ordinary citizens?

In theory at least, one advantage of localizing government is that it brings government closer to the people; it gives them an opportunity to participate in the political process, to have a direct influence on policy. Localized government conjures visions of informed citizens deciding their own political fate—the traditional New England town meeting, repeated across

municipal governments
The government units that administer a city or town.

county governments
The government units that administer a county.

school district
The government unit that administers elementary and secondary school programs.

special districts
Government units created to perform particular functions, especially when those functions are best performed across jurisdictional boundaries.

home rule
The right to enact and enforce legislation locally.

the nation. From this perspective, overlapping governments appear compatible with a majoritarian view of democracy.

The reality is somewhat different, however. Studies have shown that people are much less likely to vote in local elections than in national elections.[47] In fact, voter turnout in local contests tends to be quite low (although the influence of individual votes is thus much greater). Furthermore, the fragmentation of powers, functions, and responsibilities among national, state, and local governments makes government as a whole seem complicated, and hence incomprehensible and inaccessible, to ordinary people. In addition, most people have little time to devote to public affairs, which can be very time-consuming. These factors tend to discourage individual citizens from pursuing politics and augment the influence of organized groups, which have the resources—time, money, and know-how—to sway policymaking (see Chapter 10). Instead of bringing government closer to the people and reinforcing majoritarian democracy, the system's enormous complexity tends to encourage pluralism.

Still, the large number of governments makes it possible for government to respond to the diversity of conditions in different parts of the country. States and cities differ enormously in population, size, economic resources, climate, and other characteristics—the diverse elements that French political philosopher Montesquieu argued should be taken into account in formulating laws for a society. Smaller political units are better able to respond to particular local conditions and can generally do so more quickly than larger units. Nevertheless, smaller units may not be able to muster the economic resources to meet some challenges. And in a growing number of policy areas, from education to environmental protection to welfare provision, citizens have come to see the advantages of coordinating efforts and sharing burdens across levels of government.

Crosscutting Responsibilities

The national government continues to support state and local governments. Yet spending pressures on state and local governments are enormous. The public demands better schools, harsher sentences for criminals (and more prisons to hold them), more and better day care for children, and nursing home assistance for the elderly. Bolstered by a strong national economy, many states cut income and business taxes in 2006. Other states provided local property tax relief. However, the deep and lengthy recession that began in 2008 has added extra strains on state finances. A majority of states reported their revenues have been hurt by the housing sector slump. Most, if not all, are seeing declines in their real estate transfer or recording taxes. Higher oil prices have given Alaska a budget surplus, but that's the exception. With high unemployment, lower property values, fewer property sales, and general economic sluggishness, tax revenues have not matched state expenditures. And since state budgets must balance each year (only the national government can print money), states must either cut services, raise taxes, or borrow money. Needless to say, these are not popular options.

Whose Rules?

Grand Staircase–Escalante National Monument in southern Utah was established by presidential decree in 1996. It sits on 1.7 million acres of austere and rugged land. The decree irked local residents, who had hoped for greater industrial development, which is now barred. They have fought back by claiming ownership of hundreds of miles of dirt roads, dry washes, and riverbeds in the monument. The conflicting signs illustrate the controversy. On the left, the local government, Kane County, approves use of all-terrain vehicles. On the right, the national government signals just the opposite.

(Kevin Moloney/The New York Times/Redux)

In addition to ongoing policy development and financing the activities of government, sometimes crises press different levels of government into duty together. A tragic turn of events in October 2002 provides a case in point. During that month, the Washington, D.C., metropolitan area found itself under siege from what appeared to be random, yet chillingly precise, attacks from a rifle-wielding sniper. Before the assailants had been captured, ten people were killed and four others injured. Law enforcement agents also suggested that the Washington killings may have been related to similar murders in Alabama and Louisiana.

Officials at all levels of government in several states participated in what became a massive hunt for the killers. As the investigation unfolded, the local face that Americans became familiar with was Montgomery County (Maryland) police chief Charles Moose. His office exchanged a handful of messages with the assailants, and the chief became a regular figure on nightly news programs. Because some of the attacks also took place in Virginia, members of the Old Dominion State's local law enforcement and state police contributed their efforts. Finally, because the sniper killings came roughly one year

NYPD Meets USMS

When Pakistani-born U.S. citizen Faisal Shahzad attempted to detonate a homemade bomb near Times Square in New York City, the response by the police at all levels of government was swift and effective. Shahzad was apprehended a few days later as he attempted to leave the country. Members of NYPD were on hand at the United States Courthouse in New York City for Shaszhad's arraignment. And so were members of the United States Marshals Service, the enforcement arm of the federal courts.

(JOHN ANGELILLO/UPI/Landov)

after the attacks of 9/11, which raised the specter that they were connected to terrorism, and owing to the interstate nature of the crimes, federal law enforcement officials, including then Attorney General John Ashcroft, also participated in the hunt. Over the course of the investigation, apprehension, and trial phase of the case, the overlapping responsibilities and jurisdictions involved in the case revealed some of the strengths and weaknesses of the American federal system in action. Although many citizens were pleased to see such a comprehensive effort to halt the shootings, inevitably turf battles emerged among the various jurisdictions involved, as officials in national, state, and local government jockeyed with one another, sometimes to push for their own theories of how the case was unfolding, and, inevitably given the bright spotlight on the whole affair, to score political points with their constituents and the public at large.[48]

Federalism and the International System

In today's increasingly interconnected world, it is perhaps not surprising that federalism is more than simply a local curiosity for citizens of the United States. The dynamics of American federalism, in addition to helping shape the nation's politics, have begun to have more noticeable impacts in the international arena as well. And federalism as a system of government and governance is becoming increasingly important across the globe. In this section, we relate federalism to several evolving international issues and events.

American Federalism and World Politics

American federalism can have important impacts on how the United States deals with other nations, even in areas that clearly seem to be the prerogative of the national government. Trade policy is one good example.

Article I, Section 8, of the U.S. Constitution declares that the legislative branch shall have the power "to regulate Commerce with foreign Nations," and Section 10 prohibits individual states from entering "into any Treaty, Alliance, or Confederation," or, without Congress's consent, from laying "any Imposts or Duties on Imports or Exports, except what may be absolutely necessary for executing its inspection Laws." And even those imposts and duties "shall be for the Use of the Treasury of the United States." Article II, Section 2, reserves to the president the power to make treaties with other nations with the advice and consent of the Senate. These constitutional provisions provide the national government, but not the states, with significant justification and formal authority to develop foreign trade agreements and regulate imports and exports.

The national government also commands significant capacity to act in trade policy. The U.S. Department of Commerce, the Office of the U.S. Trade Representative, and the formal roles that the United States plays in international bodies such as the World Trade Organization provide federal officials with significant access to data and even formal decision-making power over trade-related issues on the domestic and global stages.

Despite what appears to be a clear mismatch between national and state officials on trade, state leaders do develop and advance their own trade agendas. It may come as a surprise to some readers, but trade policy has a noticeable intergovernmental component. In summarizing developments in state politics, two scholars have noted that states have become more aggressive in establishing their own outposts, so to speak, in other countries.[49] Today, all 50 states have international trade directors, and these officials coordinate several activities through an umbrella group called the State International Development Organizations (SIDO), an affiliate of the Council of State Governments. SIDO is like many other state-level groups that lobby Washington policymakers. However, the group also plays a more formal role by participating on a joint advisory panel with the U.S. Department of Commerce to help coordinate national and state export activities. Certainly, when national government officials advance agendas that would expand or restrict trade, states may see their own agendas to promote exports bolstered or challenged. Members of SIDO and other state leaders can advance their own state trade agendas by using and helping shape federal agendas in this area.[50]

State activities in the international arena extend beyond export promotion. Other dimensions of trade policy illustrate in an interesting way that state and local governments can have noticeable impacts on American foreign policy. For example, a small but not insignificant number of state and local jurisdictions have become more assertive in using their own trade activities to advance international human rights positions. A recent example involved Illinois and six other states along with six U.S. municipalities and over forty universities, which in 2006 adopted divestment measures that removed from their pension plans and other investments companies that operate in Sudan to the benefit of the Khartoum government. These laws were designed to signal concern about the genocide that has claimed the lives of hundreds of thousands in the past four years.[51] In 2007, the U.S. Senate and the U.S. House of Representatives unanimously passed the Sudan Accountability and Divestment Act, which authorizes state and local governments to divest from companies that support the Khartoum government in Sudan and also prohibits federal contracts with those companies.[52]

Federalism Across the Globe

Supreme Court Justice Anthony Kennedy once observed that "federalism was our Nation's own discovery. The Framers split the atom of sovereignty. It was the genius of their idea that our citizens would have two political capacities, one state and one federal, each protected from incursion by the other."[53] Federalism is not an obsolete nineteenth-century form of government inappropriate in the contemporary world. In fact, the concept of the nation-state, developed in the seventeenth century, may be heading for the dustbin. (A *nation-state* is a country with defined and recognized boundaries whose citizens have common characteristics, such as race, religion, customs, and language.)

Some scholars have noted that we may be moving from a world of sovereign nation-states to a world of diminished state sovereignty and increased interstate linkages of a constitutionally federal character. Among the 195 politically sovereign states in the world today, 24 are federations that together embrace about 2.5 billion people, or 40 percent of the world population. About 480 constituent or federated states serve as the building blocks of these 24 federations.[54] New versions of the federal idea continue to arise. Countries like Iraq and Sudan are transitioning to federalism, and others such as Sri Lanka are considering adoption of a federal system[55] (see "Politics of Global Change: Federalism, Iraqi Style").

The bumpy road toward the creation of a European superstate—in either a loose confederation or a binding federation—demonstrates the potential for as well as the limits of federalism to overcome long-held religious, ethnic, linguistic, and cultural divisions. The economic integration of such a superstate has created an alternative to the dominant currency, the U.S. dollar. And the creation of a single and expanding European market would serve as a magnet for buyers and sellers. The political unification of Europe seems to be more difficult to attain due to the resistance of some national populations, but European governments have not been dissuaded from their goal. They have found a new path—through the treaty—to circumvent the requirement of popular ratification and achieve the goal of a unified Europe with its own unique federal structure.

Politics of Global Change

Federalism, Iraqi Style

The United States and its coalition of willing partners deposed the Baathist regime of Saddam Hussein in Iraq. What form of government has replaced unitary dictatorial rule? In October 2005 the Iraqi people approved a new constitution that established a federal system with separate legislative, executive, and judicial functions. Whereas the United States made its transition from a highly dispersed system under the Articles of Confederation to a more centralized federal arrangement, Iraq has now moved from a highly centralized and unitary system under dictator Saddam Hussein to a more dispersed federal system under its new constitution.

The situation in Iraq is very complicated. Ethnic, tribal, and religious groups demand resources, territory, and autonomy. Arabs, Kurds, and Turkmen are the main ethnic groups. Although the population is almost entirely Muslim, the people divide into majority Shiite and minority Sunni sects. The Sunnis held sway under Saddam Hussein. Now the Shiites dominate.

Too little acknowledgment of group demands risks violent disruption. But giving too much authority to the various groups and the regions where they concentrate will fuel the very nationalisms that will divide Iraq. The

fine line between too little and too much requires compromises in reallocating economic resources, dividing power between regional and central authority, and introducing a version of democracy that rules out extremists rooted in ethnic or religious intolerance.

Former U.S. ambassador to Croatia Peter Galbraith, a critic of the Bush administration's Iraq policy but a strong defender of the new constitution, argues that "the constitution reflects the reality of the nation it is meant to serve." "There is," he says, "no meaningful Iraqi identity. In the north, you've got a pro-Western Kurdish population. In the south, you've got a Shiite majority that wants a 'pale version of an Iranian state.' And in the center you've got a Sunni population that is nervous about being trapped in a system in which it would be overrun."

These divisions over ethnic and religious lines were expressed in parliamentary elections and constitutional craftsmanship. The Kurds chose pro-autonomy leaders and opted for a constitution with strong regional control. The Shiites voted for religious parties and supported a decentralized republic along the lines of the early U.S. confederation. Many Sunnis who initially opted out of elections supported strong central government, fearing

Federalism and Pluralism

At the nation's founding, the federal system of government in the United States was designed to allay citizens' fears that they might be ruled by a majority in a distant region with whom they did not necessarily agree or share interests. By recognizing the legitimacy of the states as political divisions, the federal system also recognizes the importance of diversity. The existence and cultivation of diverse interests are the hallmarks of pluralism.

Both of the main competing theories of federalism that we have explored support pluralism, but in somewhat different ways. The layer-cake approach of dual federalism aims to maintain important powers in the states and to protect those powers from an aggressive or assertive national government.

that the Kurds and Shiites might marginalize them. In such a context, federalism is the best political tool to accommodate conflicting interests. Indeed, the Iraqi constitution provides the foundation for a loose federal system in which only fiscal and foreign affairs issues will be handled by the national government.

Five years after approving the Iraqi constitution, the country is at a stalemate. The three-way divide among Shiites, Sunni Arabs, and Kurds turns a pluralistic democracy into an unsuitable device for reaching consensus. According to the Iraqi national security adviser, Mowaffak al-Rubaie, "resolution can be achieved only through a system that incorporates regional federalism, with clear, mutually acceptable distributions of power between the regions and the central government. Such a system is in the interest of all Iraqis and is necessary if Iraq is to avoid partition or further civil strife." Critics, on the other hand, underline that the majority of Iraqis sees federalism as an imported and unwanted political solution. Scholars reunited in a symposium about Iraq's future agreed that the potential "partition of Iraq into three autonomous regions likely will lead to increased tensions between the factions" and noted "that many Iraqis associate the term partition with a western imposed division of the country." They also pointed out the challenge of incorporating Islamic beliefs into the constitution while maintaining a secular, democratic state. Nevertheless, there are reasons to be moderately optimistic about the future of democracy in the country: a poll conducted by the Brookings Institution in February 2009

shows that 64 percent of Iraqis considered that the country should be a democracy, versus the 19 percent who opted for an Islamic state. Only 14 percent claimed to prefer a government ruled by a strong leader.

The challenge of democracy is to find that delicate balance ensuring enough regional autonomy to satisfy ethnic or religious solidarity but not so much autonomy as to splinter the entire enterprise. American views of democracy may complicate the situation. An Iraq that emulates America's free-style democracy may promote the seeds of its own destruction by giving every zealot a forum. But constraining Iraqi democracy by ruling some extreme viewpoints out of bounds may call into question one of the reasons America intervened in Iraq in the first place: to plant a viable democracy in the Middle East.

Sources: Edward Wong, "The World: New Wars in Iraq; Making Compromises to Keep a Country Whole," *New York Times*, 4 January 2004, Sec. 4, p. 4; David Brooks, "Divided They Stand," *The New York Times*, 25 August 2005; "Iraq's Constitution," *Wall Street Journal*, 15 October 2005, p. A5; Mowaffak al-Rubaie, "Federalism, Not Partition; A System Devolving Power to the Regions Is the Route to a Viable Iraq," *Washington Post*, 18 January 2008, p. A19; Matthew T. Simpson and Christina J. Sheetz, "Rethinking the Future: The Next Five Years in Iraq," *American University International Law Review* 24, no. 2 (2008), available at http://ssrn.com/abstract=1319926; Thomas Sommer-Houdeville, "Six Years Later: The Political Landscape in Iraq" (Iraqi Civil Society Solidarity initiative, 25–31 March 2009); "Iraq Index: Tracking Reconstruction and Security in Post-Saddam Iraq" (Brookings Institution, 26 February 2010), available at http://www.brookings.edu/saban/iraq-index.aspx#archives.

The theory recognizes the importance of local and national standards, but it maintains that not all policy areas should be considered the same; some are more amenable to decision making and standards closer to home, while others are more appropriately national. Preserving this possible variety at the state level allows the people, if not a direct vote in policymaking, at least a choice of policies under which to live.

In contrast, the marble cake of cooperative federalism sees relations between levels of government in more fluid terms and is perfectly willing to override state standards for national ones depending on the issues at stake. Yet this view of federalism, while more amenable to national prerogatives, is highly responsive (at least in theory) to all manner of pressures from groups and policy entrepreneurs, including pressure at one level of government from those that might be unsuccessful at others. By blurring the lines of national and state responsibility, this type of federalism encourages petitioners to try their luck at whichever level of government offers them the best chance of success, or simultaneously to mount diverse sets of strategies across levels of government.

The national government has come to rely increasingly on its regulatory power to shape state policies. Through mandates and restraints, the national government has exercised a coercive form of federalism. This direction with policies flowing from Washington to the state and local levels signals a shift from a pluralist to a majoritarian model.

Summary

The government framework outlined in the Constitution is the product of political compromise, an acknowledgment of the original thirteen states' fear of a powerful central government and frustrations that the Articles of Federation produced. The division of powers sketched in the Constitution was supposed to turn over "great and aggregate" matters to the national government, leaving "local and particular" concerns to the states. The Constitution does not explain, however, what is "great and aggregate" or "what is local and particular."

Federalism comes in many varieties, two of which stand out because they capture valuable differences between the original and modern visions of a national government. Dual, or layer-cake, federalism wants to retain a strong separation between state and national powers, which, in essence, provides the states with a protective buffer against national encroachments.

Cooperative, or marble-cake, federalism sees national and state government working together to solve national problems. In its own way, each view supports the pluralist model of democracy.

One of the enduring features of American federalism has been the system's great ability to adapt to new circumstances. Several factors have produced changes in the nature of the system. National crises and demands from citizens frustrated with the responsiveness of state governments, judicial interpretations of the proper balance between states and the national government, changes in the system of grants-in-aid, and the professionalism of state governments have all contributed to changes in American federalism.

Because the Constitution treats federalism in an ambiguous and sometimes seemingly contradictory way, it is difficult to pin clear ideological labels on particular theories of federalism. Although it is common to hear political pundits and politicians associate conservatism with dual federalism and liberalism with cooperative federalism, in practice these labels do not tend to correlate as well as casual glances would suggest. Rather, it is the combination of ideology and the specific policy context—how one prioritizes freedom, order, and equality—rather than ideology alone that drives conceptions of the proper nation–state balance across several policy areas.

Although it is accurate to say that the national government's influence has grown significantly since the New Deal of the 1930s and the Great Society of the 1960s, it is also the case that citizens and elected officials alike have come to appreciate the intergovernmental nature of problems confronting the nation. Today, the answer to the question, "Which level of government is responsible?" is frequently, "All of them." Certainly there exists some separation between the national government and states—the flavors of the marble cake have not swirled together so much that they are indistinguishable. The national government's regulatory power casts a coercive shadow over all state governments. This model of coercive federalism reflects the continuing ebb and flow of power moving from states to nation to states to nation.

Still, given the mixed messages present in the Constitution and debates that date to the country's founding over the proper role for the national government and the states, for better or for worse it is likely that American federalism will remain in constant flux well into the future.

 CourseMate   Visit www.cengagebrain.com/shop/ ISBN/0495906182 for flashcards, web quizzes, videos and more!

Public Opinion and Political Socialization

Justyna Furmanczyk, 2010/Used under license from Shutterstock.com

On December 8, 2009, the state of Ohio executed Kenneth Biros in a novel way. Condemned to death for his brutal 1991 crime—sexually assaulting a woman, stabbing her 90 times, and scattering her body parts across two states—Biros was injected with a massive dose of barbiturate, the preferred method for euthanizing animals. The single drug replaced the typical three-drug execution cocktail: sodium pentothal to produce unconsciousness, pancuronium bromide to cause paralysis, and potassium chloride to stop the heart.[1] The cocktail or some variant has been used in over 1,000 lethal injections in thirty-six states since the late 1970s.[2]

Lethal injection was adopted as a more humane method of execution than alternatives (e.g., electrocution, hanging), but the three drugs are difficult to administer. Three months earlier, in fact, Ohio failed to execute Romell Broom (convicted of abduction, rape, and murder of a 14-year-old girl) after sticking him with a needle for nearly two hours, unable to find a usable vein.[3] Two Kentucky inmates had contended that the method constituted cruel and unusual punishment, outlawed by the Constitution, but the Supreme Court ruled 7 to 2 against them in April 2008.[4]

Two months later, however, an Ohio judged ruled that stricter Ohio law required "avoidance of any unnecessary risk of pain" in executions and struck down the cocktail method.[5] After the December one-drug injection produced no complications, Ohio used it again on January 7, 2010, executing Vernon Smith for killing a shopkeeper in a 1993 robbery. Experts expected that other states would soon adopt the Ohio model.[6]

The death penalty is very popular in the United States, regularly backed over several decades two to one in national surveys.[7] Nevertheless, it is outlawed in two-thirds of the world's countries, including *every* Western democracy.[8] In 2008, 93 percent of all executions were carried out in only five nations—China, Iran, Saudi Arabia, Pakistan, and the United States[9]—putting us in uncomfortable company. Since the 1990s, however, death sentences have declined in the United States, and in 2009 New Mexico became the fifteenth state to repeal the death penalty—in part due to high costs of litigation.[10]

We can learn much about the role of public opinion in America by reviewing how our government has punished violent criminals. During most of American history, government execution of people who threatened the social order was legal. In colonial times, capital punishment was imposed not just for murder but also for antisocial behavior—denying the "true" God, cursing one's parents, committing adultery, practicing witchcraft, even being a rebellious child.[11] Over the years, writers, editors, and clergy argued for abolishing the death sentence, and a few states responded by eliminating capital punishment. But the outbreak of World War I fed the public's fear of foreigners and radicals, leading to renewed support for the death penalty. The security needs of World War II and the postwar fears of Soviet communism fueled continued support for capital punishment.

After anticommunist hysteria subsided in the late 1950s, public opposition to the death penalty increased. But public opinion was neither strong enough nor stable enough to force state legislatures to outlaw it. In keeping with the pluralist model of democracy, efforts to abolish the death penalty shifted from the legislative arena to the courts. The opponents argued that the death penalty is cruel and unusual punishment and is therefore unconstitutional. Their argument apparently had some effect on public opinion: in 1966, a plurality of respondents opposed the death penalty for the first (and only) time since the Gallup Organization began polling the public on the question of capital punishment.

The states responded to this shift in public opinion by reducing the number of executions, until they stopped completely in 1968 in anticipation of a Supreme Court decision. By then, however, public opinion had again reversed in favor of capital punishment. Nevertheless, in 1972, the Court ruled in a 5–4 decision that the death penalty as imposed by existing state laws was unconstitutional.[12] The decision was not well received in many states, and thirty-five state legislatures passed new laws to get around the ruling. Meanwhile, as the nation's homicide rate increased, public approval of the death penalty jumped almost ten points and continued climbing.

In 1976, the Supreme Court changed its position and upheld three new state laws that let judges consider the defendant's record and the nature of the crime in deciding whether to impose a sentence of death.[13] The Court also rejected the argument that punishment by death in itself violates the Constitution, and it noted that public opinion favors the death penalty. Through the end of the 1970s, however, only three criminals were executed. Eventually, the states began to heed public concern about the crime rate. Over 1,000 executions have taken place since the 1976 Supreme Court ruling.[14]

Although public support for the death penalty remains high, Americans are divided on the issue. A majority of white Americans favors the death penalty for a person convicted of murder, while a majority of African Americans opposes the death penalty.[15] Conservatives are more likely than liberals to support the death penalty. In a 2009 poll, 81 percent of all Republicans favored the death penalty, versus only 48 percent of all Democrats.[16] Many Americans are concerned that innocent persons have been executed. Indeed, since 1973, over 130 death row inmates have been exonerated of their crimes with the help of DNA testing.[17]

Does the death penalty deter people from killing? A majority of the public thinks it does. **Public opinion** is simply the collective attitude of the citizens on a given issue or question. The history of public thinking on the death penalty reveals several characteristics of public opinion:

1. *The public's attitudes toward a given government policy can vary over time, often dramatically.* Opinions about capital punishment tend to fluctuate with threats to the social order. The public is more likely to favor capital punishment in times of war and when fear of foreign subversion and crime rates are high.

2. *Public opinion places boundaries on allowable types of public policy.* Stoning or beheading criminals is not acceptable to the modern American public (and surely not to courts interpreting the Constitution). Until recently, administering a lethal injection to a murderer was not controversial.[18]

3. *If asked by pollsters, citizens are willing to register opinions on matters outside their experience.* People pronounce execution by lethal injection as more humane than electrocution, asphyxiation in a gas chamber, or hanging.

public opinion
The collective attitudes of citizens concerning a given issue or question.

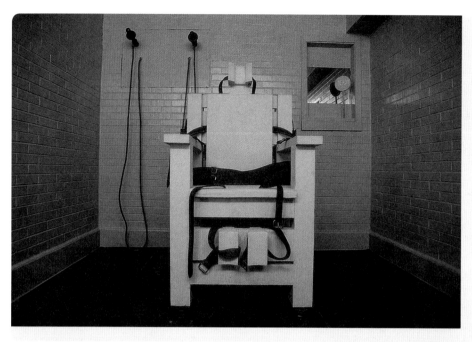

4. *Governments tend to respond to public opinion.* State laws for and against capital punishment have reflected swings in the public mood. The Supreme Court's 1972 decision against capital punishment came when public opinion on the death penalty was sharply divided; the Court's approval of capital punishment in 1976 coincided with a rise in public approval of the death penalty. Public opinion in Texas is strongly in favor of capital punishment; public opinion in states like New Jersey that have banned capital punishment is much less favorable.

5. *The government sometimes does not do what the people want.* Although public opinion overwhelmingly favors the death penalty for murder, there were only fifty-two executions in 2009 (but over sixteen thousand murders that year).

The last two conclusions bear on our understanding of the majoritarian and pluralist models of democracy discussed in Chapter 2. Here, we probe more deeply into the nature, shape, depth, and formation of public opinion in a democratic government. What is the place of public opinion in a democracy? How do people acquire their opinions? What are the major lines of division in public opinion? How do individuals' ideology and knowledge affect their opinions?

IDEALOG.ORG

One of the questions in the IDEALog self-test asks about the death penalty. After reading the information about the death penalty here, would you answer that question differently now? Take IDEALog's self-test.

Public Opinion and the Models of Democracy

Opinion polling, which involves interviewing a sample of citizens to estimate public opinion as a whole (see the feature "Sampling a Few, Predicting to Everyone"), is such a common feature of contemporary life that we often

Taking the Public Pulse

Pollsters sample households by randomly dialing telephone numbers to reach people on their land-line telephones. What happens when more and more Americans have a cell phone instead of the traditional land-line telephone? To draw valid inferences from samples with known estimates of error, every person in the population must have an equal chance of selection. Cell phone-only users constitute 16 percent of all households and tend to be younger and less well off than other respondents. Polling firms are putting together samples that include cell phone-only and land-line-only households to compensate for changes in technology.

(Spencer Grant/PhotoEdit)

IN OUR OWN WORDS

Listen to Kenneth Janda discuss the main points and themes of this chapter.

www.cengagebrain.com/shop/ISBN/0495906182

forget it is a modern invention, dating only from the 1930s (see Figure 5.1). In fact, survey methodology did not become a powerful research tool until the advent of computers in the 1950s. Before polling became a common part of the American scene, politicians, journalists, and everyone else could argue about what the people wanted, but no one really knew. Before the 1930s, observers of America had to guess at national opinion by analyzing newspaper stories, politicians' speeches, voting returns, and travelers' diaries. What if pollsters had been around when the colonists declared their independence from Britain in July 1776? We might have learned (as some historians estimate) that "40 percent of Americans supported the Revolution, 20 percent opposed it, and 40 percent tried to remain neutral."[19]

When no one really knows what the people want, how can the national government be responsive to public opinion? As we discussed in Chapter 3, the founders wanted to build public opinion into our government structure by allowing the direct election of representatives to the House and apportioning representation there according to population. The attitudes and actions of the House of Representatives, the framers thought, would reflect public opinion, especially on the crucial issues of taxes and government spending.

Feature Story

Sampling a Few, Predicting to Everyone

How can a pollster tell what the nation thinks by talking to only a few hundred people? The answer lies in the statistical theory of sampling. Briefly, the theory holds that a sample of individuals selected by chance from any population is representative of that population. This means that the traits of the individuals in the sample—their attitudes, beliefs, sociological characteristics, and physical features—reflect the traits of the whole population. Sampling theory does not claim that a sample exactly matches the population, only that it reflects the population with some predictable degree of accuracy.

Three factors determine the accuracy of a sample. The most important is how the sample is selected. For maximum accuracy, the individuals in the sample must be chosen randomly. Randomly does not mean "at whim," however; it means that every individual in the population has the same chance of being selected.

For a population as large and widespread as that of the United States, pollsters first divide the country into geographical regions. Then they randomly choose areas and sample individuals who live within those areas. This departure from strict random sampling does decrease the accuracy of polls, but by only a relatively small amount. Today, most polls conducted by the mass media are done by telephone, with computers randomly dialing numbers within predetermined calling areas. (Random dialing ensures that even people with unlisted numbers are called.)

The second factor that affects accuracy is the size of the sample. The larger the sample is, the more accurately it represents the population. For example, a sample of four hundred randomly selected individuals is accurate to (plus or minus) six percentage points 95 percent of the time. A sample of six hundred is accurate to within five percentage points. (Surprisingly, the proportion of the sample to the overall population has essentially no effect on the accuracy of most samples. A sample of, say, six hundred individuals will reflect the traits of a city, a state, or even an entire nation

with equal accuracy. Why this statement is true is better discussed in a course on statistics.)

The final factor that affects the accuracy of sampling is the amount of variation in the population. If there were no variation, every sample would reflect the population's characteristics with perfect accuracy. The greater the variation is within the population, the greater is the chance that one random sample will be different from another.

The Gallup Poll and most other national opinion polls usually survey about fifteen hundred individuals and are accurate to within three percentage points 95 percent of the time. As shown in Figure 5.1, the predictions of the Gallup Poll for nineteen presidential elections since 1936 have deviated from the voting results by less than 1.0 percentage point. Even this small margin of error can mean an incorrect prediction in a close election. But for the purpose of estimating public opinion on political issues, a sampling error of three percentage points is acceptable.

Poll results can be wrong because of problems that have nothing to do with sampling theory. For example, question wording can bias the results. A CBS News poll in August 2009 found that including the words "similar to Medicare" in asking about a government-run healthcare plan boosted support by 7 percent among persons aged 65 and older.* Survey questions are also prone to random error because interviewers are likely to obtain superficial responses from busy respondents who say anything, quickly, to get rid of them. Recently, some newspaper columnists have even urged readers to lie to pollsters outside voting booths, to confound election night television predictions. But despite the potential for abuses or distortions, modern polling has told us a great deal about public opinion in America.

---

*Katharine Q. Seelye, "Prescriptions Making Sense of the Health Care Debate; Does Public Care about Public Option?" *New York Times*, 29 November 2009, p. A27.

In practice, bills passed by a majority of elected representatives do not necessarily reflect the opinion of a majority of citizens. This would not have bothered the framers because they never intended to create a full democracy, a government completely responsive to majority opinion. Although they wanted to provide for some consideration of public opinion, they had little faith in the ability of the masses to make public policy.

The majoritarian and pluralist models of democracy differ greatly in their assumptions about the role of public opinion in democratic government. According to the classic majoritarian model, the government should do what a majority of the public wants. Indeed, polls show that 70 percent of Americans think that the views of the majority should have "a great deal" of influence on the decisions of politicians.[20] In contrast, pluralists argue that the public as a whole seldom demonstrates clear, consistent opinions on the day-to-day issues of government. At the same time, pluralists recognize that subgroups within the public do express opinions on specific matters—often and vigorously. The pluralist model requires that government institutions allow the free expression of opinions by these "minority publics." Democracy is at work when the opinions of many different publics clash openly and fairly over government policy.

Sampling methods and opinion polling have altered the debate about the majoritarian and pluralist models of democracy. One expert said, "Surveys produce just what democracy is supposed to produce—equal representation of all citizens."[21] Now that we know how often government policy runs against majority opinion, it becomes harder to defend the U.S. government as democratic under the majoritarian model. Even at a time when Americans overwhelmingly favored the death penalty for murderers, the Supreme Court decided that existing state laws applying capital punishment were unconstitutional.[22] Even after the Court approved new state laws as constitutional, relatively few murderers were actually executed. Consider, too, the case of prayer in public schools. In 1992 and again in 2000, the Supreme Court ruled against clergy-led prayers at public school graduations. Yet a 2002 survey showed that a clear majority of Americans (75 percent) did not agree with that ruling.[23] Because government policy sometimes runs against settled majority opinion, the majoritarian model is easily attacked as an inaccurate description of reality.

The two models of democracy make different assumptions about public opinion. The majoritarian model assumes that a majority of the people holds clear, consistent opinions on government policy. The pluralist model assumes that the public is often uninformed and ambivalent about specific issues, and opinion polls frequently support that claim. For example, five Gallup polls on health-care legislation showed public support fluctuating narrowly around a 50-50 split from September to December 2009.[24]

What are the bases of public opinion? What principles, if any, do people use to organize their beliefs and attitudes about politics? Exactly how do individuals form their political opinions? We will look for answers to these questions in this chapter. In later chapters, we assess the effect of public opinion on government policies. The results should help you make up your own mind about the viability of the majoritarian and pluralist models in a functioning democracy.

FIGURE 5.1   Gallup Poll Accuracy

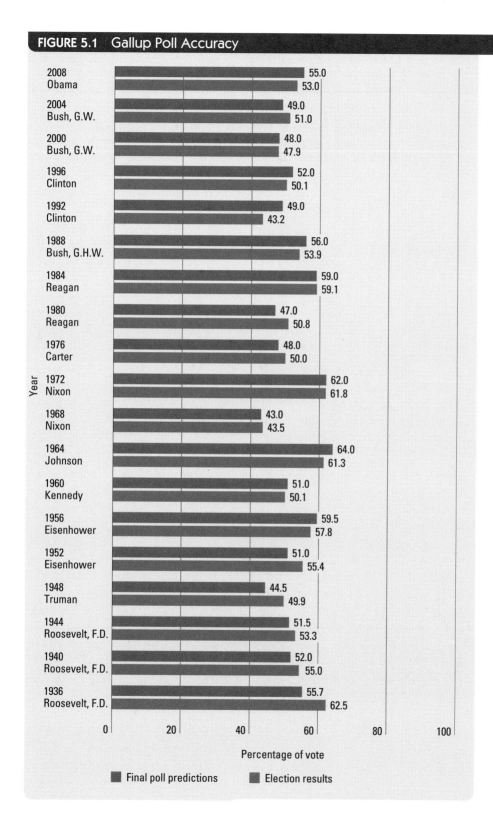

Percentage of vote

■ Final poll predictions   ■ Election results

One of the nation's oldest polls was started by George Gallup in the 1930s. The accuracy of the Gallup Poll in predicting presidential elections over sixty years is charted here. Although not always on the mark, its predictions have been fairly close. Gallup's final prediction for the 2000 election declared the race "too close to call." Indeed, the race in the electoral college remained too close to call for weeks after the election. The poll was most notably wrong in 1948, when it predicted that Thomas Dewey, the Republican candidate, would defeat the Democratic incumbent, Harry Truman, underestimating Truman's vote by 5.4 percentage points. In 1992, the Gallup Poll was off by a larger margin, but this time it identified the winner: Bill Clinton. Although third-party candidate Ross Perot was included in the presidential debates and spent vast sums on his campaign, Gallup kept with historical precedent and allocated none of the undecided vote to Perot. As a result, it overestimated Clinton's share.

Source: Gallup Organization, available at http://www.gallup.com/poll/9442/Election-Polls-Accuracy-Record-Presidential-Elections.aspx.

Stop the Presses! Oops, Too Late...

As the 1948 election drew near, few people gave President Harry Truman a chance to defeat his Republican opponent, Thomas E. Dewey. Polling was still new, and almost all the early polls showed Dewey far ahead. Most organizations simply stopped polling weeks before the election. The *Chicago Daily Tribune* believed the polls and proclaimed Dewey's victory before the votes were counted. Here, the victorious Truman triumphantly displays the most embarrassing headline in American politics. Later, it was revealed that the few polls taken closer to election day showed Truman catching up to Dewey. Clearly, polls estimate the vote only at the time they are taken.

(Bettmann/CORBIS)

The Distribution of Public Opinion

A government that tries to respond to public opinion soon learns that people seldom think alike. To understand and then act on the public's many attitudes and beliefs, government must pay attention to the way public opinion is distributed among the choices on a given issue. In particular, government must analyze the shape and the stability of that distribution.

Shape of the Distribution

The results of public opinion polls are often displayed in graphs such as those in Figure 5.2. The height of the columns indicates the percentage of those polled who gave each response, identified along the baseline. The

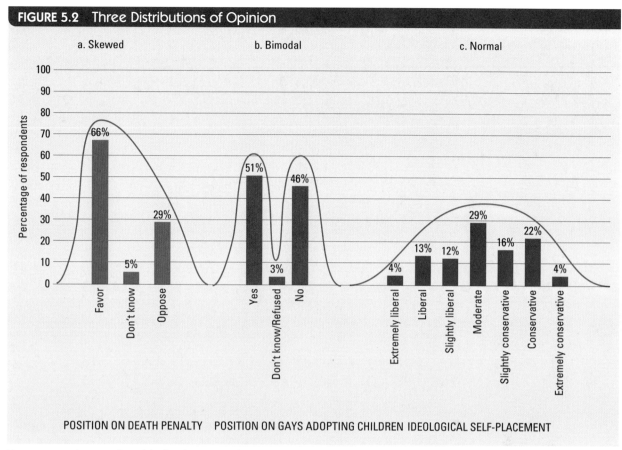

FIGURE 5.2   Three Distributions of Opinion

a. Skewed   b. Bimodal   c. Normal

POSITION ON DEATH PENALTY   POSITION ON GAYS ADOPTING CHILDREN   IDEOLOGICAL SELF-PLACEMENT

Here we superimpose three idealized patterns of distribution—skewed, bimodal, and normal—on three actual distributions of responses to survey questions. Although the actual responses do not match the ideal shapes exactly, the match is close enough that we can describe the distribution of (a) thoughts on the death penalty as skewed, (b) opinions on whether gays should adopt children as bimodal, and (c) ideological attitudes as approximately normal.

Source: 2008 American National Election Study, undertaken in collaboration by Stanford University and the University of Michigan.

shape of the opinion distribution depicts the pattern of all the responses when counted and plotted. The figure depicts three patterns of distribution: skewed, bimodal, and normal.

Figure 5.2a plots the percentages of respondents surveyed in 2008 who favored or opposed imposing the death penalty for a person convicted of murder. The most frequent response ("favor") is called the *mode*. The mode produces a prominent "hump" in this distribution. The relatively few respondents who didn't know or were opposed to the death penalty lie to one side, in its "tail." Such an asymmetrical distribution is called a **skewed distribution**.

Figure 5.2b plots responses when participants were asked whether they believed gays should be allowed to adopt children. These responses fall into a **bimodal distribution**: respondents chose two categories with equal frequency, dividing almost evenly over whether gays can be adequate parents.

skewed distribution
An asymmetrical but generally bell-shaped distribution (of opinions); its mode, or most frequent response, lies off to one side.

bimodal distribution
A distribution (of opinions) that shows two responses being chosen about as frequently as each other.

Figure 5.2c shows how respondents to a national survey in 2008 were distributed along a liberal–conservative continuum. Its shape resembles what statisticians call a **normal distribution**—a symmetrical, bell-shaped spread around a single mode, or most frequent response. Here, the mode ("moderate") lies in the center. Fewer people tended to classify themselves in each category toward the liberal and conservative extremes.

When public opinion is normally distributed on an issue, the public tends to support a moderate government policy on that issue. It will also tolerate policies that fall slightly to the left or to the right as long as they do not stray too far from the moderate center. In contrast, when opinion is sharply divided in a bimodal distribution, as it is over homosexual partners adopting a child (or Obama's health-care plan), there is great potential for political conflict. A skewed distribution, on the other hand, indicates that most respondents share the same opinion. When consensus on an issue is overwhelming, those with the minority opinion risk social ostracism and even persecution if they persist in voicing their view. If the public does not feel intensely about the issue, however, politicians can sometimes discount a skewed distribution of opinion. This is what has happened with the death penalty. Although most people favor capital punishment, it is not a burning issue for them. Thus, politicians can skirt the issue without serious consequences.

Stability of the Distribution

A **stable distribution** shows little change over time. Public opinion on important issues can change, but it is sometimes difficult to distinguish a true change in opinion from a difference in the way a question is worded. When different questions on the same issue produce similar distributions of opinion, the underlying attitudes are stable. When the same question (or virtually the same question) produces significantly different responses over time, an actual shift in public opinion probably has occurred.

We have already discussed Americans' long-standing support of the death penalty. People's descriptions of themselves in ideological terms are another distribution that has remained stable. Chapter 1 argued for using a two-dimensional ideological typology based on the trade-offs of freedom for equality and freedom for order. However, most opinion polls ask respondents to place themselves along only a single liberal–conservative dimension, which tends to force libertarians and communitarians into the middle category. Historically, the ideological distribution of the public has been skewed toward conservatism in every presidential election since 1964.[25] In surveys since 1992, the public has become marginally more conservative, with the number of those classifying themselves as such rising from 36 to 40 percent at the end of 2009. Over the same period, people have also become somewhat more liberal, with the number of those classifying themselves as such rising from 17 to 21 percent. These opposite changes occurred at the cost of moderates, who declined from 43 to 36 percent.[26]

Sometimes changes occur within subgroups that are not reflected in overall public opinion. College students, for example, were far more liberal in

normal distribution
A symmetrical bell-shaped distribution (of opinions) centered on a single mode, or most frequent response.

stable distribution
A distribution (of opinions) that shows little change over time.

FIGURE 5.3   Are Students More Conservative Than Their Parents?

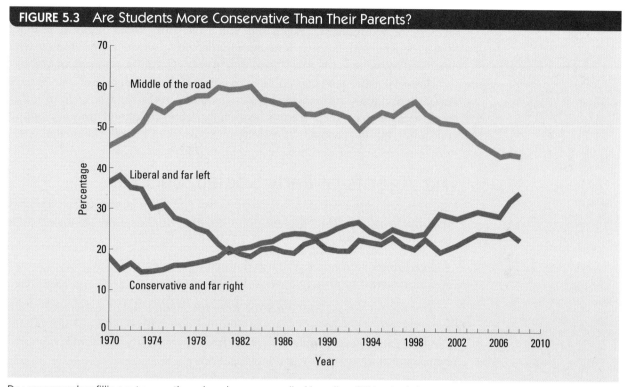

Do you remember filling out a questionnaire when you enrolled in college? If it asked about your political orientation, you may be represented in this graph. For almost four decades, researchers at the University of California at Los Angeles have collected various data on entering freshmen, including asking them to characterize their political views as far left, liberal, middle of the road, conservative, or far right. In contrast to Americans in general, who have classified themselves as more conservative over time, college students now describe themselves as markedly more liberal than they did in the mid-1980s.

Source: Higher Education Research Institute, University of California, Los Angeles, "The American Freshman: National Norms for Fall 2008," http://www.gseis.ucla.edu/heri/index.php. © 2009 The Regents of the University of California. All Rights Reserved. Used by permission.

the 1970s than in the 1980s (see Figure 5.3), but they have since turned more liberal and today are much more liberal than the general public. Moreover, public opinion in America is capable of massive change over time, even on issues that were once highly controversial. A good example is tolerance toward interracial marriage. In 1958, only 4 percent of Americans approved of it. By 2007, 77 percent approved, including 75 percent of whites.[27]

In trying to explain how political opinions are formed and how they change, political scientists cite the process of political socialization, the influence of cultural factors, and the interplay of ideology and knowledge. In the next several sections, we examine how these elements combine to create and influence public opinion.

Political Socialization

Public opinion is grounded in political values. People acquire their values through **political socialization,** a complex process through which individuals become aware of politics, learn political facts, and form political values.

political socialization
The complex process by which people acquire their political values.

Think for a moment about your political socialization. What is your earliest memory of a president? When did you first learn about political parties? If you identify with a party, how did you decide to do so? If you do not, why don't you? Who was the first liberal you ever met? The first conservative?

Obviously, the paths to political awareness, knowledge, and values vary among individuals, but most people are exposed to the same sources of influence, or agents of socialization, especially from childhood through young adulthood: family, school, community, peers, and, of course, the media.

The Agents of Early Socialization

Like psychologists, scholars of political socialization place great emphasis on early learning. Both groups point to two fundamental principles that characterize early learning:[28]

- *The primacy principle.* What is learned first is learned best.
- *The structuring principle.* What is learned first structures later learning.

The extent of the influence of any socializing agent depends on the extent of our exposure to it, our communication with it, and our receptivity to it.[29] Because most people learn first from their family, the family tends to be an important agent of early socialization.

Family. In most cases, exposure, communication, and receptivity are highest in parent–child relationships. From their parents, children learn a wide range of values—social, moral, religious, economic, and political—that help shape their opinions. It is not surprising, then, that most people link their earliest memories of politics with their family. Moreover, when parents are interested in politics and maintain a favorable home environment for studying public affairs, they influence their children to become politically interested and informed.[30]

One of the most politically important things that many children learn from their parents is party identification. They learn party identification in much the same way as they do religion. Children (very young children, anyway) imitate their parents. When parents share the same religion, children are almost always raised in that faith. When parents are of different religions, their children are more likely to follow one or the other than to choose an entirely different religion. Similarly, parental influence on party identification is greater when both parents strongly identify with the same party.[31] Overall, more than half of young American voters identify with the political party of their parents.[32] Moreover, those who change their partisanship are more likely to shift from being partisan to independent or from independent to partisan than to convert from one party to the other.[33]

Two crucial differences between party identification and religion may explain why youngsters are socialized into a religion much more reliably than into a political party. The first is that most parents care a great deal more about their religion than about their politics, so they are more deliberate about exposing their children to religion. The second is that religious institutions recognize the value of socialization; they offer Sunday schools and other activities that reinforce parental guidance. American political parties, in contrast, sponsor few activities to win the hearts of little Democrats and Republicans, which leaves children open to counterinfluences in their school and community.

School. According to some researchers, schools have an influence on political learning that is equal to or greater than that of parents.[34] Here, however, we have to distinguish between elementary and secondary schools, on the one hand, and institutions of higher education, on the other. Elementary schools prepare children in a number of ways to accept the social order. They introduce authority figures outside the family: the teacher, the principal, the police officer. They also teach the nation's slogans and symbols: the Pledge of Allegiance, the national anthem, national heroes, and holidays. And they stress the norms of group behavior and democratic decision making: respecting the opinions of others, voting for class officers. In the process, they teach youngsters about the value of political equality.

Children do not always understand the meaning of the patriotic rituals and behaviors they learn in elementary school. In fact, much of this early learning—in the United States and elsewhere—is more indoctrination than education. By the end of the eighth grade, however, children begin to distinguish between political leaders and government institutions. They become more aware of collective institutions, such as Congress and elections, than do younger children, who tend to focus on the president and other single figures of government authority.[35] In sum, most children emerge from elementary school with a sense of national pride and an idealized notion of American government.[36]

Although newer curricula in many secondary schools emphasize citizens' rights in addition to their responsibilities, high schools also attempt to build "good citizens." Field trips to the state legislature or the city council impress students with the majesty and power of government institutions. But secondary schools also offer more explicit political content in their curricula, including courses in recent U.S. history, civics, and American government. Better teachers challenge students to think critically about American government and politics; others focus on teaching civic responsibilities. The end product is a greater awareness of the political process and of the most prominent participants in that process.[37] Students who have been taught skills such as letter writing and debating are more likely to participate in politics.[38]

Political learning at the college level can be much like that in high school, or it can be quite different. The degree of difference is greater if professors (or the texts they use) encourage their students to question authority. Questioning dominant political values does not necessarily mean rejecting them. For example, this text encourages you to recognize that freedom and equality, two values idealized in our culture, often conflict. It also invites you

Bearing Global Warming

Pictures like this seem to demonstrate the reality of global warming. While opinion surveys show that most Americans believe that global warming is happening, the percentage dropped from 80 to 72 percent from 2008 to 2009. The decline occurred mainly among Republicans and independents. Increased skepticism has consequences for Democratic proposals of legislation to reduce carbon emissions.

Source: Juliet Eilperin, "Few Americans Believe in Global Warming, Poll Shows," *Washington Post*, 25 November 2009, at http://www.washingtonpost.com/wp-dyn/content/article/2009/11/24/AR2009112402989.html. *Photo:* Design Pics Inc./Alamy.

to think of democracy in terms of competing institutional models, one of which challenges the idealized notion of democracy. These alternative perspectives are meant to teach you about American political values, not to subvert those values. College courses that are intended to stimulate critical thinking have the potential to introduce students to political ideas that are radically different from those they bring to class. Most high school courses do not. Still, specialists in socialization contend that taking particular courses in college has little effect on attitude change, which is more likely to come from sustained interactions with classmates who hold different views.[39]

Community and Peers. Your community and your peers are different but usually overlapping groups. Your community is the people of all ages with whom you come in contact because they live or work near you. Peers are your friends, classmates, and coworkers. Usually they are your age and live or work within your community.

The makeup of a community has a lot to do with how the political opinions of its members are formed. Homogeneous communities—those whose members are similar in ethnicity, race, religion, or occupation—can exert strong pressures on both children and adults to conform to the dominant attitude. For example, if all your neighbors praise the candidates of one party and criticize the candidates of the other, it is difficult to voice or even hold a dissenting opinion.[40] Communities made up of one ethnic group or religion may also voice negative attitudes about other groups. Although community socialization is usually reinforced in the schools, schools sometimes introduce students to ideas that run counter to community values. (One example is sex education.)

For both children and adults, peer groups sometimes provide a defense against community pressures. Adolescent peer groups are particularly effective protection against parental pressures. In adolescence, children rely on their peers to defend their dress and their lifestyle, not their politics. At the college level, however, peer group influence on political attitudes often grows substantially, sometimes fed by new information that clashes with parental beliefs. A classic study of students at Bennington College in the 1930s found that many became substantially more liberal than their affluent and conservative parents. Two follow-up studies twenty-five and fifty years later showed that most retained their liberal attitudes, in part because their spouses and friends (peers) supported their views.[41] In another study, students who were active as protesters in college in the 1960s remained more liberal than college-educated adults who had not been protesters.[42]

Continuing Socialization

Political socialization continues throughout life. As parental and school influences wane in adulthood, peer groups (neighbors, coworkers, club members) assume a greater importance in promoting political awareness and developing political opinions.[43] Because adults usually learn about political events from the mass media—newspapers, magazines, television, radio, and the Web—the media emerge as socialization agents.[44] Older Americans are more likely to rely on newspaper and television news for political information, while younger Americans are more likely to turn to radio, magazines, or the Internet.[45] The mass media are so important in the political socialization of both children and adults that we devote a whole chapter—Chapter 6—to a discussion of their role.

Regardless of how people learn about politics, they gain perspective on government as they grow older. They are likely to measure new candidates (and new ideas) against those they remember. Their values also change, increasingly reflecting their own self-interest. As voters age, for example, they begin to see more merit in government spending for Social Security than they did when they were younger. Generational differences in values and historical experience translate into different public policy preferences. Finally, political education comes simply through exposure and familiarity. One example is voting, which people do with increasing regularity as they grow older: it becomes a habit.

Word of God?

A person's religiosity may be as important as his or her denominational identification in predicting political opinions. One measure of people's religiosity in a Christian-Judaic society is their opinion about the Bible. When asked about the nature of the Bible in 2008, about 38 percent of respondents said it was the actual word of God. About 44 percent regarded it as inspired by God but believed it should not be taken literally. The remaining 18 percent viewed it as an ancient book of history, legends, fables, and moral precepts recorded by humans. Those who believed that the Bible is the literal word of God strongly favored government action to limit abortion. They were also much more likely to think that "creationism," a theory of the origin and development of life on Earth based on a strict reading of the Bible, should be taught in public schools alongside the theory of evolution.

Source: Data from the 2008 American National Election Survey. *Photo:* Stephen Morton/Stringer/ Getty Images.

Social Groups and Political Values

No two people are influenced by precisely the same socialization agents or in precisely the same way. Each individual experiences a unique process of political socialization and forms a unique set of political values. Still, people with similar backgrounds do share similar experiences, which means they tend to develop similar political opinions. In this section, we examine the ties between people's social background and their political values. In the process, we examine the ties between background and values by looking at responses to two questions posed by the 2008 American National Election Study (ANES).[46] Many questions in the survey tap the freedom-versus-order or freedom-versus-equality dimensions. The two we chose serve to illustrate the analysis of ideological types. These specific questions do not define or exhaust the typology; they merely illustrate it.

The first question dealt with abortion. The interviewer said, "There has been some discussion about abortion during recent years. Which opinion on this page best agrees with your view? You can just tell me the number of the opinion you choose":

1. "By law, abortion should never be permitted" [15 percent agreed].
2. "The law should permit abortion only in cases of rape, incest, or when the woman's life is in danger" [27 percent agreed].
3. "The law should permit abortion for reasons other than rape, incest, or danger to the woman's life, but only after the need for the abortion has been clearly established" [18 percent agreed].
4. "By law, a woman should be able to obtain an abortion as a matter of personal choice" [40 percent agreed].[47]

Those who chose the last category most clearly valued individual freedom over order imposed by government. Evidence shows that pro-choice respondents also tend to have concerns about broader issues of social order, such as the role of women and the legitimacy of alternative life-styles.[48]

The second question posed by the 2008 ANES pertained to the role of government in guaranteeing employment:

> Some people feel the government in Washington should see to it that every person has a job and a good standard of living. Suppose that these people are at one end of the scale.... Others think the government should just let each person get ahead on his own. Suppose these people were at the other end.... Where would you put yourself on this scale, or haven't you thought much about this?

Excluding respondents who "hadn't thought much" about this question, 31 percent wanted the government to provide every person with a living, and 20 percent were undecided. That left 49 percent who wanted the government to let people "get ahead" on their own. These respondents, who opposed government efforts to promote equality, apparently valued freedom over equality.

Overall, the responses to each of these questions were divided approximately equally. Somewhat under half the respondents (42 percent) felt that government should forbid or severely restrict abortions, and a slight majority (52 percent with rounding) considered or favored guaranteeing people a job and a good standard of living. However, sharp differences in attitudes emerged for both issues when the respondents were grouped by socioeconomic factors: education, income, region, race, religion, and sex. The differences are shown in Figure 5.4 as positive and negative deviations from the national average for each question. Bars that extend to the right identify groups that are more likely than most other Americans to sacrifice freedom for order (on the left-hand side of the figure) or equality (on the right-hand side). Next, we examine the opinion patterns more closely for each socioeconomic group.

IDEALOG.ORG

What are your views on abortion? Take IDEAlog's self-test.

IDEALOG.ORG

Should the government try to improve the standard of living for all poor Americans? Take IDEAlog's self-test.

FIGURE 5.4   How Groups Differ on Two Questions of Order and Equality

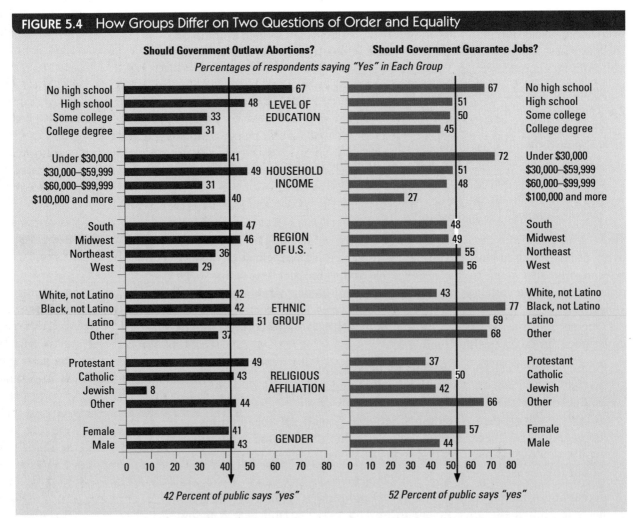

Two questions—one posing the dilemma of freedom versus order (regarding government limits on abortion) and the other the dilemma of freedom versus equality (regarding government guarantees of employment)—were asked of a national sample in 2008. Public opinion across the nation as a whole was sharply divided on each question. These two graphs show how respondents in several social groups deviated from the national mean for each question.

Source: Data from the 2008 American National Election Study, undertaken in collaboration by Stanford University and the University of Michigan.

Education

Education increases people's awareness and understanding of political issues. Higher education also promotes tolerance of unpopular opinions and behavior and invites citizens to see issues in terms of civil rights and liberties.[49] This result is clearly shown in the left-hand column of Figure 5.4, which shows that people with less education are more likely to outlaw abortions, while those with more education view abortion as a matter of a woman's choice.[50] When confronted with a choice between personal freedom and social order, college-educated individuals tend to choose freedom.

With regard to the role of government in reducing income inequality, the right-hand column in Figure 5.4 shows that people with less education favor government action to guarantee jobs and a good standard of living. Those with more education oppose government action, favoring freedom over equality. You might expect better-educated people to be humanitarian and to support government programs to help the needy. However, because educated people tend to be wealthier, they would be taxed more heavily for such government programs. Moreover, they may believe that it is unrealistic to expect government to make such economic guarantees.

Income

In many countries, differences in social class, based on social background and occupation, divide people in their politics.[51] In the United States, the vast majority of citizens regard themselves as "middle class." Yet, as Figure 5.4 shows, wealth is consistently linked to opinions favoring a limited government role in promoting equality, less consistently to opinions about order. Those with lower incomes are more likely to favor government guarantees of employment and living conditions. Those with incomes under $60,000 also favor outlawing abortions more than those earning over $60,000. For both issues, wealth and education tend to have a similar effect on opinion: the groups with more education and higher income favor freedom.

Region

Early in our country's history, regional differences were politically important— important enough to spark a civil war between the North and South. For nearly a hundred years after the Civil War, regional differences continued to affect American politics. The moneyed Northeast was thought to control the purse strings of capitalism. The Midwest was long regarded as the stronghold of isolationism in foreign affairs. The South was virtually a one-party region, almost completely Democratic. And the individualistic West pioneered its own mixture of progressive politics.

In the past, differences in wealth fed cultural differences between these regions. In recent decades, however, the movement of people and wealth away from the Northeast and Midwest to the Sunbelt states in the South and Southwest has equalized the per capita income of the various regions. One result of this equalization is that the formerly "solid South" is no longer solidly Democratic.[52] In fact, the South has tended to vote for Republican presidential candidates since 1968, and the majority of southern congressmen are now Republicans.

Figure 5.4 shows differences in public opinion on both economic and social issues in the four major regions of the United States. Respondents in the South and Midwest were more likely to favor restricting abortion. However, those in the Northeast and West were more supportive of government efforts to equalize income.

Race and Ethnicity

Over the course of American history, individuals of diverse racial and ethnic backgrounds have differed with respect to political values and opportunities.

In the early twentieth century, the major ethnic minorities in America were composed of immigrants from Ireland, Italy, Germany, Poland, and other European countries who came to the United States in waves during the late 1800s and early 1900s. These immigrants entered a nation that had been founded by British settlers more than a hundred years earlier. They found themselves in a strange land, usually without money and unable to speak the language. Moreover, their religious backgrounds—mainly Catholic and Jewish—differed from that of the predominantly Protestant earlier settlers. These urban ethnics and their descendants became part of the great coalition of Democratic voters that President Franklin Roosevelt forged in the 1930s. And for years after, the European ethnics supported liberal candidates and causes more strongly than the original Anglo-Saxon immigrants did.[53]

From the Civil War through the civil rights movement of the 1950s and 1960s, African Americans fought to secure basic political rights such as the right to vote. Initially mobilized by the Republican Party—the party of Lincoln—following the Civil War, African Americans also forged strong ties with the Democratic Party during the New Deal era. Today, African Americans are still more likely to support liberal candidates and identify with the Democratic Party. African Americans constitute 12 percent of the population, with sizable voting blocs in northern cities and in southern states like Mississippi, Georgia, and Louisiana. In 2008, large majorities of African American voters supported Barack Obama over Senator Hillary Clinton (D-N.Y.) during the Democratic primaries. In the general election, over 95 percent of African Americans voted for Obama.

According to the U.S. Census Bureau, whites comprise 79 percent of the population in 2010 and will fall to 76 percent by 2030.[54] Those figures include Latinos, people of Latin American origin. They consist of both whites and nonwhites and are commonly but inaccurately regarded as a racial group. Excluding Latinos, whites comprise 65 percent of the population in 2010 and will fall to 58 percent by 2030. Although Latinos make up only 15 percent of the nation's population in 2010, they are projected to be 20 percent in 2030. Blacks will grow slightly to 14 percent by 2030. Asians and people of other races (including Native Americans) account for about 8 percent in 2010 and will increase to 10 percent by 2030.

Latinos who speak Spanish (Haitians and Brazilians usually do not) are also known as Hispanics. At the national level, Latinos (consisting of groups as different as Cubans, Mexicans, Haitians, and Puerto Ricans) have lagged behind African Americans in mobilizing and gaining political office. However, they constitute over 45 percent of the population in New Mexico and 37 percent in California and Texas—where they have fared better in politics.[55] Both Asians and Native Americans account for another 5 percent of the population. Like other minority groups, their political impact is greatest in cities or regions where they are concentrated and greater in number. For instance, Asian Americans constitute 39 percent of the population in Hawaii and 12 percent in California; Native Americans make up 13 percent of the population of Alaska and 9 percent of New Mexico.[56]

Members of minority groups display somewhat similar political attitudes on questions pertaining to equality.[57] The reasons are twofold.[58] First, racial minorities (excepting second-generation Asians) tend to have low **socioeconomic status**, a measure of social condition that includes education, occupational status, and income. Second, minorities have been targets of prejudice and discrimination and have benefited from government actions in support of equality. The right-hand column in Figure 5.4 clearly shows the effects of race on the freedom–equality issue. All minority groups, particularly African Americans, are much more likely than whites to favor government action to improve economic opportunity. Minority groups are also more likely to express dissatisfaction with the way immigrants are treated. For instance, 71 percent of Hispanics are dissatisfied with the treatment of immigrants, while only 44 percent of non-Hispanic whites are dissatisfied.[59] The abortion issue produces less difference, although Latinos favor government restrictions on abortion more than other groups.

Religion

Since the last major wave of European immigration in the 1930s and 1940s, the religious makeup of the United States has remained fairly stable. Today, 56 percent of the population are Protestant or non-Catholic Christian, 22 percent are Catholic, 13 percent profess no religion, and fewer than 2 percent are Jewish among the 9 percent other.[60] For many years, analysts found strong and consistent differences in the political opinions of Protestants, Catholics, and Jews.[61] Protestants were more conservative than Catholics, and Catholics tended to be more conservative than Jews.

As Figure 5.4 indicates, such broad religious groupings have little effect on attitudes about economic equality but more influence on attitudes about social order. Protestants favor government action to limit abortion even more than Catholics. Jews overwhelmingly favor a woman's right to choose. Differences among religious subgroups have emerged across many contemporary social and political issues. Evangelical Protestants are also more likely than members of other religious groups to oppose gay marriage and support the death penalty while favoring the right to life over abortion. Evangelicals and Jews are more likely to express support for Israel in Middle Eastern politics. Religious beliefs have been at the center of national and local debates over issues such as stem cell research, human cloning, and the teaching of evolution or creationism as the appropriate explanation for the development of life on Earth.[62]

Gender

Men and women differ with respect to their political opinions on a broad array of social and political issues. As shown in the right-hand column of Figure 5.4, women are more likely than men to favor government actions to promote equality. Men and women differ less on the abortion issue (see the

socioeconomic status
Position in society, based on a combination of education, occupational status, and income.

Clashing Opinions on Same-Sex Marriage

In May 2008 a ruling by the Supreme Court of California allowed gays to marry. In November 2008 California voters passed Proposition 8, which amended the state constitution to invalidate the court ruling. These protesters with opposite opinions on the issue appeared outside a federal court hearing a challenge to Proposition 8.

(*left*: REUTERS/Robert Galbraith; *right*: Paul Sakuma/AP Photo)

left-hand column in Figure 5.4). Surveys show that women are consistently more supportive than men are of both affirmative action and government spending for social programs. They are consistently less supportive of the death penalty and of going to war.[63]

Since gaining the right to vote with the passage of the Nineteenth Amendment in 1919, women have been mobilized by the major political parties. Contemporary politics is marked by a "gender gap": women tend to identify with the Democratic Party more than men do (see Figure 8.5 on p. 268), and they are much more likely than men to vote for Democratic presidential candidates. In the 2008 general election, Democrat Barack Obama won the support of 56 percent of female voters, while only 43 percent of female voters supported Republican John McCain, despite having Sarah Palin as his vice-presidential running mate.

From Values to Ideology

We have just seen that differences in groups' responses to two survey questions reflect those groups' value choices between freedom and order and between freedom and equality. But to what degree do people's opinions on specific issues reflect their explicit political ideology (the set of values and beliefs they hold about the purpose and scope of government)? Political scientists generally agree that ideology influences public opinion on specific issues; they have much less consensus on the extent to which people think explicitly in ideological terms.[64] They also agree that the public's ideological thinking cannot be categorized adequately in conventional liberal–conservative terms.[65]

The Degree of Ideological Thinking in Public Opinion

Although today's media frequently use the terms *liberal* and *conservative,* some people think these terms are no longer relevant to American politics. Indeed, most voters tend not to use ideological concepts when discussing politics.[66] In one poll, voters were asked what they thought when someone was described as "liberal" or "conservative."[67] Few responded in explicitly political terms. Rather, most people gave dictionary definitions: "'liberals' are generous (a *liberal* portion). And 'conservatives' are moderate or cautious (a *conservative* estimate)." The two most frequent responses for *conservative* were "fiscally responsible or tight" (17 percent) and "closed-minded" (10 percent). For *liberal* the top two were "open-minded" (14 percent) and "free-spending" (8 percent). Only about 6 percent of the sample mentioned "degree of government involvement" in describing liberals and conservatives.

Ideological labels are technical terms used in analyzing politics, and most citizens don't play that sport. But if you want to play, you need suitable equipment. Scales and typologies, despite their faults, are essential for classification. No analysis, including the study of politics, can occur without classifying the objects being studied. The tendency to use ideological terms in discussing politics grows with increased education, which helps people understand political issues and relate them to one another. People's personal political socialization experiences can also lead them to think ideologically. For example, children raised in strong union households may be taught to distrust private enterprise and value collective action through government.

True ideologues hold a consistent set of values and beliefs about the purpose and scope of government, and they tend to evaluate candidates in ideological terms.[68] Some people respond to questions in ways that seem ideological but are not because they do not understand the underlying principles. For example, most respondents dutifully comply when asked to place themselves somewhere on a liberal–conservative continuum. The result, as shown earlier in Figure 5.2c, is an approximately normal distribution centering on "moderate," the modal category, which contains 29 percent of all respondents. But many people settle on moderate (a safe choice) when they do not clearly understand the alternatives. When allowed to say, "I haven't thought much about it"—24 percent of respondents in the survey acknowledged that they had not thought much about ideology and were excluded from the distribution.[69] The extent of ideological thinking in America, then, is even less than it might seem from responses to questions asking people to describe themselves as liberals or conservatives.[70] What conclusion should we draw from Figure 5.2c, which shows 28 percent of respondents placing themselves on the liberal side of a left–right scale, 29 percent in the middle, and 42 percent on the conservative side?

The Quality of Ideological Thinking in Public Opinion

What people's ideological self-placement means in the twenty-first century is not clear. At one time, the liberal–conservative continuum represented a single dimension: attitudes toward the scope of government activity. Liberals were in favor of more government action to provide public goods, and conservatives were in favor of less. This simple distinction is not as useful today. Many people who call themselves liberal no longer favor government activism in general, and many self-styled conservatives no longer oppose it in principle. Attitudes toward government also depend on which party controls the government.[71] As a result, many people have difficulty deciding whether they are liberal or conservative, whereas others confidently choose identical points on the continuum for entirely different reasons. People describe themselves as liberal or conservative because of the symbolic value of the terms as much as for reasons of ideology.[72]

Studies of the public's ideological thinking find that two themes run through people's minds when they are asked to describe liberals and conservatives. People associate liberals with change and conservatives with tradition. The theme corresponds to the distinction between liberals and conservatives on the exercise of freedom and the maintenance of order.[73]

The other theme has to do with equality. The conflict between freedom and equality was at the heart of President Roosevelt's New Deal economic policies (Social Security, minimum wage legislation, farm price supports) in the 1930s. The policies expanded the interventionist role of the national government to promote greater economic equality, and attitudes toward government intervention in the economy served to distinguish liberals from conservatives for decades afterward.[74] Attitudes toward government interventionism still underlie opinions about domestic *economic* policies.[75] Liberals support intervention to promote economic equality; conservatives favor less government intervention and more individual freedom in economic activities. Conservatives, however, think differently about government action on *social* policies.

In Chapter 1, we proposed an alternative system of ideological classification based on people's relative evaluations of freedom, order, and equality. We described liberals as people who believe that government should promote equality, even if some freedom is lost in the process, but who oppose surrendering freedom to government-imposed order. Conservatives do not necessarily oppose equality but put a higher value on freedom than on equality when the two conflict. Yet conservatives are not above restricting freedom when threatened with the loss of order. So both groups value freedom, but one is more willing to trade freedom for equality, and the other is more inclined to trade freedom for order. If you have trouble thinking about these trade-offs on a single dimension, you are in good company. The liberal–conservative continuum presented to survey respondents takes a two-dimensional concept and squeezes it into a one-dimensional format.[76]

Ideological Types in the United States

Our ideological typology in Chapter 1 (see Figure 1.2, p. 28) classifies people as Liberals if they favor freedom over order and equality over freedom. (Capital letters signify our ideological classification; lowercase signifies ideological self-placement.) Conversely, Conservatives favor freedom over equality and order over freedom. Libertarians favor freedom over both equality and order—the opposite of Communitarians.[77] By cross-tabulating people's answers to the two questions from the 2008 ANES about freedom versus order (abortion) and freedom versus equality (government job guarantees), we can classify respondents according to their ideological tendencies. As shown in Figure 5.5, a substantial portion of respondents falls within each of the quadrants.* This finding indicates that people do not make decisions about government activity according to a one-dimensional ideological continuum. If they did, responses to the two questions would correlate and cluster diagonally in the Liberal and Conservative boxes. In fact, the correlation is virtually zero ($r^2 = .005$). People's preferences for government action depend on what the action targets.

The Liberal pattern occurred most frequently (32 percent), with the Libertarians next (27 percent), and Conservatives (21 percent) barely outscoring Communitarians (19 percent). The size of the groups, which was determined by the particular questions, is not as important as the fact that the population divided into four significant groups in answering the questions. Indeed, the results resemble earlier findings by other researchers who conducted more exhaustive analyses involving more survey questions.[78] Of more interest are the pie charts in each quadrant. They represent the proportion of respondents in the same survey who self-described themselves as liberal, moderate, or conservative (see Figure 5.4b).

In Figure 5.5, three-quarters of *our* Conservatives (answering the questions on order and equality) also described *themselves* as conservatives, while more than half of our Liberals were also self-described liberals. In contrast, those we classified as Communitarian or Libertarian according to the order and equality questions showed less consistency in classifying themselves as liberal, moderate, or conservative.

Respondents who readily locate themselves on a single dimension running from liberal to conservative often go on to contradict their self-placement when

---

*Remember, however, that these categories—like the letter grades A, B, C, and D for courses—are rigid. The respondents' answers to both questions varied in intensity but were reduced to a simple yes or no to simplify this analysis. Many respondents would cluster toward the center of Figure 5.5 if their attitudes were represented more sensitively.

Politics of Global Change

Are Western Publics Becoming Less Conservative?

Political ideology in the United States resembles a normal distribution, centered on the middle of a scale ranging from extremely liberal to extremely conservative (see Figure 5.2c). According to national surveys, the public's ideological distribution is also fairly stable, but it can change over time. What about ideological tendencies and change in other nations? The World Values Survey organization collected social and political data from over eighty countries around the world since 1981. Giving respondents a scale from 1 to 10, they asked, "In political matters, people talk of 'the left' and 'the right.' How would you place your views on this scale, generally speaking?"

The figure here plots the average ideological self-placement for respondents in fourteen countries from surveys conducted in 1981–1983 and in 1999–2002.

During both time periods, the average ideological placements of most countries clustered around the middle of the scale, with all of the average scores somewhere between 4 and 7. The blue arrows mark movement to the left over the twenty-year period. Red arrows mark movement to the right. Every country but Italy moved to the left, though like the United States, the movement was not dramatic. Moreover, ideological self-placement was more widely distributed in the earlier period. Over two decades, average placement for all nations converged to the center. The growing influence of the European Union could have produced more similar attitudes among European publics, but some of these nations are not in the EU. Convergence in political opinions could also be consistent with the effects of globalization, which ties together people in different countries.

answering questions that trade freedom for either order or equality.[79] A two-dimensional typology such as that in Figure 5.5 allows us to analyze responses more meaningfully.[80] A single dimension does not fit their preferences for government action concerning both economic and social issues. One reason so many Americans classify themselves as conservative on a one-dimensional scale is that they have no option to classify themselves as libertarian.

The ideological typology reflects important differences between diverse social groups. Communitarians are prominent among blacks and Latinos (33 percent) and among people with no high school degree (42 percent), groups that tend to look favorably on the benefits of government. Regional differences are small among the types, except that 44 percent of respondents in the West score as Liberal. Women tend to be Liberal (38 percent) and men Libertarian (33 percent).

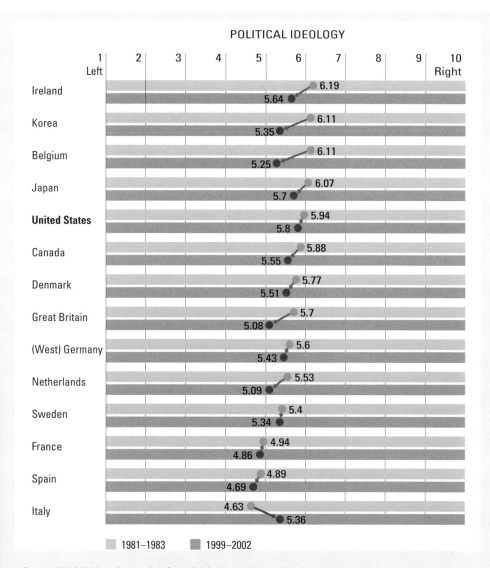

POLITICAL IDEOLOGY

Country	1981–1983	1999–2002
Ireland	6.19	5.64
Korea	6.11	5.35
Belgium	6.11	5.25
Japan	6.07	5.7
United States	5.94	5.8
Canada	5.88	5.55
Denmark	5.77	5.51
Great Britain	5.7	5.08
(West) Germany	5.6	5.43
Netherlands	5.53	5.09
Sweden	5.4	5.34
France	4.94	4.86
Spain	4.89	4.69
Italy	4.63	5.36

Source: World Values Survey data for individual countries may be found at http://worldvaluessurvey.org.

Indeed, Libertarians account for 51 percent of men making more than $100,000, who may believe that they have no need of government.

This more refined analysis of political ideology explains why even Americans who pay close attention to politics find it difficult to locate themselves on the liberal–conservative continuum. Their problem is that they are liberal on some issues and conservative on others. Forced to choose along just one dimension, they opt for the middle category, moderate. Around the world, people tend to place themselves toward the middle of the scale (see "Politics of Global Change: Are Western Publics Becoming Less Conservative?"). However, our analysis indicates that many people who classify themselves as liberal or conservative do fit these two categories in our

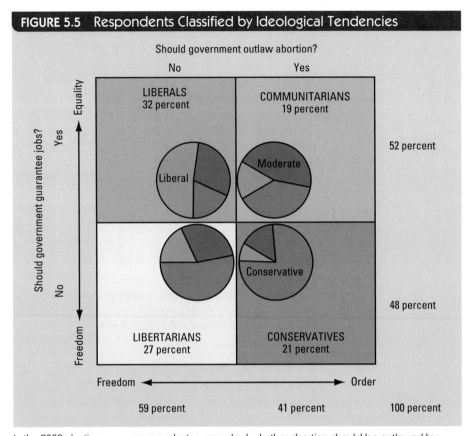

FIGURE 5.5 Respondents Classified by Ideological Tendencies

In the 2008 election survey, respondents were asked whether abortion should be outlawed by government or a matter of personal choice, and whether government should guarantee people a job and a good standard of living or people should get ahead on their own. (The questions are given verbatim on p. 155.) These two questions presented choices between freedom and order and between freedom and equality. People's responses to the two questions showed no correlation, demonstrating that these value choices cannot be explained by a one-dimensional liberal–conservative continuum. Instead, their responses can be analyzed more usefully according to four different ideological types. The pie charts in the center show the proportion of each group self-describing themselves as liberal, moderate, or conservative on the traditional one-dimensional scale.

Source: 2008 American National Election Study, undertaken in collaboration by Stanford University and the University of Michigan.

typology. There is value, then, in the liberal–conservative distinction as long as we understand its limitations.

Forming Political Opinions

We have seen that people acquire their political values through socialization and that different social groups develop different sets of political values. We have also learned that some people, but only a minority, think about politics ideologically, holding a consistent set of political attitudes and beliefs. But how do those who are not ideologues—in other words, most citizens—form political opinions? As noted at the start of the chapter, the majoritarian and pluralist models of democracy make different assumptions about public opinion. Are most people well informed about politics? What can we say about the quality of public opinion in America?

Political Knowledge

It seems reasonable to ask whether most Americans are ideologically unsophisticated yet still well informed about politics. In the United States today, education is compulsory (usually to age sixteen), and the literacy rate is relatively high. The country boasts an unparalleled network of colleges and universities, entered by two-thirds of all high school graduates. American citizens can obtain information from a variety of daily and weekly news sources in print and via the Internet. They can keep abreast of national and international affairs through cable and television news programs, which bring live coverage of world events via satellite from virtually everywhere in the world.

In a study of political knowledge, political scientists Delli Carpini and Keeter collected 3,700 individual survey items that measured some type of factual knowledge about public affairs.[81] They focused on over two thousand items that clearly dealt with political facts, such as knowledge of political institutions and processes, contemporary public figures, political groups, and policy issues. The authors found that "many of the basic institutions and procedures of government are known to half or more of the public, as are the relative positions of the parties on many major issues."[82]

Yet political knowledge is not randomly distributed within our society. "In particular, women, African Americans, the poor, and the young tend to be substantially less knowledgeable about politics than are men, whites, the affluent, and older citizens."[83] Changing news formats in the past twenty years—the emergence of twenty-four-hour cable news and the Internet—do not seem to have increased the level of political knowledge for most Americans.[84] And some researchers have suggested that survey measures of political knowledge may not be valid if respondents are not given the time or motivation to offer thoughtful answers.[85]

In general, people know more about the politics of the era in which they grew up than they know about the politics of other generations' formative years. A study of a group of people who graduated from high school in 1965 and their parents revealed that over 90 percent of the parents knew that President Franklin D. Roosevelt had been a Democrat, but only about 70 percent of their children did. However, two-thirds of this younger generation could name a country bordering Vietnam, compared with fewer than half of their parents. The author explained that for the parents, "the FDR years formed a core part of their autobiographies," whereas "the class of 1965 was inevitably affected by the [Vietnam] war and the controversy surrounding it."[86]

Researchers have not found any meaningful relationship between political sophistication and self-placement on the liberal–conservative continuum. That is, people with equivalent knowledge of public affairs and levels of conceptualization are equally likely to call themselves liberals or conservatives.[87] Nor is there any systematic relationship between Republican and Democratic partisanship and test scores on general political knowledge.[88] However, individuals who strongly believe in certain causes may be impervious to information that questions their beliefs; they may even create false memories that support their beliefs. For instance, researchers found that individuals who thought the war in Iraq was fought to eliminate that country's weapons of mass destruction were more likely to think that these weapons had been found after the start of the war.[89] They were less sensitive to news information that contradicted their initial beliefs.

Even if a portion of the public is uninformed, some researchers hold that the *collective* opinion of the public, which balances off random ignorance on both sides of an issue, can be interpreted as stable and meaningful. Political scientists Benjamin Page and Robert Shapiro analyzed the public's responses to 1,128 questions that were repeated in one or more surveys between 1935 and 1990.[90] They found that responses to more than half of the repeated policy questions "showed no significant change at all"—that is, they changed no more than six percentage points.[91] Moreover, Page and Shapiro concluded that when the public's collective opinion on public policy changes, it changes in "understandable, predictable ways."[92]

Costs, Benefits, and Cues

Perhaps people do not think in ideological terms or know a wide variety of political facts, but they can tell whether a policy is likely to directly help or hurt them. The **self-interest principle** states that people choose what benefits them personally.[93] Self-interest plays an obvious role in how people form opinions on government policies with clear costs and benefits.[94] Taxpayers tend to prefer low taxes to high taxes. Smokers tend to oppose bans on smoking in public places. Gun owners are less likely to support handgun control. Some people evaluate incumbent presidents according to whether they are better or worse off financially than they were four years ago. Group leaders often cue group members, telling them what policies they should support or oppose. (In the context of pluralist democracy, this often appears as grassroots support for or opposition to policies that affect only particular groups.)[95]

In some cases, individuals are unable to determine personal costs or benefits. This tends to be true of foreign policy, which few people interpret in terms of personal benefits. Here, many people have no opinion, or their opinions are not firmly held and are likely to change quite easily given almost any new information. For example, public approval of the war in Iraq and of former president Bush's handling of the war varied with positive news such as Iraqi elections and negative news such as the number of military casualties. (To learn more about perceptions of the United States in other countries, see "Compared with What? Exploring Our Image Around the World.")

Public opinion that is not based on a complicated ideology may also emerge from the skillful use of cues. Individuals may use heuristics—mental shortcuts that require hardly any information—to make fairly reliable political judgments.[96] For instance, citizens can use political party labels to

self-interest principle
The implication that people choose what benefits them personally.

Compared with What?

Exploring Our Image Around the World

Compared with citizens from other countries around the world, Americans have a very favorable view of their country. In 2009, the Pew Research Center asked citizens around the world if they had a favorable or unfavorable view of the United States. The figure here lists the results for twenty-five countries. Outside the United States, its image is most favorable in Kenya (home of President Obama's father), Nigeria, and South Korea. Negative views of the United States prevail in the Muslim world as well as China and Russia. Though many respondents voiced negative views of the United States when asked this general question, majorities in nearly all countries expressed admiration for U.S. science and technology. In most parts of the world, respondents also said that they liked U.S. music, movies, and television.

Percent responding Favorable (2009)

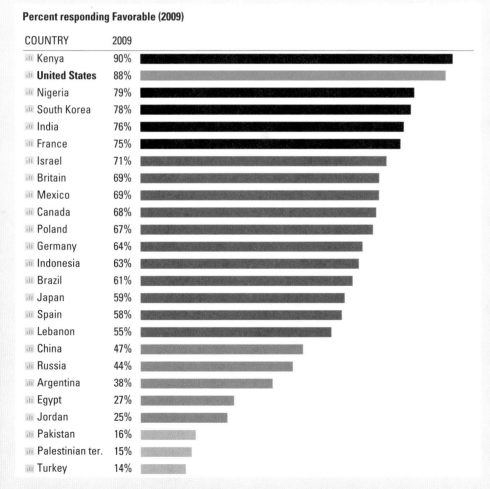

COUNTRY	2009
Kenya	90%
United States	88%
Nigeria	79%
South Korea	78%
India	76%
France	75%
Israel	71%
Britain	69%
Mexico	69%
Canada	68%
Poland	67%
Germany	64%
Indonesia	63%
Brazil	61%
Japan	59%
Spain	58%
Lebanon	55%
China	47%
Russia	44%
Argentina	38%
Egypt	27%
Jordan	25%
Pakistan	16%
Palestinian ter.	15%
Turkey	14%

Source: Pew Global Attitudes Project, "Key Indicators Database," available at http://pewglobal.org/database/?indicator=1. Copyright © 2010 Pew Research Center

compensate for low information about the policy positions of candidates. Voters may have well-developed expectations or stereotypes about political parties that structure the way they evaluate candidates and process new information.[97] They assume that Democrats and Republicans differ from each other in predictable ways. Similarly, citizens take cues from trusted government officials and interest groups regarding the wisdom of bills pending in Congress or the ideology of Supreme Court nominees.

Political Leadership

Public opinion on specific issues is molded by political leaders, journalists, and policy experts. Politicians serve as cue givers to members of the public. Citizens with favorable views of a politician may be more likely to support his or her values and policy agenda. In one study, 49 percent of respondents were uncomfortable with the statement, "I have never believed the Constitution required our schools to be religion free zones," when it was presented anonymously; only 34 percent claimed to be uncomfortable when the statement was attributed to former president Bill Clinton.[98] In a different study, African Americans were presented with a statement about the need for blacks to rely more on themselves to get ahead in society; respondents agreed with the statement when it was attributed to black politicians (Jesse Jackson, Sr., and Clarence Thomas) and disagreed when the statement was attributed to white politicians (George H. W. Bush and Ted Kennedy).[99]

Politicians routinely make appeals to the public on the basis of shared political ideology and self-interest. They collect and share information about social trends, policy options, and policy implementation. Competition and controversy among political elites provide the public with a great deal of information. But politicians are well aware that citizen understanding and support for an issue depend on its framing. In **issue framing**, politicians define the way that issues are presented, selectively invoking values or recalling history in the presentation. For example, opinion leaders might frame a reduction in taxes as "returning money to the people" or, quite differently, as "reducing government services." Politicians and other leaders can frame issues to change or reinforce public opinion. Such framing is sometimes referred to as "spin," and "spin doctors" are those who stand ready to reinforce or elaborate on the spin inherent in the framing.[100]

The ability of political leaders to influence public opinion has been enhanced enormously by the growth of the broadcast media, especially television.[101] The majoritarian model of democracy assumes that government officials respond to public opinion, but the evidence is substantial that this causal sequence is reversed—that public opinion responds to the actions of government officials.[102] If this is true, how much potential is there for public opinion to be manipulated by political leaders through the mass media? We examine the manipulative potential of the mass media in the next chapter.

issue framing
The way that politicians or interest group leaders define an issue when presenting it to others.

Summary

Public opinion does not rule in America. On most issues, it merely sets general boundaries for government policy. The shape of the distribution of opinion (skewed, bimodal, or normal) indicates how sharply the public is divided. Bimodal distributions harbor the greatest potential for political conflict. The stability of a distribution over time indicates how settled people are in their opinions. Because most Americans' ideological opinions are normally distributed around the moderate category and have been for decades, government policies can vary from left to right over time without provoking severe political conflict.

People form their values through the process of political socialization. The most important socialization agents in childhood and young adulthood are family, school, community, and peers. Members of the same social group tend to experience similar socialization processes and thus to adopt similar values. People in different social groups that hold different values often express vastly different opinions. Differences in education, race, and religion tend to produce sharper divisions of opinion today on questions of order and equality than do differences in income or region.

Most people do not think about politics in ideological terms. When asked to do so by pollsters, however, they readily classify themselves along a liberal–conservative continuum. Many respondents choose the middle category, moderate, because the choice is safe. Many others choose it because they have liberal views on some issues and conservative views on others. Their political orientation is better captured by a two-dimensional framework that analyzes ideology according to the values of freedom, order, and equality. Responses to the survey questions we used to establish our ideological typology illustrate that the American electorate may be usefully classified as Liberals, Conservatives, Libertarians, and Communitarians.

In addition to ideological orientation, many other factors affect the process of forming political opinions. When individuals stand to benefit or suffer from proposed government policies, they usually base their opinions of these policies on their own self-interest. Citizens use heuristics like political party labels to compensate for their lack of detailed information about pending legislation or political candidates. In the absence of information, respondents are particularly susceptible to cues of support or opposition from political leaders, communicated through the mass media.

Which model of democracy, the majoritarian or the pluralist, is correct in its assumptions about public opinion? Sometimes the public shows clear and settled opinions on government policy, conforming to the majoritarian model. However, public opinion is often not firmly grounded in knowledge and may be unstable on given issues. Moreover, powerful groups often divide on what they want government to do. The lack of consensus leaves politicians with a great deal of latitude in enacting specific policies, a finding that conforms to the pluralist model. Of course, politicians' actions are closely scrutinized by journalists' reporting in the mass media. We turn to the effect on politics of this scrutiny in Chapter 6.

Visit www.cengagebrain.com/shop/ ISBN/0495906182 for flashcards, web quizzes, videos and more!

CHAPTER TOPICS

Leisa Thompson, The Ann Arbor News

In February 2009, one of Denver's two major daily newspapers, the 150-year-old *Rocky Mountain News,* printed its last edition. One month later, Seattle's 146-year-old *Post-Intelligencer* became a Web-only operation. Several other newspapers across the country also stopped their presses for good or switched to Web-only content during 2008 and 2009. And many more newspapers were on the brink of financial failure. By early 2009, the owners of 33 daily newspapers in the United States—including the *Los Angeles Times,* the *Chicago Tribune,* and the *Philadelphia Inquirer*—had filed for bankruptcy. In 2010, newspapers employed 25 percent fewer people than they did in 2001.[1] Additional steps some newspapers are taking to save revenue include printing papers on fewer days per week and cutting back on home delivery services. These trends have led many people to ask, "Are newspapers dead?"

Although the Great Recession contributed to these tough times, the technological and commercial realities that led newspapers to this point have been building up for years. The development and diffusion of the Internet have been particularly significant. While circulation of printed papers has declined by over 13 percent since 2001, news readership is actually up, with most new readers accessing sources online. But Web-based audiences gain access to the news for free; most newspapers do not require paid subscriptions for their online content. Some papers, including the *New York Times* and the *Boston Herald,* have tried it, only to realize that Web users will go elsewhere rather than pay. The *Wall Street Journal* is the only major newspaper to date that has managed to charge readers for online

content successfully. The *New York Times* will try again in 2011 when it will implement a program that allows users to see a limited number articles for free but will charge for unlimited access. The rise of Craigslist.com, a free website of classified ads, has further deprived newspapers of what had traditionally been a key source of revenue.[2]

With the challenges faced by newspapers come important questions about the future of journalism, such as whether new media formats will become adequate substitutes for the local daily newspaper, whether it will become harder for readers to find objective and unbiased reporting, and whether the notion of democratic accountability itself is threatened.

On one side are people who argue that the loss of newspapers is a threat to democracy. Newspapers invest heavily in investigative reporting, following up on stories once they are no longer on the front page and sending journalists both to faraway places to report on foreign events and to local statehouses to report on state and city politics.[3] The modern journalistic norms of objectivity and accountability provide readers with accurate information that allows them to draw their own conclusions about current affairs. If and when newspapers fail, all of these services provided by the media could disappear, rendering citizens uninformed—or misinformed—and without an important check on public officials. As the T-shirts that staffers at the now defunct *Ann Arbor News* wore on their last day at work put it, "No News is bad news."

On the other side of the issue are people who find the new Web-based frontier in journalism exciting and democratizing. They argue that readers will still want investigative and local reporting and that Web-based models able to fulfill that desire will develop in time. They say that the spread of mobile technology and social networking sites, like Facebook.com, allow political information to reach ever broader audiences.[4] They also note that "citizen journalists" have begun playing an especially prominent watchdog role. During the 2008 primaries, for example, an unpaid writer for the Huffington Post political blog broke the news that Barack Obama told a group of supporters at a private event that rural voters are "bitter" and that they "cling to guns or religion."[5] This quote went on to become a major news story and was an issue throughout the rest of the campaign.

People on both sides agree on three things. The first is that the challenges facing newspapers are here to stay; we cannot put the Internet genie back in the bottle. The second is that the media continue to play a critical role in the democratic process. The third is that this critical role demands that we carefully study the scope and impact of the rapidly changing media environment.

In this chapter, we describe the origin, growth, and change of the media; assess their objectivity; and examine their influence on politics. Do the various media promote or frustrate democratic ideals? What consequences, if any, flow from liberal or conservative biases in the media? Who uses which media, and what do they learn? Do the media advance or retard equality in society? Does the concept of freedom of the press inhibit the government's effort to secure order? What new problems flow from globalization generally of the news media?

IN OUR OWN WORDS

Listen to Kenneth Janda discuss the main points and themes of this chapter.

www.cengagebrain.com/shop/ISBN/0495906182

People, Government, and Communications

"We never talk anymore" is a common lament of couples who are not getting along very well. In politics, too, citizens and their government need to communicate to get along well. *Communication* is the process of transmitting information from one individual or group to another. *Mass communication* is the process by which information is transmitted to large, heterogeneous, widely dispersed audiences. The term **mass media** refers to the means for communicating to these audiences. The mass media are commonly divided into two types:

- *Print media* communicate information through the publication of words and pictures on paper. Prime examples of print media are daily newspapers and popular magazines. Because books seldom have a large circulation relative to the general population, they are not typically classified as a mass medium.
- *Broadcast media* communicate information electronically, through sounds and images. Prime examples of broadcast media are radio and television. The worldwide network of personal computers commonly called the Internet is a broadcast technology and also qualifies as a mass medium.

Our focus here is on the role of the media in promoting communication from government to its citizens and from citizens to their government. In totalitarian governments, information flows more freely in one direction

mass media
The means employed in mass communication; often divided into print media and broadcast media.

(from government to the people) than the other. In democratic governments, information must flow freely in both directions; a democratic government can respond to public opinion only if its citizens can make their opinions known. Moreover, the electorate can hold government officials accountable for their actions only if voters know what the government has done, is doing, and plans to do. Because the mass media provide the major channels for this two-way flow of information, they have the dual capability of reflecting and shaping our political views.

The media are not the only means of communication between citizens and government. As we discussed in Chapter 5, various agents of socialization (especially schools) function as "linkage mechanisms" that promote such communication. In the next four chapters, we discuss other mechanisms for communication: voting, political parties, campaigning in elections, and interest groups. Certain linkage mechanisms communicate better in one direction than in the other. Primary and secondary schools, for example, commonly instruct young citizens about government rules and symbols, whereas voting sends messages from citizens to government. Parties, campaigns, and interest groups foster communication in both directions. The media, however, are the only linkage mechanisms that specialize in communication.

Although this chapter concentrates on political uses of five prominent mass media—newspapers, magazines, radio, television, and the Internet—political content can also be transmitted through other mass media, such as recordings and motion pictures. Popular musicians such as Green Day and U2 often express political ideas in their music. During the 2008 presidential election, Black Eyed Peas front man will.i.am produced a Web video in which he set one of Barack Obama's speeches to music and mixed Obama's spoken words with the voices of other musicians and celebrities. The video, called "Yes We Can Song," was viewed by millions of people and went on to win an Emmy Award.

Motion pictures often convey particularly intense—and consequential—political messages. Michael Moore's *Sicko,* a 2007 Oscar-nominated documentary, was a blistering attack on the health-care system in the United States. One poll found that nearly half of Americans had either seen or heard of the movie just one month after its release, and of those, nearly half said that the film made them more likely to think that health-care reform was needed.[6] Former Vice President Al Gore's *An Inconvenient Truth* warned of the perils of global warming and won an Oscar in 2007 for best documentary film feature. A *Newsweek* poll found that one quarter of Americans said the film influenced their views on global warming.[7]

The Development of the Mass Media in the United States

Although the record and film industries sometimes convey political messages, they are primarily in the business of entertainment. Our focus here is on mass media in the news industry—on print and broadcast journalism.

Figure 6.1 plots the increase in the number of Americans with access to radios, televisions, and the Internet from 1920 to the present. The growth of the country, technological inventions, and shifting political attitudes about the scope of government, as well as trends in entertainment, have shaped the development of the news media in the United States.[8]

Newspapers

When the Revolutionary War broke out in 1775, thirty-seven newspapers (all weeklies) were publishing in the colonies.[9] They had small circulations, so they were not really mass media but group media read by economic and social elites. The first newspapers were mainly political organs, financed by parties and advocating party causes. Newspapers did not move toward independent ownership and large circulations until the 1830s.

According to the 1880 census, 971 daily newspapers and 8,633 weekly newspapers and periodicals were published in the United States. Most larger cities had many newspapers: New York had twenty-nine papers; Philadelphia, twenty-four; San Francisco, twenty-one; and Chicago, eighteen. Competition for readers grew fierce among the big-city dailies. Toward the latter part of the nineteenth century, imaginative publishers sought to win readers by entertaining them with photographs, comic strips, sports sections, advice to the lovelorn, and stories of sex and crime.

FIGURE 6.1 The Growth of the Broadcast Media Since 1920

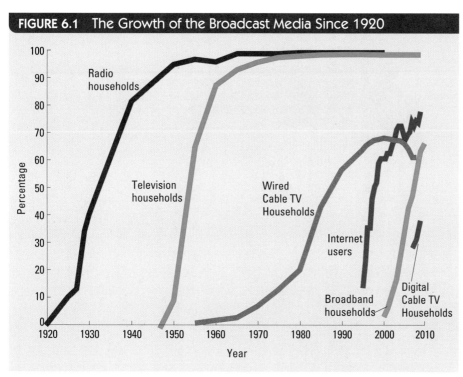

The media environment in the United States has changed dramatically over time. This graph shows the percentage of all households or adults using a particular media technology: radio, television, cable TV, Internet, or broadband. In 1950, for instance, only 9 percent of all households had a television set. Within five years, almost two-thirds of all American households owned a television set. In 1995, only 14 percent of all adults reported using the Internet. Today 70 percent of all adults report using the Internet at home or work.

Sources: For data on radio, television, and cable TV, see Northwestern University's Media Information Center website: http://www.mediainfocenter.org. Additional data on radio households in the 1920s and 1930s are reported by Steve Craig, "How America Adopted Radio," *Journal of Broadcasting and Electronic Media* 48 (June 2004): 179–195. For television and cable TV, see also http://blog.nielsen.com/nielsenwire/wp-content/uploads/2009/07/tva_2008_071709.pdf. For broadband statistics, see PEW Internet & American Life Project surveys 2000–2009, http://www.pewinternet.org/Trend-Data/Home-Broadband-Adoption.aspx. For Internet statistics, see "United States of America: Internet Usage and Broadband Usage Report," Internet World Stats, http://www.internetworldstats.com/am/us.htm.

By the 1960s, under pressure from both radio and television, intense competition among big-city dailies had nearly disappeared. New York had only three papers left by 1969, and this pattern was repeated in every other large city in the country. By 2009, only twenty-six U.S. towns or cities had two or more competing dailies under separate ownership.[10] The net result is that newspaper circulation as a percentage of the U.S. population has dropped by 55 percent since 1947.[11]

The daily paper with the largest circulation in 2009 (about 2 million copies) was the *Wall Street Journal,* followed closely by *USA Today* (1.9 million). *USA Today* used to sell over 2 million daily copies, but its circulation figures dropped more than 17 percent in 2009. The *New York Times,* which many journalists consider the best newspaper in the country, sold a little under 1 million daily copies, placing it third in circulation (see Figure 6.2). In

FIGURE 6.2	Audiences of Selected Media Sources

Different media appeal to different audiences, and what news people learn depends on their sources. The big story is the enormous growth in the Internet news audience. The print version of the *New York Times,* for instance, has a circulation of under 1 million people. Yet an average of 12 million people visits the paper's website for news every month. The major news magazines (published weekly) tend to have more readers than newspapers do, but newspapers are published daily and there are more of them. Opinion magazines reach only a small fraction of the usual television news audience.

INTERNET (Ave. per month)

Source	Value
MSNBC	39
Yahoo!News	36.6
CNN online	36.3
NY Times online	19.5
Google News	11.9

TELEVISION (Ave. per night)

Source	Value
NBC News	8.6
ABC News	8.1
CBS News	6.1
Fox News	2.0
CNN	1.3
NewsHour with Jim Lehrer	1.1

NEWS MAGAZINES

Source	Value
Time	3.4
Newsweek	2.7
U.S. News & World Report	1.8

NEWSPAPERS

Source	Value
Wall Street Journal	2.0
USA Today	1.9
NY Times	.93
LA Times	.7

OPINION MAGAZINES

Source	Value
National Review	0.2
The Nation	0.2
The New Republic	.07
The Weekly Standard	.07

Audience/circulation (in millions)

Sources: Newspaper circulation comes from Audit Bureau of Circulations. Data on the Internet, news and opinion magazines, and television are reported in "The State of the News Media 2009," http://www.stateofthemedia.org.

comparison, the weekly *National Enquirer,* which carries stories about celebrities and true crime, also sold just under 1 million copies. Neither the *Times* nor the *Wall Street Journal* carries comic strips, which no doubt limits their mass appeal. They also print more political news and news analyses than most readers want to confront.

Magazines

Magazines differ from newspapers not only in the frequency of their publication but also in the nature of their coverage. Even news-oriented magazines cover the news in a more specialized manner than do daily newspapers. Many magazines are forums for opinions, not strictly for news. The earliest public affairs magazines were founded in the mid-1800s, and two—*The Nation* and *Harper's*—are still publishing today. Such magazines were often politically influential, especially in framing arguments against slavery and later in publishing exposés of political corruption and business exploitation. Because these exposés were lengthy critiques of the existing political and economic order, they found a more hospitable outlet in magazines of opinion than in newspapers with big circulations. Yet magazines with limited readerships can wield political power. Magazines may influence **attentive policy elites**—group leaders who follow news in specific areas—and thus influence mass opinion indirectly through a **two-step flow of communication**.

As scholars originally viewed the two-step flow, it conformed ideally to the pluralist model of democracy. Once group leaders (for instance, union or industry leaders) became informed of political developments, they informed their more numerous followers, mobilizing them to apply pressure on government. Today, according to a revised interpretation of the two-step flow concept, policy elites are more likely to influence public opinion (and not just their followers) and other leaders by airing their views in the media. In this view, public deliberation on issues is mediated by these professional communicators who frame the issues in the media for popular consumption (as discussed in Chapter 5 on page 168)—that is, define the way that issues will be viewed, heard, or read.[12]

Two weekly news magazines—*Time* (founded in 1923) and *Newsweek* (1933)—enjoy big circulations in the United States (3.4 million and 2.7 million copies in 2008). Despite these large circulations, news magazine circulation has declined in recent years much as newspaper circulation has. Such declines prompted *U.S. News & World Report,* a prominent weekly magazine founded in 1933, to become a monthly magazine in 2009. In contrast to these mainstream publications, there are also explicitly political magazines such as *The New Republic* and *The Weekly Standard* that are aimed at the audience of policy elites more than the general public.

Radio

Regularly scheduled, continuous radio broadcasting began in 1920 on stations KDKA in Pittsburgh and WWJ in Detroit. Both stations claim to be the first commercial station, and both broadcast returns of the 1920 election of President Warren G. Harding. The first radio network, the National Broadcasting Company (NBC), was formed in 1926. Soon four networks were on the air, transforming radio into a national medium by linking thousands of local stations. Americans were quick to purchase and use this new technology (see Figure 6.1). Millions of Americans were able to hear President Franklin D. Roosevelt deliver his first "fireside chat" in 1933. However, the first coast-to-coast broadcast did not occur until 1937, when listeners were shocked by an eyewitness report of the explosion of the dirigible *Hindenburg* in New Jersey.

Because the public could sense reporters' personalities over radio in a way they could not in print, broadcast journalists quickly became household names. Edward R. Murrow, one of the most famous radio news personalities, broadcast news of the merger of Germany and Austria by short-wave radio from Vienna in 1938 and during World War II gave stirring reports of German air raids on London.

attentive policy elites
Leaders who follow news in specific policy areas.

two-step flow of communication
The process in which a few policy elites gather information and then inform their more numerous followers, mobilizing them to apply pressure to government.

Today there are over thirteen thousand licensed broadcast radio stations. Despite the advent of iPods, Internet radio, and podcasts, over 235 million Americans listen to a traditional AM/FM radio every week—that's more than all the audience and circulation figures from Figure 6.2 combined![13] Radio listeners tend to spend the most time tuned into stations that have news and talk radio formats, and the audience for talk radio continues to grow. Surveys show that the audience of talk radio is more Republican, most likely because the majority of talk radio hosts, like Rush Limbaugh and Bill O'Reilly, are conservative.[14] Talk radio shows have been criticized for polarizing politics by publicizing extreme views.[15]

Television

Experiments with television began in France in the early 1900s. By 1940, twenty-three television stations were operating in the United States, and—repeating radio's feat of twenty years earlier—two stations broadcast the returns of a presidential election, Roosevelt's 1940 reelection.[16] The onset of World War II paralyzed the development of television technology, but growth in the medium exploded after the war. By 1950, ninety-eight stations were covering the major population centers of the country, although only 9 percent of American households had televisions (see Figure 6.1).

The first commercial color broadcast came in 1951, as did the first coast-to-coast broadcast: President Harry Truman's address to delegates at the Japanese peace treaty conference in San Francisco. That same year, Democratic senator Estes Kefauver of Tennessee called for public television coverage of his committee's investigation into organized crime. For weeks, people with televisions invited their neighbors to watch underworld crime figures answering questions before the camera. And Kefauver became one of the first politicians to benefit from television coverage. Previously unknown and representing a small state, he nevertheless won many of the 1952 Democratic presidential primaries and became the Democrats' vice-presidential candidate in 1956.

By 1960, 87 percent of U.S. households had televisions. By 2009, the United States had more than thirteen hundred commercial and three hundred public television stations, and virtually every household (99 percent) had a television (and the majority of households had three or more sets).[17] Today, television claims the biggest news audience of all media outside the Internet (see Figure 6.2). From television's beginnings, most stations were linked into networks founded by three of the four major radio networks. Many early anchors of television network news programs came to the medium with names already made famous during their years of experience as radio broadcast journalists. Now that the news audience could actually see the broadcasters as well as hear them, networks built their evening news around an "anchorman" chosen to inspire trust in viewers.

The three broadcast networks still have huge audiences, but millions of viewers drifted to more opinionated cable networks, especially MSNBC on the left and Fox News on the right. In fact, cable news is becoming a bit of a throwback; more and more it seems analogous to the early newspapers, which

Watching the President on Television

Television revolutionized presidential politics by allowing millions of voters to look closely at the candidates' faces and judge their personalities in the process. This close-up of John Kennedy during a debate with Richard Nixon in the 1960 campaign showed Kennedy to good advantage. In contrast, close-ups of Nixon made him look as though he needed a shave. Kennedy won one of the closest elections in history; his good looks on television may have made the difference.

(MPI/Stringer/Archive Photos/Getty Images)

were blatantly political organizations. Research suggests that in today's television age, in which viewers have unprecedented choices, people who are more interested in politics increasingly desire partisan shows, while people who are less interested in politics simply avoid news programming altogether. Still, some researchers have disputed citizens' "mass migration" from traditional media, concluding instead that alternative news sources, particularly the Internet, supplement rather than displace print and broadcast sources.[18]

The Internet

What we today call the Internet began in 1969 when, with support from the U.S. Defense Department's Advanced Research Projects Agency, computers at four universities were linked to form ARPANET, which connected thirty-seven universities by 1972. New communications standards worked out in 1983 allowed these networks to be linked, creating the Internet. In its early years, the Internet was used mainly to transmit e-mail among researchers. In 1991, a group of European physicists devised a standardized system for encoding and transmitting a wide range of materials, including graphics and photographs, over the Internet, and the World Wide Web (WWW) was born. Now anyone with a computer and Internet access can read text, view images, and download data from websites worldwide. In January 1993 there were only fifty websites in existence. Today there are over 100 million sites and over 1 billion Web users.[19] (See "Compared with What? Top Thirty Nations in Internet Penetration.")

The Internet was soon incorporated into politics, and today virtually every government agency and political organization in the nation has its own

Compared with What?

Top Thirty Nations in Internet Penetration

Compared with other major countries in the world, the United States does not have the highest percentage of the population with Internet access. In fact, it ranks thirteenth. Moreover, broadband service in many countries in Europe and Asia is cheaper and faster in both download and upload speeds. The United States is the largest broadband market in terms of the current number of subscribers but ranks nineteenth in broadband penetration. People all over the world are going online and enjoying rates and speeds that U.S. Internet users envy.

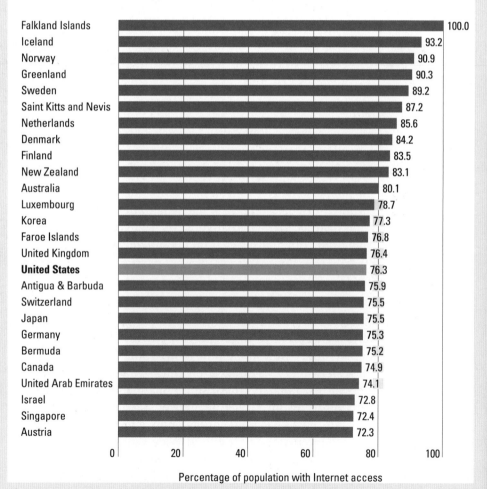

Nation	Percentage
Falkland Islands	100.0
Iceland	93.2
Norway	90.9
Greenland	90.3
Sweden	89.2
Saint Kitts and Nevis	87.2
Netherlands	85.6
Denmark	84.2
Finland	83.5
New Zealand	83.1
Australia	80.1
Luxembourg	78.7
Korea	77.3
Faroe Islands	76.8
United Kingdom	76.4
United States	76.3
Antigua & Barbuda	75.9
Switzerland	75.5
Japan	75.5
Germany	75.3
Bermuda	75.2
Canada	74.9
United Arab Emirates	74.1
Israel	72.8
Singapore	72.4
Austria	72.3

Percentage of population with Internet access

Sources: Internet data at http://www.internetworldstats.com/top25.htm. For broadband statistics, see the Organization for Economic Co-Operation and Development broadband portal at http://www.oecd.org/sti/ict/broadband.

website. Over 70 percent of Americans use the Internet, mostly people under the age of sixty-five.[20] Internet users tend to be well educated and concentrated in large cities and suburbs. Those who rely on the Internet as their main source of news tend to be very critical of traditional news media; they are much more likely to say that news organizations are politically biased.[21]

Private citizens operate their own websites on politics and public affairs, daily posting their thoughts and critical comments. An estimated 12 percent of Internet users have a so-called **blog** (for *weblog*); according to a survey of bloggers, about 35 percent of them discuss politics on their blogs.[22] Political blogs increasingly have had dramatic effects on news reporting and on politics. In 2005, conservative bloggers waited only a few minutes before criticizing President George W. Bush's nomination of Harriet Miers to replace retiring justice Sandra Day O'Connor on the Supreme Court. Their fierce opposition doomed her nomination, which Bush withdrew just three weeks later. While opposition to Supreme Court nominees is nothing new, the speed of the reaction, and the fact that the opposition originated on the president's own side of ideological spectrum, highlighted the new ways in which the blogosphere can mobilize people. Another headache for the Bush administration, congressional investigations into whether the firings of nine U.S. attorneys in 2007 were unlawfully motivated by political concerns, originated as a story on a political blog. It was eventually picked up by traditional news outlets, led to ongoing congressional hearings and court proceedings, and ultimately ushered in the resignation of Attorney General Alberto Gonzales. As these incidents illustrate, the influence of political blogs on the course of American politics to date has largely been indirect, by influencing the types of stories that get picked up by the "mainstream media"; the actual percentage of Americans who read political blogs directly is under 5 percent.[23]

Are bloggers themselves journalists? Many political bloggers say that they are. They have even formed the Media Bloggers Association, which seeks to establish formal recognition of journalist-bloggers as "real" journalists with the same credentials, access to sources, and protections against divulging sources that traditional journalists currently enjoy. In 2006, a state appeals court decided that bloggers do possess those protections. Some fear that these trends will lead to a "wild west atmosphere" in which untrained private individuals can broadcast what they wish online to millions of readers without professional, organizational, or legal concerns about its source.[24] Recent research, however, shows that many of the most prominent political bloggers "are current or former professional journalists from traditional news organizations."[25] In 2009, President Obama made history by calling on a reporter from the Huffington Post, a political blog, at his first official press conference.[26]

Laugh and Learn

Many people learn about politics by watching comedians like Jon Stewart, the host of *The Daily Show*. Almost 30 percent of adults surveyed said that they learned about the 2008 political campaign from comedy shows like *The Daily Show*, *The Colbert Report*, or *Saturday Night Live*. Studies show that watching *The Daily Show* can improve people's ability to learn real facts about politics and current affairs.

Source: Michael A. Xenos and Amy B. Becker, "Moments of Zen: Effects of *The Daily Show* on Information Seeking and Political Learning," *Political Communication* 26 (2009): 317–332. Photo: AP Photo/Jason DeCrow.

blog
A form of newsletter, journal, or "log" of thoughts for public reading, usually devoted to social or political issues and often updated daily. The term derives from weblog.

Private Ownership of the Media

In the United States, people take private ownership of the media for granted. Indeed, most Americans would regard government ownership of the media as an unacceptable threat to freedom that would interfere with the marketplace of ideas and result in one-way communication: from government to citizens. When the government controls the news flow, the people may have little chance to learn what the government is doing or to pressure it to behave differently. Certainly that is true in China. The Chinese government employs thousands of Internet police to prevent "subversive content" from being disseminated to its nearly 300 million Web users. If an Internet user in China searches for "democracy movements," she is met with a screen that reads "page cannot be displayed." In 2009, in advance of the twentieth anniversary of the 1989 pro-democracy movement in Tiananmen Square, Chinese officials blocked users' access to Twitter, Flickr, Hotmail, and YouTube.[27] In the United States, American Internet search company Google resisted government requests for records of user search queries in pornography investigations, but it agreed to limit the blogging and e-mail functions on its computer servers in China when launching Google.cn to serve that lucrative and fast-growing market.[28] Google, along with Yahoo and Microsoft, were summoned before Congress for acting as "surrogate government censors." As private companies, they defended their Chinese business policies as serving their stockholders' financial interests. Moreover, they also argued that developing the Internet in China does more good than harm.[29] In early 2010, however, Google announced that it would no longer cooperate with Chinese censors and that it might shut down its operations in that country. The announcement came after the company discovered it had been the victim of cyber attacks that originated in China and were aimed at human rights activists.[30]

In other Western democracies, the print media are privately owned, but the broadcast media often are not. In the United States, except for about three hundred public television stations (out of about fifteen hundred total) and four hundred public radio stations (out of about ten thousand), the broadcast media are privately owned.

The Consequences of Private Ownership

Just as the appearance of the newscaster became important for television viewers, so did the appearance of the news itself. Television's great advantage over radio—that it shows people and events—accounts for the influence of television news coverage. It also determines, to some extent, the news that television chooses to cover. In fact, private ownership of the mass media ensures that news is selected for its audience appeal.

Private ownership of both the print and broadcast media gives the news industry in America more political freedom than any other in the world, but it also makes the media more dependent on advertising revenues to cover their costs and make a profit. Because advertising rates are tied to audience size, the news operations of the mass media in America must appeal to the audiences they serve.

Tank Man's Fans

This iconic image of a lone pro-democracy protestor in China's Tiananmen Square in 1989 is still unknown to many people in China since the image is officially censored. On the twentieth anniversary of the protests in 2009, however, some in China were able to see the image through a Tank Man fan site on Facebook.com. Tank Man's identity—and what happened to him after he was whisked away by two men—remain worldwide mysteries.

(ARTHUR TSANG/Reuters/Landov)

The average American spends four hours watching television every day, but only about half the adult population watches any kind of news for a half-hour or more.[31] About 52 million newspapers circulate daily, but more than 60 percent of their content is advertising. After fashion reports, sports, comics, and so on, only a relatively small portion of any newspaper is devoted to news of any sort, and only a fraction of that news—excluding stories about fires, robberies, murder trials, and the like—can be classified as political. In terms of sheer volume, the entertainment content offered by the mass media in the United States can vastly overshadow the news content. In other words, the media function more to entertain than to provide news. Entertainment increases the audience, which increases advertising revenues. Thus, the profit motive creates constant pressure to increase the ratio of entertainment to news or to make the news itself more entertaining.

You might think that a story's political significance, educational value, or broad social importance determines whether the media cover it. The sad truth is that most potential news stories are not judged by such grand criteria. The primary criterion of a story's **newsworthiness** is usually its audience appeal, which is judged according to its potential impact on readers or listeners, its degree of sensationalism (exemplified by violence, conflict, disaster, or scandal), its treatment of familiar people or life situations, its close-to-home character, and its timeliness.[32] As Figure 6.3 shows, the

newsworthiness
The degree to which a news story is important enough to be covered in the mass media.

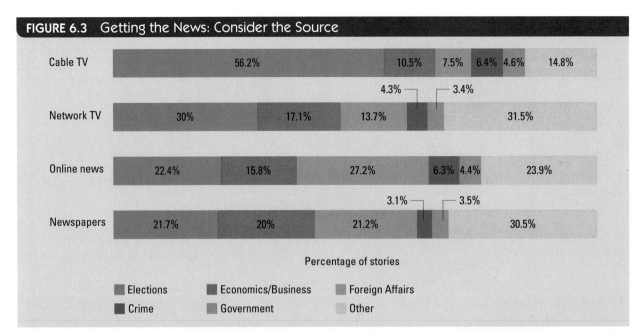

FIGURE 6.3   Getting the News: Consider the Source

An analysis of roughly 70,000 news stories in 2008 (from the front pages of newspapers, major news programs, and Internet sites) shows that just three stories dominated the news in all outlets: the 2008 presidential election, the economy, and foreign affairs. Cable TV was particularly devoted to election coverage, while online news sites and newspapers provided the most extensive coverage of foreign affairs. That these three broad issue areas dominated news coverage leads experts to conclude that the expanding range of news outlets over the past few years has paradoxically corresponded to a narrower range of topics being covered. In the current media age, a few stories are amplified and seem to drown out coverage of other events and topics.

Source: "A Year in the News, 2008," Pew Project for Excellence in Journalism, http://www.stateofthemedia.org/2009/narrative_yearinthenews_intro.php?media=2&cat=0.

content of news coverage often consists of topics that have little to do with elections, foreign affairs, government, or the economy.

The importance of audience appeal has led the news industry to calculate its audience carefully. (The bigger the audience, the higher the advertising rates.) The print media can easily determine the size of their circulations through sales figures, but the broadcast media must estimate their audience through various sampling techniques. Because both print and broadcast media might be tempted to inflate their estimated audience (to tell advertisers that they reach more people than they actually do), a separate industry has developed to rate audience size impartially. These ratings reports have resulted in a "ratings game," in which the media try to increase their ratings by adjusting the delivery or content of their news. Within the news industry, the process has been termed **market-driven journalism**—that is, both reporting news and running commercials geared to a target audience.[33] For example, the *CBS Evening News,* which has the oldest viewing audience among all network television news programs (30 percent of its viewers are over sixty-five years of age), nearly always features a health-related story and runs one or more commercials related to prescription drugs.

More citizens report watching local news than national news, and local news epitomizes market-driven journalism by matching audience demographics

market-driven journalism
Both reporting news and running commercials geared to a target audience defined by demographic characteristics.

to advertising revenue while slighting news about government, policy, and public affairs. Local television stations across the nation practice a "hook-and-hold" approach in their newscasts. They hook viewers at the start by airing eye-catching, alarming, and supposedly "live" stories based on incidents of crime, accidents, fires, and disasters. The middle of the broadcast has informative news stories about business, education, science, technology, and politics that are not considered good viewing. To hold viewers to the end, stations tease them by promising funny or unusual videos about soft topics on pop culture, human interest, and perhaps medical news or novelties. As a result, local news broadcasts from Boston, to Omaha, to Sacramento look much the same, fronted by socially diverse (but remarkably familiar) personalities dispensing political, weather, sports, and social news.[34]

At the national level, the nightly news broadcasts were once the crown jewels of independent broadcasting companies—ABC, CBS, and NBC—and valued for their public service. Now these broadcasts are cogs in huge corporate conglomerates. The Walt Disney Company, for example, owns ABC. NBC has been owned by General Electric for years. In late 2009, the cable company Comcast announced that it is planning to acquire NBC from General Electric. When complete, this merger is set to create a conglomerate that would "hold the most significant collection of cable television assets in the world."[35] News of the merger has prompted concerns about whether viewer access to certain television content will be limited to Comcast customers and about whether cable bills will rise. More broadly, the merger highlights the fact that television nightly news is no longer a public service, but a profit center. Moreover, the financial reports from network news broadcasts are not good.

From 1980 to 2008, ABC, CBS, and NBC suffered severe losses in their prime-time programming audience, dropping from 52 million viewers to 22.8 million—despite an increase in population.[36] Increasingly, viewers turned to watching cable stations instead of network programs, or they turned away from television and toward the Internet. Audience declines brought declining profits and cutbacks in network news budgets. As their parent corporations demanded that news programs "pay their way," the networks succumbed to **infotainment**—a mix of information and diversion oriented to personalities or celebrities, not linked to the day's events, and usually unrelated to public affairs or policy.[37] Over 13 million people tune in for morning shows such as ABC's *Good Morning America* and NBC's *Today Show* that have long mixed news and celebrity interviews. It is unclear whether those who consume only soft news actually learn about politics.[38]

The Concentration of Private Ownership

Media owners can make more money by increasing their audience or by acquiring additional publications or stations. There is a decided trend toward concentrated ownership of the media, increasing the risk that a few owners could control the news flow to promote their own political interests—much as political parties influenced the content of the earliest American newspapers.

infotainment
A mix of information and diversion oriented to personalities or celebrities, not linked to the day's events, and usually unrelated to public affairs or policy; often called "soft news."

In fact, the number of independent newspapers has declined as newspaper chains (owners of two or more newspapers in different cities) have acquired more newspapers. The Gannett chain, which owns *USA Today,* now also owns nearly one hundred other daily newspapers throughout the United States.[39] With the current crisis facing the newspaper industry, some observers have begun to argue that newspapers should consider rejecting the for-profit model and instead operate as nonprofits. As nonprofits, newspapers would be financed through endowments, charitable donations, dues-paying members, and even the government, similar to how PBS and NPR operate on television and radio today. To date, a number of nonprofit news organizations have emerged; some focus on local issues, others on national issues, and others track policy-specific issues, such as health care. But no major newspaper has switched to the nonprofit model ... yet.[40]

At first glance, concentration of ownership does not seem to be a problem in the television industry. Although there are only three major networks, the networks usually do not own their affiliates. About half of all the communities in the United States have a choice of ten or more stations.[41] This figure suggests that the electronic media offer diverse viewpoints and are not characterized by ownership concentration. As with newspapers, however, chains sometimes own television stations in different cities, and ownership sometimes extends across different media. As mentioned earlier, none of the three original television networks remains an independent corporation. Rupert Murdoch's News Corporation, which has worldwide interests, owns the Fox network, the *Wall Street Journal,* and the social networking website MySpace.[42]

Government Regulation of the Media

Although most of the mass media in the United States are privately owned, they do not operate free of government regulation. The broadcast media operate under more stringent regulations than the print media, initially because of technical aspects of broadcasting. In general, government regulation of the mass media addresses three aspects of their operation: technical considerations, ownership, and content.

Technical and Ownership Regulations

In the early days of radio, stations that operated on similar frequencies in the same area often jammed each other's signals, and no one could broadcast clearly. At the broadcasters' insistence, Congress passed the Federal Radio Act (1927), which declared that the public owned the airwaves and private broadcasters could use them only by obtaining a license from the Federal Radio Commission. Thus, government regulation of broadcasting was not forced on the industry by socialist politicians; capitalist owners sought it to impose order on the use of the airwaves (thereby restricting others' freedom to enter broadcasting).

Seven years later, Congress passed the Federal Communications Act of 1934, a more sweeping law that regulated the broadcast and telephone industries for more than sixty years. It created the **Federal Communications Commission (FCC)**, which has five members (no more than three from the same political party) nominated by the president for terms of five years. The commissioners can be removed from office only through impeachment and conviction. Consequently, the FCC is considered an independent regulatory commission: it is insulated from political control by either the president or Congress. (We discuss independent regulatory commissions in Chapter 13.) By law, its vague mandate is to "serve the public interest, convenience, and necessity." Accordingly, the FCC must set the social, economic, and technical goals for the communications industry and deal with philosophical issues of regulation versus deregulation.[43] Today, the FCC's charge includes regulating interstate and international communications by radio, television, telephone, telegraph, cable, and satellite.

For six decades—as technological change made television commonplace and brought the invention of computers, fax machines, and satellite transmissions—the communications industry was regulated under the basic framework of the 1934 law that created the FCC. Pressured by businesses that wanted to exploit new electronic technologies, Congress, in a bipartisan effort, swept away most existing regulations in the Telecommunications Act of 1996.

The new law relaxed or scrapped limitations on media ownership. For example, broadcasters were previously limited to owning only twelve television stations and forty radio stations. The 1996 Telecommunications Act eliminated limits on the number of television stations one company may own, just as long as their coverage didn't extend beyond 35 percent of the market nationwide. As a result, CBS, Fox, and NBC doubled or tripled the number of stations that they owned to cover or even exceed 35 percent of the viewing market allowable by law.[44] The 1996 law also set no national limits for radio ownership and relaxed local limits. In its wake, Clear Channel Communications corporation, which owned thirty-six stations, gobbled up over eleven hundred, including all six stations serving Minot, North Dakota.[45] For some local TV stations and for many local radio stations, the net effect of relaxation on media ownership was to centralize programming in one city and feed the same signals to local affiliates.[46] In addition, the FCC lifted rate regulations for cable systems, allowed cross-ownership of cable and telephone companies, and allowed local and long-distance telephone companies to compete with one another and to sell television services.[47] (For the rush to lay cable around the world, see "Politics of Global Change: The Growth of Cable in a Wireless Age.")

Thanks to the relaxed rules, media groups entered the third millennium in a flurry of megamergers. The Federal Trade Commission approved the largest of these: the $183 billion purchase of Time Warner by America Online, in 2000. The AOL/Time Warner deal merged the nation's largest Internet service provider with the second-largest cable system (which had already merged with one of the biggest publishers in the United States). The

Federal Communications Commission (FCC)
An independent federal agency that regulates interstate and international communication by radio, television, telephone, telegraph, cable, and satellite.

Politics of Global Change

The Growth of Cable in a Wireless Age

You might think that the World Wide Web relies on satellite technology. In fact, most Internet messages to distant lands run along the ocean floor. Undersea fiber-optic cables now carry most of the world's Internet, wireless, and fixed-line traffic. Over time, advances in technology have significantly reduced the costs of laying the cable and of transmission. Global bandwidth usage keeps growing and is predicted to double every 1.4 years.

As demand increases, telecommunications companies are racing to lay more cable and connect more parts of the world. New cables have been proposed for Africa, the Middle East, and even Greenland. And most countries like having more than one cable route as a backup in case one route fails. In the age of globalization, Internet-dependent businesses and nations want a reliable connection.

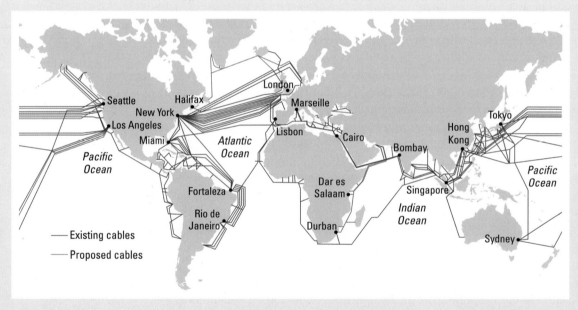

Source: Christopher Rhoads, "Internet Logjams Spur Cable Boom," *Wall Street Journal*, 8 February 2008, p. A1. Copyright 2008 by Dow Jones & Company, Inc. Reproduced with permission of Dow Jones & Company, Inc., in the format textbook via Copyright Clearance Center.

resulting conglomerate (renamed Time Warner in 2003) started with 24 million Internet customers (nearly half of the U.S. market) and 12.6 million cable subscribers. Such mergers prompted concerns that the media would be controlled by a few conglomerates.[48] The industry countered with the argument that diversity among news sources in America is great enough to provide citizens with a wide range of political ideas.[49] Indeed, some observers suggest that there might be too much diversity among news sources today and that the variation in content and quality is contributing to a population that is less informed and more polarized.[50]

In the end, the joint Internet and media venture between Time Warner and AOL failed to produce the expected profits and growth, prompting Time Warner and AOL to part ways in 2009. This outcome has led some analysts to argue that the impending Comcast/NBC union will still significant business challenges and that the media colossus might not be able to realize its alleged economic potential.

Regulation of Content

The First Amendment to the Constitution prohibits Congress from abridging the freedom of the press. Over time, *the press* has come to mean all the media, and the courts have decided many cases that define how far freedom of the press extends under the law. Chapter 15 discusses the most important of these cases, which are often quite complex. Although the courts have had difficulty defining obscenity, they have not permitted obscene expression under freedom of the press. In 1996, however, a federal court overturned an attempt to limit transmission of "indecent" (not obscene) material on the Internet, calling the attempt "profoundly repugnant to First Amendment principles."[51]

Usually the courts strike down government attempts to restrain the press from publishing or broadcasting the information, reports, or opinions it finds newsworthy. One notable exception concerns strategic information during wartime: the courts have supported censorship of information such as the sailing schedules of troop ships or the planned movements of troops in battle. Otherwise, they have recognized a strong constitutional case against press censorship. This stand has given the United States some of the freest, most vigorous news media in the world.

Because the broadcast media are licensed to use the public airwaves, they have been subject to some additional regulation, beyond what is applied to the print media, of the content of their news coverage. The basis for the FCC's regulation of content lies in its charge to ensure that radio (and, later, television) stations would "serve the public interest, convenience, and necessity." For years, the FCC operated under three rules to promote the public interest concerning political matters. The *fairness doctrine* obligated broadcasters to provide fair coverage of all views on public issues. The *equal opportunities rule* required any broadcast station that gave or sold time to a candidate for a public office to make an equal amount of time available under the same conditions to all other candidates for that office. The *reasonable access rule* required that stations make their facilities available for the expression of conflicting views on issues by all responsible elements in the community.

In 1987, under President Reagan, the FCC repealed the *fairness doctrine.* One media analyst noted that the FCC acted in the belief that competition among broadcasters, cable, radio, newspapers, and magazines would provide a vibrant marketplace of ideas. He feared, however, that the media were unlikely to supply the news and public affairs coverage needed to sustain a genuine marketplace. Moreover, because broadcasters no longer needed to cover all views, they could express ideological viewpoints, leading many stations to air conservative views on talk radio without a need to offer liberal views.[52] Prior to 1987, the news media tended to avoid controversial and partisan issues for fear of being in violation of the doctrine. The National Association of Broadcasters says that the elimination of the fairness doctrine has played a large role in the proliferation of news and opinion alternatives now available to media consumers.[53]

Then in 2000, a U.S. Court of Appeals struck down two other longstanding FCC rules. The political editorial rule required television and radio stations endorsing candidates to give free rebuttal time to the candidates' opponents. The personal attack rule required stations to notify individuals if a broadcast questioned their honesty, character, or integrity and provide free time to respond. Although these regulations seemed laudable, they were at the heart of a controversy about the deregulation of the broadcast media. Note that neither of these content regulations was imposed on the print media. In fact, one aspect of a free press is its ability to champion causes that it favors without having to argue the case for the other side. The broadcast media have traditionally been treated differently because they were licensed by the FCC to operate as semimonopolies. With the rise of one-newspaper cities and towns, however, competition among television stations is greater than among newspapers in virtually every market area. Advocates of dropping all FCC content regulations argued that the broadcast media should be just as free as the print media to decide which candidates they endorse and which issues they support.

In the United States, the mass media are in business to make money, which they do mainly by selling advertising. To sell advertising, they provide entertainment on a mass basis, which is their general function. We are more interested here in five specific functions the mass media serve for the political system: *reporting* the news, *interpreting* the news, *influencing* citizens' opinions, *setting the agenda* for government action, and *socializing* citizens about politics.[54]

Functions of the Mass Media for the Political System

Most journalists consider "news" (at least *hard* news) as an important event that has happened within the past twenty-four hours. A presidential news conference or the bombing of an embassy qualifies as news. Who decides what is important? The media, of course. In this section, we discuss how the media cover political affairs, what they choose to report (what becomes "news"), who follows the news, and what they remember and learn from it.

Reporting the News

All the major news media seek to cover political events with firsthand reports from journalists on the scene. Because so many significant political events occur in the nation's capital, Washington has by far the biggest press corps of any city in the world—nearly 7,000 congressionally accredited reporters: 2,000 from newspapers, 1,800 from periodicals, 2,500 from radio and television, and over 350 photographers. Only a few of these reporters are admitted to fill the fifty seats of the White House press briefing room.[55] Since 1902, when President Theodore Roosevelt first provided space in the White House for reporters, the press has had special access to the president (though as Figure 6.4 shows, the number of presidential news conferences with reporters has declined in recent administrations). As recently as the Truman administration, reporters enjoyed informal personal relationships with the president. Today, the media's relationship with the president is mediated primarily through the Office of the Press Secretary.

To meet their daily deadlines, White House correspondents rely heavily on information they receive from the president's staff, each piece carefully crafted in an attempt to control the news report. The most frequent form is the news release—a prepared text distributed to reporters in the hope that they will use it verbatim. A daily news briefing enables reporters to question the press secretary about news releases and allows television correspondents time to prepare their stories and film for the evening newscast. A news conference involves questioning high-level officials in the executive branch—including the president, on occasion. News conferences appear to be freewheeling, but officials tend to carefully rehearse precise answers to anticipated questions.[56]

Occasionally, information is given "on background," meaning the information can be quoted, but reporters cannot identify the source. A vague reference—"a senior official says"—is all right. Information disclosed "off the record" cannot even be printed. Journalists who violate these well-known rules risk losing their welcome at the White House. In a sense, the press corps is captive to the White House, which feeds reporters the information they need

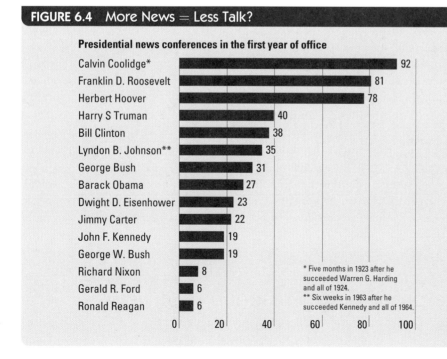

FIGURE 6.4   More News = Less Talk?

Presidential news conferences in the first year of office

Calvin Coolidge*	92
Franklin D. Roosevelt	81
Herbert Hoover	78
Harry S Truman	40
Bill Clinton	38
Lyndon B. Johnson**	35
George Bush	31
Barack Obama	27
Dwight D. Eisenhower	23
Jimmy Carter	22
John F. Kennedy	19
George W. Bush	19
Richard Nixon	8
Gerald R. Ford	6
Ronald Reagan	6

* Five months in 1923 after he succeeded Warren G. Harding and all of 1924.
** Six weeks in 1963 after he succeeded Kennedy and all of 1964.

As press conferences have become more formal and scripted, they have also become less frequent. When journalists and the president had more of a collegial relationship, press conferences were common. Except for Bill Clinton, modern presidents are clustered at the bottom of this graph, which shows the number of presidential press conferences in the first year in office since 1922.

Sources: "The Frequency of the Message is Medium," *CQ Weekly Online* 27 (July 2009): 1755. Copyright © 2009 by CQ-ROLL CALL GROUP. Reproduced with permission of CQ-ROLL CALL GROUP via Copyright Clearance Center.

to meet their deadlines and frames events so that they are covered on the evening news. Beginning with the Nixon White House, press secretaries have obliged photographers with "photo opportunities," a few minutes to take pictures or shoot film, often of the president with a visiting dignitary. The photographers can keep their editors supplied with visuals, and the press secretary ensures that the coverage is favorable by controlling the environment.

Most reporters in the Washington press corps are accredited to sit in the House and Senate press galleries, but only about 400 cover Congress exclusively. Most news about Congress comes from innumerable press releases issued by its 535 members and from an unending supply of congressional reports. A journalist, then, can report on Congress without inhabiting its press galleries. In an effort to save money in the face of tough times, many newspapers across the country, large and small, have cut the size of their Washington staff or eliminated it entirely. According to one report, "more than half the states do not have a single newspaper reporter dedicated to covering federal government."[57]

Not so long ago, individual congressional committees allowed radio and television coverage of their proceedings only on special occasions—such as the Kefauver committee's investigation of organized crime in the 1950s and the Watergate investigation in the 1970s. Congress banned microphones and cameras from its chambers until 1979, when the House permitted live coverage. Televised broadcasts of the House were surprisingly successful, thanks to C-SPAN (the Cable-Satellite Public Affairs Network), which feeds to 90 percent of the cable systems across the country and has a cultlike following among hundreds of thousands of regular viewers.[58] To share in the exposure, the Senate began television coverage in 1986. Occasionally, an event captured on C-SPAN becomes a major news story. In 2009, for example, Representative Alan Grayson (D-Fla.) argued on the floor of the House that the Republican health-care plan had two options: stay healthy or die quickly. The C-SPAN coverage was picked up on YouTube, which then led to days of political debate. It also led to a fundraising boon: in the two weeks following the broadcast, Grayson's reelection campaign raised over $150,000 from one website alone.[59]

In addition to these recognized sources of news, selected reporters occasionally benefit from leaks of information released by officials who are guaranteed anonymity. Officials may leak news to interfere with others' political plans or to float ideas ("trial balloons") past the public and other political leaders to gauge their reactions. At times, one carefully placed leak can turn into a gusher of media coverage through "pack journalism"—the tendency of journalists to adopt similar viewpoints toward the news simply because they hang around together, exchanging information and defining the day's news with one another.

Interpreting and Presenting the News

gatekeepers
Media executives, news editors, and prominent reporters who direct the flow of news.

Media executives, news editors, and prominent reporters function as **gatekeepers** in directing the news flow: they decide which events to report and how to handle the elements in those stories.[60] They not only select what topics go through the gate but also are expected to uphold standards of careful reporting and principled journalism. The rise of the Internet, however, has made more information and points of view available to the public. Most journalists think the Internet has made journalism better, mostly because it is a powerful research tool and its ability to deliver information quickly promotes competition.[61] A 2007 survey of journalists found that 59 percent said that they look to political blogs sometimes or regularly as part of their news-gathering process.[62] But the Internet also can spread factual errors and rumors. The Internet has no gatekeepers, and thus no constraints on its content.

A parade of unconnected one-minute news stories, flashing across the television screen every night, would boggle the eyes and minds of viewers. To make the news understandable and to hold viewers' attention, television editors and producers concentrate on individuals because individuals have personalities (political institutions do not—except for the presidency). A study of network news coverage of the president, Congress, and the Supreme Court in 2003–2004 found that 52 percent of the stories were about the presidency, compared with 37 percent on Congress and 10 percent on the Supreme Court.[63] Moreover, when television does cover Congress, it tries to personify the institution by focusing on prominent, quotable leaders, such as the Speaker of the House or the Senate majority leader.

During elections, personification encourages **horse race journalism**, in which media coverage becomes primarily a matter of which candidate is leading in the polls and who has raised the most money. Over three-quarters of Americans say that they want more coverage of candidates' positions on the issues; almost half would also like less coverage of who is leading in the polls.[64] Yet study after study of news coverage of presidential elections find that horse race coverage dominates and that horse race content increases as election day approaches. Journalists cover the horse race because it offers new material daily, whereas the candidates' programs remain the same.[65]

Political campaigns lend themselves particularly well to media coverage, especially if the candidates create a **media event**—a situation that is too "newsworthy" to pass up. One tried-and-true method is to conduct a statewide walking campaign. Newspapers and television can take pictures of the candidate on the highway and conduct interviews with local folks who just spoke with the political hiker. (See Chapter 9 for further discussion of the media in political campaigns.) Television is particularly partial to events that have visual impact. Organized protests and fires, for example, "show well" on television, so television tends to cover them. Violent conflict of any kind, especially unfolding dramas that involve weapons, rates especially high in visual impact.

Where the Public Gets Its News. Until the early 1960s, most people reported getting more of their news from newspapers than from any other source. Television nudged out newspapers as the public's major source of news in the early 1960s. In most countries around the world, newspaper audiences have declined, and television is dominant.[66] Today, 65 percent of Americans name television or cable news networks as their primary source for news.[67] Fourteen

horse race journalism
Election coverage by the mass media that focuses on which candidate is ahead rather than on national issues.

media event
A situation that is so "newsworthy" that the mass media are compelled to cover it. Candidates in elections often create such situations to garner media attention.

percent cite newspapers as their primary news source. Just under 11 percent of Americans claim that the Internet is their primary source of news. Over half of the public consults multiple sources of news during the day—perhaps reading the paper at breakfast, checking the Internet at work, and ending the day watching television news.[68] On average, Americans spend a little over an hour a day getting the news from one or multiple sources. Older Americans spend more time watching, reading, or listening to news; people under the age of thirty spend less.[69] Women are more likely to tune in for morning television shows and watch the nightly network news, while men are more likely to get their news from radio and online sources.[70] Some people even get their news from late-night talk shows (see Figure 6.5).[71] More and more Americans are getting news online. During the 1996 presidential election, only 3 percent of Americans said they got campaign news from the Internet. By the 2008 presidential election, that figure jumped to 36 percent.[72]

What People Remember and Know. If, as surveys indicate, about 80 percent of the public read or hear the news each day, how much political information do they absorb? By all accounts, not much. A national survey in the fall of 2009 asked respondents twelve questions about current events, including the name of the newest Supreme Court justice (Sonia Sotomayor) and the current unemployment rate (around 10 percent). On average, respondents got five questions out of twelve correct. Only 14 percent of

FIGURE 6.5   Gagging on Late-Night TV

	Number of jokes
John McCain (Republican candidate for President)	1359
George W. Bush (President)	1160
Barack Obama (Democratic candidate for President)	769
Sarah Palin (Republican candidate for Vice President)	712
Hillary Clinton (Democratic candidate for President)	709
Elliot Spitzer (ex-governor of New York)	272
Bill Clinton (ex-President)	265
Dick Cheney (Vice President)	191
Mitt Romney (Republican candidate for President)	135
Joe Biden (Democratic candidate for Vice President)	107

Polls show that many Americans get their political news from late-night television, primarily from hosts who open their programs with monologues laced with political jokes. This graph shows the most frequent joke targets in 2008 on the following popular programs: *The Tonight Show, The Late Show with David Letterman,* and *Late Night with Conan O'Brien.* The president is usually the top joke target, though in 2008 he was slightly overshadowed by John McCain, with Barack Obama coming in a distant third. The only person in the top ten who was not currently holding, formerly holding, or seeking a position in the White House was Elliot Spitzer, the former governor of New York who resigned amid revelations that he was a client of a prostitution ring.

Source: Late Night Joke Target Counts by Month (2008), http://cmpa.com/studies_humor_punchlines.htm.

respondents got ten or more correct.[73] When pollsters asked Americans to name the heads of state for Cuba, Great Britain, Russia, Mexico, and Germany, as well as the U.S. secretary of state, only 2 percent of respondents could name all six leaders; 18 percent of Americans could not name any.[74]

Numerous studies have found that those who rely on television for their news score lower on tests of knowledge about public affairs than those who rely on print media. Among media researchers, this finding has led to the **television hypothesis**—the belief that television is to blame for the low level of citizens' knowledge about public affairs.[75] This belief has a reasonable basis. We know that television tends to squeeze public policy issues into one-minute or, at most, two-minute fragments, which makes it difficult to explain candidates' positions. Television also tends to cast abstract issues in personal terms to generate the visual content that the medium needs. Thus, viewers may become more adept at visually identifying the candidates and describing their personal habits than at outlining their positions on issues. Finally, because they are regulated by the FCC, the television networks may be more concerned than newspapers, which are not regulated, about being fair and equal in covering the candidates. Recent research, however, suggests that newspapers differ from television less in content of coverage than in the amount; newspapers simply cover campaigns more extensively and intensively than television.[76] Whatever the explanation, the technological wonders of television may have contributed little to citizens' knowledge of public affairs. It may even discourage respect for different opinions since it tends to emphasize drama and conflict between political opponents.[77] It can also lead people to be less trusting of government.[78]

Additional ways in which the media cover the news can either exacerbate or diminish socioeconomic differences in levels of political knowledge. When the news is presented with lots of expert commentary—which tends to involve jargon and complex explanations—those who are more affluent and educated seem to learn more from news coverage than those Americans who are less well off. But when the news is presented in a more contextual fashion—which tends to focus on the historical and factual background of an issue—socioeconomic differences in political knowledge diminish. Contextual information "gives meaning to what otherwise might seem like disconnected events and helps people understand why issues and problems deserve their attention."[79] Contextual information reduces knowledge gaps among users of both print and television news. In our age of the 24/7 news cycle, however, there is a tendency to provide contextual information when an event is new but to rely on expert commentary in subsequent coverage. As a result, people who do not pay attention to an issue right from the start might lose a valuable chance to learn about it, since journalists quickly move on to covering experts' views on the latest developments.

Influencing Public Opinion

Americans overwhelmingly believe that the media exert a strong influence on their political institutions, and nearly nine out of ten Americans believe that

television hypothesis
The belief that television is to blame for the low level of citizens' knowledge about public affairs.

the media strongly influence public opinion.[80] However, measuring the extent of media influence on public opinion is difficult.[81] Because few of us learn about political events except through the media, it could be argued that the media create public opinion simply by reporting events. Consider the fall of Baghdad in 2003. Surely the photographs of joyous Iraqis tearing down a statue of Saddam Hussein affected American public opinion about war in Iraq.

Documenting general effects of the media on opinions about more general issues in the news is difficult. Doris Graber, a leading scholar on the media, reported several studies that carefully documented media influence. For example, more pretrial publicity for serious criminal cases leads to full trials rather than settlement through plea-bargaining; media attention to more obscure foreign policy issues tends to force them onto the policy agenda.[82] Television network coverage of the returns on the night of the 2000 presidential election may have profoundly affected public opinion toward both major candidates. In a report commissioned by cable news network CNN, three journalism experts concluded that the networks' unanimous declarations of George W. Bush's victory that night "created a premature impression" that he had defeated Al Gore before the Florida outcome had been decided. The impression carried through the postelection challenge: "Gore was perceived as the challenger and labeled a 'sore loser' for trying to steal the election."[83] Since then, network and cable news programs have been more careful about projecting winners in primary and general election contests.

Setting the Political Agenda

Despite the media's potential for influencing public opinion, most scholars believe that the media's greatest influence on politics is found in their power to set the **political agenda**—a list of issues that people identify as needing government attention. Those who set the political agenda define which issues government decision makers should discuss and debate. Like a tree that falls in the forest without anyone around to hear it, an issue that does not get on the political agenda will not get any political attention. Sometimes the media force the government to confront issues once buried in the scientific community, such as AIDS, global warming, and cloning. Other times the media move the government to deal with unpleasant social issues, such as child abuse and wrongful execution of the death penalty. However, the media can also keep high on the agenda issues that perhaps should attract fewer public resources.[84]

Crime is a good example. Local television news covers crime twice as much as any other topic.[85] Given that fear of crime today is about the same as it was in the mid-1960s, are the media simply reflecting a constantly high crime rate? Actually, crime rates have fallen in every major category (rape, burglary, robbery, assault, murder) since the 1980s.[86] As one journalist said, "Crime coverage is not editorially driven; it's economically driven. It's the easiest, cheapest, laziest news to cover."[87] Moreover, crime provides good visuals. ("If it bleeds, it leads.") So despite the falling crime rate, the public encounters a continuing gusher of crime news and believes that crime has increased over time.

political agenda
A list of issues that need government attention.

One study found varying correlations between media coverage and what the public sees as "the most important problem facing this country today," depending on the type of event. Crises such as the Vietnam War, racial unrest, and energy shortages drew extensive media coverage, and each additional news magazine story per month generated almost a one percentage point increase in citations of the event as an important problem. But public opinion was even more responsive to media coverage of recurring problems such as inflation and unemployment.[88] Additional research shows that the media are more likely to influence what the public thinks is important when they cover spectacular events such as those often related to crime or foreign policy. However, the public's enduring concern with nonspectacular issues, such as energy and the environment, can actually influence the amount of media coverage those types of issues receive. In other words, while the media often shape which issues the public thinks are important, sometimes the issues that the public thinks are important shape media coverage.[89]

The media's ability to influence public opinion by defining "the news" makes politicians eager to influence media coverage. Politicians attempt to affect not only public opinion but also the opinions of other political leaders. The president receives a daily digest of news and opinion from many sources, and other top government leaders closely monitor the major national news sources. Even journalists work hard at following the news coverage in alternative sources. In a curious sense, the mass media have become a network for communicating among attentive elites, all trying to influence one another or to assess others' weaknesses and strengths. If the White House is under pressure on some policy matter, for example, it might supply a cabinet member or other high official to appear on one of the Sunday morning talk shows, such as *Meet the Press* (NBC) or *Face the Nation* (CBS). These programs draw less than half the audience of the network news shows, but all engage the guest in lengthy discussions. The White House's goal is to influence the thinking of other insiders, who faithfully watch the program, as much as to influence the opinions of the relatively small number of ordinary citizens who watch that particular newscast.[90] Of course, other political leaders appear on these programs, and criticism of the administration's policies in one medium, especially from members of the president's own party, emboldens others to be critical in their comments to other media.

Presidents use other indirect means to try to influence political elites. In the strategy known as **going public**, the president travels around the country speaking to Americans directly about his policy agenda (see Chapter 12 for more on going public). The goal is twofold: first to generate media coverage of the speaking event, and second to motivate citizens to pressure their representatives to support the president's agenda. The strategy of going public has become more common over time. Barack Obama attempted this strategy in August 2009, when he traveled to New Hampshire, Colorado, and Montana to hold town hall meetings about health-care reform, which had stalled in Congress. By talking with Americans directly, he hoped to correct misperceptions about his reform proposals that were dominating media coverage at

going public
A strategy whereby a president seeks to influence policy elites and media coverage by appealing directly to the American people.

Just weeks into his presidency, President Obama "went public" to gain support for his proposed economic stimulus package, which was meeting stiff resistance in Congress. One of the places where he held a town hall meeting was Elkhart, Indiana, where the unemployment rate soared to 15 percent in early 2009, up from 5 percent just one year earlier. The economic proposal ultimately passed, bolstering the belief that the strategy of going public can be effective.

(AP Photo/Charles Dharapak)

the time. Such corrections, he hoped, would bolster public support for his plans and thus influence legislative action on Capitol Hill.[91]

Socializing the Citizenry

The mass media act as important agents of political socialization, at least as influential as those described in Chapter 5.[92] Young people who rarely follow the news by choice nevertheless acquire political values through the entertainment function of the broadcast media. From the 1930s to the early 1950s, children learned from dramas and comedies on the radio; now they learn from television. The average American child watches about nineteen thousand hours of television by the end of high school—and sees a lot of sex and hears countless swear words in prime time.[93] What children learned from radio was quite different from what they are learning now, however. In the golden days of radio, youngsters listening to the popular radio drama *The Shadow* heard repeatedly that "crime does not pay ... the *Shadow* knows!" In program after program—*Dragnet, Junior G-Men, Gangbusters*—the message never varied: criminals are bad; the police are good; criminals get caught and are severely punished for their crimes.

Television today does not portray the criminal justice system in the same way, even in police dramas. Consider programs such as *24* and *In Justice*, which have portrayed law enforcement officers and government agents as lawbreakers. Other series, such as *Law and Order, Prison Break,* and *The Shield*, sometimes portray a tainted criminal justice system and institutional corruption.[94] Perhaps years of television messages conveying distrust of law enforcement, disrespect for the criminal justice system, and violence shape impressionable youngsters. Certainly, one cannot easily argue that television's entertainment programs help prepare law-abiding citizens.

Some scholars argue that the most important effect of the mass media, particularly television, is to reinforce the hegemony, or dominance, of the existing culture and order. According to this argument, social control functions not through institutions of force (police, military, and prisons) but through social institutions, such as the media, that cause people to accept "the way things are."[95] By displaying the lifestyles of the rich and famous, for example, the media induce the public to accept the unlimited accumulation of private wealth. Similarly, the media socialize citizens to value "the American way," to be patriotic, to back their country, "right or wrong."

So the media play contradictory roles in the process of political socialization. On the one hand, they promote popular support for government by joining in the celebration of national holidays, heroes' birthdays, political anniversaries, and civic accomplishments. On the other hand, the media erode public confidence by detailing politicians' extramarital affairs, airing investigative reports of possible malfeasance in office, and even showing television dramas about crooked cops.[96] Some critics contend that the media also give too much coverage to government opponents, especially to those who engage in unconventional opposition (see Chapter 7). However, strikes, sit-ins, violent confrontations, and hijackings draw large audiences and thus are "newsworthy" by the mass media standards.[97] In the aftermath of September 11, nearly half the respondents to a national survey thought that news organizations were "weakening the nation's defenses" by criticizing the military while the country was involved in a global war on terror.[98]

Evaluating the Media in Government

Are the media fair or biased in reporting the news? What contributions do the media make to democratic government? What effects do they have on the pursuit of freedom, order, and equality?

Is Reporting Biased?

News reports are presented as objective reality, yet critics of modern journalism contend that the news is filtered through the ideological biases of the media owners and editors (the gatekeepers) and the reporters themselves. Even citizens tend to be skeptical of the news. Democrats and Republicans show distinct differences in which media organizations they find most credible (see Figure 6.6).

The argument that news reports are politically biased has two sides. On the one hand, news reporters are criticized in best-selling books for tilting their stories in a liberal direction, promoting social equality and undercutting social order.[99] On the other hand, wealthy and conservative media owners are suspected—in other best-selling books—of preserving inequalities and

FIGURE 6.6 — Partisanship and the Credibility of the News

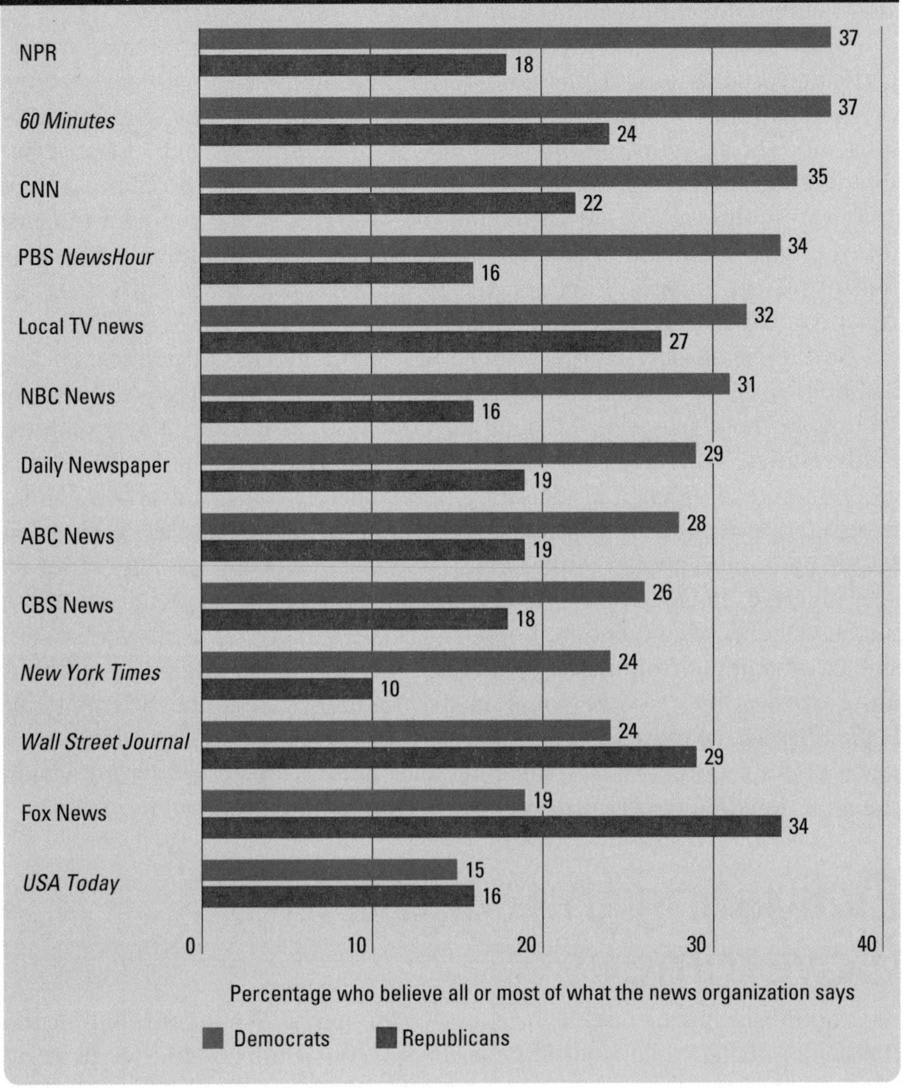

Respondents were asked to rate broadcast and print media according to whether the respondent believes "all or most" or "nothing" of what the organization says. The table here lists the results broken down by partisan identification. In general, Republicans are more skeptical of the media than Democrats are. Republicans rate the Fox News Channel and the *Wall Street Journal* most highly, while Democrats favor the PBS *NewsHour*, CNN, and National Public Radio (NPR).

News Organization	Democrats	Republicans
NPR	37	18
60 Minutes	37	24
CNN	35	22
PBS *NewsHour*	34	16
Local TV news	32	27
NBC News	31	16
Daily Newspaper	29	19
ABC News	28	19
CBS News	26	18
New York Times	24	10
Wall Street Journal	24	29
Fox News	19	34
USA Today	15	16

Percentage who believe all or most of what the news organization says

■ Democrats   ■ Republicans

Source: "Section 7: Media Credibility," in 2008 Pew Research Center for the People and the Press, News Consumption and Believability Study, 17 August 2008, http://people-press.org/reports/pdf/444.pdf, 59.

reinforcing the existing order by serving a relentless round of entertainment that numbs the public's capacity for critical analysis.[100] Let's evaluate these arguments, looking first at reporters.

Although the picture is far from clear, available evidence seems to confirm the charge of liberal leanings among reporters in the major news media. In a 2007 survey of journalists, 32 percent of the national press considered themselves "liberal," compared with only 8 percent who said they were "conservative."[101] Content analysis of the tone of ABC, CBS, and NBC network coverage of presidential campaigns from 1988 to 2004 concluded that Democratic candidates received much more "good press" than Republicans in every election but 1988, when the Republican candidate, George H. W. Bush, benefited from better press.[102] However, one news medium—talk radio—is dominated by conservative views. Rush Limbaugh alone broadcasts to more than 13 million listeners over six hundred stations. Other prominent conservative radio hosts—such as Sean Hannity and Michael Savage—reach millions more.[103] The top independent and liberal talk show hosts, in contrast, have audiences of fewer than 3 million listeners.

The counterargument is that working journalists in the national and local media often conflict with their own editors, who tend to be more conservative. This was demonstrated in a recent study of news executives in national and local media.[104] The editors, in their function as gatekeepers, tend to tone down reporters' liberal leanings by editing their stories or not placing them well in the medium. Newspaper publishers are also free to endorse candidates, and almost all daily newspapers once openly endorsed one of the two major party candidates for president. In sixteen of eighteen elections from 1932 to 2000, newspaper editorials favored the Republican candidate. In 2004, however, more editorials backed challenger John Kerry (208) than Bush (189). In 2008, the number of endorsements for Barack Obama far surpassed the number for John McCain: 287 vs. 159. That year, the *Chicago Tribune* endorsed a Democrat for the first time in its 162-year history.[105]

Without question, incumbents—as opposed to challengers—enjoy much more news coverage simply from holding office and issuing official statements. The less prominent the office, the greater the advantage from such free news coverage. Noncampaign news coverage leads to greater incumbent name recognition at election time, particularly for members of Congress (see Chapter 11). This coverage effect is independent of any bias in reporting on campaigns. For more prominent offices such as the presidency, however, a different news dynamic may come into play. When a powerful incumbent runs for reelection, journalists may feel a special responsibility to counteract his or her advantage by putting the opposite partisan spin on the news.[106] Thus, whether the media coverage of campaigns is seen as pro-Democratic (and therefore liberal) or pro-Republican (and therefore conservative) can depend on which party is in office at the time. A report of network news stories broadcast during the general election in 2008, when there was no incumbent, found that Obama received overwhelmingly positive coverage: 68 percent of stories about Obama were deemed positive. In stark contrast, only 33 percent of stories about McCain were considered positive.[107]

Of course, bias in reporting is not limited to election campaigns, and different media may reflect different understandings of political issues. An important series of surveys about perceptions of the Iraq war were taken over the summer of 2003, after Bush had announced the end of combat. Substantial portions of the public held erroneous understandings of the war just ended. For example, 27 percent in the September survey thought that world opinion supported the U.S. war against Iraq (when world opinion opposed the war), 21 percent thought that Iraq had been directly involved in the 9/11 attack (which our government never claimed and President Bush denied at a news conference),[108] and 24 percent thought that the United States had already found Iraqi weapons of mass destruction (when it had not). The researchers then analyzed which respondents held all three misperceptions by their primary source of news. Respondents who relied on the commercial television networks (Fox, CBS, ABC, CNN, or NBC) held the most misperceptions, with 45 percent of Fox viewers making all three mistakes compared with only about 15 percent for the other networks. Just 9 percent of those who relied on print media erred on all three facts. Broadcast media per se were not to blame, for a scant 4 percent of PBS viewers or listeners to National Public Radio were wrong on all items.[109]

Even the nation's outstanding newspapers display biases in reporting news. Scholars analyzed the content of thirty days' coverage of the Palestinian-Israeli conflict during ten months of 2000 and 2001 printed in the *New York Times, Washington Post,* and *Chicago Tribune.* The *Post* and the *Tribune,* while covering the conflict differently, were more similar to each other than to the *Times,* which was "the most slanted in a pro-Israeli direction, in accordance with long-standing criticisms of a pro-Israeli bias leveled against the American media by observers around the world."[110] Presumably such reporting biases affect newspaper readers.

Contributions to Democracy

As noted earlier, in a democracy, communication must move in two directions: from government to citizens and from citizens to government. In fact, political communication in the United States seldom goes directly from government to citizens without passing through the media. The point is important because news reporters tend to be highly critical of politicians; they consider it their job to search for inaccuracies in fact and weaknesses in argument—practicing **watchdog journalism.**[111] Some observers have characterized the news media and the government as adversaries—each mistrusting the other, locked in competition for popular favor while trying to get the record straight. To the extent that this is true, the media serve both the majoritarian and the pluralist models of democracy well by improving the quality of information transmitted to the people about their government.[112]

The mass media transmit information in the opposite direction by reporting citizens' reactions to political events and government actions. The press has traditionally reflected public opinion (and often created it) in the process of defining the news and suggesting courses of government action. But the media's role in reflecting public opinion has become much more refined in the information age. Since the 1820s, newspapers conducted straw polls of dubious quality that matched their own partisan inclinations.[113] After commercial polls (such as the Gallup and Roper polls) were established in the 1930s, newspapers began to report more reliable readings of public opinion. By the 1960s, the media (both national and local) began to conduct their own surveys. The *New York Times,* for example, has conducted its own polls at a rate of at least one poll per month since 2003.[114] Regularly reporting about public opinion is one of the most obvious ways in which the media can tell a story to their consumers—elites and ordinary Americans alike—about what the public believes at any point in time.

The media now have the tools to do a better job of reporting mass opinion than ever before, and they use those tools extensively, practicing

watchdog journalism
Journalism that scrutinizes public and business institutions and publicizes perceived misconduct.

"precision journalism" with sophisticated data collection and analysis techniques. The well-respected *New York Times*/CBS News Poll conducts surveys that are first aired on the *CBS Evening News* and then analyzed at length in the *Times*—the same is true for the NBC News/*Wall Street Journal* poll. Citizens and journalists alike complain that heavy reliance on polls during election campaigns causes the media to emphasize the horse race and slights the discussion of issues. But the media also use their polling expertise for other purposes, such as gauging support for going to war and for balancing the budget. Although polls sometimes create opinions just by asking questions, their net effect has been to generate more accurate knowledge of public opinion and to report that knowledge back to the public. Although widespread knowledge of public opinion does not guarantee government responsiveness to popular demands, such knowledge is necessary if government is to function according to the majoritarian model of democracy.

Effects on Freedom, Order, and Equality

The media in the United States have played an important role in advancing equality, especially racial equality. Throughout the civil rights movement of the 1950s and 1960s, the media gave national coverage to conflict in the South as black children tried to attend white schools or civil rights workers were beaten and even killed in the effort to register black voters. Partly because of this media coverage, civil rights moved up on the political agenda, and coalitions formed in Congress to pass new laws promoting racial equality. Women's rights have also been advanced by the media, which have reported instances of blatant sexual discrimination exposed by groups working for sexual equality, such as the National Organization for Women (NOW). In general, the mass media offer spokespersons for any disadvantaged group an opportunity to state their case before a national audience and to work for a place on the political agenda. Increasingly, members of minority groups have entered the media business to serve the special interests and needs of their group.

Although the media are willing to encourage government action to promote equality at the cost of some personal freedom, journalists resist government attempts to infringe on freedom of the press to promote order.[115] While the public tends to support a free press in theory, public support is not universal and wavers in practice. Asked whether it is more important "that the government be able to censor news stories it feels threaten national security OR that the news media be able to report stories they feel are in the national interest," about one-third in a 2006 national survey favored government censorship. Asked whether "it is generally right or generally wrong for the government to monitor telephone and e-mail communications of Americans suspected of having terrorist ties without first obtaining permission from the courts," more respondents (54 percent) thought it was generally right than wrong (43 percent).[116]

The media's ability to report whatever they wish and whenever they wish certainly erodes efforts to maintain order. For example, sensational media coverage of terrorist acts gives terrorists the publicity they seek;

portrayal of brutal killings and rapes on television encourages copycat crimes, committed "as seen on television." The chaos that erupted among Muslims in 2006 over Islamic cartoons published in Danish newspapers to test freedom of expression resulted in deaths and destruction across the world. Freedom of the press is a noble value and one that has been important to democratic government. But we should not ignore the fact that democracies sometimes pay a price for pursuing it without qualification.

Summary

The mass media transmit information to large, heterogeneous, and widely dispersed audiences through print and broadcasts. The mass media in the United States are privately owned and in business to make money, which they do mainly by selling space or airtime to advertisers. Both print and electronic media determine which events are newsworthy largely on the basis of audience appeal. The rise of mass-circulation newspapers in the 1830s produced a politically independent press in the United States. In their aggressive competition for readers, those newspapers often engaged in sensational reporting, a charge sometimes leveled at today's media, including the broadcast media and especially cable television.

The broadcast media operate under technical, ownership, and content regulations imposed by the government; but over the past two decades, the FCC has relaxed its rules limiting media ownership and ensuring fair and balanced representation of competing views. The main function of the mass media is entertainment, but the media also perform the political functions of reporting news, interpreting news, influencing citizens' opinions, setting the political agenda, and socializing citizens about politics.

The major media maintain staffs of professional journalists in major cities around the world. Washington, D.C., hosts the biggest press corps in the world, but only a portion of those correspondents concentrates on the presidency. Because Congress is a more decentralized institution, it is covered in a more decentralized manner. What actually gets reported in the established media depends on media gatekeepers: the publishers and editors. Professional journalists follow rules for citing sources, and these also guide their reporting, but on the Internet and in talk radio, there are few rules concerning what is covered. We are entering an era in which the gatekeepers have less control over what poses as news, in terms of both what subjects are reported on and the veracity of the reports.

Americans today get more news from television than from newspapers. Although increasing numbers of citizens turn to the Internet for news, a far smaller proportion of the public relies on online sources than on television and newspapers. Compared with television, newspapers usually do a more thorough job of informing the public about politics. Newspapers, however, have been facing unprecedented financial burdens in recent years and have been cutting back on their newsroom operations, a troubling trend for those who see newspapers as an important political institution in their own right. Despite heavy exposure to news in the print and electronic media, the ability of most people to retain much political information is shockingly low. The media's most important effect on public opinion is in setting the country's political agenda. The role of the news media may be more important for affecting interactions among attentive policy elites than in influencing public opinion. The media play more subtle, contradictory roles in political socialization, both promoting and undermining certain political and cultural values.

Reporters from the national media tend to be more liberal than the public, as judged by their tendency to vote for Democratic candidates and by their own self-descriptions. Journalists' liberal leanings are checked somewhat by the conservative inclinations of their editors and publishers. However, if journalists systematically demonstrate any pronounced bias in their news reporting, it may be against incumbents and front-runners, regardless of their party, rather than a bias that favors liberal Democrats. Numerous studies of media effects have uncovered biases of other forms, as in reporting the Iraq war and conflict in the Middle East.

From the standpoint of majoritarian democracy, one of the most important roles of the media is to facilitate communication from the people to the government through the reporting of public opinion polls. The media zealously defend the freedom of the press, even to the point of encouraging disorder by granting extensive publicity to violent protests, terrorist acts, and other threats to order.

 CourseMate

Visit www.cengagebrain.com/shop/ ISBN/0495906182 for flashcards, web quizzes, videos and more!

CHAPTER TOPICS

AP Photo/Lauren Victoria Burke

Angry citizens packed town halls across the country in the summer of 2009. They gathered to confront Democratic members of Congress over President Obama's health-care plan. The experience of Representative Tim Bishop (D-N.Y.) was typical. Videos of his June town hall meeting showed participants screaming questions and shouting him down. According to the *Wall Street Journal,* "Mr. Bishop would begin to respond to a question and a participant would yell, 'Answer the question!' At one point, Mr. Bishop yelled back, 'I'm trying to!'[1] The scene was repeated at countless meetings with Democratic members of Congress in different places—Mehlville, Missouri; Romulus, Michigan; Denver, Colorado; Morrisville, Pennsylvania; Austin, Texas; Tampa, Florida; and so on.[2]

People's anger erupted in other ways. Members of Congress were hanged in effigy, protesters carried signs linking the health plan with Nazism (and communism), demonstrations provoked fistfights, and fights led to hospitalizations.[3] On September 12, thousands of protesters traveled to Washington, filling the west lawn of the Capitol and spilling onto the National Mall.[4] It was mostly a grassroots response to Obama's policies, but with a Republican complexion. Of fifty-four demonstrators on a bus from Tallahassee, Florida, forty-four identified themselves as Republican, eight as independent, and two as Libertarian.[5] Most speakers were little-known activists, but they included Senator Jim DeMint (R-S.C.) and Representatives Mike Pence (R-Ind.), Tom Price (R-Ga.), and Marsha Blackburn (R-Tenn.).

A featured speaker was former Republican majority leader Dick Armey of Texas, now president of FreedomWorks, a Washington-based political group advocating for smaller government and lower taxes.[6] In March, FreedomWorks had launched a twenty-five-city "Tea Party Tour" to oppose Obama, the Democrats, and their alleged socialist agenda.[7] (The *tea party* term derived from the colonists' 1773 act of dumping British tea into Boston harbor in protest of Britain's new tax on tea.)[8] For the 2009 protestors, TEA reportedly stood for "Taxed Enough Already."

Republican leaders were in a quandary over how to relate to these antigovernment protesters, who persisted after the summer. On December 15, some 5,000 conservatives flocked to Washington for a "Code Red Rally" promoted by talk radio host Laura Ingraham, a featured speaker.[9] Although a national poll the same month showed that half the respondents knew "very little" or "nothing at all" about the tea party movement, about 40 percent felt "somewhat" or "very" positive about it.[10]

Republican leaders welcomed the populist opposition to Democratic plans but worried about containing the new activists' anger, often directed at Republicans too. Catherina Wojtowicz, coordinator of the Chicago tea party group, said, "Personally, I'm just as fed up with the Republican Party as the Democratic Party."[11] In the 2009 special election to fill a vacancy in New York's twenty-third congressional district, tea party activists backed the Conservative Party candidate, forcing the Republican candidate to withdraw and losing the traditional Republican seat to a Democratic challenger. Better to lose the seat to a Democrat than to elect a moderate Republican, they reasoned—and vowed to field conservative candidates in the 2010 congressional elections to oppose other moderate Republicans.

Like the colonists in 1773, tea party activists in 2009 employed unconventional forms of political protest that today are constitutionally protected. Do Americans protest more or less than citizens in other countries? What other options do people have to participate in politics? How well does political protest fit with either the pluralist or majoritarian models of democracy?

In this chapter, we try to answer these and other important questions about popular participation in government. We begin by studying participation in democratic government, distinguishing between conventional forms of political participation and unconventional forms that still comply with democratic government. Then we evaluate the nature and extent of both types of participation in American politics. Next, we study the expansion of voting rights and voting as the major mechanism for mass participation in politics. Finally, we examine the extent to which the various forms of political participation serve the values of freedom, equality, and order and the majoritarian and pluralist models of democracy.

IN OUR OWN WORDS

Listen to Kenneth Janda discuss the main points and themes of this chapter.

www.cengagebrain.com/ shop/ISBN/0495906182

Democracy and Political Participation

Government ought to be run by the people. That is the democratic ideal in a nutshell. But how much and what kind of citizen participation is necessary for democratic government? Neither political theorists nor politicians, neither idealists nor realists, can agree on an answer. Champions of direct democracy believe that if citizens do not participate directly in government affairs, making government decisions themselves, they should give up all pretense of living in a democracy. More practical observers contend that people can govern indirectly, through their elected representatives. And they maintain that choosing leaders through elections—formal procedures for voting—is the only workable approach to democracy in a large, complex nation.

Elections are a necessary condition of democracy, but they do not guarantee democratic government. Before the collapse of communism, the former Soviet Union regularly held elections in which more than 90 percent of the electorate turned out to vote, but the Soviet Union certainly did not function as a democracy because there was only one political party. Both the majoritarian and pluralist models of democracy rely on voting to varying degrees, but both models expect citizens to participate in politics in other ways. For example, they expect citizens to discuss politics, form interest groups, contact public officials, campaign for political parties, run for office, and even protest government decisions.

political participation
Actions of private citizens by which they seek to influence or support government and politics.

We define **political participation** as "those activities of citizens that attempt to influence the structure of government, the selection of government officials, or the policies of government."[12] This definition embraces both conventional and unconventional forms of political participation. In plain language, *conventional behavior* is behavior that is acceptable to the dominant culture in a given situation. Wearing a swimsuit at the beach is conventional; wearing one at a formal dance is not. Displaying campaign posters in front yards is conventional; spray-painting political slogans on buildings is not.

Figuring out whether a particular political act is conventional or unconventional can be difficult. We find the following distinction useful:

- **Conventional participation** is a relatively routine behavior that uses the established institutions of representative government, especially campaigning for candidates and voting in elections.
- **Unconventional participation** is a relatively uncommon behavior that challenges or defies established institutions or the dominant culture (and thus is personally stressful to participants and their opponents).

Voting and writing letters to public officials illustrate conventional political participation; staging sit-down strikes in public buildings and chanting slogans outside officials' windows are examples of unconventional participation. Other democratic forms of participation, such as political demonstrations, can be conventional (carrying signs outside an abortion clinic) or unconventional (linking arms to prevent entrance). Various forms of unconventional participation are often used by powerless groups to gain political benefits while working within the system.[13]

Terrorism is an extreme case of unconventional political behavior. Indeed, the U.S. legal code defines **terrorism** as "premeditated, politically motivated violence perpetrated against noncombatant targets by subnational groups or clandestine agents, usually intended to influence an audience."[14] Timothy McVeigh, a decorated veteran of the 1991 Gulf War, bombed the federal building in Oklahoma City in 1995, taking 168 lives. McVeigh said he bombed the building because the federal government had become a police state hostile to gun owners, religious sects, and patriotic militia groups.[15] In 2001, al Qaeda carried out the infamous 9/11 attack on New York and Washington, D.C., killing almost 3,000 Americans and foreign nationals. In November 2009, U.S. Army Major Nidal Malik Hasan shot to death thirteen people at Fort Hood, Texas. Political goals motivated all three acts of terrorism. McVeigh acted because of domestic politics, al Qaeda and Hasan because of international politics. Although terrorist acts are political acts by definition, they do not qualify as political *participation* because terrorists do not seek to influence government but to destroy it.

Methods of unconventional political behavior, in contrast, are used by disadvantaged groups that resort to them in lieu of more conventional forms of participation used by most citizens. These groups accept government while seeking to influence it. Let us look at both unconventional and conventional political participation in the United States.

conventional participation Relatively routine political behavior that uses institutional channels and is acceptable to the dominant culture.

unconventional participation Relatively uncommon political behavior that challenges or defies established institutions and dominant norms.

terrorism Premeditated, politically motivated violence perpetrated against noncombatant targets by subnational groups or clandestine agents.

Unconventional Participation

On Sunday, March 7, 1965, a group of about six hundred people attempted to march fifty miles from Selma, Alabama, to the state capitol at Montgomery to show their support for voting rights for blacks. (At the time, Selma had fewer than five hundred registered black voters, out of fifteen thousand eligible.)[16] Alabama governor George Wallace declared the march illegal and sent state troopers to stop it. The two groups met at the Edmund Pettus Bridge over the Alabama River at the edge of Selma. The peaceful marchers were disrupted and beaten by state troopers and deputy sheriffs—some on horseback—using clubs, bullwhips, and tear gas. The day became known as Bloody Sunday.

The march from Selma was a form of unconventional political participation. Marching fifty miles in a political protest is certainly not common; moreover, the march challenged the existing institutions that prevented blacks from voting. But they had been prevented from participating conventionally—voting in elections—for many decades, and they chose this unconventional method to dramatize their cause.

The march ended in violence because Governor Wallace would not allow even this peaceful mode of unconventional expression. In contrast to demonstrations against the Vietnam War later in the 1960s, the 1965 civil rights march posed no threat of violence. The brutal response to the marchers helped the rest of the nation understand the seriousness of the civil rights problem in the South. Unconventional participation is stressful and occasionally violent, but sometimes it is worth the risk. In 2010, thousands of blacks and whites solemnly but triumphantly reenacted the march on its forty-fifth anniversary.

March for Freedom, Forty-Five Years Later

On Sunday, March 7, 2010, thousands marched across the Edmund Pettus Bridge outside Selma, Alabama, to commemorate the "Bloody Sunday" forty-five years earlier when people were beaten during a voting rights protest.

(AP Photo/Dave Martin)

Support for Unconventional Participation

Unconventional political participation has a long history in the United States.[17] The Boston Tea Party of 1773, in which American colonists dumped three cargoes of British tea into Boston Harbor, was only the first in a long line of violent protests against British rule that eventually led to revolution. Yet we know less about unconventional than conventional participation. The reasons are twofold. First, since it is easier to collect data on conventional practices, they are studied more frequently. Second, political scientists are simply biased toward institutionalized, or conventional, politics. In fact, some basic works on political participation explicitly exclude any behavior that is "outside the system."[18] One major study of unconventional political action asked people whether they had engaged in or approved of three types of political participation other than voting: signing petitions, joining boycotts, and attending demonstrations.[19] As shown in Figure 7.1, only signing petitions was clearly regarded as conventional, in the sense that the behavior was widely practiced.

The marchers in Selma, although peaceful, were surely demonstrating against the established order. If we measure conventional participation according to the proportion of people who disapprove of the act, most demonstrations border on the unconventional, involving relatively few people. The same goes for boycotting products—for example, refusing to buy lettuce or grapes picked by nonunion farm workers. Demonstrations and boycotts are problem cases in deciding what is and is not conventional political participation.

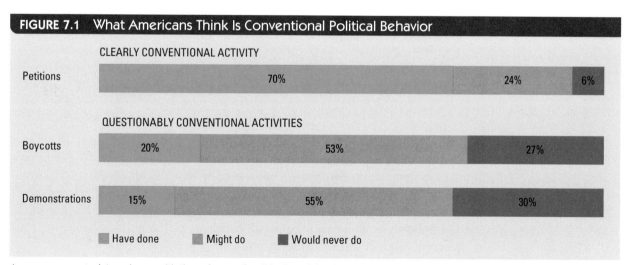

FIGURE 7.1   What Americans Think Is Conventional Political Behavior

CLEARLY CONVENTIONAL ACTIVITY

Petitions: 70% 24% 6%

QUESTIONABLY CONVENTIONAL ACTIVITIES

Boycotts: 20% 53% 27%

Demonstrations: 15% 55% 30%

■ Have done   ■ Might do   ■ Would never do

A survey presented Americans with three forms of political participation outside the electoral process and asked whether they "have done," "might do," or "would never do" any of them. The respondents approved overwhelmingly of signing petitions, which was widely done and rarely ruled out. Even attending demonstrations (a right guaranteed in the Constitution) would "never" be done by 30 percent of the respondents. Boycotting products was less objectionable and more widely practiced. According to this test, attending demonstrations and boycotting products are only marginally conventional forms of political participation in the United States.

Source: 2005–2008 World Values Survey. The World Values Survey Association, based in Stockholm, conducts representative surveys in nations across the world. See http://www.worldvaluessurvey.org.

Antiwar Protest, 1968

In August 1968, thousands of youthful antiwar protesters gathered in Chicago, where the Democrats were holding their national convention. Protests against the war had already forced President Lyndon Johnson not to seek reelection. Mayor Richard J. Daley vowed that the protesters would not disturb the impending nomination of Hubert Humphrey, Johnson's vice president. Daley's police kept the youths from demonstrating at the convention, but the resulting violence did not help Humphrey, who lost to Richard Nixon in an extremely close election. When the Democratic convention returned to Chicago in 1996, the new Mayor Daley (Richard M., the former mayor's son) faced a different situation and hosted a relatively peaceful convention.

(Bettmann/CORBIS)

Most Americans would allow public meetings for religious extremists but not for people who want to "overthrow the government."[20] When protesters demonstrating against the Vietnam War disrupted the 1968 Democratic National Convention in Chicago, they were clubbed by the city's police. Although the national television audience saw graphic footage of the confrontations and heard reporters' criticisms of the police's behavior, most viewers condemned the demonstrators, not the police.

The Effectiveness of Unconventional Participation

Vociferous antiabortion protests have discouraged many doctors from performing abortions, but they have not led to outlawing abortions. Does unconventional participation ever work (even when it provokes violence)?

Town Meetings: 1943 and 2009

The 1943 Norman Rockwell painting "Freedom of Speech" (see page 16) during the World War II era was idealized, of course. Still, it reflected civility in exercising freedom of speech that seems absent today. Consider the August 2009 photo of Democratic representative John Dingell's town hall meeting in Romulus, Michigan, to discuss health care. One wonders what reasoned ideas and insights were introduced at that discussion.

(*left*: Norman Rockwell/CORBIS; *right*: KIMBERLY P. MITCHELL/MCT/Landov)

Yes. Antiwar protesters helped convince President Lyndon Johnson not to seek reelection in 1968, and they heightened public concern about U.S. participation in the Vietnam War. American college students who disrupted campuses in the late 1960s and early 1970s helped end the military draft in 1973, and although it was not one of their stated goals, they sped passage of the Twenty-sixth Amendment, which lowered the voting age to eighteen. Ugly town hall protests and nasty Washington demonstrations against Obama's health-care plan probably contributed to public disapproval of the plan rising from 29 to 53 percent between April and December 2009.[21]

The unconventional activities of civil rights workers also produced notable successes. Dr. Martin Luther King, Jr., led the 1955 Montgomery bus boycott (prompted by Rosa Parks's refusal to surrender her seat to a white man), which sparked the civil rights movement. He used **direct action** to challenge specific cases of discrimination, assembling crowds to confront businesses and local governments and demanding equal treatment in public accommodations and government. The civil rights movement organized more than 1,000 such newsworthy demonstrations nationwide—387 in 1965 alone.[22] And like the march in Selma, many of these protests provoked violent confrontations between whites and blacks.

Denied the usual opportunities for conventional political participation, minorities used unconventional politics to pressure Congress to pass a series of civil rights laws in 1957, 1960, 1964, and 1968—each one in some way extending national protection against discrimination by reason of race,

direct action
Unconventional participation that involves assembling crowds to confront businesses and local governments to demand a hearing.

color, religion, or national origin. (The 1964 act also prohibited discrimination in employment on the basis of sex.)

In addition, the Voting Rights Act of 1965 placed some state electoral procedures under federal supervision, protecting the registration of black voters and increasing their voting rate, especially in the South, where much of the violence occurred. Black protest activity—both violent and nonviolent—has also been credited with increased welfare support for blacks in the South.[23] The civil rights movement showed that social change can occur even when it faces violent opposition at first. In 1970, fewer than fifteen hundred blacks served as elected officials in the United States. In 2006, the number was more than nine thousand, and over five thousand Hispanics held elected office.[24] In 2008, Barack Obama became the first African American to be elected President of the United States.

Although direct political action and the politics of confrontation can work, using them requires a special kind of commitment. Studies show that direct action appeals most to those who both distrust the political system and have a strong sense of political efficacy—the feeling that they can do something to affect political decisions.[25] Whether this combination of attitudes produces behavior that challenges the system depends on the extent of organized group activity. The civil rights movement of the 1960s was backed by numerous organizations across the nation.

The decision to use unconventional behavior also depends on the extent to which individuals develop a group consciousness—identification with their group and awareness of its position in society, its objectives, and its intended course of action.[26] These characteristics were present among blacks and young people in the mid-1960s and are strongly present today among blacks and, to a lesser degree, among women. Indeed, some researchers contend that black consciousness has heightened both African Americans' distrust of the political system and their sense of individual efficacy, generating more political participation by poor blacks than by poor whites.[27] The National Organization for Women (NOW) and other women's groups have also heightened women's group consciousness, which may have contributed to their increased participation in politics in both conventional and unconventional ways.

Unconventional Participation Around the World

Although most Americans disapprove of using certain forms of participation to protest government policies, U.S. citizens are about as likely to take direct action in politics as citizens of European democracies. Consider "Compared with What? Popular Participation in Politics," which shows how respondents in the United States compare with those in eight other countries on various modes of participation. Americans are just as likely as citizens of other countries to vote, sign a petition, be interested in politics, or boycott products—but they are less likely to join demonstrations. So compared with citizens in other nations, Americans are not markedly apathetic.

Is something wrong with a political system if citizens resort to unconventional—and often disapproved-of—methods of political participation? To answer this question, we must first learn how much citizens use conventional methods of participation.

Conventional Participation

A practical test of the democratic nature of any government is whether citizens can affect its policies by acting through its institutions—meeting with public officials, supporting candidates, and voting in elections. (See "Compared with What? Popular Participation in Politics.") If people must operate outside government institutions to influence policymaking, as civil rights workers had to do in the South, the system is not democratic. Citizens should not have to risk their life and property to participate in politics, and they should not have to take direct action to force the government to hear their views. The objective of democratic institutions is to make political participation conventional—to allow ordinary citizens to engage in relatively routine, nonthreatening behavior to get the government to heed their opinions, interests, and needs.

In a democracy, for a group to gather at a statehouse or city hall to dramatize its position on an issue—say, a tax increase—is not unusual. Such a demonstration is a form of conventional participation. The group is not powerless, and its members are not risking their personal safety by demonstrating. But violence can erupt between opposing groups demonstrating in a political setting, such as between pro-life and pro-choice groups. Circumstances, then, often determine whether organized protest is or is not conventional. In general, the less that the participants anticipate a threat, the more likely it is that the protest will be conventional. Town hall protests against

Compared with What?

Popular Participation in Politics

Compared with citizens in eight other nations, Americans are not noticeably apathetic when it comes to politics. Over half of American respondents report that they voted in the last election (voting overestimates are common in most countries), signed a petition, or were interested in politics. Americans are notably less likely than respondents in other countries to join demonstrations. Survey researchers have only recently begun to ask whether respondents have ever joined an Internet political forum. In the

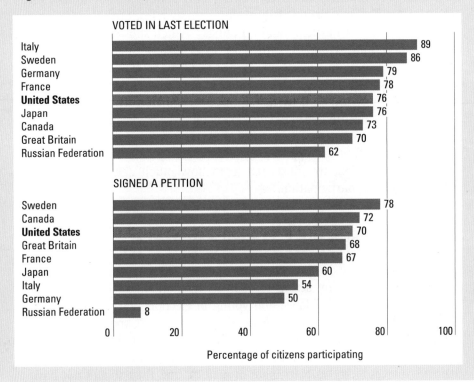

Percentage of citizens participating

health care in 2009 certainly threatened Democratic members of Congress enough for some to cancel such meetings.

Conventional political behaviors fall into two major categories: actions that show support for government policies and those that try to change or influence policies.

Supportive Behavior

supportive behavior
Action that expresses allegiance to government and country.

Supportive behavior is action that expresses allegiance to country and government. Reciting the Pledge of Allegiance and flying the American flag on holidays show support for both the country and, by implication, its political system. Such ceremonial activities usually require little effort, knowledge, or

United States, a little over 7 percent of respondents claim to have discussed politics on the Internet, which makes it a relatively infrequent act of political participation compared to these other activities.

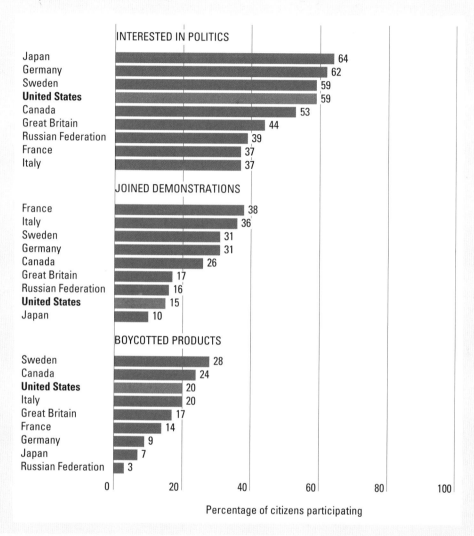

Percentage of citizens participating

personal courage; that is, they demand little initiative on the part of the citizen. The simple act of turning out to vote is in itself a show of support for the political system. Other supportive behaviors, such as serving as an election judge in a nonpartisan election or organizing a holiday parade, demand greater initiative.

At times, people's perception of patriotism moves them to cross the line between conventional and unconventional behavior. In their eagerness to support the American system, they break up a meeting or disrupt a rally of a group they believe is radical or somehow "un-American." Radical groups may threaten the political system with wrenching change, but superpatriots pose their own threat by denying to others the nonviolent means of dissent.[28]

Influencing Behavior

Citizens use **influencing behavior** to modify or even reverse government policy to serve political interests. Some forms of influencing behavior seek particular benefits from government; other forms have broad policy objectives.

Particular Benefits. Some citizens try to influence government to obtain benefits for themselves, their immediate families, or close friends. For example, citizens might pressure their alderman to rebuild the curbs on their street or vote against an increase in school taxes, especially if they have no children. Serving one's self-interest through the voting process is certainly acceptable to democratic theory. Each individual has only one vote, and no single voter can wrest particular benefits from government through voting unless a majority of the voters agrees.

Political actions that require considerable knowledge and initiative are another story. Individuals or small groups who influence government officials to advance their self-interest—for instance, to obtain a lucrative government contract—may secretly benefit without others knowing. Those who quietly obtain particular benefits from government pose a serious challenge to a democracy. Pluralist theory holds that groups ought to be able to make government respond to their special problems and needs. In contrast, majoritarian theory holds that government should not do what a majority does not want it to do. A majority of citizens might very well not want the government to do what any particular person or group seeks if it is costly to other citizens.

Citizens often ask for special services from local government. Such requests may range from contacting the city forestry department to remove a dead tree in front of a house to calling the county animal control center to deal with a vicious dog in the neighborhood. Studies of such "contacting behavior" find that it tends not to be empirically related to other forms of political activity. In other words, people who complain to city hall do not necessarily vote. Contacting behavior is related to socioeconomic status: people of higher socioeconomic status are more likely to contact public officials.[29]

Americans demand much more of their local government than of the national government. Although many people value self-reliance and individualism in national politics, most people expect local government to solve a wide range of social problems. A study of residents of Kansas City, Missouri, found that more than 90 percent thought the city had a responsibility to provide services in thirteen areas, including maintaining parks, setting standards for new home construction, demolishing vacant and unsafe buildings, ensuring that property owners clean up trash and weeds, and providing bus service. The researcher noted that "it is difficult to imagine a set of federal government activities about which there would [be] more consensus."[30] Citizens can also mobilize against a project. Dubbed the "not in my back yard," or NIMBY, phenomenon, such a mobilization occurs when citizens pressure local officials to stop undesired projects from being located near their homes.

Finally, contributing money to a candidate's campaign is another form of influencing behavior. Here, too, the objective can be particular or broad

influencing behavior
Behavior that seeks to modify or reverse government policy to serve political interests.

benefits, although determining which is which can sometimes be difficult. For example, as discussed in Chapter 9, national law limits the amount of money that an individual or organization can contribute directly to a candidate's campaign for president.

Several points emerge from this review of "particularized" forms of political participation. First, approaching government to serve one's particular interests is consistent with democratic theory because it encourages participation from an active citizenry. Second, particularized contact may be a unique form of participation, not necessarily related to other forms of participation such as voting. Third, such participation tends to be used more by citizens who are advantaged in terms of knowledge and resources. Fourth, particularized participation may serve private interests to the detriment of the majority.

Broad Policy Objectives. We come now to what many scholars have in mind when they talk about political participation: activities that influence the selection of government personnel and policies. Here, too, we find behaviors that require little initiative (such as voting) and others that require high initiative (attending political meetings, persuading others how to vote).

Even voting intended to influence government policies is a low-initiative activity. Such "policy voting" differs from voting to show support or to gain special benefits in its broader influence on the community or society. Obviously, this distinction is not sharp: citizens vote for several reasons—a mix of allegiance, particularized benefits, and policy concerns. In addition to policy voting, many other low-initiative forms of conventional participation— wearing a candidate's T-shirt, visiting a candidate's website, posting a bumper sticker—are also connected with elections. In the next section, we focus on elections as a mechanism for participation. For now, we simply note that voting to influence policy is usually a low-initiative activity. As we discuss later, it actually requires more initiative to *register* to vote in the United States than to cast a vote on election day. With a computer, it is even easier to e-mail members of Congress than to vote.

Other types of participation designed to affect broad policies require high initiative. Running for office requires the most (see Chapter 9). Some high-initiative activities, such as attending party meetings and working on campaigns, are associated with the electoral process; others, such as attending legislative hearings and writing letters to Congress, are not. Although many nonelectoral activities involve making personal contact, their objective is often to obtain government benefits for some group of people—farmers, the unemployed, children, oil producers. In fact, studies of citizen contacts in the United States show that about two-thirds deal with broad social issues and only one-third are for private gain.[31] Few people realize that using the court system is a form of political participation, a way for citizens to press for their rights in a democratic society. Although most people use the courts to serve their particular interests, some also use them, as we discuss shortly, to meet broad objectives. Going to court demands high personal initiative.[32] It also requires knowledge of the law or the financial resources to afford a lawyer.

The Twitter Revolution

After the June 2009 election in Iran, President Mahmoud Ahmadinejad was declared reelected with 62 percent of the votes—avoiding a runoff by winning more than 50 percent. Outside observers supported claims of massive voting fraud. Popular protests spread across the country, especially in Tehran, and were brutally put down. People captured the beatings on their cell phones, transmitted the images to Western media, and tweeted about the brutality. For the week of June 15–19, the tracking site TweetMeme reported that 98 percent of the links on Twitter were about Iran. Tweeting became a new form of political activity.

Source: Project for Excellence in Journalism, "140 Characters of Protest," Pew Research Center Publications, 25 June 2009, at http://pewresearch.org/pubs/1267/iran-twitter-revolution. *Image:* © Tribune Media Services, Inc. All Rights Reserved. Reprinted with permission.

class action suit
A legal action brought by a person or group on behalf of a number of people in similar circumstances.

People use the courts for both personal benefit and broad policy objectives. A person or group can bring a **class action suit** on behalf of other people in similar circumstances. Lawyers for the National Association for the Advancement of Colored People pioneered this form of litigation in the famous school desegregation case *Brown* v. *Board of Education* (1954).[33] They succeeded in getting the Supreme Court to outlaw segregation in public schools, not just for Linda Brown, who brought the suit in Topeka, Kansas, but for all others "similarly situated"—that is, for all other black students who wanted to attend desegregated schools. Participation through the courts is usually beyond the means of individual citizens, but it has proved effective for organized groups, especially those that have been unable to gain their objectives through Congress or the executive branch. Sometimes such court challenges help citizens without their knowing it. In 2009, Capital One (TV slogan: "What's in *your* wallet?") settled a class action suit over its credit cards, agreeing to drop contract language requiring customer disputes to be handled through binding arbitration instead of the legal system.[34]

Voting in Kenya

These women line up to vote in August 2010 on a referendum concerning a new constitution in Kenya that limited presidential powers and introduced a bill of rights. It was overwhelmingly approved in a peaceful election with high turnout.

(© SIGFRIED MODOLA/AFP/Getty Images)

Individual citizens can also try to influence policies at the national level by participating directly in the legislative process. One way is to attend congressional hearings, which are open to the public and are occasionally held outside Washington, D.C. Especially since the end of World War II, the national government has sought to increase citizen involvement in creating regulations and laws by making information on government activities available to interested parties. For example, government agencies are required to publish all proposed and approved regulations in the daily *Federal Register* and to make government documents available to citizens on request.

More recently, citizens have participated from their own homes, electronically. In fact, they can search the *Federal Register* online.[35] The government website USA.gov helps people find information online and offers video tutorials on standard topics. Recovery.gov was created by the Obama administration to track government spending under its 2009 economic stimulus legislation (see pages 33–34). A private site, Recovery.org, aims at the same objective, often with better results. Similarly, the private site GovTrack.us provides easier access to congressional voting records than the government site Thomas.gov.[36] Private sites also monitor more contentious issues, such as how well President Obama has kept a list of 515 campaign promises.[37] The Center for Responsible Politics covers campaign finance, lobbyists' spending, and other forms of political influence.[38] The National Institute on Money in State Politics covers similar ground for the states.[39] OMB Watch focuses on government spending and the budget deficit, while the Institute for Truth in Accounting lobbies to reduce the national debt.[40]

Using these sites, and many others, even stay-at-homes can be active citizens. Their online contribution to democracy, however, is open to question. Even before taking office, President Obama created an online "Citizen's

Briefing Book" to invite ideas to be submitted for his attention. Some 44,000 proposals were submitted and drew 1.4 million "votes" for being the best. (The idea drawing the most votes was legalizing marijuana.[41])

Conventional Participation in America

You may know someone who has testified at a congressional or administrative hearing or closely monitors governmental actions on the Internet, but the odds are that you do not. Such participation is high-initiative behavior. Relatively few people—only those with high stakes in the outcome of a decision—are willing to participate in this way. How often do Americans contact government officials and engage in other forms of conventional political participation compared with citizens in other countries?

The most common form of political behavior in most industrial democracies is voting for candidates. The rate of voting is known as **voter turnout**, the percentage of eligible voters who actually vote in a given election. Voting eligibility is hard to determine across American states, and there are different ways to estimate voter turnout.[42] However measured, voting for candidates in the United States is less common than it is in other countries, as demonstrated in "Compared with What? Voter Turnout in European and American Elections Since 1945" on page 231. When voter turnout in the United States over more than half a century is compared with historical patterns of voting in twenty-three other countries, the United States ranks at the *bottom* of the pack. This is a political paradox. On one hand, Americans are as likely as citizens in other democracies to engage in various forms of political participation. But when it comes to voting, the hand that casts the ballot, Americans rank dead last.

Other researchers noted this paradox and wrote, "If, for example, we concentrate our attention on national elections we will find that the United States is the least participatory of almost all other nations." But looking at the other indicators, they found that "political apathy, by a wide margin, is lowest in the United States. Interestingly, the high levels of overall involvement reflect a rather balanced contribution of both ... conventional and unconventional politics."[43] Clearly, low voter turnout in the United States constitutes a puzzle, to which we will return.

Participating Through Voting

The heart of democratic government lies in the electoral process. Whether a country holds elections—and if so, what kind—constitutes the critical difference between democratic and nondemocratic governments. Elections institutionalize mass participation in democratic government according to the three normative principles of procedural democracy discussed in Chapter 2: electoral rules specify *who* is allowed to vote, *how much* each person's vote counts, and *how many* votes are needed to win.

Again, elections are formal procedures for making group decisions. *Voting* is the act individuals engage in when they choose among alternatives in an election. **Suffrage** and **franchise** both mean the right to vote. By formalizing

voter turnout
The percentage of eligible citizens who actually vote in a given election.

suffrage
The right to vote. Also called the *franchise*.

franchise
The right to vote. Also called *suffrage*.

political participation through rules for suffrage and for counting ballots, electoral systems allow large numbers of people, who individually have little political power, to wield great power. Electoral systems decide collectively who governs and, in some instances, what government should do.

The simple act of holding elections is less important than the specific rules and circumstances that govern voting. According to democratic theory, everyone should be able to vote. In practice, however, no nation grants universal suffrage. All countries have age requirements for voting, and all disqualify some inhabitants on various grounds: lack of citizenship, criminal record, mental incompetence, and others. What is the record of enfranchisement in the United States?

Expansion of Suffrage

The United States was the first country to provide for general elections of representatives through "mass" suffrage, but the franchise was far from universal. When the Constitution was framed, the idea of full adult suffrage was too radical to consider seriously. Instead, the framers left the issue of enfranchisement to the states, stipulating only that individuals who could vote for "the most numerous Branch of the State Legislature" could also vote for their representatives to the U.S. Congress (Article I, Section 2).

Initially, most states established taxpaying or property-holding requirements for voting. Virginia, for example, required ownership of twenty-five acres of settled land or five hundred acres of unsettled land. The original thirteen states began to lift such requirements after 1800. Expansion of the franchise accelerated after 1815, with the admission of new "western" states (Indiana, Illinois, Alabama), where land was more plentiful and widely owned. By the 1850s, the states had eliminated almost all taxpaying and property-holding requirements, thus allowing the working class—at least its white male members—to vote. Extending the vote to blacks and women took longer.

The Enfranchisement of Blacks.
The Fifteenth Amendment, adopted shortly after the Civil War, prohibited the states from denying the right to vote "on account of race, color, or previous condition of servitude." However, the states of the old Confederacy worked around the amendment by reestablishing old voting requirements (poll taxes, literacy tests) that worked primarily against blacks. Some southern states also cut blacks out of politics through a cunning circumvention of the amendment. Because the amendment said nothing about voting rights in private organizations, these states denied blacks the right to vote in the "private" Democratic *primary* elections held to choose the party's candidates for the general election. Because the Democratic Party came to dominate politics in the South, the "white primary" effectively disenfranchised blacks, despite the Fifteenth Amendment. Finally, in many areas of the South, the threat of violence kept blacks from the polls.

The extension of full voting rights to blacks came in two phases, separated by twenty years. In 1944, the Supreme Court decided in *Smith* v. *Allwright* that laws preventing blacks from voting in primary elections were

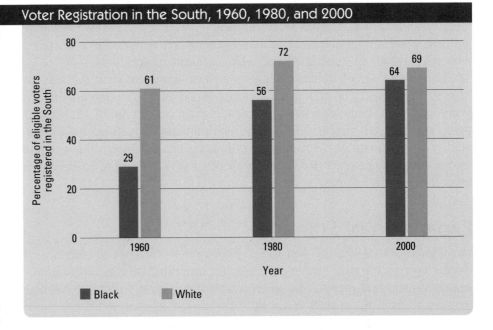

| FIGURE 7.2 | Voter Registration in the South, 1960, 1980, and 2000 |

As a result of the Voting Rights Act of 1965 and other national actions, black voter registration in the eleven states of the old Confederacy nearly doubled between 1960 and 1980. In 2000, there was very little difference between the voting registration rates of white and black voters in the Deep South.

Sources: Data for 1960 and 1980 are from U.S. Bureau of the Census, *Statistical Abstract of the United States, 1982–1983* (Washington, D.C.: U.S. Government Printing Office, 1983), p. 488; data for 2000 come from the U.S. Census Bureau, *Current Population Report*, P20–542, Table 3, Internet release, 27 February 2002.

unconstitutional, holding that party primaries are part of the continuous process of electing public officials.[44] The Voting Rights Act of 1965, which followed Selma's Bloody Sunday by less than five months, suspended discriminatory voting tests. It also authorized federal registrars to register voters in seven southern states, where less than half of the voting-age population had registered to vote in the 1964 election. For good measure, the Supreme Court ruled in 1966 in *Harper* v. *Virginia State Board of Elections* that state poll taxes are unconstitutional.[45] Although long in coming, these actions by the national government to enforce political equality in the states dramatically increased the registration of southern blacks (see Figure 7.2).

The Enfranchisement of Women. The enfranchisement of women in the United States is a less sordid story than enfranchisement of blacks but still nothing to be proud of. Women had to fight long and hard to win the right to vote. Until 1869, women could not vote anywhere in the world.[46] American women began to organize to obtain suffrage in the mid-1800s. Known then as *suffragettes*, the early feminists initially had a limited effect on politics.* Their first major victory did not come until 1869, when Wyoming, still a territory, granted women the right to vote. No state followed suit until 1893, when Colorado enfranchised women.

In the meantime, the suffragettes became more active. In 1884, they formed the Equal Rights Party and nominated Belva A. Lockwood, a lawyer

---

*The term *suffragist* applied to a person of either sex who advocated extending the vote to women, while *suffragette* was reserved primarily for women who did so militantly.

The Fight for Women's Suffrage ... and Against It

Militant suffragettes demonstrated outside the White House prior to ratification of the Nineteenth Amendment to the Constitution, which gave women the right to vote. Congress passed the proposed amendment in 1919, and it was ratified by the required number of states in time for the 1920 presidential election. Suffragettes' demonstrations were occasionally disrupted by men—and other women—who opposed extending the right to vote to women.

(Library of Congress)

(who could not herself vote), as the first woman candidate for president.[47] Between 1896 and 1918, twelve other states gave women the vote. Most of these states were in the West, where pioneer women often departed from traditional women's roles. Nationally, the women's suffrage movement intensified, often resorting to unconventional political behaviors (marches, demonstrations), which occasionally invited violent attacks from men and even other women. In 1919, Congress finally passed the Nineteenth Amendment, which prohibits states from denying the right to vote "on account of sex." The amendment was ratified in 1920, in time for the November election. A survey of Chicago voters in 1923 found that 75 percent of the men voted in the presidential election but only 46 percent of the women. Among women nonvoters, 11 percent cited "disbelief in woman's voting"; less than 2 percent cited "objection from husband."[48]

Evaluating the Expansion of Suffrage in America. The last major expansion of suffrage in the United States took place in 1971, when the Twenty-sixth Amendment lowered the voting age to eighteen. For most of its history, the United States has been far from the democratic ideal of universal suffrage. The United States initially restricted voting rights to white male taxpayers or property owners, and wealth requirements lasted until the 1850s. Through demonstrations and a constitutional amendment, women won the franchise only two decades before World War II. Through civil war, constitutional amendments, court actions, massive demonstrations, and congressional action, blacks finally achieved full voting rights only two decades after World War II. Our record has more than a few blemishes.

But compared with other countries, the United States looks pretty democratic.[49] Women did not gain the vote on equal terms with men until 1921 in Norway; 1922 in the Netherlands; 1944 in France; 1946 in Italy, Japan, and Venezuela; 1948 in Belgium; and 1971 in Switzerland. Women are still not universally enfranchised. Among the Arab monarchies, Kuwait granted full voting rights to women in 2005. Saudi Arabia did not allow women to participate in the limited municipal elections of 2005, the first there since 1960. Of course, no one at all can vote in the United Arab Emirates. In South Africa, blacks, who outnumber whites by more than four to one, were not allowed to vote freely in elections until 1994. With regard to voting age, 158 of 201 countries (almost 80 percent) allow eighteen-year-olds to vote. Another 34 countries set the minimum age at twenty or twenty-one. Fewer than a dozen allow persons under age eighteen to vote—including Austria, which allows voting at sixteen.[50]

When judged against the rest of the world, the United States, which originated mass participation in government through elections, has as good a record of providing for political equality in voting rights as other democracies and a better record than many others.

Voting on Policies

Disenfranchised groups have struggled to gain voting rights because of the political power that comes with suffrage. Belief in the ability of ordinary citizens to make political decisions and to control government through the power of the ballot box was strongest in the United States during the Progressive era, which began around 1900 and lasted until about 1925. **Progressivism** was a philosophy of political reform that trusted the goodness and wisdom of individual citizens and distrusted "special interests" (railroads, corporations) and political institutions (traditional political parties, legislatures). Although the current "tea party" movement also distrusts political institutions, its followers denounce progressivism, which they see as "national, unlimited government and the re-distribution of wealth."[51] However, their view does not match with progressivism's history.

The leaders of the Progressive movement were prominent politicians (former president Theodore Roosevelt, Senator Robert La Follette of Wisconsin) and eminent scholars (historian Frederick Jackson Turner, philosopher John Dewey). Not content to vote for candidates chosen by party leaders, the Progressives championed the **direct primary**—a preliminary election, run by the state governments, in which the voters choose the party's candidates for the general election. Wanting a mechanism to remove elected candidates from office, the Progressives backed the **recall**, a special election initiated by a petition signed by a specified number of voters. Although about twenty states provide for recall elections, this device is rarely used. Only a few statewide elected officials have actually been unseated through recall.[52] Indeed, only one state governor had ever been unseated until 2003, when California voters threw out Governor Gray Davis in a bizarre recall election that placed movie actor Arnold Schwarzenegger in the governor's mansion.

progressivism
A philosophy of political reform based on the goodness and wisdom of the individual citizen as opposed to special interests and political institutions.

direct primary
A preliminary election, run by the state government, in which the voters choose each party's candidates for the general election.

recall
The process for removing an elected official from office.

The Progressives also championed the power of the masses to propose and pass laws, approximating citizen participation in policymaking that is the hallmark of direct democracy.[53] They developed two voting mechanisms for policymaking that are still in use:

- A **referendum** is a direct vote by the people on either a proposed law or an amendment to a state constitution. The measures subject to popular vote are known as *propositions*. Twenty-four states permit popular referenda on laws, and all but Delaware require a referendum for a constitutional amendment. Most referenda are placed on the ballot by legislatures, not voters.
- The **initiative** is a procedure by which voters can propose a measure to be decided by the legislature or by the people in a referendum. The procedure involves gathering a specified number of signatures from registered voters (usually 5 to 10 percent of the total in the state) and then submitting the petition to a designated state agency. Twenty-four states provide for some form of voter initiative.

Figure 7.3 shows the West's affinity for these democratic mechanisms. Over three hundred propositions have appeared on state ballots in general elections since 2000. In 2007, six states decided the outcome of thirty-four propositions. Of these, citizens placed four on the ballot; the others were placed on the ballot by state legislatures.[54] Voters in Texas approved billions of dollars in spending for cancer research and highway improvement projects. Voters in New Jersey rejected spending for stem cell research. While most propositions concern taxes and spending, others have addressed social issues. As of 2009, thirty-one state-wide votes occurred on the issue of same-sex marriages, and thirty states (except in Arizona) voted to define marriage as a union of a man and a woman.[55]

At times, many politicians oppose the initiatives that citizens propose and approve. This was true, for example, of term limits. A referendum can also work to the advantage of politicians, freeing them from taking sides on a hot issue. In 1998, for example, voters in Maine repealed a state law that barred discrimination against gays and lesbians in employment, housing, and public accommodations. In so doing, it became the first state to repeal a gay rights law.[56]

What conclusion can we draw about the Progressives' legacy of mechanisms for direct participation in government? One seasoned journalist paints an unimpressive picture. He notes that an expensive "industry" developed in the 1980s that makes money circulating petitions and then managing the large sums of money needed to run a campaign to approve (or defeat) a referendum. In 1998, opponents of a measure to allow casino gambling on Native American land in California spent $25.8 million. This huge sum, however, pales in comparison to the $66.2 million spent during the campaign by the tribes that supported the measure. The initiative passed.[57]

Clearly, citizens can exercise great power over government policy through the mechanisms of the initiative and the referendum. What is not clear is whether these forms of direct democracy improve on the policies made by elected representatives.[58] However, recent research has shown that—especially in midterm elections, which are characterized by low turnout—ballot measures

referendum
An election on a policy issue.

initiative
A procedure by which voters can propose an issue to be decided by the legislature or by the people in a referendum. It requires gathering a specified number of signatures and submitting a petition to a designated agency.

FIGURE 7.3 Westward Ho!

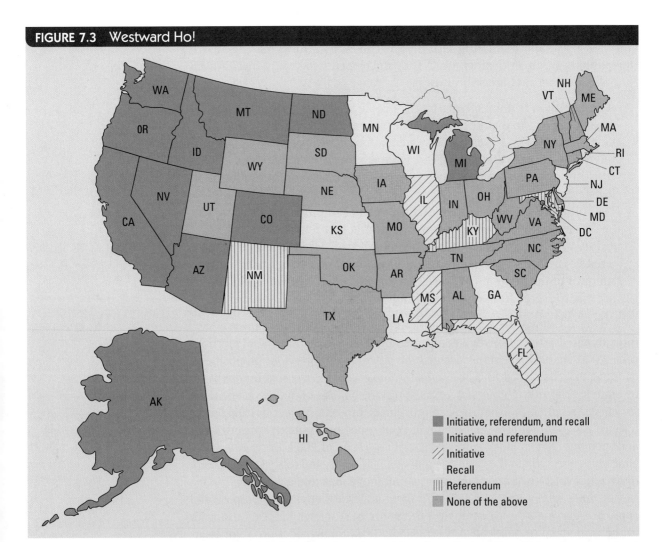

This map shows quite clearly the western basis of the initiative, referendum, and recall mechanisms intended to place government power directly in the hands of the people. Advocates of "direct legislation" sought to bypass entrenched powers in state legislatures. Established groups and parties in the East dismissed them as radicals and cranks, but they gained the support of farmers and miners in the Midwest and West. The Progressive forces usually aligned with Democrats in western state legislatures to enact their proposals, often against Republican opposition.

Source: National Conference on State Legislatures, http://www.ncsl.org/programs/legismgt/elect/irstates.htm.

tend to increase voting turnout, knowledge of issues, and campaign contributions to interest groups.[59]

If the Internet had been around during their era, Progressives certainly would have endorsed it as a mechanism of direct democracy. At an elementary level, the Internet allows ordinary citizens who seek to initiate legislation to collect on petitions the thousands of signatures needed to place the proposal on the ballot.[60] At a more advanced level, the Internet encourages much closer connections between citizens and their elected and appointed government officials, as more government agencies go online. A 2008 survey of government websites found 1,476 at the state level, 48 at the national level, and 13 for federal courts.[61] Governments, especially state governments, also tweet. In early January 2010, the website govlive.com/tweets reported 69,317 tweets from 542 agencies.

Voting for Candidates

We have saved for last the most visible form of political participation: voting to choose candidates for public office. Voting for candidates serves democratic government in two ways. First, citizens can choose the candidates they think will best serve their interests. If citizens choose candidates who are "like themselves" in personal traits or party affiliation, elected officials should tend to think as their constituents do on political issues and automatically reflect the majority's views when making public policy.

Second, voting allows the people to reelect the officials they guessed right about and to kick out those they guessed wrong about. This function is very different from the first. It makes public officials accountable for their behavior through the reward-and-punishment mechanism of elections. It assumes that officeholders are motivated to respond to public opinion by the threat of electoral defeat. It also assumes that the voters know what politicians are doing while they are in office and participate actively in the electoral process. We look at the factors that underlie voting choice in Chapter 9. Here, we examine Americans' reliance on the electoral process.

In national politics, voters seem content to elect just two executive officers—the president and vice president—and to trust the president to appoint a cabinet to round out his administration. But at the state and local levels, voters insist on selecting all kinds of officials. Every state elects a governor (and forty-five elect a lieutenant governor). Forty-two elect an attorney general; thirty-nine, a treasurer; and thirty-seven, a secretary of state. The list goes on, down through superintendents of schools, secretaries of agriculture, comptrollers, boards of education, and public utilities commissioners. Elected county officials commonly include commissioners, a sheriff, a treasurer, a clerk, a superintendent of schools, and a judge (often several). At the local level, voters elect all but about 600 of 15,300 school boards across the nation.[62] Instead of trusting state and local chief executives to appoint lesser administrators (as we do for more important offices at the national level), we expect voters to choose intelligently among scores of candidates they meet for the first time on a complex ballot in the polling booth.

Around the world, the number of countries holding regular, free, and fair elections has been rising (see "Politics of Global Change: The Growth of Electoral Democracy"). In the American version of democracy, our laws recognize no limit to voters' ability to make informed choices among candidates and thus to control government through voting. The reasoning seems to be that elections are good; therefore, more elections are better, and the most elections are best. By this thinking, the United States clearly has the best and most democratic government in the world because it is the undisputed champion at holding elections. The author of a study that compared elections in the United States with elections in twenty-six other democracies concluded:

Politics of Global Change

The Growth of Electoral Democracy

Social scientist Larry Diamond says an electoral democracy exists if its citizens "can choose and replace their leaders in regular, free, and fair elections." Using data from Freedom House, he tallied the growth of electoral democracies since 1974. The lines can be analyzed in three stages: (1) the period from 1974 to 1989 represents a "third wave" of democratization (the others were in 1828–1926 and 1943–1962) caused by social modernization and international influences; (2) the boom from 1989 to 1994 was sparked by the collapse of communism; and (3) a plateau was reached after 1995.

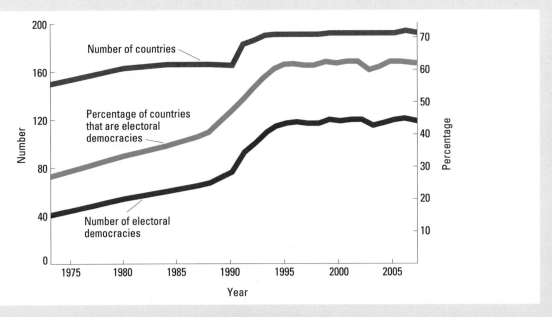

Sources: See Larry Diamond, *The Spirit of Democracy* (New York: Times Books, 2008), p. 22 and Appendix, Table 2. Freedom House supplied the data for 2007–2009.

No country can approach the United States in the frequency and variety of elections, and thus in the amount of electoral participation to which its citizens have a right. No other country elects its lower house as often as every two years, or its president as frequently as every four years. No other country popularly elects its state governors and town mayors; no other has as wide a variety of nonrepresentative offices (judges, sheriffs, attorneys general, city treasurers, and so on) subject to election.... The average American is entitled to do far more electing—probably by a factor of three or four—than the citizen of any other democracy.[63]

Compared with What?

Voter Turnout in European and American Elections 1945–2008

Compared with turnout rates in sixteen established European nations, voter turnout for American presidential elections ranks at the bottom, and turnout for American congressional elections ranks even lower. The European data show the mean percentages of the registered electorate voting in all 292 parliamentary elections from 1945 through 2008. The American data for all 31 presidential and congressional elections from 1946 to 2008 show voters as percentages of the eligible voting-age population (those eighteen and older, excluding noncitizens and ineligible felons). Turnout in U.S. elections tends to average about fifteen points higher in presidential years than in congressional years. As discussed in the text, low turnout in the United States is partly due to requiring voters to register on their own initiative. The governments in virtually all the other nations automatically register eligible citizens as voters. Note also that the United States has held more elections during that period than any other country.

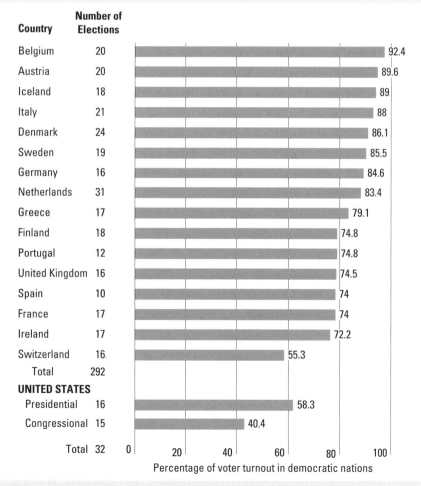

Country	Number of Elections	Percentage
Belgium	20	92.4
Austria	20	89.6
Iceland	18	89
Italy	21	88
Denmark	24	86.1
Sweden	19	85.5
Germany	16	84.6
Netherlands	31	83.4
Greece	17	79.1
Finland	18	74.8
Portugal	12	74.8
United Kingdom	16	74.5
Spain	10	74
France	17	74
Ireland	17	72.2
Switzerland	16	55.3
Total	292	
UNITED STATES		
Presidential	16	58.3
Congressional	15	40.4
Total	32	

Percentage of voter turnout in democratic nations

Source: International IDEA, "Voter Turnout," at http://idea.int/vt/index.cfm.

However, we learn from "Compared with What? Voter Turnout in European and American Elections Since 1945" that the United States ranks at the bottom of fifteen European countries in voter turnout in national elections. How do we square low voter turnout with Americans' devotion to elections as an instrument of democratic government? To complicate matters further, how do we square low voter turnout with the fact that Americans seem to participate in politics in various other ways?

Explaining Political Participation

As explained, political participation can be unconventional or conventional, can require little or much initiative, and can serve to support the government or influence its decisions. Researchers have found that people who take part in some form of political behavior often do not take part in others. For example, citizens who contact public officials to obtain special benefits may not vote regularly, participate in campaigns, or even contact officials about broader social issues. In fact, because particularized contacting serves individual rather than public interests, it is not even considered political behavior by some people.

This section examines some factors that affect the more obvious forms of political participation, with particular emphasis on voting. The first task is to determine how much patterns of participation vary within the United States over time.

Patterns of Participation over Time

Did Americans become more politically apathetic in the 2000s than they were in the 1960s? Generally not, as plots of several measures of participation from 1952 through 2008 show little variation over time in the percentage of citizens who were interested in election campaigns, talked to others about voting, worked for candidates, or attended party meetings. The only substantial dip in participation occurred in voter turnout during the 1970s and 1980s. Turnout did increase to 1960s levels in 2004 and 2008, but even then voter turnout was much lower than in most European countries. Not only is voter turnout in the United States relatively low, but turnout over two decades has decreased while other forms of participation have remained stable or even increased. What is going on? Who votes? Who does not? Why? And does it really matter?

The Standard Socioeconomic Explanation

Researchers have found that socioeconomic status is a good indicator of most types of conventional political participation. People with more education, higher incomes, and white-collar or professional occupations tend to be more aware of the effect of politics on their lives, to know what can be done to influence government actions, and to have the necessary resources (time and money) to take action. So they are more likely to participate in politics than are people of lower socioeconomic status. This relationship between socioeconomic status and conventional political involvement is called the **standard socioeconomic model** of participation.[64]

Unconventional political behavior is related to socioeconomic status, and in much the same way. Those who protest against U.S. government policies tend to be better educated. Moreover, this relationship holds in other countries too. One scholar notes: "Protest in advanced industrial democracies is not simply an outlet for the alienated and deprived; just the opposite often occurs."[65] In one major way, however, those who engage in unconventional political behavior differ from those who participate more conventionally: protesters tend to be younger.

Obviously, socioeconomic status does not account for all the differences in the ways people choose to participate in politics, even for conventional participation. Another important variable is age. Younger people are more likely to take part in demonstrations or boycotts and less likely to participate in conventional politics.[66] Younger people engage in more voluntary and charitable activities, but older Americans are more likely to vote, identify with the major political parties, and contact public officials.[67] Voting rates tend to increase as people grow older, until about age sixty-five, when physical infirmities begin to lower rates again.[68]

Two other variables—race and gender—have been related to participation in the past, but as times have changed, so have those relationships. Blacks, who had very low participation rates in the 1950s, now participate at rates comparable to whites when differences in socioeconomic status are taken into account.[69] Women also exhibited low participation rates in the past, but gender differences in political participation have virtually disappeared.[70] (The one exception is in attempting to persuade others how to vote, which women are less likely to do than men.)[71] Recent research on the social context of voting behavior has shown that married men and women are more likely to vote than those of either sex living without a spouse.[72]

Of all the social and economic variables, education is the strongest single factor in explaining most types of conventional political participation. A major study on civic participation details the impact of education:

> It affects the acquisition of skills; it channels opportunities for high levels of income and occupation; it places individuals in institutional settings where they can be recruited to political activity; and it fosters psychological and cognitive engagement with politics.[73]

Figure 7.4 shows the striking relationship between level of formal education and various types of conventional political behavior. The strong link between education and electoral participation raises questions about low voter turnout in the United States, both over time and relative to other democracies. The fact is that the proportion of individuals with college degrees is greater in the United States than in other countries. Moreover, that proportion has been increasing steadily. Why, then, is voter turnout in elections so low? And why has it been dropping over time?

standard socioeconomic model
A relationship between socioeconomic status and conventional political involvement: people with higher status and more education are more likely to participate than those with lower status.

FIGURE 7.4	Effects of Education on Political Participation

Education has a powerful effect on political participation in the United States. These data from a 2008 sample show that level of education is directly related to five different forms of conventional political participation. (Respondents tend to overstate whether they voted.)

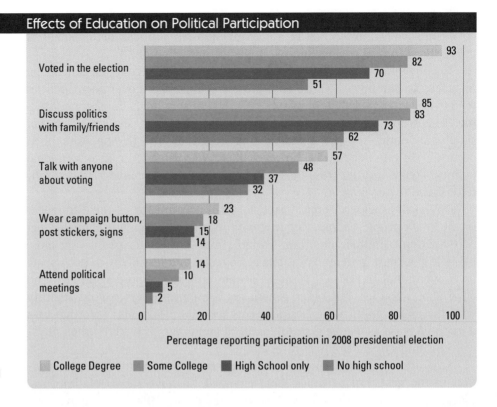

Percentage reporting participation in 2008 presidential election

■ College Degree   ■ Some College   ■ High School only   ■ No high school

Source: This analysis was based on the 2008 American National Election Time Series Study (Ann Arbor, Mich., and Palo Alto, Calif.: University of Michigan and Stanford University).

Low Voter Turnout in America

Economists wonder why people vote at all. In economic models of rational behavior, individuals avoid actions that have no payoff, and elections are rarely so close that an individual voter decides an outcome.[74] In contrast, political scientists wonder why citizens fail to vote. Voting is a low-initiative form of participation that can satisfy all three motives for political participation: showing allegiance to the nation, obtaining particularized benefits, and influencing broad policy. How then do we explain the decline in voter turnout in the United States?

The Decline in Voting over Time. The graph of voter turnout in Figure 7.5 shows that turnout in presidential elections was higher in the 1950s and 1960s than in the 1970s, 1980s, and 1990s, but it increased somewhat in 2004 and 2008.[75] The downward trend began with a sizable drop between the 1968 and 1972 elections. During this period (in 1971, actually) Congress proposed and the states ratified the Twenty-sixth Amendment, which expanded the electorate by lowering the voting age from twenty-one to eighteen. Because people younger than twenty-one are much less likely to vote, their eligibility actually reduced the overall national turnout rate (the percentage of those eligible to vote who actually vote). Although young nonvoters inevitably vote more often as they grow up, observers estimate that the enfranchisement of eighteen-year-olds accounts for about one or two percentage points in the total decline in turnout since 1952. Nevertheless, that still leaves more than ten percentage points to be explained in the lower rates since 1972.[76]

Voter turnout has declined in most established democracies since the 1980s, but not as much as in the United States. Given that educational levels are increasing virtually everywhere, the puzzle is why turnout has decreased instead of increased. Many researchers have tried to solve this puzzle.[77] Some attribute most of the decline to changes in voters' attitudes toward politics: beliefs that government is no longer responsive to citizens, that politicians are too packaged, that campaigns are too long.[78] Another is a change in attitude toward political parties, along with a decline in the extent to which citizens identify with a political party (a topic we discuss in Chapter 8).[79] According to these psychological explanations, voter turnout in the United States is not likely to increase until the government does something to restore people's faith in the effectiveness of voting—with or without political parties.

According to the age explanation, turnout in the United States is destined to remain a percentage point or two below its highs of the 1960s because of the lower voting rate of citizens younger than twenty-one. Turnout rates do increase as young people age, which suggests that voting is habit forming.[80] To increase turnout of young people, an organization called Rock the Vote was formed in 1990 within the recording industry (later incorporating the entertainment and sports communities) to mobilize young people "to create positive social and political change in their lives and communities" and "to increase youth voter turnout."[81] In 2004, almost 49 percent of those eighteen to twenty-nine years old turned out to vote.[82] In 2008, the Obama campaign made a special appeal to young voters, and youth voter turnout increased. In fact, about 62 percent of eligible voters of all ages turned out to vote, matching the high turnout rates of presidential elections in the 1960s.[83]

U.S. Turnout Versus Turnout in Other Countries. Scholars cite two factors to explain the low voter turnout in the United States compared with that in other countries. First are the differences in voting laws and administrative machinery. In a few countries, voting is compulsory, and obviously turnout is extremely high. But other methods can encourage voting: declaring election days to be public holidays or providing a two-day voting period. In 1845, Congress set election day for the first Tuesday after the first Monday in November, but a reform group—called "Why Tuesday?"—is asking Congress to change election day to a weekend.[84]

Furthermore, nearly every other democratic country places the burden of registration on the government rather than on the individual voter. This is important. Voting in the United States is a two-stage process, and the first stage (going to the proper officials to register) has required more initiative than the second stage (going to the polling booth to cast a ballot). In most American states, the registration process has been separate from the voting process in terms of both time (usually voters had to register weeks in advance of an election) and geography (often voters had to register at the county courthouse, not their polling place).[85] The nine states that do allow citizens to register and vote on the same day have consistently higher voter participation rates.[86] Turnout is higher

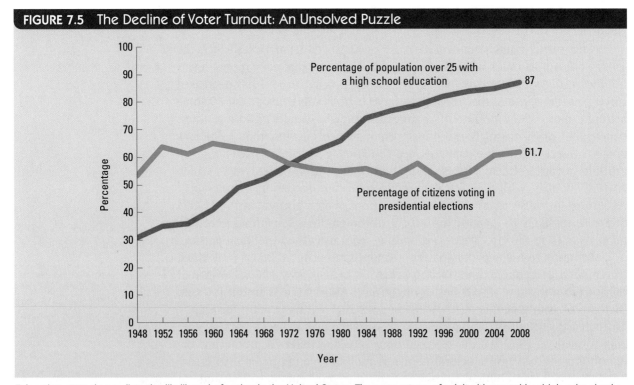

FIGURE 7.5   The Decline of Voter Turnout: An Unsolved Puzzle

Education strongly predicts the likelihood of voting in the United States. The percentage of adult citizens with a high school education or more has grown steadily since the end of World War II, but the overall rate of voter turnout trended downward from 1960 to 1996 and is still below the levels two decades after the war. Why turnout decreased as education increased is an unsolved puzzle in American voting behavior.

Sources: U.S. Census Bureau, *Statistical Abstract 1962* and *Statistical Abstract 2010*, "Table A-1. Years of School Completed by People 25 Years and Over, by Age and Sex: Selected Years 1940 to 2008," at http://www.census.gov/population/www/socdemo/educ-attn.html; Harold W. Stanley and Richard G. Niemi, *Vital Statistics on American Politics, 2009–2010* (Washington, D.C.: CQ Press, 2009), Table 1.1. The percentage voting in elections is based on the eligible voter population, not the voting-age population.

in Oregon, where everyone votes by mail.[87] No state votes by Internet, yet. In 2009, the city of Honolulu claimed to hold the first all-digital election—voting online or by phone—but it involved only about 115,000 voters.[88]

Regardless of voting ease, registration procedures for eligibility often are obscure, requiring potential voters to call around to find out what to do. People who move (and younger people move more frequently) have to reregister. In short, although voting requires little initiative, registration usually has required high initiative. If we compute voter turnout on the basis of those who are registered to vote, about 80 percent of Americans vote, a figure that moves the United States to the middle (but not the top) of all democratic nations.[89]

To increase turnout, Congress in 1993 passed the so-called motor-voter law, which aimed to increase voter registration by requiring states to permit registration by mail and when obtaining or renewing a driver's license and by encouraging registration at other facilities, such as public assistance agencies. By the 1997–1998 election cycle, over half of all voter registration took place through motor vehicle agencies and other agencies specified in the motor-voter law. Although registration rose to its highest level for a congressional election since 1970, the voting rate in 1998 declined by almost 2.4 percent below the comparable 1994 election.[90] A 2009 study showed that half of all voters are unaware that they can register at motor vehicle offices.[91]

Besides burdensome registration procedures, another factor usually cited to explain low turnout in American elections is the lack of political parties that mobilize the vote of particular social groups, especially lower-income and less educated people.[92] American parties do make an effort to get out the vote, but neither party is as closely linked to specific groups as are parties in many other countries, where certain parties work hand in hand with specific ethnic, occupational, or religious groups. Research shows that strong party–group links can significantly increase turnout.[93] One important study claims that "changing mobilization patterns by parties, campaigns, and social movements accounts for at least half of the decline in electoral participation since the 1960s."[94]

Other research suggests that although well-funded, vigorous campaigns mobilize citizens to vote, the effect depends on the type of citizens, the nature of the election, and (yes) the weather.[95] Highly educated, low-income citizens are more likely to be stimulated to vote than are less educated, high-income citizens, but lower-class citizens can be more easily mobilized to vote in presidential elections than in nonpresidential elections.[96] Some thought that the Internet would invite new classes of people to participate in politics, but well-educated and high-income people are even more apt to participate online.[97] Citizens are more likely to turn out to vote when the elections are competitive or close.[98] One study observed that college students' decision to register and vote in their home state or in their college state depended in part on which had the more competitive races.[99]

To these explanations for low voter turnout in the United States—the traditional burden of registration and the lack of strong party–group links—we add another. Although the act of voting requires low initiative, the process of learning about the scores of candidates on the ballot in American elections requires a great deal of initiative. Some people undoubtedly fail to vote simply because they feel inadequate to the task of deciding among candidates for the many offices on the ballot in U.S. elections.

Teachers, newspaper columnists, and public affairs groups tend to worry a great deal about low voter turnout in the United States, suggesting that it signifies some sort of political sickness—or at least that it gives us a bad mark for democracy. Some others who study elections closely seem less concerned.[100] One scholar argues:

> Turnout rates do not indicate the amount of electing—the frequency ...,
> the range of offices and decisions, the "value" of the vote—to which
> a country's citizens are entitled.... Thus, although the turnout rate in
> the United States is below that of most other democracies, American
> citizens do not necessarily do less voting than other citizens; most
> probably, they do more.[101]

Despite such words of assurance, the nagging thought remains that turnout ought to be higher, so various organizations mount get-out-the-vote campaigns before elections. Civic leaders often back the campaigns because they value voting for its contribution to political order.

Participation and Freedom, Equality, and Order

As we have seen, Americans do participate in government in various ways and to a reasonable extent, compared with citizens of other countries. What is the relationship of political participation to the values of freedom, equality, and order?

Participation and Freedom

From the standpoint of normative theory, the relationship between participation and freedom is clear. Individuals should be free to participate in government and politics in the way they want and as much as they want. And they should be free not to participate as well. Ideally, all barriers to participation (such as restrictive voting registration and limitations on campaign expenditures) should be abolished, as should any schemes for compulsory voting. According to the normative perspective, we should not worry about low voter turnout because citizens should have the freedom not to vote as well as to vote.

In theory, freedom to participate also means that individuals should be able to use their wealth, connections, knowledge, organizational power (including sheer numbers in organized protests), or any other resource to influence government decisions, provided they do so legally. Of all these resources, the individual vote may be the weakest—and the least important—means of exerting political influence. Obviously, then, freedom as a value in political participation favors those with the resources to advance their own political self-interest.

Participation and Equality

The relationship between participation and equality is also clear. Each citizen's ability to influence government should be equal to that of every other citizen, so that differences in personal resources do not work against the poor or the otherwise disadvantaged.[102] Elections, then, serve the ideal of equality better than any other means of political participation. Formal rules for counting ballots—in particular, one person, one vote—cancel differences in resources among individuals.

At the same time, groups of people who have few resources individually can combine their votes to wield political power. Various European ethnic groups exercised this type of power in the late nineteenth and early twentieth centuries, when their votes won them entry to the sociopolitical system and allowed them to share in its benefits. More recently, blacks, Hispanics, homosexuals, and those with disabilities have used their voting power to gain political recognition. However, minorities often have had to use unconventional forms of participation to win the right to vote. As two major scholars of political participation put it, "Protest is the great equalizer, the political action that weights intensity as well as sheer numbers."[103]

Participation and Order

The relationship between participation and order is complicated. Some types of participation (pledging allegiance, voting) promote order and so are encouraged by those who value order; other types promote disorder and so are discouraged. Many citizens—men and women alike—even resisted giving women the right to vote for fear of upsetting the social order by altering the traditional roles of men and women.

Both conventional and unconventional participation can lead to the ouster of government officials, but the regime—the political system itself—is threatened more by unconventional participation. To maintain order, the government has a stake in converting unconventional participation to conventional participation whenever possible. We can easily imagine this tactic being used by authoritarian governments, but democratic governments also use it. According to documents obtained after September 11, 2001, the FBI not only increased surveillance of groups with suspected ties to foreign terrorists but also began monitoring other groups that protested public policies.[104]

Popular protests can spread beyond original targets. Think about student unrest on college campuses during the Vietnam War. In private and public colleges alike, thousands of students stopped traffic, occupied buildings, destroyed property, boycotted classes, disrupted lectures, staged guerrilla theater, and behaved in other unconventional ways to protest the war, racism, capitalism, the behavior of their college presidents, the president of the United States, the military establishment, and all other institutions. (We are not exaggerating here. Students did such things at our home universities after members of the National Guard shot and killed four students at a demonstration at Kent State University in Ohio on May 4, 1970.)

Confronted by civil strife and disorder in the nation's institutions of higher learning, Congress took action. On March 23, 1971, it enacted and sent to the states the proposed Twenty-sixth Amendment, lowering the voting age to eighteen. Three-quarters of the state legislatures had to ratify the amendment before it became part of the Constitution. Astonishingly, thirty-eight states (the required number) complied by July 1, establishing a new speed record for ratification and cutting the old record nearly in half.[105] (Ironically, voting rights were not high on the list of students' demands.)

Testimony by members of Congress before the Judiciary Committee stated that the eighteen-year-old vote would "harness the energy of young people and direct it into useful and constructive channels," to keep students from becoming "more militant" and engaging "in destructive activities of a dangerous nature."[106] As one observer argued, the right to vote was extended to eighteen-year-olds not because young people demanded it but because "public officials believed suffrage expansion to be a means of institutionalizing youths' participation in politics, which would, in turn, curb disorder."[107]

Participation and the Models of Democracy

Ostensibly, elections are institutional mechanisms that implement democracy by allowing citizens to choose among candidates or issues. But elections also serve several other important purposes:[108]

- Elections socialize political activity. They transform what might otherwise consist of sporadic, citizen-initiated acts into a routine public function. That is, the opportunity to vote for change encourages citizens to refrain from demonstrating in the streets. This helps preserve government stability by containing and channeling away potentially disruptive or dangerous forms of mass political activity.
- Elections institutionalize access to political power. They allow ordinary citizens to run for political office or to play an important role in selecting political leaders. Working to elect a candidate encourages the campaign worker to identify problems or propose solutions to the newly elected official.
- Elections bolster the state's power and authority. The opportunity to participate in elections helps convince citizens that the government is responsive to their needs and wants, which reinforces its legitimacy.

Participation and Majoritarianism

Although the majoritarian model assumes that government responsiveness to popular demands comes through mass participation in politics, majoritarianism views participation rather narrowly. It favors conventional, institutionalized behavior—primarily voting in elections. Because majoritarianism relies on counting votes to determine what the majority wants, its bias toward equality in political participation is strong. Clearly, a class bias in voting exists because of the strong influence of socioeconomic status on turnout. Simply put, better-educated, wealthier citizens are more likely to participate in elections, and get-out-the-vote campaigns cannot counter this distinct bias.[109] Because it favors collective decisions formalized through elections, majoritarianism has little place for motivated, resourceful individuals to exercise private influence over government actions.

Majoritarianism also limits individual freedom in another way: its focus on voting as the major means of mass participation narrows the scope of conventional political behavior by defining which political actions are "orderly" and acceptable. By favoring equality and order in political participation, majoritarianism goes hand in hand with the ideological orientation of communitarianism (see Chapter 1).

Participation and Pluralism

Resourceful citizens who want the government's help with problems find a haven in the pluralist model of democracy. A decentralized and organizationally complex form of government allows many points of access and accommodates various forms of conventional participation in addition to voting. For example, wealthy people and well-funded groups can afford to hire lobbyists to press their interests in Congress. In one view of pluralist democracy, citizens are free to ply and wheedle public officials to further their own selfish visions of the public good. From another viewpoint, pluralism offers citizens the opportunity to be treated as individuals when dealing with the government, to influence policymaking in special circumstances, and to fulfill (insofar as possible in representative government) their social potential through participation in community affairs.

Summary

To have "government by the people," the people must participate in politics. Conventional forms of participation—contacting officials and voting in elections—come most quickly to mind. However, citizens can also participate in politics in unconventional ways—staging sit-down strikes in public buildings, blocking traffic, and so on. Most citizens disapprove of unconventional political behavior. Yet blacks and women used unconventional tactics to win important political and legal rights, including the right to vote.

People are motivated to participate in politics for various reasons: to show support for their country, to obtain particularized benefits for themselves or their friends, or to influence broad public policy. Their political actions may demand either little political knowledge or personal initiative, or a great deal of both.

The press often paints an unflattering picture of political participation in America. Clearly, the proportion of the electorate that votes in general elections in the United States has dropped and is far below that in other nations. The United States tends to show as much citizen participation in politics as other nations, however, when a broad range of conventional and unconventional political behavior is considered. Voter turnout in the United States suffers by comparison with that of other nations because of differences in voter registration requirements. We also lack institutions (especially strong political parties) that increase voter registration and help bring those of lower socioeconomic status to the polls.

People's tendency to participate in politics is strongly related to their socioeconomic status. Education, one component of socioeconomic status, is the single strongest predictor of conventional political participation in the United States. Because of the strong effect of socioeconomic status, the political system is potentially biased toward the interests of higher-status people. Pluralist democracy, which provides many avenues for resourceful citizens to influence government decisions, tends to increase this bias. Majoritarian democracy, which relies heavily on elections and the concept of one person, one vote, offers citizens without great personal resources the opportunity to influence government decisions through elections.

Elections also serve to legitimize government simply by involving the masses in government through voting. Whether voting means anything depends on the nature of voters' choices in elections. The range of choices available is a function of the nation's political parties, the topic of the next chapter.

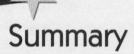 **CourseMate**

Visit www.cengagebrain.com/shop/ ISBN/0495906182 for flashcards, web quizzes, videos and more!

Political Parties

AP Photo/Ed Reinke

Visit www.cengagebrain.com/shop/
ISBN/0495906182 for flashcards, web
quizzes, videos and more!

CourseMate

In 2009, voters in the far northeast region of New York elected a Democrat to Congress for the first time since the Civil War. The story of why they switched parties begins with their 2008 reelection of Republican John M. McHugh. After comfortably winning the Twenty-third Congressional District for the fourth straight time, McHugh was appointed Secretary of the Army by President Obama in the summer of 2009. That appointment created a vacancy in Congress to be filled in a special election on November 2, which was expected to produce a Republican replacement.

Republican Party leaders in the district's counties selected as their candidate Republican New York State assemblywoman Dierdre "Dede" Scozzafava, who held moderate views on abortion and same-sex-marriage and supported the federal stimulus package. In keeping with the national party's strategy to expand its base by relaxing ideological purity,[1] local leaders passed over other possibilities, including committed social conservative Douglas Hoffman. The Republican National Committee (RNC) heartily accepted Scozzafava's candidacy and directed almost a million dollars into her campaign. Former House Speaker Newt Gingrich backed her as a Republican who could readily defeat the Democratic candidate, Bill Owens, an air force veteran.

Rejected Republican contender Doug Hoffman did not go away, however. He filed to run in November as a candidate of New York's Conservative Party, claiming that Scozzafava was a "RINO"—Republican in Name Only—and far too liberal to represent the Twenty-third District. Hoffman attracted to his cause prominent conservative Republicans—including 2008 vice-presidential candidate Sarah Palin, Minnesota governor and 2012 presidential hopeful Tim Pawlenty, and former House majority leader Dick Armey—who backed the Washington "tea party" protesters (see pages 207–208), some of whom worked for Hoffman. They were joined by conservative talk show host Rush Limbaugh, Fox TV commentator Glenn Beck, and editors of the *Wall Street Journal.* Conservatives poured money into Hoffman's campaign and attacked Scozzafava, whose polls nosedived so that she trailed both Hoffman and Owens less than one week before the election.

On October 31, the official Republican candidate suspended her campaign. Saying she was outspent and unable to address "charges that have been made about my record," she endorsed Owens, her Democratic opponent.[2] The RNC backtracked and said that it would "endorse and support the Conservative candidate, Doug Hoffman." The surprised Democratic candidate Owens took 49 percent of the vote to Hoffman's 45 percent. Republican Scozzafava (still on the ballot) got 5 percent.

Most observers attributed Hoffman's defeat to voters' resentment of outside intervention in the district. A local Republican Party leader said, "I'm seeing part of the party I never knew existed."[3] Hoffman's conservative supporters preferred losing the seat to electing a Republican who was not sufficiently conservative. Moreover, they think that fielding more conservative candidates will produce more Republican victories. Tom Davis, a former chair of the National Republican Congressional Committee, worried that his party would see more conservative challenges to moderate candidates in primary fights, which could get "very, very ugly."[4]

U.S. politics is dominated by a two-party system. The Democratic and Republican parties have dominated national and state politics for more than 125 years. Their domination is more complete than that of any pair of parties in any other democratic government. Although all democracies have some form of multiparty politics, very few have a stable two-party system, Britain being the most notable exception (see "Compared with What? Only Two to Tangle"). Most people take our two-party system for granted, not realizing that it is arguably the most distinctive feature of American politics.

Why do we have any political parties? What functions do they perform? How did we become a nation of Democrats and Republicans? Do these parties truly differ in their platforms and behavior? Are parties really necessary for democratic government, or do they just get in the way of citizens and their government? In this chapter, we answer these questions by examining political parties, perhaps the most misunderstood element of American politics.

Political Parties and Their Functions

According to democratic theory, the primary means by which citizens control their government is voting in free elections. Most Americans agree that voting is important. Of those surveyed after the 2008 presidential campaign, 89 percent felt that elections make the government "pay attention to what the people think."[5] Americans are not nearly as supportive of the role played by political parties in elections, however. When asked if Ross Perot should run for president in 1996 as "head of a third party which would also run candidates in state and local races" or "by himself as an independent candidate," 60 percent of a national sample favored his running without a party.[6] Apparently, many Americans think that politics would function better without political parties.

Nevertheless, Americans are quick to condemn as "undemocratic" countries that do not regularly hold elections contested by political parties. In truth, Americans have a love–hate relationship with political parties. They believe that parties are necessary for democratic government; at the same time, they think parties are somehow obstructionist and not to be trusted. This distrust is particularly strong among younger voters. To better appreciate the role of political parties in democratic government, we must understand exactly what parties are and what they do.

What Is a Political Party?

political party
An organization that sponsors candidates for political office under the organization's name.

nomination
Designation as an official candidate of a political party.

A **political party** is an organization that sponsors candidates for political office *under the organization's name*. The italicized part of this definition is important. True political parties select individuals to run for public office through a formal **nomination** process, which designates them as the parties' official candidates. This activity distinguishes the Democratic and Republican parties from interest groups. The AFL-CIO and the National Association of

Manufacturers are interest groups. They often support candidates, but they do not nominate them to run as their avowed representatives. If they did, they would be transformed into political parties. Because the so-called "tea party" does not nominate its own candidates, it is not a national political party, despite holding a national convention in Nashville, Tennessee, in 2010 and having some candidates on the 2010 ballot at the state level.[7] In short, the sponsoring of candidates, designated as representatives of the organization, is what defines an organization as a party.

Most democratic theorists agree that a modern nation-state cannot practice democracy without at least two political parties that regularly contest elections. In fact, the link between democracy and political parties is so firm that many people define *democratic government* in terms of competitive party politics.[8] A former president of the American Political Science Association held that even for a small nation, "democracy is impossible save in terms of parties."[9]

Party Functions

Parties contribute to democratic government through the functions they perform for the **political system**—the set of interrelated institutions that link people with government. Four of the most important party functions are nominating candidates for election to public office, structuring the voting choice in elections, proposing alternative government programs, and coordinating the actions of government officials.

Nominating Candidates. Is *every* and *any* American citizen qualified to hold public office? A few scholars have thought they were, proposing that government positions be filled "randomly"—that is, through lotteries.[10] Most observers, however, hold that political leadership requires certain abilities (if not special knowledge or public experience) and that not just anyone should be entrusted to head the government. The question then becomes, Who should be chosen among those who offer to lead? Without political parties, voters would confront a bewildering array of self-nominated candidates, each seeking votes on the basis of personal friendships, celebrity status, or name recognition. Parties can provide a form of quality control for their nominees through the process of peer review. Party insiders, the nominees' peers, usually know the strengths and faults of potential candidates much better than average voters do and thus can judge their suitability for representing the party.

In nominating candidates, parties often do more than pass judgment on potential office seekers; sometimes they go so far as to recruit talented individuals to become candidates. In this way, parties help not only to ensure a minimum level of quality among candidates who run for office but also to raise the quality of those candidates.

Structuring the Voting Choice. Political parties help democratic government by structuring the voting choice—reducing the number of candidates on the

political system
A set of interrelated institutions that links people with government.

Compared with What?

Only Two to Tangle

Compared with party systems in other countries, the U.S. two-party system is unusual indeed. Most democracies have multiparty systems in which four or five parties win enough seats in the legislature to contest for government power. Even the few countries classified as having two-party systems have minor parties that regularly contest seats and win enough votes to complicate national politics. The United Kingdom is the most notable example of a country reputed to have a two-party system. The purer U.S. pattern of two-party politics shows clearly in these graphs of votes cast for party candidates running for the U.S. House compared with votes cast for party candidates running for the British House of Commons.

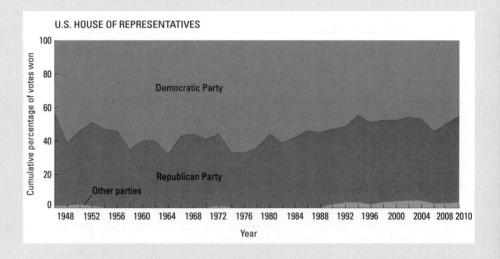

ballot to those who have a realistic chance of winning. Established parties—those with experience in contesting elections—acquire a following of loyal voters who guarantee the party's candidates a predictable base of votes. The ability of established parties to mobilize their supporters discourages nonparty candidates from running for office and new parties from forming. Consequently, the realistic choice is between candidates offered by the major parties, reducing the amount of new information that voters need to make a rational decision. Contrast the voting decision in our stable competitive two-party system (and the outcome) with Russian voters' choices in their December 2007 parliamentary election. The Russian ballot listed eleven parties. But some were formed only for the election, and some even supported President Vladimir Putin, who ran as a candidate of his own government party, United Russia. With Putin's government dominating media

Only 20 percent of Americans surveyed in 2007 agreed that our two-party system "works fairly well." Almost 30 percent thought that it is "seriously broken, and the country needs a third party.*

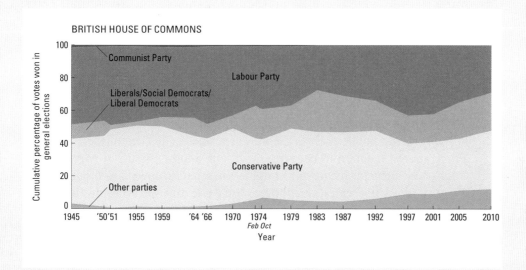

BRITISH HOUSE OF COMMONS

Sources: Thomas T. Mackie and Richard Rose, *The International Almanac of Electoral History,* 3rd ed. (Washington, D.C.: CQ Press, 1991); http://www.electionguide.org, http://www.thegreenpapers.com/G06/HouseVoteByParty.phtml, and http://news.bbc.co.uk/2/shared/election2010/results/.

---

*NBC News/Wall Street Journal Poll conducted by the polling organizations of Peter Hart (D) and Bill McInturff (R)., 14–17 December 2007. *N* = 1,008 adults nationwide. At http://www.pollingreport.com/politics.htm.

coverage, United Russia won 64 percent of the vote and 70 percent of the seats. Three other parties gained seats, but two of them were allied with United Russia.

Proposing Alternative Government Programs. Parties help voters choose among candidates by proposing alternative programs of government action—the general policies their candidates will pursue if they gain office. In a stable party system, even if voters know nothing about the qualities of the parties' candidates, they can vote rationally for the candidates of the party that has policies they favor. The specific policies advocated vary from candidate to candidate and from election to election. However, the types of policies advocated by candidates of one party tend to differ from those proposed by candidates of other parties. Although there are exceptions, candidates of the same party tend to favor policies that fit their party's underlying political philosophy, or ideology.

In many countries, parties' names, such as *Conservative* and *Socialist,* reflect their political stance. The Democrats and Republicans have ideologically neutral names, but many minor parties in the United States have used their names to advertise their policies—for example, the Libertarian Party, the Socialist Party, and the Green Party.[11] The neutrality of the two major parties' names suggests that their policies are similar. This is not true. As we shall see, they regularly adopt very different policies in their platforms.

Coordinating the Actions of Government Officials. Finally, party organizations help coordinate the actions of public officials. A government based on the separation of powers, such as that of the United States, divides responsibilities for making public policy. The president and the leaders of the House and Senate are not required to cooperate with one another. Political party organizations are the major means for bridging the separate powers to produce coordinated policies that can govern the country effectively. Parties do this in two ways. First, candidates' and officeholders' political fortunes are linked to their party organization, which can bestow and withhold favors. Second, and perhaps more important in the United States, members of the same party in the presidency, the House, and the Senate tend to share political principles and thus often voluntarily cooperate in making policy.

So why do we have parties? One expert notes that successful politicians in the United States need electoral and governing majorities and that "no collection of ambitious politicians has long been able to think of a way to achieve their goals in this democracy save in terms of political parties."[12]

A History of U.S. Party Politics

The two major U.S. parties are among the oldest in the world. In fact, the Democratic Party, founded in 1828 but with roots reaching back to the late 1700s, has a strong claim to being the oldest party in existence. Its closest rival is the British Conservative Party, formed in 1832, two decades before the Republican Party was organized in 1854. Several generations of citizens have supported the Democratic and Republican parties, and they are part of American history. They have become institutionalized in our political process.

The Preparty Period

Today we think of party activities as normal, even essential, to American politics. It was not always so. The Constitution makes no mention of political parties, and none existed when the Constitution was written in 1787. It was common then to refer to groups pursuing some common political interest as *factions*. Although factions were seen as inevitable in politics, they were also considered dangerous.[13] One argument for adopting the Constitution—proposed in *Federalist* No. 10 (see Chapter 3)—was that its federal system would prevent factional influences from controlling the government.

Factions existed even under British rule. In colonial assemblies, supporters of the governor (and thus of the Crown) were known as *Tories* or *Loyalists,* and their opponents were called *Whigs* or *Patriots.* After independence, the arguments over whether to adopt the Constitution produced a different alignment of factions. Those who backed the Constitution were loosely known as *Federalists,* their opponents as *Antifederalists.* At this stage, the groups could not be called parties because they did not sponsor candidates for election.

Elections then were vastly different from elections today. The Constitution provided for the president and vice president to be chosen by an **electoral college**–a body of electors who met in the capitals of their respective states to cast their ballots. Initially, in most states, the legislatures, not the voters, chose the electors (one for each senator and representative in Congress). Presidential elections in the early years of the nation, then, actually were decided by a handful of political leaders. (See Chapter 9 for a discussion of the electoral college in modern presidential politics.) Often they met in small, secret groups, called **caucuses**, to propose candidates for public office. Typically, they were composed of like-minded members of state legislatures and Congress. This was the setting for George Washington's election as the first president in 1789.

We can classify Washington as a Federalist because he supported the Constitution, but he was not a factional leader and actually opposed factional politics. His immense prestige, coupled with his political neutrality, left Washington unopposed for the office of president, and he was elected unanimously by the electoral college. During Washington's administration, however, the political cleavage sharpened between those who favored a stronger national government and those who wanted a less powerful, more decentralized national government.

The first group, led by Alexander Hamilton, proclaimed themselves *Federalists.* The second group, led by Thomas Jefferson, called themselves *Republicans.* (Although they used the same name, they were *not* the Republicans we know today.) The Jeffersonians chose the name *Republicans* to distinguish themselves from the "aristocratic" tendencies of Hamilton's Federalists. The Federalists countered by calling the Republicans the *Democratic Republicans,* attempting to link Jefferson's party to the disorder (and beheadings) in the French Revolution, led by "radical democrats."

The First Party System: Federalists and Democratic Republicans

Washington was reelected president unanimously in 1792, but his vice president, John Adams, was opposed by a candidate backed by the Democratic Republicans. This brief skirmish foreshadowed the nation's first party struggle over the presidency. Disheartened by the political split in his administration, Washington spoke out against "the baneful effects" of parties in his farewell address in 1796. Nonetheless, parties already existed in the political system, as Figure 8.1 shows. In the election of 1796, the Federalists supported Vice President John Adams to succeed Washington as president. The Democratic

electoral college
A body of electors chosen by voters to cast ballots for president and vice president.

caucus
A closed meeting of the members of a political party to decide questions of policy and the selection of candidates for office.

FIGURE 8.1 The Two-Party System in American History

1789	Washington unanimously elected president					PREPARTY PERIOD
1792	Washington unanimously reelected					
1796	Federalist *Adams*	Democratic Republican				
1800	—	*Jefferson*				
1804	—	*Jefferson*				FIRST PARTY SYSTEM
1808	—	*Madison*				
1812	—	*Madison*				
1816	—	*Monroe*				
1820		*Monroe*				"ERA OF GOOD FEELINGS"
1824		*J. Q. Adams*				
1828		Democratic *Jackson*		National Republican		
1832		*Jackson*		Whig		
1836	SECOND PARTY SYSTEM	*Van Buren*		—		
1840		—		*Harrison*		
1844		*Polk*		—		
1848		—		*Taylor*		
1852		*Pierce*		—		
1856		*Buchanan*			Republican	
1860	Constitutional Union Southern Democrat	—			*Lincoln*	
1864		—			*Lincoln*	
1868		—			*Grant*	
1872	THIRD PARTY SYSTEM	—			*Grant*	
1876		—			*Hayes*	
1880		—			*Garfield*	
1884		*Cleveland*			—	
1888	Rough Balance	—			*Harrison*	
1892		*Cleveland*			—	
1896		—	Populist		*McKinley*	
1900		—			*McKinley*	
1904		—			*Roosevelt, T.*	
1908		—			*Taft*	
1912	Republican Dominance	*Wilson*	Progressive		—	
1916		*Wilson*			—	
1920		—			*Harding*	
1924		—			*Coolidge*	
1928		—			*Hoover*	
1932		*Roosevelt, F. D.*			—	
1936		*Roosevelt, F. D.*			—	
1940		*Roosevelt, F. D.*			—	
1944		*Roosevelt, F. D.*			—	
1948	Democratic Dominance	*Truman*	States' Rights		—	
1952		—			*Eisenhower*	
1956		—			*Eisenhower*	
1960		*Kennedy*			—	
1964		*Johnson*			—	
1968		—	American Independent		*Nixon*	
1972		—			*Nixon*	
1976		*Carter*			—	
1980		—	Independent		*Reagan*	
1984		—			*Reagan*	
1988	Rough Balance	—			*Bush, G. H. W.*	
1992		*Clinton*	Independent		—	
1996		*Clinton*	Reform		—	
2000		—	Green		*Bush, G. W.*	
2004		—			*Bush, G. W.*	
2008		*Obama*				

Over time, the American party system has undergone a series of wrenching transformations. Since 1856, the Democrats and the Republicans have alternated irregularly in power, each party enjoying a long period of dominance.

Republicans backed Thomas Jefferson for president but could not agree on a vice-presidential candidate. In the electoral college, Adams won seventy-one votes to Jefferson's sixty-eight, and both ran ahead of other candidates. At that time, the Constitution provided that the presidency would go to the candidate who won the most votes in the electoral college, with the vice presidency going to the runner-up (like a school election). So Adams, a Federalist, had to accept Jefferson, a Democratic Republican, as his vice president. Obviously, the Constitution did not anticipate a presidential contest between candidates from opposing political parties.

The party function of nominating candidates emerged more clearly in the election of 1800. Both parties caucused in Congress to nominate candidates for president and vice president. The result was the first true party contest for the presidency. The Federalists nominated John Adams and Charles Pinckney; the Democratic Republicans nominated Thomas Jefferson and Aaron Burr. This time, both Democratic Republican candidates won. However, the new party organization worked too well. According to the Constitution, each elector had to vote by ballot for two persons. The Democratic Republican electors unanimously cast their two votes for Jefferson and Burr. The presidency was to go to the candidate with the most votes, but due to party discipline the top two candidates were tied! Although Jefferson was the party's presidential candidate and Burr its vice-presidential candidate, the Constitution empowered the House of Representatives to choose either one of them as president. After seven days and thirty-six ballots, the House decided in favor of Jefferson.

The Twelfth Amendment, ratified in 1804, prevented a repeat of the troublesome election outcomes of 1796 and 1800. It required the electoral college to vote separately for president and vice president, implicitly recognizing that parties would nominate different candidates for the two offices.

The election of 1800 marked the beginning of the end for the Federalists, who lost the next four elections. By 1820, the Federalists were no more. The Democratic Republican candidate, James Monroe, was reelected in the first presidential contest without party competition since Washington's time. (Monroe received all but one electoral vote, reportedly cast against him so that Washington would remain the only president ever elected unanimously.) Ironically, the lack of partisan competition under Monroe, in what was dubbed the "Era of Good Feelings," also fatally weakened his party, the Democratic Republicans. Lacking competition, the Democratic Republicans neglected their function of nominating candidates. In the 1824 election, the party caucus's nominee was challenged by three other Democratic Republicans, including John Quincy Adams and Andrew Jackson, who together won 70 percent of the popular and electoral vote.

Although Jackson won more of the popular vote and electoral vote than Adams, he did not win the necessary majority in the electoral college. The House of Representatives again had to decide the winner. It chose the second-place John Quincy Adams (from the established state of Massachusetts) over the voters' choice, Jackson (from the frontier state of Tennessee). The factionalism among the leaders of the Democratic Republican Party became so intense that the party split in two.

The Second Party System: Democrats and Whigs

The Jacksonian faction of the Democratic Republican Party represented the common people in the expanding South and West, and its members took pride in calling themselves simply Democrats. Jackson ran again for the presidency as a Democrat in 1828, a milestone that marked the beginning of today's Democratic Party. That election was also the first mass election in U.S. history. In earlier elections, few people were entitled to vote. States began to drop restrictive requirements for voting after 1800, and voting rights for white males expanded even faster after 1815 (see Chapter 7). With the expansion of suffrage, more states began to allow voters, rather than state legislatures, to choose the presidential electors. Although voters had directly chosen many presidential electors in 1824, the total votes cast in that election numbered fewer than 370,000. By 1828, relaxed requirements for voting (and the use of popular elections to select presidential electors in more states) had increased the vote by more than 300 percent, to more than 1.1 million.

As the electorate expanded, the parties changed. No longer could a party rely on a few political leaders in the state legislatures to control votes in the electoral college. Parties now needed to campaign for votes cast by hundreds of thousands of citizens. Recognizing this new dimension of the nation's politics, the parties responded with a new method for nominating presidential candidates. Instead of selecting candidates in a closed caucus of party representatives in Congress, the parties devised the **national convention**. At these gatherings, delegates from state parties across the nation would choose candidates for president and vice president and adopt a statement of policies called a **party platform**. The Anti-Masonic Party, which was the first "third" party in American history to challenge the two major parties for the presidency, called the first national convention in 1831. The Democrats adopted the convention idea in 1832 to nominate Jackson for a second term, as did their new opponents that year, the National Republicans.

The label *National Republicans* applied to John Quincy Adams's faction of the former Democratic Republican Party. However, the National Republicans did not become today's Republican Party. Adams's followers called themselves National Republicans to signify their old Federalist preference for a strong national government, but the symbolism did not appeal to the voters, and the National Republicans lost to Jackson in 1832.

Elected to another term, Jackson began to assert the power of the nation over the states (acting more like a National Republican than a Democrat). His policies drew new opponents, who started calling him "King Andrew." A coalition made up of former National Republicans, Anti-Masons, and Jackson haters formed the Whig Party in 1834. The name referred to the English Whigs, who opposed the powers of the British throne; the implication was that Jackson was governing like a king. For the next thirty years, Democrats and Whigs alternated in the presidency. However, the issues of slavery and sectionalism eventually destroyed the Whigs from within. Although the party had won the White House in 1848 and had taken 44 percent of the vote in

national convention
A gathering of delegates of a single political party from across the country to choose candidates for president and vice president and to adopt a party platform.

party platform
The statement of policies of a national political party.

1852, the Whigs were unable to field a presidential candidate in the 1856 election.

The Current Party System: Democrats and Republicans

In the early 1850s, antislavery forces (including some Whigs and antislavery Democrats) began to organize. At meetings in Jackson, Michigan, and Ripon, Wisconsin, they recommended the formation of a new party, the Republican Party, to oppose the extension of slavery into the Kansas and Nebraska territories. This party, founded in 1854, continues as today's Republican Party.

The Republican Party entered its first presidential election in 1856. It took 33 percent of the vote, and its candidate, John Frémont, carried eleven states—all in the North. Then, in 1860, the Republicans nominated Abraham Lincoln. The Democrats were deeply divided over the slavery issue and split into two parties. The Northern Democrats nominated Stephen Douglas. The Southern Democrats ran John Breckinridge. A fourth party, the Constitutional Union Party, nominated John Bell. Breckinridge won every southern state. Lincoln took 40 percent of the popular vote and carried every northern state.

The election of 1860 is considered the first of four critical elections under the current party system.[14] A **critical election** is marked by a sharp change in the existing patterns of party loyalty among groups of voters. Moreover, this change in voting patterns, which is called an **electoral realignment**, does not end with the election but persists through several subsequent elections.[15] The election of 1860 divided the country politically between the northern states, whose voters mainly voted Republican, and the southern states, which were overwhelmingly Democratic. The victory of the North over the South in the Civil War cemented Democratic loyalties in the South.

For forty years, from 1880 to 1920, no Republican presidential candidate won even one of the eleven states of the former Confederacy. The South's solid Democratic record earned it the nickname the "Solid South." (Today's students may be puzzled, for the South has been "solid" for Republicans throughout their lifetimes.[16] That was not true prior to 1950, and the change is addressed below.) The Republicans did not puncture the Solid South until 1920, when Warren G. Harding carried Tennessee. The Republicans won five southern states in 1928, when the Democrats ran the first Catholic candidate, Al Smith. Republican presidential candidates won no more southern states until 1952, when Dwight Eisenhower broke the pattern of Democratic dominance in the South—ninety years after that pattern had been set by the Civil War.

Eras of Party Dominance Since the Civil War

The critical election of 1860 established the Democratic and Republican parties as the dominant parties in our **two-party system**. In a two-party system, most voters are so loyal to one or the other of the major parties that independent candidates or candidates from a third party (which means any minor party) have little chance of winning office. Third-party candidates

critical election
An election that produces a sharp change in the existing pattern of party loyalties among groups of voters.

electoral realignment
The change in voting patterns that occurs after a critical election.

two-party system
A political system in which two major political parties compete for control of the government. Candidates from a third party have little chance of winning office.

tend to be more successful at the local or state level. Since the current two-party system was established, relatively few minor-party candidates have won election to the U.S. House, even fewer have won election to the Senate, and none has won the presidency.

The voters in a given state, county, or community are not always equally divided in their loyalties between the Republicans and the Democrats. In some areas, voters typically favor the Republicans, whereas voters in other areas prefer the Democrats. When one party in a two-party system regularly enjoys support from most voters in an area, it is called the *majority party* in that area; the other is called the *minority party*. Since the inception of the current two-party system, four periods (1860–1894, 1896–1930, 1932–1964, and 1968 to the present) have characterized the balance between the two major parties at the national level.

A Rough Balance: 1860–1894. From 1860 through 1894, the Grand Old Party (or GOP, as the Republican Party is sometimes called) won eight of ten presidential elections, which would seem to qualify it as the majority party. However, some of its success in presidential elections came from its practice of running Civil War heroes and from the North's domination of southern politics. Seats in the House of Representatives are a better guide to the breadth of national support. An analysis shows that the Republicans and Democrats won an equal number of congressional elections, each controlling the chamber for nine sessions between 1860 and 1894.

A Republican Majority: 1896–1930. A second critical election, in 1896, transformed the Republican Party into a true majority party. Grover Cleveland, a Democrat, occupied the White House, and the country was in a severe depression. The Republicans nominated William McKinley, governor of Ohio and a conservative, who stood for a high tariff against foreign goods and sound money tied to the value of gold. Rather than tour the country seeking votes, McKinley ran a dignified campaign from his Ohio home.

The Democrats, already in trouble because of the depression, nominated the fiery William Jennings Bryan. In stark contrast to McKinley, Bryan advocated the free and unlimited coinage of silver, which would mean cheap money and easy payment of debts through inflation. Bryan was also the nominee of the young Populist Party, an agrarian protest party that had proposed the free-silver platform Bryan adopted. The feature "The Wizard of Oz: A Political Fable" explains that the book *The Wonderful Wizard of Oz*, which you probably know as a movie, was reportedly a Populist political fable.[17] Conservatives, especially businesspeople, were aghast at the Democrats' radical turn, and voters in the heavily populated Northeast and Midwest surged toward the Republican Party, many of them permanently. McKinley carried every northern state east of the Mississippi. The Republicans also won the House, and they retained their control of it in the next six elections.

The election of 1896 helped solidify a Republican majority in industrial America and forged a link between the Republican Party and business. In the subsequent electoral realignment, the Republicans emerged as a true

majority party. The GOP dominated national politics—controlling the presidency, the Senate, and the House—almost continuously from 1896 until the Wall Street crash of 1929, which burst big business's bubble and launched the Great Depression.*

A Democratic Majority: 1932–1964. The Republicans' majority status ended in the critical election of 1932 between incumbent president Herbert Hoover and the Democratic challenger, Franklin Delano Roosevelt. Roosevelt promised new solutions to unemployment and the economic crisis of the Great Depression. His campaign appealed to labor, middle-class liberals, and new European ethnic voters. Along with Democratic voters in the Solid South, urban workers in the North, Catholics, Jews, and white ethnic minorities formed "the Roosevelt coalition." The relatively few blacks who voted at that time tended to remain loyal to the Republicans—"the party of Lincoln."

Roosevelt was swept into office in a landslide, carrying huge Democratic majorities with him into the House and Senate to enact his liberal activist programs. The electoral realignment reflected by the election of 1932 made the Democrats the majority party. Not only was Roosevelt reelected in 1936, 1940, and 1944, but also Democrats held control of both houses of Congress in most sessions from 1933 through 1964. The only exceptions were Republican control of the House and Senate in 1947 and 1948 (under President

---

*The only break in the GOP domination was in 1912, when Teddy Roosevelt's Progressive Conservative Party split from the Republicans, allowing Democrat Woodrow Wilson to win the presidency and giving the Democrats control of Congress, and again in 1916 when Wilson was reelected.

Feature Story

The Wizard of Oz: A Political Fable

Most Americans are familiar with The Wizard of Oz through the children's series or the 1939 motion picture. Some historians contend that the story was written as a political fable to promote the Populist movement around the turn of the century. Next time you see or read it, try interpreting the Tin Woodsman as the industrial worker, the Scarecrow as the struggling farmer, and the Wizard as the president, who is powerful only as long as he succeeds in deceiving the people. (Sorry, but in the book, Dorothy's ruby slippers were only silver shoes.)

The Wonderful Wizard of Oz was written by Lyman Frank Baum in 1900, during the collapse of the Populist movement. Through the Populist Party, midwestern farmers, in alliance with some urban workers, had challenged the banks, railroads, and other economic interests that squeezed farmers through low prices, high freight rates, and continued indebtedness.

The Populists advocated government ownership of railroad, telephone, and telegraph industries. They also wanted silver coinage. Their power grew during the 1893 depression, the worst in U.S. history until then, as farm prices sank to new lows, and unemployment was widespread.

In the 1894 congressional elections, the Populist Party got almost 40 percent of the vote. It looked forward to winning the presidency, and imposing the silver standard, in 1896. But in that election, which revolved around the issue of gold versus silver, Populist Democrat William Jennings Bryan lost to Republican William McKinley by ninety-five electoral votes. Bryan, a congressman from Nebraska and a gifted orator, ran again in 1900, but the Populist strength was gone.

Baum viewed these events in both rural South Dakota, where he edited a local weekly, and urban Chicago, where he wrote Oz. He mourned the destruction of the fragile alliance between the midwestern

Truman) and in 1953 and 1954 (under President Eisenhower). The Democrats also won the presidency in seven of nine elections. Moreover, national surveys from 1952 through 1964 show that Americans of voting age consistently and decidedly favored the Democratic Party.

A Rough Balance: 1968 to the Present. Scholars agree that an electoral realignment occurred after 1964, and some attribute the realignment to the turbulent election of 1968, sometimes called the fourth critical election.[18] The Republican Richard Nixon won in a very close race by winning five of the eleven southern states in the old Confederacy, while Democrat Hubert Humphrey won only one. The other five states were won by George Wallace, the candidate of the American Independent Party, made up primarily of southerners who defected from the Democratic Party. Wallace won no states outside the South.

Since 1968, Republican candidates for president have run very well in southern states and tended to win election—Nixon (twice), Reagan (twice), G. H. W. Bush, and G. W. Bush (twice). The record of party control of Congress has been more mixed since 1968. Democrats have controlled the House

farmers (the Scarecrow) and the urban industrial workers (the Tin Woodsman). Along with Bryan (the Cowardly Lion, with a roar but little else), they had been taken down the yellow brick road (the gold standard) that led nowhere. Each journeyed to Emerald City seeking favors from the Wizard of Oz (the president). Dorothy, the symbol of Everyman, went along with them, innocent enough to see the truth before the others.

Along the way, they met the Wicked Witch of the East, who, Baum tells us, had kept the little Munchkin people "in bondage for many years, making them slave for her night and day." She also had put a spell on the Tin Woodsman, once an independent and hard-working man, so that each time he swung his axe, it chopped off a different part of his body. Lacking another trade, he "worked harder than ever," becoming like a machine, incapable of love, yearning for a heart. Another witch, the Wicked Witch of the West, clearly symbolizes the large industrial corporations.

The small group heads toward Emerald City, where the Wizard rules from behind a papier-mâché façade. *Oz*, by the way, is the abbreviation for ounce, the standard measure for gold.

Like all good politicians, the Wizard can be all things to all people. Dorothy sees him as an enormous head. The Scarecrow sees a gossamer fairy. The Woodsman sees an awful beast, the Cowardly Lion "a ball of fire so fierce and glowing he could scarcely bear to gaze upon it." Later, however, when they confront the Wizard directly, they see he is nothing more than "a little man, with a bald head and a wrinkled face." "I have been making believe," the Wizard confesses. "I'm just a common man." But the Scarecrow adds, "You're more than that … you're a humbug." "It was a great mistake my ever letting you into the Throne Room," admits the Wizard, a former ventriloquist and circus balloonist from Omaha.

This was Baum's ultimate Populist message. The powers-that-be survive by deception. Only people's ignorance allows the powerful to manipulate and control them. Dorothy returns to Kansas with the magical help of her silver shoes (the silver issue), but when she gets to Kansas she realizes her shoes "had fallen off in her flight through the air, and were lost forever in the desert." Still, she is safe at home with Aunt Em and Uncle Henry, simple farmers.

Source: Peter Dreier, "The Wizard of Oz: A Political Fable," *Today Journal*, 14 February 1986. Reprinted by permission of Pacific News Service, http://www.pacificnews.org.

for most of the sessions, while the parties have split control of the Senate almost evenly.

Therefore, the period since 1968 rates as a "rough balance" between the parties, much like the period from 1860 to 1894. The razor-close election of 2000 and the close election of 2004, moreover, indicate that nationally the parties are fairly even in electoral strength.

However, the North–South coalition of Democratic voters forged by Roosevelt in the 1930s has completely crumbled. Two southern scholars wrote:

> It is easy to forget just how thoroughly the Democratic party once dominated southern congressional elections. In 1950 there were no Republican senators from the South and only 2 Republican representatives out of 105 in the southern House delegation…. A half-century later Republicans constituted *majorities* of the South's congressional delegations—13 of 22 southern senators and 71 of 125 representatives.[19]

Although party loyalty within regions has shifted inexorably, the Democratic coalition of urban workers and ethnic minorities still seems intact, if weakened. Indeed, rural voters have become decidedly more Republican.[20] Some scholars say that in the 1970s and 1980s, we were in a period of **electoral dealignment**, in which party loyalties became less important to voters as they cast their ballots. Others counter that partisanship increased in the 1990s in a gradual process of realignment not marked by a single critical election.[21] We examine the influence of party loyalty on voting in the next chapter, after we look at the operation of our two-party system.

The American Two-Party System

Our review of party history in the United States has focused on the two dominant parties. But we should not ignore the special contributions of certain minor parties, among them the Anti-Masonic Party, the Populists, and the Progressives of 1912. In this section, we study the fortunes of minor, or third, parties in American politics. We also look at why we have only two major parties, explain how federalism helps the parties survive, and describe voters' loyalty to the two major parties today.

Minor Parties in America

Minor parties have always figured in party politics in America. Most minor parties in our political history have been one of four types:[22]

- *Bolter parties* are formed by factions that have split off from one of the major parties. Six times in the thirty-eight presidential elections from the Civil War to 2008, disgruntled leaders have "bolted the ticket" and challenged their former parties by forming new parties.[23] Bolter parties have occasionally won significant proportions of the vote. However, with the exception of Teddy Roosevelt's Progressive Party in 1912 and the possible exception of George Wallace's American Independent Party in 1968, bolter parties have not affected the outcome of presidential elections.
- *Farmer-labor parties* represented farmers and urban workers who believed that they, the working class, were not getting their share of society's wealth. The People's Party, founded in 1892 and nicknamed the "Populist Party," was a prime example of a farmer-labor party. The Populists won 8.5 percent of the vote in 1892 and also became the first third party since 1860 to win any electoral votes. Flushed by success, it endorsed William Jennings Bryan, the Democratic candidate, in 1896. When he lost, the party quickly faded. Farm and labor groups revived many Populist ideas in the Progressive Party in 1924, which nominated Robert La Follette for the presidency. Although the party won 16.6 percent of the popular vote, it carried only La Follette's home state of Wisconsin and died in 1925. In 1944, however, the Minnesota Farmer-Labor Party merged with the Democrats to form the Democratic Farmer-Labor (DFL) Party. The DFL is Minnesota's Democratic Party today.
- *Parties of ideological protest* go further than farmer-labor parties in criticizing the established system. These parties reject prevailing doctrines

electoral dealignment
A lessening of the importance of party loyalties in voting decisions.

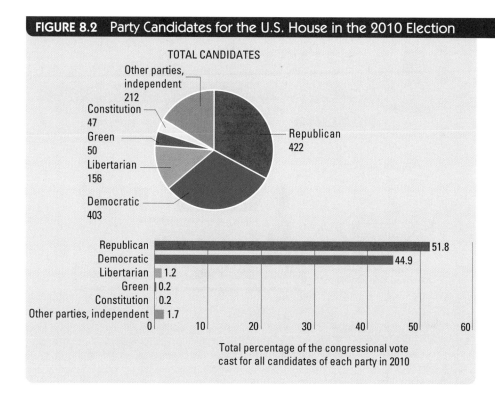

FIGURE 8.2 Party Candidates for the U.S. House in the 2010 Election

TOTAL CANDIDATES

Other parties, independent 212
Constitution 47
Green 50
Libertarian 156
Democratic 403
Republican 422

Party	Total percentage
Republican	51.8
Democratic	44.9
Libertarian	1.2
Green	0.2
Constitution	0.2
Other parties, independent	1.7

Total percentage of the congressional vote cast for all candidates of each party in 2010

In 2010, as in other recent elections, the Democratic and Republican parties each ran candidates for the House of Representatives in about 90 percent of the 435 congressional districts. Of minor parties, only the Libertarian Party, the best-organized minor party in the nation, ran candidates in more than one hundred districts. In most of those districts, however, the Libertarian candidates usually got under 1 percent of the vote. All other minor parties ran fewer candidates than the Libertarians.

Sources: http://www.votesmart. org/election_congress.php, October 8, 2010. Candidate data came from VoteSmart at http:// www.votesmart.org/election_ congress.php and election data from the *New York Times* at http://elections.nytimes.com/ 2010/results/house/big-board.

and propose radically different principles, often favoring more government activism. The Socialist Party has been the most successful party of ideological protest. Even at its high point in 1912, however, it garnered only 6 percent of the vote, and Socialist candidates for president have never won a single state. Nevertheless, the Socialist Party persists, fielding a presidential ticket again in 2008. In recent years, protest parties have tended to come from the right, arguing against government action in society. Such is the program of the Libertarian Party, which stresses freedom over order and equality (see page 260). In contrast, the Green Party protests from the left, favoring government action to preserve the environment. Together, the Libertarian and Green Parties polled less than 1 percent of the total vote for their presidential candidates in 2008. Although both parties together ran over one hundred congressional candidates, they won relatively few votes (see Figure 8.2) and no seats.

- *Single-issue parties* are formed to promote one principle, not a general philosophy of government. The Anti-Masonic parties of the 1820s and 1830s, for example, opposed Masonic lodges and other secret societies. The Free Soil Party of the 1840s and 1850s worked to abolish slavery. The Prohibition Party, the most durable example of a single-issue party, was founded to oppose the consumption of alcoholic beverages, but recently its platform has taken conservative positions: favoring right-to-life, limiting immigration, and urging withdrawal from the World Bank. Prohibition candidates

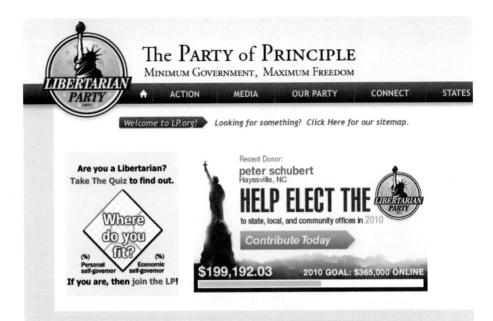

The Third-Party Theme

The Libertarian Party, founded in 1971, has run presidential candidates in every election since 1972, but no Libertarian candidate has ever won a million votes. In 2008, it ran more than 125 candidates for the 435 seats in the House of Representatives but elected none. It is true that Ron Paul, the 1988 Libertarian presidential candidate, was elected to Congress in 1996, but as a Republican. Nevertheless, the Libertarian Party's website justifiably describes itself as "America's third largest and fastest growing political party." That says something about the state of third parties in the United States.

(Libertarian National Committee, Inc.)

consistently won from 1 to 2 percent of the vote in nine presidential elections between 1884 and 1916, and the party has run candidates in every presidential election since, usually winning only a trickle of votes.

America has a long history of third parties that operate on the periphery of our two-party system. Minor parties form primarily to express some voters' discontent with choices offered by the major parties and to work for their own objectives within the electoral system.[24]

How have minor parties fared historically? As vote getters, they have not performed well. However, bolter parties have twice won more than 10 percent of the vote. (Although Ross Perot won 19 percent of the vote in 1992, he ran as an independent. When he created the Reform Party and ran as its candidate in 1996, he won only 8 percent.)[25] More significantly, the Republican Party originated in 1854 as a single-issue third party opposed to slavery in the nation's new territories. In its first election, in 1856, the party came in second, displacing the Whigs. (Undoubtedly, the Republican exception to the rule has inspired the formation of other hopeful third parties.) Although surveys repeatedly show over half the public saying they want a third major party, voters tend not to support them at the polls.[26]

As policy advocates, minor parties have a slightly better record. At times, they have had a real effect on the policies adopted by the major parties. Women's suffrage, the graduated income tax, and the direct election of senators all originated with third parties.[27] Of course, third parties may fail to win more votes simply because their policies lack popular support. The Democrats learned this lesson in 1896, when they adopted the Populists' free-silver plank in their own platform. Both their candidate and their platform went down to defeat, hobbling the Democratic Party for decades. Beginning around the 1930s, third-party voting began to decline. Research attributes the decline to the Democratic Party's leftward shift to encompass issues raised by minor parties.[28]

Most important, minor parties function as safety valves. They allow those who are unhappy with the status quo to express their discontent within the system, to contribute to the political dialogue. Surely this was the function of Ralph Nader as the Green Party candidate in 2000, when it won 2.7 percent of the vote. (By drawing votes from Democrat Al Gore in key states, Nader also denied Gore a victory over George Bush in the closest popular vote in history.) If minor parties and independent candidates are indicators of discontent, what should we make of the numerous minor parties, detailed in Figure 8.3, which took part in the 2008 election? Not much. The number of third parties that contest elections is less important than the total number of votes they receive. Despite the presence of numerous minor parties in every presidential election, the two major parties usually collect more than 95 percent of the vote, as they did in 2008 despite challenges from candidates of other parties. In the 2010 congressional elections, the tea party movement blew off steam within the Republican Party by backing more conservative candidates. In that sense, it acted like a minor party, as a safety valve.

Why a Two-Party System?

The history of party politics in the United States is essentially the story of two parties that have alternating control of the government. With relatively few exceptions, Americans conduct elections at all levels within the two-party system. Other democratic countries usually have multiparty systems—often more than three parties. Indeed, a political system with three relatively equal parties has never existed over a length of time in any country.[29] Why does the United States have only two major parties? The two most convincing answers to this question stem from the electoral system in the United States and the process of political socialization here.

In the typical U.S. election, two or more candidates contest each office, and the winner is the single candidate who collects the most votes, whether those votes constitute a majority or not. When these two principles of *single winners* chosen by a *simple plurality* of votes govern the election of the members of a legislature, the system is known as **majority representation** (despite its reliance on pluralities rather than majorities). Think about how American states choose representatives to Congress. A state entitled to ten representatives is divided into ten congressional districts, and each district

majority representation
The system by which one office, contested by two or more candidates, is won by the single candidate who collects the most votes.

FIGURE 8.3   Candidates and Parties in the 2008 Presidential Election

CANDIDATE AND PARTY*	TOTAL POPULAR VOTE	PERCENTAGE OF POPULAR VOTE
Barack Obama (Democrat)	64,413,006	52.49
John McCain (Republican)	56,733,958	46.23
Ralph Nader (Independent)	664,270	.54
Bob Barr (Libertarian)	492,294	.40
Chuck Baldwin (Constitution)	176,722	.14
Cynthia McKinney (Green)	143,884	.12
Alan Keyes (Independent)	35,294	.03
Ron Paul (Louisiana Taxpayers)	19,852	.02
Gloria La Riva (Socialism and Liberation)	7,269	.01
Roger Calero (Socialist Workers)	7,182	.01
Brian Moore (Socialist)	6,552	.01
None of these candidates	6,251	.01
Richard Duncan (Independent)	3,703	.00
James Harris (Florida Socialist Workers)	2,450	.00
Charles Jay (Boston Tea)	2,330	.00
John Joseph Polachek (New)	1,223	.00
Jeffrey Wamboldt (Independent)	771	.00
Frank McEnulty (New American Independent)	770	.00
Thomas Robert Stevens (Objectivist)	704	.00
Gene Amondson (Prohibition)	636	.00
Jeffrey Boss (Vote Here)	604	.00
George Phillies (Libertarian)	509	.00
Ted Weill (Reform)	470	.00
Donald K. Allen (Independent)	301	.00
Bradford Lyttle (Pacifist)	103	.00
Total	122,721,108	100%

*Party designations vary from state to state. Vote totals for the candidates include write-in votes.

In addition to the candidates of the two major parties, twenty-two other candidates ran in various states under banners of more than a dozen parties. All of them together, however, captured less than 2 percent of the total vote.

Source: Candidates and parties are from http://www.fec.gov/pubrec/fe2008/2008presgecands.pdf; votes cast are from http://www.cnn.com/ELECTION/2008/results/president/allcandidates, with 98 percent of precincts reporting.

elects one representative. Majority representation of voters through single-member districts is also a feature of most state legislatures.

Alternatively, a legislature might be chosen through a system of **proportional representation**, which awards legislative seats to each party in proportion to the total number of votes it wins in an election. Under this system, the state might hold a single statewide election for all ten seats, with each party presenting a rank-ordered list of ten candidates. Voters could vote for the party list they preferred, and the party's candidates would be elected from the top of each list, according to the proportion of votes won by the party. Thus, if a party got 30 percent of the vote in this example, its first three candidates would be elected.[30]

proportional representation
The system by which legislative seats are awarded to a party in proportion to the vote that party wins in an election.

Although this form of election may seem strange, more democratic countries use it than use our system of majority representation. Proportional representation tends to produce (or perpetuate) several parties because each can win enough seats nationwide to wield some influence in the legislature. In contrast, our system of elections forces interest groups of all sorts to work within the two major parties, for only one candidate in each race stands a chance of being elected under plurality voting. Therefore, the system tends to produce only two parties. Moreover, the two major parties benefit from state laws that automatically list candidates on the ballot if their party won a sizable percentage of the vote in the previous election. These laws discourage minor parties, which usually have to collect thousands of signatures to get on a state ballot.[31]

The rules of our electoral system may explain why only two parties tend to form in specific election districts, but why do the same two parties (Democratic and Republican) operate within every state? The contest for the presidency is the key to this question. A candidate can win a presidential election only by amassing a majority of electoral votes from across the entire nation. Presidential candidates try to win votes under the same party label in each state in order to pool their electoral votes in the electoral college. The presidency is a big enough political prize to induce parties to harbor uncomfortable coalitions of voters (southern white Protestants allied with northern Jews and blacks in the Democratic Party, for example) just to win the electoral vote and the presidential election.

The American electoral system may force U.S. politics into a two-party mold, but why must the same two parties reappear from election to election? In fact, they do not. The earliest two-party system pitted the Federalists against the Democratic Republicans. A later two-party system involved the Democrats and the Whigs. More than 135 years ago, the Republicans replaced the Whigs in what is our two-party system today. But with modern issues so different from the issues then, why do the Democrats and Republicans persist? This is where political socialization comes into play. The two parties persist simply because they have persisted. After more than one hundred years of political socialization, the two parties today have such a head start in structuring the vote that they discourage challenges from new parties. Third parties still try to crack the two-party system from time to time, but most have had little success. In truth, the two parties in power also write laws that make it hard for minor parties to get on the ballot, such as requiring petitions with thousands of signatures.[32]

The Federal Basis of the Party System

Focusing on contests for the presidency is a convenient and informative way to study the history of American parties, but it also oversimplifies party politics to the point of distortion. By concentrating only on presidential elections, we tend to ignore electoral patterns in the states, where elections often buck national trends. Even during its darkest defeats for the presidency, a party can still claim many victories for state offices. Victories outside the arena of presidential politics give each party a base of support that keeps its machinery oiled and ready for the next contest.[33]

Party Identification in America

The concept of **party identification** is one of the most important in political science. It signifies a voter's sense of psychological attachment to a party (which is not the same thing as voting for the party in any given election). Scholars measure party identification simply by asking, "Do you usually think of yourself as a Republican, a Democrat, an independent, or what?"[34] Voting is a behavior; identification is a state of mind. For example, millions of southerners voted for Eisenhower for president in 1952 and 1956 but continued to consider themselves Democrats. Again in the 1980s, millions of voters temporarily became "Reagan Democrats." Across the nation, more people identify with one of the two major parties than reject a party attachment. The proportions of self-identified Republicans, Democrats, and independents (no party attachment) in the electorate since 1952 are shown in Figure 8.4. Three significant points stand out:

- The number of Republicans and Democrats combined has far exceeded the independents in every year.
- The number of Democrats has consistently exceeded that of Republicans.
- The number of Democrats has shrunk over time, mainly to the benefit of independents.

Although party identification predisposes citizens to vote for their favorite party, other factors may convince them to choose the opposition candidate. If they vote against their party often enough, they may rethink their party identification and eventually switch. Apparently, this rethinking has gone on in the minds of many southern Democrats over time. In 1952, about 70 percent of white southerners thought of themselves as Democrats, and fewer than 20 percent thought of themselves as Republicans. In 2008, white southerners were only 21 percent Democratic, whereas 39 percent were Republican and 35 percent were independent.[35] Much of the nationwide growth in the proportion of Republicans and independents (and the parallel drop in the number of Democrats) stems from changes in party preferences among white southerners and from migration of northerners, which translated into substantial gains in the proportion of Republicans.[36]

Who are the self-identified Democrats and Republicans in the electorate? Figure 8.5 shows party identification by various social groups in 2008. The effects of socioeconomic factors are clear. People who have lower incomes and less education are more likely to think of themselves as Democrats than as Republicans. However, citizens with advanced degrees (such as college faculty) are slightly more Democratic. The cultural factors of religion and ethnicity produce even sharper differences between the parties. Jews are strongly Democratic compared with other religious groups, and nonwhites are more Democratic than whites. Finally, American politics has a gender gap:

party identification
A voter's sense of psychological attachment to a party.

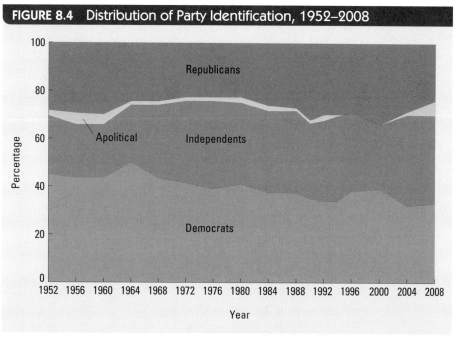

FIGURE 8.4   Distribution of Party Identification, 1952–2008

In every presidential election since 1952, voters across the nation have been asked, "Generally speaking, do you usually think of yourself as a Republican, a Democrat, an independent, or what?" Most voters think of themselves as either Republicans or Democrats, but the proportion of those who think of themselves as independents has increased over time. The size of the Democratic Party's majority has also shrunk. Nevertheless, most Americans today still identify with one of the two major parties, and Democrats still outnumber Republicans.

Sources: National Election Studies Guide to Public Opinion and Electoral Behavior, available at http://www.electionstudies.org/nesguide/nesguide.htm. The 2008 figure is from a PEW Report, "An Even More Partisan Agenda for 2008," 24 January 2008.

more women tend to be Democrats than men, and (although not shown here) this gap seems to widen with women's greater education.[37]

The influence of region on party identification has changed over time. Because of the high proportion of blacks in the South, it is still strongly Democratic (in party identity, but not in voting because of lower turnout among low-income blacks). The north-central states have slightly more Republicans than the other regions. Despite the erosion of Democratic strength in the South, we still see elements of Roosevelt's old Democratic coalition of different socioeconomic groups. Perhaps the major change in that coalition has been the replacement of white European ethnic groups by blacks, attracted by the Democrats' backing of civil rights legislation in the 1960s leading to the critical election of 1968.

Nonwhites in general have become more Democratic than Republican today, as the ethnic composition of the United States is inexorably becoming less white. Estimated at 65 percent in 2010, the non-Latino white population is projected to be only 58 percent in 2030. The Latino and nonwhite share of the population, estimated at 36 percent in 2010, is projected to be 44 percent by 2030.[38] Given that over 70 percent of blacks, Asians, and Latinos voted

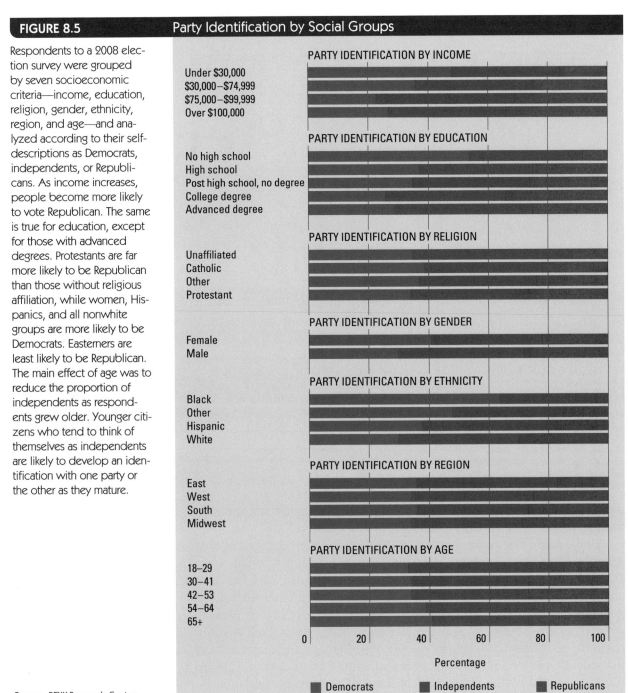

FIGURE 8.5 Party Identification by Social Groups

Respondents to a 2008 election survey were grouped by seven socioeconomic criteria—income, education, religion, gender, ethnicity, region, and age—and analyzed according to their self-descriptions as Democrats, independents, or Republicans. As income increases, people become more likely to vote Republican. The same is true for education, except for those with advanced degrees. Protestants are far more likely to be Republican than those without religious affiliation, while women, Hispanics, and all nonwhite groups are more likely to be Democrats. Easterners are least likely to be Republican. The main effect of age was to reduce the proportion of independents as respondents grew older. Younger citizens who tend to think of themselves as independents are likely to develop an identification with one party or the other as they mature.

Source: PEW Research Center Survey, 9–13 January 2008.

for Democratic candidates for Congress in 2008, the Republican Party faces problems in the partisan implications of demographic change.

Studies show that about half of all Americans adopt their parents' party. But it often takes time for party identification to develop. The youngest group of voters is most likely to be independent, but people in their thirties and forties, who were socialized during the Reagan and first Bush presidencies, are more Republican. The oldest group not only is strongly Democratic but also shows the greatest partisan commitment (fewest independents), reflecting the fact that citizens become more interested in politics as they mature.[39] While partisanship has been declining in the United States, that is true elsewhere too (see "Politics of Global Change: Fewer Citizens Are Partying").

Americans tend to find their political niche and stay there.[40] The enduring party loyalty of American voters tends to structure the vote even before an election is held, and even before the candidates are chosen. In Chapter 9, we will examine the extent to which party identification determines voting choice. But first we will explore whether the Democratic and Republican parties have any significant differences between them.

Party Ideology and Organization

George Wallace, a disgruntled Democrat who ran for president in 1968 on the American Independent Party ticket, complained that "there isn't a dime's worth of difference" between the Democrats and Republicans. Humorist Will Rogers said, "I am not a member of any organized political party—I am a Democrat." Wallace's comment was made in disgust, Rogers's in jest. Wallace was wrong; Rogers was close to being right. Here we will dispel the myth that the parties do not differ significantly on issues and explain how they are organized to coordinate the activities of party candidates and officials in government.

Differences in Party Ideology

George Wallace notwithstanding, there is more than a dime's worth of difference between the two parties. In fact, the difference amounts to many billions of dollars—the cost of the different government programs each party supports. Democrats are more disposed to government spending to advance social welfare (and hence to promote equality) than are Republicans. And social welfare programs cost money, a lot of money. Republicans decry massive social spending, but they are not averse to spending billions of dollars for the projects they consider important, among them national defense. Ronald Reagan portrayed the Democrats as big spenders, but his administration spent more than $1 trillion for defense. His Strategic Defense Initiative (the missile defense program labeled "Star Wars") cost billions before it was curtailed under the Democrats.[41] Although President George W. Bush introduced a massive tax cut, he also revived spending on missile defense, backed a $400 billion increase in Medicare, and proposed building a space platform on the moon for travel to Mars. One result was a huge increase in the budget deficit and a rare *Wall Street Journal* editorial against the GOP "spending spree."[42]

Voters and Activists. One way to examine the differences is to compare party voters with party activists. As shown in Figure 8.6, only 16 percent of Democratic

Politics of Global Change

Fewer Citizens Are Partying

A smaller percentage of U.S. citizens today identifies with one of the two major parties, compared with the early 1950s. This graph shows that the decline of partisanship is not peculiar to the United States but occurred from the 1960s to the 1990s in thirteen other Democratic nations. Only two showed slight increases in partisanship. The study's author attributes the trend to a set of common forces "that have eroded the role of parties as political institutions. Even more important, the citizenry is changing" (p. 36). More education and growing political sophistication may have decreased the need for partisanship. These trends were based on seven to twenty-one surveys in each country over several decades and estimated by slopes in regression analysis. The U.S. percentage for 2008 matches closely to the prediction line from the earlier surveys, which ended in 1998.

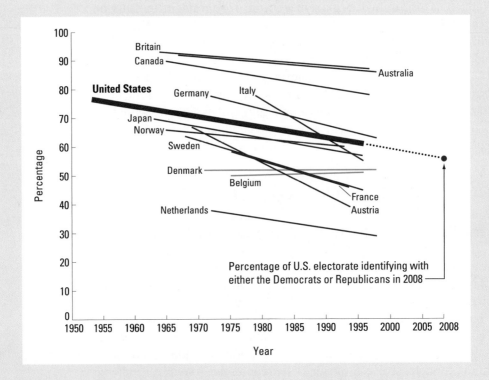

Source: Adapted from Table 2.1 in Russell J. Dalton, "The Decline of Party Identification," in *Parties Without Partisans,* ed. Russell J. Dalton and Martin P. Wattenberg (New York: Oxford University Press, 2000).

voters described themselves as conservative, compared with 63 percent of Republican voters. As we discussed in Chapter 5, relatively few ordinary voters think about politics in ideological terms, but party activists often do. The ideological gap between the parties looms even larger when we focus on party activists

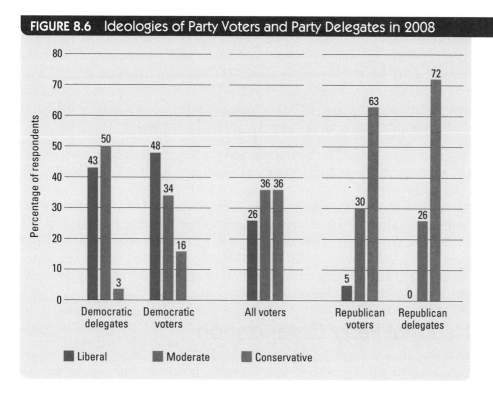

FIGURE 8.6 Ideologies of Party Voters and Party Delegates in 2008

Contrary to what many people think, the Democratic and Republican parties differ substantially in their ideological centers of gravity. When citizens were asked to classify themselves on an ideological scale, more Republicans than Democrats described themselves as conservative. When delegates to the parties' national conventions were asked to classify themselves, the differences between the parties grew even sharper.

Source: *New York Times*/CBS News Poll, 2008 Democratic National Delegate Survey and 2008 Republican National Survey, cited in *The New York Times,* 1 September 2008, p. A14.

on the left and right sides of Figure 8.6. Only 3 percent of the delegates to the 2008 Democratic convention described themselves as conservative, compared with 72 percent of the delegates to the Republican convention.

Platforms: Freedom, Order, and Equality. Surveys of voters' ideological orientation may merely reflect differences in their personal self-image rather than actual differences in party ideology. For another test of party philosophy, we can look to the platforms adopted at party conventions. Although many people feel that party platforms don't matter very much, several scholars have demonstrated, using different approaches, that winning parties tend to carry out much of their platforms when in office.[43] One study matched the parties' platform statements from 1948 to 1985 against subsequent allocations of program funds in the federal budget. Spending priorities turned out to be quite closely linked to the platform emphases of the party that won control of Congress, especially if the party also controlled the presidency.[44]

Party platforms also matter a great deal to the parties' convention delegates—and to the interest groups that support the parties.[45] The wording of a platform plank often means the difference between victory and defeat for factions within a party. Delegates fight not only over ideas but also over words.

The platforms adopted at both parties' conventions in 2008 were similar in length (about 26,500 words for the Democrats and 23,000 for the Republicans) but strikingly different in content. The Republicans mentioned "free" or "freedom" more than twice as frequently (59 to 26), while the Democrats referred to "equal" or "equality" or "inequality" more than twice as much (14 to 6). Republicans talked more about order than Democrats, mentioning "crime" or "criminals" by a wide margin (34 to 18) and swamping the Democrats with talk about "marriage" (13 to 1) and "abortion" (12 to 1). Republicans also drummed on the issue of "taxes" twice as much (98 to 42 mentions), while Democrats talked more about "poverty" (31 to 2 mentions).

Different but Similar. The Democrats and the Republicans have very different ideological orientations. Yet many observers claim that the parties are really quite similar in ideology compared to the different parties of other countries. Although both Republicans and Democrats favor a market economy over a planned economy more than parties elsewhere, Republicans do so more strongly than Democrats. A major cross-national study of party positions in Western countries since 1945 concludes that the United States experiences "a form of party competition that is as ideologically (or non-ideologically) driven as the other countries we have studied."[46]

National Party Organization

Most casual observers would agree with Will Rogers's description of the Democrats as an unorganized political party. It used to apply to the Republicans too, but this has changed since the 1970s, at least at the national level. Bear in mind the distinction between levels of party structure. American parties parallel our federal system: they have separate national and state organizations (and functionally separate local organizations, in many cases).

At the national level, each major party has four main organizational components:

- *National convention.* Every four years, each party assembles thousands of delegates from the states and U.S. territories (such as Puerto Rico and Guam) in a national convention for the purpose of nominating a candidate for president. This presidential nominating convention is also the supreme governing body of the party. It determines party policy through the platform, formulates rules to govern party operations, and designates a national committee, which is empowered to govern the party until the next convention.
- *National committee.* The **national committee**, which governs each party between conventions, is composed of party officials representing the states and territories, including the chairpersons of their party organizations. The Republican National Committee (RNC) has about 150 members, consisting of the national committeeman, national committeewoman, and a chairperson from each state and from the District of Columbia, Guam, Puerto Rico, and the Virgin Islands. The Democratic National Committee (DNC) has approximately 450 elected and appointed members, including, in addition to the national committee members and party chairs, members representing auxiliary organizations. The

national committee
A committee of a political party composed of party chairpersons and party officials from every state.

chairperson of each national committee is usually chosen by the party's presidential nominee and then duly elected by the committee. If the nominee loses the election, the national committee usually replaces the nominee's chairperson.

- *Congressional party conferences.* At the beginning of each session of Congress, the Republicans and Democrats in each chamber hold separate **party conferences** (the House Democrats call theirs a caucus) to select their party leaders and decide committee assignments. The party conferences deal only with congressional matters and have no structural relationship to each other and none with their national committees.

- *Congressional campaign committees.* Democrats and Republicans in the House and Senate also maintain separate **congressional campaign committees**, each of which raises its own funds to support its candidates in congressional elections. The separation of these organizations from the national committee tells us that the national party structure is loose; the national committee seldom gets involved with the election of any individual member of Congress. Moreover, even the congressional campaign organizations merely supplement the funds that senators and representatives raise on their own to win reelection.

It is tempting to think of the national party chairperson as sitting at the top of a hierarchical party organization that not only controls its members in Congress but also issues orders to the state committees and on down to the local level. Few ideas could be more wrong.[47] In fact, the RNC and DNC do not even really direct or control the crucial presidential campaigns. Prospective nominees hire their own campaign staffs during the party primaries to win delegates who will support them for nomination at the party conventions. Successful nominees then keep their winning staffs to contest the general election. The main role of a national committee is to support its candidate's personal campaign staff in the effort to win.

In this light, the national committees appear to be relatively useless organizations—as reflected in the 1964 book about them, *Politics Without Power*.[48] For many years, their role was essentially limited to planning for the next party convention. The committee would select the site, invite the state parties to attend, plan the program, and so on. Beginning in the 1970s, however, the roles of the DNC and RNC began to expand—but in different ways.

The Democratic story was dramatic. During the Vietnam War in 1968, an unpopular President Lyndon Johnson was challenged for renomination by prominent Democrats, including Senators Robert F. Kennedy and Eugene McCarthy. On March 31, after primary elections had begun, Johnson chose not to run for reelection. His vice president, Hubert Humphrey, then announced his candidacy. A month later Senator Kennedy was assassinated. Although Humphrey did not enter a single primary, he won the nomination over McCarthy at a riotous convention angry at the war and the role of party bosses in picking Humphrey. In an attempt to open the party to broader participation, a party commission formulated new guidelines for selecting delegates to the

party conferences
A meeting to select party leaders and decide committee assignments, held at the beginning of a session of Congress by Republicans or Democrats in each chamber.

congressional campaign committee
An organization maintained by a political party to raise funds to support its own candidates in congressional elections.

Building a Bigger Republican Tent?

In January 2009, the Republican National Committee after six ballots chose Michael Steele as its new chair by a vote of 91 to 77. Formerly head of the Maryland Republican Party, Steele vowed to fix his party's "image problem" while keeping true to his conservative views. He refused to label Obama a "socialist," as requested by some committee members, and opposed adopting ten core policy principles and denying financial support to GOP candidates who disagreed with three or more of them. This so-called purity test was sparked by the candidacy of moderate Republican Dede Scozzafava (see page 243). Political observers anticipated intraparty fights in 2010 congressional Republican primaries over the purity test. A much weaker version of the test was later adopted by the RNC. After describing the war in Afghanistan as one "of Obama's choosing," Steele was rebuked by Republican leaders who backed the war, some calling for his resignation.

Source: David Weigel, "An RNC Purity Test?" *Washington Independent,* 23 November 2009, http://washingtonindependent.com/68701/an-rnc-purity-test; Andy Barr, "Purity Test Reignites RNC Tensions," *Politico,* 25 November 2009. *Photo:* Chip Somodevilla/Getty Images.

next convention in 1972. These guidelines promised party members a "full, meaningful and timely opportunity" to participate in the process.

Many state parties rebelled at national interference with their role in selecting convention delegates, but the DNC threatened to deny seating at the 1972 convention to any state delegation that did not comply with the guidelines. Never before had a national party committee imposed such rules on a state party organization, but it worked. Even the powerful Illinois delegation, led by Chicago mayor and Democratic Party boss Richard

J. Daley, was denied seating at the 1972 convention for violating the guidelines by choosing Illinois delegates in a closed process, and an alternative delegation was seated that used open procedures. To comply with the new guidelines, many more states began to use primaries to select convention delegates.

While the Democrats were busy in the 1970s with *procedural* reforms, the Republicans were making *organizational* reforms.[49] The RNC did little to open up its delegate selection process; Republicans were not inclined to impose quotas on state parties through their national committee. Instead, the RNC strengthened its fundraising, research, and service roles. Republicans acquired their own building and their own computer system, and in 1976 they hired the first full-time chairperson in the history of either national party. (Until then, the chairperson had worked part time.) The new RNC chairman, William Brock, expanded the party's staff, launched new publications, held seminars, conducted election analyses, and advised candidates for state and legislative offices—things that national party committees in other countries had been doing for years. By the 2000 election, campaign finance analysts noted, American parties had become "an important source of funding in the race for the White House."[50]

The vast difference between the Democratic and Republican approaches to reforming the national committees shows in the funds raised by the DNC and RNC during election campaigns. During Brock's tenure as chairperson of the RNC, the Republicans raised three to four times as much money as the Democrats. Even though Republicans traditionally raised more campaign money than Democrats, they no longer relied on a relatively few wealthy contributors. As a matter of fact, the Republicans received more of their funds in small contributions (less than $100), mainly through direct-mail solicitation, than the Democrats. In short, the RNC raised far more money than the DNC, from many more citizens, as part of its long-term commitment to improving its organizational services. Its efforts have also made a difference at the state and local levels. Beginning in 2002, however, significant changes occurred in how political parties could collect money to finance their activities. These campaign finance reforms are discussed in Chapter 9.

Slow to respond to the Republican's organizational initiatives, the Democrats acquired their own building in the 1990s and enhanced their computer system for fundraising. After former Vermont governor Howard Dean became the new chair of the DNC in 2005, he pushed a program to build the party's strength in all fifty states. His plan clashed with that of Rahm Emanuel (D-Ill.), the new head of the Democratic Congressional Campaign Committee, who favored focusing resources on "winnable" races in selected states. The clash itself showed the dispersion of power in the national party organization, but the party benefited from both efforts. Thanks largely to Emanuel's work with congressional candidates, the Democrats won control of Congress in the 2006 election, and state party leaders across the nation praised Dean for improving their organizations.[51]

According to a major study of presidential party building, all Republican presidents, from Eisenhower through G. W. Bush, supported their national committee's organization efforts in order to build a Republican majority in the electorate. In contrast, Democratic presidents from Kennedy through Clinton's first term, who "were not out to build a new majority but to make use of the one they had," tended to exploit, not build, the party organization.[52] Clinton became supportive after the Republican takeover of Congress in 1995. The evidence is not in concerning Obama's role.

State and Local Party Organizations

At one time, both major parties were firmly anchored by powerful state and local party organizations. Big-city party organizations, such as the Democrats' Tammany Hall in New York City and the Cook County Central Committee in Chicago, were called *party machines.*

A **party machine** was a centralized organization that dominated local politics by controlling elections—sometimes by illegal means, often by providing jobs and social services to urban workers in return for their votes. The patronage and social service functions of party machines were undercut when the government expanded unemployment compensation, aid to families with dependent children, and other social services. As a result, most local party organizations lost their ability to deliver votes and thus to determine the outcome of elections. However, machines remained strong in certain areas. In Nassau County, New York, for example, suburban Republicans showed that they could run a machine as well as urban Democrats.[53]

The individual state and local organizations of both parties vary widely in strength, but recent research has found that "neither the Republican nor Democratic party has a distinct advantage with regard to direct campaign activities."[54] Whereas once both the RNC and the DNC were dependent for their funding on "quotas" paid by state parties, now the funds flow the other way. In the 2007–2008 election cycle, the national party campaign committees transferred over $150 million to state and local parties.[55] In addition to money, state parties also received candidate training, poll data and research, and campaigning instruction.[56] The national committees have also taken a more active role in congressional campaigns.[57]

Decentralized but Growing Stronger

Although the national committees have gained strength over the past three decades, American political parties are still among the most decentralized parties in the world.[58] Not even the president can count on loyalty from the legislative members of his party. Consider the 2009 congressional vote on reforming health care, President Obama's most important policy initiative. Although the Democrats held 258 seats in the House, the bill passed only 220–215, as 39 Democrats (15 percent) voted against it. Although all Democrats voted for the bill to reach the 60 votes needed for passage in the Senate

party machine
A centralized party organization that dominates local politics by controlling elections.

(all 39 Republicans opposed it), some Democratic Senators demanded and got changes before backing the President's plan.

Decentralization of power has always been the most distinguishing characteristic of American political parties. Moreover, the rise in the proportion of citizens who style themselves as independents suggests that our already weak parties are in further decline.[59] But there is evidence that our political parties *as organizations* are enjoying a period of resurgence. Indeed, both national parties have "globalized" their organizations, maintaining branches in over a dozen nations.[60] Both parties' national committees have never been better funded or more active in grassroots campaign activities.[61] And more votes in Congress are being decided along party lines. (See Chapter 11 for a discussion of the rise of party voting in Congress since the 1970s.) In fact, a specialist in congressional politics has concluded, "When compared to its predecessors of the past half-century, the current majority party leadership is more involved and more decisive in organizing the party and the chamber, setting the policy agenda, shaping legislation, and determining legislative outcomes."[62] However, the American parties have traditionally been so weak that these positive trends have not altered their basic character.[63] American political parties are still so organizationally diffuse and decentralized that they raise questions about how well they link voters to the government.

The Model of Responsible Party Government

According to the majoritarian model of democracy, parties are essential to making the government responsive to public opinion. In fact, the ideal role of parties in majoritarian democracy has been formalized in the four principles of **responsible party government**:[64]

1. Parties should present clear and coherent programs to voters.
2. Voters should choose candidates on the basis of party programs.
3. The winning party should carry out its program once in office.
4. Voters should hold the governing party responsible at the next election for executing its program.

How well do these principles describe American politics? You've learned that the Democratic and Republican platforms are different and that they are much more ideologically consistent than many people believe. So the first principle is being met fairly well.[65] To a lesser extent, so is the third principle: once parties gain power, they usually try to do what they said they would do. As Obama's attempt to reform health care showed, however, not every party member will necessarily support the party's position. From the standpoint of democratic theory, the real question involves principles 2 and 4: Do voters really pay attention to party platforms and policies when they cast their ballots?[66] And if so, do voters hold the governing party responsible at the next

responsible party government
A set of principles formalizing the ideal role of parties in a majoritarian democracy.

election for delivering, or failing to deliver, on its pledges? To answer these questions, we must consider in greater detail the parties' role in nominating candidates and structuring the voters' choices in elections. At the conclusion of Chapter 9, we will return to evaluating the role of political parties in democratic government.

Summary

Political parties perform four important functions in a political system: nominating candidates, structuring the voting choice, proposing alternative government programs, and coordinating the activities of government officials. Political parties have been performing these functions longer in the United States than in any other country. The Democratic Party, founded in 1828, is the world's oldest political party. When the Republican Party emerged as a major party after the 1856 election, it was the beginning of our two-party system—the oldest party system in the world.

America's two-party system has experienced four critical elections, each of which realigned the electorate for years and affected the party balance in government. The election of 1860 established the Republicans as the major party in the North and the Democrats as the dominant party in the South. Nationally, the two parties remained roughly balanced in Congress until the critical election of 1896. This election strengthened the link between the Republican Party and business interests in the heavily populated Northeast and Midwest and produced a surge in voter support that made the Republicans the majority party nationally for more than three decades. The Great Depression produced the conditions that transformed the Democrats into the majority party in the critical election of 1932. The presidential election of 1968 signaled the end of the Democrats' domination of national politics. Until that election, Republican candidates for president rarely ran well in the South. Since 1968, Republican candidates have won most presidential elections, and they relied on winning in the South when they won control of Congress in 1994. Nevertheless, the 2000 and 2004 presidential elections were extremely close, the two

houses of Congress were closely divided, and the two parties today are roughly balanced in strength.

Minor parties have not enjoyed much electoral success in America, although they have contributed ideas to the Democratic and Republican platforms. The two-party system is perpetuated in the United States by the nature of our electoral system and the political socialization process, which results in most Americans' identifying with either the Democratic or the Republican Party. The federal system of government has also helped the Democrats and Republicans survive defeats at the national level by sustaining them with electoral victories at the state level. The pattern of party identification has been changing in recent years: as more people are becoming independents and Republicans, the number of Democratic identifiers is dropping. Still, Democrats nationally outnumber Republicans, and together they far outnumber independents.

The two major parties differ in their ideological orientations. Democratic identifiers and activists are more likely to describe themselves as liberal; Republican identifiers and activists tend to be conservative. The party platforms also reveal substantial ideological differences. The 2008 Democratic Party platform showed a more liberal orientation by stressing equality over freedom; the Republican platform was more conservative, concentrating on freedom but also emphasizing the importance of restoring social order. Organizationally, the Republicans have recently become the stronger party at both the national and state levels, and both parties are showing signs of resurgence. Nevertheless, both parties are still very decentralized compared with parties in other countries.

In keeping with the model of responsible party government, American parties do tend to translate their platform positions into government policy if elected to power. As one scholar put it, "America's national parties today are at their most disciplined in congressional voting since the 1890s, and partisan polarization appears to have reached a level unprecedented in living memory."[67] But as we move to Chapter 9, it remains to be seen whether citizens pay much attention to parties and policies when casting their votes. If they do not, American parties do not fulfill the majoritarian model of democratic theory.

 Visit www.cengagebrain.com/shop/ISBN/0495906182 for flashcards, web quizzes, videos and more!

Nominations, Elections, and Campaigns

Chris Russell/Columbus Dispatch/Rapport Press/Newscom

American voters carry a heavy burden. They are asked to choose among *more* candidates for *more* offices *more* frequently than voters in any other country. Having the opportunity to choose government officials is a blessing of democracy, but learning enough about so many candidates to make informed choices is the curse of our unique and demanding electoral system.

As explained in Chapter 7, when Americans go to the polls in a general election, they are asked to choose among scores of candidates running for many different public offices at the local, state, and national levels. In the United States, an election is "general" in the sense that it includes various levels of government. In most other countries, a general election is very different and citizens have a much lighter burden in the polling booth.

Let's consider the difference between the 2010 general election in the United States and the 2010 general election in the United Kingdom, commonly called Britain. Like the United States, it is a democracy. Unlike the United States—but like most other democracies and nearly all European nations—Britain has a parliamentary, not a presidential, form of government.[1] Outlining how the British government operates illustrates how most established democracies operate.

The United Kingdom is led by a prime minister chosen by members in the elected house of parliament—the House of Commons. The party controlling the House selects the prime minister. Because a parliamentary system joins the executive and legislative powers, the prime minister becomes the head of government.[2]

British governments are limited to five-year terms in office. If the prime minister loses support of parliament, however, a general election is called to resolve the political problem. A prime minister can also hold a general election earlier if the timing looks promising for his or her party. By British law, the parliament elected in 2005 had to expire on May 10, but the prime minister could have requested the Queen to dissolve parliament earlier. British media had speculated that the election might be held in November 2007 or early in 2008.

In Britain, general elections are not held according to a fixed calendar, so no party can prepare for them far in advance. Because elections are timed to political needs (such as a vote of no confidence in the government), the campaign period is fixed and short. On April 5, Prime Minister Gordon Brown of the governing Labour Party called the 2010 election for May 6, leaving just 31 days for campaigning—matching the average campaign period for the previous 24 elections from 1918 to 2005.[3] Punished for Britain's economic downturn, Brown's Labour Party was voted out of office and replaced by the Conservative Party, led by David Cameron. Because the Conservatives failed to win a majority of seats, however, Cameron became prime minister with the support of the smaller Social Democratic Party, led by Nick Gregg. Such coalition governments are notoriously unstable, and observers expect another election to be called before long to produce a government backed by a single-party parliamentary majority.

If the United Kingdom bases its elections on the needs of politics, the United States bases its on the movement of the planets. In early November, after the Earth has traveled four times around the sun, the United States holds a presidential election. The timing is entirely predictable but has little to do with politics.[4] Predictability does carry some advantages for political stability, but it also has some negative consequences. A major negative is the multiyear length of our presidential election campaigns. Congressional candidates in both the Democratic and Republican parties began planning for the 2010 national election soon after the 2008 election—resulting in two-year campaigns for most members of Congress.

In British general elections, voters are asked *only* to choose among one small set of candidates running for a single seat in parliament. The election is general only in the sense that all members of the House are up for election; there are *no other offices or issues on the ballot.*

This difference leaps out when comparing the ballots for the United States and Britain (see "Compared with What? The Voter's Burden in the United States and United Kingdom"). This difference dramatically translates into enormous differences in the total votes that are cast by voters in the two countries. The burden of being an informed voter is much greater here than there.

In this chapter, we probe more deeply into elections in the United States. We describe the various methods that states use to count the billion votes cast in each presidential election. We also consider the role of election campaigns and how they have changed over time. We study how candidates are nominated in the United States and the factors that are important in causing voters to favor one nominee over another. We also address these important questions: How well do election campaigns inform voters? How important is money in conducting a winning campaign? What are the roles of party identification, issues, and candidate attributes in influencing voters' choices and thus election outcomes? How do campaigns, elections, and parties fit into the majoritarian and pluralist models of democracy?

IN OUR OWN WORDS

Listen to Kenneth Janda discuss the main points and themes of this chapter.

www.cengagebrain.com/
shop/ISBN/049506182

The Evolution of Campaigning

Voting in free elections to choose leaders is the main way that citizens control government. As discussed in Chapter 8, political parties help structure the voting choice by reducing the number of candidates on the ballot to those who have a realistic chance of winning or who offer distinctive policies. An **election campaign** is an organized effort to persuade voters to choose one candidate over others competing for the same office. An effective campaign requires sufficient resources to acquire and analyze information about voters' interests, develop a strategy and matching tactics for appealing to these interests, deliver the candidate's message to the voters, and get them to cast their ballots.[5]

In the past, political parties conducted all phases of the election campaign. As recently as the 1950s, state and local party organizations "felt the pulse" of their rank-and-file members to learn what was important to the voters. They chose the candidates and then lined up leading officials to

election campaign
An organized effort to persuade voters to choose one candidate over others competing for the same office.

support them and to ensure big crowds at campaign rallies. They also prepared buttons, banners, and newspaper advertisements that touted their candidates, proudly named under the prominent label of the party. Finally, candidates relied heavily on the local precinct and county party organizations to contact voters before elections, to mention their names, to extol their virtues, and—most important—to make sure their supporters voted, and voted correctly.

Today, candidates seldom rely much on political parties to conduct their campaigns. How do candidates learn about voters' interests today? By contracting for public opinion polls, not by asking the party. How do candidates plan their campaign strategy and tactics now? By hiring political consultants to devise clever sound bites (brief, catchy phrases) that will capture voters' attention on television, not by consulting party headquarters. How do candidates deliver their messages to voters? By conducting media campaigns, not by counting on party regulars to canvass the neighborhoods. Beginning with the 2004 election, presidential and congressional candidates have also relied heavily on the Internet to raise campaign funds and mobilize supporters.[6]

Increasingly, election campaigns have evolved from being party centered to being candidate centered.[7] This is not to say that political parties no longer have a role to play in campaigns, for they do. As noted in Chapter 8, the Democratic National Committee now exercises more control over the delegate selection process than it did before 1972. Since 1976, the Republicans have greatly expanded their national organization and fundraising capacity. But whereas the parties virtually ran election campaigns prior to the 1960s, now they exist mainly to support candidate-centered campaigns by providing services or funds to their candidates. Nevertheless, we will see that the party label is usually a candidate's prime attribute at election time.

Perhaps the most important change in American elections is that candidates don't campaign just to get elected anymore. Due to the Progressive movement in the 1920s that championed use of the direct primary to select party candidates (see page 226), candidates must campaign for *nomination* as well. As we said in Chapter 8, nominating candidates to run for office under the party label is one of the main functions of political parties. Party organizations once controlled that function. Even Abraham Lincoln served only one term in the House of Representatives before the party transferred the nomination for his House seat to someone else.[8] For most important offices today, however, candidates are no longer nominated *by* the party organization but *within* the party. Except when recruiting prominent individuals to challenge entrenched incumbents, party leaders seldom choose candidates; they merely organize and supervise the election process by which party *voters* choose the candidates. Because almost all aspiring candidates must first win a primary election to gain their party's nomination, those who would campaign for election must first campaign for nomination.[9]

Compared with What?

The Voter's Burden in the United States and United Kingdom

Compared with other countries, the United States puts a very heavy burden on its voters. Compare these two facsimiles of official specimen ballots for the 2010 general elections in the United States and Britain. This long U.S. ballot, which asked voters to choose among 71 candidates for 31 different offices, is just a portion of the one that confronted voters in the city of Evanston, Illinois. They also were asked to retain or terminate 65 judges also on the ballot. In addition, they voted on an amendment to the Illinois Constitution. By contrast, the straightforward British ballot for the Oxford East constituency (which includes most of Oxford University) required citizens simply to choose one from seven party candidates for the House of Commons, shown with their addresses and party affiliations. As shown by the X, the Labour candidate won, getting 43 percent of the vote compared with 34 percent for the Liberal Democrat and 19 percent for the Conservative. All four of the remaining candidates won about 5 percent. Despite the presence of seven candidates, the voters' decision was simple. Compared with Britain (and virtually all other countries), voting is very complicated in the United States.

Voter Ballot for the 2010 Election in Britain's East Oxford Constituency

Vote for One Candidate Only

1	**ARGAR** **Edward** (address in the Cities of London and Westminster constituency) The Conservative Party Candidate	
2	**CRAWFORD** **Roger Martin** The Pigling, Woodview Nurseries, Shefford Road, Meppershall, Beds, SG17 5LL Equal Parenting Alliance	
3	**DHALL** **Sushila** (address in the Oxford West and Abingdon constituency) Green Party	
4	**GASPER** **Julia Margaret** 22 Trinity Road, Oxford, OX3 8LQ UK Independence Party	
5	**GODDARD** **Steve** 60 Rosamund Road, Oxford, OX2 8NX Liberal Democrats	
6	**O'SULLIVAN** **David Andrew** (address in the Brent East constituency) Socialist Equality Party	
7	**SMITH** **Andrew** 4 Flaxfield Road, Oxford, OX4 6QD The Labour Party Candidate	X

Voter Ballot for the 2010 United States General Election
City of Evanston, Cook County, Illinois, November 2

U.S. Senator, 6 Year Term (Vote For 1)
- ☐ Mark Kirk — *Republican*
- ☐ Alexander Giannoulias — *Democratic*
- ☐ LeAlan Jones — *Green Party*
- ☐ Mike Labno — *Libertarian*

U.S. Senator, 0 Year Term (Vote For 1)
- ☐ Mark Kirk — *Republican*
- ☐ Alexander Giannoulias — *Democratic*
- ☐ LeAlan Jones — *Green Party*
- ☐ Mike Labno — *Libertarian*

Governor and Lieutenant Governor (Vote For 1)
- ☐ Bill Brady — *Republican*
- ☐ Pat Quinn — *Democratic*
- ☐ Rich Whitney — *Green Party*
- ☐ Lex Green — *Libertarian*
- ☐ Scott Cohen — *Independent*

Attorney General (Vote For 1)
- ☐ Steve Kim — *Republican*
- ☐ Lisa Madigan — *Democratic*
- ☐ David Black — *Green Party*
- ☐ Bill Malan — *Libertarian*

Secretary of State (Vote For 1)
- ☐ Robert Enriquez — *Republican*
- ☐ Jesse White — *Democratic*
- ☐ Josh Hanson — *Libertarian*

Comptroller (Vote For 1)
- ☐ Judy Topinka — *Republican*
- ☐ David Miller — *Democratic*
- ☐ R. Erika Schafer — *Green Party*
- ☐ Julie Fox — *Libertarian*

Treasurer (Vote For 1)
- ☐ Dan Rutherford — *Republican*
- ☐ Robin Kelly — *Democratic*
- ☐ Scott Summers — *Green Party*
- ☐ James Pauly — *Libertarian*

U.S. Representative, 9th District (Vote For 1)
- ☐ Joel Pollak — *Republican*
- ☐ Janice Schakowsky — *Democratic*
- ☐ Simon Ribeiro — *Green Party*

State Representative, 18th District (Vote For 1)
- ☐ Robyn Gabel — *Democratic*

Water Reclamation Commissioner (Vote For 3)
- ☐ Paul Chialdikas — *Republican*
- ☐ Jimmy Tillman — *Republican*
- ☐ Mariyana Spyropoulos — *Democratic*
- ☐ Barbara McGowan — *Democratic*
- ☐ Michael Alvarez — *Democratic*
- ☐ Diana Horton — *Green Party*
- ☐ John Ailey — *Green Party*
- ☐ Nadine Bopp — *Green Party*

Board President, Cook County (Vote For 1)
- ☐ Roger Keats — *Republican*
- ☐ Toni Preckwinkle — *Democratic*
- ☐ Thomas Tresser — *Green Party*

Clerk, Cook County (Vote For 1)
- ☐ Angel Garcia — *Republican*
- ☐ David Orr — *Democratic*

Sheriff, Cook County (Vote For 1)
- ☐ Frederick Collins — *Republican*
- ☐ Thomas Dart — *Democratic*
- ☐ Marshall Lewis — *Green Party*

Treasurer, Cook County (Vote For 1)
- ☐ Carol Morse — *Republican*
- ☐ Maria Pappas — *Democratic*

Assessor, Cook County (Vote For 1)
- ☐ Sharon Strobeck-Eckersall — *Republican*
- ☐ Joseph Berrios — *Democratic*
- ☐ Robert Grota — *Green Party*
- ☐ Forrest Claypool — *Independent*

Commissioner, 13th District (Vote For 1)
- ☐ Linda Thompson LaFianza — *Republican*
- ☐ Larry Suffredin — *Democratic*
- ☐ George Milkowski — *Green Party*

Judge, Appellate Court, 1st District (Vote For 1)
- ☐ James Epstein — *Democratic*

Judge, Appellate Court, 1st District (Vote For 1)
- ☐ Aurelia Pucinski — *Democratic*

Judge, Appellate Court, 1st District (Vote For 1)
- ☐ Mary Rochford — *Democratic*

Judge, Cook County Judicial Circuit (Vote For 1)
- ☐ William Hooks — *Democratic*

Judge, Cook County Judicial Circuit (Vote For 1)
- ☐ Terry MacCarthy — *Democratic*

Judge, Cook County Judicial Circuit (Vote For 1)
- ☐ Susan Kennedy Sullivan — *Democratic*

Judge, Cook County Judicial Circuit (Vote For 1)
- ☐ Raymond Mitchell — *Democratic*

Judge, Cook County Judicial Circuit (Vote For 1)
- ☐ John Callahan — *Democratic*

Judge, Cook County Judicial Circuit (Vote For 1)
- ☐ Maureen Masterson Pulia — *Republican*
- ☐ Daniel Gallagher — *Democratic*

Judge, Cook County Judicial Circuit (Vote For 1)
- ☐ Thomas Lyons — *Democratic*

Judge, Cook County Judicial Circuit (Vote For 1)
- ☐ Sandra Ramos — *Democratic*

Judge, 9th Subcircuit (Vote For 1)
- ☐ Geary Kull — *Democratic*

Judge, 9th Subcircuit (Vote For 1)
- ☐ Steven Bernstein — *Democratic*

Nominations

The distinguishing feature of the nomination process in American party politics is that it usually involves an election by party voters. National party leaders do not choose their party's nominee for president or even its candidates for House and Senate seats. Virtually no other political parties in the world nominate candidates to the national legislature through party elections.[10] In more than half the world's parties, local party leaders choose legislative candidates, and their national party organization must usually approve these choices.

Democrats and Republicans nominate their candidates for national and state offices in varying ways across the country, because each state is entitled to make its own laws governing the nomination process. (This is significant in itself, for political parties in most other countries are largely free of laws stating how they must select their candidates.)[11] We can classify nomination practices by the types of party elections held and the level of office sought.

Nomination for Congress and State Offices

In the United States, almost all aspiring candidates for major offices are nominated through a **primary election**, a preliminary election conducted within the party to select its candidates. Some forty states use primary elections alone to nominate candidates for all state and national offices, and primaries figure in the nomination processes of all the other states. The rules governing primary elections vary greatly by state, and they can change between elections. Hence, it is difficult to summarize the types of primaries and their incidence. Every state uses primary elections to nominate candidates for statewide office, but about ten states also use party conventions to place names on the primary ballots.[12] The nomination process, then, is highly decentralized, resting on the decisions of thousands, perhaps millions, of the party rank and file who participate in primary elections.

In both parties, only about half of the regular party voters (about one-quarter of the voting-age population) bother to vote in a given primary, although the proportion varies greatly by state and contest.[13] Early research on primary elections concluded that Republicans who voted in their primaries were more conservative than those who did not, whereas Democratic primary voters were more liberal than other Democrats. This finding led to the belief that primary voters tend to nominate candidates who are more ideologically extreme than the party as a whole would prefer. But other research, in which primary voters were compared with those who missed the primary but voted in the general election, reported little evidence that primary voters are unrepresentative of the ideological orientation of other party voters.[14] Some studies support another interpretation: although party activists who turn out for primaries and caucuses are not representative of the average party member, they subordinate their own views to select candidates "who

primary election
A preliminary election conducted within a political party to select candidates who will run for public office in a subsequent election.

will fare well in the general election."[15] Within the Republican Party in the 2010 election, however, the tea party movement worked to nominate candidates who were suitably conservative over more moderate and arguably more electable candidates. Perhaps the most significant fact about primary elections in American politics today is the decline in competition for party nominations. One major study found that only "about 25 percent of statewide candidates face serious primary competition."[16]

There are four major types of primary elections, and variants of each type have been used frequently across all states to nominate candidates for state and congressional offices.[17] At one end of the spectrum are **closed primaries**, in which voters must register their party affiliation to vote on that party's potential nominees. At the other end are **open primaries**, in which any voter, regardless of party registration or affiliation, can choose either party's ballot. In between are **modified closed primaries**, in which individual state parties decide whether to allow those not registered with either party to vote with their party registrants, and **modified open primaries**, in which all those not already registered with a party can choose any party ballot and vote with party registrants. Voters in the states of Washington (in 2004) and California (in 2010) approved a single primary open to all candidates. Called the "top two" primary because the top two vote-getters stand for the general election, the Washington system is too new to evaluate, and California's will not operate until the 2012 election.

Most scholars believe that the type of primary held in a state affects the strength of its party organizations. Open primaries weaken parties more than closed primaries, for they allow voters to float between parties rather than require them to work within one. But the differences among types of primaries are much less important than the fact that our parties have primaries at all—that parties choose candidates through elections. This practice originated in the United States and largely remains peculiar to us. Placing the nomination of party candidates in the hands of voters rather than party leaders is a key factor in the decentralization of power in American parties, which contributes more to pluralist than to majoritarian democracy.[18]

Nomination for President

The decentralized nature of American parties is readily apparent in how presidential hopefuls must campaign for their party's nomination for president. Each party formally chooses its presidential and vice-presidential candidates at a national convention held every four years in the summer prior to the November election. Until the 1960s, party delegates chose their party's nominee right at the convention, sometimes after repeated balloting over several candidates who divided the vote and kept anyone from getting the majority needed to win the nomination. In 1920, for example, the Republican National Convention deadlocked over two leading candidates after nine ballots. Party leaders then met in the storied "smoke-filled room" and compromised on

closed primaries
Primary elections in which voters must declare their party affiliation before they are given the primary ballot containing that party's potential nominees.

open primaries
Primary elections in which voters need not declare their party affiliation and can choose one party's primary ballot to take into the voting booth.

modified closed primaries
Primary elections that allow individual state parties to decide whether they permit independents to vote in their primaries and for which offices.

modified open primaries
Primary elections that entitle independent voters to vote in a party's primary.

Feature Story

Changes in the Presidential Nomination Process

When President Lyndon Johnson abruptly announced in late March 1968 that he would not run for reelection, the door opened for his vice president, Hubert Humphrey. Humphrey felt it was too late to campaign in primaries against other candidates already in the race; nevertheless, he commanded enough support among party leaders to win the Democratic nomination. The stormy protests outside the party's national convention against the "inside politics" of his nomination led to major changes in the way both parties have nominated their presidential candidates since 1972.

Presidential Nominating Process

Until 1968	Since 1972
Party Dominated The nomination decision is largely in the hands of party leaders. Candidates win by enlisting the support of state and local party machines.	**Candidate Dominated** Campaigns are independent of party establishments. Endorsements by party leaders have little effect on nomination choice.
Few Primaries Most delegates are selected by state party establishments, with little or no public participation. Some primaries are held, but their results do not necessarily determine the nominee. Primaries are used to indicate candidates' "electability."	**Many Primaries** Most delegates are selected by popular primaries and caucuses. Nominations are determined largely by voters' decisions at these contests.
Short Campaigns Candidates usually begin their public campaign early in the election year.	**Long Campaigns** Candidates begin laying groundwork for campaigns three or four years before the election. Candidates who are not well organized at least eighteen months before the election may have little chance of winning.

Warren G. Harding, who won on the tenth ballot. Harding was not among the leading candidates and had won only a single primary (in his native Ohio). The last time that either party needed more than one ballot to nominate its presidential candidate was in 1952, when the Democrats took three ballots to nominate Adlai E. Stevenson. The Republicans that year nominated Dwight Eisenhower on only one ballot, but he won in a genuine contest with Senator Robert Taft. So Eisenhower also won his nomination on the convention floor.

Although 1952 was the last year a nominating majority was constructed among delegates inside the hall, delegates to the Democratic convention in 1960 and the Republican convention in 1964 also resolved uncertain outcomes. Since 1972, both parties' nominating conventions have ratified the

Until 1968	Since 1972
Easy Money Candidates frequently raise large amounts of money quickly by tapping a handful of wealthy contributors. No federal limits on spending by candidates.	**Difficult Fundraising** Campaign contributions are limited ($1,000 per person before 2004; now $2,000 but indexed for inflation), so candidates must work endlessly to raise money from thousands of small contributors. Political action committee contributions are important in primaries. Campaign spending is limited by law, both nationally and for individual states. (If candidates forgo public funds—as most major candidates did for the primary elections in 2008—spending limits no longer apply.)
Limited Media Coverage Campaigns are followed by print journalists and, in later years, by television. But press coverage of campaigns is not intensive and generally does not play a major role in influencing the process.	**Media Focused** Campaigns are covered intensively by the media, particularly television. Media treatment of candidates plays a crucial role in determining the nominee.
Late Decisions Events early in the campaign year, such as the New Hampshire primary, are not decisive. States that pick delegates late in the year, such as California, frequently are important in selecting the nominee. Many states enter the convention without making final decisions about candidates.	**"Front-Loaded"** Early events, such as the Iowa caucuses and New Hampshire primary, are important. The nomination may even be decided before many major states vote. Early victories attract great media attention, which gives winners free publicity and greater fundraising ability.
Open Conventions National party conventions sometimes begin with the nomination still undecided. The outcome is determined by maneuvering and negotiations among party factions, often stretching over multiple ballots.	**Closed Conventions** The nominee is determined before the convention, which does little more than ratify the decision made in primaries and caucuses. Convention activities focus on creating a favorable media image of the candidate for the general election campaign.

Source: Adapted from Michael Nelson (ed.), *Congressional Quarterly's Guide to the Presidency* (Washington, D.C.: CQ Press, 1989), p. 201. Copyright © 1989 CQ Press, a division of Sage Publications, Inc. Reprinted by permission of the publisher, CQ Press.

results of the complex process for selecting the convention delegates (as described in the feature "Changes in the Presidential Nomination Process"), although the 1976 Republican convention voted narrowly on the first ballot to renominate President Gerald Ford over Ronald Reagan. Most minor parties, like the Green Party in 2008, still use conventions to choose their presidential candidates.

Selecting Convention Delegates. No national legislation specifies how the state parties must select delegates to their national conventions. Instead, state legislatures have enacted a bewildering variety of procedures, which often differ for Democrats and Republicans in the same state. The most important distinction in delegate selection is between the presidential primary and the local caucus. In 2008, both major parties in more than thirty states used primaries to select delegates to their presidential nominating conventions, and both parties in fewer than twenty states selected delegates through a combination of local caucuses and state conventions.[19]

A **presidential primary** is a special primary held to select delegates to attend a party's national nominating convention. Party supporters typically vote for the candidate they favor as their party's nominee for president, and candidates win delegates according to various formulas. Democratic presidential primaries are *proportional,* meaning that candidates win delegates in rough proportion to the votes they win. Specifically, candidates who win at least 15 percent of the vote divide the state's delegates in proportion to the percentage of their primary votes. In contrast, most Republican primaries follow the *winner-take-all* principle, which gives all the state's delegates to the candidate who wins a plurality of its vote.

The **caucus/convention** method of delegate selection has several stages. It begins with local meetings, or caucuses, of party supporters to choose delegates to attend a larger subsequent meeting, usually at the county level. Most delegates selected in the local caucuses openly back one of the presidential candidates. The county meetings select delegates to a higher level. The process culminates in a state convention, which selects the delegates to the national convention.

Primary elections were first used to select delegates to nominating conventions in 1912. Heralded as a party "reform," primaries spread like wildfire.[20] By 1916, a majority of delegates to both conventions were chosen through party elections, but presidential primaries soon dropped in popularity. From 1924 through 1960, rarely were more than 40 percent of the delegates to the national conventions chosen through primaries. Protests at the 1968 Democratic National Convention (see Chapter 8) sparked rule changes in the national party that required more "open" procedures for selecting delegates. Voting in primaries seemed the most open procedure. By 1972, this method of selection accounted for about 60 percent of the delegates at both party conventions. Now the parties in about forty states rely on presidential primaries of some form, which generate about 80 percent of the delegates.[21] Because most delegates selected in primaries are publicly committed to specific candidates, one usually can tell before a party's summer nominating convention who is going to be its nominee. Starting in 1972, we began learning the nominee's identity earlier and earlier, thanks to **front-loading** of delegate selection. This term describes the tendency during the past two decades for states to move their primaries earlier in the calendar year to gain attention from the media and the candidates. In 2008 so many states pushed their delegate selection process so early toward the beginning of the year that more than half of the delegates to both conventions were selected by February 5—when twenty-four states held simultaneous primary elections or caucuses to select convention delegates. Prior to 2000, New Hampshire's primary (the first in the nation) had never occurred that early. As a result, some scholars said the presidential nominating process had "broken" in 2008 and wrote about reforming it.[22]

presidential primary
A special primary election used to select delegates to attend the party's national convention, which in turn nominates the presidential candidate.

caucus/convention
A method used to select delegates to attend a party's national convention. Generally, a local meeting selects delegates for a county-level meeting, which in turn selects delegates for a higher-level meeting; the process culminates in a state convention that actually selects the national convention delegates.

front-loading
States' practice of moving delegate selection primaries and caucuses earlier in the calendar year to gain media and candidate attention.

Campaigning for the Nomination. The process of nominating party candidates for president is a complex, drawn-out affair that has no parallel in any other nation.[23] Would-be presidents announce their candidacy and begin campaigning many months before the first convention delegates are selected. Soon after one election ends, prospective candidates quietly begin lining up political and financial support for their likely race nearly four years later. Early in 2009, politicos speculated that former governors Mike Huckabee (Arkansas), Mitt Romney (Massachusetts), Tim Pawlenty (Minnesota), and Sarah Palin (Alaska) were positioning themselves for the 2012 Republican primaries.[24] This early, silent campaign has been dubbed the *invisible primary.*[25]

By historical accident, two small states, Iowa and New Hampshire, have become the testing ground of candidates' popularity with party voters. Accordingly, each basks in the media spotlight once every four years. The legislatures of both states are committed to leading the delegate selection process in their own way—Iowa using party caucuses and New Hampshire a direct primary—ensuring their states' share of national publicity and their bids for political history. The Iowa caucuses and the New Hampshire primary have served different functions in the presidential nominating process.[26] The contest in Iowa, attended by party activists, has traditionally tended to winnow out candidates, narrowing the field. The New Hampshire primary, typically held a week later, tests the Iowa front-runners' appeal to ordinary party voters, which foreshadows their likely strength in the general election. Because voting takes little effort by itself, more citizens are likely to vote in primaries than to attend caucuses, which can last for hours. In 2008, about 16 percent of the voting-age population participated in both parties' Iowa caucuses, whereas about 52 percent voted in both New Hampshire primaries.[27]

From 1920 to 1972, New Hampshire's primary election led the nation in selecting delegates to the parties' summer conventions. But in 1972 Iowa chose its convention delegates in caucuses held even earlier. Since then, Iowa and New Hampshire agreed to be first in their methods of delegate selection.[28] They kept that distinction in 2008, but two more states were admitted into the process with approval of the Democratic and Republican national party committees. Other states, however, tried to jump the gun by holding unapproved events, leading to uncertainty about when the delegate selection would begin and which states would participate.

Despite the confusion, the roles played by Iowa and New Hampshire in 2008 played to form—to winnow down the field—at least for the Democrats. Eight Democrats stood in the Iowa caucuses, but three (Barack Obama, Hillary Clinton, and John Edwards) took 97 percent of the delegates, with Obama winning the most. The next day, two losing candidates (Joseph Biden and Christopher Dodd) dropped out. After the New Hampshire primary gave 93 percent of the vote to Clinton, Obama, and Edwards (in that order), another candidate dropped out (Bill Richardson). So within a week the Democratic field dropped from eight candidates to five.

The story was somewhat different for the Republican candidates. Seven Republicans stood in the Iowa caucuses, and 96 percent of the vote was shared by five candidates: Mike Huckabee, Mitt Romney, Fred Thompson, John McCain, and Ron Paul, with Huckabee the surprise winner. The New Hampshire primary again saw five Republicans taking 96 percent of the vote, but this time McCain came out on top, with Romney again second.

So after Iowa and New Hampshire, only five Democrats stayed in the race for their party's nomination, while seven Republicans remained. Over the next month of primaries and caucuses the Republican race effectively dwindled to McCain, Huckabee, and Romney (see Figure 9.1), as failures in Nevada, South Carolina, and Florida forced out Duncan Hunter, Thompson, and Rudy Giuliani (who had staked everything on Florida). Although Paul remained, he was far behind. Meanwhile, the Democratic race narrowed to Obama and Clinton, as candidates Dennis Kucinich and Edwards fell short and withdrew. Although Mike Gravel remained, he was hopelessly behind.

On February 5, 2008, twenty-four states scheduled caucuses or primary elections to select delegates to the party conventions. On this "Super" Tuesday, the largest number of states would select the most delegates (about half the total in both parties) in the history of American politics. Because it was also the earliest date for holding multistate contests, many thought that it would decide the presidential nominations in both parties. In effect, that happened in the Republican Party, as McCain took a large lead in delegates, thanks to the winner-take-all rule in most of the Republican primaries. Two days later, Romney suspended his campaign. After Huckabee and Paul withdrew in early March, McCain ensured his nomination at the convention. Figure 9.1 portrays the ins and outs of the presidential hopefuls.

Super Tuesday did not settle the Democratic contest, however, because of the proportional nature of the Democratic primaries. Hillary Clinton and Barack Obama each won delegates in states that they lost in popular votes and ended nearly equal in convention delegates. The contest between a woman and an African American captured attention across the world. A professor in India said, "There's a gradual strengthening of democracy in the U.S. if so many people can accept both a black and a woman candidate. It's amazing."[29] The world also saw that the presidential selection process in the United States is extremely competitive and highly unpredictable. Among the twelve Republican presidential hopefuls in 2007, the winner was neither the most preferred at the early stages (Rudy Guiliani) nor the person with the most money (Mitt Romney). In fact, winner John McCain's campaign was almost written off as broke and hopeless in late 2007. Among the ten Democratic hopefuls, all eight white males dropped out as the race narrowed to the woman and African American candidates.

The contest for the Democratic Party nomination remained close as the rest of the states selected convention delegates from February through early June. It was not decided until Clinton withdrew on June 7, resulting in Barack Obama becoming the first African American ever nominated as a presidential candidate by a major political party.

FIGURE 9.1   From Many to Two: Presidential Hopefuls Starting and Dropping Out

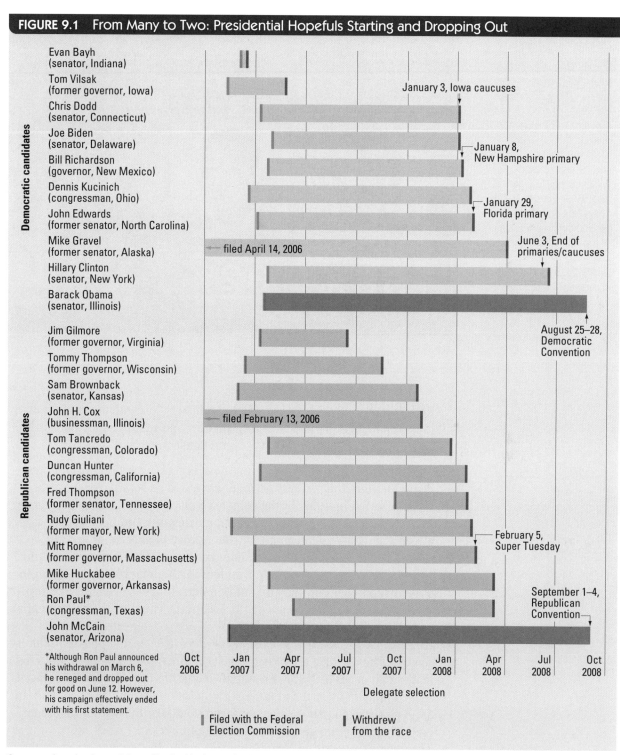

Over one hundred candidates filed with the Federal Election Commission (FEC) to run for president in 2008. The graph lists the ten Democrats and twelve Republicans who raised enough money to meet the FEC's requirement for electronic filing. As usual, some candidates withdrew before the delegate selection process began. Others dropped out for lack of support in the primaries or caucuses. By early March, McCain had captured the Republican nomination, but Clinton and Obama contested primaries into June before Clinton withdrew.

Requiring prospective presidential candidates to campaign before many millions of party voters in scores of primaries and hundreds of thousands of party activists in caucus states has several consequences:

- *When no incumbent in the White House is seeking reelection, the presidential nominating process becomes contested in both parties.* This is what occurred in 2008. In the complex mix of caucus and primary methods that states use to select convention delegates, timing and luck can affect who wins, and even an outside chance of success ordinarily attracts a half-dozen or so plausible contestants in either party lacking an incumbent president. With President Bush ineligible to run again in 2008, twelve Republicans and ten Democrats met the Federal Election Commission (FEC) requirements for electronic filing of their presidential campaigns (see Figure 9.1).
- *An incumbent president usually encounters little or no opposition for renomination within the party.* This is what happened in 2004, but challenges can occur. In 1992, President George Herbert Walker Bush faced fierce opposition for the Republican nomination from Pat Buchanan. In 1968, President Lyndon Johnson faced such hostility within the Democratic Party that he declined to seek renomination.
- *The Iowa caucuses and New Hampshire primaries do matter.* Since the first Iowa caucus in 1972, ten candidates in each party have won presidential nominations. All of the ten Republican nominees were first in either Iowa or New Hampshire, as were eight of the Democrats.[30] In 2008, former New York City mayor Rudy Giuliani neglected these early

contests to concentrate on later ones, and he lost badly. No future presidential hopeful is likely to repeat his mistake.

- *Candidates eventually favored by most party identifiers usually win their party's nomination.*[31] There have been only two exceptions to this rule since 1936, when poll data first became available: Adlai E. Stevenson in 1952 and George McGovern in 1972.[32] Both were Democrats; both lost impressively in the general election.

- *Candidates who win the nomination do so largely on their own and owe little or nothing to the national party organization, which usually does not promote a candidate.* In fact, Jimmy Carter won the nomination in 1976 against a field of nationally prominent Democrats, although he was a party outsider with few strong connections to the national party leadership. Barack Obama won in 2008 against Hillary Clinton, who had strong ties to Democratic Party leaders.

Elections

By national law, all seats in the House of Representatives and one-third of the seats in the Senate are filled in a **general election** held in early November in even-numbered years. Every state takes advantage of the national election to fill some of the nearly 500,000 state and local offices across the country, which makes the election even more "general." When the president is chosen every fourth year, the election is identified as a *presidential election*. The intervening elections are known as *congressional, midterm,* or *off-year elections*.

Presidential Elections and the Electoral College

In contrast to almost all other offices in the United States, the presidency does not go automatically to the candidate who wins the most votes. In fact, George W. Bush won the presidency in 2000 despite receiving fewer popular votes than Al Gore. Instead, a two-stage procedure specified in the Constitution decides elections for the president; it requires selection of the president by a group (college) of electors representing the states. Technically, we elect a president not in a national election but in a *federal* election.

The Electoral College: Structure. Surprising as it might seem, the term *electoral college* is not mentioned in the Constitution and is not readily found in books on American politics prior to World War II. One major dictionary defines a *college* as "a body of persons having a common purpose or shared duties."[33] The electors who choose the president of the United States became known as the electoral college largely during the twentieth century. Eventually, this term became incorporated into statutes relating to presidential elections, so it has assumed a legal basis.[34]

general election
A national election held by law in November of every even-numbered year.

The Constitution (Article II, Section 1) says, "Each State shall appoint, in such Manner as the Legislature thereof may direct, a Number of Electors, equal to the whole Number of Senators and Representatives to which the State may be entitled in the Congress." Thus, each of the fifty states is entitled to one elector for each of its senators (100 total) and one for each of its representatives (435 votes total), totaling 535 electoral votes. In addition, the Twenty-third Amendment to the Constitution awarded three electoral votes (the minimum for any state) to the District of Columbia, although it elects no voting members of Congress. The total number of electoral votes therefore is 538. The Constitution specifies that a candidate needs a majority of electoral votes, or 270 today, to win the presidency. If no candidate receives a majority, the election is thrown into the House of Representatives. The House votes by state, with each state casting one vote. The candidates in the House election are the top three finishers in the general election. A presidential election has gone to the House only twice in American history, in 1800 and 1824, before a stable two-party system had developed.

Electoral votes are apportioned among the states according to their representation in Congress, which depends largely on their population. Because of population changes recorded by the 2000 census, the distribution of electoral votes among the states changed between the 2000 and 2004 presidential elections and will not change until 2012. Figure 9.2 shows the distribution of electoral votes for the 2008 election, indicating which states have lost and gained electoral votes. The clear pattern is the systemic loss of people and electoral votes in the north-central and eastern states and the gain in the western and southern states.

The Electoral College: Politics. In 1789, the first set of presidential electors was chosen under the new Constitution. Only three states chose their electors by direct popular vote; state legislatures selected electors in the others. Selection by state legislature remained the norm until 1792. Afterward, direct election by popular vote became more common, and by 1824 voters chose electors in eighteen of twenty-four states. Since 1860, all states have selected their electors through popular vote once they had entered the Union.[35] In the disputed 2000 presidential election, the Republican Florida state legislature threatened to resolve the dispute in favor of Bush by selecting its electors itself. There was precedent to do so, but it was a pre–Civil War precedent.

Of course, the situation in Florida was itself unprecedented due to the extremely close election in 2000. Voters nationwide favored the Democratic candidate, Al Gore, by a plurality of approximately 500,000 votes out of 105 million cast. But the presidential election is a *federal* election. A candidate is not chosen president by national popular vote but by a majority of the states' electoral votes. In every state but Maine and Nebraska, the candidate who wins a plurality of its popular vote—whether by 20 votes or 20,000 votes—wins *all* of the state's electoral votes. Gore and his Republican opponent, George W. Bush, ran close races in many states across the nation. Not

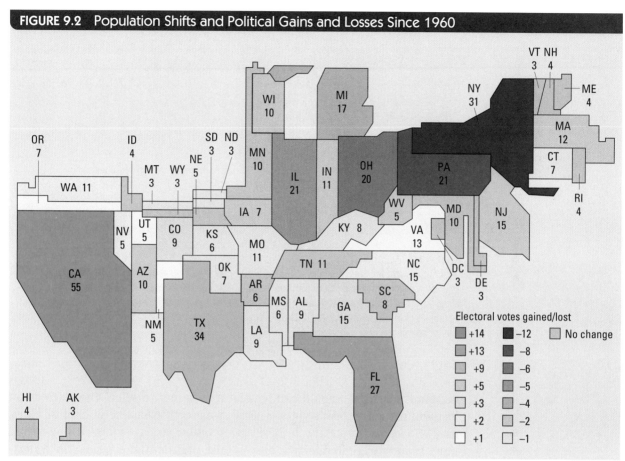

FIGURE 9.2 Population Shifts and Political Gains and Losses Since 1960

If the states were sized according to their electoral votes for the 2008 presidential election, the nation might resemble this map, on which states are drawn according to their population, based on the 2000 census. Each state has as many electoral votes as its combined representation in the Senate (always two) and the House (which depends on population). Although New Jersey is much smaller in area than Montana, New Jersey has far more people and is thus bigger in terms of "electoral geography." The coloring on this map shows the states that have gained electoral votes since 1960 (in shades of green) and those that have lost electoral votes (in shades of purple). States that have not had the number of their electoral votes changed since 1960 are blue. This map clearly reflects the drain of population (and seats in Congress) from the north-central and eastern states to the western and southern states. California, with two senators and fifty-three representatives in the 2008 election, will have fifty-five electoral votes for presidential elections until 2012, when reapportionment follows the 2010 census.

counting Florida, Gore had won 267 electoral votes, just three short of the 270 he needed to claim the presidency.

But in Florida, which had twenty-five electoral votes in 2000, the initial vote count showed an extremely close race, with Bush ahead by the slimmest of margins. If Bush outpolled Gore by just a single vote, Bush could add its 25 electoral votes to the 246 he won in the other states, for a total of 271. That was just one more than the number needed to win the presidency. Gore trailed Bush by only about 2,000 votes, close enough to ask for a recount. But the recount proved difficult due to different ballots and different methods for counting them (see Figure 9.3). After more than a month of ballot counting, recounting, more recounting, lawsuits, court

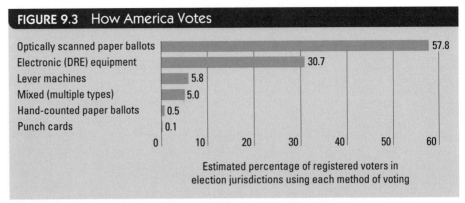

FIGURE 9.3 How America Votes

According to a study by Election Data Services of over three thousand election jurisdictions in the United States, a clear majority of the registered voters had their ballots counted by optical scanning equipment in the 2008 general election. Almost another third voted with electronic equipment. As recently as 2004, punch cards and lever machines respectively accounted for almost 20 and 15 percent of the votes cast. The change occurred because of problems counting votes in the disputed 2000 presidential election in Florida. In 2002, Congress passed the Help America Vote Act, providing funds to replace punch-card systems and mechanical-lever voting machines. Today, very few election districts rely either on punch cards or hand-counted paper ballots.

Source: Personal communication from Kimball W. Brace, President, Election Data Services, Inc.

decisions—and the Republican legislature's threat to select the electors on its own to ensure Bush's victory—Bush was certified as the winner of Florida's 25 *electoral* votes by a mere 537 *popular* votes. So ended one of the most protracted, complicated, and intense presidential elections in American history.[36]

The Electoral College: Abolish It? Between 1789 and 2000, about seven hundred proposals to change the electoral college scheme were introduced in Congress.[37] Historically, polls have shown public opinion opposed to the electoral college.[38] Following the 2000 election, letters flooded into newspapers, urging anew that the system be changed.[39]

To evaluate the criticisms, one must first distinguish between the electoral "college" and the "system" of electoral votes. Strictly speaking, the electoral college is merely the set of individuals empowered to cast a state's electoral votes. In a presidential election, voters don't actually vote for a candidate; they vote for a slate of little-known electors (their names are often not on the ballot) pledged to one of the candidates. Most critics hold that the founding fathers argued for a body of electors because they did not trust people to vote directly for candidates. But one scholar contends that the device of independent electors was adopted by the Constitutional Convention as a compromise between those who favored having legislatures cast the states' electoral votes for president and those who favored direct popular election.[40] The electoral college allowed states to choose, and—as described in Chapter 8—all states gravitated to direct election of electors by 1860. Occasionally (but rarely), electors break their pledges when they assemble to cast their written ballots at their state capitol in December (electors who do so are called "faithless electors"). Indeed, this happened in 2004, when one of the ten Minnesota electors voted not for Democrat John Kerry, who won the state, but for his running mate, John Edwards. Electors vote by secret ballot, so no one knew which one voted for Edwards instead of Kerry.[41] Such aberrations make for historical footnotes but do not affect outcomes. Today, voters have good reason to oppose a body of electors to translate their decision, and few observers defend the electoral college itself.

The more troubling criticism centers on the electoral vote *system*, which makes for a federal rather than a national election. Many reformers favor a majoritarian method for choosing the president—by nationwide direct popular vote. They argue that it is simply wrong to have a system that allows a candidate who wins the most popular votes nationally to lose the election. Until 2000, that situation had not occurred since 1888, when Grover Cleveland won the popular vote but lost the presidency to Benjamin Harrison in the electoral college. During all intervening elections, the candidate winning a plurality of the popular vote also won a majority of the electoral vote. In fact, the electoral vote generally operated to magnify the margin of victory, as Figure 9.4 shows. Some scholars argued that this magnifying effect increased the legitimacy of presidents-elect who failed to win a majority of the popular vote, which happened in the elections of Kennedy, Nixon (first time), Clinton (both times), and certainly George W. Bush (first time).

The 2000 election proved that defenders of the electoral vote system can no longer claim that a federal election based on electoral votes yields the same outcome as a national election based on the popular vote. However, three lines of argument support selecting a president by electoral votes rather than by popular vote. First, if one supports a federal form of government as embodied within the Constitution, then one may defend the electoral vote system because it gives small states more weight in the vote: they have two senators, the same as large states. Second, if one favors presidential candidates campaigning on foot and in rural areas (needed to win most states) rather than campaigning via television to the one hundred most populous market areas, then one might favor the electoral vote system.[42] Third, if you do not want to endure a *nationwide* recount in a close election (multiplying by fifty the counting problems in Florida in 2000), then you might want to keep the current system. So switching to selecting the president by popular vote has serious implications, which explains why Congress has not moved quickly to amend the Constitution.

Congressional Elections

In a presidential election, the candidates for the presidency are listed at the top of the ballot, followed by the candidates for other national offices and those for state and local offices. A voter is said to vote a **straight ticket** when she or he chooses the same party's candidates for all the offices. A voter who chooses candidates from different parties is said to vote a **split ticket**.

straight ticket
In voting, a single party's candidates for all the offices.

split ticket
In voting, candidates from different parties for different offices.

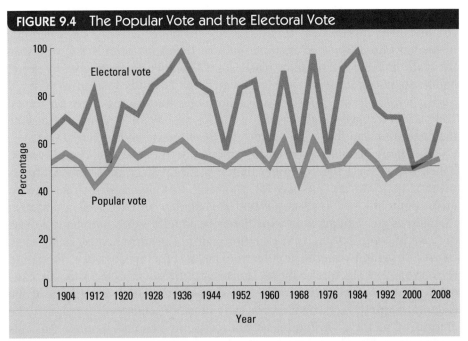

FIGURE 9.4 The Popular Vote and the Electoral Vote

Strictly speaking, a presidential election is a federal election, not a national election. A candidate must win a majority (270) of the nation's total electoral vote (538). A candidate can win a plurality of the popular vote and still not win the presidency. Until 2000, the last time a candidate won most of the popular votes but did not win the presidency was in 1888. In every election between these two, the candidate who won a plurality of the popular vote won an even larger proportion of the electoral vote. So the electoral vote system magnified the winner's victory and thus increased the legitimacy of the president-elect. As we learned from the 2000 election, that result is not guaranteed.

Source: Harold W. Stanley and Richard G. Niemi, *Vital Statistics on American Politics, 2007–2008* (Washington, D.C.: CQ Press, 2008).

About half of all voters say they split their tickets, and the proportion of voters who chose a presidential candidate from one party and a congressional candidate from the other has varied between 15 and 30 percent since 1952.[43] In the 1970s and 1980s, the common pattern was to elect a Republican as president while electing mostly Democrats to Congress. This produced a divided government, with the executive and legislative branches controlled by different parties (see Chapter 12). In the mid-1990s, the electorate flipped the pattern, electing a Democratic president but a Republican Congress. In 2008, voters elected a Democratic Congress as well as a Democratic president.

Until the 1994 election, Democrats had maintained a lock on congressional elections for decades, winning a majority of House seats since 1954 and controlling the Senate for all but six years during that period. Republicans regularly complained that inequitable districts drawn by Democrat-dominated state legislatures had denied them their fair share of seats. For example, the Republicans won 46 percent of the congressional vote in

1992 but gained only 40 percent of the seats.[44] Despite the Republicans' complaint, election specialists note that sizable discrepancies between votes won and seats won are the inevitable consequence of **first-past-the-post elections**—a British term for elections conducted in single-member districts that award victory to the candidate with the most votes. In all such elections worldwide, the party that wins the most votes tends to win more seats than projected by its percentage of the vote.* Thus in 1994, when Republicans got barely 50 percent of the House votes nationwide, they won 53 percent of the House seats. Gaining control of the House for the first time in forty years, they made no complaint. In 2004, the Republicans won 48.9 percent to the Democrats' 48.3 percent, and again the GOP took 53 percent of the seats for comfortable control. These recent election results reveal no evidence of Democratic malapportionment of congressional districts. Both parties have enjoyed, and suffered, the mathematics of first-past-the-post elections.

Heading into the 2010 congressional elections, Republicans hoped to benefit from the historical pattern of the president's party losing seats in fourteen of sixteen midterm elections from 1946 to 2006, during which the president's party avoided losses only in 1998 under President Clinton and in 2002 under President Bush. Both Clinton and Bush enjoyed approval ratings above 60 percent at election time. (See Figure 9.5.) President Obama's approval rating had dropped below 50 percent at the end of his first year, unemployment was near historic highs, and more troops were headed to fight an unpopular war in Afghanistan. Although the Democrats held about 60 percent of the seats in both the House and Senate, Republicans had aspirations of winning control of the House (as they did in the 1994 election), replacing Nancy Pelosi with John Boehner as Speaker, and cutting into the Democrats' margin in the Senate.[45] Republican hopes for 2010 soared when Republican Scott Brown, aided in his campaign by "tea party" activists, won the January election in Massachusetts to replace the late senator Ted Kennedy. Brown filled the seat held by Democrats since the election of 1952.

In the summer of 2010, the $1+ trillion budget deficit, growing national debt, and unemployment above 9 percent turned voters against the Obama administration. Four months before the November election, polls showed Republican voters far more enthusiastic than Democrats about voting in the election.[46] At that time, Republicans seemed poised to win the 39 seats needed to take control of the House and had an outside chance to regain the Senate. As it turned out, Democrats lost more than 60 House seats in the 2010 election—the most since 1938—as independent voters, who favored Democrats in 2008, flipped to Republicans in 2010. Republicans won control of the House and installed John Boehner as Speaker, but Democrats narrowly retained the Senate.

first-past-the-post elections
A British term for elections conducted in single-member districts that award victory to the candidate with the most votes.

---

*If you have trouble understanding this phenomenon, think of a basketball team that scores, on average, 51 percent of the total points in all the games it plays. Such a team usually wins more than just 51 percent of its games because it tends to win the close ones.

FIGURE 9.5 | Presidential Popularity and Party Seat Loss/Gain

American politics has shown these regularities since World War II: (1) presidents tend to lose popularity after their election, and (2) the presidential party tends to lose seats in midterm elections. As shown in the graph, presidential parties usually lose fewer seats if presidents retain their popularity at election time. In 2010, Obama's low rate of approval (48 percent) during a bad economy was accompanied by a loss of more than 60 Democratic House seats—more than any lost in a midterm election since 1938.

Sources: Jeffrey M. Jones, "Political Climate for 2010 Not as Favorable to Democrats," Gallup Poll Report, 4 November 2009. Gallup Poll Report, mid-October, 2010. House seat data as of November 4.

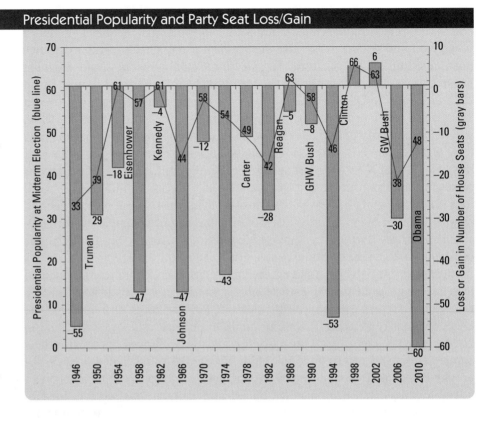

Campaigns

As political scientists Barbara Salmore and Stephen Salmore have observed, election campaigns have been studied more through anecdotes than through systematic analysis.[47] They developed an analytical framework that emphasizes the political context of the campaign, the financial resources available for conducting the campaign, and the strategies and tactics that underlie the dissemination of information about the candidate.

The Political Context

The two most important structural factors that face each candidate planning a campaign are the office the candidate is seeking and whether he or she is the *incumbent* (the current officeholder running for reelection) or the *challenger* (who seeks to replace the incumbent). Incumbents usually enjoy great advantages over challengers, especially in elections to Congress. Most congressional elections today are not very competitive. Of 2,175 congressional elections in the 2000s, only 41 (1.9 percent) were decided by 2 percentage points or fewer.[48] As explained in Chapter 11, incumbents in the House of Representatives are almost impossible to defeat, historically winning more than 95 percent of the time.[49] Incumbent senators are somewhat more vulnerable. An incumbent president is also difficult to defeat—but not impossible. Democrat Jimmy Carter was defeated for reelection in 1980, as was Republican George H. W. Bush in 1992. Of course, a nonincumbent will always triumph in an **open election**, one lacking an incumbent because of a resignation, death, or constitutional requirement.

Every candidate for Congress must also examine the characteristics of the state or district, including its physical size and the sociological makeup of its electorate. In general, the bigger and more populous the district or state and the more diverse the electorate, the more complicated and costly the campaign. Obviously, running for president means conducting a huge, complicated, and expensive campaign. By the summer of 2007, more than a year and a half before the 2008 election, both Hillary Clinton and Barack Obama had assembled campaign staffs of hundreds of people.[50]

Despite talk about the decreased influence of party affiliation on voting behavior, the party preference of the electorate is an important factor in the context of a campaign. It is easier for a candidate to get elected when her or his party matches the electorate's preference, in part because raising the money needed to conduct a winning campaign is easier. Challengers for congressional seats, for example, get far less money from organized groups than do incumbents and must rely more on their personal funds and raising money from individual donors.[51] So where candidates represent the minority party, they have to overcome not only a voting bias but also a funding bias. Finally, significant political issues—such as economic recession, personal scandals, and war—not only affect a campaign but also can dominate it and even negate such positive factors as incumbency and the advantages of a strong economy. In 2008, neither major candidate had an incumbent's advantage, and Republican John McCain was burdened by following a Republican president who presided over a weak economy.

Financing

Regarding election campaigns, former House Speaker Thomas ("Tip") O'Neill said, "There are four parts to any campaign. The candidate, the issues of the candidate, the campaign organization, and the money to run the campaign with. Without money you can forget the other three."[52] Money pays for office space, staff salaries, cell phones, computers, travel expenses, campaign literature, and, of course, advertising in the mass media. A successful campaign requires a good campaign organization and a good candidate, but enough money will buy the best campaign managers, equipment, transportation, research, and consultants—making the quality of the organization largely a function of money.[53] That may be true, but money alone does not ensure a successful campaign. By Super Tuesday, Mitt Romney had raised over $88 million—more than double the sum raised by his three remaining Republican opponents, and by January he had spent more on television ads than Clinton and Obama combined.[54] However, Romney did poorly in the early primaries and withdrew after Super Tuesday.

open election
An election that lacks an incumbent.

Nevertheless, no one can run a successful presidential campaign without raising a great deal of money. Regulations of campaign financing for state elections vary according to the state. Campaign financing for federal elections is regulated by national legislation.

Regulating Campaign Financing. Early campaign financing laws had various flaws, and none provided for adequate enforcement. In 1971, during a period of party reform, Congress passed the Federal Election Campaign Act (FECA), which limited media spending and imposed stringent new rules for full reporting of campaign contributions and expenditures. The need for strict legislation soon became clear. In 1968, before FECA was enacted, House and Senate candidates reported spending $8.5 million on their campaigns. In 1972, with FECA in force, the same number of candidates admitted spending $88.9 million.[55]

Financial misdeeds during Nixon's 1972 reelection campaign forced major amendments to the original FECA in 1974. The new legislation created the **Federal Election Commission (FEC)**, an independent agency of six members appointed by the president with approval of the Senate. No more than three members may come from the same party, and their six-year appointments are staggered over time so that no one president appoints the entire commission. The FEC is charged with enforcing limits on financial contributions to national campaigns, requiring full disclosure of campaign spending, and administering the public financing of presidential campaigns, which began with the 1976 election.

The law also limited the amounts that nonparty groups called political action committees or PACs (discussed at length in Chapter 10) could contribute to election campaigns, and it imposed limits on contributions by individuals and organizations to campaigns for federal office—that is, Congress and the presidency. The law targeted so-called **hard money** (direct contributions to candidates' election campaigns) in contrast to **soft money** (donations to party committees for buying equipment, remodeling the headquarters, or staffing regional offices). No person could contribute more than $1,000 to any candidate for federal office, but the law permitted large soft-money donations to national party committees. Later, as both parties raised very large sums of soft money, that aspect of party finance became troublesome.

Some people opposed even limits on hard-money contributions, viewing them as "free speech" and challenging the 1974 limits under the First Amendment. Although the Supreme Court upheld limits on contributions in 1976, it struck down limits on *spending* by individuals or organizations made independently on behalf of a national candidate—holding that such spending constituted free speech, protected under the First Amendment. It also limited the FEC to regulate only advertisements advocating a candidate's election or defeat with such words as "vote for" or "vote against."[56] The 1974 FECA (with minor amendments) governed national elections for almost three decades.

As campaign spending increased, some members of Congress spoke piously about strengthening campaign finance laws but feared altering the

Federal Election Commission (FEC)
A bipartisan federal agency of six members that oversees the financing of national election campaigns.

hard money
Financial contributions given directly to a candidate running for congressional office or the presidency.

soft money
Financial contributions to party committees for capital and operational expenses.

process that elected them. In 2002 a bill introduced by Republican senator John McCain (Arizona) and Democratic senator Russell Feingold (Wisconsin) finally passed as the Bipartisan Campaign Reform Act (BCRA; pronounced "bikra"). BCRA was fiercely challenged from several sources, including Republican conservatives who attacked McCain for limiting contributions and weakening the party. Nevertheless, the law was upheld by the Supreme Court in 2003 and took effect for the 2004 election.

To put BCRA into perspective, we must consider it in the light of the 1974 legislation, which it effectively replaced. In general, BCRA raised the old limits on individual spending—from $1,000 to $2,000—and indexed it for inflation in future years. However, the 2002 law did not raise the $5,000 contribution limit for PACs, which many thought already had too much influence in elections, and did not index PAC contributions for inflation. Here are the major BCRA limitations for 2009–2010 contributions by individuals, adjusted for inflation:

- $2,400 to a specific candidate in a separate election during a two-year cycle (primaries, general, and runoff elections count as separate elections);
- $10,000 per year to each state party or political committee;
- $30,400 per year to any national party committee.

BCRA also banned large soft-money contributions to political parties, which had grown over time: from $85.1 million in the 1991–1992 election cycle to $456.9 million in the 1999–2000 cycle.[57] Both parties' national committees had channeled over $200 million in soft money in 2000 to state and local party committees for registration drives and other activities not exclusively devoted to the presidential candidates but helpful to them. By outlawing large soft-money contributions, BCRA threatened both parties. It also banned organizations from running issue ads that named candidates in the weeks before an election.

However, BCRA allowed issue-advocacy groups, called **527 committees** (after Section 527 of the Internal Revenue Code, which makes them tax-exempt organizations), to spend unlimited amounts of soft money for media advertising, as long as they did not expressly advocate a candidate's election or defeat. Scholars studying campaign finance after BCRA found that spending by 527 committees increased from $151 million in 2002 to $424 million in 2004.[58]

In 2007, a more conservative Supreme Court struck down BCRA's ban of issue ads run before an election, which opened the door to massive independent campaign spending by nonparty groups. Many no longer organized as 527 committees, which were required to report their donors to the FEC, but as **501(c)4 social welfare organizations**, exploiting a legal loophole excusing them from disclosing donors.[59]

In 2010 a bitterly divided Supreme Court departed from its precedents and ruled against BCRA's ban on spending by corporations in candidate elections.[60] Conservatives viewed its decision in *Citizens United v. Federal Election Commission* as defending freedom of speech,[61] while liberals saw it

527 committees
Committees named after Section 527 of the Internal Revenue Code; they enjoy tax-exempt status in election campaigns if they are unaffiliated with political parties and take positions on issues, not specific candidates.

501(c)4 social welfare organizations
Groups named after Section 501 of the Internal Revenue Code that operate for promotion of social welfare; they are exempt from reporting donors if they spend most of their funds on issues, not candidates.

as opening the door to the corrupting influence of corporate money.[62] Beginning with the 2010 election, corporations will be free to run ads directly advocating a candidate's election for the first time since 1907, when Congress first banned using general corporate funds in federal election campaigns.[63]

Public Financing of Presidential Campaigns. The 1974 FECA provided for public funding of campaigns for presidential elections but not congressional elections, and BCRA continued the distinction. During the primary season, a presidential candidate could qualify for public funds by raising at least $5,000 in each of twenty states from private donations of no more than $250 each. The FEC matched these donations up to one-half of a preset spending limit—set in 1974 at $10 million but indexed for inflation—for each qualifying candidate. By 2008, the inflation-adjusted spending limit for primary election expenditures had risen to $42.05 million. Candidates who raised up to $21.025 million in private funds would have that amount matched by up to $21.025 million in public funds, subject to the limitation that they could not spend more than $42.05 million in their primary campaigns.

From 1976 through 1992, all major candidates seeking their party's presidential nomination accepted public matching funds for their primary election campaigns and thus adhered to the spending limits. But for the 1996 primaries, wealthy publisher Steve Forbes declined public funds, and did so again in 2000. So did Texas governor George W. Bush. Both raised and spent much more money competing for the Republican nomination than they could have by accepting public funding and its spending limits. In 2004, Democratic hopefuls Howard Dean and John Kerry, and incumbent President Bush (who had no meaningful opposition), declined public funds in the primaries. In 2008, only six of the nineteen candidates who participated in both parties' primary debates relied on matching funds.[64] Through March 2008, Obama alone had spent $183 million—far more than the $42 million limit imposed by accepting public funds.

The public funding program for presidential elections in November operated somewhat differently. First, the campaign spending limit was double that for primary elections. It began at $20 million in 1974 but stood at $84.1 million in 2008 after indexing for inflation. Second, candidates who accepted public funds had no need to raise matching funds privately. They were simply reimbursed by the government up to the spending limit. In addition, each national committee got $16.8 million of public money to run its nominating convention in 2008. Finally, each national committee was permitted to spend $19.2 million of its own money on behalf of its nominee.

From 1976 to 2004, every major party nominee for president had accepted public funds (and spending limits) for the general election. In 2008, however, the candidates clashed over the issue. Republican John McCain agreed to accept public funds and limit his campaign spending to $84.1 million. The Democratic nominee Obama refused public funds and raised far more private funds for his campaign, becoming the first candidate to do so since public funding was established over thirty years earlier. If McCain–coauthor of the McCain–Feingold campaign finance reform law (BCRA)–had not been so closely identified with limiting the role of private money in campaigns, he might also have declined public funding and the spending limit it imposed.

Private Financing of Congressional Campaigns. One might think that a party's presidential campaign would be closely coordinated with its congressional campaigns. However, campaign funds go to the presidential candidate, not to the party, and the national committee does not run the presidential campaign. Presidential candidates may join congressional candidates in public appearances for mutual benefit, but presidential campaigns are usually isolated–financially and otherwise–from congressional campaigns.

Candidates for national office raised more than $3 billion during the primary and general election campaigns in the 2007–2008 election cycle.[65] Barack Obama alone raised almost $750 million for his presidential campaign, far more than John McCain's almost $370 million.[66] The 1,544 candidates in primary and general election campaigns for the U.S. Congress in 2007–2008 raised almost $1.4 billion more.[67] Most were competing for the 435 seats in the House; only 34 Senate seats were up for election. Nevertheless, individual Senate candidates raised relatively more money because they had to compete in larger districts (states) rather than individual House districts, which average about 675,000 people.

Future Trends in Campaign Finance. Public funding of presidential campaigns was intended to equalize candidate spending as well as to limit it. After successfully equalizing and limiting spending for decades, public funding faces an uncertain future.[68] Today, prominent presidential candidates find that they can raise far more money for their campaigns than provided by public funding. Two major fundraising methods have made a huge difference. The first is the rise of contribution *bundlers* who collect legal campaign donations from individuals ($2,300 for the primary and $2,300 for the general elections in 2008) and then deliver the bundled donations to the candidate. In late 2007, the *Wall Street Journal* identified 2,045 bundlers (usually lawyers or business leaders) who "hit their friends, associates, and families for donations."[69] John Edwards, for example, had 543 bundlers contributing to him, and John McCain had 442. Taken together, they funneled over $100 million to candidates during the first nine months of the primary campaign.

The second method of fundraising is through the Internet, and it is even more lucrative. In January 2008, the month Barack Obama won contests in Iowa and South Carolina, he raised $32 million from 170,000 new contributors, mostly online.[70] Candidates need not win stunning victories to raise large sums on the Internet. Republican Ron Paul, who trailed in the polls, raised $4 million online in a single day.[71] Nor is a specific candidate required at all. A Democratic political action committee, ActBlue, set up Web pages for all Democrats who filed for elections. It promised to raise $100 million for them in the 2007–2008 election cycle.[72] Nor do you have to be in the United States to contribute. Through the first six months of 2007 and mostly through the Internet, candidates raised over $500,000 from an estimated six million American citizens living abroad.[73]

Although BCRA did ban national party committees from raising huge sums of soft money, it did not reduce the amount of money raised (and spent) for presidential campaigns. At least raising money on the Internet has a grassroots basis, in contrast to using money bundlers. But trying to prevent people from spending money to influence elections and politics is like trying to stop water flooding into a basement. Like water, money seeps around barriers. If people could no longer give massively to political parties, they gave to independent groups that campaigned for candidates separate from the parties. Studies of political contributions for the 2008 election found that 527 or 501(c)4 groups "pulled in money that the major parties used to receive."[74] Such interest groups were on track to spend over $1 billion by the election.[75] Often these independent expenditures were for ads that were not welcomed by the candidates they backed.[76] Today, the money genie has escaped from the public funding bottle, and future candidates for president are unlikely to accept the public funding limits imposed by the 1974 Federal Election Campaign Act.

Strategies and Tactics

In a military campaign, *strategy* is the overall scheme for winning the war, whereas *tactics* involve the conduct of localized hostilities. In an election campaign, strategy is the broad approach used to persuade citizens to vote for the candidate, and tactics determine the content of the messages and the way they are delivered.[77] Three basic strategies, which campaigns may blend in different mixes, are as follows:

- A *party-centered strategy,* which relies heavily on voters' partisan identification as well as on the party's organization to provide the resources necessary to wage the campaign;
- An *issue-oriented strategy,* which seeks support from groups that feel strongly about various policies;
- A *candidate-oriented strategy,* which depends on the candidate's perceived personal qualities, such as experience, leadership ability, integrity, independence, and trustworthiness.[78]

The campaign strategy must be tailored to the political context of the election. Clearly, a party-centered strategy is inappropriate in a primary because all contenders have the same party affiliation. Research suggests that a party-centered strategy is best suited to voters with little political knowledge.[79] How do candidates learn what the electorate knows and thinks about politics, and how can they use this information? Candidates today usually turn to pollsters and political consultants, of whom there are hundreds.[80] Well-funded candidates can purchase a "polling package" that includes:

- A benchmark poll, which provides "campaign information about the voting preferences and issue concerns of various groups in the electorate and a detailed reading of the image voters have of the candidates in the race";
- Focus groups, consisting of ten to twenty people "chosen to represent particular target groups (e.g., Latinos)[81] the campaign wants to reinforce or persuade ... led in their discussion by persons trained in small-group dynamics," giving texture and depth to poll results;
- A trend poll "to determine the success of the campaigns in altering candidate images and voting preferences";
- Tracking polls that begin in early October, "conducting short nightly interviews with a small number of respondents, keyed to the variables that have assumed importance."[82]

Professional campaign managers can use information from such sources to settle on a strategy that mixes party affiliation, issues, and images in its messages.[83] In major campaigns, the mass media disseminate these messages to voters through news coverage, advertising, and Internet services—around which a new industry has grown.[84]

Making the News. Campaigns value news coverage by the media for two reasons: the coverage is free, and it seems objective to the audience. If news stories do nothing more than report the candidate's name, that is important, for name recognition by itself often wins elections. To get favorable coverage, campaign managers cater to reporters' deadlines and needs.[85] Getting free news coverage is yet another advantage that incumbents enjoy over challengers, for incumbents can command attention simply by announcing political decisions—even if they had little to do with them. Members of Congress are so good at this, says one observer, that House members have made news organizations their "unwitting adjuncts."[86]

Campaigns vary in the effectiveness with which they transmit their messages through the news media. Effective tactics recognize the limitations of both the audience and the media. The typical voter is not deeply interested in politics and has trouble keeping track of multiple themes supported with details. By the same token, television is not willing to air lengthy statements from candidates. As a result, news coverage is often condensed to sound bites only a few seconds long.

The media often use the metaphor of a horse race in covering politics in the United States. In 2008, more than half the national news stories on television, in print, and online dealt with the horse race.[87] Ironically, evidence suggests that the national media focus more on campaign tactics and positioning than the state or local media do.[88] One longtime student of the media contends that reporters both enliven and simplify campaigns by describing them in terms of four basic scenarios: *bandwagons, losing ground, the front-runner,* and *the likely loser.*[89] Once the opinion polls show weakness or strength in a candidate, reporters dust off the appropriate story line.

The more time the press spends on the horse race, the less attention it gives to campaign issues. In fact, recent studies have found that in some campaigns, voters get more information from television ads than they do from television news.[90] Ads are more likely to be effective in low-visibility campaigns below the presidential level because the voters know less about the candidates at the outset and there is little "free" news coverage of the campaigns.[91]

Advertising the Candidate. In all elections, the first objective of paid advertising is name recognition. The next is to promote candidates by extolling their virtues. Finally, campaign advertising can have a negative objective: to attack one's opponent or play on emotions.[92] But name recognition is usually the most important. Studies show that many voters cannot recall the names of their U.S. senators or representatives, but they can recognize their names on a list—as on a ballot. Researchers attribute the high reelection rate for members of Congress mainly to high name recognition (see Chapter 11). Name recognition is the key objective during the primary season even in presidential campaigns, but other objectives become salient in advertising for the general election.

At one time, candidates for national office relied heavily on newspaper advertising; today, they overwhelmingly use the electronic media—primarily television. Political ads convey more substantive information than many people believe, but the amount varies by campaign. In his comprehensive study of campaign advertising in the last seven presidential elections, Darrell West found that political ads tended to mention candidates' policy preferences more in 1984, 1988, 1992, and 2000 and candidates' personal qualities more in 1996, 2004, and 2008.[93] In 1996, Bill Clinton drew fire for lack of "honesty and integrity"; in 2004, John Kerry was attacked for "flip-flopping" on issues and for false "heroism" in Vietnam; and in 2008 Obama was criticized for inexperience.

Other scholars have cautioned that the policy positions put forward in campaign ads may be misleading, if not downright deceptive.[94] West found that the 2008 presidential campaign was more positive than most recent ones, especially compared with 2004—the most negative since 1988.[95] Not all negatively toned ads qualify as *attack ads,* which advocate nothing positive. The term *contrast ads* describes those that both criticize an opponent and advocate policies of the sponsoring candidate.[96] A review of recent studies found that, ironically, both attack and contrast ads "actually carry more policy information than pure advocacy ads."[97] Regardless of whether people learn from political ads, scholars found, advertising does "a great deal to persuade potential voters" who viewed ads compared with those not seeing the ads.[98]

The media often inflate the effect of prominent ads by reporting them as news, which means that citizens are about as likely to see controversial ads during the news as in the ads' paid time slots. Although negative ads do convey information, some studies suggest that negative ads produce low voter turnout.[99] However, recent research shows that the existing level of political mistrust is more important than the negativity of the ads.[100] Moreover, negative ads seem to work differently for challengers (who show a tendency to benefit from them) than for incumbents (who tend to do better with more positive campaigns).[101] If these findings seem confusing, that's essentially the state of research on negative ads.[102] Researchers reviewing studies say that the connection between reality and perceptions is complex. Campaigns seen as negative by scholars are not necessarily viewed that way by voters.[103] BCRA contains a provision that was supposed to reduce negative ads in 2004: candidates must announce that they "approve" any ad run by their campaigns.[104] Ads run by independent groups, however, incur no such responsibility.

Using the Internet. The Internet is a relatively new medium for conducting election campaigns. It debuted in presidential campaigns in 1992, when Democratic candidate Jerry Brown, former governor of California, sent e-mail messages to supporters.[105] The first major candidate website appears to be that of Democratic senator Dianne Feinstein running for reelection from California in 1994. In 1995, the Democratic National Committee created the first website for a major party. In 2000, Democratic senator Bill Bradley raised funds online to campaign for the presidential nomination and was the first candidate to raise $1 million over the Internet; the Arizona Democratic Party held the first binding online primary election; and the Republican Party scored its own Internet first: registering 1 million activists online.

Democrats pioneered Internet usage in election campaigns, and a Democrat, Howard Dean, was the first presidential candidate to use a commercial website (www.meetup.com) to organize a meeting of campaign supporters. Using the Internet to raise large amounts of funds drew the most attention, but using it to mobilize supporters was more innovative. Dean's Internet architect, Joe Trippi, also created the first presidential campaign blog.[106] (See page 181 for more on blogs.) By 2008, presidential candidates (mainly Democrats) advertised on political blogs and were also using social networking sites—both commercial (Facebook, MySpace) and their own (for example, Obama's MyBO and McCain's McCainSpace).

Candidates like the Internet because it is fast, easy to use, and cheap—saving mailing costs and phone calls. During the first decade of its use in election campaigns, however, the Internet was not very productive, for relatively few people went online for political information or activity. Usage has steadily increased over the last decade. A national survey in December 2008 asked respondents to name two sources for "most of" their news about the presidential campaign. Most people (70 percent) named television. Although about one-third (35 percent) cited newspapers, a larger percentage (40) claimed the Internet over newspapers for the first time.[107] Young people (under 30) were equally likely to rely on the Internet as television.

Despite the increased reliance on the Internet by citizens for information and by candidates for fundraising, Internet advertising got only a "small slice of campaign spending in 2008," according to a company that tracks advertising. Because Internet users seek out what they want to view, the best way to reach average voters is still through local broadcast television.[108]

Explaining Voting Choice

Why do people choose one candidate over another? That is not easy to determine, but there are ways to approach the question. Individual voting choices can be analyzed as products of both long-term and short-term forces. Long-term forces operate throughout a series of elections, predisposing voters to choose certain types of candidates. Short-term forces are associated with particular elections; they arise from a combination of the candidates and issues of the time. Party identification is by far the most important long-term force affecting U.S. elections. The most important short-term forces are candidates' attributes and their policy positions.

Party Identification

Ever since the presidential election of 1952, when the University of Michigan's National Election Studies began, we have known that more than half the electorate decides how to vote before the party conventions end in the summer.[109] And voters who make an early voting decision generally vote according to their party identification. Despite frequent comments in the media about the decline of partisanship in voting behavior, party identification again had a substantial effect on the presidential vote in 2008, as Figure 9.6 shows. Each party's candidates, Barack Obama and John McCain, won

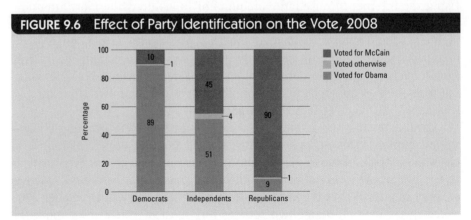

FIGURE 9.6   Effect of Party Identification on the Vote, 2008

The 2008 election showed that party identification still plays a key role in voting behavior. The chart shows the results of exit polls of thousands of voters as they left hundreds of polling places across the nation on election day. Voters were asked what party they identified with and how they voted for president. Those who identified with one of the two parties voted strongly for their party's candidate.

Source: Data from Bob Davis, "Voters Cast Their Ballots with the Economy in Mind, Exit Polls Indicate," *Wall Street Journal*, 5 November 2008, http://online.wsj.com/article/SB122584499389399483.html#articleTabs%3Dinteractive.

around 90 percent of self-described partisans of their party, with independents splitting their votes in favor of Obama.

This is a common pattern in presidential elections. The winner holds nearly all the voters who identify with his party. The loser holds most of his fellow Democrats or Republicans, but some percentage defects to the winner, a consequence of short-term forces—the candidates' attributes and the issues—surrounding the election. The winner usually gets most of the independents, who split disproportionately for him, also because of short-term forces.

In 2008, the electorate favored the Democratic candidate. But as shown in Figure 8.4 on page 265, Democrats have consistently outnumbered Republicans over the past fifty years. Why, then, have Republican candidates won more presidential elections since 1952 than Democrats? For one thing, Democrats do not turn out to vote as consistently as Republicans do. For another, Democrats tend to defect more readily from their party. Defections are sparked by the candidates' attributes and the issues, which have usually favored Republican presidential candidates since 1952. In 2008, the collapse of the economy after the party conventions was a powerful short-term factor that strongly affected voters.[110] It worked against John McCain as the candidate of the party in the White House, and for Obama—the challenger.

Issues and Policies

Candidates exploit issues that they think are important to voters. Challengers usually campaign by pointing out problems—unemployment, inflation, war, civil disorders, corruption—and promising to solve them. Incumbents compile

Hopes Dashed

Republican candidates for president, Senator John McCain, and vice president, Sarah Palin, governor of Alaska, had better days on the campaign trail. Although they lost the 2008 election, they made campaign history. When McCain chose Palin to be his running mate, she became the first woman named to the Republican presidential ticket and only the second woman vice-presidential candidate of a major party. Geraldine Ferraro ran as Walter Mondale's running mate on the Democratic ticket in 1984.

(© John Gress/Reuters/Corbis)

a record in office (for better or worse) and thus try to campaign on their accomplishments.

In January 2008, polls showed that voters, by a ratio of three to two, named the economy/jobs as a more important issue in voting for president than the war in Iraq. By the end of the party nominating conventions in early September, the situation in Iraq had improved significantly while the economy badly deteriorated. As the stock market crashed further before the election, the Iraq issue faded for voters, who became more concerned about the economy by a margin of eight to one. Polls showed that this shift in opinion greatly favored Barack Obama, who built his lead over John McCain to ten percentage points by mid-October. Obama managed to link McCain to George Bush's economic policies, with voters saying that they trusted Obama more than McCain to handle the economy.

McCain's choice for vice president also emerged as a campaign issue. Although Sarah Palin drew enthusiastic public support when she became his surprise choice as running mate and continued to excite Republican crowds, Palin's support waned in other groups after she struggled to answer questions in national interviews. Palin was lampooned several times on the television program, *Saturday Night Live*, and became viewed by a plurality of voters as not ready to serve as president.

Candidates' Attributes

Candidates' attributes are especially important to voters who lack good information about a candidate's past performance and policy stands—which means most of us. Without such information, voters search for clues about the candidates to try to predict their behavior in office.[111] Some fall back on their personal beliefs about religion, gender, and race in making political judgments.[112] Such stereotypic thinking accounts for the patterns of opposition and support met by, among others, a Catholic candidate for president (John Kennedy), a woman candidate for vice president (Geraldine Ferraro in 1984), a black contender for a presidential nomination (Jesse Jackson in 1984 and 1988), and the first Jewish vice-presidential candidate of a major party (Joe Lieberman in 2000).

In 2008, Barack Obama became the first African American presidential candidate of a major party. Opposed by some for his race and relative inexperience in government, he chose as his running mate Joe Biden, the long time senator from Delaware. John McCain, the 72-year-old war hero, surprisingly chose Sarah Palin, first-term governor of Alaska—the second woman ever nominated by a major party for vice president. The self-styled "average hockey mom" proved to be very popular among Republicans, but the public in general questioned her readiness to serve as president.

Evaluating the Voting Choice

Choosing among candidates according to their personal attributes might be an understandable approach, but it is not rational voting, according to democratic theory. According to that theory, citizens should vote according to the candidates' past performance and proposed policies. Voters who choose between candidates on the basis of their policies are voting on the issues, a behavior that fits the idealized conception of democratic theory. However, issues, candidates' attributes, and party identification all figure in the voting decision, and scholars have incorporated these factors in statistical models to explain voting.[113]

Unfortunately for democratic theory, many studies of presidential elections show that issues are less important to voters than either party identification or the candidates' attributes. One exception occurred in 1972, when voters perceived George McGovern as too liberal for their tastes and issue voting exceeded party identification.[114] Recent research has found an increase in policy-based voting.[115] Although party voting has declined somewhat since the 1950s, the relationship between voters' positions on the issues and their party identification is clearer and more consistent today. For example, Democratic Party identifiers are now more likely than Republican identifiers to describe themselves as liberal, and they are more likely than Republican identifiers to favor government spending for Social Security and health care. The more closely party identification is aligned with ideological orientation, the more sense it makes to vote by party. When citizens see differences between parties, they are less likely to vote for incumbents and more likely to justify their voting choice.[116]

Over the years, in fact, the alignment of party and ideology has increased in congressional voting such that the fit is almost perfect. Since

1981, the respected Washington weekly *National Journal* has analyzed the voting records of members of the House and Senate as predominantly liberal or conservative. In 2007, the *National Journal* ranked all one hundred members of the U.S. Senate by voting records from most conservative through centrist to most liberal. Drawing a line at the center of the rankings, one finds that only one of those with the most "conservative" records was a Democrat (Ben Nelson of Nebraska).[117] The pattern was similar for members of the House. In the absence of detailed information about candidates' positions on the issues, party labels are a handy indicator of their positions. Incidentally, Barack Obama had the highest liberal voting score among all U.S. senators in 2007.

Campaign Effects

If party identification is the most important factor in the voting decision and is also resistant to short-term changes, there are definite limits to the capacity of a campaign to influence the outcome of elections.[118] In a close election, however, changing just a few votes means the difference between victory and defeat, so a campaign can be decisive even if its effects cannot be disentangled.

The Television Campaign. Because of the propensity of television news shows to offer only sound bites, candidates cannot rely on television news to get their message out. In 2008, remarks from the two major presidential candidates on network news programs averaged only 8.9 seconds, about a second less than in the 1988 election, when sound bite timing began.[119] In truth, the networks devoted about as much airtime to the presidential campaign as in the past, but they did not give the candidates themselves much time to speak. In the average presidential campaign story, reporters spoke about 74 percent of the time compared with the candidates' 11 percent. No wonder that presidential candidates volunteer to appear on entertainment television shows: they get the chance to talk to the public![120]

Although candidates seek free coverage on news and entertainment programs, they fight their election campaigns principally through television advertisements. Both candidates in 2008 hired professional consultants to plan their ad campaigns. (As the mother lode for political consultants throughout the world—see "Politics of Global Change: The Americanization of Campaigns"—the United States has plenty to supply.) Both sides also understood that a presidential election was not truly a national election to be fought across the nation but a *federal* election whose outcome would be decided in certain "battleground" or "swing" states.[121]

During the primary season, campaign strategists mapped out sixteen battleground states that might swing from how they voted in the 2004 general election.[122] Obama hoped to pick up some states that had voted for George Bush, while McCain sought to hold all those states and win at least one (e.g., Michigan) that voted Democratic. By August, Karl Rove,

Politics of Global Change

The Americanization of Campaigns

Throughout most chapters in this book, we have discussed the process of globalization for its effects on American politics. Here we show the effect of the United States on politics and governments in other countries. Foreign scholars have used the term *Americanization of politics* to describe how politics elsewhere has been influenced by political developments in the United States. In no other aspect of politics is "Americanization" more noticeable than in election campaigns, and American influence has grown over time. A 1998 survey identified thirty-five members (half Americans) of the International Association of Political Consultants (IAPC) who worked outside the United States and Canada. Just two years later, another survey collected responses from almost six hundred campaign consultants in forty-three countries. Based on their responses, this graph shows the extent to which U.S. campaign techniques have been employed in different regions of the world. Of the forty-five IAPC officers and board directors in 2010, nineteen are from the United States. The rest spread over nineteen other countries. In the 2010 Ukrainian presidential election, three different American consulting firms advised the campaigns of the top three contenders, resulting in one U.S. firm winning.

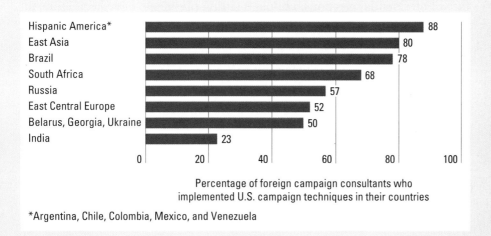

Percentage of foreign campaign consultants who implemented U.S. campaign techniques in their countries

*Argentina, Chile, Colombia, Mexico, and Venezuela

Sources: Shaun Bowler and David M. Farrell, "The Internationalization of Campaign Consultancy," in *Campaign Warriors*, ed. James A. Thurber and Candice J. Nelson (Washington, D.C.: Brookings Institution Press, 2000); Fritz Plasser and Gunda Plasser, *Global Political Campaigning: A Worldwide Analysis of Campaign Professionals and Their Practices* (Westport, Conn.: Praeger, 2002), pp. 41–43, at http://www.iapc .org; Richard Boudreaux, "Candidates Sought Guidance from American Consultants," *Wall Street Journal,* 9 February 2010, p. A10.

President Bush's campaign adviser, thought that four key states—Michigan, Colorado, Virginia, and Ohio—would decide the race.[123] By October, the collapsing economy worked against McCain almost everywhere. To conserve funds for other states, he stopped campaigning in Michigan, where polls showed he was falling behind. Meanwhile, the well-funded Obama forces kept campaigning vigorously there and in previously Republican states—for example, Colorado, Virginia, and Ohio.[124] Obama won all four battleground states.

The 2002 Bipartisan Campaign Reform Act was supposed to reduce the role of money in campaigns. Nevertheless, the 2008 presidential campaign was the most expensive in history for several reasons. First, no major presidential hopefuls in 2008 accepted matching public funds for their primary campaigns, so they did not operate under the Act's spending limits. Second, only McCain agreed to accept the $84.1 million in public funds for his general election campaign and limit spending to that amount. Third, by declining public funds Obama was free to spend as much money as he could legally raise under the 2002 Act.

Flush with funds, the Obama campaign outspent McCain's campaign on television advertising by a ratio of four to one, running ads in more states and running them more often. Although both sides ran negative ads, the University of Wisconsin analysis of television advertisements found McCain's ads to be more negative.[125] The week before the election, Obama even had funds to buy thirty minutes of broadcast time on three major networks (CBS, NBC, and Fox) for a personal and almost entirely positive appeal.

The Presidential Debates. In 1960, John F. Kennedy and Richard Nixon held the first televised presidential debate, but debates were not used again until 1976. Since then, candidate debates in some form have been a regular feature of presidential elections, although sitting presidents have been reluctant to debate except on their own terms.

Both campaign staffs in 2008 agreed to three presidential debates and one vice-presidential debate, prescribing the source of questions, length of answers, and format. In post-debate polls, viewers said Obama did a better job than McCain regardless of format: standing, roaming the floor in town-hall style, or seated. Some 60 million people watched each debate, but more than 70 million tuned into the lone vice-presidential debate, wondering how Sarah Palin would perform. She did well, but viewers said that Biden did better.[126] His showing and Obama's steady performance over all three debates were linked to a rise in their election poll ratings.

Campaigns, Elections, and Parties

Election campaigns today tend to be highly personalized, candidate centered, and conducted outside the control of party organizations. The increased use of electronic media, especially television, has encouraged candidates to personalize their campaign messages; at the same time, the decline of party identification has decreased the power of party-related appeals. Although the party affiliations of the candidates and the party identifications of the voters jointly explain a good deal of electoral behavior, party organizations are not central to elections in America, and this situation has implications for democratic government.

Parties and the Majoritarian Model

According to the majoritarian model of democracy, parties link people with their government by making government responsive to public opinion. Chapter 8 outlined the model of responsible party government in a majoritarian democracy. This model holds that parties should present clear and coherent programs to voters, that voters should choose candidates according to the party programs, that the winning party should carry out its programs once in office, and that voters should hold the governing party responsible at the next election for executing its program. As noted in Chapter 8, the Republican and Democratic parties do follow the model because they formulate different platforms and tend to pursue their announced policies when in office. The weak links in this model of responsible party government are those that connect candidates to voters through campaigns and elections.

You have not read much in this book about the role of the party platform in nominating candidates, conducting campaigns, or explaining voters' choices. In nominating presidential candidates, basic party principles (as captured in the party platform) do interact with the presidential primary process, and the candidate who wins enough convention delegates through the primaries will surely be comfortable with any platform that her or his delegates adopt. But House and Senate nominations are rarely fought over the party platform. And thoughts about party platforms usually are virtually absent from campaigning and from voters' minds when they cast their ballots.

Parties and the Pluralist Model

The way parties in the United States operate is more in keeping with the pluralist model of democracy than the majoritarian model. Our parties are not the basic mechanism through which citizens control their government; instead, they function as two giant interest groups. The parties' interests lie in electing and reelecting their candidates and in enjoying the benefits of public office. In past elections, the parties cared little about the positions or ideologies favored by their candidates for Congress or state offices. This was not true in 2010. The Republican National Committee voted to deny funding to candidates who did not agree with at least eight of its ten key policy positions, but later relented somewhat. Tea party activists within the party also pressured Republican candidates to adopt more anti-tax and anti-spending positions. Otherwise, the parties are grateful for victories by almost any candidate running under their banner. In turn, individual candidates operate as entrepreneurs, running their own campaigns as they like, without party interference, and often voting in Congress against party leadership—as some Democrats did in 2009.

Some scholars believe that stronger parties would strengthen democratic government, even if they could not meet all the requirements of the responsible party model.[127] Our parties already perform valuable functions in structuring the vote along partisan lines and in proposing alternative government policies, but stronger parties might also be able to play a more important role in coordinating government policies after elections. At present, the decentralized nature of the nominating process and campaigning for office offer many opportunities for organized groups outside the parties to identify and back candidates who favor their interests.[128] Although this is in keeping with pluralist theory, it is certain to frustrate majority interests on occasion.

Summary

Campaigning has evolved from a party-centered to a candidate-centered process. The successful candidate for public office usually must campaign first to win the party nomination, then to win the general election. A major factor in the decentralization of American parties is their reliance on primary elections to nominate candidates. Democratic and Republican nominations for president tend not to be decided in the parties' national conventions but are determined in advance through the complex process of selecting delegates pledged to particular candidates. Although candidates cannot win the nomination unless they have broad support within the party, the winners can legitimately say that they captured the nomination through their own efforts and that they owe little to the party organization.

The need to win a majority of votes in the electoral college structures presidential elections. Although a candidate can win a majority of the popular vote but lose in the electoral college, that had not happened in more than one hundred years until 2000. In fact, the electoral college usually magnifies the victory margin of the winning candidate. Since World War II, Republicans have usually won the presidency, whereas Democrats have usually controlled Congress. From 1995 to 2000, the situation was reversed: Republicans controlled Congress under a Democratic president. Following the 2006 election, Democrats controlled Congress under a Republican president. Such divided government has interfered with party control of government.

In the general election, candidates usually retain the same staff who helped them win the nomination. The dynamics of campaign financing force candidates for state offices and for Congress to rely mainly on their own resources. Public funding for presidential elections began with the 1996 election. For more than two decades, presidential candidates relied on public funds to conduct their campaigns, but recently candidates have declined public funding to raise more money on their own. Party organizations now often contribute money to congressional candidates, but the candidates must still raise most of the money themselves—increasingly online. Money is essential in running a modern campaign for major office—for conducting polls and advertising the candidate's name, qualifications, and issue positions through the media. Candidates seek free news coverage whenever possible, but most must rely on paid advertising to get their message across. Ironically, voters also get most of their campaign information from advertisements. The trend in recent years toward negative advertising seems to work, although it may contribute to voters' distaste for politics.

Voting choice can be analyzed in terms of party identification, candidates' attributes, and policy positions. Party identification is still the most important long-term factor in shaping the voting decision, but few candidates rely on it in their campaigns. Most candidates today run personalized campaigns that stress their attributes and policies. Increased use of the Internet allows candidates even more latitude in personalizing their campaigns.

The way that nominations, campaigns, and elections are conducted in America is out of keeping with the ideals of responsible party government that fit the majoritarian model of democracy. In particular, campaigns and elections do not function to link parties strongly to voters, as the model posits. American parties are better suited to the pluralist model of democracy, which sees them as major interest groups competing with lesser groups to further their own interests. At least political parties aspire to the noble goal of representing the needs and wants of most people. As we see in the next chapter, interest groups do not even pretend as much.

 Visit www.cengagebrain.com/shop/ISBN/0495906182 for flashcards, web quizzes, videos and more!

Interest Groups

Tom Williams/Roll Call/Getty Images

Visit www.cengagebrain.com/shop/
ISBN/0495906182 for flashcards, web
quizzes, videos and more!

This changing of the guard didn't take place at Buckingham Palace in London. It took place in Washington, D.C., along "K" Street and other areas where lobbyists have their offices. No sooner had Barack Obama been elected president than lobbying firms began beefing up their Democratic credentials.

Firms with a strong Republican orientation, which had done well for clients seeking access to policymakers in the George W. Bush administration, began hunting for Democratic talent. For example, during the Bush years one of the leading lobbying shops around town was BGR Holdings, which represented blue-chip clients such as Citigroup and Pfizer. One of BGR's principals was Haley Barbour, former chair of the Republican National Committee and currently the governor of Mississippi. Now, however, BGR proceeded to purchase a Democratic-leaning firm, the Westin Rinehart Group. Ed Rogers, the chairman of BGR, said, "It looks like there will be more Democrats running Washington for the foreseeable future." Rogers added, "We've done what we've done to meet that demand."[1] Republicans heading the lobbying offices in Washington of corporations such as Lockheed Martin, Boeing, and Comcast were replaced by Democrats.[2]

With Democrats firmly in control of both houses of Congress and the White House, those firms wanting to hire new lobbyists were most interested in Democrats with many years of experience in Washington and with excellent contacts to those in power. Bud Cramer, a Democrat who had served as a representative from Alabama for 18 years, had no shortage of prospective employers when he retired from Congress in 2008. He became chairman of Wexler & Walker Public Policy Associates, a well-known lobbying group. During his time in the House, Cramer had served on a number of important committees, including the Committee on Transportation and Infrastructure and the Committee on Appropriations. Surely his background is appealing to American Airlines, one of Wexler & Walker's most important clients.[3]

Although connections to policymakers are greatly valued, top lobbyists have broad skill sets. Policymaking is a continuous, long-term process, and those who want to try to influence government must develop appropriate strategies. As Michael Berman, an executive with the Duberstein Group, noted, the job of a lobbyist is "advising people on how to structure their business.... It requires knowing what's going on."[4]

Still, whatever skills a lobbyist possesses, having connections to those in power greatly enhances his or her career. Democratic lobbyists are benefiting significantly from this changing of the guard. When the tide turns and Republicans come back to power, lobbyists with ties to the Republicans will be in great demand. In Washington administrations come and go; lobbyists are always there.

In this chapter, we look at the central dynamic of pluralist democracy: the interaction of interest groups and government. In analyzing the process by which interest groups and lobbyists come to speak on behalf of different groups, we focus on several questions. How do interest groups form? Whom do they represent? What tactics do they use to convince policymakers that their views are best for the nation? Is the interest group system biased in favor of certain types of people? If so, what are the consequences?

IN OUR OWN WORDS

Listen to Jeffrey Berry discuss the main points and themes of this chapter.

www.cengagebrain.com/
shop/ISBN/0495906182

Interest Groups and the American Political Tradition

An **interest group** is an organized body of individuals who share some political goals and try to influence public policy decisions. Among the most prominent interest groups in the United States are the AFL-CIO (representing labor union members), the American Farm Bureau Federation (representing farmers), the Business Roundtable (representing big business), and Common Cause (representing citizens concerned with reforming government). Interest groups are also called **lobbies**, and their representatives are referred to as **lobbyists**.

Interest Groups: Good or Evil?

A recurring debate in American politics concerns the role of interest groups in a democratic society. Are interest groups a threat to the well-being of the political system, or do they contribute to its proper functioning? A favorable early evaluation of interest groups can be found in the writings of Alexis de Tocqueville, a French visitor to the United States in the early nineteenth century. During his travels, Tocqueville marveled at the array of organizations he found, and he later wrote that "Americans of all ages, all conditions, and all dispositions, constantly form associations."[5] Tocqueville was suggesting that the ease with which we form organizations reflects a strong democratic culture.

Yet other early observers were concerned about the consequences of interest group politics. Writing in the *Federalist* papers, James Madison warned of the dangers of "factions," the major divisions in American society. In *Federalist* No. 10, written in 1787, Madison said it was inevitable that substantial differences would develop between factions. It was only natural for farmers to oppose merchants, tenants to oppose landlords, and so on. Madison further reasoned that each faction would do what it could to prevail over other factions, that each basic interest in society would try to persuade the government to adopt policies that favored it at the expense of others. He noted that the fundamental causes of faction were "sown in the nature of man."[6]

But Madison argued against trying to suppress factions. He concluded that factions can be eliminated only by removing our freedoms because

interest group
An organized group of individuals that seeks to influence public policy. Also called a *lobby.*

lobby
See *interest group.*

lobbyist
A representative of an interest group.

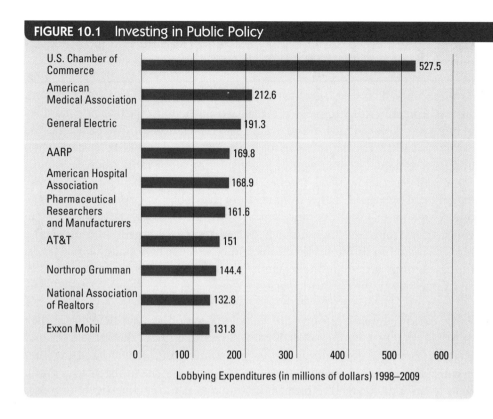

FIGURE 10.1 Investing in Public Policy

U.S. Chamber of Commerce — 527.5
American Medical Association — 212.6
General Electric — 191.3
AARP — 169.8
American Hospital Association — 168.9
Pharmaceutical Researchers and Manufacturers — 161.6
AT&T — 151
Northrop Grumman — 144.4
National Association of Realtors — 132.8
Exxon Mobil — 131.8

Lobbying Expenditures (in millions of dollars) 1998–2009

This list of the top ten spenders on lobbying over the past decade demonstrates the vast sum of money spent to influence public policy. The top spenders are, not surprisingly, predominantly business-related interest groups as a change in public policy can result in a business making or losing hundreds of millions of dollars.

Source: Center for Responsive Politics, "Top Spenders," copyright © Center for Responsive Politics. Reproduced by permission.

"Liberty is to faction what air is to fire."[7] Instead, Madison suggested that relief from the self-interested advocacy of factions should come only through controlling the effects of that advocacy. The relief would be provided by a democratic republic in which government would mediate among opposing factions. The size and diversity of the nation as well as the structure of government would ensure that even a majority faction could never come to suppress the rights of others.[8]

How we judge interest groups—as "good" or "evil"—may depend on how strongly we are committed to freedom or equality (see Chapter 1). People dislike interest groups in general because they do not offer equal representation to all; some sectors of society are better represented than others. In a poll, four out of five respondents indicated that they believe it is common for lobbyists to bribe members of Congress.[9] Recent filings with Congress listed more than $3 billion in annual spending on lobbying, and as Figure 10.1 shows, individual lobbies spend vast sums as they try to influence legislation. Interest groups have recently enjoyed unparalleled growth; many new groups have formed, and old ones have expanded. Apparently we distrust interest groups as a whole, but we like those that represent our views. Stated more bluntly, we hate lobbies—except those that speak on our behalf.

The Roles of Interest Groups

The "evil" side of interest group politics is all too apparent. Each group pushes its own selfish interests, which, despite the group's claims to the contrary, are not always in the best interest of other Americans. The "good" side of interest group advocacy may not be so clear. How do the actions of interest groups benefit our political system?[10]

Representation. Interest groups represent people before their government. Just as a member of Congress represents a particular constituency, so does a lobbyist. A lobbyist for the National Association of Broadcasters, for example, speaks for the interests of radio and television broadcasters when Congress or a government agency is considering a relevant policy decision.

Whatever the political interest—the cement industry, Social Security, endangered species—it helps to have an active lobby operating in Washington. Members of Congress represent a multitude of interests, some of them conflicting, from their own districts and states. Government administrators, too, are pulled in different directions and have their own policy preferences. Interest groups articulate their members' concerns, presenting them directly and forcefully in the political process.

Participation. Interest groups are vehicles for political participation. They provide a means by which like-minded citizens can pool their resources and channel their energies into collective political action. People band together because they know it is much easier to get government to listen to a group than to an individual. One farmer fighting against a new pesticide proposal in Congress probably will not get very far, but thousands of farmers united in an organization stand a much better chance of getting policymakers to consider their needs. Interest groups not only facilitate participation; they stimulate it as well. By asking people to write to their member of Congress or take other action, lobbies get people more involved in the political process than they otherwise would be.

Education. As part of their efforts to lobby government and increase their membership, interest groups help educate their members, the public at large, and government officials. High-tech companies were slow to set up lobbying offices in Washington and to develop a mind-set within the corporate structure that communicating with people in government was part of their job.[11] As more and more issues affecting the industry received attention from government, high-tech executives began to realize that policymakers didn't have a sufficient understanding of the rapidly changing industry. For example, as it began to grow, Google found it useful to open a Washington office and hire an outside law firm to help represent its interests before government. To gain the attention of the policymakers they are trying to educate, interest groups need to provide them with information that is not easily obtained from other sources.

Agenda Building. In a related role, interest groups bring new issues into the political limelight through a process called **agenda building**. American society has many problem areas, but public officials are not addressing all of them. Through their advocacy, interest groups make the government aware

agenda building
The process by which new issues are brought into the political limelight.

FIGURE 10.2 Labor Pains

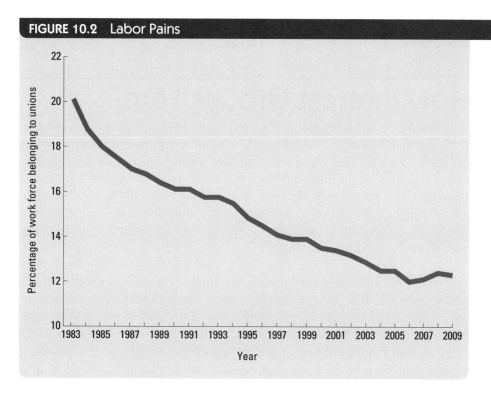

Over the years, many manufacturing jobs in the United States have migrated overseas to developing countries with lower wages. That may be good for consumers (cheaper wages mean lower-cost products), but it has been bad for labor unions because workers in heavy industry have traditionally been the most likely to be unionized. Service sector workers like restaurant employees have been much harder for unions to organize.

Source: Bureau of Labor Statistics.

of problems and then try to see to it that something is done to solve them.[12] Labor unions, for example, have historically played a critical role in gaining attention for problems that were being systematically ignored. As Figure 10.2 shows, however, union membership has declined significantly over the years.

Program Monitoring. Finally, interest groups engage in **program monitoring**. Lobbies follow government programs that are important to their constituents, keeping abreast of developments in Washington and the communities where the policies are implemented. When a program is not operating as it should, concerned interest groups push administrators to change it in ways that promote the groups' goals. They draw attention to agency officials' transgressions and even file suit to stop actions they consider unlawful. The National Federation of Independent Business, a major trade association representing small businesses, uses a computer program to estimate the cost of federal regulations. Its policy analysts monitor new regulatory proposals and are prepared to initiate action directed at trying to force government to suspend those they feel are poorly supported by available scientific data.[13]

Interest groups do, then, play some positive roles in their pursuit of self-interest. But we should not assume that the positive side of interest groups neatly balances the negative. Questions remain about the overall influence of interest groups on public policymaking. Most important, are

program monitoring
Keeping track of government programs; usually done by interest groups.

the effects of interest group advocacy being controlled, as Madison believed they should be?

How Interest Groups Form

Do some people form interest groups more easily than others? Are some factions represented while others are not? Pluralists assume that when a political issue arises, interest groups with relevant policy concerns begin to lobby. Policy conflicts are ultimately resolved through bargaining and negotiation between the involved organizations and the government. Unlike Madison, who dwelled on the potential for harm by factions, pluralists believe interest groups are a good thing—that they contribute to democracy by broadening representation within the system.

An important part of pluralism is the belief that new interest groups form as a matter of course when the need arises. David Truman outlines this idea in his classic work *The Governmental Process*.[14] He says that when individuals are threatened by change, they band together in an interest group. For example, if government threatens to regulate a particular industry, the firms that compose that industry will start a trade association to protect their financial well-being. Truman sees a direct cause-and-effect relationship in all of this: existing groups stand in equilibrium until some type of disturbance (such as falling wages or declining farm prices) forces new groups to form.

Truman's thinking on the way interest groups form is like the "invisible hand" notion of laissez-faire economics: self-correcting market forces will remedy imbalances in the marketplace. But in politics, no invisible hand, no force, automatically causes interest groups to develop. Truman's disturbance theory paints an idealized portrait of interest group politics in America. In real life, people do not automatically organize when they are adversely affected by some disturbance. A good example of "nonorganization" can be found in Herbert Gans's book *The Urban Villagers*.[15] Gans, a sociologist, moved into the West End, a low-income neighborhood in Boston, during the late 1950s. The neighborhood had been targeted for urban redevelopment; the city was planning to replace old buildings with modern ones. This meant that the people living there—primarily poor Italian Americans who very much liked their neighborhood—would have to move.

Being evicted is a highly traumatic experience, so the situation in the West End certainly qualified as a bona fide disturbance according to Truman's scheme of interest group formation. Yet the people of the West End barely put up a fight to save their neighborhood. They started an organization, but it attracted little support. Residents remained unorganized; soon they were moved, and the buildings in the neighborhood were demolished.

Disturbance theory clearly fails to explain what happened (or didn't happen) in Boston's West End. An adverse condition or change does not automatically mean that an interest group will form. What, then, is the missing ingredient? Political scientist Robert Salisbury says that the quality of interest group leadership may be the crucial factor.[16]

Interest Group Entrepreneurs

Salisbury likens the role of an interest group leader to that of an entrepreneur in the business world. An entrepreneur is someone who starts new enterprises, usually at considerable personal financial risk. Salisbury says that an **interest group entrepreneur,** or organizer, succeeds or fails for many of the same reasons a business entrepreneur succeeds or fails. The interest group entrepreneur must have something attractive to "market" in order to convince people to join.[17] Potential members must be persuaded that the benefits of joining outweigh the costs. Someone starting a new union, for example, must convince workers that the union can win them wages high enough to more than offset membership dues. The organizer of an ideological group must convince potential members that the group can effectively lobby the government to achieve their particular goals.

The development of the United Farm Workers union shows the importance of leadership in the formation of an interest group. The union is made up of men and women who pick crops in California and other parts of the country. These pickers—predominantly poor, uneducated Mexican Americans—perform backbreaking work in the hot growing season.

Their chronically low wages and deplorable living conditions made the farm workers prime candidates for organization into a labor union. And throughout the twentieth century, various unions tried to organize them. Yet for many reasons, including distrust of union organizers, intimidation by employers, and lack of money to pay union dues, all failed. Then, in 1962, the late Cesar Chavez, a poor Mexican American, began to crisscross the Central Valley of California, talking to workers and planting the idea of a union. Chavez had been a farm worker himself (he first worked as a picker at the age of ten), and he was well aware of the difficulties that lay ahead for his newly organized union.

After a strike against grape growers failed in 1965, Chavez changed his tactic of trying to build a stronger union merely by recruiting a larger membership. Copying the civil rights movement, Chavez and his followers marched 250 miles to the state capitol in Sacramento to demand help from the governor. The march and other nonviolent tactics began to draw sympathy from people who had no direct involvement in farming. Seeing the movement as a way to help poor members of the church, Catholic clergy were a major source of support. This support gave the charismatic Chavez greater credibility, and his followers cast him in the role of spiritual as well as political leader. At one point, he fasted for twenty-five days to show his commitment to nonviolence. Democratic senator Robert Kennedy of New York, one of the most popular politicians of the day, joined Chavez when he broke his fast at a mass conducted on the back of a flatbed truck in Delano, California.[18]

Chavez subsequently called for a boycott, and a small but significant number of Americans stopped buying grapes. The growers, who had bitterly fought the union, were finally hurt economically. Under this and other economic pressures, they eventually agreed to recognize and bargain with

interest group entrepreneur
An interest group organizer or leader.

No Contract, No Wine!

United Farm Workers president Arturo Rodriguez (right) leads a protest march against California's Gallo winery. The union was asking consumers to stop buying Gallo wines to pressure the company into a more generous labor contract. The recent union action was certainly intended to call to mind the successful efforts of Cesar Chavez and the public sympathy for the downtrodden farm workers in the 1960s.

(David Bacon/The Image Works)

the United Farm Workers. The union then helped its members with the wage and benefit agreements it was able to negotiate.

Who Is Being Organized?

Cesar Chavez is a good example of the importance of leadership in the formation of a new interest group. Despite many years of adverse conditions, efforts to organize farm workers had failed. The dynamic leadership of Cesar Chavez is what seems to have made the difference.

But another important element is at work in the formation of interest groups. The residents of Boston's West End and the farm workers in California were poor, uneducated or undereducated, and politically inexperienced—factors that made it extremely difficult to organize them into interest groups. If they had been well-to-do, educated, and politically experienced, they probably would have banded together immediately. People who have money, are educated, and know how the system operates are more confident that their actions can make a difference.[19] Together, these attributes give people more incentive to devote their time and ample resources to organizing and supporting interest groups.

Every existing interest group has its own history, but the three variables just discussed can help explain why groups may or may not become fully organized. First, an adverse change or disturbance can contribute to people's awareness that they need political representation. However, this alone does not ensure that an organization will form, and organizations have formed in the absence of a disturbance. Second, the quality of leadership is critical in the organization of interest groups. Some interest group entrepreneurs are more skilled than others at convincing people to join their organizations.

Third, the higher the socioeconomic level of potential members is, the more likely they are to know the value of interest groups and to participate in politics by joining them.

Finally, not all interest groups have real memberships. In this sense "group" is a misnomer; some lobbying organizations are institutions that lack members but are affected by public policy and establish lobbying offices or hire lobbyists to represent them before government. Universities and hospitals, for example, don't have members but are well represented before government. Harvard and Yale universities, for example, typically spend somewhere in the neighborhood of $400,000 to $500,000 annually on lobbying.[20] Large corporations and business trade associations are usually quite astute at understanding just how valuable it is to have lobbyists in Washington.

Because wealthy and better-educated Americans are more likely to form and join lobbies, they seem to have an important advantage in the political process. Nevertheless, as the United Farm Workers' case shows, poor and uneducated people are also capable of forming interest groups. The question that remains, then, is not *whether* various opposing interests are represented but *how well* they are represented. In terms of Madison's premise in *Federalist* No. 10, are the effects of faction—in this case, the advantages of the wealthy and well educated—being controlled? Before we can answer this question about how interest groups affect the level of political equality in our society, we need to turn our attention to the resources available to interest groups.

Interest Group Resources

The strengths, capabilities, and influence of an interest group depend in large part on its resources. A group's most significant resources are its members, lobbyists, and money, including funds that can be contributed to political candidates. The sheer quantity of a group's resources is important, and so is the wisdom with which its resources are used.

Members

One of the most valuable resources an interest group can have is a large, politically active membership. If a lobbyist is trying to convince a legislator to support a particular bill, having a large group of members who live in the legislator's home district or state is tremendously helpful. A legislator who has not already taken a firm position on a bill might be swayed by the knowledge that voters back home are kept informed by interest groups of his or her votes on key issues. The American Association of Retired Persons (AARP) has a membership of 40 million, making it a feared interest group in Washington.[21]

Members give an organization not only the political muscle to influence policy but also financial resources. The more money an organization can collect through dues and contributions, the more people it can hire to lobby government officials and monitor the policymaking process. Greater resources also allow an organization to communicate with its members more and to inform them better. And funding helps a group maintain its membership and attract new members.

Maintaining Membership. To keep the members it already has, an organization must persuade them that it is doing a good job in its advocacy. Most lobbies use a newsletter and e-mails to keep members apprised of developments in government that relate to issues of concern to them. Interest groups use these communications as public relations tools to try to keep members believing that their lobby is playing a critical role in protecting their interests. Thus, the role the organization is playing in trying to influence government always receives prominent coverage in its newsletters and e-mails.

Business, professional, and labor associations generally have an easier time holding on to members than do citizen groups, whose basis of organization is a concern for issues not directly related to their members' jobs. In many companies, corporate membership in a trade group constitutes only a minor business expense. Big individual corporations have no memberships as such, but they often open their own lobbying offices in Washington. They have the advantage of being able to use institutional financial resources to support their lobbying; they do not have to rely on voluntary contributions. Labor unions are helped in states that require workers to affiliate with the union that is the bargaining agent with their employer. In contrast, citizen groups base their appeal on members' ideological sentiments. These groups face a difficult challenge: issues can blow hot and cold, and a particularly hot issue one year may not hold the same interest to citizens the next.

Attracting New Members. All membership groups are constantly looking for new adherents to expand their resources and clout. Groups that rely on ideological appeals have a special problem because the competition in most policy areas is intense. People concerned about the environment, for example, can join a seemingly infinite number of local, state, and national groups. The National Wildlife Federation, Environmental Defense, the Natural Resources Defense Council, Friends of the Earth, the National Audubon Society, the Wilderness Society, and the Sierra Club are just some of the national organizations that lobby on environmental issues. Groups try to distinguish themselves from competitors by concentrating on a few key issues and developing a reputation as the most involved and knowledgeable about them.[22] The Sierra Club, one of the oldest and largest environmental groups, has long had a focus on protecting national parks. Some smaller organizations, such as Defenders of Wildlife and the Rainforest Action Network, have found a sufficient number of members to support their advocacy. Organizations in a crowded policy area must differentiate themselves from the competition and then aggressively market what they have to offer to potential contributors. Indeed, these groups are like businesses—their "profits" (their members and income) depend on their management's wisdom in allocating resources and choosing which issues to address.

The Internet has become an increasingly important means of soliciting new members. Compared to direct mail—an interest group sending a letter and supporting material via old-fashioned "snail mail"—e-mail is much cheaper. E-mail directed to prospects may entice them to go the organization's website to learn more and, possibly, make a contribution. Ideological citizen groups depend heavily on Internet traffic to gain new supporters. Citizen groups working to put strict conservatives on the federal courts, such as the Judicial Confirmation Network, the Committee for Justice, and the Judicial Action Network, have small offices and do not spend great sums on fundraising. Use of the Internet helps these groups keep their costs down as they compete with one another for financial support, while they also cooperate with one another to try to keep liberal jurists off the federal courts.

Interest groups also use social networking sites like Facebook for fundraising. There's no shortage of "Friends of [fill in the blank]"—postings that ask visitors to that page to make a generous contribution. These are typically ideological groups, and many try to tap the idealism of the generally youthful clientele of networking sites. The effectiveness of using social networking sites to build interest group membership is not yet clear.

The Free-Rider Problem. Interest groups' use of aggressive marketing suggests that getting people who sympathize with a group's goals to join and support it with their contributions is difficult. Economists call this difficulty the **free-rider problem**, but we might call it, more colloquially, the "let-George-do-it problem."[23] Funding for public television stations illustrates the dilemma. Almost all agree that public television, which survives in large part through viewers' contributions, is of great value. But only a fraction of those who watch public television contribute on a regular basis. Why? Because people can watch the programs whether they contribute or not. The free rider has the same access to public television as the contributor.

The same problem crops up for interest groups. When a lobbying group wins benefits, those benefits are not restricted to the members of the organization. For instance, if the U.S. Chamber of Commerce convinces Congress to enact a policy benefiting business, all businesses will benefit, not just those that actually pay the membership dues of the lobbying group. Thus, some executives may feel that their corporation doesn't need to spend the money to join the U.S. Chamber of Commerce, even though they might benefit from the group's efforts; they prefer instead to let others shoulder the financial burden.

The free-rider problem increases the difficulty of attracting paying members, but it certainly does not make the task impossible. Many people realize that if everyone decides to let someone else do it, the job simply will not get done. Millions of Americans contribute to interest groups because they are concerned about an issue or feel a responsibility to help organizations that work on their behalf. Also, many organizations offer membership benefits that have nothing to do with politics or lobbying. Business **trade associations**, for example, are a source of information about industry trends and effective management practices; they organize conventions at which members can learn,

free-rider problem
The situation in which people benefit from the activities of an organization (such as an interest group) but do not contribute to those activities.

trade association
An organization that represents firms within a particular industry.

socialize, and occasionally find new customers or suppliers. An individual firm in the electronics industry may not care that much about the lobbying done by the Electronics Industries Alliance, but it may have a vital interest in the information about marketing and manufacturing that the organization provides. Successful interest groups are adept at supplying the right mix of benefits to their target constituency.

Lobbyists

Some of the money that interest groups raise is used to pay lobbyists who represent the organizations before the government. Lobbyists make sure that people in government know what their members want and that their organizations know what the government is doing. For example, when an administrative agency issues new regulations, lobbyists are right there to interpret the content and implications of the regulations for rank-and-file members. As one lobbyist put it, "The [clients who hire me] want to know what's going down the pipe. They want to be plugged into the system."[24] Hedge funds, for example, need lobbyists to spot any proposed regulatory changes as soon as is possible. (Hedge funds are investment vehicles for wealthy individuals and institutional investors and often make investments with relatively high levels of risk.) Since a regulatory change can help or hurt a particular industry, hedge fund managers want to know of any proposals emerging in Washington so they can buy or sell their holdings accordingly.[25]

Lobbyists can be full-time employees of their organization or employees of public relations or law firms who are hired on retainer. As noted earlier, when hiring a lobbyist, an interest group looks for someone who knows her or his way around Washington. Lobbyists are valued for their experience and their knowledge of how government operates. Karen Ignagni, the chief lobbyist for America's Health Insurance Plans, an industry trade group, was at the center of the negotiations over the Obama administration's health reform proposal. Ignagni's experience, vast knowledge of health care, and skills as a bargainer made her a formidable presence as Congress struggled to formulate a bill that could pass. The stakes for the insurance companies were enormous as industry executives worried that a government-run insurance plan could cost them customers. Her stature is such that she is paid $1.6 million annually.[26]

So lucrative is lobbying that more than 40 percent of representatives and senators who leave Congress become employed as lobbyists.[27] Contacts with former colleagues can be invaluable. As one lobbyist said of her former associates on Capitol Hill, "They know you, and they return your phone calls."[28] Many lobbyists have a law degree and find their legal backgrounds useful in bargaining and negotiating over laws and regulations. Because of their location, many Washington law firms are drawn into lobbying. Expanding interest group advocacy has created a boon for Washington law firms. Corporations without their own Washington office rely heavily on law firms to lobby for them before the national government. Partners in the top law firms in Washington average more than $800,000 a year.[29] These firms can

be quite large: lobbying powerhouse Patton Boggs employs four hundred people, almost half of whom register with Congress as lobbyists. One magazine calls it "the icon of Washington's mercenary culture."[30]

The stereotype of lobbyists portrays them as people of dubious ethics because they trade on their connections and may hand out campaign donations to candidates for office as well as raise money for legislators. Lobbying is a much maligned profession, but the lobbyist's primary job is not to trade on favors or campaign contributions. It is rather to pass information on to policymakers. Lobbyists provide government officials and their staffs with a constant flow of data that support their organizations' policy goals. Lobbyist Elizabeth Moeller said of her job, "Finally, my nerdiness can pay off."[31] Lobbyists also try to build a compelling case for their goals, showing that the "facts" dictate that a particular change be made or avoided. What lobbyists are really trying to do, of course, is to convince policymakers that their data deserve more attention and are more accurate than those presented by opposing lobbyists.

Political Action Committees

One of the organizational resources that can make a lobbyist's job easier is a **political action committee (PAC)**. PACs pool campaign contributions from group members and donate the money to candidates for political office. Under federal law, a PAC can give as much as $5,000 to a candidate for Congress for each separate election. During the 2008 election cycle, roughly 3,600 PACs made donations. They contributed $413 million to candidates running for federal office, almost all of which went to congressional candidates.[32]

political action committee (PAC)
An organization that pools campaign contributions from group members and donates those funds to candidates for political office.

The greatest growth has come from corporations, which had long been prohibited from operating PACs. There has also been rapid growth in the number of nonconnected PACs, largely ideological groups that have no parent lobbying organization and are formed solely for the purpose of raising and channeling campaign funds. (Thus, a PAC can be the campaign-wing affiliate of an existing interest group or a wholly independent, unaffiliated group.) Most PACs are rather small, and 95 percent of PACs averaged just $40,000 in contributions to candidates. On the other hand, the remaining 5 percent were much larger contributors and together accounted for over half of all money donated to candidates.[33] Many PACs are large enough to gain recognition for the issues they care about. The National Association of Realtors had the largest PAC, with contributions of $4 million during the most recent two-year election cycle for which figures are available. More than twenty PACs contributed at least $2 million, including the International Brotherhood of Electrical Workers ($3.3 million), the National Beer Wholesalers ($2.9 million), the American Bankers Association ($2.8 million), and United Parcel Service ($2.1 million).[34]

Lobbyists believe that campaign contributions help significantly when they are trying to gain an audience with a member of Congress. Members of Congress and their staffers generally are eager to meet with representatives of their constituencies, but their time is limited. However, a member of Congress or staffer would find it difficult to turn down a lobbyist's request for a meeting if the PAC of the lobbyist's organization had made a significant campaign contribution in the previous election. Lobbyists also regard contributions as a form of insurance in case of issues that might arise unexpectedly. As one scholar put it, the donations are given to protect "against unforeseen future dangers as the policymaking process develops."[35]

Typically, PACs, like most other interest groups, are highly pragmatic and adaptable organizations; pushing a particular political philosophy takes second place to achieving immediate policy goals.[36] Although many corporate executives strongly believe in a free-market economy, for example, their company PACs tend to hold congressional candidates to a much more practical standard. As one lobbyist put it, "Politics are partisan; policy is bipartisan."[37] In recent elections, corporate PACs as a group have given as much as 90 percent of their contributions to incumbents (see Figure 10.3). At the same time, different sectors of the PAC universe may strongly favor one party or the other. More than nine out of every ten dollars that unions give go to Democrats, whether they are incumbents, challengers, or open-seat candidates.[38]

Critics charge that PAC contributions influence public policy, yet political scientists have not been able to document any consistent link between campaign donations and the way members of Congress vote on the floor of the House and Senate.[39] The problem is this: Do PAC contributions influence votes in Congress, or are they just rewards for legislators who would vote for the group's interests anyway because of their long-standing ideology? How do we determine the answer to this question? Simply looking for the influence of PACs in the voting patterns of members of Congress may be shortsighted; influence can also be felt before bills get to the floor of the full

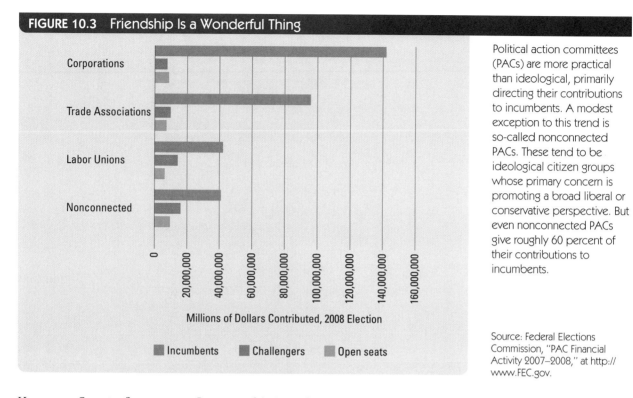

FIGURE 10.3   Friendship Is a Wonderful Thing

Millions of Dollars Contributed, 2008 Election

■ Incumbents   ■ Challengers   ■ Open seats

Political action committees (PACs) are more practical than ideological, primarily directing their contributions to incumbents. A modest exception to this trend is so-called nonconnected PACs. These tend to be ideological citizen groups whose primary concern is promoting a broad liberal or conservative perspective. But even nonconnected PACs give roughly 60 percent of their contributions to incumbents.

Source: Federal Elections Commission, "PAC Financial Activity 2007–2008," at http://www.FEC.gov.

House or Senate for a vote. Some sophisticated research shows that PAC donations do seem to influence what goes on in congressional committees. As will be discussed in Chapter 11, committees are where the bulk of the work on legislation takes place. Lobbies with PACs have an advantage in the committee process and appear to gain influence because of the additional access they receive.[40] Despite the advantages that organizations with ample resources have through PACs, there are those who defend the current system, emphasizing that interest groups and their members should have the freedom to participate in the political system through campaign donations.

Lobbying Tactics

When an interest group decides to try to influence the government on an issue, its staff and officers must develop a strategy, which may include several tactics aimed at various officials or offices. Some tactics are utilized far more frequently than others (see Figure 10.4), but all together, the tactics should use the group's resources as effectively as possible.

Keep in mind that lobbying extends beyond the legislative branch. Groups can seek help from the courts and administrative agencies as well as from Congress. Moreover, interest groups may have to shift their focus from one branch of government to another. After a bill becomes a law, for example, a group that lobbied for the legislation will probably try to influence the administrative agency responsible for implementing the new law. Some policy decisions are left unresolved by legislation and are settled through

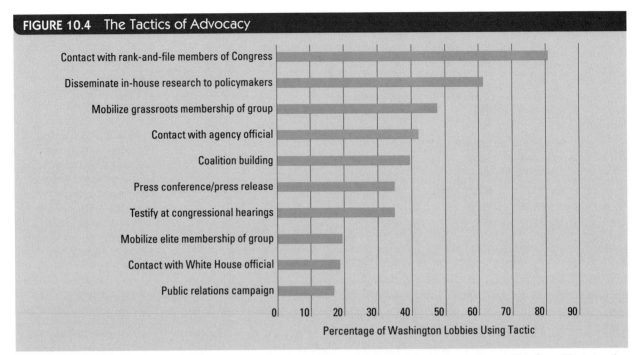

FIGURE 10.4 The Tactics of Advocacy

Interest groups can utilize a variety of tactics, including those shown here, to try to influence government. This figure illustrates the results of a random sample survey of lobbyists that asked each what tactics they were using on an issue they were currently working on. The choice of tactics is highly contingent upon the stage of the process and the institution that is targeted.

Source: Frank R. Baumgartner, Jeffrey M. Berry, Marie Hojnacki, David C. Kimball, and Beth L. Leech, *Lobbying and Policy Change* (Chicago: University of Chicago Press, 2009), p. 151. Copyright © 2009 University of Chicago Press. Reproduced by permission.

regulations. Interest groups try to influence policy through court suits as well, though litigation can be expensive, and opportunities to go to court may be narrowly structured. Lobbying Congress and agencies is more common.

We discuss three types of lobbying tactics here: those aimed at policymakers and implemented by interest group representatives (direct lobbying), those that involve group members (grassroots lobbying), and those directed at the public (information campaigns). We also examine cooperative efforts of interest groups to influence government through coalitions.[41] These tactics are not peculiar to the United States; they characterize lobbying around the world (see "Politics of Global Change: Lobbyists Swarm at the European Union").

Direct Lobbying

direct lobbying
Attempts to influence a legislator's vote through personal contact with the legislator.

Direct lobbying relies on personal contact with policymakers. This interaction occurs when a lobbyist meets with a member of Congress, an agency official, or a staff member. In their meetings, lobbyists usually convey their arguments by providing data about a specific issue. If a lobbyist from a chamber of commerce, for example, meets with a member of Congress about a bill the chamber backs, the lobbyist does not say (or even suggest), "Vote for this bill, or our people in the district will vote against you in the next election." Instead, the lobbyist might say, "If this bill is passed, we're going to see hundreds of new jobs created back home." The representative has no trouble at all figuring out that a vote for the bill can help in the next election.

Personal lobbying is a day-in, day-out process. It is not enough simply to meet with policymakers just before a vote or a regulatory decision. Lobbyists must maintain contact with congressional and agency staffers, constantly providing them with pertinent data. The basic goal is to help policymakers do their job.[42] In their meetings with policymakers and through other tactics, lobbyists are trying to frame the issue at hand in terms most beneficial to their point of view. Is a gun-control bill before Congress a policy that would make our streets and schools safer from deranged, violent individuals who should not have access to guns—or is it a bill aimed at depriving law-abiding citizens of their constitutional right to bear arms?[43] Research has shown that once an issue emerges, it is very difficult for lobbyists to reframe it—that is, to influence journalists and policymakers alike to view the issue in a new light.[44]

A tactic related to direct lobbying is testifying at committee hearings when a bill is before Congress. This tactic allows the interest group to put its views on record and make them widely known when the hearing testimony is published. Although testifying is one of the most visible parts of lobbying, it is generally considered window dressing. Most lobbyists believe that such testimony usually does little by itself to persuade members of Congress.

Another direct but somewhat different approach is legal advocacy. Using this tactic, a group tries to achieve its policy goals through litigation. Claiming some violation of law, a group will file a lawsuit and ask that a judge make a ruling that will benefit the organization. When the Army Corps of

Sanchez Reaches Out

Usually we think of lobbying as a process where groups approach a government official. But sometimes the reverse is true: a policymaker might approach an interest group to try to gain its support for a specific proposal or just to promote a good working relationship. Here, Representative Loretta Sanchez (D-Calif.) works the room at a meeting of the Hispanic Leadership Summit.

(© Ted Soqui/Corbis)

Politics of Global Change

Lobbyists Swarm at the European Union

Lobbying exists within every governmental system. In the United States that right is guaranteed by the First Amendment. At the European Union (EU), it is a matter of policy that lobbying is a valued part of the process. The administrative arm of the EU has declared that "the Commission has always been an institution open to outside input. The Commission believes this process to be fundamental to the development of its policies."

Created in 1992 by the Treaty of Maastricht, the EU has grown to twenty-seven member countries. Its primary purpose is to harmonize the economies of the member countries so that common regulatory rules level the playing

© European Union, 2010

Engineers announced plans to permit coal companies to blast off the top of mountains to facilitate their mining, environmental groups went to court alleging a violation of the Clean Water Act. The judge agreed, since the coal companies' actions would leave waste and rock deposits in adjoining streams.[45]

grassroots lobbying
Lobbying activities performed by rank-and-file interest group members and would-be members.

Grassroots Lobbying

Grassroots lobbying involves an interest group's rank-and-file members and may include people outside the organization who sympathize with its

field for all businesses within the EU. What is truly extraordinary is just how much sovereignty each member country has given over to the larger government of the EU.

The government of the EU is rather fragmented. The European Commission, located in Brussels, Belgium, is the administrative arm of the EU but also has a primary responsibility for initiating legislation. The European Parliament, headquartered in Strasbourg, France, is composed of 736 legislators who are elected within their own home countries. The Council of the European Union, composed of ministers from the individual countries, also acts in a legislative capacity. The structure of the EU, with responsibility dispersed among several institutions, facilitates a pluralistic system in which interest groups have the opportunity to influence policy at many different stages and at many different venues.

Given the power of the EU, it comes as no surprise that its governing structures are magnets for interest groups. An estimated 15,000 lobbyists swarm around EU institutions. They represent the same range of constituencies found in Washington, ranging from citizen groups like environmental lobbies to labor unions to trade associations working on behalf of large industries. There are even super trade association lobbies that represent groups of trade lobbies, such as the Union des Industries de la Communauté européenne, which represents thirty-nine national trade groups. U.S. interests are there, too. The American Chamber of Commerce to the European Union represents European companies that are subsidiaries of American corporations.

Controversy is growing over EU lobbying rules as there is little openness and few records of the interaction between interest groups and policymakers. In the United States organizations lobbying Congress must file periodic public reports that include information on what bills they are lobbying and how much they've spent on their advocacy. At the EU, however, such registration is voluntary and those that choose to file can decide what information to include. Recent filings show that there are only 2,100 registrants. Some filings reveal how much money can be involved in terms of billings. Burson-Marsteller, a worldwide public relations and lobbying firm that represents Pfizer and Continental Airlines among other corporations, indicated that it had revenues of 7 million Euros (more than $10 million in U.S. dollars) in 2007.

That so many lobbying organizations don't register or publicly reveal what they are doing raises concerns about the integrity of EU policymaking. One recent scandal involved Piia-Noora Kauppi, a member of the European Parliament from Finland. Kauppi did not willingly reveal that she went on the payroll of the Federation of Finnish Financial Services. Nevertheless, that information did come to light, and she subsequently admitted that she had introduced legislation written by the trade group that was designed to weaken banking laws it did not like.

Many things in Europe worth are emulating, but the law on lobbying there is not one of them.

Sources: Valeria Marziali, *Lobbying in Brussels* (Bonn: Center for European Integration Studies, Discussion Paper C155, 2006); Christine Mahoney, *Brussels versus the Beltway* (Washington, D.C.: Georgetown University Press, 2008); David Cronin, "And the Lobbying Award Goes to … the Worst," Inter Press Service News Agency, 10 December 2008; Simon Taylor, "Tighter Rules for Lobbyists," EuropeanVoice.com, 29 October 2009.

goals. Grassroots tactics, such as letter-writing campaigns and protests, are often used in conjunction with direct lobbying by Washington representatives. Letters, e-mails, faxes, and telephone calls from a group's members to their representatives in Congress or to agency administrators add to a lobbyist's credibility in talks with these officials. Policymakers are more concerned about what a lobbyist says when they know that constituents are really watching their decisions.

Group members—especially influential members (such as corporation presidents or local civic leaders)—occasionally go to Washington to lobby. But the most common grassroots tactic is letter writing. "Write your member of

Congress" is not just a slogan for a civics test. Legislators are highly sensitive to the content of their mail. Interest groups often launch letter-writing campaigns through their regular publications or special alerts. They may even provide sample letters and the names and addresses of specific policymakers.

The Internet facilitates mobilization as an interest group office can communicate instantaneously with its members and followers and at virtually no cost through e-mail. The Internet also allows interest groups to communicate more easily with one another, thereby reducing some of the costs in time and money to forming and maintaining coalitions.

If people in government seem unresponsive to conventional lobbying tactics, a group might resort to some form of political protest. A protest or demonstration, such as picketing or marching, is designed to attract media attention to an issue. Protesters hope that television and newspaper coverage will help change public opinion and make policymakers more receptive to their group's demands. Recall the tea party protests at town halls described at the opening of Chapter 7. The tea partiers succeeded in drawing attention to their cause as the press gave them considerable coverage. That, of course, is the immediate goal of protest: to gain press attention so a group's message is amplified beyond those immediately present.[46]

The main drawback to protesting is that policymaking is a long-term, incremental process, and a demonstration is short-lived. It is difficult to sustain anger and activism among group supporters—to keep large numbers of people involved in protest after protest. A notable exception was the civil rights demonstrations of the 1960s, which were sustained over a long period. National attention focused not only on the widespread demonstrations but also on the sometimes violent confrontations between protesters and white law enforcement officers. For example, the use of police dogs and high-power

Angry and Organized

Over the past few years, conservatives have become increasingly concerned about illegal immigration. Many conservative citizen groups have been highly vocal in trying to attract attention to the problem, such as these demonstrators in Denver. This group went out onto the streets on April 15, the day taxes are due, to add emphasis to their argument that illegal immigration has economic consequences.

(John Moore/Getty Images)

An Image That Angered a Nation

Demonstrations by blacks during the early 1960s played a critical role in pushing Congress to pass civil rights legislation. This photo of vicious police dogs attacking demonstrators in Birmingham, Alabama, is typical of scenes shown on network news broadcasts and in newspapers that helped build public support for civil rights legislation.

(Charles Moore/Black Star)

fire hoses against blacks marching in Alabama in the early 1960s angered millions of Americans who saw footage of the confrontations on television. By stirring public opinion, the protests hastened the passage of the Civil Rights Act of 1964 and the Voting Rights Act of 1965.

Information Campaigns

As the strategy of the civil rights movement shows, interest groups generally feel that public backing adds strength to their lobbying efforts. And because all interest groups believe they are absolutely right in their policy orientation, they think that they will get that backing if they can only make the public aware of their position and the evidence supporting it. To this end, interest groups launch **information campaigns**, which are organized efforts to gain public backing by bringing their views to the public's attention. The underlying assumption is that public ignorance and apathy are as much a problem as the views of competing interest groups. Various means are used to combat apathy. Some are directed at the larger public; others are directed at smaller audiences with long-standing interest in an issue.

Public relations is one information campaign tactic. A public relations campaign might involve sending speakers to meetings in various parts of the country, producing pamphlets and handouts, taking out newspaper and magazine advertising, or establishing websites. For example, labor unions and progressives have waged a public relations campaign critical of Wal-Mart.

information campaign
An organized effort to gain public backing by bringing a group's views to public attention.

The huge retailer pays relatively low wages, offers limited benefits, and aggressively fights any efforts to unionize its work force. Both Wake Up Wal-Mart and Wal-Mart Watch have publicized Wal-Mart's record on its treatment of employees. In turn, Wal-Mart has fought back with a concerted public relations campaign designed to demonstrate that it is a responsible citizen in the communities where its stores are located. The company's extensive efforts to provide water and other supplies to victims of Hurricane Katrina were particularly effective at burnishing its image.[47]

Sponsoring research is another way interest groups press their cases. When a group believes that evidence has not been fully developed in a certain area, it may commission research on the subject. In the controversy over illegal immigration, studies have proliferated as interest groups push their position forward. Lobbies on opposing sides of the issue have publicized research on matters such as the impact of illegal immigration on the overall economy, whether immigrants drive down wages, and whether undocumented aliens take jobs away from citizens who would otherwise fill them.

Coalition Building

A final aspect of lobbying strategy is **coalition building**, in which several organizations band together for the purpose of lobbying. Such joint efforts conserve or make more effective use of the resources of groups with similar views. Most coalitions are informal arrangements that exist only for the purpose of lobbying on a single issue. Coalitions most often form among groups that work in the same policy area and have similar constituencies, such as environmental groups or feminist groups. When an issue arises that several such groups agree on, they are likely to develop a coalition.

Yet coalitions often extend beyond organizations with similar constituencies and similar outlooks. Environmental groups and business groups are often thought of as dire enemies. But some businesses support the same goals as environmental lobbies because it is in their self-interest. For example, companies in the business of cleaning up toxic waste sites have worked with environmental groups to strengthen the Superfund program, the government's primary weapon for dealing with dangerous waste dumps. Lobbyists see an advantage in having a diverse coalition. In the words of one lobbyist, "You can't do anything in this town without a coalition. I mean the first question [from policymakers] is, 'Who supports this?'"[48]

Is the System Biased?

As we noted in Chapter 2, our political system is more pluralist than majoritarian. Policymaking is determined more by the interaction of groups with the government than by elections. Indeed, among Western democracies, the United States is one of the most pluralistic governments (see "Compared with What? Pluralism Worldwide"). The great advantage of majoritarianism is that it is built around the most elemental notion of fairness: what the government does is determined by what most of the people want.

coalition building
The banding together of several interest groups for the purpose of lobbying.

Compared with What?

Pluralism Worldwide

A study of democracies around the world measured the degree to which interest groups operated independent of any formal link to government. Interest groups in political systems with low scores in this chart (like Norway) run the risk of being co-opted by policymakers because of their partnerships with government. These countries tend to have fewer groups, but those groups are expected to work with government in a coordinated fashion. High scores indicate that the interest groups in those systems are clearly in a competitive position with other groups. Thus, countries with high scores (like the United States) are the most pluralistic.

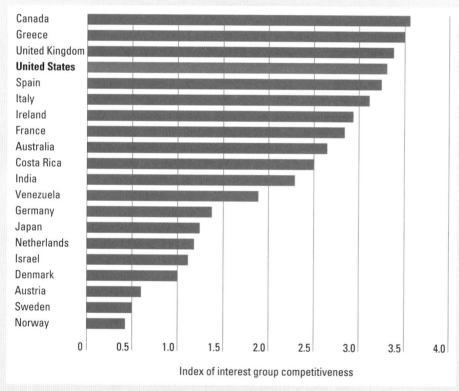

Index of interest group competitiveness

Source: Arend Lijphart, *Patterns of Democracy* (New Haven, Conn.: Yale University Press, 1999), p. 177.

How, then, do we justify the policy decisions made under a pluralist system? How do we determine whether they are fair? There is no precisely agreed-on formula, but most people would agree with the following two simple notions. First, all significant interests in the population should be adequately represented by lobbying groups. That is, if a significant number of people with similar views have a stake in the outcome of policy decisions in a particular area, they should have a lobby to speak for them. If government makes policy that affects farmers who grow wheat, for example, then wheat farmers should have a lobby.

Second, government should listen to the views of all major interests as it develops policy. Lobbies are of little value unless policymakers are willing to listen to them. We should not require policymakers to balance perfectly all competing interests, however, because some interests are diametrically opposed. Moreover, elections inject some of the benefits of majoritarianism into our system because the party that wins an election will have a stronger voice than its opponent in the making of public policy.

Membership Patterns

Public opinion surveys of Americans and surveys of interest groups in Washington can be used to determine who is represented in the interest group system. A clear pattern is evident: some sectors of society are much better represented than others.[49] As noted in the earlier discussions about the Boston West Enders and the United Farm Workers, who is being organized makes a big difference. Those who work in business or in a profession, those with a high level of education, and those with high incomes are the most likely to belong to interest groups. Even middle-income people are much more likely to join interest groups than are those who are poor.

One survey of interest groups is revealing, finding that "the 10 percent of adults who work in an executive, managerial, or administrative capacity are represented by 82 percent" of the organizations that in one way or another engage in advocacy on economic issues. In contrast, "organizations of or for the economically needy are a rarity." Thus, in terms of membership in interest groups, there is a profound bias in favor of those who are well off financially.[50]

Citizen Groups

Because the bias in interest group membership is unmistakable, should we conclude that the interest group system is biased overall? Before reaching that determination, we should examine another set of data. The actual population of interest groups in Washington surely reflects a class bias in interest group membership, but that bias may be modified in an important way. Some interest groups derive support from sources other than their membership. Thus, although they have no welfare recipients as members, the Center for Budget and Policy Priorities and the Children's Defense Fund have been effective long-term advocates working on behalf of the poor. Poverty groups gain their financial support from philanthropic foundations, government grants, corporations, and wealthy individuals.[51] Given the large numbers of Americans who benefit from welfare and social service programs, poor people's lobbies are not numerous enough. Nevertheless, the poor are represented by these and other organizations (such as labor unions and health lobbies) that regard the poor as part of the constituency they must protect.

In short, although the poor are seriously underrepresented in our system, the situation is not as bad as interest group membership patterns suggest.

Another part of the problem of membership bias has to do with free riders. The interests that are most affected by free riders are broad societal problems, such as the environment and consumer protection, in which literally everyone can be considered as having a stake in the outcome. We are all consumers, and we all care about the environment. But the greater the number of potential members of a group, the more likely it is that individuals will decide to be free riders because they believe that plenty of others can offer financial support to the organization. As noted earlier, business trade associations and professional associations do not have the same problem because they can offer many benefits that cannot be obtained without paying for membership.

Environmental and consumer interests have been chronically underrepresented in the Washington interest group community. In the 1960s, however, a strong citizen group movement emerged. **Citizen groups** are lobbying organizations built around policy concerns unrelated to members' vocational interests. People who join Environmental Defense do so because they care about the environment, not because it lobbies on issues related to their profession. If that group fights for stricter pollution control requirements, it doesn't further the financial interests of its members. The benefits to members are largely ideological and aesthetic. In contrast, a corporation fighting the same stringent standards is trying to protect its economic interests. A law that requires a corporation to install expensive antipollution devices can reduce stockholders' dividends, depress salaries, and postpone expansion. Although both the environmental group and the corporation have valid reasons for their stands, their motives are different.

As Americans have become more affluent and more secure about the future of the economy and their own personal well-being, their interest in the kind of quality-of-life issues that citizen groups pursue has increased. Organizations pursuing environmental protection, consumer protection, good government, family values, and equality for various groups in society have grown in number and collectively attract millions of members. Since these groups are not motivated by financial gain the way that business, professional, and labor groups are, they have more credibility than other types of lobbying organizations. The national press gives them considerable coverage, reinforcing the ability of these groups to get their issues on the national agenda. One study showed that citizen groups received almost half of all TV network news coverage of interest groups, even though they are a much smaller portion of the interest group universe.[52]

Business Mobilization

Because a strong public interest movement has become an integral part of Washington politics, an easy assumption is that the bias in interest group representation in favor of business has been largely overcome. What must be factored in, however, is that business has become increasingly mobilized as well. The 1970s and 1980s saw a vast increase in the number of business

citizen group
Lobbying organization built around policy concerns unrelated to members' vocational interests.

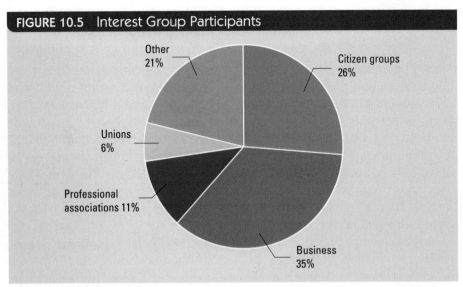

FIGURE 10.5   Interest Group Participants

One large-scale study of lobbying in Washington documented the pattern of participation by interest groups on close to a hundred issues before the federal government. Business-related groups (corporations and trade associations) made up the largest segment of all lobbies, and citizen groups constituted roughly a quarter of all organizations.

Source: Frank R. Baumgartner, Jeffrey M. Berry, Marie Hojnacki, David C. Kimball, and Beth L. Leech, *Lobbying and Policy Change* (Chicago: University of Chicago Press, 2009), p. 9. Copyright © 2009 University of Chicago Press. Reproduced by permission.

lobbies in Washington. Many corporations opened Washington lobbying offices, and many trade associations headquartered elsewhere either moved to Washington or opened branch offices there.

This mobilization was partly a reaction to the success of liberal citizen groups, which business tended to view as hostile to the free enterprise system.[53] The reaction of business also reflected the expanded scope of the national government. After the Environmental Protection Agency, the Consumer Product Safety Commission, the Occupational Safety and Health Administration, and other regulatory agencies were created, many more companies found they were affected by federal regulations. And many corporations found that they were frequently reacting to policies that were already made rather than participating in their making. They saw representation in Washington—where the policymakers are—as critical if they were to obtain information on pending government actions soon enough to act on it. Finally, the competitive nature of business lobbying fueled the increase in business advocacy in Washington. This competition exists because legislation and regulatory decisions never seem to apply uniformly to all businesses; rather, they affect one type of business or one industry more than others.

The health-care industry is a case in point. Government regulation has become an increasingly important factor in determining health-care profits. Through reimbursement formulas for Medicare, Medicaid, and other health-care programs funded by Washington, the national government limits what providers can charge. As this regulatory influence grew, more and more health-care trade associations (like the American Hospital Association) and professional associations (like the American Nurses Association) came to view

Washington lobbying as increasingly significant to the well-being of their members. The number of such lobbies has skyrocketed and health-care lobbyists cluster around Washington like locusts. In 1999 there were already over 2,300 health-care lobbyists working in the city. By 2009 the number had jumped another 50 percent to over 3,600.[54]

The advantages of business are enormous. As Figure 10.5 illustrates, there are more business lobbies (corporations and trade associations) than any other type. Professional associations—the American Dental Association, for example—tend to represent business interests as well. Beyond the numbers of groups are the superior resources of business, including lobbyists, researchers, campaign contributions, and well-connected chief executive officers. Business lobbyists, for example, are much more likely to participate in lobbying administrative agencies on proposed regulations.[55] Whereas citizen groups can try to mobilize their individual members, trade associations can mobilize the corporations that are members of the organization.

Yet the resource advantages of business make it easy to overlook the obstacles business faces in the political arena. To begin with, business is often divided, with one industry facing another. Cable companies and phone companies have frequently tangled over who will have access to what markets. And even if an industry is unified, it may face strong opposition from labor or citizen groups—sectors that have substantial resources too, even if they don't match up to those of businesses. If both sides have sufficient resources to put up a battle, simply having more money or lobbyists than the other side is unlikely to determine the outcome.[56]

A Lott of Connections

It's common for legislators to work as lobbyists after they leave the House or Senate. Two Senate heavyweights, former Republican Majority Leader Trent Lott of Mississippi (*left*) and former Democratic senator John Breaux of Louisiana (*right*) have recently formed their own lobbying firm, the Breaux Lott Leadership Group. With all their connections from their years in Congress, they'll have little trouble attracting clients.

(*left*: Jason Reed/Reuters/Corbis; *right* Scott J. Ferrell/Congressional Quarterly/Getty Images)

Reform

If the interest group system is biased, should the advantages of some groups somehow be eliminated or reduced? This is hard to do. In an economic system marked by great differences in income, great differences in the degree to which people are organized are inevitable. Moreover, as James Madison foresaw, limiting interest group activity is difficult without limiting fundamental freedoms. The First Amendment guarantees Americans the right to petition their government, and lobbying, at its most basic level, is a form of organized petitioning.

Still, some sectors of the interest group community may enjoy advantages that are unacceptable. If it is felt that the advantages of some groups are so great that they affect the equality of people's opportunity to be heard in the political system, then restrictions on interest group behavior can be justified on the grounds that the disadvantaged must be protected. Pluralist democracy is justified on exactly these grounds: all constituencies must have the opportunity to organize, and competition between groups as they press their case before policymakers must be fair.

Some critics charge that a system of campaign finance that relies so heavily on PACs undermines our democratic system. They claim that access to policymakers is purchased through the wealth of some constituencies. PAC donations come disproportionately from business and professional interests. It is not merely a matter of wealthy interest groups showering incumbents with donations; members of Congress aggressively solicit donations from PACs. Although observers disagree on whether PAC money actually influences policy outcomes, agreement is widespread that PAC donations give donors better access to members of Congress.

In January 2010, the Supreme Court ruled that government may not restrict corporations and unions from spending money in candidate elections. (Recall that PAC funds come from individual donations as well as other PACs that aggregate money and then donate it.) There is considerable concern that the Court's decision will flood the political marketplace with corporations spending unlimited funds to support their allies and oppose their enemies. Incumbents are sure to take heed. Defenders point out that the logic of the decision means that labor unions, too, can spend freely from their own treasuries, though corporate coffers dwarf labor assets.[57] (There's additional discussion of this case on pages 303–304)

Congress took an important step in campaign finance reform with the Bipartisan Campaign Finance Reform Act in 2002. Prior to its passage, corporations, labor unions, and other organizations could donate unlimited amounts of so-called soft money to the political parties. A company or union with issues before government could give a six-figure gift to the Democratic or Republican Party, even though it could make only a modest contribution to individual candidates. As noted in Chapter 9, this new law bans soft money contributions to national party committees.

A serious scandal surrounding lobbyist Jack Abramoff (subsequently convicted and sent to prison) prompted Congress to tighten its ethical rules. This modest legislation passed in 2007 bans gifts, travel, and meals paid for by lobbyists. Lobbyists must also now disclose campaign contributions that they solicit on behalf of candidates.[58] During the 2008 presidential campaign Barack Obama promised to "change the culture of Washington." On his second day in office Obama banned lobbyists from working in an agency that they had lobbied any time during the previous two years. Citizen lobbies were particularly incensed at the president's new rule, believing that since their advocacy did not financially benefit their members and donors, they should not be looked upon with the presumptive suspicion underlying the Obama policy. A coalition of citizen groups formally complained to the administration and in a letter to the White House noted that "The right to petition the government is a constitutionally protected activity."[59]

Summary

Interest groups play many important roles in our political process. They are a means by which citizens can participate in politics, and they communicate their members' views to those in government. Interest groups differ greatly in the resources at their disposal and in the tactics they use to influence government. The number of interest groups has grown sharply in recent years.

Despite the growth and change in the nature of interest groups, the fundamental problem that James Madison identified more than two hundred years ago endures. In a free and open society, groups form to pursue policies that favor them at the expense of the broader national interest. Madison hoped that the solution to the problem would come from the diversity of the population and the structure of our government.

To a certain extent, Madison's expectations have been borne out. The natural differences between groups have prevented a tyranny of any one faction. Yet the interest group system remains unbalanced, with some segments of society (particularly business, the wealthy, and the educated) considerably better organized than others. The growth of citizen groups has reduced the disparity somewhat, but significant inequalities remain in how well different interests are represented in Washington.

The inequities point to flaws in pluralist theory. There is no mechanism to automatically ensure that interest groups will form to speak for those who need representation. And when an issue arises and policymakers meet with interest groups that have a stake in the outcome, those groups may not equally represent all the constituencies that the policy changes will affect. The interest group system clearly compromises the principle of political equality stated in the maxim "one person, one vote." Formal political equality is certainly more likely to occur outside interest group politics, in elections between candidates from competing political parties, which better fits the majoritarian model of democracy.

Despite the inequities of the interest group system, little direct effort has been made to restrict interest group activity. Madison's dictum to avoid suppressing political freedoms, even at the expense of permitting interest group activity that promotes the selfish interests of narrow segments of the population, has generally guided public policy. Yet as the problem of campaign finance demonstrates, government has had to set some restrictions on interest groups. Where to draw the line on interest group donations remains a thorny issue because there is little consensus on how to balance the conflicting needs of our society. Congress is one institution that must try to balance our diverse country's conflicting interests. In the next chapter, we will see how difficult this part of Congress's job is.

CourseMate Visit www.cengagebrain.com/shop/ ISBN/0495906182 for flashcards, web quizzes, videos and more!

CHAPTER 11 Congress

CHAPTER TOPICS

During the 2008 presidential campaign, Barack Obama pledged to close the detention facility at the U.S. military base in Guantánamo Bay, Cuba, which had been used during the George W. Bush administration as a prison for people with suspected ties to international terrorist groups. Arguments for closing the prison included that prisoners were denied basic legal protections (such as being detained indefinitely without being charged with a specific crime), that they were tortured during interrogations, and that the prison itself had become a symbol used to help recruit Al Qaeda members overseas and perpetuate anti-American sentiment.[1]

Obama learned on election day that he would have large majorities in Congress to help him follow through on his campaign promises: Democrats would control nearly 60 percent of the seats in both the House and the Senate. Just two days after taking office, Obama issued an executive order calling for Guantánamo to be shut down within one year. At the time, Speaker of the House Nancy Pelosi praised the order, saying that closing Guantánamo would "ensure that terrorist suspects held by the United States are treated in ways consistent with our laws and our values."[2] Senate Majority Leader Harry Reid agreed that closing Guantánamo was the right decision. The Democratic victories certainly suggested that they could do something in Congress to enact this executive order. In theory, at least, that's how majoritarian government should work. The policies supported by the majority party are expected to become a reality. In practice, however, the majority often turns out to be more elusive than it seems.

Indeed, having the support of congressional leadership and having such a large group of fellow partisans controlling the legislature have not made it any easier for Obama to deliver on his promise to close Guantánamo. In June 2009, Congress passed a military spending bill that explicitly prohibited the use of those funds for closing the prison. A few months later, both houses passed a bill that would prohibit the transfer of Guantánamo prisoners to the United States except for prosecution. By the fall of 2009, the administration admitted that it might not be able to close the prison by January 2010 as it had ordered.[3]

Why was it so difficult for Obama to work with Congress and deliver on this campaign promise? First, divisions exist within the Democratic Party on this issue as well as on many other issues. Belonging to the same party does not guarantee agreement on key issues of the day. Second, many representatives felt that the president was crafting his detention policy without sufficient input from Congress. In short, they were annoyed about being left out of the loop; obstructing progress was a way to send the message that Obama needed to do more to solicit their input.[4] Third, members of Congress answer to their constituents as well as to their party leadership. Several members of Congress, including Democrats, were less than enthusiastic about the possibility of detainees being relocated to their states.[5] Finally, representatives have to run for reelection every two years, and Democrats in the House are concerned about being portrayed as soft on terrorism. So while a party would prefer to be the majority in Congress rather than the minority, being the majority party rarely means that the party has smooth sailing in enacting its agenda. And if the majority party fails, the minority party has a compelling theme for the next election.

In this chapter we'll examine majoritarian politics through the prism of the two congressional parties. We'll look at how the forces of pluralism work against majoritarian policymaking. We'll turn our attention to the procedures and norms that facilitate bargaining and compromise in Congress, which are key to understanding how the House and Senate operate. We'll discuss Congress's relations with the executive branch, and we'll analyze how the legislative process affects public policy. We begin by asking how the framers envisioned Congress.

The Origin and Powers of Congress

The framers of the Constitution wanted to keep power from being concentrated in the hands of a few, but they were also concerned with creating a Union strong enough to overcome the weaknesses of the government that had operated under the Articles of Confederation. They argued passionately about the structure of the new government. In the end, they produced a legislative body that was as much of an experiment as the new nation's democracy.

The Great Compromise

The U.S. Congress has two separate and powerful chambers: the House of Representatives and the Senate. A bill cannot become law unless it is passed in identical form by both chambers. During the drafting of the Constitution in the summer of 1787, "the fiercest struggle for power" centered on representation in the legislature.[6] The small states wanted all the states to have equal representation, and the more populous states wanted representation based on population; they did not want their power diluted. The Great Compromise broke the deadlock: the small states would receive equal representation in the Senate, but the number of each state's representatives in the House would be based on population and the House would have the sole right to originate revenue-related legislation.

As the Constitution specifies, each state has two senators, who serve six-year terms of office. Terms are staggered, so that one-third of the Senate is elected every two years. When it was ratified, the Constitution directed that senators be chosen by the state legislatures. However, the Seventeenth Amendment, adopted in 1913, provided for the direct election of senators by popular vote. From the beginning, the people have directly elected members of the House of Representatives. They serve two-year terms, and all House seats are up for election at the same time.

There are 435 members of the House of Representatives. Because each state's representation in the House is in proportion to its population, the Constitution provides for a national census every ten years; population shifts are handled by the **reapportionment** (redistribution) of seats among the states after each census is taken. Since recent population growth has been centered in the Sunbelt, California, Texas, and Florida have gained

reapportionment
Redistribution of representatives among the states, based on population change. The House is reapportioned after each census.

seats, while the Northeast and Midwest states like New York and Illinois have lost them. Each representative is elected from a particular congressional district within his or her state, and each district elects only one representative. The districts within a state must be roughly equal in population.

Duties of the House and Senate

Although the Great Compromise provided for considerably different schemes of representation for the House and Senate, the Constitution gives them similar legislative tasks. They share many important powers, among them the powers to declare war, raise an army and navy, borrow and coin money, regulate interstate commerce, create federal courts, establish rules for the naturalization of immigrants, and "make all Laws which shall be necessary and proper for carrying into Execution the foregoing Powers."

Of course, the constitutional duties of the two chambers are different in at least a few important ways. As noted in Chapter 3, the House alone has the right to originate revenue bills, a right that apparently was coveted at the Constitutional Convention. In practice, this power is of limited consequence because both the House and Senate must approve all bills, including revenue bills. The House of Representatives has the power of **impeachment**: the power formally to charge the president, vice president, and other "civil officers" of the national government with serious crimes. The Senate is empowered to act as a court to try impeachments, with the chief justice of the Supreme Court presiding. A two-thirds majority vote of the senators present is necessary for conviction. Prior to President Clinton's impeachment in 1998, only one sitting president, Andrew Johnson, had been impeached, and in 1868 the Senate came within a single vote of finding him guilty. Clinton was accused of both perjury and obstruction of justice concerning his relationship with a White House intern, Monica Lewinsky, but was acquitted by the Senate. The House Judiciary Committee voted to recommend impeachment of President Richard Nixon because of his involvement in the Watergate cover-up, but before the full House could vote, Nixon resigned from office.

The Constitution gives the Senate the power to approve major presidential appointments (such as to federal judgeships, ambassadorships, and cabinet posts) and treaties with foreign nations. The president is empowered to make treaties but must submit them to the Senate for approval by a two-thirds majority. Because of this requirement, the executive branch generally considers the Senate's sentiments when it negotiates a treaty. At times, a president must try to convince a doubting Senate of the worth of a particular treaty. Shortly after World War I, President Woodrow Wilson submitted to the Senate the Treaty of Versailles, which contained the charter for the proposed League of Nations. Wilson had attempted to convince the Senate that the treaty deserved its support; when the Senate refused to approve the treaty, Wilson suffered a severe setback as he had made the treaty his highest priority.

Despite the long list of congressional powers stated in the Constitution, the question of what powers are appropriate for Congress has generated substantial controversy. For example, although the Constitution gives Congress

impeachment
The formal charging of a government official with "treason, bribery, or other high crimes and misdemeanors."

the sole power to declare war, presidents have initiated military action on their own. And at times, the courts have found that congressional actions have usurped the rights of the states.

Electing Congress

If Americans are not happy with the job Congress is doing, they can use their votes to say so. With a congressional election every two years, the voters have frequent opportunities to express themselves.

The Incumbency Effect

Congressional elections offer voters a chance to show their approval of Congress's performance by reelecting **incumbents** or to demonstrate their disapproval by "throwing the rascals out."[7] The voters do more reelecting than rascal throwing. The reelection rate is astonishingly high: in the majority of elections since 1950, more than 90 percent of all House incumbents have held on to their seats (see Figure 11.1). In the 2010 congressional elections, a whopping 54 House incumbents (all but two of them Democrats) were defeated by challengers, a failure rate that is notable because of how unusual it is. It is the first time since 1974 and the fallout from Watergate that the reelection rate for House incumbents fell below 90 percent. Most House elections aren't even close; in recent elections, over 70 percent of House incumbents have won reelection by margins of greater than 60 percent of the vote.[8] Senate elections are more competitive, but incumbents still have a high reelection rate.

incumbent
A current officeholder.

FIGURE 11.1   Incumbents: Life Is Good

Despite the public's dissatisfaction with Congress in general, incumbent representatives win reelection at an exceptional rate. Incumbent senators aren't quite as successful but still do well in reelection races. Voters seem to believe that their own representatives and senators don't share the same foibles that they attribute to other members of Congress.

Sources: Various sources for 1950–2006. For 2008, Harold W. Stanley and Richard G. Niemi (eds.), *Vital Statistics on American Politics, 2009–2010* (Washington, D.C.: CQ Press, 2010), pp. 39–40. Please note that the data for 2010 are preliminary as a handful of races were still undecided at the time this edition went to press.

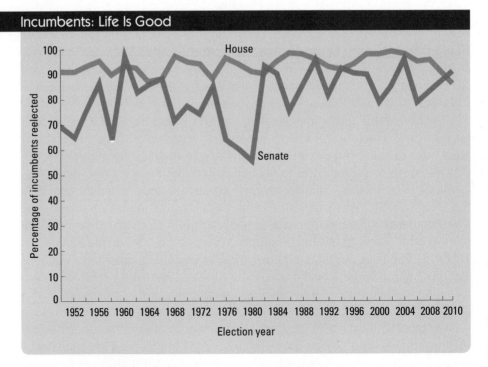

These findings may seem surprising, since the public does not hold Congress as a whole in particularly high esteem. In the past few years, Americans have been particularly critical of Congress, and some polls have shown less than one in five approving of its performance (see Figure 11.2). One reason Americans hold Congress in disdain is that they regard it as overly influenced by interest groups. A declining economy, the wars in Iraq and Afghanistan, and persistent partisan disagreements within Congress have also reduced people's confidence in the institution.[9]

Redistricting. One explanation for the incumbency effect centers on redistricting—the way states redraw House districts after a census-based reapportionment.[10] It is entirely possible for the states to draw the new districts to benefit the incumbents of one or both parties. Altering district lines for partisan advantage is commonly called **gerrymandering**.

Gerrymandering has been practiced since at least the early 1800s.[11] And with new computer software, gerrymandering is reaching new heights of precision. With an ordinary desktop computer, someone knowledgeable with the software can easily use census data and precinct voting data to manipulate boundary lines and produce districts that are optimally designed to enhance or damage a candidate's or party's chances.[12] After the 2000 census, for example, California state legislators took the solidly Republican city of San Marino out of incumbent Democrat Adam Schiff's district and put it in the adjoining district of Republican David Dreier. Instantaneously, Schiff's district became even more safely Democratic (with San Marino now gone), and Dreier's district became even more safely Republican (with San Marino now part of it). Since Dreier was the incumbent and not likely to lose anyway, the Democrats gave up little and gave themselves some insurance against Republican inroads.[13]

Some argue that gerrymandering contributes to the increasing pattern of polarization between the two parties in the House. Districts that are

gerrymandering
Redrawing a congressional district to intentionally benefit one political party.

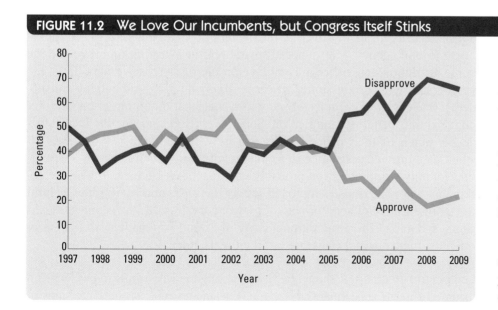

FIGURE 11.2 We Love Our Incumbents, but Congress Itself Stinks

Despite the reelection rate of incumbents reflected in Figure 11.1, public approval of Congress is far less positive. Confidence scores have never been particularly high, but opinion has turned decidedly negative in recent years. Citizens don't believe that the House and Senate are facing up to the nation's problems.

Source: NBC News/*Wall Street Journal* polls, available at http://www.pollingreport.com/CongJob1.htm.

dominated by one party or another have some tendency to be more ideologically driven. That is, with a disproportionate number of liberals or conservatives in a district, the representative will be pulled more toward a pole of the ideological spectrum than to the moderate center. Such a tendency is moderated by other factors, but representatives' behavior is influenced by the mobilization of ideologues.[14]

Name Recognition. Holding office brings with it some important advantages. First, incumbents develop significant name recognition among voters simply by being members of Congress. Congressional press secretaries help the name recognition advantage along through their efforts to get publicity for the activities and speeches of their bosses. The primary focus of such publicity seeking is on the local media back in the district, where the votes are. The local press is eager to cover what local members of Congress are saying about the issues.

Another resource available to members of Congress is the *franking privilege*—the right to send mail free of charge. Mailings work to make constituents aware of their legislators' names, activities, and accomplishments. In 2007 House members sent out 98 million pieces of mail, "many of them glossy productions filled with flattering photos and lists of the latest roads and bridges the lawmaker has brought home to the district."[15] New rules are being debated to determine appropriate ways of regulating representatives' communication with constituents via social media such as Twitter. Under current franking regulations, information about the representative's personal life and political campaign cannot be included in official mailings, but no such rules exist to govern "tweets." Currently, 33 percent of representatives have Twitter accounts and have used them to send information about sporting events, their health, and even their shopping trips.[16]

Casework. Much of the work performed by the large staffs of members of Congress is **casework**—services for constituents, such as tracking down a Social Security check or directing the owner of a small business to the appropriate federal agency. Many specialists in both the Washington office and the home district or state office are employed primarily as caseworkers. Thus, the very structure of congressional offices is largely built around helping constituents. One caseworker on a staff may be a specialist on immigration, another on veterans' benefits, another on Social Security, and so on. Legislators devote much of their office budget to casework because they assume that when they provide assistance to a constituent, that constituent will be grateful. Not only will that person probably vote for the legislator in the next election, but he or she is also sure to tell family members and friends how helpful the representative or senator was. "Casework is all profit," says one congressional scholar.[17] The growing popularity of e-mail has made it all the easier for constituents to make a request of their legislator.

casework
Solving problems for constituents, especially problems involving government agencies.

Campaign Financing. It should be clear that anyone who wants to challenge an incumbent needs solid financial backing. Challengers must spend large sums of money to run a strong campaign with an emphasis on advertising—an expensive but effective way to bring their name and record to the voters' attention. But here too the incumbent has the advantage. Challengers find raising campaign funds difficult because they have to overcome contributors' doubts about whether they can win. In the 2008 elections, incumbents raised 61 percent of all money contributed to campaigns for election to the House and the Senate. Only 23 percent went to challengers. (Those running for open seats received the rest.)[18]

PACs show a strong preference for incumbents (see Chapter 10). They tend not to want to risk offending an incumbent by giving money to a long-shot challenger. The attitude of the American Medical Association's PAC is fairly typical. "We have a friendly incumbent policy," says its director. "We always stick with the incumbent if we agree with both candidates."[19]

Successful Challengers. Clearly, the deck is stacked against challengers. As one analyst put it, "The typical House challenger is in a position similar to that of a novice athlete pitted against a world-class sprinter."[20] Yet some challengers do beat incumbents. How? The opposing party and unsympathetic PACs may target incumbents who seem vulnerable because of age, lack of seniority, a scandal, or unfavorable redistricting. Some incumbents appear vulnerable because they were elected by a narrow margin, or the ideological and partisan composition of their district does not favor their holding the seat. Vulnerable incumbents also bring out higher-quality challengers—individuals who have held elective office previously and are capable of raising adequate campaign funds. Such experienced challengers are more likely to defeat incumbents than are amateurs with little background in politics.[21] The reason Senate challengers have a higher success rate than House challengers is that they are generally higher-quality candidates. Often they are governors or members of the House who enjoy high name recognition and can attract significant campaign funds because they are regarded as credible candidates.

2010 Election. In the 2010 midterm elections, Democrats lost over 60 seats in the House and 6 in the Senate (with some races too close to call as of this writing). They retained a bare majority in the Senate but lost control of the House to Republicans. Several factors contributed to this historic change, including continuing economic uncertainty, anger over policies such as health-care reform and the economic stimulus, a mobilized Republican base (aided by the tea party movement), and a lethargic liberal base frustrated by the failure of the Obama administration to deliver on several campaign promises.

Whom Do We Elect?

The people we elect (then reelect) to Congress are not a cross-section of American society. Although nearly a third of the American labor force works in blue-collar jobs, someone currently employed as a blue-collar worker rarely wins a congressional nomination. Most members of Congress are upper-class professionals—many lawyers and businesspeople—and, at last count, 44 percent are millionaires.[22]

Women and minorities have long been underrepresented in elective office, although both groups have recently increased their representation in

Congress significantly. Seventeen women served in the Senate in the 2009–2010 session. This is a historic high, but nowhere near the proportion of women to men in the population at large. One of the reasons that the number of women elected to Congress lags behind their proportion in the population is that as women develop professionally, they are not recruited or encouraged to run in the same way that men are.[23]

Other members of Congress don't necessarily ignore the concerns of women and minorities.[24] Yet many women and minorities believe that only members of their own group—people who have experienced what they have experienced—can truly represent their interests. This is a belief in **descriptive representation**—the view that a legislature should resemble the demographic characteristics of the population it represents.[25] (See "Compared with What? Women in Legislatures" for a comparison of the representation of women in the world's national legislatures.)

During the 1980s, both Congress and the Supreme Court provided support for the principle of descriptive representation for blacks and Hispanic Americans. When Congress amended the Voting Rights Act in 1982, it encouraged the states to draw districts that concentrated minorities together so that blacks and Hispanic Americans would have a better chance of being elected to office. The Supreme Court decision in *Thornburg v. Gingles* in 1986 also pushed the states to concentrate minorities in House districts. After the 1990 census, states redrew House boundaries with the intent of creating districts with majority or near-majority minority populations. Some districts were very oddly shaped, snaking through their state to pick up black neighborhoods in various cities but leaving adjacent white neighborhoods to other districts. This effort led to a roughly 50 percent increase in the number of blacks elected to the House (see Figure 11.3).

descriptive representation
A belief that constituents are most effectively represented by legislators who are similar to them in such key demographic characteristics as race, ethnicity, religion, or gender.

The Millionaires' Club

In 2009, Representative Darrell Issa (R-Calif.) was the richest lawmaker in Congress, with an estimated net worth of $251 million. While 44 percent of lawmakers are millionaires, only about 1 percent of Americans can say the same.

Source: Erika Lovley, "Report: 237 Millionaires in Congress," *Politico,* 6 November 2009, http://dyn.politico.com/printstory .cfm?uuid=CA707571-18FE-70B2-A8721899A59ED165. *Photo:* Alex Wong/Getty Images.

Compared with What?

Women in Legislatures

The percentage of women in the world's national legislatures differs from one country to another. The number of women does not seem to be a function of the structure of the legislature or the party system in these countries. Culture does seem to make a difference, though. This figure includes fifteen European countries as well as fifteen countries from the Americas (North America, Central America, and South America) as of September 2009. Ranked by the percentage of women in the lower house of the national legislature, the European countries include, on average, a significantly higher percentage of women than the legislatures of countries in the Western Hemisphere.

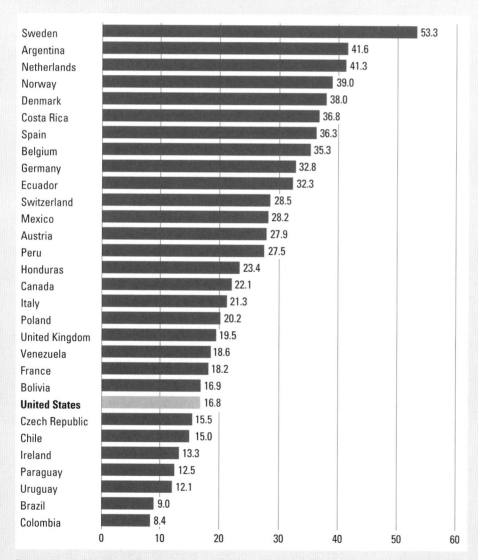

Country	Percentage
Sweden	53.3
Argentina	41.6
Netherlands	41.3
Norway	39.0
Denmark	38.0
Costa Rica	36.8
Spain	36.3
Belgium	35.3
Germany	32.8
Ecuador	32.3
Switzerland	28.5
Mexico	28.2
Austria	27.9
Peru	27.5
Honduras	23.4
Canada	22.1
Italy	21.3
Poland	20.2
United Kingdom	19.5
Venezuela	18.6
France	18.2
Bolivia	16.9
United States	16.8
Czech Republic	15.5
Chile	15.0
Ireland	13.3
Paraguay	12.5
Uruguay	12.1
Brazil	9.0
Colombia	8.4

Source: Inter-Parliamentary Union, http://www.ipu.org/wmn-e/classif.htm.

FIGURE 11.3   Minorities in Congress

Today, African Americans make up about 8 percent of the membership of the House and Senate, and Hispanics make up about 5 percent of total members. Though gains have been steady, the representation of both groups remains well below their proportions in the population at large. Hispanics constitute 14 percent of the American population; African Americans make up almost 13 percent of the total population.

Source: Updated from Greg Giroux, "A New Democratic Demographic," *CQ Weekly Online,* 20 April 2009, pp. 908–913.

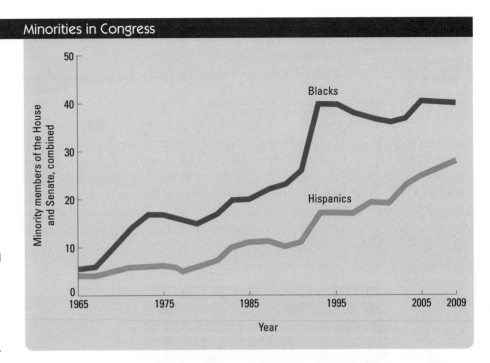

The effort to draw boundaries to promote the election of minorities has been considerably less effective for Hispanics. Hispanic representation is only about two-thirds that of African Americans, even though there are slightly more Hispanics in the United States than African Americans. Part of the reason for this inequity is that Hispanics tend not to live in such geographically concentrated areas as do African Americans. This makes it harder to draw boundaries that will likely lead to the election of a Hispanic. Another reason is that 37 percent of adult Hispanics living in the United States are ineligible to vote because they are not American citizens.[26]

In a decision that surprised many, the Supreme Court ruled in 1993 that states' efforts to increase minority representation through **racial gerrymandering** could violate the rights of whites. In *Shaw* v. *Reno*, the majority ruled in a split decision that a North Carolina district that meandered 160 miles from Durham to Charlotte was an example of "political apartheid." (In some places, the Twelfth District was no wider than Interstate 85.) In effect, the Court ruled that racial gerrymandering segregated blacks from whites instead of creating districts built around contiguous communities.[27] In a later decision, the Supreme Court ruled that the "intensive and pervasive use of race" to protect incumbents and promote political gerrymandering violated the Fourteenth Amendment and Voting Rights Act of 1965.[28] In 2001, just before the redistricting from the 2000 census was to begin in the individual states, the Court modified its earlier decisions by declaring that race was not an illegitimate consideration in drawing congressional boundaries as long as it was not the "dominant and controlling" factor.[29]

Although this movement over time to draw districts that work to elect minorities has clearly increased the number of black and Hispanic legislators,

racial gerrymandering
The drawing of a legislative district to maximize the chance that a minority candidate will win election.

almost all of whom are Democrats, it has also helped the Republican Party. As more Democratic-voting minorities have been packed into selected districts, this has diminished their numbers in other districts, leaving the remaining districts not merely "whiter" but also more Republican than they would have otherwise been.[30]

How Issues Get on the Congressional Agenda

The formal legislative process begins when a member of Congress introduces a *bill,* a proposal for a new law. In the House, members drop bills in the "hopper," a mahogany box near the rostrum where the Speaker presides. Senators give their bills to a Senate clerk or introduce them from the floor. But before a bill can be introduced to solve a problem, someone must perceive that a problem exists or that an issue needs to be resolved. In other words, the problem or issue somehow must find its way onto the congressional agenda.

Many issues Congress is working on at any given time seem to have been around forever. Foreign aid, the national debt, and Social Security have come up in just about every recent session of Congress. Other issues emerge more suddenly, especially those that are the product of technological change.[31] The issue of "cyberbullying" is one example. Just a few years ago, the term did not even exist, but in 2009, a bill was introduced in the House that would make it a federal crime to "coerce, intimidate, harass, or cause substantial emotional distress to another person, using electronic means to support severe, repeated, and hostile behavior."[32] The bill, known as the Megan Meier Cyberbullying Prevention Act, was drafted after national attention was drawn to the case of a teenage girl in St. Louis who committed suicide after being taunted by a neighbor who was pretending to be Megan's boyfriend on the social networking site MySpace.[33]

New issues reach the congressional agenda in many ways. Sometimes a highly visible event focuses national attention on a problem. When it became evident that the September 11 hijackers had little trouble boarding their planes despite carrying box cutters that they would use as weapons, Congress quickly took up the issue of airport screening procedures. It decided to create a federal work force to conduct passenger and luggage screening at the nation's airports, believing the existing workers recruited by private companies were badly trained and poorly motivated. Presidential support can also move an issue onto the agenda quickly. The media attention paid to the president gives him enormous opportunity to draw the nation's attention to problems he believes need some form of government action.

Within Congress, party leaders and committee chairs have the opportunity to move issues onto the agenda, but they rarely act capriciously, seizing on issues without rhyme or reason. They often bide their time, waiting for other members of Congress to learn about an issue as they attempt to gauge the level of support for some kind of action. At times, the efforts of an interest group spark support for action, or at least awareness of an issue. When congressional leaders—or, for that matter, rank-and-file members—sense that the time is ripe for action on a new issue, they often are spurred on by the knowledge that sponsoring an important bill can enhance their own image. In the words of one observer, "Congress exists to do things. There isn't much mileage in doing nothing."[34]

The Dance of Legislation: An Overview

The process of writing bills and getting them enacted is relatively simple in the sense that it follows a series of specific steps. What complicates the process is the many different ways legislation can be treated at each step. Here, we examine the straightforward process by which laws are made. In the next few sections, we discuss some of the complexities of that process.

After a bill is introduced in either house, it is assigned to the committee with jurisdiction over that policy area (see Figure 11.4). A banking bill, for example, would be assigned to the Financial Services Committee in the House or to the Banking, Housing, and Urban Affairs Committee in the Senate. When a committee actively considers a piece of legislation assigned to it, the bill is usually referred to a specialized subcommittee. The subcommittee may hold hearings, and legislative staffers may do research on the bill. The original bill usually is modified or revised; if passed in some form, it is sent to the full committee. A bill approved by the full committee is reported (that is, sent) to the entire membership of the chamber, where it may be debated, amended, and either passed or defeated.

Bills coming out of House committees go to the Rules Committee before going before the full House membership. The Rules Committee attaches a rule to the bill that governs the coming floor debate, typically specifying the length of the debate and the types of amendments House members can offer. On major legislation, most rules are complex and quite restrictive in terms of any amendments that can be offered. The Senate does not have a comparable committee, although restrictions on the length of floor debate can be reached through unanimous consent agreements (see the "Rules of Procedure" section later in this chapter).

Even if both houses of Congress pass a bill on the same subject, the Senate and House versions are typically different from each other. In that case, a conference committee, composed of legislators from both houses, works out the differences and develops a compromise version. This version goes back to both houses for another floor vote. If both chambers approve the bill, it goes to the president for his signature or veto.

When the president signs a bill, it becomes law. If the president **vetoes** (disapproves) the bill, he sends it back to Congress with his reasons for rejecting it. The bill becomes law only if Congress overrides the president's veto by a two-thirds vote in each house. If the president neither signs nor vetoes the

veto
The president's disapproval of a bill that has been passed by both houses of Congress. Congress can override a veto with a two-thirds vote in each house.

FIGURE 11.4 The Legislative Process

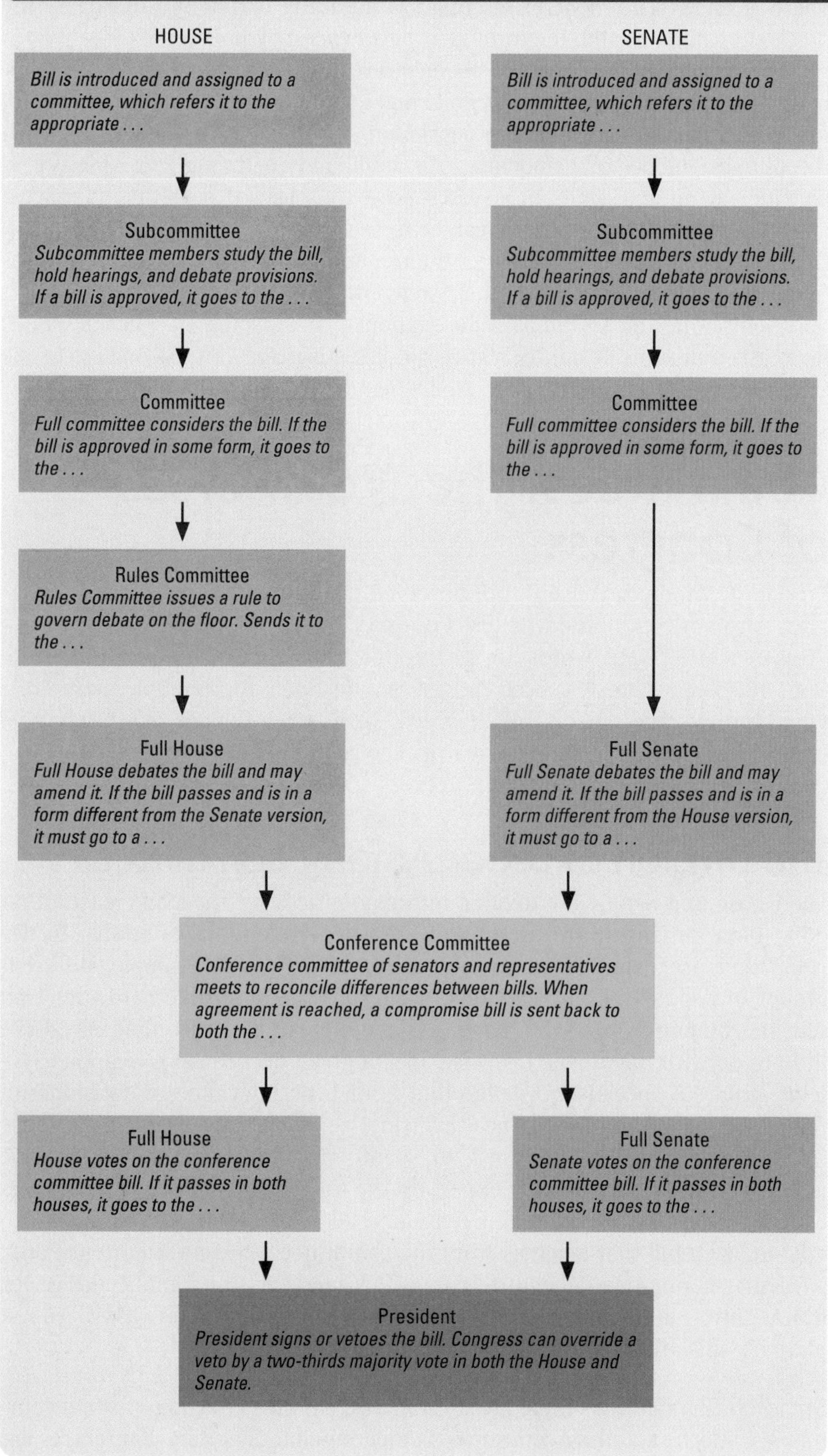

The process by which a bill becomes law is subject to much variation. This diagram depicts the typical process a bill might follow. It is important to remember that a bill can fail at any stage because of lack of support.

HOUSE

Bill is introduced and assigned to a committee, which refers it to the appropriate . . .

Subcommittee
Subcommittee members study the bill, hold hearings, and debate provisions. If a bill is approved, it goes to the . . .

Committee
Full committee considers the bill. If the bill is approved in some form, it goes to the . . .

Rules Committee
Rules Committee issues a rule to govern debate on the floor. Sends it to the . . .

Full House
Full House debates the bill and may amend it. If the bill passes and is in a form different from the Senate version, it must go to a . . .

SENATE

Bill is introduced and assigned to a committee, which refers it to the appropriate . . .

Subcommittee
Subcommittee members study the bill, hold hearings, and debate provisions. If a bill is approved, it goes to the . . .

Committee
Full committee considers the bill. If the bill is approved in some form, it goes to the . . .

Full Senate
Full Senate debates the bill and may amend it. If the bill passes and is in a form different from the House version, it must go to a . . .

Conference Committee
Conference committee of senators and representatives meets to reconcile differences between bills. When agreement is reached, a compromise bill is sent back to both the . . .

Full House
House votes on the conference committee bill. If it passes in both houses, it goes to the . . .

Full Senate
Senate votes on the conference committee bill. If it passes in both houses, it goes to the . . .

President
President signs or vetoes the bill. Congress can override a veto by a two-thirds majority vote in both the House and Senate.

bill within ten days (Sundays excepted) of receiving it, the bill becomes law. There is an exception here: if Congress adjourns within the ten days, the president can let the bill die through a *pocket veto,* by not signing it.

The content of a bill can be changed at any stage of the process in either house. Lawmaking (and thus policymaking) in Congress has many access points for those who want to influence legislation. This openness tends to fit within the pluralist model of democracy. As a bill moves through Congress, it is amended again and again, in a search for a consensus that will get it enacted and signed into law. The process can be tortuously slow, and it is often fruitless. Derailing legislation is much easier than enacting it. The process gives groups frequent opportunities to voice their preferences and, if necessary, thwart their opponents. One foreign ambassador stationed in Washington aptly described the twists and turns of our legislative process this way: "In the Congress of the U.S., it's never over until it's over. And when it's over, it's still not over."[35]

Committees: The Workhorses of Congress

President Woodrow Wilson once observed that "Congress in session is Congress on public exhibition, whilst Congress in its committee-rooms is Congress at work."[36] His words are as true today as when he wrote them more than 100 years ago. A speech on the Senate floor, for example, may convince the average citizen, but it is less likely to influence other senators. Indeed, few of them may even hear it. The real nuts and bolts of lawmaking go on in the congressional committees.

The Division of Labor Among Committees

The House and Senate are divided into committees for the same reason that other large organizations are broken into departments or divisions: to develop and use expertise in specific areas. At IBM, for example, different groups of people design computers, write software, assemble hardware, and sell the company's products. Each task requires an expertise that may have little to do with the others. Likewise, in Congress, decisions on weapons systems require a special knowledge that is of little relevance to decisions on reimbursement formulas for health insurance, for example. It makes sense for some members of Congress to spend more time examining defense issues, becoming increasingly expert on the topic as they do so, while others concentrate on health matters. Eventually, all members of Congress have to vote on each bill that emerges from the committees. Those who are not on a particular committee depend on committee members to examine the issues thoroughly, make compromises as necessary, and bring forward a sound piece of legislation that has a good chance of being passed.

standing committee
A permanent congressional committee that specializes in a particular policy area.

Standing Committees. There are several different kinds of congressional committees, but the **standing committee** is predominant. Standing committees are permanent committees that specialize in a particular area of legislation—for example, the House Judiciary Committee or the Senate Environment and Public Works Committee. Most of the day-to-day work of drafting legislation takes place in the twenty standing Senate committees and twenty-one standing House committees. Typically, sixteen to twenty senators serve on each standing Senate committee, and an average of forty-two members serve on each standing committee in the House. The proportions of Democrats and Republicans on a standing committee are controlled by the majority party in each house. The majority party gives the minority a percentage of seats that, in theory, approximates the minority party's percentage in the entire chamber. However, the majority party usually gives itself enough of a cushion to ensure that it can control each committee.

With a few exceptions, standing committees are broken down further into subcommittees. For instance, the Senate Foreign Relations committee has seven subcommittees, covering different regions of the world and issues such as international economic policy and terrorism. Subcommittees exist for the same reason parent committees exist: members acquire expertise by continually working within the same fairly narrow policy area. Typically, members of the subcommittee are the dominant force in the shaping of the content of a bill.

Other Congressional Committees. Members of Congress can also serve on joint, select, and conference committees. A **joint committee** is composed of members of both the House and the Senate. Like standing committees, the four joint committees are concerned with particular policy areas. The Joint Economic Committee, for instance, analyzes the country's economic policies. Joint committees are much weaker than standing committees because they are almost always restricted from reporting bills to the House or Senate. Thus, their role is usually that of fact finding and publicizing problems and policy issues that fall within their jurisdiction.

A **select committee** is a temporary committee created for a specific purpose. Congress establishes select committees to deal with special circumstances or with issues that either overlap or fall outside the areas of expertise of standing committees. The Senate committee that investigated the Watergate scandal, for example, was a select committee, created for that purpose only.

A **conference committee** is also a temporary committee, created to work out differences between the House and Senate versions of a specific piece of legislation. Its members are appointed from the standing committees or subcommittees from each house that originally crafted and reported the legislation. Depending on the nature of the differences and the importance of the legislation, a conference committee may meet for hours or for weeks on end.

Conference committees are not always used, however, to reconcile differing bills. Often, informal negotiations between committee leaders in the House and Senate resolve differences. The increasing partisan conflict between Democrats and Republicans has often resulted in a compromise bill devised solely by the majority party (when a single party controls both chambers).

joint committee
A committee made up of members of both the House and the Senate.

select committee
A temporary congressional committee created for a specific purpose and disbanded after that purpose is fulfilled.

conference committee
A temporary committee created to work out differences between the House and Senate versions of a specific piece of legislation.

Congressional Expertise and Seniority

Once appointed to a committee, a representative or senator has great incentive to remain on it and gain expertise over the years. Influence in Congress increases with a member's expertise. Influence also grows in a more formal way, with **seniority**, or years of consecutive service, on a committee. In their quest for expertise and seniority, members tend to stay on the same committees. However, sometimes they switch places when they are offered the opportunity to move to one of the high-prestige committees (such as Ways and Means in the House or Finance in the Senate) or to a committee that handles legislation of vital importance to their constituents.

Within each committee, the senior member of the majority party usually becomes the committee chair. Other senior members of the majority party become subcommittee chairs, whereas their counterparts from the minority party gain influence as ranking minority members. In the House and Senate combined, there are over 150 subcommittees, offering multiple opportunities for power and status. Unlike seniority, expertise does not follow simply from length of service. Ability and effort are critical factors too.

The seniority norm has been weakened considerably since the Republican Party leadership established six-year term limits for committee and subcommittee chairs, a sharp break with the tradition of unlimited tenure as a committee chair. In the wake of term limits, the opening of committee chair positions led to bargains between rank-and-file members and their party leaders.[37] Democratic Party leaders have largely adhered to the seniority system, though they have also worked to increase the representation of women, minorities, and junior members of Congress on the most prestigious congressional committees.

The way in which committees and subcommittees are led and organized within Congress is significant because much public policy decision making takes place there. The first step in drafting legislation is to collect information on the issue. Committee staffers research the problem, and committees hold hearings to take testimony from witnesses who have some special knowledge of the subject.

At times, committee hearings are more theatrical than informational, designed to draw public attention to them and to offer the majority party a chance to express its views. When President Obama nominated Sonia Sotomayor to be a Supreme Court justice, it was clear that the strong Democratic majority was all but assured of securing her confirmation. Nonetheless, Republican senators on the Judiciary Committee subjected her to intense questioning about gun control, abortion, and same-sex marriage. Some even called her radical and deceptive. In the end, Sotomayor was confirmed, but with only nine votes from Republicans.[38]

The meetings at which subcommittees and committees actually debate and amend legislation are called *markup sessions*. The process by which committees reach decisions varies. Many committees have a strong tradition of deciding by consensus. The chair, the ranking minority member, and others on these committees work hard, in formal committee sessions and in

seniority
Years of consecutive service on a particular congressional committee.

informal negotiations, to find a middle ground on issues that divide committee members. In other committees, members exhibit strong ideological and partisan sentiments. However, committee and subcommittee leaders prefer to find ways to overcome inherent ideological and partisan divisions so that they can build compromise solutions that will appeal to the broader membership of their house. The skill of committee leaders in assembling coalitions that produce legislation that can pass on the floor of their house is critically important. When committees are mired in disagreement, they lose power. Since jurisdictions overlap, other committees may take more initiative in their common policy area.

Oversight: Following Through on Legislation

There is general agreement in Washington that knowledge is power. For Congress to retain its influence over the programs it creates, it must be aware of how the agencies responsible for them are administering them. To that end, legislators and their committees engage in **oversight**, the process of reviewing agencies' operations to determine whether they are carrying out policies as Congress intended.

As the executive branch has grown and policies and programs have become increasingly complex, oversight has become more difficult. The sheer magnitude of executive branch operations is staggering. On a typical weekday, for example, agencies issue more than a hundred pages of new regulations. Even with the division of labor in the committee system, determining how good a job an agency is doing in implementing a program is no easy task.

Congress performs its oversight function in several different ways. The most visible is the hearing. Hearings may be part of a routine review or the

oversight
The process of reviewing the operations of an agency to determine whether it is carrying out policies as Congress intended.

byproduct of information that reveals a major problem with a program or with an agency's administrative practices. After the disastrous federal response to Hurricane Katrina, which destroyed much of New Orleans, congressional committees held hearings to understand why the government failed. Another way Congress keeps track of what departments and agencies are doing is by requesting reports on specific agency practices and operations. During most of the Bush administration, the Republican-controlled Congress exerted little oversight on the executive branch. After the Democrats captured Congress in the 2006 election, committees in both houses became much more aggressive in investigating ethical lapses and policy problems in the Bush administration. Hearings were held on a range of issues, including treatment of terror suspects, the deteriorating situation in Iraq, and political firings in the Department of Justice.[39] Not all oversight is so formal. A good deal of congressional oversight takes place informally, as there are ongoing contacts between committee and subcommittee leaders and agency administrators as well as between committee staffers and top agency staffers.

Oversight is often stereotyped as a process in which angry legislators bring some administrators before the hot lights and television cameras at a hearing and proceed to dress them down for some recent scandal or mistake. Some of this does go on, but the pluralist side of Congress makes it likely that at least some members of a committee are advocates of the programs they oversee because those programs serve their constituents back home. Members of the House and Senate Agriculture Committees, for example, both Democrats and Republicans, want farm programs to succeed. Thus, most oversight is aimed at trying to find ways to improve programs and is not directed at efforts to discredit them. In the last analysis, Congress engages in oversight because it is an extension of their efforts to control public policy.

Majoritarian and Pluralist Views of Committees

Government by committee vests a tremendous amount of power in the committees and subcommittees of Congress—and especially their leaders. This is particularly true in the House, which has more decentralized patterns of influence than the Senate and is more restrictive about letting members amend legislation on the floor. Committee members can bury a bill by not reporting it to the full House or Senate. The influence of committee members extends even further, to the floor debate. Many of them also make up the conference committees charged with developing compromise versions of bills.

In some ways, the committee system enhances the force of pluralism in American politics. Representatives and senators are elected by the voters in their particular districts and states, and they tend to seek membership on the committees that make the decisions most important to their constituents. Members from farm areas, for example, want membership on the House and Senate Agriculture Committees. Westerners like to serve on committees that deal with public lands and water rights. Urban liberals like committees that handle social programs. As a result, committee members tend to represent constituencies with an unusually strong interest in the committee's policy area and are predisposed to write legislation favorable to those constituencies.

The committees have a majoritarian aspect as well.[40] Although some committees have a surplus or shortage of legislators from particular kinds of districts or states, most committee members reflect the general ideological profiles of the two parties' congressional contingents. For example, Republicans on individual House committees tend to vote like all other Republicans in the House. Moreover, even if a committee's views are not in line with those of the full membership, it is constrained in the legislation it writes because bills cannot become law unless they are passed by the parent chamber and the other house. Consequently, in formulating legislation, committees anticipate what other representatives and senators will accept. The parties within each chamber also have means of rewarding members who are the most loyal to party priorities. Party committees and the party leadership within each chamber make committee assignments and respond to requests for transfers from less prestigious to more prestigious committees. Those who vote in line with the party get better assignments.[41]

Leaders and Followers in Congress

Above the committee chairs is another layer of authority in the organization of the House and Senate. The Democratic and Republican leaders in each house work to maximize the influence of their own party while trying to keep their chamber functioning smoothly and efficiently. The operation of the two houses is also influenced by the rules and norms that each chamber has developed over the years.

The Leadership Task

Republicans and Democrats elect party leaders in both the House and Senate who are charged with overseeing institutional procedures, managing legislation, fundraising, and communicating with the press. In the House of Representatives, the majority party's leader is the **Speaker of the House**, who, gavel in hand, chairs sessions from the ornate rostrum at the front of the chamber. The Speaker is a constitutional officer, but the Constitution does not list the Speaker's duties. The majority party in the House also has a majority leader, who helps the Speaker guide the party's policy program through the legislative process, and a majority whip, who keeps track of the vote count and rallies support for legislation on the floor. The minority party is led by a minority leader who is assisted by the minority whip. Democrat Nancy Pelosi was minority leader until the 2006 election gave the Democrats a majority; Pelosi then became the first woman Speaker of the House. Both parties have special committees that coordinate fundraising, develop strategy, and help with the logistics of scheduling votes and making committee assignments.

Speaker of the House
The presiding officer of the House of Representatives.

Clyburn Takes the Whip

With the Democratic takeover of the House in 2007, a new set of leaders took over in Congress. James Clyburn, who has represented South Carolina for almost twenty years in Congress, ascended to the role of majority whip. The whip's job is to keep the party united and to "whip" up votes for the party's proposed legislation. With all of the diverse viewpoints encompassed within each party, the whip's job can sometimes be quite a challenge.

(Ron Sachs/Pool/CNP/Corbis)

majority leader
The head of the majority party in the Senate; the second-highest-ranking member of the majority party in the House.

The Constitution makes the vice president of the United States the president of the Senate. But in practice the vice president rarely visits the Senate chamber, unless there is a possibility of a tie vote, in which case he can break the tie. The *president pro tempore* (president "for the time"), elected by the majority party, is supposed to chair the Senate in the vice president's absence, but by custom this constitutional position is entirely honorary. The title is typically assigned to the most senior member of the majority party.

The real power in the Senate resides in the **majority leader**. As in the House, the top position in the opposing party is that of minority leader. Technically, the majority leader does not preside over Senate sessions (members rotate in the president pro tempore's chair), but he or she does schedule legislation, in consultation with the minority leader. More broadly, party leaders play a critical role in getting bills through Congress. The most significant function that leaders play is steering the bargaining and negotiating over the content of legislation. When an issue divides their party, their house, the two houses, or their house and the White House, the leaders must take the initiative to work out a compromise.

Day in and day out, much of what leaders do is meet with other members of their house to try to strike deals that will yield a majority on the floor. It is often a matter of finding out whether one faction is willing to give up a policy preference in exchange for another concession. Beyond trying to engineer trade-offs that will win votes, the party leaders must persuade others (often powerful committee chairs) that theirs is the best deal possible. Former Speaker of the House Dennis Hastert used to say, "They call me the Speaker, but ... they really ought to call me the Listener."[42]

It is often difficult for party leaders to control rank-and-file members because they have independent electoral bases in their districts and states and receive the vast bulk of their campaign funds from nonparty sources. Contemporary party leaders are coalition builders, not autocrats. Yet party leaders can be aggressive about enforcing party discipline. When Congress was crafting health-care reform legislation in 2009, Democratic leaders wanted to include a so-called public option, essentially a government-administered health plan that would compete with private insurers. Yet Senator Max Baucus (D-Mont.), chair of the Finance Committee, was reluctant to include such an option in his committee's version of the reform bill. Senate majority leader Harry Reid insisted that a public option be included in the committee's final bill, which Baucus ultimately decided to support.[43]

Rules of Procedure

The operations of the House and Senate are structured by both formal rules and informal norms of behavior. Rules in each chamber are mostly matters of parliamentary procedure. For example, they govern the scheduling of

The Johnson Treatment

When he was Senate majority leader in the 1950s, Lyndon Johnson was well known for his style of interaction with other members. In this unusual set of photographs, we see him applying the "Johnson treatment" to Senator Theodore Francis Green (D-R.I.). Washington journalists Rowland Evans and Robert Novak offered the following description of the treatment: "Its tone could be supplication, accusation, cajolery, exuberance, scorn, tears, complaint, the hint of threat. It was all of these together. It ran the gamut of human emotions. Its velocity was breathtaking and it was all in one direction. Interjections from the target were rare. Johnson anticipated them before they could be spoken. He moved in close, his face a scant millimeter from his target, his eyes widening and narrowing, his eyebrows rising and falling. From his pockets poured clippings, memos, statistics. Mimicry, humor, and the genius of analogy made The Treatment an almost hypnotic experience and rendered the target stunned and helpless."

(Quote from Rowland Evans and Robert Novak, *Lyndon B. Johnson: The Exercise of Power* [New York: New American Library, 1966], p. 104. *Photos:* George Tames/The New York Times/ Redux Pictures)

legislation, outlining when and how certain types of legislation can be brought to the floor. Rules also govern the introduction of floor amendments. In the House, amendments must be directly germane (relevant) to the bill at hand; in the Senate, except in certain, specified instances, amendments that are not germane to the bill at hand can be proposed.

As noted earlier, an important difference between the two chambers is the House's use of its Rules Committee to govern floor debate. Lacking a similar committee to act as a "traffic cop" for legislation approaching the floor, the Senate relies on unanimous consent agreements to set the starting time and length of debate. If one senator objects to such an agreement, it does not take effect. Senators do not routinely object to unanimous consent agreements, however, because they will need them when bills of their own await scheduling by the leadership. The rules facilitate cooperation among the competing interests and parties in each house so that legislation can be voted on. However, the rules are not neutral: they are a tool of the majority party and help it control the legislative process.[44]

If a senator wants to stop a bill badly enough, she or he may start a **filibuster** and try to talk the bill to death. By historical tradition, the Senate gives its members the right of unlimited debate. During a 1947 debate, Idaho

filibuster
A delaying tactic, used in the Senate, that involves speech-making to prevent action on a piece of legislation.

Democrat Glen Taylor "spoke for $8\frac{1}{2}$ hours on fishing, baptism, Wall Street, and his children." The record for holding the floor belongs to the late Republican senator Strom Thurmond of South Carolina, however, for a twenty-four-hour, eighteen-minute marathon.[45] In the House, no member is allowed to speak for more than an hour without unanimous consent.

After a 1917 filibuster by a small group of senators killed President Wilson's bill to arm merchant ships—a bill favored by a majority of senators—the Senate finally adopted **cloture**, a means of limiting debate. A petition signed by sixteen senators initiates a cloture vote. It now takes the votes of sixty senators to invoke cloture. In today's Congress, the mere threat of a filibuster is extremely common, which means that a bill often needs the support of 60 senators instead of a simple majority in order to pass. This era of the "60-vote Senate" is often criticized for its ability to obstruct the principle of majority rule and to make the legislative process even slower than was intended by Madison and his fellow framers.[46]

Norms of Behavior

Both houses have codes of behavior that help keep them running. These codes are largely unwritten norms, although some have been formally adopted as rules. Members of Congress recognize that they must eliminate (or minimize) personal conflict, lest Congress dissolve into bickering factions unable to work together. One of the most celebrated norms is that members show respect for their colleagues in public deliberations. During floor debate, bitter opponents still refer to one another in such terms as "my good friend, the senior senator from ..." or "my distinguished colleague."

Probably the most important norm of behavior in Congress is that individual members should be willing to bargain with one another. Policymaking is a process of give and take; it demands compromise. Members of Congress are not expected to violate their conscience on policy issues simply to strike a deal. They are expected, however, to listen to what others have to say and to make every effort to reach a reasonable compromise. Obviously, if they all stick rigidly to their own view, they will never agree on anything. Moreover, few policy matters are so clear-cut that compromise destroys one's position.

The Legislative Environment

After legislation emerges from committee, it is scheduled for floor debate. How do legislators make up their minds on how to vote? In this section, we examine the broader legislative environment that affects decision making in Congress. More specifically, we look at the influence on legislators of political parties, the president, constituents, and interest groups. The first two influences, parties and the president, push Congress toward majoritarian democracy. The other two, constituents and interest groups, are pluralist influences on congressional policymaking.

cloture
The mechanism by which a filibuster is cut off in the Senate.

Political Parties

The national political parties might appear to have limited resources at their disposal to influence lawmakers. They do not control the nominations of House and Senate candidates. Candidates receive the bulk of their funds from individual contributors and political action committees, not from the national parties. Nevertheless, the parties are strong forces in the legislative process.[47] The party leaders and various party committees within each house can help or hinder the efforts of rank-and-file legislators to get on the right committees, get their bills and amendments considered, and climb on the leadership ladder themselves. Moreover, as we saw earlier, the Democrats and Republicans on a given committee tend to reflect the views of the entire party membership in the chamber. Thus, party members on a committee tend to act as agents of their party as they search for solutions to policy problems.

The most significant reason that the parties are important in Congress is that Democrats and Republicans have different ideological views.[48] Both parties have diversity, but as Figure 11.5 illustrates, Democrats tend to vote one way and Republicans the other. The primary reason that partisanship has been rising since 1980 is that the parties are becoming more homogeneous (see Chapter 8). The liberal wing of the Republican Party has practically disappeared, and the party is unified around a conservative agenda for America. Likewise, the conservative wing of the Democratic Party has declined. Republicans tend to be dominant in the South; Democrats control more seats in the Northeast and West Coast.

Majoritarianism was largely at work when Congress convened after the 2008 election. Democrats were initially united around many of their priorities, such as ending the war in Iraq, providing health insurance for children from low-income families, combating climate change, and stimulating the economy. Conversely, Republicans have stood fast, opposing the administration's initiatives.

The President

Unlike members of Congress, the president is elected by voters across the entire nation and therefore has a better claim to representing the nation than does any single member of Congress. But it can also be argued that Congress as a whole has a better claim than the president to representing the majority of voters. In fact, when Congress and the president differ, opinion surveys sometimes show that Congress's position on a given bill more closely resembles the majority view; at other times, these surveys show that the president's position accords with the majority. Nevertheless, presidents capitalize on their popular election and usually act as though they are speaking for the majority.

During the twentieth century, the public's expectations of what the president can accomplish in office grew enormously. We now expect the president to be our chief legislator: to introduce legislation on major issues and use his influence to push bills through Congress. This is much different from our early history, when presidents felt constrained by the constitutional

Source: Harold W. Stanley and Richard G. Niemi (eds.), *Vital Statistics on American Politics, 2009–2010* (Washington, D.C.: CQ Press, 2010), p. 204.

FIGURE 11.5   Rising Partisanship

Congress long relied on bipartisanship—the two parties working together—in policymaking. This often meant that the moderates of both parties were central to the development of legislation as they coalesced around the most workable compromise. More recently, behavior has turned more partisan. Increasingly, members of each party vote with each other and against the position of the other party.

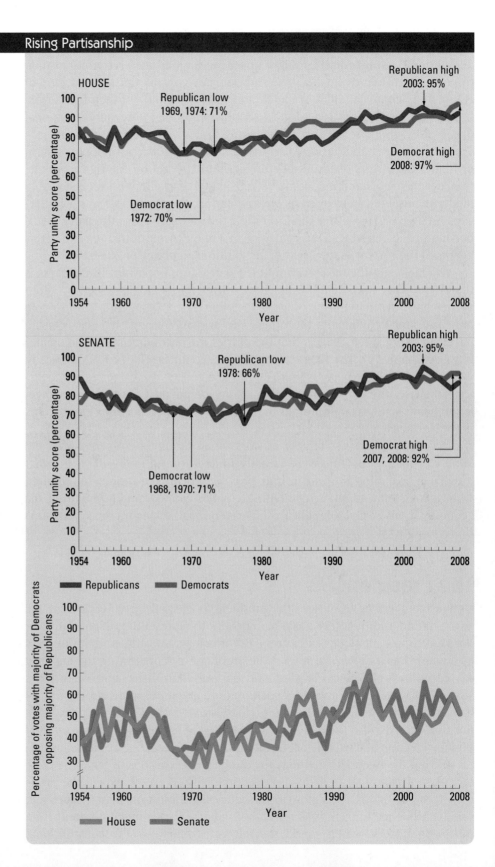

doctrine of separation of powers and had to have members of Congress work confidentially for them during legislative sessions.[49]

Today, the White House is openly involved not only in the writing of bills but also in their development as they wind their way through the legislative process. If the White House does not like a bill, it tries to work out a compromise with key legislators to have the legislation amended. On issues of the greatest importance, the president himself may meet with individual legislators to persuade them to vote a certain way. In January 2009, President Obama went to Capitol Hill to meet with Republicans in the House and the Senate to garner support for his economic stimulus plan.[50] To monitor Congress and lobby for the administration's policies, hundreds of legislative liaison personnel work for the executive branch.

Although members of Congress grant presidents a leadership role in proposing legislation, they jealously guard the power of Congress to debate, shape, and pass or defeat any legislation the president proposes. Congress often clashes sharply with the president when his proposals are seen as ill advised.

Constituents

Constituents are the people who live and vote in a legislator's district or state. Their opinions are a crucial part of the legislative decision-making process. As much as members of Congress want to please their party's leadership or the president by going along with their preferences, they have to think about what the voters back home want. If they displease enough people by the way they vote, they might lose their seat in the next election.

Constituents' influence contributes to pluralism because the diversity of America is mirrored by the geographical basis of representation in the House and Senate. A representative from Los Angeles, for instance, may need to be sensitive to issues of particular concern to constituents whose backgrounds are Korean, Vietnamese, Indian, Hispanic, African American, or Jewish. A representative from Montana will have few such constituents but must pay particular attention to issues involving minerals and mining. A senator from Nebraska will give higher priority to agricultural issues than to urban issues. Conversely, a senator from New York will be sensitive to issues involving the cities. All of these constituencies, enthusiastically represented by legislators who want to do a good job for the people back home, push and pull Congress in many different directions.

At all stages of the legislative process, the interests of the voters are on the minds of members of Congress. As they decide what to spend time on and how to vote, they weigh how different courses of action will affect their constituents' views of them, and the degree to which they feel they should follow constituency preferences.[51]

Interest Groups

As we pointed out in Chapter 10, interest groups are one way constituents influence Congress. Because they represent a vast array of vocational,

constituents
People who live and vote in a government official's district or state.

regional, and ideological groupings within our population, interest groups exemplify pluralist politics. Interest groups press members of Congress to take a particular course of action, believing sincerely that what they prefer is also best for the country. Legislators are attentive to interest groups not because of an abstract commitment to pluralist politics but because these organizations represent citizens, some of whom live back home in their district or state.

Lobbies are an indispensable source of information for members of Congress. They are also increasingly important contributors to and fundraisers for congressional campaigns. Periodic scandals raise concern, however, about potential conflicts of interest and whether legislators do special favors for lobbyists in exchange for campaign contributions or even for personal gain.[52] In one egregious case, House member Randy Cunningham (R-Calif.) resigned his seat in December 2005 and was sentenced to eight years in prison for taking $2.4 million in bribes, including yachts and a Rolls Royce, from defense contractors. Far more subtle are the entirely legal campaign contributions that individual lobbyists and political action committees (PACs) make to legislators. (Recall the discussion in Chapter 10.) Interest groups don't believe that contributions will necessarily get them what they want, but they certainly expect that significant donations will give them greater access to legislators. And access is the first step toward influencing the process.

With all these strong forces pushing and constraining legislators, it's easy to believe that they function solely in response to these external pressures. Legislators, however, bring their own views and own life experiences to Congress. The issues they choose to work on and the way they vote reflect these personal values too.[53] But to the degree that the four external sources of influence on Congress—parties, the president, constituents, and interest groups—do influence legislators, they push them in both majoritarian and pluralist directions. We'll return to the conflict between pluralism and majoritarianism at the end of this chapter.

The Dilemma of Representation

When candidates for the House and Senate campaign for office, they routinely promise to work hard for their district's or state's interests. When they get to Washington, though, they all face a troubling dilemma: what their constituents want may not be what the people across the nation want.

Presidents and Shopping Bags

In doing the research for his book *Home Style,* political scientist Richard Fenno accompanied several representatives as they worked and interacted with constituents in their home district. On one of Fenno's trips, he was in an airport with a congressional aide, waiting for the representative's plane from Washington to land. When the representative arrived, he said, "I spent fifteen minutes on the telephone with the president this afternoon. He had a plaintive tone in his voice and he pleaded with me." His side of the issue had prevailed over the president's, and he was elated by the victory. When the three men reached the aide's car, the representative saw the back seat piled high with campaign paraphernalia: shopping bags printed with his name and picture. "Back to this again," he sighed.[54]

Every member of Congress lives in two worlds: the world of presidents and the world of personalized shopping bags. A typical week in the life of a representative means working in Washington, then boarding a plane and flying back to the home district. There, the representative spends time meeting with individual constituents and talking to civic groups, church gatherings, business associations, labor unions, and others. A survey of House members during a nonelection year showed that each made an average of thirty-five trips back to her or his district, spending an average of 138 days there.[55]

Members of Congress are often criticized for being out of touch with the people they are supposed to represent. This charge does not seem justified. Legislators work extraordinarily hard at keeping in touch with voters, at finding out what is on their constituents' minds. The problem is how to act on that knowledge.

Trustees or Delegates?

Are members of Congress bound to vote the way their constituents want them to vote, even if it means voting against their conscience? Some say no. They argue that legislators must be free to vote in line with what they think is best. This view has long been associated with the eighteenth-century English political philosopher Edmund Burke (1729–1797). Burke, who served in Parliament, told his constituents in Bristol that "you choose a member, indeed; but when you have chosen him, he is not a member of Bristol, but he is a member of *Parliament.*"[56] Burke reasoned that representatives are sent by their constituents to vote as they think best. As **trustees**, representatives are obligated to consider the views of their constituents, but they are not obligated to vote according to those views if they think they are misguided.

Others hold that legislators are duty-bound to represent the majority view of their constituents—that they are **delegates** with instructions from the people at home on how to vote on critical issues. And delegates, unlike trustees, must be prepared to vote against their own policy preferences. During the fight over President Clinton's impeachment, Representative James Rogan of California knew that demographic changes were making his district less hospitable for a Republican like him. He knew that a majority of the voters back home weren't in favor of impeaching and removing Clinton from office. Rogan decided against acting as a delegate and instead voted his conscience to impeach the president. He also became one of the House managers who presented the case to the Senate. In the 2000 election, voters turned him out of office and replaced him with a Democrat.

Although the interests of their districts encourage them to act as delegates, their interpretation of the larger national interest calls on them to be trustees.[57] Given these conflicting role definitions, it is not surprising that Congress is not clearly a body of either delegates or trustees. Research has

trustee
A representative who is obligated to consider the views of constituents but is not obligated to vote according to those views if he or she believes they are misguided.

delegate
A legislator whose primary responsibility is to represent the majority view of his or her constituents, regardless of his or her own view.

Constituents Strike Back

During the summer 2009 recess, members of Congress, including Senator Arlen Specter (D-Penn.), pictured here, traveled to their home districts. Many of them attended town hall meetings where they faced angry constituents who expressed their opposition to health-care reform plans. Even though these angry voters might not be representative of the majority, their intensity proved influential. One senator, Chuck Grassley (R-Iowa) admitted that the town hall meetings convinced him to temper his support for the reforms being developed in Congress. Those who wanted to do nothing were louder than those who wanted reform, he said, adding, "I've got to listen to my people."

Source: Lori Montgomery and Perry Bacon, Jr., "Key Senator Calls for Narrower Health Reform Measure," *Washington Post,* 20 August 2009, http://www.washingtonpost.com/wp-dyn/content/article/2009/08/19/AR2009081904125.html. *Photo:* Newscom.

shown, however, that members of Congress are more likely to take the delegate role on issues that are of great concern to their constituents.[58] But much of the time, what constituents really want is not clear. Many issues are not highly visible back home. Some issues may cut across the constituency, affecting constituents in different ways. Or constituents may only partially understand them. For such issues, no delegate position is obvious.

Pluralism, Majoritarianism, and Democracy

The dilemma that individual members of Congress face in adopting the role of either delegate or trustee has broad implications for the way our country is governed. If legislators tend to act as delegates, congressional policymaking is more pluralistic, and policies reflect the bargaining that goes on among law-makers who speak for different constituencies. If, instead, legislators tend to act as trustees and vote their consciences, policymaking becomes less tied to the narrower interests of districts and states. But even here there is no guarantee that congressional decision making reflects majority interests. True majoritarian legislatures require a paramount role for political parties.

We end this chapter with a short discussion of pluralism versus majoritarianism in Congress. But first, to establish a frame of reference, we need to take a quick look at a more majoritarian type of legislature: the parliament.

Parliamentary Government

In our system of government, the executive and legislative functions are divided between a president and a Congress, each elected separately. Most other democracies—for example, Britain and Japan—have parliamentary governments. In a **parliamentary system**, the chief executive is the legislative leader whose party holds the most seats in the legislature after an election or whose party forms a major part of the ruling coalition. For instance, in Great Britain, voters do not cast a ballot for prime minister. They vote only for their member of Parliament and thus influence the choice of prime minister only indirectly, by voting for the party they favor in the local district election. Parties are unified, and in Parliament, legislators vote for their party's position, giving voters a strong and direct means of influencing public policy. Where there is a multiple party system (as opposed to just two parties), a governing coalition must sometimes be formed out of an alliance of a number of parties. (See "Politics of Global Change: Creating a Legislature.")

In a parliamentary system, government power is highly concentrated in the legislature because the leader of the majority party is also the head of the government. Moreover, parliamentary legislatures are usually composed of only one house or have a second chamber that is much weaker than the other. (In the British Parliament, the House of Commons makes the decisions of government; the other chamber, the House of Lords, is largely an honorary debating club for distinguished members of society.) And parliamentary governments usually do not have a court that can invalidate acts of the parliament. Under such a system, the government is in the hands of the party that controls the parliament. With no separation of government powers, checks on government action are few. Overall, these governments fit the majoritarian model of democracy to a much greater extent than a separation-of-powers system.

Pluralism Versus Majoritarianism in Congress

The U.S. Congress is often criticized for being too pluralist and not majoritarian enough. The federal budget deficit provides a case in point. Americans were deeply concerned about the big deficits that plagued our national budgets in recent years. And both Democrats and Republicans in Congress repeatedly called for reductions in those deficits. But when spending bills came before Congress, legislators' concern turned to what the bills would do for their district or state. Appropriations bills usually include **earmarks**, pork

parliamentary system
A system of government in which the chief executive is the leader whose party holds the most seats in the legislature after an election or whose party forms a major part of the ruling coalition.

earmarks
Federal funds appropriated by Congress for use on local projects.

Politics of Global Change

Creating a Legislature

After the fall of Saddam Hussein in 2003, Iraqis faced a daunting challenge: how to create a democratically elected legislature with free and fair elections that Iraqis see as legitimate. The problem was that this war-torn country still had a significant foreign military presence, was rocked by regular acts of violence, endured unreliable services such as electricity, and consisted of a population marked by deep and enduring divisions over religion, ethnicity, and territory. Along with the Coalition Provisional Authority (the transitional government established by the United States in 2003), Iraqis set about meeting this challenge.

One of the first decisions they needed to make was on the kind of legislature to establish. An American-style Congress with single-member districts elected by plurality rule seemed appealing at first because such a system would likely minimize the chances for extremist parties to gain seats and would produce representatives committed to their local constituency as well as to their party. But advocates for proportional representation (PR), including most of the major political factions in Iraq, prevailed. Under PR, each politically organized group can expect to be represented roughly in proportion to its support in society.

Remarkably, Iraqis held three successful elections in 2005. The first established a transitional Iraqi government, the second was a referendum for the new Iraqi constitution, and the third elected the first representatives to the new permanent government. This new government is federal in nature, with 18 provinces. Its unicameral legislature, the Council of Representatives, now stands at 325 seats. Most of the seats are divided among the provinces, much as delegations to the House of Representatives in the United States are apportioned among the states. But Iraq does not assign representatives to districts within the provinces; each province comprises a multimember district, more akin to the U.S. Senate in which two senators each represent the same territory. The remaining seats are allocated after the election, to help achieve overall proportionality among the competing parties and coalitions. In the 2005 election, voters voted for parties, not individual candidates. The party leadership got to determine which individuals would be seated. Representatives serve for four years. One of their major duties is to elect a presidential council (consisting of a president and two vice presidents), a prime minister, and a cabinet. In the 2005 election, 77 percent of registered voters voted. They gave a near majority to a coalition of Shiite groups, called the United Iraqi Alliance. Kurdish and Sunni coalitions came in second and third, respectively.

Despite the success of the 2005 elections, the Iraqi parliament remains a work in progress. The second national parliamentary election was scheduled to be held in January 2010, but disputes over how to conduct the election delayed voting until March of that year. One major dispute was whether to require that people vote for parties instead of candidates. Many Iraqis, including Shiite religious leader Grand Ayatollah Ali al-Sistani, argued that people should have the power vote for candidates. Party leaders, however, wanted to keep control over who gets seated in parliament. It was eventually decided that voters would get to select candidates directly in 2010.

While some Iraqi leaders were unconcerned about delaying the elections until these disputes were resolved,

barrel projects that benefit specific districts or states and further add to any deficit. Recent earmarks include $325,000 for the Institute for Seafood Studies in Thibodaux, Louisiana, and $1 million for potato research in Idaho, Oregon, and Washington. More expensive earmarks abound too. Representative

American officials wanted the elections to occur quickly; the pace of the withdrawal of U.S. troops will be based largely on whether the country successfully conducts a second round of parliamentary elections. The verdict is still out. The March 2010 elections have been called the most open and democratic in that nation's history, with an estimated turnout of 62 percent. But the day was still met with violence and at least 38 deaths. In addition, no party won an outright majority. The results were subject to an extended and bitter recount. By October 2010—eight months after the election—the leading parties were still unable to form a governing coalition, causing many to worry about how long the Iraqi people will tolerate a stalemate before losing faith in the legitimacy of their new democratic enterprise. *References*: Kenneth Katzman, *Iraq: Elections, Government, and Constitution, CRS Report for Congress*, RS21968; Adeed Dawisha and Larry Diamond, 2006, "Iraq's Year of Living Dangerously," *Journal of Democracy*, v17, n2, pp. 90–103; Gina Chon, "Opposition Grows to Iraqi Election Plan," *Wall Street Journal*, 12 October 2009, p. A8; Anthony Shadid and Nada Bakri, "Election Law Stalls in Iraqi Parliament," *Washington Post*, 20 October 2009, http://www.washingtonpost.com/wp-dyn/content/article/2009/10/19/AR2009101902070_pf.html; Ron Nordland, "Stalemate in Parliament Could Delay Iraqi Elections," *New York Times*, 22 October 2009, http://www.nytimes.com/2009/10/22/world/middleeast/22iraq.html; Ron Nordland, "Veto of Iraq's Election Law Could Force Delay in Vote," *New York Times*, 19 November 2009, http://www.nytimes.com/2009/11/19/world/middleeast/19iraq.html?_r=1&hp; Steven Lee Myers, "Iraqi Politicians Break Bread, But Not the Standoff," *New York Times*, 20 May 2010, http://www.nytimes.com/2010/05/21/world/middleeast/21iraq.html?ref=elections; Marina Ottaway and Danial Kaysi, "The Chess Game Continues," Carnegie Endowment for International Peace, 14 July 2010, http://carnegieendowment.org/publications/index.cfm?fa=view&id=41210; "Iraq Election Turnout 62%, Officials Say," *BBC News*, 9 March 2010, http://news.bbc.co.uk/2/hi/8556065.stm. *Photo*: Wathiq Khuzaie/Getty Images.

Bill Young (R-Fla.) secured over $90 million in earmarks for his district in fiscal year 2010 alone, making him the top earmark recipient that year.[59]

   Projects such as these get into the budget through bargaining among members; as we saw earlier in this chapter, congressional norms encourage it.

Members of Congress try to win projects and programs that will benefit their constituents and thus help them at election time. To win approval of such projects, members must be willing to vote for other legislators' projects in turn. Such a system obviously promotes pluralism (and spending).

When Democrats took control of Congress in 2007, they set about reforming the earmark process to introduce greater transparency. Now legislators need to publicize their earmark requests at least forty-eight hours before their chamber will vote, they must assert that neither they nor their family members will reap financial benefits from the earmark, and they need to identify any lobbyists who were involved in the process. Some argue that these reforms will make members of Congress request even *more* earmarks, since it will now be easier for them to claim credit for bringing resources back to their districts. At the same time, forty-eight lawmakers in the 111th Congress (forty-three of them Republicans) have sworn off earmarks entirely.[60]

It's easy to conclude that the consequence of pluralism in Congress is a lot of unnecessary spending and tax loopholes. Yet many different constituencies are well served by an appropriations process that allows pluralism. The people of each state and district pay taxes to Washington, so shouldn't Washington send some of that money back to them in the form of economic development projects?

Proponents of pluralism also argue that the makeup of Congress generally reflects that of the nation—that different members of Congress represent farm areas, oil and gas areas, low-income inner cities, industrial areas, and so on. They point out that America itself is pluralistic, with a rich diversity of economic, social, religious, and racial groups, and even if one's own representatives and senators don't represent one's particular viewpoint, it's likely that someone in Congress does.

Whatever the shortcomings of pluralism, broad-scale institutional reform aimed at reducing legislators' concern for individual districts and states is difficult. Members of Congress resist any structural changes that might weaken their ability to gain reelection. Certainly, maintaining the prerogatives of the committee system and the dominant influence of committees over legislation and pork barrel spending has proven stubbornly resistant to significant reform.[61] Nevertheless, the growing partisanship in Congress illustrated in Figure 11.5 represents a trend toward greater majoritarianism. As noted earlier, as both parties have become more ideologically homogeneous, there is greater unity around policy preferences. To the degree that voters correctly recognize the differences between the parties and are willing to cast their ballots on that basis, increasing majoritarianism will act as a constraint on pluralism in the Congress. Ironically, once in office legislators can weaken the incentive for their constituents to vote on the basis of ideology. The congressional system is structured to facilitate casework for those voters with a problem and to fund a certain amount of pork barrel spending. Both these characteristics of the modern Congress work to enhance each legislator's reputation in his or her district or state.

In short, the modern Congress is characterized by strong elements of both majoritarianism and pluralism.

Summary

Congress writes the laws of the land and attempts to oversee their implementation. It helps educate us about new issues as they appear on the political agenda. Most important, members of Congress represent us, working to ensure that interests from home and from around the country are heard throughout the policymaking process.

We count on Congress to do so much that criticism about how well it does some things is inevitable. However, certain strengths are clear. The committee system fosters expertise; representatives and senators who know the most about particular issues have the most influence over them. And the structure of our electoral system keeps legislators in close touch with their constituents.

Bargaining and compromise play important roles in the congressional policymaking process. Some find this disquieting. They want less deal making and more adherence to principle. This thinking is in line with the desire for a more majoritarian democracy. Others defend the current system, arguing that the United States is a large, complex nation, and the policies that govern it should be developed through bargaining among various interests.

There is no clear-cut answer to whether a majoritarian or a pluralist legislative system provides better representation for voters. Our system is a mix of pluralism and majoritarianism. It serves minority interests that might otherwise be neglected or even harmed by an unthinking or uncaring majority. At the same time, congressional parties work to represent the broader interests of the American people.

 CourseMate Visit www.cengagebrain.com/shop/ ISBN/0495906182 for flashcards, web quizzes, videos and more!

Lee Craker/DoD/Handout/CNP/Corbis

The not-so-secret secret war in Pakistan is one largely fought by remote control. Pilotless drones fly over the country providing live feeds from their cameras to U.S. military intelligence at bases in other countries. When instructed, the Predator drones also fire guided Hellfire missiles on terrorist targets down below them. Since 2004 the missiles fired from the Predator drones have killed an estimated 500 to 700 people.

Despite the fact that the drones are pilotless, and thus there are no direct casualties for U.S. forces, the Predator war is a dangerous one. The targets on the ground are high-ranking officials in either the Taliban or al Qaeda. Firing missiles on them invites retaliation. U.S. military forces have suffered casualties from roadside bombs and firefights in neighboring Afghanistan. Terrorist bombings are common in Pakistan, where they have killed large numbers of civilians who happened to be in the wrong place at the wrong time.

After he came into office, President Obama decided to increase the Predator strikes. As a result, the number of civilians killed has increased. In the first 13 months since he took office, approximately 100 to 175 civilians have been killed by the missiles launched from the drones.[1]

The goal of the missile firings is not to defeat the Taliban or al Qaeda—that cannot be done through bombing in Pakistan. Rather, it is aimed at disrupting the two forces. The Taliban, which are focused on ousting Western forces in Afghanistan, have used northern Pakistan (the so-called tribal areas) as a safe haven. Until recently the Pakistani government has allowed them to operate freely, as the government has little control over these areas. The Predator war is aimed at killing Taliban leaders, creating instability in their leadership, and possibly activating rivalries among competing factions trying to replace deceased leaders. The same strategy is aimed at al Qaeda, with its larger global vision of *jihad* (holy war) against the Western powers, which are regarded as infidels trying to suppress Islam. Osama bin Laden is believed to be hiding in mountainous northern Pakistan.

Pakistan's fragile government, fearful of the terrorism that plagues the country, has been hesitant to take on al Qaeda and other insurgents in its northern provinces. At the same time, Pakistan desperately needs the U.S. foreign aid it receives. Moreover, as an ostensible ally of the United States, it needs to give some appearance of fighting terrorism.

During the Obama administration, the pressure on Pakistan to do more has mounted. With the surge of U.S. troops committed to Afghanistan, it became intolerable to the U.S. military to have the Taliban ensconced just across the border in Pakistan. At some point Pakistani leaders decided that al Qaeda and its allies inside the country were a growing threat to the government itself. Publicly, the government condemns the increasing Predator missile launchings; privately, it supplies the U.S. military with intelligence about the location of Taliban and al Qaeda leaders. With better intelligence from U.S. sources and from Pakistan, the Predator strikes have become more effective and many leaders have been killed. Recently, when CIA director Leon Panetta was informed that ground intelligence had learned the whereabouts of Baitullah Meshud, he gave the go-ahead to kill him. Meshud was regarded as a major target, as he had been implicated in attacks against Americans across the border in Afghanistan. When a drone's camera spotted him, a missile was fired, killing Meshud and his wife.[2]

Although President Obama is certainly pleased with the increasing effectiveness of the Predator missile firings, questions loom before him. Exactly to what end is this war in Pakistan? Since no one in the military believes that the missile launches will put an end to terrorism,

what other steps need to be taken and can be taken? Predator missile firings kill leaders, but they also inflame the local population when innocent civilians die. Insurgents use this anger to recruit new members. And terrorism has increased inside of Pakistan. Destabilization of the Pakistani government would have serious implications. Pakistan's presumed nuclear arsenal could fall into the hands of al Qaeda. The Predator war is a small war with big question marks.[3]

IN OUR OWN WORDS

Listen to Jeffrey Berry discuss the main points and themes of this chapter.

www.cengagebrain.com/
shop/ISBN/0495906182

Like all presidents, Barack Obama faces a daunting set of challenges. American presidents are expected to offer solutions to national problems, whether waging a war or reviving a failing economy. As the nation's major foreign diplomat and commander in chief of the armed forces, they are held responsible for the security and status of America in the world. Our presidents are the focal point for the nation's hopes and disappointments.

This chapter analyzes presidential leadership, looking at how presidents try to muster majoritarian support for their domestic goals and how they must function today as global leaders. What are the powers of the presidency? How is the president's advisory system organized? What are the ingredients of strong presidential leadership: character, public relations, or a friendly Congress? Finally, what are the particular issues and problems that presidents face in foreign affairs?

The Constitutional Basis of Presidential Power

When the presidency was created, the colonies had just fought a war of independence; their reaction to British domination had focused on the autocratic rule of King George III. Thus, the delegates to the Constitutional Convention were extremely wary of unchecked power and were determined not to create an all-powerful, dictatorial presidency.

The delegates' fear of a powerful presidency was counterbalanced by their desire for strong leadership. The Articles of Confederation, which did not provide for a single head of state, had failed to bind the states together into a unified nation (see Chapter 3). In addition, the governors of the individual states had generally proved to be inadequate leaders because they had few formal powers. The new nation was conspicuously weak; its Congress had no power to compel the states to obey its legislation. The delegates knew they had to create some type of effective executive office. Their task was to provide for national leadership without allowing opportunity for tyranny.

Mourning Ford

Gerald Ford, who served as president between 1974 and 1977, died in December 2006. All living former presidents and first ladies attended a funeral service at the National Cathedral in Washington, D.C. Ford became Richard Nixon's vice president when Spiro Agnew resigned over questions about possible income tax evasion. He then assumed the presidency when Nixon resigned over the Watergate scandal. He was the only president who was never elected vice president or president.

(© Marc Wilson/Getty Images)

Initial Conceptions of the Presidency

Debates about the nature of the office began. Should there be one president or a presidential council or committee? Should the president be chosen by Congress and remain largely subservient to that body? The delegates gave initial approval to a plan that called for a single executive, chosen by Congress for a seven-year term and ineligible for reelection.[4] But some delegates continued to argue for a strong president who would be elected independently of the legislative branch.

The final structure of the presidency reflected the checks-and-balances philosophy that had shaped the entire Constitution. In the minds of the delegates, they had imposed important limits on the presidency through the powers specifically delegated to Congress and the courts. Those counterbalancing powers would act as checks, or controls, on presidents who might try to expand the office beyond its proper bounds.

The Powers of the President

The requirements for the presidency are set forth in Article II of the Constitution: the president must be a U.S.-born citizen, at least thirty-five years old, who has lived in the United States for a minimum of fourteen years. Article II also sets forth the responsibilities of presidents. In view of the importance of the office, the constitutional description of the president's duties is surprisingly brief and vague. This vagueness has led to repeated conflict about the limits of presidential power.

The delegates undoubtedly had many reasons for the lack of precision in Article II. One likely explanation was the difficulty of providing and at the same time limiting presidential power. Furthermore, the framers of the Constitution had no model—no existing presidency—on which to base their description of the office. And, ironically, their description of the presidency might have been more precise if they had had less confidence in George Washington, the obvious choice for the first president. According to one account of the Constitutional Convention, "when Dr. Franklin predicted on June 4 that 'the first man put at the helm will be a good one,' every delegate knew perfectly well who that first good man would be."[5] The delegates had great trust in Washington; they did not fear that he would try to misuse the office.

The major duties and powers that the delegates listed for Washington and his successors can be summarized as follows:

- *Serve as administrative head of the nation.* The Constitution gives little guidance on the president's administrative duties. It states merely that "the executive Power shall be vested in a President of the United States of America" and that "he shall take Care that the Laws be faithfully executed." These imprecise directives have been interpreted to mean that the president is to supervise and offer leadership to various departments, agencies, and programs created by Congress. In practice, a chief executive spends much more time making policy decisions for his cabinet departments and agencies than enforcing existing policies.
- *Act as commander in chief of the military.* In essence, the Constitution names the president as the highest-ranking officer in the armed forces. But it gives Congress the power to declare war. The framers no doubt intended Congress to control the president's military power; nevertheless, presidents have initiated military action without the approval of Congress.
- *Convene Congress.* The president can call Congress into special session on "extraordinary Occasions," although this has rarely been done. He must also periodically inform Congress of "the State of the Union."
- *Veto legislation.* The president can **veto** (disapprove) any bill or resolution enacted by Congress, with the exception of joint resolutions that propose constitutional amendments. Congress can override a presidential veto with a two-thirds vote in each house.
- *Appoint various officials.* The president has the authority to appoint federal court judges, ambassadors, cabinet members, other key policymakers, and many lesser officials. Many appointments are subject to Senate confirmation.
- *Make treaties.* With the "Advice and Consent" of at least two-thirds of those senators voting at the time, the president can make treaties with foreign powers. The president is also to "receive Ambassadors," a phrase that presidents have interpreted to mean the right to recognize other nations formally.
- *Grant pardons.* The president can grant pardons to individuals who have committed "Offenses against the United States, except in Cases of Impeachment."

veto
The president's disapproval of a bill that has been passed by both houses of Congress. Congress can override a veto with a two-thirds vote in each house.

The Expansion of Presidential Power

The framers' limited conception of the president's role has given way to a considerably more powerful interpretation. In this section, we discuss how presidential power has expanded as presidents have exercised their explicit constitutional responsibilities and boldly interpreted the ambiguities of the Constitution. First, we look at the ways in which formal powers, such as veto power, have been increasingly used over time. Second, we turn to claims that presidents make about "inherent" powers implicit in the Constitution. Finally, we discuss congressional grants of power to the executive branch.

Formal Powers

The Constitution clearly involves the president in the policymaking process through his veto power, his ability to report to Congress on the state of the Union, and his role as commander in chief. Over time, presidents have become more aggressive in their use of these formal powers. Vetoes, for instance, have become much more frequent, particularly when presidents face a Congress dominated by the opposing political party. The first sixteen presidents, from Washington to Lincoln, issued a total of 59 vetoes. Dwight Eisenhower issued 181 vetoes over the course of his two terms; Ronald Reagan vetoed legislation 78 times.[6] At least during the first part of his presidency, Barack Obama made little use of the veto as his party controlled both houses of Congress. The ability to veto legislation gives the president power even when he doesn't issue many vetoes. Veto threats shape legislation because members of Congress anticipate vetoes and modify legislation to avoid them. If a president does veto a bill and there is not enough support to override the president's veto, Congress may be forced to rewrite the bill, making concessions to the president's point of view.

Modern presidents have also taken a much more active role in setting the nation's policy agenda. The Constitution states that the president shall give Congress information on the state of the Union "from time to time." For the most part, nineteenth-century presidents sent written messages to Congress and did not publicly campaign for the passage of legislation. Early-twentieth-century presidents like Woodrow Wilson began to deliver State of the Union speeches in person before Congress, personalizing and fighting for their own policy agenda. It is now expected that the president will enter office with clear policy goals and work with his party in Congress to pass legislation.

Most controversial has been the president's use of his power as commander in chief. Several modern presidents have used their power as commander in chief to enter into foreign conflicts without appealing to Congress for a formal declaration of war.[7] The entire Vietnam War was fought without a congressional declaration of war. Complicating this issue is the nature of modern warfare. As described at the outset of this chapter, the

United States is fighting guerilla forces that the nation regards as terrorists. But there is no al Qaeda nation, nor does the Taliban hold formal power anywhere. Which country would we declare war against to try to neutralize these hostile forces?

The Inherent Powers

Several presidents have expanded the power of the office by taking actions that exceeded commonly held notions of the president's proper authority. These men justified what they had done by saying that their actions fell within the **inherent powers** of the presidency. From this broad perspective, presidential power derives not only from those duties clearly outlined in Article II but also from inferences that may be drawn from the Constitution.[8]

When a president claims a power that has not been considered part of the chief executive's authority, he forces Congress and the courts either to acquiesce to his claim or to restrict it. For instance, President Bush unilaterally established military commissions to try alleged enemy combatants captured in Afghanistan and Iraq and held at the U.S. naval base at Guantánamo Bay, Cuba. In 2006, the U.S. Supreme Court ruled that the military commissions were illegal, and the Bush administration was forced to go to Congress for the authorization to establish new commissions with new trial procedures.[9]

When presidents succeed in claiming a new power, they leave to their successors the legacy of a permanent expansion of presidential authority. During the Civil War, for example, Abraham Lincoln instituted a blockade of southern ports, thereby committing acts of war against the Confederacy without the approval of Congress. Lincoln said the urgent nature of the South's challenge to the Union forced him to act without waiting for congressional approval. His rationale was simple: "Was it possible to lose the nation and yet preserve the Constitution?"[10] In other words, Lincoln circumvented the Constitution to save the nation. Subsequently, Congress and the Supreme Court approved Lincoln's actions. That approval gave added legitimacy to the theory of inherent powers, a theory that over time has transformed the presidency.

Today, presidents routinely issue **executive orders**, presidential directives that carry the force of law.[11] The Constitution does not explicitly grant the president the power to issue an executive order. Sometimes presidents use them to see that the laws are "faithfully executed." This was the case when President Dwight Eisenhower ordered the Arkansas National Guard into service in Little Rock, Arkansas, to enforce court orders to desegregate the schools. But many times presidents issue executive orders by arguing that they may take actions in the best interest of the nation so long as the law does not directly prohibit these actions. Executive orders are issued for a wide variety of purposes, from administrative reorganization to civil rights. For instance, Harry Truman issued an executive order to end racial segregation in the armed services. To defuse a controversy over abortion that threatened passage of his health-care plan, President Obama issued an executive

inherent powers
Authority claimed by the president that is not clearly specified in the Constitution. Typically, these powers are inferred from the Constitution.

executive orders
Presidential directives that create or modify laws and public policies, without the direct approval of Congress.

order that declared that existing policies forbidding federal funding of abortions would apply to the new health-care law.

The boundaries of the president's inherent powers have been sharply debated since the September 11, 2001, attacks upon the United States. In response to an ongoing threat of terrorism, President Bush secretly authorized the National Security Agency (NSA) to wiretap telephone calls, without a warrant, between people within the United States and people overseas with suspected links to terrorism.[12] The 1978 Foreign Intelligence Surveillance Act (FISA), however, requires intelligence agencies like the NSA to obtain a warrant from a panel of judges before wiretapping the calls of U.S. citizens. When the wiretapping was revealed, critics accused Bush of putting himself above the law. Bush argued that the Constitution designates the president as the commander in chief of the armed forces; he said he could disregard FISA requirements if they hindered his ability to collect the foreign intelligence necessary to protect the nation from another terrorist attack. Criticism of warrantless wiretapping eventually led Bush to request this power from Congress, and it passed legislation that essentially authorized what the NSA had been doing.[13]

More broadly, President Bush and other members of his administration grounded his claim of expanded powers under the theory of the **unitary executive**. This interpretation of the Constitution says that since the president is given the power to see to it that the laws are "faithfully executed," his prerogatives override any efforts by Congress to give independent decision-making powers to any agency of government.[14] Thus, if the NSA were instructed by Congress to wiretap only when certain criteria were met, the president could override such instructions to the agency. The courts have yet to back such a sweeping interpretation of inherent powers, but this theory remains an ambiguous part of presidential authority.

Congressional Delegation of Power

Presidential power grows when presidents successfully challenge Congress, but in many instances, Congress willingly delegates power to the executive branch. As the American public pressures the national government to solve various problems, Congress, through a process called **delegation of powers**, gives the executive branch more responsibility to administer programs that address those problems. One example of delegation of congressional power occurred in the 1930s, during the Great Depression, when Congress gave Franklin Roosevelt's administration wide latitude to do what it thought was necessary to solve the nation's economic ills.

When Congress concludes that the government needs flexibility in its approach to a problem, the president is often given great freedom in how or when to implement policies. Richard Nixon was given discretionary authority to impose a freeze on wages and prices in an effort to combat escalating inflation. If Congress had been forced to debate the timing of the freeze, merchants and manufacturers would surely have raised their prices in anticipation of the event. Instead, Nixon was able to act suddenly, imposing the

unitary executive
A belief that the president's inherent powers allow him to overrule congressional grants of independent authority to agencies.

delegation of powers
The process by which Congress gives the executive branch the additional authority needed to address new problems.

freeze without warning. (We discuss congressional delegation of authority to the executive branch in more detail in Chapter 13.)

At other times, however, Congress believes that too much power has accumulated in the executive branch, and it enacts legislation to reassert congressional authority. During the 1970s, many representatives and senators agreed that presidents were exercising power that rightfully belonged to the legislative branch, and therefore Congress's role in the American political system was declining. The most notable reaction was the enactment of the War Powers Resolution (1973), which was directed at ending the president's ability to pursue armed conflict without explicit congressional approval (see Chapter 20).

The Executive Branch Establishment

Although we elect a single individual as president, it would be a mistake to ignore the extensive staff and resources of the entire executive branch of government. The president has a White House staff that helps him formulate policy. The vice president is another resource; his duties within the administration vary according to his relationship with the president. The president's cabinet secretaries—the heads of the major departments of the national government—play a number of roles, including the critical function of administering the programs that fall within their jurisdictions. Effective presidents think strategically about how best to use the resources available to them. Each must find ways to organize structures and processes that best suit his management style.[15]

The Executive Office of the President

The president depends heavily on key aides. They advise him on crucial political choices, devise the general strategies the administration will follow in pursuing congressional and public support, and control access to the president to ensure that he has enough time for his most important tasks. Consequently, he needs to trust and respect these top staffers; many in a president's inner circle of assistants are longtime associates. The president's personal staff constitutes the White House Office.

Presidents typically have a chief of staff, who may be a first among equals or, in some administrations, the unquestioned leader of the staff. President Obama's first chief of staff, Rahm Emanuel, earned a reputation for in-your-face aggressiveness. He pushed and prodded and was relentless in trying to gain cooperation from members of Congress and other executive branch officials. His profane manner led one of his two brothers to give him a sign for his White House desk that says, "Undersecretary for Go _____ Yourself."[16] Ultimately, Emanuel was effective, though, because Obama gave him broad authority to act on his behalf. Hamilton Jordan, President Carter's

chief of staff, was at the other end of the spectrum: Carter did not give him the authority to administer the White House with a strong hand and, not surprisingly, Jordan was not terribly effective.

Presidents also have a national security adviser to provide daily briefings on foreign and military affairs and longer-range analyses of issues confronting the administration. Similarly, the president has the Council of Economic Advisers and the National Economic Council to report on the state of the economy and advise the president on the best way to promote economic growth. Senior domestic policy advisers help determine the administration's basic approach to areas such as health, education, and social services.

Below these top aides are the large staffs that serve them and the president. These staffs are organized around certain specialties. Some staff members work on political matters, such as communicating with interest groups, maintaining relations with ethnic and religious minorities, and managing party affairs. One staff deals exclusively with the media, and a legislative liaison staff lobbies the Congress for the administration. The large Office of Management and Budget (OMB) analyzes budget requests, is involved in the policymaking process, and examines agency management practices. This extended White House executive establishment, including the White House Office, is known as the **Executive Office of the President**. The Executive Office employs around seventeen hundred individuals and has an annual budget of $800 million.[17]

No one agrees about a "right way" for a president to organize his White House staff, but scholars have identified three major advisory styles.[18]

Executive Office of the President
The president's executive aides and their staffs; the extended White House executive establishment.

Franklin Roosevelt exemplified the first system: a competitive management style. He organized his staff so that his advisers had overlapping authority and differing points of view. Roosevelt used this system to ensure that he would get the best possible information, hear all sides of an argument, and still be the final decision maker in any dispute. Dwight Eisenhower, a former general, best exemplifies a hierarchical staff model. His staff was arranged with clear lines of authority and a hierarchical structure that mirrored a military command. This places fewer demands on presidential time and energy, since the president does not participate in the details of policy discussion. Bill Clinton had more of a collegial staffing arrangement, a loose staff structure that gave many top staffers direct access to him. Clinton himself was immersed in the details of the policymaking process and brainstormed with his advisers. He was much less likely to delegate authority to others.

Above all, a president must ensure that staff members feel comfortable telling him things he may not want to hear. Telling the president of the United States he is misguided on something is not an easy thing to do. Journalists writing about George W. Bush's White House have painted him as temperamental and sometimes hostile toward aides who brought him bad news.[19] George Stephanopoulos, a close aide to President Clinton, acknowledged frankly in his memoirs that he was too eager to ingratiate himself with Clinton because he saw himself in a competitive position with other staff aides. In retrospect, he realizes that he should have confronted Clinton early in the 1992 campaign about his infidelity. But, says Stephanopoulos, "I needed Clinton to see me as his defender, not his interrogator, which made me, of course, his enabler."[20]

The Vice President

The most important duty of the vice president is to take over the presidency in the event of presidential death, disability, impeachment, or resignation. Traditionally, vice presidents were not used in any important advisory capacity. Before passage of the Twenty-fifth Amendment to the Constitution in 1965, vice presidents who became president due to the death of their predecessor did not even select a new vice president.

Vice presidents have traditionally carried out political chores—campaigning, fundraising, and "stroking" the party faithful. This is often the case because vice-presidential candidates are chosen for reasons that have more to do with the political campaign than with governing the nation. Presidential candidates often choose vice-presidential candidates who appeal to a different geographic region or party coalition. Sometimes they even join forces with a rival from their political primary campaign. New Englander John Kennedy chose Texan Lyndon Johnson. Conservative Ronald Reagan selected George H. W. Bush, his more moderate rival in the Republican primaries. Washington outsider Jimmy Carter chose the experienced Senator Walter Mondale as his vice-presidential running mate.

President Carter broke the usual pattern of relegating the vice president to political chores, relying heavily on Mondale. Carter was wise enough to

(Brendan Smialowski/Getty Images)

Next in Line

According to the Constitution, the vice president serves as president of the Senate, a largely ceremonial role, except for the ability to cast tie-breaking votes. Vice President Joe Biden knows the Senate well, having served as a senator from the state of Delaware for 36 years. In the Senate, Biden served on the Foreign Relations and Judiciary committees and wrote legislation such as the 1994 Violence against Women Act. Biden ran for the Democratic nomination for president twice before he was selected by Barack Obama to be the 2008 vice-presidential nominee.

recognize that Mondale's experience in the Senate could be of great value to him, especially because Carter had never held national office. Al Gore played a significant role in the Clinton administration and was one of the president's most influential advisers. George W. Bush's vice president, Dick Cheney, was even more influential than his predecessors. Cheney was a powerful presence in the development of Bush's foreign policy agenda, championing the war in Iraq. He also believed that the presidency had been weakened over time, and he was a forceful proponent of the unitary executive theory.[21] The incumbent vice president, Joe Biden, is an important adviser within the Obama administration and appears to have a comfortable relationship with the president.

The Cabinet

The president's **cabinet** is composed of the heads of the departments of the executive branch and a small number of other key officials, such as the head of the OMB and the ambassador to the United Nations. The cabinet has expanded greatly since George Washington formed his first cabinet, which contained an attorney general and the secretaries of state, treasury, and war. Clearly, the growth of the cabinet to fifteen departments reflects an increase in government responsibility and intervention in areas such as energy, housing, and, most recently, homeland security.

cabinet
A group of presidential advisers; the heads of the executive departments and other key officials.

In theory, the members of the cabinet constitute an advisory body that meets with the president to debate major policy decisions. In practice, however, cabinet meetings have been described as "vapid non-events in which there has been a deliberate non-exchange of information as part of a process of mutual nonconsultation."[22] Why is this so? First, the cabinet has become rather large. Counting department heads, other officials of cabinet rank, and presidential aides, it is a body of at least twenty people—a size that many presidents find unwieldy for the give-and-take of political decision making. Second, most cabinet members have limited areas of expertise and cannot contribute much to deliberations in policy areas they know little about. The secretary of defense, for example, would probably be a poor choice to help decide important issues of agricultural policy. Third, the president often chooses cabinet members because of their reputations or to give his cabinet some racial, ethnic, geographic, gender, or religious balance, not because they are personally close to the president or easy for him to work with.

Finally, modern presidents do not rely on the cabinet to make policy because they have such large White House staffs, which offer most of the advisory support they need. And in contrast to cabinet secretaries, who may be pulled in different directions by the wishes of the president and those of their clientele groups, staffers in the White House Office are likely to see themselves as being responsible to the president alone. Despite periodic calls for the cabinet to be a collective decision-making body, cabinet meetings seem doomed to be little more than academic exercises. In practice, presidents prefer the flexibility of ad hoc groups, specialized White House staffs, and the advisers and cabinet secretaries with whom they feel most comfortable.

More broadly, presidents use their personal staff and the large Executive Office of the President to centralize control over the entire executive branch. The vast size of the executive branch and the number and complexity of decisions that must be made each day pose a challenge for the White House. Each president must be careful to appoint people to top administration positions who are not merely competent but also passionate about the president's goals and skillful enough to lead others in the executive branch to fight for the president's program instead of their own agendas.[23] Ronald Reagan was especially good at communicating to his top appointees clear ideological principles that they were to follow in shaping administration policy. To fulfill more of their political goals and policy preferences, modern presidents have given their various staffs more responsibility for overseeing decision making throughout the executive branch.

Presidential Leadership

A president's influence comes not only from his assigned responsibilities but also from his political skills and from how effectively he uses the resources of his office. His leadership is a function of his own character and skill, as well as the political environment in which he finds himself. Does he work with a congressional majority that favors his policy agenda? Are his goals in

TABLE 12.1	Presidential Greatness

This table provides two "top twelve" lists of American presidents. The first ranking comes from a 2007 Gallup Poll that asked ordinary Americans to name whom they regard as the greatest U.S. president. The second ranking comes from a survey of historians and observers of the presidency, who rated presidents according to their abilities, such as public persuasion, crisis leadership, economic management, moral authority, and relations with Congress. Although the rank order is different, nine presidents appear on both lists. Ordinary Americans are more likely to name recent presidents—Carter, Clinton, and George W. Bush—with whom they have had direct experience.

Gallup Poll Ratings		Historians' Ratings	
Rank	*President*	*Rank*	*President*
1	Abraham Lincoln	1	Abraham Lincoln
2	Ronald Reagan	2	Franklin Roosevelt
3	John F. Kennedy	3	George Washington
4	Bill Clinton	4	Theodore Roosevelt
5	Franklin Roosevelt	5	Harry Truman
6	George Washington	6	Woodrow Wilson
7	Harry Truman	7	Thomas Jefferson
8	George W. Bush	8	John F. Kennedy
9	Theodore Roosevelt	9	Dwight Eisenhower
10	Dwight Eisenhower	10	Lyndon Johnson
11	Thomas Jefferson	11	Ronald Reagan
12	Jimmy Carter	12	James K. Polk

Sources: The historians' ranking is reported by the C-SPAN Survey of Presidential Leadership 2000, http://www.americanpresidents.org/survey/historians/overall.asp. Copyright 2000 C-SPAN. Gallup Poll results are reported by Lydia Saad, "Lincoln Resumes Position as Americans' Top-Rated President," 19 February 2007, http://www.gallup.com.

line with public opinion? Does he have the interpersonal skills and strength of character to be an effective leader?

Table 12.1 provides two rankings of U.S. presidents. One is based on a Gallup Poll of ordinary Americans; the other is based on a C-SPAN survey of fifty-eight prominent historians and professional observers of the presidency. In this section, we look at the factors that affect presidential performance—both those that reside in the person of the individual president and those that are features of the political context that he inherits. Why do some presidents rank higher than others?

Presidential Character

How does the public assess which presidential candidate has the best judgment and whether a candidate's character is suitable to the office? Americans must make a broad evaluation of the candidates' personalities and leadership styles. Although it's difficult to judge, character matters. One of

Lyndon Johnson's biographers argues that Johnson had trouble extricating the United States from Vietnam because of insecurities about his masculinity. Johnson wanted to make sure he "was not forced to see himself as a coward, running away from Vietnam."[24] It's hard to know for sure whether this psychological interpretation is valid. Clearer, surely, is the tie between President Nixon's character and Watergate. Nixon had such an exaggerated fear of what his "enemies" might try to do to him that he created a climate in the White House that nurtured the Watergate break-in and subsequent cover-up.

Presidential character was at the forefront of national politics when it was revealed that President Clinton engaged in a sexual relationship with Monica Lewinsky, a White House intern half his age. Many argued that presidential authority is irreparably damaged when the president is perceived as personally untrustworthy or immoral. Yet despite the disgust and anger that Clinton's actions provoked, most Americans remained unconvinced that his behavior constituted an impeachable offense. The buoyant economy and the public's general satisfaction with Clinton's leadership strongly influenced the country's views on the matter. A majority of the House of Representatives voted to impeach him, on the grounds that he had committed perjury when testifying before a federal grand jury and that he had obstructed justice by concealing evidence and encouraging others to lie about his relationship with Lewinsky. But the Senate did not have the two-thirds majority necessary to convict Clinton, so he remained in office.

The Odd Couple

Former presidents Bill Clinton and George W. Bush don't see eye-to-eye on much but they put differences aside when President Obama asked them to go to Haiti after the devastating earthquake in January 2010. Officially they were there to assess the damage to the country, but a more urgent purpose for the two presidents' visit was to encourage private donations to help Haiti rebuild.

(AP Photo/Jorge Saenz)

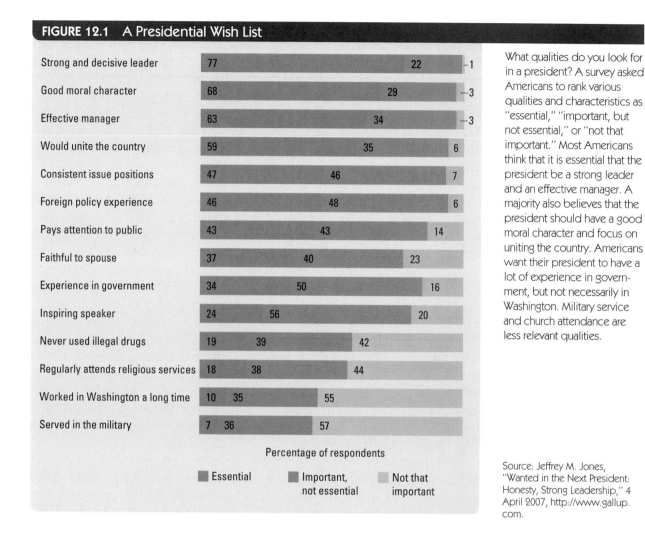

FIGURE 12.1 A Presidential Wish List

Quality	Essential	Important, not essential	Not that important
Strong and decisive leader	77	22	–1
Good moral character	68	29	–3
Effective manager	63	34	–3
Would unite the country	59	35	6
Consistent issue positions	47	46	7
Foreign policy experience	46	48	6
Pays attention to public	43	43	14
Faithful to spouse	37	40	23
Experience in government	34	50	16
Inspiring speaker	24	56	20
Never used illegal drugs	19	39	42
Regularly attends religious services	18	38	44
Worked in Washington a long time	10	35	55
Served in the military	7	36	57

Percentage of respondents

What qualities do you look for in a president? A survey asked Americans to rank various qualities and characteristics as "essential," "important, but not essential," or "not that important." Most Americans think that it is essential that the president be a strong leader and an effective manager. A majority also believes that the president should have a good moral character and focus on uniting the country. Americans want their president to have a lot of experience in government, but not necessarily in Washington. Military service and church attendance are less relevant qualities.

Source: Jeffrey M. Jones, "Wanted in the Next President: Honesty, Strong Leadership," 4 April 2007, http://www.gallup.com.

Scholars have identified personality traits such as strong self-esteem and emotional intelligence that are best suited to leadership positions like the American presidency.[25] In the media age, it often proves difficult to evaluate a candidate's personality when everyone tries to present himself or herself in a positive light. Even so, voters repeatedly claim that they care about traits such as leadership, integrity, and competence when casting their ballots (see Figure 12.1).[26]

The President's Power to Persuade

In addition to desirable character traits, individual presidents must have the interpersonal and practical political skills to get things done. A classic analysis of the use of presidential resources is offered by Richard Neustadt in his book *Presidential Power.* Neustadt develops a model of how presidents gain, lose, or maintain their influence. His initial premise is simple enough: "Presidential power is the power to persuade."[27] Presidents, for all their resources—a skilled staff, extensive media coverage of presidential actions, the great respect the country holds for the office—must depend on others' cooperation to get things done. Harry Truman echoed Neustadt's premise when he said, "I sit here all day trying to persuade people to do the things they ought to have sense enough to do without my persuading them.... That's all the powers of the President amount to."[28]

Ability in bargaining, dealing with adversaries, and choosing priorities, according to Neustadt, separates above-average presidents from mediocre ones. A president must make wise choices about which policies to push and which to put aside until he can find more support. President Nixon described such decisions as a lot like poker. "I knew when to get out of a pot," said Nixon. "I didn't stick around when I didn't have the cards."[29] The president must decide when to accept compromise and when to stand on principle. He must know when to go public and when to work behind the scenes.

A president's political skills can be important in affecting outcomes in Congress. The president must choose his battles carefully and then try to use the force of his personality and the prestige of his office to forge an agreement among differing factions. When President Lyndon Johnson needed House Appropriations chair George Mahon (D-Tex.) to support him on an issue, he called Mahon on the phone and emphasized the value of Mahon's having a good long-term relationship with him. Speaking slowly to let every point sink in, Johnson told Mahon, "I know one thing ... I know I'm right on this.... I know I mean more to you, ... and Lubbock [Texas], ... and your district, ... and your State,—and your grandchildren, than Charlie Halleck [the Republican House leader] does."[30]

Neustadt stresses that a president's influence is related to his professional reputation and prestige. When a president pushes hard for a bill that Congress eventually defeats or weakens, the president's reputation is hurt. The public perceives him as ineffective or as showing poor judgment, and Congress becomes even less likely to cooperate with him in the future. The first President Bush believed he could get very little out of the Democratic-controlled Congress that he served alongside. His agenda was not ambitious, and his lack of accomplishments on the domestic side certainly worked against him when he ran (unsuccessfully) for reelection in 1992.

The President and the Public

Neustadt's analysis suggests that a popular president is more persuasive than an unpopular one. A popular president has more power to persuade because he can use his public support as a resource in the bargaining process. Members of Congress who know that the president is highly popular back home have more incentive to cooperate with the administration. If the president and his aides know that a member of Congress does not want to be seen as hostile to the president, they can apply more leverage to achieve a favorable compromise in a legislative struggle.

A familiar aspect of the modern presidency is the effort presidents devote to mobilizing public support for their programs. A president uses televised addresses (and the media coverage surrounding them), remarks to reporters, and public appearances to speak directly to the American people and convince them of the wisdom of his policies. Scholars have coined the phrase "going public" to describe situations where the president "forces compliance from fellow Washingtonians by going over their heads to appeal to their constituents."[31] Rather than bargain exclusively with a small number of party and committee leaders in Congress, the president rallies broad coalitions of support as though undertaking a political campaign.

Since public opinion is a resource for modern presidents, they pay close attention to their standing in the polls. Presidents closely monitor their approval ratings or "popularity," which is a report card on how well they are performing their duties. Presidential popularity is typically at its highest during a president's first year in office. This "honeymoon period" affords the president a particularly good opportunity to use public support to get some of his programs through Congress.

Barack Obama entered office with very high approval ratings and great expectations. His most important domestic initiative, health-care reform, was not put front and center after his inauguration as he had first to address the dire straits of the nation's banking system and the deepening recession. Even though the Troubled Asset Relief Program (TARP), which built on a larger Bush program, succeeded in stabilizing the faltering banking system, it was unpopular. Many saw it as a taxpayer "bailout" of banks that deserved to go out of business because of their role in the subprime mortgage collapse that contributed so strongly to the recession. At this point Obama's popularity began to decline from its lofty perch when he took office.

Throughout the spring, summer, and fall, Obama tried to rally public opinion around his health proposal. At its core, its goal was to ensure that all Americans had health insurance. In raw terms that meant extending health insurance to 30 million Americans who could not afford it. To pay for this expansion of health care, the Obama plan also included regulatory measures designed to reduce health-care costs and placed a tax on the wealthy (top 5 percent of earners). Not only was the plan expansive and expensive, but also its complexity left it subject to easy distortion by its opponents. Despite Obama's energetic campaigning for the legislation, its support among the American people dropped steadily, and entering 2010, a majority of the public opposed the plan.

Still committed to health reform because of his staunch belief that all Americans should have access to health care, Obama pushed on in spite of the lack of support. With substantial majorities in Congress, the legislation was passed roughly a year after Obama began pushing for it. At the time the bill became law Obama's popularity had dropped very low, with roughly as many Americans saying they approved of the president's job performance as saying they disapproved (see Figure 12.2).[32] Unemployment and the continuing recession were more responsible for the president's decline in popularity than his health-care plan, but it contributed too.

The health-care case hardly seems like a ringing endorsement of the idea that presidents can move public opinion to pressure Congress to pass their

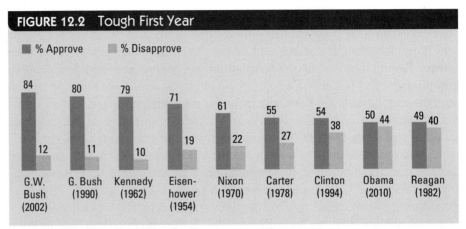

FIGURE 12.2 Tough First Year

■ % Approve   ■ % Disapprove

	G.W. Bush (2002)	G. Bush (1990)	Kennedy (1962)	Eisenhower (1954)	Nixon (1970)	Carter (1978)	Clinton (1994)	Obama (2010)	Reagan (1982)
% Approve	84	80	79	71	61	55	54	50	49
% Disapprove	12	11	10	19	22	27	38	44	40

The terrible recession and the controversy over his plan to expand health-care coverage to the uninsured drove down Barack Obama's approval ratings. At the end of his first year his rating was the second lowest among modern presidents. Yet Obama can take heart from this comparison. Bill Clinton and Ronald Reagan recovered from their low ratings to win easy reelection. In contrast George H. W. Bush, who had the second-highest rating, was defeated for reelection. George W. Bush, who had the highest end-of-first-year rating, did win reelection, albeit in a close race.

Source: Lydia Saad, "Obama Starts 2010 with 50% Approval," Gallup Poll, 6 January 2010, available at Gallup.com.

agendas. As political scientist George Edwards concludes, "Presidents cannot reshape the contours of the political landscape to pave the way for change."[33] Still, Obama's leadership did play a role in persuading members of his own party in Congress to vote for the plan in the face of public opposition.[34]

Presidents' obsessive concern with public opinion can be defended as a means of furthering majoritarian democracy: the president tries to gauge what the people want so that he can offer policies that reflect popular preferences. As discussed in Chapter 2, responsiveness to the public's views is a bedrock principle of democracy, and presidents should respond to public opinion as well as try to lead it. Some believe that presidents are too concerned about their popularity and are unwilling to champion unpopular causes or take principled stands that may affect their poll ratings. Yet research shows that presidents don't always follow public opinion and, rather, push many proposals and policies that reflect their own priorities rather than the public's.[35] Commenting on the presidential polls that first became widely used during his term, Harry Truman said, "I wonder how far Moses would have gone if he'd taken a poll in Egypt?"[36]

The Political Context

What the health-care case demonstrates is that presidents have the potential to influence public support and congressional action, but it is highly contextual. That is, a lot of different variables determine what, if any, influence a president might have in a particular situation. Political scientists try to find explanations that are simple and straightforward, but this part of the political process frustrates such analysis.

One thing we learn from this case is that the strategy of leading by courting public opinion has considerable risks. It is not easy to move public opinion, and presidents who plan to use it as leverage in dealing with Congress are left highly vulnerable if public support for their position does not materialize. We also learn that all issues are not created equal. The public cared far more about the state of the economy than it did about Obama's health-care plan. A president's popularity can also be affected by external events, such as some international calamity.

Some presidents have the benefit of working on legislation while their own political party has a majority in both chambers of Congress. Others are fortunate to serve when the economy is good. Still others have large election victories that facilitate greater policy achievements.

Partisans in Congress. Presidents vary considerably in their ability to convince Congress to enact the legislation they send to Capitol Hill. Generally, presidents have their greatest success in Congress during the period immediately following their inauguration, which is also the peak of their popularity. One of the best predictors of presidential success in Congress is the number of fellow partisans in Congress, particularly whether the president's party has a majority in each chamber. Presidential success in Congress is measured by how often the president wins his way on congressional roll call votes on which he takes a clear position. George W. Bush's success rate hovered around 75 percent during his first six years in office with a Republican Congress. After the Democrats won control of Congress in 2006, his success rate fell to 38 percent.[37] With large majorities in both the House and the Senate during his first two years in office, Barack Obama did very well with the Congress and got major pieces of legislation such as the economic stimulus package and the health-care plan enacted. (See Figure 12.3.)

The American political system poses a challenge for presidents and their policy agendas because the president is elected independently of Congress. Often this leads to **divided government**, with one party controlling the White House and the other party controlling at least one house of Congress. This may seem politically schizophrenic, with the electorate saying one thing by electing a president from one party and another by its vote for legislators of the other party. This does not appear to bother the American people, however, as divided government is fairly common.

Scholars are divided about the impact of divided government. Despite the differences in the scholarly literature, however, political scientists generally don't believe that divided government produces **gridlock**, a situation in which government is incapable of acting on important policy issues.[38] In recent years, however, there has been a pattern of increasingly partisan voting in Congress: Republicans voting in a relatively unified pattern while Democrats also vote in an increasingly unified manner.[39]

divided government
The situation in which one party controls the White House and the other controls at least one house of Congress.

gridlock
A situation in which government is incapable of acting on important issues.

Elections. In his farewell address to the nation, Jimmy Carter lashed out at the interest groups that had plagued his presidency. Interest groups, he said, "distort our purposes because the national interest is not always the sum of

Compared with What?

Hatoyama Goes Down

Barack Obama can certainly sympathize. Like Obama, Japan's new prime minister, Yukio Hatoyama, saw his popularity drop considerably after taking office. Hatoyama's descent, however, was quicker and more destructive. Starting with approval ratings of over 70 percent, he dropped 30 points in just four months. Six months into office he had the approval of only about a third of the electorate. Not much of a honeymoon.

Hatoyama came into office in a blaze of glory. After more than a half century of rule by the Liberal Democratic Party (LDP), Hatoyama's Democratic Party of Japan (DPJ) crushed the LDP in the August 2009 parliamentary elections. The DPJ won more than 60 percent of the seats in the lower house of the parliament, the Diet. The country had grown weary of the Liberal Democrats, who had ruled uninterrupted for more than a half century. The LDP's troubles led to instability, and after three LDP prime ministers in just three years, the country finally broke with the LDP and voted for the DPJ. The real source of dissatisfaction was the Japanese economy, which has slumped badly. The DPJ seemed to offer a fresh approach.

Unfortunately, Hatoyama stumbled right out of the gate, becoming embroiled in an embarrassing campaign finance scandal. For some time his mother, a wealthy heiress, had been sending 15 million yen ($167,000) a month to the DPJ. But a high-ranking Hatoyama aide had recorded these donations as coming from many different contributors, making the party look more popular and keeping Hatoyama from looking as though his success was due to an allowance from his mother. Hatoyama said he had no knowledge of the contributions and was not indicted. Still, the episode was damaging. His popularity sagged again when he went back on his campaign promise to cut taxes as the country's budget pressures made it impossible to give up revenue.

A squabble with the United States did not help. The issue involved a possible relocation of an air base on the island of Okinawa, close to the main Japanese islands. Okinawa was the last island where the Americans fought ground battles with Japanese troops in World War II before the United States dropped the atomic bombs on Hiroshima and Nagasaki. Even though the United States and Japan are now close allies, the presence of U.S. forces on Okinawa remains a touchy subject.

The economy was Hatoyama's biggest problem. Japanese unemployment has risen along with the national deficit. The growing debt has led to serious discussion of raising the nation's sales tax, hardly a step someone who campaigned on cutting taxes would have been interested in taking. Japan, of course, is caught in the same worldwide economic slowdown that plagues the United States, Europe, and other nations of the world.

Still Hatoyama had a few successes. Traditionally, the Japanese bureaucracy has been more powerful and more independent than bureaucracies in most other democracies. At the same time these bureaucratic fiefdoms were dominated by LDP sympathizers. Hatoyama forced some key resignations and instituted changes designed to make the bureaucracy more responsive to both the legislature and the public.

It was Okinawa that proved to be the final straw. In May 2010 Hatoyama came to an agreement with President Obama to extend U.S. rights to the air base. His decision sparked a firestorm of criticism. Seen as weak and irreparably damaged, members of his own party began to ask for Hatoyama's resignation. In protest a partner in the parliament, the Social Democratic Party, withdrew from the ruling coalition. Within a few days a tearful Hatoyama addressed the nation to announce that he was resigning. LDP legislators quickly elected veteran politician Naoto Kan as the new prime minister. He has his work cut out for himself.

Source: Martin Fackler, "Doubts Grow in Japan about Premier Amid Money Scandal," *New York Times,* 19 December 2009; Takashi Nakamichi, Alison Tudor, and Takashi Mochizuki, "Funding Scandal, Economy Weigh Down Hatoyama," *Wall Street Journal,* 26–27 December 2009; "Nagasaki Fallout," *The Economist,* 25 February 2010; Martin Fackler, "Rooting Out Career Bureaucrats to Plant a New Economic Formula," *New York Times,* 25 March 2010; Blaine Harden, "Japanese Prime Minister Yukio Hatoyama Resigns," *Washington Post,* 2 June 2010; and various polls from Angus Reid Global Monitor. *Photo:* AP Photo/Itsuo Inouye.

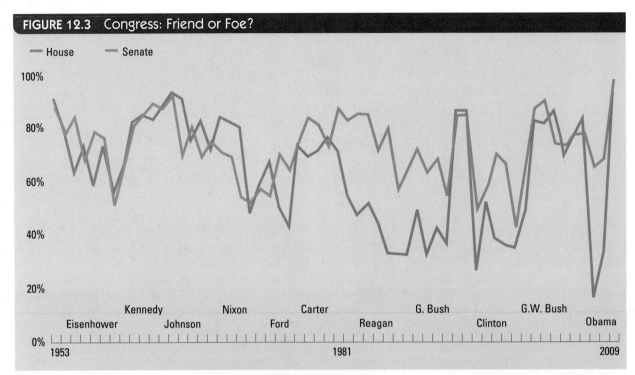

FIGURE 12.3   Congress: Friend or Foe?

— House   — Senate

The scales here measure the success rate of presidents in Congress when they had a clearly stated preference on a bill. As is evident, the success rate varies considerably over time. This reflects each president's skill to be sure, but the partisan makeup of the Congress is critical. Obama's exceptional success during his first year was built on large Democratic majorities in the House and Senate. Conversely, George W. Bush's success dropped precipitously after Republicans lost majorities in both houses in the 2006 elections.

Source: The data is from CQ and the graphic representation from Don Gonyea, "CQ: Obama's Winning Streak on Hill Unprecedented," NPR.org, January 11, 2010.

all our single or special interests." Carter noted the president's singular responsibility: "The president is the only elected official charged with representing all the people."[40] Like all other presidents, Carter quickly recognized the dilemma of majoritarianism versus pluralism after he took office. The president must try to please countless separate constituencies while trying to do what is best for the whole country.

It is easy to stand on the sidelines and say that presidents should always try to follow a majoritarian path, pursuing policies that reflect the preferences of most citizens. However, simply by running for office, candidates align themselves with particular segments of the population. As a result of their electoral strategy, their identification with activists in their party, and their own political views, candidates come into office with an interest in pleasing some constituencies more than others.

As the election campaign proceeds, each candidate tries to win votes from different groups of voters through his stand on various issues. Because issue stances can cut both ways—attracting some voters but driving others away—candidates may try to finesse an issue by being deliberately vague. Candidates sometimes hope that voters will put their own interpretations on ambiguous stances. If the tactic works, the candidate will attract some voters without offending others.

But candidates cannot be deliberately vague about all issues. A candidate who is noncommittal on too many issues appears wishy-washy. And future presidents do not build their political careers without working strongly for and becoming associated with important issues and constituencies. More-over, after the election is over, the winning candidate wants to claim that he has been given an **electoral mandate**, or endorsement, by the voters to carry out the policy platform on which he campaigned. Newly chosen presidents make a majoritarian interpretation of the electoral process, claiming that their electoral victory is an expression of the direct will of the people. For such a claim to be credible, the candidate must have emphasized some specific issues during the campaign and offered some distinctive solutions. As the franchise was extended to more ordinary citizens in the early nineteenth century, it became more credible for presidents to claim that their actions reflected a mandate of some sort. One of Andrew Jackson's biographers notes that in his first year in office Jackson claimed a mandate from voters to kill the government's national bank, and this link between votes and public policy marked "a turning point in the making of the modern presidency."[41]

Candidates who win by large margins are more likely to claim mandates and ask for major policy changes.[42] Although many presidents claim that the votes they receive at the polls are expressions of support for their policy proposals, it is often difficult to document concrete evidence of broad public support for the range of specific policies a winning candidate wants to pursue.

Political Party Systems. An individual president's election is just one in a series of contests between the major political parties in the United States. As noted in Chapter 8, American political history is marked by eras in which one of the major political parties tends to dominate national-level politics, consistently capturing the presidency and majorities in the Senate and House of Representatives. Scholars of the American presidency have noted that presidential leadership is shaped by the president's relationship to the dominant political party and its policy agenda.[43]

Presidential leadership is determined in part by whether the president is a member of the dominant political party and whether the public policies and political philosophy associated with his party have widespread support. A president will have a greater opportunity to change public policy when he is in the majority and the opposing political party is perceived to be unable to solve major national problems. Presidents who are affiliated with the dominant political party have larger majorities in Congress and more public support for their party's policy agenda.

Presidents who come to power right after critical elections have the most favorable environment for exerting strong presidential leadership. Franklin Roosevelt, for instance, came to office when the Republican Party was unable to offer solutions to the economic crisis of the Great Depression. He enjoyed a landslide victory and large Democratic majorities in Congress, and he proposed fundamental changes in government and public policy. The

electoral mandate
An endorsement by voters. Presidents sometimes argue they have been given a mandate to carry out policy proposals.

weakest presidents are those, like Herbert Hoover, who are constrained by their affiliation with a political party that is perceived to stand for worn-out ideas. Democratic presidents like Truman and Johnson, who followed FDR, were also well positioned to achieve policy success and further their party program since they were affiliated with the dominant New Deal coalition. Republicans Eisenhower and Nixon faced different leadership challenges: they needed to cultivate the support of voters and legislators in both parties in order to achieve a successful legislative program.

George W. Bush envisioned an evolution of party fortunes in which his party would become newly dominant. In the half-century since 1950 neither party had dominated the presidency, but after the terrorist attacks on the United States in September 2001 Bush saw an opportunity for the Republicans on security issues. Deciding to invade Iraq, he believed an aggressive U.S. military posture would make the Republican Party appear to be the one that would best protect the nation. Conversely, he believed the Democratic Party would be seen as weaker since it was divided over the decision to invade Iraq. But the increasingly unpopular Iraq War and the faltering economy devastated Republican fortunes in the 2006 and 2008 elections.[44]

Barack Obama envisioned a changing party landscape when he took office, and he believes that the Democrats have an opportunity to emerge as the dominant party. Democrats see demographic change helping them, as the growing proportion of minorities in the country strongly prefer the Democrats. Young voters have strongly moved toward the Democrats, there is continuing strength among urban dwellers, and the party is faring better in the suburbs than in the past. But this optimism may be premature, as the Democrats have been hurt by the faltering economy. The recession may have begun under George W. Bush, but in the reality of the political world, Obama became responsible for the economy.

The President as National Leader

With an election behind him and the resources of his office at hand, a president is ready to lead the nation. Although not every president's leadership is acclaimed, each president enters office with a general vision of how government should approach policy issues. During his term, a president spends much of his time trying to get Congress to enact legislation that reflects his general philosophy and specific policy preferences.

From Political Values ...

Presidents differ greatly in their views of the role of government. Lyndon Johnson had a strong liberal ideology concerning domestic affairs. He believed that government has a responsibility to help disadvantaged Americans. Johnson described his vision of justice in his inaugural address:

> Justice was the promise that all who made the journey would share in the fruits of the land.

In a land of wealth, families must not live in hopeless poverty. In a land rich in harvest, children just must not go hungry. In a land of healing miracles, neighbors must not suffer and die untended. In a great land of learning and scholars, young people must be taught to read and write.

For [the] more than thirty years that I have served this nation, I have believed that this injustice to our people, this waste of our resources, was our real enemy. For thirty years or more, with the resources I have had, I have vigilantly fought against it.[45]

Johnson used *justice* and *injustice* as code for *equality* and *inequality.* He used those words six times in his speech; he used *freedom* only twice. Johnson used his popularity, his skills, and the resources of his office to press for a "just" America—a "Great Society."

To achieve his Great Society, Johnson sent Congress an unprecedented package of liberal legislation. He launched projects such as the Job Corps (which created centers and camps offering vocational training and work experience to youths aged sixteen to twenty-one), Medicare (which provided medical care for the elderly), and the National Teacher Corps (which paid teachers to work in impoverished neighborhoods). Supported by huge Democratic majorities in Congress during 1965 and 1966, he had tremendous success getting his proposals through. Liberalism was in full swing.

In 1985, exactly twenty years after Johnson's inaugural speech, Ronald Reagan took his oath of office for the second time. Addressing the nation, Reagan reasserted his conservative philosophy. He emphasized freedom, using the term fourteen times, and failed to mention justice or equality once. In the following excerpt, we have italicized the term *freedom* for easy reference:

By 1980, we knew it was time to renew our faith, to strive with all our strength toward the ultimate in individual *freedom* consistent with an orderly society.... We will not rest until every American enjoys the fullness of *freedom,* dignity, and opportunity as our birthright.... Americans ... turned the tide of history away from totalitarian darkness and into the warm sunlight of human *freedom*....

Let history say of us, these were golden years—when the American Revolution was reborn, when *freedom* gained new life, when America reached for her best.... *Freedom* and incentives unleash the drive and entrepreneurial genius that are at the core of human progress.... From new *freedom* will spring new opportunities for growth.... Yet history has shown that peace does not come, nor will our *freedom* be preserved by goodwill alone. There are those in the world who scorn our vision of human dignity and *freedom*.... Human *freedom* is on the march, and nowhere more so than in our own hemisphere. *Freedom* is one of the deepest and noblest aspirations of the human spirit.... America must remain *freedom's* staunchest friend, for *freedom* is our best ally.... Every victory for human *freedom* will be a victory for world peace.... One people under God, dedicated to the dream of *freedom* that He has placed in the human heart.[46]

Different Visions

Lyndon Johnson and Ronald Reagan had strikingly different visions of American democracy and what their goals should be as president. Johnson was committed to equality for all, and major civil rights laws are among the most important legacies of his administration. He is pictured here signing the 1964 Civil Rights Act. Reagan was devoted to reducing the size of government so as to enhance freedom. He worked hard to reduce both taxes and spending.

(*left*: ASSOCIATED PRESS; *right*: Diana Walker/Time & Life Images/Getty Images)

Reagan turned Johnson's philosophy on its head, declaring that "government is not the solution to our problem. Government *is* the problem." During his presidency, Reagan worked to undo many welfare and social service programs and cut funding for programs such as the Job Corps and food stamps. By the end of his term, there had been a fundamental shift in federal spending, with sharp increases in defense spending and "decreases in federal social programs [which] served to defend Democratic interests and constituencies."[47]

... to Policy Agenda

The roots of particular policy proposals, then, can be traced to the more general political ideology of the president. Presidential candidates outline that philosophy of government during their campaign for the White House as they attempt to mobilize voters and interest groups. After the election, presidents and their staffs continue to identify and track support among different kinds of voters as they decide how to translate their general philosophy into concrete legislative proposals.

When the hot rhetoric of the presidential campaign meets the cold reality of what is possible in Washington, the newly elected president must make some hard choices about what to push for during the coming term. These choices are reflected in the bills the president submits to Congress, as well as in the degree to which he works for their passage. The president's bills, introduced by his allies in the House and Senate, always receive a good deal of initial attention. In the words of one Washington lobbyist, "When a president sends up a bill, it takes first place in the queue. All other bills take second place."[48]

The president's role in legislative leadership is largely a twentieth-century phenomenon. Not until the Budget and Accounting Act of 1921 did executive branch departments and agencies have to clear their proposed budget bills with the White House. Before this, the president did not even coordinate proposals for how much the executive branch would spend on all the programs it administered. Later, Franklin D. Roosevelt required that the White House clear all major legislative proposals by an agency or department. No longer could a department submit a bill without White House support.

Roosevelt's influence on the relationship between the president and Congress went far beyond this new administrative arrangement. With the nation in the midst of the Great Depression, Roosevelt began his first term in 1933 with an ambitious array of legislative proposals. During the first one hundred days Congress was in session, it enacted fifteen significant laws, including the Agricultural Adjustment Act, the act creating the Civilian Conservation Corps, and the National Industrial Recovery Act. Never before had a president demanded—and received—so much from Congress. Roosevelt's legacy was that the president would henceforth provide aggressive leadership of Congress through his own legislative program.

Chief Lobbyist

When Franklin D. Roosevelt and Harry Truman first became heavily involved in preparing legislative packages, political scientists typically described the process as one in which "the president proposes and Congress disposes." In other words, once the president sends his legislation to Capitol Hill, Congress decides what to do with it. Over time, though, presidents have become increasingly active in all stages of the legislative process. The president is expected not only to propose legislation but also to make sure that it passes.

The president's efforts to influence Congress are reinforced by the work of his legislative liaison staff. All departments and major agencies have legislative specialists as well. These department and agency people work with the White House liaison staff to coordinate the administration's lobbying on major issues.

The **legislative liaison staff** is the communications link between the White House and Congress. As a bill slowly makes its way through Congress, liaison staffers advise the president or a cabinet secretary on the problems that emerge. They specify what parts of a bill are in trouble and may have to be modified or dropped. They tell their boss what amendments are likely to be offered, which members of Congress need to be lobbied, and what the bill's chances for passage are with or without certain provisions. Decisions on how the administration will respond to such developments must then be reached. For example, when the Reagan White House realized that it was still a few votes short of victory on a budget bill in the House, it reversed its

legislative liaison staff
Those people who act as the communications link between the White House and Congress, advising the president or cabinet secretaries on the status of pending legislation.

opposition to a sugar price support bill. This attracted the votes of representatives from Louisiana and Florida, two sugar-growing states, for the budget bill. The White House would not call what happened a deal, but it noted that "adjustments and considerations" had been made.[49] Still, not all demands from legislators can be met.

A certain amount of the president's job consists of stereotypical arm twisting—pushing reluctant legislators to vote a certain way. The president also talks to legislators to seek their advice and takes soundings from committee chairs on what proposals can get through and what must be modified or abandoned. During Obama's first four months in office, four hundred representatives and senators were brought to the White House to speak to the president or attend meetings or other events.[50]

Yet most day-in, day-out interactions between the White House and Congress tend to be more mundane, with the liaison staff trying to build support by working cooperatively with legislators. When a congressional committee is working on a bill, liaison people talk to committee members individually to see what concerns they have and to help fashion a compromise if some differ with the president's position. This type of quiet negotiation disappeared during the 1995–1996 session of Congress, when the new Republican majority in the House, heady with excitement at controlling the chamber for the first time in forty years, briefly let the government shut down on two occasions rather than bargain with the president.

The White House also works directly with interest groups in its efforts to build support for legislation. Presidential aides hope key lobbyists will activate the most effective lobbyists of all: the voters back home. Interest groups can quickly reach the constituents who are most concerned about a bill, using their communications network to mobilize members to write, call, or e-mail their members of Congress. There are so many interest groups in our pluralist political system that they could easily overload the White House with their demands. Consequently, except for those groups most important to the president, lobbies tend to be granted access only when the White House needs them to activate public opinion. During the titanic struggle over health-care legislation, the Obama White House knew it needed a great deal of interest group support. It cut a number of deals with the insurance and pharmaceutical industries to make the president's proposal more palatable to them.

Agreement with Congress cannot always be reached, and sometimes Congress may pass a bill the president opposes. In such a case the president may veto the bill and send it back to Congress; Congress can override a veto with a two-thirds majority of those voting in each house. Presidents use their veto power sparingly, but as we noted earlier, the threat that a president will veto an unacceptable bill increases his bargaining leverage with members of Congress. We have also seen that a president's leverage with Congress is related to his standing with the American people. The ability of the president and his liaison staff to bargain with members of Congress is enhanced when he is riding high in the public opinion polls and hindered when the public is critical of his performance.

Party Leader

Part of the president's job is to lead his party.[51] This is very much an informal duty, with no prescribed tasks. In this respect, American presidents are considerably different from European prime ministers, who are the formal leaders of their party in the national legislature, as well as the head of their government. In the American system, a president and members of his party in Congress can clearly take very different positions on the issues before them.

As Congress has turned more partisan, presidents have focused more on leadership of their own party rather than trying to bridge differences between the two parties.[52] With less of a moderate middle to work with in Congress, a president needs to work hard to unify his party around his priorities. Increasingly, the public regards presidents as partisan leaders rather than unifying national leaders. Polls show that Americans have evaluated recent presidents, notably Ronald Reagan, Bill Clinton, George W. Bush, and Barack Obama, through a largely partisan prism. Republican identifiers love Republican presidents and despise Democratic ones. Likewise, Democratic identifiers like presidents of their own party and are contemptuous of Republican ones (see Figure 12.4).[53]

The president himself has become the "fundraiser in chief" for his party. Since presidents have a vital interest in more members of their party being elected to the House and Senate, they have a strong incentive to spend time raising money for congressional candidates. All incumbent presidents travel frequently to fundraising dinners in different states, where they are the main attraction. Donors pay substantial sums—$1,000 a ticket is common—to go to such a dinner. In addition to helping elect more members of his party, a

FIGURE 12.4   Through Partisan Eyes

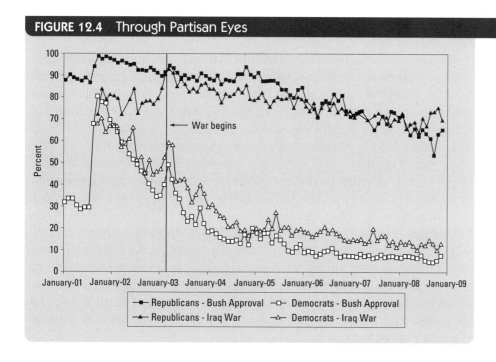

How we evaluate a president's performance is strongly shaped by our own partisan predisposition. As illustrated here, Republicans were much more likely to approve of George W. Bush's presidency than were Democrats. For their part, Democrats became quite critical of Bush after he directed the country's armed forces to invade Iraq. The same partisan pattern can be found in evaluations of Barack Obama.

Source: Gary C. Jacobson, "Perception, Memory, and Partisan Polarization on the Iraq War," *Political Science Quarterly* 152 (Spring 2010): 32.

not-so-small by-product for the president is the gratitude of legislators. It's a lot harder to say no to a president's request for help on a bill when he spoke at your fundraiser during the last election.

The President as World Leader

The president's leadership responsibilities extend beyond Congress and the nation to the international arena. Each administration tries to further what it sees as the country's best interests in its relations with allies, adversaries, and the developing countries of the world. In this role, the president must be ready to act as diplomat and crisis manager.

Foreign Relations

From the end of World War II until the late 1980s, presidents were preoccupied with containing communist expansion around the globe. Truman and Korea, Kennedy and Cuba, Johnson and Nixon and Vietnam, and Reagan and Nicaragua are just some examples of presidents and the communist crosses they had to bear. Presidents not only used overt and covert military means to fight communism but also tried to reduce tensions through negotiations. President Nixon made particularly important strides in this regard, completing an important arms control agreement with the Soviet Union and beginning negotiations with China, with which the United States had had no formal diplomatic relations.

With the collapse of communism in the Soviet Union and Eastern Europe, American presidents entered a new era in international relations, but they are still concerned with three fundamental objectives (see Chapter 20 for a more detailed discussion of American foreign policy). First is national security, the direct protection of the United States and its citizens from external threats. National security has been highlighted since the September 11 terrorist attacks.

Second is fostering a peaceful international environment. Presidents work with international organizations like the United Nations and the North Atlantic Treaty Organization (NATO) to seek an end to regional conflicts throughout the world. In some cases, like the ongoing dispute between Palestinians and Israelis, the United States has played a central role in mediating conflict and facilitating bargaining between opposing sides. In other cases, presidents send the U.S. military to participate in multinational peacekeeping forces to ensure stability, enforce negotiated peace plans, and monitor democratic elections. The United States may impose trade sanctions to discourage human rights violations.

A third objective is the protection of U.S. economic interests. The new presidential job description places much more emphasis on managing economic relations with the rest of the world. Trade relations are an especially difficult problem because presidents must balance the conflicting interests of foreign countries (many of them allies), the interests of particular American industries, the overall needs of the American economy, and the demands of the legislative branch.

Crisis Management

Periodically the president faces a grave situation in which conflict is imminent or a small conflict threatens to explode into a larger war. Because handling such episodes is a critical part of the presidency, citizens may vote for candidates who project careful judgment. One reason for Barry Goldwater's crushing defeat in the 1964 election was his warlike image and rhetoric, which scared many Americans. Fearing that Goldwater would be too quick to resort to nuclear weapons, they voted for Lyndon Johnson instead.

A president must be able to exercise good judgment and remain cool in crisis situations. John Kennedy's behavior during the Cuban missile crisis of 1962 has become a model of effective crisis management. When the United States learned that the Soviet Union had placed missiles containing nuclear warheads in Cuba, Kennedy saw those missiles as an unacceptable threat to U.S. security. He asked a group of senior aides, including top people from the Pentagon, to advise him on feasible military and diplomatic responses. Kennedy considered an invasion of Cuba and air strikes against the missiles but

Crisis in Camelot

In October 1962, people gathered in the electronics section of a store to watch President Kennedy address the nation on the Cuban missile crisis. When the United States learned that the Soviet Union was placing missile bases in Cuba, Kennedy demanded that the Soviets remove their missiles, and he ordered a naval blockade. After seven days, Soviet leader Nikita Khrushchev complied with Kennedy's demands, and direct conflict between the two major superpowers was avoided. Cuba's leader at that time, Fidel Castro, had seized power in 1959 and aligned himself with the Soviet Union during the Cold War.

(Ralph Crane/Time Life Pictures/Getty Images)

eventually chose a less dangerous response: a naval blockade. He also privately signaled to Soviet leader Nikita Khrushchev that if the Soviet Union withdrew its missiles from Cuba, the United States would remove American missiles from Turkey.[54] Although the Soviet Union complied, the world held its breath for a short time over the very real possibility of a nuclear war.

What guidelines determine what a president should do in times of crisis?[55] Drawing on a range of advisers and opinions is one. Not acting in unnecessary haste is another. A third is having a well-designed, formal review process with thorough analysis and open debate. A fourth guideline is rigorously examining the reasoning underlying all options to ensure that

Politics of Global Change

International Support for the War on Terror

All presidents inherit the legacy of their predecessor's actions in the world. President Obama took office at a time when other countries were skeptical of U.S.-led efforts to fight terrorism. In 2002, a little over six months after the September 11, 2001, terrorist attacks and the start of the war in Afghanistan, the Pew Global Attitudes Project asked respondents in various countries whether they favored or opposed U.S.-led efforts to fight terrorism. The same question was asked again in 2007, while George W. Bush was still in office and four years after

the start of the war in Iraq. Quite clearly support had dropped considerably. After Barack Obama became president, opinion across the globe turned more favorable toward the United States' efforts. The noticeable exception was the Middle East, where most respondents in the Arab countries continued to be critical of the United States.

Source: The Pew Global Attitudes Project, various polls. Available at http://pewglobal.org.

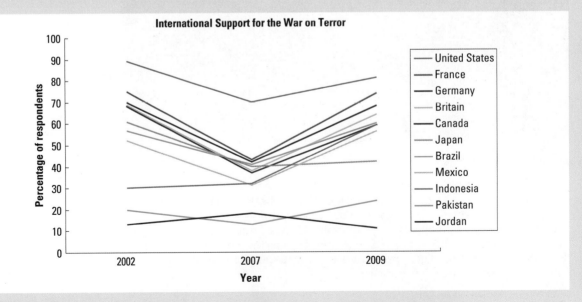

their assumptions are valid. When President Kennedy backed a CIA plan for a rebel invasion of Cuba by expatriates hostile to Fidel Castro, he did not know that its chances for success were based on unfounded assumptions of immediate uprisings by the Cuban population.

These guidelines do not guarantee against mistakes. Almost by definition, each crisis is unique. Sometimes all alternatives carry substantial risks. And almost always, time is of the essence. When Cambodia captured the American merchant ship *Mayagüez* off its coast in 1975, President Ford did not want to wait until the Cambodians moved the sailors inland, presenting little chance of rescue. So he immediately sent in the marines. Unfortunately, forty-one American soldiers were killed, "all in vain because the American captives had shortly before the attack been released and sent across the border into Thailand."[56] Even so, Ford's decision can be defended, for he did not know what the Cambodians would do. World events are unpredictable, and in the end presidents must rely on their own judgment in crisis situations.

Summary

When the delegates to the Constitutional Convention met to design the government of their new nation, they had trouble shaping the office of the president. They struggled to find a balance: an office that was powerful enough to provide unified leadership but not so strong that presidents could use their powers to become tyrants or dictators. The initial conceptions of the presidency have slowly been transformed over time, as presidents have adapted the office to meet the nation's changing needs. The trend has been to expand presidential power. Some expansion has come from presidential actions taken under claims of inherent powers. Congress has also delegated a great deal of power to the executive branch, further expanding the role of the president. The executive branch establishment has grown rapidly, and the White House has become a sizable bureaucracy.

Presidential leadership is shaped by the president's ability to bargain, persuade, and make wise choices. His influence is related to his popularity with the public because he can use his support to gain leverage with members of Congress. The president's legislative success also depends on his political party's numerical strength in Congress. Presidents who are part of a strong majority party have more resources to make bold policy changes.

New responsibilities of the presidency are particularly noticeable in the area of legislative leadership. A president is now expected to be a policy initiator for Congress as well as a lobbyist who guides his bills through the legislative process. The presidential "job description" for foreign policy has also changed considerably. Post–World War II presidents had been preoccupied with containing the spread of communism, but with the collapse of communism in the Soviet Union and Eastern Europe, presidents pay more attention to international economic relations and security issues like terrorism.

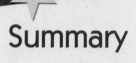 **CourseMate** Visit www.cengagebrain.com/shop/ ISBN/0495906182 for flashcards, web quizzes, videos and more!

CHAPTER 13

The Bureaucracy

AP Photo/ Lynsey Addario/VII Network

Harry Markopolos was angry. The investment adviser had been asked by his boss why the investment vehicle that Markopolos directed was producing lower earnings than a similar investment fund directed by financier Bernard Madoff. Markopolos was suspicious of the Madoff fund because year after year it consistently yielded returns of about 12 percent. Given that the stock market fluctuates and sometimes has years when it declines significantly, such steady positive returns looked highly improbable.

Markopolos began to study Madoff's stated investment strategy and eventually uncovered what turned out to be a "Ponzi scheme." This is essentially a swindle in which new investors are drawn in by the promise of very high returns. The fund manager, however, pockets the money and creates fictitious returns. If an existing investor wants to withdraw some money, he or she is paid with money coming in from new investors. This scheme is named for Charles Ponzi, the Boston con man who in 1920 began a fund that promised investors an outlandish 40 percent return over a mere 90 days. Ponzi said, falsely, that he was able to produce these returns by exploiting differences in currency exchange rates. For a short time he was extraordinarily successful, drawing $20 million (a vast sum in 1920) from investors in only a few months, until suspicions were aroused and the fund collapsed.

Markopolos continued to investigate, but without access to Madoff's books, he could not definitively prove that the fund was a Ponzi scheme. In the spring of 2000 Markopolos turned over the evidence he had collected to the Securities and Exchange Commission (SEC), the government's regulatory agency for overseeing financial markets. The SEC responded to Markopolos's detailed and well-documented complaint by doing nothing.

While the SEC slept, Madoff continued to take in money from both new and continuing investors. His Ponzi scheme would not collapse until late in 2008. Many of his investors—individuals, schools, banks, churches, synagogues, even charities—were ruined financially by his scam. It's not clear how much money was lost in the Madoff scandal. Estimates go as high as $65 billion, but some of this money may have never truly existed beyond the fantasy profits entered into the doctored financial statements mailed to clients.

When the scandal broke, questions immediately emerged as to how Madoff got away with his fraud for so long and why the SEC had failed to uncover it. As it turned out, Harry Markopolos was not the only one who filed a complaint about Madoff with the SEC. Over a 16-year period the agency received six substantive complaints about him. The SEC launched investigations in response to some of these complaints but remarkably failed to turn up anything untoward. Looking back from his jail cell in 2009, Madoff said all the SEC had to do to determine if his fund was operating honestly was check to see that the stock trades he said he was making were actually carried out. (An investment firm that makes a stock sale or purchase must go through an independent clearinghouse of some type.) Had the SEC taken this simple step, the Ponzi scheme "would have been easy for them to see," said Madoff.

The SEC launched an exhaustive review of its failures in the Madoff case—a failure that had catastrophic consequences for Madoff's investors. Its 2009 report concluded that its earlier investigations were marred by the inexperience of the staffers assigned to inspect Madoff's operations. When Madoff failed to give investigators the information they requested, they didn't follow up and insist upon it or subpoena the documents. Outside analysts looking at the SEC point out that the agency is understaffed and overwhelmed by the size of the financial markets it is meant to supervise.

The Madoff case is a painful reminder of how we depend on regulatory agencies to protect us. When those agencies fail, our health, safety, and financial well-being can be compromised. The SEC's errors in the Madoff case are surely not typical of the government's performance. However, this case does suggest that we cannot take government competence for granted and we must always look for ways to reform and improve the performance of the bureaucracy.[1]

Despite their shortcomings, we must rely on bureaucracies to administer government. In this chapter, we examine how bureaucracies operate and address many of the central dilemmas of American political life. Bureaucracies represent what Americans dislike about government, yet our interest groups lobby them to provide us with more of the services we desire. We say we want smaller, less intrusive government, but different constituencies value different agencies of government and fight fiercely to protect those bureaucracies' budgets. This enduring conflict once again represents the majoritarian and pluralist dimensions of American politics.

Organization Matters

A nation's laws and policies are administered, or put into effect, by various departments, agencies, bureaus, offices, and other government units, which together are known as its *bureaucracy*. **Bureaucracy** actually means any large, complex organization in which employees have specific job responsibilities and work within a hierarchy of authority. The employees of these government units, who are quite knowledgeable within their narrow areas, have become known somewhat derisively as **bureaucrats**.

We study bureaucracies because they play a central role in the governments of modern societies. In fact, organizations are a crucial part of any society, no matter how elementary it is. Even a preindustrial tribe is an organization. It has a clearly defined leader (a chief), senior policymakers (elders), a fixed division of labor (some hunt, some cook, some make tools), an organizational culture (religious practices, initiation rituals), and rules of governance (what kind of property belongs to families and what belongs to the tribe). How that tribe is organized is not merely a quaint aspect of its evolution; it is critical to the survival of its members in a hostile environment.

The organization of modern government bureaucracies also reflects their need to survive. The environment in which modern bureaucracies operate, filled with conflicting political demands and the ever-present threat of budget cuts, is no less hostile than that of preindustrial tribes. The way a given government bureaucracy is organized also reflects the particular needs of its clients. The bottom line, however, is that the manner in which any bureaucracy is organized affects how well it can accomplish its tasks.

IN OUR OWN WORDS

Listen to Jeffrey Berry discuss the main points and themes of this chapter.

www.cengagebrain.com/ shop/ISBN/0495906182

bureaucracy
A large, complex organization in which employees have specific job responsibilities and work within a hierarchy of authority.

bureaucrats
Employees of a bureaucracy, usually meaning a government bureaucracy.

Different approaches to fighting German submarines in World War II vividly demonstrate the importance of organization. At the beginning of the war, German submarines, or U-boats, were sinking American merchant ships off the East Coast of America at a devastating rate. One U-boat commander wrote that his task was so easy that "all we had to do was press the button." In contrast, the British had a great deal of success in defending their ships in the North Atlantic from U-boats.

The British navy used a highly centralized structure to quickly pool all incoming information on U-boat locations and just as quickly pass on what it had learned to commanders of antisubmarine ships and planes and to convoys. In contrast, the U.S. Navy's operations structure was decentralized, leaving top-line managers to decide for themselves how to allocate their resources. No one unit was coordinating antisubmarine warfare. When the U.S. Navy finally adopted a system similar to the British navy's, its success against the U-boats improved dramatically. In the eighteen months before it changed its system, the U.S. Navy sank just thirty-six U-boats. In the first six months with its centralized structure, seventy-five U-boats were destroyed.[2]

Clearly organization matters. The ways in which bureaucracies are structured to perform their work directly affect their ability to accomplish their tasks. Unfortunately, "if organization matters, it is also the case that there is no one best way of organizing."[3] Highly centralized organization, like the British navy's approach to combating U-boats, may not always be the best approach to solving a bureaucracy's performance problems. A common complaint against Washington bureaucracies is that they devise one-size-fits-all solutions to problems. In some instances, it's surely better to give local managers the flexibility to tailor their own solutions to the unique problems they face in their community or state. The study of bureaucracy, then, centers around finding solutions to the many different kinds of problems that large government organizations face.

Only 148 More Years Before He's Released from Prison. Not Clear if There's Time Off for Good Behavior.

The unconscionable fraud perpetrated by Bernard Madoff resulted in a prison sentence of 150 years. The complete failure of the Securities and Exchange Commission to uncover the scheme led to an onslaught of criticism and a demand for improved performance by the agency. While the SEC was asleep at the switch, some investors lost their life's savings.

(Mario Tama/Getty Images)

The Development of the Bureaucratic State

A common complaint voiced by Americans is that the national bureaucracy is too big and tries to accomplish too much. To the average citizen, the national government may seem like an octopus—its long arms reach just

Compared with What?

Not So Big by Comparison

Compared with other Western democracies, the U.S. government turns out to be relatively small. Measuring the size of government is difficult, but one way is to calculate the proportion of all of a nation's workers who are employed by their government.

The primary reason that the size of the bureaucracies in other democracies is larger in comparison to the United States is that they offer a much more extensive array of welfare and social service benefits to their citizens. These countries tend to have generous pension, health, and unemployment benefits. These benefits do not come cheaply, however; residents of the other advanced industrialized countries tend to pay much higher taxes than do Americans. There's no free lunch. In recent years, budget pressures have forced European governments to try to trim their spending.

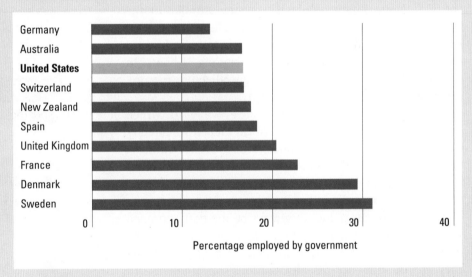

Percentage employed by government

Source: Alan R. Ball and B. Guy Peters, *Modern Politics and Government*, 7th ed. (New York: Palgrave Macmillan, 2005), p. 231.

about everywhere. Ironically, compared to other Western democracies, the size of the U.S. government is proportionally smaller (see "Compared with What? Not So Big by Comparison").

Bureaucratic Growth

American government seems to have grown unchecked since the start of the twentieth century. As one observer noted wryly, "The assistant administrator for water and hazardous materials of the Environmental Protection Agency [presides] over a staff larger than Washington's entire first administration."[4]

Yet even during George Washington's time, bureaucracies were necessary. No one argued then about the need for a postal service to deliver mail or a treasury department to maintain a system of currency.

However, government at all levels (national, state, and local) grew enormously in the twentieth century, for several major reasons. A principal cause of government expansion is the increasing complexity of society. George Washington did not have an assistant administrator for water and hazardous materials because he had no need for one. The National Aeronautics and Space Administration (NASA) was not necessary until rockets were invented.

Another reason government has grown is that the public's attitude toward business has changed. Throughout most of the nineteenth century, there was little or no government regulation of business. Business was generally autonomous, and any government intervention in the economy that might limit that autonomy was considered inappropriate. This attitude began to change toward the end of the nineteenth century as more Americans became aware that the end product of a laissez-faire approach was not always highly competitive markets that benefited consumers. Instead, businesses sometimes formed oligopolies, such as the infamous "sugar trust," a small group of companies that controlled virtually the entire sugar market.

Gradually government intervention came to be accepted as necessary to protect the integrity of markets. And if government was to police unfair business practices effectively, it needed administrative agencies. During the twentieth century, new bureaucracies were organized to regulate specific industries. Among them are the Securities and Exchange Commission (SEC), which oversees securities trading, and the Food and Drug Administration (FDA), which tries to protect consumers from unsafe food, drugs, and cosmetics. Through bureaucracies such as these, government has become a referee in the marketplace, developing standards of fair trade, setting rates, and licensing individual businesses for operation. As new problem areas have emerged, government has added new agencies, further expanding the scope of its activities. After World War II, the government created the Atomic Energy Commission—now the Nuclear Regulatory Commission—to regulate the use of nuclear materials and monitor the safety of nuclear reactors. Within months after the September 11, 2001, terrorist attacks, the government created the Transportation Security Administration (TSA) to oversee security at the nation's airports.

General attitudes about government's responsibilities in the area of social welfare have changed too. An enduring part of American culture is the belief in self-reliance. People are expected to overcome adversity on their own, to succeed on the basis of their own skills and efforts. Yet certain segments of our population are believed to deserve government support, because we either particularly value their contribution to society or have come to believe that they cannot realistically be expected to overcome adversity on their own.

This belief goes as far back as the nineteenth century. The government provided pensions to Civil War veterans because they were judged to deserve financial support. Later, programs to help mothers and children were developed.[5] Further steps toward income security came in the wake of the Great Depression, when the Social Security Act became law, creating a fund that workers pay into and then collect income from during old age. In the 1960s, the government created Head Start, Medicare, and Medicaid, programs designed to help minorities, the elderly, and the poor. As the government made these new commitments, it also made new bureaucracies and expanded existing ones.

Finally, government has grown because ambitious, entrepreneurial agency officials have expanded their organizations and staffs to take on added responsibilities. Each new program leads to new authority, and larger budgets and staffs are necessary to support that authority.

Can We Reduce the Size of Government?

Even incumbent candidates for Congress and the presidency typically "run against the government." For many Americans, government is unpopular: they have little confidence in its capabilities and feel that it wastes money and is out of touch with the people. They want a smaller government that costs less and performs better.

Most of the national government is composed of large bureaucracies, so if government is to become smaller, bureaucracies will have to be eliminated or reduced in size. Everyone wants to believe that we can shrink government by eliminating unnecessary bureaucrats. Although efficiencies can be found, serious budget cuts also require serious reductions in programs. Not surprisingly, presidents and members of Congress face opposition when they try to cut specific programs. As discussed in Chapter 17, the national government often engages in a bit of a shell game, modestly reducing the number of bureaucrats (which is popular) without reducing government programs (which is politically risky). The government often turns over the former bureaucrats' jobs to nonprofit or private contractors who do the same job but are not technically government employees.

Beneath the common rhetoric that government needs to be smaller and more efficient, serious efforts to shrink the bureaucracy have varied considerably. Ideological differences between the two parties and the gyrating size of the national budget deficit have shaped the debate. During the 1980s, President Reagan preached smaller government and made a concerted effort to reduce domestic social programs. He had only modest success, and his most ambitious proposals, like abolishing the Department of Education, didn't come close to passage by Congress. Although he was conservative in many ways, George W. Bush worked to enlarge the government. Most significantly, the 9/11 attacks and the continuing threat of terrorism led to the creation of the Department of Homeland Security and the expansion of defense- and other security-related agencies. But it wasn't just security threats that led President Bush to propose new programs and bureaucracies. He also worked to expand social welfare through a prescription drug benefit for senior citizens. Bush understood that it was not always good politics to try to downsize government and that there's an upside to providing a benefit to citizens.

Seeing the need for government to grow to address the many serious problems facing the country, President Obama proposed an expanded bureaucracy to protect the country's economy and individual consumers from the kinds of irresponsibility demonstrated by financial institutions in creating a housing bubble based on unsound mortgages. Speculators bid up the prices of real estate, assuming that prices would continue to rise, allowing quick, profitable sales. When that bubble burst, it accelerated a deep and damaging recession beginning in 2008. Obama's plan, enacted in July 2010, creates a consumer protection agency to regulate various financial products. The financial services industry opposed a new agency, believing that the government would introduce inefficiencies and higher costs into the market for financial services.[6]

Reagan and Obama represent two polar philosophies. To Reagan, small government enhanced personal freedom; to Obama, a larger government is a means of promoting equality and protecting citizens. Although government continues to grow, the tendency for big government to endure reflects the tension between majoritarianism and pluralism. Even when the public as a whole wants a smaller national government, that sentiment can be undermined by the strong desire of different segments of society for government to continue performing some valuable function for them. Lobbies that represent these segments work strenuously to convince Congress and the administration that certain agencies' funding is vital and that any cuts ought to come out of other agencies' budgets.

Bureaus and Bureaucrats

We often think of the bureaucracy as a monolith. In reality, the bureaucracy in Washington is a disjointed collection of departments, agencies, bureaus, offices, and commissions—each a bureaucracy in its own right.

The Organization of Government

By examining the basic types of government organizations, we can better understand how the executive branch operates. In our discussion, we pay particular attention to the relative degree of independence of these organizations and to their relationship with the White House.

Departments. The biggest units of the executive branch are **departments**, covering broad areas of government responsibility. As noted in Chapter 12, the secretaries (heads) of the departments, along with a few other key officials, form the president's cabinet. The current cabinet departments are State, Treasury, Defense, Interior, Agriculture, Justice, Commerce, Labor, Health and Human Services, Housing and Urban Development, Transportation, Energy, Education, Veterans Affairs, and Homeland Security (see Figure 13.1). Each of

departments
The biggest units of the executive branch, covering a broad area of government responsibility. The heads of the departments, or secretaries, form the president's cabinet.

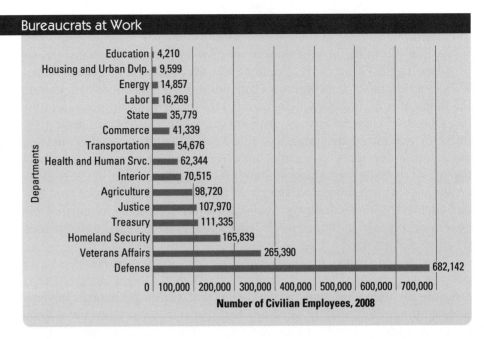

FIGURE 13.1 — Bureaucrats at Work

The size of the cabinet departments varies dramatically. That more than 1 million civilians are employed in the departments of Defense, Homeland Security, and Veterans Affairs is a reflection of the centrality of national security and war in recent American history. At the opposite end of the spectrum is the tiny Department of Education, with fewer than five thousand employees, despite the common rhetoric about the need to improve education.

Source: U.S. Census Bureau, *Statistical Abstract of the United States, 2009*, Table 487: Federal Civilian Employment by Branch and Agency, available at http://www.census.gov/compendia/statab/cats/federal_govt_finances_employment.html.

these massive organizations is broken down into subsidiary agencies, bureaus, offices, and services.

Independent Agencies. Within the executive branch are many **independent agencies** that are not part of any cabinet department. They stand alone and are controlled to varying degrees by the president. Some, among them the CIA, are directly under the president's control. Others, such as the Federal Communications Commission, are structured as **regulatory commissions.** Each commission is run by a small number of commissioners (usually an odd number, to prevent tie votes) appointed to fixed terms by the president. Some commissions were formed to guard against unfair business practices. Others were formed to protect the public from unsafe products. Although presidents don't have direct control over these regulatory commissions, they can strongly influence their direction through their appointments of new commissioners.

independent agencies
Executive agencies that are not part of a cabinet department.

regulatory commissions
Agencies of the executive branch of government that control or direct some aspect of the economy.

government corporations
Government agencies that perform services that might be provided by the private sector but that either involve insufficient financial incentive or are better provided when they are somehow linked with government.

Government Corporations. Finally, Congress has also created a small number of **government corporations.** These executive branch agencies perform services that theoretically could be provided by the private sector, but Congress has decided that the public is better served when these organizations have some link with the government. For example, the national government maintains the postal service as a government corporation because it feels that Americans need low-cost, door-to-door service for all kinds of mail, not just for profitable routes or special services. In some instances, the private sector does not have enough financial incentive to provide an essential service. This is the case with the financially troubled Amtrak passenger train line.

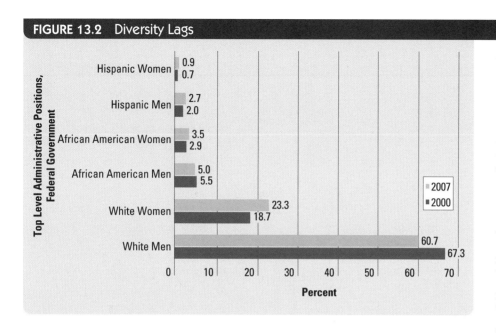

FIGURE 13.2 Diversity Lags

A top level of the federal bureaucracy is the Senior Executive Service, experienced career bureaucrats put in high positions of responsibility. These figures from the Government Accountability Office show that white women have made some modest progress in being promoted to the Senior Executive Service. African Americans and Hispanics lag badly compared to their share of the general population, and progress is limited.

Source: Joe Davidson, "Room at the Top for More Diversity," *Washington Post,* 2 December 2008.

The Civil Service

The national bureaucracy is staffed by nearly 2.8 million civilian employees, who account for about 2 percent of the U.S. work force.[7] Americans have a tendency to stereotype all government workers as faceless paper pushers, but the public sector work force is quite diverse. Government workers include forest rangers, FBI agents, typists, foreign service officers, computer programmers, policy analysts, public relations specialists, security guards, librarians, administrators, engineers, plumbers, and people from literally hundreds of other occupations. (For the diversity balance among top career officials in departments and agencies, see Figure 13.2.)

An important feature of the national bureaucracy is that most of its workers are hired under the requirements of the **civil service**. The civil service was created after the assassination of President James Garfield, who was killed by an unbalanced and dejected job seeker. Congress responded by passing the Pendleton Act (1883), which established the Civil Service Commission (now the Office of Personnel Management). The objective of the act was to reduce patronage–the practice of filling government positions with the president's political allies or cronies. The civil service fills jobs on the basis of merit and sees to it that workers are not fired for political reasons. Over the years, job qualifications and selection procedures have been developed for most government positions.

The tidal wave of criticism of the federal bureaucracy–that it's unresponsive, too big, and too inefficient–has raised concerns that the government has become a less appealing place to work. As one study concluded, "The federal bureaucracy became the symbol of big government's problems–rarely of its success."[8] The quality of the civil service could decline as agencies may find fewer superior candidates for job openings. Surveys find that younger

civil service
The system by which most appointments to the federal bureaucracy are made, to ensure that government jobs are filled on the basis of merit and that employees are not fired for political reasons.

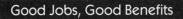

FIGURE 13.3	Good Jobs, Good Benefits

Despite tight budgets, jobs in the federal government maintain good pay and benefits. In this figure, those jobs listed below the 100 percent line pay better if they are in the government than in the private sector. For two people holding the same type of job listed above the 100 percent line, the one employed in the private sector will receive higher pay.

Source: Reprinted by permission of the publisher from *The Warping of Government Work* by John D. Donahue, p. 47, Cambridge, Mass.: Harvard University Press, Copyright © 2008 by the President and Fellows of Harvard College.

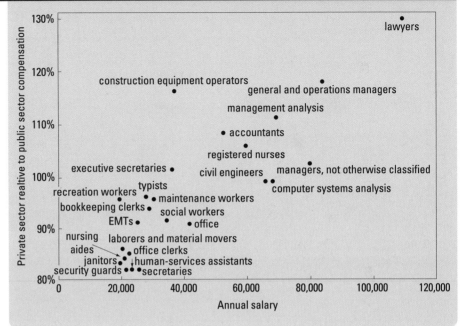

people seem less interested in working for the government, preferring private sector employment instead. One appealing strength of government sector work is that pay and benefits compare favorably to the private sector, especially for jobs at the lower end of the skills range (see Figure 13.3).[9] Research has demonstrated that along a range of indicators, the quality of civil servants has not declined over time.[10] Those civil servants passionate about the mission of their agency are particularly motivated and goal oriented.[11]

Presidential Control over the Bureaucracy

Civil service and other reforms have effectively insulated the vast majority of government workers from party politics.[12] An incoming president can appoint only about three thousand people to jobs in his administration, less than 1 percent of all executive branch employees. These presidential appointees fill the top policymaking positions in government, and about a thousand of the president's appointees require Senate confirmation.[13] Each new president, then, establishes an extensive personnel review process to find appointees who are both politically compatible and qualified in their field. Although the president selects some people from his campaign staff, most political appointees have not been campaign workers. Instead, cabinet secretaries, assistant secretaries, agency heads, and the like tend to be drawn directly from business, universities, nonprofits, and government itself.

Presidents find that the bureaucracy is not always as responsive as they might like, for several reasons.[14] Principally, pluralism can pull agencies in a direction other than that favored by the president. The Department of Transportation may want to move toward more support for mass transit, but politically it cannot afford to ignore the preferences of highway builders. An agency administrator must often try to broker a compromise between conflicting groups rather than pursue a position that holds fast and true to the president's ideology. Bureaucracies must also follow—at least in general terms—the laws governing the programs they are entrusted with, even if the president doesn't agree with some of those statutes. In this regard, bureaucracies are full of experienced careerists who are effective at running their programs. It is difficult for political appointees to ignore the careerists' preferences because of their long experience in the agency.[15]

Even with the constraints imposed by interest group preferences and by what the statutes require, presidents still have considerable influence over agency policymaking. They appoint administrators sympathetic to their policy goals who work to adapt the president's philosophy to both pending issues and new initiatives. Presidential aides review agency policymaking to ensure that it is in line with their preferences, often setting up a process requiring agencies to submit draft regulations to a White House office like the Office of Management and Budget. As will be explored in the next section, in varying degrees agencies have the authority to set policy under the laws passed by Congress authorizing an agency to administer a program. After President Obama took office and appointed Inez Moore Tennenbaum as head of the Consumer Product Safety Commission, Tennenbaum instructed staffers there to write a new safety requirement for off-road recreational vehicles, which sometimes flip over on uneven terrain and have been blamed for the deaths of 59 riders. Tennenbaum's predecessor prompted manufacturers to offer repairs aimed at design flaws that may have caused the flipping problem, but Tennenbaum didn't think that went far enough and required manufacturers to make changes.[16]

Congress always has the prerogative to override regulations that it doesn't like or that it feels distort its intent. When a president faces a Congress controlled by the opposition party, this constraint is more significant. When the president's party also controls both houses, it is much easier for him to implement regulations that are in line with his preferences. Whatever party controls Congress, the White House and agency administrators have an incentive to consult with committee chairs to minimize conflict and gain a sense of what might provoke a hostile response on the part of a committee overseeing a particular agency.[17] A committee can punish an agency by cutting its budget, altering a key program, or (for Senate committees) holding up confirmation of a nominee to a top agency post.

Administrative Policymaking: The Formal Processes

Many Americans wonder why agencies sometimes actually make policy rather than merely carry it out. Administrative agencies are, in fact, authoritative policymaking bodies, and their decisions on substantive issues are legally binding on the citizens of this country.

Administrative Discretion

What are executive agencies set up to do? To begin with, cabinet departments, independent agencies, and government corporations are creatures of Congress. Congress creates a new department or agency by enacting a law that describes the organization's mandate, or mission. As part of that mandate, Congress grants the agency the authority to make certain policy decisions. Congress recognized long ago that it has neither the time nor the technical expertise to make all policy decisions. Ideally, it sets general guidelines for policy and expects agencies to act within those guidelines. The latitude that Congress gives agencies to make policy in the spirit of their legislative mandate is called **administrative discretion.**

Critics of the bureaucracy frequently complain that agencies are granted too much discretion because Congress commonly gives vague directives in its initial enabling legislation. Congress charges agencies with protecting "the public interest" but leaves them to determine on their own what policies best serve the public. Critics believe that members of Congress delegate too much of their responsibility for difficult policy choices to appointed administrators.

Congress often is vague about its intent when setting up a new agency or program. At times, a problem is clear-cut, but the solution is not; yet Congress is under pressure to act. So it creates an agency or program to show that it is concerned and responsive, but it leaves to administrators the work of developing specific solutions. For example, the 1934 legislation that established the Federal Communications Commission (FCC) recognized a need for regulation in the burgeoning radio industry. The growing number of stations and overlapping frequencies would soon have made it impossible to listen to the radio. But Congress avoided tackling several sticky issues by giving the FCC the ambiguous directive that broadcasters should serve the "public interest, convenience, and necessity."[18]

When agency directives are vague, bureaucrats work out the policy details. For instance, Congress gives the FCC the power to fine broadcasters for violating decency standards. The FCC's operating definition for "indecent" is language or material that is offensive "as measured by community standards."[19] Some cases of indecency are fairly straightforward: the FCC fined CBS stations after the singer Janet Jackson's "wardrobe malfunction" caused exposure of her breasts during a Super Bowl halftime show. (It's not clear whether the "malfunction" was an accident or occurred accidentally on purpose.) But even after the Super Bowl controversy, members of Congress could not agree on a more concrete definition of *indecency*; they agreed only to increase the amount of fines for violations of the current law. Affected industries often have an interest in curbing the growth of administrative discretion. After the Super Bowl incident, the National Cable and Telecommunications Association announced a $250 million campaign to educate consumers about channel-blocking tools; they did not want lawmakers to give the FCC the power to regulate cable and satellite TV.[20]

administrative discretion
The latitude that Congress gives agencies to make policy in the spirit of their legislative mandate.

Congress grants the broadest discretion to those agencies that are involved in domestic and global security. Both the FBI and the CIA have enjoyed a great deal of freedom from formal and informal congressional constraints because of the legitimate need for secrecy in their operations. The National Security Agency (NSA) was formed to centralize the work of breaking foreign codes and protecting sensitive government information systems. It also monitors foreign communications. After September 11, 2001, President Bush directed the NSA to wiretap telephone conversations between people within the United States and people overseas who have suspected links with terrorists without first obtaining a warrant as required by the 1978 Foreign Intelligence Surveillance Act. NSA bureaucrats followed the secret orders of the president, without the knowledge of members of Congress.[21] Congress has since amended the law, actually expanding the authority of the government to eavesdrop.[22] (For more on this controversy, see Chapter 15.)

Tarmac Hell

Flying these days has its share of challenges but government regulation has resulted in some modest improvements. The airlines' practice of keeping passengers on their plane on the tarmac while waiting for bad weather to clear is now subject to restrictions. If an airline keeps a plane on the tarmac for more than three hours it is subject to a heavy fine. In June 2009, 268 flights sat for more than three hours. By way of comparison with the regulations subsequently put into effect, there were only three such incidents in June 2010.

(Rolf Adlercreutz/Alamy)

Rule Making

Agencies exercise their policymaking discretion through formal administrative procedures, usually rule making. **Rule making** is the administrative process that results in the issuance of regulations. **Regulations** are rules that guide the operation of government programs. When an agency issues regulations, it is using the discretionary authority granted to it by Congress to implement a program or policy enacted into law. Rule making itself follows procedural guidelines requiring that proposed regulations first be published so that interested parties—typically interest groups—have a chance to comment on them, making any recommendations they see as appropriate.[23]

Because they are authorized by congressional statutes, regulations have the effect of law. When Congress created the Department of Transportation in 1966 it was given authority to write regulations relevant to the safety, accessibility, and efficiency of various transportation industries. Controversy has swirled for years around a practice of airlines to keep passengers on board an aircraft that has pulled away from the gate but cannot take off (usually due to inclement weather). Horror stories abound. In August 2009, an ExpressJet flight with forty-seven passengers on board stayed overnight on the tarmac at the airport in Rochester, New York. It doesn't take long before a plane runs out of food and water and bathrooms become fouled.

Whenever Congress threatened to enact a "passenger bill of rights" to forbid such unconscionable tarmac delays, the airlines promised to improve their service. At the end of 2009, however, the Department of Transportation

rule making
The administrative process that results in the issuance of regulations by government agencies.

regulations
Administrative rules that guide the operation of a government program.

Politics of Global Change

And Now for a Real Challenge, Regulate the World

It is difficult for a government to regulate its own country, and an effort by an international body to try to regulate the world may be a fool's errand. It seems like an impossible task in all but the direst of emergencies.

Yet many scientists believe that global warming is, indeed, an emergency with dire consequences for the planet. The culprit is industrialization. As countries develop they build factories, use automobiles for transportation, and heat residences and buildings with carbon-based fuels. All these sources emit greenhouse gases into the atmosphere. Data collected by the U.S. National Aeronautics and Space Administration (NASA)

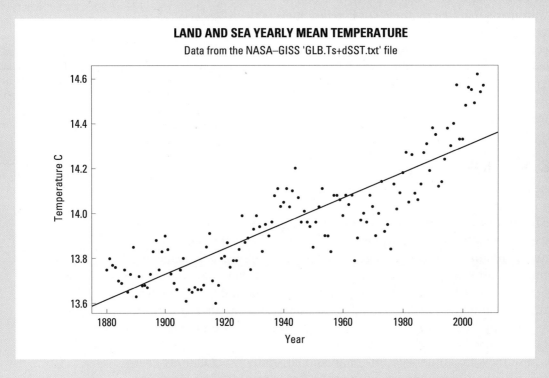

LAND AND SEA YEARLY MEAN TEMPERATURE
Data from the NASA–GISS 'GLB.Ts+dSST.txt' file

announced a new set of rules, limiting tarmac waits to no more than three hours. If that much time elapses, the plane must return to the gate and give passengers the option of deplaning. Airlines claimed there would be unintended consequences and even longer delays as ground crews removed luggage and searched for bags belonging to passengers who deplaned. Passenger rights organizations were ecstatic and believed that airlines would improve their service to keep from further alienating their customers.[24]

The regulatory process is controversial because regulations often require individuals and corporations to act against their own self-interest. (On

show a general rise in global surface temperature since 1880, but there is considerable annual variation in temperature. These variations support those who argue that the world has always undergone periods of warming and cooling. Other observers acknowledge the reality of warming but throw doubt on the long-term implications.

International cooperation is necessary to fight global warming because greenhouse gas emissions know no borders. Pollution goes into the atmosphere, where it can cross political boundaries with impunity. Damage to the atmosphere, such as thinning the ozone layer, affects us all no matter where we live.

Some countries have tried to reduce greenhouse gases on their own, but their efforts have been insufficient as the amount of carbon-based emissions continues to grow. Thus, over the years there have been attempts to negotiate a global reduction in greenhouse gases. An agreement of sorts was reached at the summit in Kyoto, Japan, in 1997, but it had no enforcement mechanism and the United States refused to implement it.

The United States' refusal reflected in part an enduring problem of fairness in such pollution treaties. The nub of the problem is this: poorer, developing countries don't want to limit industrialization because they believe doing so will hinder efforts to improve the standard of living for their citizens. Yet developed nations are often reluctant to require their citizens to make changes in their lifestyles in order to reduce greenhouse gas emissions if the developing world is just going to pollute more as it industrializes.

Expectations were high when the heads of state of 115 countries met in Copenhagen, Denmark, in 2009, to try to hammer out a new agreement. The equity problem was partially addressed by the developed countries' pledge of $100 billion in aid to poorer countries. But the sticking point in a broad treaty was an enforcement provision for implementing any agreed-on reductions.

China, with its huge industrialized economy, has been particularly resistant to the establishment of any mechanism for monitoring emissions levels, much less creating a body with enforcement powers. In what may be a window into world politics of the future, President Obama and Chinese premier Wen Jiabao negotiated privately. China subsequently made a modest concession: the Copenhagen agreement would require monitoring and public reporting of emissions, though it would be done domestically rather than by outside bodies and no enforcement mechanism would be established. This was a small step forward, and it is possible that the world will move incrementally toward limiting greenhouse gases. On the other hand, there is no assurance that any country will take steps to curb emissions.

Sources: John Whalley and Sean Walsh, "Bringing the Copenhagen Global Climate Change Negotiations to Conclusion," *CESifo Economic Studies* 55 (April 2009): 255–285; Michele B. Battig and Thomas Bernauer, "National Institutions and Global Public Goods: Are Democracies More Cooperative in Climate Change Policy?" *International Organization* 63 (Spring 2009): 281–308; Darren Samuelsohn and Lisa Freeman, "Obama Tries to Rally U.N. Climate Conference, but Deadlock Persists," *New York Times*, 18 December 2009; Anthony Faiola, Juliet Eilperin, and John Pomfret, "Copenhagen Climate Deal Shows New World Order May Be Led by U.S., China," *Washington Post*, 20 December 2009.

regulating across nations and the problem of self-interest, see "Politics of Global Change: And Now for a Real Challenge, Regulate the World.") The airline regulations are a classic case of freedom versus order. The airline companies believed they needed the greater freedom to conduct business in a way that they found most efficient. Consumer groups preferred that the government put more of a premium on maintaining order (preserving the health and well-being of passengers). Administrative rule making gives agencies the flexibility as they try to find a balance between conflicting pressures.

Administrative Policymaking: Informal Politics

When an agency is considering a new regulation and all the evidence and arguments have been presented, how does an administrator reach a decision? Because policy decisions typically address complex problems that lack a single satisfactory solution, these decisions rarely exhibit mathematical precision and efficiency.

The Science of Muddling Through

In his classic analysis of policymaking, "The Science of Muddling Through," Charles Lindblom compared the way policy might be made in the ideal world with the way it is formulated in the real world.[25] The ideal, rational decision-making process, according to Lindblom, begins with an administrator's tackling a problem by ranking values and objectives. After clarifying the objectives, the administrator thoroughly considers all possible solutions to the problem. He or she comprehensively analyzes alternative solutions, taking all relevant factors into account. Finally, the administrator chooses the alternative that appears to be the most effective means of achieving the desired goal and solving the problem.

Lindblom claims that this "rational-comprehensive" model is unrealistic. Policymakers have great difficulty defining precise values and goals. Administrators at the U.S. Department of Energy, for example, want to be sure that supplies of home heating oil are sufficient each winter. At the same time, they want to reduce dependence on foreign oil. Obviously, the two

When It Rains, It Pours

The Federal Emergency Management Agency (FEMA) came under fire when the federal government was slow to help the victims of Hurricane Katrina, which struck the Gulf Coast on August 29, 2005. Bureaucrats at the FEMA command center in Washington, D.C., shown here, were uncertain about conditions on the ground in New Orleans, not knowing the extent of the flooding or the number of residents who needed to be evacuated.

(*left*: Tim Sloan/AFP/Getty Images; *right*: Marko Georgiev/Getty Images)

goals are not fully compatible. How should these administrators decide which goal is more important? And how should they relate them to the other goals of the nation's energy policy?

Real-world decision making parts company with the ideal in another way: the policy selected cannot always be the most effective means to the desired end. Even if a tax at the gas pump is the most effective way to reduce gasoline consumption during a shortage, motorists' anger would make this theoretically "right" decision politically difficult. So the "best" policy is often the one on which most people can agree. However, political compromise may mean that the government is able to solve only part of a problem.

Finally, critics of the rational-comprehensive model point out that policymaking can never be based on truly comprehensive analyses. A secretary of energy cannot possibly find the time to read a comprehensive study of all alternative energy sources and relevant policy considerations for the future. A truly thorough investigation of the subject would produce thousands of pages of text. Instead, administrators usually rely on short staff memos that outline a limited range of feasible solutions to immediate problems. Time is of the essence, and problems are often too pressing to wait for a complete study. According to Lindblom, policymaking tends to be characterized by **incrementalism**, with policies and programs changing bit by bit, step by step. Decision makers are constrained by competing policy objectives, opposing political forces, incomplete information, and the pressures of time. They choose from a limited number of feasible options that are almost always modifications of existing policies rather than wholesale departures from them.

Because policymaking proceeds by means of small modifications of existing policies, it is easy to assume that incrementalism describes a process that is intrinsically conservative, sticking close to the status quo. Yet even if policymaking moves in small steps, those steps may all be in the same direction. Over time, a series of incremental changes can significantly alter a program. Moreover, although Lindblom offered a more realistic portrayal of the policymaking process, incrementalism is not ubiquitous. There are a minority of cases where decisions are made that move a policy in a significantly new direction. The Obama administration's intervention to resuscitate a collapsing banking industry could not accurately be labeled an incremental change, even though in the past the government has on occasion intervened to shore up an industry in trouble. The staggering sums the government loaned to failed or fragile financial institutions and the level of control the government exerted were without real precedent. It's certainly true that virtually all policy changes have antecedents in current policy, but some changes are considerable in scope.[26]

The Culture of Bureaucracy

How an agency makes decisions and performs its tasks is greatly affected by the people who work there: the bureaucrats. Americans often find their interactions with bureaucrats frustrating because bureaucrats are inflexible

incrementalism
Policymaking characterized by a series of decisions, each instituting modest change.

(they go by the book) or lack the authority to get things done. Top administrators too can become frustrated with the bureaucrats who work for them.

Why do people act bureaucratically? Individuals who work for large organizations cannot help but be affected by the culture of bureaucracy.[27] Part of that culture is the development of **norms**, an organization's informal, unwritten rules that guide individual behavior. For example, the Individuals with Disabilities Act (IDEA) requires that every child with qualifying disabilities receive an Individualized Education Plan that provides for the necessary, appropriate services. However, school administrators implementing this law frequently offer families fewer services than the law arguably calls for. The reason is not that school administrators don't want to do the maximum for disabled children but that they don't have enough money to provide all services to all qualifying students in their school or district. Norms develop about how to allocate scarce resources even though the law assumes adequate services will be offered.[28]

Bureaucracies are often influenced in their selection of policy options by the prevailing customs, attitudes, and expectations of the people working within them. Departments and agencies commonly develop a sense of mission, where a particular objective or a means for achieving it is emphasized. The Army Corps of Engineers, for example, is dominated by engineers who define the agency's objective as protecting citizens from floods by building dams. There could be other objectives, and there are certainly other methods of achieving this one, but the engineers promote the solutions that fit their conception of what the agency should be doing.

When Leon Panetta became head of the CIA in 2009, he faced an especially delicate and difficult task in trying to change behavior in a bureaucracy with a powerful sense of mission. During the war on terror under the Bush administration, many suspected terrorists who were captured were taken to secret prisons and subjected to waterboarding and other forms of torture. Some of these people were truly evil, while others were not terrorists but victims of mistaken identity. For Panetta the challenge was more than developing new legal standards to replace the ones that permitted torture. Rather, he had to change the mindset of the agency, as many bureaucrats there believed that the CIA needed to do whatever was necessary to protect the United States from another 9/11. Panetta wanted to instill the belief that the agency could fight terrorism within the rule of law.[29]

Bureaucrats are often criticized for being rigid, for going by the book when some flexibility might be a better option. Bureaucrats go by the book because the "book" is actually the law they administer, and they are obligated to enforce the law. The regulations under those laws are often broad standards intended to cover a range of behavior. Yet sometimes those laws and regulations don't seem to make sense. Take the case of Tommy McCoy, who was the batboy for the Savannah Cardinals, then a farm team for the Major League Atlanta Braves. An investigator for the Department of Labor discovered that Tommy was only fourteen years old and was working at night games. Child labor laws forbid fourteen-year-olds from working past 7:00 p.m. on school nights, and the Department of Labor inspector

norms
An organization's informal, unwritten rules that guide individual behavior.

threatened to fine the team unless they stopped employing Tommy. The Cardinals went to bat for Tommy, scheduling a "Save Tommy's Job" night at the stadium. The publicity about Tommy's imminent firing made the Department of Labor look ridiculous. When ABC News asked Secretary of Labor Robert Reich to comment on the situation, he knew he was facing a public relations disaster. But when he asked his staff how they could permit Tommy to keep his job, he was told, "There's nothing we can do. The law is the law."[30]

Reich overrode his staff, deciding that new regulations would exempt batboys and batgirls. That may seem to be a happy ending to a story of a bureaucracy gone mad, but it's not that simple. Child labor laws are important. Before this country had such laws, children were exploited in factories that paid them low wages and subjected them to unsanitary working conditions. The exploitation of child labor is still a problem in many parts of the world. It made sense for Congress to pass a law to forbid child labor abuses, and it made sense for the Department of Labor to write a blanket regulation that forbids work after 7:00 p.m. for all children age fourteen and under. The alternative was to try to determine an evening curfew for every type of job that a youngster might have. Although Reich's exemption made sense from a public relations point of view, it was nonsensical as public policy. How about kids working as peanut vendors at the Cardinals' games? Why didn't Reich write a new regulation exempting them as well? And if he wrote an exemption for children who worked for a baseball team, how about children who scoop ice cream at the local creamery? Why should Tommy McCoy be treated with favoritism?

Bureaucrats often act bureaucratically because they are trying to apply the laws of this country in a manner that treats everyone equally. Sometimes, as in the case of Tommy McCoy, equal application of the law doesn't seem to make sense. Yet it would be unsettling if government employees interpreted rules as they pleased. Americans expect to be treated equally before the law, and bureaucrats work with that expectation in mind.

Problems in Implementing Policy

The development of policy in Washington is the end of one phase of the policymaking cycle and the beginning of another. After policies have been developed, they must be implemented. **Implementation** is the process of putting specific policies into operation. Ultimately, bureaucrats must convert policies on paper into policies in action. It is important to study implementation because policies do not always do what they were designed to do.

Implementation may be difficult because the policy to be carried out is not clearly stated. Policy directives to bureaucrats sometimes lack clarity and leave them with too much discretion. We have already mentioned the example of the FCC enforcing standards of "decency." Implementation can also be problematic because it often involves many different agencies and different layers of government. Take, for example, the case of reducing air

implementation
The process of putting specific policies into operation.

pollution in Los Angeles, a city that was afflicted with horrible smog. In 1977 Congress amended the Clean Air Act, which among other things shifted a great deal of responsibility to state, regional, and local institutions. The Environmental Protection Agency (EPA) still retained much authority and continued to issue regulations specifying standards. To implement these regulations in the Los Angeles region, the state of California created the South Coast Air Quality Management District. However, considerable jurisdiction over many sources of pollution lay with another body, the California Air Resources Board. Implementation also involved many city governments in the Los Angeles basin along with a number of transportation agencies.

Despite these challenges of divided responsibilities, considerable progress was made in reducing pollution and smog. But the national government then changed regulatory philosophies and in 1993 the EPA issued a new set of instructions. The new approach was to move away from "command and control" regulations (basically orders to be carried out) to market incentives. Both businesses and consumers were to be offered incentives to move toward less polluting technologies. Progress in reducing pollution was made through this approach as well. Los Angeles is now at the beginning of a third approach, one aimed at "sustainability." This approach aims at achieving an equilibrium in which pollution is offset by gains that improve the environment. In one analyst's words, this "would be a fundamental transformation in what Los Angelenos value in their personal and professional lives."[31] The implementation challenges are no less daunting.

Effective implementation takes time as processes must be established and continually improved so all stakeholders can negotiate and communicate effectively. There's a great deal of trial and error as bureaucrats learn what works and what doesn't, and what's efficient and what is too costly or

too slow. Trying to implement a program with little time for trial and error is an imposing problem. As noted earlier, when President Obama took office in January of 2009 the economy was in terrible shape and the housing market was in free fall. As housing prices plummeted, many owners found that they owed more money than the current worth of their homes and chose to default on their mortgages. For example, why continue to make payments on a $400,000 mortgage when the home's market value has dropped to $250,000? Others didn't want to default but could not make the payments because they'd lost their jobs.

The flood of foreclosed homes depressed prices further—the supply swamped the demand. Obama policymakers reasoned that there were many homeowners who wanted to stay in their homes rather than walk away from their mortgages, if only their monthly payments could be brought in line with what they could pay and the current value of the home. After all, for a bank that $400,000 mortgage was really worth only the $250,000 value of the house on the market if the owner defaulted. Moreover, the bank holding the mortgage would lose many months of payments between the time that an owner stopped making payments and was evicted and the time the house sold to new owners with a newly written mortgage.

Under enormous pressure from the Obama administration, banks agreed to a mortgage relief program. The banks then proceeded to run it abysmally. By December 2009, only 31,000 mortgages out of the 700,000 that banks had accepted into the program had been reconstituted into new mortgages with lower monthly payments. The program was floundering for several reasons. For one, the banks were implementing a policy they had little stake in seeing succeed. The banks received up to $3,000 for each mortgage successfully modified, but this was not a strong incentive as the bank could still repossess homes if no modification emerged. In addition, the banks didn't have systems set up to take on huge numbers of distressed properties. Their task was complicated because they had to determine which owners could meet lower payments and which were deadbeats and shouldn't be accepted into the program. The banks also blamed mortgage holders for not submitting all the paperwork required after a three-month trial modification.[32]

Clearly the sheer complexity of public policy problems makes implementation a challenge. The more organizations and levels of government involved, the more difficult it is to coordinate implementation. Moreover, many policies are implemented at the last stage not by government bureaucracies but by nonprofit or for-profit organizations hired under a contract to deliver a specific service. As will be discussed in the next section, "outsourcing" of government programs is very common. Government agencies devise, fund, and oversee programs but hire some other entity to run them. That adds another layer of participants and more opportunities for miscommunication, poor performance, and coordination problems.

Obstacles to effective implementation can create the impression that nothing the government does succeeds, but programs can and do work.[33] Problems in implementation demonstrate why patience and continual analysis are necessary ingredients of successful policymaking. The Los Angeles clean air example shows that implementation can succeed, even when the problem is complex. To return to a term we used earlier, implementation is by its nature an *incremental* process, in which trial and error eventually lead to policies that work. Even the mortgage relief program, poorly as it has performed, can be made to work if government and the banks make a commitment to improve it, with both necessary resources and attention to organizational processes.

Reforming the Bureaucracy: More Control or Less?

As we saw at the beginning of this chapter, organization matters. How bureaucracies are designed directly affects how effective they are in accomplishing their tasks. People in government constantly tinker with the structure of bureaucracies, trying to find ways to improve their performance. Administrative reforms have taken many different approaches as criticism of government has mounted.

In recent years three basic approaches to reforming the bureaucracy have attracted the most attention. First, advocates of *deregulation* envision eliminating layers of bureaucracy and reducing the rules that govern business markets with the market forces of supply and demand. Let consumer preferences dictate what products and services are offered. A second approach is directed at waste and inefficiency in government and promotes *competition* so that government services are offered by the lowest bidder from the public or private sector. Instead of a bureaucracy having a monopoly over a particular task, create incentives for that bureaucracy to continually find ways of doing the job more cheaply, thus saving the taxpayers money. Third, a range of reforms focuses on measuring agency performance. Instituting clear *performance standards* and holding bureaucrats accountable for meeting those standards should improve the quality and efficiency of government services.[34]

Deregulation

Many people believe that government is too involved in **regulation**, intervening in the natural working of business markets to promote some social goal. For example, government might regulate a market to ensure that products pose no danger to consumers. Through **deregulation**, the government reduces its role and lets the natural market forces of supply and demand take over. Conservatives have championed deregulation because they see freedom in the marketplace as the best route to an efficient and growing economy. Indeed, nothing is more central to capitalist philosophy than the belief that the free market will efficiently promote the balance of supply and demand. Considerable deregulation took place in the 1970s and 1980s, notably in the airline, trucking, financial services, and telecommunications industries.

In telecommunications, for example, consumers used to have no role in choosing a long-distance vendor—one could call on the Bell system or not call at all. After an out-of-court settlement broke up the Bell system in 1982, AT&T was awarded the right to sell the long-distance services that had previously been provided by that system, but it now had to face competition from newly emergent long-distance carriers. Deregulation for local phone service followed some years later, and consumers have benefited from the vigorous competition for their business in both realms. Few sectors of the economy have shown as much innovation and appeal as today's telephones and handhelds like iPhones and BlackBerries, which are essentially small computers that can be put in a pocket, backpack, or purse.

Deciding on an appropriate level of deregulation is especially difficult for health and safety issues. Companies within a particular industry may legitimately claim that health and safety regulations are burdensome, making it difficult for them to earn sufficient profits or compete effectively with foreign manufacturers. But the FDA's drug licensing procedures illustrate the potential danger of deregulating such policy areas. The thorough and lengthy process that the FDA uses to evaluate drugs has as its ultimate validation the thalidomide case. The William S. Merrell Company purchased the license to market this sedative, already available in Europe, and filed an application with the FDA in 1960. The company then began a protracted fight with an FDA bureaucrat, Dr. Frances Kelsey, who was assigned to evaluate the thalidomide application. She demanded that the company abide by all FDA drug testing requirements, despite the fact that the drug was already in use in other countries. She and her superiors resisted pressure from the company to bend the rules a little and expedite approval. Before Merrell had conducted all the FDA tests, news came pouring in from Europe that some women who had taken thalidomide during pregnancy were giving birth to babies without arms, legs, or ears. Strict adherence to government regulations protected Americans from the same tragic consequences.

regulation
Government intervention in the workings of a business market to promote some socially desired goal.

deregulation
A bureaucratic reform by which the government reduces its role as a regulator of business.

Some agencies have tried to move beyond rules that simply increase or decrease the amount of government control to regulatory processes that offer firms flexibility in meeting standards while at the same time protecting health and safety concerns. For example, the EPA has instituted flexible caps on air pollution at some manufacturing plants. Instead of having to request permits on new equipment and processes, plants are given an overall pollution cap and can decide on their own how to meet that limit. The overall caps are stricter than would otherwise be the case, but manufacturers gain by not having to wait for approvals for any changes and do not face uncertainty concerning the EPA's response.[35]

Efforts aimed at making organizations, typically corporations, more transparent and accountable in their actions are also gaining favor as another regulatory approach. For example, food manufacturers are now required to disclose information in packaging labels as to the quantity of trans-fats in the product. Regulations do not limit the amount of trans-fatty acids but, rather, give consumers the information and then let them decide how much is too much.[36] Transparency also extends to government, though not exclusively to regulatory issues. As noted in Chapter 2, e-government is expanding. Government bureaucracies at all levels are increasingly putting their working documents online so citizens can better understand policymaking choices.[37]

A strong case can be made for deregulated business markets, in which free and unfettered competition benefits consumers and promotes productivity. The strength of capitalist economies comes from the ability of individuals and firms to compete freely in the marketplace, and the regulatory state places restrictions on this freedom. But without regulation, nothing ensures that marketplace participants will act responsibly.

Competition and Outsourcing

Conservative critics of government have long complained that bureaucracies should act more like businesses, meaning they should try to emulate private sector practices that promote efficiency and innovation. Many recent reformers advocate something more drastic: unless bureaucracies can demonstrate that they are as efficient as the private sector, turn those agencies' functions over to the private sector. Underlying this idea is the belief that competition will make government more dynamic and more responsive to changing environments and will weaken the ability of labor unions to raise wages beyond those of nonunion employees.[38]

One widespread adaptation of competitive bidding to administer government programs has come in the area of social services. Over time government welfare programs have increasingly emphasized social services—giving people training and noncash support—rather than income maintenance (cash support). Social services are labor intensive, and state and local governments have found it efficient to outsource programs to nongovernmental organizations, principally nonprofit organizations like community health centers and day-care centers for elderly persons. Recently, for-profit companies have started to compete for the grants and contracts that the government awards through competitive

(Bettman/Corbis)

Bureaucratic Heroine

The government recognized Dr. Frances Kelsey's courageous work to keep Thalidomide off the American market with the President's Award for Distinguished Federal Civilian Service. The medal is being affixed here by President John F. Kennedy in 1962. In 2010, the Food and Drug Administration awarded its first annual Frances Kelsey Award to honor a staff member of the agency. Its first recipient: Dr. Frances Kelsey, now 96 years old.

grants or bidding. For example, the for-profit company Maximus holds a contract from the state of Connecticut to manage the state's program for providing child-care slots to poor families seeking such assistance.[39]

This movement toward **competition and outsourcing** continues to grow. More and more government jobs are open to bidding from nongovernment competitors, and sometimes a government bureau or office competes for the jobs and programs that they used to "own." As the number of federal government employees has declined while the population of Americans increases, some wonder if our country is building a "hollow state." By this, critics mean a government that is distinct from the programs it funds, disengaged from interaction with the people it serves.

Performance Standards

Another approach to improving the bureaucracy's performance is to focus on performance: To what degree does any individual agency accomplish the objectives that have been set for it? In this view, each agency is held accountable for reaching quantifiable goals each year or budget cycle. Under such a system, congressional and White House overseers examine each agency to see if it meets its objectives, and they reward or punish agencies accordingly. As one analyst noted, this is a philosophy of "*making* the managers manage."[40]

A major initiative to hold agencies accountable for their performance is the **Government Performance and Results Act**. Passed by Congress, it requires each agency to identify specific goals, adopt a performance plan, and develop quantitative indicators of agency progress in meeting its goals.[41] The law requires that agencies publish reports with performance data on each measure established. This is no small challenge. A case in point is the Healthy Start program funded by the Health Resources and Services Administration

competition and outsourcing
Procedures that allow private contractors to bid for jobs previously held exclusively by government employees.

Government Performance and Results Act
A law requiring each government agency to implement quantifiable standards to measure its performance in meeting stated program goals.

(HRSA) and intended to improve infant mortality rates and infant health generally. Among the specific goals are increasing the number of mothers receiving prenatal care during the first trimester and reducing the number of low-weight births. These are measurable, and the hospitals and health centers receiving federal funding for Healthy Start must report the appropriate data to HRSA. More complicated is the degree to which this program makes a difference since infant health can be influenced by many factors.[42]

Another problem is that since agencies set their own goals and know they'll be judged on meeting them, they may select indicators where they know they'll do best.[43] Or if standards that have been set prove to be too difficult to achieve, standards may be lowered, sometimes under the guise of "reform," to make them work better. The Department of Education's No Child Left Behind program was envisioned as a means for forcing underperforming schools to raise their students up to the reading and math standards prescribed for each grade level. Although the law is that of the national government, states were allowed to implement the program in their own way. Over time many states reduced their standards because their schools could not improve enough to meet the model guidelines of a national test of students. Between 2005 and 2007, fifteen states lowered the bar for student performance. Other states had already lowered their standards (see Figure 13.4). In short,

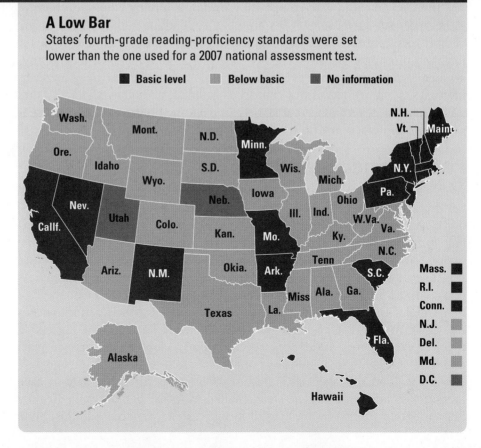

FIGURE 13.4   Meeting Performance Standards a Problem? Just Lower Them

School districts across the country have had trouble meeting performance standards designed to push individual schools to change priorities and revise their curricula. As a result, many states have simply lowered their standards so that more school districts in the state meet requirements under the No Child Left Behind Act.

A Low Bar
States' fourth-grade reading-proficiency standards were set lower than the one used for a 2007 national assessment test.

■ Basic level   ■ Below basic   ■ No information

Source: John Hechninger, "Some States Drop Testing Bar," *Wall Street Journal,* 30 October 2009.

performance-based management runs the risk of perverting an agency's incentives toward what it can achieve rather than what would be most valuable to achieve.

Despite the relative appeal of these different approaches to improving the bureaucracy, each has serious shortcomings. There is no magic bullet. The commitment of the government to solve a problem is far more important than management techniques. Still, to return to a theme that we began with, organization does matter. Trying to find ways of improving the bureaucracy is important because bureaucracies affect people's lives, and enhancing their performance, even at the margins, has real consequences.

Summary

As the scope of government activity has grown during the twentieth and early twenty-first centuries, so too has the bureaucracy. The executive branch has evolved into a complex set of departments, independent agencies, and government corporations. The way in which the various bureaucracies are organized matters a great deal because their structure affects their ability to carry out their tasks.

Operating under the administrative discretion granted them by Congress, these bodies make policy decisions through rules that have the force of law. In making policy choices, agency decision makers are influenced by their external environment, especially the White House, Congress, and interest groups. Internal norms and the need to work cooperatively with others both inside and outside their agencies also influence decision makers.

The most serious charge facing the bureaucracy is that it is unresponsive to the will of the people. In fact, the White House, Congress, interest groups, and public opinion act as substantial controls on the bureaucracy. Still, to many Americans, the bureaucracy seems too big, too costly, and too intrusive. Reducing the size and scope of bureaucratic activity is difficult because pluralism characterizes our political system. The entire executive branch may appear too large, and each of us can point to agencies that we believe should be reduced or eliminated. Yet each bureaucracy has its supporters. The Department of Agriculture performs vital services for farmers. Unions care a great deal about the Department of Labor. Scholars want the National Science Foundation protected. And home builders do not want Housing and Urban Development programs cut back. Bureaucracies survive because they provide important services to groups of people, and those people—no matter how strong their commitment to shrinking the government—are not willing to sacrifice their own benefits.

Plans for reforming the bureaucracy to make it work better are not in short supply. Broad-scale reforms include deregulation, competition and outsourcing, and performance standards. Each has merits and offers plausible mechanisms for improving government efficiency and responsiveness. Each has shortcomings as well, and advocates often overlook the tradeoffs and problems associated with these reforms. Yet it is important to keep trying to find ways of improving government because most people continue to believe that the overall management of bureaucracies is poor and that government needs to be more customer-driven.

CourseMate   Visit www.cengagebrain.com/shop/ISBN/0495906182 for flashcards, web quizzes, videos and more!

CHAPTER

14 The Courts

Matthew Cavanaugh/epa/Corbis

W hen Chief Justice Fred M. Vinson died unexpectedly in September 1953, his colleague Associate Justice Felix Frankfurter commented, "This is the first solid piece of evidence I've ever had that there really is a God."[1] Frankfurter despised Vinson as a leader and disliked him as a person. Vinson's sudden death would bring a new colleague—and perhaps new hope—to the school desegregation cases known collectively as *Brown* v. *Board of Education*. The issue of segregated schools had arrived in the Supreme Court in late 1951. Although the Court had originally scheduled oral argument for October 1952, the justices elected a postponement until December and merged several similar cases. When a law clerk expressed puzzlement at the delay, Frankfurter explained that the Court was holding the cases for the outcome of the national election in 1952. "I thought the Court was supposed to decide without regard to elections," declared the clerk. "When you have a major social political issue of this magnitude," replied Frankfurter, "we do not think this is the time to decide it."[2]

The justices were at loggerheads following the December argument, with Vinson unwilling to invalidate racial segregation in public education. Because the justices were not ready to reach a decision, they scheduled the cases for reargument the following year. The justices asked the attorneys to address the history of the Fourteenth Amendment and the potential remedies if the Court ruled against segregation.

Frankfurter's caustic remark about Vinson's death reflected the critical role Vinson's replacement would

play when the Court again tackled the desegregation issue. In his first appointment to the nation's highest court, President Dwight D. Eisenhower chose California's Republican governor, Earl Warren, as chief justice. The president would later regret his choice.

When the Court heard the reargument of *Brown* v. *Board of Education* in late 1953, the new chief justice led his colleagues from division to unanimity on the issue of public school segregation. Unlike his predecessor, Warren began the secret conference to decide the segregation issue with a strong statement: that segregation was contrary to the Thirteenth, Fourteenth, and Fifteenth amendments to the Constitution. "Personally," remarked the new chief justice, "I can't see how today we can justify segregation based solely on race."[3] Moreover, if the Court were to uphold segregation, he argued, it could do so only on the theory that blacks were inherently inferior to whites. As the discussion proceeded, Warren's opponents were cast in the awkward position of appearing to support racism.

Five justices were clearly on Warren's side, making six votes; two were prepared to join the majority if Warren's reasoning satisfied them. With only one clear holdout, Warren set about the task of responding to his colleagues' concerns. In the months that followed, he met with them individually in their chambers, reviewing the decision and the justification that would accompany it. Finally, in April 1954, Warren approached Justice Stanley Reed, whose vote would make the opinion unanimous. "Stan," said the chief justice, "you're all by yourself in this now. You've got to decide whether it's really the best thing for the country." Ultimately, Reed joined the others. On May 17, 1954, the Supreme Court unanimously ruled against racial segregation in public schools, signaling the end of legally created or government-enforced segregation of the races in the United States.[4]

Judges confront conflicting values in the cases before them, and in crafting their decisions, they—especially Supreme Court justices—make policy. Their decisions become the precedents other judges use to rule in similar cases. One judge in one court makes public policy to the extent that she or he influences other decisions in other courts.

The power of the courts to shape public policy creates a difficult problem for democratic theory. According to that theory, the power to make law resides only in the people or the people's elected representatives. When judges undo the work of elected majorities (which was surely the case with government-sponsored racial separation), they risk depriving the people of the right to make the laws or to govern themselves.

Court rulings—especially Supreme Court rulings—extend far beyond any particular case. Judges are students of the law, but they remain human beings. They have their own opinions about the values of freedom, order, and equality. And although all judges are constrained by statutes and precedents from imposing their personal will on others through their decisions, some judges are more prone than others to interpreting the law in the light of those beliefs.

America's courts are deeply involved in the life of the country and its people. Some courts, such as the Supreme Court, make fundamental policy decisions vital to the preservation of freedom, order, and equality. Through checks and balances, the elected branches link the courts to democracy, and the courts link the elected branches to the Constitution. But does this system work? Can the courts exercise political power within the pluralist model? Or are judges simply sovereigns in black robes, making decisions independent of popular control? In this chapter, we examine these questions by exploring the role of the courts in American political life.

National Judicial Supremacy

Section 1 of Article III of the Constitution creates "one supreme Court." The founders were divided on the need for other national courts, so they deferred to Congress the decision to create a national court system. Those who opposed the creation of national courts believed that such a system would usurp the authority of state courts.[5] Congress considered the issue in its first session and, in the Judiciary Act of 1789, gave life to a system of federal (that is, national) courts that would coexist with the courts in each state but be independent of them. Federal judges would also be independent of popular influences because the Constitution provided for their lifetime appointment.

In the early years of the Republic, the federal judiciary was not a particularly powerful branch of government. It was especially difficult to recruit

IN OUR OWN WORDS

Listen to Jerry Goldman discuss the main points and themes of this chapter.

www.cengagebrain.com/
shop/ISBN/0495906182

"Keep Away from the Doors!"

On May 4, 2010, the Supreme Court shut its grand bronze doors, with their panels depicting the development of law, to those seeking to enter the building. For security reasons, entry has been directed to the ground level. It will still be possible to exit through the bronze doors. Justice Stephen G. Breyer, joined by Justice Ruth Bader Ginsburg, issued a statement expressing regret at the policy. "This court's main entrance and front steps," he wrote, "are not only a means to, but also a metaphor for, access to the court itself."

(STEPHEN CROWLEY/The New York Times/Redux Pictures)

and keep Supreme Court justices. They spent much of their time as individual traveling judges ("riding circuit"); disease and poor transportation were everyday hazards. The justices met as the Supreme Court only for a few weeks in February and August.[6] John Jay, the first chief justice, refused to resume his duties in 1801 because he concluded that the Court could not muster the "energy, weight, and dignity" to contribute to national affairs.[7] Several distinguished statesmen refused appointments to the Court, and several others, including Oliver Ellsworth, the third chief justice, resigned. But a period of profound change began in 1801 when President John Adams appointed his secretary of state, John Marshall, to the position of chief justice.

Judicial Review of the Other Branches

Shortly after Marshall's appointment, the Supreme Court confronted a question of fundamental importance to the future of the new republic: If a law enacted by Congress conflicts with the U.S. Constitution, which should prevail? The question arose in the case of *Marbury* v. *Madison* (1803), which involved a controversial series of last-minute political appointments.[8]

**Chief Justice
John Marshall**

John Marshall (1755–1835) clearly ranks as the Babe Ruth of the Supreme Court. Both Marshall and the Bambino transformed their respective games and became symbols of their institutions. Scholars now recognize both men as originators—Marshall of judicial review and Ruth of the modern age of baseball.

(National Portrait Gallery, Smithsonian Institution/Art Resource, NY)

The case began in 1801 when an obscure Federalist, William Marbury, was designated a justice of the peace in the District of Columbia. Marbury and several others were appointed to government posts created by Congress in the last days of John Adams's presidency, but the appointments were never completed. The newly arrived Jefferson administration had little interest in delivering the required documents; qualified Jeffersonians would welcome the jobs.

To secure their jobs, Marbury and the other disgruntled appointees invoked an act of Congress to obtain the papers. The act authorized the Supreme Court to issue orders against government officials. Marbury and the others sought such an order in the Supreme Court against the new secretary of state, James Madison, who held the crucial documents.

Marshall observed that the act of Congress that Marbury invoked to sue in the Supreme Court conflicted with Article III of the U.S. Constitution, which did not authorize such suits. In February 1803, the Court delivered its opinion.*

Must the Court follow the law or the Constitution? The High Court held, in Marshall's forceful argument, that the Constitution was "the fundamental and paramount law of the nation" and that "an act of the legislature, repugnant to the constitution, is void." In other words, when an act of the legislature conflicts with the Constitution—the nation's highest law—that act is invalid. Marshall's argument vested in the judiciary the power to weigh the validity of congressional acts:

> It is emphatically the province and duty of the judicial department to say what the law is. Those who apply the rule to particular cases, must of necessity expound and interpret that rule.... So if a law be in opposition to the constitution; if both the law and the constitution apply to a particular case, so that the court must either decide that case conformably to the law, disregarding the constitution; or conformably to the constitution, disregarding the law; the court must determine which of these conflicting rules governs the case. This is of the very essence of judicial duty.[9]

The decision in *Marbury* v. *Madison* established the Supreme Court's power of **judicial review**—the power to declare congressional acts invalid if they violate the Constitution.† Subsequent cases extended the power to cover presidential acts as well.[10]

---

*Courts publish their opinions in volumes called *reporters*. Today, the *United States Reports* is the official reporter for the U.S. Supreme Court. For example, the Court's opinion in the case of *Brown* v. *Board of Education* is cited as 347 U.S. 483 (1954). This means that the opinion in *Brown* begins on page 483 of Volume 347 in *United States Reports*. The citation includes the year of the decision, in this case, 1954.

Before 1875, the official reports of the Supreme Court were published under the names of private compilers. For example, the case of *Marbury* v. *Madison* is cited as 1 Cranch 137 (1803). This means that the case is found in Volume 1, compiled by reporter William Cranch, starting on page 137, and that it was decided in 1803.

†The Supreme Court had earlier upheld an act of Congress in *Hylton* v. United States (3 Dallas 171 [1796]). *Marbury* v. Madison was the first exercise of the power of a court to invalidate an act of Congress.

judicial review
The power to declare congressional (and presidential) acts invalid because they violate the Constitution.

Marshall expanded the potential power of the Supreme Court to equal or exceed the power of the other branches of government. Should a congressional act (or, by implication, a presidential act) conflict with the Constitution, the Supreme Court claimed the power to declare the act void. The judiciary would be a check on the legislative and executive branches, consistent with the principle of checks and balances embedded in the Constitution. Although Congress and the president may sometimes wrestle with the constitutionality of their actions, judicial review gave the Supreme Court the final word on the meaning of the Constitution. The exercise of judicial review—an appointed branch's checking of an elected branch in the name of the Constitution—appears to run counter to democratic theory. But in more than two hundred years of practice, the Supreme Court has invalidated only about 160 provisions of national law. Only a small number have had great significance for the political system.[11] (Since 1994, with conservative justices in the majority, the Court has struck down more than 30 acts of Congress, several of them important expressions of public policy.) The Constitution provides mechanisms to override judicial review (constitutional amendments) and to control excesses of the justices (impeachment), but these steps are more theoretical than practical. In addition, the Court can respond to the continuing struggle among competing interests (a struggle that is consistent with the pluralist model) by reversing itself. It has done so only 230 times in its entire history.[12]

Judicial Review of State Government

The establishment of judicial review of national laws made the Supreme Court the umpire of the national government. When acts of the national government conflict with the Constitution, the Supreme Court can declare those acts invalid. But suppose state laws conflict with the Constitution, national laws, or federal treaties: Can the U.S. Supreme Court invalidate them as well?

The Court answered in the affirmative in 1796. The case involved a British creditor who was trying to collect a debt from the state of Virginia.[13] Virginia law canceled debts owed to British subjects, yet the Treaty of Paris (1783), in which Britain formally acknowledged the independence of the colonies, guaranteed that creditors could collect such debts. The Court ruled that the Constitution's supremacy clause (Article VI), which embraces national laws and treaties, nullified the state law.

The states continued to resist the yoke of national supremacy. Advocates of strong states' rights conceded that the supremacy clause obligates state judges to follow the Constitution when state law conflicts with it; however, they maintained that the states were bound only by their own interpretation of the Constitution. The Supreme Court said no, ruling that it had the authority to review state court decisions calling for the interpretation of national law.[14] National supremacy required the Supreme Court to impose uniformity on national law; otherwise, the Constitution's meaning would vary from state to state. The people, not the states, had ordained the Constitution, and the people had subordinated state power to establish a viable national government. In time, the Supreme Court would use its judicial review power in nearly twelve hundred instances to invalidate state and local laws, on issues as diverse as abortion, the death penalty, the rights of the accused, and reapportionment.[15]

The Exercise of Judicial Review

These early cases, coupled with other historic decisions, established the components of judicial review:

- The power of the courts to declare national, state, and local laws invalid if they violate the Constitution
- The supremacy of national laws or treaties when they conflict with state and local laws
- The role of the Supreme Court as the final authority on the meaning of the Constitution

This political might—the power to undo decisions of the representative branches of the national and state governments—lay in the hands of appointed judges, that is, people who were not accountable to the electorate. Did judicial review square with democratic government?

Alexander Hamilton had foreseen and tackled the problem in *Federalist* No. 78. Writing during the ratification debates surrounding the adoption of the Constitution (see Chapter 3), Hamilton maintained that despite the power of judicial review, the judiciary would be the weakest of the three branches of government because it lacked the strength of the sword or the purse. The judiciary, wrote Hamilton, had "neither FORCE nor WILL, but merely judgment."

Although Hamilton was defending legislative supremacy, he argued that judicial review was an essential barrier to legislative oppression.[16] He recognized that the power to declare government acts void implied the superiority of the courts over the other branches. But this power, he contended, simply reflects the will of the people, declared in the Constitution, as opposed to the will of the legislature, expressed in its statutes. Judicial independence, guaranteed by lifetime tenure and protected salaries, frees judges from executive and legislative control, minimizing the risk of their deviating from the law established in the Constitution. If judges make a mistake, the people or their elected representatives have the means to correct the error, through constitutional amendments and impeachment.

Their lifetime tenure does free judges from the direct influence of the president and Congress. And although mechanisms to check judicial power are in place, these mechanisms require extraordinary majorities and are rarely used. When they exercise the power of judicial review, then, judges can and occasionally do operate counter to majoritarian rule by invalidating the actions of the people's elected representatives.

The Organization of Courts

The American court system is complex, partly as a result of our federal system of government. Each state runs its own court system, and no two states' courts are identical. In addition, we have a system of courts for the national government. The national, or federal, courts coexist with the state courts (see Figure 14.1). Individuals fall under the jurisdiction of both court systems. They can sue or be sued in either system, depending mostly on what their case is about. Litigants file nearly all cases (99 percent) in state courts. State trial courts receive on average one civil, domestic relations, criminal, juvenile, or traffic case for every three citizens. The volume of state court cases continues to rise at about 1 percent a year, due largely to contract disputes.[17]

Some Court Fundamentals

Courts are full of mystery to citizens uninitiated in their activities. Lawyers, judges, and seasoned observers understand the language, procedures, and norms associated with legal institutions. Let's start with some fundamentals.

Criminal and Civil Cases. A crime is a violation of a law that forbids or commands an activity. Criminal laws are created, amended, and repealed by state legislatures. These laws and the punishments for violating them are recorded in each state's penal code. Some crimes—murder, rape, arson—are on the books of every state. Others—marijuana use, for example—are considered crimes in certain states but not all. Because crime is a violation of public order, the government prosecutes **criminal cases**. Maintaining public order through the criminal law is largely a state and local function. Criminal cases brought by the national government represent only a small fraction of all criminal cases prosecuted in the United States. In theory, the national penal code is limited by the principle of federalism. The code is aimed at activities that fall under the delegated and implied powers of the national government, enabling the government, for example, to criminalize tax evasion or the use of computers and laser printers to counterfeit money, bank checks, or even college transcripts.

Fighting crime is popular, and politicians sometimes outbid one another in their efforts to get tough on criminals. National crime-fighting measures have begun to usurp areas long viewed to be under state authority. Since 1975, Congress has added hundreds of new federal criminal provisions covering a wide range of activities once thought to be within the states' domain, including carjacking, willful failure to pay child support, and crossing state lines to engage in gang-related street crime.[18]

Courts decide both criminal and civil cases. **Civil cases** stem from disputed claims to something of value. Disputes arise from accidents, contractual obligations, and divorce, for example. Often the parties disagree over tangible issues (possession of property, custody of children), but civil cases can involve more abstract issues too (the right to equal accommodations,

criminal cases
Court cases involving a crime, or violation of public order.

civil cases
Court cases that involve a private dispute arising from such matters as accidents, contractual obligations, and divorce.

FIGURE 14.1   The Federal and State Court Systems, 2008–2009

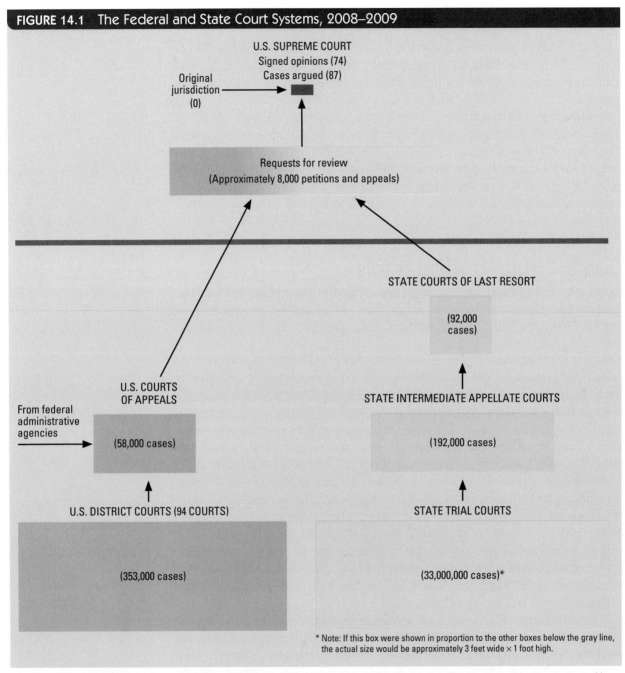

U.S. SUPREME COURT
Signed opinions (74)
Cases argued (87)

Original jurisdiction (0)

Requests for review
(Approximately 8,000 petitions and appeals)

STATE COURTS OF LAST RESORT

(92,000 cases)

U.S. COURTS OF APPEALS

From federal administrative agencies

(58,000 cases)

STATE INTERMEDIATE APPELLATE COURTS

(192,000 cases)

U.S. DISTRICT COURTS (94 COURTS)

(353,000 cases)

STATE TRIAL COURTS

(33,000,000 cases)*

* Note: If this box were shown in proportion to the other boxes below the gray line,
the actual size would be approximately 3 feet wide × 1 foot high.

The federal courts have three tiers: district courts, courts of appeals, and the Supreme Court. The Supreme Court was created by the Constitution; all other federal courts were created by Congress. State courts dwarf federal courts, at least in terms of case load. There are more than one hundred state cases for every federal case filed. The structure of state courts varies from state to state; usually there are minor trial courts for less serious cases, major trial courts for more serious cases, intermediate appellate courts, and supreme courts. State courts were created by state constitutions.

Sources: John Roberts, "The 2009 Year-End Report on the Federal Judiciary," Dec. 31, 2009, http://www.supremecourt.gov/publicinfo/year-end/2009year-endreport.pdf; *Federal Court Management Statistics 2009,* http://www.uscourts.gov/fcmstat/index.html; Court Statistics Project, *State Court Caseload Statistics, 2007* (Williamsburg, Va.: National Center for State Courts, 2009), Table 10, p. 153, http://www.ncsconline.org/D_Research/csp/CSP_Main_Page.html.

compensation for pain and suffering). The government can be a party to civil disputes, called on to defend its actions or to allege wrongdoing.

Procedures and Policymaking. Most civil and criminal cases never go to trial. In most criminal cases, the defendant's lawyer and the prosecutor **plea-bargain**, negotiating the severity and number of charges to be brought against the defendant. In a civil case, one side may only be using the threat of a lawsuit to exact a concession from the other. Often the parties *settle* (or resolve the dispute between themselves) because of the uncertainties in litigation. Though rare, settlement can occur even at the level of the Supreme Court. And sometimes the initiating parties (the plaintiffs in civil cases) may simply abandon their efforts, leaving disputes unresolved.

When cases are neither settled nor abandoned, they end with an *adjudication,* a court judgment resolving the parties' claims and enforced by the government. When trial judges adjudicate cases, they may offer written reasons to support their decisions. When the issues or circumstances of cases are novel, judges may publish *opinions,* explanations justifying their rulings.

Judges make policy in two different ways. The first is through their rulings on matters that no existing legislation addresses. Such rulings set precedents that judges rely on in future, similar cases. We call this body of rules the **common, or judge-made, law**. The roots of the common law lie in the English legal system. Contracts, property, and torts (injuries or wrongs to the person or property of another) are common-law domains. The second area of judicial lawmaking involves the application of statutes enacted by legislatures. The judicial interpretation of legislative acts is called *statutory construction.* The proper application of a statute is not always clear from its wording. To determine how a statute should be applied, judges look for the legislature's intent, reading reports of committee hearings and debates. If these sources do not clarify the statute's meaning, the court does so. With or without legislation to guide them, judges look to the relevant opinions of higher courts for authority to decide the issues before them.

The federal courts are organized in three tiers, as a pyramid. At the bottom of the pyramid are the **U.S. district courts**, where litigation begins. In the middle are the **U.S. courts of appeals**. At the top is the Supreme Court of the United States. To *appeal* means to take a case to a higher court. The courts of appeals and the Supreme Court are appellate courts; with few exceptions, they review only cases that have already been decided in lower courts. Most federal courts hear and decide a wide array of civil and criminal cases.

The U.S. District Courts

There are ninety-four federal district courts in the United States. Each state has at least one district court, and no district straddles more than one state.[19] In 2006, there were 678 full-time federal district judgeships, and they received over 353,000 new criminal and civil cases.[20]

plea bargain
A defendant's admission of guilt in exchange for a less severe punishment.

common, or judge-made, law
Legal precedents derived from previous judicial decisions.

U.S. district courts
Courts within the lowest tier of the three-tiered federal court system; courts where litigation begins.

U.S. courts of appeals
Courts within the second tier of the three-tiered federal court system, to which decisions of the district courts and federal agencies may be appealed for review.

The district courts are the entry point for the federal court system. When trials occur in the federal system, they take place in the federal district courts. Here is where witnesses testify, lawyers conduct cross-examinations, and judges and juries decide the fate of litigants. More than one judge may sit in each district court, but each case is tried by a single judge, sitting alone. U.S. magistrate judges assist district judges, but they lack independent judicial authority. Magistrate judges have the power to hear and decide minor offenses and conduct preliminary stages of more serious cases. District court judges appoint magistrate judges for eight-year (full-time) or four-year (part-time) terms. In 2009, there were 466 full-time and 60 part-time magistrate judges.[21]

Sources of Litigation. Today the authority of U.S. district courts extends to the following:

- Federal criminal cases, as defined by national law (for example, robbery of a nationally insured bank or interstate transportation of stolen securities)
- Civil cases, brought by individuals, groups, or the government, alleging violation of national law (for example, failure of a municipality to implement pollution-control regulations required by a national agency)
- Civil cases brought against the national government (for example, a vehicle manufacturer sues the motor pool of a government agency for its failure to take delivery of a fleet of new cars)
- Civil cases between citizens of different states when the amount in controversy exceeds $75,000 (for example, when a citizen of New York sues a citizen of Alabama in a U.S. district court in Alabama for damages stemming from an auto accident that occurred in Alabama)

The U.S. Courts of Appeals

All cases resolved in a U.S. district court and all decisions of federal administrative agencies can be appealed to one of the twelve regional U.S. courts of appeals. These courts, with 167 full-time judgeships, received nearly 58,000 new cases in 2009.[22] Each appeals court hears cases from a geographical area known as a *circuit*. The U.S. Court of Appeals for the Seventh Circuit, for example, is located in Chicago; it hears appeals from the U.S. district courts in Illinois, Wisconsin, and Indiana. The United States is divided into twelve circuits.*

Appellate Court Proceedings. Appellate court proceedings are public, but they usually lack courtroom drama. There are no jurors, witnesses, or cross-examinations; these are features only of the trial courts. Appeals are based strictly on the rulings made and procedures followed in the trial courts.

---

*The thirteenth court, the U.S. Court of Appeals for the Federal Circuit, is not a regional court. It specializes in appeals involving patents, contract claims against the national government, and federal employment cases.

Suppose, for example, that in the course of a criminal trial, a U.S. district judge allows the introduction of evidence that convicts a defendant but was obtained under questionable circumstances. The defendant can appeal on the grounds that the evidence was obtained in the absence of a valid search warrant and so was inadmissible. The issue on appeal is the admissibility of the evidence, not the defendant's guilt or innocence. If the appellate court agrees with the trial judge's decision to admit the evidence, the conviction stands. If the appellate court disagrees with the trial judge and rules that the evidence is inadmissible, the defendant must be retried without the incriminating evidence or be released.

The courts of appeals are regional courts. They usually convene in panels of three judges to render judgments. The judges receive written arguments known as *briefs* (which are also sometimes submitted in trial courts). Often the judges hear oral arguments and question the lawyers to probe their arguments.

Precedents and Making Decisions. Following review of the briefs and, in many appeals, oral arguments, the three-judge panel meets to reach a judgment. One judge attempts to summarize the panel's views, although each judge remains free to disagree with the judgment or the reasons for it. When an appellate opinion is published, its influence can reach well beyond the immediate case. For example, a lawsuit turning on the meaning of the Constitution produces a ruling, which then serves as a **precedent** for subsequent cases; that is, the decision becomes a basis for deciding similar cases in the future in the same way. Thus, judges make public policy to the extent that they influence decisions in other courts. Although district judges sometimes publish their opinions, it is the exception rather than the rule. At the appellate level, however, precedent requires that opinions be written.

Making decisions according to precedent is central to the operation of our legal system, providing continuity and predictability. The bias in favor of existing decisions is captured by the Latin expression *stare decisis,* which means "let the decision stand." But the use of precedent and the principle of **stare decisis** do not make lower-court judges cogs in a judicial machine. "If precedent clearly governed," remarked one federal judge, "a case would never get as far as the Court of Appeals: the parties would settle."[23]

Judges on the courts of appeals direct their energies to correcting errors in district court proceedings and interpreting the law (in the course of writing opinions). When judges interpret the law, they often modify existing laws. In effect, they are making policy. Judges are politicians in the sense that they exercise political power, but the black robes that distinguish judges from other politicians signal constraints on their exercise of power.

Uniformity of Law. Decisions by the courts of appeals ensure a measure of uniformity in the application of national law. For example, when similar issues are dealt with in the decisions of different district judges, the decisions may be inconsistent. The courts of appeals harmonize the decisions within their region so that laws are applied uniformly.

precedent
A judicial ruling that serves as the basis for the ruling in a subsequent case.

stare decisis
Literally, "let the decision stand"; decision making according to precedent.

The regional character of the courts of appeals undermines uniformity somewhat because the courts are not bound by the decisions of other circuits. A law may be interpreted differently in different courts of appeals. For example, the Internal Revenue Code imposes identical tax burdens on similar individuals. But thanks to the regional character of the courts of appeals, national tax laws may be applied differently throughout the United States. The percolation of cases up through the federal system of courts virtually guarantees that at some point, two or more courts of appeals, working with similar sets of facts, are going to interpret the same law differently. However, the problem of conflicting decisions in the intermediate appellate courts can be corrected by review in the Supreme Court, where policymaking, not error correction, is the paramount goal.

The Supreme Court

Above the west portico of the Supreme Court building are inscribed the words EQUAL JUSTICE UNDER LAW. At the opposite end of the building, above the east portico, are the words JUSTICE THE GUARDIAN OF LIBERTY. The mottos reflect the Court's difficult task: achieving a just balance among the values of freedom, order, and equality. Consider how these values came into conflict in two controversial issues the Court has faced.

Flag burning as a form of political protest pits the value of order, or the government's interest in maintaining a peaceful society, against the value of freedom, including the individual's right to vigorous and unbounded political expression. In two flag-burning cases, the Supreme Court affirmed constitutional protection for unbridled political expression, including the emotionally charged act of desecrating a national symbol.[24] Because under a pluralist system no decision is ever truly final, the flag-burning decisions hardly quelled the demand for laws to punish flag desecration. In 2006, Congress inched ever so close to a constitutional amendment banning flag desecration. The proposal passed by more than a two-thirds vote in the House but failed by a single vote in the Senate.

School desegregation pits the value of equality against the value of freedom. In *Brown* v. *Board of Education* (1954), the Supreme Court carried the banner of racial equality by striking down state-mandated segregation in public schools. The decision helped launch a revolution in race relations in the United States. The justices recognized the disorder their decision would create in a society accustomed to racial bias, but in this case, equality clearly outweighed freedom. Twenty-four years later, the Court was still embroiled in controversy over equality when it ruled that race could be a factor in university admissions (to diversify the student body).[25] Having secured equality for blacks, the Court in 2003 faced the charge by white students who sought admission to the University of Michigan that it was denying whites the freedom to compete for admission. A slim Court majority concluded that the equal protection clause of the Fourteenth Amendment did not prohibit the narrowly tailored use of race as *a* factor in law school admissions but

The Supreme Court, 2010 Term: The Lineup

The justices of the Supreme Court of the United States. Seated are (left to right) Clarence Thomas, Antonin Scalia, Chief Justice John G. Roberts, Jr., Anthony Kennedy, and Ruth Bader Ginsburg. Standing are Sonia Sotomayor, Stephen J. Breyer, Samuel A. Alito, and Elena Kagan.

(Steve Petteway, Collection of the Supreme Court of the United States)

rejected the automatic use of racial categories to award fixed points toward undergraduate admissions.[26]

The Supreme Court makes national policy. Because its decisions have far-reaching effects on all of us, it is vital that we understand how it reaches those decisions. With this understanding, we can better evaluate how the Court fits within our model of democracy. Great Britain is the latest democracy to establish a supreme court (see Compared with What? A Supreme Court of Its Own).

IDEALOG.ORG

Do you support or oppose affirmative action? After reading the material here, would your answer be the same? Take IDEAlog's self-test.

Access to the Court

There are rules of access that must be followed to bring a case to the Supreme Court. Also important is a sensitivity to the justices' policy and ideological preferences. The notion that anyone can take a case all the way to the Supreme Court is true only in theory, not fact.

The Supreme Court's cases come from two sources. A few arrive under the Court's **original jurisdiction**, conferred by Article III, Section 2, of the Constitution, which gives the Court the power to hear and decide "all Cases affecting Ambassadors, other public Ministers and Consuls, and those in which a State shall be Party." Cases falling under the Court's original jurisdiction are tried and decided in the Court itself; the cases begin and end there. For example, the Court is the first and only forum in which legal disputes between states are resolved. It hears few original jurisdiction cases today, however, usually referring them to a special master, often a retired

original jurisdiction
The authority of a court to hear a case before any other court does.

Compared with What?

A Supreme Court of Its Own

The opening of the United Kingdom's Supreme Court marks the culmination of a long process of separation of the judiciary from the legislature and the executive.[1]

Jack Straw, Justice Secretary and Lord Chancellor

More than two centuries after its inception, the American model of separation of powers continues to influence the structure of government. Its influence is not confined to new democracies. The United Kingdom—one of the oldest democracies in the world—recently created a Supreme Court to decide on all matters under English, Welsh, and Northern Irish law and under Scottish civil law.[2] Prior to October 2009, a committee of the House of Lords (the upper chamber of the British Parliament) exercised these judicial functions, coupling the legislative and judicial branches of government.

The new twelve-member court is now independent of Parliament and is located at a highly symbolic location, "balancing judiciary and legislature across the open

Newscom

judge, who reviews the parties' contentions and recommends a resolution that the justices are free to accept or reject.

Most cases enter the Supreme Court from the U.S. courts of appeals or the state courts of last resort. This is the Court's **appellate jurisdiction**. These cases have been tried, decided, and reexamined as far as the law permits in other federal or state courts. The Court exercises judicial power under its

appellate jurisdiction
The authority of a court to hear cases that have been tried, decided, or reexamined in other courts.

space of Parliament Square, with the other two sides occupied by the executive (the Treasury building) and the church (Westminster Abbey)."[3] According to Lord Phillips of Worth Matravers, the president of the Supreme Court, "This is the last step in the separation of powers in this country.... We have come to it fairly gently and gradually, but we have come to the point where the judges are completely separated from the legislature and executive."[4]

A steady process of policy devolution has accompanied the decoupling of judicial and legislative functions from London to the regional administrations of Scotland, Wales, and Northern Ireland. This devolution signals an increasing "federalization" of the United Kingdom, in the sense that regional jurisdictions are becoming more autonomous from the central government. The new Supreme Court is also the final court of appeal for all devolution matters, "that is, issues about whether the devolved executive and legislative authorities in Scotland, Wales and Northern Ireland have acted or propose to act within their powers or have failed to comply with any other duty imposed on them."[5]

Supporters of the Supreme Court celebrate the transparency of their new institution. Hearings will be open to the public and broadcast on television. (The U.S. Supreme Court continues to resist televising its proceedings.) Opponents, on the other hand, consider the change mainly a cosmetic makeover and emphasize that the workings of the recently created Court will be the same as they were when the House of Lords was in charge.[6] One observer commented ominously: "The danger is that you muck around with a constitution like the British Constitution at your peril because you do not know what the consequences of any change will be."[7] Time will tell whether the Supreme Court plays a vital role in the United Kingdom's internal affairs and its relationship with Europe. Conflicts between freedom and order and between freedom and equality will arise in its chambers. Balancing these values remains the challenge of this democracy.

---

[1]Speech given at the official opening of the U.K. Supreme Court, 16 October 2009, available at the Ministry of Justice website, http://www.justice.gov.uk/news/speech161009a.htm (accessed 2 December 2009).

[2]The U.K. Supreme Court has no jurisdiction over criminal proceedings from the High Court of Justiciary or any other court in Scotland. Supreme Court of the United Kingdom, *Practice Direction 1*, Article 1.2.10, http://www.supremecourt.gov.uk/docs/pd01.pdf (accessed 2 December 2009).

[3]Information available at the website of the U.K. Supreme Court, http://www.supremecourt.gov.uk/docs/pd01.pdf (accessed 2 December 2009).

[4]"UK Supreme Court Judges Sworn In," BBC News Online Edition, 1 October 2009, http://news.bbc.co.uk/2/hi/uk_news/8283939.stm (accessed 2 December 2009).

[5]Ibid.

[6]Nevertheless, the new justices are unable to sit and vote in the House of Lords. A selection commission will make subsequent judicial appointments.

[7]Joshua Rozenberg, "Fear over UK Supreme Court Impact," BBC News, http://news.bbc.co.uk/2/hi/uk_news/8237855.stm.

---

appellate jurisdiction only because Congress gives it the authority to do so. Congress may change (and, perhaps, eliminate) the Court's appellate jurisdiction. This is a powerful but rarely used weapon in the congressional arsenal of checks and balances.

Litigants in state cases who invoke the Court's appellate jurisdiction must satisfy two conditions. First, the case must have reached the end of the

FIGURE 14.2 Access to and Decision Making in the U.S. Supreme Court, 2008 Term

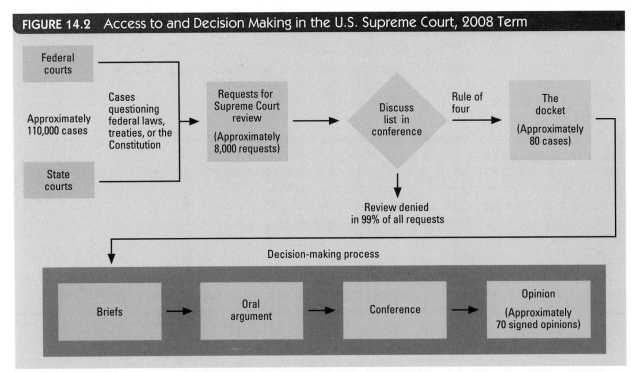

State and national appeals courts churn out thousands of decisions each year. Only a fraction ends up on the Supreme Court's docket. This chart sketches the several stages leading to a decision from the High Court.

Source: John G. Roberts, Jr., "The 2009 Year-End Report on the Federal Judiciary," http://www.supremecourt.gov/publicinfo/year-end/2009year-endreport.pdf.

federal question
An issue covered by the U.S. Constitution, national laws, or U.S. treaties.

docket
A court's agenda.

rule of four
An unwritten rule that requires at least four justices to agree that a case warrants consideration before it is reviewed by the U.S. Supreme Court.

line in the state court system. Litigants cannot jump at will from a state to the national arena of justice. Second, the case must raise a **federal question**, that is, an issue covered by the Constitution, federal laws, or national treaties. But even cases that meet both of these conditions do not guarantee review by the Court.

Since 1925, the Court has exercised substantial (today, nearly complete) control over its **docket**, or agenda (see Figure 14.2). The Court selects a handful of cases (fewer than one hundred) for full consideration from the eight thousand or more requests filed each year. These requests take the form of petitions for *certiorari*, in which a litigant seeking review asks the Court "to become informed" of the lower-court proceeding. For the vast majority of cases, the Court denies the petition for *certiorari*, leaving the decision of the lower court undisturbed. No explanations accompany these denials, so they have little or no value as Court rulings.

The Court grants a review only when four or more justices agree that a case warrants full consideration. This unwritten rule is known as the **rule of four**. With advance preparation by their law clerks, who screen petitions and prepare summaries, all nine justices make these judgments at secret conferences held twice a week.[27] During the conferences, justices vote on previously argued cases and consider which new cases to add to the docket. The chief justice circulates a "discuss list" of worthy petitions. Cases on the list are then subject to the rule of four. Though it takes only four votes to place a case on the docket, it may ultimately take an enormous leap to garner a fifth, and deciding, vote on the merits of the appeal. This is especially true if the Court is sharply split ideologically. Thus, a minority of justices in favor of an appeal may oppose review if they are not confident the outcome will be to their satisfaction.[28]

It is important to note that business cases represent a substantial portion of the Court's docket, though they receive far less attention than cases addressing social issues such as the death penalty, affirmative action, and school prayer. Business disputes are less emotional and the issues more technical. But business cases involve billions of dollars, have enormous consequences for the economy, and affect people's lives more often than the social issues that tend to dominate public debate and discussion.[29]

The Solicitor General

Why does the Court decide to hear certain cases but not others? The best evidence scholars have adduced suggests that agenda setting depends on the individual justices, who vary in their decision-making criteria, and on the issues raised by the cases. Occasionally justices weigh the ultimate outcome of a case when granting or denying review. At other times, they grant or deny review based on disagreement among the lower courts or because delay in resolving the issues would impose alarming economic or social costs.[30] The solicitor general plays a vital role in the Court's agenda setting.

The **solicitor general** represents the national government before the Supreme Court, serving as the hinge between an administration's legal approach and its policy objectives. Appointed by the president, the solicitor general is the third-ranking official in the U.S. Department of Justice (after the attorney general and the deputy attorney general). Today, the acting solicitor general is Neal Katyal, who succeeded Elena Kagan, the first woman to hold the office. President Obama tapped Kagan to replace Supreme Court Justice John Paul Stevens, who retired in June 2010.

The solicitor general's duties include determining whether the government should appeal lower-court decisions; reviewing and modifying, when necessary, the briefs filed in government appeals; and deciding whether the government should file an **amicus curiae brief*** in any appellate court.[31] The objective is to create a cohesive program for the executive branch in the federal courts.

Solicitors general play two different, and occasionally conflicting, roles. First, they are advocates for the president's policy preferences; second, as officers of the Court, they traditionally defend the institutional interests of the national government.

solicitor general
The third highest official of the U.S. Department of Justice, and the one who represents the national government before the Supreme Court.

amicus curiae brief
A brief filed (with the permission of the court) by an individual or group that is not a party to a legal action but has an interest in it.

---

*Amicus curiae is Latin for "friend of the court." Amicus briefs can be filed with the consent of all the parties or with the permission of the court. They allow groups and individuals who are not parties to the litigation but have an interest in it to influence the court's thinking and, perhaps, its decision.

Solicitors general usually act with considerable restraint in recommending to the Court that a case be granted or denied review. By recommending only cases of general importance, they increase their credibility and their influence.

By carefully selecting the cases it presses, the solicitor general's office usually maintains a very impressive record of wins in the Supreme Court. Solicitors general are a "formidable force" in the process of setting the Supreme Court's agenda.[32] Their influence in bringing cases to the Court and arguing them there has earned them the informal title of "the tenth justice."

Decision Making

Once the Court grants review, attorneys submit written arguments (briefs). The justices follow an unwritten rule to avoid discussing cases with one another before oral argument. Should the rule be violated, the justices will inform their colleagues in an effort to avoid "little cliques or cabals or little groups that lobby each other before [argument]."[33] Oral argument, typically limited to thirty minutes for each side, is the first time the justices know what their colleagues might be thinking. From October through April, the justices spend two to three hours a day, five or six days a month, hearing arguments. Experience seems to help. Like the solicitor general, seasoned advocates enjoy a greater success rate, regardless of the party they represent.[34] The justices like crisp, concise, conversational presentations; they disapprove of attorneys who read from a prepared text. Some justices are aggressive, relentless questioners who frequently interrupt the lawyers; others are more subdued. In a 1993 free speech case, an attorney who offered an impassioned plea on the facts of the case was soon "awash in a sea of judicial impatience that at times seemed to border on anger.... 'We didn't take this case to determine who said what in the cafeteria,'" snapped one justice.[35]

Court protocol prohibits the justices from addressing one another directly during oral arguments, but they often debate obliquely through the questions they pose to the attorneys. The justices reach no collective decision at the time of oral arguments. They reach a tentative decision only after they have met in conference.

Our knowledge of the dynamics of decision making on the Supreme Court is all secondhand. Only the justices attend the Court's Wednesday and Friday conferences. By tradition, the justices first shake hands prior to conference and to going on the bench, a gesture of harmony. The handshaking was introduced by Melville Fuller when he was chief justice from 1888 to 1910.[36] The chief justice then begins the presentation of each case with a discussion of it and his vote, which is followed by a discussion and vote from each of the other justices, in order of their seniority on the Court. Justice Antonin Scalia, who joined the Court in 1986, remarked that "not much conferencing goes on." By *conferencing,* Scalia meant efforts to persuade others to change their views by debating points of disagreement. "To call our discussion of a case a conference," he said, "is really something of a misnomer.

Journey of a Lifetime

President Barack Obama congratulates Sonia Sotomayor prior to her investiture ceremony at the Supreme Court on September 8, 2009. Other members of the Court and Vice President Joe Biden are in the background.

(Official White House Photo by Pete Souza)

It's much more a statement of the views of each of the nine Justices, after which the totals are added and the case is assigned" for an opinion.[37]

Judicial Restraint and Judicial Activism. How do the justices decide how to vote on a case? According to some scholars, legal doctrines and previous decisions explain their votes. This explanation, which is consistent with the majoritarian model, anchors the justices closely to the law and minimizes the contribution of their personal values. This view is embodied in the concept of **judicial restraint**, which maintains that the people's elected representatives, not judges, should make the laws. Judges are said to exercise judicial restraint when they defer to decisions of other governmental actors. Other scholars contend that the value preferences and resulting ideologies of the justices provide a more powerful interpretation of their voting.[38] This view is embodied in the concept of **judicial activism**, which maintains that judges should not give deference to the elected branches but should use their judicial power to promote the judges' preferred social and political goals. The concept of judicial activism and its cognate, judicial restraint, has many strands, and scholars sometimes disagree on its many meanings.[39] But at its core, all would agree that judges are activists when their decisions run counter to the will of the other branches of government, in effect substituting their own judgment for the judgment of the people's representatives. By interjecting personal values into court decisions, activist judging is more consistent with the pluralist model.

The terms *judicial restraint* and *judicial activism* describe different relative degrees of judicial assertiveness. Judges acting according to an extreme model of judicial restraint would never question the validity of duly enacted laws but would defer to the superiority of other government institutions in

judicial restraint
A judicial philosophy by which judges tend to defer to decisions of the elected branches of government.

judicial activism
A judicial philosophy by which judges tend not to defer to decisions of the elected branches of government, resulting in the invalidation or emasculation of those decisions.

FIGURE 14.3   Measuring Judicial Activism

Votes to strike down congressional acts, 1994–2008 (percentage)

Thomas	61
Kennedy	60
Scalia	53
Souter	43
Ginsburg	39
Stevens	37
Breyer	29

The terms *activism* and *restraint* are not tied to a particular ideology. They simply describe a behavior. Conservatives and liberals are equally capable of exercising activism or restraint. One universally accepted measure of activism is the extent to which judges are inclined to strike down congressional acts. Of course, judicial invalidation of legislation may be appropriate, but that judgment is independent of the label "activist judge." From 1994 through 2009, seven Supreme Court justices voted to uphold or strike down congressional acts in 75 cases. The figure shows that the conservative justices were more inclined to activism than their more moderate to liberal colleagues.

Sources: Data from Paul Gewirtz and Chad Golder, "So Who Are the Activists?" *New York Times,* 6 July 2005, p. A19; data through the end of the 2008 Term kindly provided by Amanda Bryan, Charles Gregory, and Timothy R. Johnson (University of Minnesota).

construing the laws. Judges acting according to an extreme model of judicial activism would be an intrusive and ever-present force that would dominate other government institutions. Actual judicial behavior lies somewhere between these two extremes.

From the 1960s through the 1980s, many activist judges tended to support liberal values, thus linking judicial activism with liberalism. But the critical Supreme Court case of *Bush* v. *Gore* suggests to many critics that conservative jurists can also be judicial activists, promoting their preferred political goals. Had a majority deferred to the Florida courts on the issue of the recount, the decision would have been hailed as an example of judicial restraint. But overturning the Florida courts and delivering a victory for the Republicans have labeled the majority in *Bush* v. *Gore* as conservative judicial activists (see also Figure 14.3). By overturning a raft of federal statutes, the Rehnquist and Roberts Courts now link judicial activism with conservatism.

Judgment and Argument. The voting outcome is the **judgment,** the decision on who wins and who loses. The justices often disagree not only on the winner and loser, but also on the reasons for their judgment. This should not be surprising, given nine independent minds and issues that can be approached in several ways. Voting in the conference does not end the justices' work or resolve their disagreements. Votes remain tentative until the Court issues an opinion announcing its judgment.

judgment
The judicial decision in a court case.

After voting, the justices in the majority must draft an opinion setting out the reasons for their decision. The **argument** is the kernel of the opinion—its logical content, as distinct from supporting facts, rhetoric, and procedures. If all justices agree with the judgment and the reasons supporting it, the opinion is unanimous. Agreement with a judgment for different reasons from those set forth in the majority opinion is called a **concurrence**. Or a justice can **dissent** if she or he disagrees with a judgment. Both concurring and dissenting opinions may be drafted, in addition to the majority opinion.

The Opinion. After the conference, the chief justice or most senior justice in the majority (in terms of years of service on the Court) decides which justice will write the majority opinion. He or she may consider several factors in assigning the crucial opinion-writing task, including the prospective author's workload, expertise, public opinion, and (above all) ability to hold the majority together. (Remember that the votes are only tentative at this point.) On the one hand, if the drafting justice holds an extreme view on the issues in a case and is not able to incorporate the views of more moderate colleagues, those justices may withdraw their votes. On the other hand, assigning a more moderate justice to draft an opinion could weaken the argument on which the opinion rests. Opinion-writing assignments can also be punitive. Justice Harry Blackmun once commented, "If one's in the doghouse with the Chief [former Chief Justice Warren Burger], he gets the crud."[40]

Opinion writing is the justices' most critical function. It is not surprising, then, that they spend much of their time drafting opinions. The justices usually call on their law clerks—top graduates of the nation's elite law schools—to help them prepare opinions and carry out other tasks. The commitment can be daunting. All of the justices now rely on their clerks to shoulder substantial responsibilities, including the initial drafts of opinions.[41]

The writing justice distributes a draft opinion to all the justices, who then read it and circulate their criticisms and suggestions. An opinion may have to be rewritten several times to accommodate colleagues who remain unpersuaded by the draft. Justice Felix Frankfurter was a perfectionist; some of his opinions went through thirty or more drafts. Justices can change their votes, and perhaps alter the judgment, until the decision is officially announced. Often, the most controversial cases pile up as coalitions on the Court vie for support or sharpen their criticisms. When the Court announces a decision, the justices who wrote the opinion read or summarize their views in the courtroom.

Justices in the majority frequently try to muffle or stifle dissent to encourage institutional cohesion. Since the mid-1940s, however, unity has been more difficult to obtain.[42] Gaining agreement from the justices today is akin to negotiating with nine separate law firms. It may be more surprising that the justices ever agree. In 2006, for example, the Court spoke without dissent in more than half of its cases. The conservative shift occasioned by the appointments of Roberts and Alito has infused cohesion among dissenters,

argument
The heart of a judicial opinion; its logical content separated from facts, rhetoric, and procedure.

concurrence
The agreement of a judge with the Supreme Court's majority decision, for a reason other than the majority reason.

dissent
The disagreement of a judge with a majority decision.

who have tended to join a single opinion. And the Court's genteel etiquette appears strained as once collegial justices voice their views publicly and forcefully from the bench.[43]

The justices remain aware of the slender foundation of their authority, which rests largely on public respect. That respect is tested whenever the Court ventures into controversial areas. Banking, slavery, and Reconstruction policies embroiled the Court in the nineteenth century. Freedom of speech and religion, racial equality, the right to privacy, the 2000 election, and the extent of presidential power have led the Court into controversy in the past sixty years.

Strategies on the Court

The Court is more than the sum of its formal processes. The justices exercise real political power. If we start with the assumption that the justices attempt to stamp their own policy views on the cases they review, we should expect typical political behavior from them. Cases that reach the Supreme Court's docket pose difficult choices. Because the justices are grappling with conflict on a daily basis, they probably have well-defined ideologies that reflect their values. Scholars and journalists have attempted to pierce the veil of secrecy that shrouds the Court from public view and analyze the justices' ideologies.[44]

The beliefs of most justices can be located on the two-dimensional model of political values discussed in Chapter 1 (see Figure 1.2). Liberal justices, such as Ruth Bader Ginsburg, choose freedom over order and equality over freedom. Conservative justices—Antonin Scalia and Clarence Thomas, for example—choose order over freedom and freedom over equality. These choices translate into clear policy preferences.

As in any other group of people, the justices also vary in their intellectual ability, advocacy skills, social graces, temperament, and other characteristics. For example, Chief Justice Charles Evans Hughes (1930–1941) had a photographic memory and came to each conference armed with well-marked copies of Supreme Court opinions. Few justices could keep up with him in debates. Then, as now, justices argue for the support of their colleagues, offering information in the form of drafts and memoranda to explain the advantages and disadvantages of voting for or against an issue. And justices make occasional, if not regular, use of friendship, ridicule, and appeals to patriotism to mold their colleagues' views.

A justice might adopt a long-term strategy of encouraging the appointment of like-minded colleagues to marshal additional strength on the Court. Chief Justice (and former president) William Howard Taft, for example, bombarded President Warren G. Harding with recommendations and suggestions whenever a Court vacancy was announced. Taft was especially determined to block the appointment of anyone who might side with the "dangerous twosome," Justices Oliver Wendell Holmes and Louis D. Brandeis. Taft said he "must stay on the court in order to prevent the Bolsheviki from getting control."[45]

The Chief Justice

The chief justice is only one of nine justices, but he has several important functions based on his authority. Apart from his role in forming the docket and directing the Court's conferences, the chief justice can also be a social leader, generating solidarity within the group. Sometimes a chief justice can embody intellectual leadership. Finally, the chief justice can provide policy leadership, directing the Court toward a general policy position. Perhaps only John Marshall could lay claim to possessing social, intellectual, and policy leadership. Warren E. Burger, who resigned as chief justice in 1986, was reputed to be a lackluster leader in all three areas.[46]

When presiding at the conference, the chief justice can control the discussion of issues, although independent-minded justices are not likely to acquiesce to his views. Moreover, justices today rarely engage in a debate of the issues in the conference. Rather, they communicate by memoranda, not e-mail; they use their law clerks as ambassadors between justices' chambers and, in effect, "run the Court without talking to one another."[47]

Judicial Recruitment

Neither the Constitution nor national law imposes formal requirements for appointment to the federal courts. Once appointed, district and appeals judges must reside in the district or circuit to which they are appointed.

The president appoints judges to the federal courts, and all nominees must be confirmed by majority vote in the Senate. Congress sets, but cannot lower, a judge's compensation. In 2010, salaries were as follows:

Chief justice of the Supreme Court	$223,500
Associate Supreme Court justices	213,900
Courts of appeals judges	184,500
District judges	174,000
Magistrate judges	160,080

By comparison, in 2009 the average salary of a state supreme court judge was $150,633. The average for a state trial judge was $134,826.[48] Although annual compensation for equity partners in major law firms exceeds $1 million, employment prospects for lawyers have eroded in the Great Recession of 2009.[49] Still, Supreme Court clerks entering private practice earn more than the justices who hired them. No wonder some lawyers find the judicial path unappealing, though the power and prestige of judicial office remains a compelling lure, with no shortage of applicants.

In more than half the states, the governor appoints the state judges, often in consultation with judicial nominating commissions. In many of these states, voters decide whether the judges should be retained in office. Other states select their judges by partisan, nonpartisan, or (rarely) legislative election.[50] In some states, nominees must be confirmed by the state legislature. Contested elections for judgeships are unusual, though at the extreme,

Compared with What?

Selecting Judges Around the World

In at least half of the U.S. states, judges run for election. In fact, nearly 90 percent of all state judges face the voters. This practice is in stark contrast to the rest of the world, where judges are appointed, either by the executive branch (with or without recommendations from a judicial selection commission), by the judicial selection commission itself, or by the legislative branch. In a few countries the civil service offers a professional career path leading to a judgeship. In these countries judges are selected through examinations and school programs. In only two nations—Switzerland and Japan—judicial elections hold sway, but only in a very limited way: (1) Some smaller Swiss cantons (subnational units) elect judges, and (2) appointed justices of the Japanese Supreme Court may face retention elections, though scholars regard the practice as a mere formality. Hans A. Linde, a retired justice of the Oregon Supreme Court, captured the essence of the American exception when he observed: "To the rest of the world, American adherence to judicial elections is as incomprehensible as our rejection of the metric system."

The table here shows the judicial selection process used in countries around the world. Some countries use more than one method; the table lists the primary one.

Executive Appointment without Commission	Executive Appointment with Commission	Appointment by Commission	Legislative Appointment	Career Judiciary
Afghanistan	Albania	Algeria	China	Czech Republic
Argentina	Canada	Andorra	Cuba	France
Australia	Dominican Republic	Angola	Laos	Germany
Bangladesh	England	Bulgaria	Macedonia	Italy
Belarus	Greece	Croatia	Montenegro	Japan
Belgium	Namibia	Cyprus		Poland
Cambodia	Russia	Israel		Portugal
Chad	Scotland	Lebanon		Spain
Egypt	South Africa	Mexico		Turkey
New Zealand	Ukraine	Rwanda		
Uzbekistan	Zimbabwe	Yemen		

Source: Adam Liptak, "American Exception: Rendering Justice, with One Eye on Re-election," *New York Times*, 25 May 2008, http://www.nytimes.com/2008/05/25/us/25exception.html?pagewanted=1&_r=1.

such contests may call a judge's impartiality into question. In 2009, the U.S. Supreme Court ruled that the newly elected chief justice of the West Virginia Supreme Court, Brent Benjamin, had to disqualify himself from deliberations in a case involving a coal company chief executive who had spent $3 million to elect Benjamin.[51] In most other countries, judges are appointed, not elected (see Compared with What? Selecting Judges Around the World).

The Appointment of Federal Judges

The Constitution states that federal judges shall hold their commission "during good Behaviour," which in practice means for life.* A president's judicial appointments, then, are likely to survive his administration, providing a kind of political legacy. The appointment power assumes that the president is free to identify candidates and appoint judges who favor his policies. President Franklin D. Roosevelt had appointed nearly 75 percent of all sitting federal judges by the end of his twelve years in office. In contrast, President Ford appointed fewer than 13 percent in his three years in office. Presidents Reagan and George H. W. Bush together appointed more than 60 percent of all federal judges. During his administration, President Clinton appointed more than 40 percent of the 852 federal judges at all levels. President George W. Bush appointed 38 percent (or 325) of all federal judges during his tenure.

Judicial vacancies occur when sitting judges resign, retire, or die. Vacancies also arise when Congress creates new judgeships to handle increasing case loads. In both cases, the president nominates a candidate, who must be confirmed by the Senate. Under President Barack Obama, the Office of White House Counsel is deeply involved in this screening process. The president also had the help of the Justice Department, primarily through its Office of Legal Policy, which screens candidates before the formal nomination, subjecting serious contenders to FBI investigation. The White House and the Justice Department formed a Judicial Selection Committee as part of this vetting process. The White House and the Senate vie for control in the approval of district and appeals court judges.

The "Advice and Consent" of the Senate. For district and appeals court vacancies, the nomination "must be acceptable to the home state senator from the president's party"[52] (or to the state's House delegation from the president's party if no senator is from the president's party). The Judicial Selection Committee consults extensively with home state senators from which the appointment will be made.[53] Senators' influence is greater for appointments to district court than for appointments to the court of appeals.

This practice, called **senatorial courtesy**, forces presidents to share the nomination power with members of the Senate. The Senate will not confirm a nominee who is opposed by the senior senator from the nominee's state if that senator is a member of the president's party. The Senate does not actually reject the candidate. Instead, the chairman of the Senate Judiciary Committee, which reviews all judicial nominees, will not schedule a confirmation hearing, effectively killing the nomination.

---

*As of 2010, fourteen federal judges have been impeached. Of these, seven were convicted in the Senate and removed from office. Three judges were removed from office by the Senate in the 1980s. Judge Thomas Porteous was impeached by the House in 2010; his trial is pending in the Senate.

senatorial courtesy
A norm under which a nomination must be acceptable to the home state senator from the president's party.

Although the Justice Department is still sensitive to senatorial prerogatives, senators can no longer submit a single name to fill a vacancy. The department searches for acceptable candidates and polls the appropriate senator for her or his reaction to them. President George H. W. Bush asked Republican senators to seek more qualified female and minority candidates. Bush made progress in developing a more diverse bench, and President Clinton accelerated the change.[54] President George W. Bush had a better track record of appointing women and minorities to the bench than did either his father or Ronald Reagan, but he lagged behind Clinton. Ideology remains the dominant motivating force behind judicial appointments.[55]

The Senate Judiciary Committee conducts a hearing for each judicial nominee. The committee chair exercises a measure of control in the appointment process that goes beyond senatorial courtesy. If a nominee is objectionable to the chair, he or she can delay a hearing or hold up other appointments until the president and the Justice Department find an alternative. Such behavior does not win a politician much influence in the long run, however. So committee chairs of the president's party are usually loath to place obstacles in a president's path, especially when they may want presidential support for their own policies and constituencies.

Beginning with the Carter administration, judicial appointments below the Supreme Court have proved a new battleground, with a growing proportion of nominees not confirmed and increasing delays in the process. These appointments were once viewed as presidential and party patronage, but that old-fashioned view has given way to a focus on the president's policy agenda through judicial appointments. This perspective has enlarged the ground on which senators have opposed judicial nominees to include matters of judicial policy (for example, abortion) and theory (for example, delving into a nominee's approach when interpreting the meaning of a statute). Beginning in 2003, Democratic senators used the filibuster to prevent confirmation votes for judicial candidates they deemed "outside the mainstream." This behavior provoked ire from the majority Republicans, who threatened to end the filibuster practice entirely. The parties reached an uneasy compromise in 2005 to invoke a judicial filibuster only for "extraordinary circumstances," thus ending its use to scuttle most presidential nominations.

The American Bar Association. The American Bar Association (ABA), the biggest organization of lawyers in the United States, has been involved in screening candidates for the federal bench since 1946.[56] Its role is defined by custom, not law. At the president's behest, the ABA's Standing Committee on the Federal Judiciary routinely rates prospective appointees using a three-value scale: "well qualified," "qualified," and "not qualified." The association no longer has advance notice of possible nominees. The George W. Bush administration considered the ABA too liberal, posing an unnecessary impediment to the confirmation of conservative judges.[57] Nonetheless, the association continued to evaluate the professional qualifications of nominees after they were nominated. President Obama restored the ABA's prenomination review in March 2009.[58]

Recent Presidents and the Federal Judiciary

Since the presidency of Jimmy Carter, chief executives have tended—more or less—to make appointments to the federal courts that are more diverse in racial, ethnic, and gender terms than in previous administrations. President Bill Clinton took the lead on diversity. For the first time in history, more than half of the president's judicial appointments were women or minorities. Clinton's chief judge selector, Assistant Attorney General Eleanor Acheson, followed through on Clinton's campaign pledge to make his appointees "look like America."

The racial and ethnic composition of the parties themselves helps to explain much of the variation between the appointments of presidents of different parties. It seems clear that political ideology, not demographics, lies at the heart of judicial appointments. Reagan and George H. W. Bush sought nominees with particular policy preferences who would leave their stamp on the judiciary well into the twenty-first century. When it comes to ideological preferences as revealed by judicial choices, Carter's judges carry off the honors. A review of more than twenty-five thousand federal court decisions from 1968 to 1995 concluded that Carter-appointed judges were the most liberal, whereas Reagan- and Bush-appointed judges were the least liberal. (Carter had an advantage in his efforts to mold the bench because his appointees were reviewed by a Democratic-led Senate. Reagan, George H. W. Bush, Clinton, and George W. Bush contended with a Senate in the hands of the opposing party for part of their administrations.) Clinton-appointed judges were somewhat less liberal than Carter's but decidedly more liberal than the legacy of Nixon, Ford, Reagan, or George H. W. Bush.[59] And George W. Bush's judges are among the most conservative on record when it comes to civil rights and liberties.[60] One general rule seems clear: presidents are likely to appoint judges who share similar values.[61]

Appointment to the Supreme Court

The announcement of a vacancy on the High Court usually causes quite a stir. Campaigns for Supreme Court seats are commonplace, although the public rarely sees them. Hopefuls contact friends in the administration and urge influential associates to do the same on their behalf. Some candidates never give up hope. Judge John J. Parker, whose nomination to the Court was defeated in 1930, tried in vain to rekindle interest in his appointment until he was well past the age—usually the early sixties—that appointments are made.[62]

The president is not shackled by senatorial courtesy when it comes to nominating a Supreme Court justice. However, appointments to the Court attract more intense public scrutiny than do lower-level appointments, effectively narrowing the president's options and focusing attention on the Senate's advice and consent.

Of the 156 men and 6 women nominated to the Court, 11 names have been withdrawn, and 25 have failed to receive Senate confirmation. (Seven confirmed justices declined to serve.)[63] Only 6 such fumbles have occurred since 1900. The last one was George W. Bush's nomination of Harriet Miers in 2005

Welcome to the Club!

Chief Justice John G. Roberts, Jr. (right) congratulated Elena Kagan (left), after administering the judicial oath to Kagan on August 7, 2010, making her the 112th justice of the U.S. Supreme Court. (Jeffrey Minear, counselor to the Chief Justice, held the Bible.) In prepared remarks afterward, Kagan pledged to support judicial restraint and a "modest" role for the court.

(Paul J. Richards/AFP/Getty Images)

to fill the vacancy created by the retirement of Sandra Day O'Connor. Miers, who was White House counsel, withdrew her candidacy after coming under withering criticism, largely from conservatives, for her lack of clarity on issues likely to come before the Court.

The most important factor in the rejection of a nominee is partisan politics. Thirteen candidates lost their bids for appointment because the presidents who nominated them were considered likely to become lame ducks: the party in control of the Senate anticipated victory for its candidate in an upcoming presidential race and sought to deny the incumbent president an important political appointment.[64]

Nineteen of the twenty-six successful Supreme Court nominees since 1950 have had prior judicial experience in federal or state courts. This tendency toward "promotion" from within the judiciary may be based on the idea that a judge's previous opinions are good predictors of his or her future opinions on the High Court. After all, a president is handing out a powerful lifetime appointment, so it makes sense to want an individual who is sympathetic to his views. Federal or state court judges holding lifetime appointments are likely to state their views frankly in their opinions. In contrast, the policy preferences of High Court candidates who have been in legal practice or in political office can only be guessed at, based on the conjecture of professional associates or on speeches they have given to local Rotary Clubs, on the floor of a legislature, and elsewhere.

After a vacancy drought of more than eleven years, President George W. Bush put his stamp on the Supreme Court with two appointments in 2005. He nominated federal judge John G. Roberts, Jr., in July 2005 to replace Associate Justice Sandra Day O'Connor (after the withdrawal of Harriet Miers). But with the death of Chief Justice William H. Rehnquist in September, Bush withdrew Roberts's nomination as associate justice and resubmitted him for the position of chief justice. Roberts was confirmed 78–22. Democrats were evenly split: 22 for and 22 against. Bush then nominated federal judge Samuel A. Alito for the seat vacated by O'Connor. His confirmation hearing was far more contentious, with the Democrats aiming to paint him as "outside the mainstream." The effort failed, as did a last-minute call to filibuster the nomination. Alito was confirmed by the Senate by a narrow margin, 58–42 (nearly all Democrats were opposed), and he took his seat as the 110th justice in January 2006.

The results of the Roberts and Alito appointments were soon apparent. In the 2006 Term (October 2006 to June 2007), the first full term with Roberts and Alito on the bench, the Court moved in a decidedly conservative direction. One-third of all the cases were decided by 5–4 votes, almost triple the proportion of close votes from the previous term. In each case, Justice Anthony Kennedy cast the deciding vote. He joined the majority in all twenty-four 5–4 decisions, siding more often with his conservative colleagues. Subsequently, Kennedy has left his mark by authoring the majority opinion or providing the deciding vote across a range of hot-button issues: declaring the death penalty unconstitutional for the rape of a child, ensuring Guantánamo detainees a constitutional right to challenge their detention in federal courts, supporting a constitutional right for individuals to own a gun for personal use, and removing restrictions on corporate spending in election campaigns.

The hearts of many a lawyer and loyal Democrat fluttered when Justice David H. Souter announced his decision to retire from the Supreme Court effective June 29, 2009. This gave President Obama the opportunity to appoint a second woman to the Supreme Court, federal judge Sonia Sotomayor

Justices at Bat

At his confirmation hearings in 2005 to become the 17th chief justice of the United States, John G. Roberts, Jr., declared, "[I]t's my job to call balls and strikes and not to pitch or bat." But bat he did, moving the Court in a more conservative direction in 2010 by voting in a landmark, 5-to-4 decision to strike down campaign finance legislation that had prohibited corporations and unions from broadcasting "electioneering communications."

(Toles © 2010 The Washington Post. Reprinted by permission of Universal Uclick. All rights reserved.)

of New York. Sotomayor, the first Latina to be nominated to the Court, possessed a sterling résumé with a compelling personal story. Raised by her widowed mother in a Bronx housing project, Sotomayor went on to earn top honors at Princeton and distinction at Yale Law School. She spent years as a federal prosecutor and in private legal practice before she was appointed by Republican president George H. W. Bush to the federal district court in 1992. President Bill Clinton appointed her to the federal appellate court in 1998.

Republicans on the Senate Judiciary Committee tried to derail Sotomayor's nomination, pouring over everything she had written or said. Some senators focused on a comment she made in 2001, that a wise Latina woman "would more often than not reach a better conclusion than a white male who hasn't lived that life."[65] In opposing Sotomayor, some Republicans risked the ire of Hispanic voters, whose role in American politics is destined to grow. As illustrated in Figure 14.4, by 2050, the percentage of Hispanics in the population is expected to increase from 15 to 30 percent.

Sotomayor deflected the attacks and stuck to her well-rehearsed script, declaring that her core guiding principle was "fidelity to the law." That bromide kept her opponents at bay. In the end, she was confirmed by a vote of 68 to 31, largely along party lines. Given her record as a moderate, Sotomayor's appointment will not be a game-changer since she replaced a moderate justice.

As for future Supreme Court appointments, liberal justice John Paul Stevens announced in April 2010 that he would retire at the end of the current term in June 2010. President Obama nominated Elena Kagan, his solicitor general, to fill the seat. In a departure from recent practice, Obama did not find his choice in the minor leagues of the federal judiciary. Rather, Kagan

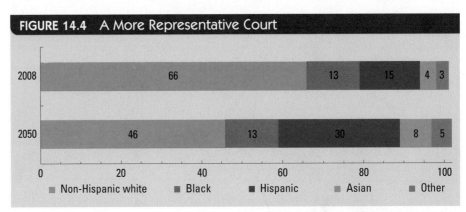

FIGURE 14.4   A More Representative Court

Legend: Non-Hispanic white | Black | Hispanic | Asian | Other

2008: 66, 13, 15, 4, 3
2050: 46, 13, 30, 8, 5

Before President Obama appointed Sonia Sotomayor to the Supreme Court, the Court had only one woman, one African American, and no Hispanics among its nine members. Although the Court remained overwhelmingly male (78 percent) after her appointment, it did move toward becoming more demographically representative of the nation. Its composition (11 percent African American and 11 percent Hispanic) put it close to the national ethnic breakdown in 2008. Over the next generation, the Hispanic percentage is expected to double, arguing for the political significance of Sotomayor's appointment.

Source: Sam Roberts, "In a Generation, Minorities May Be the U.S. Majority," *New York Times,* 13 August 2008, http://www.nytimes.com/2008/08/14/washington/14census.html.

made her mark as a law professor and law school administrator (and a coveted clerkship with Supreme Court justice Thurgood Marshall). In a 1995 book review, Kagan wrote that confirmation hearings were "a vapid and hollow charade."[66] But when it was her turn to be interrogated by the Senate Judiciary Committee, she chose the well-worn path of avoiding answers to serious questions. Her bromide: the Court's role "must...be a modest one—properly deferential to the decisions of the American people and their elected representatives."[67] The Senate confirmed Kagan by a vote of 63 to 37. On August 7, 2010, she became the 112th justice—and the 4th woman—to serve on Court.

One of the great prizes of any presidency is the ability to appoint federal judges. These are lifetime appointments, enabling presidents to extend their legacies well beyond their terms of office. As of October 2010, President Obama has appointed a total of 43 federal judges and nominated 43 others to fill 103 vacancies on the federal courts. In all likelihood, Obama will also fill at least 18 anticipated vacancies resulting from announced retirements. Obama has taken a decidedly go-slow approach, but given the increased partisanship and rancor in the Senate, it would not be surprising for the Republicans to use the filibuster threat and a parliamentary procedure known as a "secret hold" to block or delay additional appointments.

The Consequences of Judicial Decisions

Judicial rulings represent the tip of the iceberg in terms of all the legal conflicts and disputes that arise in this country. Most cases never surface in court. The overwhelming majority of lawsuits end without a court judgment. Many civil cases are settled, or the parties give up, or the courts dismiss the suits because they are beyond the legitimate bounds of judicial resolution. Most criminal cases end in a plea bargain, with the defendant admitting his or her guilt in exchange for a less severe punishment. Only about 10 percent of criminal cases in the federal district courts are tried; an equally small percentage of civil cases are adjudicated.

Furthermore, the fact that a judge sentences a criminal defendant to ten years in prison or a court holds a company liable for billions in damages does not guarantee that the defendant will lose his or her freedom or the company will give up any assets. In the case of the criminal defendant, the road of seeking an appeal following trial and conviction is well traveled and, if nothing else, serves to delay the day when he or she must go to prison. In civil cases as well, an appeal may be filed to delay the day of reckoning.

Supreme Court Rulings: Implementation and Impact

When the Supreme Court makes a decision, it relies on others to implement it—to translate policy into action. How a judgment is implemented depends in good measure on how it was crafted. Remember that the justices, in preparing their opinions, must work to hold their majorities together, to gain greater, if not unanimous, support for their arguments. This forces them to compromise in their opinions, to moderate their arguments, which introduces ambiguity into many of the policies they articulate. Ambiguous opinions affect the implementation of policy. For example, when the Supreme Court issued its unanimous order in 1955 to desegregate public school facilities "with all deliberate speed,"[68] judges who opposed the Court's policy dragged their feet in implementing it. In the early 1960s, the Supreme Court prohibited prayers and Bible reading in public schools. Yet state court judges and attorneys general reinterpreted the High Court's decision to mean that only compulsory prayer or Bible reading was unconstitutional and that state-sponsored voluntary prayer or Bible reading was acceptable.[69]

Because the Supreme Court confronts issues freighted with deeply felt social values or fundamental political beliefs, its decisions have influence beyond the immediate parties in a dispute. The Court's decision in *Roe* v. *Wade,* legalizing abortion, generated heated public reaction. The justices were barraged with thousands of angry letters. Groups opposing abortion vowed to overturn the decision; groups favoring the freedom to obtain an abortion moved to protect the right they had won. Within eight months of the decision, more than two dozen constitutional amendments had been introduced in Congress, although none managed to carry the extraordinary majority required for passage. Still, the antiabortion faction achieved a modest victory with the passage of a provision forbidding the use of national government funds for abortions except when the woman's life is in jeopardy. (Since 1993, the exception has also included victims of rape or incest.)

Abortion opponents have also directed their efforts at state legislatures, hoping to load abortion laws with enough conditions to discourage women from terminating their pregnancies. For example, one state required that women receive detailed information about abortions, then wait at least twenty-four hours before consenting to the procedure. The information listed every imaginable danger associated with abortion and included a declaration that fathers are liable to support their children financially. A legal challenge to these new restrictions reached the Supreme Court, and in 1989, it abandoned its strong defense of abortion rights.[70] The Court continued to support a woman's right to abortion, but in yet another legal challenge in 1992, it recognized the government's power to further limit the exercise of that right.[71] In 2000, in a 5–4 vote, it struck down a state law banning late-term abortions. But in 2007, the Roberts Court reversed course and in a 5–4 vote upheld a nearly identical federal late-term abortion ban.[72]

IDEALOG.ORG

What are your views on abortion? Take IDEAlog's self-test.

Public Opinion and the Supreme Court

Democratic theorists have a difficult time reconciling a commitment to representative democracy with a judiciary that is not accountable to the electorate yet has the power to undo legislative and executive acts. The difficulty may simply be a problem for theorists, however. The policies coming from the Supreme Court, although lagging years behind public opinion, rarely seem out of line with the public's ideological choices.[73] Surveys in several controversial areas reveal that an ideologically balanced Court seldom departs from majority sentiment or trends.[74] "What history shows," wrote Professor Barry Friedman in the most recent and thorough study in this area, "is assuredly not that Supreme Court decisions always are in line with popular opinion, but rather that they come into line with one another over time."[75] That alignment has yet to materialize nearly five decades later on the issue of school prayer, since the Court struck down the recitation of a nondenominational public school prayer in 1961.[76] A majority of Americans then and now do not agree with the Court's position. And so long as much of the public continues to want prayer in schools, the controversy will continue.

New research has shed valuable light on public knowledge and understanding of the judiciary. It turns out that Americans know more about the Supreme Court than pundits had previously acknowledged. As citizens gain knowledge about the judiciary, they are at the same time confronted with important symbols of judicial power such as the wearing of judicial robes, the use of a privileged form of address (e.g., "Your Honor"), and the requirement to rise when judges enter a court room. These symbols tend to emphasize a special role for the courts. "To know more about courts may not be to love them," wrote James L. Gibson and Gregory A. Caldeira, "but to know them is to learn and think that they are different from other political institutions (and often therefore more worthy of trust, respect, and legitimacy)."[77]

As recently as 2009, the Gallup Poll showed that nearly six out of ten Americans are much more likely to approve than disapprove of the job the Supreme Court is doing.[78] Following the 2000 presidential election, polling organizations documented a large gap in the Court's approval ratings between Democrats and Republicans. Oddly, the gap flip-flopped in 2009. Court approval surged for Democrats and declined for Republicans even as the Court continued its conservative direction.[79]

The judicial process is imperfect, so it is not surprising that the Court will continue to step into minefields of public criticism. In 2005 the Court ruled that the Constitution did not forbid a city from taking private property for private development.[80] The outrage across the ideological spectrum was enormous and immediate. State legislatures and courts acted swiftly to give greater protection to private property. This was strong evidence that the Court's measured opinion was out of step with conventional wisdom.

IDEALOG.ORG

Do you believe that public schools should allow or ban prayer? Take IDEAlog's self-test.

The Courts and Models of Democracy

How far should judges stray from existing statutes and precedents? Supporters of the majoritarian model would argue that the courts should adhere to the letter of the law, that judges must refrain from injecting their own values into their decisions. If the law places too much (or not enough) emphasis on equality or order, the elected legislature, not the courts, can change the law.

Politics of Global Change

The Right to Die

In June 1997, the Supreme Court ended its long silence on the constitutionality of a right to suicide, rejecting two separate challenges to state laws prohibiting assisted suicide. In 1996, the U.S. Court of Appeals for the Ninth Circuit relied on the Supreme Court's abortion decisions to strike down a Washington State law against aiding or abetting suicide. The circuit court reasoned from the High Court's abortion rulings that the Fourteenth Amendment's due process clause protects the individual's right "to define one's own concept of existence, of meaning, of the universe, and of the mystery of life." The Supreme Court, however, in *Washington* v. *Glucksberg*, unanimously rejected the circuit court's reasoning in no uncertain terms stressing that suicide is not a "fundamental right" that is "deeply rooted in our legal tradition." Unlike abortion, suicide has been all but universally condemned in the law.

In another 1996 decision, the U.S. Court of Appeals for the Second Circuit adopted a different line of reasoning to invalidate a New York law banning physician-assisted suicide. The court held that the law violated the Fourteenth Amendment's equal protection clause because it treated those who needed a physician's

help to administer lethal doses of prescription drugs (which is criminalized by law) differently from those who can demand removal of life-support systems (which is allowed under prior Supreme Court cases). In June 1997, the Supreme Court unanimously rejected this argument in *Vacco* v. *Quill*. The Court held that the New York law does not result in similar cases being treated differently. "The distinction between letting a patient die and making that patient die is important, logical, rational, and well established," the majority declared.

The Supreme Court displayed an acute awareness of the ongoing debate in the states about assisted suicide. Because the Court determined only that the U.S. Constitution does not protect a right to assisted suicide, the states may still establish such a right by statute or state constitutional amendments.

Only Oregon and Washington State, under their Death with Dignity Acts, have established a limited right to assisted suicide. The laws specify detailed sets of conditions that individuals and their doctors must follow in order to implement physician-assisted suicide. From 1998 to 2009, 460 people died in this fashion

In contrast, those who support the pluralist model maintain that the courts are a policymaking branch of government. It is thus legitimate for the individual values and interests of judges to mirror group interests and preferences and for judges to attempt consciously to advance group interests as they see fit. However, judges at all levels find it difficult to determine when, where, and how to proceed (see "Politics of Global Change: The Right to Die").

The argument that our judicial system fits the pluralist model gains support from a legal procedure called a **class action**. A class action is a device for assembling the claims or defenses of similarly situated individuals so that they can be heard in a single lawsuit. A class action makes it possible for people with small individual claims and limited financial resources to aggregate their claims and resources and thus make a lawsuit viable. The class action also permits the case to be tried by representative parties, with

class action

A procedure by which similarly situated litigants may be heard in a single lawsuit.

in Oregon. In Washington State, since the act became law in 2009, 47 people died out of 63 who were dispensed the medication. The data in both states suggest that terminally ill older patients with higher education are more likely to use physician-assisted suicide than younger patients.

In a much more complicated case, the Supreme Court spoke through its silence. In 1990, Terri Schiavo suffered cardiac arrest that led to irreversible brain damage. In the ensuing fifteen years, she was aided by a feeding tube to provide nutrition and hydration. Her husband (and legal guardian) received state court approval to remove the tube and hasten her death. The U.S. Supreme Court refused to get involved after a federal court turned down a plea by her family to reinsert the feeding tube. The Florida governor, the Florida legislature, the U.S. Congress, and President George W. Bush all sought to intervene and encroach on judicial authority, but to no avail. Schiavo died without regaining consciousness.

Other industrial democracies have tacked in a different direction by decriminalizing the right to die, also known as euthanasia or "good death." The Netherlands, Belgium, and Switzerland have adopted distinct laws that regulate the right to a mercy death. Physician-assisted suicide is legal in the Netherlands, whereas Swiss law decriminalizes assisted suicide only when physicians are not involved. The Swiss legislation on assisted suicide is one of the most liberal in the world, and "many terminally ill foreigners ... now travel to Switzerland to commit suicide." In Belgium, since 2005 pharmacists can supply doctors with fatal doses of medicines, permitting assisted suicide. The euthanasia debate is active in Spain after several high-profile cases of assisted suicide. Only recently, in March 2010, the legislature of the southern province of Andalucía enacted the first Death with Dignity Law in Spain with support from parties representing the whole ideological spectrum. The Oscar-winning movie *The Sea Inside* ("Mar Adentro") tells one such real-life story of a Spanish quadriplegic in a legal and human quest to achieve his right to end his life with dignity.

Sources: *Washington* v. *Glucksberg*, 521 U.S. 793 (1997); *Vacco* v. *Quill*, 521 U.S. 702 (1997); *Compassion in Dying* v. *Washington*, 79 F.3d 790 (9th Cir. 1996); *Quill* v. *Vacco*, 80 F.3d 716 (2d Cir. 1996); State of Oregon Department of Human Services, *Twelfth Annual Report on Oregon's Death with Dignity Act*, March 2010, http://www.oregon.gov/DHS/ph/pas/docs/yr12-tbl-1.pdf; Janet I. Tu, "Assisted Suicide Measure Passes," *Seattle Times*, 4 November 2008, http://seattletimes.nwsource.com/html/localnews/2008352033_1000prop05m.html; Washington State Department of Health, *2009 Death with Dignity Act Report in Washington State*, March 2010, http://www.doh.wa.gov/dwda/forms/DWDA_2009.pdf; K. L. Cerminara and K. W. Goodman, *Key Events in the Case of Theresa Marie Schiavo*, http://www.miami.edu/ethics/schiavo/timeline.htm; Ted Barrett et al., "Schiavo Parents Back in Federal Court. Supreme Court, State Judge Deny Appeals to Resume Feeding," CNN.com, 25 March 2005, http://www.cnn.com/2005/LAW/03/24/schiavo; Ursula Smartt, "Euthanasia and the Law," BBC News, 21 February 2007, http://cdnedge.bbc.co.uk/1/hi/health/2600923.stm; Reyes Rincon, "El Parlamento andaluz aprueba la primera ley de muerte digna en España," *El País.com*, 17 March 2010, http://www.elpais.com/articulo/sociedad/Parlamento/andaluz/aprueba/primera/ley/muerte/digna/Espana/elpepusoc/20100317elpepusoc_2/Tes.

the judgment binding on all. Decisions in class action suits can have broader impact than decisions in other types of cases. Since the 1940s, class action suits have been the vehicles through which groups have asserted claims involving civil rights, legislative apportionment, and environmental problems. For example, schoolchildren have sued (through their parents) under the banner of class action to rectify claimed racial discrimination on the part of school authorities, as in *Brown* v. *Board of Education*.

Abetting the class action is the resurgence of state supreme courts' fashioning policies consistent with group preferences. Informed Americans often look to the U.S. Supreme Court for protection of their rights and liberties. In many circumstances, that expectation is correct. But state courts may serve as the staging areas for legal campaigns to change the law in the nation's highest court. They also exercise substantial influence over the policies that affect citizens daily, including the rights and liberties enshrined in state constitutions, statutes, and common law.[81]

Furthermore, state judges need not look to the U.S. Supreme Court for guidance on the meaning of certain state rights and liberties. If a state court chooses to rely solely on national law in deciding a case, that case is reviewable by the U.S. Supreme Court. But a state court can avoid review by the U.S. Supreme Court by basing its decision solely on state law or by plainly stating that its decision rests on both state and federal law. If the U.S. Supreme Court is likely to render a restrictive view of a constitutional right and the judges of a state court are inclined toward a more expansive view, the state judges can use the state ground to avoid Supreme Court review. In a period when the nation's highest court is moving in a decidedly conservative direction, some state courts have become safe havens for liberal values. And individuals and groups know where to moor their policies.

The New Jersey Supreme Court has been more aggressive than most other state supreme courts in following its own liberal constitutional path. It has gone further than the U.S. Supreme Court in promoting equality at the expense of freedom by prohibiting discrimination against women by private employers and by striking down the state's public school financing system, which had perpetuated vast disparities in public education within the state. The court has also preferred freedom over order in protecting the right to terminate life-support systems and in protecting free speech against infringement.[82] The New Jersey judges have charted their own path, despite the similarity in language between sections of the New Jersey Constitution and the U.S. Constitution. And the New Jersey judges have parted company with their national cousins even when the constitutional provisions at issue were identical.[83]

For example, the U.S. Supreme Court ruled in 1988 that warrantless searches of curbside garbage are constitutionally permissible. Both the New Jersey Constitution and the U.S. Constitution bar unreasonable searches and seizures. Yet in a 1990 decision expanding constitutional protections, the New Jersey court ruled that police officers need a search warrant before they can rummage through a person's trash. The court claimed that the New Jersey Constitution offers a greater degree of privacy than the U.S. Constitution. Because the decision rested on an interpretation of the state constitution, the existence of a similar right in the national charter had no bearing. The New Jersey court cannot act in a more restrictive manner than the U.S. Supreme Court allows, but it can be—and is—less restrictive.[84] State supreme courts can turn to their own state constitutions to "raise the ceiling of liberty above the floor created by the federal Bill of Rights."[85]

When judges reach decisions, they pay attention to the views of other courts—and not just those above them in the judicial hierarchy. State and federal court opinions are the legal storehouse from which judges regularly draw their ideas. Often the issues that affect individual lives—property, family, contracts—are grist for state courts, not federal courts. For example, when a state court faces a novel issue in a contract dispute, it will look at how other state courts have dealt with the problem. (Contract disputes are not a staple of the federal courts.) And if courts in several states have addressed an issue and the direction of the opinion is largely one-sided, the weight and authority of those opinions may move the court in that direction.[86] Courts that confront new issues with cogency and clarity are likely to become leaders of legal innovation.

State courts continue to serve as arenas for political conflict, with litigants, individually or in groups, vying for their preferred policies. The multiplicity of the nation's court system, with overlapping state and national responsibilities, provides alternative points of access for individuals and groups to present and argue their claims. This description of the courts fits the pluralist model of government.

Summary

The power of judicial review, claimed by the Supreme Court in 1803, placed the judiciary on an equal footing with Congress and the president. The principle of checks and balances can restrain judicial power through several means, such as constitutional amendments and impeachment. But restrictions on that power have been infrequent, leaving the federal courts to exercise considerable influence through judicial review and statutory construction.

The federal court system has three tiers. At the bottom are the district courts, where litigation begins and most disputes end. In the middle are the courts of appeals. At the top is the Supreme Court. The ability of judges to make policy increases as they move up the pyramid from trial courts to appellate courts to the Supreme Court.

The Supreme Court, free to draft its agenda through the discretionary control of its docket, harmonizes conflicting interpretations of national law and articulates constitutional rights. It is helped at this crucial stage by the solicitor general, who represents the executive branch of government before the High Court. The solicitor general's influence with the justices affects their choice of cases to review.

Political allegiance and complementary values are necessary conditions for appointment by the president to the coveted position of judge. The president and senators from the same party share appointment power

in the case of federal district and appellate judges. The president has more leeway in nominating Supreme Court justices, although all nominees must be confirmed by the Senate.

Courts inevitably fashion policy, for each of the states and for the nation. They provide multiple points of access for individuals to pursue their preferences and so fit the pluralist model of democracy. Furthermore, the class action enables people with small individual claims and limited financial resources to pursue their goals in court, reinforcing the pluralist model.

Judges confront both the original and the modern dilemmas of government. The impact of their decisions can extend well beyond a single case. Some democratic theorists are troubled by the expansion of judicial power. But today's courts fit within the pluralist model and usually are in step with what the public wants.

As the U.S. Supreme Court marches in a more conservative direction, some state supreme courts have become safe havens for more liberal policies on civil rights and civil liberties and for legal innovation generally. The state court systems have overlapping state and national responsibilities, offering groups and individuals many access points to present and argue their claims.

 CourseMate

Visit www.cengagebrain.com/shop/ ISBN/0495906182 for flashcards, web quizzes, videos and more!

NICHOLAS KAMM/AFP/Newscom

In public school classrooms around the country, students stand each day, salute the flag, and recite the Pledge of Allegiance. The Pledge has been part of classroom culture since 1892, when President Benjamin Harrison issued a proclamation celebrating the 400th anniversary of Christopher Columbus's discovery of America. In January 2010, a student at Roberto Clemente Middle School in Germantown, Maryland, did not stand, salute, and pledge. She refused her teacher's command to stand and was escorted from the classroom by a school security guard and sent to a counselor's office, where she was threatened with detention. She returned to school the next day and again refused to participate and was again escorted from the classroom to a counselor's office. Her mother objected, demanding an apology from the teacher. He refused. The assistant principal countered, suggesting that the student apologize to the teacher. As a last straw, the mother contacted the local chapter of the American Civil Liberties Union (ACLU).[1]

The ACLU intervened, explaining that the law has been crystal clear since 1943, when the U.S. Supreme Court ruled that students with religious objections are not required to recite the Pledge or salute the flag.[2] Subsequent decisions have clarified further that a student's rights to free expression—as well as freedom from forced expression—are protected by the Constitution, regardless of the source of a student's beliefs.[3] This student exercised her freedom of expression, though to be more exact, it was her freedom not to speak or participate that was at issue. But the price of her exercise was steep: she was humiliated and embarrassed repeatedly by her Pledge-reciting classmates.[4]

Can school officials ever require student expression? May those officials suppress student expression? More generally, how well do the courts respond to clashes that pit freedom against order or freedom against equality? Is freedom, order, or equality ever unconditional? In this chapter, we explore some value conflicts that the judiciary has resolved. You will be able to judge from the decisions in these cases whether American government has met the challenge of democracy by finding the appropriate balance between freedom and order and between freedom and equality.

To Pledge or Not to Pledge, That Is the Question

Every day, students across the United States stand, place their right hands over their hearts, and recite the Pledge of Allegiance while facing the American flag. The pledge exercise began in 1892, when Francis Bellamy proposed the right-hand-extended gesture to accompany the Pledge of Allegiance, which he authored. President Franklin D. Roosevelt instituted the hand-over-heart gesture in 1943 to avoid confusion with the Roman salute (right hand extended) used by the Italian fascists and quickly copied by the German Nazis. The picture on the left shows March 1943 grade school students saluting the flag. The picture on the right shows contemporary grade school students saluting the flag.

Some students hold religious beliefs that conflict with saluting the flag or reciting the pledge. Though the Supreme Court has long recognized the freedom to decline the pledge recitation and salute, that ruling was forgotten or ignored in Germantown, Maryland in 2010.

(*left*: Library of Congress; *right*: Michael Newman/PhotoEdit)

The value conflicts described in this chapter revolve around claims or entitlements that rest on law. Although we concentrate on conflicts over constitutional issues, the Constitution is not the only source of people's rights. Government at all levels creates rights through laws written by legislatures and regulations issued by bureaucracies.

We begin this chapter with the Bill of Rights and the freedoms it protects. Then we take a closer look at the role of the First Amendment in the original conflict between freedom and order. Next, we turn to the Fourteenth Amendment and the limits it places on the states. Then we examine the Ninth Amendment and its relationship to issues of personal autonomy. In Chapter 16, we will look at the Fourteenth Amendment's promise of equal protection, which sets the stage for the modern dilemma of government: the struggle between freedom and equality.

The Bill of Rights

You may remember from Chapter 3 that, at first, the framers of the Constitution did not include a list of individual liberties—a bill of rights—in the national charter. They believed that a bill of rights was not necessary because the Constitution spelled out the extent of the national government's power. But during the ratification debates, it became clear that the omission of a bill of rights was the most important obstacle to the adoption of the Constitution by the states. Eventually, the First Congress approved twelve amendments and sent them to the states for ratification. In 1791, the states ratified ten of the twelve amendments, and the nation had a bill of rights.

The Bill of Rights imposed limits on the national government but not on the state governments.* During the next seventy-seven years, litigants pressed the Supreme Court to extend the amendments' restraints to the states, but the Court refused until well after the adoption of the Fourteenth Amendment in 1868. Before then, protection from repressive state government had to come from state bills of rights.

The U.S. Constitution guarantees Americans numerous liberties and rights. In this chapter we explore a number of them. We will define and distinguish civil liberties and civil rights. (On some occasions, we use the terms interchangeably.) **Civil liberties**, sometimes referred to as "negative rights," are freedoms that are guaranteed to the individual. The guarantees take the form of restraints on government. For example, the First Amendment declares that "Congress shall make no law ... abridging the freedom of speech." Civil liberties declare what the government cannot do. The opening example of this chapter illustrates the civil liberties claim that government (in the form of the public school) cannot require students to salute and recite the Pledge.

In contrast, civil rights, sometimes called "positive rights," declare what the government must do or provide. **Civil rights** are powers and privileges that are guaranteed to the individual and protected against arbitrary removal at the hands of the government or other individuals. The right to vote and the right to a jury trial in criminal cases are civil rights embedded in the Constitution. Today, civil rights also embrace laws that further certain values. The Civil Rights Act of 1964, for example, furthered the value of equality by establishing the right to nondiscrimination in public accommodations and the right to equal employment opportunity. (See the feature "Examples of Positive and Negative Rights: Constitutional Rights and Human Rights" for examples in U.S. and U.N. contexts.) Civil liberties are the subject of this chapter; we discuss civil rights and their ramifications in Chapter 16.

The Bill of Rights lists both civil liberties and civil rights. When we refer to the rights and liberties of the Constitution, we mean the protections that are enshrined in the Bill of Rights and the first section of the Fourteenth Amendment.[5] The list includes freedom of religion, freedom of speech and of the press, the rights to assemble peaceably and to petition the government, the right to bear arms, the rights of the criminally accused, the requirement of due process, and the equal protection of the laws. The idea of a written enumeration of rights seems entirely natural to Americans today. Lacking a written constitution, Great Britain has started to provide written guarantees for human rights (see "Compared with What? Britain's Bill of Rights").

IN OUR OWN WORDS

Listen to Jerry Goldman discuss the main points and themes of this chapter.

www.cengagebrain.com/shop/ISBN/0495906182

civil liberties
Freedoms guaranteed to individuals taking the form of restraint on government.

civil rights
Powers or privileges guaranteed to individuals and protected from arbitrary removal at the hands of government or individuals.

---

*Congress considered more than one hundred amendments in its first session. One that was not approved would have limited power of the states to infringe on the rights of conscience, speech, press, and jury trial in criminal cases. James Madison thought this amendment was the "most valuable" of the list, but it failed to muster a two-thirds vote in the Senate.

Feature Story

Examples of Positive and Negative Rights: Constitutional Rights and Human Rights

	U.S. Constitution	United Nations Universal Declaration of Human Rights
Civil liberties, or "negative rights"	"Congress shall make no *law ... abridging the* freedom of speech, or of the press." (First Amendment) "Excessive bail *shall not be* required, nor excessive fines imposed, nor cruel and unusual punishments inflicted." (Eighth Amendment)	"*No one shall be* held in slavery or servitude; slavery and the slave trade shall be prohibited in all their forms." (Article 4) "*No one shall be* subjected to arbitrary arrest, detention or exile." (Article 9)
Civil rights, or "positive rights"	"In all criminal prosecutions, the accused shall enjoy *the right to* a speedy and public trial, ... and to have the assistance of counsel for his defense." (Sixth Amendment)	"Everyone has *the right to* a standard of living adequate for the health and well-being of himself and of his family, including food, clothing, housing and medical care and necessary social services, and the right to security in the event of unemployment, sickness, disability, widow-hood, old age or other lack of livelihood in circumstances beyond his control." (Article 25.1) "Everyone has *the right to* work, to free choice of employment, to just and favourable conditions of work and to protection against unemployment." (Article 23.1)

Some additional distinctions will prove useful in this and subsequent chapters. Persons possess *rights,* and governments possess *powers.* If governments may lawfully regulate a person's behavior (for example, requiring that you possess a valid license to drive a car), then that behavior is a privilege. Thus, you do not have a right to drive, but merely a privilege subject to reasonable restrictions by government. Although some rights may be spelled out in absolute language, generally no right is absolute. However, government limitations on rights are exceptional: they require a higher burden of proof and must be minimal in scope.[6]

Freedom of Religion

Congress shall make no law respecting an establishment of religion, or prohibiting the free exercise thereof.

Religious freedom was important to the colonies and later to the states. That importance is reflected in its position among the ratified amendments that we know as the Bill of Rights: first, in the very first amendment. The First Amendment guarantees freedom of religion in two clauses: the **establishment clause**, which prohibits laws establishing religion, and the **free-exercise clause**, which prevents the government from interfering with the exercise of religion. Together, they ensure that the government can neither promote nor inhibit religious beliefs or practices.

At the time of the Constitutional Convention, many Americans, especially in New England, maintained that government could and should foster religion, specifically Protestantism. However, many more Americans agreed that this was an issue for state governments, that the national government had no authority to meddle in religious affairs. The religion clauses were drafted in this spirit.[7]

The Supreme Court has refused to interpret the religion clauses definitively. The result is an amalgam of rulings, the cumulative effect of which is that freedom to believe is unlimited, but freedom to practice a belief can be limited. Religion cannot benefit directly from government actions (for example, government cannot make contributions to churches or synagogues), but it can benefit indirectly from those actions (for example, government can supply books on secular subjects for use in all schools—public, private, and parochial).

Religion is much more important to Americans than to citizens of other advanced nations.[8] Most Americans identify with a particular religious faith, and 40 percent attend church in a typical week. The vast majority believe in God or a supreme being, in far greater proportion than people in France, Britain, or Italy. (See Figure 15.1.)

Majoritarians might argue, then, that government should support religion. They would agree that the establishment clause bars government support of a single faith, but they might maintain that government should support all faiths. Such support would be consistent with what the majority wants and true to the language of the Constitution. In its decisions, the Supreme Court has rejected this interpretation of the establishment clause, leaving itself open to charges of undermining democracy. Those charges may be true with regard to majoritarian democracy, but the Court can justify its protection in terms of the basic values of democratic government.

The Establishment Clause

The provision that "Congress shall make no law respecting an establishment of religion" bars government sponsorship or support of religious activity. The Supreme Court has consistently held that the establishment clause requires government to maintain a position of neutrality toward religions and to maintain that position in cases that involve choices between religion and nonreligion. However, the Court has never interpreted the clause as barring all assistance that incidentally aids religious institutions.

Government Support of Religion. In 1879, the Supreme Court contended, quoting Thomas Jefferson, that the establishment clause erected "a wall of separation between church and State."[9] That wall was breached somewhat

establishment clause
The first clause in the First Amendment, which forbids government establishment of religion.

free-exercise clause
The second clause in the First Amendment, which prevents the government from interfering with the exercise of religion.

Compared with What?

Britain's Bill of Rights

Unlike the United States, Britain has no single document or law known as "the constitution." Instead, it has an "unwritten constitution"—a combination of important documents and laws passed by Parliament (the British legislature), court decisions, customs, and conventions. Britain's "constitution" has no existence apart from ordinary law. In contrast to the American system of government, Britain's Parliament may change, amend, or abolish its fundamental laws and conventions at will. No special procedures or barriers must be overcome to enact such changes.

According to government leaders, Britain has done very well without a written constitution, or at least that was the position of Prime Minister Margaret Thatcher when she was presented with a proposal for a written constitution in 1989. Thatcher observed that despite Britain's lack of a bill of rights and an independent judiciary, "our present constitutional arrangements continue to serve us well.... Furthermore, the government does not feel that a written constitution in itself changes or guarantees anything."

In 1995, a nationwide poll revealed that the British people held a different view. Three-fourths of British adults thought that it was time for a written constitution, and even more maintained that the country needed a written bill of rights. These high levels of public support and the election of a new government in 1997 helped build momentum for important changes in Britain's long history of rule by unwritten law. In October 2000, England formally began enforcing the Human Rights Act, a key component of the government's political program, which incorporated into British law sixteen guarantees of the European Convention on Human Rights. Thus, the nation that

in 1947, when the justices upheld a local government program that provided free transportation to parochial school students.[10] The breach seemed to widen in 1968, when the Court held constitutional a government program in which parochial school students borrowed state-purchased textbooks.[11] The objective of the program, reasoned the majority, was to further educational opportunity. The students, not the schools, borrowed the books, and the parents, not the church, realized the benefits.

But in 1971, in *Lemon* v. *Kurtzman*, the Court struck down a state program that would have helped pay the salaries of teachers hired by parochial schools to give instruction in secular subjects.[12] The justices proposed a three-pronged test for determining the constitutionality of government programs and laws under the establishment clause:

- They must have a secular purpose (such as lending books to parochial school students).
- Their primary effect must not be to advance or inhibit religion.
- They must not entangle the government excessively with religion.

has been the source of some of the world's most significant ideas concerning liberty and individual freedom finally put into writing guarantees to ensure these fundamental rights for its own citizens. Legal experts hailed the edict as the largest change to British law in three centuries.

The Charter of Fundamental Rights, a text that is in harmony with the provisions stipulated in the European Convention on Human Rights, was to achieve legally binding status assuming that all European Union countries ratified the current Reform Treaty. The United Kingdom and Poland, skittish about the imposition of European values in their courts, opted out from the Charter provisions. Questions remain whether the opt-out language is sufficient to achieve the desired objective. So it is uncertain whether the Human Rights Act will, in the words of one former minister in the Thatcher government, "rob us of freedoms we have had for centuries" or, as British human rights lawyer Geoffrey Robertson sees it, "help produce a better culture of liberty." A 2008 report by a joint committee of Parliament endorsed the idea of a consensus-based U.K. Bill of Rights and Freedoms emphasizing civil liberties rather than civil rights. But in doing so, the committee firmly rejected the idea that such a Bill of Rights would empower courts to strike down legislation, as in the power of judicial review. "We consider this to be fundamentally at odds with this country's tradition of parliamentary democracy," concluded the committee.

Sources: Andrew Marr, *Ruling Britannia: The Failure and Future of British Democracy* (London: Michael Joseph, 1995); Will Hutton, *The State We're In* (London: Cape, 1995); Fred Barbash, "The Movement to Rule Britannia Differently," *Washington Post,* 23 September 1995, p. A27; "Bringing Rights Home," *Economist,* 26 August 2000, pp. 45–46; Sarah Lyall, "209 Years Later, the English Get American-Style Bill of Rights," *New York Times,* 2 October 2000, p. A3; Suzanne Kapner, "Britain's Legal Barriers Start to Fall," *New York Times,* 4 October 2000, p. W1; Joint Committee on Human Rights, *A Bill of Rights for the UK? Twenty-ninth Report of Session 2007–08* (London: Stationery Office, Ltd., 10 August 2008), http://www.publications.parliament.uk/pa/jt200708/jtselect/jtrights/165/165i.pdf.

The program in *Lemon* did not satisfy the last prong. The government would have had to monitor the program constantly, thus ensuring an excessive entanglement with religion. The *Lemon* test, as it became known, governed the Supreme Court's interpretation of such cases for twenty-five years. Then in 1997, the Court dramatically loosened its application of the test in a case reminiscent of the one that gave rise to it. The future of the test now seems uncertain.

Agostini v. *Felton* involved the use of public school teachers to teach congressionally mandated remedial courses to disadvantaged students in New York parochial schools. This time, the Court emphasized that only government *neutrality* toward religion was required by the First Amendment. Moreover, only *excessive* entanglements will be deemed to violate the establishment clause. By a vote of 5–4, it held that religion was neither hindered nor helped by parochial schools' using public school teachers at taxpayers' expense to teach secular subjects.[13] Although the opinion was narrowly written, the Court appears to have lowered the wall separating church and state.

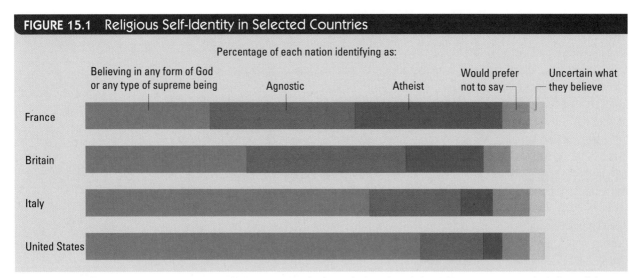

FIGURE 15.1 Religious Self-Identity in Selected Countries

Percentage of each nation identifying as:

Believing in any form of God or any type of supreme being — Agnostic — Atheist — Would prefer not to say — Uncertain what they believe

France
Britain
Italy
United States

Most Americans believe in God or a supreme being compared to people in Italy, Britain, or France. France and Britain each have proportionally more atheists than people in Italy or the United States.

Source: *New York Times,* 5 September 2007.

The Court provided additional support in 2002 for its tolerant position regarding the establishment clause when it upheld a state school-voucher program in which secular or sectarian schools could participate. In *Zelman* v. *Simmons-Harris,* the justices, dividing 5–4, maintained that the program did not favor religious schools over nonreligious ones when the aid went to the student or parent who then chose the school.[14]

Consider another thorny issue. Does the display of religious artifacts on public property violate the establishment clause? In *Lynch* v. *Donnelly* (1984), the court said no, by a vote of 5–4.[15] At issue was a publicly funded nativity scene on public property, surrounded by commercial symbols of the Christmas season such as Santa and his sleigh. Although he conceded that a crèche has religious significance, Chief Justice Warren E. Burger, writing for the majority, maintained that the display had a legitimate secular purpose: the celebration of a national holiday. Second, the display did not have the primary effect of benefiting religion; the religious benefits were "indirect, remote and incidental." And third, the display led to no excessive entanglement of religion and government. The justices hinted at a relaxation of their interpretation of the establishment clause by asserting an "unwillingness to be confined to any single test or criterion in this sensitive area." The upshot of *Lynch* was an acknowledgment of the religious heritage of the majority of Americans, although the Christmas holiday is a vivid reminder to religious minorities and the nonreligious of their separateness from the dominant Christian culture.

The *Lynch* decision led to a proliferation of closely decided cases testing the limits of government-sponsored religious displays. The latest ones in 2005 involved a forty-year-old monument displaying the Ten Commandments on the Texas state capitol and a display of the Ten Commandments in two Kentucky county courthouses. In separate 5–4 rulings, the justices upheld the Texas display because of the monument's "secular purpose,"[16] but on the same day, the Court struck down the Kentucky courthouse displays because they were not integrated into a secular presentation and so had a primarily religious purpose.[17]

The Court continued to struggle with the limits of government entanglement with religious symbols. In 2010, a badly splintered 5–4 ruling that generated six separate opinions held that a five-by-eight-foot cross—originally made of wood but more recently made of four-inch metal pipe—erected by the Veterans of Foreign Wars on federal land to honor World War I veterans did not violate the establishment clause.[18] The federal government faced a dilemma: leaving the cross in place would violate the establishment clause, but removing the cross would show "disrespect for those the cross was seen as honoring," wrote Justice Anthony M. Kennedy for the majority. The solution at issue in the case was a land swap in which the government traded the public land for private property, enabling the cross to remain. But the land trade could be viewed as promoting religion, argued Justice John Paul Stevens in dissent. Such cases are sure to continue as the Court's membership, and perhaps the majority coalition, changes.

School Prayer. The Supreme Court has consistently equated prayer in public schools with government support of religion. In 1962, it struck down the daily reading of this twenty-two-word nondenominational prayer in New York's public schools: "Almighty God, we acknowledge our dependence upon Thee, and we beg Thy blessings upon us, our parents, our teachers and our country." Justice Hugo L. Black, writing for a 6–1 majority, held that official state approval of prayer was an unconstitutional attempt on the part of the state to establish a religion. This decision, in *Engel* v. *Vitale,* drew a storm of protest that has yet to subside.[19]

The Crux of the Matter

A crucifix on national park land honored World War I veterans. The government swapped the small plot for private land to avoid a possible violation of the First Amendment's Establishment Clause. A splintered Supreme Court ruling in 2010 allowed the trade. A few weeks later, thieves stole the eight-foot-high cross.

(Eric Nystrom)

IDEALOG.ORG

Should prayer in school be required? Take IDEAlog's self-test.

The following year, the Court struck down a state law calling for daily Bible reading and recitation of the Lord's Prayer in Pennsylvania's public schools.[20] The school district defended the reading and recitation on the grounds that they taught literature, perpetuated traditional institutions, and inculcated moral virtues. But the Court held that the state's involvement violated the government's constitutionally imposed neutrality in matters of religion.

In 1992, the Court struck down the offering of nonsectarian prayers at official public school graduations. In a 5–4 decision, the Court held that government involvement creates "a state-sponsored and state-directed religious exercise in a public school."[21] The justices said that the establishment clause means that government may not conduct a religious exercise in the context of a school event. Yet school prayer persists.

In 2000, the football gridiron was the latest battlefield in the conflict. By a 6–3 vote, the Supreme Court struck down the practice of organized, student-led prayer at public high school football games. The majority maintained that "the delivery of a pregame prayer had the improper effect of coercing those present to participate in an act of religious worship." It reaffirmed that "fundamental rights may not be submitted to vote; they depend on the outcome of no elections."[22]

Team Religion Moves from Field to Stands

Friday night football is a big deal for high school students and their families. Following 9/11, cheerleaders at a Fort Oglethorpe, Georgia, high school wanted to embrace the Bible as part of Friday night football. For eight seasons, players charged on to the field with banners declaring "Commit for Christ." But recognizing that it was deep in a constitutional hole, the school board banned the practice in 2009. Parents and cheerleaders responded by moving their banners to the stands, where they now cheer on their team and fans with inspirations from scripture. Their freedom of expression seems secure, as long as it is not exercised on the playing field.

(The New York Times/Redux Picture)

Religious training during public school is out-of-bounds, but religious training after school now passes constitutional muster. In 2001, the Supreme Court ruled that public schools must open their doors to after-school religious activities on the same basis as other after-school programs such as the debate club. To do otherwise would constitute viewpoint discrimination in violation of the free speech clause of the First Amendment.

The issue of school prayer remains. In 2008, the Indian River school district in Sussex County, Delaware, agreed to revise its policies that had tolerated Christian prayer at school functions in clear violation of prior Supreme Court rulings. The settlement, which arose from a lawsuit by two Jewish families, created enormous ill will. One family was forced to move after facing threats and harassment when Christian community members viewed the lawsuit as an effort to limit their free exercise of religion.[23]

The establishment clause creates a problem for government. Support for all religions at the expense of nonreligion seems to pose the least risk to social order. Tolerance of the dominant religion at the expense of other religions risks minority discontent, but support for no religion (neutrality between religion and nonreligion) risks majority discontent.

The Free-Exercise Clause

The free-exercise clause of the First Amendment states that "Congress shall make no law ... prohibiting the free exercise [of religion]." The Supreme Court has struggled to avoid absolute interpretations of this restriction and thus avoid its complement, the establishment clause. An example: suppose Congress grants exemptions from military service to individuals who have religious scruples against war. These exemptions could be construed as a

Let Us Pray

Although school prayer and religious activity in the Indian River school district in Sussex County, Delaware, may have been resolved as a matter of policy, the invocation of a prayer at the start of school board meetings continues. Here, board member Nina Lou Bunting bows her head in prayer at a 2005 meeting. A Delaware federal court rebuffed an establishment clause challenge to the practice in 2010.

(News Journal File/Scott Nathan)

violation of the establishment clause because they favor some religious groups over others. But if Congress forced conscientious objectors to fight—to violate their religious beliefs—the government would run afoul of the free-exercise clause. In fact, Congress has granted military draftees such exemptions. But the Supreme Court has avoided a conflict between the establishment and free-exercise clauses by equating religious objection to war with any deeply held humanistic opposition to it. This solution leaves unanswered a central question: Does the free-exercise clause require government to grant exemptions from legal duties that conflict with religious obligations, or does it guarantee only that the law will be applicable to religious believers without discrimination or preference?[24]

In the free-exercise cases, the justices have distinguished religious beliefs from actions based on those beliefs. Beliefs are inviolate, beyond the reach of government control. But the First Amendment does not protect antisocial actions. Consider conflicting values about working on the Sabbath.

Working on the Sabbath. The modern era of free-exercise thinking began with *Sherbert* v. *Verner* (1963). Adeil Sherbert, a Seventh-Day Adventist, lost her mill job because she refused to work on Saturday, her Sabbath. She filed for unemployment compensation and was referred to another job, which she declined because it also required Saturday work. Because she declined the job, the state disqualified her from receiving unemployment benefits. In a 7–2 decision, the Supreme Court ruled that the disqualification imposed an impermissible burden on Sherbert's free exercise of religion. The First Amendment, declared the majority, protects observance as well as belief. A neutral law that burdens the free exercise of religion is subject to **strict scrutiny**. This means that the law may be upheld only if the government can demonstrate that (1) the law is justified by a "compelling governmental interest," (2) the law is narrowly tailored to achieve a legitimate goal, and (3) the law in question is the least restrictive means for achieving that interest.[25] Scholars had long maintained that strict scrutiny was "strict in theory but fatal in fact." A recent empirical study debunked this claim, finding that in all strict scrutiny cases from 1990 to 2003, the federal courts upheld nearly one-third of the challenged laws.[26] The strict scrutiny standard sets a high bar but not an insurmountable one.

The *Sherbert* decision prompted religious groups and individual believers to challenge laws that conflict with their faith. We have seen how conflicts arise from the imposition of penalties for refusing to engage in religiously prohibited conduct. But conflicts may also arise from laws that impose penalties for engaging in religiously motivated conduct.[27]

strict scrutiny
A standard used by the Supreme Court in deciding whether a law or policy is to be adjudged constitutional. To pass strict scrutiny, the law or policy must be justified by a "compelling governmental interest," must be narrowly tailored, and must be the least restrictive means for achieving that interest.

Freedom of Expression

Congress shall make no law ... abridging the freedom of speech, or of the press; or the right of the people peaceably to assemble, and to petition the Government for a redress of grievances.

James Madison introduced the original versions of the speech clause and the press clause of the First Amendment in the House of Representatives in June 1789. One early proposal provided that "the people shall not be deprived of their right to speak, to write, or to publish their sentiments, and the freedom of the press, as one of the great bulwarks of liberty, shall be inviolable." That version was rewritten several times, then merged with the religion and peaceable assembly clauses to yield the First Amendment.

The spare language of the First Amendment seems perfectly clear: "Congress shall make no law ... abridging the freedom of speech, or of the press." Yet a majority of the Supreme Court has never agreed that this "most majestic guarantee" is absolutely inviolable.[28] Historians have long debated the framers' intentions regarding these **free-expression clauses**, the press and speech clauses of the First Amendment. The dominant view is that the clauses confer a right to unrestricted discussion of public affairs.[29] Other scholars, examining much the same evidence, conclude that few, if any, of the framers clearly understood the clause; moreover, they insist that the First Amendment does not rule out prosecution for seditious statements (statements inciting insurrection).[30]

The license to speak freely does not move multitudes of Americans to speak out on controversial issues. Americans have woven subtle restrictions into the fabric of our society: the risk of criticism or ostracism by family, peers, or employers tends to reduce the number of people who test the limits of free speech to individuals ready to bear the burdens. The middle school student who sat through the Pledge of Allegiance in 2010 bore that burden. As Mark Twain once remarked, "It is by the goodness of God that in our country we have three unspeakably precious things: freedom of speech, freedom of conscience, and the prudence never to practice either of them."[31]

Today, the clauses are deemed to bar most forms of **prior restraint**—censorship before publication as well as after-the-fact prosecution for political and other discourse. The Supreme Court has evolved two approaches to the resolution of claims based on the free-expression clauses. First, government can regulate or punish the advocacy of ideas, but only if it can prove an intent to promote lawless action and demonstrate that a high probability exists that such action will occur.[32] Second, government may impose reasonable restrictions on the means for communicating ideas, restrictions that can incidentally discourage free expression. Hence, people have the right to protest but not if their physical presence would block the entrance to an occupied public building.

Suppose, for example, that a political party advocates nonpayment of personal income taxes. Government cannot regulate or punish that party for advocating tax nonpayment because the standards of proof—that the act be directed at inciting or producing imminent lawless action and that the act be likely to produce such action—do not apply. But government can impose restrictions on the way the party's candidates communicate what they are advocating. Government can bar them from blaring messages from loudspeakers in residential neighborhoods at 3:00 A.M.

free-expression clauses
The press and speech clauses of the First Amendment.

prior restraint
Censorship before publication.

Freedom of Speech

The starting point for any modern analysis of free speech is the **clear and present danger test**, formulated by Justice Oliver Wendell Holmes in the Supreme Court's unanimous decision in *Schenck* v. *United States* (1919). Charles T. Schenck and his fellow defendants were convicted under a federal criminal statute for attempting to disrupt World War I military recruitment by distributing leaflets claiming that conscription was unconstitutional. The government believed this behavior threatened the public order. At the core of the Court's opinion, Holmes wrote, was the view that

> the character of every act depends upon the circumstances in which it is done.... The most stringent protection of free speech would not protect a man in falsely shouting fire in a theatre, and causing a panic.... The question in every case is whether the words used are used in such circumstances and are of such a nature as to create *a clear and present danger* that they will bring about the substantive evils that Congress has a right to prevent. It is a question of proximity and degree. When a nation is at war many things that might be said in time of peace are such a hindrance to its effort that their utterance will not be endured so long as men fight, and that no court could regard them as protected by any constitutional right [emphasis added].[33]

Because the actions of the defendants in *Schenck* were deemed to create a clear and present danger to the United States at that time, the Supreme Court upheld the defendants' convictions. The clear and present danger test helps to distinguish the advocacy of ideas, which is protected, from incitement, which is not. However, Holmes later frequently disagreed with a majority of his colleagues in applying the test.

In an often quoted dissent in *Abrams* v. *United States* (1919), Holmes revealed his deeply rooted resistance to the suppression of ideas. The majority had upheld Jacob Abrams's criminal conviction for distributing leaflets that denounced the war and U.S. opposition to the Russian Revolution. Holmes wrote:

> When men have realized that time has upset many fighting faiths, they may come to believe ... that the ultimate good desired is better reached by free trade in ideas—that the best test of truth is the power of the thought to get itself accepted in the competition of the market, and that truth is the only ground upon which their wishes safely can be carried out. That at any rate is the theory of our Constitution.[34]

clear and present danger test
A means by which the Supreme Court has distinguished between speech as the advocacy of ideas, which is protected by the First Amendment, and speech as incitement, which is not protected.

In 1925, the Court issued a landmark decision in *Gitlow* v. *New York*.[35] Benjamin Gitlow was arrested for distributing copies of a "left-wing manifesto" that called for the establishment of socialism through strikes and working-class uprisings of any form. Gitlow was convicted under a state criminal anarchy law; Schenck and Abrams had been convicted under a federal law. For the first time, the Court assumed that the First Amendment speech and press provisions applied to the states through the due process clause of the Fourteenth Amendment. Still, a majority of the justices affirmed Gitlow's conviction. Justices

Holmes and Louis D. Brandeis argued in dissent that Gitlow's ideas did not pose a clear and present danger. "Eloquence may set fire to reason," conceded the dissenters. "But whatever may be thought of the redundant discourse before us, it had no chance of starting a present conflagration."

The protection of advocacy faced yet another challenge in 1948, when eleven members of the Communist Party were charged with violating the Smith Act, a federal law making the advocacy of force or violence against the United States a criminal offense. The leaders were convicted, although the government introduced no evidence that they had actually urged people to commit specific violent acts. The Supreme Court mustered a majority for its decision to uphold the convictions under the act, but it could not get a majority to agree on the reasons in support of that decision. The biggest bloc, of four justices, announced the plurality opinion in 1951, arguing that the government's interest was substantial enough to warrant criminal penalties.[36] The justices interpreted the threat to the government to be the gravity of the advocated action, "discounted by its improbability." In other words, a single soap-box orator advocating revolution stands little chance of success. But a well-organized, highly disciplined political movement advocating revolution in the tinderbox of unstable political conditions stands a greater chance of success. In broadening the "clear and present danger" test to the "grave and probable danger" test, the Court held that the government was justified in acting preventively rather than waiting until revolution was about to occur.

By 1969, the pendulum had swung back in the other direction: the justices began to put more emphasis on freedom. That year, in *Brandenburg* v. *Ohio*, a unanimous decision extended the freedom of speech to new limits.[37] Clarence Brandenburg, the leader of the Ohio Ku Klux Klan, had been convicted under a state law for advocating racial strife at a Klan rally. His comments, which had been filmed by a television crew, included threats against government officials.

The Court reversed Brandenburg's conviction because the government had failed to prove that the danger was real. The Court went even further and declared that threatening speech is protected by the First Amendment unless the government can prove that such advocacy is "directed to inciting or producing imminent lawless action and is likely to incite or produce such action." The ruling offered wider latitude for the expression of political ideas than ever before in the nation's history.

The United States stands alone when it comes to protection for hateful speech. Several democratic nations—including Canada, England, France, Germany, the Netherlands, South Africa, Australia, and India—have laws or have signed international conventions banning such speech. Nazi swastikas and flags are forbidden for sale in Israel and France but not in the United States. Anyone who denies the Holocaust in Canada, Germany, and France is subject to criminal prosecution but not in the United States. Some scholars have begun to urge a relaxation of our stringent speech protections because we now live "in an age when words have inspired acts of mass murder and terrorism."[38]

Symbolic Expression. Symbolic expression, or nonverbal communication, generally receives less protection than pure speech. But the courts have upheld certain types of symbolic expression. *Tinker* v. *Des Moines Independent County School District* (1969) involved three public school students who wore black armbands to school to protest the Vietnam War. Principals in their school district had prohibited the wearing of armbands on the grounds that such conduct would provoke a disturbance; the district suspended the students. The Supreme Court overturned the suspensions. Justice Abe Fortas declared for the majority that the principals had failed to show that the forbidden conduct would substantially interfere with appropriate school discipline:

> Undifferentiated fear or apprehension of disturbance is not enough to overcome the right to freedom of expression. Any departure from absolute regimentation may cause trouble. Any variation from the majority's opinion may inspire fear. Any word spoken, in class, in the lunchroom, or on the campus, that deviates from the views of another person may start an argument or cause a disturbance. But our Constitution says we must take this risk.[39]

Order Versus Free Speech: Fighting Words and Threatening Expression. Fighting words are a notable exception to the protection of free speech. In *Chaplinsky* v. *New Hampshire* (1942), Walter Chaplinsky, a Jehovah's Witness, convicted under a state statute for calling a city marshal a "God-damned racketeer" and "a damned fascist" in a public place, appealed to the Supreme Court.[40] The Supreme Court upheld Chaplinsky's conviction on the theory that **fighting words**—words that "inflict injury or tend to incite an immediate breach of the peace"—do not convey ideas and thus are not subject to First Amendment protection.

The Court sharply narrowed the definition of *fighting words* just seven years later. Arthur Terminiello, a suspended Catholic priest from Alabama and a vicious anti-Semite, addressed the Christian Veterans of America, a right-wing extremist group, in a Chicago hall. Terminiello called the jeering crowd of fifteen hundred angry protesters outside the hall "slimy scum" and ranted on about the "communistic, Zionistic" Jews of America, evoking cries of "kill the Jews" and "dirty kikes" from his listeners. The crowd outside the hall heaved bottles, bricks, and rocks, while the police attempted to protect Terminiello and his listeners inside. Finally, the police arrested Terminiello for disturbing the peace.

Terminiello's speech was far more incendiary than Walter Chaplinsky's. Yet the Supreme Court struck down Terminiello's conviction on the ground that provocative speech, even speech that stirs people to anger, is protected by the First Amendment. "Freedom of speech," wrote Justice William O. Douglas in the majority opinion, "though not absolute ... is nevertheless protected against censorship or punishment, unless shown likely to produce a clear ... and present danger of a serious substantive evil that rises far above public inconvenience, annoyance, or unrest."

fighting words
Speech that is not protected by the First Amendment because it inflicts injury or tends to incite an immediate disturbance of the peace.

This broad view of protection brought a stiff rebuke in Justice Robert Jackson's dissenting opinion:

> The choice is not between order and liberty. It is between liberty with order and anarchy without either. There is danger that, if the court does not temper its doctrinaire logic with a little practical wisdom, it will convert the constitutional Bill of Rights into a suicide pact.[41]

The times seem to have caught up with the idealism that Jackson criticized in his colleagues. In *Cohen* v. *California* (1971), a nineteen-year-old department store worker expressed his opposition to the Vietnam War by wearing a jacket in the hallway of a Los Angeles county courthouse emblazoned with the words "FUCK THE DRAFT. STOP THE WAR." The young man, Paul Cohen, was charged in 1968 under a California statute that prohibits "maliciously and willfully disturb[ing] the peace and quiet of any neighborhood or person [by] offensive conduct." He was found guilty and sentenced to thirty days in jail. On appeal, the U.S. Supreme Court reversed Cohen's conviction.

The Court reasoned that the expletive he used, while provocative, was not directed at anyone in particular; besides, the state presented no evidence that the words on Cohen's jacket would provoke people in "substantial numbers" to take some kind of physical action. In recognizing that "one man's vulgarity is another's lyric," the Supreme Court protected two elements of speech: the emotive (the expression of emotion) and the cognitive (the expression of ideas).[42]

The Supreme Court will confront these kinds of questions again as challenges to intimidating speech on the World Wide Web make their way through the nation's legal system. In 1996, Congress passed the Communications Decency Act, which made it a crime for a person knowingly to circulate "patently offensive" sexual material to Internet sites accessible to those under eighteen years old. Is this an acceptable way to protect children from offensive material, or is it a muzzle on free speech? A federal court quickly declared the act unconstitutional. In an opinion of over two hundred pages, the Court observed that "just as the strength of the Internet is chaos, so the strength of our liberty depends on the chaos and cacophony of the unfettered speech the First Amendment protects."[43]

The Supreme Court upheld the lower court's ruling in June 1997 in *Reno* v. *ACLU*.[44] Its nearly unanimous opinion was a broad affirmation of free speech rights in cyberspace, arguing that the Internet was more analogous to print media than to television, and thus even indecent material on the Internet was entitled to First Amendment protection.

How far does free expression extend? Very far, so far. The justices in 2010 struck down on free expression grounds a federal law that banned depictions of animal cruelty.[45] The Court also agreed to decide whether California's ban on the sale of violent video games to minors is an unconstitutional limitation on freedom of speech.[46]

Freedom of the Press

The First Amendment guarantees that government "shall make no law ... abridging the freedom ... of the press." Although the free press guarantee was originally adopted as a restriction on the national government, the Supreme Court has held since 1931 that it applies to state and local governments as well.

The ability to collect and report information without government interference was (and still is) thought to be essential to a free society. The print media continue to use and defend the freedom conferred on them by the framers. However, the electronic media have had to accept some government regulation stemming from the scarcity of broadcast frequencies (see Chapter 6).

Defamation of Character. Libel is the written defamation of character.* A person who believes his or her name and character have been harmed by false statements in a publication can institute a lawsuit against the publication and seek monetary compensation for the damage. Such a lawsuit can impose limits on freedom of expression; at the same time, false statements impinge on the rights of individuals. In a landmark decision in *New York Times* v. *Sullivan* (1964), the Supreme Court declared that freedom of the press takes precedence—at least when the defamed individual is a public official.[47] The Court unanimously agreed that the First Amendment protects the publication of all statements—even false ones—about the conduct of

---

*Slander is the oral defamation of character. The durability of the written word usually means that libel is a more serious accusation than slander.

public officials, except statements made with actual malice (with knowledge that they are false or in reckless disregard for their truth or falsity).

Three years later, the Court extended this protection to apply to suits brought by any public figure, whether a government official or not. **Public figures** are people who assume roles of prominence in society or thrust themselves to the forefront of public controversies, including officials, actors, writers, and television personalities. These people must show actual malice on the part of the publication that printed false statements about them. Because the burden of proof is so great, few plaintiffs prevail. And freedom of the press is the beneficiary.

What if the damage inflicted is not to one's reputation but to one's emotional state? Government seeks to maintain the prevailing social order, which prescribes proper modes of behavior. Does the First Amendment restrict the government in protecting citizens from behavior that intentionally inflicts emotional distress? This issue arose in a parody of a public figure in *Hustler* magazine. The target was the Reverend Jerry Falwell, a televangelist who founded the Moral Majority. The parody had Falwell—in an interview—discussing a drunken, incestuous rendezvous with his mother in an outhouse, saying, "I always get sloshed before I go out to the pulpit." Falwell won a $200,000 award for "emotional distress." The magazine appealed, and the Supreme Court confronted the issue of social order versus free speech in 1988.[48]

In a unanimous decision, the Court overturned the award. In his sweeping opinion for the Court, Chief Justice William H. Rehnquist gave wide latitude to the First Amendment's protection of free speech. He observed that "graphic depictions and satirical cartoons have played a prominent role in public and political debate" throughout the nation's history and that the First Amendment protects even "vehement, caustic, and sometimes unpleasantly sharp attacks." Free speech protects criticism of public figures, even if the criticism is outrageous and offensive.

Prior Restraint and the Press. As discussed above, in the United States, freedom of the press has primarily meant protection from prior restraint, or censorship. The Supreme Court's first encounter with a law imposing prior restraint on a newspaper was in *Near* v. *Minnesota* (1931).[49] In Minneapolis, Jay Near published a scandal sheet in which he attacked local officials, charging that they were in league with gangsters.[50] Minnesota officials obtained an injunction to prevent Near from publishing his newspaper, under a state law that allowed such action against periodicals deemed "malicious, scandalous, and defamatory."

The Supreme Court struck down the law, declaring that prior restraint places an unacceptable burden on a free press. Chief Justice Charles Evans Hughes forcefully articulated the need for a vigilant, unrestrained press: "The fact that the liberty of the press may be abused by miscreant purveyors of scandal does not make any the less necessary the immunity of the press from previous restraint in dealing with official misconduct." Although the Court acknowledged that prior restraint may be permissible in exceptional circumstances, it did not specify those circumstances, nor has it yet done so.

public figures
People who assume roles of prominence in society or thrust themselves to the forefront of public controversy.

Consider another case, which occurred during a war, a time when the tension between government-imposed order and individual freedom is often at a peak. In 1971, Daniel Ellsberg, a special assistant in the Pentagon's Office of International Security Affairs, delivered portions of a classified U.S. Department of Defense study to the *New York Times* and the *Washington Post*. By making the documents public, he hoped to discredit the Vietnam War and thereby end it. The U.S. Department of Justice sought to restrain the *Times* and the *Post* from publishing the documents, which became known as the Pentagon Papers, contending that their publication would prolong the war and embarrass the government. The case was quickly brought before the Supreme Court, which delayed its summer adjournment to hear oral arguments.

Three days later, in a 6–3 decision in *New York Times* v. *United States* (1971), the Court concluded that the government had not met the heavy burden of proving that immediate, inevitable, and irreparable harm would follow publication of the documents.[51] The majority expressed its view in a brief, unsigned opinion; individual and collective concurring and dissenting views added nine additional opinions to the decision. Two justices maintained that the First Amendment offers absolute protection against government censorship, no matter what the situation. But the other justices left the door ajar for the imposition of prior restraint in the most extreme and compelling of circumstances. The result was hardly a ringing endorsement of freedom of the press or a full affirmation of the public's right to all the information that is vital to the debate of public issues.

Freedom of Expression Versus Maintaining Order. The courts have consistently held that freedom of the press does not override the requirements of law enforcement. A grand jury called on a Louisville, Kentucky, reporter who had researched and written an article about drug-related activities to identify people he had seen in possession of marijuana or in the act of processing it. The reporter refused to testify, maintaining that freedom of the press shielded him from this inquiry. In a closely divided decision, the Supreme Court in 1972 rejected this position.[52] The Court declared that no exception, even a limited one, is permissible to the rule that all citizens have a duty to give their government whatever testimony they are capable of giving.

Consider the 1988 case of a St. Louis high school principal who deleted articles on divorce and teenage pregnancy from the school's newspaper on the grounds that the articles invaded the privacy of students and families who were the focus of the stories. Three student editors filed suit in federal court, claiming that the principal had violated their First Amendment rights. They argued that the principal's censorship interfered with the newspaper's function as a public forum, a role protected by the First Amendment. The principal maintained that the newspaper was just an extension of classroom instruction and thus was not protected by the First Amendment.

In a 5–3 decision, the Supreme Court upheld the principal's actions in sweeping terms. Educators may limit speech within the confines of the school curriculum, including speech that might seem to bear the approval of

the school, provided their actions serve any "valid educational purpose." Student expression beyond school property took a hit in 2007 when an increasingly conservative Supreme Court upheld the suspension of a high school student in Juneau, Alaska, who had displayed a banner ("Bong Hits 4 Jesus") at an outside school event. School officials may prohibit speech, wrote Chief Justice John G. Roberts, Jr., if it could be interpreted as promoting illegal drug use.[53]

The Rights to Assemble Peaceably and to Petition the Government

The final clause of the First Amendment states that "Congress shall make no law ... abridging ... the right of the people peaceably to assemble, and to petition the Government for a redress of grievances." The roots of the right of petition can be traced to the Magna Carta, the charter of English political and civil liberties granted by King John at Runnymede in 1215. The right of peaceable assembly arose much later. The framers meant that the people have the right to assemble peaceably *in order to* petition the government. Today, however, the right to assemble peaceably is equated with the right to free speech and a free press, independent of whether the government is petitioned. Precedent has merged these rights and made them indivisible.[54] Government cannot prohibit peaceful political meetings and cannot brand as criminals those who organize, lead, and attend such meetings.[55]

The clash of interests in cases involving these rights illustrates the continuing nature of the effort to define and apply fundamental principles. The need for order and stability has tempered the concept of freedom. And when freedom and order conflict, the justices of the Supreme Court, who are responsible only to their consciences, strike the balance. Such clashes are certain to occur again and again. Freedom and order conflict when public libraries become targets of community censors, when religious devotion interferes with military service, and when individuals and groups express views or hold beliefs at odds with majority sentiment.

The Right to Bear Arms

The Second Amendment declares:

> A well-regulated militia, being necessary to the security of a free State, the right of the people to keep and bear arms, shall not be infringed.

This amendment has created a hornet's nest of problems for gun-control advocates and their opponents. Gun-control advocates assert that the amendment protects the right of the states to maintain *collective* militias. Gun-use advocates assert that the amendment protects the right of *individuals* to own and use guns. There are good arguments on both sides.

Federal firearms regulations did not come into being until Prohibition, so the Supreme Court had little to say on the matter before then. In 1939, however, a unanimous Court upheld a 1934 federal law requiring the taxation and registration of machine guns and sawed-off shotguns. The Court held that the Second Amendment protects a citizen's right to own ordinary militia weapons; sawed-off shotguns did not qualify for protection.[56]

In 2008, the Court squarely considered whether the Second Amendment protects an individual's right to gun ownership or is simply a right tied to service in a militia. *District of Columbia* v. *Heller* was a challenge to the strictest gun-control statute in the country. It barred private possession of handguns and required the disassembly or use of trigger locks on rifles and shotguns. In a landmark decision, the Court ruled 5–4 that there is a personal constitutional right to keep a loaded handgun at home for self-defense. Justice Antonin Scalia, writing for the conservative majority, acknowledged the problem of handgun violence. "But the enshrinement of constitutional rights," declared Scalia, "necessarily takes certain policy choices off the table.... It is not the role of this court to pronounce the Second Amendment extinct."[57]

The ruling overturned the ban, but it left a host of issues unanswered. Here are three:

1. The Court expressly left open whether the individual right to keep and bear arms in the Second Amendment should be brought into or incorporated into the Fourteenth Amendment to apply against the states. (The District of Columbia is a creation of the federal government; it is not a state.)
2. The justices suggested that personal handgun possession did not extend to unusual weapons like submachine guns or assault rifles, but that issue was not squarely before them.

3. The opinion did not set out the standard that would be used to evaluate future challenges to gun regulations that stop short of prohibition.

The Court addressed only the first of these issues in *McDonald* v. *Chicago* (2010), leaving the matter of gun regulation for another day.[58] In five separate opinions covering more than 200 pages, the justices held, 5–4, that an individual's right to bear arms is fundamental and cannot be prohibited by state or local government. The majority could not agree on the exact Fourteenth Amendment clause that enabled this application. Four justices—Chief Justice John G. Roberts, Jr., and Associate Justices Antonin Scalia, Anthony M. Kennedy, and Samuel A. Alito, Jr.—argued that the due process clause served this function. Justice Clarence Thomas maintained that the quiescent privileges and immunities clause should carry the freight.

How much regulation will the Court tolerate when it comes to the right to bear arms? New cases now in the legal pipeline will test the waters on what is permissible and what is not.

Rallying for a Right

Second Amendment activists gathered around the country on April 19, 2010, also known as Patriots Day, to demonstrate the right to bear arms. The date commemorates the battles of Lexington and Concord during the Revolutionary War. One protester wore his holstered unloaded pistol while attending such a rally in Sacramento, California. He and others objected to a proposed state law that would ban gun owners from openly carrying unloaded guns in public. In June 2010, the U.S. Supreme Court held that state and local governments may not forbid individual gun ownership. The Court has yet to decide how far government may go in regulating gun ownership.

(AP Photo/Rich Pedroncelli)

Applying the Bill of Rights to the States

The major purpose of the Constitution was to structure the division of power between the national government and the state governments. Even before it was amended, the Constitution set some limits on both the nation and the states with regard to citizens' rights. It barred both governments from passing **bills of attainder,** laws that make an individual guilty of a crime without a trial. It also prohibited them from enacting **ex post facto laws,** which declare an action a crime after it has been performed. And it barred both nation and states from impairing the **obligation of contracts,** the obligation of the parties in a contract to carry out its terms.

Although initially the Bill of Rights seemed to apply only to the national government, various litigants pressed the claim that its guarantees also applied to the states. In response to one such claim, Chief Justice John Marshall affirmed what seemed plain from the Constitution's language and "the history of the day" (the events surrounding the Constitutional Convention): the provisions of the Bill of Rights served only to limit national authority. "Had the framers of these amendments intended them to be limitations on the powers of the state governments," wrote Marshall, "they would have ... expressed that intention."[59]

Change came with the Fourteenth Amendment, which was adopted in 1868. The due process clause of that amendment is the linchpin that holds the states to the provisions of the Bill of Rights.

The Fourteenth Amendment: Due Process of Law

> *Section 1....* No State shall make or enforce any law which shall abridge the privileges or immunities of citizens of the United States; nor shall any State deprive any person of life, liberty, or property, without due process of law.

Most freedoms protected in the Bill of Rights today function as limitations on the states. And many of the standards that limit the national government serve equally to limit state governments. The changes have been achieved through the Supreme Court's interpretation of the due process clause of the Fourteenth Amendment: "nor shall any State deprive any person of life, liberty, or property, without due process of law." The clause has two central meanings. First, it requires the government to adhere to appropriate procedures. For example, in a criminal trial, the government must establish the defendant's guilt beyond a reasonable doubt. Second, it forbids unreasonable government action. For example, at the turn of the twentieth century, the Supreme Court struck down a state law that forbade bakers from working more than sixty hours a week. The justices found the law unreasonable under the due process clause.[60]

bills of attainder
A law that pronounces an individual guilty of a crime without a trial.

ex post facto laws
Laws that declare an action to be criminal after it has been performed.

obligation of contracts
The obligation of the parties to a contract to carry out its terms.

The Supreme Court has used the first meaning of the due process clause as a sponge, absorbing or incorporating the procedural specifics of the Bill of Rights and spreading or applying them to the states. The history of due process cases reveals that unlikely litigants often champion constitutional guarantees and that freedom is not always the victor.

The Fundamental Freedoms

In 1897, the Supreme Court declared that the states are subject to the Fifth Amendment's prohibition against taking private property without providing just compensation.[61] The Court reached that decision by absorbing the prohibition into the due process clause of the Fourteenth Amendment, which explicitly applies to the states. Thus, one Bill of Rights protection—but only that one—applied to both the states and the national government, as illustrated in Figure 15.2. In 1925, the Court assumed that the due process clause protected the First Amendment speech and press liberties from impairment by the states.[62]

The inclusion of other Bill of Rights guarantees within the due process clause faced a critical test in *Palko* v. *Connecticut* (1937).[63] Frank Palko had been charged with homicide in the first degree. He was convicted of second-degree murder, however, and sentenced to life imprisonment. The state of Connecticut appealed and won a new trial; this time, Palko was found guilty of first-degree murder and sentenced to death. Palko appealed the second conviction on the grounds that it violated the protection against double jeopardy guaranteed to him by the Fifth Amendment. This protection applied to the states, he contended, because of the Fourteenth Amendment's due process clause.

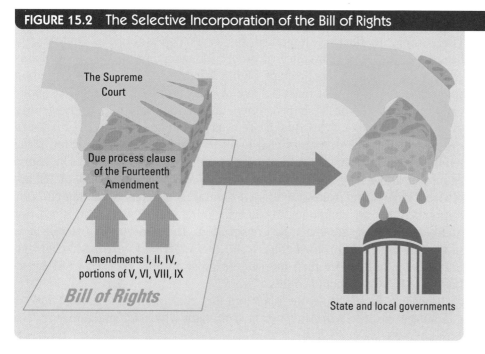

FIGURE 15.2   The Selective Incorporation of the Bill of Rights

The Supreme Court

Due process clause of the Fourteenth Amendment

Amendments I, II, IV, portions of V, VI, VIII, IX

Bill of Rights

State and local governments

The Supreme Court has used the due process clause of the Fourteenth Amendment as a sponge, absorbing most of the provisions in the Bill of Rights and applying them to state and local governments. All provisions in the Bill of Rights apply to the national government.

The Supreme Court upheld Palko's second conviction. In his opinion for the majority, Justice Benjamin N. Cardozo formulated principles that were to guide the Court's actions for the next three decades. He reasoned that some Bill of Rights guarantees, such as freedom of thought and speech, are fundamental and that these fundamental rights are absorbed by the Fourteenth Amendment's due process clause and are therefore applicable to the states. These rights are essential, argued Cardozo, because "neither liberty nor justice would exist if they were sacrificed." Trial by jury and other rights, although valuable and important, are not essential to liberty and justice and therefore are not absorbed by the due process clause. "Few would be so narrow or provincial," Cardozo claimed, "as to maintain that a fair and enlightened system of justice would be impossible" without these other rights. In other words, only certain provisions of the Bill of Rights—the "fundamental" provisions—were absorbed selectively into the due process clause and made applicable to the states. Because protection against double jeopardy was not one of them, Palko died in Connecticut's gas chamber in 1938.

The next thirty years saw slow but perceptible change in the standard for determining whether a Bill of Rights guarantee was fundamental. The reference point changed from the idealized "fair and enlightened system of justice" in *Palko* to the more realistic "American scheme of justice" thirty years later.[64] Case after case tested various guarantees that the Court found to be fundamental. By 1969, when *Palko* was finally overturned, the Court had found most of the Bill of Rights applicable to the states. (Recall that the Court made the Second Amendment's "right to keep and bear arms" fully applicable to the states in 2010.)

Criminal Procedure: The Meaning of Constitutional Guarantees

"The history of liberty," remarked Justice Felix Frankfurter, "has largely been the history of observance of procedural safeguards."[65] The safeguards embodied in the Fourth through Eighth Amendments to the Constitution specify how government must behave in criminal proceedings. Their application to the states has reshaped American criminal justice in the past thirty years in two stages. The first stage was the judgment that a guarantee asserted in the Bill of Rights also applied to the states. The second stage required that the judiciary give specific meaning to the guarantee. The courts could not allow the states to define guarantees themselves without risking different definitions from state to state—and thus differences among citizens' rights. If rights are fundamental, their meaning cannot vary. But life is not quite so simple under the U.S. Constitution. The concept of federalism is sewn into the constitutional fabric, and the Supreme Court has recognized that there may be more than one way to prosecute the accused while heeding his or her fundamental rights.

Consider, for example, the right to a jury trial in criminal cases, which is guaranteed by the Sixth Amendment. This right was made obligatory for the states in *Duncan* v. *Louisiana* (1968). The Supreme Court later held that the right applied to all nonpetty criminal cases—those in which the penalty for conviction was more than six months' imprisonment.[66] But the Court did not require that state juries have twelve members, the number required for federal criminal proceedings. The Court permits jury size to vary from state to state, although it has set the minimum number at six. Furthermore, it has not imposed on the states the federal requirement of a unanimous jury verdict. As a result, even today, many states do not require unanimous verdicts for criminal convictions. Some observers question whether criminal defendants in these states enjoy the same rights as defendants in unanimous-verdict states.

In contrast, the Court left no room for variation in its definition of the fundamental right to an attorney, also guaranteed by the Sixth Amendment. Clarence Earl Gideon was a penniless vagrant accused of breaking into and robbing a pool hall. Because Gideon could not afford a lawyer, he asked the state to provide him with legal counsel for his trial. The state refused and subsequently convicted Gideon and sentenced him to five years in the Florida State Penitentiary. From his cell, Gideon appealed to the U.S. Supreme Court, claiming that his conviction should be struck down because the state had denied him his Sixth Amendment right to counsel.[67]

In its landmark decision in *Gideon* v. *Wainwright* (1963), the Court set aside Gideon's conviction and extended to defendants in state courts the Sixth Amendment right to counsel.[68] The state retried Gideon, who this time had the assistance of a lawyer, and the court found him not guilty.

In subsequent rulings that stretched over more than a decade, the Court specified at which points in the course of criminal proceedings a defendant is entitled to a lawyer (from arrest to trial, appeal, and beyond). These pronouncements are binding on all states. In state as well as federal proceedings, the government must furnish legal assistance to those who do not have the means to hire their own attorney. During this period, the Court also came to grips with another procedural issue: informing suspects of their constitutional rights. Without this knowledge, procedural safeguards are meaningless. Ernesto Miranda was arrested in Arizona in connection with the kidnapping and rape of an eighteen-year-old woman. After the police questioned him for two hours and the woman identified him, Miranda confessed to the crime. An Arizona court convicted him based on that confession—although he was never told that he had the right to counsel and the right not to incriminate himself. Miranda appealed his conviction, which was overturned by the Supreme Court in 1966.[69]

The Court based its decision in *Miranda* v. *Arizona* on the Fifth Amendment privilege against self-incrimination. According to the Court, the police had forced Miranda to confess during in-custody questioning, not with physical force but with the coercion inherent in custodial interrogation without counsel. The Court said that warnings are necessary to dispel that coercion. The Court does not require warnings if a person is only held in custody without being questioned or is only questioned without being arrested. But in *Miranda,* the Court found the combination of custody and interrogation sufficiently intimidating to require warnings before questioning. These statements are known today as the *Miranda* **warnings:**

- You have the right to remain silent.
- Anything you say can be used against you in court.
- You have the right to talk to a lawyer of your own choice before questioning.
- If you cannot afford to hire a lawyer, a lawyer will be provided without charge.

In each area of criminal procedure, the justices have had to grapple with two steps in the application of constitutional guarantees to criminal defendants: the extension of a right to the states and the definition of that right. In *Duncan,* the issue was the right to jury trial, and the Court allowed variation in all states. In *Gideon,* the Court applied the right to counsel uniformly in all states. Finally, in *Miranda,* the Court declared that all governments—national, state, and local—have a duty to inform suspects of the full measure of their constitutional rights. In one of its most important cases in 2000, the Court reaffirmed this protection in a 7–2 decision, holding that *Miranda* had "announced a constitutional rule" that Congress could not undermine through legislation.[70]

The problems in balancing freedom and order can be formidable. A primary function of government is to maintain order. What happens when the government infringes on individuals' freedom for the sake of order? Consider the guarantee in the Fourth Amendment: "The right of the people to be secure in their persons, houses, papers, and effects, against unreasonable searches and seizures, shall not be violated." The Court made this right applicable to the states in *Wolf* v. *Colorado* (1949).[71] Following the reasoning in *Palko,* the Court found that the core of the amendment—security against arbitrary police intrusion—is a fundamental right and that citizens must be protected from illegal searches by state and local governments. But how? The federal courts had long followed the **exclusionary rule,** which holds that evidence obtained from an illegal search and seizure cannot be used in a trial. If that evidence is critical to the prosecution, the case dissolves. But the Court refused to apply the exclusionary rule to the state courts. Instead, it allowed the states to decide on their own how to handle the fruits of an illegal search. The decision in *Wolf* stated that obtaining evidence by illegal means violated the Constitution and that states could fashion their own rules of evidence to give effect to this constitutional decree. The states were not bound by the exclusionary rule.

The justices considered the exclusionary rule again twelve years later, in *Mapp* v. *Ohio.*[72] An Ohio court had found Dolree Mapp guilty of possessing obscene materials after an admittedly illegal search of her home for a fugitive. The Ohio Supreme Court affirmed her conviction, and she appealed to the U.S. Supreme Court. Mapp's attorneys argued for a reversal based primarily on freedom of expression, contending that the First Amendment protected the confiscated materials. However, the Court elected to use the decision in *Mapp* to give meaning to the constitutional guarantee against unreasonable search and seizure. In a 6–3 decision, the justices declared that

Miranda **warnings**
Statements concerning rights that police are required to make to a person before he or she is subjected to in-custody questioning.

exclusionary rule
The judicial rule that states that evidence obtained in an illegal search and seizure cannot be used in trial.

"all evidence obtained by searches and seizures in violation of the Constitution is, by [the Fourth Amendment], inadmissible in a state court." Ohio had convicted Mapp illegally; the evidence should have been excluded.

The decision was historic. It placed the exclusionary rule under the umbrella of the Fourth Amendment and required all levels of government to operate according to the provisions of that amendment. Failure to do so could result in the dismissal of criminal charges against guilty defendants.

Mapp launched a divided Supreme Court on a troubled course of determining how and when to apply the exclusionary rule. For example, the Court has continued to struggle with police use of sophisticated electronic eavesdropping devices and searches of movable vehicles. In each case, the justices have confronted a rule that appears to handicap the police and to offer freedom to people whose guilt has been established by the illegal evidence. In the Court's most recent pronouncements, order has triumphed over freedom.

The struggle over the exclusionary rule took a new turn in 1984, when the Court reviewed *United States* v. *Leon*.[73] In this case, the police obtained a search warrant from a judge on the basis of a tip from an informant of unproved reliability. The judge issued a warrant without firmly establishing probable cause to believe the tip. The police, relying on the warrant, found large quantities of illegal drugs. The Court, by a vote of 6–3, established the **good faith exception** to the exclusionary rule. The justices held that the state could introduce at trial evidence seized on the basis of a mistakenly issued search warrant. The exclusionary rule, argued the majority, is not a right but a remedy against illegal police conduct. The rule is costly to society. It excludes pertinent valid evidence, allowing guilty people to go unpunished and generating disrespect for the law. These costs are justifiable only if the exclusionary rule deters police misconduct. Such a deterrent effect was not a factor in *Leon:* the police acted in good faith. Hence, the Court decided, there is a need for an exception to the rule.

The Court recognized another exception in 2006. When police search a home with a warrant, they have been required to "knock and announce" before entering. But the Supreme Court held that when the police admittedly fail to "knock and announce," the evidence obtained from such a search may still be admitted into evidence, thus creating a new exception to the exclusionary rule. The case was a close one: decided 5–4 with Justice Scalia writing the majority opinion and implying that the exclusionary rule should not be applied in other illegal search circumstances.[74]

As a more conservative coalition has taken shape, the exclusionary rule has come under close scrutiny as the preference for order outweighs the value in freedom. In yet another exception, the Supreme Court held in 2009 that evidence obtained through police negligence would not bar the introduction of that evidence at trial.[75]

The Internet and information technology have had enormous, positive impacts on American life. But they come at a price. For example, personal privacy is surely compromised when e-mail and text messages can be retrieved and shared. But Internet-based telephone conversations may overprotect privacy. (See "Politics of Global Change: Wiretapping in the Digital Age.")

good faith exception
An exception to the Supreme Court exclusionary rule, holding that evidence seized on the basis of a mistakenly issued search warrant can be introduced at trial if the mistake was made in good faith, that is, if all the parties involved had reason at the time to believe that the warrant was proper.

Politics of Global Change

Wiretapping in the Digital Age

In the pre-Internet world, telephone calls followed a continuous path between two parties. Armed with a search warrant from a state or federal court, investigators could select a point somewhere along the line to tap the call. But with the advent of the Internet, calls can be placed online. The emergence of VoIP (voice over Internet protocol) has dropped the cost of long-distance and international telephone calls to all-time lows. Some services like Skype provide such services for free. Lawbreakers have reason to rejoice.

The Communications Assistance for Law Enforcement Act (CALEA) governs wiretap requests in the United States. It imposes requirements on telecom companies to cooperate with lawful intercepts. Congress enacted the law in 1994, at the dawn of the Internet. The growth of VoIP telephony left the FBI, the Drug Enforcement Administration, and the Department of Justice powerless. The agencies successfully lobbied the Federal Communications Commission (the agency that oversees implementation of CALEA) to extend the rules to cover VoIP telecoms.

Civil libertarians cried foul, claiming that CALEA targeted only traditional telephone wiretaps. But the fight against terrorism trumped these objections. Today, all broadband-Internet and VoIP providers must comply with the new rules. These firms are required to intercept calls such that suspects cannot tell that they are under surveillance. That's no easy task for at least three reasons.

First, complying with CALEA is complicated because the device at the end of the line today is a computer, not a telephone. A reasonably sophisticated caller can tell if her calls are intercepted by simply measuring the "latency" of the connection, that is, the time taken for a single packet of data to travel from a local machine to a computer elsewhere on the Internet. Inserting a bugging device into the chain increases the

The USA-PATRIOT Act

More than fifty years ago, Justice Robert H. Jackson warned that exceptional protections for civil liberties might convert the Bill of Rights into a suicide pact. The national government decided, after the September 11 terrorist attacks, to forgo some liberties in order to secure greater order, through bipartisan passage of the USA-PATRIOT Act. This landmark law greatly expanded the ability of law enforcement and intelligence agencies to tap phones, monitor Internet traffic, and conduct other forms of surveillance in pursuit of terrorists. In 2006, Congress extended with a few minor changes sixteen expiring provisions of the act.

Shortly after the bill became law, then Attorney General John Ashcroft declared: "Let the terrorists among us be warned: If you overstay your visas, even by one day, we will arrest you. If you violate a local law, we will hope that you will, and work to make sure that you are put in jail and kept in custody as long as possible. We will use every available statute. We will seek every prosecutorial advantage. We will use all our weapons within the law and under the Constitution to protect life and enhance security for America."[76]

latency, signaling a possible tap. To address this problem, Internet companies, siding with regulators, now leave lawful-intercept equipment permanently in place to be activated as required. In effect, there is now a back door into everyone's connection.

Second, another issue created by VoIP telephony is the enormous volume of data passing along the Internet. Traditional telephone taps required an agent to switch on a recorder to collect evidence. Today's digital eavesdropping requires the collection of hundreds upon hundreds of gigabytes of data and then making sense of the material. Standards for formatting and delivering data to investigators still need resolution to work across national borders.

Third, perhaps the biggest issue remains encryption. Not all VoIP calls are encrypted. But even those who do encrypt their calls must provide law enforcement agencies with the appropriate decryption keys. The one exception is Skype, the most popular VoIP service, with over 520 million users. Skype is a "peer-to-peer" system, routing calls entirely over the public Internet. Skype cannot provide investigators with access to a suspect's calls because Skype does not handle any of the traffic itself. Even if investigators could intercept a Skype call, they would still face the task of unraveling the strong encryption used for those calls. Only the chief spy agency, the National Security Agency, has the computing power to unravel Skype packets. NSA's resources focus on intelligence gathering, not law enforcement. Skype, based in Luxembourg but partially owned by the American company eBay, "cooperates fully with all lawful requests," but it remains to be seen whether CALEA requests are "lawful" from the perspective of a European-based company.

One way around the problem of strong encryption is to grab decryption keys directly from a suspect's computer. A German court has ruled this approach would be inadmissible, prompting German legislators to draft a change in the law.

In a world made ever smaller by technology, eavesdropping on criminals today will require governments to be nimble in lawmaking and persuasive in their efforts to secure cooperation from other nations. This probably means that governments will lag behind in their efforts to eavesdrop as part of law enforcement. Telephony technology may prove a bulwark for personal privacy, but at what cost to the need for order?

Source: "Bugging the Cloud," *Economist Technology Quarterly*, 8 March 2008, pp. 28–30.

In this shift toward order, civil libertarians worry. "These new and unchecked powers could be used against American citizens who are not under criminal investigation," said Gregory T. Nojeim, associate director of the American Civil Liberties Union's Washington office.[77]

The USA-PATRIOT Act runs over three hundred pages. Some parts engender strong opposition; others are benign. More than 150 communities have passed resolutions denouncing the act as an assault on civil liberties. Consider one of the key provisions: Section 215, dealing with rules for searching private records such as you might find in the library, video store, or doctor's office. Prior to the act, the government needed, at minimum, a warrant issued by a judge and probable cause to access such records. (Foreign intelligence information could justify a warrantless search, but judges still reviewed the exception.) Now, under the USA-PATRIOT Act, the government need only certify without substantiation that its search protects against terrorism, which turns judicial oversight into a rubber stamp. With the bar lowered, more warrantless searches are likely to follow. In 2005, the FBI conducted more than thirty-five hundred such searches of U.S. citizens and legal residents, a significant jump from previous years.[78]

IDEALOG.ORG

Do you believe that the USA-PATRIOT Act is needed to protect the country from terrorism? Take IDEAlog's self-test.

To complicate matters, a gag order bars the person turning over the records from disclosing the search to anyone. You may never know that your records were searched. In a fig leaf to civil libertarians, the renewed provision allows those served with such gag orders to challenge them in court after a year's wait. But in order to prevail, they must prove that the government acted in "bad faith."[79]

Detainees and the War on Terrorism

In 2004, the Supreme Court addressed some of the difficult issues in the war on terrorism in two cases in which war detainees had been designated "enemy combatants." President Bush, relying on a series of World War II–era opinions, maintained that the detainees were not entitled to basic legal requirements such as attorneys or hearings and that his actions could not be reviewed in the courts.[80] The Supreme Court rejected his position. Regardless of the location of their detention—hundreds of foreign detainees are being held at a naval base in Guantánamo Bay, Cuba—the Court said in the first case that they are entitled to challenge their designation as "enemy combatants" before a federal judge or other neutral decision maker.[81]

In the second case, a Saudi Arabian resident, who was born in the United States and thus a citizen, was picked up on an Afghan battlefield and detained as an enemy combatant. In an 8–1 vote, the Court declared that he is entitled by the due process clause of the Fifth Amendment to a "meaningful opportunity" to contest the basis for his detention. In blunt language, Justice Sandra Day O'Connor, speaking for herself and three other justices, rebuffed the president's claim: "We have long since made clear that a state of war is not a blank check for the President when it comes to the rights of the Nation's citizens."[82]

In 2006, the Court rejected by a vote of 5–3 the president's claim of unbounded authority in the creation and use of military commissions for enemy combatants imprisoned at Guantánamo Bay, Cuba. In *Hamdan* v. *Rumsfeld,* the justices held that the commissions were unauthorized by Congress and that they violated a provision of international law. The opinion rebuking presidential authority also established minimum procedures for any future commissions.[83] Shortly after, the Bush administration complied with the decision by announcing that terror suspects held by the United States would have a right to basic legal and human protections under international law.

In 2008, the Court issued yet another rebuke to the Bush administration when it ruled 5–4 in *Boumediene* v. *Bush* that prisoners at Guantánamo have a right to challenge their detentions in the federal courts.[84] The president continued to claim he could do as he wished with prisoners he designated as "enemy combatants," expecting the justices to side with him during armed conflicts. But the Court's repeated rejection of presidential authority is likely the result of an unusually aggressive position on executive power. Rather than narrowing its claims after its losses, the administration continued to assert that the 1940s precedents gave it a free hand. That was the wrong lesson.

The Ninth Amendment and Personal Autonomy

> The enumeration in the Constitution, of certain rights, shall not be construed to deny or disparage others retained by the people.

The working and history of the Ninth Amendment remain an enigma; the evidence supports two different views: the amendment may protect rights that are not enumerated, or it may simply protect state governments against the assumption of power by the national government.[85] The meaning of the amendment was not an issue until 1965, when the Supreme Court used it to protect privacy, a right that is not enumerated in the Constitution.

Controversy: From Privacy to Abortion

In *Griswold* v. *Connecticut* (1965), the Court struck down, by a vote of 7–2, a seldom-enforced Connecticut statute that made the use of birth control devices a crime.[86] Justice Douglas, writing for the majority, asserted that the "specific guarantees in the Bill of Rights have penumbras [partially illuminated regions surrounding fully lit areas]" that give "life and substance" to broad, unspecified protections in the Bill of Rights. Several specific guarantees in the First, Third, Fourth, and Fifth amendments create a zone of privacy, Douglas argued, and this zone is protected by the Ninth Amendment and is applicable to the states by the due process clause of the Fourteenth Amendment.

Three justices gave further emphasis to the relevance of the Ninth Amendment, which, they contended, protects fundamental rights derived from those specifically enumerated in the first eight amendments. This view contrasted sharply with the position expressed by the two dissenters, Justices Black and Stewart. In the absence of some specific prohibition, they argued, the Bill of Rights and the Fourteenth Amendment do not allow judicial annulment of state legislative policies, even if those policies are abhorrent to a judge or justice.

Griswold established the principle that the Bill of Rights as a whole creates a right to make certain intimate, personal choices, including the right of married people to engage in sexual intercourse for reproduction or pleasure. This zone of personal autonomy, protected by the Constitution, was the basis of a 1973 case that sought to invalidate state antiabortion laws. But rights are not absolute, and in weighing the interests of the individual against the interests of the government, the Supreme Court found itself caught up in a flood of controversy that has yet to subside.

In *Roe* v. *Wade* (1973), the Court, in a 7–2 decision, declared unconstitutional a Texas law making it a crime to obtain an abortion except for the purpose of saving the woman's life.[87]

Justice Harry A. Blackmun, who wrote the majority opinion, could not point to a specific constitutional guarantee to justify the Court's ruling. Instead, he based the decision on the right to privacy protected by the due process clause of the Fourteenth Amendment. In effect, state abortion laws were unreasonable and hence unconstitutional. The Court declared that in the first three months of pregnancy, the abortion decision must be left to the woman and her physician. In the interest of protecting the woman's health, states may restrict but not prohibit abortions in the second three months of pregnancy. Finally, in the last three months of pregnancy, states may regulate or even prohibit abortions to protect the life of the fetus, except when medical judgment determines that an abortion is necessary to save the woman's life. In all, the Court's ruling affected the laws of forty-six states.

The dissenters—Justices Byron R. White and Rehnquist—were quick to assert what critics have frequently repeated since the decision: the Court's judgment was directed by its own dislikes, not by any constitutional compass. In the absence of guiding principles, they asserted, the majority justices simply substituted their views for the views of the state legislatures whose abortion regulations they invalidated.[88] In a 1993 television interview, Blackmun insisted that "*Roe* versus *Wade* was decided ... on constitutional grounds."[89] It was as if Blackmun were trying, by sheer force of will, to turn back twenty years' worth of stinging objections to the opinion he had crafted.

The composition of the Court shifted under President Ronald Reagan. His elevation of Rehnquist to chief justice in 1986 and his appointment of Scalia in 1986 and Kennedy in 1988 raised new hope among abortion foes and old fears among advocates of choice.

A perceptible shift away from abortion rights materialized in *Webster* v. *Reproductive Health Services* (1989). The case was a blockbuster, attracting voluminous media coverage. In *Webster,* the Supreme Court upheld the constitutionality of a Missouri law that denied the use of public employees or publicly funded facilities in the performance of an abortion unless the woman's life was in danger.[90] Furthermore, the law required doctors to perform tests to determine whether fetuses twenty weeks and older could survive outside the womb. This was the first time that the Court upheld significant government restrictions on abortion.

The justices issued five opinions, but no single opinion captured a majority. Four justices (Blackmun, Brennan, Thurgood Marshall, and John Paul Stevens) voted to strike down the Missouri law and hold fast to *Roe*. Four justices (Kennedy, Rehnquist, Scalia, and White) wanted to overturn *Roe* and return to the states the power to regulate abortion. The remaining justice, Sandra Day O'Connor, avoided both camps. Her position was that state abortion restrictions are permissible provided they are not "unduly burdensome." She voted with the conservative plurality to uphold the restrictive Missouri statute on the grounds that it did not place an undue burden on women's rights. But she declined to reconsider (and overturn) *Roe*.

The Court has since moved cautiously down the road toward greater government control of abortion. In 1990, the justices split on two state parental notification laws. The Court struck down a state requirement that compelled unwed minors to notify both parents before having an abortion. In another case, however, the Court upheld a state requirement that a physician notify one parent of a pregnant minor of her intent to have an abortion. In both cases, the justices voiced widely divergent opinions, revealing a continuing division over abortion.[91]

The abortion issue pits freedom against order. The decision to bear or beget children should be free from government control. Yet government has a legitimate interest in protecting and preserving life, including fetal life, as part of its responsibility to maintain an orderly society. Rather than choose between freedom and order, the majority on the Court has loosened constitutional protections of abortion rights and cast the politically divisive issue into the state legislatures, where elected representatives can thrash out the conflict.

Many groups defending or opposing abortion have now turned to state legislative politics to advance their policies. This approach will force candidates for state office to debate the abortion issue and then translate electoral outcomes into legislation that restricts or protects abortion. If the abortion issue is deeply felt by Americans, pluralist theory would predict that the strongest voices for or against abortion will mobilize the greatest support in the political arena.

With a clear conservative majority, the Court seemed poised to reverse *Roe* in 1992. But a new coalition—forged by Reagan and Bush appointees O'Connor, Souter, and Kennedy—reaffirmed *Roe* yet tolerated additional restrictions on abortions. In *Planned Parenthood* v. *Casey,* a bitterly divided bench opted for the O'Connor "undue burden" test. Eight years later, in 2000, O'Connor sided with a coalition of liberal and moderate justices in a 5–4 decision striking down a Nebraska law that had banned so-called partial-birth abortion, illustrating the Court's continuing and deep division on the abortion issue.[92]

Let's view the abortion controversy through our lens of value conflicts. Presidents try to appoint justices whose values coincide with their own. Justices appointed by conservative presidents Reagan and George H. W. Bush weakened abortion as a constitutional right, putting more weight on order. President Clinton's appointees (Ruth Bader Ginsburg and Stephen G. Breyer) fulfilled his liberal campaign promise to protect women's access to abortion from further assault, putting more weight on freedom. President George W. Bush's conservative appointees—John G. Roberts, Jr., and Samuel A. Alito, Jr.—have tipped the balance toward order. In 2007, the Court by a 5–4 vote upheld a federal law banning partial-birth abortion.[93] The law was nearly identical to the one struck down by the Court years before. Today, order trumps freedom. An ideological shift in the White House may be insufficient to produce a different result unless conservative justices leave the Court. And none have expressed the intention to do so.

Personal Autonomy and Sexual Orientation

The right-to-privacy cases may have opened a Pandora's box of divisive social issues. Does the right to privacy embrace private homosexual acts between consenting adults? Consider the case of Michael Hardwick, who was arrested in 1982 in his Atlanta bedroom while having sex with another man. In a standard approach to prosecuting homosexuals, Georgia charged him under a state criminal statute with the crime of sodomy, which means oral or anal intercourse. The police said that they had gone to his home to arrest him for failing to pay a fine for drinking in public. Although the prosecutor dropped the charges, Hardwick sued to challenge the law's constitutionality. He won in the lower courts, but the state pursued the case.

The conflict between freedom and order lies at the core of the case. "Our legal history and our social traditions have condemned this conduct uniformly for hundreds and hundreds of years," argued Georgia's attorney.

Constitutional law, he continued, "must not become an instrument for a change in the social order." Hardwick's attorney, a noted constitutional scholar, said that government must have a more important reason than "majority morality to justify regulation of sexual intimacies in the privacy of the home." He maintained that the case involved two precious freedoms: the right to engage in private sexual relations and the right to be free from government intrusion in one's home.[94]

More than half the states have eliminated criminal penalties for private homosexual acts between consenting adults. The rest still outlaw homosexual sodomy, and many outlaw heterosexual sodomy as well. As a result, homosexual rights groups and some civil liberties groups followed Hardwick's case closely. Fundamentalist Christian groups and defenders of traditional morality expressed deep interest in the outcome too.

In a bitterly divided ruling in 1986, the Court held in *Bowers* v. *Hardwick* that the Constitution does not protect homosexual relations between consenting adults, even in the privacy of their own homes.[95] The logic of the findings in the privacy cases involving contraception and abortion would seem to have compelled a finding of a right to personal autonomy—a right to make personal choices unconstrained by government—in this case as well. But the 5–4 majority maintained that only heterosexual choices—whether and whom to marry, whether to conceive a child, whether to have an abortion—fall within the zone of privacy established by the Court in its earlier rulings. "The Judiciary necessarily takes to itself further authority to govern the country without express constitutional authority" when it expands the list of fundamental rights not rooted in the language or design of the Constitution, wrote Justice White, the author of the majority opinion.

The arguments on both sides of the privacy issue are compelling. This makes the choice between freedom and order excruciating for ordinary citizens and Supreme Court justices alike. At the conference to decide the merits of the *Bowers* case, Justice Lewis Powell cast his vote to extend privacy rights to homosexual conduct. Later, he joined with his conservative colleagues, fashioning a new majority. Four years after the *Bowers* decision, Powell revealed another change of mind: "I probably made a mistake," he declared, speaking of his decision to vote with the conservative majority.[96]

Justice White's majority opinion was reconsidered in 2003 when the Court considered a challenge to a Texas law that criminalized homosexual but not heterosexual sodomy. This time, in *Lawrence and Garner* v. *Texas,* a new coalition of six justices viewed the issue in a different light. May a majority use the power of government to enforce its views on the whole society through the criminal law? Speaking through Justice Kennedy, the Court observed "an emerging awareness that liberty gives substantial protection to adult persons in deciding how to conduct their private lives in matters pertaining to sex." Since the Texas law furthered no legitimate state interest but intruded into the intimate personal choices of individuals, the law was void. Kennedy along with four other justices then took the unusual step of reaching back in time to declare that the *Bowers* decision was wrong and should be overruled.[97]

Justice Antonin Scalia, joined by Chief Justice Rehnquist and Justice Clarence Thomas, issued a stinging dissent. Scalia charged the majority with "signing on to the homosexual agenda" aimed at eliminating the moral opprobrium traditionally attached to homosexual conduct. The consequence is that the Court would be departing from its role of ensuring that the democratic rules of engagement are observed. He continued:

> What Texas has chosen to do is well within the range of traditional democratic action, and its hand should not be stayed through the invention of a brand-new "constitutional right" by a Court that is impatient of democratic change. It is indeed true that "later generations can see that laws once thought necessary and proper in fact serve only to oppress," ... and when that happens, later generations can repeal those laws. But it is the premise of our system that those judgments are to be made by the people, and not imposed by a governing caste that knows best.[98]

The challenge of democracy calls for the democratic process to sort out value conflicts whenever possible. And, according to Scalia, the majority has moved from its traditional responsibility of umpiring the system to favoring one side over another in the struggle between freedom and order.

Issues around sexual orientation have shifted toward the states. In anticipation of state-approved same-sex unions, Congress moved affirmatively in 1996 to bar the effects of homosexual marriage through passage of the Defense of Marriage Act. President Clinton signed the bill into law. The law defines marriage as a union between people of opposite sexes and declares that states are not obliged to recognize gay marriages performed elsewhere. The law does not ban such unions; it only protects states from having to recognize same-sex marriage sanctioned by other states. President Obama favors repeal of the act. In July 2010, a federal trial court struck down the marriage-defining section of the Act on the ground that it violated the concept of equality inherent in the Fifth Amendment.[99]

Some states have been innovators in legitimizing homosexuality. Same-sex couples may now marry in fives states (Connecticut, Iowa, Massachusetts, New Hampshire, and Vermont) plus the District of Columbia. Additional states have recognized same-sex "unions" but not same-sex marriages. The difference between a union and a marriage may prove to be a distinction without a difference.

Same-sex marriage still remains a flashpoint for political conflict. In 2009, Maine voters relying on a public referendum became the thirty-first state to ban such marriages. About the same time, the New York State legislature failed to adopt a same-sex marriage law despite a concerted campaign to assure passage.

In 2008, the California Supreme Court, relying on state constitutional provisions, opened the door to same-sex marriage by striking down legislation limiting marriage to opposite-sex couples (see Chapter 16). But opponents struck back with an initiative—known as Proposition 8—asking voters to ban same-sex marriage. It passed with 52 percent of the vote that same year. In the interim, 18,000 couples married and their marriages are duly recognized by the state.

In 2010, federal judge Vaughn Walker struck down the initiative as a violation of the due process and equal protection clauses of the Fourteenth

Adam and Eve or Adam and Steve?

Protesters against same-sex marriage rallied outside the Massachusetts State House in Boston as state legislators contemplated amending the state constitution in 2004 to ban such unions. The state's highest court had ruled that only full, equal marriage rights for same-sex couples satisfied the state constitution. The amendment effort failed.

(Rick Friedman/Corbis)

Amendment, rather than follow the ambiguous line of privacy-related decisions.[100] Anticipating that the decision will be appealed eventually to the Supreme Court, Judge Walker crafted his analysis to model the reasoning of Supreme Court Justice Anthony M. Kennedy, the critical fifth vote in cases favorable to gay rights decided in the last decade. Walker concluded that California lacked a rational basis to deny gays and lesbians marriage licenses.

Today, twenty-four states have constitutional amendments barring the recognition of same-sex marriage and confining civil marriage to the union of a man and a woman. The pluralist model provides one solution for groups dissatisfied with rulings from the nation's courts. State courts and state legislatures have demonstrated their receptivity to positions that are probably untenable in the federal courts. Pluralist mechanisms like the initiative and referendum offer counterweights to judicial intervention. However, state-by-state decisions offer little comfort to Americans who believe the U.S. Constitution protects them in their most intimate decisions and actions, regardless of where they reside.

IDEALOG.ORG

Do you support a constitutional amendment that would bar marriages between gay and lesbian couples? Take IDEAlog's self-test.

Summary

When they established the new government of the United States, the states and the people compelled the framers, through the Bill of Rights, to protect their freedoms. In interpreting these ten amendments, the courts, especially the Supreme Court, have taken on the task of balancing freedom and order.

The First Amendment protects several freedoms: freedom of religion, freedom of speech and of the press, and the freedom to assemble peaceably and to petition the government. The establishment clause demands government neutrality toward religions and between the religious and the nonreligious. According to judicial interpretations of the free-exercise clause, religious beliefs are inviolable, but the Constitution does not protect antisocial actions in the name of religion. Extreme interpretations of the religion clauses could bring the clauses into conflict with each other.

Freedom of expression encompasses freedom of speech, freedom of the press, and the right to assemble peaceably and to petition the government. Freedom of speech and freedom of the press have never been held to be absolute, but the courts have ruled that the Bill of Rights gives the people far greater protection than other freedoms. Exceptions to free speech protections include some forms of symbolic expression, fighting words, and obscenity. Press freedom has enjoyed broad constitutional protection because a free society depends on the ability to collect and report information without government interference. The rights to assemble peaceably and to petition the government stem from the guarantees of freedom of speech and of the press. Each freedom is equally fundamental, but the right to exercise them is not absolute.

After nearly seventy years of silence, the Supreme Court declared that the right to bear arms protects an individual right to own a gun for personal use. New legal challenges will determine the standard that should apply when judging the appropriateness of gun regulations. For now, however, government may not prohibit individual gun ownership. The adoption of the Fourteenth Amendment in 1868 extended the guarantees of the Bill of Rights to the states. The due process clause became the vehicle for applying specific provisions of the Bill of Rights—one at a time, case after case—to the states. The designation of a right as fundamental also called for a definition of that right. The Supreme Court has tolerated some variation from state to state in the meaning of certain constitutional rights. It has also imposed a duty on governments to inform citizens of their rights so that they are equipped to exercise them.

As it has fashioned new fundamental rights from the Constitution, the Supreme Court has become embroiled in controversy. The right to privacy served as the basis for the right of women to terminate a pregnancy, which in turn suggested a right to personal autonomy. The abortion controversy is still raging, and the justices, relying in part on the abortion cases, have extended protections against state criminal prosecution of private consensual sexual behavior for homosexuals.

These are controversial judicial decisions, and they raise a basic issue. By offering constitutional protection to certain public policies, the courts may be threatening the democratic process, the process that gives the people a voice in government through their elected representatives. And should elected representatives fail to heed the public, the public may act on its own through mechanisms such as the referendum or initiative. One thing is certain: the challenge of democracy requires the constant balancing of freedom and order.

KEY CASES

Lemon v. *Kurtzman* (religious establishment)
Sherbert v. *Verner* (religious free exercise)
Brandenburg v. *Ohio* (free speech)
Tinker v. *Des Moines Independent County School District* (symbolic speech)
Morse v. *Frederick* (limit on student expression)
Cohen v. *California* (free expression)
Reno v. *ACLU* (obscenity)
New York Times v. *Sullivan* (free press)
New York Times v. *United States* (prior restraint)
District of Columbia v. *Heller* and *McDonald* v. *Chicago* (right to bear arms)
Palko v. *Connecticut* (Bill of Rights)
Gideon v. *Wainwright* (assistance of counsel)
Griswold v. *Connecticut* (privacy)
Miranda v. *Arizona* (self-incrimination)
Roe v. *Wade* (abortion)
Gonzales v. *Carhart* (abortion restrictions)
Lawrence and Garner v. *Texas* (gay rights)
Hamdan v. *Rumsfeld* (presidential authority; procedural protections at trial)
Boumediene v. *Bush* (constitutional right to challenge detention)

 CourseMate Visit www.cengagebrain.com/shop/ISBN/0495906182 for flashcards, web quizzes, videos and more!

AP Photo/Danny Moloshok

"When we want you, we'll call you; when we don't, git."[1] A rancher's sentiment toward his Mexican workers summarizes the treatment of illegal immigrants, many of them Mexicans or Latin Americans, who routinely cross our southern border in search of better wages and the possibility of a better life. The swings of the economy often signal whether illegal immigrants will be welcomed or sent packing. To be sure, illegal immigrants have provided the United States with cheap labor for a hundred years, undertaking tasks that few, if any, Americans would care to shoulder and providing goods and services at a far lower price than we would otherwise have to pay. They pick our fruit and vegetables, butcher our meat and poultry, clean our homes, flip our burgers, and mow our lawns. But illegal immigrants have also taken up jobs and better pay in other trades, including construction and manufacturing. "Better pay" is relative; it may be better for the illegal immigrant, but it is likely to drive down wages for everyone else. In a strong economy, a rising tide lifts all boats, including illegal ones. But in the Great Recession of today, illegal immigrants can become easy targets in the ebbing economic tide.

All governments provide for the general welfare, which embraces health, education, and fire and police protection. For example, public hospitals cannot decline care; public schools must admit and educate every student. These services ensure a measure of equality, a floor beneath which no one need fall. But does the floor exist for illegal immigrants and their children? Should illegal immigrants or their children be denied public education or health care?

In this chapter, we consider the different ideals of equality and the quest to realize them through government action. We begin with the struggle for racial equality, which continues to cast a long shadow in government policies. This struggle has served as a model for the diverse groups that chose to follow in the same path.*

---

*The effort to staunch the flow of illegal immigration also pits individual freedom against social order. In this chapter, we focus attention on the modern dilemma of government, the conflict between freedom and equality.

Two Conceptions of Equality

Most Americans support **equality of opportunity**, the idea that people should have an equal chance to develop their talents and that effort and ability should be rewarded equitably. This form of equality offers all individuals the same chance to get ahead; it glorifies personal achievement and free competition and allows everyone to play on a level field where the same rules apply to all. Special recruitment efforts aimed at identifying qualified minority or female job applicants, for example, ensure that everyone has the same chance starting out. Low-bid contracting illustrates equality of opportunity because every bidder has the same chance to compete for work.

Americans are far less committed to **equality of outcome**, which means greater uniformity in social, economic, and political power among different social groups. For example, schools and businesses aim at equality of outcome when they allocate admissions or jobs on the basis of race, gender, or disability, which are unrelated to ability. (Some observers refer to these allocations as *quotas;* others call them *goals*. The difference is subtle. A quota *requires* that a specified proportional share of some benefit go to a favored group. A goal *aims* for proportional allocation of benefits, without requiring it.) The government seeks equality of outcome when it adjusts the rules to handicap some bidders or applicants and favor others. The vast majority of Americans, however, consistently favor low-bid contracting and merit-based admissions and employment over preferential treatment.[2] Quota or goal-based policies muster only modest support in national opinion polls, ranging from 10 to 30 percent of the population, depending on how poll questions are worded.[3] The most recent surveys signal a significant decline in support for such egalitarian policies.[4]

Some people believe that equality of outcome can occur in today's society only if we restrict the free competition that is the basis of equality of opportunity. In 1978, Supreme Court Justice Harry Blackmun articulated this controversial position on a divided bench: "In order to get beyond racism, we must first take account of race. There is no other way. And in order to treat some persons equally, we must treat them differently."[5] In 2007, Chief Justice John G. Roberts, Jr., cast the issue in reverse on a divided bench: "The way to stop discrimination on the basis of race is to stop discriminating on the basis of race."[6] Quota policies generate the most opposition because they confine competition and create barriers to personal achievement. Quotas limit advancement for some individuals and ensure advancement for others. They alter the results by taking into account factors unrelated to ability. Equal outcomes policies that benefit minorities, women, or people with disabilities at the expense of whites, men, or the able-bodied create strong opposition because quotas seem to be at odds with individual initiative. In other words, equality clashes with freedom. To understand the ways government resolves this conflict, we have to understand the development of civil rights in this country.

The history of civil rights in the United States is primarily the story of a search for social and economic equality. This search has persisted for more than a century and is ongoing. It began with the battle for civil rights for black citizens, whose prior subjugation as slaves had roused the passions of the

equality of opportunity
The idea that each person is guaranteed the same chance to succeed in life.

equality of outcome
The concept that society must ensure that people are equal, and governments must design policies to redistribute wealth and status so that economic and social equality is actually achieved.

nation and brought about its bloodiest conflict, the Civil War. The struggle of blacks has been a beacon lighting the way for Native Americans, immigrant groups of which Latinos represent the largest component, women, people with disabilities, and homosexuals. Each of these groups has confronted **invidious discrimination**. Discrimination is simply the act of making or recognizing distinctions. When making distinctions among people, discrimination may be benign (that is, harmless) or invidious (harmful). Sometimes this harm has been subtle, and sometimes it has been overt. Sometimes it has even come from other minorities. Each group has achieved a measure of success in its struggle by pressing its interests on government, even challenging it. These challenges and the government's responses to them have helped shape our democracy.

Remember that **civil rights** are powers or privileges guaranteed to the individual and protected from arbitrary removal at the hands of the government or other individuals. Sometimes people refer to civil rights as "positive rights" (see the feature "Examples of Positive and Negative Rights: Constitutional Rights and Human Rights" in Chapter 15). In this chapter, we concentrate on the rights guaranteed by the constitutional amendments adopted after the Civil War and by laws passed to enforce those guarantees. Prominent among them is the right to equal protection of the laws. This right remained a promise rather than a reality well into the twentieth century.

The Civil War Amendments

The Civil War amendments were adopted to provide freedom and equality to black Americans. The Thirteenth Amendment, ratified in 1865, provided that

> neither slavery nor involuntary servitude ... shall exist within the United States, or any place subject to their jurisdiction.

The Fourteenth Amendment was adopted three years later. It provides first that freed slaves are citizens:

> All persons born or naturalized in the United States, and subject to the jurisdiction thereof, are citizens of the United States and of the State wherein they reside.

As we saw in Chapter 15, it also prohibits the states from abridging the "privileges or immunities of citizens of the United States" or depriving "any person of life, liberty, or property, without due process of law." The amendment then goes on to guarantee equality under the law, declaring that no state shall

> deny to any person within its jurisdiction the equal protection of the laws.

The Fifteenth Amendment, adopted in 1870, added a measure of political equality:

> The right of citizens of the United States to vote shall not be denied or abridged by the United States or by any State on account of race, color, or previous condition of servitude.

invidious discrimination
Discrimination against persons or groups that works to their harm and is based on animosity.

civil rights
Powers or privileges guaranteed to individuals and protected from arbitrary removal at the hands of government or individuals.

American blacks were thus free and politically equal—at least according to the Constitution. But for many years, the courts sometimes thwarted the efforts of the other branches to protect their constitutional rights.

Congress and the Supreme Court: Lawmaking Versus Law Interpreting

In the years after the Civil War, Congress went to work to protect the rights of black citizens. In 1866, lawmakers passed a civil rights act that gave the national government some authority over the treatment of blacks by state courts. This legislation was a response to the **black codes**, laws enacted by the former slave states to restrict the freedom of blacks. For example, vagrancy and apprenticeship laws forced blacks to work and denied them a free choice of employers. One section of the 1866 act that still applies today grants all citizens the right to make and enforce contracts; the right to sue others in court (and the corresponding ability to be sued); the duty and ability to give evidence in court; and the right to inherit, purchase, lease, sell, hold, or convey property. Later, in the Civil Rights Act of 1875, Congress attempted to guarantee blacks equal access to public accommodations (parks, theaters, and the like).

Although Congress enacted laws to protect the civil rights of black citizens, the Supreme Court weakened some of those rights. In 1873, the Court ruled that the Civil War amendments had not changed the relationship between the state and national governments.[7] State citizenship and national citizenship remained separate and distinct. According to the Court, the Fourteenth Amendment did not obligate the states to honor the rights guaranteed by U.S. citizenship.

In subsequent years, the Court's decisions narrowed some constitutional protections for blacks. In 1876, the justices limited congressional attempts to protect the rights of blacks.[8] A group of Louisiana whites had used violence and fraud to prevent blacks from exercising their basic constitutional rights, including the right to assemble peaceably. The justices held that the rights allegedly infringed on were not nationally protected rights and that therefore Congress was powerless to punish those who violated them. On the very same day, the Court ruled that the Fifteenth Amendment did not guarantee all citizens the right to vote; it simply listed grounds that could not be used to deny that right.[9] And in 1883, the Court struck down the public accommodations section of the Civil Rights Act of 1875.[10] The justices declared that the national government could prohibit only *government* action that discriminated against blacks; private acts of discrimination or acts of omission by a state were beyond the reach of the national government. For example, a person who refused to serve blacks in a private club was outside the control of the national government because the discrimination was a private—not a governmental— act. The Court refused to see racial discrimination as an act that the national government could prohibit. In many cases, the justices tolerated racial discrimination. In the process, they abetted **racism**, the belief that there are inherent differences among the races that determine people's achievement and that one's own race is superior to and thus has a right to dominate others.

black codes
Legislation enacted by former slave states to restrict the freedom of blacks.

racism
A belief that human races have distinct characteristics such that one's own race is superior to, and has a right to rule, others.

The Court's decisions gave the states ample room to maneuver around civil rights laws. In the matter of voting rights, for example, states that wanted to bar black men from the polls simply used nonracial means to do so. One popular tool was the **poll tax**, first imposed by Georgia in 1877. This was a tax of $1 or $2 on every citizen who wanted to vote. The tax was not a burden for most whites. But many blacks were tenant farmers, deeply in debt to white merchants and landowners; they had no extra money for voting. Other bars to black suffrage included literacy tests, minimum education requirements, and a grandfather clause that restricted suffrage to men who could establish that their grandfathers were eligible to vote before 1867 (three years before the Fifteenth Amendment declared that race could not be used to deny individuals the right to vote).[11] White southerners also used intimidation and violence to keep blacks from the polls.

The Roots of Racial Segregation

From well before the Civil War, **racial segregation** had been a way of life in the South: blacks lived and worked separately from whites. After the war, southern states began to enact Jim Crow laws to reinforce segregation. (*Jim Crow* was a derogatory term for a black person.) Once the Supreme Court took the teeth out of the Civil Rights Act of 1875, such laws proliferated. They required blacks to live in separate (generally inferior) areas and restricted them to separate sections of hospitals; separate cemeteries; separate drinking and toilet facilities; separate schools; and separate sections of trains, jails, and parks.

In 1892, Homer Adolph Plessy, who was seven-eighths Caucasian, took a seat in a "whites-only" car of a Louisiana train. He refused to move to the car reserved for blacks and was arrested. Plessy argued that Louisiana's law mandating racial segregation on its trains was an unconstitutional infringement on both the privileges and immunities guaranteed by the Fourteenth Amendment and its equal protection clause. The Supreme Court disagreed. The majority in *Plessy* v. *Ferguson* (1896) upheld state-imposed racial segregation.[12] They based their decision on what came to be known as the **separate-but-equal doctrine,** which held that separate facilities for blacks and whites satisfied the Fourteenth Amendment as long as they were equal. (The Court majority used the phrase "equal but separate" to describe the requirement. Justice John Marshall Harlan's dissenting opinion cast the phrase as "separate but equal," the way we have come to refer to the doctrine.)

Three years later, the Supreme Court extended the separate-but-equal doctrine to the schools.[13] The justices ignored the fact that black educational facilities (and most other "colored-only" facilities) were far from equal to those reserved for whites.

By the end of the nineteenth century, legal racial segregation was firmly entrenched in the American South. Although constitutional amendments and national laws to protect equality under the law were in place, the Supreme Court's interpretation of those amendments and laws rendered them ineffective. Several decades would pass before any change was discernible.

poll tax
A tax of $1 or $2 on every citizen who wished to vote, first instituted in Georgia in 1877. Although it was no burden on most white citizens, it effectively disenfranchised blacks.

racial segregation
Separation from society because of race.

separate-but-equal doctrine
The concept that providing separate but equivalent facilities for blacks and whites satisfies the equal protection clause of the Fourteenth Amendment.

Separate and Unequal

The Supreme Court gave constitutional protection to racial separation on the theory that states could provide "separate but equal" facilities for blacks. The facilities here appear equal, but the harm inherent in racial separation lies beneath the surface. Separating people by race is inherently unequal, declared the Supreme Court, in its landmark 1954 ruling, *Brown* v. *Board of Education*.

(Bettmann/Corbis)

The Dismantling of School Segregation

Denied the right to vote and to be represented in the government, blacks sought access to power through other parts of the political system. The National Association for the Advancement of Colored People (NAACP), founded in 1909 by W. E. B. Du Bois and others, both black and white, with the goal of ending racial discrimination and segregation, took the lead in the campaign for black civil rights. The plan was to launch a two-pronged legal and lobbying attack on the separate-but-equal doctrine: first by pressing for fully equal facilities for blacks, then by proving the unconstitutionality of segregation. The process would be a slow one, but the strategies involved did not require a large organization or heavy financial backing; at the time, the NAACP had neither.[*]

Pressure for Equality...

By the 1920s, the separate-but-equal doctrine was so deeply ingrained in American law that no Supreme Court justice would dissent from its continued application to racial segregation. But a few Court decisions offered hope that change would come. In 1935, Lloyd Gaines graduated from Lincoln University, a black college in Missouri, and applied to the state law school.

---

[*]In 1939, the NAACP established an offshoot, the NAACP Legal Defense and Education Fund, to work on legal challenges while the parent organization concentrated on lobbying.

The law school rejected him because he was black. Missouri refused to admit blacks to its all-white law school; instead, the state's policy was to pay the costs of blacks admitted to out-of-state law schools. With the support of the NAACP, Gaines appealed to the courts for admission to the University of Missouri Law School. In 1938, the U.S. Supreme Court ruled that he must be admitted.[14] Under the *Plessy* ruling, Missouri could not shift to other states its responsibility to provide an equal education for blacks.

Later cases helped reinforce the requirement that segregated facilities must be equal in all major respects. One was brought by Heman Sweatt, again with the help of the NAACP. The all-white University of Texas Law School had denied Sweatt entrance because of his race. A federal court ordered the state to provide a black law school for him; the state responded by renting a few rooms in an office building and hiring two black lawyers as teachers. Sweatt refused to attend the school and took his case to the Supreme Court.[15]

The Court ruled on *Sweatt* v. *Painter* in 1950. The justices unanimously found that the facilities were inadequate: the separate "law school" provided for Sweatt did not approach the quality of the white state law school. The University of Texas had to give Sweatt full student status. But the Court avoided reexamining the separate-but-equal doctrine.

...and Pressure for Desegregation

These decisions suggested to the NAACP that the time was right for an attack on segregation itself. In addition, public attitudes toward race relations were slowly changing from the predominant racism of the nineteenth and early twentieth centuries toward greater tolerance. Black groups had fought with honor—albeit in segregated military units—in World War II. Blacks and whites were working together in unions and in service and religious organizations. Social change and court decisions suggested that government-imposed segregation was vulnerable.

President Harry S. Truman risked his political future with his strong support of blacks' civil rights. In 1947, he established the President's Committee on Civil Rights. The committee's report, issued later that year, became the agenda for the civil rights movement during the next two decades. It called for national laws prohibiting racially motivated poll taxes, segregation, and brutality against minorities and for guarantees of voting rights and equal employment opportunity. In 1948, Truman ordered the **desegregation** (the dismantling of authorized racial segregation) of the armed forces.

In 1947, the U.S. Department of Justice had begun to submit briefs to the courts in support of civil rights. The department's most important intervention probably came in *Brown* v. *Board of Education*.[16] This case was the culmination of twenty years of planning and litigation on the part of the NAACP to invalidate racial segregation in public schools.

Linda Brown was a black child whose father had tried to enroll her in a white public school in Topeka, Kansas. The white school was close to Linda's home; the walk to the black school meant that she had to cross a dangerous

desegregation
The ending of authorized segregation, or separation by race.

set of railroad tracks. Brown's request was refused because of Linda's race. A federal district court found that the black public school was equal in quality to the white school in all relevant respects; therefore, according to the *Plessy* doctrine, Linda was required to go to the black public school. Brown appealed the decision.

Brown v. *Board of Education* reached the Supreme Court in late 1951. The justices delayed argument on the sensitive case until after the 1952 national election. *Brown* was merged with four similar cases into a class action, a device for combining the claims or defenses of similar individuals so that they can be tried in a single lawsuit (see Chapter 14). The class action was supported by the NAACP and coordinated by Thurgood Marshall, who would later become the first black justice to sit on the Supreme Court. The five cases squarely challenged the separate-but-equal doctrine. By all tangible measures (standards for teacher licensing, teacher–pupil ratios, library facilities), the two school systems in each case—one white, the other black—were equal. The issue was legal separation of the races.

On May 17, 1954, Chief Justice Earl Warren, who had only recently joined the Court, delivered a single opinion covering four of the cases. (See Chapter 14.) Warren spoke for a unanimous Court when he declared that "in the field of public education the doctrine of 'separate but equal' has no place. Separate educational facilities are inherently unequal,"[17] depriving the plaintiffs of the equal protection of the laws. Segregated facilities generate in black children "a feeling of inferiority ... that may affect their hearts and minds in a way unlikely ever to be undone."[18] In short, the nation's highest court found that state-imposed public school segregation violated the equal protection clause of the Fourteenth Amendment.

A companion case to *Brown* challenged the segregation of public schools in Washington, D.C.[19] Segregation there was imposed by Congress. The equal protection clause protected citizens only against state violations; no equal protection clause restrained the national government. It was unthinkable for the Constitution to impose a lesser duty on the national government than on the states. In this case, the Court unanimously decided that the racial segregation requirement was an arbitrary deprivation of liberty without due process of law, a violation of the Fifth Amendment. In short, the concept of liberty encompassed the idea of equality.

The Court deferred implementation of the school desegregation decisions until 1955. Then, in *Brown* v. *Board of Education II,* it ruled that school systems must desegregate "with all deliberate speed" and assigned the task of supervising desegregation to the lower federal courts.[20]

Some states quietly complied with the *Brown* decree. Others did little to desegregate their schools. And many communities in the South defied the Court, sometimes violently. Some white business and professional people formed "white citizens' councils." The councils put economic pressure on blacks who asserted their rights by foreclosing on their mortgages and denying them credit at local stores. Georgia and North Carolina resisted desegregation by paying tuition for white students attending private schools. Virginia and other states ordered that desegregated schools be closed.

Anger Erupts in Little Rock

In 1957, the Little Rock, Arkansas, school board attempted to implement court-ordered desegregation: nine black teenagers were to be admitted to Little Rock Central High School. Governor Orval Faubus ordered the National Guard to bar their attendance. A mob blocked a subsequent attempt by the students. Finally, President Dwight D. Eisenhower ordered federal troops to escort the students to the high school. Among them was fifteen-year-old Elizabeth Eckford (*right*). Hazel Brown (*left*) angrily taunted her from the crowd. This image seared the nation's conscience. The violence and hostility led the school board to seek a postponement of the desegregation plan. The Supreme Court, meeting in special session, affirmed the decision in *Brown* v. *Board of Education* and ordered the plan to proceed. Fifty years later, a federal judge declared Little Rock's schools desegregated. But the school district remains riven by racial strife, as a new black majority on the school board clashed with the black school superintendent over jobs, not education.

(ullstein bild/The Image Works)

This resistance, along with the Supreme Court's "all deliberate speed" order, placed a heavy burden on federal judges to dismantle what was the fundamental social order in many communities.[21] Gradual desegregation under *Brown* was in some cases no desegregation at all. In 1969, a unanimous Supreme Court ordered that the operation of segregated school systems stop "at once."[22]

Two years later, the Court approved several remedies to achieve integration, including busing, racial quotas, and the pairing or grouping of noncontiguous school zones. In *Swann* v. *Charlotte-Mecklenburg County Schools*, the Supreme Court affirmed the right of lower courts to order the busing of children to ensure school desegregation.[23] But these remedies applied only to **de jure segregation**, government-imposed segregation (for example, government assignment of whites to one school and blacks to another within the same community). Court-imposed remedies did not apply to **de facto segregation**, which is not the result of government action (for example, racial segregation resulting from residential patterns).

The busing of schoolchildren came under heavy attack in both the North and the South. Desegregation advocates saw busing as a potential remedy in many northern cities, where schools had become segregated as white families left the cities for the suburbs. This "white flight" had left inner-city schools predominantly black and suburban schools almost all white. Public opinion strongly opposed the busing approach, and Congress sought to impose limits on busing as a remedy to segregation. In 1974, a closely divided Court ruled that lower courts could not order busing across school district boundaries unless each district had practiced racial discrimination or school district lines had been deliberately drawn to achieve racial segregation.[24] This ruling meant an end to large-scale school desegregation in metropolitan areas.

The Civil Rights Movement

Although the NAACP concentrated on school desegregation, it also made headway in other areas. The Supreme Court responded to NAACP efforts in the late 1940s by outlawing whites-only primary elections in the South, declaring them to be in violation of the Fifteenth Amendment. The Court also declared segregation on interstate bus routes to be unconstitutional and desegregated restaurants and hotels in the District of Columbia. Despite these and other decisions that chipped away at existing barriers to equality, states still were denying black citizens political power, and segregation remained a fact of daily life.

Dwight D. Eisenhower, who became president in 1953, was not as concerned about civil rights as his predecessor had been. He chose to stand above the battle between the Supreme Court and those who resisted the Court's decisions. He even refused to reveal whether he agreed with the Court's decision in *Brown* v. *Board of Education.* "It makes no difference," Eisenhower declared, because "the Constitution is as the Supreme Court interprets it."[25] Eisenhower did enforce school desegregation when the safety of schoolchildren was involved, but he appeared unwilling to do much more to advance racial equality. That goal seemed to require the political mobilization of the people—black and white—in what is now known as the **civil rights movement**.

Black churches served as the crucible of the movement. More than places of worship, they served hundreds of other functions. In black communities, the church was "a bulletin board to a people who owned no organs of communication, a credit union to those without banks, and even a kind of people's court."[26] Some of its preachers were motivated by fortune, others by saintliness. One would prove to be a modern-day Moses.

de jure segregation
Government-imposed segregation.

de facto segregation
Segregation that is not the result of government influence.

civil rights movement
The mass mobilization during the 1960s that sought to gain equality of rights and opportunities for blacks in the South and to a lesser extent in the North, mainly through nonviolent, unconventional means of participation.

Civil Disobedience

Rosa Parks, a black woman living in Montgomery, Alabama, sounded the first call to action. That city's Jim Crow ordinances were tougher than those in other southern cities, where blacks were required to sit in the back of the bus while whites sat in the front, both races converging as the bus filled with passengers. In Montgomery, bus drivers had the power to define and redefine the floating line separating blacks and whites: drivers could order blacks to vacate an entire row to make room for one white or order blacks to stand even when some seats were vacant. Blacks could not walk through the white section to their seats in the back; they had to leave the bus after paying their fare and reenter through the rear.[27] In December 1955, Parks boarded a city bus on her way home from work and took an available seat in the front of the bus; she refused to give up her seat when the driver asked her to do so. She was arrested and fined $10 for violating the city ordinance.

Montgomery's black community responded to Parks's arrest with a boycott of the city's bus system. A **boycott** is a refusal to do business with a company or individual as an expression of disapproval or a means of coercion. Blacks walked or carpooled or stayed at home rather than ride the city's buses. As the bus company moved close to bankruptcy and downtown merchants suffered from the loss of black business, city officials began to harass blacks, hoping to frighten them into ending the boycott. But Montgomery's black citizens now had a leader, a charismatic twenty-six-year-old Baptist minister named Martin Luther King, Jr. King urged the people to hold out, and they did. A year after the boycott began, a federal court ruled that segregated transportation systems violated the equal protection clause of the Constitution. The boycott had proved to be an effective weapon.

In 1957, King helped organize the Southern Christian Leadership Conference to coordinate civil rights activities. He was totally committed to nonviolent action to bring racial issues into the light. To that end, he advocated **civil disobedience**, the willful but nonviolent breach of unjust laws.

One nonviolent tactic was the sit-in. On February 1, 1960, four black freshmen from North Carolina Agricultural and Technical College in Greensboro sat down at a whites-only lunch counter. They were refused service by the black waitress, who said, "Fellows like you make our race look bad." The young men stayed all day and promised to return the next morning to continue what they called a "sit-down protest." Other students soon joined in, rotating shifts so that no one missed classes. Within two days, eighty-five students had flocked to the lunch counter. Although abused verbally and physically, the students would not move. Finally, they were arrested. Soon people held similar sit-in demonstrations throughout the South and then in the North.[28] The Supreme Court upheld the actions of the demonstrators, although the unanimity that had characterized its earlier decisions was gone. (In this decision, three justices argued that even bigots had the right to call on the government to protect their property interests.)[29]

boycott
A refusal to do business with a firm, individual, or nation as an expression of disapproval or as a means of coercion.

civil disobedience
The willful but nonviolent breach of laws that are regarded as unjust.

The Civil Rights Act of 1964

In 1961, a new administration, headed by President John F. Kennedy, came to power. At first Kennedy did not seem to be committed to civil rights. But his stance changed as the movement gained momentum and as more and more whites became aware of the abuse being heaped on sit-in demonstrators, freedom riders (who protested unlawful segregation on interstate bus routes), and those who were trying to help blacks register to vote in southern states. Volunteers were being jailed, beaten, and even killed for advocating activities among blacks that whites took for granted.

In late 1962, President Kennedy ordered federal troops to ensure the safety of James Meredith, the first black to attend the University of Mississippi. In early 1963, Kennedy enforced the desegregation of the University of Alabama. In April 1963, television viewers were shocked to see civil rights marchers in Birmingham, Alabama, attacked with dogs, fire hoses, and cattle prods. (The idea of the Birmingham march was to provoke confrontations with white officials in an effort to compel the national government to intervene on behalf of blacks.) Finally, in June 1963, Kennedy asked Congress for legislation that would outlaw segregation in public accommodations.

Two months later, Martin Luther King, Jr., joined in a march on Washington, D.C. The organizers called the protest "A March for Jobs and Freedom," signaling the economic goals of black America. More than 250,000 people, black and white, gathered peaceably at the Lincoln Memorial to hear King speak. "I have a dream," the great preacher extemporized, "that my little children will one day live in a nation where they will not be judged by the color of their skin but by the content of their character."[30]

Congress had not yet enacted Kennedy's public accommodations bill when he was assassinated on November 22, 1963. His successor, Lyndon B. Johnson, considered civil rights his top legislative priority. Johnson's long congressional experience and exceptional leadership ability as Senate majority leader were put to good use in overcoming the considerable opposition to the legislation. Within months, Congress enacted the Civil Rights Act of 1964, which included a vital provision barring segregation in most public accommodations. This congressional action was in part a reaction to Kennedy's death. But it was also almost certainly a response to the brutal treatment of blacks throughout the South. Viewed from afar, it is probably fair to say that King's efforts were necessary but not sufficient to ensure passage of the law. And Johnson's efforts were sufficient but not necessary to ensure passage. Together, their efforts were necessary and sufficient to ensure enactment.

Congress had enacted civil rights laws in 1957 and 1960, but they dealt primarily with voting rights. The 1964 act was the most comprehensive legislative attempt ever to erase racial discrimination in the United States. Among its many provisions, the act

- Entitled all persons to "the full and equal enjoyment" of goods, services, and privileges in places of public accommodation, without discrimination on the grounds of race, color, religion, or national origin (the inclusion of "national origin" or place of birth would set in motion plans for immigration reform the following year)

- Established the right to equality in employment opportunities
- Strengthened voting rights legislation
- Created the Equal Employment Opportunity Commission (EEOC) and charged it with hearing and investigating complaints of job discrimination*
- Provided that funds could be withheld from federally assisted programs administered in a discriminatory manner

The last of these provisions had a powerful effect on school desegregation when Congress enacted the Elementary and Secondary Education Act in 1965. That act provided billions of federal dollars for the nation's schools; the threat of losing that money spurred local school boards to formulate and implement new plans for desegregation.

The 1964 act faced an immediate constitutional challenge. Its opponents argued that the Constitution does not forbid acts of private discrimination—the position the Supreme Court itself had taken in the late nineteenth century. But this time, a unanimous Court upheld the law, declaring that acts of discrimination impose substantial burdens on interstate commerce and thus are subject to congressional control.[31] In a companion case, Ollie McClung, the owner of a small restaurant, had refused to serve blacks. McClung maintained that he had the freedom to serve whomever he wanted in his own restaurant. The justices, however, upheld the government's prohibition of McClung's racial discrimination on the grounds that a substantial portion of the food served in his restaurant had moved in interstate commerce.[32] Thus, the Supreme Court vindicated the Civil Rights Act of 1964 by reason of the congressional power to regulate interstate commerce rather than on the basis of the Fourteenth Amendment. Since 1937, the Court had approved ever-widening authority to regulate state and local activities under the commerce clause. It was the most powerful basis for the exercise of congressional power in the Constitution.

President Johnson's goal was a "great society." Soon a constitutional amendment and a series of civil rights laws were in place to help him meet his goal:

- The Twenty-fourth Amendment, ratified in 1964, banned poll taxes in primary and general elections for national office.
- The Economic Opportunity Act of 1964 provided education and training to combat poverty.

When Leaders Confer

Martin Luther King, Jr., was a Baptist minister who believed in the principles of nonviolent protest practiced by India's Mohandas (Mahatma) Gandhi. This photograph captures King at a meeting with President Lyndon Johnson and other civil rights leaders in the White House cabinet room on March 18, 1966. King later joked that he was instructed to reach the White House south gate by "irregular routes," chuckling that he "had to sneak in the back door." King, who won the Nobel Peace Prize in 1964, was assassinated in 1968 in Memphis, Tennessee.

(LBJ Library/Photo by Yoichi R. Okamoto)

---

*Since 1972, the EEOC has had the power to institute legal proceedings on behalf of employees who allege that they have been victims of illegal discrimination.

- The Voting Rights Act of 1965 empowered the attorney general to send voter registration supervisors to areas in which fewer than half the eligible minority voters had been registered. This act has been credited with doubling black voter registration in the South in only five years.[33]
- The Fair Housing Act of 1968 banned discrimination in the rental and sale of most housing.

The Continuing Struggle over Civil Rights

In the decades that followed, it became clear that civil rights laws on the books do not ensure civil rights in action. In 1984, for example, the Supreme Court was called on to interpret a law forbidding sex discrimination in schools and colleges that receive financial assistance from the national government: Must the entire institution comply with the regulations, or only those portions of it that receive assistance?

In *Grove City College* v. *Bell,* the Court ruled that government educational grants to students implicate the institution as a recipient of government funds; therefore, it must comply with government nondiscrimination provisions. However, only the specific department or program receiving the funds (in Grove City's case, the financial aid program), not the whole institution, was barred from discriminating.[34] Athletic departments rarely receive such government funds, so colleges had no obligation to provide equal opportunity for women in their sports programs.

The *Grove City* decision had widespread effects because three other important civil rights laws were worded similarly. The implication was that any law barring discrimination on the basis of race, sex, age, or disability would be applicable only to programs receiving federal funds, not to the entire institution. So a university laboratory that received federal research grants could not discriminate, but other departments that did not receive federal money could. The effect of *Grove City* was to frustrate enforcement of civil rights laws. In keeping with pluralist theory, civil rights and women's groups shifted their efforts to the legislative branch.

Congress reacted immediately, exercising its lawmaking power to check the law-interpreting power of the judiciary. Congress can revise national laws to counter judicial decisions; in this political chess game, the Court's move is hardly the last one. Legislators protested that the Court had misinterpreted the intent of the antidiscrimination laws, and they forged a bipartisan effort to make that intent crystal clear: if any part of an institution gets federal money, no part of it can discriminate. Their work led to the Civil Rights Restoration Act, which became law in 1988 despite a presidential veto by Ronald Reagan.

Although Congress tried to restore and expand civil rights enforcement, the Supreme Court weakened it again. The Court restricted minority contractor **set-asides** of state public works funds, an arrangement it had approved in 1980. (A set-aside is a purchasing or contracting provision that reserves a certain percentage of funds for minority-owned contractors.) The five-person majority held that past societal discrimination alone cannot serve as the basis for rigid quotas.[35]

set-aside
A purchasing or contracting provision that reserves a certain percentage of funds for minority-owned contractors.

Buttressed by Republican appointees, the Supreme Court continued to narrow the scope of national civil rights protections in a string of decisions that suggested the ascendancy of a new conservative majority more concerned with freedom than equality.[36] To counter the Court's changing interpretations of civil rights laws, liberals turned to Congress to restore and enlarge earlier Court decisions by writing them into law. The result was a comprehensive new civil rights bill. The Civil Rights Act of 1991 reversed or altered twelve Court decisions that had narrowed civil rights protections. The new law clarified and expanded earlier legislation and increased the costs to employers for intentional, illegal discrimination. Continued resentment generated by equal outcomes policies would move the battle back to the courts, however.

Racial Violence and Black Nationalism

Increased violence on the part of those who demanded their civil rights and those who refused to honor them marked the mid- and late 1960s. Violence against civil rights workers was confined primarily to the South, where volunteers continued to work for desegregation and to register black voters. Among the atrocities that incensed even complacent whites were the bombing of dozens of black churches; the slaying of three young civil rights workers in Philadelphia, Mississippi, in 1964 by a group of whites, among them deputy sheriffs; police violence against demonstrators marching peacefully from Selma, Alabama, to Montgomery in 1965; and the assassination of Martin Luther King, Jr., in Memphis in 1968.

Black violence took the form of rioting in northern inner cities. Civil rights gains had come mainly in the South. Northern blacks had the vote and were not subject to Jim Crow laws, yet most lived in poverty. Unemployment was high, opportunities for skilled jobs were limited, and earnings were low. The segregation of blacks into the inner cities, although not sanctioned by law, was nevertheless real; their voting power was minimal because they constituted a small minority of the northern population. The solid gains made by southern blacks added to their frustration. Beginning in 1964, northern blacks took to the streets, burning and looting. Riots in 168 cities and towns followed King's assassination in 1968, and many were met with violent responses from urban police forces and the National Guard.

The lack of progress toward equality for northern blacks was an important factor in the rise of the black nationalist movement in the 1960s. The Nation of Islam, or Black Muslims, called for separation from whites rather than integration and for violence in return for violence. Malcolm X was their leading voice until he distanced himself from the Muslims shortly before his assassination by fellow Muslims in 1965. The militant Black Panther Party generated fear with its denunciation of the values of white America. In 1966, Stokely Carmichael, then chairman of the Student Nonviolent Coordinating Committee (SNCC), called on blacks to assert, "We want black power," in their struggle for civil rights. Organizations that had espoused integration and nonviolence now argued that blacks needed power more than white friendship.

IDEALOG.ORG

Have we gone too far in pushing equal rights ... or not far enough? After reading the material in this chapter, would you answer that question differently? Take IDEAlog's self-test.

The movement had several positive effects. Black nationalism instilled and promoted pride in black history and black culture. By the end of the decade, U.S. colleges and universities were beginning to institute black studies programs. More black citizens were voting than ever before, and their voting power was evident: increasing numbers of blacks were winning election to public office. In 1967, Cleveland's voters elected Carl Stokes, the first black mayor of a major American city. And by 1969, black representatives formed the Congressional Black Caucus. These achievements were incentives for other groups that also faced barriers to equality.

Civil Rights for Other Minorities

Recent civil rights laws and court decisions protect members of all minority groups. The Supreme Court underscored the breadth of this protection in an important decision in 1987.[37] The justices ruled unanimously that the Civil Rights Act of 1866 (known today as Section 1981) offers broad protection against discrimination to all minorities. Previously, members of white ethnic groups could not invoke the law in bias suits. Under the 1987 decision, members of any ethnic group can recover money damages if they prove they have been denied a job, excluded from rental housing, or subjected to another form of discrimination prohibited by the law. The 1964 Civil Rights Act offers similar protections but specifies strict procedures for filing suits that tend to discourage litigation. Moreover, the remedies in most cases are limited. In job discrimination, for example, back pay and reinstatement are the only remedies. Section 1981 has fewer hurdles and allows litigants to seek punitive damages (damages awarded by a court as additional punishment for a serious wrong). In some respects, then, the older law is a more potent weapon than the newer one in fighting discrimination.

Clearly, the civil rights movement has had an effect on all minorities. Here we examine the civil rights struggles of four groups: Native Americans, immigrant groups (the largest of which are Latinos), people with disabilities, and homosexuals.

Native Americans

During the eighteenth and nineteenth centuries, the U.S. government took Indian lands, isolated Native Americans on reservations, and denied them political and social rights. The government's dealings with the Indians were often marked by violence and broken promises. The agencies responsible for administering Indian reservations kept Native Americans poor and dependent on the national government.

The national government switched policies at the beginning of the twentieth century, promoting assimilation instead of separation. The government banned the use of native languages and religious rituals; it sent Indian children to boarding schools and gave them non-Indian names. In 1924, Indians received U.S. citizenship. Until that time, they had been considered members of tribal nations whose relations with the U.S. government were determined by treaties. The Native American population suffered badly during the Great Depression, primarily because the poorest Americans were affected most severely but also because of the inept administration of Indian reservations. (Today, Native Americans make up less than 1 percent of the population.) Poverty persisted on the reservations well after the Depression was over, and Indian land holdings continued to shrink through the 1950s and into the 1960s—despite signed treaties and the religious significance of portions of the lands they lost. In the 1960s, for example, a part of the Hopi Sacred Circle, which is considered the source of all life in the Hopi tribal religion, was strip-mined for coal.

Anger bred of poverty, unemployment, and frustration with an uncaring government exploded in militant action in late 1969, when several American Indians seized Alcatraz Island, an abandoned island in San Francisco Bay. The group cited an 1868 Sioux treaty that entitled them to unused federal lands; they remained on the island for a year and a half. In 1973, armed members of the American Indian Movement seized eleven hostages at Wounded Knee, South Dakota, the site of an 1890 massacre of two hundred Sioux (Lakota) by U.S. cavalry troops. They remained there, occasionally exchanging gunfire with federal marshals, for seventy-one days, until the government agreed to examine the treaty rights of the Oglala Sioux.[38]

In 1946, Congress enacted legislation establishing an Indian claims commission to compensate Native Americans for land that had been taken from them. In the 1970s, the Native American Rights Fund and other groups used that legislation to win important victories in the courts. The tribes won the return of lands in the Midwest and in the states of Oklahoma, New Mexico, and Washington. In 1980, the Supreme Court ordered the national government to pay the Sioux $117 million plus interest for the Black Hills of South Dakota, which had been stolen from them a century before. Other cases, involving land from coast to coast, are still pending.

The special status accorded Indian tribes in the Constitution has proved attractive to a new group of Indian leaders. Some of the 565 recognized tribes have successfully instituted casino gambling on their reservations, even in the face of state opposition to their plans. The tribes pay no taxes on their profits, which has helped them make gambling a powerful engine of economic growth for themselves and has given a once impoverished people undreamed-of riches and responsibilities. Congress has allowed these developments, provided that the tribes spend their profits on Indian assistance programs.

It is important to remember that throughout American history, Native Americans have been coerced physically and pressured economically to assimilate into the mainstream of white society. The destiny of Native Americans as viable groups with separate identities depends in no small measure on curbing their dependence on the national government.[39] The wealth created by casino gambling and other ventures funded with gambling profits may prove to be Native Americans' most effective weapon for regaining their heritage.

Immigrant Groups

The Statue of Liberty stands at the entrance to New York harbor, a gift from the people of France to commemorate the centennial of the United States. It is an icon of the United States in the world, capturing the belief that this country is a beacon of liberty for countless immigrants far and wide. We are a nation of immigrants. But the truth is more complex. Until 1965, the laws that governed immigration were rooted in invidious discrimination. Liberty's beacon drew millions of undocumented or illegal immigrants. Efforts to stem this tide brought unanticipated consequences, but further reform has failed to stop the flow of illegal immigrants to these shores.

For most of the first half of the twentieth century, immigration rules established a strict quota system that gave a clear advantage to Northern and Western Europeans and guaranteed that few Southern or Eastern Europeans, Asians, Africans, and Jews would enter the country by legal means. This was akin to the same unjustified discrimination that had subjugated blacks since the end of the Civil War. In the same spirit that championed civil rights for African Americans, a once reluctant Congress changed the rules to end discrimination on the basis of national origin. In 1965, President Lyndon Johnson signed a new immigration bill into law at the Statue of Liberty. Henceforth, the invidious quota system was gone; everyone was supposed to have an equal chance of immigrating to the United States. Upon signing the bill, Johnson remarked that there was nothing revolutionary about the law. "It will not reshape the structure of our daily lives or add importantly to either our wealth or our power." Within a few years, Johnson's prediction proved fundamentally wrong.

One purpose of the new law was to reunite families. It gave preference to relatives of immigrants already here, but since the vast majority of these legal immigrants came from Northern or Western Europe, the expectation was that reuniting families would continue the earlier preferences. Another provision gave preference in much smaller numbers to immigrants with much needed skills, such as doctors and engineers. It never occurred to the law's designers that African doctors, Indian engineers, Philippine nurses, or Chinese software programmers would be able to immigrate. Word trickled out to those newly eligible to come. Once here, these immigrants petitioned for their relatives to come. And those family members petitioned for yet others. As a result of this "chain migration," entire extended families established themselves in the United States, and the law did nothing to staunch the flow of illegal immigrants.

The demand for cheap labor in agriculture and manufacturing proved an enticing lure to many of the poor with access to America's southern border. The personal risk in crossing the border illegally was often outweighed by the possible gain in employment and a new, though illegal, start. There was no risk of imprisonment, merely a return to south of the border and perhaps another attempt to cross into a "promised land." During the post-1965 period, millions of men and women chose personal risk for the possibility of a better future.

In 1986, Congress sought to fix a system that by all accounts was broken. It sought to place the burden of enforcement on employers by imposing fines for hiring undocumented workers and then by offering amnesty to resident illegal immigrants who were in the United States for at least five years. But lax government enforcement and ease in obtaining falsified worker documents such as a "green card" doomed the enforcement strategy. Illegal immigrants continued to enter the United States, the majority from Mexico (see Figure 16.1).

By 2006, politicians were ready for another round of reform, motivated by over 11 million illegal immigrants in the United States (triple the number since the previous reform effort twenty years earlier); state and local governments in border states that were hit hard for the cost of public services (for example, health and education) for illegal immigrants; and the threat to national security in a post-9/11 world posed by porous, unguarded borders.

While the public is opposed to illegal immigrants obtaining driver's licenses or health care, it is important to note that in 2005, illegal immigrants paid an estimated $7 billion in Social Security taxes with little or nothing in return from the government.

FIGURE 16.1   Illegal Immigrants in the United States, 2009

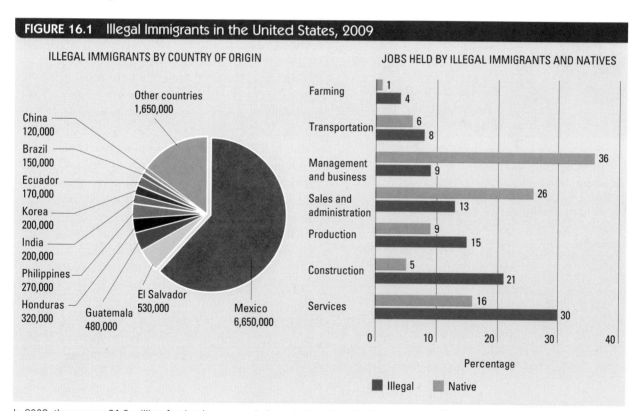

In 2009, there were 31.2 million foreign-born people living in America. The Department of Homeland Security "estimates that the unauthorized immigrant population living in the United States decreased to 10.8 million in January 2009 from 11.6 million in January 2008. Between 2000 and 2009, the unauthorized population grew by 27 percent."

Sources: Michael Hoefer, Nancy Rytina, and Bryan C. Baker, "Estimates of the Unauthorized Immigrant Population Residing in the United States: January 2009," Office of Immigration Statistics of the DHS, January 2010, http://www.dhs.gov/xlibrary/assets/statistics/publications/ois_ill_pe_2009.pdf; Jeffrey S. Passel and D'Vera Cohn, "Table 5: Comparing Occupations of US-Born and Unauthorized Immigrant Workers, 2008," in *A Portrait of Unauthorized Immigrants in the United States* (Washington, D.C.: Pew Hispanic Center, 14 April 2009), http://pewhispanic.org/files/reports/107.pdf.

Arizonans Protest

Protesters gathered outside the Arizona Capitol Saturday, May 1, 2010 in Phoenix to demonstrate their opposition to Arizona's controversial new immigration bill. A federal judge held key provisions void on federalism grounds shortly before the law was to take effect.

(AP Photo/Matt York)

Taking a lesson from the civil rights struggle for African Americans, immigrant organizers in 2006 publicly voiced their opposition to new legislation that would fence off large sections of the U.S.-Mexican border and make illegal aliens criminals who face penalties in excess of a year in prison. Immigrants from a wide range of ethnic communities responded with large-scale, peaceful protests across the United States. Their point was to demonstrate their quest for legal status and their deep resistance to the concept that their mere presence was to be taken as a criminal act. But a major overhaul of immigration policy orchestrated by the Bush administration and Senate Democrats failed in 2007. Republicans abandoned the president as conservative critics, abetted by talk radio programs, insisted on labeling the effort a form of amnesty for lawbreakers. For their part, Democrats brought the bill to the Senate floor without committee hearings, hoping that any bill would be better than no bill. Senator Edward M. Kennedy (D-Mass.), the bill's chief Democratic architect, said many senators "voted their fears, not their hopes."

Frustration brought about by hard economic times tends to make illegal immigrants easy targets. This is especially the case in Arizona, which experiences the greatest number of illegal border crossings from Mexico and has a large Hispanic population. With a surge in violence resulting from drug smuggling and human trafficking at its border, the Arizona legislature—backed by strong public opinion—adopted the strictest state immigration law in the nation in 2010. Among its many provisions, the Support Our Law Enforcement and Safe Neighborhoods Act makes it a crime for an alien to be in Arizona without carrying legal documents and obligates the police to determine a person's immigration status if there's a reasonable suspicion that the person is an illegal alien. It also steps up state and local law enforcement of federal immigration laws and cracks down on those sheltering, hiring, and transporting illegal aliens. In July 2010, a federal judge in Phoenix struck down key provisions of the law on federalism grounds, citing Article I, Section 8, of the Constitution, which vests exclusive power over naturalization (the process of citizenship)—and by implication over exclusion and deportation of aliens—in the national government, not the states. (See Chapter 4.)

Many Latinos have a rich and deep-rooted heritage in America, but until the 1920s, that heritage was largely confined to the southwestern states, particularly California. Then unprecedented numbers of Mexican immigrants came to the United States in search of employment and a better life.

Businesspeople who saw in them a source of cheap labor welcomed them. Many Mexicans became farm workers; others settled mainly in crowded, low-rent, inner-city districts in the Southwest, forming their own barrios, or neighborhoods, within the cities, where they maintained the customs and values of their homeland.

Like blacks who had migrated to northern cities, most new Latino immigrants found poverty and discrimination. And like poor blacks and Native Americans, they suffered disproportionately during the Great Depression. About one-third of the Mexican American population (mainly those who had been migratory farm workers) returned to Mexico during the 1930s.

World War II gave rise to another influx of Mexicans, who this time were primarily courted to work farms in California. But by the late 1950s, most farm workers—blacks, whites, and Hispanics—were living in poverty. Latinos who lived in cities fared little better. Yet millions of Mexicans continued to cross the border into the United States, both legally and illegally. The effect was to depress wages for farm labor in California and the Southwest.

In 1965, Cesar Chavez led a strike of the United Farm Workers union against growers in California. The strike lasted several years and eventually, in combination with a national boycott, resulted in somewhat better pay, working conditions, and housing for farm workers.

In the 1970s and 1980s, the Latino population continued to grow, and to grow rapidly. The 20 million Latinos living in the United States in the 1970s were still mainly Puerto Rican and Mexican American, but they were joined by immigrants from the Dominican Republic, Colombia, Cuba, and Ecuador. Although civil rights legislation helped them to an extent, they were among the poorest and least educated groups in the United States. Their problems were similar to those faced by other nonwhites, but most also had to overcome the further difficulty of learning and using a new language.

One effect of the language barrier is that voter registration and voter turnout among Hispanics are lower than among other groups. The creation of nine Hispanic-majority congressional districts ensured a measure of representation. These majority minority districts remain under scrutiny as a result of Supreme Court decisions prohibiting race-based districting. Also, voter turnout depends on effective political advertising, and Hispanics have not been targeted as often as other groups with political messages in Spanish. But despite these stumbling blocks, Hispanics have started to exercise a measure of political power.

Hispanics occupy positions of power in national and local arenas. Hispanics or Latinos constitute nearly 13 percent of the population and 4 percent of Congress. The 109th Congress (2005–2007) convened with a diverse group of twenty-six members of Hispanic descent: twenty-four in the House and two in the Senate. The National Hispanic Caucus of State Legislators, which has over three hundred members, is an informal bipartisan group dedicated to voicing and advancing issues affecting Hispanic Americans. The appointment of Sonia Sotomayor to the U.S. Supreme Court in 2009, and the growing number of Hispanics appointed to the lower federal courts, signaled yet another milestone in the quest for equality for America's largest minority group.

Americans with Disabilities

Minority status is not confined to racial and ethnic groups. After more than two decades of struggle, 43 million Americans with disabilities gained recognition in 1990 as a protected minority with the enactment of the Americans with Disabilities Act (ADA). The law extends the protections embodied in the Civil Rights Act of 1964 to people with physical or mental disabilities, including people with AIDS, alcoholism, and drug addiction. It guarantees them access to employment, transportation, public accommodations, and communication services.

The roots of the disabled rights movement stem from the period after World War II. Thousands of disabled veterans returned to a country and a society that were insensitive to their needs. Institutionalization seemed the best way to care for people with disabilities, but this approach came under increasing fire as people with disabilities and their families sought care at home.

Advocates for persons with disabilities found a ready model in the existing civil rights laws. Opponents argued that the changes mandated by the 1990 law (such as access for those confined to wheelchairs) could cost billions of dollars, but supporters replied that the costs would be offset by an equal or greater reduction in federal aid to people with disabilities, who would rather be working.

The law's enactment set off an avalanche of job discrimination complaints filed with the national government's discrimination watchdog agency, the EEOC. By 2005, the EEOC had received almost 220,000 ADA-related complaints. Curiously, most complaints came from already employed people, both previously and recently disabled. They charged that their employers failed to provide reasonable accommodations as required by the law. The disabilities cited most frequently were back problems, mental illness, heart trouble, neurological disorders, and substance abuse.[40]

A deceptively simple question lies at the heart of many ADA suits: What is the meaning of *disability?* According to the EEOC, a disability is "a physical or mental impairment that substantially limits one or more major life activities." This deliberately vague language has thrust the courts into the role of providing needed specificity, a path that politicians have feared to tread.[41]

Congress moved a step closer in 2008 to passing a revision to the ADA. The legislation would increase protections for people with disabilities by making it easier for workers to prove discrimination. The legislation would give protection to people with epilepsy, diabetes, cancer, cerebral palsy, multiple sclerosis, and other ailments. Federal court decisions had denied protection under the ADA because the disabling conditions were controlled by medication or were in remission. The House passed the bill by a wide margin, but the legislation remained stalled in the Senate.

A change in the nation's laws, no matter how welcome, does not ensure a change in people's attitudes. Laws that end racial discrimination do not extinguish racism, and laws that ban biased treatment of people with disabilities cannot mandate their acceptance. But civil rights advocates predict that bias against people with disabilities, like similar biases against other minorities, will wither as they become full participants in society.

Homosexual Americans

June 27, 1969, marked the beginning of an often overlooked movement for civil rights in the United States. On that Friday evening, plainclothes officers of the New York City police force raided a gay bar in Greenwich Village known as the Stonewall Inn. The police justified the raid because of their suspicions that Stonewall had been operating without a proper liquor license. In response, hundreds of citizens took to the streets in protest. Violent clashes and a backlash against the police involving hundreds of people ensued for several nights, during which cries of "Gay power!" and "We want freedom!" could be heard. The event became known as the Stonewall Riots and served as the touchstone for the gay liberation movement in the United States.[42]

Stonewall led to the creation of several political interest groups that have fought for the civil liberties and civil rights of members of the gay and lesbian communities. One in particular, the National Gay and Lesbian Task Force (NGLTF), successfully lobbied the U.S. Civil Service Commission in 1973 to allow gay people to serve in public employment. More recently, in 1999, the NGLTF founded the Legislative Lawyering Program, designed to work for progressive legislation at both the federal and state levels. Another organization, the Human Rights Campaign, founded in 1980, today boasts a membership of over 700,000. One of its current priorities is to seek passage of an employment nondiscrimination act to prevent U.S. citizens from being fired from their jobs for being gay.

Although once viewed as being on the fringe of American society, the gay community today maintains a visible presence in national politics. Two openly gay members serve in the U.S. House of Representatives (110th Congress): Barney Frank (D-Mass.) and Tammy Baldwin (D-Wisc.). But gay and lesbian issues seem less paramount than other issues to the American public. In the 2004 election, the economy and the Iraq war were more important to voters than same-sex marriage.[43] Financial support for candidates and groups favoring gay and lesbian rights has declined since 2000.[44]

Gays and lesbians have made significant progress since the early 1970s, but they still have a long way to go to enjoy the complete menu of civil rights now written into laws that protect other minority groups. In addition to some of the civil liberties concerns noted in Chapter 15, gays and lesbians are still unable to serve openly in the U.S. military, despite attempts by the Clinton administration, and later the Bush administration, to improve conditions through its "don't ask, don't tell" policy, which some observers maintain has actually made things worse for homosexuals in uniform. In 2010, President Obama indicated his plan to repeal the policy within a year through a coordinated effort with Congress and the military.[45] Also, because domestic partner benefits are not recognized uniformly across the United States, same-sex partners are unable to take full advantage of laws that allow citizens to leave their personal estates to family members. And finally, they often cannot sign onto their partner's health-care plans (except when company policies allow it); heterosexual couples enjoy this employment benefit almost without exception.

The demand for equality found a new voice in 2003 when the highest court in Massachusetts held, in a 4–3 ruling, that same-sex couples have a state constitutional right to the "protections, benefits, and obligations of civil marriage." The majority rested its holding on the Massachusetts Constitution, which affirms the dignity and equality of all individuals. The justices acknowledged that the Massachusetts Constitution is more protective of equality and liberty than the federal Constitution, enabling actions that the U.S. Supreme Court might be unwilling or unable to take.[46]

The decision challenged the state legislature, which sought a compromise to avoid an affirmation of same-sex marriage. The High Court rejected this maneuver, setting the stage for a state constitutional amendment limiting marriages to unions between a man and a woman. At least thirty-seven states prohibit recognition of marriages between same-sex couples. Only residents of states that recognize the validity of same-sex marriage may legally marry today in Massachusetts. But it will be years before the lengthy amendment process runs its course.

In 2008, the California Supreme Court ruled 4–3 that same-sex couples have a state constitutional right to marry. State law and a statewide initiative approved in 2000 defined marriage as a union between a man and a woman. The question before the court was whether those laws violated provisions of the state constitution protecting equality and the right to marry. "In view of the substance and significance of the fundamental constitutional right to form a family relationship," wrote Chief Justice Ronald

Going to the Chapel

Julie and Hillary Goodridge, along with their daughter, Annie, were the first gay couple to obtain a marriage license from Boston registrar Judith A. McCarthy in May 2004. After affirming the truth of the information they provided and paying the requisite fee, they headed to the altar. Armed with their license, a minister pronounced the couple "fully and legally married." Marital bliss ran out for the Goodridges two years later. They filed for divorce in 2006.

(DAVID L. RYAN/Boston Globe/ Landov)

M. George, "the California Constitution properly must be interpreted to guarantee this basic civil right to all Californians, whether gay or heterosexual, and to same-sex couples as well as to opposite-sex couples."[47]

The ruling was celebrated in San Francisco's large gay community and denounced by religious and conservative groups throughout the state who supported a ballot initiative that would amend the state constitution to ban same-sex marriages and overturn the decision. The initiative passed in 2008, overturning the ruling by defining marriage in the state constitution as a union between one man and one woman. The initiative is now under constitutional challenge in the federal courts, and it is likely that the U.S. Supreme Court will finally decide the matter. While conceding that Californians could define their own rules, attorney Theodore Olson argued that those rules could not take away a fundamental right. The case boils down to marriage and equality. Is marriage a fundamental constitutional right? If so, then everyone is entitled to exercise that right unless the government has compelling reasons to curtail it.[48]

A 2000 Supreme Court decision, *Boy Scouts of America* v. *Dale,* illustrates both the continuing legal struggles of gays and lesbians for civil rights and the modern conflict between freedom and equality. James Dale began his involvement in scouting in 1978 and ten years later achieved the esteemed rank of Eagle Scout. In 1989, he applied to and was accepted for the position of assistant scoutmaster of Troop 73 in New Jersey. Shortly after, in 1990, the Boy Scouts revoked Dale's membership in the organization when it learned that he had become a campus activist with the Rutgers University Lesbian/Gay Alliance. The Boy Scouts argued that because homosexual conduct was inconsistent with its mission, the organization enjoyed the right to revoke his membership. Dale argued that the Scouts' actions violated a New Jersey law that prohibited discrimination on the basis of sexual orientation in places of public accommodation. The U.S. Supreme Court resolved this conflict in a narrow 5–4 decision and sided with the Scouts. The majority opinion, authored by Chief Justice William H. Rehnquist, maintained that New Jersey's public accommodations law violated the Boy Scouts' freedom of association, outweighing Dale's claim for equal treatment. The dissenters, led by Justice John Paul Stevens, maintained that equal treatment outweighed free association. They reasoned that allowing Dale to serve as an assistant scoutmaster did not impose serious burdens on the Scouts or force the organization "to communicate any message that it does not wish to endorse."[49]

IDEALOG.ORG

Do you support a constitutional amendment that would bar marriages between gay and lesbian couples? Take IDEAlog's self-test.

Gender and Equal Rights: The Women's Movement

Together with unconventional political activities such as protests and sit-ins, conventional political tools such as the ballot box and the lawsuit have brought minorities in America a measure of equality. The Supreme Court, once responsible for perpetuating inequality for blacks, has expanded the array of legal tools available to all minorities to help them achieve social equality. Women, too, have benefited from this change.

Protectionism

Until the early 1970s, laws that affected the civil rights of women were based on traditional views of the relationship between men and women. At the heart of these laws was **protectionism**—the notion that women must be sheltered from life's harsh realities. Thomas Jefferson, author of the Declaration of Independence, believed that "were our state a pure democracy there would still be excluded from our deliberations women, who, to prevent deprivation of morals and ambiguity of issues, should not mix promiscuously in gatherings of men."[50] And "protected" they were, through laws that discriminated against them in employment and other areas. With few exceptions, women were also "protected" from voting until early in the twentieth century.

The demand for women's rights arose from the abolition movement and later was based primarily on the Fourteenth Amendment's prohibition of laws that "abridge the privileges or immunities of citizens of the United States." However, the courts consistently rebuffed challenges to protectionist state laws. In 1873, the Supreme Court upheld an Illinois statute that prohibited women from practicing law. The justices maintained that the Fourteenth Amendment had no bearing on a state's authority to regulate admission of members to the bar.[51]

Protectionism reached a peak in 1908, when the Court upheld an Oregon law limiting the number of hours women could work.[52] The decision was rife with assumptions about the nature and role of women, and it gave wide latitude to laws that "protected" the "weaker sex." It also led to protectionist legislation that barred women from working more than forty-eight hours a week and from working at jobs that required them to lift more than thirty-five pounds. (The average work week for men was sixty hours or longer.) In effect, women were locked out of jobs that called for substantial overtime (and overtime pay) and were shunted to jobs that men believed suited their abilities.

Protectionism can take many forms. Some employers hesitate to place women at risk in the workplace. Some have excluded women of childbearing age from jobs that involve exposure to toxic substances that could harm a developing fetus. Usually such jobs offer more pay to compensate for their higher risk. Although they too face reproductive risks from toxic substances, men have experienced no such exclusions.

In 1991, the Supreme Court struck down a company's fetal protection policy in strong terms. The Court relied on amendments to the 1964 Civil Rights Act providing for only a very few narrow exceptions to the principle that unless some workers differ from others in their ability to work, they must be treated the same as other employees. "In other words," declared the majority, "women as capable of doing their jobs as their male counterparts may not be forced to choose between having a child and having a job."[53]

protectionism
The notion that women must be protected from life's cruelties; until the 1970s, the basis for laws affecting women's civil rights.

Political Equality for Women

With a few exceptions, women were not allowed to vote in this country until 1920. In 1869, Francis and Virginia Minor sued a St. Louis, Missouri, registrar for not allowing Virginia Minor to vote. In 1875, the Supreme Court held that the Fourteenth Amendment's privileges and immunities clause did not confer the right to vote on all citizens or require that the states allow women to vote.[54]

The decision clearly slowed the movement toward women's suffrage, but it did not stop it. In 1878, Susan B. Anthony, a women's rights activist, convinced a U.S. senator from California to introduce a constitutional amendment requiring that "the right of citizens of the United States to vote shall not be denied or abridged by the United States or by any State on account of sex." The amendment was introduced and voted down several times over the next twenty years. Meanwhile, as noted in Chapter 7, a number of states, primarily in the Midwest and West, did grant limited suffrage to women.

The movement for women's suffrage became a political battle to amend the Constitution. In 1917, police arrested 218 women from twenty-six states when they picketed the White House, demanding the right to vote. Nearly one hundred went to jail, some for days and others for months. The movement culminated in the adoption in 1920 of the **Nineteenth Amendment**, which gave women the right to vote. Its wording was that first suggested by Anthony.

The right of women to vote does not ensure that women representatives will be elected to public office. Beginning in the 1990s, several countries sought to ensure elected representation of women by the use of gender quotas. The results have been mixed. (See "Politics of Global Change: Gender Quotas for Representatives in Lower Legislative Houses.")

Meanwhile, the Supreme Court continued to act as the benevolent protector of women. Women entered the work force in significant numbers during World War I and did so again during World War II, but they received lower wages than the men they replaced. Again, the justification was the "proper" role of women as mothers and homemakers. Because society expected men to be the principal providers, it followed that women's earnings were less important to the family's support. This thinking perpetuated inequalities in the workplace. Economic equality was closely tied to social attitudes. Because society expected women to stay at home, the assumption was that they needed less education than men did. Therefore, they tended to qualify only for low-paying, low-skilled jobs with little chance for advancement.

Prohibiting Sex-Based Discrimination

The movement to provide equal rights to women advanced a step with the passage of the Equal Pay Act of 1963, which required equal pay for men and women doing similar work. However, state protectionist laws still had the effect of restricting women to jobs that men usually did not want. Where employment was stratified by sex, equal pay was an empty promise. To remove the restrictions of protectionism, women needed equal opportunity for employment. They got it in the Civil Rights Act of 1964 and later legislation.

The objective of the Civil Rights Act of 1964 was to eliminate racial discrimination in America. The original wording of Title VII of the act prohibited employment discrimination based on race, color, religion, and national

Nineteenth Amendment
The amendment to the Constitution, adopted in 1920, that ensures women of the right to vote.

Politics of Global Change

Gender Quotas for Representatives in Lower Legislative Houses

One way to assure the election of women to public office is to mandate it. Several countries have taken this step, with mixed results. One approach is to establish a quota system that women must constitute a certain percentage or number of elective positions. The philosophical justification behind this idea is tied to the

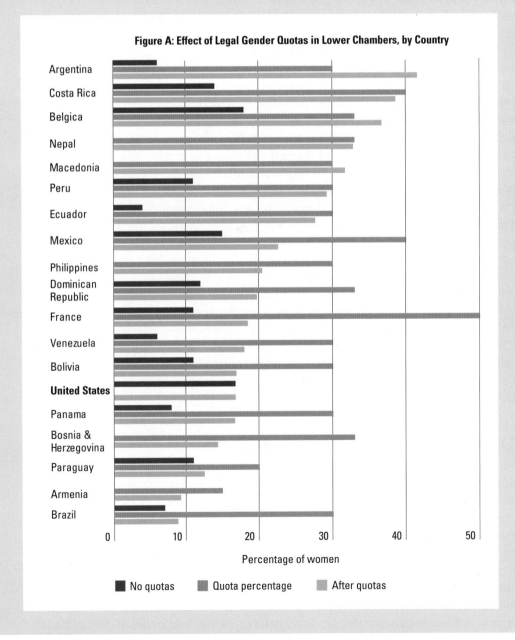

Figure A: Effect of Legal Gender Quotas in Lower Chambers, by Country

Percentage of women

■ No quotas   ■ Quota percentage   ■ After quotas

notion of equality of outcome. While women constitute 50 percent of the population, they tend to be under represented in political offices. The establishment of legal quotas aims at solving this disparity.

But not all gender quota systems are created equal. Some nations, such as Nepal and the Philippines, include quotas in their constitutions. Other nations, such as most of Latin America, include quotas in their electoral laws. And in some cases—Germany, Italy, Norway, and Sweden, for example—several political parties advance a voluntary quota system regardless of their country's legislation. Gender quota systems vary also according to the level at which they are applied. In some cases they regulate the number of candidacies that must be held by women, whereas in others they mandate the number or percentage of elected positions held by women.

Have these quota systems achieved their desired level of gender equality? Figure A identifies eighteen countries with gender quota systems (and the United States, which lacks such a system), their gender goals,

and in thirteen cases the pre- and post-quota results. First, only in two cases (Argentina and Nepal) did actual electoral results match the established quota. Second, note the wide variance regarding the ultimate effectiveness of gender quotas. Women's representation increased significantly in some countries such as Argentina, Costa Rica, and Ecuador, but in most countries, the result is not as spectacular (an increase of less than 10 percent). What explains this disparity among cases? Figure B offers a hint. The main reason is the electoral system itself. Quotas are most effective in proportional representation systems with closed lists of candidates, provided women are positioned in competitive places. Quotas are least effective in majoritarian electoral systems. Electoral systems combining features of majoritarian and proportional representation schemes fit in the middle. However, women's representation has steadily increased in the past decade. Whether this trend is explained by means of institutional engineering or by societal transformations remains a matter of continuing research.

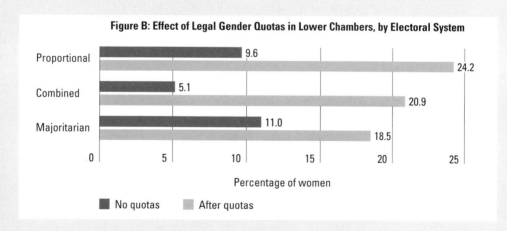

Figure B: Effect of Legal Gender Quotas in Lower Chambers, by Electoral System

Proportional: No quotas 9.6, After quotas 24.2
Combined: No quotas 5.1, After quotas 20.9
Majoritarian: No quotas 11.0, After quotas 18.5

Percentage of women

■ No quotas   ■ After quotas

origin—but not gender. In an effort to scuttle the provision during House debate, Democrat Howard W. Smith of Virginia proposed an amendment barring job discrimination based on sex. Smith's intention was to make the law unacceptable; his effort to ridicule the law brought gales of laughter to the debate. But Democrat Martha W. Griffiths of Michigan used Smith's strategy against him. With her support, Smith's amendment carried, as did the act.[55] Congress extended the jurisdiction of the EEOC to cover cases of invidious sex discrimination, or **sexism**.

Subsequent women's rights legislation was motivated by the pressure for civil rights, as well as by a resurgence of the women's movement, which

sexism
Invidious sex discrimination.

had subsided in 1920 after the adoption of the Nineteenth Amendment. One particularly important law was Title IX of the Education Amendments of 1972, which prohibited sex discrimination in federally aided education programs. Another boost to women came from the Revenue Act of 1972, which provided tax credits for child-care expenses. In effect, the act subsidized parents with young children so that women could enter or remain in the work force. However, the high-water mark in the effort to secure women's rights was the equal rights amendment, as we shall explain shortly.

In 2007, a conservative Supreme Court tightened the rules over pay discrimination lawsuits under Title VII.[56] The case involved a woman who did not learn of the pay disparity with sixteen men in her office until years later because salary information is secret. But the law required her to file a complaint within 180 days of pay setting. The 5–4 decision prompted a bitter oral dissent by Justice Ruth Bader Ginsburg.

True to the pluralist character of American democracy, the Obama administration and a Democratic Congress reversed the 2007 decision by passing the Lilly Ledbetter Fair Pay Act. The act allows the filing of complaints beyond the 180-day period.[57] Pay equity for women still remains a hope, not a reality.

Stereotypes Under Scrutiny

After nearly a century of protectionism, the Supreme Court began to take a closer look at gender-based distinctions. In 1971, it struck down a state law that gave men preference over women in administering the estate of a person who died without naming an administrator.[58] The state maintained that the law reduced court workloads and avoided family battles; however, the

A Journey of a Thousand Miles Begins with the First Step

With his final pen stroke on the very first piece of legislation of his administration, the president handed the pen to one of its proponents. Standing fourth from the left is Lilly Ledbetter. The law extends the period for filing equal-pay complaints; it does not mandate equal pay for equal work.

(Stephen Crowley/The New York Times/Redux)

Court dismissed those objections, because they were not important enough to justify making gender-based distinctions between individuals. Two years later, the justices declared that paternalism operated to "put women not on a pedestal, but in a cage."[59] They then proceeded to strike down several laws that either prevented or discouraged departures from traditional sex roles. In 1976, the Court finally developed a workable standard for reviewing such laws: gender-based distinctions are justifiable only if they serve some important government purpose.[60]

The objective of the standard is to dismantle laws based on sexual stereotypes while fashioning public policies that acknowledge relevant differences between men and women. Perhaps the most controversial issue is the idea of *comparable worth,* which requires employers to pay comparable wages for different jobs, filled predominantly by one sex or the other, that are of about the same worth to the employer. Absent new legislation, the courts remain reluctant and ineffective vehicles for ending wage discrimination.[61]

The courts have not been reluctant to extend to women the *constitutional* guarantees won by blacks. In 1994, the Supreme Court extended the Constitution's equal protection guarantee by forbidding the exclusion of potential jurors on the basis of their sex. In a 6–3 decision, the justices held that it is unconstitutional to use gender, and likewise race, as a criterion for determining juror competence and impartiality. "Discrimination in jury selection," wrote Justice Harry A. Blackmun for the majority, "whether based on race or on gender, causes harm to the litigants, the community, and the individual jurors who are wrongfully excluded from participation in the judicial process."[62] The 1994 decision completed a constitutional revolution in jury selection that began in 1986 with a bar against juror exclusions based on race.

In 1996, the Court spoke with uncommon clarity when it declared that the men-only admissions policy of the Virginia Military Institute (VMI), a state-supported military college, violated the equal protection clause of the Fourteenth Amendment. Virginia defended the school's policy on the grounds that it was preserving diversity among America's educational institutions.

In an effort to meet women's demands to enter VMI—and stave off continued legal challenges—Virginia established a separate-but-equal institution, the Virginia Women's Institute for Leadership (VWIL). The program was housed at Mary Baldwin College, a private liberal arts college for women, and students enrolled in VWIL received the same financial support as students at VMI.

The presence of women at VMI would require substantial changes in the physical environment and the traditional close scrutiny of the students. Moreover, the presence of women would alter the manner in which cadets interact socially. Was the uniqueness of VMI worth preserving at the expense of women who could otherwise meet the academic, physical, and psychological stress imposed by the VMI approach?

In a 7–1 decision, the High Court voted no. Writing for a six-member majority in *United States* v. *Virginia,* Justice Ruth Bader Ginsburg applied a demanding test she labeled "skeptical scrutiny" to official acts that deny individuals rights or responsibilities based on their sex. "Parties who seek to defend gender-based government action," she wrote, "must demonstrate an 'exceedingly persuasive justification' for that action." Ginsburg declared that "women seeking and fit for a VMI-quality education cannot be offered anything less, under the State's obligation to afford them genuinely equal protection." Ginsburg went on to note that the VWIL program offered no cure for the "opportunities and advantages withheld from women who want a VMI education and can make the grade."[63] The upshot is that distinctions based on sex are almost as suspect as distinctions based on race.

Three months after the Court's decision, VMI's board of directors finally voted 9–8 to admit women. This ended VMI's distinction as the last government-supported single-sex school. However, school officials made few allowances for women. Buzz haircuts and fitness requirements remained the standard for all students. "It would be demeaning to women to cut them slack," declared VMI's superintendent.[64]

The Equal Rights Amendment

Policies protecting women, based largely on gender stereotypes, have been woven into the legal fabric of American life. This protectionism has limited the freedom of women to compete with men socially and economically on an equal footing. However, the Supreme Court has been hesitant to extend the principles of the Fourteenth Amendment beyond issues of race. When judicial interpretation of the Constitution imposes a limit, then only a constitutional amendment can overcome it.

The National Women's Party, one of the few women's groups that did not disband after the Nineteenth Amendment was enacted, introduced the proposed **equal rights amendment (ERA)** in 1923. The ERA declared that "equality of rights under the law shall not be denied or abridged by the United States or any State on account of sex." It remained bottled up in committee in every Congress until 1970, when Representative Martha Griffiths filed a discharge petition to bring it to the House floor for a vote. The House passed the ERA, but the Senate scuttled it by attaching a section calling for prayer in the public schools.

A national coalition of women's rights advocates generated enough support to get the ERA through Congress in 1972. Its proponents then had seven years to get the amendment ratified by thirty-eight state legislatures, as required by the Constitution. By 1977, they were three states short of that goal, and three states had rescinded their earlier ratification. Then, in an unprecedented action, Congress extended the ratification deadline. It didn't help. The ERA died in 1982, still three states short of adoption.

equal rights amendment (ERA)
A failed constitutional amendment introduced by the National Women's Party in 1923, declaring that "equality of rights under the law shall not be denied or abridged by the United States or any State on account of sex."

Why did the ERA fail? There are several explanations. Its proponents mounted a national campaign to generate approval, while its opponents organized state-based anti-ERA campaigns. ERA proponents hurt their cause by exaggerating the amendment's effects; such claims only gave ammunition to the amendment's opponents. For example, the puffed-up claim that the amendment would make wife and husband equally responsible for their family's financial support caused alarm among the undecided. As the opposition grew stronger, especially from women who wanted to maintain their traditional role, state legislators began to realize that supporting the amendment involved risk. Given the exaggerations and counter-exaggerations, lawmakers ducked. Because it takes an extraordinary majority to amend the Constitution, it takes only a committed minority to thwart the majority's will.

Despite its failure, the movement to ratify the ERA produced real benefits. It raised the consciousness of women about their social position, spurred the formation of the National Organization for Women (NOW) and other large organizations, contributed to women's participation in politics, and generated important legislation affecting women.[65]

The failure to ratify the ERA stands in stark contrast to the quick enactment of many laws that now protect women's rights. Such legislation had little audible opposition. If years of racial discrimination called for government redress, then so did years of gender-based discrimination. Furthermore, laws protecting women's rights required only the amending of civil rights bills or the enactment of similar bills.

Some scholars argue that for practical purposes, the Supreme Court has implemented the equivalent of the ERA through its decisions. It has struck down distinctions based on sex and held that stereotyped generalizations about sexual differences must fall.[66] In recent rulings, the Court has held that states may require employers to guarantee job reinstatement to women who take maternity leave, that sexual harassment in the workplace is illegal, and that the existence of a hostile work environment may be demonstrated by a reasonable perception of abuse rather than by proven psychological injury.[67]

But the Supreme Court can reverse its decisions, and legislators can repeal statutes. Without an equal rights amendment, argue some feminists, the Constitution will continue to bear the sexist imprint of a document written by men for men. Until the ERA becomes part of the Constitution, said the late feminist Betty Friedan, "We are at the mercy of a Supreme Court that will interpret equality as it sees fit."[68]

Affirmative Action: Equal Opportunity or Equal Outcome?

In his vision of a Great Society, President Johnson linked economic rights with civil rights and equality of outcome with equality of opportunity. "Equal opportunity is essential, but not enough," he declared. "We seek not just legal equity but human ability, not just equality as a right and a theory but equality as a fact and equality as a result."[69] This commitment led to affirmative action programs to expand opportunities for women, minorities, and people with disabilities.

Affirmative action is a commitment by a business, employer, school, or other public or private institution to expand opportunities for women, blacks, Hispanic Americans, and members of other minority groups. Affirmative action aims to overcome the effects of present and past discrimination. It embraces a range of public and private programs, policies, and procedures, including special recruitment, preferential treatment, and quotas in job

affirmative action
Any of a wide range of programs, from special recruitment efforts to numerical quotas, aimed at expanding opportunities for women and minority groups.

training and professional education, employment, and the awarding of government contracts. The point of these programs is to move beyond equality of opportunity to equality of outcome.

Establishing numerical goals (such as designating a specific number of places in a law school for minority candidates or specifying that 10 percent of the work on a government contract must be subcontracted to minority-owned companies) is the most aggressive form of affirmative action, and it generates more debate and opposition than any other aspect of the civil rights movement. Advocates claim that such goal setting for college admissions, training programs, employment, and contracts will move minorities, women, and people with disabilities out of their second-class status. President Johnson explained why aggressive affirmative action was necessary:

> You do not take a person who for years has been hobbled by chains, liberate him, bring him up to the starting line of a race, and then say, "You are free to compete with all the others," and still justly believe that you have been completely fair. Thus, it is not enough just to open the gates of opportunity; all our citizens must have the ability to walk through those gates.[70]

Arguments for affirmative action programs (from increased recruitment efforts to quotas) tend to use the following reasoning: certain groups have historically suffered invidious discrimination, denying them educational and economic opportunities. To eliminate the lasting effects of such discrimination, the public and private sectors must take steps to provide access to good education and jobs. If the majority once discriminated to hold groups back, discriminating to benefit those groups is fair. Therefore, quotas are a legitimate means to provide a place on the ladder to success.[71]

Affirmative action opponents maintain that quotas for designated groups necessarily create invidious discrimination (in the form of reverse discrimination) against individuals who are themselves blameless. Moreover, they say, quotas lead to the admission, hiring, or promotion of the less qualified at the expense of the well qualified. In the name of equality, such policies thwart individuals' freedom to succeed.

Government-mandated preferential policies probably began in 1965 with the creation of the Office of Federal Contract Compliance. Its purpose was to ensure that all private enterprises doing business with the federal government complied with nondiscrimination guidelines. Because so many companies do business with the federal government, a large portion of the American economy became subject to these guidelines. In 1968, the guidelines required "goals and timetables for the prompt achievement of full and equal employment opportunity." By 1971, they called for employers to eliminate "underutilization" of minorities and women, which meant that employers had to hire minorities and women in proportion to the government's assessment of their availability.[72]

Preferential policies are seldom explicitly legislated. More often, such policies are the result of administrative regulations, judicial rulings, and initiatives in the private sector to provide a remedial response to specific discrimination or to satisfy new legal standards for proving nondiscrimination. Quotas or goals enable administrators to assess changes in hiring, promotion, and admissions policies. Racial quotas are an economic fact of life today. Employers engage in race-conscious preferential treatment to avoid litigation. Cast in value terms, equality trumps freedom. Do preferential policies in other nations offer lessons for us? (See "Compared with What? How Others Struggle with Affirmative Action" to learn the answer.)

Reverse Discrimination

The Supreme Court confronted an affirmative action quota program for the first time in *Regents of the University of California* v. *Bakke.*[73] Allan Bakke, a thirty-five-year-old white man, had twice applied for admission to the University of California Medical School at Davis and was rejected both times. As part of the university's affirmative action program, the school had reserved sixteen places in each entering class of one hundred for qualified minority applicants in an effort to redress long-standing and unfair exclusion of minorities from the medical profession. Bakke's academic qualifications exceeded those of all the minority students admitted in the two years his applications were rejected. Bakke contended, first in the California courts and then in the Supreme Court, that he was excluded from admission solely on the basis of his race. He argued that the equal protection clause of the Fourteenth Amendment and the Civil Rights Act of 1964 prohibited this reverse discrimination.

The Court's decision in *Bakke* contained six opinions and spanned 154 pages, but no opinion commanded a majority. Despite the confusing multiple opinions, the Court struck down the school's rigid use of race, thus admitting Bakke, and it approved of affirmative action programs in education that use race as a *plus* factor (one of many such factors) but not as the *sole* factor. Thus, the Court managed to minimize white opposition to the goal of equality (by finding for Bakke) while extending gains for racial minorities through affirmative action.

True to the pluralist model, groups opposed to affirmative action continued their opposition in federal courts and state legislatures. They met with some success. The Supreme Court struck down government-mandated set-aside programs in the U.S. Department of Transportation.[74] Lower federal courts took this as a signal that other forms of affirmative action were ripe for reversal.

By 2003—twenty-five years after *Bakke*—the Supreme Court reexamined affirmative action in two cases, both challenging aspects of the University of Michigan's racial preferences policies. In *Gratz* v. *Bollinger,* the Court considered the university's undergraduate admissions policy, which conferred 20 points automatically to members of favored groups (100 points guaranteed admission). In a 6–3 opinion, Chief Justice William H. Rehnquist argued that such a policy violated the equal protection clause because it lacked the narrow tailoring required for permissible racial preferences and it

Compared with What?

How Others Struggle with Affirmative Action

Compared with other countries around the world, Americans are not alone in their disagreements over affirmative action. Controversies, even bloodshed, have arisen where the government treats certain groups of citizens preferentially. One study found several common patterns among countries that had enacted preferential policies. Although begun as temporary measures, preferential policies tended to persist and even to expand to include more groups. The policies usually sought to improve the situation of disadvantaged groups as a whole, but they often benefited the better-off members of such groups more so than the worse-off members. Finally, preferential policies tended to increase antagonisms among different groups within a country.

Of course, there were variations across countries in terms of who benefited from such policies, what types of benefits were bestowed, and even the names the policies were given. In India, such policies carry the label "positive discrimination." But that isn't the only way India differs from the United States when it comes to preferential policies.

Although India is the world's largest democracy, its society is rigidly stratified into groups called castes. The government forbids caste-based discrimination, but members of the lower castes (the lowest being the Dalits, or "untouchables") were historically restricted to the least prestigious and lowest-paying jobs. To improve their status, India has set aside government jobs for the lower castes, who make up half of India's population of 1 billion. India now reserves 27 percent of government jobs for the lower castes and an additional 23 percent for untouchables and remote tribe members. Gender equality has also improved since a 1993 constitutional amendment that set aside one-third of all seats in local government councils for women. By 2004, 900,000 women had been elected to public office, and 80,000 of them now lead local governing bodies. Positive discrimination in India has intensified tensions between the lower and upper castes. In 1990, soon after the new quotas were established, scores of young upper-caste men and women set themselves ablaze in protest. And when Indian courts issued a temporary injunction against the positive-discrimination policies, lower-caste terrorists bombed a train and killed dozens of people. Adding further strain, a 2010 proposal to create a one-third set-aside for women in the parliament and state legislatures has met stiff resistance from the political parties representing the lower castes. The Dalits view the proposal as a threat to their monopoly quota. Lower-caste women oppose the idea while feminists from higher-caste parties support it. The issue is not the use of quotas but which group should benefit from quotas. No longer considered temporary, quotas have become a fact of life in the world's largest democracy.

In Brazil, the state of Rio de Janeiro set aside racial quotas for black and native Brazilians applying to the state university system in 2000. However, the initiative backfired when many white students claimed African heritage to benefit from the quotas in a very competitive setting. Brazil is a mixed-race society: 42 percent of its population is racially mixed. Critics of affirmative action argue that it is difficult to determine with precision "to which race each Brazilian belongs." A former minister of education, Paulo Renato Souza, claims that the real task is to improve access to public education for poor Brazilians and therefore racial quotas are misleading. Other critics argue that with 42 percent of the population identifying as mixed race, a quota would turn Brazil into a two-color nation. Supporters of the affirmative action program oddly include a private college in São Paulo that sets aside 50 percent of its places for black students. The president of the university says that a "large part of the public, if they didn't have this opportunity, would find it difficult to study elsewhere." The legitimacy of racial quotas at the University of Brasília is now under review by the federal Supreme Court.

In South Africa, the gradual development of policies of affirmative action for blacks ended with the establishment of the Broad-Based Black Economic Empowerment Act, which aims at promoting equality in the workplace. Government employment legislation sets aside 80 percent of new jobs for black people and favors black-owned companies as subcontractors. Supporters of these policies argue that opponents still share the mind-set prevailing during the apartheid regime and that "many of these people cannot accept the fact that now we are all equal." Critics underline that the blacks that have been empowered by these policies "have largely been senior members of the ruling African National Congress. The bulk of the 'empowerment' seems to involve just four very rich men, three of them contenders for the presidency in 2009."

All governments broker conflict to varying degrees. Under a majoritarian model, group demands could lead quickly to conflict and instability because majority rule leaves little room for compromise. A pluralist model allows different groups to get a piece of the pie. By parceling out benefits, pluralism mitigates disorder in the short term. But in the long term, repeated demands for increased benefits can spark instability. A vigorous pluralist system should provide acceptable mechanisms (legislative, executive, bureaucratic, judicial) to vent such frustrations and yield new allocations of benefits.

Sources: Trudy Rubin, "Will Democracy Survive in India?" *Record* (Bergen County, N.J.), 19 January 1998, p. A12; Alex Spillius, "India's Old Warriors to Launch Rights Fight," *Daily Telegraph*, 20 October 1997, p. 12; Robin Wright, "World's Leaders: Men, 187, Women, 4," *Los Angeles Times*, 30 September 1997, p. A1; "Indian Eunuchs Demand Government Job Quotas," *Agence France Presse*, 22 October 1997; Juergen Hein and M. V. Balaji, "India's First Census of New Millennium Begins on February 9," *Deutsche Presse-Agentur*, 7 February 2001; Gillian Bowditch, "You Can Have Meritocracy or Equality, but Not Both," *Sunday Times*, Features Section: Scotland News, 19 January 2003, p. 21; Press Trust of India, "About a Million Women Elected to Local Bodies in India," 10 February 2004; Somini Sengupta, "Quotas to Aid India's Poor vs. Push for Meritocracy," *New York Times*, 23 May 2006, p. A3; "Caste in Doubt," *The Economist*, 12 June 2010, p. 46; Robert Plummer, "Black Brazil Seeks a Better Future," *BBC News*, 25 September 2006, http://news.bbc.co.uk/2/hi/americas/5357842.stm; Pueng Vongs, "Around the World, Countries Grapple with Affirmative Action," *New America Media*, 10 July 2003, http://news.newamericamedia.org/news/view—article.html?article—id=3e26118fcdf4fba57da467da3eeb43d0; Robert Guest, "The World's Most Extreme Affirmative Action Program: Aiming for Prosperity Would Be Better," *Wall Street Journal*, 26 December 2004, http://www.opinionjournal.com/extra/?id=110006066; Simon Woods, "Race against Time," *Observer Magazine*, 22 January 2006, http://observer.guardian.co.uk/magazine/story/0,,1691343,00.html; Rafael Ribeiro, "Cotas estão paradas no Congresso: Projeto propõe critérios raciais e sociais para ingresso na universidade," *Diário de São Paulo*, 10 April 2010, http://www.diariosp.com.br/Noticias/Dia-a-dia/3379/Cotas+estao+paradas+no+Congresso; Shikha Dalmia, "India's Government by Quota," *Wall Street Journal*, 1–2 May 2010, p. A13.

failed to provide for individualized consideration of each candidate.[75] In the second case, *Grutter* v. *Bollinger,* the Court considered the University of Michigan's law school admissions policy, which gave preference to minority applicants with lower GPAs and standardized test scores over white applicants. This time, the Court, in a 5–4 decision authored by Justice Sandra Day O'Connor, held that the equal protection clause did not bar the school's narrowly tailored use of racial preferences to further a compelling interest that flowed from a racially diverse student body.[76] Since each applicant is judged individually on his or her merits, race remains only one among many factors that enter into the admissions decision.

The issue of race-based classifications in education arose again in 2007 when parents challenged voluntary school integration plans based on race in *Parents Involved in Community Schools* v. *Seattle School District No. 1.*[77] Chief Justice John G. Roberts, Jr., writing for the 5–4 majority on a bitterly divided bench, invalidated the plans, declaring that the programs were "directed only to racial balance, pure and simple," which the equal protection clause of the Fourteenth Amendment forbids. "The way to stop discrimination on the basis of race is to stop discriminating on the basis of race," he said.

Justice Anthony Kennedy, who cast the fifth and deciding vote, wrote separately to say that achieving racial diversity and avoiding racial isolation were "compelling interests" that schools could constitutionally pursue as long as they "narrowly tailored" their programs to avoid racial labeling and sorting of individual children. Kennedy's opinion, and his key role as the "swing" vote, will likely determine the design of such programs to pass legal muster. In a broader sense, Kennedy's vote may prove to be the most important vote in a growing number of 5–4 decisions.

Justice Stephen G. Breyer, writing for the minority and speaking from the bench, used pointed language, declaring: "This is a decision that the Court and the nation will come to regret." A sign of growing frustration among the justices is the increased frequency with which they have read their dissents aloud, a tactic used to express great distress with the majority opinion.

The Politics of Affirmative Action

A comprehensive review of nationwide surveys conducted over the past twenty-five years reveals an unsurprising truth: that blacks favor affirmative action programs and whites do not. The gulf between the races was wider in the 1970s than it is today, but the moderation results from shifts among blacks, not whites. Perhaps the most important finding is that "whites' views have remained essentially unchanged over twenty-five years."[78]

How do we account for the persistence of equal outcomes policies? A majority of Americans have consistently rejected explicit race or gender preferences for the awarding of contracts, employment decisions, and college admissions, regardless of the groups such preferences benefit. Nevertheless, preference policies have survived and thrived under both Democrats and Republicans because they are attractive. They encourage unprotected groups to strive for inclusion. The list of protected groups includes African Americans,

Hispanic Americans, Native Americans, Asian Pacific Americans, and subcontinent Asian Americans.[79] Politicians have a powerful motive–votes–to expand the number of protected groups and the benefits such policies provide.

Recall that affirmative action programs began as temporary measures, ensuring a jump-start for minorities shackled by decades or centuries of invidious discrimination. For example, fifty years ago, minority racial identity was a fatal flaw on a medical or law school application. Today it is viewed as an advantage, encouraging applicants to think in minority-group terms. Thinking in group terms and conferring benefits on such grounds generates hostility from members of the majority, who see the deck stacked against them for no other reason than their race. It is not surprising that affirmative action has become controversial, since many Americans view it as a violation of their individual freedom.

Recall Lyndon Johnson's justification for equal outcomes policies. Though free to compete, a person once hobbled by chains cannot run a fair race. Americans are willing to do more than remove the chains. They will support special training and financial assistance for those who were previously shackled. The hope is that such efforts will enable once-shackled runners to catch up with those who have forged ahead. But Americans stop short at endorsing equal outcomes policies because they predetermine the results of the race.[80]

The conflict between freedom and equality will continue as other individuals and groups continue to press their demands through litigation and legislation. The choice will depend on whether and to what extent Americans still harbor deep-seated racial prejudice.

Summary

Americans want equality, but they disagree on the extent to which government should guarantee it. At the heart of this conflict is the distinction between equal opportunities and equal outcomes. Today, immigrant groups are vocal advocates for a share of the American dream, including tax-paying illegal immigrants and their children who may require health care and public education. Their quest follows the long path toward equality forged by African Americans.

Congress enacted the Civil War amendments—the Thirteenth, Fourteenth, and Fifteenth amendments—to provide full civil rights to black Americans. In the late nineteenth century, however, the Supreme Court interpreted the amendments very narrowly, declaring that they did not restrain individuals from denying civil rights to blacks and did not apply to the states. The Court's rulings had the effect of denying the vote to most blacks and of institutionalizing racism, making racial segregation a fact of daily life.

Through a series of court cases spanning two decades, the Court slowly dismantled segregation in the schools. The battle for desegregation culminated in the *Brown* cases in 1954 and 1955, in which a now-supportive Supreme Court declared segregated schools to be inherently unequal and therefore unconstitutional. The Court also ordered the desegregation of all schools and upheld the use of busing to do so.

Gains in other spheres of civil rights came more slowly. The motivating force was the civil rights movement, led by Martin Luther King, Jr., until his assassination in 1968. King believed strongly in civil disobedience and nonviolence, strategies that helped secure for blacks equality in voting rights, public accommodations, higher education, housing, and employment opportunity.

Civil rights activism and the civil rights movement worked to the benefit of all minority groups—in fact, they benefited all Americans. Native Americans obtained some redress for past injustices. Immigrant groups press government for a stake in the American experience as they work to gain a better life in jobs that few citizens will do. Latinos have come to recognize the importance of group action to achieve economic and political equality. Disabled Americans won civil rights protections enjoyed by African Americans and others. And civil rights legislation removed the protectionism that was, in effect, legalized discrimination against women in education and employment. Homosexuals aim to follow the same path, but their quest for equality has been trumped by occasional conflicts with freedom.

Despite legislative advances in the area of women's rights, the states did not ratify the equal rights amendment. Still, the struggle for ratification produced several positive results, heightening awareness of women's roles in society and mobilizing their political power. And legislation and judicial rulings implemented much of the amendment's provisions in practice. The Supreme Court now judges sex-based discrimination with "skeptical scrutiny," meaning that distinctions based on sex are almost as suspect as distinctions based on race.

Government and business instituted affirmative action programs to counteract the results of past discrimination. These provide preferential treatment for women, minorities, and people with disabilities in a number of areas that affect individuals' economic opportunity and well-being. In effect, such programs discriminate to remedy earlier discrimination. But in a major reversal beginning in 2007, government acts of racial discrimination, however well intentioned, are out of bounds for all but the most compelling reasons. When programs make race the determining factor in awarding contracts, offering employment, or granting admission to educational institutions, the courts will be increasingly skeptical of their validity. However, the politics of affirmative action suggest that such programs are likely to remain persistent features on our political landscape.

We can guarantee equal outcomes only if we restrict the free competition that is an integral part of equal opportunity. Many Americans object to policies that restrict individual freedom, such as quotas and set-asides that arbitrarily change the outcome of the race. The challenge of pluralist democracy is to balance the need for freedom with demands for equality.

KEY CASES

Plessy v. *Ferguson* (racial segregation constitutional, 1896)

Brown v. *Board of Education* (racial segregation unconstitutional, 1954)

Brown v. *Board of Education II* (racial desegregation implementation, 1955)

Regents of the University of California v. *Bakke* (affirmative action, 1978)

United States v. *Virginia* (gender equality, 1996)

Boy Scouts of America v. *Dale* (association rights, Boy Scouts versus gays, 2000)

Gratz v. *Bollinger* (affirmative action, 2003)

Grutter v. *Bollinger* (affirmative action, 2003)

Parents Involved in Community Schools v. *Seattle School District No. 1* (public school racial diversity, 2007)

CourseMate

Visit www.cengagebrain.com/shop/ISBN/0495906182 for flashcards, web quizzes, videos and more!

CHAPTER
17

Policymaking

CHAPTER TOPICS

Andrew Harrer/Bloomberg/Getty Images

Seventeen-year-old Phoenix high school student Karen Cordova sometimes texts her friends while driving home from her part-time job. She does this even though it's illegal to text while driving in the city of Phoenix. She does it because she's bored and lonely late at night in the car. Asked if she might give up texting while driving if a national law banning the practice was enacted, Cordova said she'd keep doing it anyway. "Nobody is going to listen," she rationalized.

Texting while driving is dangerous—very dangerous. As drivers multitask, they pay less attention to the road. Using a cell phone while driving reduces the amount of brain activity focused on actually driving the car by 37 percent. A texting driver's reaction time is roughly the same as that of a driver who is legally intoxicated.

Yet large numbers of Americans text while driving. Stuck in bumper-to-bumper traffic, late for something, or just plain bored, excuses abound. We all think accidents happen to other people, not to us.

As driving-while-texting accidents have made the newspapers and TV news, Americans have come to believe that texting while driving is a serious problem and something ought to be done about it. A poll taken by CBS News and the *New York Times* showed remarkable unity on this score: 97 percent of respondents believe texting while driving should be against the law.

Despite this rare unanimity of opinion, texting while driving remains legal in most states. Momentum is building across the country, however, to do something about what is a highly preventable problem. More than a dozen states have now banned the practice (see Figure 17.1).

Some states and cities have gone further to make it illegal to talk on a cell phone while driving. Maine has banned driving while "distracted." Under Maine law this means that any activity in the car that is not necessary to driving the vehicle and impairs the ability to drive is against the law. The push for such legislation in Maine got a boost when a state trooper said he saw a driver watching the *Gilmore Girls* on a laptop as she drove through a toll booth. President Obama issued an executive order banning texting while driving for government employees while they're on the job. The federal government also banned texting by commercial truck and bus drivers.

As more laws are passed banning texting and other distracting practices, a key to actually stopping the practice is to make the punishment significant and to make sure that people understand the penalties. In England, a driver causing a fatality in a crash while texting must receive prison time, and the judge must consider the traffic offense as a more significant crime. Phillipa Curtis is serving time in a British prison for killing a driver in another car. When she crashed into a vehicle on the side of the road, Curtis was texting a friend that earlier in the evening she had served a pop singer at the restaurant where she worked as a waitress.

Texting while driving is a relatively new issue, and Congress has not yet passed a law banning the practice. It's possible that national legislation will be enacted, but at present, only some states have faced up to the issue. Others haven't. The lack of a forceful, national response makes our roads less safe than they need to be. Watch out next time you're in a car. Someone behind you might be texting.[1]

FIGURE 17.1	No Worries! I Can Drive without Watching the Road

States vary considerably in their attitude toward texting while driving. A number of states without such laws are considering legislation to confront the problem. There is no national law forbidding texting while driving.

DRIVING LEGISLATION IN OTHER STATES
Accurate as of Dec. 31, 2009

■ States with bans on **texting** while driving

■ States with **both** texting bans and elderly-driver provisions

Previous chapters have focused on individual institutions of government. Here we look at government more broadly and ask how policymaking takes place across institutions. We first identify different types of public policies and then analyze the stages in the policymaking process. Because different institutions and different levels of government (national, state, and local) frequently work on the same issues, policymaking is often fragmented. How can better coordination be achieved?

IN OUR OWN WORDS

Listen to Jeffrey Berry discuss the main points and themes of this chapter.

www.cengagebrain.com/
shop/ISBN/0495906182

Government Purposes and Public Policies

In Chapter 1, we noted that virtually all citizens are willing to accept limitations on their personal freedom in return for various benefits of government. We defined the major purposes of government as maintaining order, providing public benefits, and promoting equality. Different governments place different values on each broad purpose, and those differences are reflected in their public policies. A **public policy** is a general plan of action adopted by a government to solve a social problem, counter a threat, or pursue an objective.

At times, governments choose not to adopt a new policy to deal with a troublesome situation; instead, they just muddle through, hoping the problem

public policy
A general plan of action adopted by the government to solve a social problem, counter a threat, or pursue an objective.

will go away or diminish in importance. This too is a policy decision because it amounts to choosing to maintain the status quo. Sometimes government policies are carefully developed and effective. Sometimes they are hastily drawn and ineffective, even counterproductive. But careful planning is no predictor of success. Well-constructed policies may result in total disaster, and quick fixes may work just fine.

Whatever their form and effectiveness, however, all policies have this in common: they are the means by which government pursues certain goals in specific situations. People disagree about public policies because they disagree about one or more of the following elements: the goals government should have, the means it should use to meet them, and how the situation at hand should be perceived.

The Policymaking Process

When people inside and outside government disagree on goals, that disagreement is often rooted in a basic difference in values. As emphasized throughout this book, such value conflict is often manifested as disputes pitting freedom against order or freedom against equality. The roots of the values we hold can run deep, beginning with childhood socialization as parents transmit their values to their children. Disputes involving values are in many ways the hardest to bridge since they reflect a basic worldview and go to the core of one's sense of right and wrong.

The problem of illegal drugs illustrates how different core values lead us to prefer different public policies. Everyone agrees that government should address the problems created by drugs. Yet views of what should be done differ sharply. Recall from Chapter 1 that libertarians put individual freedom above all else and want to limit government as much as possible. Many libertarians argue that drugs should be decriminalized; if people want to take drugs, they should be free to do so, just as they are free to drink alcohol if they want. If drugs were decriminalized, they could be sold openly, prices would fall dramatically, and the crime associated with illegal drugs would largely evaporate. Conservatives' value system places considerable emphasis on order. In their minds, a decent, safe, and civilized society does not allow people to debase themselves through drug abuse, and the government should punish those who violate the law. Liberals place greater emphasis on treatment as a policy option. They regard drug addiction as a medical or emotional problem and believe that government should offer the services that addicts can use to stop their self-destructive behavior. Liberals value equality, and their view on this issue is that government should be expansive so that it can help people in need. Many drug offenders are impoverished because of their spending on drugs and cannot pay for private treatment.

Types of Policies

Although values underlie choices, analysis of public policy does not usually focus explicitly on core beliefs. Political scientists often try to categorize public policy choices by their objectives. That is, in the broad scheme of things, what are policymakers trying to do by choosing a particular policy direction? One common purpose is to allocate resources so that some segment of society or region of the country can receive a service or benefit. We can call these **distributive policies**. Democratic representative John Murtha, who died in early 2010, was known as the "King of Pork" for his ability to bring grants to his Pennsylvania district. As chairman of the House Appropriations Defense Subcommittee, Murtha wrote a series of grants and contracts into bills that were restricted to specific companies in his district. These earmarks were intended to stimulate the economy in the depressed southwestern area of Pennsylvania he represented. Some of these contracts have worked out well. Concurrent Technologies got off the ground thanks to Murtha's earmarks and now employs 800 workers. On the other hand, despite more than $150 million in grants, Caracal, Inc., never employed more than 10 people and went out of business.[2]

Distributional policies are not all projects or new buildings. Some are social programs designed to help a disadvantaged group in society. What distributional policies have in common is that all of us pay through our taxes to support those who receive the benefit, presumably because that benefit works toward the common good, such as stronger security, a better-trained work force, or a cleaner environment. In contrast, **redistributional policies** are explicitly designed to take resources from one sector of society and transfer them to another (reflecting the core value of greater equality). In a rather unusual redistributional proposal in Seattle, Washington, proponents of early childhood education programs succeeded in getting an initiative on a citywide ballot that would have added a 10-cent tax on every cup of espresso sold in the coffee-crazed city. The new revenues brought in by this tax were to fund early childhood programs, and, as such, the plan was to redistribute revenues from espresso drinkers to families with small children. The voters rejected the initiative, and no such redistribution took place.[3]

A broader, more far-reaching redistributive tax plan was put forth by the Republican governor of Alabama, Bob Riley. Alabama is unusual in that it taxes the wealthy at an effective rate of only 3 percent, one of the lowest rates among the fifty states. At the other end of the spectrum, it begins taxing citizens when they reach just $4,600 in income and then taxes the poorest Alabamians at an effective tax rate of 12 percent. The reason to compare the *effective rate*—what people actually pay as opposed to the stated tax rate—is that there are many deductions and exceptions in the tax code, such as taxing investment income lower than salaried income. Wealthy people have more deductions and more investment income. Alabama schools reflect the revenue problems produced by its tax code: the state ranks dead last in per capita expenditures per student. Governor Riley pushed for a new tax code designed to be redistributive, giving tax relief to poor and working-class Alabamians while taxing the wealthy at a higher rate. Also, some of the new revenue was not to be redistributed to those at the lower end of the income scale but was to be put into the state's schools. Under the state's constitution, a tax change must be approved by the voters, and a statewide

distributive policies
Government policies designed to confer a benefit on a particular institution or group.

redistributional policies
Policies that take government resources, such as tax funds, from one sector of society and transfer them to another.

FIGURE 17.2   Who Is Paying Their Fair Share?

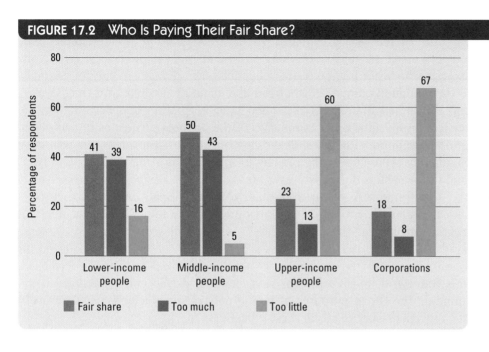

According to the Gallup Poll, Americans strongly believe that upper-income Americans and corporations pay too little in the way of taxes. A battle over federal income taxes looms as tax cuts enacted by Congress at the behest of President Bush expire at the end of 2010. The two parties differ sharply over what tax rates should be and what constitutes "fair" taxes.

Source: Gallup Poll, 6–9 April 2009.

referendum was held on Riley's plan. The redistribution plan was defeated: many lower-income Alabamians were not persuaded that a conservative Republican was really going to help them. The antitax coalition also ran a more persuasive and much better funded campaign.[4] (For public opinion on federal taxes, see Figure 17.2.)

Another basic policy approach is **regulation**. In Chapter 13, we noted that regulations are the rules that guide the operation of government programs. When regulations apply to business markets, they are an attempt to structure the operations of that market in a particular way. Government intersperses itself as a referee, setting rules as to what kinds of companies can participate in what kinds of market activities. Trucking is a case in point. The United States used to restrict the entrance of Mexican trucks into this country, barring them from traveling more than twenty miles into the United States. Truckers would have to unload their cargo at a transfer station, where it would be placed on an American carrier that would take the merchandise to its destination. The United States said it forbade Mexican trucks from traveling on their own to wherever their cargo was headed because they weren't always safe and they polluted more than American trucks. An international trade panel determined, however, that these regulatory rules violated the North American Free Trade Agreement. In response, Congress passed a new law providing inspection stations at border crossings to ensure that the Mexican trucks were safe and that their drivers met the same licensing standards as American drivers.

Americans disagree over the degree to which markets should operate freely, some believing government should be only minimally involved. Others believe that markets usually need close supervision because competitive pressures can lead individual businesses to cut corners on the safety of

regulation
Government intervention in the workings of a business market to promote some socially desired goal.

their products or the integrity of their conduct. On the one hand, the decisions on how to regulate or whether to reduce regulation (to *deregulate*) may involve many technical questions and seem to be matters best left to the experts who work for the relevant bureaucratic agencies. What, for example, is the minimum amount of tire tread that should be required for trucks entering the United States? On the other hand, regulation and deregulation are subject to the same pulls and pushes of the political process as distributional and redistributional policies. In the case of the Mexican trucks, the restrictive regulations were largely the product of lobbying by American trucking firms and the Teamsters union, which wanted to preserve business for themselves.[5]

This framework of distributional, redistributional, and regulatory policies is rather general, and there are surely policy approaches that don't fit neatly into one of these categories.[6] As you will see in Chapter 20, some kinds of foreign policies, such as the regulation of international trade, fit this framework better than other issues, like national security. Nevertheless, this framework is a useful prism to examine public policymaking. Understanding the broad purposes of public policy allows a better evaluation of the tools necessary to attain these objectives.

Public Policy Tools

Just as there are different objectives in public policy, there are different ways of achieving those objectives. If the goal is to redistribute wealth, different approaches can accomplish the same goal. As in the Alabama referendum, one way is to tax the wealthy more and working-class people less. A more politically palatable approach may be simply to institute more tax exemptions for working-class people so their effective tax rate drops. An example would be a child tax credit of $500 for those with incomes below $35,000. This is still redistributive, since a higher percentage of the state's overall revenue must come from those with a higher income who do not receive the deductions.

One of the most basic of policy tools are *incentives*. A fundamental element of human behavior is that we can be induced to do certain things if the rewards become substantial enough. We should all give to charity because we're generous and caring people. To promote more giving, the government provides taxpayers who file an itemized tax return a substantial tax deduction for donating to a nonprofit with charitable status. For a taxpayer with a marginal tax rate of 30 percent, a donation of $1,000 to a charity like the American Cancer Society or the Alzheimer's Association effectively costs her only $700. (The deduction for this taxpayer is 30 percent of the $1,000, or $300.) Although we can all agree that giving to charity is a good thing, there's no free lunch. Incentives that come in the form of money saved by those who take advantage of the incentive constitute a *tax expenditure*. Since government loses revenue on the charity deduction, it is effectively spending those funds and must make up revenue elsewhere. This tax expenditure is quite substantial: Americans give over $300 billion a year in charity.[7]

The flip side of incentives are *disincentives*—policies that discourage particular behavior. A tax on pollution, for example, is a disincentive for a factory to continue using the same (high-polluting) manufacturing process. State taxes on cigarettes are meant to discourage smoking (see "Compared with What? Greeks Smoke a Lot. Bulgarians Too."). New York City put forth a proposal to discourage drivers from entering Manhattan by instituting congestion pricing. Cars entering the demarcated area would need a transponder, and the registered owners would be billed $8 for the day ($21 for trucks). A similar system in London has succeeded in reducing traffic by 21 percent, and, conversely, ridership on the city's subway system is up significantly.[8] The New York State legislature refused to approve the congestion pricing plan, and drivers can still enter Manhattan without fee.

Much of what policymakers want to accomplish cannot be done through a set of incentives or disincentives. Often government must provide a service or program. That is, rather than coaxing or discouraging behavior, it must take responsibility itself to establish a program. Government's largest expenditures—for health care, education, social services, and defense—come from government's direct payments to its employees or vendors.

Finally, a common policy tool is to set rules. Much of what government does in the form of regulation is to set rules as to what various businesses or individuals can do in the marketplace. To preserve the integrity of pensions, government agencies set rules to try to ensure that companies protect such funds so that money is available when employees retire. What kind of investments can pension funds be invested in? How much pension money can a company invest in its own stock? Rules are set on such matters. Each day the federal government issues new or revised rules on a variety of policy questions.

Gridlock Proposal Gridlocked

Rising fuel prices, traffic congestion, and air pollution have all led cities to try to find creative solutions to these problems. As a disincentive to driving into New York City, Mayor Michael Bloomberg proposed a significant fee on all vehicles entering central Manhattan. The New York State legislature, however, balked at the plan, and the city continues to choke on its traffic.

(© Robert Landau/Corbis)

Whatever the policy objectives of government, the main tools are thus incentives and disincentives, direct provision of services, and rule setting. They are often combined to achieve a particular goal, and over time one approach may fall out of favor and another may be tried. Policies aimed at specific problems are not static; means, goals, and situations change.

A Policymaking Model

Clearly, different approaches to solving policy problems affect the policymaking process, but common patterns do underlie most processes. Political scientists have produced many models of the policymaking process to distinguish the different types of policy. They also distinguish different stages of the policymaking process and try to identify patterns in the way people attempt to influence decisions and in the way decisions are reached.

Compared with What?

Greeks Smoke a Lot. Bulgarians Too.

In the United States smoking has declined considerably. Smoking rates among Americans were around 40 percent of all adults in the early 1970s. Today just one in five Americans smokes. Smoking rates in Europe are, on average, considerably higher, but countries there have begun to mirror the United States in using public policy tools to try to dissuade their citizens from smoking. Many European countries have raised taxes; some countries have raised them significantly. Ireland, for example, imposes a tax of around $9 on a pack of cigarettes. The European Union (EU) has just mandated a rise in the minimum tax on cigarettes for member countries. At least 60 percent of the price of a pack must be taxes. Research has shown that increasing the price of smoking lowers the number of people who light up.

Regulatory restrictions on where one can smoke differ greatly by country. In Greece 62 percent of workers say there are weak or no restrictions on smoking in the workplace. Thus, in many places nonsmoking coworkers are exposed to secondary smoke, which is dangerous to them. But in Sweden and England, less than 10 percent of workers report weak or no restrictions on smoking at their place of employment. Across Europe more emphasis is being placed on education to try to persuade people that smoking is dangerous. Using these different public policy approaches is leading to progress against smoking. A recent EU report concluded that "Smoking is becoming less and less socially acceptable."

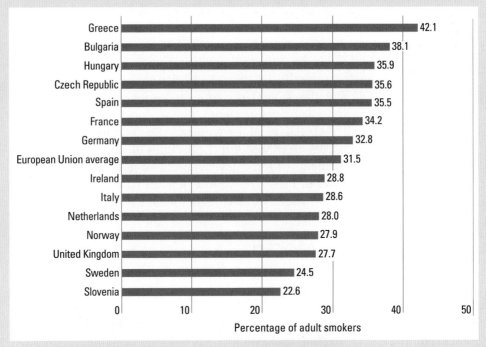

Sources: Eurobarometer, *Survey on Tobacco: Analytical Report* (Budapest: European Commission, Directorate-General for Health and Consumers, March 2009); Directorate-General for Health and Consumers, *Tobacco Control in the EU* (Brussels: European Commission, 2009); Gallup Poll, "U.S. Smoking Rates Still Coming Down," 24 July 2008.

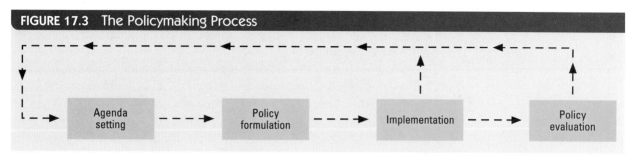

FIGURE 17.3   The Policymaking Process

This model, one of many possible ways to depict the policymaking process, shows four policymaking stages. Feedback on program operations and performance from the last two stages stimulates new cycles of the process.

We can separate the policymaking process into four stages: agenda setting, policy formulation, implementation, and policy evaluation. Figure 17.3 shows the four stages in sequence. Note, however, that the process does not end with policy evaluation. Policymaking is a circular process; the end of one phase is really the beginning of another.

Agenda Setting. When we think of the political agenda, we usually think of the broad set of policy areas that are central to American life. This broad, systemic agenda changes over time as conditions change. For a number of years the war in Iraq was of major concern to Americans, but today it's the economy that is the top priority of Americans.

Political scientists not only study what's on the agenda at any one time but also maintain a strong interest in **agenda setting**, the part of the process in which problems are defined as political issues. Many problems confront Americans in their daily lives, but government is not actively working to solve them all. Consider Social Security, for example. Today the old-age insurance program seems a hardy perennial of American politics, but it was not created until the New Deal. The problem of poverty among the elderly did not suddenly arise during the 1930s—there had always been poor people of all ages—but that is when inadequate income for the elderly was defined as a political problem. During this time, people began arguing that it was government's responsibility to create a system of income security for the aged rather than leaving old people to fend for themselves. When the government begins to consider acting on an issue it has previously ignored, we say that the issue has become part of the political agenda.

Why does an existing social problem become redefined as a political problem? There is no single reason; many different factors can stimulate new thinking about a problem. Sometimes highly visible events or developments push issues onto the agenda. Examples are great calamities (such as a terrible oil spill, showing a need for safer offshore drilling rigs), the effects of technology (such as air pollution, requiring clean-air regulations), or irrational human behavior (such as airline hijackings, pointing to the need for greater airport security).[9] The probability that a certain problem will move onto the agenda is also affected by who controls the government and by broad ideological shifts. Presidential and congressional candidates run

agenda setting
The stage of the policymaking process during which problems get defined as political issues.

for office, promising to put neglected issues on the policy agenda. The political parties also take up new issues to promote their candidates for office and respond to public opinion.

Technology is one of the major factors explaining the rise of new issues. New discoveries and applications emerge quickly, and technologies may be adopted before the consequences of their use are fully understood. When an al Qaeda sympathizer tried to blow up a Northwest Airline flight from Amsterdam to Detroit, pressure quickly built for broad-scale use of body scanners at airports. These machines can rapidly produce an X-ray-like image of a traveler's entire body. Yet the privacy issues of such electronic examinations of our bodies have not been fully debated. In Germany some demonstrators showed up at the Berlin airport in their underwear to protest what they saw as a wholesale invasion of their personal privacy.[10]

Political scientists analyze the agenda of a particular political institution over time to try to understand political change. Health care has always been of critical importance, but the government's role in health policy has expanded significantly, and Congress spends more and more time on an array of health matters. One of the sharpest trends is the increased amount of time and resources that Congress has devoted to quality-of-life issues, such as environmental protection and consumer protection. Such issues involve protecting wildlife and wilderness, ensuring the integrity of markets so that consumers are not taken advantage of, establishing the rights of vulnerable segments of society, and reforming the procedures of government so that it works better.[11]

Part of the politics of agenda building is not just which new issues emerge and which issues decline in visibility, but the way the substantive problem at the heart of an issue is conceived. **Issue definition** is the way we think about a problem. As individuals, our conception of an issue is influenced by our own values and the way we see the political world. Interest groups and political parties try to persuade Americans of a broad world view, which, if accepted, influences the kinds of policy solutions that seem feasible. Over the years conservatives have pushed hard to make us think of policy problems in terms of market approaches. If we accept that a market approach is generally better, then we'll shy away from strong regulation by government bureaucracies.[12]

Citizens' views are also colored by what they regard as a government responsibility. Consider autism. If we define autism strictly as a *disease*, then we might see a very limited role for government—primarily as a funder of scientific research. But if we define autism as a *disability*, our issue definition will likely be broader. In the United States, persons with disabilities are guaranteed certain protections, and government has the responsibility to fight relevant forms of discrimination. Some advocates on behalf of those with autism claim that a preservative in vaccines is related to the onset of autism. This is a highly controversial idea, but if research confirms this claim as fact, then the issue definition will also include government regulation of medication.[13] When interest groups believe that it would be better if an issue of concern were defined differently, they can try to change it. In the language of Washington, they can try to change the spin on the story. This is hard to do, however, because there is no coordinating mechanism that

issue definition
Our conception of the problem at hand.

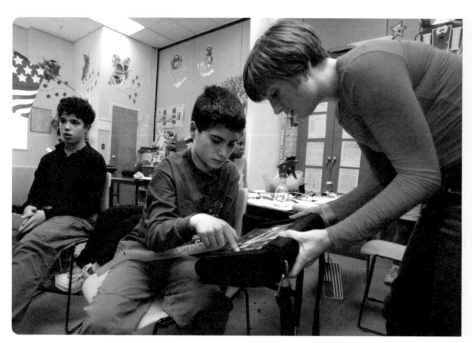

determines how we define problems. Even a wealthy group that can buy a lot of advertising has an uphill struggle to change the way a problem is broadly perceived. For most issues, the initial definitions endure over time, changing in incremental ways, if at all.

The most likely form of change in terms of issue definition occurs when an additional *frame* emerges. That is, in addition to the existing sides of a policy dispute, a new side comes to the fore. For example, for many years the dominant arguments or issue frames concerning the death penalty involved what is just punishment and morality. Some argued that the death penalty is a just punishment for a heinous crime. Those on the other side of the issue typically argued that the death penalty was immoral—that the state didn't have the right to take a life. In the late 1990s, though, many stories began to emerge in the press about people who were unjustly convicted and sentenced to death (see Figure 17.4). DNA laboratory testing became an increasing source of exculpatory evidence, demonstrating that the DNA of a number of people convicted was not found on the victim's body, clothes, or elsewhere at the crime scene. This so-called innocence frame became part of the debate over the death penalty, and support for the death penalty began to drop in public opinion polls.[14]

Since the emergence of a new frame can alter policymaking around an issue, interest groups make concerted efforts to try to reshape policy debate when the dominant frames work to their disadvantage. However, it is very difficult for interest groups to reshape a debate.[15] Existing frames are difficult to dislodge, and the quick rise of the innocence frame is more the exception than the rule. Most change in issue framing is evolutionary and reflects both changes in the world and long-term interest group advocacy.

Although there is no specific limit to how many issues can be on a government institution's agenda, there is limited space. A congressional committee or

FIGURE 17.4

The Innocence Frame Gains Traction

The way the news media cover the death penalty has evolved over time. As cases have emerged in which evidence was later uncovered proving that a convicted individual was actually innocent, or other serious flaws in trials were revealed, an "innocence frame" became an important part of the debate over the fairness of capital punishment.

Source: Frank R. Baumgartner, Suzanna L. DeBoef, and Amber E. Boydstun, *The Decline of the Death Penalty and the Discovery of Innocence* (New York: Cambridge University Press, 2008), p. 120. Copyright © 2008 Frank R. Baumgartner; Suzanna L. DeBoef; Amber E. Boydstun. Reprinted with the permission of Cambridge University Press.

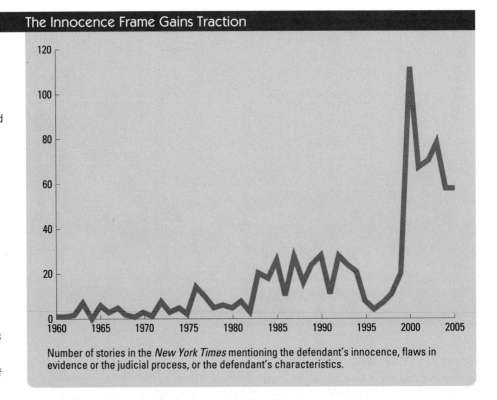

Number of stories in the *New York Times* mentioning the defendant's innocence, flaws in evidence or the judicial process, or the defendant's characteristics.

an agency can pay attention to only so many issues and have the resources to work on only some of those problems that fall under their jurisdictions. For this reason a considerable amount of lobbying in Washington is trying to convince policymakers simply to pay attention to a particular problem and to put it on their institution's agenda.

Policy Formulation. **Policy formulation** is the stage of the policymaking process in which formal policy proposals are developed and officials decide whether to adopt them. The most obvious kind of policy formulation is the proposal of a measure by the president or the development of legislation by Congress. Administrative agencies also formulate policy, through the regulatory process. Courts formulate policy too, when their decisions establish new interpretations of the law. We usually think of policy formulation as a formal process with a published document (a statute, regulation, or court opinion) as the final outcome. In some instances, however, policy decisions are not published or otherwise made explicit. Presidents and secretaries of state may not always fully articulate their foreign policy decisions, for example, because they want some wiggle room for adapting policy to changing conditions.

Although policy formulation is depicted in Figure 17.3 as a single continuous process, it can actually take place over several separate stages and across different levels of government. Congress passed legislation that requires states to compile registries of sexual offenders. Disclosure of such information differs by state, and bureaucracies in each state must try to develop policies as to just how much information should be made public. Is

policy formulation
The stage of the policymaking process during which formal proposals are developed and adopted.

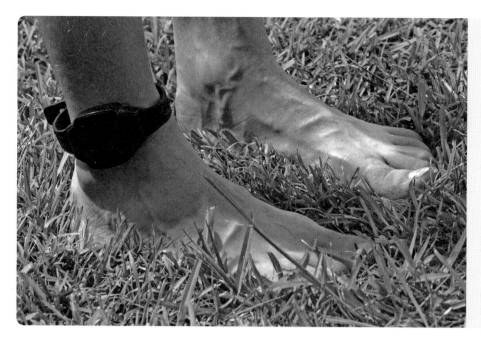

Tracking Sex Offenders

A difficult public policy problem is what to do with convicted sex offenders once they've served any incarceration. Understandably, no one wants them living in their neighborhood. In some cities, like Fayetteville, North Carolina (where this offender lives), those released into the community must wear an electronic tracking device. This type of ankle bracelet allows police to monitor any movement into areas where children congregate.

(AP Photo/Gerry Broome)

it enough to identify where a sex offender lives, or should more about the individual be revealed? Courts are called in as such decisions are contested. A number of states have passed laws that allow them to continue to hold sexually violent prisoners after they serve their terms if they are regarded as too dangerous to be returned to the community. These laws have generated considerable litigation as there is some inherent ambiguity as to what constitutes being too dangerous to be let out of prison.

As noted in Chapter 13, policy formulation tends to be *incremental.* As policies are being debated, the starting point is the existing policy in that area, and if new policy is adopted, it is usually a modification of what was in place previously. Figure 17.3 depicts how this process works. At the very end of the Clinton administration, the Forest Service adopted a new set of regulations that banned the construction of new roads into one-third of all national forests. This change effectively banned any logging in these areas because roads are necessary to take the timber out. On one level, this new departure was important because it marked a change in the way the Forest Service calculated the costs and benefits of logging versus the preservation of wilderness. On another level, however, this policy had its roots in policies on wilderness formulated in the late 1970s by the Carter administration. In another twist, shortly after taking office, the Bush administration modified the Clinton rules, instituting a new regulation that allowed each forest plan to be reviewed on a case-by-case basis. Thus, the ban in these forests could be lifted if officials in Washington believe more logging (and road building) is warranted.[16] The Obama administration may change them yet again.

Keep in mind that policy formulation is only the development of proposals designed to solve a problem. Some issues reach the agenda and stimulate new proposals but then fail to win enactment because political opposition mobilizes. In the early 1980s, for example, a movement arose to freeze the development of nuclear weapons. Although a freeze resolution gained significant support in Congress, it never gained enough votes to pass. The nuclear freeze movement quickly withered away and disappeared from sight. Thus, the move from proposal to policy requires the approval of some authoritative policymaking body.

Implementation. Policies are not self-executing; **implementation** is the process by which they are carried out. When agencies in Washington issue regulations, some government bodies must then put those policies into effect. This process begins with notifying the intended targets of agency actions of new or changed regulations. During the Clinton administration a far-reaching reform was instituted for procurement. Previously, purchasing in the area of information technology was centralized by the national government. Centralization created a bottleneck as Washington needed to understand the unique demands of federal government agencies and offices throughout the country. The Clinton-era reform freed these units of government from centralized purchasing and let them buy computers on their own. This reform may seem simple enough to implement, but there are somewhere around 27,000 purchasing officers in the federal government. They all needed to understand the new procedures and be instructed on what they were free to do and what went beyond the bounds of the new law. Despite these difficulties, the law was successfully implemented.[17]

Some policy programs encounter more practical difficulties than others. In 2003, President Bush signed into law the Medicare Prescription Drug, Improvement, and Modernization Act, expanding Medicare to offer prescription drug coverage for senior citizens. According to the new law, a number of private companies are authorized to sell insurance plans offering prescription drug coverage to senior citizens. Over 30 million seniors are enrolled in the program.

Implementation of the prescription drug program was marked by several problems. First, every county in every state offers a different type and number of prescription drug plans. Many seniors had difficulty sorting out their options. And seniors who made a decision often had to wait well over thirty minutes to reach a customer service representative to sign up for a prescription plan.[18] To make matters worse, federal officials found that some insurers were publishing misleading information about which prescription drugs would be covered and which would not. When the law finally went into effect in January 2006, some senior citizens could not get their medication because Medicare databases had not been adequately updated. State governments stepped in to pay for medication for these individuals while state and federal bureaucrats sorted out the problems. In another computer glitch, premiums that were supposed to be withheld from Social Security checks were not, with the result that drug companies were billing seniors directly for months of premiums and threatening to drop their coverage altogether.[19]

The drug plan falls under the jurisdiction of the Centers for Medicare and Medicaid Services (CMS) in the Department of Health and Human Services. The agency acknowledged the need for better data transmission of patient information to private companies and for more surveillance to

implementation
The process of putting specific policies into operation.

ensure that private companies are complying with the law.[20] Over time, however, administrators have made changes and improved their management of the program, and seniors' overall satisfaction with it has grown.

Although it may sound highly technical, implementation is very much a political process. It involves a great deal of bargaining and negotiation among different groups of people in and out of government. The difficulty of implementing complex policies in a federal system, with multiple layers of government, that is also a pluralistic system, with multiple competing interests, seems daunting. Yet there are incentives for cooperation, not the least of which is to avoid blame if a policy fails. (We will discuss coordination in more detail later in the chapter.)

Policy Evaluation. How does the government know whether a policy is working? In some cases, success or failure may be obvious, but at other times, experts in a specific field must tell government officials how well a policy is working. **Policy evaluation** is the analysis of the results of public policy. Although there is no one method of evaluating policy, evaluation tends to draw heavily on approaches used by academics, including cost-effectiveness analysis and various statistical methods designed to provide concrete measurements of program outcomes. Although technical, the studies can be quite influential in decisions on whether to continue, expand, alter, reduce, or eliminate programs.

A beginning point for a new policy is coming to some understanding of how it is working in practice in contrast to the underlying suppositions that led to its enactment. A case in point is the college admissions policy in Texas. When the courts overturned the affirmative action program for higher education in Texas, officials there were faced with a difficult problem. Now forbidden to use any race-related criteria as part of the admissions process, educational administrators predicted that the percentage of minorities at the state's top institutions could drop dramatically if no other change was made. Texas is a majority-minority state, meaning that non-Hispanic whites constitute less than half the population.[21] Minority students are disproportionately low in income and disproportionately live in areas where schools are not as strong as they are in wealthy suburban districts.

As a response to the court's decision, the state legislature passed the so-called top 10 percent law, guaranteeing college admission to all high school students who finish in the top tenth of their graduating class. This policy was designed to ensure that a significant number of minority students from modest- and low-income areas would be admitted to the state's two flagship universities, the University of Texas and Texas A&M University.

Parents whose children went to strong high schools and whose academic records placed them just below the top 10 percent began to complain that their children would leave the state for college if unable to get into a top Texas school. Two Princeton University researchers tested this so-called brain drain thesis. Did the new policy result in students from suburban schools being more likely to leave the state if they were outside the top 10 percent? The results disproved the brain drain thesis. Students just below the

policy evaluation
Analysis of a public policy so as to determine how well it is working.

top 10 percent (those ranking between 11 and 20 percent) at suburban schools ended up going to Texas schools and out-of-state schools at the same rate as students in the top tenth.[22]

Evaluation is part of the policymaking process because it helps identify problems and issues that arise from current policy. In other words, evaluation studies provide **feedback** to policymakers on program performance. The dotted line in Figure 17.3 represents a feedback loop. Problems that emerge during the implementation stage also provide feedback to policymakers. Feedback can be positive or negative.[23]

Commonly, a number of studies must be conducted over the years before a consensus emerges. Studies may disagree because the behavior being measured is complex and may be influenced by many different causes.[24] Comparison can be difficult because different programs aimed at the same problem are constructed differently. Abstinence-only sex education programs, which are generally based on the idea that teaching students birth control options weakens the message that sex before marriage is wrong and risks pregnancy, provide an interesting example. The message of such programs has generally been "wait until marriage." Research shows that these programs, whose message can be moralistic in tone, are ineffective. One rigorous study of four programs aimed at students at either the elementary or middle school level revealed that they had no impact on rates of sexual activity when researchers gathered data from those students four to six years after their courses. Students from the abstinence-only programs were just as likely to engage in sexual activity as those from the control group of students who were not exposed to these programs.[25] As such studies were published, support for abstinence-only sex education weakened. Concluding that they were ineffective, the Obama administration eliminated funding for abstinence-only programs in its first budget.

To the surprise of those who had been convinced that abstinence only didn't work, a study published in early 2010 demonstrated that a certain type of abstinence approach was effective. This program differed from others, however. It was not moralistic and did not tell students that they needed to wait until marriage. Rather, the message was "wait until you're ready." There were other differences as well, but this evaluation demonstrated something important: subtle differences in the design of programs can be the difference between success and failure (see Figure 17.5).[26]

Feedback, positive or negative, reflects the dynamic nature of policymaking. By drawing attention to emerging problems, policy evaluation influences the political agenda. The end of the process—evaluating whether the policy is being implemented as it was envisioned when it was formulated—is the beginning of a new cycle of public policymaking.

Fragmentation and Coordination

The policymaking process encompasses many different stages and includes many different participants at each stage. Here we examine some forces that pull the government in different directions and make problem solving less

feedback
Information received by policymakers about the effectiveness of public policy.

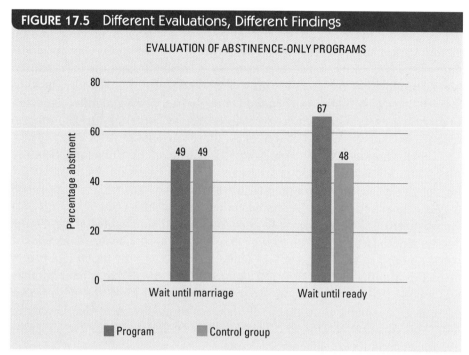

FIGURE 17.5   Different Evaluations, Different Findings

EVALUATION OF ABSTINENCE-ONLY PROGRAMS

Evaluation studies on the same type of policy approach or program can turn up significantly different findings. These two studies of abstinence-only sex education programs were both conducted by highly respected researchers who used rigorous methodologies. Human behavior is complex and can be influenced by many different factors.

Sources: Christopher Trenholm et al., *Impacts of Four Title V, Section 510 Abstinence Education,* report to the U.S. Department of Health and Human Services (Princeton, N.J.: Mathematica Policy Research, 2007); John B. Jemmott III, Loretta S. Jemmott, and Geoffrey T. Fong, "Efficacy of a Theory-Based Abstinence-Only Intervention over 24 Months," *Archives of Pediatric & Adolescent Medicine* 164 (February 2010): 152–159.

coherent than it might otherwise be. In the next section, we look at some structural elements of American government that work to coordinate competing and sometimes conflicting approaches to the same problems.

Multiplicity and Fragmentation

A single policy problem may be attacked in different and sometimes competing ways by government for many reasons. At the heart of this **fragmentation** of policymaking is the fundamental nature of government in America. The separation of powers divides authority among the branches of the national government, and federalism divides authority among the national, state, and local levels of government. These multiple centers of power are, of course, a primary component of pluralist democracy. Different groups try to influence different parts of the government; no one entity completely controls policymaking.

Fragmentation is often the result of many different agencies being created at different times to address different problems. Over time, however, as those problems evolve and change, they can become more closely related even as the different agencies do little or nothing to try to coordinate their

fragmentation
In policymaking, the phenomenon of attacking a single problem in different and sometimes competing ways.

efforts. Many of the intelligence and operational failures associated with the September 11 disaster can be traced in part to the lack of coordination among various security-related agencies. In the area of border and transportation security, for example, responsibility was split among the Immigration and Naturalization Service, the Transportation Security Agency, the Customs Service, the Coast Guard, the Federal Protective Services, and other agencies. In other words, lots of agencies were in charge of border and transportation security, but no one was in charge of all those agencies.

The formation of the cabinet-level Department of Homeland Security (DHS) in 2002 was an attempt to create a centralized administrative structure to overcome policy fragmentation in this area. Yet fragmentation still plagues homeland security. As noted earlier, on Christmas Day 2009, a Nigerian member of al Qaeda, Umar Farouk Abdulmutallab, boarded a flight from Amsterdam to Detroit with an explosive sewn into his underwear. Fortunately, when he tried to set off the device while the plane was in flight, it failed to detonate. Months earlier, U.S. intelligence had learned that Abdulmutallab was a potential terrorist, but the security agencies that knew this never managed to get his name onto the no-fly list. A furious President Obama vented that "This was not a failure to collect intelligence, it was a failure to integrate and understand the intelligence."[27]

Congress is also characterized by a diffusion of authority. For instance, when the DHS was created, sixty-one House and Senate committees and subcommittees possessed some degree of jurisdiction over the agencies that were incorporated into the new organization.[28] Congressional committees

Unusual Underwear

Umar Farouk Abdulmutallab tried to blow up a Northwest Airlines flight from Amsterdam to Detroit by sewing a packet of explosive powder into his underwear. Although the bomb did not go off, the incident created an uproar. For all the effort and new equipment designed to keep people with weapons or explosives off of airlines, Abdulmutallab demonstrated that there is still a problem. Policymakers are still trying to find foolproof methods for screening airline passengers.

(ABC News/Getty Images)

jealously guard their prerogatives and ardently fight reorganizations that will reduce their authority.

Differing policies among the states and between states and the federal government cause confusion because of the fragmented approach of the different levels of government. Frustrated because the federal government had taken no action regarding the poisoning of small children who unknowingly drink out of containers of antifreeze, California and Oregon passed laws requiring manufacturers to add a bitter-tasting ingredient to the mix. Thus, a child who made the mistake of starting to drink antifreeze would quickly stop because it tasted so horrible. But this legislation meant that different states required different things from manufacturers.[29]

As we'll discuss below, the multiplicity of institutional participants is partly the product of the complexity of public policy issues. Since a broad public policy issue can create multiple problems that must each be addressed and these problems may change over time, it's not surprising that the responsibilities of agencies and committees overlap. But why are responsibilities not parceled out more precisely to clarify jurisdictions and eliminate overlap? Such reorganizations create winners and losers, and agencies fearing the loss of jurisdiction over an issue become highly protective of their turf.

The Pursuit of Coordination

How does the government overcome fragmentation so that it can make its public policies more coherent? Coordination of different elements of government is not impossible, and fragmentation often creates a productive pressure to rethink jurisdictions.

The Office of Management and Budget (OMB) is a means that the White House can use to try to foster coordination within the executive branch. OMB can do much more than review budgets and look for ways to improve management practices. The Reagan administration used OMB to clear regulations before they were proposed publicly by the administrative agencies. It initiated OMB's regulatory review role to centralize control of the executive branch. Various presidents have modified this approach in different ways to suit their needs.[30]

The White House often goes beyond trying to improve coordination within the executive branch to enhancing control over other parts of government. In our federal system, states possess some degree of autonomy, but just how much autonomy is always subject to change. American federalism is often lauded because the states can be "fifty laboratories" for developing policy alternatives. Yet this can be frustrating to the White House because various states may develop policies at odds with those of the administration. This happened to the Bush White House as more liberal states began to push more aggressively on environmental protection. From the states' point of view, the Bush administration was remiss in moving slowly to combat global climate change. In contrast, the Bush White House believed that since it had won the presidency twice, it had the prerogative to set national policy, and states should not be free to set their own environmental standards.

The White House ordered the Environmental Protection Agency to clamp down on states, such as California, that tried to adopt their own approach to major environmental problems.[31]

As illustrated with the case of homeland security, reorganization of disparate parts of government working in related areas is a fundamental approach to enhancing coordination. Despite the obstacles that administrators trying to protect their turf put up, reorganization across agencies is possible. The involvement and commitment of the president is often critical as his status and willingness to expend political capital can put reorganizations on the agenda and push them forward.

Reorganizations within a single agency are easier to accomplish, though far from simple. A highly visible problem, a scandal, or a critical report (forms of negative feedback) can catalyze agency restructuring and minimize the ability of managers within that agency to work against changes they oppose. The Federal Emergency Management Agency (FEMA) was an independent agency formed in 1979 to unify the nation's disaster response programs. In 2002, FEMA was one of the many agencies incorporated into the Department of Homeland Security. This reorganization resulted in budget cuts for FEMA as well as the departure of many experienced FEMA employees. When the nation's new disaster response bureaucracy was put to the test by Hurricane Katrina, which devastated New Orleans in August 2005, it failed miserably. There was little coordination among FEMA officials, DHS officials, the White House, and state and local politicians.[32] After Katrina, politicians moved to change the structure of FEMA; some even argued that FEMA should be abolished and a new emergency preparedness agency built from scratch.

Over its history, Congress has repeatedly made efforts to promote greater coordination among all its disparate, decentralized parts. A major problem is that as agendas change with the emergence of new issues, the overlap in committee jurisdictions worsens. As noted above, many committees and subcommittees can claim some jurisdiction over the same problem. In recent years, both the Republican and Democratic congressional leaderships have worked to centralize power so that their parties could respond to broad policy issues in a more coordinated, coherent fashion.

Finally, the policy fragmentation created by federalism may be solved when an industry asks the national government to develop a single regulatory policy. In the antifreeze case discussed above, the state actions convinced the industry trade group that represents antifreeze manufacturers that it should drop its opposition to federal safety regulations.[33] Although an industry may prefer no regulation at all, it generally prefers one master to fifty.

The effect of pluralism on the problem of coordination is all too evident. In a decentralized, federal system of government with large numbers of interest groups, fragmentation is inevitable. Beyond the structural factors is the natural tendency of people and organizations to defend their base of power. Government officials understand, however, that mechanisms of coordination are necessary so that fragmentation does not overwhelm policymaking. Mechanisms such as interagency task forces, reorganizations, and White House review can bring some coherence to policymaking.

Government by Policy Area

Another counterweight to the fragmentation of a pluralist system with many different parts of government, each making policy, and many different sets of participants with differing objectives, is the working relationships that develop among these participants. We noted earlier that policy formulation takes place across different institutions. Participants from these institutions do not patiently wait their turn as policymaking proceeds from one institution to the next. Rather, they try to influence policy at whatever stage they can. Suppose that Congress is considering amendments to the Clean Air Act. Because Congress does not function in a vacuum, the other parts of government that will be affected by the legislation participate in the process too. The Environmental Protection Agency (EPA) has an interest in the outcome because it will have to administer the law. The White House is concerned about any legislation that affects such vital sectors of the economy as the steel and coal industries. As a result, officials from both the EPA and the White House work with members of Congress and the appropriate committee staffs to try to ensure that their interests are protected. At the same time, lobbyists representing corporations, trade associations, and environmental groups do their best to influence Congress, agency officials, and White House aides. Trade associations might hire public relations firms to sway public opinion toward their industry's point of view. Experts from think tanks and universities might be asked to testify at hearings or to serve in an informal advisory capacity in regard to the technical, economic, and social effects of the proposed amendments.

The various individuals and organizations that work in a particular policy area form a loosely knit community. The boundaries and membership of an **issue network** are hardly precise, but participants share expertise in a policy domain and interact frequently.[34] In general terms, such networks include members of Congress, committee staffers, agency officials, lawyers, lobbyists, consultants, scholars, and public relations specialists. Overall, a network can be quite large. One study identified over twelve hundred interest groups that had some contact with government officials in Washington in relation to health care over a five-year period.[35] But the real working relationships develop in specific policy areas, not throughout the entire policy community. The drug companies and their trade groups work with legislators and administrators on issues involving pharmaceuticals. Insurance companies work on other issues with other officials. It is within these more limited networks that ongoing working relationships emerge. Although network participants try to reach consensual agreements that an agency or congressional committee can act on, conflict within a network is common. On a regulatory issue, environmental or consumer groups may be lined up against an industry. Different parts of an industry often have conflicting views on an issue. Small businesses, for example, may have different views on regulatory matters than do large corporations in the same field.

The common denominator in a network is not the same political outlook but policy expertise. One must have the necessary expertise to enter the

issue network
A shared-knowledge group consisting of representatives of various interests involved in some particular aspect of public policy.

community of activists and politicians who influence policymaking in an issue area. Consider Medicare. The program is crucial to the health of the elderly, and with millions of baby boomers rapidly approaching retirement age, it needs to be restructured to make sure there will be enough money available to care for them all. But to enter the political debate on this issue requires specialized knowledge. What is the difference between "global capitation" and "fee for service"? What's the "doughnut hole" in Medicare Part D? "Advance directives" and "withholds for never events" may be grating jargon to the uninitiated, but they are meaningful terms to those in this network. In short, members of an issue network speak the same language. They can participate in the negotiation and compromise of policymaking because they can offer concrete, detailed solutions to the problems at hand. They understand the substance of policy, the way Washington works, and one another's viewpoints.

In a number of ways, issue networks promote pluralist democracy. They are open systems, populated by a wide range of interest groups. Decision making is not centralized in the hands of a few key players; policies are formulated in a participatory fashion. But there is still no guarantee that all relevant interests are represented, and those with greater financial resources have an advantage. Nevertheless, issue networks provide access to government for a diverse set of competing interests and thus further the pluralist ideal.

For those who prefer majoritarian democracy, however, issue networks are an obstacle to achieving their vision of how government should operate. The technical complexity of contemporary issues makes it especially difficult for the public at large to exert control over policy outcomes. When we think of the complexity of issues such as nuclear power, toxic wastes, air pollution, poverty, and drug abuse, it is easy to understand why majoritarian democracy is so difficult to achieve. The more complex an issue, the more elected officials must depend on a technocratic elite for policy guidance. And technical expertise is a chief characteristic of participants in issue networks.

At first glance, having technical experts play a key role in policymaking may seem highly desirable. After all, who but the experts should be making decisions about toxic wastes? This works to the advantage of government bureaucracies, which are full of people hired for their technical expertise.[36] But governmental dependence on technocrats also helps interest groups, which use policy experts to maximize their influence with government. Seen in this light, issue networks become less appealing. Interest groups—at least those with which we do not personally identify—are seen as selfish. They pursue policies that favor their constituents rather than the national interest.

Finally, although issue networks promote pluralism, majoritarian influences on policymaking are still significant. The broad contours of public opinion can be a dominant force on highly visible issues. Policymaking on civil rights, for example, has been sensitive to shifts in public opinion. Elections, too, send messages to policymakers about the most widely discussed campaign issues. What issue networks have done, however, is facilitate pluralist politics in policy areas in which majoritarian influences are weak.

The Nonprofit Sector

Community-based organizations are important participants in the policy-making process. Although they are not officially part of the government, these organizations may receive government funds and use them to implement a government program. Often assisted by many volunteers, they provide social services and offer the government valuable feedback about policy implementation at the local level. These organizations are **nonprofits**. Nonprofits are neither governmental organizations nor private sector organizations, and, as the term *nonprofit* denotes, they may not distribute profits to shareholders or to anyone else.[37]

There are many different types of nonprofits, but when we use the term, we are usually referring to organizations that are considered "public charities" by the Internal Revenue Service. They are not charities in the sense that they necessarily have to distribute money or goods to the needy; rather, they perform some public good. Of those nonprofits with an annual income of at least $25,000, the greatest number are involved in social services (see Figure 17.6). Social service nonprofits might distribute meals, offer after-school activities to low-income children, administer shelters for abused women or runaway children, or provide hospice care for the terminally ill.

Such organizations include the Salvation Army, a nonprofit with sixty thousand employees that provides services to 30 million people a year, as well as smaller organizations like the Genesis Women's Shelter in Dallas, where women and their children can find safe haven from an abusive situation at home; Beyond Shelter, a Los Angeles organization that works to find housing for the homeless and provides social services to them; and the Transitional Work Corporation of Philadelphia, which offers job training to hard-core unemployed.[38] Nonprofits offer vitally important services, and all communities are highly dependent on them. Indeed, all countries depend on them (see "Politics of Global Change: A Lifeline in Haiti"). As one scholar notes, they are "the glue that holds civil society together."[39]

nonprofits
Organizations that are not part of government or business and cannot distribute profits to shareholders or to anyone else.

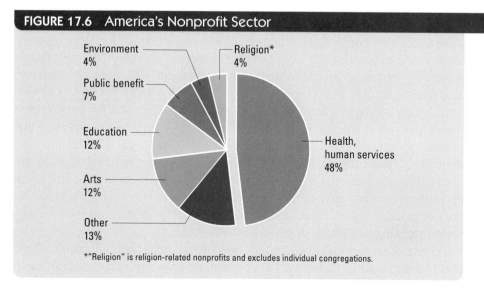

FIGURE 17.6 America's Nonprofit Sector

Environment 4%
Public benefit 7%
Education 12%
Arts 12%
Other 13%
Religion* 4%
Health, human services 48%

*"Religion" is religion-related nonprofits and excludes individual congregations.

Of all nonprofits large enough to file a tax return, close to half work in the fields of human services or health care. The numbers of nonprofits have skyrocketed as Americans increasingly turn to them for social services. Nonprofits employ 9 percent of the nation's work force.

Source: Jeffrey M. Berry with David F. Arons, *A Voice for Nonprofits* (Washington, D.C.: Brookings Institution, 2003), p. 5. Reprinted by permission.

Politics of Global Change

A Lifeline in Haiti

Even in the best of times Haiti is a tough place to live. It is characterized by grinding, persistent poverty. Its infrastructure is inadequate at best. It has little in the way of natural resources or industry. Indeed, it's the poorest country in the entire western hemisphere.

And then the earthquake came.

On January 12, 2010, an intense earthquake shook the country. In Port-au-Prince, the nation's capital, the devastation was particularly widespread. Much of the city was flattened, literally. Buildings and homes collapsed and killed and maimed residents. The death toll is estimated at more than 200,000; most of those were buried alive.

Frantz Verdieu was lucky in that he wasn't killed by a collapsing roof or wall. But he was injured and needed someone to fix his broken arm. In Port-au-Prince, with rubble everywhere, there was nowhere for Verdieu, a 34-year-old teacher, to go for help. He began walking toward Cange, a city of 30,000 in the mountains roughly 60 miles from Port-au-Prince. People

in shock, newly homeless, poured out of Port-au-Prince and a number headed toward Cange.

Why Cange? Verdieu knew that the Boston-based nonprofit, Partners in Health, ran a hospital there. He could get high-quality care there, as he could at any of the ten small hospitals Partners in Health ran in Haiti. The nonprofit operates in many developing countries and is highly respected for its expertise and effectiveness in providing medical care to those who would not otherwise have access to doctors and other medical professionals.

The U.S. government immediately sent military personnel to Haiti to provide food, water, and other emergency services, but it wasn't practical for the United States to keep its military in Haiti for an extended period. As the focus turned to longer-range plans to rebuild the shattered country, it was clear that nonprofits would play a central role in Haiti's redevelopment.

There was already a strong nonprofit presence throughout Haiti, and nonprofit organizations had

Not all the nonprofits that qualify as public charities are social service providers. Other nonprofits include symphony orchestras, PTAs, Little Leagues, museums, and foundations. All of these groups provide something valuable to society by engaging people in their communities, offering them a chance to appreciate art, creating opportunities for volunteering, and providing recreation to children and adults alike. These activities enrich society, and it's important to design policies to encourage people to become involved in nonprofits. Nonprofits are rewarded for these valuable endeavors with tax deductibility for donors. As noted earlier, individuals who contribute money to public charity nonprofits can deduct that money from their taxable income. This tax break encourages people to give money because government is essentially subsidizing the contribution. (Recall the earlier discussion of tax expenditures—tax provisions that cause a loss of government revenue.)

Often the relationship between government agencies and nonprofits is that of a partnership. Agency officials distribute grants to nonprofit applicants

both immediate relief and long-term reconstruction. Hundreds of millions of dollars poured into Partners in Health, the Red Cross, Catholic Relief Services, Doctors without Borders, and many other widely respected nonprofits. Many smaller nonprofits work in Haiti as well. On an annual budget of just $500,000, the Lord of Life Lutheran Church from Virginia operates three schools and orphanages for 700 children in Haiti.

Today, as industrialized countries look for ways to assist the developing world, they turn to nonprofits to devise and implement programs. The number of nonprofits is growing to meet this demand. One analyst concludes that there is a "massive upsurge of … voluntary activity in literally every corner of the world." Internationally oriented nonprofits are now lifelines in poverty-stricken areas. Nonprofit scholar Alan Abramson notes that such organizations "are the ones who know the neighborhood and are connected with the people in need."

people on the ground in Haiti who had been providing services to the impoverished Haitians on an ongoing basis. The nonprofit workers had substantial experience in addressing the country's enduring problems. They understood the culture and many spoke Creole, the country's primary language. Nonprofit organizations operate with low overhead because of the commitment and compassion of their workers, who work for low wages, and the presence of volunteers who come to Haiti to work for nonprofits for varying lengths of time.

In the wake of the catastrophe in Haiti, people across the world donated to nonprofits to help with

Sources: Stephen Smith and James F. Smith, "Rising to Meet an Infinite Need," *Boston Globe,* 24 January 2010; Damian Cave, "More Than 150,000 Have Been Buried, Government Says," *New York Times,* 24 January 2010; William Wan, "Haiti's Logistical Hurdles Are Thwarting Small Hospitals," *Washington Post,* 22 January 2010; Matthew Hay Brown, "With Click of a Mouse, Haiti Aid Grows," *Baltimore Sun,* 25 January 2010; Lester Salamon et al., *Global Civil Society* (Baltimore: Center for Civil Society Studies, 1999). *Photo:* AP Photo/Andres Leighton.

and then oversee the performance of those nonprofits in providing services.[40] However, the typical nonprofit working in social services is supported by a mix of private and government funds. One of the advantages for government from using nonprofits to administer social service programs is that substantial amounts of funding come from contributions made by individuals. Although the government is subsidizing those contributions through the tax deductibility of donations, it benefits by not having to pay for all those services itself.

The government also gets more social services than would be the case if there were no nonprofits and the government had to provide more direct services through its bureaucracies at the national, state, and local levels. Government is under substantial pressure to keep expenditures down. Indeed, nonprofits are growing in importance because government has found it desirable to shift more administration of social services to this sector. This allows elected officials to appear to cut the size of government

Curious George Takes a Job

The nonprofit group Helping Hands trains capuchin monkeys to help people who are paralyzed. Monkeys can turn lights on and off, put on a CD, and warm up food in the microwave. It costs roughly $35,000 to train each monkey, but no fee is charged to the recipients of their services.

(Melanie Stetson Freeman/The Christian Science Monitor via Getty Images)

by reducing the number of bureaucrats while at the same time not angering people who depend on social services.[41]

Nonprofits are also inexpensive ways to deliver services because they make considerable use of volunteer labor. America is a nation of volunteers; one survey showed that 27 percent of the adult population, approximately 61 million people, volunteered. On average, volunteers contribute just over 200 hours a year, and much of this volunteering is channeled through nonprofits.[42] It's not clear what percentage of this volunteering is devoted to helping paid staff deliver social services, but it is an enormously significant means of support in our social welfare system. A primary reason that people volunteer for nonprofits is that they find helping others is meaningful and rewarding to them.

Nonprofits may sound too good to be true, and in a sense they are because they can't do all that we might like them to. During the recession that took hold in 2008, states and cities were forced to make significant budget cuts. This meant that some services they offered were reduced. Those in need turned in greater numbers to nonprofits. Yet many nonprofits have had their government grants reduced and have found themselves struggling to deliver the same level of services they were offering before the recession hit.

Given the importance of nonprofits in providing social services, it's clear that they have a role to play in developing policy as well as in implementing it. In many policy areas, they've become part of the policymaking communities that dominate the debate over the political issues relevant to their concerns.

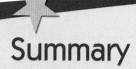

Summary

Underlying policy choices are basic values—the core beliefs about how government should work. But values must be translated into policy choices. The basic objectives of government tend to be distributional, redistributional, and regulatory. To achieve a policy objective, those in government usually rely on one or more of the most basic tools or approaches: incentives and disincentives, direct provision of services, or rule setting.

Although there is much variation in the policymaking process, we can conceive of it as consisting of four stages. The first stage is agenda setting, the process by which problems become defined as political issues worthy of government attention. Once people in government feel that they should be doing something about a problem, an attempt at policy formulation will follow. All three branches of the national government formulate policy. Once policies have been formulated and ratified, administrative units of government must implement them. Finally, once policies are being carried out, they need to be evaluated. Implementation and program evaluation influence agenda building because program shortcomings become evident during these stages. Thus, the process is really circular, with the end often marking the beginning of a new round of policymaking.

Our policymaking system is also characterized by forces that push it toward fragmentation and by institutional structures intended to bring some element of coordination to government. The multiplicity of participants in policymaking, the diffusion of authority within both Congress and the executive branch, the separation of powers, and federalism are chief causes of conflict and fragmentation in policymaking.

To try to reduce fragmentation, presidents and congressional leaders have pushed for various reforms designed to bring greater coordination to policymaking and program implementation. Presidents continually tinker with the organization of the executive branch, reorganizing agencies and offices within the constraints of political feasibility. In varying degrees, presidents have also relied on central clearance of proposed agency regulations.

The fragmentation of government accentuates the forces of pluralism. The structure of the policymaking process facilitates the participation of interest groups. This in turn works in favor of well-organized, aggressive constituencies and against the broader but more passive public at large. There are certainly majoritarian counterweights to the advantages to pluralism inherent in the structure of our government, but such forces as public opinion and political party stands work best on national issues of great concern to the public. On the mundane, day-to-day issues of government, pluralism is aided by the complexity of public policy and the fragmentation of responsibility.

CourseMate   Visit www.cengagebrain.com/shop/ ISBN/0495906182 for flashcards, web quizzes, videos and more!

CHAPTER

18

Economic Policy

CHAPTER TOPICS

United States Office of Management and Budget

"This Bud's for you!" was the slogan of Anheuser-Busch, the St. Louis-based brewery that had made Budweiser beer since 1876. Today, Bud is made by the foreign owner who bought the company in 2008 and created Anheuser-Busch InBev, the world's largest brewery.[1] Based in Leuven, Belgium, the new owner still maintains a St. Louis office, but fewer workers are employed there.[2] Want to buy a purely American beer? Don't look to Miller Lite or High Life, for Miller Brewing was sold to a South African brewery in 1999 to create SABMiller. Don't look to Coors either; it was bought by Molson of Canada in 2005. These international breweries are now investing in China, the world's largest beer market and producer.[3]

Want to visit the world's tallest building? You'd have to go to Dubai in the United Arab Emirates, where the 2,700-foot-tall Khalifa Tower opened in 2010, succeeding Taiwan's Taipei 101 tower (2004), which topped the Petronas Twin Towers in Kuala Lumpur, Malaysia (1998). For more than a decade, the world's tallest buildings have stood outside the United States, once famous for the highest skyscrapers—the Empire State Building (1931), the twin towers of the World Trade Center (1973), and the Sears Tower (1973). Today, nine of the eleven tallest buildings in the world are in Asia or the Middle East.[4]

Want to buy a Hummer, or Pontiac, or Saturn? Too bad, General Motors—the bankrupt carmaker rescued by the U.S. government in 2009—had to scrap the lines to save money. Instead, how about a Town & Country SUV from Chrysler? Also bankrupt and rescued by the government, Chrysler was bought by the Italian company Fiat, which may or may not continue to build the SUV. Ford Motors did not go bankrupt but raised cash in 2010 by selling its Volvo division (bought from a Swedish group in 1999) to the Chinese company Zhejiang Geely. China had already surpassed the United States in car sales in 2009.

Maybe you fancy riding at 150 mph between New York and Boston on the new Acela Express high-speed train. Unfortunately, the tracks are so poor that the train averages only half that speed. In France, a TGV train runs at sustained speeds of 133 mph between Paris and Lyon. Japan's bullet trains average about 180 mph on multiple routes. The German company Siemens is building a train to run between Moscow and St. Petersburg at more than 200 mph.[5] China already runs a train from Guangzhou to Wuhan at 215 mph.[6] In the United States—a land built around railroad transportation—rail passenger service today is distinctly inferior to that in many other countries. Very few trains run faster than 79 mph, and some travel at slower speeds than seventy-five years ago.

Maybe the United States can lead the world in manufacturing alternative energy sources. That's unlikely. In 2009, China became the largest manufacturer of wind turbines (passing tiny Denmark) and the largest maker of solar panels (passing Japan). A century ago, the United States led in exporting windmills—engineered to pump water and generate electricity for millions of American farms.[7] Today, the Chinese government, through its National Energy Commission, is committed to making sure that most of the world's energy equipment "will carry a brass plate, 'Made in China.'"[8]

It may be unimportant that the top American breweries were bought by foreign firms. It hurts our pride more than our pocketbook that the tallest skyscrapers are rising in Asia and the Middle East. It is troubling, however, that we no longer lead in making automobiles and moving people by rail, and it is critical that the United States lags behind in manufacturing alternative energy sources. In his 2010 State of the Union address, President Obama said that government

> can put Americans to work today building the infrastructure of tomorrow. From the first railroads to the Interstate Highway System, our

nation has always been built to compete. There's no reason Europe or China should have the fastest trains, or the new factories that manufacture clean energy products.

Is it proper for government to assist economic growth in targeted areas? Or is that socialism, as critics charge? Would economic conditions be improved if government did not try to intervene in the economy? Did the government do right in keeping General Motors and Chrysler in business, or should they have collapsed into unstructured bankruptcy?

How much control of the domestic economy can government really exercise through the judicious use of economic theory? How much is the economy influenced by events that lie outside governmental control? More concretely, how is the national budget formulated, and why did the deficit grow so large and prove so difficult to control against spending appetites of Congress? What effects do government taxing and spending policies have on the economy and on economic equality? We address these questions in this chapter. As we shall see, no one person or organization controls the American economy; multiple actors have a voice in economic conditions. And not all of these actors are public—or American.

Theories of Economic Policy

Government efforts to control the economy rely on theories about how the economy responds to government taxing and spending policies and its control of the money supply. How policymakers tax and spend, and loosen and tighten interest rates, depends on their beliefs about how the economy functions and the proper role of government in the economy. The American economy is so complex that no one knows exactly how it works. Policymakers rely on economic theories to explain its functioning, and there are nearly as many theories as there are economists. Unfortunately, different theories (and economists) often predict different outcomes. One source of differing predictions is the different assumptions that underlie competing economic theories. Another problem is the differences between abstract theories and the real world. Still, despite disagreement among economists, a knowledge of basic economics is necessary to understand how government approaches public policy.[9]

We are concerned here with economic policy in a market economy—one in which the prices of goods and services are determined through the interaction of sellers and buyers (that is, through supply and demand). This kind of economy is typical of the consumer-dominated societies of Western

Europe and the United States. A nonmarket economy relies on government planners to determine both the prices of goods and the amounts that are produced. The old Soviet economy is a perfect example; the government owned and operated the major means of production.

Market economies are loosely called *capitalist economies*: they allow private individuals to own property; sell goods for profit in free, or open, markets; and accumulate wealth, called *capital*. Market economies often exhibit a mix of government and private ownership. For example, Britain has had more government-owned enterprises (railroads, broadcasting, and housing) than has the United States. China today contends that it has a *socialist market economy*, which depends on the private sector for economic growth but also directs and supports state-owned enterprises.[10] Competing economic theories differ largely on how free they say the markets should be—in other words, on government's role in directing the economy (see "Politics of Global Change: We Buy More, and We Borrow More").

Laissez-Faire Economics

The French term *laissez faire*, introduced in Chapter 1 and discussed again in Chapter 13, describes the absence of government control. The economic doctrine of laissez faire likens the operation of a free market to the process of natural selection. Economic competition weeds out the weak and preserves the strong. In the process, the economy prospers, and everyone eventually benefits.

Advocates of laissez-faire economics are fond of quoting Adam Smith's *The Wealth of Nations*. In his 1776 treatise, Smith argued that each individual, pursuing his own selfish interests in a competitive market, was "led by an invisible hand to promote an end which was no part of his intention." Smith's "invisible hand" has been used for two centuries to justify the belief that the narrow pursuit of profits serves the broad interests of society.[11] Strict advocates of laissez faire maintain that government interference with business tampers with the laws of nature, obstructing the workings of the free market. Mainstream economists today favor market principles but do recognize that "governments can sometimes improve market outcomes."[12] Within the last century, a companion principle, the **efficient market hypothesis**, has held that financial markets are informationally efficient—they quickly absorb all relevant information about securities into their prices. It implies that securities are priced and traded at their fair value, meaning that investors cannot "beat the market." If the market is rational, attempts to regulate it become irrational.[13]

Keynesian Theory

According to laissez-faire economics, our government should have done nothing when markets across the world crashed in February 2008 and threatened our economy. Laissez-faire economics holds that government should do little about **economic depression** (a period of high unemployment and business failures); or raging **inflation** (price increases that decrease the value of currency); or—for that matter—**stagflation** (the joint occurrence of slow growth,

efficient market hypothesis
Financial markets are informationally efficient—they quickly absorb all relevant information about securities into their prices.

economic depression
A period of high unemployment and business failures; a severe, long-lasting downturn in a business cycle.

inflation
An economic condition characterized by price increases linked to a decrease in the value of the currency.

stagflation
The joint occurrence of slow growth, unemployment, and inflation.

Politics of Global Change

We Buy More, and We Borrow More

Globalization produces economic interdependence among nations. Over the past four decades, Americans have been buying more goods and services from other countries than we are selling to them. Foreigners have been using their profits to buy U.S. government secur-

ities, thus acquiring increasing shares of our public debt, which totaled over $7.5 trillion in 2009. (That number excludes over $4 billion in intragovernmental debts. See page 609.) In effect, foreigners have been lending us money to buy their goods and services.

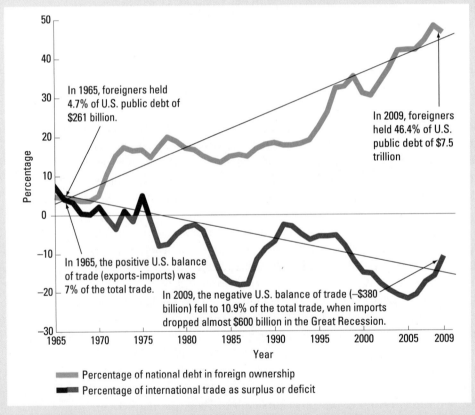

In 1965, foreigners held 4.7% of U.S. public debt of $261 billion.

In 2009, foreigners held 46.4% of U.S. public debt of $7.5 trillion

In 1965, the positive U.S. balance of trade (exports-imports) was 7% of the total trade.

In 2009, the negative U.S. balance of trade (–$380 billion) fell to 10.9% of the total trade, when imports dropped almost $600 billion in the Great Recession.

Percentage of national debt in foreign ownership
Percentage of international trade as surplus or deficit

Sources: Office of Management and Budget, "Table 6.7: Foreign Holdings of Federal Debt," in *Analytical Perspectives: Budget of the U.S. Government, Fiscal Year 2011* (Washington, D.C.: U.S. Government Printing Office, 2010); U.S. Census Bureau, Foreign Trade Division, "U.S. Trade in Goods and Services, Balance of Payments (BOP) Basis," http://www.census.gov/foreign-trade/statistics/historical/gands.txt; U.S. Census Bureau, Foreign Trade Division, "Historical Series," http://www.census.gov/foreign-trade/statistics/historical/index.html.

business cycles
Expansions and contractions of business activity, the first accompanied by inflation and the second by unemployment.

unemployment, and inflation of the 1970s). Inflation is ordinarily measured by the consumer price index (CPI), explained in the feature "The Consumer Price Index." Since the beginning of the Industrial Revolution, capitalist economies have suffered through many cyclical fluctuations. Since 1857, the United States has experienced more than thirty of these **business cycles:**

Economists Getting Data for Predictions

The forecast you get depends on the economist you ask.

(Used with permission by Susan MacNelly and the Estate of Jeff MacNelly)

expansions and contractions of business activity, the first stage accompanied by inflation and the second stage by unemployment.[14] No widely accepted theory explained these cycles until the Great Depression of the 1930s.

That was when John Maynard Keynes, a British economist, theorized that business cycles stem from imbalances between aggregate demand and productive capacity. **Aggregate demand** is the total income that consumers, business, and government wish to spend on goods and services. **Productive capacity** is the total value of goods and services that can be produced when the economy is working at full capacity. The value of the goods and services actually produced is called the **gross domestic product (GDP)**. When demand exceeds productive capacity, people are willing to pay more for available goods, which leads to price inflation. When productive capacity exceeds demand, producers cut back on their output of goods, which leads to unemployment. When many people are unemployed for an extended period, the economy is in a depression. Keynes theorized that government could stabilize the economy (and smooth out or eliminate business cycles) by controlling the level of aggregate demand.

Keynesian theory holds that aggregate demand can be adjusted through a combination of fiscal and monetary policies.[15] **Fiscal policies**, which are enacted by the president and Congress, involve changes in government spending and taxing. When demand is too low, according to Keynes, government should either spend more itself, hiring people and thus giving them money, or cut taxes, giving people more of their own money to spend. When demand is too great, the government should either spend less or raise taxes, giving people less money to spend. **Monetary policies**, which are largely determined by the Federal Reserve Board, involve changes in the money supply and operate less directly on the economy. Increasing the amount of money in circulation increases aggregate demand and thus increases price inflation. Decreasing the money supply decreases aggregate demand and inflationary pressures.

aggregate demand
The total income that consumers, businesses, and government wish to spend for goods and services.

productive capacity
The total value of goods and services that can be produced when the economy works at full capacity.

gross domestic product (GDP)
The total value of the goods and services produced by a country during a year.

Keynesian theory
An economic theory stating that the government can stabilize the economy—that is, can smooth business cycles—by controlling the level of aggregate demand, and that the level of aggregate demand can be controlled by means of fiscal and monetary policies.

fiscal policies
Economic policies that involve government spending and taxing.

monetary policies
Economic policies that involve control of, and changes in, the supply of money.

Feature Story

The Consumer Price Index

Inflation in the United States is usually measured in terms of the consumer price index (CPI), which is calculated by the U.S. Bureau of Labor Statistics (BLS). The CPI is based on prices paid for food, clothing, shelter, transportation, medical services, and other items necessary for daily living. Data are collected from eighty-seven areas across the country, from over fifty thousand homes and more than twenty thousand businesses. The CPI is thoroughly reviewed about every ten years, most recently in 1998. Moreover, the BLS has since made many adjustments in the index.

The CPI is not a perfect measure of inflation. For example, it does not differentiate between inflationary price increases and other price increases. An automobile bought in 1990 is not the same as one bought in 2010. Any price increase for the same model reflects an improved product as well as a decrease in the value of the dollar. Another problem is the CPI's delay in reflecting changes in buying habits. VCRs were around for several years before they were included among the hundreds of items in the index; the prices of cell phones were not in the 2009 index.

These are minor issues compared with the changing weight given to the cost of housing. Before 1983, the cost of purchasing and financing a home accounted for 26 percent of the CPI, which neglected the reality that few people buy a home every year—and many people

rent. Since 1983, the BLS figured the cost of renting equivalent housing as only 15 percent of the CPI. In recent years, the BLS has released a "core" CPI that excludes the costs of food and energy, which fluctuate more widely than what has become known as the standard, or "headline," CPI.

The government incorporates the standard CPI in cost-of-living adjustments for civil service and military pension payments and Social Security benefits. Moreover, union wage contracts with private businesses are often indexed (tied) to the CPI. As the CPI tends to rise each year, so do payments that are tied to it. In this way, CPI indexing promotes both the growth of government spending and inflation itself. The United States is one of the few nations that also ties its tax brackets to a price index, which reduces government revenues by eliminating the effect of inflation on taxpayer incomes.

Despite its faults, the CPI is at least a consistent measure of prices, and it is likely to continue as the basis for adjustments to wages, benefits, and payments affecting millions of people.

Sources: Bureau of Labor Statistics, "The Consumer Price Index—December 2009," http://www.bls.gov/news.release/pdf/cpi.pdf. Unfortunately, the CPI captures costs of goods better than costs of services, such as medical care, insurance, and education. Thus, many citizens complain of rising prices while the CPI stays low. See Jon E. Hilsenrath, "America's Pricing Paradox," *Wall Street Journal*, 16 May 2003, p. B1.

deficit financing
The Keynesian technique of spending beyond government income to combat an economic slump. Its purpose is to inject extra money into the economy to stimulate aggregate demand.

Despite some problems with the assumptions of Keynesian theory, capitalist countries have widely adopted it in some form.[16] At one time or another, virtually all have used the Keynesian technique of **deficit financing**— spending in excess of tax revenues—to combat an economic slump. Because a slump lowers profits and wages, it reduces tax revenues—thus generating a budget deficit all by itself. Prior to Keynes, economists prescribed raising taxes and cutting spending to bring the budget back into balance. That only reduced aggregate demand and worsened the recession. The objective of deficit financing is to increase demand for goods and services, either directly by increasing government purchases or indirectly by cutting taxes to generate more after-tax income to spend. Most deficits are financed with funds borrowed through the issuing of government bonds, notes, or other securities. The theory holds that deficits can be paid off with budget surpluses after the economy recovers.

Because Keynesian theory requires government to play an active role in controlling the economy, it runs counter to laissez-faire economics. Before Keynes, no administration in Washington would shoulder responsibility for maintaining a healthy economy. In 1946, the year Keynes died, Congress passed an employment act establishing "the continuing responsibility of the national government to ... promote maximum employment, production and purchasing power." It also created the **Council of Economic Advisers (CEA)** within the Executive Office of the President to advise the president on maintaining a stable economy. The CEA normally consists of three economists (usually university professors) appointed by the president with Senate approval. Aided by a staff of about twenty-five people (mostly economists), it helps the president prepare his annual economic report, also a provision of the 1946 act. The CEA's importance lessened under President Clinton in 1993 with the creation of the broader National Economic Council (NEC), consisting of key cabinet secretaries and advisers, including the chair of the CEA. As NEC director under President Obama, Larry Summers emerged as a major spokesperson for economic policy, along with Treasury Secretary Timothy Geithner and CEA chair Christina Romer.[17]

The Employment Act of 1946, which reflected Keynesian theory, had a tremendous effect on government economic policy. Many people believe it was the primary source of "big government" in America. Even Richard Nixon, a conservative president, admitted in 1971 that "we are all Keynesians now," by accepting government responsibility for the economy. But not all conservatives buy into that philosophy. In a 2008 editorial, "We're All Keynesians Now," the *Wall Street Journal* deplored Bush's $168 billion fiscal stimulus package of tax rebates to forestall a recession as taking money from one pocket (those with high income) and handing it to another (those with low to moderate income).[18] Obama's $787 billion stimulus package in 2009 drew even heavier fire, but even conservative economists credit it with saving millions of jobs and contributing to 5.7 percent economic growth by the end of the year.[19] New books appeared praising Keynes.[20]

Monetary Policy

Although most economists accept Keynesian theory in its broad outlines, they depreciate its political utility. Some especially question the value of fiscal policies in controlling inflation and unemployment. They argue that government spending programs take too long to enact in Congress and to implement through the bureaucracy. As a result, jobs are created not when they are needed but years later, when the crisis may have passed and government spending needs to be reduced.

Also, government spending is easier to start than to stop because the groups that benefit from spending programs tend to defend them even when

Council of Economic Advisers (CEA)
A group that works within the executive branch to provide advice on maintaining a stable economy.

Chairman of the Board

Appointed by President George W. Bush, Ben S. Bernanke became chairman of the Federal Reserve Board on February 1, 2006. As an economics professor, he was known for his analysis of the Great Depression in the 1930s. Previous studies blamed contraction of the money supply for the depression, but he concluded that it was due to widespread bank failures. Bernanke implied that the Fed's main task is not to tune the economy through monetary policy but to respond to financial crises, which he did promptly when global markets crashed in January 2008. Two months later, he took even bolder actions to avoid a credit collapse, allowing investment banks to borrow from the Fed. By September, Bernanke and Treasury Secretary Henry Paulson engineered a $700 billion plan to rescue the financial system. *Time* named Bernanke "Person of the Year" for what did not happen: the financial system did not collapse. Nevertheless, critics decried his actions prior to the crisis as well as his "bailout" of Wall Street. Obama reappointed Bernanke chairman, and he was confirmed by the Senate—but by the lowest margin in the Fed's ninety-six-year history.

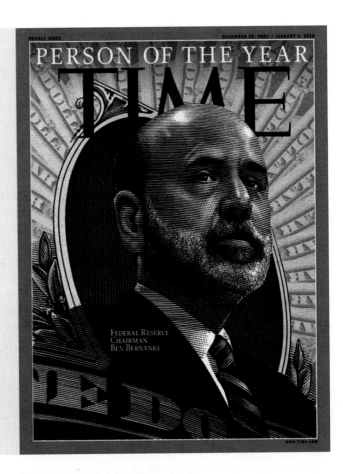

they are no longer needed. A similar criticism applies to tax policies. Politically, it is much easier to cut taxes than to raise them. In other words, Keynesian theory requires that governments be able to begin and end spending quickly and to cut and raise taxes quickly. But in the real world, these fiscal tools are easier to use in one direction than the other.

Recognizing these limitations of fiscal policies, **monetarists** argue that government can control the economy's performance simply by controlling the nation's money supply.[21] Staunch monetarists, like Nobel Laureate Milton Friedman, favor a long-range policy of small but steady growth in the amount of money in circulation rather than frequent manipulation of monetary policies.

Monetary policies in the United States are under the control of the **Federal Reserve System**, which acts as the country's central bank. Established in 1913, the Fed by law has three major goals: controlling inflation, maintaining maximum employment, and insuring moderate interest rates.[22] The Fed is not a single bank but a system of banks. At the top of the system is the board of governors, seven members appointed by the president for staggered terms of fourteen years. The president designates one member of the board to be its chairperson, who serves a four-year term that extends beyond the president's term of office. This complex arrangement was intended to make the board independent of the president and even of Congress. An independent board, the

monetarists
Those who argue that government can effectively control the performance of an economy mainly by controlling the supply of money.

Federal Reserve System
The system of banks that acts as the central bank of the United States and controls major monetary policies.

reasoning went, would be able to make financial decisions for the nation without regard to their political implications.[23] Following the Fed's bold actions taken to combat the financial crisis in 2008, however, members of Congress proposed auditing Fed decisions for the first time. By the summer of 2010, when President signed the sweeping Dodd-Frank financial reform bill, the Fed was granted even greater powers to regulate large complex financial firms.[24]

The Fed controls the money supply, which affects inflation, in three ways. Most important, the Fed can sell and buy government securities (such as U.S. Treasury bills) on the open market. When the Fed sells securities, it takes money out of circulation, thereby making money scarce and raising the interest rate. When the Fed buys securities, the process works in reverse, lowering interest rates. The Fed also sets a target for the *federal funds rate,* which banks charge one another for overnight loans and which is usually cited when newspapers write, "The Fed has decided to lower [or raise] interest rates." Less frequently (for technical reasons), the Fed may change its *discount rate,* the interest rate that member banks have to pay to borrow money from a Federal Reserve bank. Finally, the Fed can change its *reserve requirement,* which is the amount of cash that member banks must keep on deposit in their regional Federal Reserve bank. An increase in the reserve requirement reduces the amount of money banks have available to lend.[25]

Basic economic theory holds that interest rates should be raised to discourage borrowing and spending when the economy is growing too quickly (this combats inflation) and lowered when the economy is sluggish (thus increasing the money flow to encourage spending and economic growth). Historically, the Fed has adjusted interest rates to combat inflation rather than to stimulate economic growth, which would maximize employment.[26] (A former Fed chairman once said its task was "to remove the punch bowl when the party gets going.")[27] That is, the Fed would dampen economic growth before it leads to serious inflation.

Accordingly, some charge that the Fed acts to further interests of the wealthy (who fear rampant inflation) more than interests of the poor (who fear widespread unemployment). Why so? Although all classes of citizens complain about increasing costs of living, inflation usually harms upper classes (creditors) more than lower classes (debtors). To illustrate, suppose someone borrows $20,000, to be repaid after ten years, during which the inflation rate was 10 percent. When the loan is due, the $20,000 borrowed is "worth" only $18,000. Debtors find the cheaper money easier to raise, and creditors are paid less than the original value of their loan. Hence, wealthy people fear severe inflation, which can erode the value of their saved wealth. As one Federal Reserve bank bluntly stated: "Debtors gain when inflation is unexpectedly high, and creditors gain when it is unexpectedly low."[28]

Formally, the president is responsible for the state of the economy, and voters hold him accountable. As the economy deteriorated in 2008, more people blamed President Bush for its poor performance than blamed Congress, multinational corporations, or financial institutions.[29] However, the president neither determines interest rates (the Fed does) nor controls spending (Congress does). In this respect, all presidents since 1913 have had to work with a Fed made independent of both the president and Congress, and all have had to deal with the fact that Congress ultimately controls spending. These restrictions on presidential authority are consistent with the pluralist model of democracy, but a president held responsible for the economy may not appreciate that theoretical argument.

Although the Fed's economic policies are not perfectly insulated from political concerns, they are sufficiently independent that the president is not able to control monetary policy without the Fed's cooperation. This means that the president cannot be held completely responsible for the state of the economy. Nevertheless, the public blames presidents for poor economic conditions and votes against them in elections. Naturally, a strong economy favors the incumbent party. When people are optimistic about the economic future and feel that they are doing well, they typically see no reason to change the party controlling the White House. But when conditions are bad or worsening, voters often decide to seek a change.

The Fed's activities are essential parts of the government's overall economic policy, but they lie outside the direct control of the president—and directly in the hands of the chair of the Federal Reserve Board. This makes the Fed chair a critical player in economic affairs and can create problems in coordinating economic policy. For example, the president might want the Fed to lower interest rates to stimulate the economy, but the Fed might resist for fear of inflation. Such policy clashes can pit the chair of the Federal Reserve Board directly against the president. So presidents typically court the Fed chair, even one who served a president of the other party.

Appointed Fed chair in 2006 by President Bush, Ben Bernanke replaced Alan Greenspan, who held the post for almost twenty years and was praised for overseeing an economy with low inflation, low unemployment, and strong growth. Greenspan, who believed that markets knew best and should be left unregulated (in keeping with the "efficient market hypothesis"), was later blamed for the financial crisis of 2008. Called before a House committee in October, Greenspan admitted that his "whole intellectual edifice collapsed in the summer," when banks held nearly worthless securities that had tumbled from dizzyingly high values.[30] Criticized for his complacency prior to the crisis, Bernanke acted boldly during it to rescue the economy, stretching the Fed's authority by arranging bank purchases, emergency loan programs, and the lowest interest rates in American history.[31] Named *Time* magazine "Person of the Year" in 2009, Bernanke was reappointed by Obama and confirmed in 2010 for another term.

Historical evidence suggests that government can indeed slow down and smooth out the booms and busts of business cycles through active use of monetary and fiscal policies. From 1855 through World War II—prior to the active employment of Keynesian theory—the nation suffered through economic recessions 42 percent of the time, with each recession averaging twenty-one months. Since then and through June 2007, the nation was in a recession only 16 percent of the time, and the average duration lasted only ten months.[32] The Great Recession that began in December 2007 lasted for 18 months, officially ending in June 2009.

Supply-Side Economics

When Reagan came to office in 1981, he embraced a school of thought called **supply-side economics** to deal with the stagflation (both unemployment and inflation) that the nation was experiencing. Keynesian theory argues that inflation results when consumers, businesses, and governments have more money to spend than there are goods and services to buy. The standard Keynesian solution is to reduce demand (for example, by increasing taxes). Supply-siders argue that inflation can be lowered more effectively by increasing the supply of goods (that is, they stress the supply side of the economic equation). Specifically, they favor tax cuts to stimulate investment (which leads to the production of more goods) and less government regulation of business (again, to increase productivity—which they hold will yield more, not less, government revenue). Supply-siders also argue that the rich should receive larger tax cuts than the poor because the rich have more money to invest. The benefits of increased investment will then "trickle down" to working people in the form of additional jobs and income.

In a sense, supply-side economics resembles laissez-faire economics because it prefers fewer government programs and regulations and less taxation. Supply-siders believe that government interferes too much with the efforts of individuals to work, save, and invest. Inspired by supply-side theory, Reagan proposed (and got) massive tax cuts in the Economic Recovery Tax Act of 1981. The act reduced individual tax rates by 23 percent over a three-year period and cut the marginal tax rate for the highest income group from 70 to 50 percent. Reagan also launched a program to deregulate business. According to supply-side theory, these actions would generate extra government revenue, making spending cuts unnecessary to balance the budget. Nevertheless, Reagan also cut funding for some domestic programs, including Aid to Families with Dependent Children. Contrary to supply-side theory, he also proposed hefty increases in military spending. This blend of tax cuts, deregulation, cuts in spending for social programs, and increases in spending for defense became known, somewhat disparagingly, as *Reaganomics.*

How well did Reaganomics work? Inflation, which ran over 13 percent in 1981, was lowered to about 3 percent by 1983, but that was due mostly to Federal Reserve chair Paul Volcker raising interest rates to 20 percent. Although Reaganomics worked largely as expected in the area of industry deregulation, unemployment increased to 9.6 percent in 1983, and it failed massively to reduce the budget deficit. Contrary to supply-side theory, the 1981 tax cut was accompanied by a massive drop in tax revenues. Shortly after taking office, Reagan promised that his economic policies would balance the national budget by 1984. In fact, lower tax revenues and higher defense spending produced the largest budget deficits to that time, as shown in Figure 18.1.[33] Budget deficits continued until 1998, when a booming U.S. economy—plus increased tax rates (see below)—generated the first budget surplus since 1969. Economist Gregory Mankiw, who became head of President Bush's CEA, said that history failed to confirm the main conjecture of supply-side economics: that lower tax revenues would raise tax revenues: "When Reagan cut taxes after he was elected, the

supply-side economics Economic policies aimed at increasing the supply of goods (as opposed to decreasing demand); consists mainly of tax cuts for possible investors and less regulation of business.

FIGURE 18.1   Budget Deficits and Surpluses over Time

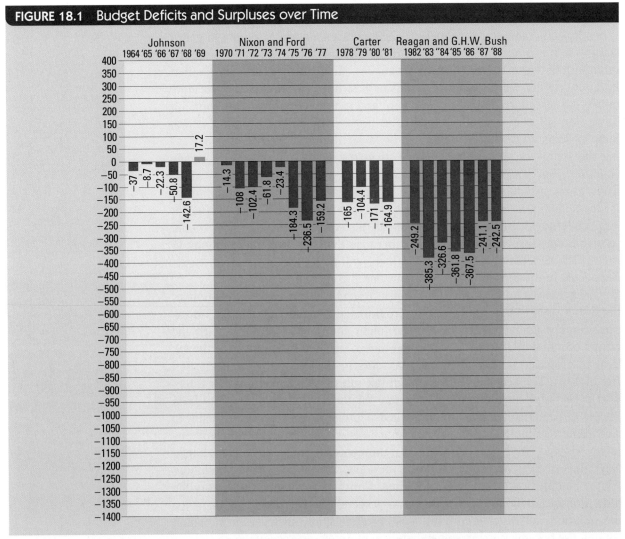

This chart shows the actual deficits and surpluses in constant 2005 dollars incurred under administrations from Johnson to Barack Obama. Even computed this way, the deficits were enormous under Reagan, George H. W. Bush, and even during Clinton's early years. Budget deficits were eventually eliminated under Clinton and replaced by surpluses. Larger deficits in constant dollars appeared again under George W. Bush.

Source: Executive Office of the President, *Budget of the United States Government, Fiscal Year 2011: Historical Tables* (Washington, D.C.: U.S. Government Printing Office, 2010), Table 1.3.

result was less tax revenue, not more."[34] Nevertheless, the supply-side idea that cutting taxes raises more revenue is still popular.[35]

Public Policy and the Budget

To most people the national budget is B-O-R-I-N-G. To national politicians, it is an exciting script for high drama. The numbers, categories, and percentages that numb normal minds cause politicians' nostrils to flare and their

FIGURE 18.1 (Continued)

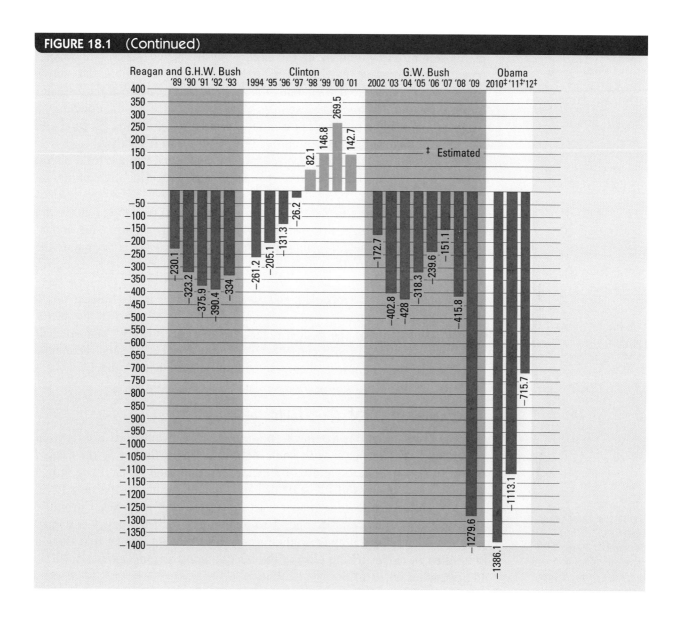

hearts to pound. The budget is a battlefield on which politicians wage war over the programs they support.

Control of the budget is important to members of Congress because they are politicians, and politicians want to wield power, not watch someone else wield it. Also, the Constitution established Congress, not the president, as the "first branch" of government and the people's representatives. Unfortunately for Congress, the president has emerged as the leader in shaping the budget. Although Congress often disagrees with presidential spending priorities, it has been unable to mount a serious challenge to presidential authority by presenting a coherent alternative budget.

Today, the president prepares the budget, and Congress approves it. This was not always the case. Before 1921, Congress prepared the budget under its constitutional authority to raise taxes and appropriate funds. The budget was formed piecemeal by enacting a series of laws that originated in the many committees involved in the highly decentralized process of raising revenue, authorizing expenditures, and appropriating funds. Executive agencies even submitted their budgetary requests directly to Congress, not to the president. No one was responsible for the big picture—the budget as a whole. The president's role was essentially limited to approving revenue and appropriations bills, just as he approved other pieces of legislation.

Congressional budgeting (such as it was) worked well enough for a nation of farmers, but not for an industrialized nation with a growing population and an increasingly active government. Soon after World War I, Congress realized that the budget-making process needed to be centralized. With the Budget and Accounting Act of 1921, it thrust the responsibility for preparing the budget onto the president. The act established the Bureau of the Budget to prepare the *president's* budget to be submitted to Congress each January. Congress retained its constitutional authority to raise and spend funds, but now Congress would begin its work with the president's budget as its starting point. And all executive agencies' budget requests had to be funneled for review through the Bureau of the Budget (which became the Office of Management and Budget in 1970); those consistent with the president's overall economic and legislative program were incorporated into the president's budget.

The Nature of the Budget

The national budget is complex. But its basic elements are not beyond understanding. We begin with some definitions. The *Budget of the United States Government* is the annual financial plan that the president is required to submit to Congress at the start of each year. It applies to the *next* **fiscal year**, the interval the government uses for accounting purposes. Currently, the fiscal year runs from October 1 to September 30. The budget is named for the year in which it *ends*, so the fiscal year (FY) 2011 budget that Obama submitted in early 2010 applies to the twelve months from October 1, 2010, to September 30, 2011.

Broadly, the budget defines **budget authority** (how much government agencies are authorized to spend on current and future programs); **budget outlays,** or expenditures (how much agencies are expected to spend this year, which includes past authorizations); and **receipts** (how much is expected in taxes and other revenues). President Obama's FY 2011 budget contained *authority* for expenditures of $3,691 billion, but it provided for *outlays* of $3,834 billion (including some previous obligations). His budget also anticipated *receipts* of $2,567 billion in current dollars, leaving an estimated *deficit* of $1,267 billion—the difference between receipts and outlays.

When the U.S. government runs a deficit, it borrows funds on a massive scale to finance its operation that fiscal year, thus limiting the supply of loanable funds for business investment. The long-run impact of Bush's budget deficits worried fiscal conservatives, who complained about the "GOP spending spree."[36] But the Bush administration seemed unconcerned;

fiscal year
The twelve-month period from October 1 to September 30 used by the government for accounting purposes. A fiscal year budget is named for the year in which it ends.

budget authority
The amounts that government agencies are authorized to spend for current and future programs.

budget outlays
The amounts that government agencies are expected to spend in the fiscal year.

receipts
For a government, the amount expected or obtained in taxes and other revenues.

Vice President Dick Cheney reportedly told the secretary of the treasury, "Reagan proved deficits don't matter."[37]

Indeed, economists seemed more concerned about the accumulated government debt, not the annual deficit.[38] A deficit in the annual budget is different from the **public debt**, which represents the sum of all unpaid government deficits. On July 25, 2010, the total public debt was $13.2 trillion.[39] Various "public debt clocks" calculate real-time estimates of the total public debt.[40] However, about $4.5 billion of the total debt is "intragovernmental"—money that one part of the government owes to another part. Defining public debt as money owed to lenders outside the government, the public debt was a staggering $8.7 *trillion*. Of this amount, almost 50 percent was held by institutions or individuals in other countries (see page 598).[41] If foreign lenders were to stop financing America's governmental annual deficit and national debt, the economy could suffer a serious blow, a prospect discussed frequently in financial pages, especially in the *Wall Street Journal*.[42]

Preparing the President's Budget

The budget that the president submits to Congress each winter is the end product of a process that begins the previous spring under the supervision of the **Office of Management and Budget (OMB)**. The OMB is located within the Executive Office of the President and is headed by a director appointed by the president, with the approval of the Senate. The OMB, with a staff of more than five hundred, is the most powerful domestic agency in the bureaucracy, and its director, who attends meetings of the president's cabinet, is one of the most powerful figures in government. The federal budget, with appendixes, is now available electronically on the OMB website.[43] Thousands of pages long, the budget contains more than numbers. It also explains individual spending programs in terms of national needs and agency objectives, and it analyzes proposed taxes and other receipts. Each year, reporters, lobbyists, and political analysts anxiously await publication of the president's budget, eager to learn his plans for government spending in the coming year.

The OMB initiates the budget process each spring by meeting with the president to discuss the economic situation and his budgetary priorities. It then sends broad budgeting guidelines to every government agency and requests their initial projection of how much money they will need for the next fiscal year. The OMB assembles this information and makes recommendations to the president, who then develops more precise guidelines describing how much each is likely to get. By summer, the agencies are asked to prepare budgets based on the new guidelines. By fall, they submit their formal budgets to the OMB, where budget analysts scrutinize agency requests, considering both their costs and their consistency with the president's legislative program. A lot of politicking goes on at this stage, as agency heads try to circumvent the OMB by pleading for their pet projects with presidential advisers and perhaps even the president himself.

Political negotiations over the budget may extend into the early winter—and often until it goes to the printer. The voluminous document looks very

public debt
The accumulated sum of past government borrowing owed to lenders outside the government.

Office of Management and Budget (OMB)
The budgeting arm of the Executive Office; prepares the president's budget.

much like a finished product, but the figures it contains are not final. In giving the president the responsibility for preparing the budget in 1921, Congress simply provided itself with a starting point for its own work. And even with this head start, Congress has a hard time disciplining itself to produce a coherent, balanced budget.

Passing the Congressional Budget

The president's budget must be approved by Congress. Its process for doing so is a creaky conglomeration of traditional procedures overlaid with structural reforms from the 1970s, external constraints from the 1980s, and changes introduced by the 1990 Budget Enforcement Act. The cumbersome process has had difficulty producing a budget according to Congress's own timetable.

The Traditional Procedure: The Committee Structure. Traditionally, the tasks of budget making were divided among a number of committees, a process that has been retained. Three types of committees are involved in budgeting:

- **Tax committees** are responsible for raising the revenues to run the government. The Ways and Means Committee in the House and the Finance Committee in the Senate consider all proposals for taxes, tariffs, and other receipts contained in the president's budget.
- **Authorization committees** (such as the House Armed Services Committee and the Senate Banking, Housing, and Urban Affairs Committee) have jurisdiction over particular legislative subjects. The House has about twenty committees that can authorize spending and the Senate about fifteen. Each pores over the portions of the budget that pertain to its area of responsibility. However, in recent years, power has shifted from the authorization committees to the appropriations committees.
- **Appropriations committees** decide which of the programs approved by the authorization committees will actually be funded (that is, given money to spend). For example, the House Armed Services Committee might propose building a new line of tanks for the army, and it might succeed in getting this proposal enacted into law. But the tanks will never be built unless the appropriations committees appropriate funds for that purpose. Thirteen distinct appropriations bills are supposed to be enacted each year to fund the nation's spending.

Two serious problems are inherent in a budgeting process that involves three distinct kinds of congressional committees. First, the two-step spending process (first authorization, then appropriation) is complex; it offers wonderful opportunities for interest groups to get into the budgeting act in the spirit of pluralist democracy. Second, because one group of legislators in each house plans for revenues and many other groups plan for spending, no one is responsible for the budget as a whole. In the 1970s, Congress added a new committee structure that combats the pluralist politics inherent in the old procedures and allows

tax committees
The two committees of Congress responsible for raising the revenue with which to run the government.

authorization committees
Committees of Congress that can authorize spending in their particular areas of responsibility.

appropriations committees
Committees of Congress that decide which of the programs passed by the authorization committees will actually be funded.

budget choices to be made in a more majoritarian manner, by votes in both chambers. In the 1980s, Congress tried to force itself to balance the budget by setting targets. In the 1990s, Congress introduced some belt-tightening reforms and passed important tax increases that led to a balanced budget. In the early 2000s, Congress allowed some reforms to lapse and cut taxes, recreating budget deficits. Here is a brief account of these developments.

Three Decades of Budgetary Reforms. Congress surrendered considerable authority in 1921 when it gave the president the responsibility of preparing the budget. During the next fifty years, attempts by Congress to regain control of the budgeting process failed because of jurisdictional squabbles between the revenue and appropriations committees.

In the 1970s, Congress added a new committee structure to combat the pluralist politics inherent in the old procedures and make budget choices in a more majoritarian manner, by roll-call votes in both chambers. The Budget and Impoundment Control Act of 1974 retained all the tax and appropriations committees (and chairpersons), while superimposing new House and Senate budget committees over the old committee structure. It created **budget committees** to supervise a comprehensive budget review process, aided by a new **Congressional Budget Office (CBO)**, with a staff of more than two hundred, to supply budgetary expertise equal to the president's OMB, so it can prepare credible alternative budgets for Congress.

The 1974 reforms also set up a timetable for the congressional budgeting process—that is, certain steps were to be taken by certain dates. This process worked reasonably well for the first few years, but it broke down when President Reagan submitted annual budgets heavy with military spending and huge deficits. The Democratic Congress refused to propose a tax increase to reduce the deficit without the president's cooperation, and Congress encountered increasing difficulty in enacting its budget resolutions according to its own timetable.

In the 1980s, Congress tried to force itself to balance the budget by setting annual targets to gradually lower the deficit. If Congress did not meet the deficit level in any year, a law would trigger across-the-board budget cuts. The very first year, Congress failed to meet its deficit target but did not pull the trigger on cutting spending. Unable to make the deficit meet the law again in 1987, Congress and the president simply changed the law to match the deficit, demonstrating that Congress lacked the will to force itself to balance the budget by an orderly plan of deficit reduction.

In the 1990s, Congress introduced some belt-tightening reforms and passed important tax increases that led to a balanced budget. Threatened by another huge deficit for FY 1991, Congress and President George H. W. Bush agreed on a new package of reforms and deficit targets in the **Budget Enforcement Act (BEA)** of 1990. The BEA defined two types of spending: **mandatory spending** and **discretionary spending**. Spending is mandatory for programs that have become **entitlements** (such as Social Security and veterans' pensions), which provide benefits to individuals legally entitled to them (see Chapter 19) and cannot be reduced without changing the law.

budget committees
One committee in each house of Congress that supervises a comprehensive budget review process.

Congressional Budget Office (CBO)
The budgeting arm of Congress, which prepares alternative budgets to those prepared by the president's OMB.

Budget Enforcement Act (BEA)
A 1990 law that distinguished between mandatory and discretionary spending.

mandatory spending
In the Budget Enforcement Act of 1990, expenditures required by previous commitments.

discretionary spending
In the Budget Enforcement Act of 1990, authorized expenditures from annual appropriations.

entitlements
Benefits to which every eligible person has a legal right and that the government cannot deny.

Discretionary spending entails expenditures authorized by annual appropriations, such as for the military. The law also established "pay-as-you-go"—called **pay-go**—restrictions on spending: any proposed expansion of an entitlement program must be offset by cuts to another program or by a tax increase. Similarly, any tax cut must be offset by a tax increase somewhere else or by spending cuts.[44] The law also imposed limits, or caps, on discretionary spending.

To get the Democratic Congress to pass the BEA, President George H. W. Bush accepted some modest tax increases—despite having vowed at the 1988 Republican National Convention: "Read my lips: no new taxes." The tax hike may have cost him reelection in 1992. Nevertheless, the 1990 law did limit discretionary spending and slowed unfinanced entitlements and tax cuts. The 1993 Deficit Reduction Act under Clinton made even more progress in reducing the deficit by cutting spending and raising taxes. By 1997, the deficit declined to $22 billion.[45]

The 1990 and 1993 budget agreements, both of which encountered strong opposition in Congress, helped pave the way for the historic **Balanced Budget Act (BBA)** that President Clinton and Congress negotiated in 1997. The BBA accomplished what most observers thought was beyond political possibility. It not only led to the balanced budget it promised but actually produced a budget surplus ahead of schedule—the first surplus since 1969.

The End of Budgetary Reform, 2000–Present. In the early 2000s, President Bush and Republicans in Congress advocated using the budget surplus for large across-the-board tax cuts to return money to taxpayers.[46] Although the caps on discretionary spending and pay-go requirements, established by the 1990 Budget Enforcement Act, helped balance the budget entering 2000, many members of Congress in both parties resented its restrictions on their freedom to make fiscal decisions. Accordingly, Congress allowed the caps on discretionary spending and the pay-go requirements to expire at the end of 2002.[47] Since 2002, the government has run budget deficits, not surpluses. In 2010, Congress, at Obama's request, reinstituted the pay-go rules in an effort to reduce the deficit.[48]

Tax Policies

So far, we have been concerned mainly with the spending side of the budget, for which appropriations must be enacted each year. The revenue side of the budget is governed by overall tax policy, which is designed to provide a continuous flow of income without annual legislation. A major text on government finance says that tax policy is sometimes changed to accomplish one or more of several objectives:

- To adjust overall revenue to meet budget outlays
- To make the tax burden more equitable for taxpayers
- To help control the economy by raising taxes (thus decreasing aggregate demand) or by lowering taxes (thus increasing demand)[49]

pay-go
The requirement that any tax cut or expansion of an entitlement program must be offset by a tax increase or other savings.

Balanced Budget Act (BBA)
A 1997 law that promised to balance the budget by 2002.

If those were the only objectives, the tax code might be simple, but tax policy also reflects two conflicting philosophies for distributing the costs of government: whether citizens should be taxed according to their ability to pay or for benefits they receive. Tax policy is further complicated because it is also used to advance social goals (such as home ownership through the deduction for mortgage interest) or to favor certain industries. To accommodate such deductions and incentives, the tax code (which is available over the Internet) runs over seven thousand pages.[50] Almost 95 percent of the government revenue in FY 2011 was expected from three major sources: individual income taxes (44 percent), social insurance taxes (36 percent), and corporate income taxes (12 percent).[51] Because the income tax accounts for most government revenue, discussion of tax policy usually focuses on that source.

Reform

Tax reform proposals are usually so heavily influenced by interest groups looking for special benefits that they end up working against their original purpose.[52] Without question, the tax code is complex. Before 1987, people paid different tax rates depending on where they fit in fourteen income brackets. President Reagan backed a sweeping reform that reduced the number of brackets to two and the rate for the top bracket from 70 to 28 percent. By eliminating many tax brackets, the new tax policy approached the idea of a flat tax—one that requires everyone to pay at the same rate.

We Gave at the Bureaucracy

One of many clerks working at the Cincinnati Internal Revenue Service Center in Covington, Kentucky, one of the ten centers operated by the Internal Revenue Service to process tax forms and taxpayer requests. Each processes millions of forms each year.

(© Mike Simons/Stringer/Getty Images)

A flat tax has the appeal of simplicity, but it violates the principle of **progressive taxation**, under which the rich pay proportionately higher taxes than the poor. The ability to pay has long been a standard of fair taxation, and surveys show that citizens favor this idea in the abstract.[53] In practice, however, they have different opinions, as we will see. Nevertheless, most democratic governments rely on progressive taxation to redistribute wealth and thus promote economic equality. Although wealthy people finance redistributive programs, they also benefit if redistribution alleviates extreme inequalities and prevents poor people from revolting.

In general, the greater the number of tax brackets, the more progressive a tax can be, for higher brackets can be taxed at higher rates. To deal with a budget deficit in 1990, President George H. W. Bush violated his campaign pledge of "no new taxes" by creating a third tax rate, 31 percent, for those with the highest incomes. In 1993, Clinton created a fourth level, 39.6 percent, moving toward a more progressive tax structure, although still less progressive than before 1987. Both presidents acted to increase revenue to reduce a soaring deficit.

Campaigning for president, George W. Bush promised to cut taxes. Soon after his election, he got Congress to pass a complex $1.35 trillion tax cut, with a top personal tax rate of 35 percent. Intended to stimulate the economy, the tax cut also reduced the revenue needed to match government spending.[54] Budget deficits quickly returned under Bush, owing to reduced revenue, a downturn in the stock market, and unanticipated expenses for homeland defense and military action following the September 11 attacks on America. The deficit zoomed to over a trillion dollars in Bush's last budget (see Figure 18.1), which reflected costs of his $168 billion stimulus package and his $700 billion Troubled Assets Relief Program (TARP; see pages 4 and 401). The deficit grew further with Obama's $787 billion stimulus package in 2009.

Comparing Tax Burdens

No one likes to pay taxes, so politicians find it popular to criticize the agency that collects taxes: the Internal Revenue Service. The income tax itself—and taxes in general—are also popular targets for U.S. politicians who campaign on getting government off the backs of the people. Is the tax burden on U.S. citizens truly too heavy? Compared with what? One way to compare tax burdens is to examine taxes over time in the same country; another is to compare taxes in different countries at the same time. By comparing taxes over time in the United States, we find that the total tax burden on U.S. citizens has not grown much since the 1950s. The federal tax rate for a family of four with the median household income was 20 percent in 1955 and 22.7 percent in 2008.[55] The largest increases have come in social insurance taxes, which have risen steadily to pay for the government's single largest social welfare program: aid to the elderly (see Figure 18.2 and Chapter 19).

Another way to compare tax burdens is to examine tax rates in different countries. By nearly two to one, more respondents in a post-2000 national survey thought that Americans pay a higher percentage of their income

progressive taxation
A system of taxation whereby the rich pay proportionately higher taxes than the poor; used by governments to redistribute wealth and thus promote equality.

Compared with What?

Tax Burdens in Thirty Countries

Compared with other nations, the tax burden in the United States is relatively low. Are you surprised? This graph compares tax burdens in 2007 in thirty countries as a percentage of gross domestic product (GDP), which is the market value of goods produced inside the country by workers, businesses, and government. The percentages encompass national, state, and local taxes and Social Security contributions. By this measure, the U.S. government extracts less in taxes from its citizens than do the governments of all Western democratic nations. At the top of the list stand Denmark and Sweden, well known for providing heavily for social welfare. Despite its low ranking in tax burden, the United States also supports the world's largest military force, to which it allocates about 3 percent of its GDP, or nearly 10 percent of its total tax receipts.

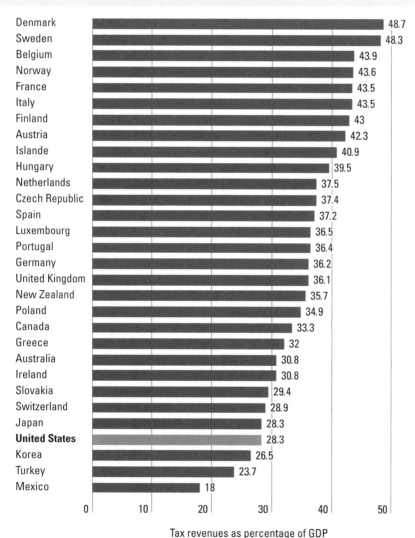

Denmark — 48.7
Sweden — 48.3
Belgium — 43.9
Norway — 43.6
France — 43.5
Italy — 43.5
Finland — 43
Austria — 42.3
Islande — 40.9
Hungary — 39.5
Netherlands — 37.5
Czech Republic — 37.4
Spain — 37.2
Luxembourg — 36.5
Portugal — 36.4
Germany — 36.2
United Kingdom — 36.1
New Zealand — 35.7
Poland — 34.9
Canada — 33.3
Greece — 32
Australia — 30.8
Ireland — 30.8
Slovakia — 29.4
Switzerland — 28.9
Japan — 28.3
United States — 28.3
Korea — 26.5
Turkey — 23.7
Mexico — 18

Tax revenues as percentage of GDP

Source: Organization for Economic Development and Cooperation, available at http://www.oecd.org/document/47/0,3343,en_2649_ 34533_44115887_1_1_1_37427,00.html.

in taxes than citizens in Western Europe.[56] They were flat wrong. Despite Americans' complaints about high taxes, the U.S. tax burden is not large compared with that of other democratic nations. As shown in "Compared with What? Tax Burdens in Thirty Countries," Americans' taxes are quite low in general compared with those in twenty-nine other democratic nations. Primarily because they provide their citizens with more generous social benefits (such as health care and unemployment compensation), almost every democratic nation taxes more heavily than the United States does.[57]

IDEALOG.ORG

Do you favor tax cuts for the wealthy or tax cuts for all? Take IDEAlog's self-test.

Spending Policies

The FY 2011 budget projects spending over $3,800,000,000,000—that's almost 4 trillion dollars (or 4,000 billion, if you prefer). Where does all that money

---

FIGURE 18.2   Federal Spending in 2011, by Function

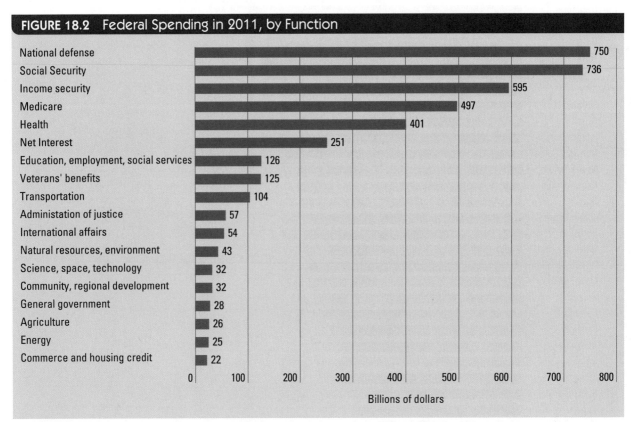

Function	Billions of dollars
National defense	750
Social Security	736
Income security	595
Medicare	497
Health	401
Net Interest	251
Education, employment, social services	126
Veterans' benefits	125
Transportation	104
Administation of justice	57
International affairs	54
Natural resources, environment	43
Science, space, technology	32
Community, regional development	32
General government	28
Agriculture	26
Energy	25
Commerce and housing credit	22

Billions of dollars

Federal budget authorities and outlays are organized into about twenty categories, some of which are mainly for bookkeeping purposes. This graph shows expected outlays for each of eighteen substantive functions in President Obama's FY 2011 budget. The final budget differed somewhat from this distribution because Congress amended some of the president's spending proposals. The graph makes clear the huge differences among spending categories. Military spending accounts for the largest share of the budget (20 percent) and is the largest amount in inflation-adjusted dollars since World War II. About 35 percent of government outlays are for Social Security and income security—that is, payments to individuals. Health costs (including Medicare) account for almost 25 percent more, and net interest consumes about 7 percent. This leaves relatively little for transportation, agriculture, justice, science, and energy—matters often regarded as important centers of government activity.

Source: Executive Office of the President, *Budget of the United States Government, Historical Tables, Fiscal Year 2011* (Washington, D.C.: U.S. Government Printing Office, 2010), Table 3–1.

go? Figure 18.2 breaks down the $3.8 trillion in proposed outlays in President Obama's FY 2011 budget by eighteen major governmental functions. The largest amount (20 percent of the total budget) was targeted for national defense.

From World War II to FY 1993, national defense (military spending) accounted for most spending under these categories, but it fell to second place after the collapse of communism and stayed there until FY 2009. Medicare and health, the fourth and fifth largest categories, together account for almost 24 percent of all budgetary outlays, which underscores the importance of controlling the costs of health care. The third largest, income security, encompasses various programs that provide a social safety net, including unemployment compensation, food for low-income parents and children, help for blind and disabled persons, and assistance for the homeless. The sixth largest category is interest on the accumulated national debt, which alone consumes over 6 percent of all national government spending. Some people think that money spent on "foreign aid" is a huge drain on our treasury. However, the $54 billion outlay for international affairs constitutes only about 1 percent of the total—and one-quarter of that is for the State Department and our embassies abroad.

Consider the relative shares of expenditures over time in broad categories, as in Figure 18.3. The effect of World War II is clear: spending for national defense rose sharply after 1940, peaked at about 90 percent of the budget in 1945, and fell to about 30 percent in peacetime. The percentage

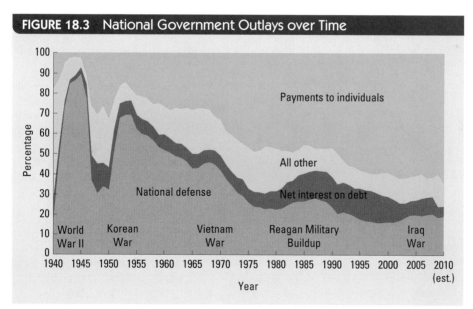

FIGURE 18.3 National Government Outlays over Time

This chart plots the percentage of the annual budget devoted to four major expense categories over time. It shows that significant changes have occurred in national spending since 1940. During World War II, defense spending consumed more than 80 percent of the national budget. Defense again accounted for most national expenditures during the Cold War of the 1950s. Following the collapse of communism in the 1990s, the military's share of the budget declined but rose again with the war in Iraq. The major story, however, has been the growth in payments to individuals—for example, in the form of Social Security benefits and health care.

Source: Executive Office of the President, *Budget of the United States Government, Fiscal Year 2011: Historical Tables* (Washington, D.C.: U.S. Government Printing Office, 2011), Table 6–1.

for defense rose again in the early 1950s, reflecting rearmament during the Cold War with the Soviet Union. Thereafter, defense's share of the budget decreased steadily (except for the bump during the Vietnam War in the late 1960s). This trend was reversed by the Carter administration in the 1970s and then shot upward during the Reagan presidency. Defense spending decreased under George H. W. Bush and continued to decline under Clinton. Following the September 11 attacks, President George W. Bush increased military spending 22 percent in FY 2003 over spending in 2001. Throughout his administration, military spending increased by 30 percent.[58] The Iraq war alone cost an estimated $600 billion over five years.[59]

Government payments to individuals (e.g., Social Security checks) consistently consumed less of the budget than national defense until 1971. Since then, payments to individuals have accounted for the largest portion of the national budget, and they have been increasing. Net interest payments also increased substantially during the years of budget deficits. Pressure from payments for national defense, individuals, and interest on the national debt has squeezed all other government outlays.

One might expect government expenditures to increase steadily, if only because of price inflation. In fact, national spending has barely outstripped inflation over fifty years. Figure 18.4 graphs government receipts and

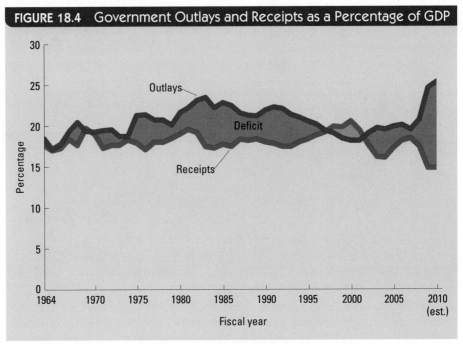

FIGURE 18.4 Government Outlays and Receipts as a Percentage of GDP

In this graph, outlays and receipts are each expressed as a percentage of the gross domestic product (GDP). The area between the two lines represents years of deficits or (rarely) surpluses. The graph portrays outlays and receipts in the context of economic growth (as some economists favor). It shows that—relative to the size of the economy—the national government (until the 2008 financial crisis) was spending about what it spent half a century ago, about 20 percent of the GDP. It also shows how large the deficit grew in 2009, relative to the economy.

Source: Executive Office of the President, *Budget of the United States Government, Fiscal Year 2011: Historical Tables* (Washington, D.C.: U.S. Government Printing Office, 2010), Table 1.3.

outlays as a percentage of the GDP, which eliminates the effect of inflation. It shows that national spending was about 20 percent of the GDP in the early 1950s and about the same until the Great Recession starting in 2007.

There are two major explanations for the general trend of increasing government spending. One is bureaucratic, the other political.

Incremental Budgeting ...

The bureaucratic explanation for spending increases involves **incremental budgeting**: bureaucrats, in compiling their funding requests for the following year, traditionally ask for the amount they got in the current year plus some incremental increase to fund new projects. Because Congress has already approved the agency's budget for the current year, it pays little attention to the agency's current size (the largest part of its budget) and focuses instead on the extra money (the increment) requested for the next year. As a result, few agencies are ever cut back, and spending continually goes up.

Incremental budgeting generates bureaucratic momentum that continually raises spending. Once an agency is created, it attracts a clientele that defends its existence and supports its requests for extra funds year after year. Because budgeting is a two-step process, agencies that get cut back in the authorizing committees sometimes manage (assisted by their interest group clientele) to get funds restored in the appropriations committees—and if not in the House, then perhaps in the Senate. Often appropriations committees approve spending for a specific purpose, known as an **earmark**. The practice of earmarking funds for "congressional pork" has greatly increased since the early 1990s.[60]

The Obama administration promised to publicize earmarks, thus hoping to reduce them. The OMB produced a website for that purpose, but it is not as useful as the private site run by Washingtonwatch.com.[61] Most earmark leaders are unapologetic. Illinois senator Democrat Dick Durbin said, "I can't wait to put out a press release to tell people what I have done," including targeting $300,000 to commemorate the Lincoln–Douglas debates.[62] How earmarks are viewed depends to some extent on how one views the role of a member of Congress. Senator Durbin and others think their role is to represent their constituents' interests. Viewed that way, earmarks are another manifestation of pluralist politics, which lives comfortably with the congressional budget-making process. In FY 2008 Congress passed appropriations bills that contained over eleven thousand earmarks, such as "$1 million for a river walk in Massachusetts, $200,000 for a hunting and fishing museum in Pennsylvania, and $213,000 for olive-fruit-fly research in France."[63]

... and Uncontrollable Spending

Earmarks are examples of **discretionary outlays** that Congress can choose to make. Most spending is enshrined in law and uncontrollable unless the law is changed. For example, Social Security legislation guarantees certain benefits to program participants when they retire. Medicare and veterans' benefits also entitle citizens to certain payments. These represent **mandatory outlays**. In Obama's FY 2011 budget, over 60 percent of all budget outlays

incremental budgeting
A method of budget making that involves adding new funds (an increment) onto the amount previously budgeted (in last year's budget).

earmark
Federal funds appropriated by Congress for use on local projects.

discretionary outlays
Payments made by legislators' choice and based on annual appropriations.

mandatory outlays
Payments that government must make by law.

were uncontrollable or relatively uncontrollable—mainly payments to individuals under Social Security, Medicare, and public assistance; interest on the public debt; and farm price supports. About half of the rest went for national defense or homeland security, leaving about 15 percent for domestic discretionary spending—excluding homeland security.[64]

To be sure, Congress could change the laws to abolish entitlement payments, and it does modify them through the budgeting process. But politics argues against large-scale reductions. What spending cuts would be acceptable to or even popular with the public? In the abstract, voters favor cutting government spending, but they tend to favor maintaining "government programs that help needy people and deal with important national problems."[65] Substantial majorities favor spending the same or even more on Social Security, Medicare, education, job training, programs for poor children, and the military. In fact, when a national poll asked whether respondents thought federal spending should be "increased, decreased, or kept about the same" for twelve different purposes—highwayslfare, public schools, crime, child care, border security, terrorism, aid to the poor, Social Security, science and technology, the environment, and foreign aid—respondents favored increasing or keeping about the same level of spending for *every* purpose![66]

In truth, a perplexed Congress, trying to reduce the budget deficit, faces a public that favors funding most programs at even higher levels than those favored by most lawmakers.[67] Moreover, spending for the most expensive of these programs—Social Security and Medicare—is uncontrollable. Americans have grown accustomed to certain government benefits, but they do not like the idea of raising taxes to pay for them.

IDEALOG.ORG

Do you prefer a bigger government with more services or smaller government with fewer services? Would you answer that question differently based on what you have learned about spending for federal programs? Take IDEAlog's self-test.

Taxing, Spending, and Economic Equality

As we noted in Chapter 1, the most controversial purpose of government is to promote equality, especially economic equality. Economic equality comes about only at the expense of economic freedom, for it requires government action to redistribute wealth from the rich to the poor. One means of redistribution is government tax policy, especially the progressive income tax. The other instrument for reducing inequalities is government spending through welfare programs. The goal in both cases is not to produce equality of outcome; it is to reduce inequalities by helping the poor.

The national government introduced an income tax in 1862 to help finance the Civil War. That tax was repealed in 1871, and the country relied on revenue from tariffs on imported goods to finance the national government. The tariffs acted as a national sales tax imposed on all citizens, and many manufacturers—themselves taxed at the same rate as a laborer—grew rich from undercutting foreign competition.[68] Followers of a new political movement, the Populists (see Chapter 8), decried the inequities of wealth and called for a more equitable form of taxation, an income tax. An income tax law passed in 1894 was declared unconstitutional by the Supreme Court the next year. The Democratic Party and the Populists accused the Court of defending wealth against equal taxation and called for amending the Constitution to permit an income tax in their 1896 platforms. A bill to do so was introduced in 1909 and ratified in 1913 as the Sixteenth Amendment.

The Sixteenth Amendment gave government the power to levy a tax on individual incomes, and it has done so every year since 1914.[69] From 1964 to 1981, people who reported taxable incomes of $100,000 or more were taxed at least 70 percent on all income above that figure or margin. Individuals with lower incomes paid taxes at progressively lower marginal rates. (Figure 18.5 shows how the top marginal rate has fluctuated over the years.) Let us look at the overall effect of government spending and tax policies on economic equality in America.

Government Effects on Economic Equality

We begin by asking whether government spending policies have any measurable effect on income inequality. Economists refer to a government payment to individuals through Social Security, unemployment insurance, food stamps, and other programs, such as agricultural subsidies, as a **transfer payment**. Transfer payments need not always go to the poor. In fact, one problem with the farm program is that the wealthiest farmers have often received the largest subsidies.[70] Nevertheless, most researchers have determined that transfer payments have had a definite effect on reducing income inequality.

A study of the poverty-reducing effects of taxes and transfer payments from 1979 to 2002 found that government policies cut the poverty rate almost in half for the years studied. For example, 20 percent of the population was below or at the poverty rate in 2002 based on income before taxes and transfer payments, but only 10.6 percent was at or below that rate after the government policies were figured into their situation.[71]

According to the principle of progressive taxation, tax rates are supposed to take more revenue from the rich than from the poor. Did that happen more at some times than others? A study of tax rates in 1979 (before the Reagan tax cuts), in 1989 (after the cuts), and in 2001 (after Clinton raised the rates) concluded, "The progressivity of federal tax rates varied substantially over the period."[72] In 1979, the 20 percent of households in the top income level paid 27.5 percent of their income in taxes, compared with 8.0 percent for the lowest income quintile—that is, the wealthy paid 3.4 times more than the poor. But with the lower top tax rate in 1989, the wealthy paid only 3.0 times more. After Clinton raised the top rate, the wealthiest 20 percent paid 4.4 times more in 2001 than the poorest 20 percent.[73]

Although the effective rates have varied during the recent past, the wealthy were always taxed at higher rates than the poor, in line with the principle of progressive taxation. Some oppose progressive taxation as a tool for redistributing income rooted in an "obsession" with inequality.[74] They can point out that the richest 1 percent of taxpayers paid 40 percent of all taxes in 2007.[75] Perhaps they paid so much because they *made* so much. If

transfer payment
A payment by government to an individual, mainly through Social Security or unemployment insurance.

FIGURE 18.5   The Ups and Downs of Top National Tax Rates

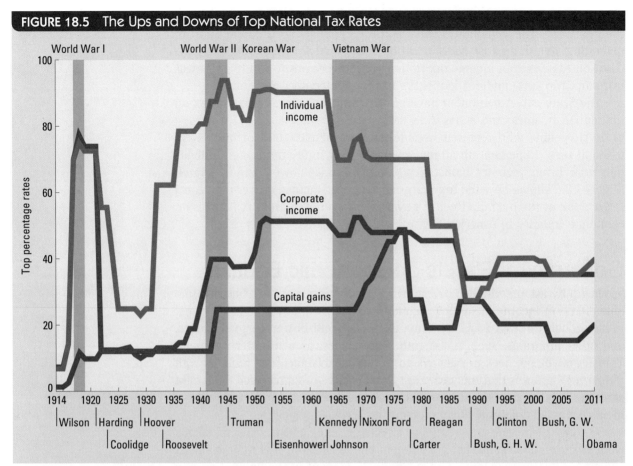

In 1913, the Sixteenth Amendment empowered the national government to collect taxes on income. Since then, the government has levied taxes on individual and corporate income and on capital gains realized by individuals and corporations from the sale of assets, such as stocks or real estate. Typically, incomes above certain levels are taxed at higher rates than incomes below those levels. This chart, which lists only the maximum tax rates, shows that these top tax rates have fluctuated wildly over time, from less than 10 percent to more than 90 percent. (They tend to be highest during periods of war.) During the Reagan administration, the maximum individual income tax rate fell to the lowest level since the Coolidge and Hoover administrations in the late 1920s and 1930s. The top rate increased slightly for 1991, to 31 percent, as a result of a law enacted in 1990, and jumped to 39.6 percent for 1994 under Clinton's 1993 budget package. The top rate was reduced in stages to 35 percent by Bush's tax plans in 2001 and 2003. Obama's 2011 budget restored the 39.6 rate for top earners, but its fate was undecided at press time.

Sources: *Wall Street Journal,* 18 August 1986, p. 10. Copyright 1986 by Dow Jones & Company, Inc. Reproduced with permission of Dow Jones & Company, Inc., in the format textbook via Copyright Clearance Center. Additional data from the Tax Policy Center, which reports tax brackets for individual years at http://www.taxpolicycenter.org, and from Brown, Kaplan & Liss, LLP.

the richest 1 percent of all taxpayers took in 23 percent of all income in the nation (which they did), some think that they should pay twice that percentage in taxes (which they almost did).[76]

However, the national income tax is only part of the story. In some cases, poorer citizens pay a larger share of their income in taxes than wealthier citizens. (As reported on YouTube, the world's third-richest man, Warren Buffett, paid 18 percent in income taxes in 2006 while his secretary paid 30 percent.) How can people in the lowest income group pay a higher percentage of their income in taxes than do those in the very highest group? The answer has to do with the combination of national, state, and local tax policies. Only the national income tax is progressive, with rates rising as income rises. The national payroll tax, which funds Social Security and Medicare, has two components—12.4 points go to Social Security and 2.9 to Medicare—for a total tax of 15.3 percent. The tax is regressive: its effective rate decreases as income increases beyond a certain point. Because employers typically pay half, the effective rate for taxpayers is usually 7.65 percent. However, the larger Social Security component is levied on only the first $106,800 of a person's income (in 2009), and there is no Social Security tax at all on wages over that amount. So the effective rate of the Social Security tax is higher for lower-income groups than for the very top group. In fact, 98 percent of employees in the lowest 20 percent paid more payroll tax than income tax, compared with only 8 percent of employees in the upper 20 percent.[77]

Most state and local sales taxes are equally regressive. Poor and rich usually pay the same flat rate on their purchases. But the poor spend almost everything they earn on purchases, which are taxed, whereas the rich are able to save. A study showed that the effective sales tax rate for the lowest income group was thus about 7 percent, whereas that for the top 1 percent was only 1 percent.[78]

In general, the nation's tax policies at all levels have historically favored not only those with higher incomes, but also the wealthy—those who draw income from capital (wealth) rather than labor—for example:

- There is no national tax at all on investments in certain securities, including municipal bonds (issued by local governments for construction projects).
- The tax on earned income (salaries and wages) is withheld from paychecks by employers under national law; the tax on unearned income (interest and dividends) is not.
- The tax on income from the sale of real estate or stocks (called *capital gains*) has typically been lower than the highest tax on income from salaries. (Income from selling property or from receiving stock dividends is taxed at 15 percent, while income from salaries is taxed at twice that rate.)

Effects of Taxing and Spending Policies over Time

In 1966, at the beginning of President Johnson's Great Society programs, the poorest fifth of American families received 4 percent of the nation's income after taxes, whereas the richest fifth received 46 percent. Forty years later, after many billions of dollars had been spent on social programs, the income gap between the rich and poor had actually *grown,* as illustrated in Figure 18.6. This is true despite the fact that many households in the lowest category had about one-third more earners, mainly women, going to work and that the average American worked ninety-three more hours (two full work weeks) per year in 2000 than in 1989.[79]

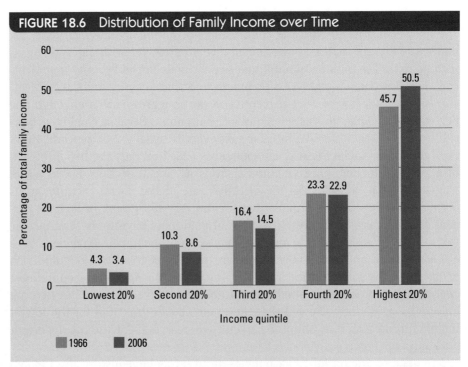

FIGURE 18.6 Distribution of Family Income over Time

Over the past four decades, the 20 percent of U.S. families with the highest incomes received over 45 percent of all income, and their share has increased over time. This distribution of income is one of the most unequal among Western nations. At the bottom end of the scale, the poorest 20 percent of families received less than 5 percent of total family income, and their share has decreased over time.

Sources: For the 1966 data, see Joseph A. Pechman, *Who Paid the Taxes, 1966–1985?* (Washington, D.C.: Brookings Institution, 1985), p. 74; the 2006 data come from the U.S. Census Bureau, "Income, Poverty, and Health Insurance Coverage in the United States: 2006," *Current Population Reports* (Washington, D.C.: U.S. Government Printing Office, August 2007), Table 2.

In a capitalist system, some degree of inequality is inevitable. Is there some mechanism that limits how much economic equality can be achieved and prevents government policies from further equalizing income, no matter what is tried? To find out, we can look to other democracies to see how much equality they have been able to sustain. A study of household inequality in eighteen developed countries found that the United States had the most unequal distribution of income. The median income of U.S. households in the top ninetieth percentile had 5.4 times the median income of the bottom tenth percentile. Italy was next most unequal, with the top group of Italians having 4.8 times the income of the bottom group. The average ratio for all nations was 3.8.[80] Other studies also show that our society has more economic inequality than other advanced nations.[81] The question is, Why?

Democracy and Equality

Although the United States is a democracy that prizes political equality for its citizens, its record in promoting economic equality is not as good. In fact, its distribution of wealth—which includes not only income but also ownership of savings, housing, automobiles, stocks, and so on—is strikingly unequal. According to the Federal Reserve, the wealthiest 1 percent of American families control about 33 percent of the nation's household wealth (property, stock holdings, bank accounts).[82] Moreover, the distribution of wealth among ethnic groups is alarming. The typical white family has an annual income almost 1.5 times that of both blacks and Hispanics.[83] If democracy means government "by the people," why aren't the people sharing more equally in the nation's wealth? If one of the supposed purposes of government is to promote equality, why are government policies not working that way?

One scholar theorizes that interest group activity in a pluralist democracy distorts government's efforts to promote equality. His analysis of pluralism sees "corporations and organized groups with an upper-income slant as exerting political power over and above the formal one-man-one-vote standard of democracy."[84] As you learned in Chapters 10 and 17, the pluralist model of democracy rewards groups that are well organized and well funded.

What would happen if national tax policy were determined according to principles of majoritarian rather than pluralist democracy? Perhaps not much, if public opinion is any guide. In a string of Gallup polls from 1985 to 2008, clear majorities consistently said that the distribution of wealth is not fair and favor some redistribution—but not through heavy taxes on the rich.[85] The people of the United States are not eager to redistribute wealth by increasing the only major progressive tax, the income tax. If national taxes must be raised, Americans favor a national sales tax over increased income taxes.[86] But a sales tax is a flat tax, paid by rich and poor at the same rate, and it would have a regressive effect on income distribution, promoting inequality. In one poll, the public also preferred a weekly $10 million national lottery to an increase in the income tax.[87] Because the poor are willing to chance more of their income on winning a fortune through lotteries than are rich people, lotteries (run by about forty states) also contribute to wealth inequality.[88]

Majoritarians might argue that most Americans fail to understand the inequities of the national tax system, which hides regressiveness in sales taxes and Social Security taxes. According to a national survey, Americans in the highest income categories (earning over $150,000 a year) understand the tax system much better than those at the lower income levels.[89] In Alabama, for example, income above $4,600 for a family of four went untaxed—meaning that most poor and all rich paid the same income tax, and the state relied mainly on sales and property taxes. In 2003, the conservative Republican governor of Alabama proposed a more progressive system of higher tax rates, mainly on the wealthy, only to have voters reject his reforms 2 to 1.[90] A black preacher and advocate of tax reform said that his parishioners like the (regressive) sales tax because they pay it in small increments.[91]

Will Do Finances for Food

Unemployment during the Great Recession that started in December 2007 peaked at 10.2 percent in October 2009 and hit all categories of employees—unskilled, semiskilled, skilled, and professional. This white middle-age professional man did not expect to hit the street to get a job.

(John Woodworth / Alamy)

So majoritarians cannot argue that the public demands "fairer" tax rates that take from richer citizens to help poorer ones. If the public did, the lowest-income families might receive a greater share of the national income than they do. Instead, economic policy is determined mainly through a complex process of pluralist politics that returns nearly half the national income to only 20 percent of the nation's families.

Summary

There are conflicting theories about how market economies work best. Laissez-faire economics holds that the government should keep its hands off the economy. Keynesian theory holds that government should take an active role in dealing with inflation and unemployment, using fiscal and monetary policies to produce desired levels of aggregate demand. Monetarists believe fiscal policies are unreliable; they opt instead to use the money supply to affect aggregate demand. Supply-side economists, who wielded influence on economic policy during the Reagan administration, focus on controlling the supply of goods and services rather than the demand for them. The remarkable growth of the U.S. economy in the mid- to late 1990s convinced many economists of the omniscience of free markets versus the evils of government regulation. The financial crisis of 2008 and its accompanying Great Recession led to a rethinking of economic principles. Meanwhile, the continuing process of globalization has eroded government's ability to manage its own economy completely.

Congress alone prepared the budget until 1921, when it thrust the responsibility onto the president. After World War II, Congress tried unsuccessfully to regain control of the process. Later, Congress managed to restructure the process under the House and Senate budget committees. The new process worked well until it confronted the huge budget deficits of the 1980s. Because so much of the budget involves military spending and uncontrollable payments to individuals, balancing the budget by reducing what remains—mainly spending for nonentitlement domestic programs—was

regarded as impossible. Unwilling to accept responsibility for passing a tax increase, Congress passed a deficit-reduction law in 1985. Under that law, deficits were to be reduced in stages, through automatic across-the-board cuts if necessary, until the budget was balanced by FY 1991. The deficit problem proved so intractable, however, that Congress had to amend the law in 1987 to extend the deadline to 1993—and the budget still wasn't balanced.

President George H. W. Bush promised "no new taxes" when campaigning for office in 1988, but he needed revenue to cut huge deficits and had to accept a 1990 law that raised the income tax. The 1990 act also amended Reagan's 1986 tax reform bill, which had drastically reduced the number of tax brackets to two and added a third bracket, at 31 percent, still much lower than the top rate before Reagan's reforms. In 1993, President Clinton won approval for a fourth bracket, at 40 percent. Responding to increased revenue and a hold on spending, the deficit declined. Aided by a growth economy, Clinton engineered taxing and spending changes in 1997 that produced a budget surplus in FY 1998—the first since 1969. The budget surplus disappeared in FY 2002 after President George W. Bush cut taxes and increased defense spending to combat terrorism. The budget deficit ballooned beyond $1 trillion in FY 2009 due to President Bush spending $189 billion to stimulate the economy and $700 billion to rescue financial institutions. The deficit expanded further in FY 2010 owing to reduced revenue from the bad economy and President Obama's $787 billion stimulus program to combat high unemployment.

Despite public complaints about high taxes, current U.S. tax rates are lower than those in most other major countries and lower than they have been since the Great Depression of the 1930s. But even with the heavily progressive tax rates of the past, the national tax system has done little to redistribute income. Government transfer payments to individuals have helped reduce some income inequalities, but the distribution of income is less equal in the United States than in most major Western nations.

Pluralist democracy as practiced in the United States has allowed well-organized, well-financed interest groups to manipulate taxing and spending policies to their benefit. The result is that a larger and poorer segment of society is paying the price. Taxing and spending policies in the United States are tipped in the direction of freedom rather than equality.

CourseMate Visit www.cengagebrain.com/shop/ ISBN/0495906182 for flashcards, web quizzes, videos and more!

Domestic Policy

Brendan Smialowski/Getty Images

Providing affordable health care for all. That goal was a central theme of Barack Obama's presidential campaign. He told one audience, "We'll guarantee health care for anyone who needs it [and] make it affordable for anyone who wants it. And we're not going to do it 20 years from now or 10 years from now; we're going to do it by the end of my first term as president."[1] Why the urgency? For starters, about 16 percent of America's gross domestic product (GDP) is currently spent on health care, a number that experts say will continue to rise (see "Compared with What? Health Spending and Its Possible Effects"). In 2007, the average American household spent 6 percent of its income on health care. The elderly and the poor spent closer to 10 percent of their incomes on health-related costs.[2] The rises in health-care costs and in premiums for private coverage in recent years have far outpaced inflation and increases in income.[3] Moreover, these cost increases mean that more and more small businesses are unable offer health insurance to their employees.[4]

Then there's the human side of this issue. According to one study, "an American family filed for bankruptcy in the aftermath of illness every 90 seconds" in 2007. Over 60 percent of all personal bankruptcies that year were attributed to medical costs. Most of those debtors actually had health insurance and were considered to be solidly middle class, but once they became ill, either they realized that their insurance plans weren't as comprehensive as they thought (the fine print on most plans can make one's head spin) or their illnesses kept them out of work for so long that they lost their jobs and the health insurance that came along with it.[5]

According to one analyst, most Americans are "one diagnosis away from financial collapse."[6] Lawrence Yurdin, a sixty-four-year-old computer specialist, is but one example. His insurance policy claimed to cover $150,000 per year in hospital care, but the fine print indicated that only his hospital room and board were covered, not the actual treatment that he received there for heart procedures. His bills ended up reaching $200,000, and he had to file for bankruptcy.[7]

Then there's the issue of the uninsured, who account for roughly 16 percent of the population, or about 46 million people (one study found that nearly 87 million people—almost one in three Americans under sixty-five years old—went without insurance at some point during 2007 and 2008).[8] Among their ranks are countless people who have tried to purchase private health insurance but have been denied coverage due to so-called pre-existing conditions. In many cases, these conditions are both severe and expensive to treat, such as heart disease. But in many other cases, the conditions that lead someone to be denied seem so trivial that it would be comical were the stakes not so high. Alex Lange, for example, is a four-month-old baby in Colorado who was denied coverage because his weight was in the ninety-ninth percentile. "I could understand if we could control what he's eating," said his father, "[but] he's breastfeeding. We can't put him on the Atkins diet or on a treadmill." Many others have been denied coverage for other seemingly absurd reasons, including acne, bunions, allergies, and toenail fungus.[9]

Denying coverage to people who are likely to incur high medical bills because of illnesses like cancer or diabetes makes sense from an economic perspective in private enterprise. But in modern democracies, the United States included, many people feel that the government should provide basic social services so that no one's quality of life falls below a certain level. The notion that only the wealthy or the healthy have access both to routine and life-saving medical care is at odds with modern understandings of the role of government. For most of the past ten years, well over half of the American public has believed that it is the responsibility of the federal government to make sure that all Americans have health-care coverage, though the extent of support declined somewhat when Congress began debating reform proposals in earnest in 2009.[10]

Yet solving the health-care problem in America is by no means straightforward. Challenges include the long-standing American aversion to "big government" (despite simultaneous support for government aid for those in need), figuring out how to control costs, determining which types of procedures should be covered, crafting a policy that garners enough votes in Congress to pass, and devising a way to pay for and implement these new programs, just to name a few. Despite these challenges, many observers say the health-care crisis in America is simply too dire to ignore. The future of the nation's economy demands that we find solutions, as does the ability to live up to the very preamble of the Constitution: to promote the general welfare.

IN OUR OWN WORDS

Listen to Jerry Goldman discuss the main points and themes of this chapter.

www.cengagebrain.com/shop/ISBN/0495906182

public policy
A general plan of action adopted by the government to solve a social problem, counter a threat, or pursue an objective.

General plans of action adopted by government to solve a social problem, counter a threat, or pursue an objective, that is, a **public policy**, often appear promising or frightening in theory, but what matters most is how they behave in practice. The debate about health-care reform is a textbook example that is both promising and frightening. In Chapter 17 we examined the policymaking process in general; in this chapter, we look at specific domestic social policies, that is, government plans of action targeting concerns internal to the United States. These are among the most enduring and costly programs that the government has launched on behalf of its citizens. Four key questions guide our inquiry: What are the origins and politics of specific domestic policies? What are the effects of these policies once they are implemented? Why do some policies succeed and others fail? Finally, are disagreements about policy really disagreements about values?

Public policies sometimes seem as numerous as fast-food restaurants, offering something for every appetite and budget. Despite this wide range of policies worth exploring, we focus our efforts in this chapter on a few key areas: Social Security, public assistance, health care, education, and immigration. These policies deserve special consideration for four reasons. First, government expenditures in these areas represent more than half the national budget.[11] All citizens ought to know how their resources are allocated and why. Second, one goal of social welfare policies is to alleviate some consequences of economic inequality. Nevertheless, poverty remains a fixture of American life, and we must try to understand why. Third, these policies pose some vexing questions involving the conflicts between freedom and order and between freedom and equality. Fourth, despite increasing concerns about terrorism and the war in Iraq, social welfare issues (along with the economy) have remained at the forefront of the nation's agenda. In 2009, health care, education, unemployment, and immigration were among the top ten issues mentioned in surveys that asked Americans to name the nation's most important problem.[12] Many Americans report being dissatisfied with the availability of affordable health care, the Social Security system, and the nation's efforts to deal with poverty and homelessness.[13]

This chapter concentrates on policies based on the authority of the national government to tax and spend for the general welfare. But it is important to recognize that state and local governments play a vital role in shaping and directing the policies that emanate from Washington. It is not an understatement to say that the success of several national domestic initiatives depends in large part on the capacities of governments at lower levels to effectively carry them out.

The Development of the American Welfare State

The most controversial purpose of government is to promote social and economic equality. To do so may conflict with the freedom of some citizens because it requires government action to redistribute income from rich to poor. This choice between freedom and equality constitutes the modern dilemma of government; it has been at the center of many conflicts in U.S. public policy since World War II. On one hand, most Americans believe that government should help the needy. On the other hand, they do not want to sacrifice their own standard of living to provide government handouts to those whom they may perceive as shiftless and lazy.

At one time, governments confined their activities to the minimal protection of people and property—to ensuring security and order. Now, almost every modern nation may be characterized as a **welfare state** serving as the provider and protector of individual well-being through economic and social programs. **Social welfare programs** are government programs designed to provide the minimum living conditions necessary for all citizens. Income for the elderly, health care, public assistance, and education are among the concerns addressed by government social welfare programs.

Social welfare policy is based on the premise that society has an obligation to provide for the basic needs of its members. The term *welfare state* describes this protective role of government. Moreover, the public wants government to shoulder some of this responsibility. In national surveys, a majority of Americans regularly agrees that money and wealth should be more evenly distributed and that the federal government should do more to combat poverty.[14]

America today is far from being a welfare state on the order of Germany or Great Britain; those nations provide many more medical, educational, and unemployment benefits to their citizens than does the United States. However, the United States does have several social welfare functions. To understand American social welfare policies, you must first understand the significance of a major event in U.S. history—the Great Depression—and the two presidential plans that extended the scope of the government, the New Deal and the Great Society. The initiatives that flowed from those presidential programs

welfare state
A nation in which the government assumes responsibility for the welfare of its citizens by providing a wide array of public services and redistributing income to reduce social inequality.

social welfare programs
Government programs that provide the minimum living standards necessary for all citizens.

dominated national policy until changes in the 1980s and 1990s produced retrenchment in important aspects of the American welfare state. They established the idea that it is the role of the federal government to help meet the basic needs of its citizens, though debates about the extent of the government's obligations in this regard remain vibrant to this day.

The Great Depression

Throughout its history, the U.S. economy has experienced alternating good times and hard times, generally referred to as business cycles (see Chapter 18). The **Great Depression** was by far the longest and deepest setback that the American economy has ever experienced. It began with the stock market crash on October 24, 1929, a day known as Black Thursday, and did not end until the start of World War II. By 1933, one out of every four U.S. workers was unemployed, and millions more were underemployed. To put that number into perspective, the average annual U.S. unemployment rate since the end of World War II has never topped 10 percent.[15] No other event, with the exception of World War II perhaps, has had a greater effect on the thinking and the institutions of government in the twentieth and twenty-first centuries than the Great Depression.

Great Depression
The longest and deepest setback the American economy has ever experienced. It began with the stock market crash on October 24, 1929, and did not end until the start of World War II.

In the 1930s, the forces that had stemmed earlier business declines were no longer operating. There were no more frontiers, no growth in export markets, no new technologies to boost employment. Unchecked, unemployment spread like an epidemic, and the crisis fueled itself. Workers who lost their source of income could no longer buy the food, goods, and services that kept the economy going. Thus, private industry and commercial farmers tended to produce more than they could sell profitably. Closed factories, surplus crops, and idle workers were the consequences.

The industrialized nations of Europe were also hit hard. The value of U.S. exports fell, and the value of imports increased; this led Congress to impose high tariffs, which strangled trade and fueled the Depression. From 1929 to 1932, more than 44 percent of the nation's banks failed when unpaid loans exceeded the value of bank assets. Farm prices fell by more than half in the same period. The uprooted—tens of thousands of dispossessed farm families—headed West with their possessions atop their cars and trucks in a hopeless quest for opportunity. Author John Steinbeck described the plight of these desperate poor in his Pulitzer Prize–winning novel, *The Grapes of Wrath* (1939).

The New Deal

In his speech accepting the presidential nomination at the 1932 Democratic National Convention, Franklin Delano Roosevelt, then governor of New York, made a promise: "I pledge you, I pledge myself to a new deal for the American people." Roosevelt did not specify the contents of his **New Deal**, but the term was later applied to measures Roosevelt's administration undertook to stem the Depression. Some scholars regard these measures as the most imaginative burst of domestic policy in the nation's history. Others see them as the source of massive government growth without matching benefits.

President Roosevelt's New Deal had two phases. The first, which ended in 1935, was aimed at boosting prices and lowering unemployment through programs like the Civilian Conservation Corps (CCC), which provided short-term jobs for young men. The second phase, which ended in 1938, was aimed at aiding the forgotten people: the poor, the aged, unorganized working men and women, and farmers. The hallmark of this second phase is the Social Security program.

Poverty and unemployment persisted despite the best efforts of Roosevelt and his massive Democratic majorities in Congress. By 1939, 17 percent of the work force (more than 9 million people) was still unemployed. Only World War II was able to provide the economic surge needed to yield lower unemployment and higher prices, the elusive goals of the New Deal.

Roosevelt's overwhelming popularity did not translate into irresistibly popular policy or genuine popularity for government. Public opinion polls revealed that Americans were divided over New Deal policies through the early 1940s. Eventually, the New Deal became the status quo, and Americans grew satisfied with it. But Americans remained wary of additional growth in the power of the national government.[16]

New Deal
The measures advocated by the Franklin D. Roosevelt administration to alleviate the Depression.

Economists still debate whether the actual economic benefits of the New Deal reforms outweighed their costs. It is clear, however, that New Deal policies initiated a long-range trend toward government expansion. And another torrent of domestic policymaking burst forth three decades later.

The Great Society

John F. Kennedy's election in 1960 brought to Washington a corps of public servants sensitive to the needs of the poor and minorities. This raised expectations that national government policies would benefit these groups. But Kennedy's razor-thin margin of victory was far from a mandate to improve the plight of the poor and dispossessed.

In the aftermath of Kennedy's assassination in November 1963, his successor, Lyndon Baines Johnson, received enormous support for a bold policy program designed to foster equality (see Chapter 12). After winning the 1964 presidential election in a landslide over his opponent, Barry Goldwater, LBJ entered 1965 committed to pushing an aggressive and activist domestic agenda. In his 1965 State of the Union address, President Johnson offered his own version of the New Deal: the **Great Society**, a broad array of programs designed to redress political, social, and economic inequality. In contrast to the New Deal, few, if any, of Johnson's programs were aimed at short-term relief; most were targeted at chronic ills requiring a long-term commitment by the national government.

A vital element of the Great Society was the **War on Poverty**. The major weapon in this war was the Economic Opportunity Act (1964); its proponents promised that it would eradicate poverty in ten years. The act encouraged a variety of local community programs to educate and train people for employment. Among them were college work-study programs, summer employment for high school and college students, loans to small businesses, a domestic version of the Peace Corps (called VISTA, for Volunteers in Service to America), educational enrichment and nutrition for preschoolers through Head Start, and legal services for the poor. It offered opportunity: a hand up rather than a handout.

Retrenchment and Reform

Despite the declining national poverty rate that ensued after the passage of major domestic legislation of the 1960s, in subsequent years critics seized on the perceived shortcomings of the growing American welfare state. Perhaps these counterarguments were the predictable result of the high standards that LBJ and his team had set, such as their promise to eliminate poverty in a decade. The fact that poverty still persisted (even though it had declined) and had become more concentrated in areas that the Great Society had targeted (inner cities and rural areas) suggested to some observers that the Johnson effort was a failure. In the War on Poverty, these critics claimed, poverty had won.

Those arguments began to take hold in the latter part of the 1970s and in part helped Ronald Reagan capture the White House in 1980. Reagan's

Great Society
President Lyndon Johnson's broad array of programs designed to redress political, social, and economic inequality.

War on Poverty
A part of President Lyndon Johnson's Great Society program, intended to eradicate poverty within ten years.

overwhelming victory and his landslide reelection in 1984 forced a reexamination of social welfare policy. In office, the president professed support for the "truly needy" and for preserving a "reliable safety net of social programs," by which he meant the core programs begun in the New Deal. Nevertheless, his administration abolished several social welfare programs and redirected others.

In a dramatic departure from his predecessors (Republicans as well as Democrats), Reagan shifted emphasis from economic equality to economic freedom (Presidents Johnson and Reagan are compared in Chapter 12). He questioned whether government alone should continue to be responsible for guaranteeing the economic and social well-being of less fortunate citizens. And he maintained that to the extent that government should bear this responsibility, state and local governments could do so more efficiently than the national government.

Congress, controlled by Democrats, blocked some of Reagan's proposed cutbacks, and many Great Society programs remained in force, although with less funding. Overall spending on social welfare programs (as a proportion of the gross national product) fell to about mid-1970s levels. But the dramatic growth in the promotion of social welfare that began with the New Deal ended with the Reagan administration. It remained in repose during George H. W. Bush's term in the White House.

After Bush's term in office, the rest of the 1990s produced important reforms to the American welfare state. Recognizing persistent concerns that federal welfare policy made recipients dependent on government rather than helping them to live independent lives, President Bill Clinton entered office in 1993 hoping to reform the system while simultaneously protecting the basic fabric that was the nation's safety net. Charting that middle course suited Clinton's political tendencies. It also became absolutely necessary after 1994 when Republicans took control of Congress. By the end of Clinton's two terms, important reforms emerged in public assistance, which we describe later in this chapter. Then the George W. Bush administration led the greatest expansion of welfare benefits for seniors with the passage of the Medicare drug program. President Obama, in turn, enacted the biggest welfare state reform since the New Deal, with the passage of health-care reform in 2010.

Social Security

Insurance is a device for protecting against loss. Since the late nineteenth century, there has been a growing tendency for governments to offer **social insurance**, which is government-backed protection against loss by individuals, regardless of need. The most common forms of social insurance offer health protection and guard against losses from worker sickness, injury, and disability; old age; and unemployment. The first example of social insurance in the United States was workers' compensation. Beginning early in the twentieth century, most states created systems of insurance that compensated workers who lost income because they were injured in the workplace.

social insurance
A government-backed guarantee against loss by individuals without regard to need.

Social insurance benefits are distributed to recipients without regard to their economic status. Old-age benefits, for example, are paid to workers—rich or poor—provided that they have enough covered work experience and have reached the required age. Thus, social insurance programs are examples of entitlements. Today, national entitlement programs consume about half of every dollar of government spending; the largest entitlement program is **Social Security**.

As a general concept, Social Security is social insurance that provides economic assistance to people faced with unemployment, disability, or old age. In most social insurance programs, employees and employers contribute to a fund from which employees later receive payments. If you examine your end-of-year W2 wage and tax statement from your employer, you should be able to find your contributions to two specific programs for social insurance in the United States: Social Security and Medicare. The Social Security tax, which was assessed at a rate of 6.20 percent for the first $106,800 of wages earned in 2010, supports disability, survivors', and retirement benefits. The Medicare tax finances much (but not all) of the Medicare program and was assessed at 1.45 percent of all wages in 2010.[17]

Origins of Social Security

Compared with its international peers, the idea of Social Security came late to the United States. As early as 1883, Germany enacted legislation to protect workers against the hazards of industrial life. Most European nations adopted old-age insurance after World War I; many provided income support for the disabled and income protection for families after the death of the principal wage earner. In the United States, however, the needs of the elderly and the unemployed were left largely to private organizations and individuals. Although twenty-eight states had old-age assistance programs by 1934, neither private charities nor state and local governments—nor both together—could cope with the prolonged unemployment and distress that resulted from the Great Depression. It became clear that a national policy was necessary to deal with a national crisis.

The first important step came on August 14, 1935, when President Franklin Roosevelt signed the **Social Security Act**, which remains the cornerstone of the modern American welfare state. The act's framers developed three approaches to the problem of dependence. The first provided social insurance in the form of old-age and surviving-spouse benefits and cooperative state-national unemployment assistance. To ensure that the elderly did not retire into poverty, it created a program to provide income to retired workers. Its purpose was to guarantee that the elderly would have a reliable base income after they stopped working. (Most Americans equate Social Security with this part of the Social Security Act.) An unemployment insurance program, financed by employers, was also created to provide payments for a limited time to workers who were laid off or dismissed for reasons beyond their control.

The second approach provided aid to the destitute in the form of grants-in-aid to the states. The act represented the first permanent national commitment

Social Security
Social insurance that provides economic assistance to persons faced with unemployment, disability, or old age. It is financed by taxes on employers and employees.

Social Security Act
The law that provided for Social Security and is the basis of modern American social welfare.

to provide financial assistance to the needy aged, needy families with dependent children, the blind, and (since the 1950s) the permanently and totally disabled. By the 1990s, the disabled category had grown to include those who are learning disabled and those who are drug and alcohol dependent.

The third approach provided health and welfare services through federal aid to the states. Included were health and family services for disabled children and orphans and vocational rehabilitation for the disabled.

How Social Security Works

Although the Social Security Act encompasses many components, when most people think of "Social Security," they have the retirement security element of the law in mind. Specifically, revenues for old-age retirement security go into their own *trust fund* (each program contained in the Social Security Act has a separate fund). The fund is administered by the Social Security Administration, which became an independent government agency in 1995. Trust fund revenue can be spent only for the old-age benefits program. Benefits, in the form of monthly payments, begin when an employee reaches retirement age, which today is sixty-five. (People can retire as early as age sixty-two but with reduced benefits.) The age at which full benefits are paid is now sixty-seven for persons born in 1960 or later.

Many Americans believe that each person's Social Security contributions are set aside specifically for his or her retirement, like a savings account.[18] But Social Security doesn't operate like that at all. Instead, the Social Security taxes collected today pay the benefits of today's retirees with surpluses held over, in theory at least, to help finance the retirement of future generations. Thus, Social Security (and social insurance in general) is not a form of savings; it is a pay-as-you-go tax system. Today's workers support today's elderly and other program beneficiaries.

When the Social Security program began, it had many contributors and few beneficiaries. The program could thus provide relatively large benefits with low taxes. In 1937, for example, the tax rate was 1 percent, and the Social Security taxes of nine workers supported each beneficiary. As the program matured and more people retired or became disabled, the ratio of workers to recipients decreased. In 2008, the Social Security system paid benefits of $615 billion to 51 million people and collected tax revenue from 162 million, a ratio of roughly 3.2 workers for every beneficiary. By 2030, the ratio will decline to just over 2.0 workers for every beneficiary.[19]

The solvency of the Social Security program will soon be tested. As the baby-boom generation retires beginning in about 2010, politicians will face an inevitable dilemma: lower benefits and generate the ire of retirees, or raise taxes and generate the ire of taxpayers. To put off this day of reckoning, policymakers built up the trust funds' assets in anticipation of the growth in the number of retirees. But based on projections of the most recent report of the trustees of the Social Security system, the program's assets will be exhausted by 2037 under intermediate economic and demographic assumptions (see Figure 19.1 and the section on "Social Security Reform," p. 639).[20]

At one time, federal workers, members of Congress, judges, and even the president were omitted from the Social Security system. Today there are few exceptions. Because the system is a tax program, not a savings program, universal participation is essential. If participation were not compulsory, revenue would be insufficient to provide benefits to current retirees. Government—the only institution with the authority to coerce—requires all employees and their employers to contribute, thereby imposing restrictions on freedom.

People who currently pay into the system will receive retirement benefits financed by future participants. As with a pyramid scheme or a chain letter, success depends on the growth of the base. If the birthrate remains steady or grows, future wage earners will be able to support today's contributors when they retire. If the economy expands, there will be more jobs, more income, and a growing wage base to tax for increased benefits to retirees. But suppose the birthrate falls, or mortality declines, or unemployment rises and the economy falters. Then contributions could decline to the point at which benefits exceed revenues. The pyramidal character of Social Security is its Achilles' heel.

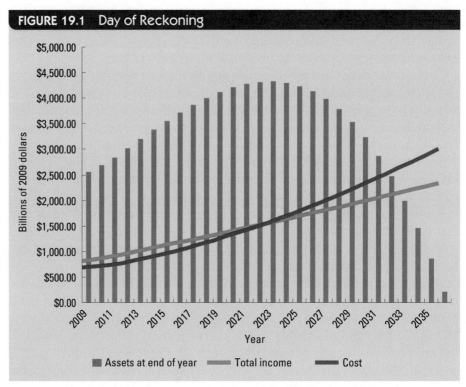

FIGURE 19.1   Day of Reckoning

■ Assets at end of year   ▬ Total income   ▬ Cost

Social security tax revenues plus interest exceed benefits paid out. But as of 2010, tax revenues alone were no longer sufficient to meet the cost of Social Security. With bankruptcy of the system looming so predictably, the debate over change boils down to two questions that politicians politely decline to answer: How soon will the national government change the current system, and how much will it change it?

Source: Social Security Administration, "Operations of the Combined OASI and DI Trust Funds, in Current Dollars," in *The 2009 Annual Report of the Board of Trustees of the Federal Old-Age and Survivors Insurance and Federal Disability Insurance Trust Funds* (Washington, D.C.: U.S. Government Printing Office, 12 May 2009), http://www.ssa.gov/OACT/TR/2009/lr6f8.html.

Who Pays? Who Benefits?

"Who pays?" and "Who benefits?" are always important questions in government policymaking, and they continue to shape Social Security policy. In 1968, the Republican Party platform called for automatic increases in Social Security payments as the cost of living rose. The theory was simple: as the cost of living rises, so should retirement benefits; otherwise, benefits are paid in "shrinking dollars" that buy less and less. Cost-of-living adjustments (COLAs) became a political football in 1969 as Democrats and Republicans tried to outdo each other by suggesting larger increases for retirees. The result was a significant expansion in benefits, far in excess of the cost of living. The beneficiaries were the retired, who were beginning to flex their political muscle. Politicians knew that alienating this constituency could lose them an election.[21]

In 1972, Congress adopted automatic adjustments in benefits and in the dollar amount of contributors' wages subject to tax, so that revenue would expand as benefits grew. This approach set Social Security on automatic pilot. When most economists criticized the COLA as overly generous, Congress tempered it. The 2009 COLA was 5.8 percent. Due to the Great Recession that began in late 2007, the consumer price index did not rise in 2009, which meant that there was no COLA in 2010. This marked the first time that benefits did not rise since adjustments were made automatic in the 1970s. Benefits will remain stagnant in 2011 as well.[22]

When stagflation (high unemployment coupled with high inflation) took hold in the 1970s, it jeopardized the entire Social Security system. Stagflation produced an economic vise: unemployment meant a reduction in revenue; high inflation meant automatically growing benefits. This one-two punch drained Social Security Trust Fund reserves to critically low levels in the late 1970s and early 1980s. Meanwhile, other troubling factors were becoming clear. A lower birthrate meant that in the future, fewer workers would be available to support the pool of retirees. And the number of retirees would grow as average life spans lengthened and the baby-boom generation retired. Higher taxes, an unpopular political move, loomed as one alternative. Another was to pay for Social Security out of general revenues—that is, income taxes. Social Security would then become a public assistance program, similar to welfare, which some people believed would deal a political blow to the program. In 1983, shortly before existing Social Security benefit funds would have become exhausted, Congress and President Reagan agreed to a solution that called for two painful adjustments: increased taxes and reduced benefits.

Social Security Reform

The changes enacted in 1983 prolonged the life of the Social Security system. However, future economic conditions will determine its success or failure. Concern over the future survival of Social Security is reflected in public opinion polls. For example, in a nationwide poll conducted in February 2009, 61 percent of adults said that they were not confident that Social Security would have the money available to pay for their benefits throughout their retirement.[23]

In the 2000 and 2004 presidential election campaigns, both major parties sought to capitalize on Social Security reform as an issue. The Republicans argued that if the system is not changed, the country will be faced with "three bitter choices": raising taxes, reducing benefits, or adding to the national debt. As an alternative, Republicans proposed a plan that would allow individual workers to invest their own payroll taxes in the stock market in hopes of earning a higher rate of return than currently paid to the Social Security Trust Funds. However, people who wanted to stay in the current Social Security system could choose to do so.[24] The Democrats also proposed a private investment program, but theirs would have been in addition to the existing program rather than a reform of it. The positions of both parties illustrated how each side, in attempting to extend the life of the Social Security program, emphasized different values. The Republicans relied more on choice and freedom as values in their proposed reforms. The Democrats professed a commitment to greater equality as a value.

President Bush pushed hard for the Republican version of Social Security reform, especially during his second term. But he was unable to generate enough public support for privatizing Social Security. Support was especially low if the survey question specifically called attention to the increased risk associated with investing in the stock market and the fact that the level of one's benefits would become more dependent on fluctuations in values of stocks.[25] Moreover, Bush's party lost control of Congress in 2006. Thus, one of Bush's major domestic policy agendas went unaddressed, and the problem of the program's impending insolvency remains.

When Obama took office in 2009, addressing the economic recession became his first priority, and reforming Social Security returned to the back burner, though Obama has stated that he "stands firmly opposed to privatization."[26] It is unlikely that Congress will simply let the Social Security fund run dry, which means that the issues of raising taxes, raising the retirement age, reducing benefit levels, and devising alternative means of controlling the fund will return to the agenda. Yet given the unpopularity of all of these options, decision makers will be reluctant to act until it becomes absolutely necessary.

IDEALOG.ORG

Should the government invest Social Security taxes in the stock market? Take IDEAlog's self-test.

Public Assistance

Most people mean **public assistance** when they use the term *welfare* or *welfare payments*; it is government aid to individuals who demonstrate a need for that aid. Although much public assistance is directed toward those who lack the ability or the resources to provide for themselves or their families, the poor are not the only recipients of welfare. Corporations, farmers, and college students are among the many recipients of government aid in the form of tax breaks, subsidized loans, and other benefits.

Public assistance programs instituted under the Social Security Act, in contrast to the retirement security components of the law, are known today

public assistance
Government aid to individuals who can demonstrate a need for that aid.

as *categorical assistance programs*. They include (1) old-age assistance for the needy elderly not covered by old-age pension benefits, (2) aid to the needy blind, (3) aid to needy families with dependent children, and (4) aid to the totally and permanently disabled. Adopted initially as stop-gap measures during the Great Depression, these programs have become **entitlements**– benefits to which every eligible person has a legal right and that the government cannot deny. They are administered by the states, but the bulk of the funding comes from the national government's general tax revenues. Because the states also contribute to the funding of their public assistance programs, the benefits and some of the standards that define eligibility can vary widely from state to state.

Poverty in the United States

Until 1996, the national government imposed national standards on state welfare programs. It distributed funds to each state based on the proportion of its population that was living in poverty. That proportion is determined on the basis of a federally defined **poverty level**, or poverty threshold, which is the minimum cash income that will provide for a family's basic needs. The poverty level varies by family size and is calculated as three times the cost of a minimally nutritious diet for a given number of people over a given time period. The threshold is computed in this way because research suggested that poor families of three or more persons spend approximately one-third of their income on food.[27]

The poverty level is fairly simple to apply, but it is only a rough measure for distinguishing the poor from the nonpoor. Using it is like using a wrench as a hammer: it works, but not very well. For instance, the poverty level has been fairly constant since the early 1970s, even though other indicators of public well-being, like the infant mortality rate, the quality of housing, and the percentage of adults with a high school diploma, show dramatic improve-ment in that same time period.[28] Policymakers have considered different approaches to determine how much a family of four needs to live in the United States, but they have been reluctant to abandon a measure that has been in use since the 1960s. Critics of the current formula argue that a more accurate measure of the poverty level would show higher levels of poverty in the United States, since the proportion of income spent on food has declined as the costs of housing, child care, health care, and other daily expenses have increased.[29] We attach importance to the poverty-level figure, despite its inaccuracies, because measuring poverty is a means of measuring how the American prom-ise of equality stands up against the performance of our public policies.

The poverty rate in the United States has declined since the mid-1960s. It rose slightly in the 1980s, then declined again after that. In 2008, the U.S. Census Bureau estimated that 39.8 million people, or roughly 13.2 percent of the population, were living in poverty in the United States.[30] The poverty rate jumped in 2009 to 14.3 percent, as a result of the Great Recession. Poverty was once a condition of old age. Social Security changed that. Today, poverty is still related to age, but in the opposite direction: it is largely a predicament of

entitlements
Benefits to which every eligi-ble person has a legal right and that the government cannot deny.

poverty level
The minimum cash income that will provide for a family's basic needs; calculated as three times the cost of a market basket of food that provides a minimally nutritious diet.

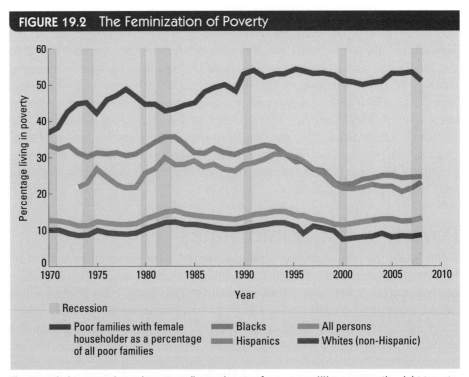

FIGURE 19.2   The Feminization of Poverty

The twentieth century brought extraordinary changes for women. Women won the right to vote and to own property, and they gained a measure of legal and social equality (see Chapter 16). But increases in the rates of divorce, marital separation, and adolescent pregnancy have cast more women into the head-of-household role, a condition that tends to push women and children into poverty. In the absence of a national child-care policy, single women with young children face limited employment opportunities and lower wages in comparison to full-time workers. These factors and others contribute to the feminization of poverty—the fact that a growing percentage of all poor Americans are women or the dependents of women.

Sources: Barbara Ehrenreich and Frances Fox Piven, "The Feminization of Poverty," *Dissent* (Spring 1984): 162–170; Harrell R. Rodgers, Jr., *Poor Women, Poor Families: The Economic Plight of America's Female-Headed Households*, 2nd ed. (Armonk, N.Y.: M. E. Sharpe, 1990); U.S. Census Bureau, *Income, Poverty, and Health Insurance Coverage in the United States: 2008* (Washington, D.C.: U.S. Government Printing Office, September 2009), Table 4, http://www.census.gov/prod/2009pubs/p60-236.pdf.

the young. In 2008, 19.0 percent of persons under eighteen years of age were in poverty, compared with about 9.7 percent of people over age sixty-five.[31]

Another trend in the United States, which we describe in Figure 19.2, is the concentration of poverty in households headed by single women. One in every two poor Americans resides in a family in which a woman is the sole householder, or head of the household. Thirty years ago, only one in every four poor people lived in such a family. Researchers have labeled this trend toward greater poverty among women the **feminization of poverty**, as a growing percentage of all poor Americans are women or dependents of women.

The poverty level is adjusted each year to reflect changes in consumer prices. One measure, the poverty *threshold,* determines the number of people who live below the threshold. (A second measure, the poverty *guideline,* determines the income level at which families qualify for government assistance.) In 2008, the poverty threshold for a family of four was a cash income

feminization of poverty
The term applied to the fact that a growing percentage of all poor Americans are women or the dependents of women.

below $22,025.[32] Some critics believe that factors other than income should be considered in computing the poverty level. Assets (home, cars, possessions), for example, are excluded from the definition. The computation also fails to take into account noncash benefits such as food stamps, health benefits (Medicaid), and subsidized housing. Presumably, the inclusion of these noncash benefits as income would reduce the number of individuals seen as living below the poverty level.

The use of the poverty line as a social indicator reflects a fundamental ambiguity in the notion of equality. Consider, for example, that greater equality of incomes can be achieved in two completely different ways: those lowest in the income distribution could be raised up by increasing their income, or those at the top could be brought down by the government's taking a greater share of their income. Doing the latter alone would not help the worst off at all if the money taken from the wealthiest were not transferred to the poorest. Using a concept like the poverty threshold, which reflects a social commitment that no citizen should live below a certain standard, is intended to ensure that our progress toward equality improves the absolute condition of the least well off among us.

Welfare Reform

It is relatively easy to draw a portrait of the poor. It is much more difficult to craft policies that move them out of destitution. In the wake of Johnson's Great Society programs, critics of social welfare spending argued that antipoverty policies made poverty more attractive by removing incentives to work. During Reagan's campaign for the presidency, he blamed such policies for creating Cadillac-driving "welfare queens."[33] The 1990s represented an important turning point in this debate. In 1996, the Republican-led Congress sought a fundamental revision of the welfare system and managed to enlist the president in their cause. When President Clinton signed the Personal Responsibility and Opportunity to Work Act into law on August 22, 1996, he joined forces with the Republican-led Congress "to end welfare as we know it." The act abolished the sixty-one-year-old Aid to Families with Dependent Children (AFDC) program, which since the 1930s had provided a federal guarantee of cash assistance that had kept millions of citizens afloat during difficult times, and replaced it with the **Temporary Assistance for Needy Families (TANF)** program.

Critics of AFDC had complained that for some recipients, floating had become a way of life and that government aid discouraged individuals from swimming on their own. The program was also quite unpopular. In 1994, 59 percent of Americans thought that "welfare recipients were taking advantage of the system."[34] Although originally established with widowed mothers in mind, at a time when divorce and out-of-wedlock births were rare, AFDC grew rapidly beginning in the 1960s as divorce and single motherhood increased (see Figure 19.3). By the time AFDC was abolished, 4 million adults and almost 9 million children were on the welfare rolls, and 24 million Americans were receiving food stamps. The end of AFDC significantly changed the lives of more than one-fifth of American families.

Temporary Assistance for Needy Families (TANF) A 1996 national act that abolished the longtime welfare policy, AFDC (Aid for Families with Dependent Children). TANF gives the states much more control over welfare policy.

FIGURE 19.3	Families on Welfare, 1955–2008

Beginning in the 1950s, the number of families on welfare skyrocketed as divorce and single motherhood increased. The welfare rolls stabilized during the late 1970s and 1980s but again lurched upward in the early 1990s. The sharp decline at the end of the 1990s represents the "end of welfare as we know it" by legislation and the demand for workers fueled by a strong domestic economy in the 1990s, reaching a new stability through 2008.

Source: Department of Health and Human Services, Administration for Children and Families, "Caseload Data," http://www.acf.hhs.gov/programs/ofa/data-reports/caseload/caseload_recent.html.

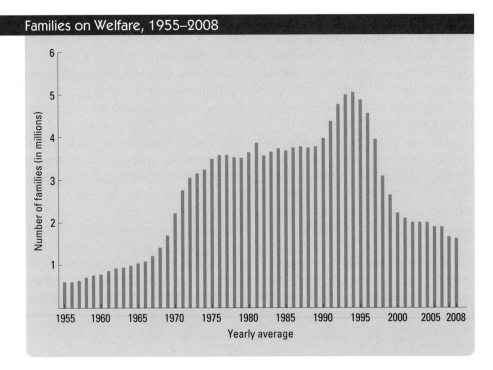

Under TANF, adult recipients of welfare payments have to become employed within two years. The law places the burden of job creation on the states. Families can receive no more than a total of five years of benefits in a lifetime, and the states can set a lower limit. Even before signing the bill, Clinton had granted waivers permitting states to offer extensions beyond the five-year limit as long as recipients continue to look for work. Republicans countered that such waivers effectively undermined the law.[35]

Nonetheless, for the 328 House members and 74 senators who voted for the bill (Republicans heavily in favor, Democrats split), devolving power to the states proved a prime force in the reform effort. President Clinton's own desire to permit states to act as laboratories for welfare reform provided ample ammunition for advocates of change. When the bill was signed into law, some forty-five states had already begun experimenting with their welfare systems.[36]

How has the welfare reform bill of 1996 affected the states? As envisioned, there are now fifty new welfare systems under the plan of federal block, or lump-sum, grants to the states. Initially, at least, some state officials were concerned by the stringent work requirements imposed by the new law and confused by some of its provisions. The extent to which states would be able to count job training as work is an issue that state and federal officials have debated since 1996. As in any other complicated piece of domestic legislation, the process of writing regulations and offering guidance to help states implement the law has consumed significant time. Overall, though, despite their several specific complaints, state leaders generally have been pleased with the increased flexibility that TANF has provided when compared to policy on the books prior to 1996.

TANF was reauthorized in 2006 and was supposed to be reexamined again in 2010. During the reauthorization process, Congress debates whether to make changes to both the funding levels and the rules that affect how and under what conditions the funds may be spent. When Congress turns its attention to TANF, the debates will likely center on how the program fared during the Great Recession and the extent to which job training and education can be counted as work when determining a potential recipient's eligibility for aid.[37]

In terms of funding, federal support for the law has been implemented through block grants to the states totaling $16.5 billion per year. President Obama's economic stimulus plan (the American Recovery and Reinvestment Act of 2009) included a provision for an emergency fund of $5 billion to supplement the block grants in states that saw an increase in their assistance caseloads and expenditures due to the Great Recession.[38]

What about welfare recipients themselves? How have they fared under the law? Now that TANF has begun to build up a track record during a time period that included a national economic recession (something that observers noted would provide a strong test of the law's ability to provide assistance to the needy), some general results have begun to emerge. Most clearly, as Figure 19.3 illustrates, the number of families on welfare has declined and remained relatively low when compared to the pre-TANF period. And the good news is that large numbers of former welfare recipients have been able to find steady work. Also, one of the biggest fears of TANF's critics, that employers would find former welfare recipients undesirable employees and that there would be few jobs available in major urban areas, appears not to have materialized.[39] Supporters of the law have cheered these results and celebrated specific success stories of people who have moved from welfare to work. As a result, Americans' opposition to welfare spending has declined in recent years, and their attitudes about welfare recipients have improved.[40]

Other findings are less promising and raise issues that members of Congress have been considering as they debate how to reauthorize TANF. Despite former welfare recipients' increased levels of employment, most have not been able to find jobs that pay good wages and offer valuable benefits, such as health care. Thus, many former TANF recipients still live below or close to the poverty level. Moreover, studies have consistently found that these jobs often require workers to travel great distances (such as long commutes from urban centers to the suburbs), which creates added stress as parents need to secure child care during their long workday commutes.[41] One source of confusion among TANF recipients and state officials alike has been the extent to which recipients still maintain eligibility for other federal programs, such as Medicaid, even as they move into full-time employment. Reaching out to individuals as they make the transition from welfare to work, to help make them aware of these opportunities, has been a challenge for policymakers and private or nonprofit contractors on the front lines who are implementing the law.

Other challenges became particularly acute during the Great Recession. Emerging data suggest that many Americans hit hard by the recession have had difficulty assessing their eligibility for different programs, and there is wide variation from state to state in the types of aid that people in similar circumstances can receive. Moreover, people who are working while on welfare are finding that if they lose their jobs, they also lose a range of essential benefits that had come with meeting the work requirements of TANF, such as subsidies for child care. Some analysts say that during tough economic times, Congress may need to make changes to TANF, such as lowering the state-level work requirements (the current requirement is a 50 percent work participation rate for TANF recipients) and simply increasing the grants made to states.[42] From 2008 to 2009, TANF caseloads increased in 38 states. In some states, the caseload increased by 20 percent or more, leading one architect of the 1996 reforms to note, "To me it's good news. This is exactly what should happen [at a time of added need]."[43] Yet others worry that the increased caseloads mean that much of the available funds are going toward cash assistance at the expense of funding for job training programs. The Great Recession was the most significant test of TANF's ability to meet demands of the needy; it is still too early to tell whether it passed or failed.

Health Care

It is hard to imagine a modern welfare state that does not protect the health of its population. Yet the United States is the only major industrialized nation without a universal health-care system. Rather, the United States has had what is perhaps best described as a patchwork system of care designed to cover different segments of the population. In addition to private insurance, which many Americans receive as a benefit of employment, government programs to provide health care include Medicare, primarily for the elderly; Medicaid, for the qualifying poor; and the Children's Health Insurance Program (CHIP) for children in needy families. This section discusses Medicare, Medicaid, and the health-care bill enacted by the Obama administration in 2010.

Cost and Access

Nearly everyone maintains that the U.S. health-care system needs fixing. To better understand the American patchwork system of health care and possibilities for future reforms, it is important to consider two issues that have animated the nation's health-care debate for several years: access to care and cost.[44] First, many Americans have no health insurance. In 2008, nearly 47 million people in America, roughly 16 percent of all Americans, had no health insurance. The number of uninsured people varies according to factors such as age, race, and income.[45] People under the age of thirty-five are less likely to have insurance. African Americans and Hispanics are more likely to be uninsured than whites. Immigrants are less likely to have insurance. Families with an income under $50,000 are much less likely to have insurance. Figure 19.4 lists the states with the highest percentages of uninsured residents. About two-thirds of Americans with health insurance are insured through their employer or have some type of private plan. The

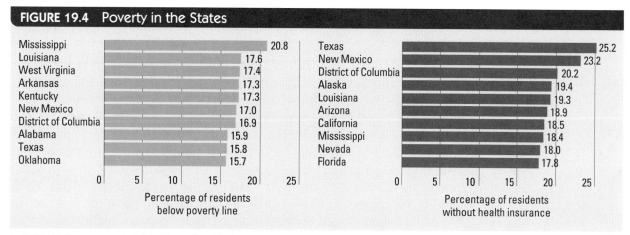

FIGURE 19.4 Poverty in the States

Percentage of residents below poverty line:
- Mississippi — 20.8
- Louisiana — 17.6
- West Virginia — 17.4
- Arkansas — 17.3
- Kentucky — 17.3
- New Mexico — 17.0
- District of Columbia — 16.9
- Alabama — 15.9
- Texas — 15.8
- Oklahoma — 15.7

Percentage of residents without health insurance:
- Texas — 25.2
- New Mexico — 23.2
- District of Columbia — 20.2
- Alaska — 19.4
- Louisiana — 19.3
- Arizona — 18.9
- California — 18.5
- Mississippi — 18.4
- Nevada — 18.0
- Florida — 17.8

In 2008, 13.2 percent of all Americans lived below the poverty line; 15.4 percent had no health insurance. These national figures mask important differences across states. In Connecticut and New Hampshire, for example, less than 10 percent of the population lives in poverty; in Mississippi, almost 21 percent of state residents live in poverty. In Hawaii, Massachusetts, and Wisconsin, less than 9 percent of state residents are without health insurance, yet a quarter of Texans don't have health insurance. Variations are due to state laws and social problems, immigration, and local job opportunities. In this figure, we list the top ten states according to the percentage of state residents who live below the poverty line and who are without health insurance (as of 2008).

Sources: U.S. Census Bureau, "Small Area Income and Poverty Estimates," 2008; Kaiser Family Foundation, "Health Insurance Coverage of the Total Population, States (2007-2008), U.S. (2008)," 2008, http://www.statehealthfacts.org/comparetable.jsp?ind=125&cat=3.

remainder is insured through the government, with programs such as Medicaid, Medicare, and the military.[46]

Access to health care depends on more than simply having insurance coverage. As described at the start of this chapter, many Americans with insurance are actually underinsured, with plans that do not adequately meet their true health-care needs. And even with adequate private or public health insurance of some kind, many Americans lack easy access to doctors or hospitals. The supply of physicians in the United States simply does not meet the demand. Any legislation that insures more Americans will only make the problem worse. One study projects that with greater use of medical services, the United States will need 159,000 additional physicians by 2025.[47]

The second major issue confronting the nation's health-care system is cost. Overall, the health-care sector is a significant portion of the U.S. economy. In 2008, public and private spending on health care reached an all-time high of $2.4 trillion, which was more than 16 percent of GDP.[48] Given the aging of the American population and the development of newer medical technologies, those numbers are projected to increase in the future. By 2018, for example, health care is expected to account for 20.3 percent of GDP.[49] Looking at the factors driving these increasing costs, the fastest-growing segment of the nation's health-care bill is in the area of prescription drugs.

Among advanced industrial nations, the United States spends the largest proportion of its economy on health care. In 2007, it spent more than other nations with comprehensive systems of coverage, including Switzerland (10.8 percent of GDP), Germany (10.4 percent), Canada (10.1 percent), and France (11.0 percent).[50] These numbers have raised concerns for some observers who

IDEALOG.ORG

Do you believe that health care is a government responsibility? Take IDEAlog's self-test.

note that the benefits to the entire nation of higher health-care spending may be elusive (see "Compared with What? Health Spending and Its Possible Effects").

The two central problems of health care, access and cost, give rise to two key goals and a familiar dilemma. First, any reform should democratize health care—that is, it should make health care available to more people, ideally everyone. But by providing broad access to medical care, we will increase the amount we spend on such care and increase the amount of regulations we place on private insurance companies. Second, any reform must control the ballooning cost of health care. But controlling costs requires restricting the range of procedures and providers available to patients. Thus, both of the central problems of the health-care issue go to the heart of the modern dilemma of government: we must weigh greater equality in terms of universal coverage and cost controls against a loss of freedom in markets for health care and in choosing a doctor.

The dilemma of controlling costs without inhibiting the freedom to choose one's doctor applies not just to public health care. The same financial pressures affecting Medicare and Medicaid have also affected privately provided health coverage. Over the past quarter of a century, the health insurance industry has undergone tremendous change.

Most Americans used to carry what was called catastrophic care insurance, which provided hospital coverage for serious illnesses only. As the cost of medical care ballooned, numerous scholars and health-care providers realized that preventing illness through regular physical examinations and appropriate lifestyle changes was far cheaper than curing illnesses after onset. Thus, health insurance providers began to offer extended coverage of routine, preventive care in return for limiting an individual's freedom to choose when and what type of medical specialist to see. Health insurance providers also became increasingly concerned with the amount of risk they were taking on by providing insurance. As discussed at the start of this chapter, they became more interested in covering healthy people who were likely to consume fewer services and less interested in covering people with existing—and expensive—medical conditions.

Medicare

In 1962, the Senate considered extending Social Security benefits to provide hospitalization and medical care for the elderly. Democratic senator Russell Long of Louisiana opposed the extension and declared, "We are not staring at a sweet old lady in bed with her kimono and nightcap. We are looking into the eyes of the wolf that ate Red Riding Hood's grandma."[51] Long was concerned that costs would soar without limit. Other opponents echoed the fears of the American Medical Association (AMA), which saw virtually any form of government-provided medical care as a step toward government control of medicine. Long and his compatriots won the battle that day. Three years later, however, on the heels of Lyndon Johnson's sweeping victory in the 1964 presidential election, the Social Security Act was amended to provide **Medicare**, a health insurance program for all people aged sixty-five and older.

Medicare
A health insurance program serving primarily persons sixty-five and older.

Compared with What?

Health Spending and Its Possible Effects

Compared to other nations, the United States spends a great deal of money on health care. In 2007, the United States spent more than 16 percent of its GDP on health care.* Most of American health-care spending was in the private sector. Public health spending is far less, both as a proportion of the GDP and in comparison to other nations.

What does health spending achieve? Measures of health spending outcomes are too numerous for inclusion here. Let's focus on just one: longevity. Overall, life expectancy in large-population nations reveals very little variation. Babies born in the United States in 2007 can expect to live on average to age seventy-eight. In contrast, also for 2007, babies born in Japan can expect to live to age eighty-three, and those born in Australia are likely to reach age eighty-one. Despite the fact that Americans outspend other nations on health care, the payoff in life expectancy has not yet been realized.

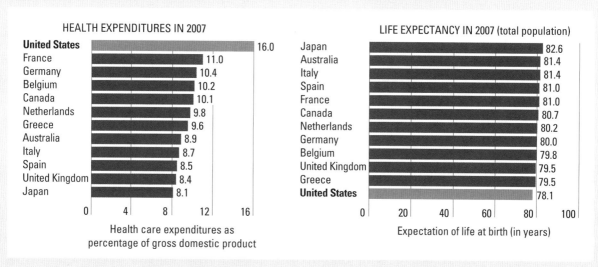

HEALTH EXPENDITURES IN 2007

United States	16.0
France	11.0
Germany	10.4
Belgium	10.2
Canada	10.1
Netherlands	9.8
Greece	9.6
Australia	8.9
Italy	8.7
Spain	8.5
United Kingdom	8.4
Japan	8.1

Health care expenditures as percentage of gross domestic product

LIFE EXPECTANCY IN 2007 (total population)

Japan	82.6
Australia	81.4
Italy	81.4
Spain	81.0
France	81.0
Canada	80.7
Netherlands	80.2
Germany	80.0
Belgium	79.8
United Kingdom	79.5
Greece	79.5
United States	78.1

Expectation of life at birth (in years)

Source: Organization for Economic Co-operation and Development, "OECD Health Data 2009," http://www.oecd.org/document/16/0,3343,en_2649_34631_2085200_1_1_1_1,00.html.

*See National Health Expenditure data at http://www.cms.hhs.gov/NationalHealthExpendData/Downloads/proj2008.pdf.

As early as 1945, public opinion had clearly supported some form of national health insurance, and President Harry Truman proposed such a program during his administration. However, that idea became entangled in Cold War politics—the growing crusade against communism in America.[52] The AMA, representing the nation's physicians, mounted and financed an all-out campaign to link national health insurance (so-called socialized medicine) with socialism; the campaign was so successful that the prospect of a national health-care policy vanished.

Both proponents and opponents of national health insurance tried to link their positions to deeply rooted American values: advocates emphasized equality and fairness; opponents stressed individual freedom. In the absence of a clear mandate on the kind of insurance (publicly funded or private) the public wanted, the AMA was able to exert its political influence to prevent any national insurance at all.[53] After the 1960 election, however, the terms of the debate changed. It no longer focused on the clash between freedom and equality. Democrats cast the issue of health insurance in terms of providing assistance to the aged, and a groundswell of support brought it back to the national agenda.[54]

The Democratic victory in 1964 and the advent of President Johnson's Great Society made some form of national health-care policy almost inevitable. On July 30, 1965, with Harry Truman at his side, Johnson signed a bill that provided a number of health benefits to the elderly and the poor. Fearful of the AMA's power to punish its opponents, rather than pushing for a comprehensive program such as the one Truman had advocated while in office, the Democrats in 1965 confined their efforts to a compulsory hospitalization insurance plan for the elderly (known today as Part A of Medicare). In addition, the bill contained a version of an alternative Republican plan that called for voluntary government-subsidized insurance to cover physicians' fees (known today as Part B of Medicare).

Medicare was designed as a health insurance program for the elderly, and today almost 85 percent of the program's beneficiaries are aged sixty-five and older. A small portion of two other groups can also qualify for the program even though they might not have reached retirement age: those who are disabled, who make up 16 percent of the beneficiary pool, and a small number (less than 1 percent) of citizens who suffer from end-stage renal disease, a kidney disorder. In 2010, almost 47 million people were enrolled in the program at a total cost of roughly $513 billion.[55]

Medicare is compulsory insurance that covers certain hospital services for people aged sixty-five and older. Workers pay a tax, and for certain parts of the program other than Part A, retirees pay premiums deducted from their Social Security payments. Payments for necessary services are made by the national government directly to participating hospitals and other qualifying facilities. Citizens who enjoy Medicare coverage may also possess or purchase private insurance for additional services that the program may not cover or may cover only in less generous ways. Seniors who receive health insurance as part of their employment retirement packages, for example, are not required to give up those benefits because of Medicare; they can enjoy coverage from both Medicare and their private plans.

The program still contains its original components, Part A and Part B, but over the years, Medicare has also expanded to cover more kinds of services and to provide program participants with additional health-care options. Today, Part A essentially pays for care in facilities, such as inpatient hospital visits, care in skilled nursing facilities, hospice, and some home health care. Part B pays for doctors' services and outpatient hospital care. Services under Part A come at no cost to beneficiaries, but Part B services require participants to pay a premium (just under $100 in 2010); the remaining cost of Part B is picked up by the federal government.

Taken together, Part A and Part B are referred to as the Original Medicare Plan. Because that plan may not cover all services that program participants may desire, and because some may not have access to additional health insurance options as a part of their private retirement packages, the Medicare program has expanded to attempt to meet additional health-care needs. The program now offers a series of supplemental plans, known as Medigap plans, that are run by private insurance companies and that seniors pay for through a premium, which varies by type of plan.

The most recent change in Medicare occurred in 2003 with the passage of the Medicare Prescription Drug, Improvement, and Modernization Act. Rather than a single program with simple rules, the new drug plan (known as Part D) encouraged private insurers to offer competing plans. In some locations, seniors may have the option of thirty or more plans from which to choose, each with a different combination of costs, deductibles, participating pharmacies, and formularies (covered medications). It should come as no surprise that only a small proportion of seniors initially signed up for any plan, since the list of different plans, options, and prices was overwhelming. Like other aspects of Medicare, the costs of the program continue to increase at rates in excess of the cost of living. In 2009, 10 percent of government spending on Medicare was devoted to the prescription plan (see section on Health Care Reform for new provisions related to Medicare).[56]

Medicaid

In addition to Medicare, another important part of the nation's health-care patchwork is **Medicaid,** the nation's main program to provide health care to Americans with low incomes. Like Medicare, this program was also the product of Lyndon Johnson's Great Society effort; it passed as yet another amendment to the Social Security Act. In 1965, the program was relatively small and enrolled 4 million people at an annual cost of $0.4 billion. By 2008, it had grown to become the single largest public program in the nation, enrolling more than 62 million people at a cost of $336 billion (federal and state expenditures combined).[57]

The program's scope is vast. According to one author, "It insures one-fifth of the nation's children and pays for one-third of all childbirths. It finances nearly 40 percent of all long-term care expenses, more than one-sixth of all drug costs, and half of states' mental health services. It is ... the 'workhorse' of the U.S. health system."[58]

Although Medicaid is designed primarily to cover citizens with low incomes, the pool of potentially eligible people can vary significantly across the country. That is because, unlike Medicare, which is solely a federal program, Medicaid is jointly run and financed by the federal government and the states. In 2008, for instance, the federal share of Medicaid costs was $192 billion, just 57 percent of the total cost.[59] Federal law defines a certain minimum level of benefits that states must offer through Medicaid, but

Medicaid
A need-based comprehensive medical and hospitalization program.

states have much leeway to determine income levels and other criteria to define eligibility.

This sharing of cost and administration in the American federal system can leave some Medicaid beneficiaries in challenging circumstances. For example, citizens who might be eligible for Medicaid services in one state may lose eligibility if they move elsewhere. Also, because Medicaid expenditures are typically one of the top expenses in state budgets (usually just ahead of or behind spending on education), benefits are frequently cut when states experience difficult budgetary situations, as has occurred since the Great Recession began. By the end of 2008, for example, in order to contain Medicaid costs and reduce state budget deficits, seven states reported restricting eligibility, fifteen reduced benefits, and five increased the copayments required of program participants. Several more states planned similar cutbacks for 2010.[60]

Medicaid participants essentially fall into four groups: children under age twenty-one (29.8 million in 2008, or 48 percent of all Medicaid participants), adults (16.5 million), those who are blind and disabled (9.6 million), and those aged sixty-five and over (6.1 million).[61] Don't be confused by that last group. Senior citizens qualify for Medicare, but they can also participate in Medicaid if their incomes fall below a certain level. Finally, although their numbers are relatively small compared to other participants in the program, those who are blind and disabled and the elderly account for over half of Medicaid expenditures. Thus, the cost of the program appears to be driven by the high cost of medical care for these two groups rather than other factors.[62]

Health-Care Reform

On March 23, 2010, President Obama signed sweeping health-care reform legislation into law, delivering on a major campaign promise. The new law, called the Patient Protection and Affordable Care Act, has been described as the most wide-ranging policy change in a generation, comparable the creation of Social Security and Medicare.

In passing this bill, Obama achieved what presidents as far back as Truman have advocated: he enacted a plan designed to provide insurance to as many Americans as possible. To achieve this victory, he had to scale back some initial ideas (such as offering a health insurance plan administered by the federal government), create new taxes, and ensure that federal funds would not be used to cover the costs of abortions. The year-long legislative battle pitted arguments about equality of access to care against arguments about freedom from government intervention. The arguments about equality won the day, but battles about the scope of this legislation may have only just begun.

The more notable aspects of the legislation are the following: By 2014, insurance providers can no longer deny people coverage because of pre-existing conditions. Until then, people with pre-existing conditions can gain coverage through a high-risk pool. To make it possible for insurers to pay for the needs of high-cost treatments, what is perhaps the most controversial aspect of the reform was added, namely that all individuals are required to have health insurance by 2014 or pay a fine (some are exempt from this so-called *individual mandate*, including Native Americans and people with religious objections or financial hardship). There are significant opportunities for people to get government subsidies to help them obtain coverage, and the bill also expands eligibility for Medicaid. It is estimated that legislation will lead to near-universal coverage by 2019. Employers will be subjected to mandates as well. By 2014, all employers with 50 or more employees must offer health insurance or pay a fine. Tax credits are available to some small businesses that begin to offer health plans to their workers. Finally, states must set up insurance marketplaces, called *exchanges*, by 2014 where people and small businesses can shop for competitively priced health plans.[63]

One of the biggest concerns about this bill is how much it will cost: approximately $940 billion in the first ten years. While that figure leads to sticker-shock for some, others argue that the reform will pay for itself. In fact, the Congressional Budget Office estimates that the bill will reduce deficits by $143 billion over ten years. These savings are possible because of other controversial features of the legislation: it places new taxes on high-cost health plans, places new Medicare taxes on wealthy Americans, creates a new tax on indoor tanning, charges fees to employers and private health insurance companies, and reforms some aspects of Medicare spending (including the creation of an advisory commission that can alter how Medicare is administered and the introduction of program in which doctors are paid for the quality of treatment instead of the quantity). The state insurance exchanges will also lower health-care costs; because private insurers will have new competition, insurance premiums are expected to decrease.[64]

That the reform is not expected to add to the deficit in the long term does not necessarily silence critics. For people who are wary of "big government," any program that results in more bureaucracy, more regulation, and more taxes is problematic Additionally, many patients and hospitals harbor fears about how reforms to Medicare will play out despite assurances from Obama that benefits will not be affected. In addition to concerns about costs and the expanded role of government, other opponents simply charge that it is unconstitutional for the government to require that all individuals purchase health insurance. Several states have filed lawsuits in federal court to challenge the new law.[65]

While there is much uncertainty about how the implementation of health care reform will play out, one thing is certain: debates about its effectiveness, its economic impact, and its constitutionality will be a feature of American politics for years to come.

Elementary and Secondary Education

Although it is no less important, education is unlike the other public policies discussed in this chapter given that responsibility for children's schooling resides primarily in state and local governments in the United States. Since Horace Mann introduced mandatory public schooling in Massachusetts in the second quarter of the nineteenth century, public elementary and secondary schools have been a highly visible part of local government. And at no time in the nation's history has the federal government contributed more than 10 percent to finance the nation's K–12 education bill; today, Washington's contribution hovers around 8 percent.[66] Although federal policy in education dates back to the earliest days of the nation, significant national involvement in education has been more recent.

Concerns Motivating Change

Two main factors, related to freedom, order, and equality, have prompted greater federal involvement in the nation's elementary and secondary schools during the last half century.

Equity. The overriding and persistent concern has been educational equity. An important part of Lyndon Johnson's Great Society was the traditional American belief that social and economic equality could be attained through equality of educational opportunity. The justices of the U.S. Supreme Court argued as much in their landmark decision in *Brown* v. *Board of Education* (1954). Legislatively, the **Elementary and Secondary Education Act of 1965 (ESEA)**, yet another product of the Great Society, was the first major federal effort to address educational equity in a systematic way. The law, which has been reauthorized periodically since its original enactment, provided direct national government aid to local school districts in order to improve the educational opportunities of the economically disadvantaged.

The ESEA began as a relatively short bill of around thirty pages in 1965, but it has grown to encompass hundreds of pages and dozens of federal programs, with nearly all devoted to improving educational opportunities for disadvantaged groups. The original law focused on economic disadvantage; later iterations recognized more explicitly other groups, such as students for whom English is a second language and Native American students. A separate law altogether, the Individuals with Disabilities Education Act (IDEA), which originally passed with a different name in the 1970s, is designed to improve educational opportunities for students of all ages (elementary school through college and graduate school) with physical or other disabilities.

Despite the efforts of federal policy, the promised improvements in educational, and thus social and economic, equality have been elusive. Differences in student achievement between advantaged and disadvantaged groups have declined since the 1960s. However, as data from the 2007 National Assessment of Educational Progress, a federally sponsored test also known as the "nation's report card," show, significant gaps still remain in key subject areas such as reading and math as well as in overall graduation rates.[67] These test score gaps are important because they tend to correlate with future educational and economic opportunities.[68]

Elementary and Secondary Education Act of 1965 (ESEA)
The federal government's primary law to assist the nation's elementary and secondary schools. It emerged as part of President Lyndon Johnson's Great Society program.

National Security and Prosperity. Concern over educational achievement is not limited to issues of social equality at home. In an increasingly competitive global economy with fewer barriers to international investment and plant relocation, countries are competing to offer—and attract—highly educated and skilled workers. Thus, a desire to keep the United States competitive with other nations, both economically and militarily, is one reason that politicians, business leaders, and American citizens more generally see education as a key public policy area.

In fact, the connection between national security and federal education policy is not recent. It dates back at least as far as the 1950s when the Eisenhower administration supported and helped to push into law the National Defense Education Act of 1958 (NDEA). The law is typically considered to be a response to the Soviet Union's launch of a tiny satellite known as *Sputnik,* the first such craft to orbit the earth. This Soviet success, which many interpreted to mean that the United States was losing the "brain race" against its rival, set off calls for improving the nation's stock of scientists and engineers, as well as its cadre of foreign language speakers, to counter the communist threat around the globe. Funding from the NDEA supported efforts in all of these areas at the elementary, secondary, and postsecondary levels.

A desire to improve American economic competitiveness has been the most recent force prompting greater efforts to improve the nation's education system. These concerns date back to the 1970s, when state governors became increasingly attuned to the link between their own states' economic fortunes and the quality of their schools. These state-level concerns foreshadowed subsequent debates at the national level that forged a similar link between the competitiveness of the entire nation and the educational preparation of the country's young people.

These state- and national-level concerns coalesced in a famous report entitled *A Nation at Risk,* which was released in 1983 by the National Commission on Excellence in Education. The commission was the brainchild of the nation's second secretary of education, Terrell Bell. The report, along with improved data comparing American students with their international counterparts, through projects such as the Trends in International Mathematics and Science Study (TIMSS), created significant momentum for public officials at all levels of government to support improving the nation's schools.

Values and Reform

At the center of the current debate over education is the dilemma of freedom versus equality. The American belief in equality is heavily weighted toward equality of opportunity, and equality of opportunity depends on equal access to a good education. Thus, several advocates suggest that important components of any future reforms must include measures to provide better teachers and funding commensurate with educational needs in the nation's urban and rural areas.

At the same time, the American belief in freedom is perhaps nowhere expressed more vigorously than in the freedom to choose both where to live and what one's children will be taught in school. Advocates of this view see greater educational success tied to plans to increase educational opportunities for students and their parents. Popular among these proposals are charter schools, which are public schools of choice that have been freed from several state and local regulations. Others would go still further and support school voucher programs, which would enable parents to choose to send their children to any school—public or private, secular or religious—at tax-payers' expense. Choice would not only improve opportunities for these parents and children, proponents argue, but would also provide a jolt of competition that would improve public schools more generally.

As the national and international challenges we face grow in technological and scientific sophistication, the dilemmas of education reform will become more pressing. The questions of who will pay for reform, who will benefit, and how best to improve student learning have all come to a head in the most recent reauthorization of the ESEA, known as the **No Child Left Behind Act of 2001 (NCLB)**.

The No Child Left Behind Act of 2001

In 2000, Republican candidate George W. Bush made education one of the most important issues in his campaign for the White House.[69] Once in Office, Bush wasted no time in offering up his vision to reform the Elementary and Secondary Education Act. The fact that Bush and his team pressed the issue, even after the attacks on the United States of 9/11, illustrated the importance that the president placed on achieving significant education reform in his first year in office. With much fanfare, President Bush signed the measure into law in January 2002.

Although Bush, members of Congress, and observers in the press called the bill a historic breakthrough, it actually extended several initiatives that the previous reauthorization of the ESEA from 1994 had set in motion. Most significant among NCLB's numerous components is the law's requirement that states guarantee that all of their students are performing at proficient levels in reading and math by 2014. Along the way, schools will have to show that they are making what the law calls Adequate Yearly Progress among all student groups, be they economically disadvantaged, weak in English language skills, or disabled. Schools need to demonstrate that progress through annual testing in reading and math for students in grades 3 through 8 and then once again in tests administered in grades 10, 11, and 12.

The law also includes several other provisions to help schools and offer more public school choices to parents whose children attend schools that persistently fail to meet Adequate Yearly Progress targets. In an effort to improve the nation's stock of classroom teachers, NCLB also calls on school districts to hire only highly qualified teachers in the core subjects of reading and math.

NCLB was initially praised for highlighting educational inequality in the United States and for asserting that all students deserve qualified teachers. But the implementation of NCLB was controversial.[70] Critics charged that the emphasis on testing led teachers to "teach to the test" and ignore subjects that were not tested, like music and social studies. Others, including the American Federation of Teachers (AFT), charged that the federal government did not spend enough money to help schools live up to the standards that it set. The funding allocated by NCLB did not make up for the existing

No Child Left Behind Act of 2001 (NCLB)
The latest reauthorization of the Elementary and Secondary Education Act.

inequalities in per pupil spending across school districts. Some charged that low-achieving students were being pushed out of schools for the sake of increasing test scores.

When the NCLB law came up for reauthorization in 2007, the Bush administration wanted to expand the law to include testing for high school students and merit pay for teachers. Democrats in Congress opposed the new changes, however, and members of the House Education and Labor Committee could not agree on a compromise bill. NCLB was not reauthorized. The Obama administration plans to put its own stamp on the legislation, including stricter requirements for teacher quality, but critics maintain that the fundamental flaws, such as the reliance on standardized testing, will remain.[71]

Immigration

Along with health care and education, illegal immigration is also consistently cited as one of the most important problems facing the country.[72] Immigrants today make up around 13 percent of the population (see "Politics of Global Change: Nations of Immigrants"). It is estimated that about 30 percent of the 38 million immigrants (or about 4 percent of the total American population) is here illegally.[73] Most Americans want to stem the tide of illegal immigrants; over 50 percent of Americans regularly say that the level of immigration should be decreased.[74] But they have mixed opinions on the question of what to do about the illegal immigrants who are already in the United States. Illegal immigrants are among the poorest and most vulnerable individuals. Whereas 15.8 percent of all Americans are without health insurance, 45 percent of foreign-born noncitizens lack health insurance. Twenty-three percent of noncitizens live below the poverty line.[75] Should they have access to the benefits of the social welfare state such as health care and education? Should they be eligible to earn citizenship?

Foreigners who wish to work in the United States for an extended period of time need to apply for and receive a permanent resident card, or "green card." Individuals with a green card are known as "lawful permanent residents," and they may eventually apply to become U.S. citizens. In 2008, the United States granted permanent admission to around 1.1 million noncitizens.[76] Federal immigration policy places a cap on the total number of people who can receive permanent residency status every year. As we noted in Chapter 16, priority is given to reuniting families, admitting workers in occupations with strong demand for labor, providing a refuge for people who face persecution in their home countries, and providing admission to people from a diverse set of countries.[77] Prior to the 1996 welfare reforms (discussed earlier in this chapter), legal immigrants were eligible for most public benefits on the same terms as citizens. The 1996 reforms, however, prohibit legal immigrants from participating in safety net programs such as Food Stamps, Medicaid, and TANF until they have been in the country for five years. States are free to enroll legal immigrants sooner, provided that state funds—and not federal funds—are used to supply the benefit.[78]

But it is the illegal immigrants who get most of the attention in policy debates. If caught, these individuals may be offered the chance to leave the country voluntarily, or they may be fined, imprisoned, deported, and prohibited from returning to the United States. In 2008, about 350,000 people were deported, and around 811,000 chose to leave voluntarily.[79] Most of the illegal immigrants in the United States come from Mexico and other Latin American countries. They tend to be geographically concentrated in western states and large urban areas, where they provide cheap labor in agriculture and manufacturing industries.[80]

Illegal immigrants have always been ineligible for the safety net programs discussed in this chapter (their American-born children are eligible), but they enroll in public schools and get treated in hospital emergency rooms, both of which come at a cost to American taxpayers. Most public policy debates about illegal immigration focus on how best to increase border security with Mexico, how to get employers to stop hiring undocumented workers, and whether illegal immigrants currently in the United States should be allowed to become legal residents. State governments have worked out their own plans.[81] Employers in several states are required to check their workers' residency status, using a federal program called E-Verify, and could be fined if they knowingly hire illegal immigrants. State governments have also passed legislation about the distribution of government benefits, the role of state law enforcement in detaining illegal immigrants, and education.

In 2007, President Bush and members of the Senate attempted to work out a bipartisan bill that would allow illegal immigrants to stay in the United States and earn citizenship after several years if they paid fines, passed English and civics exams, and remained employed.[82] When the bill was made public, however, conservative groups complained that it was "offering amnesty" to people who had broken the law. Immigrant groups did not like another feature of the bill, which would have created a temporary worker program that allowed people to work in the United States for three years but forced them to return to their home country for a year before reapplying for a temporary permit. The proposed law also shifted preference away from extended families toward entry for those with more education, work experience, and English skills. Union groups feared that legal temporary workers would drive down wages and take jobs away from American workers. Liberals did not like yet another aspect of the proposed reform, which would have required employers to use E-Verify to check the immigration status of current and future employees. With no consensus, the bipartisan bill failed.

Despite the bill's failure, majorities of the American public consistently supported the major provisions of the bill, including creating a so-called path to citizenship for illegal immigrants. Majorities supported creating such a path even when it was described as providing "amnesty."[83] President Obama likewise supports the major provisions of the Bush administration's efforts and has vowed to attempt immigration reform along similar lines. Some doubt, however, whether Obama's efforts can be successful in light of the economic challenges facing the country during his administration. Given

Undocumented Santa

Santa Claus is a resident of the North Pole who works in the United States every year on one night in December. Technically, he is an illegal immigrant, and protesters are using his image in demonstrations against the crackdown on illegal immigration. This particular "undocumented" Santa is protesting a decision by the mayor of Phoenix, Arizona, to allow police officers to ask people about their immigration status during routine encounters. Advocates of the move say this will help to enforce immigration laws, while critics say that it will ruin cooperation with local police in communities with large immigrant populations.

(© Jack Kurtz/The Arizona Republic)

its tough battles with enacting health-care reform, some also question whether the Democratic majority in Congress has the political will to delve into yet another controversial policy overhaul.[84]

Benefits and Fairness

As we have seen, the national government provides many Americans with benefits. There are two kinds of benefits: cash, such as a retiree's Social Security check, and noncash, such as food stamps. Some benefits are conditional. **Means-tested benefits** impose an income test to qualify. For example, free or low-cost school lunch programs and Pell college grants are available to households with an income that falls below a designated threshold. **Non-means-tested benefits** impose no such income test; benefits such as Medicare and Social Security are available to all, regardless of income.

Some Americans question the fairness of non-means-tested benefits. After all, benefits are subsidies, and some people need them more than

means-tested benefits
Conditional benefits provided by government to individuals whose income falls below a designated threshold.

non-means-tested benefits
Benefits provided by government to all citizens, regardless of income; Medicare and Social Security are examples.

Politics of Global Change

Nations of Immigrants

The United States is widely celebrated as a "nation of immigrants," but many other Western democracies rival or surpass the U.S. in the percentage of its population that is foreign born. Some countries, such as Spain and Sweden, not only match the United States in this regard but have also seen their percentage of foreign-born residents increase at more dramatic rates than the United States has over the past 10 years. And it would perhaps be more appropriate to call Canada and Australia,

two other countries with colonial ties to England, nations of immigrants than the United States. Australia's foreign-born population as a percentage of the total population is more than double that in the United States.

Source: OECD International Migration Data, 2009, Table A.1.4, http://www.oecd.org/document/52/0,3343,en_2649_33931_42274676_1_1_1_37415,00.html.

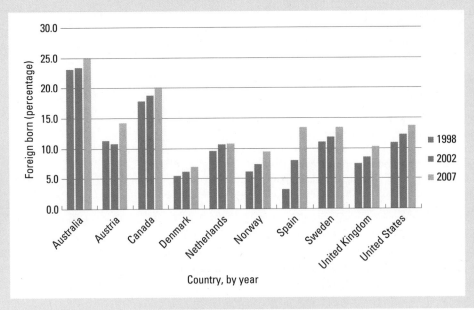

others do. If the size of the benefit pie remains fixed, imposing means tests on more benefits has real allure. For example, all elderly people now receive the same basic Medicare benefits, regardless of their income. Fairness advocates maintain that the affluent elderly should shoulder a higher share of Medicare costs, shifting more benefits to the low-income elderly.

If the idea of shifting benefits gains support in the future, reform debates will focus on the income level below which a program will apply. Thus, the question of fairness is one more problem for policymakers to consider as they try to reform social insurance, public assistance, health care, and education programs.

Summary

In this chapter, we have examined several different domestic policies—general plans of action adopted by the government to solve a social problem, counter a threat, or pursue an objective within the country's own borders. Often, disagreements about public policy are disagreements about values. Some of the oldest and most costly domestic policies, such as Social Security and Medicare, pose choices between freedom and equality.

Many domestic policies that provide benefits to individuals and promote economic equality were instituted during the Great Depression. Today, the government plays an active role in providing benefits to the poor, the elderly, and the disabled. The object of these domestic policies is to alleviate conditions that individuals are powerless to prevent. This is the social welfare function of the modern state. Recent health-care reform is a reflection of the modern dilemma of democracy: universal coverage and cost controls versus a loss of freedom in health-care choices.

Government confers benefits on individuals through social insurance and public assistance. Social insurance is not based on need; public assistance (welfare) hinges on proof of need. In one form of social insurance— old-age benefits—a tax on current workers pays retired workers' benefits. Aid for the poor, by contrast, comes from the government's general tax revenues.

Programs to aid the elderly and the poor have been gradually transformed into entitlements, or rights that accrue to eligible persons. These government programs have reduced poverty among some groups, especially the elderly. However, poverty retains a grip on certain segments of the population. Social and demographic changes have feminized poverty, and there is little prospect of reversing that trend soon.

Bill Clinton and a Republican-led Congress reformed the welfare system. The biggest entitlement program (Aid to Families with Dependent Children, or AFDC) is gone. Thanks to Temporary Assistance for Needy Families (TANF), individual state programs substitute for a single national policy. Work requirements and time limits on welfare may break the cycle of dependency, but the reforms run the risk of endangering the neediest among us. Time and experience will tell whether this grand experiment will produce better outcomes.

In contrast to social insurance and public assistance programs, significant federal involvement in education is of relatively recent origin, dating from the Great Society initiatives of the 1960s. Even today, education remains largely a state and local endeavor, with the federal government providing less than 10 percent of the funds for primary and secondary education. Traditionally, the federal government's education policy has centered on providing equal access to a good education for all Americans. That goal of achieving educational equity still remains important. With efforts such as the No Child Left Behind Act, we can see how policymakers have begun to link equity with educational excellence. In short, financial equity in education has little meaning if students do not achieve at comparable levels.

For a long time, the federal government has limited the number of immigrants who can become permanent legal residents of the United States. Federal immigration policy focuses on stemming the tide of illegal immigration through measures such as increased border security. At the same time, however, the federal government must address the needs of illegal immigrants in the United States; they are among the nation's poorest and most vulnerable individuals.

Some government subsidy programs provide means-tested benefits, for which eligibility hinges on income. Non-means-tested benefits are available to all, regardless of income. As the demand for such benefits exceeds available resources, policymakers have come to question their fairness. Subsidies for rich and poor alike are the basis for a broad national consensus. A departure from that consensus in the name of fairness may very well be the next challenge of democracy.

 CourseMate   **Visit www.cengagebrain.com/shop/ ISBN/0495906182 for flashcards, web quizzes, videos and more!**

CHAPTER

20

Global Policy

Feng Li/Getty Images

On August 27, 1883, the volcanic island of Krakatoa, between Sumatra and Java in the (then) Dutch East Indies, was destroyed by an eruption thousands of times stronger than the atomic bomb that devastated Hiroshima in 1945. Over 35,000 people were killed by the explosion and accompanying tsunami waves. On January 12, 2010, the Caribbean nation of Haiti suffered a major earthquake measuring 7.0 on the Richter scale. Over 200,000 inhabitants died under collapsed buildings. How nations and people of the world responded to these two natural disasters illustrates the phenomenon of globalization and its impact on international relations.

In Chapter 1 we defined globalization as the increasing interdependence of citizens and nations across the world, which means that people everywhere are somehow connected to one another and that we all are responsible for helping others, even those in foreign countries.[1] The world embraced this principle in responding to the Haiti disaster in 2010 but not to the Krakatoa catastrophe in 1883.

True, communications improved immensely over the century separating the events. But telegraphy began in the 1830s, and the Dutch capital of Batavia in Java (now Jakarta, Indonesia) was connected to the world by international cable by 1870. In his absorbing book *Krakatoa*, Simon Winchester said that humankind was "able to learn and know about" the enormous eruption "in detail, within days or even hours of its very happening":

It would not be stretching a point to suggest that *the Global Village* … coined by Marshall McLuhan in 1960 … was essentially born with the worldwide apprehension of, and fascination with, the events in Java that began in the summer of 1883.[2]

Thanks largely to the fledgling British news service, Reuters, the story appeared in major newspapers in England, Holland, the United States, South Africa, India, France, and Germany, among other countries.[3] People across the world were fascinated by the catastrophe but unmoved to help those who suffered it. According to Winchester, local Dutch officials buried bodies, drained swamps, and removed wreckage: "The king back in Holland opened a fund. Dutch mothers sent blankets, tents, food. A flotilla of ships traveled east to see what could be done." He says, "The Dutch were quite generously helping the people who were worst affected"—if only to restore profits of Dutch-owned businesses. Winchester makes no mention of aid coming from other countries where newspaper readers avidly followed stories about the Krakatoa eruption.[4]

As with Krakatoa, news of the earthquake in Haiti circled the globe almost immediately. People thousands of miles away watched video replays of shaking buildings in Port-au-Prince. In real time, they witnessed property devastation, human suffering, and heroic rescues. But the world's reactions to the disaster in Haiti were dramatically different. Outsiders were more than fascinated by the unfolding horror story; they were moved to help. Governments, international relief organizations, and private aid groups mobilized the next day to deliver food, medicine, supplies, and money to Haiti.[5] By Friday after the Tuesday earthquake, the United Nations listed forty-five countries that had pledged aid.[6]

For example, China flew in a rescue team with supplies and promised $4.4 million; Israel sent a rescue team and medical personnel; Cuba sent thirty doctors; Norway contributed $4.9 million, a field hospital, and tents.

Within ten days after the earthquake, the U.S. government had pledged $163 million in aid; other foreign governments pledged another $1 billion; and private individuals and nongovernmental organizations vowed $106 million (see pages 590–591).[7] People across the world contributed cash by going to websites or by sending text messages authorizing phone providers to send $10 to relief funds. On January 22, movie actor George Clooney hosted a "Hope for Haiti" telethon, featuring music and film celebrities. Broadcast internationally, the telethon raised more than $55 million from viewers worldwide.

What can account for the world's active response to the earthquake in Haiti versus its passive curiosity concerning the eruption in Krakatoa? Today, as a result of globalization, people and nations are aware of their interdependence and are willing to give (and expect) help in times of need. But globalization is not all positive. The economies of distant countries can have a strong impact on others. Free movement of goods and capital across borders leads to investing in developing countries where goods can be produced more cheaply. Often the result is the loss of jobs and wages in developed countries (e.g., the United States) while international corporate profits increase.

How should the U.S. government deal with the public's concerns over problems of globalization? Should it try to intervene actively in international affairs? If so, to what end? Should it favor economic growth at home over human rights elsewhere? Concerning our need for foreign oil, should the U.S. government favor regime stability in oil-rich countries over their citizens' civil liberties?

The ideological framework in Chapter 1, which runs through this book, was devised for analyzing ideological attitudes in domestic politics. One can adapt it to international affairs, as shown in Figure 20.1.[8] President George W. Bush probably fits in the International Libertarian category. Pope Benedict XVI's encyclical proposing a "true world authority" to work for the "common good" suggests he is an International Communitarian.[9] Protestant minister Pat Robertson seems to be an International Conservative.[10] President Obama qualifies as an International Liberal.

Although the president is held accountable for international affairs, many other actors are involved. We begin our discussion of global policy by establishing the constitutional bases of governmental authority for making American foreign policy in the military, economic, and social arenas.

IN OUR OWN WORDS

Listen to Kenneth Janda discuss the main points and themes of this chapter.

www.cengagebrain.com/
shop/ISBN/0495906182

Making Foreign Policy: The Constitutional Context

foreign policy
The general plan followed by a nation in defending and advancing its national interests, especially its security against foreign threats.

A nation's **foreign policy** is its general plan to defend and advance national interests, especially its security against foreign threats. The Constitution uses the word *foreign* in only five places. Four are in the section dealing with Congress, which is entrusted to "regulate commerce among foreign nations"; to "regulate the value ... of foreign coin"; to approve any gift or title to a government official "from any king, prince, or foreign state"; and to approve "any compact or agreement" between a state and "a foreign power"

FIGURE 20.1 A Two-Dimensional Framework of International Ideologies

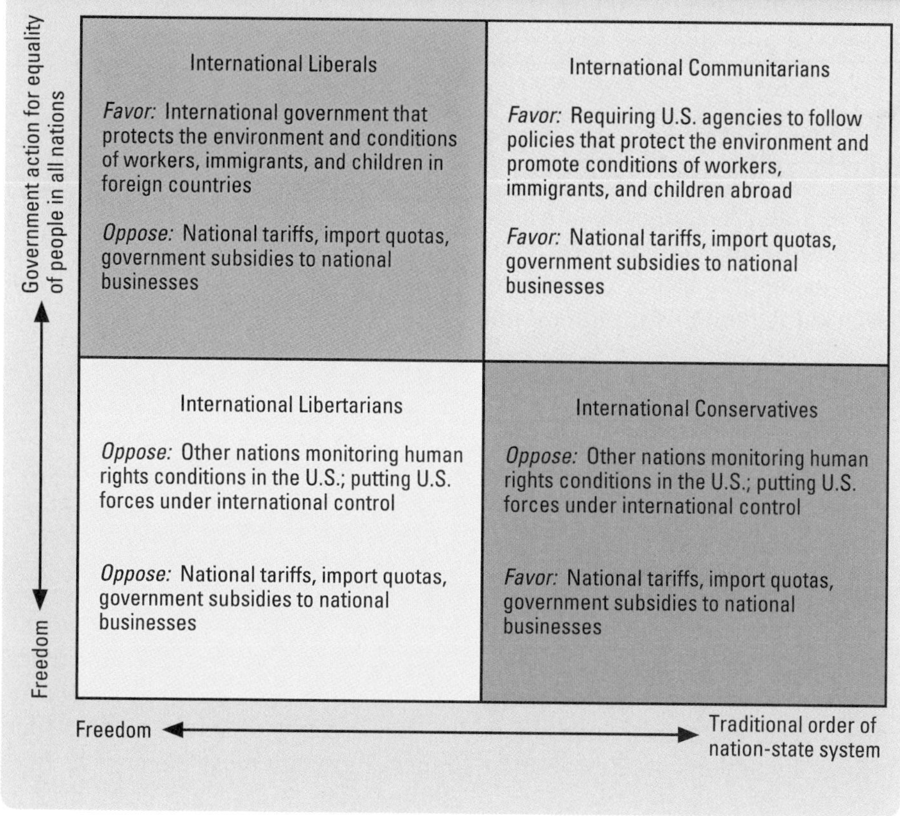

As in Figure 1.2 in Chapter 1, the four ideological types here are defined by the values that they favor in balancing the values of freedom and order with freedom and equality in international affairs. In this typology, however, order is tied to the defense of national sovereignty within the traditional nation-state system of international relations.

in time of war. The fifth mention gives the courts jurisdiction over cases arising "between a state ... and foreign states." The Constitution never uses *foreign* in its article describing the executive branch, and yet the presidency has emerged as the dominant actor in foreign policy. Why?

Constitutional Bases of Presidential Authority in Foreign Policy

One must read between the lines of the Constitution to understand how presidents have derived their authority in foreign policy. The Constitution creates the executive in Article II, which provides that the president

- is commander in chief of the armed forces.
- has the power to make treaties (subject to the consent of the Senate).
- appoints U.S. ambassadors and the heads of executive departments (also with the advice and consent of the Senate).
- receives (or refuses to receive) ambassadors from other countries.

Over time, the president has parlayed these constitutional provisions—plus laws passed by Congress, Supreme Court decisions, and precedents created by bold action and political acceptance—to emerge as the leading actor in American foreign policy. But as in a play, there are other actors in the foreign policy drama, and Congress plays a strong supporting role—sometimes even upstaging the star performer.

Constitutional Bases of Congressional Authority in Foreign Policy

As noted above, Congress already claims most uses of the word *foreign* in the Constitution, and, as in the case of the presidency, the Constitution gives Congress additional powers in foreign policy without mentioning the term. Specifically, the Constitution establishes that Congress is empowered to

- legislate.
- declare war.
- raise revenue and dispense funds.
- support, maintain, govern, and regulate the army and navy.
- call out the state militias to repel invasions.
- regulate commerce with foreign nations.
- define and punish piracy and offenses against the law of nations.

The most salient power for foreign policy on this list is the power to declare war, but Congress has used this power only five times.[11] It has relied more on its other powers to influence foreign policy. Using its legislative power, Congress can involve the nation in programs of international scope or limit the actions of the executive branch. Probably most important, Congress has used the power of the purse to provide funds for the activities it supports—and to prohibit funds for those it opposes. The Constitution also ascribes some powers to the Senate alone, which has made the U.S. Senate the leading chamber of Congress on foreign policy issues. The Constitution requires that the Senate

- give advice and consent to treaties made by the president.
- give advice and consent to the appointment of ambassadors and various other public officials involved in foreign policy.

The Senate has used its special powers to check presidential initiatives in foreign policy. Whereas only the president can *make* treaties, the Senate can *break* treaties—in the sense of rejecting those made by the president.

The Senate and Major Treaties. In truth, the Senate rarely defeats a treaty, having defeated only twenty-one of the thousands it has considered.[12] Some of the defeats have been historically significant, however, establishing the Senate as a force in foreign policy. A hard-hearted Senate lorded its veto power over a very ill Democratic President Woodrow Wilson in 1919. At the end of World War I, Wilson proposed and championed a plan for an international organization—the League of Nations—to eliminate future wars. To enter the League, however, Wilson's treaty had to be approved by two-thirds of the Senate. Wilson, an idealistic, international liberal, was opposed by a group of mostly Republican, internationally conservative senators. After eight months of debate, the Senate rejected his treaty, and the United States never joined the League of Nations. Some attribute the weakness of the League of Nations, which failed to prevent a second world war, to the absence of the United States.

In the early days of World War II, President Franklin D. Roosevelt and British prime minister Winston Churchill revived Wilson's idea for collective security and proposed a new international organization—the United Nations—after the war. By the time the U.N. treaty went to the Senate in the summer of 1945, Roosevelt had died. It fell to President Harry Truman, also a Democrat and mindful of Wilson's failure with the League of Nations, to win acceptance of the U.N. treaty by a Republican-controlled Senate. In public hearings on the treaty, several representatives of isolationist groups spoke against it, fearing loss of American sovereignty to a world government.[13] But by then, both parties in Congress widely accepted U.S. international involvement, and Republican senator Arthur H. Vandenberg, chair of the Foreign Relations Committee, led his party and the Senate to approve the treaty by a vote of 89–2 after only five days of debate. Without the Senate's approval, the United States would not have entered the United Nations.

The twenty-first and most recent treaty rejection by the Senate occurred on October 13, 1999, on the Comprehensive Nuclear Test Ban Treaty. This treaty, signed by President Clinton in 1996, would have effectively outlawed all nuclear weapons testing. Almost all arms control agreements since Eisenhower's administration have been proposed by presidents of both parties and opposed by conservatives in Congress from both parties. True to form, the Nuclear Test Ban Treaty failed to get the required two-thirds majority. All Democratic senators voted for it, and all but four Republicans voted against it.[14]

Governmental leaders around the world reacted angrily to the defeat of a treaty that had been decades in the making. One overseas newspaper editorialized, "If the United States, the sole superpower, refuses stubbornly to ratify a global nuclear test ban treaty that will make the world safer for all, why on earth would any other country want to do it?"[15] In the United States, however, Senator Jon Kyl (R-Ariz.) said that the treaty rejection shows "that our constitutional democracy, with its shared powers and checks and balances, is alive and well."[16]

Skirting the Senate Through Executive Agreements. An **executive agreement** is a pact between heads of countries concerning their joint activities. The Supreme Court has ruled that executive agreements are within the inherent powers of the president and have the legal status of treaties.[17] Executive agreements must conform to the Constitution, existing treaties, and the laws of Congress.[18] Like treaties, executive agreements have the force of law; unlike treaties, they do not require Senate approval. Until 1972 the texts of these agreements did not even have to be reported to Congress. Legislation passed that year required the president to send copies to the House and Senate Foreign Relations committees. This requirement has not seriously affected the use of executive agreements, which has escalated dramatically, outnumbering treaties by about ten to one since the 1930s.[19]

executive agreement
A pact between the heads of two countries.

After NAFTA, CAFTA

CAFTA is a free trade agreement with Central American countries patterned after NAFTA, an agreement among the United States, Canada, and Mexico. Among their other objectives, these agreements were designed to improve the Mexican and Central American economies, resulting in less illegal immigration. Organized labor denounced both agreements, saying they cost American jobs transferred to those countries while not slowing illegal immigration that takes jobs.

(© Darr Beiser/USA TODAY/Copyright May 12, 2005 USA TODAY. Reprinted with permission.)

Most executive agreements deal with minor bureaucratic business that would not interest a busy Senate. On occasion, presidents have resorted to executive agreements on important issues that were unlikely to win Senate consent. In 1992, President George H. W. Bush negotiated an accord with Canada and Mexico that facilitated free trade among the three countries by reducing national tariffs on imported goods. This plan, which reflected a free-market international libertarian ideology, was widely favored by economists but bitterly opposed by trade protectionists and international conservatives.

Instead of proposing the arrangement as a treaty, President Bush framed it as an executive agreement: the North American Free Trade Agreement (NAFTA), which required only simple majorities in both houses to pass.[20] President Clinton inherited the pending NAFTA legislation and—despite opposition from organized labor—shepherded NAFTA through passage with more support from Republicans than Democrats. In 1993, President Clinton signed the NAFTA agreement negotiated by President George H. W. Bush.

In 2004, President George W. Bush signed CAFTA—the Central American Free Trade Agreement—with Costa Rica, the Dominican Republic, El Salvador, Guatemala, Honduras, and Nicaragua. Similar to NAFTA, it drew similar criticisms but was approved in 2005 after close votes in Congress. In 2006, President Bush implemented CAFTA through a presidential **proclamation**, declaring that the trade agreement was in effect. Once associated with official observances (like Mother's Day), presidential proclamations concerning trade have become common as Congress cedes authority to the president in this area.[21]

Constitutional Roots of Statutory Powers in Foreign Policy

Within the framework of the powers the Constitution grants to the executive, Congress has conferred other responsibilities to the presidency through laws—and creative presidents have expanded on these grants of authority. For example, Congress has allowed the presidency certain leeway on the use of *discretionary funds*—large sums of cash that may be spent on unforeseen needs to further the national interest. Similarly, the president's *transfer authority,* or the reprogramming of funds, allows him to take money that Congress has approved for one purpose and spend it on something else. The executive branch also has control over the disposal of excess government stocks, including surplus or infrequently used equipment. The Central Intelligence Agency (CIA) has been an important beneficiary of excess stock disposal.

As commander in chief of the armed forces, several presidents have committed American troops in emergency situations, thus involving the United States in undeclared wars. America's undeclared wars, police actions, and similar interventions have outnumbered its formal, congressionally declared wars by about forty to one. Since the last declared war ended in 1945, over 100,000 American members of the military have died in locations ranging from Korea and Vietnam to Grenada, Somalia, Iraq, and Afghanistan.

Reacting to casualties from the undeclared Vietnam War, Congress passed the War Powers Resolution in 1973 over Nixon's veto. It required that the president "consult" with Congress in "every possible instance" before involving U.S. troops in hostilities and notify Congress within forty-eight hours of committing troops to a foreign intervention. If troops are deployed, they may not stay for more than sixty days without congressional approval (although the president may take up to thirty days more to remove them "safely"). Some critics of the legislation claimed that it did not restrict presidential power as much as extend a free hand to wage war for up to sixty days.[22] The actual impact of the War Powers Resolution is probably quite minimal. Nixon's successors in the White House (like Nixon) have all questioned its constitutionality, and no president has ever been punished for violating its provisions.

After September 11, 2001, President George W. Bush had to work within the War Powers Resolution to build his "global coalition against terrorism." Congress promptly authorized the president to "use all necessary and appropriate force against those nations, organizations or persons he determines planned, authorized, committed or aided the terrorist attacks … or harbored such organizations or persons."[23] Bush relied on this joint resolution to attack

proclamation
An official declaration or statement of action or recognition.

al Qaeda in Afghanistan and to defeat the Taliban regime there in late 2001, prior to the Taliban's resurgence in 2006.

A year later, Congress was not as quick to support the president's use of military force against Saddam Hussein. Bush again sought authorization through a joint resolution in October 2002 that allowed the president

> to use the Armed Forces of the United States as he determines to be necessary and appropriate in order to (1) defend the national security of the United States against the continuing threat posed by Iraq; and (2) enforce all relevant United Nations Security Council Resolutions regarding Iraq.

Although the resolution passed with strong support in both chambers, it was opposed by more than half the Democrats in the House and nearly half in the Senate.

As presidents have expanded their role in the foreign policy drama, the Senate sought to enlarge its part, interpreting quite broadly its power to "advise and consent" on presidential appointments to offices involved in foreign affairs. Senators have used confirmation hearings to prod the administration for more acceptable appointments. Sometimes presidents exploit a quirk in the Constitution that allows appointments when Congress is not in session. In 2007, Bush used such a "recess appointment" to name a major party donor as ambassador to Belgium.[24] Fearing being bypassed with another appointment over the Christmas recess, the Senate did not adjourn when nearly all members went home for the holidays in 2007. One lonely Democratic senator each day formally opened and then closed the session, without transacting any business.[25]

Making Foreign Policy: Organization and Cast

Although American foreign policy originates within the executive branch, the organizational structure for policymaking is created and funded by Congress and is subject to congressional oversight. When the United States acquired its superpower status after World War II, Congress overhauled the administration of foreign policy with the 1947 National Security Act, which established three new organizations—the Department of Defense, the National Security Council, and the CIA—to join the Department of State in the organizational structure. Following 9/11, new legislation sought to coordinate the intelligence activities of all three new organizations.

The Department of State

During its very first session in 1789, Congress created the Department of Foreign Affairs as the government's first executive department. Within two months, it was renamed the State Department.[26] The State Department helps formulate American foreign policy and then executes and monitors it throughout the world. The department's head, the secretary of state, is the highest-ranking official in the cabinet; he or she is also, in theory at least, the president's most important foreign policy adviser. However, some chief executives, like John Kennedy, preferred to act as their own secretary of state and appointed relatively weak figures to the post. Others, such as Dwight Eisenhower, appointed stronger individuals (Eisenhower chose John Foster Dulles) to the post. President Obama surprised everyone by picking his presidential campaign rival, Hillary Clinton. She surprised everyone by accepting. Comfortable dealing with world leaders, she stood against Vice President Biden in supporting the 2009 troop buildup in Afghanistan. In 2010, Secretary Clinton committed the United States to oppose Internet censorship and to punish states for cyberattacks.[27]

Presidents often come to the Oval Office promising to rely on the State Department and its head to play a leading role in formulating and carrying out foreign policy. The reality that emerges is usually somewhat different and prompts analysts to bemoan the chronic weakness of the department.[28] One wrote that in 2008 there were more "lawyers at the Defense Department than the entire U.S. diplomatic corps" and "more musicians in military bands than there are U.S. diplomats."[29]

Like other executive departments, the State Department is staffed by political appointees and permanent employees selected under the civil service merit system. Political appointees include deputy secretaries and undersecretaries of state and some—but not all—ambassadors. Permanent employees include approximately four thousand foreign service officers, at home and abroad, who staff and service U.S. embassies and consulates throughout the world. They have primary responsibility for representing America to the rest of the world and caring for American citizens and interests abroad. Although the foreign service is highly selective (fewer than two hundred of the fifteen thousand candidates who take the annual examination are appointed), the State Department is often charged with lacking initiative and creativity. Critics claim that bright young foreign service officers quickly realize that conformity is the best path to career advancement.[30]

The State Department also lacks a strong domestic constituency to exert pressure in support of its policies. The Department of Agriculture, by contrast, can mobilize farmers to support its activities, and the Department of Defense can count on help from defense industries and veterans' groups. In a pluralist democracy, the lack of a natural constituency is a serious drawback for an agency or department. Exacerbating this problem is the changing character of global political issues. As economic and social issues emerge in foreign affairs, executive agencies with pertinent domestic policy expertise have become more involved in shaping global policy.

The Department of Defense

In 1947, Congress replaced two venerable cabinet-level departments—the War Department and the Department of the Navy—with the Department of Defense, intending to promote unity and coordination among the armed forces and to provide the modern bureaucratic structure needed to manage

America's greatly expanded peacetime military. In keeping with the U.S. tradition of civilian control of the military, the new department was given a civilian head—the secretary of defense, a cabinet member with authority over the military. Later reorganizations of the department (in 1949 and 1958) have given the secretary greater budgetary powers; control of defense research; and the authority to transfer, abolish, reassign, and consolidate functions among the military services.

The role of the defense secretary depends on the individual's vision of the job and willingness to use the tools available. Strong secretaries, including Robert McNamara (under Kennedy and Johnson), Melvin Laird (under Nixon), James Schlesinger (under Nixon and Ford), and Caspar Weinberger (under Reagan), wielded significant power. President George W. Bush chose Donald Rumsfeld, who had previously served as secretary of defense under President Ford but who clashed with Secretary of State Colin Powell over planning and handling the Iraq war.[31] Bush later replaced Rumsfeld with Robert M. Gates, former director of the CIA. Gates proved to be so effective that Democratic president Obama reappointed him. Gates opposed costly weapons systems, like the expensive F-22 Raptor fighter plane, to refocus military strategy on smaller-scale guerrilla warfare.[32]

Below the defense secretary are the civilian secretaries of the army, navy, and air force; below them are the military commanders of the individual branches of the armed forces, who make up the Joint Chiefs of Staff. The Joint Chiefs meet to coordinate military policy among the different branches; they also serve as the primary military advisers to the president, the secretary of defense, and the National Security Council, helping to shape policy positions on matters such as alliances, plans for nuclear and conventional war, and arms control and disarmament.

The National Security Council

The National Security Council (NSC) is made up of a group of advisers who help the president mold a coherent approach to foreign policy by integrating and coordinating details of domestic, foreign, and military affairs that relate to national security. The statutory members of the NSC are the president, the vice president, and the secretaries of state and defense. NSC discussions can cover a wide range of issues, such as the formulation of U.S. policy in the Middle East. In theory, at least, NSC discussions offer the president an opportunity to solicit advice and allow key participants in the foreign policymaking process to keep abreast of the policies and capabilities of other departments.

In practice, the role played by the NSC has varied considerably under different presidents. Truman and Kennedy seldom met with it; Eisenhower and Nixon brought it into much greater prominence. During the Nixon administration, the NSC was critically important in making foreign policy. Much of this importance derived from Nixon's reliance on Henry Kissinger, his assistant for national security affairs (the title of the head of the NSC staff). President George W. Bush picked as head of the NSC Condoleezza Rice, who later became secretary of state. Obama's first choice, retired Marine General James Jones, was replaced by his deputy, Tom Donilon.

The Intelligence Community

Conducting an effective foreign policy requires accurate information—termed "intelligence" in international affairs.[33] Raw data on foreign countries, observations of politics abroad, and inside information are merged into finished intelligence for policymakers through activities spread across sixteen agencies in the executive branch known as the **Intelligence Community**.[34] Of these agencies listed in the photo caption on page 674, the two most prominent are the Central Intelligence Agency (CIA) and the National Security Agency (NSA). The CIA is an independent agency, while the NSA is part of the Department of Defense (DOD), as are the National Reconnaissance Office (NRO); the National Geospatial-Intelligence Agency (NGA); the Defense Intelligence Agency (DIA); and the intelligence operations of the Army, Navy, Marine Corps, Coast Guard, and Air Force—which explains why 80 percent of the intelligence budget is controlled by the DOD.[35]

Many attributed the 9/11 attacks on America to a failure of intelligence, and Congress created an independent commission to investigate the charge. Known as the 9/11 Commission, its 2004 report proposed sweeping reorganization of intelligence agencies and responsibilities. Here is a brief account of its three main elements.

The Director of National Intelligence. Responding to the 9/11 Report, Congress passed the Intelligence Reform and Terrorism Prevention Act of 2004. It amended the 1947 National Security Act, restructured the Intelligence Community, and created an Office of Director of National Intelligence to coordinate all intelligence activities. The law also stripped the title of director of central intelligence (DCI) from the head of the CIA. The new director of

Intelligence Community
Sixteen agencies in the executive branch that conduct the various intelligence activities that make up the total U.S. national intelligence effort.

Agencies of Intelligence

The Office of the Director of National Intelligence is charged with coordinating the intelligence operations of all sixteen agencies whose seals are arrayed here in two rows in alphabetical order: (*top row*) Air Force Intelligence, Army Intelligence, Central Intelligence Agency, Coast Guard Intelligence, Defense Intelligence Agency, Department of Energy, Department of Homeland Security, Department of State; (*bottom row*) Department of the Treasury, Drug Enforcement Administration, Federal Bureau of Investigation, Marine Corps Intelligence, National Geospatial-Intelligence Agency, National Reconnaissance Office, National Security Agency, and Navy Intelligence.

(Office of the Director of National Intelligence)

national intelligence (DNI) assumed all the coordinating functions of the DCI and became the principal adviser to the president and the National Security Council. The DNI also oversees and directs the National Intelligence Program. Critics warned that the DNI lacked the budget and clout to succeed. Indeed, the post became a revolving door, filled by four people in five years. President Obama originally chose as its director Dennis Blair, a retired four-star admiral. He was replaced in 2010 by Lieutenant General James R. Clapper.

The Central Intelligence Agency. Before World War II, the United States had no permanent agency specifically charged with gathering intelligence about the actions and intentions of foreign powers. After the war, when America began to play a much greater international role and feared the spread of communism, Congress created the Central Intelligence Agency (CIA) to collect information and to draw on intelligence activities in other departments and agencies.

Most material obtained by the CIA comes from readily available sources: statistical abstracts, books, and newspapers. The agency's Intelligence Director-ate is responsible for these overt (open) activities in collecting and processing information. The CIA's charter also empowers it "to perform such other functions and duties related to intelligence affecting the national security as the National Security Council shall direct." This vague clause has been used to justify the agency's covert (secret) activities undertaken in foreign countries by its Operations Directorate. These activities have included espionage, coups, assassination plots, wiretaps, interception of mail, and infiltration of protest groups.

Covert operations raise both moral and legal questions for a democracy. Allen Dulles, President Eisenhower's CIA director (and brother of John Foster Dulles, secretary of state), once called these operations "an essential part of the free world's struggle against communism." Are they equally important in a post–Cold War world? Can they be reconciled with the principle of checks and balances in American government? When government engages in clandestine actions, are the people able to hold their government accountable for its actions? Prior to the September 11 terrorist attacks, one analyst argued that "the Cold War may be over, but the U.S. need for accurate information about the world remains acute."[36]

After September 11, some accused the CIA of neglecting covert intelligence activities (such as infiltrating terrorist organizations abroad), and blame centered on director George J. Tenet, who had mobilized the agency for the successful war in Afghanistan.[37] Tenet said it was a "slam dunk case" that Iraq had weapons of mass destruction.[38] When the U.S. chief weapons inspector failed to find major stockpiles of weapons of mass destruction, Tenet's position deteriorated, and he resigned in 2004.[39] Later, he was succeeded by Air Force General Michael V. Hayden, former director of the National Security Agency. In 2007 Hayden ordered release of "the family jewels"—a disturbing 702-page report on domestic wiretapping, spying on journalists and protesters, and failed assassination plots in the 1960s and 1970s.[40] President Obama chose someone outside the Intelligence Community to head the CIA: Leon Panetta, former congressman from California and President Clinton's chief of staff. Panetta soon learned of and ended a controversial CIA program to assassinate terrorists.[41] The program proved less

MORI DocID: 1451843

SECRET
EYES ONLY   Attachment A

"FAMILY JEWELS"

1.

2. Johnny Roselli -- The use of a member of the Mafia in an attempt to assassinate Fidel Castro.

3. Project MOCKINGBIRD -- During the period from 12 March 1963 to 15 June 1963, this Office installed telephone taps on two Washington-based newsmen who were suspected of disclosing classified information obtained from a variety of governmental and congressional sources.

4. Yuriy Ivanovich Nosenko -- A KGB defector who from the period 13 August 1965 to 27 October 1967 was confined in a specially constructed "jail" at[   ] He was literally confined in a cell behind bars with nothing but a cot in it for this period.

5. Various Surveillance and Support Activities -- These are briefly summarized and range from the surveillance of newsmen to the provision of specialized support of local police officials in the Metropolitan area. I believe that each one is self-explanatory and, therefore, no further comment is needed here.

6. Equipment Support to Local Police -- Attached is a list provided me by the Director of Logistics (he will simply report these items in his report) which we have provided local police in the Metropolitan D. C. area over the past four or five years on indefinite loan. During the period when the Agency's installations in this area appeared to be a target of dissident elements

SECRET
EYES ONLY   00005

Revealing the CIA's "Family Jewels"

In June 2007, the CIA released 702 pages of documents known informally as its "family jewels"—fifteen years after the National Security Archive at George Washington University sought them under the Freedom of Information Act. These pages detail the CIA's previously secret but suspected activities of domestic wiretapping; spying on journalists, protesters, and social leaders; mind-control experiments; and failed plots to assassinate foreign leaders. Here is page 5 of the documents, with some sections blanked out.

(CIA National Archives)

effective than killing terrorists using missiles fired from pilotless drone aircraft operated by the CIA in Pakistan, Afghanistan, and Yemen.[42]

The National Security Agency. Created in 1952, the National Security Agency (NSA) today conducts SIGINT–SIGnals INTelligence–using super-computers, satellites, and other high-tech equipment for *foreign* (outside the United States) electronic intelligence surveillance. (This activity contrasts with the CIA's focus on HUMINT–HUMan INTelligence.) NSA's work is highly secret; the joke is that NSA stands for "No Such Agency." Although it keeps a lower profile than the CIA, NSA has more employees and a much larger budget. Located in the Defense Department, its directors have always been high-ranking military officers. Lieutenant General Michael Hayden headed NSA from 1999 to 2005, during which period he acquiesced in secret electronic eavesdropping on U.S. citizens without court warrants and then vigorously defended the program when it became public.[43] In May 2006, *USA Today* revealed that NSA had also secretly collected billions of *domestic* (not foreign) phone call records of millions of Americans from AT&T, Verizon, and BellSouth.[44] Hayden was succeeded by Lieutenant General Keith Alexander, whom Obama reappointed to head NSA.

The Intelligence Community is less communal than feudal. All the agencies—especially the DNI, CIA, and FBI—jealously guard their turf. For example, Obama had to step in to decide who had the power to appoint the top spy—the CIA as in the past or the new DNI, organizationally over the CIA. Obama sided with the CIA.[45]

Other Parts of the Foreign Policy Bureaucracy

Government agencies outside the Intelligence Community provide input to making foreign policy. Due to globalization and the interdependence of social, environmental, and economic issues with political matters, many departments and agencies other than those described above now find themselves involved in global policy. For some, foreign affairs constitute their chief concern. The Agency for International Development (AID) oversees aid programs to nations around the globe. In doing so, AID works with a full range of other departments and agencies, including the Defense Department, the CIA, the Peace Corps, and the Department of Agriculture. Soon after the Haiti earthquake in 2010, AID had established a website, "Help for Haiti," to facilitate assistance.[46]

Other departments and agencies primarily concerned with domestic issues have become more active in the foreign policy arena. For example, the Department of Agriculture provides agricultural assistance to other countries and promotes American farm products abroad. The Department of Commerce tries to expand overseas markets for nonagricultural U.S. goods. In addition, the Department of Commerce administers export control laws to prevent other nations from gaining access to American technologies connected with national security (such as computers and military equipment). As trade has become a more important aspect of foreign policy, the role of the Commerce Department in promoting American business abroad has also grown. The Department of Energy monitors nuclear weapons programs internationally and works with foreign governments and international agencies such as the International Atomic Energy Agency to coordinate international energy programs. Recently it has also supported American energy companies trying to do business abroad.

An array of government corporations, independent agencies, and quasi-governmental organizations also participate in the foreign policy arena. These include the National Endowment for Democracy, an independent nonprofit organization, funded by Congress, to promote democracy in other countries; the Export-Import Bank, a government corporation that subsidizes the export of American products; and the Overseas Private Investment Corporation, an independent agency that helps American companies invest abroad. In addition, private companies hold military contracts to supply food and services to troops abroad—and even to guard convoys and military bases. In Afghanistan in 2009, there were more private contractors than U.S. troops.[47]

This list of bureaucratic entities with foreign policy interests is by no means exhaustive, but it does suggest the complexity of the foreign policymaking machinery. Furthermore, as social and economic issues become more prominent on the global policy agenda, we can expect an increase in the involvement of agencies not traditionally preoccupied with foreign policy. Finally, states and localities have also begun to pay attention to international matters. Most state governments now have separate offices, bureaus, or divisions for promoting the export of state goods and attracting overseas investment into their state.[48] In 2007, for example, the governor of Nebraska, Republican Dave Heineman, signed an $11 million wheat deal with Cuba.[49] All this suggests that the line between domestic and foreign policy will become even more blurred.

A Review of U.S. Foreign Policy

Presidents come to office with an ideological orientation for interpreting and evaluating international events, and they tend to be more internationalist than most members of Congress. Presidents also tend to fill the offices of secretary of state, secretary of defense, national security adviser, and director of the CIA with individuals who are tuned to the presidential wavelength. However, presidents must accept advice and receive consent from Congress. The political result is the nation's foreign policy. Of course, foreign policies change according to presidential and congressional views of "national interests" and according to whatever actions are thought appropriate for defending and advancing those interests. In examining America's role in foreign affairs, it is helpful to structure the review in terms of presidents and the shorthand labels attached to the nation's policies during their administrations.

Emerging from Isolationism

For most of the nineteenth century, American interests were defined by the Monroe Doctrine of 1823, in which the United States rejected European

The Same in Any Language

These three World War I posters (from France, Great Britain, and the United States) were used to persuade men to join the army. Interestingly, all employed the same psychological technique: pointing at viewers to make each individual feel the appeal personally.

(*left*: Swim Ink 2, LLC/CORBIS; *middle*: Lordprice Collection / Alamy; *right*: Library of Congress. Washington, D.C. [LC-USZC4-3859])

intervention in the Western Hemisphere and agreed not to involve itself in European politics. Throughout the 1800s, U.S. presidents practiced a policy of **isolationism,** or withdrawal from the political entanglements of Europe. American isolationism was never total, however. As the nineteenth century wore on, the United States expanded from coast to coast and became a regional power that was increasingly involved in Pacific and Latin American nations. Still, America's defense establishment and foreign policy commitments remained limited.

World War I was the United States's first serious foray into European politics. The idealistic rhetoric that surrounded our entry into the war in 1917—"to make the world safe for democracy"—cloaked America's effort to advance its interest in freedom of the seas. Such moralism has often characterized America's approach to international politics, and it was certainly reflected in Wilson's plan for U.S. entry into the League of Nations. When the Senate failed to ratify the treaty needed for entry, America's brief moment of internationalism ended. Until World War II, America continued to define its security interests narrowly and needed only a small military establishment to defend them.

World War II dramatically changed America's orientation toward the rest of the world. The United States emerged from the war a superpower, and its national security interests extended across the world. The country also confronted a new rival: its wartime ally, the Soviet Union. In the fight against Hitler, the Soviets overran much of Eastern Europe. After the war,

isolationism
A foreign policy of withdrawal from international political affairs.

the Soviets solidified their control over these lands, spreading their communist ideology. To Americans, Soviet communism aimed to destroy freedom, and the prospect of Soviet expansion in Europe threatened international order. European conflicts had drawn the United States into war twice in twenty-five years. American foreign policy experts believed that the Soviets, if left unchecked, might soon do it again.

Cold War and Containment

To frustrate Soviet expansionist designs, Americans prepared to wage a new kind of war: not an actual shooting war, or "hot war," but a **Cold War**, characterized by suspicion, rivalry, mutual ideological revulsion, and a military buildup between the two superpowers, but no shooting. The United States waged its Cold War on a policy of **containment**, or holding Soviet power in check.[50]

The policy of containment had military, economic, and political dimensions. Militarily, the United States committed itself to high defense expenditures, including maintaining a large fighting force with troops stationed around the world. Economically, the United States backed the establishment of an international economic system that relied on free trade, fixed currency exchange rates, and America's ability to act as banker for the world. This system, plus an aid program to rebuild Europe (the Marshall Plan), fueled recovery and reduced the economic appeal of communism. Politically, the United States forged numerous alliances against Soviet aggression. The first treaty of alliance (1949) created the **North Atlantic Treaty Organization (NATO)**, dedicated to the defense of member countries in Europe and North America. In addition, the United States tried to use international institutions such as the United Nations as instruments of containment. Because the Soviets had veto power in the U.N. Security Council, the United States was rarely able to use the United Nations as anything more than a sounding board to express anti-Soviet feelings. (Ironically, the September 11, 2001, attack on America triggered the treaty's defense clause for the first time, but NATO supplied troops for war against terrorism, not communism.)

In the first decades of the Cold War, the United States relied on its weapons superiority to implement a policy of nuclear deterrence. It discouraged Soviet expansion by threatening to use nuclear weapons to retaliate against Soviet power, which had also acquired nuclear capabilities. By the late 1960s, both nations had enough weapons to destroy each other. This led to a MAD (mutual assured destruction) situation: a first strike from either nation would result in the complete annihilation of both sides.

In the 1950s and 1960s, many countries in the developing world were seeking independence from colonial control by Western nations, and the Soviets were paying close attention to these developing nations. They offered to help forces involved in these "wars of national liberation," that is, wars fought to end colonialism. To counter the Soviets, the United States followed policies aimed at **nation building**: strengthening the opponents of communism in newly emerging nations (the so-called Third World) by promoting democratic reforms and shoring up their economies.

Cold War
A prolonged period of adversarial relations between the two superpowers, the United States and the Soviet Union. During the Cold War, which lasted from the late 1940s to the late 1980s, many crises and confrontations brought the superpowers to the brink of war, but they avoided direct military conflict with each other.

containment
The basic U.S. policy toward the Soviet Union during the Cold War, according to which the Soviets were to be contained within existing boundaries by military, diplomatic, and economic means, in the expectation that the Soviet system would decay and disintegrate.

North Atlantic Treaty Organization (NATO)
An organization including nations of Western Europe, the United States, and Canada, created in 1949 to defend against Soviet expansionism.

nation building
A policy to shore up countries economically and democratically, thereby making them less likely to collapse or be taken over.

Vietnam and the Challenge to the Cold War Consensus

Soviet support for wars of national liberation conflicted with American nation building in Vietnam. There, the United States tried to strengthen non-communist institutions in South Vietnam to prevent a takeover by Soviet-backed forces from North Vietnam and their communist allies in the south, the Viet Cong. The Cold War turned hot in Vietnam by the mid-1960s. Over 58,000 American lives were lost before the United States withdrew in 1973. The Vietnam War badly damaged the Cold War consensus on containment, both abroad and at home. Some American critics charged that the government lacked the will to use enough military force to win. Others argued that America relied on military force to solve what were really political problems. Still others objected that America was intervening in a civil war rather than blocking Soviet expansion. In short, Americans disagreed passionately on what to do in Vietnam and how to do it. After signing a peace agreement in 1973, the United States pulled its forces out of Vietnam, and in 1975, north and south were joined under a communist regime.

As the war in Vietnam wore on, President Nixon and his chief foreign policy adviser (and later secretary of state), Henry Kissinger, overhauled American foreign policy under the **Nixon Doctrine**. Now the United States would intervene only where "it makes a real difference and is considered in our interest."[51] A student of European diplomatic history, Kissinger believed that peace prevailed when the great nations maintained a balance of power among themselves. Nixon and Kissinger sought to create a similar framework for peace among the world's most powerful nations. To this end, they pursued a policy of **détente** (a relaxing of tensions between rivals) with the Soviet Union and ended decades of U.S. hostility toward communist China. The brief period of détente saw the conclusion of a major arms agreement, the Strategic Arms Limitation Treaty (SALT I), in 1972. This pact limited the growth of strategic nuclear weapons. The thaw in the Cold War also witnessed greater cooperation between the United States and the Soviet Union in other spheres, including a joint space mission.

President Jimmy Carter's stance on foreign policy from 1977 to 1979 differed substantially from that of his predecessors. He downplayed the Soviet threat, seeing revolutions in Nicaragua and Iran as products of internal forces, not Soviet involvement. In contrast to Nixon and Kissinger, Carter was criticized as being overly idealistic. He emphasized human rights, admonishing both friends and enemies with poor human rights records. He usually leaned toward open rather than secret diplomacy. Nonetheless, his greatest foreign policy achievement—peace between Egypt and Israel—resulted from closed negotiations he arranged between Egyptian president Anwar Sadat and Israeli premier Menachem Begin at Camp David.

In many ways, Carter's foreign policy reflected the influence of the Vietnam syndrome—a crisis of confidence that resulted from America's failure in Vietnam and the breakdown of the Cold War consensus about America's role in the world. For example, his administration deemphasized the use of

Nixon Doctrine
Nixon's policy, formulated with assistance from Henry Kissinger, that restricted U.S. military intervention abroad absent a threat to its vital national interests.

détente
A reduction of tensions. This term is particularly used to refer to a reduction of tensions between the United States and the Soviet Union in the early 1970s during the Nixon administration.

military force but could offer no effective alternatives in late 1979 when Iranians took American diplomats hostage and when the Soviets invaded Afghanistan.

The End of the Cold War

Carter's successor, Ronald Reagan, came to the Oval Office in 1981 untroubled by the Vietnam syndrome. He believed that the Soviets were responsible for most of the evil in the world. Attributing instability in Central America, Africa, and Afghanistan to Soviet meddling, he argued that the best way to combat the Soviet threat was to renew and demonstrate American military strength—a policy of **peace through strength**. Increased defense spending focused on major new weapons systems, such as the Strategic Defense Initiative (dubbed the "Star Wars" program), a new space-based missile defense system (expensive and never implemented). The Reagan administration argued that its massive military buildup was both a deterrent and a bargaining chip to use in talks with the Soviets. During this period, the Cold War climate once again grew chilly. Things changed when Mikhail Gorbachev came to power in the Soviet Union in 1985. Gorbachev wished to reduce his nation's commitments abroad so it could concentrate on needed domestic reforms. By the end of Reagan's second term, the United States and the Soviet Union had concluded agreements outlawing intermediate-range nuclear forces (the INF Treaty) and providing for a Soviet military pullout from Afghanistan.[52]

In 1989, only months after Reagan left office, the Berlin Wall was torn down, symbolizing the end of the Cold War. The conventional view is that the Cold War ended and America won.[53] Some believe that communism collapsed because of Reagan's policies. Others insist that the appeal of Western affluence, Gorbachev's own new thinking, and a shared interest in overcoming the nuclear threat led to the end of the Cold War.[54] Still others argue that both superpowers had lost by spending trillions of dollars on defense while neglecting other sectors of their economies.[55] Regardless of its explanation, the Soviet threat ended—until the Russian incursion into Georgia in August 2008. Once again, Moscow's actions threatened the United States.

Foreign Policy Without the Cold War

In 1990, soon after George H. W. Bush became president, Saddam Hussein invaded Kuwait. Not only did Iraq attack an American friend, but it also threatened the U.S. supply of oil. Bush emphasized multilateral action, building a coalition of nations that included America's Western allies, Eastern European nations, many Arab states, and other developing countries. The United States also won approval for actions against Iraq from the U.N. Security Council. During the Cold War, the Security Council usually proved ineffective because the United States and U.S.S.R. could veto the other's action. However, the two superpowers cooperated against Saddam in this

peace through strength
Reagan's policy of combating communism by building up the military, including aggressive development of new weapons systems.

post–Cold War crisis. After the coalition launched its counterattack in January 1991, the war lasted less than two months. By the end of February 1991, Iraqi troops were driven out of Kuwait and into Iraq, but the cease-fire left Saddam Hussein in power.

Iraq's invasion of Kuwait constituted a visible, vital threat to U.S. interests and galvanized Americans in support of President Bush's military action to repel the invasion. President Clinton, who came to the White House in 1993 with no foreign policy experience, enjoyed no galvanizing challenge and struggled to provide clear, coherent foreign policy leadership. Clinton's presidential campaign emphasized domestic concerns, but he soon found that messy crises in Somalia, Bosnia, Haiti, and then Kosovo absorbed much of his time. His administration replaced the Cold War policy of containment with a policy of **enlargement and engagement.** "Enlargement" meant increasing the number of democracies with market economies and also adding to the membership of NATO. "Engagement" meant rejecting isolationism and striving to achieve greater flexibility in a chaotic global era. But critics worried that the policy did not provide adequate guidelines about when, where, and why the United States should be engaged.[56] Even when Clinton acted with NATO to stop the genocidal violence in Kosovo, his policy was criticized. Nevertheless, Clinton himself drew praise for his efforts to end the fighting in Northern Ireland and for working to broker a peaceful end to the Israeli–Palestinian conflict.

The Hot War on Terrorism

Entering the presidency in 2001, George W. Bush had something in common with Bill Clinton: no foreign policy experience. The attacks on America on September 11, 2001, transformed Bush's presidency, testing him in foreign affairs as no other previous president had been tested.[57] Addressing Congress on September 20, Bush vowed to eliminate the threat to order posed by international terrorism. The sovereignty of other nations would not limit the United States from acting as world policeman to eliminate terrorism.

Bush made international affairs the centerpiece of his administration.[58] He also presided over a brilliant campaign against al Qaeda in Afghanistan. The president and his advisers spent three weeks after 9/11 lining up international support (mainly from NATO countries) and planning for a military response before launching air strikes on October 7 to support anti-Taliban militias.[59] The war against the Taliban (which cost very few U.S. casualties) was effectively over by December 6. On December 20, Hamid Karzai arrived in Kabul to head an interim government with British Royal Marines in the vanguard of a United Nations force.

Flushed with genuine success in Afghanistan, President Bush announced in September 2002 a new doctrine of **preemptive action:** "to act alone, if necessary, to exercise our right of self-defense by acting preemptively against ... terrorists to prevent them from doing harm against our people and our country."[60] Bush explicitly scrapped the doctrine of containment in

enlargement and engagement
Clinton's policy, following the collapse of communism, of increasing the spread of market economies and increasing the U.S. role in global affairs.

preemptive action
The policy of acting against a nation or group that poses a severe threat to the United States before waiting for the threat to occur; sometimes called the "Bush doctrine."

2003 as invoked in his controversial doctrine of preemption and launched war on Iraq.[61]

The war in Iraq dragged on for more than seven years, cost over 4,000 American lives, and produced little success apart from toppling Saddam Hussein. No weapons of mass destruction were destroyed (or found), and Iraq remained a place of violent death with an unstable government, dismal oil production, and crumbling infrastructure. American public opinion turned against the president on Iraq three years after the war began. In May 2003, when Bush had declared that "combat operations were over," 74 percent of the public approved of the way he was handling the situation in Iraq. In May 2006, his approval fell to 29 percent.[62]

President Bush nevertheless defended his decision to invade Iraq.[63] Early in 2007, he authorized a "surge" of about 30,000 additional troops for Iraq, raising the force level to about 160,000. By the end of the year, the extra troops helped reduce the violence in Iraq, and the Iraqi parliament passed some laws to improve the political situation. Nevertheless, the U.S. public's approval of Bush's handling of the situation increased only slightly, to 31 percent.[64] In *Plan of Attack,* Bob Woodward's book on the decision to invade Iraq, Bush is quoted as saying that "it would take about ten years to understand the impact and true significance of the war."[65]

In his election campaign, Barack Obama described the war in Iraq as a "war of choice" (Bush's choice) while the war in Afghanistan against al Qaeda was a "war of necessity." As president, Obama quickly implemented the Iraq exit strategy outlined by the Bush administration and pledged to withdraw all combat forces by August 2010.[66] Lasting 89 months from the invasion in March 2003 to the withdrawal of combat troops, the Iraq war was second to the Vietnam War as the longest in American history.[67]

In Afghanistan, Obama twice ordered troop increases, almost tripling the number to nearly 100,000.[68] While favoring the buildup, most Americans at the end of 2009 opposed the war itself.[69] As more troops engaged Taliban forces, the American death toll rose, as shown in Figure 20.2. The figure shows as well that the 40,000 NATO forces also incurred far more deaths than allied forces did in Iraq. Begun in October 2001, the Afghanistan war had already lasted 105 months by August 2010, when combat troops left Iraq. By then, the war in Afghanistan had become our longest war, surpassing the 103 months of fighting in Vietnam.[70] Authors wrote books about whether Afghanistan would become "another Vietnam."[71]

Even as he sent more troops to fight in Afghanistan, Obama sought to distance his presidency from the unilateral action of the previous administration. In his September 2009 speech to the United Nations, he said, "America will live its values" and promised to lead by example. The Norwegian Nobel Committee referred to that speech when surprisingly awarding Obama the 2009 Nobel Peace Prize "for his extraordinary efforts to strengthen international diplomacy and cooperation between peoples."[72] (See "Compared with What? Who Will Do the 'Right Thing' in World Affairs? 2008 and 2009.")

FIGURE 20.2　　A Tale of Two Wars

The wars in Afghanistan and Iraq had different origins and different combatants. The war in Afghanistan began in 2001 as a direct response to al Qaeda's 9/11 attack on America. Our NATO allies soon sent troops to help under the terms of our common defense treaty. By 2009, foreign NATO troops numbered about 40,000, compared with 100,000 U.S. troops, and accounted for 40 percent of allied deaths. The war in Iraq began in 2003 to eliminate Saddam Hussein's "weapons of mass destruction," which were never found. The Iraq war was not supported by NATO. Although President Bush assembled a multinational coalition, only Britain supplied substantial numbers of combat troops. Consequently, U.S. troops suffered over 90 percent of allied deaths in Iraq. By the end of 2009, combat deaths had dropped sharply in Iraq and risen substantially in Afghanistan.

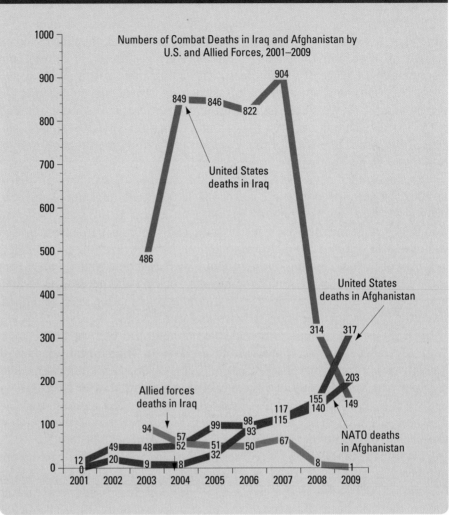

Numbers of Combat Deaths in Iraq and Afghanistan by U.S. and Allied Forces, 2001–2009

Source: Iraq Coalition Casualty Count, http://icasualties.org.

From Foreign Policy to Global Policy

The end of the Cold War and the process of globalization have resulted in a fundamental shift in the nature of foreign policy. For the first time, U.S. foreign policy has taken on a truly *global* focus. We apply the term **global policy**, like *foreign policy*, to a general plan to defend and advance national interests, but global policy embraces a broader view of national interests. Whereas foreign policy focuses on security against foreign threats (mainly military but also economic threats), global policy adds social and environmental concerns to matters of national interest. Whereas foreign policy typically deals with disputes between leaders, ideologies, or states, global policy confronts more silent, cumulative effects of billions of individual choices made by people everywhere around the globe.

Inevitably, global policy requires global action. The players are no longer competing alliances among nations but international organizations that

global policy
Like foreign policy, it is a plan for defending and advancing national interests, but—unlike foreign policy—it includes social and environmental concerns among national interests.

Who Will Do the "Right Thing" in World Affairs? 2008 and 2009

Compared with George W. Bush, Barack Obama inspired more confidence to do the "right thing" in world affairs in respondents from fourteen of fifteen countries surveyed in 2008 and 2009. Indeed, people in Western European countries had more confidence in Obama than Americans did. In every country but Israel, respondents were far more likely to trust him than Bush. Worldwide, it seems, people welcomed Obama's less confrontational approach to foreign policy.

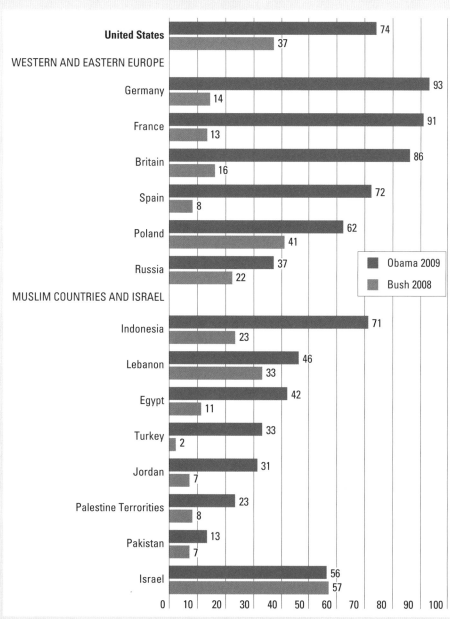

Sources: PEW survey of over 20,000 respondents in twenty-five nations during May and June 2009, available at Pew Research Center, "Highlights from 2009 Pulse of Europe Survey," 2 November 2009, http://pewglobal.org/docs/?DocID=12; report at Pew Research Center, "Confidence in Obama Lifts U.S. Image around the World," 23 July 2009, http://pewglobal.org/reports/display.php?ReportID=264.

cooperate on a worldwide scale. For example, the Internet Corporation for Assigned Names and Numbers (ICANN) meeting in Seoul, Korea, allowed use of Internet addresses in non-Latin characters beginning in 2010.[73] The Russian-language site Kremlin.ru became Кремль.рф.[74] As another example, the International Skating Union relaxed its citizenship rules for pairs and dance ice-skaters. Of forty-two pairs of skaters in the 2010 European championships, fifteen had skaters who started their careers competing for other countries.[75]

The most prominent international organization is the United Nations, which grew in membership from 51 at the founding in 1945 to its present size of 192. As the United Nations expanded its membership to include many newly independent states, the United States frequently found itself outvoted. Fearing loss of sovereignty, the United States reduced its commitment to international institutions such as the United Nations and the International Court of Justice (commonly called the World Court) when they acted in ways that ran counter to American interests. For example, the World Court ruled in 2004 that the state of Texas could not execute a Mexican citizen for murder because he was denied contact with Mexican consular officials until after his conviction—contrary to our treaty obligations. However, the U.S. Supreme Court in 2008 allowed the execution to proceed without a new hearing, contending that the World Court's ruling "is not domestic law."[76]

After the Cold War ended, the United States briefly acted as the world leader and repelled Iraq's invasion of Kuwait in 1991. Soon afterward, the international political agenda shifted toward issues such as world trade, world poverty, the environment, human rights, and emerging democracy—and American leadership was less evident. The September 11, 2001, attacks refocused attention on military action, with the United States leading the war against terrorism in Afghanistan. The invasion of Iraq cost the United States some of its moral authority, and U.S. efforts to combat the nuclear ambitions of North Korea and Iran were often blocked in the United Nations Security Council by China and Russia, which also differed with America concerning other global problems.[77]

Global Policy Issue Areas

Global issues like world poverty and environmental degradation have always existed, and they have moved up on national policy agendas because of globalization, the increased interdependence among nations. Nations today understand not only that their economies are tied to one another, but also that the air we breathe, the illnesses we contract, and even the climate we experience can be affected by events in other countries. In addition to terrorism, globalization (according to one author) involves fighting five other festering wars: against illegal international trade, drugs, arms, transportation of aliens, and theft of intellectual property.[78] Consequently, global policy deals with issues that blend international and domestic concerns. Because global policy requires global action, domestic policies and practices become subject to policies and rules of international organizations.

Conservative opponents of international organizations regard this global interaction as compromising their nation's sovereignty. Not only does global policy present different challenges to policymaking, but also those challenges threaten the very concept of sovereignty that lies at the basis of national interest in traditional foreign policy. In this section, we choose to study only three broad topics within global interdependence: investment and trade, human rights and foreign aid, and the environment. International approaches to all topics involve salient threats to the sovereignty of the nations that take on global policies.

Investment and Trade

At the end of World War II, the United States dominated the world's economy. Half of all international trade involved the United States, and the dollar played a key role in underwriting economic recovery in Europe and Asia. America could not expect to retain the economic dominance it enjoyed in the late 1940s and 1950s, but it was able to invest heavily abroad even through the 1970s, prompting European concern that both profits and control of European-based firms would drain away to America.

During the Cold War, the economically dominant United States often made tactical use of economic policy in foreign policy. To shore up anti-Soviet forces in Western Europe and Japan, the United States lowered trade barriers for those countries. Meanwhile, the United States forbade the export to communist countries of products with possible military uses.[79] These policies were thought to produce security gains that outweighed their economic costs. In the 1980s, however, a combination of tax cuts and increases in defense spending created gaping deficits in the federal budget. These deficits were partly financed by selling U.S. treasury obligations to foreigners. As they bought up American government debt, the value of the dollar soared, making American goods very expensive on the world market and foreign goods relatively cheap. The result was a shift in our balance of trade: the United States began to import more than it exported. And we continued to borrow heavily. With the recession in the late 1980s and declining interest rates, foreign firms became less interested in investing in the United States.

When foreign capital rushed backed into the United States in the 1990s, we feared that foreigners owned too much of our national debt (see page 598), making us dependent on their continued financial support. Then there was the new fear of huge foreign **sovereign wealth funds** (SWFs), very large pools of government money saved from budget surpluses and reserved for investment. About twenty nations—rich from oil or exports—have a sovereign wealth fund (SWF). Examples are Saudi Arabia, Kuwait, United Arab Emirates, and Norway (from oil), and China and Singapore (from exports).[80] SWF investments, which are controlled by foreign governments, can be made or withdrawn for political rather than economic reasons.[81] In 2008, the U.S. Department of the Treasury began negotiations to oversee the behavior of such foreign government funds without discouraging their investments, a delicate task indeed.[82]

sovereign wealth funds
A government-owned fund of financial assets built from budget surpluses and reserved for investment purposes.

Entering the 2010s, the United States no longer dominates the world economy as it did decades earlier. In 1960, the United States generated about 45 percent of the entire world's gross domestic product. By 2008, it accounted for less than 30 percent.[83] Moreover, it had new economic rivals. As late as 1999, the largest economies after the United States were, respectively, Japan, Germany, Britain, France, and Italy—followed by China in seventh place. By 2010, China had leaped to second.[84] The American public sensed the changing situation, seeing the United States as less important in 2009 than it had been a decade earlier and regarding China as a major threat.[85] Moreover, Brazil, Russia, India, and China (known as the BRIC nations) began to demand more say in the global economic order because of their growth and resources.[86]

An increasingly severe problem is American dependence on oil imports. In 1960, the United States produced 7 million barrels of oil a day (more than Saudi Arabia and all the Persian Gulf states combined) and met over 80 percent of its own needs.[87] Due to increasing demand for oil and decreasing domestic supply, the United States today imports about two-thirds of the oil it consumes (see "Politics of Global Change: Growing Dependence on Foreign Oil"). As other nations (especially China) increased their oil consumption, the price climbed and fluctuated wildly, pressuring all countries to seek alternative sources of energy.

As the United States became entangled in the global web of international finance, it became more closely tied to other countries through international trade. In 1970, the value of U.S. foreign trade came to 11.2 percent of the nation's GDP; today, it is about 25 percent.[88] As foreign trade became more important to the American economy, policymakers faced alternative responses. Among them are free trade, fair trade, managed trade, and protectionism.

A true **free-trade** policy would allow for the unfettered operation of the free market—nations would not impose tariffs or other barriers to keep foreign goods from being sold in their countries. All trading partners would benefit under free trade, which would allow the principle of **comparative advantage** to work unhindered. According to this principle, all trading nations gain when each produces goods it can make comparatively cheaply and then trades them to obtain funds for the items it can produce only at a comparatively higher cost.

Although the United States has not embraced a pure form of free trade, it generally favored a liberal international trade regime in the last decades of the twentieth century. (In this case, the word *liberal* is used in its classic political sense to mean "free.") American critics of free-trade policies complain that free trade has too often been a one-way street. America's trading partners could sell their goods in the United States while restricting their own markets through an array of tariffs and nontariff barriers (NTBs)—regulations that make importation of foreign goods difficult or impossible by outlining stringent criteria that an imported product must meet in order to be offered for sale. The Japanese, for example, have been criticized for excessive use of NTBs. In one instance, American-made baby bottles were barred from the

free trade
An economic policy that allows businesses in different nations to sell and buy goods without paying tariffs or other limitations.

comparative advantage
A principle of international trade that states that all nations will benefit when each nation specializes in those goods that it can produce most efficiently.

Politics of Global Change

Growing Dependence on Foreign Oil

In 1960, the United States supplied nearly all its petroleum needs from its own oil wells. By 1995, the United States imported more oil from foreign sources than it produced. In 1960, the United States accounted for 46 percent of the world's oil consumption of 21 million barrels. Despite doubling its own use by 2008, the U.S. share dropped to 25 percent of the world's use of over 85 million barrels. As demand for oil rose across the world, so did oil prices, leading to increased costs for our increasing energy needs and expanded quests for alternative sources.

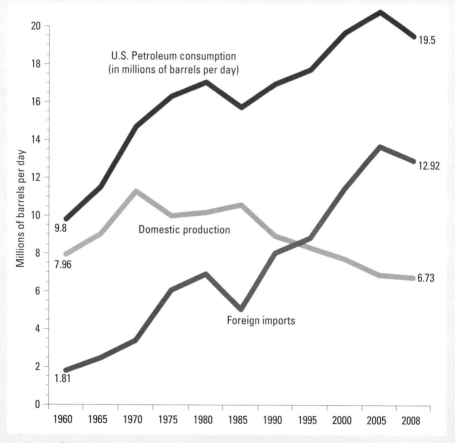

Source: U.S. Government, Bureau of Transportation Statistics, "National Transportation Statistics," Table 4.1, http://www.bts.gov/publications/national_transportation_statistics/#front_matter.

Japanese market because the bottles provided gradation marks in ounces as well as centiliters.[89]

Although the United States has sought to make trade freer by reducing tariffs and nontariff barriers, Americans want more than freedom in the world market; they want order too. Policymakers committed to the idea of **fair trade** have worked to create order through international agreements outlawing unfair business practices. These practices include bribery; pirating intellectual property such as software, CDs, and films; and "dumping," a practice in which a country sells its goods below cost in order to capture the market for its products in another country. The World Trade Organization (WTO) was created in 1995 to regulate trade among member nations. Headquartered in Geneva, Switzerland, it has a staff of 600 to administer trade agreements signed by its 153 member nations and ratified in their parliaments. According to the WTO, "These agreements are the legal ground-rules for international commerce. Essentially, they are contracts, guaranteeing member countries important trade rights. They also bind governments to keep their trade policies within agreed limits."[90] Originally, conservatives in the United States feared that the WTO's dispute settlement authority could be used to erode America's sovereignty and international trading position. Indeed, the WTO has ruled that some U.S. laws violated its regulations, but the rulings were highly technical and with limited impact. For example, in early 2000, the WTO ruled against certain tax breaks to American exporters, and the United States offered to change its tax laws.[91] The WTO has been criticized also from the left for its secretive decision making and for neglecting labor rights and environmental concerns in making purely business decisions.[92]

Free trade and fair trade are not the only approaches to trade that American policymakers consider. America began the 1980s as the world's leading creditor and ended the decade as the world's leading debtor. For years the nation has run up huge balance-of-payments deficits with other nations. The largest of these deficits is with China, which has become our largest trading partner after Canada.[93] The trade acts mentioned above are ways the United States has tried to redress trade imbalances. Another method is **managed trade**, in which the government intervenes in trade policy in order to achieve a specific result, a clear departure from a free-trade system.

Domestic political pressure often bears on trade issues. Although free traders claim that the principle of comparative advantage ensures that eliminating trade barriers would make everyone better off in the long run, their opponents argue that imports threaten American industries and jobs. To guard against these hazards, **protectionists** want to retain barriers to free trade. For example, most unions and many small manufacturers opposed NAFTA and CAFTA. They believed that if tariffs were removed, Mexico, with its low labor costs, would be able to undersell American producers and thus run them out of business or force them to move their operations to Mexico. Either alternative threatened American jobs. At the same time, many Americans were eager to take advantage of new opportunities in a growing Mexican market for goods and services. They realized that protectionism can be a double-edged sword. Countries whose products are kept out of the United States retaliate by refusing to import American goods. And protectionism enormously complicates the process of making foreign policy. It is a distinctly unfriendly move toward nations that may be our allies.

fair trade
Trade regulated by international agreements outlawing unfair business practices.

managed trade
Government intervention in trade policy in order to achieve a specific result.

protectionists
Those who wish to prevent imports from entering the country and therefore oppose free trade.

Nevertheless, there is a growing backlash against globalization, which has not only reduced jobs and wages in developed nations but also increased inequality in developing countries.[94] Even in states such as Iowa, which benefited from expanded exports for its crops and farm equipment, people lament the decline of high-paid factory jobs.[95]

Human Rights, Poverty, and Foreign Aid

NATO's campaign against ethnic cleansing in the Balkans in the late 1990s made clear that the Western democracies would go to war to protect human rights. This is especially true of America, which has long championed democracy and human rights. Support for moral ideals such as freedom, democracy, and human rights fits well with U.S. interests. These elements of liberal democracy permeate our political culture, and we relate better to nations that share them. But the relationship between America's human rights policy goals and its economic policy goals has often been problematic.

The ten big emerging markets (BEMs) that seem especially promising for U.S. investments and trade are the Chinese economic area (the People's Republic of China, Taiwan, and Hong Kong), Indonesia, India, South Korea, Mexico, Brazil, Argentina, South Africa, Turkey, and Poland. These nations have large areas and populations, are growing rapidly, are influential in their region, and buy the types of goods and services America has to sell. The Commerce Department took the lead in helping American businesses win contracts in these nations.[96] But engagement with these countries raises questions that go beyond America's economic interests. Some of the BEMs have dubious records in the areas of human rights, workers' rights, and child labor. Some are lax about environmental standards, intellectual property protection, or nuclear nonproliferation. To what extent should development of commercial ties with these nations override other policy objectives?

In addition to granting nations favorable trade terms, the United States can use other economic tools to pursue its policy objectives. These include development aid, debt forgiveness, and loans with favorable credit terms (see Figure 20.3). Assistance to developing countries also takes the form of donations of American goods, which directly benefits the American businesses that supply the products. Inequality between rich nations and poor nations is growing. Figures show an increasing gap in income between the industrialized states of the North and the nonindustrialized states of the South.[97] This income gap between nations provokes arguments in international politics, just as issues of social inequality motivate those who favor social equality for minorities in domestic politics. Many people believe it is unjust for the developed world to enjoy great wealth while people in the global South, or Third World, are deprived. Sheer self-interest may also motivate policymakers to address this problem. Great disparities in wealth between the developed and developing nations may lead to political instability and disorder, and thus threaten the interests of the industrially developed democracies.

In times of fiscal austerity, foreign aid is an easy target for budget cuts. Foreign aid tends to be unpopular, partly because recipients do not vote in

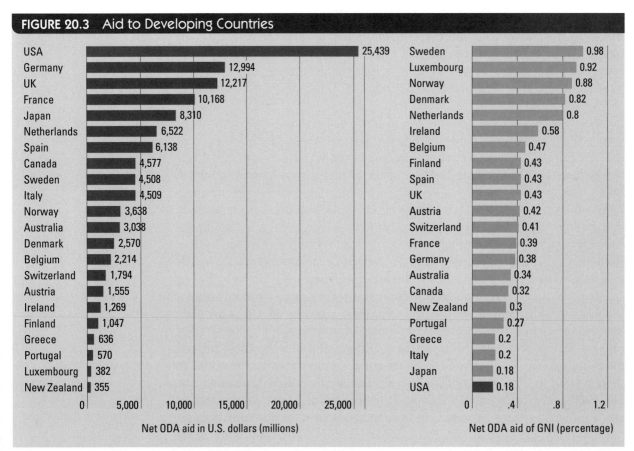

FIGURE 20.3 Aid to Developing Countries

This graph compares U.S. aid to developing countries in 2008 with aid given by the other twenty-one member countries of the Development Assistance Committee of the Organization of Economic Co-operation and Development (OECD). These figures are reported for Official Development Assistance (ODA), a standard measure of grants and loans to a designated list of recipient nations. The data show the amount of aid in absolute dollars given by each country and the amount of aid as a percentage of the country's gross national income (GNI). Although the United States gave the most in dollars to assist developing countries, it gave the least in percentage of national income.

Source: Global Issues website, "Foreign Aid Numbers in Charts and Graphs," April 2010, http://www.globalissues.org/article/35/us-and-foreign-aid-assistance#ForeignAidNumbersinChartsandGraphs.

American elections and because American citizens overestimate what the nation spends on aid. In repeated national surveys, about half the respondents believe that at least 15 percent of the federal budget goes to foreign aid. Half also think it would be appropriate to devote 5 percent of the budget to foreign aid and that 3 percent would be too little. In actuality, far less than 1 percent of the federal budget goes to foreign aid.[98] Figure 20.3 shows how America's aid to developing countries stacks up against the contributions of other developed nations. However, the United States deserves credit for some humanitarian programs, especially in Africa. President George W. Bush championed a $15 billion program to fight HIV/AIDS and $1.2 billion for the prevention of malaria, mainly for millions of bed nets to protect against mosquitoes. Even his critics praised these actions.[99]

Late in his administration, Clinton signed a treaty to establish the International Criminal Court, the world's first standing court with jurisdiction over individuals charged with genocide and other crimes against humanity. Conservatives and the armed services feared that American troops abroad could be vulnerable to prosecution as a result of military operations. George W. Bush not only failed to submit the treaty to the Senate but also announced that he "unsigned" it in 2002 when the sixtieth nation ratified the treaty and the International Criminal Court became a reality.[100] In 2009, 110 countries—but not the United States—were members.[101] However, President Obama and Secretary of State Clinton indicated that they would review the issue of membership.[102]

The Environment

Environmental issues pose new and vexing challenges for those making foreign policy. First, some terms in the debate: Biodiversity and climate change are distinct but intertwined concepts. Biodiversity (biological diversity) refers to the complex interactions between living organisms and their environment.[103] Climate change is one factor that affects biodiversity. The term *global warming* has become a politicized term referring to one aspect of climate change.[104] Even some who doubt that their environment has grown warmer may believe that it suffers more from drought, rain, or wind than earlier in their lifetime. The question is whether human beings have contributed to global climate change. Most scientists think they have.[105] In 2010, the United Nation's Intergovernmental Panel on Climate Change determined that 2000–2009 was "the warmest decade in the instrumental record."[106] If the world really is warming, what can, or should, be done about it?

The value conflict of freedom versus order, which we have seen in domestic politics, surfaces when dealing with the global environment. In the prototypical example, wealthy industrialized nations, which polluted the world in the process of industrializing, tell Third World nations that *they* cannot burn fossil fuels to develop themselves because doing so would further pollute the environment. Leaders in developing countries do not appreciate limits on their freedom to industrialize—limits that serve the developed world's definition of global order.

The 1992 United Nations Conference on Environment and Development in Rio de Janeiro produced the Biodiversity Treaty aimed at conserving the Earth's diverse biological resources through the development of national strategies for conservation, creation of protected areas, and protection of ecosystems and natural habitats. President George H. W. Bush thought the Biodiversity Treaty limited U.S. patent rights in biotechnology and failed to protect U.S. intellectual property rights, so he refused to sign it. Although President Clinton later signed the treaty and sent it to the Senate, the Senate did not vote on it, so the United States is not a party to the treaty. The 1997 Kyoto Protocol set binding greenhouse gas reductions for industrialized countries but not developing countries, including major polluters China and India.[107] It too was signed by Clinton but was never sent to a hostile Senate.

Summit Meeting

In early December 2009, all twenty-one members of the Nepalese cabinet flew by helicopter to near the Mount Everest base camp at an altitude of 17,000 feet. They met there days prior to the Copenhagen conference on climate change to dramatize the reduced snowfall and melting glaciers attributed to global warming. In October, the government of the Maldives, an island country in the Indian Ocean, held an underwater cabinet meeting to dramatize the threat of rising sea levels.

Source: Joanna Jolly, "Nepal Cabinet Holds Meeting on Mount Everest," BBC News, 4 December 2009, http://news.bbc.co.uk/2/hi/8394452.stm. *Photo*: AP Photo/Gemunu Amarasinghe.

The 2009 Copenhagen agreement on climate change, signed by President Obama, required nations only to state intended amounts of reduced emissions.[108] Nations were not ready to submit to global regulations.

The Public and Global Policy

The president and Congress have always considered public opinion when making foreign policy: both had to face the public's wrath if blamed for policy failures. Historically, the public has paid little attention to traditional concerns of foreign policy—alliances, military bases abroad, and general diplomacy.[109] Except for issues of war and peace, the spread of communism, acts of terrorism, and other matters of national security, public opinion on foreign policy seldom affected domestic politics in any major way.

Today, globalization has made nations more interdependent in economic and social spheres, and major events in other countries can have a direct impact on life in the United States. If gangsters in Russia and China cooperate with mobs in Nigeria and Italy, the United States will soon experience an increase in smuggled aliens, drugs, and counterfeit goods.[110] The globalized media immediately communicate foreign affairs to the American audience. If the economy collapses in Asian countries, Wall Street reacts literally within hours. Accordingly, one might expect the U.S. public to pay much more attention to foreign affairs now than it did thirty years ago. Alas, this is not so.

The Public and the Majoritarian Model

To assess the state of public knowledge of and interest in foreign affairs, we draw on a 2008 survey by the Chicago Council on Global Affairs (CCGA), one in a series begun in 1974.[111] The CCGA surveys permit comparisons of public attitudes over time. Immediately after 9/11, the 2002 survey showed a spike in the percentage of the public that was "very interested" in news of other countries, rising to 62 percent above the range of 44 to 53 percent in previous surveys. The 2008 survey, however, fell below pre-9/11 levels, with only 31 percent being "very interested" in foreign news. It asked specifically about globalization: whether "the increasing connections of our economy with others around the world" is "mostly good or mostly bad for the United States." Most of the public (58 percent) thought that globalization was mostly good, but 65 percent thought that it was bad for American workers' job security. Only 17 percent thought it was "very important" to help "bring a democratic form of government to other nations," which had been a cornerstone of President Bush's foreign policy.

The majoritarian model of democracy posits that a nation's foreign policy should conform to public opinion. Is public opinion up to the task? In a major study involving hundreds of survey questions from nine national surveys from 1974 to 2004, two scholars found the public's collective responses to the questions were "coherent and mutually consistent, durable over time, and (given the information available to the citizenry) sensible." They concluded that the average citizen

> is able to form coherent, reasonable views on many matters of foreign policy—presumably through historical learning, talking things over, and making simple use of heuristics and media-reported collective deliberation.[112]

Nevertheless, a separate study found that public opinion has little unique effect on foreign policy; the most important direct effect comes from internationally minded business organizations and their leaders.[113] This finding fits instead with the pluralist model of democracy.

Interest Groups and the Pluralist Model

What would be the nature of policies in a global society made under the pluralist model, in which government responds to competing groups? Ordinary citizens can become interested in foreign affairs when they learn how events in foreign lands can affect their economic interests or values. Often citizens learn from the more knowledgeable leaders of groups to which they belong.

Both labor and business leaders in the auto industry may urge their followers to favor import restrictions on Japanese cars. Church leaders may warn of religious persecution abroad. Aroused citizens often have their positions argued to lawmakers in Washington by group representatives.

As described in Chapter 10, thousands of interest groups maintain offices in Washington, D.C. Even foreign firms, groups, and governments have hired lobbying firms to represent their interests in the U.S. capital. The influence of these groups varies with the issue. Interest groups are more effective at maintaining support for the status quo than at bringing about policy changes.[114] Because global policies often respond to new events abroad, one might expect these policies to form with little impact from interest groups. However, lobbying is also more effective when it deals with noncrisis issues of little importance to the public at large and can take place behind the scenes. Because the public has little interest in foreign affairs, interest groups can wield a great deal of influence on global policies outside matters of national security.

Interest groups focus their attention on foreign policy leaders—including elected and appointed government officials and prominent figures in business, academia, the media, labor unions, and religious organizations. The same major study cited above also compared such policy leaders' responses with the public's responses to identical foreign policy questions. The authors found disagreements between a majority of leaders and a majority of the public on 26 percent of the items.[115] Moreover, actual government policy differed from public opinion on several important issues. For example, most of the public in 2002 favored the Comprehensive Nuclear Test Ban Treaty, supported a treaty to ban land mines, backed an agreement to establish an International Criminal Court to try individuals for war crimes, and endorsed the Kyoto treaty on global warming. The administration opposed all, and none were put into effect.[116]

Sometimes even the current administration does not get its way. Consider the purchase of military aircraft. Since 2006, the secretary of defense and other Pentagon officials have tried to end production of the F-22 Raptor fighter jet, the Air Force's most advanced and expensive weapon, which costs about $160 million apiece. This jet was designed for superpower conflict and was never used in Iraq or Afghanistan.[117] The Pentagon preferred continuing to produce the $77 million F-35 Joint Strike Fighter, used heavily in Iran and Afghanistan. Nevertheless, Congress insisted on building the far more costly plane, and it remains in production. Why? It is supported by a powerful lobby consisting of the Air Force, Lockheed Martin (the primary contractor), and key members of Congress from Georgia (where the plane is assembled) and from Connecticut (where its engines are made).[118] Many other members benefit from the plane's subcontractors scattered across their districts.[119] Military spending clearly fits the pluralist model. Interest groups (both business and labor) want the contracts, and members vote their districts. Congress values the profits and jobs from building the plane more than it respects the Pentagon's case—argued by Defense Secretary Roberts Gates under Republican and Democratic administrations—that it is not militarily useful.

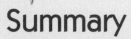

Summary

The ideological orientations of key players on the stage affect the nation's global policy. The president is the leading actor, but Congress, and especially the U.S. Senate, has a strong supporting role. With shared responsibility among Congress, the executive branch, and various agencies, foreign policy can change from drama to farce if the cast is not reading from the same script. For two decades following World War II, from which America emerged as a superpower, there was a clear consensus: communism was the threat, and the goal was to contain Soviet expansion. The Vietnam War challenged that consensus, and Democrats and Republicans began to argue over foreign policy. In the post–Cold War era, international issues and domestic concerns became more closely entwined as a result of globalization, and foreign policy became embraced within broader issues of global policy. Strict notions of national sovereignty eroded as international organizations emerged to deal with global policies.

The September 11, 2001, terrorist attacks on America shifted attention back to military options for dealing with international threats. Although most American citizens want broad international backing for military action, the public supported President George W. Bush's 2003 invasion of Iraq (aided by British troops) to eliminate the threat from Saddam Hussein's weapons of mass destruction. When no such weapons were found after Hussein's defeat, the Bush administration was accused of acting with incorrect intelligence. *The 9/11 Commission Report* severely criticized the performance of the CIA, FBI, and Intelligence Community in the war on terrorism and proposed sweeping reforms that culminated in the creation of a Director of National Intelligence.

Global policy embraces more than military actions. Globalization has involved the nation more deeply than ever before in international investments and foreign trade—especially as the U.S. government depends increasingly on foreign investments and the nation incurs increasing deficits in foreign trade. Issues of human rights and poverty in other countries are now linked more specifically to U.S. foreign aid, which tends to be lower (as a percentage of gross national income) than aid given by other developed countries. Environmental issues, such as global warming, often pit the United States (as the largest source of gaseous emissions) against other countries in negotiating and implementing international treaties (such as the Kyoto treaty) to deal with worldwide health threats.

Generally, the majoritarian model of democratic policymaking does not fit well with foreign policy and fits even less well with global policy, because most citizens do not pay much attention to foreign affairs. Opinion leaders are closely attuned to globalization, however, and global policy tends to be hammered out on the anvil of competing groups, according to the pluralist model.

Visit www.cengagebrain.com/shop/ ISBN/0495906182 for flashcards, web quizzes, videos and more!

Appendix

The Declaration of Independence, July 4, 1776

The Constitution of the United States of America

The Articles of Confederation, *Federalist* No. 10, *Federalist* No. 51, Presidents of the United States, Justices of the Supreme Court Since 1900, and Party Control of the Presidency and Congress, 1901–2007, are available on the Student Website Resources at www.cengagebrain.com/shop/ISBN/0495906182.

The Declaration of Independence, July 4, 1776

The unanimous Declaration of the thirteen United States of America

When in the course of human events, it becomes necessary for one people to dissolve the political bands which have connected them with another, and to assume, among the powers of the earth the separate and equal station to which the Laws of Nature and of Nature's God entitle them, a decent respect to the opinions of mankind requires that they should declare the causes which impel them to the separation.

We hold these truths to be self-evident, that all men are created equal, that they are endowed by their Creator with certain unalienable rights, that among these are life, liberty, and the pursuit of happiness. That to secure these rights, governments are instituted among men, deriving their just powers from the consent of the governed. That whenever any form of government becomes destructive of these ends, it is the right of the people to alter or to abolish it, and to institute new government, laying its foundation on such principles, and organizing its power in such form, as to them shall seem most likely to effect their safety and happiness. Prudence, indeed, will dictate that governments long established should not be changed for light and transient causes; and accordingly all experience hath shown, that mankind are more disposed to suffer, while evils are sufferable, than to right themselves by abolishing the forms to which they are accustomed. But when a long train of abuses and usurpations, pursuing invariably the same object evinces a design to reduce them under absolute despotism, it is their right, it is their duty, to throw off such government, and to provide new guards for their future security. Such has been the patient sufferance of these Colonies; and such is now the necessity which constrains them to alter their former systems of government. The history of the present King of Great Britain is a history of repeated injuries and usurpations, all having in direct object the establishment of an absolute tyranny over these States. To prove this, let facts be submitted to a candid world.

He has refused his assent to laws, the most wholesome and necessary for the public good.

He has forbidden his governors to pass laws of immediate and pressing importance, unless suspended in their operation till his assent should be obtained; and, when so suspended, he has utterly neglected to attend to them.

He has refused to pass other laws for the accommodation of large districts of people, unless those people would relinquish the right of representation in the legislature, a right inestimable to them, and formidable to tyrants only.

He has called together legislative bodies at places unusual, uncomfortable, and distant from the depository of their public records, for the sole purpose of fatiguing them into compliance with his measures.

He has dissolved representative houses repeatedly, for opposing, with manly firmness, his invasions on the rights of the people.

He has refused for a long time, after such dissolutions, to cause others to be elected; whereby the legislative powers, incapable of annihilation, have returned to the people at large for their exercise; the State remaining, in the meantime exposed to all the dangers of invasions from without and convulsions within.

He has endeavored to prevent the population of these States; for that purpose obstructing the laws for naturalization of foreigners; refusing to pass others to encourage their migration hither, and raising the conditions of new appropriations of lands.

He has obstructed the administration of justice, by refusing his assent to laws for establishing judiciary powers.

He has made judges dependent on his will alone, for the tenure of their offices, and the amount and payment of their salaries.

He has erected a multitude of new offices, and sent hither swarms of officers to harass our people, and eat out their substance.

He has kept among us, in times of peace, standing armies, without the consent of our legislatures.

He has affected to render the military independent of and superior to the civil power.

He has combined with others to subject us to a jurisdiction foreign to our constitution, and unacknowledged by our laws; giving his assent to their acts of pretended legislation: For quartering large bodies of armed troops among us; For protecting them, by a mock trial, from punishment for any murders which they should commit on the inhabitants of these states; For cutting off our trade with all parts of the world; For imposing taxes on us without our consent; For depriving us, in many cases, of the benefits of trial by jury; For transporting us beyond seas, to be tried for pretended offenses; For abolishing the free system of English laws in a neighboring province, establishing therein an arbitrary government, and enlarging its boundaries, so as to render it at once an example and fit instrument for introducing the same absolute rule into these Colonies; For taking away our Charters, abolishing our most valuable laws, and altering fundamentally the forms of our governments; For suspending our own Legislatures, and declaring themselves invested with power to legislate for us in all cases whatsoever.

He has abdicated government here, by declaring us out of his protection and waging war against us.

He has plundered our seas, ravaged our coasts, burned our towns, and destroyed the lives of our people.

He is at this time transporting large armies of foreign mercenaries to complete the works of death, desolation, and tyranny, already begun with circumstances of cruelty and perfidy scarcely paralleled in the most barbarous ages, and totally unworthy the head of a civilized nation.

He has constrained our fellow-citizens taken captive on the high seas to bear arms against their country, to become the executioners of their friends and brethren, or to fall themselves by their hands.

He has excited domestic insurrection among us, and has endeavored to bring on the inhabitants of our frontiers the merciless Indian savages, whose known rule of warfare is an undistinguished destruction of all ages, sexes, and conditions.

In every stage of these oppressions we have petitioned for redress in the most humble terms: our repeated petitions have been answered only by repeated injury. A prince whose character is thus marked by every act which may define a tyrant, is unfit to be the ruler of a free people.

Nor have we been wanting in our attentions to our British brethren. We have warned them, from time to time, of attempts by their Legislature to extend an unwarrantable jurisdiction over us. We have reminded them of the circumstances of our emigration and settlement here. We have appealed to their native justice and magnanimity, and we have conjured them by the ties of our common kindred to disavow these usurpations, which would inevitably interrupt our connections and correspondence. They too have been deaf to the voice of justice and of consanguinity. We must, therefore, acquiesce in the necessity, which denounces our separation, and hold them, as we hold the rest of mankind, enemies in war, in peace friends.

We, therefore, the Representatives of the United States of America, in General Congress assembled, appealing to the Supreme Judge of the world for the rectitude of our intentions, do, in the name, and by the authority of the good people of these Colonies, solemnly publish and declare, That these United Colonies are, and of right ought to be, FREE AND INDEPENDENT STATES; that they are absolved from all allegiance to the British Crown, and that all political connection between them and the State of Great Britain is, and ought to be, totally dissolved; and that, as Free and Independent States they have full power to levy war, conclude peace, contract alliances, establish commerce, and do all other acts and things which independent States may of right do. And for the support of this declaration, with a firm reliance on the protection of Divine Providence, we mutually pledge to each other our lives, our fortunes and our sacred honor.

JOHN HANCOCK
and fifty-five others

The Constitution of the United States of America*

[Preamble: outlines goals and effect]

We the people of the United States, in order to form a more perfect Union, establish Justice, insure domestic Tranquility, provide for the common defence, promote the general Welfare, and secure the Blessings of Liberty to ourselves and our Posterity, do ordain and establish this Constitution for the United States of America.

Article I

[The legislative branch]

[Powers vested]

Section 1 All legislative Powers herein granted shall be vested in a Congress of the United States, which shall consist of a Senate and a House of Representatives.

---

*Passages no longer in effect are printed in italic type.

[House of Representatives: selection, term, qualifications, apportionment of seats, census requirement, exclusive power to impeach]

Section 2 The House of Representatives shall be composed of Members chosen every second Year by the people of the several States, and the Electors in each State shall have the Qualifications requisite for Electors of the most numerous Branch of the State Legislature.

No person shall be a Representative who shall not have attained to the Age of twenty five Years, and been seven Years a Citizen of the United States, and who shall not, when elected, be an Inhabitant of that State in which he shall be chosen.

Representatives and direct Taxes shall be apportioned among the several States which may be included within this Union, according to their respective numbers, which shall be determined by adding to the whole Number of free Persons, including those bound to Service for a Term of Years and excluding Indians not taxed, three-fifths of all other Persons. The actual Enumeration shall be made within three Years after the first Meeting of the Congress of the United States, and within every subsequent Term of ten Years, in such Manner as they shall by Law direct. The number of Representatives shall not exceed one for every thirty Thousand, but each State shall have at Least one Representative; *and until such enumeration shall be made, the State of New Hampshire shall be entitled to choose three, Massachusetts eight, Rhode Island and Providence Plantations one, Connecticut five, New York six, New Jersey four, Pennsylvania eight, Delaware one, Maryland six, Virginia ten, North Carolina five, South Carolina five, and Georgia three.*

When vacancies happen in the Representation from any State, the Executive Authority thereof shall issue Writs of Election to fill such Vacancies.

The House of Representatives shall chuse their Speaker and other Officers; and shall have the sole Power of Impeachment.

[Senate: selection, term, qualifications, exclusive power to try impeachments]

Section 3 The Senate of the United States shall be composed of two Senators from each State, *chosen by the Legislature thereof,* for six years; and each Senator shall have one Vote.

Immediately after they shall be assembled in Consequence of the first Election, they shall be divided as equally as may be into three Classes. The Seats of the Senators of the first Class shall be vacated at the Expiration of the second Year, of the second Class at the expiration of the fourth Year, and of the third Class at the expiration of the sixth Year, so that one-third may be chosen every second Year; and if Vacancies happen by Resignation or otherwise, during the Recess of the Legislature of any State, the Executive thereof may make temporary Appointments until the next meeting of the legislature, which shall then fill such Vacancies.

No person shall be a Senator who shall not have attained to the Age of thirty Years, and been nine Years a Citizen of the United States, and who shall not, when elected, be an Inhabitant of that State for which he shall be chosen.

The Vice-President of the United States shall be President of the Senate, but shall have no Vote, unless they be equally divided.

The Senate shall choose their other officers, and also a President pro tempore, in the absence of the Vice-President, or when he shall exercise the Office of President of the United States.

The Senate shall have the sole Power to try all impeachments. When sitting for that purpose, they shall be on Oath or Affirmation. When the President of the United States is tried, the Chief Justice shall preside: and no Person shall be convicted without the Concurrence of two-thirds of the members Present.

Judgment in Cases of Impeachment shall not extend further than to removal from the Office, and disqualification to hold and enjoy any Office of honor, Trust or Profit under the United States: but the Party convicted shall nevertheless be liable and subject to Indictment, Trial, Judgment and Punishment, according to Law.

[Elections]

Section 4 The Times, Places and Manner of holding Elections for Senators and Representatives shall be prescribed in each State by the Legislature thereof; but the Congress may at any time by Law make or alter such regulations, except as to the Places of chusing Senators.

The Congress shall assemble at least once in every Year, and such meeting *shall be on the first Monday in December, unless they shall by Law appoint a different Day.*

[Powers and duties of the two chambers: rules of procedure, power over members]

Section 5 Each House shall be the Judge of the Elections, Returns and Qualifications of its own Members, and a Majority of each shall constitute a Quorum to do Business; but a smaller Number may adjourn from day to day, and may be authorized to compel the Attendance of absent Members, in such Manner, and under such Penalties as each House may provide.

Each House may determine the Rules of its proceedings, punish its Members for disorderly behaviour, and with the Concurrence of two thirds, expel a Member.

Each House shall keep a Journal of its Proceedings, and from time to time publish the same, excepting such Parts as may in their Judgment require Secrecy; and the Yeas and Nays of the Members of either House on any question shall, at the Desire of one fifth of those Present, be entered on the Journal.

Neither House, during the Session of Congress, shall, without the Consent of the other, adjourn for more than three days, nor to any other Place than that in which the two Houses shall be sitting.

[Compensation, privilege from arrest, privilege of speech, disabilities of members]

Section 6 The Senators and Representatives shall receive a Compensation for their services, to be ascertained by Law, and paid out of the Treasury of the United States. They shall in all Cases, except Treason, Felony and Breach of the Peace, be privileged from Arrest during their Attendance at the Session of their respective Houses, and in going to and returning from the same; and for any Speech or Debate in either House, they shall not be questioned in any other Place.

No Senator or Representative shall, during the Time for which he was elected, be appointed to any civil Office under the Authority of the United States, which shall have been created, or the Emoluments whereof shall have been increased, during such time; and no Person holding any Office under the United States, shall be a Member of either House during his Continuance in Office.

[Legislative process: revenue bills, approval or veto power of president]

Section 7 All bills for raising Revenue shall originate in the House of Representatives; but the Senate may propose or concur with Amendments as on other Bills.

Every Bill which shall have passed the House of Representatives and the Senate, shall, before it become a Law, be presented to the President of the United States; if he approve he shall sign it, but if not he shall return it with Objections to that House in which it originated, who shall enter the Objections at large on their journal, and proceed to reconsider it. If after such Reconsideration two thirds of that House shall agree to pass the Bill, it shall be sent, together with the Objections, to the other House, by which it shall likewise be reconsidered, and, if approved by two thirds of that house, it shall become a Law. But in all such Cases the Votes of both houses shall be determined by yeas and Nays, and the Names of the Persons voting for and against the Bill shall be entered on the journal of each House respectively. If any Bill shall not be returned by the President within ten Days (Sundays excepted) after it shall have been presented to him, the Same shall be a Law, in like Manner as if he had signed it, unless the Congress by their Adjournment prevent its Return, in which Case it shall not be a Law.

Every Order, Resolution, or Vote to which the Concurrence of the Senate and House of Representatives may be necessary (except on a question of Adjournment) shall be presented to the President of the United States; and before the Same shall take Effect, shall be approved by him, or being disapproved by him, shall be repassed by two thirds of the Senate and House of Representatives, according to the Rules and Limitations prescribed in the Case of a Bill.

[Powers of Congress enumerated]

Section 8 The Congress shall have Power

To lay and collect Taxes, Duties, Imposts, and Excises, to pay the Debts and provide for the common Defence and general Welfare of the United States; but all Duties, Imposts and Excises shall be uniform throughout the United States;

To borrow Money on the credit of the United States;

To regulate Commerce with foreign Nations, and among the several States, and with the Indian tribes;

To establish an uniform Rule of Naturalization, and uniform Laws on the subject of Bankruptcies throughout the United States;

To coin Money, regulate the Value thereof, and of foreign Coin, and fix the Standard of Weights and Measures;

To provide for the Punishment of counterfeiting the Securities and current Coin of the United States;

To establish Post Offices and post Roads;

To promote the Progress of Science and useful Arts by securing for limited Times to Authors and Inventors the exclusive Right to their respective Writings and Discoveries;

To constitute Tribunals inferior to the supreme Court;

To define and punish Piracies and Felonies committed on the high Seas, and offenses against the Law of Nations;

To declare War, grant Letters of Marque and Reprisal, and make Rules concerning Captures on Land and Water;

To raise and support Armies, but no Appropriation of Money to that Use shall be for a longer Term than two Years;

To provide and maintain a Navy;

To make rules for the Government and Regulation of the land and naval Forces;

To provide for calling forth the Militia to execute the Laws of the Union, suppress Insurrections, and repel Invasions;

To provide for organizing, arming, and disciplining the Militia, and for governing such Part of them as may be employed in the Service of the United States, reserving to the States respectively the Appointment of the Officers, and the Authority of training the Militia according to the discipline prescribed by Congress;

To exercise exclusive Legislation in all Cases whatsoever, over such District (not exceeding ten Miles square) as may, by cession of particular States, and the Acceptance of Congress, become the Seat of Government of the United States, and to exercise like Authority over all places purchased by the Consent of the Legislature of the State in which the Same shall be, for Erection of Forts, Magazines, Arsenals, dockYards, and other needful Buildings;—And

[Elastic clause]

To make all Laws which shall be necessary and proper for carrying into Execution the foregoing Powers, and all other powers vested by this Constitution in the Government of the United States, or in any Department or Officer thereof.

[Powers denied Congress]

Section 9 *The Migration or Importation of such persons as any of the States now existing shall think proper to admit, shall not be prohibited by the Congress prior to the Year 1808; but a Tax or duty may be imposed on such Importation, not exceeding $10 for each Person.*

The Privilege of the Writ of Habeas Corpus shall not be suspended, unless when in Cases of Rebellion or Invasion the public Safety may require it.

No Bill of Attainder or ex post facto Law shall be passed.

No Capitation, or other direct, Tax shall be laid, unless in Proportion to the Census or Enumeration herein before directed to be taken.

No Tax or Duty shall be laid on Articles exported from any State.

No Preference shall be given by any Regulation of Commerce or Revenue to the Ports of one State over those of another; nor shall Vessels bound to, or from, one State, be obliged to enter, clear, or pay Duties in another.

No Money shall be drawn from the Treasury, but in Consequence of Appropriations made by Law; and a regular Statement and Account of the receipts and Expenditures of all public Money shall be published from time to time.

No Title of Nobility shall be granted by the United States: And no Person holding any Office or Profit or trust under them, shall, without the Consent of the Congress, accept of any present, Emolument, Office, or Title, of any kind whatever, from any King, Prince, or foreign State.

[Powers denied the states]

Section 10 No State shall enter into any Treaty, Alliance, or Confederation; grant Letters of Marque and Reprisal; coin Money; emit Bills of Credit; make any Thing but gold and silver Coin a Tender in Payment of Debts; pass any Bill of Attainder, ex post facto law, or Law impairing the obligation of Contracts, or grant any Title of Nobility.

No State shall, without the Consent of Congress, lay any Imposts or Duties on Imports or Exports, except what may be absolutely necessary for executing its inspection Laws: and the net Produce of all duties and imposts, laid by any State on Imports or Exports, shall be for the Use of the Treasury of the United States; and all such Laws shall be subject to the Revision and Controul of the Congress.

No State shall, without the consent of Congress, lay any Duty of Tonnage, keep Troops or Ships of War in time of Peace, enter into any Agreement or Compact with another State, or with a foreign Power, or engage in War, unless actually invaded, or in such imminent Danger as will not admit of delay.

Article II

[The executive branch]

[The president: power vested, term, electoral college, Qualifications, presidential succession, compensation, oath of Office]

Section 1 The executive Power shall be vested in a President of the United States of America. He shall hold his Office during the Term of four Years, and, together with the Vice President, chosen for the same Term, be elected as follows:

Each State shall appoint, in such Manner as the Legislature thereof may direct, a Number of Electors, equal to the whole Number of Senators and Representatives to which the State may be entitled in the Congress; but no Senator or Representative, or Person holding an Office of Trust or Profit under the United States, shall be appointed an Elector.

The Electors shall meet in their respective States, and vote by Ballot for two Persons, of whom one at least shall not be an inhabitant of the same State with themselves. And they shall make a List of all the Persons voted for, and of the Number of Votes for each: which List they shall sign and certify, and transmit sealed to the Seat of Government of the United States, directed to the President of the Senate. The President of the Senate shall, in the presence of the Senate and House of Representatives, open all the Certificates, and the Votes shall then be counted. The Person having the greatest Number of Votes shall be the President, if such Number be a Majority of the whole number of Electors appointed; and if there be more than one who have such Majority, and have an equal Number of Votes, then the House of Representatives shall immediately chuse by Ballot one of them for President; and if no Person have a Majority, then from the five highest on the List said House shall in like Manner chuse the President. But in chusing the President the Votes shall be taken by States, the Representation from each State having one Vote; a quorum for this purpose shall consist of a Member or Members from two thirds of the States, and a Majority of all the States shall be necessary to a Choice. In every Case, after the Choice of the President, the person having the greatest Number of Votes of the Electors shall be the Vice President. But if there should remain two or more who have equal Votes, the Senate shall chuse from them by Ballot the Vice President.

The Congress may determine the Time of chusing the Electors and the Day on which they shall give their Votes; which Day shall be the same throughout the United States.

No person except a natural born Citizen, or a Citizen of the United States at the time of the Adoption of this Constitution, shall be eligible to the Office of President; neither shall any Person be eligible to that Office who shall not have attained to the age of thirty-five Years, and been fourteen Years a Resident within the United States.

In cases of the Removal of the President from Office or of his Death, Resignation, or Inability to discharge the Powers and Duties of the said Office, the same shall devolve on the Vice President, and the Congress may by law provide for the case of Removal, Death, Resignation, or inability, both of the President and Vice President, declaring what Officer shall then act as President, and such Officer shall act accordingly, until the Disability be removed, or a President shall be elected.

The President shall, at stated Times, receive for his Services, a Compensation, which shall neither be increased nor diminished during the Period for which he shall have been elected, and he shall not receive within that Period any other emolument from the United States, or any of them.

Before he enter on the Execution of his Office, he shall take the following Oath or Affirmation:—"I do solemnly swear (or affirm) that I will faithfully execute the Office of the President of the United States, and will to the best of my Ability preserve, protect and defend the Constitution of the United States."

[Powers and duties: as commander in chief, over advisers, to pardon, to make treaties and appoint officers]

Section 2 The President shall be Commander in Chief of the Army and Navy of the United States, and of the Militia of the several States, when called into the actual service of the United States; he may require the Opinion, in writing, of the principal Officer in each of the executive Departments, upon any Subject relating to the Duties of their respective Offices, and he shall have Power to grant Reprieves and Pardons for Offences against the United States, except in Cases of Impeachment.

He shall have Power, by and with the Advice and Consent of the Senate, to make Treaties, provided two-thirds of the Senators present concur; and he shall nominate, and by and with the Advice and Consent of the Senate, shall appoint Ambassadors, other public Ministers and Consuls, Judges of the supreme Court, and all other Officers of the United States, whose Appointments are not herein otherwise provided for, and which shall be established by Law: but Congress may by Law vest the Appointment of such inferior Officers, as they think proper, in the President alone, in the courts of Law, or in the Heads of Departments.

The President shall have Power to fill up all Vacancies that may happen during the Recess of the Senate, by granting Commissions which shall expire at the end of their next Session.

[Legislative, diplomatic, and law-enforcement duties]

Section 3 He shall from time to time give to the Congress Information of the State of the Union, and recommend to their Consideration such Measures as he shall judge necessary and expedient; he may, on extraordinary Occasions, convene both Houses, or either of them, and in Case of Disagreement between them, with Respect to the Time of Adjournment, he may adjourn them to such Time as he shall think proper; he shall receive Ambassadors and other public Ministers; he shall take Care that the Laws be faithfully executed, and shall Commission all the Officers of the United States.

[Impeachment]

Section 4 The President, Vice President and all civil Officers of the United States shall be removed from Office on Impeachment for, and on Conviction of, Treason, Bribery, or other high Crimes and Misdemeanors.

Article III

[The judicial branch]

[Power vested; Supreme Court; lower courts; judges]

Section 1 The judicial Power of the United States shall be vested in one supreme Court, and in such inferior Courts as the Congress may from time to time ordain and establish. The Judges, both of the supreme and inferior Courts, shall hold their Offices during good Behaviour, and shall, at stated Times, receive for their Services a Compensation which shall not be diminished during their Continuance in Office.

[Jurisdiction; trial by jury]

Section 2 The judicial Power shall extend to all Cases, in Law and Equity, arising under this Constitution, the Laws of the United States, and Treaties made, or which shall be made, under their Authority;—to all Cases affecting Ambassadors, other public Ministers and Consuls;—to all Cases of admiralty and maritime Jurisdiction;—to Controversies to which the United States shall be a Party;—to controversies between two or more States;— *between a State and Citizens of another State;*—between Citizens of different States— between Citizens of the same State claiming Lands under grants of different States, and between a State, or the Citizens thereof, and foreign States, Citizens or Subjects.

In all cases affecting Ambassadors, other public Ministers and Consuls, and those in which a State shall be Party, the supreme Court shall have original Jurisdiction. In all the other Cases before mentioned, the supreme Court shall have appellate Jurisdiction, both as to Law and Fact, with such Exceptions, and under such Regulations, as the Congress shall make.

The Trial of all Crimes, except in cases of Impeachment, shall be by Jury; and such Trial shall be held in the State where said Crimes shall have been committed;

but when not committed within any State, the Trial shall be at such Place or Places as the Congress may by Law have directed.

[Treason: definition, punishment]

Section 3 Treason against the United States shall consist only in levying War against them, or in adhering to their Enemies, giving them Aid and Comfort. No Person shall be convicted of Treason unless on the Testimony of two Witnesses to the same overt Act, or on confession in open Court.

The Congress shall have power to declare the Punishment of Treason, but no Attainder of Treason shall work Corruption of Blood, or Forfeiture except during the Life of the Person attainted.

Article IV
[States' relations]

[Full faith and credit]

Section 1 Full Faith and Credit shall be given in each State to the public Acts, Records, and judicial Proceedings of every other State. And the Congress may by general laws prescribe the Manner in which such Acts, Records, and Proceedings shall be proved, and the Effect thereof.

[Interstate comity, rendition]

Section 2 The Citizens of each State shall be entitled to all Privileges and Immunities of Citizens in the several States.

A Person charged in any State with Treason, Felony, or other Crime, who shall flee from Justice, and be found in another State, shall on Demand of the executive Authority of the State from which he fled, be delivered up, to be removed to the State having Jurisdiction of the Crime.

No person held to Service or Labor in one State, under the Laws thereof, escaping into another, shall, in consequence of any Law or Regulation therein, be discharged from such Service or Labor, but shall be delivered up on Claim of the Party to whom such Service or Labor may be due.

[New states]

Section 3 New States may be admitted by the Congress into this Union; but no new State shall be formed or erected within the Jurisdiction of any other State; nor any State be formed by the Junction of two or more States, or parts of States, without the Consent of the Legislatures of the States concerned as well as of the Congress.

The Congress shall have Power to dispose of and make all needful Rules and Regulations respecting the Territory or other Property belonging to the United States; and nothing in this Constitution shall be so construed as to Prejudice any Claims of the United States, or of any particular State.

[Obligations of the United States to the states]

Section 4 The United States shall guarantee to every State in this Union a Republican Form of Government, and shall protect each of them against Invasion; and on Application of the Legislature, or of the Executive (when the Legislature cannot be convened), against domestic Violence.

Article V
[Mode of amendment]

The Congress, whenever two-thirds of both Houses shall deem it necessary, shall propose Amendments to this Constitution, or, on the Application of the Legislatures of two-thirds of the several States, shall call a Convention for proposing Amendments, which, in either Case, shall be valid to all Intents and Purposes, as part of this Constitution, when ratified by the legislatures of three-fourths of the several States, or by Conventions in three-fourths thereof, as the one or the other Mode of Ratification may be proposed by the Congress; Provided *that no Amendment which may be made prior to the Year One thousand eight hundred and eight shall in any Manner affect the first and fourth clauses in the Ninth Section of the first Article;* and that no State, without its Consent, shall be deprived of its equal suffrage in the Senate.

Article VI

[Prior debts, supremacy of Constitution, oaths of Office]

All Debts contracted and Engagements entered into, before the Adoption of this Constitution, shall be as valid against the United States under this Constitution, as under the Confederation.

This Constitution, and the Laws of the United States which shall be made in Pursuance thereof; and all Treaties made, or which shall be made, under the Authority of the United States, shall be the supreme Law of the Land; and the judges in every State shall be bound thereby, anything in the Constitution or Laws of any State to the Contrary notwithstanding.

The Senators and Representatives before mentioned, and the Members of the several State Legislatures, and all executive and judicial Officers, both of the United States and of the several States, shall be bound by Oath or Affirmation to support this Constitution; but no religious test shall ever be required as a Qualification to any Office or public Trust under the United States.

Article VII

[Ratification]

The ratification of the Conventions of nine States shall be sufficient for the Establishment of this Constitution between the States so ratifying the Same.

Done in Convention by the Unanimous Consent of the States present, the seventeenth day of September in the Year of our Lord one thousand seven hundred and eighty-seven and of the Independence of the United States of America the twelfth. In WITNESS whereof We have hereunto subscribed our Names.

GEORGE WASHINGTON
and thirty-seven others

Amendments to the Constitution
[The first ten amendments—the Bill of Rights—were adopted in 1791.]

Amendment I

[Freedom of religion, speech, press, assembly]

Congress shall make no law respecting an establishment of religion, or prohibiting the free exercise thereof; or abridging the freedom of speech, or of the press; or the right of the people peaceably to assemble, and to petition the Government for a redress of grievances.

Amendment II

[Right to bear arms]

A well-regulated militia being necessary to the security of a free State, the right of the people to keep and bear arms shall not be infringed.

Amendment III

[Quartering of soldiers]

No Soldier shall, in time of peace, be quartered in any house without the consent of the Owner, nor in time of war, but in a manner to be prescribed by law.

Amendment IV

[Searches and seizures]

The right of the people to be secure in their persons, houses, papers, and effects, against unreasonable searches and seizures, shall not be violated, and no Warrants shall issue but upon probable cause, supported by Oath or Affirmation, and particularly describing the place to be searched, and the persons or things to be seized.

Amendment V

[Rights of persons: grand juries, double jeopardy, self-incrimination, due process, eminent domain]

No person shall be held to answer for a capital, or otherwise infamous crime, unless on a presentment or indictment of a Grand Jury, except in cases arising in the land or naval forces, or in the Militia, when in actual service in time of War or public danger; nor shall any person be subject for the same offense to be twice put in jeopardy of life or limb; nor shall be compelled in any criminal case to be a witness against himself, nor be deprived of life, liberty, or property, without due process of law; nor shall private property be taken for public use without just compensation.

Amendment VI

[Rights of accused in criminal prosecutions]

In all criminal prosecutions, the accused shall enjoy the right to a speedy and public trial, by an impartial jury of the State and district wherein the crime shall have been committed, which district shall have been previously ascertained by law, and to be informed of the nature and cause of the accusation; to be confronted with the witnesses against him; to have compulsory process for obtaining Witnesses in his favor, and to have the assistance of counsel for his defence.

Amendment VII

[Civil trials]

In Suits at common law, where the value in controversy shall exceed twenty dollars, the right of trial by jury shall be preserved, and no fact tried by a jury shall be otherwise reexamined in any Court of the United States, than according to the rules of the common law.

Amendment VIII

[Punishment for crime]

Excessive bail shall not be required, nor excessive fines imposed, nor cruel and unusual punishments inflicted.

Amendment IX

[Rights retained by the people]

The enumeration in the Constitution, of certain rights, shall not be construed to deny or disparage others retained by the people.

Amendment X
[Rights reserved to the states]
The powers not delegated to the United States by the Constitution, nor prohibited by it to the States, are reserved to the States respectively, or to the people.

Amendment XI
[Suits against the states; adopted 1798]
The Judicial power of the United States shall not be construed to extend to any suit in law or equity, commenced or prosecuted against one of the United States by Citizens of another state, or by Citizens or Subjects of any Foreign State.

Amendment XII
[Election of the president; adopted 1804]
The electors shall meet in their respective States, and vote by ballot for President and Vice-President, one of whom, at least, shall not be an inhabitant of the same state with themselves; they shall name in their ballots the person voted for as President, and in distinct ballots the person voted for as Vice-President, and they shall make distinct lists of all persons voted for as President, and of all persons voted for as Vice-President, and of the number of votes for each, which lists they shall sign and certify, and transmit sealed to the seat of government of the United States, directed to the President of the Senate;—the President of the Senate shall, in the presence of the Senate and House of Representatives, open all the certificates and the votes shall then be counted;—the person having the greatest number of votes for President shall be the President, if such number be a majority of the whole number of electors appointed; and if no person have such majority, then from the persons having the highest numbers not exceeding three on the list of those voted for as President, the House of Representatives shall choose immediately, by ballot, the President. But in choosing the President, the votes shall be taken by States, the representation from each State having one vote; a quorum for this purpose shall consist of a member or members from two-thirds of the States, and a majority of all the States shall be necessary to a choice. And if the House of Representatives shall not choose a President whenever the right of choice shall devolve upon them, before *the fourth day of March* next following, then the Vice-President shall act as President, as in the case of the death or other constitutional disability of the President.—The person having the greatest number of votes as Vice-President shall be the Vice-President, if such number be a majority of the whole number of electors appointed; and if no person have a majority, then from the two highest numbers on the list the Senate shall choose the Vice-President; a quorum for the purpose shall consist of two-thirds of the whole number of Senators, and a majority of the whole number shall be necessary to a choice. But no person constitutionally ineligible to the Office of President shall be eligible to that of Vice-President of the United States.

Amendment XIII
[Abolition of slavery; adopted 1865]

Section 1 Neither slavery nor involuntary servitude, except as a punishment for crime whereof the party shall have been duly convicted, shall exist within the United States, or any place subject to their jurisdiction.

Section 2 Congress shall have power to enforce this article by appropriate legislation.

Amendment XIV

[Adopted 1868]

[Citizenship rights; privileges and immunities; due process; equal protection]

Section 1 All persons born or naturalized in the United States, and subject to the jurisdiction thereof, are citizens of the United States and of the State wherein they reside. No State shall make or enforce any law which shall abridge the privileges or immunities of citizens of the United States; nor shall any State deprive any person of life, liberty, or property, without due process of law; nor deny to any person within its jurisdiction the equal protection of the laws.

[Apportionment of representation]

Section 2 Representatives shall be apportioned among the several States according to their respective numbers, counting the whole number of persons in each State, excluding Indians not taxed. But when the right to vote at any election for the choice of Electors for President and Vice-President of the United States, Representatives in Congress, the Executive and Judicial officers of a State, or the members of the Legislature thereof, is denied to any of the male inhabitants of such State, being twenty-one years of age and citizens of the United States, or in any way abridged, except for participation in rebellion, or other crime, the basis of representation therein shall be reduced in the proportion which the number of such male citizens shall bear to the whole number of male citizens twenty-one years of age in such State.

[Disqualification of Confederate officials]

Section 3 No person shall be a Senator or Representative in Congress, or Elector of President and Vice-President, or hold any Office, civil or military, under the United States, or under any State, who, having previously taken an oath, as a member of Congress, or as an officer of the United States, or as a member of any State legislature, or as an executive or judicial officer of any State, to support the Constitution of the United States, shall have engaged in insurrection or rebellion against the same, or given aid or comfort to the enemies thereof. Congress may, by a vote of two-thirds of each house, remove such disability.

[Public debts]

Section 4 The validity of the public debt of the United States, authorized by law, including debts incurred for payment of pensions and bounties for services in suppressing insurrection or rebellion, shall not be questioned. But neither the United States nor any State shall assume or pay any debt or obligation incurred in aid of insurrection or rebellion against the United States, or any claim for the loss of emancipation of any slave; but all such debts, obligations, and claims shall be held illegal and void.

[Enforcement]

Section 5 The Congress shall have power to enforce, by appropriate legislation, the provisions of this article.

Amendment XV

[Extension of right to vote; adopted 1870]

Section 1 The right of citizens of the United States to vote shall not be denied or abridged by the United States or by any State on account of race, color, or previous condition of servitude.

Section 2 The Congress shall have power to enforce this article by appropriate legislation.

Amendment XVI
[Income tax; adopted 1913]
The Congress shall have power to lay and collect taxes on incomes, from whatever source derived, without apportionment among the several States, and without regard to any census or enumeration.

Amendment XVII
[Popular election of senators; adopted 1913]

Section 1 The Senate of the United States shall be composed of two Senators from each State, elected by the people thereof, for six years; and each Senator shall have one vote. The electors in each State shall have the Qualifications requisite for electors of the most numerous branch of the State legislatures.

Section 2 When vacancies happen in the representation of any State in the Senate, the executive authority of such State shall issue writs of election to fill such vacancies: Provided, that the Legislature of any State may empower the executive thereof to make temporary appointments until the people fill the vacancies by election as the Legislature may direct.

Section 3 This amendment shall not be so construed as to affect the election or term of any Senator chosen before it becomes valid as part of the Constitution.

Amendment XVIII
[Prohibition of intoxicating liquors; adopted 1919, repealed 1933]

Section 1 After one year from the ratification of this article the manufacture, sale or transportation of intoxicating liquors within, the importation thereof into, or the exportation thereof from the United States and all territory subject to the jurisdiction thereof, for beverage purposes, is hereby prohibited.

Section 2 The Congress and the several States shall have concurrent power to enforce this article by appropriate legislation.

Section 3 This article shall be inoperative unless it shall have been ratified as an amendment to the Constitution by the legislatures of the several States, as provided by the Constitution, within seven years from the date of the submission thereof to the States by the Congress.

Amendment XIX
[Right of women to vote; adopted 1920]

Section 1 The right of citizens of the United States to vote shall not be denied or abridged by the United States or by any State on account of sex.

Section 2 The Congress shall have power to enforce this article by appropriate legislation.

Amendment XX

[Commencement of terms of Office; adopted 1933]

Section 1 The terms of the President and Vice-President shall end at noon on the 20th day of January, and the terms of Senators and Representatives at noon on the 3d day of January, of the years in which such terms would have ended if this article had not been ratified; and the terms of their successors shall then begin.

Section 2 The Congress shall assemble at least once in every year, and such meetings shall begin at noon on the 3d day of January, unless they shall by law appoint a different day.

[Extension of presidential succession]

Section 3 If, at the time fixed for the beginning of the term of the President, the President-elect shall have died, the Vice-President-elect shall become President. If a President shall not have been chosen before the time fixed for the beginning of his term, or if the President-elect shall have failed to qualify, then the Vice-President-elect shall act as President until a President shall have qualified; and the Congress may by law provide for the case wherein neither a President-elect nor a Vice-President-elect shall have qualified, declaring who shall then act as President, or the manner in which one who is to act shall be selected, and such persons shall act accordingly until a President or Vice-President shall have qualified.

Section 4 The Congress may by law provide for the case of the death of any of the persons from whom the House of Representatives may choose a President whenever the right of choice shall have devolved upon them, and for the case of the death of any of the persons from whom the Senate may choose a Vice-President whenever the right of choice shall have devolved upon them.

Section 5 Sections 1 and 2 shall take effect on the 15th day of October following the ratification of this article.

Section 6 This article shall be inoperative unless it shall have been ratified as an amendment to the Constitution by the Legislatures of three-fourths of the several States within seven years from the date of its submission.

Amendment XXI

[Repeal of Eighteenth Amendment; adopted 1933]

Section 1 The eighteenth article of amendment to the Constitution of the United States is hereby repealed.

Section 2 The transportation or importation into any State, Territory, or Possession of the United States for delivery or use therein of intoxicating liquors, in violation of the laws thereof, is hereby prohibited.

Section 3 This article shall be inoperative unless it shall have been ratified as an amendment to the Constitution by conventions in the several States, as provided in the Constitution, within seven years from the date of submission thereof to the States by the Congress.

Amendment XXII

[Limit on presidential tenure; adopted 1951]

Section 1 No person shall be elected to the Office of President more than twice, and no person who has held the Office of President, or acted as President, for more than two years of a term to which some other person was elected President shall be elected to the Office of President more than once. But this article shall not apply to any person holding the Office of President when this article was proposed by the Congress, and shall not prevent any person who may be holding the Office of President, or acting as President, during the term within which this article becomes operative from holding the Office of President or acting as President during the remainder of such term.

Section 2 This article shall be inoperative unless it shall have been ratified as an amendment to the Constitution by the legislatures of three-fourths of the several States within seven years from the date of its submission to the States by the Congress.

Amendment XXIII

[Presidential electors for the District of Columbia; adopted 1961]

Section 1 The District constituting the seat of Government of the United States shall appoint in such manner as the Congress may direct: A number of electors of President and Vice President equal to the whole number of Senators and Representatives in Congress to which the District would be entitled if it were a State, but in no event more than the least populous State; they shall be in addition to those appointed by the States, but they shall be considered for the purposes of the election of President and Vice President, to be electors appointed by a State; and they shall meet in the District and perform such duties as provided by the twelfth article of amendment.

Section 2 The Congress shall have the power to enforce this article by appropriate legislation.

Amendment XXIV

[Poll tax outlawed in national elections; adopted 1964]

Section 1 The right of citizens of the United States to vote in any primary or other election for President or Vice President, for electors for President or Vice President, or for Senator or Representative in Congress, shall not be denied or abridged by the United States or any State by reason of failure to pay any poll tax or other tax.

Section 2 The Congress shall have the power to enforce this article by appropriate legislation.

Amendment XXV

[Presidential succession; adopted 1967]

Section 1 In case of the removal of the President from Office or of his death or resignation, the Vice President shall become President.

[Vice-presidential vacancy]

Section 2 Whenever there is a vacancy in the Office of the Vice President, the President shall nominate a Vice President who shall take Office upon confirmation by a majority vote of both Houses of Congress.

Section 3 Whenever the President transmits to the President pro tempore of the Senate and the Speaker of the House of Representatives his written declaration that he is unable to discharge the powers and duties of his Office, and until he transmits to them a written declaration to the contrary, such powers and duties shall be discharged by the Vice President as Acting President.

[Presidential disability]

Section 4 Whenever the Vice President and a majority of either the principal officers of the executive departments or of such other body as Congress may by law provide, transmit to the President pro tempore of the Senate and the Speaker of the House of Representatives their written declaration that the President is unable to discharge the powers and duties of his Office, the Vice President shall immediately assume the powers and duties of the Office as Acting President.

Thereafter, when the President transmits to the President pro tempore of the Senate and the Speaker of the House of Representatives his written declaration that no inability exists, he shall resume the powers and duties of his Office unless the Vice President and a majority of either the principal officers of the executive department(s) or of such other body as Congress may by law provide, transmit within four days to the President pro tempore of the Senate and the Speaker of the House of Representatives their written declaration that the President is unable to discharge the powers and duties of his Office. Thereupon Congress shall decide the issue, assembling within forty-eight hours for that purpose if not in session. If the Congress, within twenty-one days after receipt of the latter written declaration, or, if Congress is not in session, within twenty-one days after Congress is required to assemble, determines by two-thirds vote of both Houses that the President is unable to discharge the powers and duties of his Office, the Vice President shall continue to discharge the same as Acting President; otherwise, the President shall resume the powers and duties of his Office.

Amendment XXVI

[Right of eighteen-year-olds to vote; adopted 1971]

Section 1 The right of citizens of the United States, who are eighteen years of age or older, to vote shall not be denied or abridged by the United States or by any State on account of age.

Section 2 The Congress shall have power to enforce this article by appropriate legislation.

Amendment XXVII

[Congressional pay raises; adopted 1992]

No law, varying the compensation for the services of the Senators and Representatives shall take effect, until an election of Representatives shall have intervened.

Glossary

administrative discretion The latitude that Congress gives agencies to make policy in the spirit of their legislative mandate. (13)

affirmative action Any of a wide range of programs, from special recruitment efforts to numerical quotas, aimed at expanding opportunities for women and minority groups. (16)

agenda building The process by which new issues are brought into the political limelight. (10)

agenda setting The stage of the policymaking process during which problems get defined as political issues. (17)

aggregate demand The total income that consumers, businesses, and government wish to spend for goods and services. (18)

amicus curiae brief A brief filed (with the permission of the court) by an individual or group that is not a party to a legal action but has an interest in it. (14)

anarchism A political philosophy that opposes government in any form. (1)

appellate jurisdiction The authority of a court to hear cases that have been tried, decided, or reexamined in other courts. (14)

appropriations committees Committees of Congress that decide which of the programs passed by the authorization committees will actually be funded. (18)

argument The heart of a judicial opinion; its logical content separated from facts, rhetoric, and procedure. (14)

Articles of Confederation The compact among the thirteen original states that established the first government of the United States. (3)

attentive policy elites Leaders who follow news in specific policy areas. (6)

authorization committees Committees of Congress that can authorize spending in their particular areas of responsibility. (18)

autocracy A system of government in which the power to govern is concentrated in the hands of one individual. (2)

Balanced Budget Act (BBA) A 1997 law that promised to balance the budget by 2002. (18)

bill of attainder A law that pronounces an individual guilty of a crime without a trial. (15)

Bill of Rights The first ten amendments to the Constitution. They prevent the national government from tampering with fundamental rights and civil liberties, and emphasize the limited character of national power. (3)

bimodal distribution A distribution (of opinions) that shows two responses being chosen about as frequently as each other. (5)

black codes Legislation enacted by former slave states to restrict the freedom of blacks. (16)

block grants Grants-in-aid awarded for general purposes, allowing the recipient great discretion in spending the grant money. (4)

blog A form of newsletter, journal, or "log" of thoughts for public reading, usually devoted to social or political issues and often updated daily. The term derives from weblog. (6)

boycott A refusal to do business with a firm, individual, or nation as an expression of disapproval or as a means of coercion. (16)

budget authority The amounts that government agencies are authorized to spend for current and future programs. (18)

budget committees One committee in each house of Congress that supervises a comprehensive budget review process. (18)

Budget Enforcement Act (BEA) A 1990 law that distinguished between mandatory and discretionary spending. (18)

budget outlays The amounts that government agencies are expected to spend in the fiscal year. (18)

bureaucracy A large, complex organization in which employees have specific job responsibilities and work within a hierarchy of authority. (13)

bureaucrats Employees of a bureaucracy, usually meaning a government bureaucracy. (13)

business cycles Expansions and contractions of business activity, the first accompanied by inflation and the second by unemployment. (18)

cabinet A group of presidential advisers; the heads of the executive departments and other key officials. (12)

capitalism The system of government that favors free enterprise (privately owned businesses operating without government regulation). (1)

casework Solving problems for constituents, especially problems involving government agencies. (11)

categorical grants Grants-in-aid targeted for a specific purpose by either formula or project. (4)

caucus A closed meeting of the members of a political party to decide questions of policy and the selection of candidates for office. (8)

caucus/convention A method used to select delegates to attend a party's national convention. Generally, a local meeting selects delegates for a county-level meeting, which in turn selects delegates for a higher-level meeting; the process culminates in a state convention that actually selects the national convention delegates. (9)

checks and balances A government structure that gives each branch some scrutiny of and control over the other branches. (3)

citizen group Lobbying organization built around policy concerns unrelated to members' vocational interests. (10)

civil cases Court cases that involve a private dispute arising from such matters as accidents, contractual obligations, and divorce. (14)

civil disobedience The willful but nonviolent breach of laws that are regarded as unjust. (16)

civil liberties Freedoms guaranteed to individuals taking the form of restraint on government. (15)

civil rights Powers or privileges guaranteed to individuals and protected from arbitrary removal at the hands of government or individuals. (15, 16)

civil rights movement The mass mobilization during the 1960s that sought to gain equality of rights and opportunities for blacks in the South and to a lesser extent in the North, mainly through nonviolent, unconventional means of participation. (16)

civil service The system by which most appointments to the federal bureaucracy are made, to ensure that government jobs are filled on the basis of merit and that employees are not fired for political reasons. (13)

class action A procedure by which similarly situated litigants may be heard in a single lawsuit. (14)

class action suit A legal action brought by a person or group on behalf of a number of people in similar circumstances. (7)

clear and present danger test A means by which the Supreme Court has distinguished between speech as the advocacy of ideas, which is protected by the First Amendment, and speech as incitement, which is not protected. (15)

closed primaries Primary elections in which voters must declare their party affiliation before they are given the primary ballot containing that party's potential nominees. (9)

cloture The mechanism by which a filibuster is cut off in the Senate. (11)

coalition building The banding together of several interest groups for the purpose of lobbying. (10)

coercive federalism A view holding that the national government may impose its policy preferences on the states through regulations in the form of mandates and restraints. (4)

Cold War A prolonged period of adversarial relations between the two superpowers, the United States and the Soviet Union. During the Cold War, which lasted from the late 1940s to the late 1980s, many crises and confrontations brought the super-powers to the brink of war, but they avoided direct military conflict with each other. (20)

commerce clause The third clause of Article I, Section 8, of the Constitution, which gives Congress the power to regulate commerce among the states. (4)

common, or judge-made, law Legal precedents derived from previous judicial decisions. (14)

communism A political system in which, in theory, ownership of all land and productive facilities is in the hands of the people, and all goods are equally shared. The production and distribution of goods are controlled by an authoritarian government. (1)

communitarians Those who are willing to use government to promote both order and equality. (1)

comparative advantage A principle of international trade that states that all nations will benefit when each nation specializes in those goods that it can produce most efficiently. (20)

competition and outsourcing Procedures that allow private contractors to bid for jobs previously held exclusively by government employees. (13)

concurrence The agreement of a judge with the Supreme Court's majority decision, for a reason other than the majority reason. (14)

confederation A loose association of independent states that agree to cooperate on specified matters. (3)

conference committee A temporary committee created to work out differences between the House and Senate versions of a specific piece of legislation. (11)

Congressional Budget Office (CBO) The budgeting arm of Congress, which prepares alternative budgets to those prepared by the president's OMB. (18)

congressional campaign committee An organization maintained by a political party to raise funds to support its own candidates in congressional elections. (8)

conservatives Those who are willing to use government to promote order but not equality. (1)

constituents People who live and vote in a government official's district or state. (11)

containment The basic U.S. policy toward the Soviet Union during the Cold War, according to which the Soviets were to be contained within existing boundaries by military, diplomatic, and economic means, in the expectation that the Soviet system would decay and disintegrate. (20)

conventional participation Relatively routine political behavior that uses institutional channels and is acceptable to the dominant culture. (7)

cooperative federalism A view holding that the Constitution is an agreement among people who are citizens of both state and nation, so there is much overlap between state powers and national powers. (4)

Council of Economic Advisers (CEA) A group that works within the executive branch to provide advice on maintaining a stable economy. (18)

county governments The government units that administer a county. (4)

criminal cases Court cases involving a crime, or violation of public order. (14)

critical election An election that produces a sharp change in the existing pattern of party loyalties among groups of voters. (8)

de facto segregation Segregation that is not the result of government influence. (16)

de jure segregation Government-imposed segregation. (16)

Declaration of Independence Drafted by Thomas Jefferson, the document that proclaimed the right of the colonies to separate from Great Britain. (3)

deficit financing The Keynesian technique of spending beyond government income to combat an economic slump. Its purpose is to inject extra money into the economy to stimulate aggregate demand. (18)

delegate A legislator whose primary responsibility is to represent the majority view of his or her constituents, regardless of his or her own view. (11)

delegation of powers The process by which Congress gives the executive branch the additional authority needed to address new problems. (12)

democracy A system of government in which, in theory, the people rule, either directly or indirectly. (2)

democratic socialism A socialist form of government that guarantees civil liberties such as freedom of speech and religion. Citizens determine the extent of government activity through free elections and competitive political parties. (1)

democratization A process of transition as a country attempts to move from an authoritarian form of government to a democratic one. (2)

departments The biggest units of the executive branch, covering a broad area of government responsibility. The heads of the departments, or secretaries, form the president's cabinet. (13)

deregulation A bureaucratic reform by which the government reduces its role as a regulator of business. (13)

descriptive representation A belief that constituents are most effectively represented by legislators who are similar to them in such key demographic characteristics as race, ethnicity, religion, or gender. (11)

desegregation The ending of authorized segregation, or separation by race. (16)

détente A reduction of tensions. This term is particularly used to refer to a reduction of tensions between the United States and the Soviet Union in the early 1970s during the Nixon administration. (20)

direct action Unconventional participation that involves assembling crowds to confront businesses and local governments to demand a hearing. (7)

direct lobbying Attempts to influence a legislator's vote through personal contact with the legislator. (10)

direct primary A preliminary election, run by the state government, in which the voters choose each party's candidates for the general election. (7)

discretionary outlays Payments made by legislators' choice and based on annual appropriations. (18)

discretionary spending In the Budget Enforcement Act of 1990, authorized expenditures from annual appropriations. (18)

dissent The disagreement of a judge with a majority decision. (14)

distributive policies Government policies designed to confer a benefit on a particular institution or group. (17)

divided government The situation in which one party controls the White House and the other controls at least one house of Congress. (12)

docket A court's agenda. (14)

dual federalism A view holding that the Constitution is a compact among sovereign states, so that the powers of the national government and the states are clearly differentiated. (4)

earmark Federal funds appropriated by Congress for use on local projects. (11, 18)

economic depression A period of high unemployment and business failures; a severe, long-lasting downturn in a business cycle. (18)

efficient market hypothesis Financial markets are informationally efficient—they quickly absorb all relevant information about securities into their prices. (18)

E-government Online communication channels that enable citizens to easily obtain information from government and facilitate the expression of opinions to government officials. (2)

elastic clause The last clause in Article I, Section 8, of the Constitution, which gives Congress the means to execute its enumerated powers. This clause is the basis for Congress's implied powers. Also called the *necessary and proper clause*. (4)

election campaign An organized effort to persuade voters to choose one candidate over others competing for the same office. (9)

electoral college A body of electors chosen by voters to cast ballots for president and vice president. (3, 8)

electoral dealignment A lessening of the importance of party loyalties in voting decisions. (8)

electoral mandate An endorsement by voters. Presidents sometimes argue they have been given a mandate to carry out policy proposals. (12)

electoral realignment The change in voting patterns that occurs after a critical election. (8)

Elementary and Secondary Education Act of 1965 (ESEA) The federal government's primary law to assist the nation's elementary and secondary schools. It emerged as part of President Lyndon Johnson's Great Society program. (19)

elite theory The view that a small group of people actually makes most of the important government decisions. (2)

enlargement and engagement Clinton's policy, following the collapse of communism, of increasing the spread of market economies and increasing the U.S. role in global affairs. (20)

entitlements Benefits to which every eligible person has a legal right and that the government cannot deny. (18, 19)

enumerated powers The powers explicitly granted to Congress by the Constitution. (3)

equal rights amendment (ERA) A failed constitutional amendment introduced by the National Women's Party in 1923, declaring that "equality of rights under the law shall not be denied or abridged by the United States or any State on account of sex." (16)

equality of opportunity The idea that each person is guaranteed the same chance to succeed in life. (1, 16)

equality of outcome The concept that society must ensure that people are equal, and governments must design policies to redistribute wealth and status so that economic and social equality is actually achieved. (1, 16)

establishment clause The first clause in the First Amendment, which forbids government establishment of religion. (15)

ex post facto laws Laws that declare an action to be criminal after it has been performed. (15)

exclusionary rule The judicial rule that states that evidence obtained in an illegal search and seizure cannot be used in trial. (15)

executive agreement A pact between the heads of two countries. (20)

executive branch The law-enforcing branch of government. (3)

Executive Office of the President The president's executive aides and their staffs; the extended White House executive establishment. (12)

executive orders Presidential directives that create or modify laws and public policies, without the direct approval of Congress. (12)

extraordinary majority A majority greater than the minimum of 50 percent plus one. (3)

fair trade Trade regulated by international agreements outlawing unfair business practices. (20)

Federal Communications Commission (FCC) An independent federal agency that regulates interstate and international communication by radio, television, telephone, telegraph, cable, and satellite. (6)

Federal Election Commission (FEC) A bipartisan federal agency of six members that oversees the financing of national election campaigns. (9)

federal question An issue covered by the U.S. Constitution, national laws, or U.S. treaties. (14)

Federal Reserve System The system of banks that acts as the central bank of the United States and controls major monetary policies. (18)

federalism The division of power between a central government and regional governments. (3, 4)

feedback Information received by policymakers about the effectiveness of public policy. (17)

feminization of poverty The term applied to the fact that a growing percentage of all poor Americans are women or the dependents of women. (19)

fighting words Speech that is not protected by the First Amendment because it inflicts injury or tends to incite an immediate disturbance of the peace. (15)

filibuster A delaying tactic, used in the Senate, that involves speechmaking to prevent action on a piece of legislation. (11)

first-past-the-post elections A British term for elections conducted in single-member districts that award victory to the candidate with the most votes. (9)

fiscal policies Economic policies that involve government spending and taxing. (18)

fiscal year The twelve-month period from October 1 to September 30 used by the government for accounting purposes. A fiscal year budget is named for the year in which it ends. (18)

501(c)4 social welfare organizations Groups named after Section 501 of the Internal Revenue Code that operate for promotion of social welfare; they are exempt from reporting donors if they spend most of their funds on issues, not candidates. (9)

527 committees Committees named after Section 527 of the Internal Revenue Code; they enjoy tax-exempt status in election campaigns if they are unaffiliated with political parties and take positions on issues, not specific candidates. (9)

foreign policy The general plan followed by a nation in defending and advancing its national interests, especially its security against foreign threats. (20)

formula grants Categorical grants distributed according to a particular set of rules, called a formula, that specify who is eligible for the grants and how much each eligible applicant will receive. (4)

fragmentation In policymaking, the phenomenon of attacking a single problem in different and sometimes competing ways. (17)

franchise The right to vote. Also called *suffrage*. (7)

free trade An economic policy that allows businesses in different nations to sell and buy goods without paying tariffs or other limitations. (20)

freedom from Immunity, as in *freedom from want*. (1)

freedom of An absence of constraints on behavior, as in *freedom of speech* or *freedom of religion*. (1)

free-exercise clause The second clause in the First Amendment, which prevents the government from interfering with the exercise of religion. (15)

free-expression clauses The press and speech clauses of the First Amendment. (15)

free-rider problem The situation in which people benefit from the activities of an organization (such as an interest group) but do not contribute to those activities. (10)

front-loading States' practice of moving delegate selection primaries and caucuses earlier in the calendar year to gain media and candidate attention. (9)

gatekeepers Media executives, news editors, and prominent reporters who direct the flow of news. (6)

general election A national election held by law in November of every even-numbered year. (9)

gerrymandering Redrawing a congressional district to intentionally benefit one political party. (11)

global policy Like foreign policy, it is a plan for defending and advancing national interests, but—unlike foreign policy—it includes social and environmental concerns among national interests. (20)

globalization The increasing interdependence of citizens and nations across the world. (1)

going public A strategy whereby a president seeks to influence policy elites and media coverage by appealing directly to the American people. (6)

good faith exception An exception to the Supreme Court exclusionary rule, holding that evidence seized on the basis of a mistakenly issued search warrant can be introduced at trial if the mistake was made in good faith, that is, if all the parties involved had reason at the time to believe that the warrant was proper. (15)

government The legitimate use of force to control human behavior; also, the organization or agency authorized to exercise that force. (1)

government corporations Government agencies that perform services that might be provided by the private sector but that either involve insufficient financial incentive or are better provided when they are somehow linked with government. (13)

Government Performance and Results Act A law requiring each government agency to implement quantifiable standards to measure its performance in meeting stated program goals. (13)

grant-in-aid Money provided by one level of government to another to be spent for a given purpose. (4)

grassroots lobbying Lobbying activities performed by rank-and-file interest group members and would-be members. (10)

Great Compromise Submitted by the Connecticut delegation to the Constitutional Convention of 1787, and thus also known as the Connecticut Compromise, a plan calling for a bicameral legislature in which the House of Representatives would be apportioned according to population and the states would be represented equally in the Senate. (3)

Great Depression The longest and deepest setback the American economy has ever experienced. It began with the stock market crash on October 24, 1929, and did not end until the start of World War II. (19)

Great Society President Lyndon Johnson's broad array of programs designed to redress political, social, and economic inequality. (19)

gridlock A situation in which government is incapable of acting on important issues. (12)

gross domestic product (GDP) The total value of the goods and services produced by a country during a year. (18)

hard money Financial contributions given directly to a candidate running for congressional office or the presidency. (9)

home rule The right to enact and enforce legislation locally. (4)

horse race journalism Election coverage by the mass media that focuses on which candidate is ahead rather than on national issues. (6)

impeachment The formal charging of a government official with "treason, bribery, or other high crimes and misdemeanors." (11)

implementation The process of putting specific policies into operation. (13, 17)

implied powers Those powers that Congress needs to execute its enumerated powers. (3, 4)

incremental budgeting A method of budget making that involves adding new funds (an increment) onto the amount previously budgeted (in last year's budget). (18)

incrementalism Policymaking characterized by a series of decisions, each instituting modest change. (13)

incumbent A current officeholder. (11)

independent agencies Executive agencies that are not part of a cabinet department. (13)

inflation An economic condition characterized by price increases linked to a decrease in the value of the currency. (18)

influencing behavior Behavior that seeks to modify or reverse government policy to serve political interests. (7)

information campaign An organized effort to gain public backing by bringing a group's views to public attention. (10)

infotainment A mix of information and diversion oriented to personalities or celebrities, not linked to the day's events, and usually unrelated to public affairs or policy; often called "soft news." (6)

inherent powers Authority claimed by the president that is not clearly specified in the Constitution. Typically, these powers are inferred from the Constitution. (12)

initiative A procedure by which voters can propose an issue to be decided by the legislature or by the people in a referendum. It requires gathering a specified number of signatures and submitting a petition to a designated agency. (7)

Intelligence Community Sixteen agencies in the executive branch that conduct the various intelligence activities that make up the total U.S. national intelligence effort. (20)

interest group An organized group of individuals that seeks to influence public policy. Also called a *lobby*. (2, 10)

interest group entrepreneur An interest group organizer or leader. (10)

invidious discrimination Discrimination against persons or groups that works to their harm and is based on animosity. (16)

isolationism A foreign policy of withdrawal from international political affairs. (20)

issue definition Our conception of the problem at hand. (17)

issue framing The way that politicians or interest group leaders define an issue when presenting it to others. (5)

issue network A shared-knowledge group consisting of representatives of various interests involved in some particular aspect of public policy. (17)

joint committee A committee made up of members of both the House and the Senate. (11)

judgment The judicial decision in a court case. (14)

judicial activism A judicial philosophy by which judges tend not to defer to decisions of the elected branches of government, resulting in the invalidation or emasculation of those decisions. (14)

judicial branch The law-interpreting branch of government. (3)

judicial restraint A judicial philosophy by which judges tend to defer to decisions of the elected branches of government. (14)

judicial review The power to declare congressional (and presidential) acts invalid because they violate the Constitution. (3, 14)

Keynesian theory An economic theory stating that the government can stabilize the economy—that is, can smooth business cycles—by controlling the level of aggregate demand, and that the level of aggregate demand can be controlled by means of fiscal and monetary policies. (18)

laissez faire An economic doctrine that opposes any form of government intervention in business. (1)

legislative branch The law-making branch of government. (3)

legislative liaison staff Those people who act as the communications link between the White House and Congress, advising the president or cabinet secretaries on the status of pending legislation. (12)

liberalism The belief that states should leave individuals free to follow their individual pursuits. Note that this differs from the definition of *liberal* later in this chapter. (1)

liberals Those who are willing to use government to promote equality but not order. (1)

libertarianism A political ideology that is opposed to all government action except as necessary to protect life and property. (1)

libertarians Those who are opposed to using government to promote either order or equality. (1)

lobby See *interest group*. (10)

lobbyist A representative of an interest group. (10)

majoritarian model of democracy The classical theory of democracy in which government by the people is interpreted as government by the majority of the people. (2)

majority leader The head of the majority party in the Senate; the second-highest-ranking member of the majority party in the House. (11)

majority representation The system by which one office, contested by two or more candidates, is won by the single candidate who collects the most votes. (8)

majority rule The principle—basic to procedural democratic theory—that the decision of a group must reflect the preference of more than half of those participating; a simple majority. (2)

managed trade Government intervention in trade policy in order to achieve a specific result. (20)

mandate A requirement that a state undertake an activity or provide a service, in keeping with minimum national standards. (4)

mandatory outlays Payments that government must make by law. (18)

mandatory spending In the Budget Enforcement Act of 1990, expenditures required by previous commitments. (18)

market-driven journalism Both reporting news and running commercials geared to a target audience defined by demographic characteristics. (6)

mass media The means employed in mass communication; often divided into print media and broadcast media. (6)

means-tested benefits Conditional benefits provided by government to individuals whose income falls below a designated threshold. (19)

media event A situation that is so "newsworthy" that the mass media are compelled to cover it. Candidates in elections often create such situations to garner media attention. (6)

Medicaid A need-based comprehensive medical and hospitalization program. (19)

Medicare A health insurance program serving primarily persons sixty-five and older. (19)

minority rights The benefits of government that cannot be denied to any citizen by majority decisions. (2)

***Miranda* warnings** Statements concerning rights that police are required to make to a person before he or she is subjected to in-custody questioning. (15)

modified closed primaries Primary elections that allow individual state parties to decide whether they permit independents to vote in their primaries and for which offices. (9)

modified open primaries Primary elections that entitle independent voters to vote in a party's primary. (9)

monetarists Those who argue that government can effectively control the performance of an economy mainly by controlling the supply of money. (18)

monetary policies Economic policies that involve control of, and changes in, the supply of money. (18)

municipal governments The government units that administer a city or town. (4)

nation building A policy to shore up countries economically and democratically, thereby making them less likely to collapse or be taken over. (20)

national committee A committee of a political party composed of party chairpersons and party officials from every state. (8)

national convention A gathering of delegates of a single political party from across the country to choose candidates for president and vice president and to adopt a party platform. (8)

national sovereignty A political entity's externally recognized right to exercise final authority over its affairs. (1)

necessary and proper clause The last clause in Section 8 of Article I of the Constitution, which gives Congress the means to execute its enumerated powers. This clause is the basis for Congress's implied powers. Also called the *elastic clause.* (3)

New Deal The measures advocated by the Franklin D. Roosevelt administration to alleviate the Depression. (19)

New Jersey Plan Submitted by the head of the New Jersey delegation to the Constitutional Convention of 1787, a set of nine resolutions that would have, in effect, preserved the Articles of Confederation by amending rather than replacing them. (3)

newsworthiness The degree to which a news story is important enough to be covered in the mass media. (6)

Nineteenth Amendment The amendment to the Constitution, adopted in 1920, that ensures women of the right to vote. (16)

Nixon Doctrine Nixon's policy, formulated with assistance from Henry Kissinger, that restricted U.S. military intervention abroad absent a threat to its vital national interests. (20)

No Child Left Behind Act of 2001 (NCLB) The latest reauthorization of the Elementary and Secondary Education Act. (19)

nomination Designation as an official candidate of a political party. (8)

non-means-tested benefits Benefits provided by government to all citizens, regardless of income; Medicare and Social Security are examples. (19)

nonprofits Organizations that are not part of government or business and cannot distribute profits to shareholders or to anyone else. (17)

normal distribution A symmetrical bell-shaped distribution (of opinions) centered on a single mode, or most frequent response. (5)

norms An organization's informal, unwritten rules that guide individual behavior. (13)

North Atlantic Treaty Organization (NATO) An organization including nations of Western Europe, the United States, and Canada, created in 1949 to defend against Soviet expansionism. (20)

obligation of contracts The obligation of the parties to a contract to carry out its terms. (15)

Office of Management and Budget The budgeting arm of the Executive Office; prepares the president's budget. (18)

oligarchy A system of government in which power is concentrated in the hands of a few people. (2)

open election An election that lacks an incumbent. (9)

open primaries Primary elections in which voters need not declare their party affiliation and can choose one party's primary ballot to take into the voting booth. (9)

order Established ways of social behavior. Maintaining order is the oldest purpose of government. (1)

original jurisdiction The authority of a court to hear a case before any other court does. (14)

oversight The process of reviewing the operations of an agency to determine whether it is carrying out policies as Congress intended. (11)

parliamentary system A system of government in which the chief executive is the leader whose party holds the most seats in the legislature after an election or whose party forms a major part of the ruling coalition. (11)

participatory democracy A system of government where rank-and-file citizens rule themselves rather than electing representatives to govern on their behalf. (2)

party conference A meeting to select party leaders and decide committee assignments, held at the beginning of a session of Congress by Republicans or Democrats in each chamber. (8)

party identification A voter's sense of psychological attachment to a party. (8)

party machine A centralized party organization that dominates local politics by controlling elections. (8)

party platform The statement of policies of a national political party. (8)

pay-go The requirement that any tax cut or expansion of an entitlement program must be offset by a tax increase or other savings. (18)

peace through strength Reagan's policy of combating communism by building up the military, including aggressive development of new weapons systems. (20)

plea bargain A defendant's admission of guilt in exchange for a less severe punishment. (14)

pluralist model of democracy An interpretation of democracy in which government by the people is taken to mean government by people operating through competing interest groups. (2)

police power The authority of a government to maintain order and safeguard citizens' health, morals, safety, and welfare. (1)

policy entrepreneurs Citizens, members of interest groups, or public officials who champion particular policy ideas. (4)

policy evaluation Analysis of a public policy so as to determine how well it is working. (17)

policy formulation The stage of the policymaking process during which formal proposals are developed and adopted. (17)

political action committee (PAC) An organization that pools campaign contributions from group members and donates those funds to candidates for political office. (10)

political agenda A list of issues that need government attention. (6)

political equality Equality in political decision making: one vote per person, with all votes counted equally. (1, 2)

political ideology A consistent set of values and beliefs about the proper purpose and scope of government. (1)

political participation Actions of private citizens by which they seek to influence or support government and politics. (7)

political party An organization that sponsors candidates for political office under the organization's name. (8)

political socialization The complex process by which people acquire their political values. (5)

political system A set of interrelated institutions that links people with government. (8)

poll tax A tax of $1 or $2 on every citizen who wished to vote, first instituted in Georgia in 1877. Although it was no burden on most white citizens, it effectively disenfranchised blacks. (16)

poverty level The minimum cash income that will provide for a family's basic needs; calculated as three times the cost of a market basket of food that provides a minimally nutritious diet. (19)

precedent A judicial ruling that serves as the basis for the ruling in a subsequent case. (14)

preemption The power of Congress to enact laws by which the national government assumes total or partial responsibility for a state government function. (4)

preemptive action The policy of acting against a nation or group that poses a severe threat to the United States before waiting for the threat to occur; sometimes called the "Bush doctrine." (20)

presidential primary A special primary election used to select delegates to attend the party's national convention, which in turn nominates the presidential candidate. (9)

primary election A preliminary election conducted within a political party to select candidates who will run for public office in a subsequent election. (9)

prior restraint Censorship before publication. (15)

procedural democratic theory A view of democracy as being embodied in a decision-making process that involves universal participation, political equality, majority rule, and responsiveness. (2)

proclamation An official declaration or statement of action or recognition. (20)

productive capacity The total value of goods and services that can be produced when the economy works at full capacity. (18)

program monitoring Keeping track of government programs; usually done by interest groups. (10)

progressive taxation A system of taxation whereby the rich pay proportionately higher taxes than the poor; used by governments to redistribute wealth and thus promote equality. (18)

progressivism A philosophy of political reform based on the goodness and wisdom of the individual citizen as opposed to special interests and political institutions. (7)

project grants Categorical grants awarded on the basis of competitive applications submitted by prospective recipients to perform a specific task or function. (4)

proportional representation The system by which legislative seats are awarded to a party in proportion to the vote that party wins in an election. (8)

protectionism The notion that women must be protected from life's cruelties; until the 1970s, the basis for laws affecting women's civil rights. (16)

protectionists Those who wish to prevent imports from entering the country and therefore oppose free trade. (20)

public assistance Government aid to individuals who can demonstrate a need for that aid. (19)

public debt The accumulated sum of past government borrowing owed to lenders outside the government. (18)

public figures People who assume roles of prominence in society or thrust themselves to the forefront of public controversy. (15)

public goods Benefits and services, such as parks and sanitation, that benefit all citizens but are not likely to be produced voluntarily by individuals. (1)

public opinion The collective attitudes of citizens concerning a given issue or question. (5)

public policy A general plan of action adopted by the government to solve a social problem, counter a threat, or pursue an objective. (17, 19)

racial gerrymandering The drawing of a legislative district to maximize the chance that a minority candidate will win election. (11)

racial segregation Separation from society because of race. (16)

racism A belief that human races have distinct characteristics such that one's own race is superior to, and has a right to rule, others. (16)

reapportionment Redistribution of representatives among the states, based on population change. The House is reapportioned after each census. (11)

recall The process for removing an elected official from office. (7)

receipts For a government, the amount expected or obtained in taxes and other revenues. (18)

redistributional policies Policies that take government resources, such as tax funds, from one sector of society and transfer them to another. (17)

redistricting The process of redrawing political boundaries to reflect changes in population. (4)

referendum An election on a policy issue. (7)

regulation Government intervention in the workings of a business market to promote some socially desired goal. (13, 17)

regulations Administrative rules that guide the operation of a government program. (13)

regulatory commissions Agencies of the executive branch of government that control or direct some aspect of the economy. (13)

representative democracy A system of government where citizens elect public officials to govern on their behalf. (2)

republic A government without a monarch; a government rooted in the consent of the governed, whose power is exercised by elected representatives responsible to the governed. (3)

republicanism A form of government in which power resides in the people and is exercised by their elected representatives. (3)

responsible party government A set of principles formalizing the ideal role of parties in a majoritarian democracy. (8)

responsiveness A decision-making principle, necessitated by representative government, that implies that elected representatives should do what the majority of people wants. (2)

restraint A requirement laid down by act of Congress, prohibiting a state or local government from exercising a certain power. (4)

rights The benefits of government to which every citizen is entitled. (1)

rule making The administrative process that results in the issuance of regulations by government agencies. (13)

rule of four An unwritten rule that requires at least four justices to agree that a case warrants consideration before it is reviewed by the U.S. Supreme Court. (14)

school district The government unit that administers elementary and secondary school programs. (4)

select committee A temporary congressional committee created for a specific purpose and disbanded after that purpose is fulfilled. (11)

self-interest principle The implication that people choose what benefits them personally. (5)

senatorial courtesy A norm under which a nomination must be acceptable to the home state senator from the president's party. (14)

seniority Years of consecutive service on a particular congressional committee. (11)

separate-but-equal doctrine The concept that providing separate but equivalent facilities for blacks and whites satisfies the equal protection clause of the Fourteenth Amendment. (16)

separation of powers The assignment of lawmaking, law-enforcing, and law-interpreting functions to separate branches of government. (3)

set-aside A purchasing or contracting provision that reserves a certain percentage of funds for minority-owned contractors. (16)

sexism Invidious sex discrimination. (16)

skewed distribution An asymmetrical but generally bell-shaped distribution (of opinions); its mode, or most frequent response, lies off to one side. (5)

social contract theory The belief that the people agree to set up rulers for certain purposes and thus have the right to resist or remove rulers who act against those purposes. (3)

social equality Equality in wealth, education, and status. (1)

social insurance A government-backed guarantee against loss by individuals without regard to need. (19)

Social Security Social insurance that provides economic assistance to persons faced with unemployment, disability, or old age. It is financed by taxes on employers and employees. (19)

Social Security Act The law that provided for Social Security and is the basis of modern American social welfare. (19)

social welfare programs Government programs that provide the minimum living standards necessary for all citizens. (19)

socialism A form of rule in which the central government plays a strong role in regulating existing private industry and directing the economy, although it does allow some private ownership of productive capacity. (1)

socioeconomic status Position in society, based on a combination of education, occupational status, and income. (5)

soft money Financial contributions to party committees for capital and operational expenses. (9)

solicitor general The third highest official of the U.S. Department of Justice, and the one who represents the national government before the Supreme Court. (14)

sovereign wealth funds A government-owned fund of financial assets built from budget surpluses and reserved for investment purposes. (20)

sovereignty The quality of being supreme in power or authority. (4)

Speaker of the House The presiding officer of the House of Representatives. (11)

special districts Government units created to perform particular functions, especially when those functions are best performed across jurisdictional boundaries. (4)

split ticket In voting, candidates from different parties for different offices. (9)

stable distribution A distribution (of opinions) that shows little change over time. (5)

stagflation The joint occurrence of slow growth, unemployment, and inflation. (18)

standard socioeconomic model A relationship between socioeconomic status and conventional political involvement: people with higher status and more education are more likely to participate than those with lower status. (7)

standing committee A permanent congressional committee that specializes in a particular policy area. (11)

stare decisis Literally, "let the decision stand"; decision making according to precedent. (14)

states' rights The idea that all rights not specifically conferred on the national government by the U.S. Constitution are reserved to the states. (4)

straight ticket In voting, a single party's candidates for all the offices. (9)

strict scrutiny A standard used by the Supreme Court in deciding whether a law or policy is to be adjudged constitutional. To pass strict scrutiny, the law or policy must be justified by a "compelling governmental interest," must be narrowly tailored, and must be the least restrictive means for achieving that interest. (15)

substantive democratic theory The view that democracy is embodied in the substance of government policies rather than in the policymaking procedure. (2)

suffrage The right to vote. Also called the *franchise*. (7)

supply-side economics Economic policies aimed at increasing the supply of goods (as opposed to decreasing demand); consists mainly of tax cuts for possible investors and less regulation of business. (18)

supportive behavior Action that expresses allegiance to government and country. (7)

supremacy clause The clause in Article VI of the Constitution that asserts that national laws take precedence over state and local laws when they conflict. (3)

tax committees The two committees of Congress responsible for raising the revenue with which to run the government. (18)

television hypothesis The belief that television is to blame for the low level of citizens' knowledge about public affairs. (6)

Temporary Assistance for Needy Families (TANF) A 1996 national act that abolished the longtime welfare policy AFDC (Aid for Families with Dependent Children). TANF gives the states much more control over welfare policy. (19)

terrorism Premeditated, politically motivated violence perpetrated against noncombatant targets by subnational groups or clandestine agents. (7)

totalitarianism A political philosophy that advocates unlimited power for the government to enable it to control all sectors of society. (1)

trade association An organization that represents firms within a particular industry. (10)

transfer payment A payment by government to an individual, mainly through Social Security or unemployment insurance. (18)

trustee A representative who is obligated to consider the views of constituents but is not obligated to vote according to those views if he or she believes they are misguided. (11)

two-party system A political system in which two major political parties compete for control of the government. Candidates from a third party have little chance of winning office. (8)

two-step flow of communication The process in which a few policy elites gather information and then inform their more numerous followers, mobilizing them to apply pressure to government. (6)

U.S. courts of appeals Courts within the second tier of the three-tiered federal court system, to which decisions of the district courts and federal agencies may be appealed for review. (14)

U.S. district courts Courts within the lowest tier of the three-tiered federal court system; courts where litigation begins. (14)

unconventional participation Relatively uncommon political behavior that challenges or defies established institutions and dominant norms. (7)

unitary executive A belief that the president's inherent powers allow him to overrule congressional grants of independent authority to agencies. (12)

universal participation The concept that everyone in a democracy should participate in governmental decision making. (2)

veto The president's disapproval of a bill that has been passed by both houses of Congress. Congress can override a veto with a two-thirds vote in each house. (11, 12)

Virginia Plan A set of proposals for a new government, 1submitted to the Constitutional Convention of 1787; included separation of the government into three branches, division of the legislature into two houses, and proportional representation in the legislature. (3)

voter turnout The percentage of eligible citizens who actually vote in a given election. (7)

War on Poverty A part of President Lyndon Johnson's Great Society program, intended to eradicate poverty within ten years. (19)

watchdog journalism Journalism that scrutinizes public and business institutions and publicizes perceived misconduct. (6)

welfare state A nation in which the government assumes responsibility for the welfare of its citizens by providing a wide array of public services and redistributing income to reduce social inequality. (19)

References

Chapter 1 / Freedom, Order, or Equality? / pages 2–31

1. Federal Deposit Insurance Corporation, "Managing the Crisis: The FDIC and RTC Experience," at http://www.fdic.gov/bank/historical/managing/Chron/pre-fdic.

2. U.S. Bureau of the Census, *Historical Statistics of the United States, Colonial Times to 1957* (Washington, D.C.: U.S. Government Printing Office, 1960), p. 70.

3. "NBER Makes It Official: Recession Started in December 2007," *Wall Street Journal,* 1 December 2008.

4. Catherine Rampell, "'Great Recession': A Brief Etymology," *New York Times,* 11 March 2009, at http://economix.blogs.nytimes.com/2009/03/11/great-recession-a-brief-etymology.

5. Kelly Evans and Kris Maher, "Yearly Job Loss Worst Since 1945," *Wall Street Journal,* 10 January 2009, p. A1.

6. Peter S. Goodman, "85,000 More Jobs Cut in December, Fogging Outlook," *New York Times,* 9 January 2010, pp. A1, A3.

7. Sam Roberts, "Figures Look at Families in Recession," *New York Times,* 17 January 2010, p. A18.

8. "The Shifting Job Market," *Wall Street Journal,* 9 January 2010, p. A5.

9. Michael Luo and Megan Thee-Brenan, "Emotional Havoc Wreaked on Workers and Family," *New York Times,* 15 December 2009, pp. A1, A26.

10. For the 1930s estimates of bank failures see http://www.livinghistoryfarm.org/farminginthe30s/money_08.html; for 2009 see http://www.calculatorplus.com/savings/advice_failed_banks.html.

11. Richard B. Morris (ed.), *Encyclopedia of American History* (New York: Harper, 1961), p. 403.

12. The next day, the *Wall Street Journal* ran a story subtitled "Mortgage Bailout Marks the Return of Federal Activism." See Bob Davis and Jon Hilsenrath, "U.S. Poised for Bigger Role: Mortgage Bailout Marks the Return of Federal Activism," *Wall Street Journal,* 8 September 2008, p. A15.

13. See http://useconomy.about.com/od/candidatesandtheeconomy/a/Obama_Stimulus.htm.

14. James R. Hagerty and Jon Hilsenrath, "Stimulus Fueled Much of Expansion," *Wall Street Journal,* 30 October 2009, p. A2; Jackie Calmes and Michael Cooper, "New Consensus Views Stimulus as Worthy Step," *New York Times,* 21 November 2009, p. 1.

15. John Hilsenrath, "Lack of Credit," *Wall Street Journal,* 20 January 2010, p. R3.

16. Louis Uchitelle, "Another Shifting Industry," *New York Times,* 19 January 2010, pp. B1, B5.

17. There are more elaborate definitions. A recent book defines globalization as "the intensification of cross-national interactions that promote the establishment of trans-national structures and the global integration of cultural, economic, environmental, political, technological and social processes on global, supra-national, national, regional and local levels," in Axel Dreher, Noel Gaston, and Pim Martens, *Measuring Globalisation: Gauging Its Consequences* (New York: Springer, 2008), p. 15.

18. Mark Andreas Kayser, "How Domestic Is Domestic Politics? Globalization and Elections," *Annual Review of Political Science* 10 (2007): 341–362.

19. 2008 American National Election Study, undertaken in collaboration by Stanford University and the University of Michigan.

20. David Easton, *The Political System* (New York: Knopf, 1953), p. 65.

21. Thomas Biersteker and Cynthia Weber (eds.), *State Sovereignty as Social Construct* (Cambridge: Cambridge University Press, 1996), p. 12. For distinctions among four different types of sovereignty, see Stephen D. Krasner, "Abiding Sovereignty," *International Political Science Review* 22 (July 2001): 229–251.

22. William T. R. Fox and Annette Baker Fox, "International Politics," in *International Encyclopedia of the Social Sciences* (New York: Macmillan and Free Press, 1968), 8:50–53.

23. Safeer Tariq Bhatti, "How Has the Conflict in Darfur Impacted Notions of Sovereignty" (unpublished paper, Berkeley Electronic Press, 2007). Available at http://works.bepress.com/safeer_bhatti/1.

24. Nick Timiraos, "Arctic Thaw Defrosts a Sea Treaty," *Wall Street Journal,* 3 November 2007, p. 11.

25. "The new administration will be well packed with LOST boys and girls," said the Let Freedom Ring USA website, at http://www.letfreedomringusa.com/news/read/334.

26. Jess Bravin, "U.S. to Pull Out of World Court on War Crimes," *Wall Street Journal*, 6 May 2002, p. A4.

27. Charles M. Madigan and Colin McMahon, "A Slow, Painful Quest for Justice," *Chicago Tribune*, 7 September 1999, pp. 1, 8.

28. Tom Hundley, "Europe Seeks to Convert U.S. on Death Penalty," *Chicago Tribune*, 26 June 2000, p. 1; Salim Muwakkil, "The Capital of Capital Punishment," *Chicago Tribune*, 12 July 1999, p. 18.

29. Joseph Winter, "Living in Somalia's Anarchy," BBC News, 18 November 2004, at http://news.bbc.co.uk/2/hi/4017147.stm; Alemayehu Fentaw, "Anarchy, Terrorism, and Piracy in Somalia: New Rules of Engagement for the International Community," *American Chronicle*, 27 May 2009, at http://www.americanchronicle.com/articles/view/103942.

30. Liberalism constitutes a nebulous doctrine for theorists. Louis Hartz, in his classic *The Liberal Tradition in America* (New York: Harcourt, Brace & World, 1955), says it is an "even vaguer term" than *feudalism* (pp. 3–4). David G. Smith calls it "too ecumenical and too pluralistic to be called, properly, an ideology" in *The International Encyclopedia of the Social Sciences* (New York: Macmillan and Free Press, 1968), 9:276. More recently, Robert Eccleshall admitted that "in everyday usage," *liberalism* "often stands for little more than a collection of values and principles which no decent person would reject" but then proceeds to find substance in an "incoherent doctrine." In *Political Ideologies: An Introduction*, 3rd ed. (London: Routledge, 2003), p. 18.

31. Edward Cody, "Chinese Lawmakers Approve Measure to Protect Private Property Rights," *Washington Post*, 17 March 2007, p. A10.

32. Karl Marx and Friedrich Engels, *Critique of the Gotha Programme* (New York: International Publishers, 1938), p. 10. Originally written in 1875 and published in 1891.

33. Abby Goodnough, "Gay Rights Rebuke May Bring Change in Tactics," *New York Times*, 5 November 2009, pp. A1, A4.

34. One scholar holds that freedom came from northern European languages, liberty from Latin, and the words originally had opposite meanings. Liberty meant separation and freedom meant connection. See David Hackett Fischer, *Liberty and Freedom: A Visual History of America's Founding Ideas* (New York: Oxford University Press, 2005), pp. 1–15.

35. For a philosophical analysis, see Robert E. Goodin and Frank Jackson, "Freedom from Fear," *Philosophy and Public Affairs* 35 (2007): 249–265.

36. See the argument in Amy Gutman, *Liberal Equality* (Cambridge: Cambridge University Press, 1980), pp. 9–10.

37. See John H. Schaar, "Equality of Opportunity and Beyond," in *Equality, NOMOS IX*, ed. J. Roland Pennock and John W. Chapman (New York: Atherton Press, 1967), pp. 228–249.

38. Lyndon Johnson, "To Fulfill These Rights," commencement address at Howard University, 4 June 1965, available at http://www.hpol.org/record.asp?id=54.

39. Jean Jacques Rousseau, *The Social Contract and Discourses*, trans. G. D. H. Cole (New York: Dutton, 1950), p. 5.

40. Gallup Poll, 1–4 October 2009, at http://www.gallup.com/poll/1603/Crime.aspx.

41. Tamara Audi and Gary Fields, "L.A. Is Latest City to See Crime Drop," *Wall Street Journal*, 7 January 2010, p. A8.

42. Pew Global Attitudes Project, "Two Decades after the Wall's Fall: End of Communism Cheered but Now with More Reservations," 2 November 2009.

43. Centers for Disease Control and Prevention, *Basic Statistics*, 26 February 2009, at http://www.cdc.gov/hiv/topics/surveillance/basic.htm#ddaids.

44. Milton Friedman, *Capitalism and Freedom* (Chicago: University of Chicago Press, 1962).

45. Joseph Khan, "Anarchism, the Creed That Won't Stay Dead," *New York Times*, 5 August 2000, p. A15.

46. For a similar approach, see Scott Keeter and Gregory A. Smith, "In Search of Ideologues in America," Pew Research Center for the People & the Press, 11 April 2006, at http://pewresearch.org/pubs/17/in-search-of-ideologues-in-america.

47. The communitarian category was labeled "populist" in the first four editions of this book. We have relabeled it for two reasons. First, we believe that *communitarian* is more descriptive of the category. Second, we recognize that the term *populist* has been used increasingly to refer to the political styles of candidates such as Pat Buchanan and Ralph Nader. In this sense, a populist appeals to mass resentment against those in power. Given the debate over what *populist* really means, we have decided to use *communitarian*, a less familiar term with fewer connotations. See Michael Kazin, *The Populist Persuasion: An American History* (New York: Basic Books, 1995).

48. Keeter and Smith call this grouping "Populist."

49. The communitarian movement was founded by a group of ethicists and social scientists who met in Washington, D.C., in 1990 at the invitation of sociologist Amitai Etzioni and political theorist William Galston to discuss what they viewed as the declining state of morality and values in the United States. Etzioni became the leading spokesperson for the movement. See his *Rights and the Common Good: The Communitarian Perspective* (New York: St. Martin's Press, 1995), pp. iii–iv. The communitarian political movement should be distinguished from communitarian thought in political philosophy, which is associated with theorists such as Alasdair MacIntyre,

Michael Sandel, and Charles Taylor, who wrote in the late 1970s and early 1980s. In essence, communitarian theorists criticized liberalism, which stressed freedom and individualism, as excessively individualistic. Their fundamental critique was that liberalism slights the values of community life. See Allen E. Buchanan, "Assessing the Communitarian Critique of Liberalism," *Ethics* 99 (July 1989): 852–882, and Patrick Neal and David Paris, "Liberalism and the Communitarian Critique: A Guide for the Perplexed," *Canadian Journal of Political Science* 23 (September 1990): 419–439. Communitarian philosophers attacked liberalism over the inviolability of civil liberties. In our framework, such issues involve the trade-off between freedom and order. Communitarian and liberal theorists differ less concerning the trade-off between freedom and equality. See William R. Lund, "Communitarian Politics and the Problem of Equality," *Political Research Quarterly* 46 (September 1993): 577–600. But see also Susan Hekman, "The Embodiment of the Subject: Feminism and the Communitarian Critique of Liberalism," *Journal of Politics* 54 (November 1992): 1098–1119.

50. Etzioni, *Rights and the Common Good*, p. iv; Etzioni, "Communitarian Solutions/What Communitarians Think," *Journal of State Government* 65 (January–March 1992): 9–11. For a critical review of the communitarian program, see Jeremiah Creedon, "Communitarian Manifesto," *Utne Reader* (July–August 1992): 38–40.

51. Etzioni, "Communitarian Solutions/What Communitarians Think," p. 10. Dana Milbank, "Catch-Word for Bush Ideology; 'Communitarianism' Finds Favor," *Washington Post*, 1 February 2001, p. A1. See also Lester Thurow, "Communitarian vs. Individualistic Capitalism," in Etzioni, *Rights and the Common Good*, pp. 277–282. Note, however, that government's role in dealing with issues of social and economic inequality is far less developed in communitarian writings than is its role in dealing with issues of order. In the same volume, an article by David Osborne, "Beyond Left and Right: A New Political Paradigm" (pp. 283–290), downplays the role of government in guaranteeing entitlements.

52. Etzioni, *Rights and the Common Good*, p. 17.

53. Ibid., p. 22.

54. On the philosophical similarities and differences between communitarianism and socialism, see Alexander Koryushkin and Gerd Meyer (eds.), *Communitarianism, Liberalism, and the Quest for Democracy in Post-Communist Societies* (St. Petersburg: St. Petersburg University Press, 1999).

55. Researchers who have studied populations in Western and Eastern Europe find that the model fits citizens in Western Europe better than those in Eastern Europe.

See Hulda Thorisdottir, John T. Jost, Ido Liviatan, and Patrick E. Shrout, "Psychological Needs and Values Underlying Left-Right Political Orientation: Cross-National Evidence from Eastern and Western Europe," *Public Opinion Quarterly* 71 (Summer 2007): 175–203.

Chapter 2 / Majoritarian or Pluralist Democracy? / pages 32–57

1. Jonathan Martin and Carol E. Lee, "Obama to GOP: 'I Won,'" *Politico*, 23 January 2009.

2. Martin and Lee, "Obama to GOP."

3. Jackie Calmes, "House Passes Stimulus Plan with No G.O.P. Votes," *New York Times*, 29 January 2009; David M. Herszenhorn, "Senate Approves Stimulus Plan," *New York Times*, 11 February 2009.

4. Jeanne Cummings, "Business Eyes Stimulus Goodies," *Politico*, 27 January 2009.

5. Kenneth Janda, "What's in a Name? Party Labels across the World," in *The CONTA Conference: Proceedings of the Conference of Conceptual and Terminological Analysis of the Social Sciences*, ed. F. W. Riggs (Frankfurt: Indeks Verlage, 1982), pp. 46–62.

6. The 2004 data is from the National Election Study of that year.

7. William Roberts Clark, Matt Golder, and Sona Nadenichek Golder, *Principles of Comparative Politics* (Washington, D.C.: CQ Press, 2009), p. 152.

8. Richard F. Fenno, Jr., *The President's Cabinet* (New York: Vintage, 1959), p. 29.

9. See Carmen Siriana, *Investing in Democracy* (Washington, D.C.: Brookings Institution, 2009).

10. Robert A. Dahl, *Democracy and Its Critics* (New Haven, Conn.: Yale University Press, 1989), pp. 13–23.

11. Jeffrey M. Berry, Kent E. Portney, and Ken Thomson, *The Rebirth of Urban Democracy* (Washington, D.C.: Brookings Institution, 1993).

12. Archon Fung, *Empowered Participation* (Princeton, N.J.: Princeton University Press, 2004).

13. Shaun Bowler, Todd Donovan, and Jeffrey A. Karp, "Enraged or Engaged? Preferences for Direct Citizen Participation in Affluent Democracies," *Political Research Quarterly* 60 (September 2007): 351–361.

14. Berry, Portney, and Thomson, *Rebirth of Urban Democracy*, p. 77.

15. Darrell M. West, *State and Federal Electronic Government in the United States, 2008*, Brookings Institution, available at http://www.brookings.edu/~/media/Files/rc/reports/2008/0826_egovernment_west/0826_egovernment_west.pdf.

16. https://www.ago.mo.gov/cgi-bin/Environment/complaint.cgi.

17. See James A. Stimson, Michael B. MacKuen, and Robert S. Erikson, "Dynamic Representation," *American Political Science Review* 89 (September 1995):

543–565; G. Bingham Powell, Jr., "The Chain of Responsiveness," *Journal of Democracy* 15 (October 2004): 91–105.

18. Dietrich Rueschemeyer, "Address Inequality," *Journal of Democracy* 15 (October 2004): 76–90.

19. Russell J. Dalton, Doh C. Shin, and Willy Jou, "Popular Conceptions of the Meaning of Democracy," (Irvine: Center for the Study of Democracy, University of California, Irvine, 18 May 2007), available at http://escholarship.org/uc/item/2j74b860.

20. See Robert A. Dahl, "What Political Institutions Does Large-Scale Democracy Require?" *Political Science Quarterly* 120 (2005): 187–197.

21. Kenneth Janda, "Do Our People's Republics Work?" *Newsday,* 6 August 2003.

22. Deborah Ball and Nicholas Birch, "Swiss Ban Minarets in Controversial Vote," *Wall Street Journal* 30 November 2009.

23. Gallup Poll, "More Americans Plugged Into Political News," 28 September 2009, available at http://www.gallup.com/poll/123203/Americans-Plugged-Into-Political-News.aspx.

24. John R. Hibbing and Elizabeth Theiss-Morse, *Stealth Democracy: Americans' Beliefs about How Government Should Work* (Cambridge: Cambridge University Press, 2002), p. 7.

25. Robert A. Dahl, *Pluralist Democracy in the United States* (Chicago: Rand McNally, 1967), p. 24.

26. Robert D. Putnam, *Bowling Alone* (New York: Simon & Schuster, 2000).

27. Stephen Macedo et al., *Democracy at Risk* (Washington, D.C.: Brookings Institution, 2005).

28. The classic statement on elite theory is C. Wright Mills, *The Power Elite* (New York: Oxford University Press, 1956).

29. Jeffrey A. Winters and Benjamin I. Page, "Oligarchy in the United States?" *Perspectives on Politics* 7 (December 2009): 731–751.

30. On the difficulty of documenting the link between advocacy and policy outcomes, see Jeffrey M. Berry, "An Ever Fainter Voice," in *The Future of Political Science,* ed. Gary King, Kay Lehman Schlozman, and Norman Nie (New York: Routledge, 2009), pp. 98–100.

31. Powerful arguments on the subtlety of elite domination can be found in Peter Bachrach and Morton S. Baratz, "Two Faces of Power," *American Political Science Review* 56 (December 1962): 947–952; and John Gaventa, *Power and Powerlessness* (Urbana: University of Illinois Press, 1980).

32. Frank R. Baumgartner, Jeffrey M. Berry, Marie Hojnacki, David C. Kimball, and Beth L. Leech, *Lobbying and Policy Change* (Chicago: University of Chicago Press, 2009).

33. See Larry M. Bartels, *Unequal Democracy* (Princeton, N.J.: Princeton University Press, 2009).

34. See, for example, David Beetham, Edzia Carvalho, Todd Landman, and Stuart Weir (eds.), *Assessing the Quality of Democracy: A Practical Guide* (Stockholm: International Institute for Democracy and Electoral Assistance, 2008), available at http://www.idea.int/publications/aqd/index.cfm.

35. *Freedom in the World 2009* (Washington, D.C.: Freedom House, 2009).

36. Abraham Diskin, Hanna Diskin, and Reuven Y. Hazan, "Why Democracies Collapse: The Reasons for Democratic Failure and Success," *International Political Science Review* 26 (July 2005): 291–309.

37. Jeffrey Gettleman, "In Africa, Clinton May Face a Kenyan Crisis," *New York Times,* 4 August 2009.

38. Larry P. Goodson, "Afghanistan in 2003: The Taliban Resurface and a New Constitution Is Born," *Asian Survey* 44 (January/February 2004): 14–22; Nazif M. Shahrani, "War, Factionalism, and the State in Afghanistan," *American Anthropologist* 104 (September 2002): 715–722.

39. The classic treatment of the conflict between freedom and order in democratizing countries is Samuel P. Huntington, *Political Order in Changing Societies* (New Haven, Conn.: Yale University Press, 1968).

40. See Henry Teune, "The Consequences of Globalization on Local Democracy: An Assessment" (paper presented at the International Political Science Association, Durban, South Africa, July 2003); *Human Development Report 2002: Deepening Democracy in a Fragmented World* (New York: United Nations, 2002), pp. 51–61; Yi Feng, *Democracy, Governance, and Economic Performance: Theory and Evidence* (Cambridge, Mass.: MIT Press, 2003), pp. 296–299; and Adam Przeworski and Fernando Limongi, "Modernization: Theories and Facts," *World Politics* 49 (January 1997): 155–183.

41. "Obama Approval on Afghanistan, at 35%, Trails Other Issues," Gallup Poll, 1 December 2009, available at http://www.gallup.com/poll/124520/Obama-Approval-Afghanistan-Trails-Issues.aspx.

42. Susan J. Pharr and Robert D. Putnam (eds.), *Disaffected Democracies* (Princeton, N.J.: Princeton University Press, 2000).

43. Hari Kumar and Heather Timmons, "Violence in India Is Fueled by Religious and Economic Divide," *New York Times,* 4 September 2008.

44. "India: International Religious Freedom Report 2009," U.S. Department of State, 26 October 2009.

45. E. E. Schattschneider, *The Semi-Sovereign People* (New York: Holt, Rinehart, & Winston, 1960), p. 35.

46. See Nolan McCarty, Keith T. Poole, and Howard Rosenthal, *Polarized America* (Cambridge, Mass.: MIT Press, 2006); and Steven S. Smith, *Party Influence in Congress* (New York: Cambridge University Press, 2007).

47. Jacob S. Hacker and Paul Pierson, *Off Center* (New Haven, Conn.: Yale University Press, 2005).

48. Jeffrey Berry and Sarah Sobieraj, "The Outrage Industry" (paper presented at the conference on Going to Extremes: The Fate of the Political Center in American Politics, Rockefeller Center, Dartmouth College, 19–21 June 2008).

Chapter 3 / The Constitution / pages 58–99

1. Introductory speech by President V. Giscard d'Estaing to the Convention on the Future of Europe, 28 February 2002, http://gandalf.aksis.uib.no/~brit/EXPORT-EU-Constitution/Export-Document-CONV/CONV-004-02-03-05-EN/ANNEX4Chairmanofthe EuropeanConvention,Mr.html.

2. Letter from George Washington to James Madison, 31 March 1787, http://gwpapers.virginia.edu/documents/constitution/1787/madison3.html.

3. Elaine Sciolino, "French No Vote on Constitution Rattles Europe," *New York Times,* 31 May 2005.

4. Günter Burghardt, "The Development of the European Constitution from the U.S. Point of View," in Esther Brimmer (ed.), *The European Union Constitutional Treaty: A Guide for Americans* (Washington, D.C.: Center for Transatlantic Relations, Johns Hopkins University, 2004).

5. Charles Forelle and Quentin Fottrell, "Irish Vote Decisively to Support EU Reform," *Wall Street Journal,* 4 October 2009, http://online.wsj.com/article/SB125456184521661679.html?mod=WSJ_hp-s_LEFTWhatsNews, accessed 4 October 2009.

6. Samuel Eliot Morison, *Oxford History of the American People* (New York: Oxford University Press, 1965), p. 172.

7. Richard Walsh, *Charleston's Sons of Liberty: A Study of the Artisans, 1763–1789* (Columbia: University of South Carolina Press, 1959).

8. Mary Beth Norton, *Liberty's Daughters* (Boston: Little, Brown, 1980), pp. 155–157.

9. Morison, *Oxford History,* p. 204.

10. David McCullough, *John Adams* (New York: Simon & Schuster, 2001).

11. John Plamentz, *Man and Society,* rev. ed., ed. M. E. Plamentz and Robert Wokler, vol. 1, *From the Middle Ages to Locke* (New York: Logan, 1992), pp. 216–218.

12. Pauline Maier, *American Scripture: Making the Declaration of Independence* (New York: Knopf, 1997), pp. 133–134.

13. Jack N. Rakove (ed.), *The Annotated U.S. Constitution and Declaration of Independence* (Boston: Belknap Press of Harvard University Press, 2009), p. 23.

14. Joseph Ellis, *American Sphinx: The Character of Thomas Jefferson* (New York: Vintage Books, 1998), p. 59.

15. Charles H. Metzger, *Catholics and the American Revolution: A Study in Religious Climate* (Chicago: Loyola University Press, 1962).

16. Extrapolated from U.S. Department of Defense, *Selected Manpower Statistics, FY 1982* (Washington, D.C.: U.S. Government Printing Office, 1983), Table 2-30, p. 130; and U.S. Bureau of the Census, *1985 Statistical Abstract of the United States* (Washington, D.C.: U.S. Government Printing Office, 1985), Tables 1 and 2, p. 6.

17. Maya Jasanoff, "Loyal to a Fault," *New York Times Magazine,* 1 July 2007, pp. 20–22.

18. McCullough, *John Adams,* pp. 165–385.

19. Joseph T. Keenan, *The Constitution of the United States* (Homewood, Ill.: Dow-Jones-Irwin, 1975).

20. Rakove, *Annotated U.S. Constitution,* p. 30.

21. David P. Szatmary, *Shays' Rebellion: The Making of an Agrarian Insurrection* (Amherst: University of Massachusetts Press, 1980), pp. 82–102.

22. As cited in Morison, *Oxford History,* p. 304.

23. "The Call for the Federal Constitutional Convention, Feb. 21, 1787," in *The Federalist,* ed. Edward M. Earle (New York: Modern Library, 1937), p. 577.

24. Robert H. Jackson, *The Struggle for Judicial Supremacy* (New York: Knopf, 1941), p. 8.

25. John Dickinson of Delaware, as quoted in Morison, *Oxford History,* p. 270.

26. Catherine Drinker Bowen, *Miracle at Philadelphia* (Boston: Little, Brown, 1966), p. 122.

27. Forrest McDonald, *Novus Ordo Seclorum: The Intellectual Origins of the Constitution* (Lawrence: University Press of Kansas, 1985), pp. 205–209.

28. It may be overstating the case to refer to this small shift as "a compromise," as there was hardly consensus or general agreement, but that is how historians have characterized it.

29. U.S. Constitution, Article V.

30. Donald S. Lutz, "The Preamble to the Constitution of the United States," *This Constitution* 1 (September 1983): 23–30.

31. Charles O. Jones, "The Separated Presidency—Making It Work in Contemporary Politics," in *The New American Political System,* 2nd ed., ed. Anthony King (Washington, D.C.: American Enterprise Institute, 1990).

32. Charles A. Beard, *An Economic Interpretation of the Constitution of the United States* (New York: Macmillan, 1913).

33. Leonard W. Levy, *Constitutional Opinions* (New York: Oxford University Press, 1986), p. 101.

34. Robert E. Brown, *Charles Beard and the Constitution* (Princeton, N.J.: Princeton University Press, 1956); Levy, *Constitutional Opinions,* pp. 103–104; Forrest McDonald, *We the People: Economic Origins of the Constitution* (Chicago: University of Chicago Press, 1958).

35. Compare Eugene D. Genovese, *The Political Economy of Slavery: Studies in the Economics and Society of the Slave South* (Middletown, Conn.: Wesleyan University Press, 1989), and Robert William Fogel, *Without Contract or Consent: The Rise and Fall of American Slavery* (New York: Norton, 1989).

36. Robert A. Goldwin, letter to the editor, *Wall Street Journal,* 30 August 1993, p. A11.

37. Bernard Bailyn, *Faces of Revolution: Personalities and Themes in the Struggle for American Independence* (New York: Knopf, 1990), pp. 221–222.

38. Walter Berns, *The First Amendment and the Future of Democracy* (New York: Basic Books, 1976), p. 2.

39. Herbert J. Storing, ed., *The Complete Anti-Federalist,* 7 vols. (Chicago: University of Chicago Press, 1981).

40. Alexis de Tocqueville, *Democracy in America,* ed. J. P. Mayer and Max Lerner (1835–1839, reprint, New York: Harper & Row, 1966), p. 102.

41. Russell L. Caplan, *Constitutional Brinkmanship: Amending the Constitution by National Convention* (New York: Oxford University Press, 1988), p. 162.

42. Daniel Okrent, *Last Call: The Rise and Fall of Prohibition* (New York: Scribners, 2010), p. 3.

43. Seth Lipsky, *The Citizen's Constitution: An Annotated Guide* (New York: Basic Books, 2009), p. 286.

44. Richard L. Berke, "1789 Amendment Is Ratified but Now the Debate Begins," *New York Times,* 8 May 1992, p. A1.

45. The interpretation debate is fully explored in John H. Garvey and T. Alexander Aleinikoff, *Modern Constitutional Theory: A Reader,* 2nd ed. (Minneapolis, Minn.: West Publishing Co., 1991). A classic statement on judicial decision making, composed before he became a member of the U.S. Supreme Court in 1932, is Benjamin N. Cardozo's *The Nature of the Judicial Process* (New Haven, Conn.: Yale University Press, 1921).

46. International Institute, *Birth of Democracy: Twelve Constitutions of Central and Eastern Europe,* 2nd ed. rev. (Amsterdam: Council of Europe, 1996).

47. Jerold L. Waltman, *Political Origins of the U.S. Income Tax* (Jackson: University Press of Mississippi, 1985), p. 10.

Chapter 4 / Federalism / pages 100–135

1. Alan Dean Foster, "Garden Variety Javelinas," *New York Times,* 7 Aug 2010, p. WK10.

2. Daniel B. Wood, "Opinion polls show broad support for tough Arizona immigration law," *The Christian Science Monitor,* 30 April 2010, http://www.csmonitor.com/USA/Society/2010/0430/Opinion-polls-show-broad-support-for-tough-Arizona-immigration-law.

3. 8 U.S.C. § 1302 and § 1304(e).

4. SB1070, http://www.azleg.gov/legtext/49leg/2r/bills/sb1070s.pdf.

5. Randal C. Archibold, "Arizona Law Is Stoking Unease Among Latinos," *New York Times,* 28 May 2010, p. A11.

6. *United States of America* v. *Arizona,* CV 10-1413-PHX-SRB (USDC AZ)(28 July 2010), http://www.azd.uscourts.gov/azd/courtinfo.nsf/983700DFEE44B56B0725776E005D6CCB/$file/10-1413-87.pdf.

7. William H. Stewart, *Concepts of Federalism* (Lanham, Md.: University Press of America, 1984).

8. Martha Derthick, *Keeping the Compound Republic: Essays on American Federalism* (Washington, D.C.: Brookings Institution Press, 2001), p. 153.

9. Edward Corwin, "The Passing of Dual Federalism," *University of Virginia Law Review* 36 (1950): 1–24.

10. See Daniel J. Elazar, *The American Partnership* (Chicago: University of Chicago Press, 1962); Morton Grodzins, *The American System* (Chicago: Rand McNally, 1966).

11. James T. Patterson, *The New Deal and the States: Federalism in Transition* (Princeton, N.J.: Princeton University Press, 1969).

12. See, for example, Eric Lichtblau and Adam Liptak, "Bush Presses On in Legal Defense for Wiretapping," *New York Times,* 28 January 2006, p. A1.

13. John Dinan and Shama Gamkhar, "The State of American Federalism 2008–2009: The Presidential Election, the Economic Downturn, and the Consequences for Federalism," *Publius: The Journal of Federalism* 39, no. 3 (2009): 369–407.

14. *McCulloch* v. *Maryland,* 4 Wheat. 316 (1819).

15. *Dred Scott* v. *Sandford,* 19 How. 393, 426 (1857).

16. Jeff Shesol, *Supreme Power: Franklin Roosevelt vs. the Supreme Court* (New York: W.W. Norton, 2010).

17. Raoul Berger, *Federalism: The Founders' Design* (Norman: University of Oklahoma Press, 1987), pp. 61–62.

18. *United States* v. *Lopez,* 514 U.S. 549 (1995).

19. *Printz* v. *United States,* 521 U.S. 898 (1997).

20. *United States* v. *Morrison,* 120 S. Ct. 1740 (2000).

21. *Lawrence and Garner* v. *Texas,* 539 U.S. 558 (2003). This decision overturned *Bowers* v. *Hardwick,* 478 U.S. 186 (1986).

22. *Atkins* v. *Virginia,* 536 U.S. 304 (2002).

23. *Roper* v. *Simmons,* 343 U.S. 551 (2005).

24. *Baze* v. *Rees,* 553 U.S. (2008).

25. Historical Tables, *Budget of the United States Government,* FY2009 (Washington, D.C.: U.S. Government Printing Office, 2008), Table 12.1.

26. *South Dakota* v. *Dole,* 483 U.S. 203 (1987).

27. Jonathan D. Silver, "Clinton Signs Lower Drunk Driving Limit; States That Don't Adopt 0.08 Rule Would Lose Federal Highway Aid," *Pittsburgh Post-Gazette,* 24 October 2000, p. A1.

28. Terry Sanford, *Storm over the States* (New York: McGraw-Hill, 1967).

29. Quoted in Cynthia J. Bowling and Deil S. Wright, "Public Administration in the Fifty States: A Half-Century Administrative Revolution," *State and Local Government Review* 30 (Winter 1998): 52.

30. David M. Hedge, *Governance and the Changing American States* (Boulder, Colo.: Westview Press, 1998).

31. U.S. Department of Labor, Bureau of Labor Statistics, "State and Local Government, Excluding Education and Hospitals," in *Career Guide to Industries, 2010-11 Edition,* http://www.bls.gov/oco/cg/cgs042.htm.

32. Paul Manna, *School's In: Federalism and the National Education Agenda* (Washington D.C.: Georgetown University Press, 2006).

33. Ronald Reagan, "Statement on Signing Executive Order Establishing the Presidential Advisory Committee on Federalism," 1981 *Public Papers of the President* 341, 8 April 1981.

34. Dinan and Gamkhar, "The State of American Federalism 2008–2009," p. 370.

35. Internet Tax Nondiscrimination Act of 2004.

36. Joseph Zimmerman, "Congressional Preemption during the George W. Bush Administration," *Publius* 37 (2007): 432–452.

37. Ibid., p. 436.

38. Ibid., p. 432.

39. John Kincaid, "American Federalism: The Third Century," *Annals of the American Academy of Political and Social Science* 509 (1990): 139–152.

40. "Unfunded Federal Mandates," *Congressional Digest* (March 1995): 68.

41. Paul Posner, "The Politics of Coercive Federalism," *Publius* 37 (2007): 390–412.

42. National Conference of State Legislatures, "State Legislatures Face Unsettled Conditions in 2008," *NCSL News,* 14 December 2007, http://www.ncsl.org/default.aspx?tabid=16893.

43. National Conference of State Legislatures, "State Lawmakers Intercept Shipment of Federal Unfunded Mandates and Cost-Shifts," *NCSL News,* 5 August 2007, http://www.ncsl.org/PressRoom/StateLawmakersInterceptShipmentofFederalUnfu/tabid/16981/Default.aspx.

44. C. David Kotok, "Cheney Lends a Hand in Iowa, Vice President Rallies GOP Voters: A Day with the V.P.," *Omaha World Herald,* 1 November 2002, p. 1A; Raymond Hernandez, "Bush Swings Through Three States to Build Support for the GOP," *New York Times,* 1 November 2002, p. A27; James Harding, "Bush Finds Time for Diplomacy on Campaign Trail," *Financial Times* (London), 25 October 2002, p. 10; John Broder, "The 2006 Elections: Democrats Take Senate," *New York Times,* 10 November 2006 (online edition).

45. U.S. Department of Justice, "Guidance Concerning Redistricting in Retrogression under Section 5 of the Voting Rights Act 42 U.S.C., 1973c," *Federal Register,* 18 January 2001; David E. Rosenbaum, "Fight over Political Map Centers on Race," *New York Times,* 21 February 2002, p. A20.

46. U.S. Census Bureau, *2007 Census of Governments,* http://www.census.gov/govs/cog/GovOrgTab03ss.html.

47. Nancy Burns, *The Formation of American Local Governments: Private Values in Public Institutions* (New York: Oxford University Press, 1994), pp. 11–13; Garrick L. Percival, Mary Currin-Percival, Shaun Bowler, and Henk van der Kolk, "Taxing, Spending, and Voting: Voter Turnout Rates in Statewide Elections in Comparative Perspective," *State & Local Government Review* 39, no. 3 (2007): 131–143.

48. CNN, "Sniper Attacks: A Trail of Terror," 2002, http://web.archive.org/web/20031208191803/www.cnn.com/SPECIALS/2002/sniper/.

49. Bowling and Wright, "Public Administration in the Fifty States," pp. 57–58.

50. SIDO maintains a presence at http://www.sidoamerica.org.

51. Information available at the website of U.S. Senator Dick Durbin (D-Ill.): http://durbin.senate.gov/showRelease.cfm?releaseId=270383.

52. *Darfur Scores,* available at http://www.genocideintervention.net/darfurscoresorg (accessed 11 March 2010).

53. *U.S. Term Limits* v. *Thornton,* 514 U.S. 779 (1995).

54. Ann L. Griffiths and Karl Nerenberg (eds.), *Handbook of Federal Countries* (Montreal and Kingston, Canada: McGill-Queens University Press, 2005).

55. Information available at the *Forum of Federations* at http://www.forumfed.org/en/federalism/by_country/index.php (accessed 11 March 2010).

Chapter 5 / Public Opinion and Political Socialization / pages 136–169

1. "A Three Drug Cocktail," *Washington Post,* 26 September 2007, available at http://www.washingtonpost.com/wp-dyn/content/graphic/2007/09/26/GR2007092600116.html.

2. Ian Urbina, "Ohio Killer Is First Inmate in U.S. to Be Executed with a Single Drug," *New York Times,* 9 December 2009, p. A16.

3. Ian Urbina, "Ohio Is First to Change to One Drug in Executions," *New York Times,* 14 November 2009, p. A10.

4. *Baze and Bowling* v. *Rees,* at http://www.oyez.org/cases/2000-2009/2007/2007_07_5439.

5. Ian Urbina, "Ohio Finds Itself Leading the Way to a New Execution Method," *New York Times,* 18 November 2009, p. A21.

6. Tony Rizzo, "Ohio Uses Single-Drug Execution for Second Time," *St. Paul Pioneer Press,* 8 January 2010, p. 16.

7. Frank Newport, "In U.S., Two-Thirds Continue to Support Death Penalty: Little Change in Recent Years despite International Opposition," Gallup Poll Report, 13 October 2009, at http://www.gallup.com/poll/123638/in-u.s.-two-thirds-continue-support-death-penalty.aspx.

8. InfoPlease, "The Death Penalty Worldwide," http://www.infoplease.com/ipa/A0777460.html.

9. Amnesty International, "The Death Penalty in 2008," http://www.amnesty.org/en/death-penalty/death-sentences-and-executions-in-2008.

10. John Schwartz, "Death Sentences Dropped, but Executions Rose in '09," New York Times, 18 December 2009, p. A22.

11. Warren Weaver, Jr., "Death Penalty a 300-Year Issue in America," New York Times, 3 July 1976.

12. Furman v. Georgia, 408 U.S. 238 (1972).

13. Gregg v. Georgia, 248 U.S. 153 (1976).

14. U.S. Department of Justice, Bureau of Justice Statistics, "Number of Persons Executed in the U.S. 1930–2007," http://www.ojp.usdoj.gov/bjs/glance/tables/exetab.htm; the Death Penalty Information website, "Facts about the Death Penalty, January 2, 2008," http://www.deathpenaltyinfo.org.

15. Seventy percent of whites favor the death penalty while 56 percent of African Americans oppose it. Lydia Saad, "Racial Disagreement over Death Penalty Has Varied Historically," Gallup News Service, 30 July 2007, http://www.gallup.com. For a discussion of the effects of the disenfranchisement of felons, see Jeff Manza and Christopher Uggen, Locked Out: Felon Disenfranchisement and American Democracy (New York: Oxford University Press, 2006).

16. Frank Newport, "In U.S., Two-Thirds Continue to Support Death Penalty."

17. Death Penalty Information website, "Facts about the Death Penalty, January 8, 2010."

18. David Masci, "An Impassioned Debate: An Overview of the Death Penalty in America," Pew Forum on Religion and Public Life, 19 December 2007, http://pewforum.org/docs/?DocID=270.

19. E. Wayne Carp, "If Pollsters Had Been Around during the American Revolution" (letter to the editor), New York Times, 17 July 1993, p. 10.

20. "Government by the People," results of the 2001 Henry J. Kaiser Family Foundation/Public Perspective Polling and Democracy Survey, http://www.ropercenter.uconn.edu/pubper/pdf/pp12_4b.pdf.

21. Sidney Verba, "The Citizen as Respondent: Sample Surveys and American Democracy," American Political Science Review 90 (March 1996): 3. For a historical discussion of the search for the "average" citizen, see Sarah E. Igo, The Averaged American: Surveys, Citizens, and the Making of a Mass Public (Cambridge, Mass.: Harvard University Press, 2007).

22. For more on the relationship between Supreme Court decisions and public opinion, see Nathan Persity, Jack Citrin, and Patrick Egan (eds.), Public Opinion and Constitutional Controversy (New York: Oxford University Press, 2008).

23. Linda Lyons, "The Gallup Brain: Prayer in Public Schools," Gallup News Service, 10 December 2002, http://www.gallup.com/poll/7393/Gallup-Brain-Prayer-Public-Schools.aspx

24. Jeffrey M. Jones, "Majority of Americans Still Not Backing Healthcare Bill: Forty-six Percent Would Advise Their Member to Vote for It, or Lean in That Direction," Gallup Poll Report, 16 December 2009, at http://www.gallup.com/poll/124715/Majority-Americans-Not-Backing-Healthcare-Bill.aspx.

25. Warren E. Miller and Santa A. Traugott, American National Election Studies Sourcebook, 1952–1986 (Cambridge, Mass.: Harvard University Press, 1989), pp. 94–95; Richard Niemi, John Mueller, and Tom Smith, Trends in Public Opinion: A Compendium of Survey Data (Westport, Conn.: Greenwood Press, 1989), p. 19.

26. Lydia Saad, "Conservatives Finish 2009 as No. 1 Ideological Group," Gallup Poll Report, 7 January 2010.

27. Joseph Carroll, "Most Americans Approve of Interracial Marriages," Gallup Poll Report, 16 August 2007, at http://www.gallup.com/poll/28417/Most-Americans-Approve-Interracial-Marriages.aspx.

28. Steven A. Peterson, Political Behavior: Patterns in Everyday Life (Newbury Park, Calif.: Sage, 1990), pp. 28–29. See also David O. Sears and Sheri Levy, "Childhood and Adult Political Development," in Oxford Handbook of Political Psychology, ed. David O. Sears, Leonie Huddy, and Robert Jervis (New York: Oxford University Press, 2003).

29. Paul Allen Beck, "The Role of Agents in Political Socialization," in Handbook of Political Socialization Theory and Research, ed. Stanley Allen Renshon (New York: Free Press, 1977), pp. 117–118; see also James G. Gimpel, J. Celeste Lay, and Jason E. Schuknecht, Cultivating Democracy: Civic Environments and Political Socialization in America (Washington, D.C.: Brookings Institution Press, 2003).

30. Hugh McIntosh, Daniel Hart, and James Youniss, "The Influence of Family Political Discussion on Youth Civic Development: Which Parent Qualities Matter?" PS: Political Science and Politics 40 (2007): 495–499; Richard G. Niemi and Jane Junn, Civic Education: What Makes Students Learn (New Haven, Conn.: Yale University Press, 1998). But some researchers have argued that political attitudes and behaviors may have a genetic component rather than being purely a function of the learning environment at home. See John Alford, Carolyn Funk,

and John R. Hibbing, "Are Political Orientations Genetically Transmitted?" *American Political Science Review* 99 (2005): 153–167.

31. M. Kent Jennings and Richard G. Niemi, *The Political Character of Adolescence: The Influence of Families and Schools* (Princeton, N.J.: Princeton University Press, 1974), p. 39. See also Stephen E. Frantzich, *Political Parties in the Technological Age* (New York: Longman, 1989), p. 152. Frantzich presents a table showing that more than 60 percent of children in homes in which both parents have the same party preference will adopt that preference. When parents are divided, the children tend to be divided among Democrats, Republicans, and independents.

32. Recent research on twins separately raised confirms that party identification "is driven almost entirely by familial socialization," but there appears to be a genetic propensity for twins "to be intense or apathetic" regardless of which party they were raised to support. See Peter K. Hatemi et al., "Is There a 'Party' in Your Genes?" *Political Research Quarterly* 62 (September 2009): 584–600.

33. In a panel study of parents and high school seniors in 1965 and in 1973, some years after their graduation, Jennings and Niemi found that 57 percent of children shared their parents' party identification in 1965, but only 47 percent did by 1973. See Jennings and Niemi, *Political Character*, pp. 90–91. See also Robert C. Luskin, John P. McIver, and Edward G. Carmines, "Issues and the Transmission of Partisanship," *American Journal of Political Science* 33 (May 1989): 440–458. They found that children are more likely to shift between partisanship and independence than to "convert" to the other party. When conversion occurs, it is more likely to be based on economic issues than on social issues.

34. Robert D. Hess and Judith V. Torney, *The Development of Political Attitudes in Children* (Chicago: Aldine, 1967). But other researchers disagree. See Jerry L. Yeric and John R. Todd, *Public Opinion: The Visible Politics* (Itasca, Ill.: F. E. Peacock, 1989), pp. 45–47, for a summary of the issues. For a critical evaluation of the early literature on political socialization, see Pamela Johnston Conover, "Political Socialization: Where's the Politics?" in *Political Science: Looking to the Future,* vol. 3, *Political Behavior,* ed. William Crotty (Evanston, Ill.: Northwestern University Press, 1991), pp. 125–152.

35. David Easton and Jack Dennis, *Children in the Political System* (New York: McGraw-Hill, 1969).

36. Jarol B. Manheim, *The Politics Within* (New York: Longman, 1982), pp. 83, 125–151.

37. Niemi and Junn, *Civic Education.*

38. Cliff Zukin et al., *A New Engagement: Political Participation, Civic Life, and the Changing American Citizen* (New York: Oxford University Press, 2006), pp. 142–144.

39. Janie S. Steckenrider and Neal E. Cutler, "Aging and Adult Political Socialization: The Importance of Roles and Transitions," in *Political Learning in Adulthood: A Sourcebook of Theory and Research,* ed. Roberta S. Sigel (Chicago: University of Chicago Press, 1989), pp. 56–88.

40. See Robert Huckfeldt and John Sprague, *Citizens, Politics, and Social Communication* (Cambridge: Cambridge University Press, 1995), Chap. 7. The authors' study of voting in neighborhoods in South Bend, Indiana, found that residents who favored the minority party were acutely aware of their minority status.

41. Theodore M. Newcomb et al., *Persistence and Social Change: Bennington College and Its Students After Twenty-Five Years* (New York: Wiley, 1967); Duane F. Alwin, Ronald L. Cohen, and Theodore M. Newcomb, *Political Attitudes over the Life Span: The Bennington Women After Fifty Years* (Madison: University of Wisconsin Press, 1991).

42. Sears and Levy, "Childhood and Adult Political Development," p. 85.

43. See Roberta S. Sigel (ed.), *Political Learning in Adulthood: A Sourcebook of Theory and Research* (Chicago: University of Chicago Press, 1989).

44. One study found that additional media coverage of political issues did not change the impact of education on political knowledge. See Benjamin Highton, "Political Knowledge Gaps and Changes in the Information Environment: The Case of Education" (paper presented at the annual meeting of the Midwest Political Science Association, Chicago, 2008).

45. Pew Research Center, "The Internet's Broader Role in Campaign 2008," 11 January 2008, http://pewresearch.org.

46. The American National Election Studies are jointly done by Stanford University and the University of Michigan, with funding by the National Science Foundation.

47. Other scholars have analyzed opinion on abortion using six questions from the General Social Survey. See R. Michael Alvarez and John Brehm, "American Ambivalence toward Abortion Policy," *American Journal of Political Science* 39 (1995): 1055–1082; Elizabeth Adell Cook, Ted G. Jelen, and Clyde Wilcox, *Between Two Absolutes: Public Opinion and the Politics of Abortion* (Boulder, Colo.: Westview Press, 1992).

48. Although some people view the politics of abortion as "single-issue" politics, the issue has broader political significance. In their book on the subject, Cook, Jelen, and Wilcox say, "Although embryonic life is one important value in the abortion debate, it is not

the only value at stake." They contend that the politics is tied to alternative sexual relationships and traditional roles of women in the home, which are "social order" issues. See *Between Two Absolutes,* pp. 8–9.

49. Russell J. Dalton, *The Good Citizen* (Washington, D.C.: Congressional Quarterly Press, 2008), Chap. 5.

50. Ibid., p. 50.

51. For years, scholars have been debating whether the increasing wealth in industrialized societies is replacing class conflict with conflict over values. See the exchange between Ronald Inglehart and Scott C. Flanagan, "Value Change in Industrial Societies," *American Political Science Review* 81 (December 1987): 1289–1319.

52. Earl Black and Merle Black, *The Vital South* (Cambridge, Mass.: Harvard University Press, 1992), and *The Rise of Southern Republicans* (Cambridge, Mass.: Harvard University Press, 2002); David Lublin, *The Republican South: Democratization and Partisan Change* (Princeton, N.J.: Princeton University Press, 2004); Nicholas Valentino and David O. Sears, "Old Times There Are Not Forgotten: Race and Partisan Realignment in the Contemporary South," *American Journal of Political Science* 49 (2005): 672–688.

53. Nathan Glazer, "The Structure of Ethnicity," *Public Opinion* 7 (October–November 1984): 4.

54. U.S. Census Bureau, International Data Base, Table 094, http://www.census.gov/ipc/www.idbprint.html.

55. Infoplease, "Hispanic Americans by the Numbers," http://www.infoplease.com/spot/hhmcensus1.html.

56. U.S. Census Bureau, American Fact Finder, Section on Race and Ethnicity, http://factfinder.census.gov/servlet/GRTSelectServlet?ds_name-ACS_2007_1YR_G00_&_lang=en&_ts=281548554033.

57. Michael Dawson, *Black Visions: The Roots of Contemporary African American Political Ideologies* (Chicago: University of Chicago Press, 2001); John Garcia, *Latino Politics in America* (Lanham, Md.: Rowman & Littlefield, 2003); Thomas Kim, *The Racial Logic of Politics: Asian Americans and Party Competition* (Philadelphia: Temple University Press, 2007); Pei-te Lien, M. Margaret Conway, and Janelle Wong, *The Politics of Asian Americans* (New York: Routledge, 2004); Katherine Tate, *Black Faces in the Mirror: African Americans and Their Representatives in the U.S. Congress* (Princeton, N.J.: Princeton University Press, 2003).

58. Glazer, "Structure of Ethnicity," p. 5; Dennis Chong and Dukhong Kim, "The Experiences and Effects of Economic Status among Racial and Ethnic Minorities," *American Political Science Review* 100 (August 2006): 335–351.

59. Jeffrey M. Jones, "Only 4 in 10 Americans Satisfied with Treatment of Immigrants," 15 August 2007, http://www.gallup.com.

60. Frank Newport, "This Christmas, 78% of Americans Identify as Christian," Gallup Poll Report, 24 December 2009; http://www.gallup.com/poll/124793/This-Christmas-78-Americans-Identify-Christian.aspx.

61. See David C. Leege and Lyman A. Kellstedt (eds.), *Rediscovering the Religious Factor in American Politics* (Armonk, N.Y.: M. E. Sharpe, 1993); and "Many Americans Uneasy with Mix of Religion and Politics," Pew Forum on Religion and Public Life, 24 August 2006, http://pewforum.org/docs/DocID=153.

62. Some scholars have argued that Americans are not as polarized as the news media would have us think. See Morris P. Fiorina, *Culture War? The Myth of a Polarized America* (Upper Saddle River, N.J.: Longman, 2004).

63. Fact Sheet, "The Gender Gap: Attitudes on Public Policy Issues," Center for American Women and Politics, Eagleton Institute of Politics, Rutgers, August 1997, http://www.cawp.rutgers.edu.

64. John Robinson, "The Ups and Downs and Ins and Outs of Ideology," *Public Opinion* 7 (February–March 1984): 12.

65. For a more positive interpretation of ideological attitudes within the public, see William G. Jacoby, "The Structure of Ideological Thinking in the American Electorate," *American Journal of Political Science* 39 (1995): 314–335. Jacoby analyzes data for the 1984 and 1988 elections and concludes "that there is a systematic, cumulative structure underlying liberal-conservative thinking in the American public" (p. 315).

66. When asked to describe the parties and candidates in the 1956 election, only about 12 percent of respondents volunteered responses that contained ideological terms (such as *liberal, conservative,* and *capitalism*). Most respondents (42 percent) evaluated the parties and candidates in terms of "benefits to groups" (farmers, workers, or businesspeople, for example). Others (24 percent) spoke more generally about "the nature of the times" (for example, inflation, unemployment, and the threat of war). Finally, a good portion of the sample (22 percent) gave answers that contained no classifiable issue content. See Angus Campbell, Philip E. Converse, Warren E. Miller, and Donald E. Stokes, *The American Voter* (New York: Wiley, 1960), Chap. 10.

67. Marjorie Connelly, "A 'Conservative' Is (Fill in the Blank)," *New York Times,* 3 November 1996, sec. 4, p. 5.

68. See William G. Jacoby, "Levels of Conceptualization and Reliance on the Liberal-Conservative Continuum," *Journal of Politics* 48 (May 1986): 423–432. We also know that certain political actors, such as

delegates to national party conventions, hold far more consistent and durable beliefs than does the general public. See M. Kent Jennings, "Ideological Thinking among Mass Publics and Political Elites," *Public Opinion Quarterly* 56 (Winter 1992): 419–441.

69. American National Election Study, 2008.

70. However, citizens can have ideologically consistent attitudes toward candidates and perceptions about domestic issues without thinking about politics in explicitly liberal and conservative terms. See Jacoby, "The Structure of Ideological Thinking."

71. Pew Research Center for the People and the Press, "Opinion of State Governments Drops with the Economy, Budget Gaps: New Administration Changes Partisan Views of Federal Government," 11 August 2009, at http://pewresearch.org/pubs/1307/state-government-favorability-falls-partisan-split-federal-government.

72. Pamela Johnston Conover, "The Origins and Meaning of Liberal-Conservative Self-Identifications," *American Journal of Political Science* 25 (November 1981): 621–622, 643.

73. A relationship between liberalism and political tolerance was found by John L. Sullivan et al., "The Sources of Political Tolerance: A Multivariate Analysis," *American Political Science Review* 75 (March 1981): 102. See also Robinson, "Ups and Downs," pp. 13–15.

74. Herbert Asher, *Presidential Elections and American Politics,* 5th ed. (Upper Saddle River, N.J.: International Thomson Publishing Group, 1997). Asher also constructs a two-dimensional framework, distinguishing between "traditional New Deal" issues and "new lifestyle" issues.

75. John E. Jackson, "The Systematic Beliefs of the Mass Public: Estimating Policy Preferences with Survey Data," *Journal of Politics* 45 (November 1983): 840–865.

76. Milton Rokeach also proposed a two-dimensional model of political ideology grounded in the terminal values of freedom and equality. See *The Nature of Human Values* (New York: Free Press, 1973), especially Chap. 6. Rokeach found that positive and negative references to the two values permeate the writings of socialists, communists, fascists, and conservatives and clearly differentiate the four bodies of writing from one another (pp. 173–174). However, Rokeach built his two-dimensional model around only the values of freedom and equality; he did not deal with the question of freedom versus order.

77. In our framework, opposition to abortion is classified as a communitarian position. However, the communitarian movement led by Amitai Etzioni adopted no position on abortion (personal communication from Vanessa Hoffman by e-mail, in reply to a query of 5 February 1996).

78. William S. Maddox and Stuart A. Lilie, *Beyond Liberal and Conservative: Reassessing the Political Spectrum* (Washington, D.C.: Cato Institute, 1984), p. 68. From 1993 to 1996, the Gallup Organization, in conjunction with CNN and *USA Today,* asked national samples two questions: (1) whether individuals or government should solve our country's problems and (2) whether the government should promote traditional values. Gallup constructed a similar ideological typology from responses to these questions and found a similar distribution of the population into four groups. See Gallup's "Final Top Line" for 12–15 January 1996, pp. 30–31.

79. See W. Russell Neuman, *The Paradox of Mass Politics: Knowledge and Opinion in the American Electorate* (Cambridge, Mass.: Harvard University Press, 1986), p. 81. See also Aaron Wildavsky, "Choosing Preferences by Constructing Institutions: A Cultural Theory of Preference Formation," *American Political Science Review* 81 (March 1987): 13.

80. The same conclusion was reached in a major study of British voting behavior. See Hilde T. Himmelweit et al., *How Voters Decide* (New York: Academic Press, 1981), pp. 138–141. See also Wildavsky, "Choosing Preferences," p. 13; and Stanley Feldman and Christopher Johnston, "Understanding Political Ideology" (paper presented at the annual meeting of the American Political Science Association, Toronto, Canada, 2009).

81. Michael X. Delli Carpini and Scott Keeter, *What Americans Know about Politics and Why It Matters* (New Haven, Conn.: Yale University Press, 1996).

82. Ibid., p. 269. For more on this topic, see Scott L. Althaus, *Collective Preferences in Democratic Politics: Opinion Surveys and the Will of the People* (New York: Cambridge University Press, 2003).

83. Carpini and Keeter, *What Americans Know,* p. 271.

84. "Public Knowledge of Current Affairs Little Changed by News and Information Revolution: What Americans Know 1989–2007," Pew Research Center for the People and the Press, 15 April 2007, http://people-press.org/reports/display.php3?ReportID=319.

85. Markus Prior and Arthur Lupia, "Money, Time, and Political Knowledge: Distinguishing Quick Recall and Political Learning Skills," *American Journal of Political Science* 52 (2008): 169–183.

86. M. Kent Jennings, "Political Knowledge over Time and Across Generations," *Public Opinion Quarterly* 60 (Summer 1996): 239, 241.

87. Neuman, *Paradox,* p. 81.

88. Pew Research Center for the People and the Press, "Who Knows News? What You Read or View Matters, but Not Your Politics," 15 October 2008, at

http://pewresearch.org/pubs/993/who-knows-news-what-you-read-or-view-matters-but-not-your-politics.

89. Stephan Lewandowsky, Werner Stritzke, Klaus Oberauer, and Michael Morales, "Memory for Fact, Fiction, and Misinformation: The Iraq War 2003," *Psychological Science* 16 (March 2005): 190–195.

90. Benjamin I. Page and Robert Y. Shapiro, *The Rational Public* (Chicago: University of Chicago Press, 1992).

91. Ibid., p. 45.

92. Ibid., p. 385. The argument for a rational quality in public opinion by Page and Shapiro was supported by Stimson's massive analysis of swings in the liberal–conservative attitudes of the U.S. public from 1956 to 1990. Analyzing more than 1,000 attitude items, he found that the public mood had already swung away from liberalism when Ronald Reagan appeared on the scene to campaign for president as a conservative. See James A. Stimson, *Public Opinion in America: Moods, Cycles, and Swings* (Boulder, Colo.: Westview Press, 1992), and *Tides of Consent: How Public Opinion Shapes American Politics* (Cambridge: Cambridge University Press, 2004). But for a more cynical view of citizen competence, see Althaus, *Collective Preferences,* and James Kuklinski and Paul Quirk, "Reconsidering the Rational Public," in *Elements of Reason,* ed. A. Lupia, M. McCubbins, and S. Popkin (Cambridge: Cambridge University Press, 2000), pp. 153–182.

93. Self-interest is often posed as the major alternative to choice based on general orientations such as political ideology and moral values. A significant literature exists on the limitations of self-interest in explaining political life. See Jane J. Mansbridge (ed.), *Beyond Self-Interest* (Chicago: University of Chicago Press, 1990). A literature is also developing on the role of emotions in the process of political judgment. See G. E. Marcus, W. R. Neuman, and M. Mackuen, *Affective Intelligence and Political Judgment* (Chicago: University of Chicago Press, 2000); and George E. Marcus, *The Sentimental Citizen: Emotion in Democratic Politics* (University Park, Pa.: Pennsylvania State University Press, 2002).

94. Richard D. Dixon et al., "Self-Interest and Public Opinion toward Smoking Policies," *Public Opinion Quarterly* 55 (1991): 241–254; David O. Sears and Jack Citrin, *Tax Revolt: Something for Nothing in California* (Cambridge, Mass.: Harvard University Press, 1985); Robin Wolpert and James Gimpel, "Self-Interest, Symbolic Politics, and Public Attitudes toward Gun Control," *Political Behavior* 20 (1998): 241–262.

95. Wildavsky, "Choosing Preferences," pp. 3–21.

96. Henry Brady and Paul Sniderman, "Attitude Attribution: A Group Basis for Political Reasoning," *American Political Science Review* 79 (1985): 1061–1078; Samuel Popkin, *The Reasoning Voter,* 2nd ed. (Chicago: University of Chicago Press, 1994); P. Sniderman, R. Brody, and P. Tetlock, *Reasoning and Choice* (Cambridge: Cambridge University Press, 1991). Psychologists have tended to emphasize the distorting effects of heuristics. See D. Kahneman, P. Slovic, and A. Tversky (eds.), *Judgment under Uncertainty: Heuristics and Biases* (Cambridge: Cambridge University Press, 1982); and R. Nisbett and L. Ross, *Human Inference: Strategies and Shortcomings of Social Judgment* (Englewood Cliffs, N.J.: Prentice-Hall, 1980).

97. Political psychologists refer to beliefs that guide information processing as opinion "schemas." See Pamela Johnston Conover and Stanley Feldman, "How People Organize the Political World: A Schematic Model," *American Journal of Political Science* 28 (February 1984): 95–127; M. Lodge and K. M. McGraw, *Political Judgment: Structure and Process* (Ann Arbor: University of Michigan Press, 1995). For an excellent review of schema structures in contemporary psychology, especially as they relate to political science, see Reid Hastie, "A Primer of Information-Processing Theory for the Political Scientist," in *Political Cognition,* ed. Richard R. Lau and David O. Sears (Hillsdale, N.J.: Erlbaum, 1986), pp. 11–39.

98. Pew Center for the People and the Press, "Religion and Politics: Contention and Consensus," 24 July 2003, http://people-press.org/reports/display.php3?ReportID=189.

99. J. Kuklinski and N. L. Hurley, "On Hearing and Interpreting Political Messages," *Journal of Politics* 56 (1994): 729–751.

100. On framing, see Dennis Chong and James N. Druckman, "Framing Public Opinion in Competitive Democracies," *American Political Science Review* 101 (November 2007): 637–655; James N. Druckman, "Political Preference Formation: Competition, Deliberation, and the (Ir)relevance of Framing Effects," *American Political Science Review* 98 (November 2004): 671–686; and Michael W. Wagner, "The Utility of Staying on Message: Competing Partisan Frames and Public Awareness of Elite Differences on Political Issues," *The Forum* 5, no. 3 (2007), http://www.bepress.com/forum/vol15/iss3/art8. On political spin, see Lawrence R. Jacobs and Robert Y. Shapiro, *Politicians Don't Pander* (Chicago: University of Chicago Press, 2000).

101. Benjamin I. Page, Robert Y. Shapiro, and Glenn R. Dempsey, "What Moves Public Opinion?" *American Political Science Review* 81 (March 1987): 23–43.

102. Michael Margolis and Gary A. Mauser, *Manipulating Public Opinion: Essays on Public Opinion as a Dependent Variable* (Pacific Grove, Calif.: Brooks/Cole, 1989).

Chapter 6 / The Media / pages 170–205

1. Bloomberg News, "Seattle Newspaper Ends Print Edition," 17 March 2009, http://www.boston.com/business/articles/2009/03/17/seattle_newspaper_ends_print_edition; Michael Liedke and Andrew Vanacore, "Newspaper Upheaval Seen with Filings," Associated Press, 24 February 2009, http://www.boston.com/ae/media/articles/2009/02/24/newspaper_upheaval_seen_with_filings; David Cook, "Monitor Shifts from Print to Web-Based Strategy," *Christian Science Monitor,* 28 October 2009, http://www.csmonitor.com/2008/1029/p25s01-usgn.html; "Albuquerque Tribune to Cease Publication," Scripps Press Release, 20 February 2008, http://pressreleases.scripps.com/release/1003; Lynn DeBruin and Lisa Ryckman, "Rocky Mountain News to Close, Publish Final Edition Friday," *Rocky Mountain News,* 26 February 2009, http://www.rockymountainnews.com/news/2009/feb/26/rocky-mountain-news-closes-friday-final-edition; Pew Research Center's Project for Excellence in Journalism, "The State of the News Media 2009," http://www.stateofthemedia.org/2009/index.htm.

2. Alex S. Jones, *Losing the News* (New York: Oxford University Press, 2009); Tom Price, "Future of Journalism," *CQ Researcher* 19, no. 12 (27 March 2009): 273–295; Pew Project for Excellence in Journalism, http://www.stateofthemedia.org/2009/narrative_newspapers_audience.php?media=4&cat=2.

3. Alex S. Jones, *Losing the News.*

4. Richard Davis, *Typing Politics: The Role of Blogs in American Politics* (New York: Oxford University Press, 2009); Tom Price, "Future of Journalism"; Pew Project for Excellence in Journalism, http://www.stateofthemedia.org/2009/narrative_online_audience.php?media=5&cat=2.

5. Ed Pilkington, "Obama Angers Midwest Voters with Guns and Religion Remark," *Guardian,* 14 April 2008, http://www.guardian.co.uk/world/2008/apr/14/barackobama.uselections2008.

6. "Michael Moore's *Sicko:* Broad Reach and Impact Even without the Popcorn?" Press release from Kaiser Family Foundation, 27 August 2007, http://www.kff.org/kaiserpolls/pomr082707nr.cfm.

7. Survey by Newsweek and Princeton Survey Research Associates International, iPOLL Databank, Roper Center for Public Opinion Research, University of Connecticut, 1–2 August 2007, http://www.ropercenter.uconn.edu/data_access/ipoll/ipoll.html.

8. See Markus Prior, *Post-Broadcast Democracy* (New York: Cambridge University Press, 2007).

9. S. N. D. North, *The Newspaper and Periodical Press* (Washington, D.C.: U.S. Government Printing Office, 1884), p. 27. This source provides much of the information reported here about newspapers and magazines before 1880.

10. Editor & Publisher, *International Year Book,* 2009 (New York: Editor & Publisher, 2009), p. xi.

11. In 1947, a total of 1,854 daily papers had a circulation of 53.3 million; in 2007, a total of 1,422 newspapers had a circulation of 50.1 million. See Harold W. Stanley and Richard G. Niemi (eds.), *Vital Statistics on American Politics, 2009–2010* (Washington, D.C.: CQ Press, 2010), p. 157. For a brief history of the newspaper business, see Paul E. Steiger, "Read All about It: How Newspapers Got into Such a Fix and Where They Go from Here," *Wall Street Journal,* 29–30 December 2007, p. 1.

12. On framing in the media, see Stephen D. Reese, Oscar H. Gandy, Jr., and August E. Grant (eds.), *Framing Public Life: Perspectives on Media and Our Understanding of the Social World* (Mahwah, N.J.: Erlbaum, 2001). More generally on how leaders mediate public deliberation on issues, see Doris A. Graber, *Media Power in Politics,* 7th ed. (Washington, D.C.: CQ Press, 2005).

13. See radio statistics at "The State of the News Media 2009," http://www.stateofthenewsmedia.org.

14. Ibid.

15. David Barker and Kathleen Knight, "Political Talk Radio and Public Opinion," *Public Opinion Quarterly* 64 (Summer 2000): 149–170; David C. Barker, *Rushed to Judgment: Talk Radio, Persuasion, and American Political Behavior* (New York: Columbia University Press, 2003).

16. Dana R. Ulloth, Peter L. Klinge, and Sandra Eells, *Mass Media: Past, Present, Future* (St. Paul, Minn.: West, 1983), p. 278.

17. 2009 Television Bureau of Advertising data, http://www.tvb.org/rcentral/mediatrendstrack/tvbasics; Nielson, "Television Audience 2008," http://blog.nielsen.com/nielsenwire/wp-content/uploads/2009/07/tva_2008_071709.pdf.

18. Douglas Ahers, "News Consumption and the New Electronic Media," *Harvard International Journal of Press/Politics* 11 (Winter 2006): 29–52; Bill Carter, "CNN Last in TV News on Cable," *New York Times,* 27 October 2009, http://www.nytimes.com/2009/10/27/business/media/27rating.html?emc=eta1; Markus Prior, *Post-Broadcast Democracy.*

19. Marsha Walton, CNN, "Web Reaches New Milestone: 100 Million Sites," 1 November 2006, http://www.cnn.com/2006/TECH/internet/11/01/100millionwebsites/index.html; Internet World

Stats, "Top 58 Countries with the Highest Internet Penetration Rate," http://www.internetworldstats .com/top25.htm.

20. "Demographics of Internet Users," Pew Internet and American Life 2007 survey, http://www.pewinternet .org.

21. "Internet News Audience Highly Critical of News Organizations," Pew Research Center for the People and the Press, 9 August 2007, http://people-press.org.

22. Richard Davis, *Typing Politics* (New York: Oxford University Press, 2009); Technorati State of the Blogosphere 2008, http://technorati.com/blogging/ feature/state-of-the-blogosphere-2008.

23. Richard Davis, *Typing Politics*; Michael Fletcher and Charles Babington, "Miers, Under Fire from Right, Withdrawn as Court Nominee," *Washington Post,* 28 October 2005, http://www.washingtonpost.com/wp-dyn/content/article/2005/10/27/ AR2005102700547.html; Stephen Lee Myers and Philip Shenon, "Embattled Attorney General Resigns," *New York Times,* 27 August 2007, http:// www.nytimes.com/2007/08/27/washington/27cnd-gonzales.html.

24. Katharine Q. Seelye, "Take That, Mr. Newsman!" *New York Times,* 1 January 2006, p. C1.

25. Matthew Hindman, *The Myth of Digital Democracy* (Princeton, N.J.: Princeton University Press, 2009).

26. Belinda Luscombe, "The HuffPo Gets to Question Obama—Making History," *Time,* 10 February 2009, http://www.time.com/time/nation/article/ 0,8599,1878625,00.html.

27. Paul Wiseman, "Cracking the 'Great Firewall' of China's Web Censorship," *USA Today,* 23 April 2008, http://www.usatoday.com/tech/news/techpolicy/ 2008-04-22-InternetBandits_N.htm; Michael Wines and Andrew Jacobs, "To Shut Off Tiananmen Talk, China Disrupts Sites," *New York Times,* 2 June 2009, http://www.nytimes.com/2009/06/03/world/asia/ 03china.html.

28. Katie Hafner and Matt Richtel, "U.S. Is Pressing Google for Data on Searches," *New York Times,* 20 January 2006, p. 1; Kevin J. Delaney, "Google to Launch Service in China," *Wall Street Journal,* 25 January 2006, p. B2.

29. Amy Schatz, "Tech Firms Defend China Web Policies," *Wall Street Journal,* 16 February 2006, p. A2.

30. Andrew Jacobs and Miguel Helft, "Google, Citing Attack, Threatens to Exit China," *New York Times,* 12 January 2010, http://www.nytimes.com/2010/ 01/13/world/asia/13beijing.html.

31. Pew Research Center for the People and the Press, "Online Papers Modestly Boost Newspaper Readership," 30 July 2006, http://people-press.org.

32. Doris A. Graber, *Mass Media and American Politics,* 7th ed. (Washington, D.C.: CQ Press, 2005),

pp. 98–101. See also W. Lance Bennett, *News: The Politics of Illusion,* 3rd ed. (White Plains, N.Y.: Longman, 1996), Chap. 2.

33. John H. McManus, *Market-Driven Journalism: Let the Citizen Beware?* (Thousand Oaks, Calif.: Sage, 1994), p. 85.

34. David D. Kurplus, "Bucking a Trend in Local Television News," *Journalism* 4 (2003): 77–94.

35. Bill Carter and Brian Stelter, "In NBC Universal Bid, Comcast Seeks an Empire," *New York Times,* 1 October 2009, http://www.nytimes.com/2009/10/02/ business/media/02nbc.html.

36. Pew Research Center's Project for Excellence in Journalism, "The State of the News Media 2009," http:// www.stateofthemedia.org/2009/narrative_ networktv_audience.php?media=6&cat=2.

37. Thomas E. Patterson, *Doing Well and Doing Good: How Soft News and Critical Journalism Are Shrinking the News Audience and Weakening Democracy— and What News Outlets Can Do about It* (Cambridge, Mass.: Harvard University, Joan Shorenstein Center for Press, Politics, and Public Policy, 2000), pp. 2–5.

38. Learning from soft news was argued by Matthew A. Baum, "Sex, Lies, and War: How Soft News Brings Foreign Policy to the Inattentive Public," *American Political Science Review* 96 (2002): 91–110. The study that found otherwise was by Markus Prior, "Any Good News in Soft News? The Impact of Soft News Preferences on Political Knowledge," *Political Communication* 20 (2003): 149–171.

39. Editor & Publisher, *International Year Book,* 2009.

40. Tom Price, "Future of Journalism."

41. Kelvin Childs, "End the Cross-Owner Ban," *Editor & Publisher* 30, no. 26 (28 June 1997): 11.

42. Jonathan R. Laing, "Harvest Time: After Years of Stumbles, News Corp.'s Big Bets Finally Pay Off," *Barron's,* 20 October 2003, pp. 28–31.

43. Graber, *Mass Media and American Politics,* pp. 43–47.

44. Matthew Rose and Joe Flint, "Behind Media-Ownership Fight, an Old Power Struggle Is Raging," *Wall Street Journal,* 15 October 2003, p. 1. In 2003 the Federal Communications Commission (FCC) voted to increase the percentage share of the market to 45 percent. In 2007, the FCC ruled that no company can control more than 30 percent of the cable television market and relaxed newspaper–broadcast cross-ownership rules in the nation's twenty largest media markets. See Stephen Labaton, "F.C.C. Reshapes Rules Limiting Media Industry," *New York Times,* 19 December 2007, p. A1.

45. Jennifer Lee, "On Minot, N.D., Radio, a Single Corporate Voice," *New York Times,* 31 March 2003, p. C7.

46. Jim Rutenberg with Micheline Maynard, "TV News That Looks Local, Even If It's Not," *New York Times,* 2 June 2003, pp. C1, C9.

47. For a clear summary of very complex developments, see Robert B. Horowitz, "Communications Regulations in Protecting the Public Interest," in *The Institutions of American Democracy: The Press,* ed. Geneva Overholser and Kathleen Hall Jamieson (New York: Oxford University Press, 2005), pp. 284–302.

48. Mark Crispin Miller, "Free the Media," *Nation,* 3 June 1996, pp. 9–15; see also Stephen Labaton, "It's a World of Media Plenty. Why Limit Ownership?" *New York Times,* 12 October 2003, sec. 4, p. 4.

49. Jim Rutenberg, "Fewer Media Owners, More Media Choices," *New York Times,* 2 December 2002, p. C1. See also Edwin Baker, *Media Concentration and Democracy: Why Ownership Matters* (New York: Cambridge University Press, 2006); and Eric Klinenberg, *Fighting for Air: The Battle to Control America's Media* (New York: Holt, 2008).

50. See Markus Prior, *Post-Broadcast Democracy.*

51. Jared Sandberg, "Federal Judges Block Censorship on the Internet," *Wall Street Journal,* 13 June 1996, p. B1.

52. Robert Entman, *Democracy without Citizens: Media and the Decay of American Politics* (New York: Oxford University Press, 1989), pp. 103–108; John Leland, "Why the Right Rules the Radio Waves," *New York Times,* 8 December 2003, sec. 4, p. 7.

53. Wes Allison, "Are Democrats Really Trying to Hush Rush?" *St. Petersburg Times,* 20 February 2009, p. 1A.

54. For an alternative view of the functions of the media, see Graber, *Mass Media and American Politics,* pp. 5–12.

55. For a view from the point of view of a reporter who covered Washington for over sixty years, see Helen Thomas, *Watch-dogs of Democracy? The Waning Washington Press Corps and How It Has Failed the Public* (New York: Scribner, 2006).

56. For a discussion of the Bush years, see Scott McClellan, *What Happened: Inside the Bush White House and Washington's Culture of Deception* (New York: PublicAffairs Books, 2008). For a discussion of Obama, see Adriel Bettelheim, "Meeting the Press Less Than Half Way." *CQ Weekly Online,* 20 July 2009, pp. 1700–1701, http://library.cqpress.com/cqweekly/weeklyreport111-000003170492.

57. Pew Research Center's Project for Excellence in Journalism, "The State of the News Media 2009," http://www.stateofthemedia.org/2009/narrative_newspapers_newsinvestment.php?media=4&cat=4.

58. Warren Weaver, "C-SPAN on the Hill: 10 Years of Gavel to Gavel," *New York Times,* 28 March 1989, p. 10; Francis X. Clines, "C-SPAN Inventor Offers More Politics Up Close," *New York Times,* 31 March 1996, p. 11.

59. ActBlue, "Alan Grayson," http://www.actblue.com/entity/fundraisers/18665.

60. Jon Garfunkel, "The New Gatekeepers Part 1: Changing the Guard," *Civilities: Media Structures Research,* 4 April 2005, http://civilities.net/TheNewGatekeepers-Changing.

61. "Press Going Too Easy on Bush," The State of the News Media 2007, http://www.stateofthemedia.org.

62. Richard Davis, *Typing Politics.* Also see the Media Bloggers Association website: http://www.mediabloggers.org.

63. Graber, *Mass Media and American Politics,* p. 253. For weekly content analysis of news topics, see the Project for Excellence in Journalism's "News Coverage Index," http://www.journalism.org.

64. "Summary of Findings: Modest Interest in 2008 Campaign News," Pew Research Center for the People and the Press, 23 October 2007, http://people-press.org.

65. Stephen J. Farnsworth and S. Robert Lichter, "The Nightly News Nightmare Revisited: Network Television's Coverage of the 2004 Presidential Election" (paper presented at the annual meeting of the Washington, D.C. American Political Science Association, 2005); "Contest Lacks Content," *Media Tenor* 1 (2005): 12–15; Cristina Alsina, Philip John Davies, and Bruce Gronbeck, "Preference Poll Stories in the Last 2 Weeks of Campaign 2000," *American Behavioral Scientist* 44, no. 12 (2001): 2288–2305; C. Anthony Broh, "Horse-Race Journalism: Reporting the Polls in the 1976 Presidential Election," *Public Opinion Quarterly* 44 (1980): 514–529; David Paletz, Jonathan Short, Helen Baker, Barbara Cookman Campbell, Richard Cooper, and Rochelle Oeslander, "Polls in the Media: Content, Credibility, and Consequences," *Public Opinion Quarterly* 44 (1980): 495–513.

66. "World Publics Welcome Global Trade—But Not Immigration," Nation Pew Global Attitudes Survey, 4 October 2007, http://www.pewglobal.org.

67. "Television: Primary Media Sources for News," TVB, Nielsen Media Research Survey 2008, Media Information Center, http://www.mediainfocenter.org/television/content/leading_news.asp.

68. "Online Papers Modestly Boost Newspaper Readership," Pew Research Center for the People and the Press, 30 July 2006, http://people-press.org.

69. Ibid.

70. Pew Research Center Publications, "Where Men and Women Differ in Following the News," 6 February 2008, http://pewresearch.org. Women are also more interested in weather and crime news. Men are more likely to closely follow sports, science, and business news.

71. Geoffrey Baym, "Representation and the Politics of Play: Stephen Colbert's *Better Know a District,*" *Political Communication* 24 (October 2007): 359–376.

72. Harold W. Stanley and Richard G. Niemi, *Vital Statistics on American Politics, 2009–2010,* p. 169.

73. Pew Research Center for the People and the Press, "Well Known: Public Option, Sonia Sotomayor; Little Known: Cap and Trade, Max Baucus," 14 October 2009, http://people-press.org/report/554/news-iq-knowledge-quiz.

74. Jeffrey Jones, "Gallup Quizzes Americans on Knowledge of World Leaders," 20 February 2006, Gallup News Service, http://www.gallup.com.

75. W. Russell Neuman, Marion R. Just, and Ann N. Crigler, *Common Knowledge: News and the Construction of Political Meaning* (Chicago: University of Chicago Press, 1992), p. 10. See also Debra Gersh Hernandez, "Profile of the News Consumer," *Editor & Publisher,* 18 January 1997, pp. 6, 7. Respondents who said that newspapers were their primary source of information correctly answered more factual questions than those who used other media. For a more optimistic assessment of television's instructional value, see Doris A. Graber, *Processing Politics: Learning from Television in the Internet Age* (Chicago: University of Chicago Press, 2001), esp. pp. 120–128. Another negative note is sounded by Alan B. Krueger, "Economic Scene," *New York Times,* 1 April 2004, p. C2.

76. James N. Druckman, "Media Matter: How Newspapers and Television News Cover Campaigns and Influence Voters," *Political Communication* 22 (October–December 2005): 463–481. For a complementary study finding that television news has little effect on campaign learning, see Stephen C. Craig, James G. Kane, and Jason Gainous, "Issue-Related Learning in a Gubernatorial Campaign: A Case Study," *Political Communication* 22 (October–December 2005): 483–503.

77. Diana Mutz, "Effects of 'In-Your-Face' Television Discourse on Perceptions of a Legitimate Opposition," *American Political Science Review* 101 (November 2007): 621–635.

78. James M. Avery, "Videomalaise or Virtuous Circle? The Influence of the News Media on Political Trust," *International Journal of Press/Politics* 14, no. 4 (2009): 410–433.

79. Jennifer Jerit, "Understanding the Knowledge Gap: The Role of Experts and Journalists," *The Journal of Politics* 71, no. 2 (2009): 444.

80. Laurence Parisot, "Attitudes about the Media: A Five-Country Comparison," *Public Opinion* 10 (January–February 1988): 60.

81. Farnsworth and Lichter, in "The Nightly News Nightmare Revisited" (pp. 16–21), consider three models of media influence: (1) "hypodermic needle"—quick effect, like a shot; (2) "minimal effects"—the two-step flow, which may work only as the media focus on the activity; and (3) "more-than-minimal effects," primarily through setting the agenda for discussion.

82. Graber, *Media Power in Politics,* pp. 278–279.

83. Daniel J. Wakin, "Report Calls Networks' Election Night Coverage a Disaster," *New York Times,* 3 February 2001, p. A8.

84. Maxwell McCombs, "The Agenda-Setting Function of the Press," in Overholser and Jamieson, *Institutions of American Democracy,* pp. 156–168.

85. Danilo Yanich, "Kids, Crime, and Local TV News," a report of the Local TV News Media Project (Newark: University of Delaware, January 2005). See also Jeremy H. Lipschultz and Michael L. Hilt, *Crime and Local Television News: Dramatic, Breaking, and Live from the Scene* (Mahwah, N.J.: Erlbaum, 2002).

86. Lipschultz and Hilt, *Crime and Local Television News,* p. 2.

87. Lawrie Mifflin, "Crime Falls, But Not on TV," *New York Times,* 6 July 1997, sec. 4, p. 4.

88. W. Russell Neuman, "The Threshold of Public Attention," *Public Opinion Quarterly* 54 (Summer 1990): 159–176.

89. Joseph E. Uscinski, "When Does the Public's Issue Agenda Affect the Media's Issue Agenda (and Vice Versa)? Developing a Framework for Media-Public Influence," *Social Science Quarterly* 80, no. 4 (2009): 796–815.

90. John Tierney, "Talk Shows Prove Key to White House," *New York Times,* 21 October 2002, p. A13.

91. Samuel Kernell, *Going Public: New Strategies of Presidential Leadership,* 4th ed. (Washington D.C.: CQ Press, 2006); Janet Adamy, "Obama Heads to Town-Hall Meetings," *Wall Street Journal,* 11 August 2009, http://online.wsj.com/article/SB124994653098120945.html.

92. Doris Graber reviews some studies of socially undesirable effects on children and adults in *Processing Politics,* pp. 91–95.

93. Richard Zoglin, "Is TV Ruining Our Children?" *Time,* 5 October 1990, p. 75. Moreover, much of what children see is advertisements. See "Study: Almost 20% of Kid TV Is Ad-Related," *Chicago Tribune,* 22 April 1991, p. 11. See also Stephen Seplow and Jonathan Storm, "Reviews Mixed on Television's Effect on Children," *St. Paul Pioneer Press,* 28 December 1997, p. 9A; and Nell Minow, "Standards for TV Language Rapidly Going Down the Tube," *Chicago Tribune,* 7 October 2003, sec. 5, p. 2.

94. John J. O'Connor, "Soothing Bromides? Not on TV," *New York Times,* 28 October 1990, Arts & Leisure section, pp. 1, 35. Some people watched *The X-Files* because it involved sinister government activities. See Alanna Nash, "Confused or Not, the X-Philes Keep Coming," *New York Times,* 11 January 1998, p. 41.

95. Douglas Kellner, *Television and the Crisis of Democracy* (Boulder, Colo.: Westview Press, 1990), p. 17.

96. James Fallows, *Breaking the News: How the Media Undermine American Democracy* (New York: Pantheon Books, 1996). Americans don't have much confidence in the news media either. See Paul Gronke and Timothy Cook, "Disdaining the Media," *Political Communication* 24 (July 2007): 259–281.

97. For a discussion of how the media affect our collective memory of such events, see Jill A. Edy, *Troubled Pasts: News and the Collective Memory of Social Unrest* (Philadelphia: Temple University Press, 2006).

98. Katharine Q. Seelye, "Survey on News Media Finds Wide Displeasure," *New York Times,* 27 June 2005, p. C5.

99. See Bernard Goldberg, *Bias: A CBS Insider Exposes How the Media Distort the News* (Washington, D.C.: Regnery Publishing, 2002); and Ann Coulter, *Slander: Liberal Lies about the American Right* (New York: Crown, 2002).

100. See Eric Alterman, *What Liberal Media? The Truth about Bias and the News* (New York: Basic Books, 2003); and Al Franken, *Lies and the Liars Who Tell Them ... a Fair and Balanced Look at the Right* (New York: Penguin, 2003).

101. Pew Research Center of the People and the Press, "Financial Woes Now Overshadow All Other Concerns for Journalists," 17 March 2008, http://people-press.org/reports/pdf/403.pdf.

102. Farnsworth and Lichter, "The Nightly News Nightmare Revisited," p. 31.

103. William G. Mayer, "Why Talk Radio Is Conservative," *Public Interest* (Summer 2004): 86–103. For audience figures, see "Talk Radio," The State of the News Media 2007, http://stateofthemedia.org.

104. *The People, the Press, and Their Leaders* (Washington, D.C.: Times-Mirror Center for the People and the Press, 1995). See also Pew Research Center, "Self Censorship: How Often and Why," a survey of nearly three hundred journalists and news executives in February–March 2000, released 30 April 2000.

105. Stanley and Niemi, *Vital Statistics on American Politics, 2007–2008*; Greg Mitchell, "Barack the Vote: 2008 Broke with Tradition," *Editor & Publisher,* 1 December 2008.

106. Maura Clancey and Michael J. Robinson, "General Election Coverage: Part I," *Public Opinion* 7 (December–January 1985): 54. Some journalists take their watchdog role seriously. See Pew Research Center, "Striking the Balance, Audience Interests, Business Pressures and Journalists' Values," 30 March 1999, http://people-press.org/reports/display.php3?ReportID=67.

107. Center for Media and Public Affairs, "Election Watch: Campaign 2008 Final," *Media Monitor* 23, no. 1 (Winter 2009): http://www.cmpa.com/pdf/media_monitor_jan_2009.pdf.

108. Bob Kemper, "Bush: No Iraqi Link to Sept. 11," *Chicago Tribune,* 18 September 2003, pp. 1–6.

109. Steven Kull and others, "Misperceptions, the Media, and the Iraq War," Program on International Policy Attitudes (PIPA), 2 October 2003, http://www.pipa.org.

110. Barbie Zelizer, David Park, and David Gudelunas, "How Bias Shapes the News: Challenging *The New York Times'* Status as a Newspaper of Record on the Middle East," *Journalism* 3 (2002): 303.

111. W. Lance Bennett and William Serrin, "The Watchdog Role," in Overholser and Jamieson, *Institutions of American Democracy,* pp. 169–188.

112. For a critique of the press on these grounds, see W. Lance Bennett, Regina G. Lawrence, and Steven Livingston, *When the Press Fails* (Chicago: University of Chicago Press, 2007).

113. For a historical account of efforts to determine voters' preferences before modern polling, see Tom W. Smith, "The First Straw? A Study of the Origin of Election Polls," *Public Opinion Polling* 54 (Spring 1990): 21–36. See also Susan Herbst, *Numbered Voices: How Opinion Polling Has Shaped American Politics* (Chicago: University of Chicago Press, 1993), Chap. 4.

114. See New York Times Polls Index: http://www.nytimes.com/ref/us/polls_index.html.

115. William Schneider and I. A. Lewis, "Views on the News," *Public Opinion* 8 (August–September 1985): 6–11, 58–59. For similar findings from a 1994 study, see Times-Mirror Center for the People and the Press, "Mixed Message about Press Freedom on Both Sides of the Atlantic," press release, 16 March 1994, p. 65. See also Thomas E. Patterson, "News Decisions: Journalists as Partisan Actors" (paper presented at the annual meeting of the American Political Science Association, 1996), p. 21.

116. Pew Research Center for the People and the Press, News Interest Final Topline, 1–5 February 2006, http://peoplepress.org/reports/display.php3?ReportID=270.

Chapter 7 / Participation and Voting / pages 206–241

1. Janet Adamy and Naftali Bendavid, "Lawmakers Rethink Town Halls," *Wall Street Journal,* 8 August 2009, p. A5.

2. Ian Urbina, "Beyond Beltway, Halt Debate Turns Hostile," *New York Times,* 8 August 2009, pp. A1, A10.

3. Ibid.

4. Jeff Zeleny, "Thousands Attend Broad Protest of Government," *New York Times,* 13 September 2009, p. 33.

5. Adamy and Bendavid, "Lawmakers Rethink Town Halls."

6. Michael M. Phillips, "FreedomWorks Harnesses Growing Activism on the Right," *Wall Street Journal,* 5 October 2009, p. A4.

7. Rob Jordan, "FreedomWorks Launches Nationwide 'Tea Party' Tour," 9 March 2009, at http://www .freedomworks.org/publications/freedomworks-launches-nationwide-%E2%80%9Ctea-party%E2% 80%9D-tour.

8. Justin Quinn, "A Tea Party Revival," About.com Guide to US Conservative Politics, 16 December 2009, at http://usconservatives.about.com/b/2009/ 12/16/a-tea-party-revival.htm.

9. Laura Ingraham, "Momentum Building for Code Red Rally," 8 December 2009, at http://www .lauraingraham.com/b/Code-Red-Rally/ 405052069012270353.html.

10. NBC News/Wall Street Journal Survey, Study #6099, December 2009.

11. Naftali Bendavid, "Tea-Party Activists Complicate Republican Comeback Strategy," *Wall Street Journal,* 16 October 2009, p. 1.

12. M. Margaret Conway, *Political Participation in the United States,* 3rd ed. (Washington, D.C.: CQ Press, 2000), p. 3.

13. Michael Lapsky, "Protest as a Political Resource," *American Political Science Review* 62 (December 1968): 1145.

14. U.S. Department of State, "Patterns of Global Terrorism 2001" (Washington, D.C.: U.S. Department of State, May 2002), p. 17. The definition is contained in Title 22 of the U.S. Code, Section 2656f(d). On the problem of defining terrorism, see Walter Laquer, *No End to War: Terrorism in the 21st Century* (New York: Continuum International, 2003), esp. the appendix.

15. Lou Nichel and Dan Herbeck, *American Terrorist: Timothy McVeigh and the Oklahoma City Bombing* (New York: HarperCollins, 2001), pp. 350–354.

16. William E. Schmidt, "Selma Marchers Mark 1965 Clash," *New York Times,* 4 March 1985.

17. Frances Fox Piven, *Challenging Authority: How Ordinary People Change America* (Lanham, Md.: Rowman & Littlefield, 2006).

18. See Sidney Verba and Norman H. Nie, *Participation in America: Political Democracy and Social Equality* (New York: Harper & Row, 1972), p. 3.

19. 2005–2008 World Values Survey. The World Values Survey Association, based in Stockholm, conducts representative surveys in nations across the world. See http://www.worldvaluessurvey.org.

20. International Social Survey Programme (ISSP) 2004: Citizenship Survey, http://www.zacat.gesis.org.

21. ABC News/Washington Post Poll, 10–13 December 2009.

22. Jonathan D. Casper, *Politics of Civil Liberties* (New York: Harper & Row, 1972), p. 90.

23. David C. Colby, "A Test of the Relative Efficacy of Political Tactics," *American Journal of Political Science* 26 (November 1982): 741–753. See also Frances Fox Piven and Richard Cloward, *Poor People's Movements* (New York: Vintage, 1979).

24. U.S. Census Bureau, *2010 Statistical Abstract,* http:// www.census.gov/compendia/statab/cats/elections/ elected_public_officials–characteristics.html.

25. Stephen C. Craig and Michael A. Magiotto, "Political Discontent and Political Action," *Journal of Politics* 43 (May 1981): 514–522. But see Mitchell A. Seligson, "Trust Efficacy and Modes of Political Participation: A Study of Costa Rican Peasants," *British Journal of Political Science* 10 (January 1980): 75–98, for a review of studies that came to different conclusions.

26. Arthur H. Miller et al., "Group Consciousness and Political Participation," *American Journal of Political Science* 25 (August 1981): 495. See also Susan J. Carroll, "Gender Politics and the Socializing Impact of the Women's Movement," in *Political Learning in Adulthood: A Sourcebook of Theory and Research,* ed. Roberta S. Sigel (Chicago: University of Chicago Press, 1989), p. 307.

27. Richard D. Shingles, "Black Consciousness and Political Participation: The Missing Link," *American Political Science Review* 75 (March 1981): 76–91. See also Lawrence Bobo and Franklin D. Gilliam, Jr., "Race, Sociopolitical Participation, and Black Empowerment," *American Political Science Review* 84 (June 1990): 377–393; and Jan Leighley, "Group Membership and the Mobilization of Political Participation," *Journal of Politics* 58 (May 1996): 447–463.

28. See James L. Gibson, "The Policy Consequences of Political Intolerance: Political Repression during the Vietnam War Era," *Journal of Politics* 51 (February 1989): 13–35. Gibson found that individual state legislatures reacted quite differently in response to antiwar demonstrations on college campuses, but the laws passed to discourage dissent were not related directly to public opinion within the state.

29. See Verba and Nie, *Participation in America,* p. 69. Also see John Clayton Thomas, "Citizen-Initiated Contacts with Government Agencies: A Test of Three Theories," *American Journal of Political Science* 26 (August 1982): 504–522; and Elaine B. Sharp, "Citizen-Initiated Contacting of Government Officials and Socioeconomic Status: Determining

the Relationship and Accounting for It," *American Political Science Review* 76 (March 1982): 109–115.

30. Elaine B. Sharp, "Citizen Demand Making in the Urban Context," *American Journal of Political Science* 28 (November 1984): 654–670, esp. pp. 654, 665.

31. Verba and Nie, *Participation in America*, p. 67; Sharp, "Citizen Demand Making," p. 660.

32. See Joel B. Grossman et al., "Dimensions of Institutional Participation: Who Uses the Courts and How?" *Journal of Politics* 44 (February 1982): 86–114; Frances Kahn Zemans, "Legal Mobilization: The Neglected Role of the Law in the Political System," *American Political Science Review* 77 (September 1983): 690–703.

33. *Brown* v. *Board of Education,* 347 U.S. 483 (1954).

34. "Capital One Settles Litigation over Card Disputes," http://www.dailyherald.com/story/?id=345003.

35. http://www.gpoaccess.gov/fr.

36. Victoria McGrane, "Online Voting Records User Unfriendly," *Politico,* 27 April 2009, at http://dyn.politico.com/printstory.cfm?uuid=E4D92857-18FE-70B2-A844894C6FC926C9.

37. http://www.politifact.com/truth-o-meter.

38. http://www.opensecrets.org.

39. http://www.followthemoney.org.

40. http://www.ombwatch.org and http://truthin accounting.org.

41. See Anand Girigharadas, "'Athens' on the Net," *New York Times,* 13 September 2009, p. WK1. The full set of ideas and votes is available at http://www.whitehouse.gov/assets/documents/Citizens_Briefing_Book_Final.pdf.

42. See Michael P. MacDonald and Samuel L. Popkin, "The Myth of the Vanishing Voter," *American Political Science Review* 95 (December 2001): 963–974. Traditionally, turnout had been computed by dividing the number of voters by the voting-age population, which included noncitizens and ineligible felons. Recent research excludes these groups in estimating voter turnout and has revised the U.S. turnout rates upward by three to five points in elections since 1980. For a study of felon disenfranchisement, see Jeff Manza and Christopher Uggen, *Locked Out: Felon Disenfranchisement and American Democracy* (New York: Oxford University Press, 2006).

43. Max Kaase and Alan Marsh, "Political Action: A Theoretical Perspective," in *Political Action: Mass Participation in Five Western Democracies,* ed. Samuel H. Barnes and Max Kaase (Beverly Hills, Calif.: Sage, 1979), p. 168.

44. *Smith* v. *Allwright,* 321 U.S. 649 (1944).

45. *Harper* v. *Virginia State Board of Elections,* 383 U.S. 663 (1966).

46. Everett Carll Ladd, *The American Polity* (New York: Norton, 1985), p. 392.

47. Gorton Carruth et al. (eds.), *The Encyclopedia of American Facts and Dates* (New York: Crowell, 1979), p. 330. For an eye-opening account of women's contributions to politics before gaining the vote, see Robert J. Dinkin, *Before Equal Suffrage: Women in Partisan Politics from Colonial Times to 1920* (Westport, Conn.: Greenwood Press, 1995).

48. Jodie T. Allen, "Reluctant Suffragettes: When Women Questioned Their Right to Vote," Pew Research Center, 18 March 2009, at http://pewresearch.org/pubs/1156/women-reluctant-voters-after-suffrage-19th-amendment.

49. Ivor Crewe, "Electoral Participation," in *Democracy at the Polls: A Comparative Study of Competitive National Elections,* ed. David Butler, Howard R. Penniman, and Austin Ranney (Washington, D.C.: American Enterprise Institute, 1981), pp. 219–223.

50. International IDEA, "Frequently Asked Questions," https://www.cia.gov/library/publications/the-world-factbook/fields/2123.html.

51. See the Tea Party Handbook at http://teapartyhandbook.blogspot.com/2010/01/what-you-should-know-about.html.

52. Thomas E. Cronin, *Direct Democracy: The Politics of Initiative, Referendum, and Recall* (Cambridge, Mass.: Harvard University Press, 1989), p. 127.

53. For an early history, see Thomas Goebel, *A Government by the People: Direct Democracy in America, 1890–1940* (Chapel Hill: University of North Carolina Press, 2007).

54. Ian Urbina, "Voters Split on Spending Initiatives on States' Ballots," *New York Times,* 8 November 2007, p. A25; Initiative and Referendum Institute, *Ballot-Watch,* http://www.iandrinstitute.org.

55. Initiative and Referendum Institute, "Same-Sex Marriage: Breaking the Firewall in California?" *Ballotwatch* (October 2008); Amy Goodnough, "Gay Rights Rebuke May Bring Change in Tactics," *New York Times,* 5 November 2009, pp. A1, A24.

56. "Gay Rights Law Faces Reversal in Maine Vote," *Chicago Tribune,* 11 January 1998, p. 16.

57. David S. Broder, *Democracy Derailed: Initiative Campaigns and the Power of Money* (New York: Harcourt, 2000); David S. Broder, "A Snake in the Grass Roots," *Washington Post,* 26 March 2000, pp. B1, B2.

58. One could also select special bodies of citizens to decide policies. One scholar proposes creating large "citizens assemblies" consisting of randomly selected citizens statistically representative of the population to decide very critical issues. See James H. Snider, "Using Citizens Assemblies to Reform the Process of Democratic Reform," Joan Shorenstein Center on the Press, Politics and Public Policy, Spring 2008.

59. Caroline J. Tolbert, Ramona S. McNeal, and Daniel A. Smith, "Enhancing Civic Engagement: The Effect of Direct Democracy on Political Participation and Knowledge," *State Politics and Policy Quarterly* 3 (Spring 2003): 23–41. For a more critical look at initiatives as undermining representative government, see Bruce E. Cain and Kenneth P. Miller, "The Populist Legacy: Initiatives and the Undermining of Representative Government," in *Dangerous Democracy? The Battle over Ballot Initiatives in America,* ed. Larry J. Sabato, Howard R. Ernst, and Bruce A. Larson (Lanham, Md.: Rowman & Littlefield, 2001), pp. 33–62. For the role of interest groups in ballot issue campaigns, see Robert M. Alexander, *Rolling the Dice with State Initiatives* (Westport, Conn.: Praeger, 2002).

60. For the impact of the Internet on ballot measures (not all good), see Richard J. Ellis, *Democratic Delusions: The Initiative Process in America* (Lawrence: University of Kansas Press, 2002), esp. pp. 198–203.

61. Darrell M. West, "State and Federal Electronic Government in the United States, 2008," http://www .insidepolitics.org. The list of state websites is at that address. Also see Elaine Ciulla Kamarack and Joseph S. Nye, Jr. (eds.), *Governance.com: Democracy in the Information Age* (Washington, D.C.: Brookings Institution Press, 2002); and David Schlosberg, Stephen Zavestoski, and Stuart W. Shulman, "Democracy and E-Rulemaking: Web-Based Technologies, Participation, and the Potential for Deliberation," *Journal of Information Technology and Politics* 4, no. 1 (2007): http://jitp.net/files/JITP4-1.pdf.

62. Data on the elected state officials come from *The Book of the States 2003* (Lexington, Ky.: Council of State Governments, 2003), p. 201. Estimates of the number of elected school board members come from *Chicago Tribune,* 10 March 1985.

63. Crewe, "Electoral Participation," p. 232. A rich literature has grown to explain turnout across nations. See Pippa Norris, *Democratic Phoenix: Reinventing Political Activism* (Cambridge: Cambridge University Press, 2002), Chap. 3; Mark N. Franklin, "The Dynamics of Electoral Participation," in *Comparing Democracies 2: New Challenges in the Study of Elections and Voting,* ed. Lawrence LeDuc, Richard G. Niemi, and Pippa Norris (London: Sage, 2002), pp. 148–168.

64. Verba and Nie, *Participation in America,* p. 13.

65. Russell J. Dalton, *Citizen Policies,* 3rd ed. (New York: Seven Bridges, 2002), pp. 67–68. For the argument that greater economic inequality leads to greater political inequality, see Frederick Solt, "Economic Inequality and Democratic Political Engagement," *American Journal of Political Science* 52 (January 2008): 48–60.

66. Russell J. Dalton, *The Good Citizen: How a Younger Generation Is Reshaping American Politics* (Washington, D.C.: Congressional Quarterly Press, 2008).

67. Cliff Zukin et al., *A New Engagement?* (New York: Oxford University Press, 2006), pp. 188–191.

68. For a concise summary of the effect of age on voting turnout, see William H. Flanigan and Nancy H. Zingale, *Political Behavior of the American Electorate,* 11th ed. (Washington, D.C.: CQ Press, 2005).

69. Ibid., pp. 46–47.

70. M. Margaret Conway, Gertrude A. Steuernagel, and David W. Ahern, *Women and Political Participation: Cultural Change in the Political Arena* (Washington, D.C.: CQ Press, 1997), pp. 79–80.

71. Ronald B. Rapoport, "The Sex Gap in Political Persuading: Where the 'Structuring Principle' Works," *American Journal of Political Science* 25 (February 1981): 32–48. Perhaps surprisingly, research fails to show any relationship between a wife's role in her marriage and her political activity. See Nancy Burns, Kay Lehman Schlozman, and Sidney Verba, "The Public Consequences of Private Inequality: Family Life and Citizen Participation," *American Political Science Review* 91 (June 1997): 373–389.

72. Bruce C. Straits, "The Social Context of Voter Turnout," *Public Opinion Quarterly* 54 (Spring 1990): 64–73.

73. Sidney Verba, Kay Lehman Scholzman, and Henry E. Brady, *Voice and Equality: Civic Voluntarism in American Politics* (Cambridge, Mass.: Harvard University Press, 1995), p. 433.

74. Stephen J. Dubner and Steven D. Levitt, "Why Vote?" *New York Times Magazine,* 6 November 2005, pp. 30–31. The classic formulation of the rational choice theory of turnout is Anthony Downs, *An Economic Theory of Democracy* (New York: Harper and Row, 1957). For an empirical test of economic models, see David Levine and Thomas Palfry, "The Paradox of Voter Participation? A Laboratory Study," *American Political Science Review* 101 (February 2007): 143–158.

75. Associated Press, "Voter Turnout Tops Since 1968," *St. Paul Pioneer Press,* 14 December 2008, p. A4.

76. Stephen D. Shaffer, "A Multivariate Explanation of Decreasing Turnout in Presidential Elections, 1960–1976," *American Journal of Political Science* 25 (February 1981): 68–95; Paul R. Abramson and John H. Aldrich, "The Decline of Electoral Participation in America," *American Political Science Review* 76 (September 1981): 603–620. However, one scholar argues that this research suffers because it looks only at voters and nonvoters in a single election. When the focus shifts to people who vote sometimes but not at other times, the models do not fit so well. See M. Margaret Conway and John E. Hughes,

"Political Mobilization and Patterns of Voter Turnout" (paper presented at the annual meeting of the American Political Science Association, Washington, D.C., September 1993).

77. Apparently, Richard A. Brody was the first scholar to pose this problem as a puzzle. See his "The Puzzle of Political Participation in America," in *The New American Political System,* ed. Anthony King (Washington, D.C.: American Enterprise Institute, 1978), pp. 287–324. Since then, a sizable literature has attempted to explain the decline in voter turnout in the United States. One scholar contends that postindustrial societies experience a "ceiling effect" that blunts increased voting due to increased education; see Norris, *Democratic Phoenix,* Chap. 3. Another finds that the perceived importance of electoral contests and the closeness of the vote are the major factors explaining differences in turnout; see Franklin, "The Dynamics of Electoral Participation," pp. 148–168.

78. See Jack Doppelt and Ellen Shearer, *America's No-Shows: Non-voters* (Washington, D.C.: Medill School of Journalism, 2001); Thomas E. Patterson, *The Vanishing Voter* (New York: Vintage Books, 2003); Deborah J. Brooks and John Geer, "Beyond Negativity: The Effects of Incivility on the Electorate," *American Journal of Political Science* 51 (January 2007): 1–16.

79. Some scholars argue that Americans generally have become disengaged from social organizations (not just political parties), becoming more likely to act "alone" than to participate in group activities. See Robert D. Putnam, *Bowling Alone: The Collapse and Revival of American Community* (New York: Simon & Schuster, 2000).

80. See Eric Pultzer, "Becoming a Habitual Voter: Inertia, Resources, and Growth in Young Adulthood," *American Political Science Review* (March 2002): 41–56; Alan S. Gerber, Donald P. Green, and Ron Shachar, "Voting May Be Habit-Forming: Evidence from a Randomized Field Experiment," *American Journal of Political Science* (July 2003): 540–550; and David Dreyer Lassen, "The Effect of Information on Voter Turnout: Evidence from a Natural Experiment," *American Journal of Political Science* 49 (January 2005): 103–111. For the argument that turnout may be genetic, see Charles Q. Choi, "The Genetics of Politics," *Scientific American,* November 2007.

81. Obtained 11 July 1996 from Rock the Vote home page at http://www.rockthevote.org.

82. Center for Information and Research on Civil Learning and Engagement (CIRCLE) at the University of Maryland School of Public Policy, "The 2004 Youth Vote," http://www.civicyouth.org.

83. For the latest analysis of voting trends in the United States, see the research done by Michael McDonald at http://elections.gmu.edu/voter_turnout.htm.

84. Visit the Why Tuesday? website at http://www.whytuesday.org.

85. The negative effect of registration laws on voter turnout is argued in Frances Fox Piven and Richard Cloward, "Government Statistics and Conflicting Explanations of Nonvoting," *PS: Political Science and Politics* 22 (September 1989): 580–588. Their analysis was hotly contested in Stephen Earl Bennett, "The Uses and Abuses of Registration and Turnout Data: An Analysis of Piven and Cloward's Studies of Nonvoting in America," *PS: Political Science and Politics* 23 (June 1990): 166–171. Bennett showed that turnout declined 10 to 13 percent after 1960, despite efforts to remove or lower legal hurdles to registration. For their reply, see Frances Fox Piven and Richard Cloward, "A Reply to Bennett," *PS: Political Science and Politics* 23 (June 1990): 172–173. You can see that reasonable people can disagree on this matter. Moreover, cross-national research has found that compulsory voter registration (not voluntary, as in the United States) did not increase turnout across nations. See Franklin, "The Dynamics of Electoral Participation," p. 159.

86. "High Turnout with Iowa's Election Day Registration Law," http://www.866ourvote.org/newsroom/news?id=0191.

87. Ruth Goldway, "The Election Is in the Mail," *New York Times,* 6 December 2006; Randal C. Archibold, "Mail-in Voters Become the Latest Prize," *New York Times,* 14 January 2008.

88. "Hawaii's Internet Vote is 1st in Nation," *St. Paul Pioneer Press,* 24 May 2009, p. 5A.

89. David Glass, Peverill Squire, and Raymond Wolfinger, "Voter Turnout: An International Comparison," *Public Opinion* 6 (December–January 1984): 52. Wolfinger says that because of the strong effect of registration on turnout, most rational choice analyses of voting would be better suited to analyzing turnout of only registered voters. See Raymond E. Wolfinger, "The Rational Citizen Faces Election Day," *Public Affairs Report* 6 (November 1992): 12.

90. Federal Election Commission, *The Impact of the National Voter Registration Act of 1993 on the Administration of Elections for Federal Office 1997–1998* (Washington, D.C.: Federal Election Commission, 1999), http://www.fec.gov/press/press1999/mtrvtr99.htm.

91. Pew Center on the States, "Bringing Elections into the 21st Century: Voter Registration Modernization," Issue Brief (August 2009), p. 2.

92. American parties don't work hard at voter mobilization. See Raymond V. Carman, Jr., Ian M. Farrell,

and Jonathan S. Krasno, "The Parties as Mobilizers: Party Efforts to Get Out the Vote in the 2000 and 2004 Elections" (paper presented at the 66th Annual Midwest Political Science Association Conference, Chicago, 3–6 April 2007). That activity seems more important to parties elsewhere. See Aníbal Pérez-Liñán, "Neoinstitutional Accounts of Voter Turnout: Moving Beyond Industrial Democracies," *Electoral Studies* 20 (2001): 281–297.

93. Recent research finds that "party contact is clearly a statistically and substantively important factor in predicting and explaining political behavior." See Peter W. Wielhouwer and Brad Lockerbie, "Party Contacting and Political Participation, 1952–1990" (paper presented at the annual meeting of the American Political Science Association, Chicago, 1992), p. 14. Of course, parties strategically target the groups that they want to see vote in elections. See Peter W. Wielhouwer, "Strategic Canvassing by Political Parties, 1952–1990," *American Review of Politics* 16 (Fall 1995): 213–238.

94. Steven J. Rosenstone and John Mark Hansen, *Mobilization, Participation, and Democracy in America* (New York: Macmillan, 1993), p. 213.

95. For the differences between national and local elections, see J. Eric Oliver and Shang E. Ha, "Vote Choice in Suburban Elections," *American Political Science Review* 101 (August 2007): 393–408; Brad T. Gomez, Thomas G. Hansford, and George A. Krause, "The Republicans Should Pray for Rain: Weather, Turnout, and Voting in U.S. Presidential Elections," *Journal of Politics* 69 (August 2007): 649–663.

96. See Robert A. Jackson, "Voter Mobilization in the 1986 Midterm Election," *Journal of Politics* 55 (November 1993): 1081–1099; Kim Quaile Hill and Jan E. Leighley, "Political Parties and Class Mobilization in Contemporary United States Elections," *American Journal of Political Science* 40 (August 1996): 787–804; Janine Parry et al., "Mobilizing the Seldom Voter: Campaign Contact and Effects in High Profile Elections," *Political Behavior* 30 (March 2008): 97–113.

97. Aaron Smith, "Civic Engagement Online: Politics as Usual," Pew Internet & American Life Project, 1 September 2009, at http://pewresearch.org/pubs/1328/online-political-civic-engagement-activity.

98. Nonprofit Voter Engagement Network, "America Goes to the Polls: A Report on Voter Turnout in the 2006 Election," http://www.nonprofitvote.org.

99. Richard Niemi and Michael Hanmer, "Voter Registration and Turnout among College Students" (paper presented at the annual meeting of the American Political Science Association, 2006). Students at Northwestern University in 2008 were more likely to register and vote absentee if they came from a "swing" state. See Kim Castle, Janice Levy, and Michael Peshkin, "Local and Absentee Voter Registration Drives on a College Campus," CIRCLE Working Paper 66, October 2009.

100. See Charles Krauthammer, "In Praise of Low Voter Turnout," *Time,* 21 May 1990, p. 88. Krauthammer says, "Low voter turnout means that people see politics as quite marginal to their lives, as neither salvation nor ruin…. Low voter turnout is a leading indicator of contentment." A major study in 1996 that compared 1,000 likely nonvoters with 2,300 likely voters found that 24 percent of the nonvoters, versus 5 percent of likely voters, said they "hardly ever" followed public affairs. See Dwight Morris, "No-Show '96: Americans Who Don't Vote," summary report to the Medill News Service and WTTW Television, Northwestern University School of Journalism, 1996. For a critical view of nonvoting, see Patterson, *The Vanishing Voter,* pp. 11–13.

101. Crewe, "Electoral Participation," p. 262.

102. For research showing that economic inequality depresses political engagement of the citizenry, see Frederick Solt, "Economic Inequality and Democratic Political Engagement," *American Journal of Political Science* 52 (2008): 48–60.

103. Barnes and Kaase, *Political Action,* p. 532.

104. Eric Lichtblau, "F.B.I. Watched Activist Groups, New Files Show," *New York Times,* 20 December 2005, p. 1.

105. *1971 Congressional Quarterly Almanac* (Washington, D.C.: CQ Press, 1972), p. 475.

106. Benjamin Ginsberg, *The Consequences of Consent: Elections, Citizen Control, and Popular Acquiescence* (Reading, Mass.: Addison-Wesley, 1982), p. 13.

107. Ibid., pp. 13–14.

108. Ibid., pp. 6–7.

109. Some people have argued that the decline in voter turnout during the 1980s served to increase the class bias in the electorate because people of lower socioeconomic status stayed home. But later research has concluded that "class bias has not increased since 1964." Jan E. Leighley and Jonathan Nagler, "Socioeconomic Class Bias in Turnout, 1964–1988: The Voters Remain the Same," *American Political Science Review* 86 (September 1992): 734. Nevertheless, Rosenstone and Hansen, in *Mobilization, Participation, and Democracy in America,* say, "The economic inequalities in political participation that prevail in the United States today are as large as the racial disparities in political participation that prevailed in the 1950s. America's leaders today face few incentives to attend to the needs of the disadvantaged" (p. 248).

Chapter 8 / Political Parties / pages 242–277

1. Alan K. Ota, "Will Cornyn's 'Big Tent' Strategy Collapse?" CQ Today Online News, 5 November 2009, at http://www.cqpolitics.com.

2. Jeremy W. Peters and Adam Nagourney, "G.O.P. Candidate Pressed by Right, Ends Upstate Bid," *New York Times,* 1 November 2009, pp. 1, 34.

3. Jonathan Weisman and Naftali Bendavid, "Late Moves Jumble House Race," *Wall Street Journal,* 2 November 2009, p. A3.

4. Charles Mahtesian and Alex Isenstadt, "Uncivil War: Conservatives to challenge a dozen GOP candidates," *Politico,* 3 November 2009, at http://www.politico.com.

5. The American National Election 2008 Time Series Study, http://www.electionstudies.org.

6. David W. Moore, "Perot Supporters: For the Man, Not a Third Party," *Gallup Organization Newsletter Archive,* 7 August 1995.

7. The tea party qualified to appear on the Florida ballot in 2010. See *Ballot Access News* 25 (1 March 2010): 6; and a candidate in Nevada qualified to run for the U.S. Senate under the tea party of Nevada.

8. See, for example, Peter Mair, "Comparing Party Systems," in *Comparing Democracies 2: New Challenges in the Study of Elections and Voting,* ed. Lawrence LeDuc, Richard G. Niemi, and Pippa Norris (London: Sage, 2002), pp. 88–107.

9. E. E. Schattschneider, *Party Government* (New York: Holt, 1942).

10. See Lyn Carson and Brian Martin, *Random Selection in Politics* (Westport, Conn.: Praeger, 1999). They say: "The assumption behind random selection in politics is that just about anyone who wishes to be involved in decision making is capable of making a useful contribution, and that the fairest way to ensure that everyone has such an opportunity is to give them an equal chance to be involved" (p. 4).

11. See James M. Snyder, Jr., and Michael M. Ting, "An Informational Rationale for Political Parties," *American Journal of Political Science* 46 (January 2002): 90–110. They formalize the argument that political parties acquire "brand names" that help voters make sense of politics.

12. John H. Aldrich, *Why Parties? The Origin and Transformation of Political Parties in America* (Chicago: University of Chicago Press, 1995), p. 296.

13. See John Kenneth White and Daniel M. Shea (eds.), *New Party Politics: From Jefferson and Hamilton to the Information Age* (Boston: Bedford/St. Martin's, 2000), for essays on the place of political parties in American history.

14. See Jerome M. Clubb, William H. Flanigan, and Nancy H. Zingale, *Partisan Realignment: Voters, Parties, and Government in American History* (Beverly Hills, Calif.: Sage, 1980), p. 163. Once central to the analysis of American politics, the concept of critical elections has been discounted by some scholars in recent years. See Larry M. Bartels, "Electoral Continuity and Change," *Electoral Studies* 17 (September 1998): 301–326; and David R. Mayhew, *Electoral Realignments: A Critique of an American Genre* (New Haven, Conn.: Yale University Press, 2002). However, the concept has been defended by other scholars. See Peter F. Nardulli, "The Concept of a Critical Realignment, Electoral Behavior, and Political Change," *American Political Science Review* 89 (March 1995): 10–22; and Norman Schofield, Gary Miller, and Andrew Martin, "Critical Elections and Political Realignments in the USA: 1860–2000," *Political Studies* 51 (2003): 217–240.

15. See Gerald M. Pomper, "Classification of Presidential Elections," *Journal of Politics* 29 (August 1967): 535–566. See also Walter Dean Burnham, *Critical Elections and the Mainsprings of American Politics* (New York: Norton, 1970). Decades later, an update of Gerald Pomper's analysis of presidential elections through 1996 determined that 1960, 1964, and 1968 all had realigning characteristics. See Jonathan Knuckley, "Classification of Presidential Elections: An Update," *Polity* 31 (Summer 1999): 639–653.

16. See Ronald Brownstein, "For GOP, a Southern Exposure," *National Journal Online,* at http://www.nationaljournal.com/njonline/no_20090523_3656.php?.

17. For more extensive treatments, see Henry M. Littlefield, "The Wizard of Oz: Parable on Populism," *American Quarterly* 16 (Spring 1964): 47–58; and David B. Parker, "The Rise and Fall of *The Wonderful Wizard of Oz* as a 'Parable on Populism,' " *Journal of the Georgia Association of Historians* 15 (1994): 49–63.

18. In "Realignment in Presidential Politics: South and North?" (paper presented at the Citadel Symposium on Southern Politics, 4–5 March 2004), William Crotty argues that a political realignment definitely occurred in the South around 1968 that affected presidential politics and national voting behavior.

19. Earl Black and Merle Black, *The Rise of Southern Republicans* (Cambridge, Mass.: Harvard University Press, 2002), pp. 2–3.

20. Seth C. McKeen, "Rural Voters and the Polarization of American Presidential Elections," *PS: Political Science and Politics* 41 (January 2008): 101–108.

21. Jeffrey M. Stonecash, *Political Parties Matter: Realignment and the Return of Partisan Voting* (Boulder, Colo.: Lynne Rienner, 2006), pp. 129–130.

22. The discussion that follows draws heavily on Austin Ranney and Willmoore Kendall, *Democracy and the American Party System* (New York: Harcourt, Brace, 1956), Chaps. 18, 19. For later analyses of multiparty

politics in America, see Steven J. Rosenstone, Roy L. Behr, and Edward H. Lazarus, *Third Parties in America: Citizen Response to Major Party Failure,* 2nd ed. (Princeton, N.J.: Princeton University Press, 1996); and John F. Bibby and L. Sandy Maisel, *Two Parties—or More?* (Boulder, Colo.: Westview Press, 1998).

23. The seven candidates who bolted from their former parties and ran for president on a third-party ticket were Theodore Roosevelt (1912), Robert La Follette (1924), Henry A. Wallace (1948), Strom Thurmond (1948), George Wallace (1968), John Anderson (1980), and Pat Buchanan (2000). Thurmond and both Wallaces had been Democrats; the others had originally been elected to office as Republicans. Note that Harry Truman won reelection in 1948 despite facing opposition from former Democrats running as candidates of other parties.

24. J. David Gillespie, *Politics at the Periphery: Third Parties in a Two-Party America* (Columbia: University of South Carolina Press, 1993). Surveys of public attitudes toward minor parties are reported in Christian Coller, "Trends: Third Parties and the Two-Party System," *Public Opinion Quarterly* 60 (Fall 1996): 431–449. For a spirited defense of having a strong third party in American politics, see Theodore J. Lowi, "Toward a More Responsible Three-Party System: Deregulating American Democracy," in *The State of the Parties,* 4th ed., ed. John C. Green and Rick Farmer (Lanham, Md.: Rowman & Littlefield, 2003), pp. 354–377. For an analysis of third-party presidential campaigns in 2008, see Brian J. Brox, "Running Nowhere: Third Party Presidential Campaigns in 2008" (paper presented at the annual meeting of the Midwest Political Science Association, Chicago, 3–6 April 2008).

25. Ronald B. Rapoport and Walter J. Stone, *Three's a Crowd: The Dynamics of Third Parties, Ross Perot, and Republican Resurgence* (Ann Arbor: University of Michigan Press, 2005).

26. In a June 18–29, 2008, Pew Research Center Poll, 56 percent of the respondents agreed that "we should have a third major political party in this country in addition to the Democrats and Republicans." See also Shigeo Hirano and James M. Snyder, Jr., "The Decline of Third-Party Voting in the United States," *The Journal of Politics* 69 (February 2007): 1–16.

27. Rosenstone, Behr, and Lazarus, *Third Parties in America,* p. 8.

28. Shigeo Hirano and James M. Snyder, Jr., "The Decline of Third-Party Voting in the United States," *Journal of Politics* 69 (February 2007): 1–6. See also Rapoport and Stone, *Three's a Crowd.*

29. In his study of party systems, Jean Blondel noticed that most three-party systems had two major parties and a much smaller third party, which he called two-and-a-half-party systems. (Britain, for example, has two major parties—Labour and Conservative—and a smaller Social Democratic Party. Germany has followed a similar pattern.) Blondel said, "While it would seem theoretically possible for three-party systems to exist in which all three significant parties were of about equal size, there are in fact no three-party systems of this kind among Western democracies." He concluded that "genuine three-party systems do not normally occur because they are essentially transitional, thus unstable, forms of party systems." See his "Types of Party System," in *The West European Party System,* ed. Peter Mair (New York: Oxford University Press, 1990), p. 305.

30. See Douglas J. Amy, *Real Choices, New Voices: The Case for Proportional Representation in the United States,* 2nd ed. (New York: Columbia University Press, 2002).

31. The most complete report of these legal barriers is contained in monthly issues of *Ballot Access News,* http://www.ballot-access.org. State laws and court decisions may systematically support the major parties, but the U.S. Supreme Court seems to hold a more neutral position toward major and minor parties. See Lee Epstein and Charles D. Hadley, "On the Treatment of Political Parties in the U.S. Supreme Court, 1900–1986," *Journal of Politics* 52 (May 1990): 413–432; and E. Joshua Rosenkranz, *Voter Choice 96: A 50-State Report Card on the Presidential Elections* (New York: New York University School of Law, Brennan Center for Justice, 1996), p. 24.

32. Samuel Issacharoff, Pamela S. Karlan, and Richard H. Pildes, *The Law of Democracy,* rev. 2nd ed. (New York: Foundation Press, 2002), pp. 417–436.

33. See James Gimpel, *National Elections and the Autonomy of American State Party Systems* (Pittsburgh, Pa.: University of Pittsburgh Press, 1996).

34. Measuring the concept of party identification has had its problems. For insights into the issues, see R. Michael Alvarez, "The Puzzle of Party Identification," *American Politics Quarterly* 18 (October 1990): 476–491; and Donald Philip Green and Bradley Palmquist, "Of Artifacts and Partisan Instability," *American Journal of Political Science* 34 (August 1990): 872–902.

35. The American National Election 2008 Time Series Study, http://www.electionstudies.org.

36. Rhodes Cook, "GOP Shows Dramatic Growth, Especially in the South," *Congressional Quarterly Weekly Report,* 13 January 1996, pp. 97–100.

37. Susan Page, "Highly Educated Couples Often Split on Candidates," *USA Today,* 18 December 2002, pp. 1–2.

38. U.S. Census, Table 1a, Projected Population of the United States, by Race and Hispanic Origin: 2000 to 2050, available at http://www.census.gov/population/www/projections/usinterimproj.

39. The relationship between age and party identification is quite complicated, but research finds that it becomes more stable as people age. See Elias Dinas and Mark Franklin, "The Development of Partisanship during the Life-Course" (paper presented at the Midwest Political Science Association 67th Annual National Conference, Palmer House Hilton, Chicago, 2 April 2009), http://www.allacademic.com/meta/p363000_index .html.

40. Two scholars on voting behavior describe partisanship as "the feeling of sympathy for and loyalty to a political party that an individual acquires—sometimes during childhood—and holds through life, often with increasing intensity." See William H. Flanigan and Nancy H. Zingale, *Political Behavior of the American Electorate,* 10th ed. (Washington, D.C.: CQ Press, 2002), p. 60.

41. Bill Keller, "As Arms Buildup Eases, U.S. Tries to Take Stock," *New York Times,* 14 May 1985; Ed Gillespie and Bob Schellhas, *Contract with America* (New York: Times Books, 1994), p. 107.

42. "The GOP's Spending Spree," *Wall Street Journal,* 25 November 2003, p. A18.

43. See, for example, Gerald M. Pomper, *Elections in America* (New York: Dodd, Mead, 1968); Benjamin Ginsberg, "Election and Public Policy," *American Political Science Review* 70 (March 1976): 41–50; and Jeff Fishel, *Presidents and Promises* (Washington, D.C.: CQ Press, 1985).

44. Ian Budge and Richard I. Hofferbert, "Mandates and Policy Outputs: U.S. Party Platforms and Federal Expenditures," *American Political Science Review* 84 (March 1990): 111–131.

45. See Terri Susan Fine, "Economic Interests and the Framing of the 1988 and 1992 Democratic and Republican Party Platforms," *American Review of Politics* 16 (Spring 1995): 79–93.

46. Ian Budge et al., *Mapping Policy Preferences: Estimates for Parties, Electors, and Governments 1945–1998* (Oxford: Oxford University Press, 2001), p. 49.

47. See Ralph M. Goldman, *The National Party Chairmen and Committees: Factionalism at the Top* (Armonk, N.Y.: M. E. Sharpe, 1990). The subtitle is revealing.

48. Cornelius P. Cotter and Bernard C. Hennessy, *Politics without Power: The National Party Committees* (New York: Atherton Press, 1964).

49. Phillip A. Klinkner, "Party Culture and Party Behavior," in *The State of the Parties,* 3rd ed., ed. Daniel M. Shea and John C. Green (Lanham, Md.: Rowman & Littlefield, 1999), pp. 275–287; Phillip A. Klinkner, *The Losing Parties: Out-Party National Committees, 1956–1993* (New Haven, Conn.: Yale University Press, 1994).

50. Anthony Corrado, Sarah Barclay, and Heitor Gouvea, "The Parties Take the Lead: Political Parties and the Financing of the 2000 Presidential Election," in *The State of the Parties,* 4th ed., ed. John C. Green and Rick Farmer (Lanham, Md.: Rowman & Littlefield, 2003), p. 97; Klinkner, *The Losing Parties.*

51. Jeff Zeleny, "His Meteoric Days Behind Him, a Less Fiery Dean Leads Party," *New York Times,* 21 October 2007, pp. 1, 16; Naftali Bendavid, "The House That Rahm Built," *Chicago Tribune,* Special Report, 12 November 2007.

52. Daniel J. Galvin, *Presidential Party Building: Dwight D. Eisenhower to George W. Bush* (Princeton, N.J.: Princeton University Press, 2010), pp. ix–x.

53. Dan Barry, "Republicans on Long Island Master Science of Politics," *New York Times,* 8 March 1996, p. A1S. Recent research suggests that when both major parties have strong organizations at the county level, the public has more favorable attitudes toward the parties. See John J. Coleman, "Party Organization Strength and Public Support for Parties," *American Journal of Political Science* 40 (August 1996): 805–824.

54. John Frendreis et al., "Local Political Parties and Legislative Races in 1992," in Shea and Green, *The State of the Parties,* p. 139.

55. Federal Election Commission, *National Party Transfers to State/Local Party Committees, January 1,* 2007–*December 31,* 2008. Available at http://www.fec.gov/ press/press2009/05282009Party/20090528Party .shtml.

56. Raymond J. La Raja, "State Parties and Soft Money: How Much Party Building?" in Green and Farmer, *The State of the Parties,* p. 146.

57. Robert Biersack, "Hard Facts and Soft Money: State Party Finance in the 1992 Federal Elections," in Shea and Green, *The State of the Parties,* p. 114.

58. See the evidence presented in Robert Harmel and Kenneth Janda, *Parties and Their Environments* (New York: Longman, 1982), Chap. 5, and the more recent assessment in Nicol C. Rae, "Be Careful What You Wish For: The Rise of Responsible Parties in American National Politics," *Annual Review of Political Science* 10 (2007): 169–191.

59. Martin P. Wattenberg, *The Decline of American Political Parties, 1952–1994* (Cambridge, Mass.: Harvard University Press, 1996).

60. Taylor Dark III, "The Rise of a Global Party? American Party Organizations Abroad," *Party Politics* 9 (March 2003): 241–255.

61. In 1996, the Democratic National Committee mounted an unprecedented drive to organize up to sixty thousand precinct captains in twenty states, while the new Republican candidate for U.S. senator from Illinois, Al Salvi, fired his own campaign manager and replaced him with someone from the National Republican Senatorial Campaign Committee. See Sue Ellen Christian,

"Democrats Will Focus on Precincts," *Chicago Tribune*, 29 June 1996; and Michael Dizon, "Salvi Fires Top Senate Race Aides," *Chicago Tribune*, 24 May 1996, sec. 2, p. 3.

62. Barbara Sinclair, "The Congressional Party: Evolving Organizational, Agenda-Setting, and Policy Roles," in *The Parties Respond: Changes in American Parties and Campaigns*, 3rd ed., ed. L. Sandy Maisel (Boulder, Colo.: Westview Press, 1998), p. 227.

63. David M. Farrell, "Political Parties in a Changing Campaign Environment," in *Handbook of Party Politics*, ed. Richard S. Katz and William Crotty (London: Sage, 2006), p. 124.

64. The model is articulated most clearly in a report by the American Political Science Association, "Toward a More Responsible Two-Party System," *American Political Science Review* 44 (September 1950): Part II. See also Gerald M. Pomper, "Toward a More Responsible Party System? What, Again?" *Journal of Politics* 33 (November 1971): 916–940. See also the seven essays in the symposium "Divided Government and the Politics of Constitutional Reform," *PS: Political Science and Politics* 24 (December 1991): 634–657.

65. Within the American states, parties also differ on policies, but to varying degrees. See John H. Aldrich and James S. Coleman Battista, "Conditional Party Government in the States," *American Journal of Political Science* 46 (January 2002): 164–172.

66. Recent research finds that voters do differentiate between policies backed by the president and by congressional candidates. See David R. Jones and Monika L. McDermott, "The Responsible Party Government Model in House and Senate Elections," *American Journal of Political Science* 48 (January 2004): 1–12.

67. Rae, "Be Careful What You Wish For," p. 171.

Chapter 9 / Nominations, Elections, and Campaigns / pages 278–319

1. See Arend Lijphart, *Patterns of Democracy: Government Forms and Performance in Thirty-six Countries* (New Haven, Conn.: Yale University Press, 1999), pp. 116–121. Of Lijphart's thirty-six democracies, only six have had presidential forms of government at some time in their history, while Colombia, Costa Rica, Venezuela, and the United States have been consistently presidential.

2. The British parliament has a House of Lords, but it is an appointive body with limited legislative powers.

3. Computed from data in Oonagh Gay and Isobel White, "Election Timetables" (House of Commons Library, Research Paper 07/31, 22 March 2007), p. 14.

4. For a philosophical discussion of "temporal properties" of American elections, see Dennis F. Thompson, "Election Time: Normative Implications of the Electoral Process in the United States," *American Political Science Review* 98 (February 2004): 51–64.

5. This is essentially the framework for studying campaigns set forth in Barbara C. Salmore and Stephen A. Salmore, *Candidates, Parties, and Campaigns: Electoral Politics in America*, 2nd ed. (Washington, D.C.: CQ Press, 1989). For a more recent review of campaigns, see James A. Thurber and Candice J. Nelson (eds.), *Campaigns and Elections American Style*, 3rd ed. (Boulder, Colo.: Westview Press, 2010).

6. Adam Nagourney, "Internet Injects Sweeping Change into U.S. Politics," *New York Times*, 2 April 2006, pp. 1, 17.

7. David Menefree-Libey, *The Triumph of Campaign-Centered Politics* (New York: Chatham House, 2000).

8. Stephen E. Frantzich, *Political Parties in the Technological Age* (New York: Longman, 1989), p. 105.

9. "It is probable that no nation has ever experimented as fully or as fitfully with mechanisms for making nominations as has the United States," say William J. Keefe and Marc J. Hetherington, *Parties, Politics, and Public Policy in America*, 9th ed. (Washington, D.C.: CQ Press, 2003), p. 59.

10. Reuven Y. Hazan and Gideon Rahat, "Candidate Selection: Methods and Consequences," in Richard S. Katz and William Crotty, *Handbook of Party Politics* (London: Sage, 2006), p. 109. See also Krister Lundell, "Determinants of Candidate Selection: The Degree of Centralization in Comparative Perspective," *Party Politics* 10 (January 2004): 25–47.

11. Kenneth Janda, "Adopting Party Law," in *Political Parties and Democracy in Theoretical and Practical Perspectives* (Washington, D.C.: National Democratic Institute for International Affairs, 2005). This is a series of research papers.

12. *The Book of the States*, 2009 (Lexington, Ky.: Council of State Governments, 2009), pp. 295–296.

13. Voting turnout in almost twenty states holding primaries on Super Tuesday, 2 February 2008, set a new record of 27 percent. See Katharine Q. Seelye, "Records for Turnout," *New York Times*, 7 February 2008, p. A24.

14. See John G. Geer, "Assessing the Representativeness of Electorates in Presidential Elections," *American Journal of Political Science* 32 (November 1998): 929–945; Barbara Norrander, "Ideological Representativeness of Presidential Primary Voters," *American Journal of Political Science* 33 (August 1989): 570–587.

15. James A. McCann, "Presidential Nomination Activists and Political Representation: A View from the Active Minority Studies," in *Pursuit of the White House: How We Choose Our Presidential Nominees*, ed. William G. Mayer (Chatham, N.J.: Chatham House, 1996), p. 99.

16. James M. Snyder, Jr., et al., "The Decline of Competition in U.S. Primary Elections, 1908–2004" (unpublished paper, MIT, Cambridge, Mass., June 2005), p. 22.

17. Talar Aslanian et al., "Recapturing Voter Intent: The Nonpartisan Primary in California" (capstone seminar report, Pepperdine University, April 2003), Appendix C, http://publicpolicy.pepperdine.edu/master-public-policy/capstone.htm.

18. Nicol C. Rae, "Exceptionalism in the United States," in Katz and Crotty, *Handbook of Party Politics,* p. 201. See also Lawrence LeDuc, "Democratizing Party Leadership Selection," *Party Politics* 7 (May 2001): 323–341.

19. See "The Green Papers" website at http://www.thegreenpapers.com for information on state methods of delegate selection in 2008.

20. Alan Ware, *The American Direct Primary: Party Institutionalization and Transformation in the North* (Cambridge: Cambridge University Press, 2002). Ware argues that the primary system resulted less from the reform movement than the unwieldy nature of the caucus/convention system for nominating candidates.

21. Harold W. Stanley and Richard G. Niemi, *Vital Statistics on American Politics, 1788–2008* (Washington, D.C.: CQ Press, 2008). According to state-by-state delegate totals in "The Green Papers" website, about 15 percent of the delegates to each party's 2008 presidential nominating convention were selected through the caucus/convention system.

22. See the symposium, "Reforming the Presidential Nomination Process," in *PS: Political Science & Politics* 42 (January 2009): 27–79.

23. See Rhodes Cook, *The Presidential Nominating Process: A Place for Us?* (Lanham, Md.: Rowman & Littlefield, 2004), Chap. 5. Nations that have copied the U.S. model have experienced mixed results. See James A. McCann, "The Emerging International Trend toward Open Presidential Primaries," in *The Making of the Presidential Candidates 2004,* ed. William G. Mayer (Lanham, Md.: Rowman & Littlefield, 2004), pp. 265–293.

24. Rachel Kapochunas, "In Some Ways, 2012 Presidential Race Already Underway," CQ Today Online News – Politics, 5 September 2009.

25. Arthur T. Hadley, *The Invisible Primary* (Englewood Cliffs, N.J.: Prentice-Hall, 1976). For a test of some of Hadley's assertions, see Emmett H. Buell, Jr., "The Invisible Primary," in *In Pursuit of the White House,* ed. William G. Mayer (Chatham, N.J.: Chatham House, 1996), pp. 1–43. More recently, see Cook, *The Presidential Nominating Process,* pp. 83–89. An analogous concept for presidents in office is the "permanent campaign"; see Brendan J. Doherty, "Elections: The Politics of the Permanent Campaign: Presidential Travel and the Electoral College, 1977–2004," *Presidential Studies Quarterly* 37 (December 2007): 749–773.

26. Gary R. Orren and Nelson W. Polsby (eds.), *Media and Momentum: The New Hampshire Primary and Nomination Politics* (Chatham, N.J.: Chatham House, 1987), p. 23.

27. These figures, calculated for voting-eligible population (VEP), come from elections. http://elections.gmu.edu/voter_turnout.htm. VEP is lower than voting-age population (VAP) because VEP excludes those ineligible to vote, usually noncitizens and felons.

28. Richard L. Berke, "Two States Retain Roles in Shaping Presidential Race," *New York Times,* 29 November 1999, p. 1; Leslie Wayne, "Iowa Turns Its Presidential Caucuses into a Cash Cow, and Milks Furiously," *New York Times,* 5 January 2000, p. A16. See also Adam Nagourney, "Iowa Worries about Losing Its Franchise," *New York Times,* 18 January 2004, sec. 4, p. 3.

29. Laurie Goering, "Race Watched Round the World," *Chicago Tribune,* 29 February 2008, pp. 1, 16.

30. In general, Democratic winners are less predictable. See Wayne P. Steger, "Who Wins Nominations and Why? An Updated Forecast of the Presidential Primary Vote," *Political Research Quarterly* 60 (March 2007): 91–99.

31. One scholar holds that early popularity is more important for Republican presidential hopefuls. See D. Jason Berggren, "Two Parties, Two Types of Nominees, Two Paths to Winning a Presidential Nomination, 1972–2004," *Presidential Studies Quarterly* 37 (June 2007): 203–227.

32. See James R. Beniger, "Winning the Presidential Nomination: National Polls and State Primary Elections, 1936–1972," *Public Opinion Quarterly* 40 (Spring 1976): 22–38.

33. *The American Heritage Dictionary of the English Language,* 4th ed. (Boston: Houghton Mifflin, 2000), p. 362. Indeed, the entry on "Electoral College" in the 1989 *Oxford English Dictionary* does not note any usage in American politics up to 1875, when it cites a reference in connection with the Germanic Diet.

34. References to the electoral college in the U.S. Code can be found through the Legal Information Institute website, http://www4.law.cornell.edu/uscode/3/ch1.html.

35. Michael Nelson, *Congressional Quarterly's Guide to the Presidency* (Washington, D.C.: CQ Press, 1989), pp. 155–156. Colorado selected its presidential electors through the state legislature in 1876, but that was the year it entered the Union.

36. Who would have become president if the 538 electoral votes had been divided equally, at 269 each?

According to the Constitution, the House of Representatives would have chosen the president, for no candidate had a majority. One way to avoid tied outcomes in the future is to create an odd number of electoral votes. To do this, one scholar proposes making the District of Columbia a state. That would give Washington three electoral votes—the same number as it has now without congressional representation. The Senate would increase to 102 members, while the House would remain fixed at 435. (Presumably, Washington's seat would come from one of the other states after decennial reapportionment.) This clever solution would produce an electoral college of 537, an odd number that could not produce a tie between two candidates. See David A. Crockett, "Dodging the Bullet: Election Mechanics and the Problem of the Twenty-third Amendment," *PS: Political Science and Politics* 36 (July 2003): 423–426.

37. Shlomo Slonim, "The Electoral College at Philadelphia: The Evolution of an Ad Hoc Congress for the Selection of a President," *Journal of American History* 73 (June 1986): 35. For a recent critique and proposal for reform, see David W. Abbott and James P. Levine, *Wrong Winner: The Coming Debacle in the Electoral College* (New York: Praeger, 1991). For a reasoned defense, see Walter Berns (ed.), *After the People Vote: A Guide to the Electoral College* (Washington, D.C.: American Enterprise Institute, 1992). For a detailed analysis of a congressional failure to enact proportional distribution of state electoral votes, see Gary Bugh, "Normal Politics and the Failure of the Most Intense Effort to Amend the Presidential Election System" (paper presented at the annual meeting of the Northeastern Political Science Association, Boston, 2006).

38. Gallup News Service, "Americans Have Historically Favored Changing Way Presidents Are Elected," *Poll Releases,* 10 November 2000, www.gallup.com/poll/releases/pr001110.asp. See also Frank Newport, "Americans Support Proposal to Eliminate Electoral College System," *Poll Releases,* 5 January 2001, www.gallup.com/poll/releases/pr010105.asp.

39. For the most recent review, see Gary Bugh (ed.), Electoral College Reform: Challenges and Possibilities (Burlington, VT: Ashgate, 2010).

40. Walter Berns (ed.), *After the People Vote: A Guide to the Electoral College* (Washington, D.C.: American Enterprise Institute, 1992), pp. 45–48. The framers had great difficulty deciding how to allow both the people and the states to participate in selecting the president. This matter was debated on twenty-one different days before they compromised on the electoral college, which, Slonim says, "in the eyes of its admirers ... represented a brilliant scheme for successfully blending national and federal elements in the selection of the nation's chief executive" ("The Electoral College at Philadelphia," p. 58).

41. Observers suspect that the vote for Edwards instead of Kerry was cast by error. See http://news.minnesota.publicradio.org/features/2004/12/13_ap_electors.

42. See Alexis Simendinger, James A. Barnes, and Carl M. Cannon, "Pondering a Popular Vote," *National Journal,* 18 November 2000, pp. 3650–3656.

43. Harold W. Stanley and Richard G. Niemi, *Vital Statistics on American Politics, 1999–2008* (Washington, D.C.: CQ Press, 2009), Table 3.10.

44. Rhodes Cook, "House Republicans Scored a Quiet Victory in '92," *Congressional Quarterly Weekly Report,* 17 April 1993, p. 966.

45. In fact, the *New York Times* profiled John Boehner in a long article weeks before the election. See Jennifer Steinhauer and Carl Hulse, "Boehner's Path to Power Began in Small-Town Ohio," *New York Times,* 14 October 2010, p. A1.

46. Lydia Saad, "Democrats Jump into Six-Point Lead on Generic Ballot," *Gallup Report,* 19 July 2010, http://www.gallup.com/poll/141440/Democrats-Jump-Six-Point-Lead-Generic-Ballot.aspx.

47. Salmore and Salmore, *Candidates, Parties, and Campaigns,* p. 1. Also see Paul S. Herrnson, *Congressional Elections: Campaigning at Home and in Washington* (Washington, D.C.: CQ Press, 2008).

48. Nate Silver and Andrew Gelman, "No Country for Close Calls," *New York Times,* 19 April 2009, p. WK11.

49. See Edward I. Sidlow, *Challenging the Incumbent: An Underdog's Undertaking* (Washington, D.C.: CQ Press, 2004), for the engaging account of the unsuccessful 2000 campaign by a young political scientist, Lance Pressl, against the most senior Republican in the House, Phil Crane, in Illinois' Sixth District. Sidlow's book invites readers to ponder what the high reelection rate of incumbents means for American politics.

50. Brody Mullins, "Inside Clinton Campaign, a Potent Political Machine," *Wall Street Journal,* 9 April 2007, pp. A1, A11; John McCormick, "Chicago Is Heart, Brain Center of Obama Campaign," *Chicago Tribune,* 11 June 2007, p. 4.

51. See Peter L. Francia et al., *The Financiers of Congressional Elections* (New York: Columbia University Press, 2003).

52. Quoted in E. J. Dionne, Jr., "On the Trail of Corporation Donations," *New York Times,* 6 October 1980.

53. Salmore and Salmore, *Candidates, Parties, and Campaigns,* p. 11. See also David Himes, "Strategy and Tactics for Campaign Fund-Raising," in *Campaigns and Elections: American Style,* ed. James A. Thurber and Candice J. Nelson (Boulder, Colo.: Westview Press, 1995), pp. 62–77.

54. Mike Dorning, "Romney's Big Ad Buys Don't Pre-Empt Foes," *Chicago Tribune,* 25 December 2007,

pp. 1, 29; and Center for Responsive Politics, "Banking on Becoming President," http://www.opensecrets.org/pres08/index.asp.

55. Federal Election Commission, *The First Ten Years: 1975–1985* (Washington, D.C.: Federal Election Commission, 14 April 1985), p. 1.

56. Michael J. Malbin, "Assessing the Bipartisan Campaign Reform Act," in *The Election After Reform: Money, Politics and the Bipartisan Campaign Reform Act,* ed. Michael J. Malbin (Lanham, Md.: Rowman & Littlefield, 2006).

57. Center for Responsive Politics, at http://www.opensecrets.org/parties/softsource.php.

58. Steve Weissman and Ruth Hassan, "BCRA and the 527 Groups," in Malbin, *The Election After Reform.*

59. Brody Mullins, "Stealthy Groups Shake Up Races," *Wall Street Journal,* 4 February 2008, p. A12.

60. Adam Liptak, "Justices, 5–4, Reject Corporate Campaign Spending Limit," *New York Times,* 22 January 2010, pp. A1, A16.

61. Editorial, "A Free Speech Landmark," *Wall Street Journal,* 22 January 2010, p. A18.

62. Editorial, "The Court's Blow to Democracy," *New York Times,* 22 January 2010, p. A20.

63. "Changing the Rules," *Wall Street Journal,* 22 January 2010, p. A6.

64. James A. Barnes, "Matching Funds, R.I.P.," *National Journal,* 26 April 2008, p. 75.

65. Federal Election Commission, "2008 Presidential Campaign Financial Activity Summarized: Receipts Nearly Double 2004 Total," News Release, 8 June 2009.

66. Center for Responsive Politics, "Banking on Becoming President," http://www.opensecrets.org/pres08/index.php.

67. Center for Responsive Politics, "Price of Admission," http://www.opensecrets.org/bigpicture/stats.php?cycle=2008.

68. David D. Kirkpatrick, "Death Knell May Be Near for Public Election Funds," *New York Times,* 23 January 2007, pp. A1, A16.

69. Brody Mullins, "Donor Bundling Emerges as Major Ill in '08 Race," *Wall Street Journal,* 18 October 2007, pp. A1, A14.

70. Leslie Wayne and Jeff Zeleny, "Enlisting New Donors, Obama Reaped $32 Million in January," *New York Times,* 1 February 2008, pp. A1, A14.

71. Katharine Q. Seelye and Leslie Wayne, "The Web Finds Its Man, and Takes Him for a Ride," *New York Times,* 11 November 2007, p. 22.

72. Leslie Wayne, "A Fund-Raising Rainmaker Arises Online," *New York Times,* 29 November 2008, p. A22.

73. Russ Buettner and Marc Santora, "In '08 Campaign, Money Chase Circles the Globe," *New York Times,* 22 September 2007, pp. 1, 12; Taylor E. Dark III, "Americans Abroad: The Challenge of a Globalized Electorate," *PS: Political Science and Politics* 36 (October 2003): 733–740.

74. Brody Mullins, "Parties Lose Ground in Political Cash Quest," *Wall Street Journal,* 19 December 2007, pp. A1, A17.

75. T. W. Farnam and Brody Mullins, "Inter-Group Campaign Spending Nears Record," *Wall Street Journal,* 5 February 2008, p. A13.

76. Brody Mullins, "Stealthy Groups Shake Up Races," *Wall Street Journal,* 4 February 2008, p. A12.

77. David A. Dulio, "Strategic and Tactical Decisions in Campaigns," in *Guide to Political Campaigns in America,* ed. Paul S. Herrnson (Washington, D.C.: CQ Press, 2005), pp. 231–243.

78. Salmore and Salmore, *Candidates, Parties, and Campaigns,* p. 11.

79. According to Brian F. Schaffner and Matthew J. Streb, less educated respondents are less likely to express a vote preference when party labels are not available. See "The Partisan Heuristic in Low-Information Elections," *Public Opinion Quarterly* 66 (Winter 2002): 559–581.

80. See the "Marketplace: Political Products and Services" section in monthly issues of the magazine *Campaigns and Elections.* These classified ads list scores of names, addresses, and telephone numbers for people who supply "political products and services"—from "campaign schools" to "voter files and mailing lists." For an overview, see Philip Kotler and Neil Kotler, "Political Marketing: Generating Effective Candidates, Campaigns, and Causes," in *Handbook of Political Marketing,* ed. Bruce I. Newman (Thousand Oaks, Calif.: Sage, 1999), pp. 3–18.

81. See Matt A. Barreto et al., "Bulls Eye or Ricochet? Ethnically Targeted Campaign Ads in the 2008 Election" (paper presented at the Chicago Area Behavioral Workshop, Evanston, Ill., 8 May 2009); and Michael G. Hagenand and Robin Kolodny, "Microtargeting: Campaign Advertising on Cable Television" (paper presented at the annual meeting of the Midwest Political Science Association, Chicago, 3–6 April 2008).

82. Salmore and Salmore, *Candidates, Parties, and Campaigns,* pp. 115–116. See also Eric W. Rademacher and Alfred J. Tuchfarber, "Preelection Polling and Political Campaigns," in Newman, *Handbook of Political Marketing,* pp. 197–221.

83. Bruce I. Newman, "A Predictive Model of Voter Behavior," in Newman, *Handbook of Political Marketing,* pp. 259–282. For studies on campaign consultants at work, see James A. Thurber and Candice J. Nelson (eds.), *Campaign Warriors: The Role of*

Political Consultants in Elections (Washington, D.C.: Brookings Institution Press, 2000).

84. A major player in the new Internet election campaign industry is Election Advantage, which describes its offerings at http://www .campaignadvantage.com.

85. James Warren, "Politicians Learn Value of Sundays—Too Well," *Chicago Tribune,* 22 October 1990, p. 1.

86. Timothy E. Cook, *Making Laws and Making News: Media Strategies in the U.S. House of Representatives* (Washington, D.C.: Brookings Institution, 1989). Subsequent research into media effects on Senate and House elections finds that in low-information elections, which characterize House more than Senate elections, the media coverage gives an advantage to incumbents, particularly among independent voters. See Robert Kirby Goidel, Todd G. Shields, and Barry Tadlock, "The Effects of the Media in United States Senate and House Elections: A Comparative Analysis" (paper presented at the annual meeting of the American Political Science Association, Washington, D.C., September 1993).

87. Stephen J. Farnsworth and S. Robert Lichter, *The Nightly News Nightmare: Media Coverage of U.S. Presidential Elections, 1988–2008* (Lanham, MD: Rowman & Littlefield, 2010), p. 52

88. Julianne F. Flowers, Audrey A. Haynes, and Michael H. Crispin, "The Media, the Campaign, and the Message," *American Journal of Political Science* 47 (April 2003): 259–273.

89. Ann N. Crigler, Marion R. Just, and Timothy E. Cook, "Local News, Network News and the 1992 Presidential Campaign" (paper presented at the annual meeting of the American Political Science Association, Washington, D.C., September 1993), p. 9.

90. Stephen Ansolabehere and Shanto Iyengar, *Going Negative: How Political Advertisements Shrink and Polarize the Electorate* (New York: Free Press, 1995), p. 145.

91. Darrell M. West, *Air Wars: Television Advertising in Election Campaigns, 1952–2004,* 4th ed. (Washington, D.C.: CQ Press, 2010), p. 23.

92. Ted Brader, "Striking a Responsive Chord: How Political Ads Motivate and Persuade Voters by Appealing to Emotions," *American Journal of Political Science* 49 (April 2005): 388–405.

93. Darrell M. West, *Air Wars: Television Advertising in Election Campaigns, 1952–2009,* 5th ed. (Washington, D.C.: CQ Press, 2010), pp. 51–52.

94. This theme runs throughout Kathleen Hall Jamieson's *Dirty Politics: Distraction, and Democracy* (New York: Oxford University Press, 1992). See also John Boiney, "You Can Fool All of the People ... Evidence on the Capacity of Political

Advertising to Mislead" (paper presented at the annual meeting of the American Political Science Association, Washington, D.C., September 1993).

95. West, *Air Wars,* 5th ed., p. 159.

96. Kathleen Hall Jamieson, Paul Waldman, and Susan Sheer, "Eliminate the Negative? Categories of Analysis for Political Advertisements," in *Crowded Airwaves: Campaign Advertising in Elections,* ed. James A. Thurber, Candice J. Nelson, and David A. Dulio (Washington, D.C.: Brookings Institution Press, 2000), p. 49.

97. David A. Dulio, Candice J. Nelson, and James A. Thurber, "Summary and Conclusions," in Thurber, Nelson, and Dulio, *Crowded Airwaves,* p. 172. Laboratory research found that even "uncivil" exchanges between candidates can be handled by the public. See Deborah Jordan Brooks and John G. Geer, "Beyond Negativity: The Effects of Incivility on the Electorate," *American Journal of Political Science* 51 (January 2007): 1–16.

98. Gregory A. Huber and Kevin Arceneaux, "Identifying the Persuasive Effects of Presidential Advertising," *American Journal of Political Science* 51 (2007): 957–977.

99. Ansolabehere and Iyengar, *Going Negative,* p. 112.

100. West, however, takes issue with the Ansolabehere and Iyengar analysis in *Going Negative,* saying that turnout is more dependent on mistrust than on negativity of ads. See West, *Air Wars,* pp. 71–72.

101. Richard R. Lau and Gerald M. Pomper, "Effectiveness of Negative Campaigning in U.S. Senate Elections," *American Journal of Political Science* 46 (January 2002): 47–66.

102. Richard R. Lau, Lee Sigelman, and Ivy Brown Rovner, "The Effects of Negative Political Campaigns: A Meta-Analytic Reassessment," *Journal of Politics* 69 (November 2007): 1176–1209.

103. Lee Sigelman and Mark Kugler, "Why Is Research on the Effects of Negative Campaigning So Inconclusive? Understanding Citizens' Perceptions of Negativity," *Journal of Politics* 65 (February 2003): 142–160; Richard R. Lau, Lee Sigelman, and Ivy Brown Rovner, "The Effects of Negative Political Campaigns: A Meta-Analytic Reassessment," *The Journal of Politics* 69 (November 2007): 1176–1209.

104. Jeanne Cummings, "Attacking Is Riskier in 2004 Campaign," *Wall Street Journal,* 23 March 2004, p. A4.

105. The information on early campaign websites comes from Jill Zuckerman, "Candidates Spin Web of Support on Cybertrail," *Chicago Tribune,* 3 December 2003, p. 13.

106. Jeanne Cummings, "Behind Dean Surge: A Gang of Bloggers and Webmasters," *Wall Street Journal,* 14 October 2003, pp. A1, A14.

107. PEW Research Report, "Internet Overtakes Newspapers as News Outlet," 23 December 2008.

108. Emily Steel, "Why Web Campaign Spending Trails TV," *Wall Street Journal,* 14 December 2008, p. B4.

109. See the website for the American National Election Studies at http://www.electionstudies.org/.

110. Michael S. Lewis-Beck, Richard Nadeau, and Angelo Elias, "Economics, Party, and the Vote: Causality Issues and Panel Data," *American Journal of Political Science* 52 (2008): 84–95.

111. Pamela Johnston Conover and Stanley Feldman, "Candidate Perception in an Ambiguous World: Campaigns, Cues, and Inference Processes," *American Journal of Political Science* 33 (November 1989): 912–940.

112. Kira Sanbonmatsu, "Gender Stereotypes and Vote Choice," *American Journal of Political Science* 46 (January 2002): 20–34. Sanbonmatsu contends that some voters have a "baseline preference" for men or women candidates and that women are more likely to hold the preference than men. See also Kathleen A. Dolan, *Voting for Women: How the Public Evaluates Women Candidates* (Boulder, Colo.: Westview Press, 2004).

113. See Herbert F. Weisberg and Clyde Wilcox (eds.), *Models of Voting in Presidential Elections: The 2000 U.S. Election* (Stanford: Stanford University Press, 2004), for a set of studies explaining voting behavior in the presidential election. See also Jean-François Godbout and Éric Bélanger, "Economic Voting and Political Sophistication in the United States: A Reassessment," *Political Research Quarterly* 60 (September 2007): 541–554.

114. Michael M. Gant and Norman R. Luttbeg, *American Electoral Behavior* (Itasca, Ill.: Peacock, 1991), pp. 63–64. Ideology appears to have played little role in the 2000 election. See William G. Jacoby, "Ideology in the 2000 Election: A Study in Ambivalence," in Weisberg and Wilcox, *Models of Voting in Presidential Elections,* pp. 103–104.

115. Martin Gilens, Lynn Vavreck, and Martin Cohen, "The Mass Media and the Public's Assessments of Presidential Candidates, 1952–2000," *Journal of Politics* 69 (November 2007): 1160–1175.

116. Craig Goodman and Gregg R. Murray, "Do You See What I See? Perceptions of Party Differences and Voting Behavior," *American Politics Research* 35 (November 2007): 905–931.

117. "Most Liberal, Most Conservative," *National Journal,* 8 March 2008, pp. 28–31.

118. For a thorough review of studies on campaign effects, see Rian J. Brox and Daron R. Shaw, "Political Parties, American Campaigns, and Effects on Outcomes," in Katz and Crotty, *Handbook of Party Politics,* pp. 146–150.

119. Farnsworth and Lichter, *The Nightly News Nightmare,* p. 64.

120. Matthew A. Baum, "Talking the Vote: Why Presidential Candidates Hit the Talk Show Circuit," *American Journal of Political Science* 49 (April 2005): 213–234.

121. Electorates tend to be more engaged by campaigning in "battleground" states. See James G. Gimpel et al., "Battleground States versus Blackout States: The Behavioral Implications of Modern Presidential Campaigns," *Journal of Politics* 69 (August 2007): 786–797.

122. Laura Meckler, "Campaigns Throw Out Traditional Political Map," *Wall Street Journal,* 8 May 2008, p. A6.

123. Karl Rove, "I See Four Key Battleground States," *Wall Street Journal,* 14 August 2008, p. A11.

124. Laura Meckler and Easha Anand, "Obama Camp's Travel Seems a Factor in Recent Leads in Battleground States," *Wall Street Journal,* 13 October 2008, p. A13.

125. Jim Rutenberg, "Nearing Record, Obama Ad Effort Swamps McCain," *New York Times,* 18 October 2008, pp. A1, A14.

126. CNNPolitics.com, "Poll: Debate Watchers Say Obama Wins," http://www.cnn.com/2008/POLITICS/10/15/debate.poll/index.html.

127. But for a contrary view, see Nicol C. Rae, "Be Careful What You Wish For: The Rise of Responsible Parties in American National Politics," *Annual Review of Political Science* 10 (2007): 169–191.

128. See Peter Kobrak, *Cozy Politics: Political Parties, Campaign Finance, and Compromised Governance* (Boulder, Colo.: Lynne Rienner, 2002), for an indictment of the flow of money in politics from interest groups untempered by the aggregating influence of political parties.

Chapter 10 / Interest Groups / pages 320–349

1. Elizabeth Williamson and Brody Mullins, "Lobbyists Put Democrats Out Front as Winds Shift," *Wall Street Journal,* 5 November 2008.

2. Matthew Mosk, "Democrats Benefitting from Post-election Lobby Boom," *Washington Post,* 14 November 2008.

3. Jonathan D. Salant, "Obama's Spending Spurs Former U.S. Lawmakers to Join Lobbyists," Bloomberg.com, 9 April 2009; "Robert (Bud) Cramer," http://www.wexlergroup.com/bud-cramer.html.

4. Mosk, "Democrats Benefitting from Post-election Lobby Boom."

5. Alexis de Tocqueville, *Democracy in America, 1835–1839,* ed. Richard D. Heffner (New York: Mentor Books, 1956), p. 79.

6. *The Federalist Papers* (New York: Mentor Books, 1961), p. 79.

7. Ibid., p. 78.

8. See Robert A. Dahl, *A Preface to Democratic Theory* (Chicago: University of Chicago Press, 1956), pp. 4–33.

9. The poll was taken by the Pew Research Center for the People and the Press, 1–5 February 2006, http://www.pollingreport.com/politics.htm.

10. This discussion follows from Jeffrey M. Berry and Clyde Wilcox, *The Interest Group Society,* 5th ed. (New York: Longman, 2009), pp. 7–8.

11. Ken Auletta, "The Search Party," *New Yorker,* 14 January 2008, pp. 30–37.

12. See Frank R. Baumgartner, "Interest Groups and Agendas," in *The Oxford Handbook of American Political Parties and Interest Groups,* ed. L. Sandy Maisel and Jeffrey M. Berry (Oxford, UK: Oxford University Press, 2010), pp. 519–533.

13. Rebecca Adams, "Federal Regulations Face Assault on Their Foundation," *CQ Weekly,* 10 August 2002, p. 2183.

14. David B. Truman, *The Governmental Process* (New York: Knopf, 1951).

15. Herbert Gans, *The Urban Villagers* (New York: Free Press, 1962).

16. Robert H. Salisbury, "An Exchange Theory of Interest Groups," *Midwest Journal of Political Science* 13 (February 1969): 1–32.

17. See Mancur Olson, Jr., *The Logic of Collective Action* (New York: Schocken, 1968).

18. Marshall Ganz, *Why David Sometimes Wins* (New York: Oxford University Press, 2009).

19. Kay Lehman Schlozman et al., "Inequalities of Political Voice," in *Inequality and American Democracy,* ed. Lawrence R. Jacobs and Theda Skocpol (New York: Russell Sage Foundation, 2005), pp. 19–87.

20. Center for Responsive Politics, "Harvard University," http://www.opensecrets.org/lobby/clientsum.php?lname=Harvard+University&year=, and "Yale University," http://www.opensecrets.org/lobby/clientsum.php?lname=Yale+University&year=2008.

21. For a skeptical view of the AARP's prowess, see Christopher Howard, *The Welfare State Nobody Knows* (Princeton, N.J.: Princeton University Press, 2007), pp. 125–149.

22. Christopher J. Bosso, *Environment, Inc.* (Lawrence: University Press of Kansas, 2005).

23. See Olson, *The Logic of Collective Action.*

24. Anthony J. Nownes, *Total Lobbying* (New York: Cambridge University Press, 2006), p. 44.

25. Brody Mullins and Kara Acannell, "Hedge Funds Hire Lobbyists to Gather Tips in Washington," *Wall Street Journal,* 8 December 2008, p. A1.

26. "Health Lobbyist Has Great Sway," Associated Press, 24 May 2009.

27. *Congressional Revolving Doors* (Washington, D.C.: Public Citizen, 2005), p. 6.

28. Jeffrey H. Birnbaum, *The Lobbyists* (New York: Times Books, 1992), pp. 128–129.

29. Berry and Wilcox, *The Interest Group Society,* p. 112.

30. Berry and Wilcox, *The Interest Group Society,* p. 114.

31. Suzy Khimm, "Transformers," *New Republic,* 24 December 2008, p. 13.

32. Federal Election Commission, "Growth in PAC Financial Activity Slows," http://fec.gov/press/press2009/20090415PAC/20090424PAC.shtml.

33. Ibid.

34. Federal Election Commission, "Top 50 PACs Contributions to Candidates," http://fec.gov/press/press2009/20090415PAC/documents/10top50paccontrib2008.pdf.

35. Rogan Kersh, "To Donate or Not to Donate?" (paper delivered at the annual meeting of the American Political Science Association, Philadelphia, August 2003), p. 2.

36. Michael M. Franz, *Choices and Changes* (Philadelphia: Temple University Press, 2008).

37. Michael Forsythe and Kristin Jensen, "Democratic Lobbyists Relish Return to Washington's Power Elite," Bloomberg.wire service, 10 November 2006.

38. Federal Election Commission, "PAC Financial Activity," http://www.fec.gov/press/press2009/20090415PAC/documents/1summary2008.pdf.

39. Stephen Ansolabehere, John de Figueredo, and James M. Snyder, Jr., "Why Is There So Little Money in U.S. Politics?" *Journal of Economic Perspectives* 17 (Winter 2003): 161–181; Mark Smith, *American Business and Political Power* (Chicago: University of Chicago Press, 2000), pp. 115–141.

40. Marie Hojnacki and David Kimball, "PAC Contributions and Lobbying Access in Congressional Committees," *Political Research Quarterly* 54 (March 2001): 161–180; John R. Wright, "Contributions, Lobbying, and Committee Voting in the U.S. House of Representatives," *American Political Science Review* 84 (June 1990): 417–438; Richard L. Hall and Frank W. Wayman, "Buying Time: Money Interests and the Mobilization of Bias in Congressional Committees," *American Political Science Review* 84 (September 1990): 797–820.

41. On tactics generally, see Beth L. Leech, *Conflict and Cooperation: Interest Group Lobbying Strategies in Washington* (Princeton, N.J.: Princeton University Press, forthcoming).

42. Richard L. Hall and Alan V. Deardorff, "Lobbying as Legislative Subsidy," *American Political Science Review* 100 (February 2006): 69–84.

43. See Kristin A. Goss, *Disarmed* (Princeton, N.J.: Princeton University Press, 2006).

44. Frank R. Baumgartner Jeffrey M. Berry, Marie Hojnacki, David C. Kimball, and Beth L. Leech, *Lobbying and Policy Change* (Chicago: University of Chicago Press, 2009), pp. 166–189.

45. Eric Pianin, "For Environmentalists, Victories in the Courts," *Washington Post*, 27 January 2003, p. A3.

46. Jeffrey M. Berry and Sarah Sobieraj, "The Outrage Industry" (paper presented at the Going to Extremes Conference: The Fate of the Political Center in American Politics, Rockefeller Center, Dartmouth College, June 2008).

47. Clay Risen, "Store Lobby," *New Republic*, 25 July 2005, pp. 10–11.

48. Dara Z. Strolovitch, *Affirmative Advocacy* (Chicago: University of Chicago Press, 2007), p. 181.

49. The best available data on this can be found in Kay L. Schlozman, "Who Sings in the Heavenly Chorus? The Shape of the Organized Interest Group System," in *The Oxford Handbook of American Political Parties and Interest Groups*, ed. Maisel and Berry, pp. 425–450.

50. Kay Lehman Schlozman, Traci Burch, and Samuel Lampert, "Still an Upper-Class Accent?" (paper presented at the annual meeting of the American Political Science Association, September 2004), pp. 16, 25.

51. Such nonprofits have obstacles created by their status as tax-deductible public charities. See Jeffrey M. Berry with David F. Arons, *A Voice for Nonprofits* (Washington, D.C.: Brookings Institution, 2003); and Elizabeth T. Boris and C. Eugene Steurele (eds.), *Nonprofits and Government*, 2nd ed. (Washington, D.C.: Urban Institute Press, 2006).

52. Jeffrey M. Berry, *The New Liberalism* (Washington, D.C.: Brookings Institution, 1999), pp. 120–130.

53. Mark A. Smith, *The Right Talk* (Princeton, N.J.: Princeton University Press, 2007).

54. These figures are the authors' calculations, derived from the Center for Responsive Politics at OpenSecrets.org. The number of lobbyists is the aggregate of the categories under "Industry" for pharmaceuticals/health products, hospitals/nursing homes, and health professionals. Figures are current as of 10 November 2009.

55. Jason Webb Yackee and Susan Webb Yackee, "A Bias towards Business? Assessing Interest Group Influence on the U.S. Bureaucracy," *Journal of Politics* 68 (February 2006): 128–139.

56. Baumgartner et al., *Lobbying and Policy Change*, pp. 190–214.

57. *Citizens United* v. *Federal Election Commission, 558 U.S. ___ (2010)*.

58. Jeff Zeleny and Carl Hulse, "Congress Votes to Tighten Rules on Lobbyist Ties," *New York Times*, 3 August 2007, p. A1.

59. Suzanne Perry, "Nonprofit Lobbyists Protest Restrictions Imposed by Obama Administration," *Chronicle of Philanthropy*, 23 April 2009, p. 35; Dan Eggen, "Lobbying Rules Keep Some Activists Out of Government," *Washington Post*, 22 March 2009, p. A1.

Chapter 11 / Congress / pages 350–383

1. Mark Mazzetti and William Glaberson, "Obama Issues Directive to Shut Down Guantánamo," *New York Times,* 22 January 2009, http://www.nytimes.com/2009/01/22/us/politics/22gitmo.html.

2. Nancy Pelosi, "Pelosi Statement on Obama Executive Orders on Closing Guantanamo and Revising Interrogation Policies," press release, 22 January 2009, http://www.speaker.gov/newsroom/pressreleases?id=0972.

3. "House Puts New Restrictions on Gitmo Closing," Associated Press, 18 June 2009; Tim Starks and Joanna Anderson, "Senate Clears Bill That Would Limit Moving Detainees from Guantanamo," *CQ Weekly Online,* 12 October 2009; Anne Kornblut and Dafna Linzer, "White House Regroups on Guantanamo," *Washington Post,* 25 September 2009, http://www.washingtonpost.com/wp-dyn/content/article/2009/09/24/AR2009092404893_pf.html.

4. Keith Perine, "Detainees' Future Tied Up in Policy," *CQ Weekly Online,* 10 August 2009.

5. Mark Mazzetti and Scott Shane, "Where Will Detainees from Guantánamo Go?" *New York Times,* 23 January 2009, http://www.nytimes.com/2009/01/24/us/politics/24intel.html.

6. Clinton Rossiter, *1787: The Grand Convention* (New York: Mentor, 1968), p. 158.

7. Monika McDermott and David Jones, "Do Public Evaluations of Congress Matter? Retrospective Voting in Congressional Elections," *American Politics Research* 31, no. 2 (2003): 155–177.

8. Harold W. Stanley and Richard G. Niemi (eds.), *Vital Statistics on American Politics, 2009–2010* (Washington, D.C.: CQ Press, 2010), p. 46.

9. For more on public opinion about Congress, see John Hibbing and Elizabeth Theiss-Morse, *Congress as Public Enemy: Public Attitudes toward American Political Institutions* (Cambridge: Cambridge University Press, 1995); John Hibbing and Elizabeth Theiss-Morse, *Stealth Democracy: Americans' Beliefs about How Government Should Work* (Cambridge: Cambridge University Press, 2002).

10. Alan Abramowitz, Brad Alexander, and Matthew Gunning, "Incumbency, Redistricting, and the Decline of Competition in U.S. House Elections," *Journal of Politics* 68 (February 2006): 75–88.

11. Gary W. Cox and Jonathan N. Katz, *Elbridge Gerry's Salamander* (Cambridge: Cambridge University Press, 2002).

12. Micah Altman, Karin MacDonald, and Michael McDonald, "Pushbutton Gerrymanders? How Computing Has Changed Redistricting," in *Party Lines,* ed. Thomas E. Mann and Bruce E. Cain (Washington, D.C.: Brookings Institution, 2005), pp. 51–66; Mark Monmonier, *Bushmanders and Bullwinkles* (Chicago: University of Chicago Press, 2001).

13. John Harwood, "House Incumbents Tap Census, Software to Get a Lock on Seats," *Wall Street Journal,* 19 June 2002, p. A1.

14. Thomas E. Mann, "Polarizing the House of Representatives: How Much Does Gerrymandering Matter?" in *Red and Blue Nation*, ed. Pietro S. Nivola and David W. Brady (Washington, D.C.: Brookings Institution and Hoover Institution, 2006), pp. 263–283. For a contrasting view, see Nolan McCarty, Keith Poole, and Howard Rosenthal, "Does Gerrymandering Cause Polarization?" *American Journal of Political Science* 53, no. 3 (2009): 666–680.

15. Dennis Conrad, "House Spends Big on Home Mailings," *Boston Globe,* 28 December 2007, p. A2; Michael Glassman, "Franking Privilege: An Analysis of Member Mass Mailings in the House, 1997–2007," *CRS Report for Congress,* 16 April 2008.

16. Jordan Fabian, "Critics Say Franking Rules Should Change to Suit the Age of Twitter," *The Hill,* 14 October 2009, http://thehill.com/homenews/senate/62969-critics-say-franking-rules-should-change-for-twitter.

17. Morris P. Fiorina, as cited in Roger H. Davidson and Walter J. Oleszek, *Congress and Its Members,* 11th ed. (Washington, D.C.: CQ Press, 2008), p. 144.

18. Center for Responsive Politics, "Incumbent Advantage," http://www.opensecrets.org/bigpicture/incumbs.php?cycle=2008.

19. Larry Sabato, *PAC Power* (New York: Norton, 1984), p. 72.

20. Paul S. Herrnson, *Congressional Elections,* 5th ed. (Washington, D.C.: CQ Press, 2008), p. 252.

21. Walter J. Stone and L. Sandy Maisel, "The Not-So-Simple Calculus of Winning: Potential U.S. House Candidates' Nomination and General Election Prospects," *Journal of Politics* 65 (November 2003): 951–977.

22. Herrnson, *Congressional Elections,* pp. 65–66; Erika Lovley, "Report: 237 Millionaires in Congress," *Politico,* 6 November 2009, http://dyn.politico.com/printstory.cfm?uuid=CA707571-18FE-70B2-A8721899A59ED165.

23. Jennifer L. Lawless and Richard L. Fox, *It Takes a Candidate* (New York: Cambridge University Press, 2005).

24. See Beth Reingold, *Representing Women* (Chapel Hill, N.C.: University of North Carolina Press, 2000); Michele L. Swers, *The Difference Women Make* (Chicago: University of Chicago Press, 2002).

25. Hanna Fenichel Ptikin, *The Concept of Representation* (Berkeley: University of California Press, 1967), pp. 60–91; Jane Mansbridge, "Should Blacks Represent Blacks and Women Represent Women? A Contingent 'Yes,'" *Journal of Politics* 61 (1999): 628–657.

26. Mark Hugo Lopez and Paul Taylor, "Dissecting the 2008 Electorate: The Most Diverse in U.S. History," *Pew Hispanic Center Report,* 30 April 2009, http://www.pewhispanic.org/files/reports/108.pdf.

27. *Shaw* v. *Reno,* 509 U.S. 630 (1993).

28. *Bush* v. *Vera,* 116 S. Ct. 1941 (1996).

29. *Easley* v. *Cromartie,* 532 U.S. 234 (2001).

30. See David Lublin, *The Paradox of Representation* (Princeton, N.J.: Princeton University Press, 1997). See, *contra,* Kenneth W. Shotts, "Does Racial Redistricting Cause Conservative Policy Outcomes?" *Journal of Politics* 65 (2003): 216–226.

31. See Frank R. Baumgartner et al., *Advocacy and Policy Change* (Chicago: University of Chicago Press, 2009).

32. H.R. 1966, available at http://thomas.loc.gov.

33. "Megan's Law: Cyber-bullying and the Courts," *The Economist,* 11 July 2009.

34. John W. Kingdon, *Agendas, Alternatives, and Public Policies,* 2nd ed. (New York: HarperCollins, 1995), p. 38.

35. David Shribman, "Canada's Top Envoy to Washington Cuts Unusually Wide Swath," *Wall Street Journal,* 29 July 1985, p. 1.

36. Woodrow Wilson, *Congressional Government* (Boston: Houghton Mifflin, 1885), p. 79.

37. Veronika Oleksyn, "Seniority, Loyalty and Political Needs Shape Makeup of Committee," *CQ Weekly,* 11 April 2005, p. 894; Allison Stevens, "More Power to the Senate's Majority Leader?" *CQ Weekly,* 6 November 2004, p. 2605.

38. Paul Kane, Robert Barnes, and Amy Goldstein, "Senate Republicans Won't Block Vote on Sotomayor," *Washington Post,* 17 July 2009, p. A1; Amy Goldstein and Paul Kane, "Democrats Rally for Sotomayor," *Washington Post,* 6 August 2009, p. A3; Janet Hook, "Republicans Seeking Alternate Paths to Block Sotomayor," *Los Angeles Times,* 28 May 2009, p. A15; Amy Goldstein and Paul Kane, "Sotomayor Wins Confirmation," *Washington Post,* 7 August 2009, p. A1.

39. Dan Eggen and Paul Kane, "2 Former Aides to Bush Get Subpoenas," *Washington Post,* 14 June 2007, p. A01; Lolita Blakdor, "Pace to Lose Post as Joint Chiefs Head," *Washington Post,* 9 June 2007.

40. See Steven S. Smith, *Party Influence in Congress* (New York: Cambridge University Press, 2007).

41. Gary W. Cox and Mathew D. McCubbins, *Legislative Leviathan* (Berkeley: University of California Press,

1993); Keith Krehbiel, *Information and Legislative Organization* (Ann Arbor: University of Michigan Press, 1992).

42. Jonathan Franzen, "The Listener," *New Yorker,* 6 October 2003, p. 85.

43. David Herszenhorn and Robert Pear, "Democrats Divided over Reid Proposal for Public Option," *New York Times,* 27 October 2009, http://www.nytimes.com/2009/10/28/health/policy/28health.html.

44. Cox and McCubbins, *Legislative Leviathan.*

45. Charles O. Jones, *The United States Congress* (Homewood, Ill.: Dorsey Press, 1982), p. 322.

46. Norman Ornstein, "Our Broken Senate," *The American,* May/April 2008, http://www.american.com/archive/2008/march-april-magazine-contents/our-broken-senate; Barbara Sinclair, "The 60 Vote Senate," in *U.S. Senate Exceptionalism,* ed. Bruce Oppenheimer (Columbus: Ohio State University Press, 2002), pp. 241–261.

47. Gary W. Cox and Mathew D. McCubbins, *Setting the Agenda: Responsible Party Government in the U.S. House of Representatives* (New York: Cambridge University Press, 2005); Smith, *Party Influence in Congress.*

48. These ideological views affect policy outcomes as well as the structure of the institution itself. See Nelson Polsby, *How Congress Evolves: Social Bases of Institutional Change* (New York: Oxford University Press, 2004).

49. James Sterling Young, *The Washington Community* (New York: Harcourt, Brace, 1964).

50. Rick Klein et al., "Obama Meets with Wary GOP on Stimulus," ABCNews.com, 27 January 2009.

51. Joshua D. Clinton, "Representation in Congress: Constituents and Roll Calls in the 106th House," *Journal of Politics* 68 (May 2006): 397–409.

52. See John Cochran, "The Influence Implosion," *CQ Weekly,* 16 January 2006, p. 174; Susan Ferrechio, "2005 Legislative Summary: House Ethics Investigations," *CQ Weekly,* 2 January 2006, p. 31.

53. Barry C. Burden, *The Personal Roots of Representation* (Princeton, N.J.: Princeton University Press, 2007).

54. Richard F. Fenno, Jr., *Home Style* (Boston: Little, Brown, 1978), p. xii.

55. Ibid., p. 32.

56. Louis I. Bredvold and Ralph G. Ross (eds.), *The Philosophy of Edmund Burke* (Ann Arbor: University of Michigan Press, 1960), p. 148.

57. For an alternative and more highly differentiated set of representation models, see Jane Mansbridge, "Rethinking Representation," *American Political Science Review* 97 (November 2003): 515–528.

58. Warren E. Miller and Donald E. Stokes, "Constituency Influence in Congress," *American Political Science Review* 57 (March 1963): 45–57.

59. Taxpayers for Common Sense, 17 February 2010, http://www.taxpayer.net.

60. Michael Mezey, *Representative Democracy: Legislators and Their Constituents* (Lanham, Md.: Rowman & Littlefield, 2008); Club for Growth, http://www.clubforgrowth.org.

61. E. Scott Adler, *Why Congressional Reforms Fail* (Chicago: University of Chicago Press, 2002).

Chapter 12 / The Presidency / pages 384–417

1. Ian S. Livingston and Michael O'Hanlon, *Pakistan Index* (Washington, D.C.: Brookings Institution, 12 February 2010).

2. Peter Finn and Joby Warrick, "Under Panetta, a More Aggressive CIA," *Washington Post,* 21 March 2010.

3. Daniel Byman, "Taliban vs. Predator," *Foreign Affairs,* at http://www.foreignaffairs.com/articles/64901/daniel-byman/taliban-vs-predator; Jane Mayer, "The Predator War," *New Yorker,* 26 October 2009, pp. 36–45; Mark Hosenball, "U.S. Increases Drone Use in Pakistan," *Newsweek,* 27 October 2009; Finn and Warrick, "Under Panetta."

4. Clinton Rossiter, *1787: The Grand Convention* (New York: Mentor, 1968), p. 148.

5. Ibid., pp. 190–191.

6. The Federal Register Executive Order Disposition Tables, http://www.archives.gov/federal-register/executive-orders/disposition.html.

7. Louis Fisher, *Presidential War Power* (Lawrence: University Press of Kansas, 1995); Donald R. Kelley (ed.), *Divided Power: The Presidency, Congress, and the Formation of American Foreign Policy* (Fayetteville: University of Arkansas Press, 2005); Andrew Rudalevige, *The New Imperial Presidency: Renewing Presidential Power After Watergate* (Ann Arbor: University of Michigan Press, 2005); Arthur M. Schlesinger, Jr., *War and the American Presidency* (New York: W. W. Norton, 2004) and *The Imperial Presidency* (Boston: Houghton Mifflin, 2004).

8. For an in-depth look at inherent powers, see *Presidential Studies Quarterly* 37 (March 2007), a special issue on invoking inherent presidential powers.

9. *Hamdan* v. *Rumsfeld,* 548 U.S. 557 (2006).

10. Wilfred E. Binkley, *President and Congress,* 3rd ed. (New York: Vintage, 1962), p. 155.

11. William G. Howell, *Power without Persuasion: The Politics of Direct Presidential Action* (Princeton, N.J.: Princeton University Press, 2003); Kenneth R. Mayer, *With the Stroke of a Pen: Executive Orders and Presidential Power* (Princeton, N.J.: Princeton University Press, 2001); Adam Warber, *Executive Orders and the Modern Presidency* (Boulder, Colo.: Lynne Rienner, 2005).

12. James Risen and Eric Lichtblau, "Bush Lets U.S. Spy on Callers without Courts," *New York Times,* 16 December 2005, p. A1; Lauren Etter, "Is Someone Listening to Your Phone Calls?" *Wall Street Journal,* 7 January 2006, p. A5.

13. James P. Pfiffner, *Power Play* (Washington, D.C.: Brookings Institution, 2008), pp. 190–191.

14. An expansive defense of this doctrine is offered by Bush Justice Department aide John Yoo in *Crisis and Command: A History of Executive Power from George Washington to George W. Bush* (New York: Kaplan Publishing, 2010).

15. See Peri Arnold, *Making the Managerial Presidency,* 2nd ed. (Lawrence: University of Kansas Press, 1998); Bradley H. Patterson, *The White House Staff* (Washington, D.C.: Brookings Institution Press, 2000); James Pfiffner (ed.), *The Managerial Presidency,* 2nd ed. (College Station: Texas A&M University Press, 1999).

16. Noam Scheiber, "The Chief," *New Republic,* 25 March 2010, pp. 17–21; Ryan Lizza, "The Gatekeeper," *New Yorker,* 2 March 2009, pp. 24–29.

17. *2010 Statistical Abstract of the United States,* Table 487: "Federal Civilian Employment by Branch and Agency: 1990 to 2008" and Table 460: "Federal Budget Outlays by Agency: 1990 to 2009."

18. Richard Tanner Johnson, *Managing the White House* (New York: Harper & Row, 1974); John P. Burke, *The Institutional Presidency* (Baltimore: Johns Hopkins University Press, 1992).

19. Dan Froomkin, "Now They Tell Us," *Washington Post,* 12 September 2005, http://busharchive.froomkin .com/BL2005091200806_pf.html.

20. George Stephanopoulos, *All Too Human* (Boston: Back Bay Books, 1999), p. 61.

21. Barton Gellman, *Angler: The Cheney Vice Presidency* (New York: Penguin, 2008).

22. Edward Weisband and Thomas M. Franck, *Resignation in Protest* (New York: Penguin, 1975), p. 139, quoted in Thomas E. Cronin, *The State of the Presidency,* 2nd ed. (Boston: Little, Brown, 1980), p. 253.

23. David E. Lewis, "Staffing Alone: Unilateral Action and the Politicization of the Executive Branch," *Presidential Studies Quarterly* 35 (September 2005): 496–514. For an excellent discussion of Lincoln's appointment of his political rivals to his cabinet, see Doris Kearns Goodwin, *Team of Rivals* (New York: Simon & Schuster, 2005).

24. Doris Kearns, *Lyndon Johnson and the American Dream* (New York: Signet, 1977), p. 363.

25. James David Barber, *Presidential Character,* 4th ed. (Englewood Cliffs, N.J.: Prentice Hall, 1992); Fred I. Greenstein, *The Presidential Difference: Leadership Style from FDR to Clinton* (Princeton, N.J.: Princeton University Press, 2000); David G. Winter, "Things I've Learned about Personality from Studying Political Leadership at a Distance," *Journal of Personality* 73 (2005): 557–584.

26. Donald Kinder, "Presidential Character Revisited," in *Political Cognition,* ed. Richard Lau and David O. Sears (Hillsdale, N.J.: Erlbaum, 1986), pp. 233–255; W. E. Miller and J. M. Shanks, *The New American Voter* (Cambridge, Mass.: Harvard University Press, 1996); Frank Newport and Joseph Carroll, "Analysis: Impact of Personal Characteristics on Candidate Support," Gallup News Service, 13 March 2007, http://www .gallup.com.

27. Richard E. Neustadt, *Presidential Power* (New York: Wiley, 1980), p. 10.

28. Ibid., p. 9.

29. Chad Roedemeier, "Nixon Kept Softer Self Off Limits, Tape Shows," *Boston Globe,* 8 July 2000, p. A4.

30. Terry Sullivan, "I'll Walk Your District Barefoot" (paper presented at the MIT Conference on the Presidency, Cambridge, Mass., 29 January 2000), p. 6.

31. Samuel Kernell, *Going Public: New Strategies of Presidential Leadership,* 4th ed. (Washington, D.C.: CQ Press, 2007).

32. Jeffrey M. Jones, "Obama Job Approval at 51% After Healthcare Vote," Gallup Poll, 25 March 2010, http:// www.gallup.com/poll/126989/Obama-Job-Approval- 51-After-Healthcare-Vote.aspx.

33. George C. Edwards III, *The Strategic President* (Princeton: Princeton University Press, 2009), p. 188.

34. Sheryl Gay Stolberg, Jeff Zeleny, and Carl Hulse, "The Long Road Back," *New York Times,* 21 March 2010, p. A1.

35. B. Dan Wood, *The Myth of Presidential Representation* (New York: Cambridge University Press, 2009); Lawrence C. Jacobs and Robert Y. Shapiro, *Politicians Don't Pander* (Chicago: University of Chicago Press, 2000).

36. David McCullough, *Truman* (New York: Simon & Schuster, 1992), p. 914.

37. Clea Benson, "Presidential Support: The Power of No," *Congressional Quarterly Weekly Report,* 14 January 2008, p. 137.

38. See Sarah H. Binder, "The Dynamics of Legislative Gridlock, 1947–96," *American Political Science Review* 93 (September 1999): 519–534.

39. Sean M. Theriault, *Party Polarization in Congress* (New York: Cambridge University Press, 2008); Nolan McCarty, Keith T. Poole, and Howard Rosenthal, *Polarized America* (Cambridge, Mass.: MIT Press, 2008).

40. "Prepared Text of Carter's Farewell Address," *New York Times,* 15 January 1981, p. B10.

41. Jon Meacham, *American Lion* (New York: Random House, 2008), p. 267.

42. Patricia Conley, *Presidential Mandates: How Elections Shape the National Agenda* (Chicago: University of Chicago Press, 2001).

43. Stephen Skowronek, *The Politics Presidents Make,* 2nd ed. (Cambridge, Mass.: Harvard University Press, 1997).

44. Gary C. Jacobson, "George W. Bush, Polarization, and the War in Iraq," in *The George W. Bush Legacy,* ed. Colin Campbell, Bert A. Rockman, and Andrew Rudalevige (Washington, D.C.: CQ Press, 2008), pp. 62–91.

45. *Public Papers of the President, Lyndon B. Johnson, 1965,* vol. 1 (Washington, D.C.: U.S. Government Printing Office, 1966), p. 72.

46. "Transcript of Second Inaugural Address by Reagan," *New York Times,* 22 January 1985, p. 72. For a historical study of how presidents use the symbol of freedom, see Kevin Coe, "The Language of Freedom in the American Presidency, 1933–2006," *Presidential Studies Quarterly* 37 (September 2007): 375–398.

47. Kevin Phillips, *The Politics of Rich and Poor* (New York: Random House, 1990), p. 88.

48. John W. Kingdon, *Agendas, Alternatives, and Public Policies,* 2nd ed. (New York: HarperCollins, 1995), p. 23.

49. Seth King, "Reagan, in Bid for Budget Votes, Reported to Yield on Sugar Prices," *New York Times,* 27 June 1981, p. A1.

50. Matt Bai, "Taking the Hill," *New York Times Magazine,* 7 June 2009, p. 35.

51. Sidney M. Milkis and Jesse H. Rhodes, "The President, Party Politics, and Constitutional Development," in *The Oxford Handbook of American Political Parties and Interest Groups,* ed. L. Sandy Maisel and Jeffrey M. Berry (Oxford, UK: Oxford University Press, 2010), pp. 377–402.

52. Richard M. Skinner, "George W. Bush and the Partisan Presidency," *Political Science Quarterly* 123 (Winter 2008–09): 605–622.

53. Jeffrey M. Jones, "Obama's Approval Most Polarized for First-Year President," Gallup Poll, 25 January 2010, available at http://www.gallup.com.

54. Ernest R. May and Philip D. Zelikow (eds.), *The Kennedy Tapes: Inside the White House during the Cuban Missile Crisis* (Cambridge, Mass.: Harvard University Press, 1997), pp. 498–499, 498–501, 512–513, 663–666.

55. For example, see Richard M. Pious, *Why Presidents Fail* (Lanham, Md.: Rowman & Littlefield, 2008).

56. Theodore J. Lowi, *The Personal President* (Ithaca, N.Y.: Cornell University Press, 1985), p. 185.

Chapter 13 / The Bureaucracy / pages 418–445

1. Gregory Zuckerman and Kara Scannell, "Madoff Misled SEC in '06, Got Off," *Wall Street Journal,* 18 December 2008; Diana Henriques, "'Lapses Helped Scheme,' Madoff Told Investigators," *New York Times,* 31 October 2009; Liz Moyer, "Why the SEC Missed Madoff," *Forbes,* 17 December 2008; Binyamin Appelbaum and David S. Hilzenrath, "SEC Didn't Act on Madoff Tips," *Washington Post,* 16 December 2008; U.S. Securities and Exchange Commission, Office of Investigations, *Investigation of Failure of the SEC to Uncover Bernard Madoff's Ponzi Scheme* (Washington, D.C.: U.S. Department of Health and Human Services, Office of Inspector General, 31 August 2009).

2. Malcolm Gladwell, "The Talent Myth," *New Yorker,* 22 July 2002, p. 32.

3. James Q. Wilson, *Bureaucracy* (New York: Basic Books, 1989), p. 25.

4. Bruce D. Porter, "Parkinson's Law Revisited: War and the Growth of American Government," *Public Interest* 60 (Summer 1980): 50.

5. Theda Skocpol, *Protecting Soldiers and Mothers: The Political Origins of Social Policy in the United States* (Cambridge, Mass.: Harvard University Press, 1992).

6. Damian Paletta, "Fight Over Consumer Agency Looms as Overhaul Is Signed," *Wall Street Journal,* 22 July 2010.

7. Data from the Bureau of the Census, "Federal Government Civilian Employment by Function: December 2008," December 2009, http://www2.census.gov/govs/apes/08fedfun.pdf.

8. Joel D. Aberbach and Bert A. Rockman, *In the Web of Politics* (Washington, D.C.: Brookings Institution, 2000), p. 162.

9. John D. Donohue, *The Warping of Government Work* (Cambridge, Mass.: Harvard University Press, 2008), pp. 16–50.

10. Aberbach and Rockman, *In the Web of Politics.*

11. Bradley E. Wright, "Public Service and Motivation: Does Mission Matter?" *Public Administration Review* 67 (January–February 2007): 54–63.

12. On the challenges of trying to loosen the strictures and protections of civil service, see Norma Riccucci and Frank J. Thompson, "The New Public Management, Homeland Security, and the Politics of Civil Service Reform," *Public Administration Review* 68 (September–October 2008): 877–890.

13. Stephen Hess, *What Do We Do Now?* (Washington, D.C.: Brookings Institution, 2008).

14. See Kenneth J. Meier and Laurence J. O'Toole, Jr., *Bureaucracy in a Democratic State* (Baltimore: Johns Hopkins University Press, 2006).

15. David E. Lewis, "Testing Pendleton's Premise: Do Political Appointees Make Worse Bureaucrats?" *Journal of Politics* 69 (November 2007): 1073–1088.

16. Lyndsey Layton, "A Vigorous Push from Federal Regulators," *Washington Post,* 13 October 2009.

17. Though formally located within the executive branch, the bureaucracy is "caught in the middle" between Congress and the president. See Barry Weingast,

"Caught in the Middle: The President, Congress, and the Political-Bureaucratic System," in *The Executive Branch,* ed. J. Aberbach and M. Peterson (New York: Oxford University Press, 2005), pp. 312–343.

18. Alliance for Better Campaigns et al., *Public Interest Obligations Proposed Processing Guidelines,* 7 April 2004, http://www.campaignlegalcenter.org/attachments/1591.pdf.

19. Amol Sharma and Jennifer Dlouhy, "A New Indecency Standard: Lost in Terminal Vagueness?" *CQ Weekly,* 10 July 2004, p. 1668.

20. Amol Sharma, "2005 Legislative Summary: Broadcast Indecency Penalties," *CQ Weekly,* 2 January 2006, p. 55.

21. Lauren Etter, "Is Someone Listening to Your Phone Calls?" *Wall Street Journal,* 7 January 2006, p. A5; James Risen and Eric Lichtblau, "Bush Lets U.S. Spy on Callers without Courts," *New York Times,* 16 December 2005, p. A1.

22. Tom A. Peter, "Warrantless Wiretaps Expanded," *Christian Science Monitor,* 7 August 2007; Lawrence Wright, "The Spymaster," *New Yorker,* 21 January 2008, pp. 42–59.

23. Stuart Shapiro, "The Role of Procedural Controls in OSHA's Ergonomics Rulemaking," *Public Administration Review* 67 (July–August 2007): 688–701.

24. Department of Transportation, "New DOT Consumer Rule Limits Airline Tarmac Delays," press release, http://www.dot.gov/affairs/2009/dot19909.htm; Matthew L. Wald, "Stiff Fines Are Set for Long Wait on Tarmac," *New York Times,* 22 December 2009.

25. Charles E. Lindblom, "The Science of Muddling Through," *Public Administration Review* 19 (Spring 1959): 79–88.

26. Bryan D. Jones and Frank R. Baumgartner, *The Politics of Attention* (Chicago: University of Chicago Press, 2005).

27. "Bureaucratic culture" is a particularly slippery concept but can be conceived of as the interplay of artifacts, values, and underlying assumptions. See Celeste Watkins-Hayes, *The New Welfare Bureaucrats* (Chicago: University of Chicago Press, 2009); Irene Lurie and Norma Riccucci, "Changing the 'Culture' of Welfare Offices," *Administration and Society* 34 (January 2003): 653–677; and Marissa Martino Golden, *What Motivates Bureaucrats?* (New York: Columbia University Press, 2000).

28. Jay P. Greene and Stuart Buck, "The Case for Special Education Vouchers," *Education Next* (Winter 2010): 36–43.

29. Jane Mayer, "The Secret History," *New Yorker,* 22 June 2009, pp. 50–59; Jane Mayer, *The Dark Side* (New York: Anchor Books, 2009).

30. Robert B. Reich, *Locked in the Cabinet* (New York: Vintage, 1998), pp. 115–118.

31. Daniel A. Mazmanian, "Los Angeles' Clean Air Saga—Spanning the Three Epochs," in *Toward Sustainable Communities,* ed. Daniel A. Mazmanian and Michael E. Kraft (Cambridge, Mass.: MIT Press, 2009), p. 107.

32. Jim Puzzanghera, "Few Troubled Mortgages Being Modified Permanently," *Los Angeles Times,* 11 December 2009.

33. See generally Eric M. Patashnik, *Reforms at Risk* (Princeton, N.J.: Princeton University Press, 2008).

34. See Donald Kettl et al., *Managing for Performance: A Report on Strategies for Improving the Results of Government* (Washington, D.C.: Brookings Institution, 2006).

35. Daniel J. Fiorino, *The New Environmental Regulation* (Cambridge, Mass.: MIT Press, 2006).

36. Archon Fung, Mary Graham, and David Weil, *Full Disclosure* (New York: Cambridge University Press, 2007).

37. Darrell M. West, *State and Federal Electronic Government in the United States,* 2008 (Washington, D.C.: Brookings Institution, 2008), http://www.brookings.edu/~/media/Files/rc/reports/2008/0826_egovernment_west/0826_egovernment_west.pdf.

38. See generally Philip J. Cooper, *Government by Contract* (Washington, D.C.: CQ Press, 2003).

39. Steven Rathgeb Smith, "Social Services," in *The State of Nonprofit America,* ed. Lester M. Salamon (Washington, D.C.: Brookings Institution and Aspen Institute, 2002), p. 165.

40. Donald F. Kettl, "The Global Revolution in Public Management: Driving Themes, Missing Links," *Journal of Policy Analysis and Management* 16 (1997): 448.

41. Beryl A. Radin, *Challenging the Performance Movement* (Washington, D.C.: Georgetown University Press, 2006).

42. David G. Frederickson and H. George Frederickson, *Measuring the Performance of the Hollow State* (Washington, D.C.: Georgetown University Press, 2006), pp. 56–57.

43. Vassia Gueorguieva et al., "The Program Assessment Rating Tool and the Government Performance and Results Act," *The American Review of Public Administration* 39 (May 2009): 225–245.

Chapter 14 / The Courts / pages 446–483

1. Philip Elman (interviewed by Norman Silber), "The Solicitor General's Office, Justice Frankfurter, and Civil Rights Litigation, 1946–1960: An Oral History," *Harvard Law Review* 100 (1987): 840.

2. David O'Brien, *Storm Center,* 2nd ed. (New York: Norton, 1990), p. 324.

3. Bernard Schwartz, *The Unpublished Opinions of the Warren Court* (New York: Oxford University Press, 1985), p. 446.

4. Ibid., pp. 445–448.

5. Felix Frankfurter and James M. Landis, *The Business of the Supreme Court* (New York: Macmillan, 1928), pp. 5–14; Julius Goebel, Jr., *The History of the Supreme Court of the United States,* vol. 1, *Antecedents and Beginnings to 1801* (New York: Macmillan, 1971).

6. Maeva Marcus (ed.), *The Documentary History of the Supreme Court of the United States, 1789–1800,* vol. 3, *The Justices on Circuit, 1795–1800* (New York: Columbia University Press, 1990).

7. Robert G. McCloskey, *The United States Supreme Court* (Chicago: University of Chicago Press, 1960), p. 31.

8. Cliff Sloan and David McKean, *The Great Decision: Jefferson, Adams, Marshall, and the Battle for the Supreme Court* (New York: PublicAffairs, 2009).

9. *Marbury* v. *Madison,* 1 Cranch 137 at 177, 178 (1803).

10. Interestingly, the term *judicial review* dates only to 1910; it was apparently unknown to Marshall and his contemporaries. Robert Lowry Clinton, *Marbury* v. *Madison and Judicial Review* (Lawrence: University Press of Kansas, 1989), p. 7.

11. Lee Epstein et al., *The Supreme Court Compendium,* 4th ed. (Washington, D.C.: CQ Press, 2006), Table 2-15.

12. *Constitution of the United States of America: Annotated and Interpreted* (2008 Supplement), http://www.gpoaccess.gov/constitution/browse2002.html#08supp.

13. *Ware* v. *Hylton,* 3 Dallas 199 (1796).

14. *Martin* v. *Hunter's Lessee,* 1 Wheat. 304 (1816).

15. Epstein et al., *The Supreme Court Compendium,* Table 2-16.

16. Garry Wills, *Explaining America: The Federalist* (Garden City, N.Y.: Doubleday, 1981), pp. 127–136.

17. Court Statistics Project, *Examining the Work of State Courts, 2006* (Williamsburg, Va.: National Center for State Courts, 2007), http://www.ncsconline.org/d_research/csp/CSP_Main_Page.html.

18. William P. Marshall, "Federalization: A Critical Overview," *DePaul Law Review* 44 (1995): 722–723.

19. Charles Alan Wright, *Handbook on the Law of Federal Courts,* 3rd ed. (St. Paul, Minn.: West, 1976), p. 7.

20. *Judicial Business of the United States Courts, 2009,* pp. 9–11, http://www.uscourts.gov/Statistics/JudicialBusiness/JudicialBusiness.aspx?doc=/uscourts/Statistics/JudicialBusiness/2009/JudicialBusiness2009.pdf.

21. http://www.fjc.gov/history/home.nsf/page/judges_magistrate.html.

22. *Judicial Business of the United States Courts, 2009,* pp. 5–8, http://www.uscourts.gov/Statistics/JudicialBusiness/JudicialBusiness.aspx?doc=/uscourts/Statistics/JudicialBusiness/2009/JudicialBusiness2009.pdf.

23. Linda Greenhouse, "Precedent for Lower Courts: Tyrant or Teacher?" *New York Times,* 29 January 1988, p. B7.

24. *Texas* v. *Johnson,* 491 U.S. 397 (1989); *United States* v. *Eichmann,* 496 U.S. 310 (1990).

25. *Regents of the University of California* v. *Bakke,* 438 U.S. 265 (1978).

26. *Grutter* v. *Bollinger,* 539 U.S. 244 (2003); *Gratz* v. *Bollinger,* 539 U.S. 306 (2003).

27. "Reading Petitions Is for Clerks Only at High Court Now," *Wall Street Journal,* 11 October 1990, p. B7.

28. H. W. Perry, Jr., *Deciding to Decide: Agenda Setting in the United States Supreme Court* (Cambridge, Mass.: Harvard University Press, 1991); Linda Greenhouse, "Justice Delayed; Agreeing Not to Agree," *New York Times,* 17 March 1996, sec. 4, p. 1.

29. Jeffrey Rosen, "Supreme Court Inc.: How the Nation's Highest Court Has Come to Side with Business," *New York Times Magazine,* 16 March 2008, pp. 38 et seq.

30. Perry, *Deciding to Decide;* Gregory A. Caldiera and John R. Wright, "The Discuss List: Agenda Building in the Supreme Court," *Law and Society Review* 24 (1990): 807.

31. Doris M. Provine, *Case Selection in the United States Supreme Court* (Chicago: University of Chicago Press, 1980), pp. 74–102.

32. Perry, *Deciding to Decide,* p. 286.

33. Justice Anthony M. Kennedy, quoted in Adam Liptak, "No Vote-Trading Here," *New York Times: Week in Review,* 16 May 2010, p. 4.

34. Kevin T. McGuire, "Repeat Players in the Supreme Court: The Role of Experienced Lawyers in Litigation Success," *Journal of Politics* 57 (1995): 187–196.

35. Michael Kirkland, "Court Hears 'Subordinate' Speech Debate," 1 December 1993, NEWSNET News Bulletin Board. The oral argument in the case, *Waters* v. *Churchill,* can be found at http://www.oyez.org/cases/1990-1999/1993/1993_92_1450.

36. William H. Rehnquist, "Remarks of the Chief Justice: My Life in the Law Series," *Duke Law Journal* 52 (2003): 787–805.

37. "Rising Fixed Opinions," *New York Times,* 22 February 1988, p. 14. See also Linda Greenhouse, "At the Bar," *New York Times,* 28 July 1989, p. 21.

38. Jeffrey A. Segal and Harold J. Spaeth, *The Supreme Court and the Attitudinal Model* (Cambridge: Cambridge University Press, 1993).

39. Stefanie A. Lindquist and Frank B. Cross, *Measuring Judicial Activism* (New York: Oxford University Press), pp. 1–28.

40. Stuart Taylor, Jr., "Lifting of Secrecy Reveals Earthy Side of Justices," *New York Times,* 22 February 1988, p. A16.

41. Richard A. Posner, "The Courthouse Mice," *New Republic,* 12 June 2006, http://www.tnr.com/article/the-courthouse-mice.

42. Thomas G. Walker, Lee Epstein, and William J. Dixon, "On the Mysterious Demise of Consensual Norms in the United States Supreme Court," *Journal of Politics* 50 (1988): 361–389.

43. Linda Greenhouse, "Roberts Is at Court's Helm, but He Isn't Yet in Control," *New York Times,* 2 July 2006, sec. 1, p. 1. See also John P. Kelsh, "The Opinion Delivery Practices of the United States Supreme Court, 1790–1945," *Washington University Law Quarterly* 77 (1999): 137–181. For more on the Roberts Court, see Linda Greenhouse, "Oral Dissents Give Ginsberg New Voice," *New York Times,* 31 May 2007, p. A1; Jeffrey Toobin, "Five to Four," *New Yorker,* 25 June 2007, pp. 35–37.

44. See, for example, Walter F. Murphy, *Elements of Judicial Strategy* (Chicago: University of Chicago Press, 1964); Bob Woodward and Scott Armstrong, *The Brethren* (New York: Simon & Schuster, 1979).

45. Henry J. Abraham, *Justices and Presidents: A Political History of Appointments to the Supreme Court,* 2nd ed. (New York: Oxford University Press, 1985), pp. 183–185.

46. Stephen L. Wasby, *The Supreme Court in the Federal Judicial System,* 3rd ed. (Chicago: Nelson-Hall, 1988), p. 241.

47. Greenhouse, "At the Bar," p. 21.

48. National Center for State Courts, "Survey of Judicial Salaries," http://contentdm.ncsconline.org/cgi-bin/showfile.exe?CISOROOT=/judicial&CISOPTR=288.

49. Jane Genova, "The Model [Almost]: Winston & Strawn's Revenue Down, Profits Flat." Newstex Weblogs (Law and More), 2 March 2010 (accessed from Lexis.com 23 March 2010).

50. Lawrence Baum, *American Courts: Process and Policy,* 3rd ed. (Boston: Houghton Mifflin, 1994), pp. 114–129.

51. *Caperton* v. *A. T. Massey Coal Co.,* 558 U.S. ___ (2009).

52. Tajuana D. Massie, Thomas G. Hansford, and David R. Songer, "The Timing of Presidential Nominations to Lower Federal Courts," *Political Research Quarterly* 57 (2004): 145–154.

53. Sheldon Goldman et al., "Picking Judges in a Time of Turmoil: W. Bush's Judiciary during the 109th Congress," *Judicature* 90 (May–June 2007): 252–283.

54. Paul Barrett, "More Minorities, Women Named to U.S. Courts," *Wall Street Journal,* 23 December 1993, p. B1; Sheldon Goldman and Elliot Slotnick, "Clinton's Second Term Judiciary: Picking Judges under Fire," *Judicature* 82 (May–June 1999): 264–284.

55. Kenneth L. Manning and Robert A. Carp, "The Decision-Making Ideology of George W. Bush's Judicial Appointees: An Update" (paper presented at the annual meeting of the American Political Science Association, Chicago, 2–5 September 2004).

56. Wasby, *Supreme Court,* pp. 107–110.

57. Jeffrey Toobin, *The Nine: Inside the Secret World of the Supreme Court* (New York: Doubleday, 2007), p. 269.

58. State News Service, "Statement of H. Thomas Wells Jr., President, American Bar Association re: American Bar Association Standing Committee on Federal Judiciary," 17 March 2009.

59. Ronald Stidham, Robert A. Carp, and Donald R. Songer, "The Voting Behavior of Judges Appointed by President Clinton" (paper presented at the annual meeting of the Southwestern Political Science Association, Houston, Texas, March 1996). See also Susan B. Haire, Martha Anne Humphries, and Donald R. Songer, "The Voting Behavior of Clinton's Courts of Appeals Appointees," *Judicature* 84 (March–April 2001): 274–281.

60. Robert A. Carp, Ronald Stidham, and Kenneth L. Manning, "The Voting Behavior of George W. Bush's Judges: How Sharp a Turn to the Right?" in *Principles and Practice of American Politics: Classic and Contemporary Readings,* 3rd ed., ed. Samuel Kernell and Steven S. Smith (Washington, D.C.: CQ Press, 2006).

61. Sheldon Goldman, "Obama and the Federal Judiciary," *The Forum* 7 no. 1 (2009): article 9.

62. Peter G. Fish, "John J. Parker," in *Dictionary of American Biography,* supp. 6, *1956–1980* (New York: Scribner's, 1980), p. 494.

63. Ibid.

64. *Congressional Quarterly's Guide to the U.S. Supreme Court,* 2nd ed. (Washington, D.C.: CQ Press, 1990), pp. 655–656.

65. "Supreme Court Nominee Sonia Sotomayor's Speech at Berkeley Law in 2001," *Berkeley La Raza Law Journal* (2002), http://www.law.berkeley.edu/4982.htm.

66. Kagan, "Confirmation Messes: Old and New," *The University of Chicago Law Review,* Vol. 62, No. 2 (Spring, 1995), pp. 919–942, http://www.scotusblog.com/wp-content/uploads/2010/03/Confirmation-Messes.pdf.

67. "Transcript: Kagan's Opening Statement," http://m.npr.org/news/front/128171860?page=3.

68. *Brown* v. *Board of Education II,* 349 U.S. 294 (1955).

69. Charles A. Johnson and Bradley C. Canon, *Judicial Policies: Implementation and Impact* (Washington, D.C.: CQ Press, 1984).

70. *Webster* v. *Reproductive Health Services,* 492 U.S. 490 (1989).

71. *Planned Parenthood* v. *Casey,* 505 U.S. 833 (1992).

72. *Stenberg* v. *Carhart,* 530 U.S. 914 (2000); *Gonzales* v. *Carhart,* 550 U.S. 124 (2007).

73. Alexander M. Bickel, *The Least Dangerous Branch* (Indianapolis, Ind.: Bobbs-Merrill, 1962); Robert A. Dahl,

"Decision-Making in a Democracy: The Supreme Court as a National Policy-Maker," *Journal of Public Law* 6 (1962): 279.

74. William Mishler and Reginald S. Sheehan, "The Supreme Court as a Countermajoritarian Institution? The Impact of Public Opinion on Supreme Court Decisions," *American Political Science Review* 87 (1993): 87–101.

75. Barry Friedman, *The Will of the People* (New York: Farrar, Straus and Giroux, 2009).

76. *Engel* v. *Vitale,* 367 U.S. 643 (1961).

77. James L. Gibson and Gregory A. Caldeira, "Knowing about Courts" (paper presented at the Second Annual Conference on Empirical Legal Studies, 20 June 2007), available at http://ssrn.com/abstract=956562 (accessed 27 June 2008).

78. Gallup Poll, "High Court to Start Term with Near Decade-High Approval," http://www.gallup.com/poll/122858/High-Court-Start-Term-Near-Decade-High-Approval.aspx?CSTS=alert.

79. See note 72.

80. *Kelo* v. *City of New London,* 545 U.S. 469 (2005).

81. William J. Brennan, Jr., "State Supreme Court Judge versus United States Supreme Court Justice: A Change in Function and Perspective," *University of Florida Law Review* 19 (1966): 225.

82. G. Alan Tarr and M. C. Porter, *State Supreme Courts in State and Nation* (New Haven, Conn.: Yale University Press, 1988), pp. 206–209.

83. John B. Wefing, "The Performance of the New Jersey Supreme Court at the Opening of the Twenty-first Century: New Cast, Same Script," *Seton Hall Law Review* 32 (2003): 769.

84. Dennis Hevesi, "New Jersey Court Protects Trash from Police Searches," *New York Times,* 19 July 1990, p. A9.

85. Kermit L. Hall, "The Canon of American Constitutional History in Comparative Perspective" (keynote address to the Supreme Court Historical Society, Washington, D.C., 16 February 2001).

86. Baum, *American Courts,* pp. 319–347.

Chapter 15 / Order and Civil Liberties / pages 484–523

1. Jenna Jones, "Pledge of Allegiance Dispute Results in Md. Teacher Having to Apologize," *Washington Post,* 24 February 2010, http://www.washingtonpost.com/wp-dyn/content/article/2010/02/23/AR2010022303889.html.

2. *West Virginia Board of Education* v. *Barnette,* 319 U.S. 642 (1943).

3. *Street* v. *New York,* 394 U.S. 576 (1969).

4. Deborah A. Jeon, Legal Director, ACLU of Maryland, to Mrs. Khadija F. Barkley, Acting Principal, *Washington Post,* 5 February 2010, http://media.washingtonpost.com/wp-srv/metro/documents/Pledge02-2310.pdf.

5. Learned Hand, *The Bill of Rights* (Boston: Atheneum, 1958), p. 1.

6. Richard E. Berg-Andersson, "Of Liberties, Rights and Powers (Part One): Just How Far Is Too Far—for Both Governments and Persons?" Green Papers Commentary, 27 April 2006, http://www.thegreenpapers.com/PCom/?20060427-0.

7. Leonard W. Levy, *The Establishment Clause: Religion and the First Amendment* (New York: Macmillan, 1986); Leo Pfeffer, *Church, State, and Freedom* (Boston: Beacon Press, 1953); Leonard W. Levy, "The Original Meaning of the Establishment Clause of the First Amendment," in *Religion and the State,* ed. James E. Wood, Jr., (Waco, Tex.: Baylor University Press, 1985), pp. 43–83.

8. Pew Research Center for the People and the Press, "U.S. Stands Alone in Its Embrace of Religion," Washington, D.C., 19 December 2002.

9. *Reynolds* v. *United States,* 98 U.S. 145 (1879).

10. *Everson* v. *Board of Education,* 330 U.S. 1 (1947).

11. *Board of Education* v. *Allen,* 392 U.S. 236 (1968).

12. *Lemon* v. *Kurtzman,* 403 U.S. 602 (1971).

13. *Agostini* v. *Felton,* 96 U.S. 552 (1997).

14. *Zelman* v. *Simmons-Harris,* 536 U.S. 639 (2002).

15. *Lynch* v. *Donnelly,* 465 U.S. 668 (1984).

16. *Van Orden* v. *Perry,* 545 U.S. 677 (2005).

17. *McCreary County* v. *ACLU of Kentucky,* 545 U.S. 844 (2005).

18. *Salazar* v. *Buono,* 559 U.S. ___ (2010).

19. *Engle* v. *Vitale,* 370 U.S. 421 (1962).

20. *Abington School District* v. *Schempp,* 374 U.S. 203 (1963).

21. *Lee* v. *Weisman,* 505 U.S. 577 (1992).

22. *Sante Fe Independent School District* v. *Doe,* 530 U.S. 290 (2000), quoting *West Virginia Board of Education* v. *Barnette,* 319 U.S. 624, 638 (1943).

23. Neela Banerjee, "School Board to Pay in Jesus Prayer Suit," *New York Times,* 28 February 2008, p. A16.

24. Michael W. McConnell, "The Origins and Historical Understanding of the Free Exercise of Religion," *Harvard Law Review* 103 (1990): 1409.

25. *Sherbert* v. *Verner,* 374 U.S. 398 (1963).

26. Adam Winkler, "Fatal in Theory and Strict in Fact: An Empirical Analysis of Strict Scrutiny in the Federal Courts," *Vanderbilt Law Review* 59 (2006): 793.

27. McConnell, "Origins and Historical Understanding."

28. Laurence Tribe, *Treatise on American Constitutional Law,* 2nd ed. (St. Paul, Minn.: West, 1988), p. 566.

29. Zechariah Chafee, *Free Speech in the United States* (Cambridge, Mass.: Harvard University Press, 1941).

30. Leonard W. Levy, *The Emergence of a Free Press* (New York: Oxford University Press, 1985).

31. Mark Twain, *Following the Equator* (Hartford, Conn.: American Publishing, 1897).
32. *Brandenburg* v. *Ohio*, 395 U.S. 444 (1969).
33. *Schenck* v. *United States*, 249 U.S. 47 (1919).
34. *Abrams* v. *United States*, 250 U.S. 616 (1919).
35. *Gitlow* v. *New York*, 268 U.S. 652 (1925).
36. *Dennis* v. *United States*, 341 U.S. 494 (1951).
37. *Brandenburg* v. *Ohio*, 395 U.S. 444 (1969).
38. Anthony Lewis, *Freedom for the Thought That We Hate: A Biography of the First Amendment* (New York: Basic Books, 2008).
39. *Tinker* v. *Des Moines Independent County School District*, 393 U.S. 503, at 508 (1969).
40. *Chaplinsky* v. *New Hampshire*, 315 U.S. 568 (1942).
41. *Terminiello* v. *Chicago*, 337 U.S. 1, 37 (1949).
42. *Cohen* v. *California*, 403 U.S. 15 (1971).
43. *ACLU* v. *Reno*, 929 F. Supp. 824 (E.D. Penn., 1996).
44. *Reno* v. *ACLU*, 521 U.S. 844 (1997).
45. *United States* v. *Stevens*, 559 U.S. ___ (2010).
46. *Schwarzenegger* v. *Entertainment Merchants Assn.* (No. 08-1448).
47. *New York Times* v. *Sullivan*, 376 U.S. 254 (1964).
48. *Hustler Magazine* v. *Falwell*, 485 U.S. 46 (1988).
49. *Near* v. *Minnesota*, 283 U.S. 697 (1931).
50. For a detailed account of *Near*, see Fred W. Friendly, *Minnesota Rag* (New York: Random House, 1981).
51. *New York Times* v. *United States*, 403 U.S. 713 (1971).
52. *Branzburg* v. *Hayes*, 408 U.S. 665 (1972).
53. *Hazelwood School District* v. *Kuhlmeier*, 484 U.S. 260 (1988); *Morse* v. *Frederick*, 551 U.S. 393 (2007).
54. *United States* v. *Cruikshank*, 92 U.S. 542 (1876); *Constitution of the United States of America: Annotated and Interpreted* (Washington, D.C.: U.S. Government Printing Office, 1973), p. 1031.
55. *DeJonge* v. *Oregon*, 299 U.S. 353 (1937).
56. *United States* v. *Miller*, 307 U.S. 174 (1939).
57. *District of Columbia* v. *Heller*, 554 U.S. 290 (2008).
58. *McDonald* v. *Chicago*, 561 U.S. ___ (2010).
59. *Barron* v. *Baltimore*, 32 U.S. (7 Pet.) 243 (1833).
60. *Lochner* v. *New York*, 198 U.S. 45 (1905).
61. *Chicago B&Q Railroad* v. *Chicago*, 166 U.S. 226 (1897).
62. *Gitlow* v. *New York*, 268 U.S. 652, 666 (1925).
63. *Palko* v. *Connecticut*, 302 U.S. 319 (1937).
64. *Duncan* v. *Louisiana*, 391 U.S. 145 (1968).
65. *McNabb* v. *United States*, 318 U.S. 332 (1943).
66. *Baldwin* v. *New York*, 399 U.S. 66 (1970).
67. Anthony Lewis, *Gideon's Trumpet* (New York: Random House, 1964).
68. *Gideon* v. *Wainwright*, 372 U.S. 335 (1963).
69. *Miranda* v. *Arizona*, 384 U.S. 436 (1966).
70. *Dickerson* v. *United States*, 530 U.S. 428 (2000).
71. *Wolf* v. *Colorado*, 338 U.S. 25 (1949).
72. *Mapp* v. *Ohio*, 367 U.S. 643 (1961).
73. *United States* v. *Leon*, 468 U.S. 897 (1984).
74. *Hudson* v. *Michigan*, 547 U.S. 586 (2006).
75. *Herring* v. *United States*, 555 U.S. ___ (2009).
76. Liane Hansen, "Voices in the News This Week," *NPR Weekend Edition*, 28 October 2001 (NEXIS transcript).
77. Dan Eggen, "Tough Anti-Terror Campaign Pledged: Ashcroft Tells Mayors He Will Use New Law to Fullest Extent," *Washington Post*, 26 October 2001, p. A1.
78. "Security: FBI Sought 3,500 Records without Subpoenas," *National Journal's Technology Daily*, 1 May 2006.
79. Michael Sandler, "Anti-Terrorism Law on Final Tack," *CQ Weekly*, 3 March 2006, p. 600.
80. *Ex parte Quirin*, 317 U.S. 1 (1942); *In re Yamashita*, 327 U.S. 1 (1946); *Hirota* v. *MacArthur*, 338 U.S. 197 (1949); *Johnson* v. *Eisentrager*, 339 U.S. 763 (1950).
81. *Rasul* v. *Bush*, 542 U.S. 466 (2004).
82. *Hamdi* v. *Rumsfeld*, 542 U.S. 507 (2004).
83. *Hamdan* v. *Rumsfeld*, 548 U.S. 557 (2006).
84. *Boumediene* v. *Bush*, 553 U.S. 723 (2008).
85. Paul Brest, *Processes of Constitutional Decision-making* (Boston: Little, Brown, 1975), p. 708.
86. *Griswold* v. *Connecticut*, 381 U.S. 479 (1965).
87. *Roe* v. *Wade*, 410 U.S. 113 (1973).
88. See John Hart Ely, "The Wages of Crying Wolf: A Comment on Roe v. Wade," *Yale Law Journal* 82 (1973): 920.
89. Justice Harry Blackmun, interview by Ted Koppel and Nina Totenberg, *Nightline*, ABC, 2 December 1993.
90. *Webster* v. *Reproductive Health Services*, 492 U.S. 490 (1989).
91. *Hodgson* v. *Minnesota*, 497 U.S. 417 (1990); *Ohio* v. *Akron Center for Reproductive Health*, 497 U.S. 502 (1990).
92. *Steinberg* v. *Carhart*, 530 U.S. 914 (2000).
93. *Gonzales* v. *Carhart*, 550 U.S. 124 (2007).
94. Stuart Taylor, "Supreme Court Hears Case on Homosexual Rights," *New York Times*, 1 April 1986, p. A24.
95. *Bowers* v. *Hardwick*, 478 U.S. 186 (1986).
96. Linda Greenhouse, "Washington Talk: When Second Thoughts Come Too Late," *New York Times*, 5 November 1990, p. A9.
97. *Lawrence and Garner* v. *Texas*, 539 U.S. 558 (2003).
98. Ibid.
99. *Gill* v. *Office of Personnel Management*, No. 1:09-cv-10309 (U.S. Dist. Ct., D. Mass.).
100. *Perry* v. *Schwarzenegger*, No C 09-2292 VRW (U.S. Dist. Ct., N.D. Cal.), 4 August 2010, https://ecf.cand.uscourts.gov/cand/09cv2292/files/09cv2292-ORDER.pdf.

Chapter 16 / Equality and Civil Rights / pages 524–565

1. Nina Bernstein, "100 Years in the Back Door, Out the Front," *New York Times,* 21 May 2006, sec. 4, p. 4, quoted in Aristide Zolberg, *A Nation by Design: Immigration Policy in the Fashioning of America* (New York: Russell Sage, 2006).

2. Jack Citrin, "Affirmative Action in the People's Court," *Public Interest* 122 (1996): 40–41; Sam Howe Verhovek, "In Poll, Americans Reject Means but Not Ends of Racial Diversity," *New York Times,* 14 December 1997, sec. 1, p. 1; "Aid to Blacks and Minorities, 1970–2004," in *National Election Studies Guide to Public Opinion and Electoral Behavior,* 27 November 2005, http://www.electionstudies.org/nesguide/text/tab4b_4.txt.

3. David W. Moore, "Americans Today Are Dubious about Affirmative Action," *Gallup Poll Monthly* (March 1995): 36–38; Charlotte Steeh and Maria Krysan, "Affirmative Action and the Public, 1970–1995," *Public Opinion Quarterly* 60 (1996): 128–158; Gallup Poll, 25–28 October 2000: "Would you vote … for or against a law which would allow your state to give preferences in job hiring and school admission on the basis of race?" For, 13 percent; against, 85 percent; no opinion, 2 percent.

4. *Gallup Brain* question: "Do you generally favor or oppose affirmative action programs for racial minorities?" 12–15 June 2003: For, 58 percent; against, 34 percent; don't know/refused, 8 percent. 6–26 June 2005: For, 50 percent; against, 42 percent; don't know/refused, 8 percent. Available at http://brain.gallup.com.

5. *Regents of the University of California* v. *Bakke,* 438 U.S. 265, 407 (1978).

6. *Parents Involved in Community Schools* v. *Seattle School District No. 1,* 551 U.S. 701 (2007).

7. *The Slaughterhouse Cases,* 83 U.S. 36 (1873).

8. *United States* v. *Cruikshank,* 92 U.S. 542 (1876).

9. *United States* v. *Reese,* 92 U.S. 214 (1876).

10. *Civil Rights Cases,* 109 U.S. 3 (1883).

11. Mary Beth Norton et al., *A People and a Nation: A History of the United States,* 3rd ed. (Boston: Houghton Mifflin, 1990), p. 490.

12. *Plessy* v. *Ferguson,* 163 U.S. 537 (1896).

13. *Cummings* v. *County Board of Education,* 175 U.S. 528 (1899).

14. *Missouri ex rel. Gaines* v. *Canada,* 305 U.S. 337 (1938).

15. *Sweatt* v. *Painter,* 339 U.S. 629 (1950).

16. *Brown* v. *Board of Education,* 347 U.S. 483 (1954).

17. Ibid., 347 U.S. 483, 495 (1954).

18. Ibid., 347 U.S. 483, 494 (1954).

19. *Bolling* v. *Sharpe,* 347 U.S. 497 (1954).

20. *Brown* v. *Board of Education II,* 349 U.S. 294 (1955).

21. Jack W. Peltason, *Fifty-Eight Lonely Men,* rev. ed. (Urbana: University of Illinois Press, 1971).

22. *Alexander* v. *Holmes County Board of Education,* 396 U.S. 19 (1969).

23. *Swann* v. *Charlotte-Mecklenburg County Schools,* 402 U.S. 1 (1971).

24. *Milliken* v. *Bradley,* 418 U.S. 717 (1974).

25. Richard Kluger, *Simple Justice* (New York: Knopf, 1976), p. 753.

26. Taylor Branch, *Parting the Waters: America in the King Years, 1955-1963* (New York: Simon & Schuster, 1988), p. 3.

27. Ibid., p. 14.

28. Ibid., p. 271.

29. *Bell* v. *Maryland,* 378 U.S. 226 (1964).

30. Norton et al., *People and a Nation,* p. 943.

31. *Heart of Atlanta Motel* v. *United States,* 379 U.S. 241 (1964).

32. *Katzenbach* v. *McClung,* 379 U.S. 294 (1964).

33. But see Abigail M. Thernstrom, *Whose Vote Counts? Affirmative Action and Minority Voting Rights* (Cambridge, Mass.: Harvard University Press, 1987).

34. *Grove City College* v. *Bell,* 465 U.S. 555 (1984).

35. *Richmond* v. *J. A. Croson Co.,* 488 U.S. 469 (1989).

36. *Martin* v. *Wilks,* 490 U.S. 755 (1989); *Wards Cove Packing Co.* v. *Atonio,* 490 U.S. 642 (1989); *Patterson* v. *McLean Credit Union,* 491 U.S. 164 (1989); *Price Waterhouse* v. *Hopkins,* 490 U.S. 228 (1989); *Lorance* v. *AT&T Technologies,* 490 U.S. 900 (1989); *EEOC* v. *Arabian American Oil Co.,* 499 U.S. 244 (1991).

37. *Saint Francis College* v. *Al-Khazraji,* 481 U.S. 604 (1987).

38. Dee Brown, *Bury My Heart at Wounded Knee: An Indian History of the American West* (New York: Holt, Rinehart & Winston, 1971).

39. Francis Paul Prucha, *The Great Father: The United States Government and the American Indian,* vol. 2 (Lincoln: University of Nebraska Press, 1984).

40. U.S. Equal Employment Opportunity Commission, "Americans with Disabilities Act of 1990 (ADA) FY 1992–FY 2005," information available at http://www.eeoc.gov/stats/ada-charges.html.

41. Lisa J. Stansky, "Opening Doors," *ABA Journal* 82 (1996): 66–69.

42. "Stonewall and Beyond: Lesbian and Gay Culture," Columbia University Libraries exhibition, 25 May–17 September 1994, http://www.columbia.edu/cu/libraries/events/sw25/.

43. See, generally, *PS: Political Science and Politics* 38 (April 2005).

44. "Gay/Lesbian Rights: Long-Term Contribution Trends," http://www.opensecrets.org/industries/indus.asp?Ind=J7300.

45. Barack Obama, "State of the Union Address, 2010," http://stateoftheunionaddress.org/2010-barack-obama.

46. *Goodridge & Others* v. *Department of Public Health,* 440 Mass. 309 (2003); Opinions of the Justices to the Senate, 440 Mass. 1201 (2004).

47. *In re Marriage Cases,* Calif. Sup. Ct., No. S147999, 15 May 2008.

48. Jesse McKinley, "Tart Questions at Same-Sex Marriage Trial's Closing," *New York Times,* 17 June 2010, p. A15.

49. *Boy Scouts of America* v. *Dale,* 530 U.S. 610 (2000).

50. Cited in Martin Gruberg, *Women in American Politics* (Oshkosh, Wisc.: Academic Press, 1968), p. 4.

51. *Bradwell* v. *Illinois,* 83 U.S. 130 (1873).

52. *Muller* v. *Oregon,* 208 U.S. 412 (1908).

53. *International Union, United Automobile, Aerospace and Agricultural Implement Workers of America* v. *Johnson Controls, Inc.,* 499 U.S. 187 (1991).

54. *Minor* v. *Happersett,* 88 U.S. 162 (1875).

55. John H. Aldrich et al., *American Government: People, Institutions, and Policies* (Boston: Houghton Mifflin, 1986), p. 618.

56. *Ledbetter* v. *Goodyear Tire and Rubber Company,* 550 U.S. (2007).

57. Sheryl Gay Stolberg, "Obama Signs Equal-Pay Legislation," *New York Times,* 30 January 2009.

58. *Reed* v. *Reed,* 404 U.S. 71 (1971).

59. *Frontiero* v. *Richardson,* 411 U.S. 677 (1973).

60. *Craig* v. *Boren,* 429 U.S. 190 (1976).

61. Paul Weiler, "The Wages of Sex: The Uses and Limits of Comparable Worth," *Harvard Law Review* 99 (1986): 1728; Paula England, *Comparable Worth: Theories and Evidence* (New York: Aldine de Gruyter, 1992).

62. *J.E.B.* v. *Alabama ex rel. T.B.,* 511 U.S. 127 (1994).

63. *United States* v. *Virginia,* slip op. 94–1941 and 94–2107 (decided 26 June 1996).

64. Mike Allen, "Defiant V.M.I. to Admit Women but Will Not Ease Rules for Them," *New York Times,* 22 September 1996, sec. 1, p. 1.

65. Jane J. Mansbridge, *Why We Lost the ERA* (Chicago: University of Chicago Press, 1986).

66. Melvin I. Urofsky, *A March of Liberty* (New York: Knopf, 1988), p. 902.

67. *Harris* v. *Forklift Systems,* 510 U.S. 17 (1993).

68. *Time,* 6 July 1987, p. 91.

69. *Facts on File* 206B2, 4 June 1965.

70. As quoted in Melvin I. Urofsky, *A Conflict of Rights: The Supreme Court and Affirmative Action* (New York: Scribner's, 1991), p. 17.

71. Ibid., p. 29.

72. Thomas Sowell, *Preferential Policies: An International Perspective* (New York: Morrow, 1990), pp. 103–105.

73. *Regents of the University of California* v. *Bakke,* 438 U.S. 265 (1978).

74. *Adarand Constructors, Inc.* v. *Peña,* 518 U.S. 200 (1995).

75. *Gratz* v. *Bollinger,* 539 U.S. 244 (2003).

76. *Grutter* v. *Bollinger,* 539 U.S. 306 (2003).

77. *Parents Involved in Community Schools* v. *Seattle School District No. 1,* 551 U.S. (2007).

78. Stephen Earl Bennett et al., *Americans' Opinions about Affirmative Action* (Cincinnati, Ohio: University of Cincinnati, Institute for Policy Research, 1995), p. 4; Lawrence Bobo, "Race and Beliefs about Affirmative Action," in *Racialized Politics: The Debate about Racism in America,* ed. David O. Sears, Jim Sidanius, and Lawrence Bobo (Chicago: University of Chicago Press, 2000), pp. 137–164.

79. For example, see the eligibility standards of the Small Business Administration for "small disadvantaged business," http://www.sba.gov/sdb/indexaboutsdb.html.

80. Seymour Martin Lipset, "Two Americas, Two Systems: Whites, Blacks, and the Debate over Affirmative Action," *New Democrat* (May–June 1995): 9–15, http://www.ndol.org/documents/May95TND.pdf.

Chapter 17 / Policymaking / pages 566–593

1. U.S. Department of Transportation, "Statistics and Facts about Distracted Driving," http://www.distraction.gov/stats-and-facts; Glenn Adams, "Maine Outlaws 'Distracted' Driving," *Boston Globe,* 13 September 2009; Marjorie Connelly, "Many in U.S. Want Texting at the Wheel to Be Illegal," *New York Times,* 2 November 2009; Elisabeth Rosenthal, "When Texting Kills, Britain Offers Path to Prison," *New York Times,* 2 November 2009; Dan Whitcomb, "U.S. Teens Ignore Laws against Texting While Driving," Reuters wire service, 11 December 2009; Matt Richtel, "Bills to Curb Distracted Driving Gain Momentum across Nation," *New York Times,* 2 January 2010; Angela Greiling Keane, "Texting Banned for Truckers and Bus Drivers in U.S.," Bloomberg wire service, 27 January 2010.

2. Carol D. Leonnig, "Rep. Murtha's Earmarks Lead to Fewer Jobs than Promised," *Washington Post,* 31 December 2009.

3. "Espresso Tax Is Defeated," *New York Times,* 18 September 2003, p. A17.

4. Jason Zengerle, "Not a Prayer," *New Republic,* 22 September 2003, pp. 13–15.

5. Steven Greenhouse, "Mexican Trucks Gain Approval to Haul Cargo Throughout U.S.," *New York Times,* 28 November 2002, p. A1.

6. This typology is adapted from Theodore Lowi's classic article, "American Business, Public Policy Case Studies, and Political Theory," *World Politics* 16 (July 1964): 677–715.

7. Since not all charitable contributions are claimed as deductions on taxes, the actual tax expenditure is less than $300 billion. See Grant Williams, "Deductions Rose Slightly in 2007, IRS Says," *The Chronicle of Philanthropy,* 14 January 2010, p. 20.

8. Ken Belson, "Importing a Decongestant for Midtown Streets," *New York Times,* 16 March 2008.

9. Roger W. Cobb and Charles D. Elder, *Participation in American Politics,* 2nd ed. (Baltimore, Md.: Johns Hopkins University Press, 1983), p. 14.

10. Matt Phillips, "From Granny to Nearly Nude Germans, Everyone's Raising Cane at the Airport," *Wall Street Journal,* 11 January 2010.

11. Jeffrey M. Berry, *The New Liberalism* (Washington, D.C.: Brookings Institution, 1999).

12. Lawrence D. Brown and Lawrence R. Jacobs, *The Private Abuse of the Public Interest* (Chicago: University of Chicago Press, 2008).

13. Dana Lee Baker and Shannon Stokes, "Brain Politics: Aspects of Administration in the Comparative Issue Definition of Autism-Related Policy," *Public Administration Review* 67 (July–August 2007): 757–767.

14. Frank R. Baumgartner, Suzanna L. De Boef, and Amber E. Boydstun, *The Decline of the Death Penalty and the Discovery of Innocence* (New York: Cambridge University Press, 2008).

15. Frank R. Baumgartner Jeffrey M. Berry, Marie Hojnacki, David C. Kimball, and Beth L. Leech, *Lobbying and Policy Change* (Chicago: University of Chicago Press, 2009), pp. 166–189.

16. Douglas Jehl, "Bush Will Modify Ban on New Roads in Federal Lands," *New York Times,* 4 May 2001, p. A1.

17. Eric M. Patashnik, *Reforms at Risk* (Princeton, N.J.: Princeton University Press, 2008), pp. 91–109.

18. Robert Pear, "Deadline Near, Jams Are Seen for Drug Plan," *New York Times,* 24 April 2006, p. A1.

19. Ibid., p. A14.

20. Kate Schuler, "New Medicare Drug Plan Gets Off to Rocky Start," *CQ Weekly,* 30 January 2006, p. 267.

21. U.S. Census Bureau, "State & County QuickFacts: Texas," http://quickfacts.census.gov/qfd/states/48000.html.

22. Marta Tienda and Sunny Xinchun Niu, "Flagships, Feeders, and the Texas Top 10% Law: A Test of the 'Brain Drain' Hypothesis," *Journal of Higher Education* 77 (July–August 2006): 712–739.

23. Frank R. Baumgartner and Bryan D. Jones, "Positive and Negative Feedback in Politics," in *Policy Dynamics,* ed. Frank R. Baumgartner and Bryan D. Jones (Chicago: University of Chicago Press, 2002), pp. 3–28.

24. On the politicization of the evaluation process, see Jeffrey R. Henig, *Spin Cycle* (New York: Russell Sage Foundation and Century Foundation, 2008).

25. Christopher Trenholm et al., *Impacts of Four Title V, Section 510 Abstinence Education,* report to the U.S.

26. John B. Jemmott III, Loretta S. Jemmott, and Geoffrey T. Fong, "Efficacy of a Theory-Based Abstinence-Only Intervention over 24 Months," *Archives of Pediatric & Adolescent Medicine* 164 (February 2010): 152–159.

27. Karen DeYoung and Michael A. Fletcher, "Attempt to Bomb Airliner Could Have Been Prevented, Obama Says," *Washington Post,* 6 January 2010.

28. Derek Willis, "Turf Battles Could Lie Ahead in Fight to Oversee Homeland Department," *CQ Weekly,* 16 November 2002, p. 3006.

29. Eric Lipton and Gardiner Harris, "In Turnaround, Industries Seek U.S. Regulations," *New York Times,* 16 September 2007.

30. On the first steps by the Obama administration, see Beryl A. Radin, "The Relationship between OMB and the Agencies in the Obama Administration," *International Journal of Public Administration* 32 (2009): 781–785.

31. Barry Rabe, "Environmental Policy and the Bush Era: The Collision between the Administrative Presidency and State Experimentation," *Publius* 37 (Summer 2007): 413–431.

32. Marc Landy, "Mega-Disasters and Federalism," in "The Winter Commission Report Reconsidered: 21st Century Challenges Confronting State and Local Governance—and How Performance Can Be Improved," ed. Frank J. Thompson, special issue, *Public Administration Review* 68 (December 2008): S186–S198.

33. Lipton and Harris, "In Turnaround."

34. Jeffrey M. Berry and Clyde Wilcox, *The Interest Group Society,* 5th ed. (New York: Pearson Longman, 2009), pp. 155–176.

35. Michael T. Heaney, "Coalitions and Interest Group Influence over Health Care Policy" (paper presented at the annual meeting of the American Political Science Association, Philadelphia, August 2003), p. 16.

36. Robert Agranoff, *Managing Within Networks* (Washington, D.C.: Georgetown University Press, 2007).

37. John Simon, Harvey Dale, and Laura Chisolm, "The Federal Tax Treatment of Charitable Organizations," in *The Nonprofit Sector,* 2nd ed., ed. Walter W. Powell and Richard Steinberg (New Haven, Conn.: Yale University Press, 2006), p. 268.

38. Jeffrey M. Berry with David F. Arons, *A Voice for Nonprofits* (Washington, D.C.: Brookings Institution, 2003), pp. 1–2.

39. William Gorham, "Foreword," in *Nonprofits and Government,* ed. Elizabeth T. Boris and C. Eugene Steuerle (Washington, D.C.: Urban Institute, 1999), p. xi.

40. Beth Gazley and Jeffrey L. Brudney, "The Purpose (and Perils) of Government-Nonprofit Partnership," *Nonprofit and Voluntary Sector Quarterly* 36 (September 2007): 389–415.

41. Paul C. Light, *The True Size of Government* (Washington, D.C.: Brookings Institution, 1999); "Fact Sheet on the New True Size of Government," Center for Public Service, Brookings Institution, 5 September 2003, http://www.brookings.edu/gs/cps/light20030905.htm.

42. Kennard T. Wing, Thomas H. Pollak, and Amy Blackwood, *The Nonprofit Almanac,* 2008 (Washington, D.C.: Urban Institute Press, 2008), pp. 83, 97.

Chapter 18 / Economic Policy / pages 594–627

1. Michael J. de la Merced, "Anheuser-Busch Agrees to Be Sold to a Belgian Brewer for $52 Billion," *New York Times,* 17 July 2008, p. A13.

2. David Kesmodel and Suzanne Vranica, "Unease Brewing at Anheuser as New Owners Slash Costs," *Wall Street Journal,* 29 April 2009, pp. A1, A4.

3. Gilles Guillaume, "China Car Sales Top U.S.," Reuters, 11 January 2010, http://www.reuters.com/article/idUSTRE60A1BQ20100111.

4. "Trump Tower Now the World's Sixth-Tallest," *Chicago Tribune,* 18 November 2009, p. 3.

5. Andrew E. Kramer, "Siemens Fills Need for High-Speed Trains in Russia," *New York Times,* 25 September 2009, p. B1.

6. Tom Mitchell, "Chinese High-Speed Train Sets New Record," CNN, 27 December 2009, http://www.cnn.com/2009/BUSINESS/12/27/china.speed.train.ft/index.html.

7. Richard L. Hills, *Power from Wind: A History of Windmill Technology* (Cambridge, UK: Cambridge University Press, 1994), pp. 258–259.

8. Keith Bradsher, "China Leading Race to Make Clean Energy," *New York Times,* 31 January 2010, p. A1, A8.

9. You won't learn basic economics in this chapter. For a quick summary of "ten principles of economics," see N. Gregory Mankiw, *Principles of Economics,* 3rd ed. (Mason, Ohio: Thomson South-Western, 2004), pp. 3–14. Mankiw served as chairman of the Council of Economic Advisers under George W. Bush.

10. Yingyi Qian and Jinglian Wu, "China's Transition to a Market Economy: How Far across the River?" (paper presented at the Conference on Policy Reform in China at the Center for Research on Economic Development and Policy Reform, Stanford University, 18–20 November 1999), http://elsa.berkeley.edu/~yqian/how%20far%20across%20the%20river.pdf.

11. Dan Usher, in *Political Economy* (Malden, Mass.: Blackwell Publishing, 2003), offers this interpretation of Adam Smith's "invisible hand" metaphor: "Self-interested people are guided by market-determined prices to deploy the resources of the world to produce what people want to consume. This assertion, made commonplace by repetition, is so extraordinary and so completely counter-intuitive that it cannot be strictly and unreservedly true. A central task of economics is to show when the assertion is true, when public intervention in the economy might be helpful, and when markets are best left alone because public intervention is likely to do more harm than good" (p. xiv).

12. Two of the ten principles of economics that Mankiw cites in *Principles of Economics* are "#6: Markets are usually a good way to organize economic activity" and "#7: Governments can sometimes improve market outcomes" (pp. 9–11).

13. Justin Fox, *The Myth of the Rational Market* (New York: HarperCollins, 2009), pp. xii–xiii.

14. National Bureau of Economic Research, "Business Cycle Expansions and Contractions," 1 December 2008, http://www.nber.org/cycles.html.

15. Paul Peretz, "The Politics of Fiscal and Monetary Policy," in *The Politics of American Economic Policy Making,* 2nd ed., ed. Paul Peretz (Armonk, N.Y.: M. E. Sharpe, 1996), pp. 101–113.

16. Shaun P. Hargraves Heap, "Keynesian Economics," in *Routledge Encyclopedia of International Political Economy,* vol. 2, ed. R. J. Barry Jones (London: Routledge, 2001), pp. 877–878.

17. The inner workings of the White House economic team are described at length by Ryan Lizza, "Inside the Crisis, *The New Yorker,* 12 October 2009.

18. *Wall Street Journal,* 18 January 2008, p. A12.

19. Jackie Calmes and Michael Cooper, "New Consensus Views Stimulus as Worthy Step," *New York Times,* 21 November 2009, pp. A1, A10; Alec MacGillis, "Economic Stimulus Has Created or Saved Nearly 2 Million Jobs, White House Says," *Washington Post,* 13 January 2010, p. A13.

20. For example, Peter Clarke, *Keynes: The Rise, Fall, and Return of the 20th Century's Most Influential Economist* (London: Bloomsbury Press, 2009); and Robert Skidelsky, *Keynes: The Return of the Master* (New York: Public Affairs Books, 2009).

21. Kathleen R. McNamara, "Monetarism," in *Routledge Encyclopedia of International Political Economy,* pp. 1035–1037.

22. The Federal Reserve Act (as amended over the years) cites "maximum employment, stable prices, and moderate long-term interest rates," http://www.federalreserve.gov/GeneralInfo/fract/sect02a.htm.

23. See Allan H. Meltzer, *A History of the Federal Reserve,* vol. 1, *1913–1951* (Chicago: University of Chicago Press, 2003). Meltzer writes that the leading banks in 1913 were privately owned institutions with public responsibilities. Fears were that they would place their interests above the public interest, but there was also concern about empowering government to control money. "President Woodrow Wilson offered a solution

that appeared to reconcile competing public and private interests. He proposed a public-private partnership with semiautonomous, privately funded reserve banks supervised by a public board" (p. 3).

24. Luca LiLeo, "Fed Gets More Power, Responsibility," *Wall Street Journal,* 16 July 2010, p. A5.

25. See the discussion of Federal Reserve policy actions in John B. Taylor, *Economics,* 4th ed. (Boston: Houghton Mifflin, 2004), Chap. 32.

26. Greg Ip and Jon E. Hilsenrath, "Having Defeated Inflation, Fed Girds for New Foe: Falling Prices," *Wall Street Journal,* 19 May 2003, p. A1.

27. The quote, attributed to William McChesney Martin, Jr., is in Martin Mayer, *The Fed* (New York: Free Press, 2001), p. 165.

28. Federal Reserve Bank of San Francisco, *Weekly Letter 96–08,* 23 February 1996.

29. Pew Research Center, "Economic Discontent Deepens as Inflation Concerns Rise," news release, 14 February 2008.

30. Fox, *The Myth of the Rational Market,* pp. xi–xii.

31. Edmund L. Andrews, "Bernanke, a Hero to His Own, Still Faces Fire in Washington, *New York Times,* 20 August 2009, pp. A1, B4; David Wessel, "Inside Dr. Bernanke's E.R.," *Wall Street Journal,* 24 July 2009, p. W3.

32. Charles Duhigg, "Depression You Say? Check Those Safety Nets," *New York Times,* 23 March 2008, sec. 4, pp. 1, 4.

33. Jonathan Rauch, Lawrence J. Haas, and Bruce Stokes, "Payment Deferred," *National Journal,* 14 May 1988, p. 1256.

34. Mankiw, *Principles of Economics,* pp. 170–171.

35. See the editorial "How to Raise Revenue," *Wall Street Journal,* 24 August 2007, p. A14; and Austan Goolsbee, "Is the New Supply Side Better Than the Old?" *New York Times,* 20 January 2008, p. BU6.

36. "The GOP's Spending Spree," *Wall Street Journal,* 25 November 2005, p. A18.

37. William Neikirk, "Budget Deficits Have Weight," *Chicago Tribune,* 8 February 2004, sec. 2, pp. 1–6.

38. Ibid.; David Leonhardt, "That Big Fat Budget Deficit. Yawn," *New York Times,* 8 February 2004, sec. 3, p. 1.

39. U.S. Department of Treasury, "The Debt to the Penny and Who Holds It," http://www.treasurydirect.gov/NP/BPDLogin?application=np.

40. One such "public debt clock" is at http://www.usdebtclock.org.

41. Justin Murray and Marc Labonte, "Foreign Holdings of Federal Debt," Congressional Research Service, RS22331, 17 March 2009. Many financial analysts think that the national debt seriously understates the *real* debt by several trillion dollars. See the website operated by the Institute for Truth in Accounting: http://www.truthinaccounting.org.

42. See, for example, these articles: Christopher Rhoads et al., "A Growing Global Unease," *Wall Street Journal,* 22 January 2004, pp. A10–11; Phillip Day and Hae Won Choi, "Asian Central Banks Consider Alternatives to Big Dollar Holdings," *Wall Street Journal,* 5 February 2004, pp. A1, A8; David Wessel, "U.S. to Rest of the World: Charge It!" *Wall Street Journal,* 12 February 2004, p. A2.

43. For the FY 2011 federal budget, go to http://www.whitehouse.gov/omb.

44. For a concise discussion of the 1990 budget reforms, see James A. Thurber, "Congressional-Presidential Battles to Balance the Budget," in *Rivals for Power: Presidential-Congressional Relations,* ed. James A. Thurber (Washington, D.C.: CQ Press, 1996), pp. 196–202.

45. For a brief account of presidential attempts, from Carter to Clinton, to deal with budget deficits, see Alexis Simendinger et al., "Sky High," *National Journal,* 7 February 2004, pp. 370–373.

46. Ibid., p. 377; Concord Coalition, "Budget Process Reform: An Important Tool for Fiscal Discipline, but Not a Magic Bullet," *Issue Brief,* 5 February 2004.

47. Concord Coalition, "Budget Process Reform," p. 3.

48. J. Taylor Rushing, "Obama Signs Pay-Go Law but Also Raises Federal Debt Ceiling," *The Hill,* 13 February 2010, http://thehill.com/homenews/administration/80981-obama-pay-as-you-go-rules-necessary-and-now-law-along-with-higher-debt-ceiling?tmpl=component&print=1&layout=default&page=.

49. Richard A. Musgrave and Peggy B. Musgrave, *Public Finance in Theory and Practice,* 2nd ed. (New York: McGraw-Hill, 1976), p. 42.

50. If you can spare 24 megabytes of storage, you can download the complete text of the U.S. Internal Revenue Code, Title 26 of the U.S. Code, at http://www.fourmilab.ch/uscode/26usc. If you print the tax code, expect more than 7,500 pages.

51. Office of Management and Budget, "Historical Tables, FY 2011 Budget," Table 2-2, http://www.whitehouse.gov/omb/budget/Historicals.

52. David Cay Johnston, "Talking Simplicity, Building a Maze," *New York Times,* 15 February 2004, Money and Business section, pp. 11, 14.

53. Michael L. Roberts, Peggy A. Hite, and Cassie F. Bradley, "Understanding Attitudes toward Progressive Taxation," *Public Opinion Quarterly* 58 (Summer 1994): 167–168. A Gallup Poll on 3–5 April 2005 found that respondents favored the current system over a flat tax 55 to 39 percent. And a Gallup Poll on 2–5 April 2007 found that 66 percent of respondents said "upper-income people" paid "too little" in taxes while 45 percent said "lower-income people" paid "too much."

54. Jill Barshay, "'Case of the Missing Revenue' Is Nation's Troubling Mystery," *CQ Weekly,* 17 January 2004, p. 144.

55. Tax Policy Center, "Historical Combined Income and Employee Tax Rates for a Family of Four," 9 April 2009, http://taxpolicycenter.org/taxfacts/displayafact.cfm?DocID=228&Topic2id=20&Topic3id=22.

56. Pew Research Center for the People and the Press, "Economic Inequality Seen as Rising, Boom Bypasses Poor," *Survey Report,* 21 June 2001.

57. Spending as percentage of GDP is a common way of measuring social welfare benefits, but it is not the only way. If spending is measured by dollars per capita, the United States, with a very high GDP, rates much more favorably. See Christopher Howard, "Is the American Welfare State Unusually Small?" *PS: Political Science and Politics* 36 (July 2003): 411–416.

58. Thom Shanker, "Proposed Military Spending Is Highest Since WWII," *New York Times,* 4 February 2008, p. A10.

59. David Herszenhorn, "Estimates of Iraq War Cost Were Not Close to Ballpark," *New York Times,* 19 March 2008, p. A9.

60. Jackie Calmes, "In Search of Presidential Earmarks," *Wall Street Journal,* 21 February 2006, p. A6.

61. The Office of Management and Budget website for earmarks is at http://earmarks.omb.gov. The superior private site for earmarks is at http://www.washingtonwatch.com/bills/earmarks.

62. Carl Hulse, "The Earmark Bounces Back," *New York Times,* 20 December 2007, pp. A1, A26.

63. John D. McKinnon, "Bush's Drive against 'Earmarks' Gains Steam," *Wall Street Journal,* 22 December 2008, p. A6.

64. Executive Office of the President, *Budget of the United States Government, Fiscal Year 2011: Historical Tables* (Washington, D.C.: U.S. Government Printing Office, 2010), Table 8.1.

65. Times-Mirror Center for the People and the Press, "Voter Anxiety Dividing GOP: Energized Democrats Backing Clinton," press release, 14 November 1995, p. 88.

66. These questions were asked in the 2008 American National Election Survey conducted by Stanford University and the University of Michigan.

67. Fay Lomax Cook et al., *Convergent Perspectives on Social Welfare Policy: The Views from the General Public, Members of Congress, and AFDC Recipients* (Evanston, Ill.: Center for Urban Affairs and Policy Research, Northwestern University, 1988), Table 4-1.

68. Cynthia Crossen, "Not Too Long Ago, Some People Begged for an Income Tax," *Wall Street Journal,* 4 June 2003, p. B1.

69. B. Guy Peters, *The Politics of Taxation: A Comparative Perspective* (Cambridge, Mass.: Basil Blackwell, 1991), p. 228.

70. Elizabeth Becker, "U.S. Subsidizes Companies to Buy Subsidized Cotton," *New York Times,* 4 November 2003, p. C1.

71. Lawrence Mishel, Jared Bernstein, and Sylvia Allegretto, *The State of Working America, 2004–2005* (Ithaca, N.Y.: Cornell University Press, 2005), pp. 338–340.

72. Ibid., p. 79.

73. Ibid., p. 62.

74. Arthur C. Brooks, "The Left's 'Inequality' Obsession," *Wall Street Journal,* 19 July 2007, p. A15. Federal income taxes do make income distribution slightly more equal. See David Wessel, "Fishing Out the Facts on the Wealth Gap," *Wall Street Journal,* 15 February 2007, p. A10.

75. Gerald Prante, "Summary of Latest Federal Individual Income Tax Data," *Fiscal Facts* (Washington, D.C.: Tax Foundation), 30 July 2009.

76. Ibid.

77. Tax Policy Center, "Effective Tax Rate by Size of Income, 2000–2006," 4 June 2009, http://taxpolicycenter.org/taxfacts/displayafact.cfm?Docid=366&Topic2id=48.

78. Joseph A. Pechman, *Who Paid the Taxes, 1966–1985?* (Washington, D.C.: Brookings Institution, 1985), p. 80. See also Lawrence Mishel, Jared Bernstein, and Heather Boushey, *The State of Working America, 2002–2003* (Ithaca, N.Y.: Cornell University Press, 2003), p. 66.

79. Mishel et al., *The State of Working America, 2002–2003,* p. 118.

80. Lawrence Mishel, Jared Bernstein, and Sylvia Allegretto, *The State of Working America, 2006–2007* (Ithaca, N.Y.: Cornell University Press, 2007), Table 8.16.

81. For a general discussion, see Vita Tanzi and Ludger Schuknecht, *Public Spending in the Twentieth Century: A Global Perspective* (Cambridge: Cambridge University Press, 2000), pp. 94–98.

82. Christopher Conkey, "Wealthiest American Families Add to Their Share of U.S. Net Worth," *Wall Street Journal,* 5 April 2006, p. A4; Arthur B. Kennickell, "Currents and Undercurrents: Changes in the Distribution of Wealth, 1989–2004," Federal Reserve Board, 30 January 2006, Table 5.

83. U.S. Bureau of the Census, *Statistical Abstract of the United States 2009* (Washington, D.C.: U.S. Government Printing Office, 2010), Table 674.

84. Benjamin I. Page, *Who Gets What from Government?* (Berkeley: University of California Press, 1983), p. 213.

85. Frank Newport, "Americans Split on Redistributing Wealth by Taxing the Rich," Gallup Poll Report, 30 October 2008.

86. A 2003 survey reported 36 percent of respondents favoring changing from an income tax to a flat-rate tax, with only 32 percent opposed; cited in Robert J. Blendon et al., "Tax Uncertainty: A Divided America's

Uninformed View of the Federal Tax System," *Brookings Review* 21 (Summer 2003): 28–31. Data from the National Conference of State Legislatures show that states raised income taxes by $8.2 billion from 1990 through 1993, which had a greater impact on wealthy than on poor residents. But from 1994 to 1997, the states reduced income taxes by $9.8 billion. In contrast, sales and excise taxes, which weigh more on those with lower incomes, were raised by $11.7 billion from 1990 through 1993 and cut by only $200 million from 1994 to 1997. See David Cay Johnston, "Taxes Are Cut, and Rich Get Richer," *New York Times,* 5 October 1997, p. 16.

87. James Sterngold, "Muting the Lotteries' Perfect Pitch," *New York Times,* 14 July 1996, sec. 4, p. 1.

88. "Taxes: What's Fair?" *Public Perspective* 7 (April–May 1996): 40–41. Similar findings were found in experiments involving undergraduate students in advanced tax classes at two public universities; see Roberts et al., "Understanding Attitudes toward Progressive Taxation."

89. Blendon et al., "Tax Uncertainty."

90. Jason White, "Taxes and Budget," *State of the States: 2004* (Washington, D.C.: Pew Center on the States, 2004), p. 30.

91. Shailagh Murray, "Seminary Article in Alabama Sparks Tax-Code Revolt," *Wall Street Journal,* 12 February 2003, pp. A1, A8.

Chapter 19 / Domestic Policy / pages 628–661

1. McCain–Obama speeches at the Ninety-ninth NAACP Convention, 12 July 2008.

2. RAND Corporation, "Consumer Financial Risk," RAND Report on Health Care, 2010, http://www .randcompare.org/current/dimension/consumer_ financial_risk.

3. Kaiser Family Foundation, "Health Care Costs: A Primer," March 2009, http://www.kff.org/insurance/ upload/7670_02.pdf.

4. Associated Press, "Small Firms Scrapping, Scaling Back Health Plans," 18 November 2009, http:// abcnews.go.com/Business/wireStory?id=9112244.

5. David Himmelstein et al., "Medical Bankruptcy in the United States, 2007: Results of a National Study," *The American Journal of Medicine* 122, no. 8 (2009): 741–746.

6. Reed Abelson, "Insured, but Bankrupted by Health Crises," *New York Times,* 1 July 2009, http:// www.nytimes.com/2009/07/01/business/01meddebt .html.

7. Ibid.

8. "Americans at Risk: One in Three Uninsured," *Families USA,* March 2009, http://www.familiesusa.org/

resources/publications/reports/americans-at-risk-findings.html.

9. Nancy Lofholm, "Heavy Infant in Grand Junction Denied Health Insurance," *Denver Post,* 10 October 2009, http://www.denverpost.com/ci_13530098; David Hilzenrath, "Acne, Pregnancy among Disqualifying Conditions," *Washington Post,* 19 September 2009, p. A03.

10. Frank Newport, "More in U.S. Say Health Coverage Is Not Gov't Responsibility," Gallup, 13 November 2009, http://www.gallup.com/poll/124253/Say-Health-Coverage-Not-Gov-Responsibility.aspx.

11. In 2008, for example, 21 percent of the federal budget was allocated for Social Security alone. Another 33 percent went to Medicare, Medicaid, and other domestic spending programs. Congressional Budget Office estimates provided by Michael Phillips and John McKinnon, "Legacy of Deficits Will Constrain Bush's Successor," *Wall Street Journal,* 1 February 2008, p. A3.

12. Jeffrey Jones, "Economy, Health Care Top Most Important Problems List," Gallup.com, 9 September 2009, http://www.gallup.com/poll/122885/Economy-Healthcare-Top-Important-Problem-List.aspx.

13. Lydia Saad, "State of the Union: Both Good and Bad," *Gallup Poll Report,* 24 January 2008, http://www .gallup.com/poll/103918/Americans-State-Union-Ratings-All-Bad.aspx; Jeffrey Jones, "Greater Optimism about U.S. Health System Coverage, Costs," Gallup, 19 November 2009, http://www.gallup.com/poll/ 124415/Greater-Optimism-U.S.-Health-System-Coverage-Costs.aspx.

14. "Economy, Jobs Trump All Other Policy Priorities in 2009," Pew Research Center for the People and the Press, January 2009, http://people-press.org/report/ 485/economy-top-policy-priority; *Survey by USA Today and Gallup Organization, March 27–March 29, 2009.* Retrieved 3 December 2009 from the iPOLL Databank, Roper Center for Public Opinion Research, University of Connecticut.

15. Data available from U.S. Department of Labor, Bureau of Labor Statistics, http://www.bls.gov/cps/prev_yrs .htm.

16. Linda L. M. Bennett and Stephen Earl Bennett, *Living with Leviathan: Americans Coming to Terms with Big Government* (Lawrence: University Press of Kansas, 1990), pp. 21–24.

17. Information available at the website of the U.S. Social Security Administration: http://www.ssa.gov/OACT/ COLA/cbb.html and http://www.ssa.gov/OACT/ ProgData/taxRates.html.

18. Paul C. Light, *Artful Work: The Politics of Social Security Reform* (New York: Random House, 1985), p. 63.

19. Social Security Administration, *The 2009 Annual Report of the Board of Trustees of the Federal Old-Age*

and *Survivors Insurance and Disability Insurance Trust Funds* (Washington, D.C.: U.S. Government Printing Office, 12 May 2009), http://www.ssa.gov/OACT/TR/2009/trTOC.html.

20. Ibid.

21. Martha Derthick, *Policymaking for Social Security* (Washington, D.C.: Brookings Institution, 1979), pp. 346–347.

22. Robert Pear, "Social Security Benefits Not Expected to Rise in '10," *New York Times,* 2 May 2009, http://www.nytimes.com/2009/05/03/us/politics/03benefits.html.

23. The Polling Report, "Social Security," ABC News/Washington Post Poll, 19–22 February 2009, http://pollingreport.com/social.htm.

24. *Retirement Security and Quality Health Care: Our Pledge to America,* n.d., GOP Platform, found at: http://abcnews.go.com/Politics/story?id=123296&page=1.

25. Lydia Saad, "Bush Fails to Ignite Public Support for Reform," Gallup.com, 4 May 2005, http://www.gallup.com/poll/16153/Bush-Fails-Ignite-Public-Support-Reform.aspx; Frank Newport and Lydia Saad, "Americans Appear Open to Arguments on Privatizing Social Security," Gallup.com, 7 February 2005, http://www.gallup.com/poll/14815/Americans-Appear-Open-Arguments-Privatizing-Social-Security.aspx.

26. "Seniors & Social Security," http://www.whitehouse.gov/issues/seniors-and-social-security.

27. Although it has been the source of endless debate, today's definition of poverty retains remarkable similarity to its precursors. As early as 1795, a group of English magistrates "decided that a minimum income should be the cost of a gallon loaf of bread, multiplied by three, plus an allowance for each dependent." See Alvin L. Schorr, "Redefining Poverty Levels," *New York Times,* 9 May 1984, p. 27; and Louis Uchitelle, "How to Define Poverty? Let Us Count the Ways," *New York Times,* 26 May 2001, http://www.nytimes.com/2001/05/26/arts/how-to-define-poverty-let-us-count-the-ways.html?pagewanted=1.

28. Nicholas Eberstadt, "The Mismeasure of Poverty," *Policy Review* 138 (August–September 2006): 1–21.

29. Sarah Fass, "Measuring Poverty in the United States," National Center for Children in Poverty, April 2009, http://www.nccp.org/publications/pdf/text_876.pdf; "Mismeasuring Poverty," *The American Prospect,* 16 September 2009, http://www.prospect.org/cs/articles?article=mismeasuring_poverty.

30. Alimayehu Bishaw and Trudi J. Renwick, "Poverty: 2007 and 2008 American Community Surveys," U.S. Census Bureau, September 2009, http://www.census.gov/prod/2009pubs/acsbr08-1.pdf.

31. U.S. Census Bureau, *Income, Poverty, and Health Insurance Coverage in the United States: 2008* (Washington, D.C.: U.S. Government Printing Office, 2009), http://www.census.gov/prod/2009pubs/p60-236.pdf.

32. U.S. Census Bureau, "Poverty Thresholds 2008," http://www.census.gov/hhes/www/poverty/data/threshld/thresh08.html. The poverty guideline for that year was slightly lower, at $21,200 (see the 2008 HHS Poverty Guidelines at http://aspe.hhs.gov/poverty/08Poverty.shtml).

33. Juan Williams, "Reagan, the South, and Civil Rights," National Public Radio, 10 June 2004, http://www.npr.org/templates/story/story.php?storyId=1953700.

34. Andrea Hetling, Monika McDermott, and Mingus Mapps, "Symbolism vs. Policy Learning: Public Opinion of the 1996 U.S. Welfare Reforms," *American Politics Research* 36, no. 3 (2008): 335–357.

35. Francis X. Clines, "Clinton Signs Bill Cutting Welfare," *New York Times,* 23 August 1996, p. A1.

36. Peter T. Kilborn, "With Welfare Overhaul Now Law, States Grapple with the Consequences," *New York Times,* 23 August 1996, p. A10.

37. Liz Schott, "Policy Basics: An Introduction to TANF," Center on Budget and Policy Priorities, 22 November 2002, http://www.cbpp.org/cms/?fa=view&id=936.

38. Department of Health and Human Services Office of Family Assistance, "TANF Factsheet," http://www.acf.hhs.gov/opa/fact_sheets/tanf_factsheet.html.

39. Alan Weil and Kenneth Feingold (eds.), *Welfare Reform: The Next Act* (Washington, D.C.: Urban Institute, 2002).

40. Hettling et al., "Symbolism vs. Policy Learning"; Joshua Dyck and Laura Hussey, "The End of Welfare As We Know It? Durable Attitudes in a Changing Information Environment," *Public Opinion Quarterly* 72, no. 4 (2008): 589–618.

41. Eugenie Hildebrandt and Patricia Stevens, "Impoverished Women with Children and No Welfare Benefits: The Urgency of Researching Failures of the Temporary Assistance for Needy Families Program," *American Journal of Public Health* 99, no. 5 (2009): 793–801; Robert Wood, Quinn Moore, and Anu Rangarajan, "Two Steps Forward, One Step Back: The Uneven Economic Progress of TANF Recipients," *Social Service Review* 82, no. 1 (2008): 3–28.

42. Jason DeParle, "For Victims of Recession, Patchwork of State Aid," *New York Times,* 10 May 2009, http://www.nytimes.com/2009/05/10/us/10safetynet.html; Sheila Zedlewski, "The Role of Welfare during a Recession," Urban Institute, December 2008, http://www.urban.org/publications/411809.html.

43. Sara Murray, "Numbers on Welfare See Sharp Increase," *Wall Street Journal,* 22 June 2009, http://online.wsj.com/article/SB124562449457235503.html.

44. Public opinion polls show that access and cost are the top two health-care problems for Americans. In 2008,

these were also the issues that likely voters wanted to hear the presidential candidates talk about. See Gallup Report, "'Access' Gains as Top Perceived US Health Problem," 3 December 2007, http://www.gallup.com; and Elizabeth Wasserman, "May the Best Health Care Plan Win," *Congressional Quarterly Weekly Report,* 25 February 2008, p. 506.

45. U.S. Census Bureau, *Income, Poverty, and Health Insurance Coverage in the United States: 2008* (Washington, D.C.: U.S. Government Printing Office, 2009).

46. Ibid.

47. Rebecca Adams, "Health Care: After the Reform," *CQ Weekly Online,* 28 September 2009, pp. 2156–2166.

48. See National Health expenditure data at http://www.cms.hhs.gov/NationalHealthExpendData/Downloads/proj2008.pdf.

49. Ibid.

50. Organization for Economic Co-operation and Development, "OECD Health Data 2009," http://www.oecd.org/document/16/0,3343,en_2649_34631_2085200_1_1_1_1,00.html.

51. Derthick, *Policymaking,* p. 335.

52. Paul Starr, *The Social Transformation of American Medicine* (New York: Basic Books, 1982), pp. 279–280.

53. Ibid., p. 287.

54. Theodore Marmor, *The Politics of Medicare* (Chicago: Aldine, 1973).

55. "Medicare: A Primer," Kaiser Family Foundation. April 2010. http://www.kff.org/medicare/upload/7615-03.pdf., http://www.cms.hhs.gov/DataCompendium/16_2008_Data_Compendium.asp#TopOfPage.

56. Kaiser Family Foundation Fast Facts, "Medicare Benefit Payments, by Type of Service, 2009," http://facts.kff.org/chart.aspx?ch=379.

57. Centers for Medicare and Medicaid Services, "Brief Summaries of Medicare and Medicaid," 1 November 2008, http://www.cms.hhs.gov/medicareprogramratesstats/02_summarymedicaremedicaid.asp.

58. Alan Weil, "There's Something about Medicaid," *Health Affairs* 22 (January–February 2003): 13.

59. Centers for Medicare and Medicaid Services, 2008 Compendium; Centers for Medicare and Medicaid Services, "Brief Summaries of Medicare and Medicaid."

60. "Critical Care: The Economic Recovery Package and Medicaid," FamiliesUSA, January 2009, http://www.familiesusa.org/assets/pdfs/critical-care.pdf.

61. Centers for Medicare and Medicaid Services, 2008 Compendium.

62. Centers for Medicare and Medicaid Services, *2005 CMS Statistics,* "Table 34: Medicaid/Payments by Eligibility Status," accessed 22 January 2006 at http://www.cms.hhs.gov/MedicareMedicaidStatSupp/downloads/2005_CMS_Statistics.pdf; also see Kaiser Family Foundation

Fast Facts, "Medicaid Enrollees and Expenditures by Enrollment Group," 2009, http://facts.kff.org/chart.aspx?ch=465.

63. "Health Timeline 2010–2015," *CQ Weekly*, April 5, 2010, p. 818; Robert Pear and David M. Herszenhorn, "Obama Hails Vote on Health Care as Answering 'the Call of History," *New York Times*, March 21, 2010, http://www.nytimes.com/2010/03/22/health/policy/22health.html?scp=1&sq=obama%20hails%20vote%20on%20helath%20care&tst=cse; "Health Care Reform, at Last," *New York Times*, March 22, 2010, http://www.nytimes.com/2010/03/22/opinion/22mon5.html?scp=1&sq=health%20care%20reform,%20at%20last&tst=cse.

64. Kerry Young, "Controlling Medicare Costs," *CQ Weekly*, April 5, 2010, p. 826; "How Health Care Reform Reduces the Deficit in 5 Not-So-Easy Steps," *Newsweek*, March 20, 2010, http://www.newsweek.com/2010/03/20/how-health-care-reform-reduces-the-deficit-in-5-not-so-easy-steps.html; Peter Grier, "Health Care Reform Bill 101: Who Will Pay for Reform?" *Christian Science Monitor*, March 21, 2010, http://www.csmonitor.com/USA/Politics/2010/0321/Health-care-reform-bill-101-Who-will-pay-for-reform.

65. Kevin Sack, "Florida Suit Poses a Challenge to Health Care Law," *New York Times*, May 10, 2010, http://www.nytimes.com/2010/05/11/health/policy/11lawsuit.html?_r=1&ref=health_care_reform.

66. U.S. Department of Education, "Federal Role in Education," http://www.ed.gov/about/overview/fed/role.html.

67. National Center for Education Statistics, *The Nation's Report Card* (Washington, D.C.: U.S. Department of Education, October 2009), http://nationsreportcard.gov/math_2009/math_2009_report; National Center for Education Statistics, "White, Black, Hispanic, and Asian/Pacific Islander Fourth-Graders Scored Higher in 2007 Than in 1992," http://nationsreportcard.gov/reading_2007/r0009.asp.

68. Christopher Jencks and Meredith Phillips (eds.), *The Black-White Test Score Gap* (Washington, D.C.: Brookings Institution Press, 1998).

69. Paul Manna, "Federalism, Agenda Setting, and the Development of Federal Education Policy, 1965–2001" (Ph.D. diss., University of Wisconsin–Madison, 2003).

70. For an overview, see Linda Darling-Hammond, "Evaluating No Child Left Behind," *The Nation,* 21 May 2007; and Libby George, "His Permanent Record: Bush Mints a Legacy," *Congressional Quarterly Weekly Report,* 18 February 2008, p. 427.

71. Michael Sandler, "2007 Legislative Summary: No Child Left Behind Reauthorization," *CQ Weekly*

Report, 7 January 2008, p. 42; Sam Dillon, "Democrats Make Bush School Act an Election Issue," *New York Times,* 23 December 2007, p. A1; "No Child Left Behind Act," *New York Times,* Times Topics, October 2009, http://topics.nytimes.com/top/reference/timestopics/subjects/n/no_child_left_behind_act/index.html.

72. Jeffrey Jones, "Economy, Healthcare Top 'Most Important Problem' List," Gallup, 9 September 2009, http://www.gallup.com/poll/122885/Economy-Healthcare-Top-Important-Problem-List.aspx.

73. Aaron Terrazas and Jeanne Batalova, "Frequently Requested Statistics on Immigrants and Immigration in the United States," Migration Policy Institute, October 2009, http://www.migrationinformation.org/USfocus/display.cfm?ID=747#9a.

74. Lymari Morales, "Americans Return to Tougher Immigration Stance," Gallup, 5 August 2009, http://www.gallup.com/poll/122057/Americans-Return-Tougher-Immigration-Stance.aspx.

75. U.S. Census Bureau, *Income, Poverty, and Health Insurance Coverage in the United States: 2008,* (Washington, D.C.: U.S. Government Printing Office, 2008), Table 6.

76. Terrazas and Batalova, "Frequently Requested Statistics on Immigrants and Immigration in the United States."

77. Congressional Budget Office, *Immigration Policy in the United States,* February 2006, p. 4.

78. Migration Policy Institute, "Public Benefits Use," http://www.migrationinformation.org/integration/publicbenefits.cfm.

79. Department of Homeland Security, "Immigrant Enforcement Actions: 2008," Annual Report, July 2009, http://www.dhs.gov/xlibrary/assets/statistics/publications/enforcement_ar_08.pdf.

80. Almost 30 percent of California's residents are foreign born. Twenty percent of the residents of New York and New Jersey are foreign born. Florida, Texas, Nevada, and New Jersey also have rates of foreign born that exceed the national average. See Migration Policy Institute, "2008 American Community Survey and Census Data on the Foreign Born by State," MPI Data Hub, http://www.migrationinformation.org/DataHub/acscensus.cfm.

81. Alan Greenblatt, "Local Officials Bypassing the Beltway," *Congressional Quarterly Weekly Report,* 19 November 2007, p. 3470; also see National Conference of State Legislators, "State Laws Related to Immigrants and Immigration," Immigration Policy Project, http://www.ncsl.org/default.aspx?tabid=18030.

82. Michael Sandler, "2007 Legislative Branch: Immigration: Immigration Policy Overhaul," *Congressional Quarterly Weekly Report,* 7 January 2008, p. 50; Jonathan Weisman, "Immigration Overhaul, Bill Stalls in Senate," *Washington Post,* 8 June 2007, p. A1.

83. Scott Keeter, "Where the Public Stands on Immigration Reform," Pew Research Center, 23 November 2009, http://pewresearch.org/pubs/1421/where-the-public-stands-on-immigration-reform.

84. Julia Preston, "White House Plan on Immigration Includes Legal Status," *New York Times,* 13 November 2009, http://www.nytimes.com/2009/11/14/us/politics/14immig.html?scp=3&sq=obama%20and%20immigration&st=cse; Tim Gaynor, "Busy Agenda Clouds Hope for Immigration Reform," Reuters, 19 November 2009, http://www.reuters.com/article/idUSTRE5AI5CX20091119.

Chapter 20 / Global Policy / pages 662–697

1. The World Wildlife Federation defines interdependence as "The concept that everything in nature is connected to each other, and cannot survive without the help of other plants, animals and abiotic factors (such as sun, soil, water and air) around it." See http://www.worldwildlife.org/climate/curriculum/item5957.html. Other definitions are similar.

2. Simon Winchester, *Krakatoa: The Day the World Exploded: August 27, 1883* (New York: HarperCollins, 2003), p. 182.

3. Ibid., pp. 193–194.

4. Ibid., pp. 316–318.

5. Corey Dade and Chris Herring, "International Aid Groups Mobilize," *Wall Street Journal,* 14 January 2010, p. A8.

6. "Providing Relief: Who Is Contributing Aid to Haiti," *Wall Street Journal,* 16 January 2010, p. A8.

7. Peter Spiegel, "U.S. Leads Way in Aid Pledges, with Tally Likely to Skyrocket," *Wall Street Journal,* 22 January 2010, p. A9.

8. For an alternative analysis, see Hanspeter Kriesi, "Globalization and the Transformation of the National Political Space: Six European Countries Compared," *European Journal of Political Research* 45 (2006): 921–956.

9. Rachel Donaldio and Laurie Goodstein, "Pope Urges Forming New World Economic Order to Work for the 'Common Good,'" *New York Times,* 8 July 2009, p. A6.

10. See his website at http://www.patrobertson.com/speeches/ConservatismWillTriumph.asp.

11. John Yoo, who worked in the Office of Legal Counsel for President George W. Bush, distinguishes between the power to "declare" war, given to Congress, and the power to "make" war, which inheres in the president, in *Crisis and Command: The History of Executive Power from George Washington to George W. Bush* (New York: Kaplan Publishing, 2009).

12. The official Senate website lists twenty-one having been rejected, including the 1999 nuclear test ban

treaty: http://www.senate.gov/artandhistory/
history/common/briefing/Treaties.htm.

13. "Pros and Cons Testify at Charter Hearings," *Life,* 30 July 1945, pp. 22–23.

14. *Congressional Quarterly Weekly Report,* 16 October 1999, p. 2477. See also R. W. Apple, "The G.O.P. Torpedo," *New York Times,* 14 October 1999, p. 1.

15. Barbara Crossette, "Around the World, Dismay over Senate Vote on Treaty," *New York Times,* 15 October 1999, p. A1. The article quotes *The Straits Times of Singapore.*

16. Chuck McCutcheon, "Treaty Vote a 'Wake-Up Call,'" *Congressional Quarterly Weekly Report,* 16 October 1999, p. 2435.

17. *United States* v. *Curtiss-Wright Export Corporation,* 299 U.S. 304 (1936); *United States* v. *Belmont,* 301 U.S. 324 (1937); Jack C. Plano and Roy Olton, *The International Relations Dictionary* (New York: Holt, Rinehart and Winston, 1969), p. 149.

18. Plano and Olton, *The International Relations Dictionary,* p. 149.

19. Lyn Ragsdale, *Vital Statistics on the Presidency* (Washington, D.C.: CQ Press, 1998), pp. 317–319. After 1984, government reports eliminated the clear distinction between treaties and executive agreements, making it difficult to determine the ratio. Indeed, other nations have criticized the reluctance of the United States to sign binding treaties. See Barbara Crossette, "Washington Is Criticized for Growing Reluctance to Sign Treaties," *New York Times,* 4 April 2002, p. A5.

20. Ragsdale, *Vital Statistics on the Presidency,* p. 298.

21. Brandon Rottinghaus and Jason Maier, "The Power of Decree: Presidential Use of Executive Proclamations, 1977–2005," *Political Research Quarterly* 60 (June 2007): 338–343.

22. These critics included both conservative Republican senator Barry Goldwater of Arizona and liberal Democratic senator Thomas Eagleton of Missouri. Eagleton's feelings were succinctly summarized in the title of his book: *War and Presidential Power: A Chronicle of Congressional Surrender* (New York: Liveright, 1974).

23. Miles A. Pomper, "In for the Long Haul," *CQ Weekly Report,* 15 September 2001, p. 2118.

24. Jim Rutenberg, "Bush Uses Recess to Fill Envoy Post and 2 Others," *New York Times,* 5 April 2007, p. A12.

25. David M. Herszenhorn, "Gone for the Holidays, but Leaving a Light On (Got It, Mr. President?)," *New York Times,* 21 December 2007, p. A22.

26. Richard Morris (ed.), *Encyclopedia of American History: Bicentennial Edition* (New York: Harper & Row, 1976), p. 146.

27. Mark Landler, "Clinton Makes Case for Internet Freedom as a Plank of American Foreign Policy," *New York Times,* 22 January 2010, p. A6.

28. Duncan Clarke, "Why State Can't Lead," *Foreign Policy* 66 (Spring 1987): 128–142. See also Steven W. Hook, "Domestic Obstacles to International Affairs: The State Department under Fire at Home," *PS: Political Science and Politics* 36 (January 2003): 23–29.

29. J. Anthony Holmes, "Where Are the Civilians? How to Rebuild the U.S. Foreign Service," *Foreign Affairs* 88 (January–February 2009): 148–160.

30. Harry Crosby [pseudonym], "Too at Home Abroad: Swilling Beer, Licking Boots and Ignoring the Natives with One of Jim Baker's Finest," *Washington Monthly* (September 1991): 16–20.

31. See Steven R. Weisman, "The Battle Lines Start in Washington," *New York Times,* 27 April 2003, sec. 4, p. 2; Gerald F. Seib and Carla Anne Robbins, "Powell-Rumsfeld Feud Now Hard to Ignore," *Wall Street Journal,* 25 April 2003, p. A4.

32. August Cole and Yochi J. Dreazen, "Pentagon Shifts Its Strategy to Small-Scale Warfare," *New York Times,* 30 January 2010, p. A4.

33. From "The Intelligence Cycle," in *CIA Factbook on Intelligence,* http://www.fas.org/irp/cia/product/facttell/index.html.

34. The Intelligence Community was defined in the Intelligence Reform and Terrorism Prevention Act of 2004. See http://www.intelligence.gov.

35. Merle D. Kellerhals, Jr., "Negroponte Nominated to Become Director of National Intelligence," announcement of the U.S. Department of State, International Information Programs, 17 February 2005, http://florence.usconsulate.gov/viewer/article.asp?article=/file2005_02/alia/a5021702.htm.

36. Loch K. Johnson, "Now That the Cold War Is Over, Do We Need the CIA?" in *The Future of American Foreign Policy,* ed. Charles Kegley and Eugene Wittkopf (New York: St. Martin's Press, 1992), p. 306.

37. David S. Cloud, "Caught Off-Guard by Terror, the CIA Fights to Catch Up," *Wall Street Journal,* 14 April 2002, p. 1.

38. Quoted in Bob Woodward, *Plan of Attack* (New York: Simon & Schuster, 2004), p. 249; and David S. Cloud, "Tenet's Mission: Devising an Exit Strategy," *Wall Street Journal,* 28 January 2004, p. A4.

39. Bob Kemper, "Bush De-emphasizes Weapons Claim," *Chicago Tribune,* 28 January 2004, p. 9.

40. Stephen J. Hedges and John Crewdson, "Bungled Plots, Wire Taps, Leaks," *Chicago Tribune,* 27 June 2007, p. 1.

41. Richard A. Clarke, "Targeting the Terrorists," *Wall Street Journal,* 18 July 2009, pp. W1, W2.

42. Scott Shane, "C.I.A. Expanding Drone Assaults inside Pakistan," *New York Times,* 4 December 2009,

pp. A1, A14; Mark Mazzetti, "C.I.A. Takes on Expanded Role on Front Lines," *New York Times,* 1 January 2010, pp. A1, A12.

43. Elisabeth Bumiller and Carl Hulse, "C.I.A. Pick Names as White House Takes Up Critics," *New York Times,* 8 May 2006, pp. A1, A21.

44. Leslie Cauley, "NSA Has Massive Database of Americans' Phone Calls," *USA Today,* 11 May 2006, p. 1.

45. Mark Mazzetti, "White House Sides with the C.I.A. in a Spy Turf Battle," *New York Times,* 13 November 2009, p. A12. Earlier in the year, the Senate backed the DNI; see Walter Pincus, "Senate Panel Backs DNI in Turf Battle with CIA," *Washington Post,* 23 July 2009.

46. At http://www.usaid.gov/haiti, people could donate cash and offer volunteer medical service, nonmedical service, or other assistance.

47. August Cole, "Afghanistan Contractors Outnumber Troops," *Wall Street Journal,* 22 August 2009, p. A6.

48. Dag Ryen, "State Action in a Global Framework," in *The Book of the States* (Lexington, Ky.: Council of State Governments, 1996), pp. 524–536.

49. James C. McKinley, Jr., "For U.S. Exporters in Cuba, Business Trumps Politics," *New York Times,* 12 November 2007, p. A3.

50. X [George F. Kennan], "The Sources of Soviet Conduct," *Foreign Affairs* 25 (July 1947): 575.

51. Richard M. Nixon, *U.S. Foreign Policy for the 1970s: A New Strategy for Peace* (Washington, D.C.: U.S. Government Printing Office, 1970), p. 2.

52. Thomas Halverson, *The Last Great Nuclear Debate: NATO and Short-Range Nuclear Weapons in the 1980s* (New York: St. Martin's Press, 1995).

53. See, for example, Francis Fukuyama, *The End of History and the Last Man* (New York: Free Press, 1992).

54. Daniel Deudney and C. John Ikenberry, "Who Won the Cold War?" *Foreign Policy* 87 (Summer 1992): 128–138.

55. See, for example, Paul Kennedy, *Preparing for the Twenty-first Century* (New York: Random House, 1993), especially Chap. 13.

56. Richard H. Ullman, "A Late Recovery," *Foreign Policy* 101 (Winter 1996): 76–79; James M. McCormick, "Assessing Clinton's Foreign Policy at Midterm," *Current History* 94 (November 1995): 370–374; Michael Mandelbaum, "Foreign Policy as Social Work," *Foreign Affairs* (January–February 1996): 16–32.

57. Frank Bruni, "Bush, and His Presidency, Are Transformed," *New York Times,* 22 September 2001, p. 1.

58. David E. Sanger, "On the Job, Bush Has Mastered Diplomacy 101, His Aides Say," *New York Times,* 22 May 2002, p. 1.

59. Bob Woodward, *Bush at War* (New York: Simon & Schuster, 2002). Woodward was given access to contemporaneous notes taken during more than fifty meetings of the National Security Council and other personal notes, memos, and so on from participants in planning the war in Afghanistan.

60. The 19 September 2002 document is "The National Security Strategy of the United States." Extracts were published in the *New York Times,* 20 September 2002, p. A10. The full version is at http://georgewbush-whitehouse.archives.gov/nsc/nss/2002/.

61. In a news conference, Bush said, "After September 11, the doctrine of containment just doesn't hold any water, as far as I'm concerned." Quoted in the *New York Times,* 1 February 2003, p. A8.

62. Adam Nagourney and Megan Thee, "Poll Gives Bush Worst Marks Yet on Major Issues," *New York Times,* 10 May 2006, pp. A1, A18. Poll results are at http://nytimes.com/ref/us/polls_index.html.

63. The National Security Strategy of the United States of America, March 2006, http://www.whitehouse.gov/nsc/nss/2006.

64. CBS News/*New York Times* Poll, 20–24 February 2008.

65. Bob Woodward, *Plan of Attack: The Definitive Account of the Decision to Invade Iraq* (New York: Simon & Schuster, 2004), p. 443.

66. Peter Baker, "With Pledges to Troops and Iraqis, Obama Details Pullout," *New York Times,* 27 February 2009, p. A1.

67. "Longest Wars," *New York Times,* 7 October 2009, p. A10.

68. Peter Spiegel, Jonathan Weisman, and Yochi J. Dreazen, "Obama Bets Big on Troop Surge," *Wall Street Journal,* 2 December 2009, pp. A1, A7.

69. CNN/Opinion Research Corporation Poll, 16–20 December 2009.

70. Thomas Nagorski, "Editor's Notebook: Afghan War Now Country's Longest," *ABC News/Politics* http://abcnews.go.com/Politics/afghan-war-now-longest-war-us-history/story?id=10849303.

71. Peter Spiegel and Jonathan Weisman, "Behind Afghan War Debate, a Battle of Two Books Rages," *Wall Street Journal,* 7 October 2009, p. 1. The books were *A Better War,* by Lewis Sorley, and *Lessons in Disaster,* by Gordon M. Goldstein.

72. Nobel Committee, "The Nobel Peace Prize for 2009," press release, 9 October 2009, http://nobelprize.org/nobel_prizes/peace/laureates/2009/press.html.

73. Choe Sang-Hun, "In 2010, Web Addresses to Come in Any Language," *New York Times,* 31 October 2009, p. B3.

74. The Latin "ru" cannot transliterate as "PY" for that is too close to ".py" in Latin for Paraguay. See DomainNews.com, ".РП Internationalised Domain Name Will Translate DNS in Russian," 23 November 2009, http://www.domainnews.com/en/%D0%A0%

D0%A4-internationalised-domain-name-will-translate-dns-in-russian.html.

75. Christopher Clarey, "Now Skating for (Insert Country)," *New York Times,* 28 January 2010, p. B13.

76. Linda Greenhouse, "Justices Block New Hearing for Mexican," *New York Times,* 26 March 2008, p. A19.

77. See Joseph S. Nye, Jr., "U.S. Power and Strategy After Iraq," *Foreign Affairs* (July–August 2003): 60–73. For a contrasting view, see Grenville Byford, "The Wrong War," *Foreign Affairs* (July–August 2002): 34–43.

78. See Moisés Naím, "The Five Wars of Globalization," *Foreign Policy* (January–February 2003): 29–37. For problems in combating terrorism, see Thomas Homer-Dixon, "The Rise of Complex Terrorism," *Foreign Policy* (January–February 2002): 52–62.

79. Michael Mastanduno, "Trade Policy," in *U.S. Foreign Policy: The Search for a New Role,* ed. Robert J. Art and Seyom Brown (New York: Macmillan, 1993), p. 142.

80. Nick Timiraos, "Will Overseas Funds Be a Juggernaut?" *Wall Street Journal,* 1 December 2007, p. A11.

81. Steven R. Weisman, "A Fear of Foreign Investments," *New York Times,* 21 August 2007, p. C1; and "Sovereign Impunity," *Wall Street Journal,* 1 December 2007, p. A12.

82. Bob Davis, "U.S. Pushes Sovereign Funds to Open to Outside Scrutiny," *Wall Street Journal,* 26 February 2008, pp. A1, A16.

83. NationMaster.com, "GDP by Country," http://www.nationmaster.com/red/pie/eco_gdp-economy-gdp&date=1960.

84. Terence Poon and Andrew Batson, "China Targets Inflation as Economy Runs Hot," *Wall Street Journal,* 22 January 2010, p. A11.

85. Pew Research Center for the People and the Press, *America's Place in the World 2009* (Washington, D.C.: Pew Research Center, December 2009), p. 2, http://people-press.org/reports/pdf/569.pdf.

86. Andrew E. Kramer, "Four Nations Seek More Diversity in Global Economic Order," *New York Times,* 17 June 2009, p. A8.

87. U.S. Energy Information Administration, "Table 11.5: World Crude Oil Production, 1960–2008," in *Annual Energy Review* (Washington, D.C.: Department of Energy, 26 June 2009), http://www.eia.doe.gov/emeu/aer/txt/ptb1105.html.

88. Statistics derived from Office of Trade and Economic Analysis, International Trade Administration, U.S. Department of Commerce, "GDP and U.S. International Trade in Goods and Services, 1976–2004," available at http://www.trade.gov/td/industry/otea/usfth/tabcon.html.

89. "Hills, in Japan, Stirs a Baby-Bottle Dispute," *New York Times,* 14 October 1989, p. 35.

90. Information from the World Trade Organization, "Members and Observers," http://www.wto.org/english/thewto_e/whatis_e/tif_e/org6_e.htm; and "WTO in Brief," http://www.wto.org/english/thewto_e/whatis_e/inbrief_e/inbr00_e.htm.

91. "WTO Rules against U.S. Dumping Laws," *Wall Street Journal,* 7 June 2000, p. A2.

92. R. C. Longworth, "WTO Deserves Some but Not All of the Criticism It's Getting," *Chicago Tribune,* 2 December 1999, p. 25.

93. Greg Hitt, "China Focus May Stall Bush's Trade Plans," *Wall Street Journal,* 31 December 2007, p. A3. For 2009 data, see http://www.census.gov/foreign-trade/top/index.html#2009.

94. Deborah Solomon, "Seeking to Soften Blows of Globalization," *Wall Street Journal,* 26 June 2007, p. A8; Chicago Council on Global Affairs, "Economic Worries Undermining Americans' Global Confidence," 14 October 2008, p. 2.

95. Deborah Solomon and Greg Hitt, "A Globalization Winner Joins in Trade Backlash," *Wall Street Journal,* 21 November 2007, pp. A1, A16.

96. John Stremlau, "Clinton's Dollar Diplomacy," *Foreign Policy* 97 (Winter 1995): 18–35.

97. R. C. Longworth, "A 'Grotesque' Gap," *Chicago Tribune,* 12 July 1999, p. 1.

98. Steven Kull, "What the Public Knows That Washington Doesn't," *Foreign Policy* 101 (Winter 1995–1996): 102–115.

99. Bay Fang, "Bush Gets Restrained Praise on Africa," *Chicago Tribune,* 16 February 2008, p. 9.

100. Barbara Crossette, "War Crimes Tribunal Becomes Reality, without U.S. Role," *New York Times,* 12 April 2002, p. A3; Neil A. Lewis, "U.S. Rejects All Support for New Court on Atrocities," *New York Times,* 7 May 2002, p. A9.

101. For membership of the International Criminal Court, see http://www.globalsolutions.org/issues/icc.

102. See Citizens for Global Solutions, "Presidential Policy Statements on the ICC," http://www.globalsolutions.org/issues/international_criminal_court/Bush_Policy.

103. Connexions, "Definition of Biodiversity," http://cnx.org/content/m12151/latest.

104. John M. Broder, "Struggling to Save the Planet, with a Thesaurus," *New York Times,* 2 May 2009, pp. A1, A11.

105. See the 2007 report of the Intergovernmental Panel on Climate at http://www.ipcc.ch. Critics, however, claimed bias in this report. For an analysis, see Gautam Naik and Keith Johnson, "Controversies Create Opening for Critics," *Wall Street Journal,* 17 February 2010, p. A4.

106. Gautam Naik, "Climate Study Cites 2000s as Warmest Decade," *Wall Street Journal,* 29 July 2010, p. A4.

107. See UNFCCC, "Kyoto Protocol," http://unfccc.int/kyoto_protocol/items/2830.php.

108. Andrew C. Revkin and John M. Broder, "Grudging Accord on Climate, Along with Plenty of Discord," *New York Times*, 20 December 2009, pp. A1, A4.

109. See Paul R. Brewer et al., "International Trust and Public Opinion about World Affairs," *American Journal of Political Science* 48 (January 2004): 93, 109. They say, "Most Americans see the realm of international relations as resembling the 'state of nature' described by Hobbes. Put more simply, they see it as a 'dog-eat-dog' world" (p. 105).

110. Joseph Kahn and Judith Miller, "Getting Tough on Gangsters, High Tech and Global," *New York Times*, 15 December 2000, p. A7.

111. *Global Views 2008* (Chicago: Chicago Council on Global Affairs, 2008). The report is available at http://www.thechicagocouncil.org/curr_pos.php.

112. Benjamin I. Page and Marshall M. Bouton, *The Foreign Policy Disconnect: What Americans Want from Our Leaders but Don't Get* (Chicago: University of Chicago Press, 2006), p. 227.

113. Lawrence R. Jacobs and Benjamin I. Page, "Who Influences U.S. Foreign Policy?" *American Political Science Review* 99 (February 2005): 107–123.

114. Charles Kegley and Eugene Wittkopf, *American Foreign Policy: Pattern and Process,* 4th ed. (New York: St. Martin's Press, 1991), pp. 272–273.

115. Page and Bouton, p. 241.

116. Ibid., pp. 162–163.

117. U.S. Politics Online, "USAF Wants Big Bucks to Keep Flying," forum commentary, 18–25 February 2008, http://www.uspoliticsonline.com/breaking-news-politics/43985-usaf-wants-big-bucks-keep-flying.html.

118. August Cole, "Fight over F-22's Future to Test Defense Overhaul," *Wall Street Journal,* 8 April 2009, p. A5.

119. Leslie Wayne, "Air Force Jet Wins Battle in Congress," *New York Times,* 28 September 2006, p. C1.

Index of References

Index

California Politics
and Government

California Politics and Government

A Practical Approach

ELEVENTH EDITION

LARRY N. GERSTON
San Jose State University

TERRY CHRISTENSEN
San Jose State University

Australia • Brazil • Japan • Korea • Mexico • Singapore • Spain • United Kingdom • United States

WADSWORTH
CENGAGE Learning

California Politics and Government: A Practical Approach, Eleventh Edition
Larry N. Gerston, Terry Christensen

Senior Publisher: Suzanne Jeans

Executive Editor: Carolyn Merrill

Marketing Manager: Lydia Lestar

Editorial Assistant: Nina Wasserman

Media Editor: Laura Hildebrand

Marketing Coordinator: Josh Hendrick

Marketing Communications Manager: Heather Baxley

Content Project Manager: Susan Miscio

Senior Art Director: Linda Helcher

Production Technology Analyst: Jeff Joubert

Print Buyer: Fola Orekoya

Senior Rights Acquisition Manager, Text: Katie Huha

Production Service: Macmillan Publishing Services

Cover Designer: Lou Ann Thesing

Cover Image: Golden gate bridge ©Cheng Chang/ istockphoto
Beach ©Lee Pettet/istockphoto
Wind Turbine ©EuToch/istockphoto
Flag ©Lee Pettet/istockphoto
Buildings ©S. Greg Panosian/istockphoto
Surfers ©DNY59/istockphoto
Vineyard ©Galina Barskaya/istockphoto
Jerry Brown © Justin Sullivan/©Getty Images

Compositor: MPS Limited, a Macmillan Company

For product information and technology assistance, contact us at **Cengage Learning Customer & Sales Support, 1-800-354-9706**

For permission to use material from this text or product, submit all requests online at **www.cengage.com/permissions**.
Further permissions questions can be e-mailed to **permissionrequest@cengage.com**

Library of Congress Control Number: 2010939141

ISBN-13: 978-0-495-91345-0
ISBN-10: 0-495-91345-6

Wadsworth
20 Channel Center Street
Boston, MA 02210
USA

Cengage Learning is a leading provider of customized learning solutions with office locations around the globe, including Singapore, the United Kingdom, Australia, Mexico, Brazil and Japan. Locate your local office at **international.cengage.com/region**

Cengage Learning products are represented in Canada by Nelson Education, Ltd.

For your course and learning solutions, visit **www.cengage.com**.
Purchase any of our products at your local college store
or at our preferred online store
www.cengagebrain.com.

Printed in the United States of America
1 2 3 4 5 6 7 14 13 12 11 10

*To the futures of Adam and Marisa, Lee, and Rachel Gerston
and
the memories of Anna and Teter Christensen and Tillie and Chester Welliever*

Contents

Preface

Whe n we published the first edition of *California Politics and Government: A Practical Approach* twenty years ago, we promised a book that emphasized the "nuts and bolts" of the state's political processes and institutions. We remain equally committed to that objective in this, our eleventh, edition. Within the complexities of cumbersome institutions, competing interests, and over-the-top personalities exists a state government responsible to a population of more than 38 million people. Our task then and our task today remains the same: to help explain how these two entities interact in the political collage otherwise known as California.

Our fascination grows with every edition. The more we observe California, the more we realize that the state doesn't fit any single neat pattern or formula. Rather, it is an awkward combination of historic traditions and contemporary extremes perched atop a wobbly governmental foundation of dysfunctional institutions. The more reformers attempt to pull the state's politics and policies in a new direction, the more vested interests protect their turfs by exercising a variety of strategies. Sometimes amazed, sometimes aghast, and often apathetic, Californians struggle to make sense of this perplexing picture.

Our ongoing effort is to clarify confusion—not an easy task, given California's composition. Some themes persist year after year with great certainty. Conflicts between the governor and legislature, Democrats and Republicans, and tax cutters and government boosters are standard fare. Other topics, such as immigration, gay rights, and education reform, sometimes clog the agenda, only to disappear until they reappear. Through it all, the state's policymakers struggle to meet ever-swelling needs with too few resources. All this takes place in a state where the "haves" and "have-nots" seem to grow farther apart each year. Still, California moves, even if the direction is tentative and the beat irregular.

All of which takes us to the eleventh edition. As with the past editions, we honor the timeless topics that have historically defined our reporting. We touch on institutions, their leaders, and issues that affect most of us one way or another.

Perennial themes such as gridlock, direct democracy, and contentious relations with the federal government receive attention because they are, well, perennial! At the same time, we flow with the action on current themes such as soaring interest group influence, the power of money, deteriorating infrastructure, and a state on the verge of bankruptcy.

Specifically, we focus on election changes in the executive and legislative branches, along with new appointments to the courts. We are also drawn to the growing fiscal crisis at the local government level, the soaring campaign contributions of interest groups, and the increasing power of the Latino vote in a state where racial and ethnic minorities now comprise a solid majority. In addition, we discuss the impact of the 2010 congressional elections; although the national Republican wave stopped at the Sierras, California's role in Washington was impacted greatly by the switch from Democratic to Republican control in the House of Representatives.

But just because we focus on these themes today doesn't mean the same combination of issues will persist tomorrow. Like the changes with a twist of a kaleidoscope, California is always on the move. Our challenge is to keep up and explain the state's many mysteries.

This book is an effort to move us along that path. Because we focus on nuts and bolts, we offer extended opportunities at the end of each chapter to explore topics through books and various Web sites online. We also include a Glossary that contains definitions of the key terms, offices, institutions, and events printed in bold throughout the book. Combined, these tools provide access to and elaboration about the many themes discussed in *California Politics and Government*.

Many have assisted us on our journey. Our friends in politics, elected office, and the media, as well as fellow academics, have provided valuable information and insights at numerous junctures. We would especially like to thank the following reviewers whose comments helped mold this edition: Maria Sampanis, California State University, Sacramento; Robert Melsh, Mt. San Jacinto College; Ted Lempert, University of California, Berkeley; and Alex Yamato, San José State University. Most of all, we continue to benefit from our students who, with their penetrating questions and thoughtful comments, push us to examine topics that we might not have considered otherwise. Some have themselves gone on to their own political careers and have made us equally proud.

Finally, we are indebted to the attentive production staff at Cengage, who artfully managed an incredibly tight schedule to facilitate production within weeks of the November 2, 2010, election. They include Carolyn Merrill, executive editor; Lydia LeStar, marketing manager; Susan Miscio, content project manager; and Charu Khanna of MPS Ltd. who patiently and efficiently worked with us from manuscript to page proofs. All these people and others helped us to complete this project to the best of our abilities. Of course, in the end we assume full responsibility for the product.

Larry N. Gerston
Terry Christensen
December 31, 2010

About the Authors

Larry N. Gerston professor of political science at San Jose State University, interacts with the political process as both an author and an observer. As an author, he has written nine academic books in addition to *California Politics and Government: A Practical Approach*, including *Making Public Policy: From Conflict to Resolution* (1983), *Politics in the Golden State* (with Terry Christensen, 1984), *The Deregulated Society* (with Cynthia Fraleigh and Robert Schwab, 1988), *American Government: Politics, Process and Policies* (1993), *Public Policy: Process and Principles* (1987), *Public Policymaking in a Democratic Society: A Guide to Civic Engagement* (2002), *Recall! California's Political Earthquake* (with Christensen, 2004), *American Federalism: A Concise Introduction* (2007), and *Confronting Reality: Ten Issues Threatening to Implode American Society and How We Can Fix It* (2009). On a lighter note, Gerston has written *The Costco Experience: An Unofficial Survivor's Guide* (2003). As an observer, Gerston serves as the political analyst for NBC11, a San Francisco Bay Area television station. He has written more than a hundred op-ed pieces for newspapers throughout the nation and appears regularly as a motivational speaker. Gerston is a consultant for the Center for Civic Education, where he frequently leads seminars for the Project Citizen public policy program.

Terry Christensen was named San Jose State University's Outstanding Professor in 1998. He has also won awards for his scholarship and his service to the university. He is the author or co-author of nine books and frequent newspaper op-ed pieces. Local and national media regularly call on him for analysis of politics in California and Silicon Valley. In addition to other books co-authored with Larry Gerston, his works include *Projecting Politics: Political Messages in American Films* (2005), co-authored by Peter Haas, and *Local Politics: A Practical Guide to Governing at the Grassroots* (2006), co-authored by Tom Hogen-Esch. Christensen is experienced in practical politics at the local level as an advocate of policy proposals, an adviser to grassroots groups, and an adviser and mentor to candidates for local office—many of whom are his former students. He has served on numerous civic committees and commissions. Most recently, he served as the founding executive director of CommUniverCity San Jose (www.communivercitysanjose.org), a partnership between the City of San Jose, San Jose State University, and adjacent neighborhoods. Through CommUniverCity, hundreds of students are learning about life and politics in their community through service projects selected by neighborhood residents and supported by the city.

1

California's People, Economy, and Politics: Yesterday, Today, and Tomorrow

CHAPTER CONTENTS

Colonization, Rebellion, and Statehood

Railroads, Machines, and Reform

The Workingmen's Party

The Progressives

The Great Depression and World War II

Growth, Change, and Political Turmoil

California Today

California's People, Economy, and Politics

Is California a failed state? That term is usually applied to collapsed nation-states like Somalia—places that lack a cohesive central government and often are caught up in civil war. But after a decade of budget deficits and gridlock in the California state capital, many observers, including even California loyalists like historian Kevin Starr, were asking that question.[1] To many, California politics seems turbulent and unpredictable. Political leaders rise and fall precipitately. Wealthy candidates and special interests are accused of "buying" elections. The governor and the legislature can't agree on a budget on schedule, as a prolonged recession grips the economy. While state government stalls in gridlock, issues are referred to the voters, who are often confused by complex and sometimes obscure ballot measures. Some say this is democracy gone mad; others have concluded that California is ungovernable.

But however volatile or dysfunctional California politics may seem, it is serious business that affects us all, and it can be understood by examining the history and present characteristics of our state—especially its changing population and economy. Wave after wave of immigrants have made California a diverse, multicultural society, while new technologies repeatedly transform the state's economy. The resulting disparate demographic and economic interests compete for the benefits and protections conferred by government and thus shape the state's politics. To understand California today—and tomorrow—we need to know a little about its past and about the development of the competing interests within the state.

COLONIZATION, REBELLION, AND STATEHOOD

The first Californians probably were immigrants like the rest of us who followed. Archaeologists believe that the ancestors of American Indians crossed an ice or land bridge or traveled by sea from Asia to Alaska thousands of years ago and then headed south. Europeans began exploring the California coast in the early 1500s, but colonization didn't start until 1769, when the Spanish established a string of missions and military outposts. About 300,000 Native Americans were living here then, mostly near the coast.

These native Californians were brought to the missions as Catholic converts and workers, but European diseases and the destruction of the native culture reduced their numbers to about 100,000 by 1849. Disease and massacres wiped out entire tribes, and the Indian population continued to diminish throughout the nineteenth century. Today, less than 1 percent of California's population is Native American, and many feel alienated from a society that has overwhelmed their peoples, cultures, and traditions. Chronic poverty, however, has been alleviated for some by the development of casinos on native lands, a phenomenon that has also made some tribes major players in state politics.

Apart from building missions, the Spaniards did little to develop their faraway possession. Not much changed when Mexico, which included California within its boundaries, declared its independence from Spain in 1822. A few thousand Mexicans quietly raised cattle on vast ranches and continued to build the province's small towns around their central plazas.

Meanwhile, expansionist interests in the United States coveted California's rich lands and access to the Pacific Ocean. When Mexico and the United States went to war over Texas in 1846, Yankee immigrants to California seized the moment and declared independence from Mexico. After the U.S. victory, Mexico surrendered its claim to lands extending from Texas to California. By this time, foreigners already outnumbered Californians of Spanish ancestry 9,000 to 7,500.

In 1848 gold was discovered, and the '49ers who started arriving the next year brought the nonnative population to 264,000 by 1852. Many immigrants came directly from Europe. The first Chinese people also arrived to work in the mines, which yielded more than a billion dollars' worth of gold in five years.

The surge in population and commerce moved the new Californians to political action. A constitutional convention consisting of forty-eight delegates (only seven of whom were native Californians) threw together the **Constitution of 1849** by cutting and pasting from the constitutions of existing states; the convention requested statehood, which the U.S. Congress quickly granted. The constitutional structure of the new state was remarkably similar to what we have today, with a two-house legislature; a supreme court; and an executive branch consisting of a governor, lieutenant governor, controller, attorney general, and superintendent of public instruction. The constitution also included a bill of rights, but only white males were allowed to vote. California's Chinese, African American, and Native American residents were soon prohibited by law from owning land, testifying in court, or attending public schools.

The voters approved the constitution, and San Jose became the first state capital. With housing in short supply, many newly elected legislators had to lodge in tents, and the primitive living conditions were exacerbated by heavy rain and flooding. Despite these conditions, the partying politicians became known—and discredited—as "the legislature of a thousand drinks." The state capital soon moved on to Vallejo and Benicia, finally settling in 1854 in Sacramento—closer to the gold fields.

As the gold rush ended, a land rush began. While small homesteads were common in other states because of federal ownership of land, much of California had been divided into huge tracts by Spanish and Mexican land grants. As early as 1870, a few hundred men owned most of the farmland. Their ranches were the forerunners of the agribusiness corporations of today, and as the mainstay of the state's economy, they exercised even more clout than their modern successors.

In less than fifty years, California had belonged to three different nations. During the same period, its economy and population had changed dramatically as hundreds of thousands of immigrants from all over the world came to claim their share of the "Golden State." The pattern of a rapidly evolving, multicultural polity was set.

RAILROADS, MACHINES, AND REFORM

Technology wrought the next transformation in the form of railroads. In 1861 Sacramento merchants Charles Crocker, Mark Hopkins, Collis Huntington, and Leland Stanford founded the railroad that would become the **Southern Pacific Railroad**. They persuaded Congress to provide millions of dollars in land grants and loan subsidies for a railroad linking California with the eastern United States, thus greatly expanding the market for California's products. Stanford, then governor, used his influence to provide state assistance. Cities and counties also contributed—under the threat of being bypassed by the railroad. To obtain workers at cheap rates, the railroad builders imported 15,000 Chinese laborers.

When the transcontinental track was completed in 1869, the Southern Pacific expanded its system throughout the state by building new lines and buying up existing ones. The railroad crushed competitors by cutting its shipping charges, and by the 1880s it had become the state's dominant transportation company, as well as its largest private landowner, in possession of 11 percent of the entire state. With its business agents doubling as political representatives in almost every California city and county, the Southern Pacific soon developed a formidable political machine. "The Octopus," as novelist Frank Norris called the railroad, placed allies in state and local offices through its control of both the Republican and Democratic parties. Once there, these officials protected the interests of the Southern Pacific if they wanted to continue in office. County tax assessors who were supported by the political machine set favorable tax rates for the railroad and its allies, while the machine-controlled legislature ensured a hands-off policy by state government.

THE WORKINGMEN'S PARTY

People in small towns and rural areas who were unwilling to support the machine lost jobs, business, and other benefits. Some moved to cities, especially San Francisco, where manufacturing jobs were available. Chinese workers who had been brought to California to build the railroad also sought work in the cities when it was completed. But when a depression in the 1870s made jobs scarce, these newcomers faced hostile treatment from earlier immigrants. Led by Denis Kearney, Irish immigrants became the core of the **Workingmen's Party**, a political organization that blamed economic difficulties on the railroad and the Chinese.

Small farmers who opposed the railroad united through the Grange movement. In 1879 the Grangers and the Workingmen's Party called California's second constitutional convention in hopes of breaking the railroad's hold on the state. The **Constitution of 1879** mandated regulation of railroads, utilities, banks, and other corporations. An elected State Board of Equalization was set up to ensure the fairness of local tax assessments on railroads and their friends, as well as their enemies. The new constitution also prohibited the Chinese from owning land, voting, or working for state or local government.

The railroad soon reclaimed power, however, gaining control of the very agencies that were created to regulate it. Nonetheless, the efforts made during this period to regulate big business and control racial relations became recurring themes in California life and politics, and much of the Constitution of 1879 remains intact today.

THE PROGRESSIVES

The growth fostered by the railroad eventually produced a new middle class, encompassing merchants, doctors, lawyers, teachers, and skilled workers, who were not dependent on the railroad. They objected to the corrupt practices and favoritism of the railroad's political machine, which they thought was restraining economic development in their communities. The new middle class demanded honesty and competence, which they called "good government." In 1907 a number of these crusaders established the Lincoln-Roosevelt League, a reform group within the Republican Party, and became part of the national Progressive movement. Their leader, Hiram Johnson, was elected governor in 1910; they also captured control of the state legislature.

To break the power of the machine, the **Progressives** introduced a wave of reforms that shape California politics to this day. Predictably, they created a new regulatory agency for the railroads and utilities, the Public Utilities Commission (PUC). Most of their reforms, however, aimed at weakening the political parties as tools of bosses and machines. Instead of party bosses handpicking candidates at party conventions, the voters now were given the power to select their party's nominees for office in primary elections. Cross-filing further diluted party power by allowing candidates to file for and win the nominations of more than one political party. The Progressives made city and county elections "nonpartisan" by removing party labels from local ballots altogether. They also created a civil service system to select state employees on the basis of their qualifications rather than their political connections.

Finally, the Progressives introduced direct democracy, which allowed the voters to amend the constitution and create laws through initiatives and referenda and to recall, or remove, elected officials before their terms expired. Supporters of an initiative, referendum, or recall must circulate petitions and collect a specified number of signatures of registered voters before it becomes a ballot measure or proposition.

Like the Workingmen's Party before them, the Progressives were concerned about immigration. Antagonism toward recent Japanese immigrants (who numbered 72,000 by 1910) resulted in Progressive support for a ban on land ownership by aliens and the National Immigration Act of 1924, which effectively halted Asian immigration. Other, more positive changes by the Progressives included giving women the right to vote, passing child labor and workers' compensation laws, and implementing conservation programs to protect natural resources.

Thanks largely to the Progressive reforms, the railroad's political machine eventually died; California's increasingly diverse economy had also weakened the machine, however, as the emerging oil, automobile, and trucking industries gave the state alternative means of transportation and shipping. These and other growing industries ultimately restructured economic and political power in California.

The reform movement waned in the 1920s, but the Progressive legacy of weak political parties and direct democracy opened up California's politics to its citizens, as well as to powerful interest groups and individual candidates with strong personalities. A long and detailed constitution is also part of the legacy. The Progressives instituted their reforms by amending (and thus lengthening) the Constitution of 1879 rather than calling for a new constitutional convention.

Direct democracy subsequently enabled voters and interest groups to amend the constitution, which has become an extraordinarily lengthy document over time.

THE GREAT DEPRESSION AND WORLD WAR II

California's population grew by more than 2 million in the 1920s (see Table 1.1). Most of the newcomers headed for Los Angeles, where employment opportunities in shipping, filmmaking, and manufacturing (of clothing, automobiles, and aircraft) abounded. Then came the Great Depression of the 1930s, which saw the unemployment rate soar from 3 percent in 1925 to 33 percent by 1933. Even so, more than a million people still came to California, including thousands of poor white immigrants from the "dust bowl" of the drought-impacted Midwest. Many wandered through California's great Central Valley in search of work, displacing Mexicans—who earlier had supplanted the Chinese and Japanese—as the state's farm workers. Racial antagonism ran high, and many Mexicans were arbitrarily sent back to Mexico. Labor unrest reached a crescendo in the early 1930s, as workers on farms, in canneries, and on the docks of San Francisco and Los Angeles fought for higher wages and an eight-hour workday.

The immigrants and union activists of the 1920s and 1930s also changed California politics. Many registered as Democrats, thus challenging the dominant Republicans. The Depression and President Franklin Roosevelt's popular New Deal helped the Democrats become California's majority party in registration, although winning elections proved more difficult. Their biggest boost came from Upton Sinclair, a novelist, a socialist, and the Democratic candidate for governor in 1934.

T A B L E 1.1 California's Population Growth, Selected Decades, 1850–2010

Year	Population	Percentage of U.S. Population
1850	93,000	0.4
1900	1,485,000	2.0
1950	10,643,000	7.0
1960	15,863,000	8.8
1970	20,039,000	9.8
1980	23,780,000	10.5
1990	29,733,000	11.7
2000	33,871,648	12.0
2010	38,648,090	12.6

SOURCE: California Department of Finance and U.S. Census.

Sinclair's End Poverty in California (EPIC) movement almost led to an election victory, but the state's conservative establishment spent an unprecedented $10 million to defeat him. The Democrats finally gained the governorship in 1938, but their candidate, Culbert Olson, was the only Democratic winner between 1894 and 1958.

World War II revived the economic boom. The federal government spent $35 billion in California between 1940 and 1946, creating 500,000 jobs in defense industries. California's radio, electronics, and aircraft industries grew at phenomenal rates. The jobs brought new immigrants, including many African Americans, whose proportion of the state's population quadrupled during the 1940s. African Americans were nevertheless on the periphery of the state's racial conflicts—unlike Japanese and Mexican Americans. During the war, more than 100,000 Japanese Americans, suspected of loyalty to their ancestral homeland, were sent to prison camps (officially called internment centers). Antagonism toward Mexican Americans resulted in the Zoot Suit Riots in Los Angeles in 1943, when Anglo sailors and police attacked Mexican Americans wearing distinctive suits featuring long jackets with wide lapels, padded shoulders, and high-waisted, pegged pants.

While the cities boomed, with defense industries becoming permanent fixtures and aerospace and electronics adding to the momentum, the Central Valley bloomed, thanks to water projects initiated by the state and federal governments during the 1930s. Dams and canals brought water to the desert and reaffirmed agriculture as a mainstay of California's economy.

Although the voters chose a Democratic governor during the Great Depression, they returned to the Republican fold as the economy revived. Earl Warren, one of a new breed of moderate, urbane Republicans, was elected governor in 1942, 1946, and 1950, becoming the only individual to win the office three times until Jerry Brown was elected in 2010. Warren used cross-filing to win the nominations of both parties and staked out a relationship with the voters that he claimed was above party politics. A classic example of California's personality-oriented politics, Warren left the state in 1953 to become chief justice of the United States Supreme Court.

GROWTH, CHANGE, AND POLITICAL TURMOIL

In 1958 the Republican Party was in disarray because of infighting. Californians elected a Democratic governor, Edmund G. "Pat" Brown, and a Democratic majority in the state legislature. To prevent Republicans from taking advantage of cross-filing again, the state's new leaders immediately outlawed that electoral device.

In control of both the governor's office and the legislature for the first time in the twentieth century, Democrats moved aggressively to develop the state's infrastructure. Completion of the massive California Water Project, construction of the state highway network, and creation of an unparalleled higher education system were among the advances to accommodate a growing population.

Meanwhile, in the 1960s, California's black and Latino minorities became more assertive, pushing for civil rights, desegregation of schools, access to higher education, and improved treatment for California's predominantly Latino farm workers.

The demands of minority groups alienated some white voters, however, and the Democratic programs were expensive. After opening their purse strings during the eight-year tenure of Pat Brown, Californians became more cautious about the state's direction. Race riots precipitated by police brutality in Los Angeles, along with student unrest over the Vietnam War, also turned the voters against liberal Democrats such as Brown.

In 1966 Republican Ronald Reagan was elected governor; he moved the state in a more conservative direction before going on to serve as president. His successor as governor, Democrat Edmund G. "Jerry" Brown, Jr., was the son of the earlier governor Brown and a liberal on social issues. Like Reagan, however, the younger Brown led California away from spending on growth-inducing infrastructure, such as highways and schools. In 1978 the voters solidified this change with the watershed tax-cutting initiative, Proposition 13 (see Chapter 8). Although Democrats have long outnumbered Republicans among California's registered voters, Brown was followed by Republicans George Deukmejian in 1982 and Pete Wilson in 1990, each of whom served two terms in office.

In 1998 California elected Gray Davis, its first Democratic governor in sixteen years. He was reelected in 2002 despite voter concerns about an energy crisis, a recession, and a growing budget deficit. As a consequence of these crises and what some perceived as an arrogant attitude, Davis faced an unprecedented recall election in October 2003. The voters removed him from office and replaced him with Republican Arnold Schwarzenegger, who was reelected in 2006.

In 2010, former governor Jerry Brown attempted a comeback and made history as California's youngest and oldest governor when he defeated former eBay chief executive Meg Whitman, a Republican who broke the U.S. campaign spending record for any office other than the presidency.

Democrats have had more consistent success in the state legislature and the congressional delegation, where they have been the dominant party since 1960. California voters have also opted for Democrats in every presidential election since 1988.

The challenges of governing California have been exacerbated by recurring conflicts between a Democratic legislature and Republican governors, as well as by the constitutional requirement for a supermajority to enact the state budget. Meanwhile, the voters have become increasingly involved in policymaking by initiative and referendum (see Chapter 2). Amendments to California's constitution, which require voter approval, appear on almost every state ballot. As a consequence, California's Constitution of 1879 has been amended over five hundred times; the U.S. Constitution includes just twenty-seven amendments.

Throughout these changes the state's population continued to grow, outpacing most other states so much that the California delegation to the U.S. House of Representatives now numbers fifty-three—more than twenty-one other states combined. Much of this growth was the result of a new wave of immigration facilitated by more flexible national immigration laws during the 1960s and 1970s. Immigration from Asia—especially from Southeast Asia after the Vietnam War—increased greatly. A national amnesty for undocumented residents also enabled many Mexicans to gain citizenship and bring their families from Mexico. In all, 85 percent of the 6 million newcomers and births in California in the 1980s were Asian, Latino, or black. Growth slowed in the 1990s, as 2 million more people left the state than came to it from other states, but California's population continued to increase as a result of births and immigration from abroad. In 1990 whites made up 57 percent of the state's population; by 2000 they were 47 percent.

Constantly increasing diversity enlivened California's culture and provided a steady flow of new workers, but it also increased tensions. Some affluent Californians retreated to gated communities; others fled the state. Racial conflict broke out between gangs on the streets and in prisons. As in difficult economic times throughout California's history, a recession during the early 1990s led many Californians, including Governor Wilson, to blame immigrants, especially those who were in California illegally. A series of ballot measures raised divisive race-related issues such as illegal immigration, bilingualism, and affirmative action. The issue of immigration enflames California politics to this day, although the increasing electoral clout of minorities and big public demonstrations in support of immigrants have provided some balance.

CALIFORNIA TODAY

If California were an independent nation, its economy would rank eighth in the world, with an annual gross national product exceeding $1.8 trillion. Much of the state's strength stems from its economic diversity (see Table 1.2). The elements of this diversity also constitute powerful political interests in state politics.

Half of California—mostly desert and mountains—is owned by the state and federal governments. In the rural areas, a few big farm corporations control much of the state's rich farmlands. These enormous corporate farms, known as agribusinesses, make California the nation's leading farm state, producing more than four hundred crops and providing nearly half of the vegetables, fruits, and nuts and a quarter of the dairy products consumed nationally. Grapes and wine are also top products, with 4,600 growers and 2,843 wineries.

State politics affects this huge economic force in many ways, but most notably in labor relations, environmental regulation, and water supply. Farmers and their employees have battled for decades over issues ranging from wages to safety. Under the leadership of Cesar Chavez and the United Farm Workers union, laborers organized. Supported by public boycotts of certain farm products, they achieved some improvements in working conditions, but the struggle continues today. California's agricultural industry is also caught up in environmental

T A B L E 1.2 California's Economy

Industrial Sector	Employees	Amount (in millions)
Professional and business services	2,035,300	$ 260,133
Education and health services	1,766,600	131,067
Leisure and hospitality services	1,483,600	75,639
Other services	477,300	42,196
Information	447,600	112,752
Government	2,482,000	216,764
Trade, transportation, and utilities	2,580,100	299,645
Manufacturing	1,237,200	181,134
Finance, insurance, and real estate	777,800	416,324
Construction	553,800	67,770
Mining and natural resources	24,700	43,333
Agriculture	389,100	36,600
Total, all sectors	14,255,100	$1,883,357

SOURCE: California Employment Development Department, www.edd.ca.gov (accessed May 2010); and U.S. Department of Commerce, Bureau of Economic Analysis, *Survey of Current Business*, June 2010.

issues, including the use of pesticides and the pollution of water supplies. In addition, booming growth in the Central Valley has urbanized some farmland, bringing "city" problems such as traffic and crowded schools to once-rural areas. The biggest issue, however, is always water. Most of California's cities and farmlands must import water from other parts of the state. Thanks to government subsidies, farmers claim 80 percent of the state's water supply at prices so low that they have little reason to improve inefficient irrigation systems. Meanwhile, the growth of urban areas is limited by their water supplies. Today, agriculture is in the thick of California politics as the state strives to balance an essential and powerful industry with the interests of its other citizens.

Agriculture is big business, but many more Californians work in manufacturing, especially in the aerospace, defense, and high-tech industries. Employment in manufacturing, however, has been declining in California for some years, especially after the federal government reduced military and defense spending in the 1990s when the collapse of communism in the Soviet Union brought an end to the Cold War. Employment in California shifted to postindustrial occupations such as retail sales, tourism, and services, although jobs in these sectors often pay low wages. Government policies on growth, the environment, and taxation affect all of these employment sectors, and all suffer when any one sector goes into a slump.

But the salvation of California's economy is its innovation, especially in telecommunications, entertainment, medical equipment, international trade, and above all, high-tech businesses spawned by the defense and aerospace companies that withered in the early 1990s. At the peak of the high-tech boom, California hosted one-fourth of the nation's high-tech firms, which provided nearly a million jobs.

Half of the nation's computer engineers worked in **Silicon Valley**, named after the silicon chip that revolutionized the computer industry. Running between San Jose and San Francisco, Silicon Valley became a center for innovation in technology from technical instruments, computer chips, networking equipment, workstations, and software to Internet-based dot-com businesses. Biomedical and pharmaceutical companies also proliferated, further contributing to California's transformation.

Computer technology also spurred rapid expansion of the entertainment industry, long a key component of California's economy. This growth particularly benefited the Los Angeles area, which had been hit hard by cuts in defense spending. Together, entertainment and tourism provide more than 500,000 jobs for Californians. Half of these are in film and television, but tourism remains a bastion of the economy, with California regularly ranking first among the states in visitors. Along with agriculture, high-tech, telecommunications, and other industries, these businesses have made California a leader in both international and domestic trade. All these industries are part of a globalized economy, which has bolstered and sustained California's economy. Much of this trade goes through the massive port complex of Los Angeles/Long Beach, as well as the San Francisco Bay Port of Oakland; much is also shipped by air.

The California economy has been on a roller coaster for the past few years, though. It has been in and out of recession—first in the early 1990s, and then again after the terrible events of September 11, 2001, when the California-centered Internet boom went bust as thousands of dot-com companies failed to generate projected profits. High-tech industry went into decline, and tens of thousands of workers lost their jobs, some of which were "off-shored" (moved to other countries). At about the same time, an energy crisis hit California. The state had deregulated energy suppliers in 1996 at the urging of industry, but by 2000, prices for gas and electricity had risen and parts of the state experienced shortages of electrical power. Belatedly, Governor Davis took action to resolve the crisis, but his initial caution and the exorbitant prices the state paid to ensure supplies caused his popularity to slump. All these factors combined to push California into a recession, with unemployment reaching 7 percent statewide and 9 percent in Silicon Valley in 2003 (the national rate was 5.9 percent).

When tax revenues rose during the heady days of the dot-coms, Governor Davis and the legislature had expanded programs and cut some fees and taxes. But when the boom ended, tax revenues declined precipitously, producing a state budget deficit that ultimately exceeded $30 billion. The deficit and other issues plunged California into a crisis that continued beyond the recall of Governor Davis in 2003. After a brief resurgence in 2006–2007, California's economy slipped back toward recession as unemployment reached 12.4 percent in 2010 (the U.S. rate was 9.7 percent). California had lost hundreds of thousands of manufacturing jobs since the 1990s as employers migrated to other states. By 2010, however, employment in all sectors, even film and television production, was in decline. The national home finance and foreclosure crisis also hit the California housing market and construction industry hard. Governor Schwarzenegger found himself faced with even bigger budget deficits than his predecessor—and nearly the same low public approval ratings.

Throughout its history, California has experienced economic ups and downs like these, recovered, reinvented itself, and moved on thanks to the diversity of its economy and its people and their ability to adapt to change. While some businesses have forsaken California for other states, complaining of burdensome regulation and the high cost of doing business in California, the Public Policy Institute of California reports that the skill and higher productivity of the state's workforce, access to capital, and quality of life compensate for such costs and keep the state attractive to many businesses.[2] Innovation continues to be an economic mainstay as well. Nanotechnology companies, for example, are concentrated in the San Francisco Bay Area, while biotechnology thrives in the San Diego region and green industry (for example, solar power and electric cars) booms throughout California. Small businesses—many of which are minority owned—form the backbone of the California economy, and while many struggle, others thrive. Most other states lack these advantages; some are dependent on a single industry or product, and none can match the energy and optimism brought by California's constant flow of immigrants eager to take jobs in the state's new and old industries.

California's globalized economy consistently attracts more immigrants than any other state; as of 2010, 26.6 percent of the state's population was foreign born, down slightly from a peak of 27.4 percent in 2007.[3] For perspective, the foreign-born share of the U.S. population was 12.2 percent. Fifty-six percent of California's immigrants are from Latin America (mostly Mexico), and 34 percent are from Asia (especially the Philippines, China, Vietnam, India, and Korea). Significantly for the California economy, 75 percent of the state's immigrant population is of working age (twenty-five to sixty-four).[4] An estimated 3 million immigrants are in California illegally. As a consequence of so much immigration, nearly 40 percent of all Californians over the age of five speak a language other than English at home, resulting in a major challenge for California schools. As in past centuries, immigration and language have been hot-button political issues in California in recent years.

The extent of California's ethnic diversity is indicated in Table 1.3. Although non-Latino whites remain the single largest group, they are no longer a majority. Overall, the black and white proportions of California's population have decreased, while Asian and Latino numbers have grown rapidly since the 1970s, slowly producing a shift in political power. As of 2008, 70.6 percent of students in California's public schools were nonwhite.[5]

The realization of the California dream is not shared equally among these groups. Although the median household income as of 2009 was $58,931 according the U.S. Census Bureau, the income of 15.3 percent of Californians fell below the federal poverty level—slightly above the national average—but the state's rate is considerably higher when the cost of living in California is factored in. Over half the students in California schools qualify for free or reduced-price meals.[6] The gap between rich and poor in California is among the largest in the United States and is still growing. Poverty is worst among Latinos, blacks, and Southeast Asians, who tend to hold low-paying service jobs; other Asians, along with Anglos, predominate in the more comfortable professional classes.

T A B L E 1.3 California's Racial and Ethnic Diversity

	1990	2000	2010
Non-Latino white	57.1%	47.3%	42.0%
Latino	26.0	32.4	37.1
Asian/Pacific Islander	9.2	11.4	12.4
Black	7.1	6.5	5.8
Native American	0.6	0.5	0.6
Mixed race	N.A.	1.9	2.1

SOURCE: U.S. Census; California Department of Finance, *Population Projections by Race/Ethnicity for California and Its Counties, 2000–2050,* www.dof.ca.gov (accessed June 18, 2010).

As the poor grow in number, some observers fear that California's middle class is vanishing. Once a majority, many of the middle class have slipped down the economic ladder, and others have simply fled the state. Instead of a class structure with a great bulge in the center, California now exhibits an "**hourglass economy**," with many people doing very well at the top, many barely getting by at the bottom, and fewer and fewer in the middle. Recent growth has concentrated in low- and high-wage jobs, and the income gap continues to widen.[7]

The costs of housing and health care are at the heart of this problem. The housing crisis of 2008–2010 increased the affordability of home ownership for some families, but many more suffered substantial losses of equity in their homes, and some lost their homes to foreclosure. With a median home price of $306,230 in 2010 compared with the U.S. median of $175,000, Californians still spent more of their income on housing than the national average, and fewer families were able to afford to own homes, especially in the coastal counties from San Diego to San Francisco. Homes were more affordable in inland California, however.[8] Overall, home ownership in California lags well behind the national average, especially for Latinos and blacks. Health care is also a problem for poor and working Californians. Over 24 percent (8.2 million) have no health insurance,[9] although coverage for children was expanded under the state's Healthy Families program established in 2001.

Geographic divisions complicate California's economic and ethnic diversity. In the past, the most pronounced of these divisions was between the northern and southern portions of the state. The San Francisco Bay Area tended to be diverse, liberal, and in elections, Democratic, while Southern California was staunchly Republican and much less diverse. However, with growth and greater diversity, Los Angeles also began voting Democratic. Today, the greatest division is between the coastal and inland regions of the state (see Figure 2-3). Democrats now outnumber Republicans in San Diego, for example, and even notoriously conservative Orange County has elected a Latina Democrat to Congress.

But even as the differences between northern and southern California fade, the contrast between coastal and inland California has increased.[10] The state's vast Central Valley has led the way in population and job growth, with cities from Sacramento to Fresno to Bakersfield gobbling up farmland. The Inland Empire, from Riverside to San Bernardino, has grown even more rapidly since the late 1990s. Although still sparsely populated, California's northern coast, Sierra Nevada, and southern desert regions are also growing, while retaining their own distinct identities. Water, agriculture, and the environment are major issues in all these areas. Except for Sacramento, inland California is more conservative than the coastal region of the state. Perhaps ironically, a recent study showed that the liberal counties of the coast contribute more per capita in state taxes, and the conservative inland counties receive more per capita for social service programs.[11] While coastal California remains politically dominant, the impact of inland areas on California politics increases with every election.

CALIFORNIA'S PEOPLE, ECONOMY, AND POLITICS

All these elements of California's economic, demographic, and geographic diversity vie with one another for political influence in the context of political structures that were created more than a hundred years ago. Dissatisfaction with this system has resulted in dozens of reforms by ballot measure, a recall election, and more recently, calls for a constitutional convention. Voter frustration is at a peak. As of 2010, only 18 percent of Californians felt the state was "going in the right direction" (compared with 55 percent in 2007); only 23 percent approved of the governor's performance (compared with 57 percent in 2007); and 16 percent approved of the performance of the legislature (compared with 41 percent in 2007).[12] Perhaps people see California as a failed state, or maybe they're just frustrated with the current leadership. A majority, however, support constitutional reform,[13] which could be done piecemeal through ballot measures or more comprehensively through a constitutional convention. A convention can be proposed by a two-thirds vote of the state legislature (which some consider unlikely) and then approved by the voters. In the chapters that follow, we'll see how the diverse interests of our state operate in the current political system and gain an understanding of how it all works, why voters and others may feel frustration, and what some are doing to bring about change even as others resist.

NOTES

1. Quoted in Paul Harris, "Will California Become America's First Failed State?" *Guardian.co.uk,* October 5, 2009, www.guardian.co.uk/world/2009/oct/04/california-failing-state-debt (accessed June 14, 2010). See also www.newsweek.com/2010/01/25/california-america-s-first-failed-state.html (accessed June 14, 2010). Googling "California as a failed state" produces 2,870,000 hits.

2. Jed Kolko, "California Economy: Planning for a Better Future," July 2009, www.ppic.org (accessed June 18, 2010).

3. USC Population Dynamics Research Group, School of Policy, Planning and Development, "The New Place of Birth Profile of Los Angeles and California Residents in 2010," www.usc.edu/schools/sppd/research/popdynamics/futures (accessed June 18, 2010).

4. Public Policy Institute of California, "Just the Facts: Immigrants in California," June 2008, www.ppic.org (accessed June 21, 2010).

5. Southern Education Foundation, January 31, 2010, www.southerneducation.org/pdf/New%20Diverse%20Majority-Summary.pdf (accessed June 21, 2010).

6. *Ibid.*

7. California Budget Project, "A Generation of Widening Inequality," August 2007, www.cpb.org (accessed June 21, 2010); and California Budget Project, "Policy Points: New Data Show That California's Income Gaps Continue to Widen," June 2009, www.cpb.org (accessed June 21, 2010).

8. For information about regional variation in housing costs, see the National Association of Home Builders (NAHB)/Wells Fargo Housing Opportunity Index (HOI), www.nahb.org/reference_list.aspx?sectionID=135 (accessed June 13, 2010).

9. UCLA Center for Health and Policy Research, reported in "The Uninsured," *San Jose Mercury News,* March 17, 2010, p. A1.

10. See Frederick Douzet and Kenneth P. Miller, "California's East-West Divide," in *The New Political Geography of California,* ed. Frederick Douzet, Thad Kousser, and Kenneth P. Miller (Berkeley: Berkeley Public Policy Press, Institute of Governmental Studies, University of California, 2008).

11. Report from the Legislative Analyst's Office cited in "California's Unequal Give and Take," *San Jose Mercury News,* June 21, 2010.

12. Public Policy Institute of California, "Statewide Survey Time Trends," www.ppic.org (accessed June 21, 2010).

13. Public Policy Institute of California, "Statewide Survey," September 9, 2009. Thirty-three percent supported major constitutional change, 36 percent supported minor changes, 24 percent thought California's constitution was fine as is, and 7 percent don't know.

LEARN MORE ON THE WEB

The California Constitution:
www.leginfo.ca.gov/const-toc.html

Events and personalities from California's past at the California Historical Society's online historical guide:
www.californiahistoricalsociety.org/timeline

Demographic data:
www.dof.ca.gov/research/demographic

Demographic and business comparisons between California and the United States:
www.quickfacts.census.gov/qfd/states/06000.html
quickfacts.census.gov/qfd

Digitized photographs, documents, newspapers, political cartoons, works of art, diaries, oral histories, advertising, and other cultural artifacts:
www.calisphere.universityofcalifornia.edu

LEARN MORE AT THE LIBRARY

Sandra Bass and Bruce M. Cain, eds. *Racial and Ethnic Politics in California*. Berkeley: Berkeley Public Policy Press, Institute of Governmental Studies, University of California, 2008.

Frederick Douzet, Thad Kousser, and Kenneth P. Miller, eds. *The New Political Geography of California*. Berkeley: Berkeley Public Policy Press, Institute of Governmental Studies, University of California, 2008.

Carey McWilliams. *California: The Great Exception*. Berkeley: University of California Press, 1949.

Frank Norris. *The Octopus*. New York: Penguin, 1901. A novel of nineteenth-century California.

Peter Schrag. *California: America's High-Stakes Experiment*. Berkeley: University of California Press, 2006. Especially good on the impact of immigration.

Kevin Starr. *California: A History*. New York: Modern Library, 2005.

2

California's Political Parties
and Direct Democracy

CHAPTER CONTENTS

In many states, political parties are strong organizations that control the selection of their nominees for public office, set out policy agendas based on their political ideologies, and can count on the loyalty of their voters. They link citizens to government, building coalitions of different interests and helping candidates make their case to the voters. This doesn't always happen in California, where party organizations are weak and voters make policy through the initiative process. As we'll learn in Chapter 5, political parties and party discipline are strong in the California state legislature, but that's not usually true of local or statewide party organizations. History tells us why: the Progressive reformers intentionally weakened political parties in order to rid California of the railroad-dominated political machine. In doing so, they unintentionally made candidate personalities, media manipulation, and fat campaign war chests as important in elections as political parties—and sometimes more so.

The Progressives also introduced **direct democracy**. Through the initiative, referendum, and recall, California voters gained the power to make law and even to overrule elected officials or remove them between elections. The reformers' intent was to empower citizens, but in practice, interest groups and politicians are more likely to use—and sometimes abuse—direct democracy.

Weak party organizations and direct democracy are fixtures of the state constitution and modern California politics. Some political observers argue that this combination promotes political disarray, governmental gridlock, and voters who are confused or turned off. Others believe that the system reflects a body of political values that eschews structured authority and maximizes opportunities for democratic decision making.

THE PROGRESSIVE LEGACY

To challenge the dominance of the Southern Pacific Railroad's political machine, Progressive reformers from both the Democratic and Republican parties focused on the machine's control of party conventions, where party leaders picked their candidates for various offices. Republican reformers scored the first breakthrough in 1908, when they succeeded in electing many antirailroad candidates to the state legislature. In 1909 the reform legislators replaced party conventions with **primary elections**, in which the registered voters of each party choose the nominee. Candidates who win their party's primary in these elections face the nominees of other parties in the November **general elections**. By instituting this system, the reformers ended the machine's control of the nomination process.

In 1910 Progressives won elections for both governor and the legislature. They introduced direct democracy to give policymaking authority to the people. They also replaced the party column ballot—which had permitted bloc voting for all the candidates of a single party by making just one mark—with separate balloting for each office. In addition, Progressive reformers introduced **cross-filing**, which permitted candidates of one party to seek the nominations of rival parties. Finally, the Progressives instituted **nonpartisan elections**, which eliminated party labels in contests to elect judges, school board members, and local government officials.

These changes reduced the railroad's control of the political parties, but they also sapped the strength of the party organizations. By allowing the voters to circumvent an unresponsive legislature, direct democracy paved the way for interest groups to dominate policymaking. Deletion of the party column ballot encouraged voters to cast their ballots for members of different parties for different offices (split-ticket voting), increasing the likelihood of a divided-party government (see Chapter 7). Nonpartisan local elections made it difficult for the parties to build their organizations at the grassroots level as well.

Party leaders tried to regain control of nominations by settling on favored candidates before the primary elections. Ultimately, however, such **preprimary endorsements** were also outlawed. Then in 1959, when Democrats gained control of the legislature for the first time in more than forty years, they outlawed cross-filing, which had been disproportionately helpful to Republican incumbents. This marked a return to the system in which candidates file for nomination for their own party only.

PARTY ORGANIZATION—STRUCTURE AND SUPPORTERS

Thanks to the Progressive reforms, political parties in California operate under unusual constraints. Although the original reformers have long since departed from the scene, the reform mentality remains very much a part of California's political culture.

Official Party Structures

According to the California State Elections Code, political parties can place candidates on the ballot by registering a number of members equal to 1 percent of the state vote in the most recent gubernatorial election or by submitting a petition with signatures amounting to 10 percent of that vote. After a party is qualified, if it retains the registration of at least 1 percent of the voters or if at least one of its candidates for any statewide office receives 2 percent of the votes cast, that party will be on the ballot in the next election. By virtue of their sizes, the Democratic and Republican parties have been fixtures on the ballot almost since statehood.

Minor parties, sometimes called **third parties**, are another story. Some have been on the ballot for decades; others have had brief political lives. In the 2006 general election, the Green, Libertarian, and Peace and Freedom parties each secured the minimum 2 percent of the vote for one of their statewide candidates, guaranteeing them positions on the ballot in 2010. No statewide candidates for the American Independent Party reached the 2 percent threshold, but enough voters are registered as American Independents to keep the party on the ballot. The total number of parties qualified for the 2010 California ballot, including Democrats and Republicans, is six.

Nonetheless, breaking the hold of the two major political parties has proved difficult. The Democratic and Republican candidates for governor garnered 95 percent of the vote in 2010—slightly less than the 98.2 percent shared by the Democratic and Republican candidates for president in 2008. Among the smaller parties, the Greens have been the most successful at winning elections. They have earned one seat in the state legislature and several seats at the local level.

California voters choose their party when they register to vote, which must be done fifteen or more days before the election. In 2010, 75.2 percent were registered as either Democrats or Republicans, 4.6 percent signed up with the

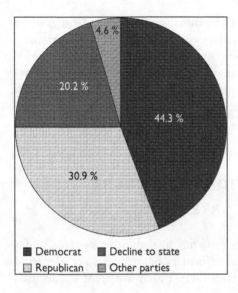

4.6 %

20.2 %

44.3 %

30.9 %

■ Democrat   ■ Decline to state
▣ Republican   ▨ Other parties

FIGURE 2.1 Party Registration in California, 2010. (Courtesy of Terry Christensen)
SOURCE: California Secretary of State.

other parties, and 20.2 percent declared themselves independent (officially known as "decline to state")—see Figure 2.1. The independent percentage has more than doubled since 1986, when it was just 9 percent.

For most of its history, California used **closed primary** elections to select the nominees of each party for state elective office and the U.S. Congress. Voters who are registered with a political party cast their ballots in the primary only for that party's nominees for various offices. The winners of each party's primary election face off in the November general election, when all voters are free to cast their ballots for the candidate of any of the parties. But in 2010, voters approved a "top two" or **open primary** system to go into effect in 2012. In an open primary, no matter what their own party, voters may choose their preferred candidate from any party; the top two vote getters face off in the November election, even if they're from the same party. Advocates of this system hope that instead of concentrating their appeals on the core of their own parties (liberals for Democrats and conservatives for Republicans), candidates will reach out to independent and moderate voters and that those elected will be more moderate and thus more willing to compromise when they get to Sacramento. In theory, this system could break the gridlock in the state capital, but whether it will do so remains to be seen. Meanwhile, the political parties have complained that the open primary system takes away the right of voters registered with their party to choose their own candidates, and it will almost certainly mean that candidates of the minor parties never appear on general election ballots. It's likely that the open primary system will be challenged in court.

Before the Great Depression, California was steadfastly Republican, but during the 1930s a Democratic majority emerged. Since then, the Democrats have dominated in voter registration (see Figure 2.2), although their lead declined from a peak of 60 percent of registered voters in 1942 to a low of 42.7 percent in 2006. Since then, partly due to an exciting presidential election in 2008, Democratic registration has risen slightly—to 44.5 percent in 2010. Meanwhile,

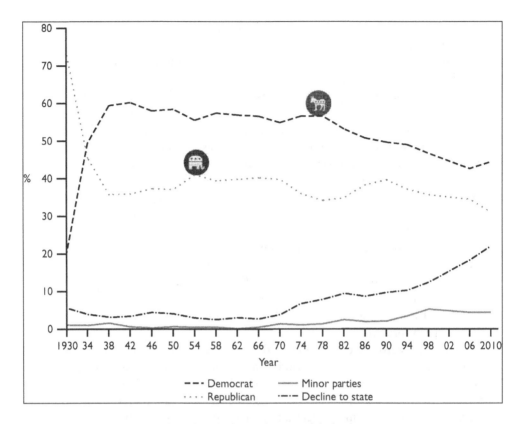

FIGURE 2.2 Party Registration during Gubernatorial Election Years
SOURCE: California Secretary of State

Republican registration has slipped to 30.9 percent. The independent percentage, however, has more than doubled since 1986, when it was just 9 percent. Despite their registration margin, the Democrats did not gain a majority in both houses of the state legislature until 1958. More dramatically, Republican candidates have won eight of the last thirteen gubernatorial elections.

State law dictates party organization, as it does registration and voting. Today's Democratic and Republican parties have similar structures, although the Democrats elect a few more party officials. The state **central committee** is the highest-ranking body in each party. All party candidates and officeholders are automatically members, along with county chairpersons. Officeholders and nominees of each party also appoint members. In addition, Democratic voters elect members from each assembly district, and Republican county central committees elect or appoint members. Each party's state central committee elects a state chair, who functions mainly as the party spokesperson. Although the position traditionally has been powerless, competition for it is sometimes intense.

Beneath the state central committee are county central committees. The voters registered with each party choose committee members every two years in the primary election. The party's nominees for state legislature are also members, as are those who win election. Critics say this system enables officeholders to dominate the grassroots members, but it also ensures that the two levels of party leadership are linked. The state and county party committees play an important role in generating volunteers and contributions for party candidates. They also draft policy positions for party platforms, although candidates and elected officials often ignore these. Despite their low public profile, county committees are sometimes sites of intense conflict among activists. Liberals usually dominate Democratic county central committees, whereas conservatives rule Republican committees. The religious right gained influence in the Republican Party during the 1990s by taking over a majority of the party's county central committees, but since then, moderate Republicans have regained influence in some counties.

California's political parties had an opportunity to strengthen their role in choosing party nominees when the United States Supreme Court overturned the state ban on preprimary endorsements in 1990. California Democrats responded quickly by establishing a preprimary endorsement process that required a candidate to secure at least 60 percent of the delegates at their state convention. The Republican Party declined such endorsements until 2005, when Governor Arnold Schwarzenegger won an early endorsement for reelection and avoided a divisive party primary.

Despite assertions of strengthened party organization, preprimary endorsements don't always matter to California voters. Since the court ruling, Democratic voters have rejected several statewide candidates officially endorsed by their party in primaries, while most party-endorsed candidates who succeeded were incumbents seeking reelection with no opposition in their own party. In 2010, however, the Democratic convention's preprimary endorsement of Assemblyman Dave Jones helped him win the Democratic nomination for state insurance commissioner in an otherwise low-profile race. The influence of such endorsements is limited by the inability of the parties to deliver organizational support to the chosen candidates and by high-spending campaigns and the media, but preprimary endorsements may become more significant when the open primary system goes into effect in 2012.

Party Supporters

Besides the official party organizations, a variety of caucuses and clubs are associated with both major parties. The California Republican Assembly is a staunchly conservative statewide grassroots organization that has dominated the Republican Party, thanks to an activist membership. Republican governor Arnold Schwarzenegger, a moderate, had difficulty with the conservatives in his own party. At the 2007 state party convention, he chastised his fellow California Republicans "for their insularity and narrowness," to which they responded "that they'd rather be ideologically principled than pander to moderates."[1] On the Democratic side, liberals dominate through the California Democratic Council, which comprises hundreds of local Democratic clubs organized by geography, gender, race, ethnicity, or sexual orientation.

Party activists such as these are a tiny percentage of the electorate, however. The remaining support base comes from citizens who designate their party affiliations when they register to vote and usually cast their ballots accordingly. Public opinion polls tell us that voters who prefer the Democratic Party tend to be sympathetic to the poor and immigrants; concerned about health care, education, and the environment; in favor of gay rights, gun control, and abortion rights; and supportive of tax increases to provide public services. Those who prefer the Republican Party are more likely to oppose these views and to worry more about big government and high taxes. Of course, many people mix these positions.[2]

Both major parties enjoy widespread support, but the more liberal Democratic Party fares better with blacks; city dwellers; union members; and residents of Los Angeles, Sacramento, and the San Francisco Bay Area (see Figure 2.3). Latino voters also favor Democrats, a tendency that was strengthened by Republican support for several statewide initiatives relating to immigration and affirmative action. Voters among most Asian nationalities identify themselves as Democratic, but some (notably Chinese and Vietnamese) lean Republican. Voters with ties to China, India, and Vietnam are also more likely to register as independents than are other Californians. As with Latinos, Asian loyalties to the California Republican Party were weakened by its sponsorship of initiatives perceived as anti-immigrant in the 1990s. Thanks in large part to the failure of Republicans to win support from minority voters, Democrats currently enjoy majorities in the state legislature and congressional delegation, and California is considered a solidly "blue" (Democratic) state—despite occasional Republican victories for statewide offices.

The more conservative Republican Party does better with whites, suburbanites, rural voters, and in Orange County, the Central Valley, and inland California, as well as with older, more affluent voters and with Christian conservatives. These constituencies are more likely to turn out to vote than those that support Democrats, which is why Republicans sometimes win statewide elections despite their registration disadvantage.

In the past, Republican candidates were also successful because they could often win the support of Democratic voters thanks to cross-filing (until 1958), charismatic candidates, clever campaigns, and split-ticket voting. But in the 1990s, ticket splitting declined, and instead, voters increasingly voted a straight party-line ticket—either all Democratic or all Republican.[3] This includes decline-to-state voters, who, contrary to common wisdom, are not necessarily "independent": 42 percent lean Democratic, and 28 percent lean Republican.[4] Some observers assert that the rightward thrust of the Republican Party drove independent voters to the Democrats and was even more important to the Democratic Party's continued success than was winning over minority voters.[5] Republicans who can present themselves as moderates, as did gubernatorial candidates Arnold Schwarzenegger in 2003 and Meg Whitman in 2010, may have proved this thesis by winning the votes of many independents and some Democrats, thus demonstrating that Californians will still indulge in split-ticket voting, at least on occasion.

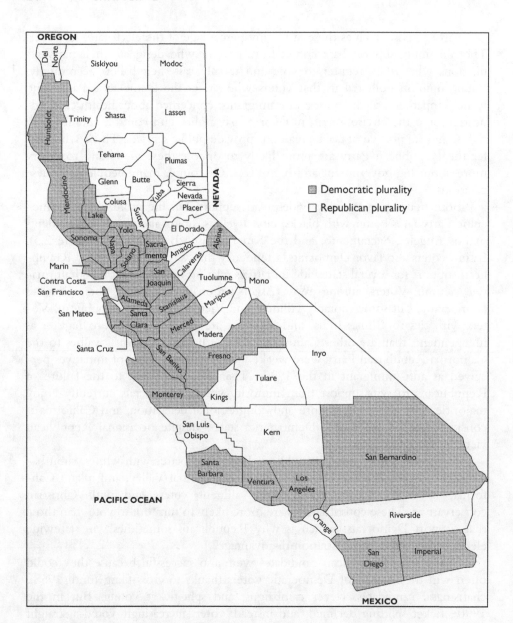

FIGURE 2.3 California's Partisan Division by County, 2010. (Courtesy of Terry Christensen)

SOURCE: California Secretary of State

DIRECT DEMOCRACY

Party politics is only one way Californians participate in the political process. To counter the railroad machine's control of state and local government, the Progressive reformers also guaranteed the people a say through the mechanisms of direct democracy introduced in Chapter 1: the recall, the referendum, and the initiative. Referenda and initiatives appear on our ballots as "propositions," with numbers assigned by the secretary of state; local measures are assigned letters by the county clerk.

The Recall

The least-used form of direct democracy is the **recall**, by which the voters can remove officeholders at all levels of government between scheduled elections. Advocates circulate a recall petition with a statement of their reasons for wanting the official in question to be removed from office. They must collect a specific number of voter signatures within a specific period. The numbers vary with the office in question. At the local level, for example, the number of signatures required to qualify a recall for the ballot varies between 10 and 30 percent of those who voted in the previous local election; these signatures must be collected over periods that vary between 40 and 160 days. A recall petition for a judge or a legislator requires signatures equaling 20 percent of the vote in the last state election, while for state executive officeholders, the figure is 12 percent. In all these cases, petitioners have 160 days to collect the signatures. If enough signatures are collected by advocates and validated by the secretary of state (for a state officeholder) or by the county clerk (for a local officeholder), an election is held. The ballot is simple: "Shall [name] be removed from the office of [title]?" The recall takes effect if a majority of voters vote yes, and then either an election or an appointment—whichever state or local law requires—fills the vacancy for the office. Elected officials who are recalled cannot be candidates in the replacement election.

Recalling state officeholders is easier in California than in the other seventeen states where recall is possible. All but one of these states require more signatures, and while any reason suffices in California, most other states require corruption or malfeasance by the officeholder. Nevertheless, recalls are rare in California, where the process has been used most extensively and successfully in local government, particularly by parents who are angry with school board members. Even so, only a dozen or so recalls are on local ballots in any given year, and only about half of the officials who face recall are removed from office. Two of California's state senators were recalled in 1913, but no other state officeholders were removed until 1995, when two legislators were recalled during a struggle between Democrats and Republicans over control of the state assembly.

Then, spectacularly, Governor Gray Davis was recalled in 2003. Davis had narrowly won reelection in November 2002; three months later, opponents launched their recall petition. Thirty-one previous attempts to recall a California governor had failed to make the ballot, and most political observers assumed that the petitioners would fail to acquire the 897,158 valid signatures required to qualify for an election. But they underestimated voter discontent, not only with Davis but also with the general condition of California politics. Despite his reelection, Davis's approval rating in public opinion polls had sunk to just 24 percent when signature gathering began.[6] His decline in popularity was a result of his cautious leadership during the state's energy crisis in 2001, a recession, a huge budget deficit, and the inability of the legislature and the governor to agree on solutions to these problems. Davis's aloof personality also contributed to his problems. His recall opponents discovered a groundswell of support, facilitated by conservative talk radio hosts and the availability of the Internet to circulate petitions. Even so, signature gathering was slow until Republican congressman Darrell Issa contributed $2 million to pay for professionals to assist.

In July 2003, the secretary of state certified that 1.3 million valid signatures had been gathered—far more than required—and the election was set for October. Ultimately, 135 candidates qualified to run, including actor Arnold Schwarzenegger. His seventy-five-day campaign took the state by storm, gaining far more media and public attention than any regular election in recent memory—thanks in part to his status as a movie star. On Election Day, 55.4 percent of the voters said yes to recall, and Schwarzenegger easily outpaced all other replacement candidates with 48.6 percent of the vote. For the first time in California history—and only the second time ever in the United States—a governor had been recalled.

The Referendum

The **referendum** is another form of direct democracy. A referendum allows the voters to nullify acts of the legislature. Referendum advocates have ninety days after the legislature makes a law to collect a number of signatures equal to 5 percent of the votes cast for governor in the previous election (510,756 based on the 2010 vote). Referenda are even rarer than recalls. Of the forty-seven referenda on California ballots since 1912, voters have rejected acts of the legislature twenty-eight times. In 2004, business groups qualified a referendum on health-care legislation approved in Governor Davis's last days in office. The hard-fought campaign pitted liberals, unions, and Democrats who supported the program against conservatives, business leaders, and Republicans. In the end, the voters narrowly rejected the health-care legislation, even though nearly 20 percent of Californians lacked health insurance. In 2008, competing gambling interests challenged the state's tribal gaming agreements in referenda, but the voters approved the agreements.

The Initiative

Recalls and referenda are reactions to what elected officials do; in contrast, the **initiative** allows citizens to make policy themselves by drafting a new law or a constitutional amendment and then circulating petitions to get it onto the ballot. Qualifying a proposed law requires a number of signatures equal to 5 percent of the votes cast for governor in the last election; constitutional amendments require a number of signatures equal to 8 percent (817,215 based on California's 2010 election). If enough valid signatures are obtained within 150 days, the initiative goes to the voters at the next election or, on rare occasions, in a special election called by the governor.

The subjects of initiatives vary wildly and are often controversial. In the past, voters have approved limits on bilingual education, banned the slaughter of horses for human consumption, and defined marriage as a relationship between a man and a woman only. Other recent propositions have dealt with tribal gambling

TABLE 2.1 The Track Record of State Initiatives

Time Period	Number	Number Adopted	Rejected
1912–1919	31	8	23
1920–1929	34	10	24
1930–1939	37	10	27
1940–1949	20	7	13
1950–1959	11	1	10
1960–1969	10	3	7
1970–1979	24	7	17
1980–1989	52	25	27
1990–1999	50	20	30
2000–2009	65	20	45
2010	11	4	7
Total	345	115 (33.3%)	230 (66.7%)

SOURCE: California Secretary of State.

(repeatedly), redistricting (repeatedly), stem cell research, DNA sampling, and mental health services. In 2010 voters considered legalization of marijuana, redistricting (again), suspension of air-pollution control laws, funding of local governments, and a vehicle license fee to support state parks—and more.

Twenty-three other states provide for the initiative, but few rely on it as heavily as California. Initiatives were common between 1912 and 1939, but declined in number during the next four decades (see Table 2.1). Then **political consultants**, interest groups, and governors rediscovered the initiative, and ballot measures proliferated. The 1988 and 1990 election year ballots witnessed an explosion, with eighteen initiatives on each. In 2010 voters faced a total of fourteen propositions in the primary and general elections, including both citizen-generated and legislative initiatives.

Legislative Initiatives, Constitutional Amendments, and Bonds

Propositions can also be placed on the ballot by the state legislature. Such **legislative initiatives** can include new laws that the legislature prefers to put before the voters rather than enact on its own, or proposed **constitutional amendments**, for which voter approval is compulsory. The 2010 open primary measure, for example, was put on the ballot by the legislature as part of a deal to win the vote of a Republican senator for the proposed budget.

Voter approval is also required when the governor or the legislature seeks to issue **bonds** (borrowing money) to finance parks, schools, transportation, or other capital-intensive projects. Few of these proposals are controversial, and more than 60 percent pass with minimal campaigning or spending. In the 2006 and 2008 elections, voters approved $29 billion in bonds for projects ranging from high-speed trains to aid for veterans.

THE POLITICS OF BALLOT PROPOSITIONS

The proliferation of ballot propositions is hardly the result of a sudden surge in democratic participation. Rather, it stems largely from the opportunism of special interests, individual politicians, and public relations firms. One man, hoping for cures to diseases suffered by his mother and son, provided the $3 million that funded the initiative to support stem cell research in 2004. Hundreds of millions of dollars have been spent on ballot measures regulating casinos on Native American lands, the most recent of which appeared on the ballot in 2008. In 2010, Pacific Gas and Electric and Mercury Insurance single-handedly funded separate initiatives that were clearly in their self-interest, and both the Chamber of Commerce and the Democratic Party funded measures affecting their own pet causes.

Although intended as mechanisms for citizens to shape policy, even the most grassroots-driven initiatives cost half a million dollars to qualify and millions more to mount a successful campaign. "If you pay enough," declared Ronald George, then chief justice of the California Supreme Court, "you can get anything on the ballot. You pay a little bit more and you get it passed."[7] In 2006 the pro and con campaigns on a proposition that would have imposed a modest fee on oil extraction spent $152 million, with oil companies spending $93 million on the measure. The campaigns for and against the 2008 proposition banning same-sex marriage spent a total of $83 million—much of it coming from out of state, because California is often seen as setting precedents for campaigns elsewhere. Total spending for proposition campaigns in any given election year now averages nearly $300 million. Much of it comes from corporations and unions. According to the California Fair Political Practices Commission, "These interests have spent hundreds of millions of dollars for and against ballot measures. They often win by spending money to defeat measures, which has the effect of maintaining the status quo... . The conclusion is inescapable: A handful of special interests have a disproportionate amount of influence on California elections and public policy."[8]

Besides wealthy individuals such as international financier George Soros (a supporter of drug decriminalization) and high-tech executive Tim Draper (a supporter of school vouchers), politicians have also discovered initiatives as a way to further their own careers or shape public policy. Republican governor Pete Wilson helped secure reelection in 1994 by sponsoring a successful measure on illegal immigration. In 2002 then movie star Arnold Schwarzenegger sponsored an initiative to fund after-school programs, advancing both that cause and his political career. As governor, Schwarzenegger tried to use ballot measures to further his agenda when thwarted by the Democratic majority in the legislature. In a succession of elections, he put forward initiatives addressing political and budget reforms, as well as bond measures. The bond measures passed, but most of the reforms were rejected by the voters, much to the disappointment of the governor.

Others also take advantage of direct democracy. Public relations firms and **political consultants**, virtual "guns for hire," have developed lucrative careers managing initiative and referenda campaigns; they offer expertise in public opinion polling, computer-targeted mailing, and television advertising—the staples of modern campaigns. Some firms generate initiatives themselves by conducting test mailings and preliminary polls in hopes of snagging big contracts from proposition sponsors. With millions of dollars in campaign spending hanging in the balance, big economic interests gain an advantage over grassroots efforts—surely not what the Progressives intended.

Nevertheless, direct democracy offers hope to the relatively powerless by enabling them to take their case to the public. In 2004 voters showed sympathy for those with little power when they approved Proposition 63, which increased taxes on the rich to fund mental health programs. In 2008, a proposition on the treatment of farm animals passed, despite the strong opposition of agribusiness. In 2010, environmentalists got a measure to fund state parks on the ballot and local governments qualified an initiative restricting state's ability to "take back" local funds at will (see Chapter 9). The former proposition was soundly defeated, but the latter passed easily. Almost every California ballot includes initiatives generated by grassroots groups. Although these initiatives are often defeated by well-funded corporate interests, at least direct democracy provides such groups an opportunity to make their cases.

Unfortunately, direct democracy does not necessarily result in good laws. Because self-interested sponsors draft initiatives and media masters run campaigns, careful and rational deliberation is rare. Flaws or contradictions in successful initiatives may take years to resolve. Sometimes this is done through the implementation of the measures by government agencies or through the legislative process. Increasingly, however, disputes about initiatives are resolved in state and federal courts, which must rule on whether the initiatives are consistent with other laws and with the state and federal constitutions. In recent years, courts have overturned all or parts of initiatives dealing with illegal immigration, campaign finance, and same-sex marriage, for example (see Chapter 6). Although such rulings seem to deny the will of the voters, the electorate cannot make laws that contradict the state or federal constitutions.

The increased use of direct democracy has also had an impact on the power of our elected representatives. Although we expect them to make policy, their ability to do so has been constrained by a sequence of initiatives in recent decades. This is particularly the case with the state budget, much of which is dictated by past ballot measures rather than the legislature or the governor.

The proliferation of initiatives, expensive and deceptive campaigns, flawed laws, and court interventions have annoyed voters and policymakers alike. Perhaps as a consequence, two-thirds of all initiatives are rejected (see Table 2–1). Although Californians express anger and frustration with the initiative process, a solid majority of survey respondents support direct democracy in concept. At the same time, a majority favors reforms such as a review of ballot language and legal issues before initiatives are placed on the ballot.[9]

POLITICAL PARTIES AND DIRECT DEMOCRACY

Authors Mark Baldassare and Cheryl Katz argue that California has evolved into a unique "hybrid democracy," with power divided between elected representatives and the public.[10] Partisan gridlock in Sacramento, voter distrust, and powerful interest groups (see Chapter 4) have resulted in the increased reliance on direct democracy to resolve issues, albeit often imperfectly. California's political parties can't break the gridlock or even control the choice of their own candidates in an electoral system in which money seems to trump party organization. Once elected, our officials seem unable to resolve the issues that confront us. Direct democracy provides an alternative—for political leaders, moneyed interests, and citizens—yet the proliferation of propositions further confounds voters. Does California have too much democracy? Sometimes it seems so. Some voters feel overwhelmed and turned off, but most manage to sift through complex initiatives and seductive campaigns to find the candidates and policies that suit their preferences.

NOTES

1. Peter Schrag, "On Race and Gender, the GOP's Tent Is Teeny," *Sacramento Bee,* September 19, 2007.

2. See Public Policy Institute of California, "California Voter and Party Profiles," *Just the Facts,* September 2009, www.ppic.org (accessed June 24, 2010); and past reports of the PPIC Statewide Survey, also at www.ppic.org.

3. See Gary C. Jacobson, "Partisanship and Ideological Polarization in the California Electorate," *State Politics and Policy Quarterly* 4 (2004): 113–139.

4. Public Policy Institute of California, "California's Likely Voters," *Just the Facts*, September 2009, www.ppic.org (accessed June 24, 2010).

5. Morris P. Fiorina and Samuel J. Abrams, "Is California Really a Blue State?" in *The New Political Geography of California,* ed. Frederick Douzet, Thad Kousser, and Kenneth P. Miller (Berkeley: Berkeley Public Policy Press, Institute of Governmental Studies, University of California, 2008).

6. "State of the Golden State," Public Policy Institute of California, San Francisco: Public Policy Institute of California, August 2003, www.ppic.org.

7. Ronald George, "Promoting Judicial Independence," *The Commonwealth*, February 2006, p. 9.

8. California Fair Political Practices Commission, *Big Money Talks*, March 2010, p. 6, www.fppc.ca.gov/reports/Report38104.pdf (accessed June 25, 2010).

9. Public Policy Institute of California, "Californians and Their Government," Statewide Survey, December 2008, www.ppic.org (accessed June 25, 2010).

10. Mark Baldassare and Cheryl Katz, *The Coming Age of Direct Democracy* (New York: Rowman & Littlefield, 2008).

LEARN MORE ON THE WEB

Polling data, including archives:
> www.field.com/fieldpoll or www.ppic.org

California's political parties:
> American Independent Party: www.aipca.org
> California Democratic Party: www.cadem.org
> California Republican Party: www.cagop.org
> Green Party of California: www.cagreens.org
> Libertarian Party of California: www.ca.lp.org
> Peace and Freedom Party: www.peaceandfreedom.org

Information on electoral reform:
> www.cgs.org

Information on ballot propositions:
> www.calvoter.org or www.ss.ca.gov

LEARN MORE AT THE LIBRARY

John Allswang. *The Initiative and Referendum in California, 1897–1998.* Stanford, Calif.: Stanford University Press, 2000.

Mark Baldassare and Cheryl Katz. *The Coming Age of Direct Democracy.* New York: Rowman & Littlefield, 2008.

Center for Government Studies. *Democracy by Initiative.* 2d ed. 2008. www.cgs.org (accessed June 24, 2010).

Larry N. Gerston and Terry Christensen, *Recall! California's Political Earthquake.* Armonk, N.Y.: M. E. Sharpe, 2004.

3

California Elections, Campaigns, and the Media

CHAPTER CONTENTS

A typical California ballot requires voters to make decisions about more than twenty elective positions and propositions. Even the best-informed citizens sometimes find it difficult to choose among candidates for offices they know little about and to decide on obscure and complicated propositions. Political party labels provide some guidance, but candidates, campaigns, and the media are also crucial in the California elections.

Campaigns and the media are especially important because of the mobility and rootlessness that characterize California society. More than half of all Californians were born elsewhere, and many voters in every California state election are participating for the first time. Residents also move frequently within the state, reducing the political influence of families, friends, and peer groups and boosting that of campaigns and the media.

THE VOTERS

California citizens who are eighteen years or older are eligible to vote unless they are in prison or a mental institution. Those eligible must **register to vote**, which must be done at least fifteen days before an election by completing a form available at post offices, fire stations, libraries, and public places where party activists eagerly solicit new voters. Registration forms are also available with applications for driver's licenses and at social service agencies or online at www.sos. ca.gov/nvrc/dedform. Once registered, those who cast their ballots regularly stay on the voter rolls indefinitely. Occasionally, however, voter lists are "purged" of voters who have not participated for some time or who have died or moved.

Altogether, nearly 23.4 million Californians are eligible to vote. Only 17 million (72.4 percent) were registered in 2010, however, and as few as 8 million actually vote in some elections—somewhat below the national average. In the gubernatorial election of 2010, turnout among those registered to vote was 59 percent. Turnout is higher in presidential elections. In 2008, 79.4 percent of the state's registered voters participated, a rate that was higher than the national average. In the 2010 primary election, however, only 33.3 percent of those registered actually participated—a record low for a gubernatorial primary election.

Traditionally, voters go to designated polling places to cast their ballots, but today nearly half **vote by mail**, having requested absentee ballots from their county registrar of voters. Those who prefer to cast their ballots this way can sign up as "permanent" absentee voters so that ballots are automatically sent to them for every election. In the 2010 gubernatorial primary election, a record 58 percent of those who voted did so by absentee ballot. Most of these people simply prefer the convenience of voting by mail given their busy lives; many prefer to deal with the complex ballots at their leisure; and still others vote absentee because campaigns push identified supporters to vote by mail to ensure their participation. With so many more people voting absentee—up to three weeks before Election Day—campaigns have had to change their tactics. Rather than a big push in the last few days, they must spread their resources and extend their messages over a longer period.

Voting by mail may have increased participation slightly, but even with this convenience, many Californians choose not to vote. Some don't get around to registering. Millions more who are registered still don't vote. Some are apathetic, some are unaware, and others feel too uninformed to act. Still others believe that voting is a charade because politics "is controlled by special interests." Some people say election information is "too hard to understand," and others are bewildered by all the messages that bombard them during a typical California election. But the reason that people most frequently give for not voting is that they are too busy.[1]

Yet political campaigns are designed to motivate voters to support candidates and causes. This task is complicated, though, because those who vote are not a representative cross section of the actual population. Non-Latino whites, for example, make up 42 percent of the population but 65 percent of the electorate.

Although Latinos, African Americans, and Asians constitute 58 percent of California's population, they are only 35 percent of the voters in primary and general elections.[2] This disparity in turnout means that California's voting electorate is not representative of the state's population. The lower participation rate among Latinos and Asians is partly explained by the relative youth of these populations (about one-third of Latinos, for example, are too young to vote) and by the fact that many are not yet citizens.

Language, culture, and socioeconomic status may also be barriers to registration and voting among minority groups. This situation is changing, however; Latinos were just 8 percent of the state's registered voters in 1978 but are more than 21 percent today,[3] and the number continues to rise. Still, voter registration lags among Latino citizens, with only about half of those eligible currently registered to vote.[4]

Differences in the levels of voter participation do not end with ethnicity. The people most likely to vote are suburban homeowners and Republicans, who tend to be richer, better educated, and older. Lower levels of participation are usually found among poorer, less educated, and younger inner-city residents and Democrats.[5] According to recent reports, 78 percent of adults over the age of sixty-five are "likely voters," while just 24 percent of adults aged eighteen to

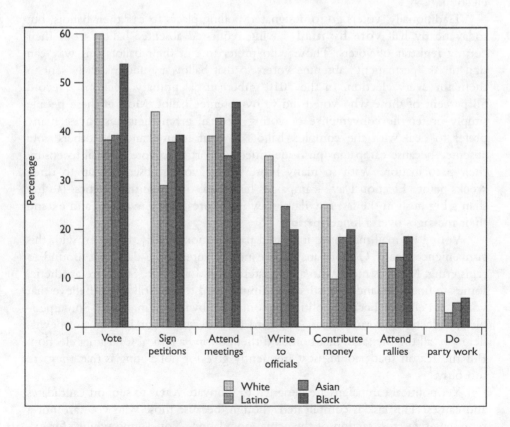

FIGURE 3.1 Political Participation by Ethnic Groups

SOURCE: From Public Policy Institute of California, "The Ties That Bind," 2004. Reprinted with permission.

twenty-four are "likely to participate in elections."[6] All this adds up to a voting electorate that is more conservative than the population as a whole, which explains how Republicans sometimes win statewide elections despite the Democratic edge in registration and why liberal ballot measures rarely pass.

Of course, voting is only one form of political participation. Many people sign petitions, attend public meetings, write letters or e-mails to officials, and contribute money to campaigns. But as we see in Figure 3.1, the number participating diminishes with each form of engagement, and differences among ethnic groups persist. As with voting, those who participate most are white, older, more affluent, homeowners, and more highly educated. Does the differential in voting and other forms of participation matter? It seems self-evident that elected officials pay more attention to the concerns of those who participate than those who do not.

THE CANDIDATES

When we vote, we choose among candidates, but where do candidates come from? Some are encouraged to run by political parties or interest groups seeking to advance their causes. Political leaders looking for allies recruit others, although weak political parties make such overtures less common in California than elsewhere. Most California candidates are self-starters with an interest in politics who decide to run and then seek support. The rising cost and increasing negativity of campaigns have discouraged some people from running, although wealthy individuals who can fund their own campaigns have frequently appeared as candidates in recent years. Most candidates start at the bottom of the political ladder, running for school board or city council, and work their way up, building support as they go. Others gain experience as staff members for elected officials, eventually running for their boss's job. Wealthy candidates sometimes skip such apprenticeships and run directly for higher office, but the voters are sometimes skeptical about their lack of political experience.

Historically, candidates in California have been even less representative of the population than the electorate. Most have been educated white males of above-average financial means. The 1990s brought change, however. Underrepresented groups such as women, racial and ethnic minorities, and gay men and lesbians grew in strength and organization, and structural changes facilitated their candidacies. A 1990 initiative limited the number of terms that legislators could serve, thus ensuring greater turnover in the state legislature. In addition, the redistricting decisions after the censuses of 1990 and 2000 resulted in redrawn legislative and congressional districts that gave minority candidates new opportunities at both levels. This could happen again with the redistricting that will follow the 2010 census, when district boundaries will be revised by a citizens' commission created by initiative rather than by the legislators themselves.

Latinos have gained the most from these changes, obtaining a sizable delegation in the state legislature and the California congressional delegation. Latinos have also gained representation at the local level, electing more than 1,200 of California's county supervisors, city council members, mayors, and school board members.[7] Most Latino officeholders are Democrats.

Although a smaller minority, African Americans gained a foothold in state politics earlier, including the statewide positions of lieutenant governor and superintendent of public instruction. Three African Americans have served as speaker of the assembly (its most powerful leader), but overall, black representation has shrunk as that of other minorities has increased.

Asian Americans remain the most underrepresented of California's racial minorities. In the past, Asian Americans have won election to statewide offices, including U.S. senator, secretary of state, and state treasurer. John Chiang, a Democrat of Chinese descent, was elected state controller in 2006 and re-elected in 2010. Electing candidates has been difficult for Asian Americans, however, because many are recent immigrants who are not yet rooted in the state's political system and because of cultural and political differences among the Chinese, Japanese, Vietnamese, Filipinos, Koreans, Indo-Americans, and others. But these groups have generated more candidates in every recent election. Many [Asians] have won local offices on city councils and school boards, and nine serve in the state legislature.

Women candidates have been more successful. Both of California's U.S. senators are now women. Women have been elected to statewide office in the past, although only one, Secretary of State Deborah Bowen, is currently serving. A substantial number of women are in the state legislature, however, including Assembly Majority Leader Fiona Ma. Many of California's city council members, mayors, and county supervisors also are women.

Lesbians and gay men achieved elected office later than any of these groups. Greater bias may be a factor, and in the past, the closeted status of many homosexuals—including candidates and elected officials—weakened organizing efforts and made gay and lesbian elective successes invisible. Nevertheless, eighty openly gay and lesbian individuals have won election to local offices (including sixteen judges),[8] and seven serve in the state legislature. Some, such as Assembly Speaker John Perez a Democrat from Los Angeles, have risen to leadership positions.

Racism and sexism partly explain the underrepresentation of all these groups, but other factors contribute as well. Many members of these groups are economically disadvantaged, which makes it hard to participate in politics, let alone to take on the demands of a candidacy. Women, minorities, and gay men and lesbians are usually not plugged in to the network of lobbyists, interest groups, and big donors that provide funds for California's expensive campaigns. Minorities also have difficulty winning support outside their own groups and may alienate their natural constituencies in the process. The fact that minorities are less likely to vote than Anglos further reduces their candidates' potential. Nevertheless, organizations within each of these constituencies work to recruit, train, and support candidates, and the diversity of California candidates and elected officials increases with each election.

THE MONEY

The introduction of primary elections in 1909 shifted the focus of campaigns from political parties to individual candidates. Political aspirants must raise money, recruit workers, research issues, and plot strategy on their own or with the help of expensive consultants rather than with that of political parties, which contribute little in the way of money or staff. California campaigns thus tend to focus on the personalities of the candidates more than on parties or policies.

Weak parties mean that candidates must promote themselves, so the cost of running for state assembly or senate often exceeds $1 million. Spending on races for the legislature totaled $97.7 million in the 2007–2008 election cycle.[9] Campaigns for statewide offices are even more expensive. The top two candidates for governor spent over $210 million in 2010.

Interest groups, businesses, and wealthy individuals provide the money. Much campaign financing is provided by **political action committees (PACs)**, which interest groups use to direct money to preferred campaigns. Legislative leaders such as the speaker of the assembly and the president pro tem of the senate raise huge sums from such sources and channel the money to their allies in the legislature; individual candidates raise money by asking potential contributors for donations directly and by organizing special fund-raising events, which range from coffees and barbecues to banquets and concerts. They also solicit contributions from specific audiences through targeted mailings and the Internet.

Increasingly, however, it appears that candidates must be wealthy enough to finance their own campaigns. Arnold Schwarzenegger provided more than $10 million for his campaigns in 2003 and 2006, but Republican Meg Whitman broke state and national records by spending $71 million of her own money to win the Republican nomination for governor in 2010 and then spending another $71 million in the general election. Voters are skeptical about wealthy candidates who self-finance their campaigns, however, and in the past, most such candidates have lost.

Worried about the influence of money and turned off by campaign advertising, Californians have approved a series of initiatives aimed at regulating campaign finance. The **Political Reform Act of 1974** required public disclosure of all donors and expenditures through the **Fair Political Practices Commission (FPPC)**. Since then, reformers have tried repeatedly to limit the amount that individuals and groups can contribute, but several initiatives approved by the voters were invalidated by the courts on grounds that they limited free speech. In 2000 voters approved Proposition 34, a legislative initiative setting higher contribution limits for individuals and committees (see Table 3.1).

Proposition 34 also set voluntary spending limits for candidates (see Table 3.2). Those who accept the limits have their photo and candidate statements published in the official ballot booklets that go to all voters; candidates who decline the limits are excluded from the booklet. Most candidates for the legislature and statewide offices other than governor comply with the spending limits; those who don't lose the moral high ground to those who do, which may influence voters. There is no limit,

TABLE 3.1 Proposition 34 Limits on Contributions to State Candidates, 2009–2010

Contributor	Legislature	Statewide except Governor	Governor
Person	$3,900	$ 6,500	$25,000
Small contributor committee	$7,800	$12,900	$25,900
Political party	No limit	No limit	No limit

SOURCE: California Fair Political Practices Commission, www.fppc.ca.gov.

TABLE 3.2 Voluntary Expenditure Ceilings for Candidates for State Offices, 2009–2010

Office	Primary	General Election
Assembly	$518,000	$906,000
Senate	777,000	1,165,000
Governor	7,768,000	12,946,000
Other statewide offices	5,178,000	7,768,000

SOURCE: California Fair Political Practices Commission, www.fppc.ca.gov.

however, on how much a candidate can contribute to his or her own campaign, which enables candidates such as Whitman to substantially fund their campaigns.

Like most reforms, Proposition 34 has had unintended consequences. Money is given to political parties to spend on behalf of candidates rather than to the candidates themselves, which may ultimately increase the power of the parties—and such contributions jumped dramatically after Proposition 34. More significantly, the new spending limits have been subverted by **independent expenditures** by PACs or groups specially organized by political consultants in support of candidates. Since Proposition 34, over $110 million has been spent in this way, including $32 million for the gubernatorial candidates in 2010. Jerry Brown, the victor, was the primary beneficiary.[10] Top independent expenditure groups include the prison guards' union, Indian gaming interests, and the California Teachers Association.[11] In some campaigns, independent expenditures exceed those of the candidates. The only restriction on independent expenditures is that they cannot be coordinated with the campaigns of the candidates they support. Because they are not directly associated with the candidates, "independent" mailings and television ads often feature the most vicious attacks on opponents.

Between various loopholes in Proposition 34, independent expenditures, PACs with names that cloak their real purpose and backers, and PACs that contribute to other PACs to obscure the individuals and interests who contribute the money, the Proposition 34 regulations have been condemned as "ineffective hypocrisy,"[12] even as reformers seek ways to close the loopholes. Twenty-five other states limit the impact of money on politics by providing some form of public financing for campaigns, but Californians rejected initiatives proposing such a system in the 2006 and 2010 elections.

CAMPAIGNING CALIFORNIA STYLE

Campaign contributors hope to elect allies who will support their interests. They also expect their money to buy immediate access and long-term influence. Candidates deny making specific deals, however, insisting that they and their contributors merely share views on key issues. Millions of dollars flow into candidates' coffers through this murky relationship. In the 2010 election, for example, labor unions generously supported Democrat Jerry Brown, while business interests gave to Meg Whitman. Some donors give to candidates of both parties, just to cover their bases.

So much money is needed because California campaigns, whether local or statewide, are highly professionalized. To supplement political party support, candidates hire political consultants and management firms to perform a variety of functions, including recruiting workers, raising money, advertising, conducting public opinion polls, and performing virtually all other campaign activities. These specialists understand the workings of California's volatile electorate and use their knowledge to a candidate's benefit. California's top-ranked political consultants include Gale Kaufman and Garry South, who work for Democratic candidates, and Frank Schubert, who works for Republicans.[13]

Television has made campaign management firms indispensable, allowing candidates instant entry into voters' homes. It also enables candidates to put their message across at the exact moment of their choosing—on broadcast or cable TV, between wrestling bouts, during the local news or *Oprah,* or just after *American Idol,* depending on the targeted audience. The efficacy of the medium is proved repeatedly when relatively unknown candidates spend big money on television commercials and become major contenders, as eBay billionaire Meg Whitman did when she saturated the airwaves beginning in late 2009 in the 2010 race for governor. A statewide advertising buy on television costs at least $1 million—and one round of ads is never enough. Although initially a leader in the Republican race for the U.S. Senate nomination in 2010, former congressman Tom Campbell was effectively eliminated when he lacked funds to compete on television.

More than in smaller, more compact states where people are more connected, Californians rely heavily on television for political information. As a consequence, television advertising accounts for as much as 80 percent of all spending for statewide races in California. In such a big state, it is the only way to reach the mass of voters. At the height of the gubernatorial campaigns, candidates run hundreds of ads a day in California's major media markets. Well-funded initiative campaigns also rely almost exclusively on television advertising.

Television is too costly for most candidates for legislative and local offices, however. A thirty-second prime-time spot can cost more than $20,000 in Los Angeles, and because most television stations broadcast to audiences much larger than a legislative district, the message is wasted on many viewers. Advertising during the day or on cable is cheaper, however, and many legislative candidates have turned to these alternatives. Most, however, have found a more efficient way to spend their money: **direct mail**. Computers have revolutionized political mail by enabling campaign strategists to target selected voters with personal messages.

Direct-mail experts develop lists of voters and their characteristics and then send special mailings to people who share particular qualities. In addition to listing voters by party registration and residence, these experts compile data banks that identify various groups, including liberals and conservatives, ethnic voters, retired people, homeowners and renters, union members, women, gay men and lesbians, and those most likely to vote. Campaigns even do data mining on consumer interests that might predict the political or policy concerns of voters so their mailing can be microtargeted. Once the targets have been identified, campaign strategists can develop just the right message to send to them. Conservatives may be told of the candidate's opposition to gay marriage; liberals may be promised action on the environment. For the price of a single thirty-second television spot, local or legislative candidates can send multiple mailings to their selected audiences.

Television and direct mail dominate California campaigns because they reach the most voters, but the use of these media is not without problems. Because television and direct mail are expensive, campaign costs have risen, as has the influence of major donors. Candidates who are unable to raise vast sums of money are usually left at the starting gate. Incumbent officeholders, who are masters at fund-raising and are well connected to major contributors, become invincible. Furthermore, these media are criticized for oversimplifying issues and emphasizing the negative. Television commercials for ballot measures reduce complicated issues to emotional thirty-second spots aimed at uninformed voters. Candidates' ads and mailings indulge in the same oversimplification, often in the form of attacks on opponents. When the candidates portray each other negatively, voters may feel that they must choose the lesser evil rather than make a decision on the policies and positive traits of the candidates. Voters have grown skeptical of such attacks, yet they are hard to resist. Campaign consultants, who are usually blamed for the phenomenon, point out that campaigns had a nasty edge even a century ago and that the public pays more attention to negative messages than to positive ones.

Candidates also take their campaigns to the Internet, with Web sites and e-mail lists to communicate with the media and with supporters. Former eBay executive Meg Whitman, perhaps not surprisingly given her background, spent nearly $3 million on website development and information technology during the 2010 gubernatorial primary, building what was described as the "Cadillac" Web site.[14] The political impact of Internet campaigning is unclear, however.

Whereas television and mail enable candidates to reach us whether we're interested or not, voters must initiate contact on the Internet, which limits the audience to those who are already engaged. Interest groups, however, can use e-mail to send campaign messages to their members, and some candidates have targeted e-mails to particular constituencies, such as Christian conservatives. The Internet can also help candidates recruit volunteers and solicit donations.

Overall, California's media-oriented campaigns reinforce both the emphasis on candidates' personalities and voter cynicism. Some people blame such campaigns for declining voter turnout. Contemporary campaigns may also depress voter turnout by aiming all their efforts at regular voters and ignoring those who are less likely to vote—often minority voters. Although this is a sensible way to use campaign resources, it is not a way to stimulate democracy.

Some candidates try to revive old-fashioned door-to-door or telephone campaigns and get-out-the-vote drives on Election Day. Labor union volunteers have become a force in elections in Los Angeles and San Jose, for example, and the Democratic and Republican parties rely on volunteers to turn out voters for their candidates. Grassroots campaigns have a long and honorable tradition in California, but even in small-scale, local races, they are often up against not only big-money opponents but also the California lifestyle: few people are at home to be contacted, and those who are may let calls go to voice mail or be mistrustful of strangers at their door. For good or ill, candidates need money for their campaigns; those with the most money don't always win, but those with too little rarely even become contenders.

Many of the traditional means of contacting voters were tossed out in the recall election of 2003, when the brevity of the campaign and the candidacy of Arnold Schwarzenegger changed everything. State law required a single election, rather than a primary and a general election, to be held within sixty to eighty days of the certification of the recall petition. Normally, statewide elections sprawl over at least a year, but when the election was set for October 7, Governor Davis and the candidates to replace him had just seventy-five days to make their cases, resulting in the most intense campaign in California history. Candidates who were well known or who could raise funds quickly, such as Democratic lieutenant governor Cruz Bustamante and Republican Arnold Schwarzenegger, had an immediate head start. But Schwarzenegger had another advantage. As an internationally famous and glamorous movie star, he attracted massive—and free—coverage by the news media within California and beyond.

Although media coverage of the brief campaign was different, some elements of the recall were not. The major candidates relied on television ads and mailings more than ever because time was too short to organize more traditional outreach efforts. Even in so short a campaign, more than $85 million was spent. Schwarzenegger ultimately succeeded by appealing to independent voters and many labor and Latino Democrats; his campaign balanced the funds going to other candidates, especially from labor unions and tribal gaming interests, with nearly $9 million of his own money and massive free media.[15]

THE NEWS MEDIA AND CALIFORNIA POLITICS

From candidates and campaigns to public policy, almost everything Californians know about politics—which is not necessarily very much—comes from the news media. They have a profound impact on ideas, issues, and leaders. Until the 1950s, a few family-owned newspapers dominated the media. Then television gave the newspapers some competition while expanding the cumulative clout of the mass media. Today, new media like the Internet and a plethora of ethnic publications also play a role.

Paper Politics

California's great newspapers were founded in the nineteenth century by ambitious men such as Harrison Gray Otis of the *Los Angeles Times,* William Randolph Hearst of the *San Francisco Examiner,* and James McClatchy of the *Sacramento Bee.* These print-media moguls used their newspapers to boost their communities, their political candidates, and their favored causes. Most were like Otis, an ardent conservative who fought labor unions and pushed for growth while making a fortune in land investments. In the heyday of bosses and machines, his *Los Angeles Times* supported the Southern Pacific Railroad's political machine and condemned Progressive leader Hiram Johnson as a demagogue, as did many other newspapers in the state. Other journalists, however, helped found the Lincoln-Roosevelt League and led the campaign for reform.

After reform triumphed over the machine, newspapers continued to play a crucial role in California politics. In Los Angeles, San Francisco, Oakland, San Jose, and San Diego, Republican publishers used the power of the press—on editorial and news pages—to promote their favorite candidates and causes. They were instrumental in keeping Republicans in office long after the Democrats gained a majority of registered voters.

Change came in the 1970s, when most of California's family-owned newspapers became part of corporate chains. The new managers brought in more professional editors and reporters. News coverage became more objective, and opinion was more consistently confined to the editorial pages, which became distinctly less conservative.

Such editorials, expressing the opinion of the publisher or, more commonly, an editorial board made up of journalists, have been extremely influential in California politics. Voters often follow editorial recommendations on candidates and issues for lack of alternative sources of advice, especially on lower-profile races and ballot measures. For example, by winning newspaper editorials throughout the state, Larry Aceves, a little-known former school superintendent, beat two prominent legislators to come in first in the 2010 primary election for superintendent of public instruction. Despite these endorsements, however, he was defeated in the November election. Nevertheless, today's editorial pages are less influential than they once were as the number of newspapers and their circulation have declined.

At one time, there were hundreds of newspapers in California, with several competing with one another in most large cities. Today, less than a hundred survive, and most cities have just one. But that's not the only change. As a result of the loss of readers and advertisers to other media, the surviving newspapers have shrunk in both news coverage and staffing. The *Los Angeles Times,* for example, employed more than 1,300 journalists in 1998 but was down to 600 by 2009.[16] As a consequence of these changes, newspaper coverage of California politics is less extensive than it once was. Newspapers now share reporters or rely on the Associated Press or the *Los Angeles Times,* which still maintains the largest and most respected Sacramento bureau. Other media, including television and the Internet, have become more important to many people.

Television Politics

Public opinion surveys report that 37 percent of Californians say they get their news and information about state politics from television, with 15 percent citing newspapers, 10 percent radio, and 24 percent the Internet.[17] But television coverage of California politics leaves a lot to be desired.

Before Arnold Schwarzenegger was elected governor, not one of California's television stations, other than those based in Sacramento, operated a news bureau in the state capital. Television news editors avoided state political coverage because they believed that viewers wanted big national stories or local features. The minimal television coverage of state politics—a tiny percentage of newscast time, according to various studies—was mainly drawn from newspaper articles, wire service stories, or events staged by politicians, who struggled to gain any coverage at all. Even candidates for governor had a hard time making local news broadcasts, and most television stations declined to broadcast live candidate debates out of fear of low ratings. Cynics pointed out that if television doesn't provide news coverage, candidates are forced to buy advertising time—on television. As a consequence, candidate ads take up more time than news coverage of campaigns during the nightly news on California television stations—and provide a major source of revenue for the stations.

Nevertheless, television coverage of state politics has improved somewhat in the twenty-first century. A movie star governor and his carefully staged media events brought the cameras back to Sacramento. Coverage also increased with the advent of transmission by satellite vans, which made it easier for television stations to send reporters to cover breaking news and major events "live from the Capitol!" without the necessity of investing in permanent Sacramento bureaus. Ongoing conflict between the Republican governor and Democratic majorities in the legislature added drama, as did the state's persistent budget crisis.

Californians who prefer their politics raw—without reporters or commentary—can watch their government in action on the California Channel, now available on 114 cable systems.

New Media

The traditional print and broadcast media still dominate, but in recent years more alternative sources of news and information have become available to

Californians. Nearly seven hundred ethnic broadcasting outlets and publications now serve Californians in Spanish, Vietnamese, Mandarin, and many other languages.[18] Latino newspapers and television and radio stations reach major audiences, especially in Southern California. Many of these ethnic media are virtually obsessed with politics as their communities generate candidates or factional conflict.

Talk radio has also become a political fixture, especially in a state where people spend so much time in their cars. Fifty percent of Californians say they listen to opinion-filled radio shows "regularly" or "sometimes."[19] Politics is a hot topic on talk radio, which played a crucial role in stirring up the recall of Governor Gray Davis in 2003.

But the medium with the most spectacular recent impact on politics is the Internet. Access to news and information on the Internet has given audiences exponentially more information and sources and diverted audiences and advertisers from more traditional media, especially newspapers. Thousands of Web sites focus on state or local politics and give citizens direct access to their governments. Blogs by political junkies offer news and opinion and often break stories. Listservs and social networking keep members of traditional interest groups in touch with one another and create whole new communities. Seventy-five percent of Californians use a computer at home, work, or school, and 70 percent regularly use the Internet; 55 percent report that they get news on the Internet. Latinos, elders, and lower-income residents are less likely to have access to computers or use the Internet, however, so access is not equally distributed.[20]

ELECTIONS, CAMPAIGNS, AND THE MEDIA

The influence of money and the media is greater in California politics than in most other states. Politicians must organize their own campaigns, raise vast sums of money, and then take their cases to the people via direct mail and television. Such campaigns are inevitably personality oriented, with substantive issues taking a back seat to puff pieces or attacks on opponents. The media provide a check of sorts, but declining coverage limits its impact.

All of this takes us back to the issue of declining voter turnout. The recall election of 2003 and the presidential election of 2008 increased turnout, but only momentarily. Turnout in succeeding elections has been much lower. Could stronger parties, more news coverage, and public-financed, issue-oriented campaigns revive voter participation? Maybe, but campaign consultants and the media say they are already giving the public what it wants.

NOTES

1. California Voter Foundation, "California Voter Participation Survey," March 2005, www.calvoter.org.
2. "The Changing California Electorate," *California Opinion Index,* August 2009, www.fieldpoll.com (accessed June 27, 2010).

3.   *Ibid.*

4.   Ricardo Ramirez and Luis Fraga, "Continuity and Change: Latino Political Incorporation in California since 1990," in *Racial and Ethnic Politics in California*, ed. Sandra Bass and Bruce E. Cain (Berkeley: Berkeley Public Policy Press, Institute of Governmental Studies, University of California, 2008).

5.   Public Policy Institute of California, "California's Likely Voters," *Just the Facts,* September 2009, www.ppic.org.

6.   Public Policy Institute of California, "The Age Gap in California Politics," *Just the Facts*, August 2008, www.ppic.org.

7.   National Association of Latino Elected Officials, "2010 Latino Electoral Profile: California State Primary Election," www.naleo.org (accessed June 28, 2010).

8.   Gay and Lesbian Leadership Institute, www.glli.org/leadership (accessed June 27, 2010).

9.   California Fair Political Practices Commission, "The Billion Dollar Money Train," April 2009, www.fppc.ca.gov (accessed June 29, 2010).

10. *Ibid.*

11. California Fair Political Practices Commission, "Independent Expenditures: The Giant Gorilla in Campaign Finance," June 2008, www.fppc.ca.gov (accessed June 29, 2010).

12. Dan Walters, "Proposition 34 Only Gave the Appearance of Reform," *San Jose Mercury News*, June 6, 2010. For more on how PACs shuffle funds and obscure sources, see "Campaign Spending Harder to Track," *San Jose Mercury News,* June 28, 2010.

13. "Capitol Weekly's Top 100 List, Parts I and II," *Capitol Weekly,* April 16 and 23, 2009, www.capitolweekly.net (accessed June 29, 2010).

14. "Whitman Digs Deep into Tech's Toolbox," *San Jose Mercury News,* July 2, 2010, p. 1A.

15. For a full discussion of the recall campaign, see Larry N. Gerston and Terry Christensen, *Recall! California's Political Earthquake* (Armonk, N.Y.: M. E. Sharpe, 2004).

16. "As Cities Downsize from Two Newspapers to Just One, Some Talk of Zero," *New York Times*, March 12, 2009.

17. Public Policy Institute of California, *Statewide Survey*, October 2010, www.ppic.org (accessed November 5, 2010).

18. Marcelo Ballve et al., *Profiles of Ethnic Media: California's New Civic Communicators* (San Francisco: New California Media, 2002).

19. Public Policy Institute of California, *Statewide Survey*, October 2004, www.ppic.org.

20. Public Policy Institute of California, *Statewide Survey*, June 2008, www.ppic.org.

LEARN MORE ON THE WEB

Public opinion polls:
    Public Policy Institute of California: www.ppic.org
    The Field Poll: www.fieldpoll.com

Elections, political reform, and campaign finance:
  California Secretary of State: www.sos.ca.gov
  California Fair Political Practices Commission: www.fppc.ca.gov
  California Voter Foundation: www.calvoter.org
  League of Women Voters: www.ca.lwv.org
  Smart Voter: www.smartvoter.org
  National Institute on Money in State Politics: www.followthemoney.org

News on state politics, campaigns, and elections:
  Capitol Weekly: www.capitolweekly.net
  California Report (radio): www.californiareport.org
  Rough & Tumble (links to news articles on California politics): www.rtumble.com

Listings of publications and broadcast media in California:
  ABYZ News Links: www.abyznewslinks.com/uniteca.htm
  California Voter Foundation: http://www.calvoter.org/issues/votereng/votpart/index.html

Blogs—for lively opinion and information on California politics:
  www.calbuzz.com
  www.calitics.com (progressive)
  www.californiarepublic.org (conservative)
  www.californiaprogressreport.com (progressive)
  www.flashreport.org (conservative)

LEARN MORE AT THE LIBRARY

Mark Baldassare. *A California State of Mind: The Conflicted Voter in a Changing World*. Berkeley: University of California Press, 2002. Developments in public opinion.

Greg Mitchell. *The Campaign of the Century*. New York: Random House, 1992. Upton Sinclair's 1934 campaign for governor.

Ethan Rarick, ed. *California Votes: The 2006 Governor's Race*. Berkeley: Berkeley Public Policy Press, Institute of Governmental Studies, University of California, 2007.

4

Interest Groups: The Power behind the Dome

CHAPTER CONTENTS

Many people belong to one or more **interest groups**—organizations formed to protect and promote the shared political objectives of their members. Existing in all shapes and sizes, interest groups range from labor unions, ethnic organizations, and business associations to student unions, environmental entities, and automobile clubs. Whatever their differences, interest groups share the same goal of seeing their visions and values incorporated into the actions of public policymakers.

In California, interest groups have prospered and proliferated, and in some ways cases become more important than political parties. That's because weak political parties and the state's election system provide a fertile political environment for organized groups to exercise influence. Weak political parties make candidates dependent on groups for financing, while direct democracy often enables groups to take their issues directly to the voters, circumventing the legislature and other elected policymakers in the process.

Interest groups come in all shapes and sizes. More people pay dues to the California Teachers Association (CTA) or the California Chamber of Commerce, for example, than contribute to the state Republican or Democratic parties. All groups are not equal, however; depending on resources and issues, some are far more successful than others. Just because groups are large does not automatically mean they are the most successful in having their way.

Besides exercising their influence through campaign contributions and use of direct democracy, interest groups also influence legislators in the lobbies beneath the capitol dome. Some observers view these efforts as assisting the legislative process; others see them as manipulating that process.

THE EVOLUTION OF GROUP POWER
IN CALIFORNIA

The astonishing length of California's constitution attests to the historical clout of the state's interest groups. In other states, groups gain advantages such as tax exemptions through acts of the legislature, which can be changed at any time. In California, such protections are often written into the constitution, making alteration difficult because constitutional amendments require the approval of the electorate. Among California's constitutionally favored interests are dozens of crops (protecting organized agriculture), trees less than forty years old (protecting the timber industry), and ships for passengers or freight (protecting the shipping industry). These "safeguards" were not responses to public demands. Instead, interest groups pushed them through for their own benefit either at the time the California Constitution was written or in subsequent elections.

Different interests have benefited throughout California's colorful history. In the early days, the mining industry and ranchers dominated the state's public policy environment. From about 1870 to 1910, the Southern Pacific Railroad monopolized California's economy and politics, with incredible control over both of California's major political parties.[1] Land development, shipping, and horse racing interests next dominated the political landscape through the mid-twentieth century, followed by the automobile and defense industries. Agricultural interests have remained strong through all these periods.

These days, banking and service businesses tower over manufacturing, while high-tech industries have surpassed defense and aerospace. Insurance companies, teachers' associations, physicians' and attorneys' groups, and other vocation-related associations also routinely lobby state government. Agribusiness also remains influential, particularly with respect to water policy and land use. Organized labor and business interests—almost always at odds—continue to battle for preeminence with the legislature and voters. They have been joined by the California Nations Indian Gaming Association, the largest contributor to the 2003 recall campaign and the largest contributor to a series of ballot propositions in 2008 that ratified gaming agreements between the tribes and the state. Single-issue groups, such as Gun Owners of California and Mothers Against Drunk Driving (MADD), have entered the fray, along with evangelical, pro-choice, right-to-life, minority, feminist, and gay and lesbian groups. Public interest groups, such as the League of Women Voters, Common Cause, and The Utility Reform Network (TURN), are also part of the ever-growing interest group mix. Pressured by these many groups and their financial contributions, California politicians often find themselves responding to the demands of interest groups rather than governing them.

THE GROUPS

Interest groups vary in size, resources, and goals. At one extreme, groups that pursue narrow and targeted economic benefits tend to have relatively small memberships but a great deal of financial resources. At the other end of the spectrum public interest groups often have large memberships but little money. A few, such as the Consumer Attorneys of California (CAC), whose membership consists of 3,000 trial lawyers, have the dual advantage of being both large and well funded. Others, such as the Consumers for Auto Reliability and Safety (CARS), operate on a shoestring.

Economic Groups

Economic groups that seek various financial gains or hope to prevent losses dominate the state's interest group environment. Every major corporation in the state, from Southern California Edison to the California Northern Railroad, is represented in Sacramento either by its own lobbyists or by lobbying firms hired to present the corporation's cases to policymakers. Often, individual corporations or businesses with similar goals form broad-based associations to further their general objectives. These umbrella organizations include the California Manufacturers and Technology Association, the California Business Alliance (for small enterprises), the California Bankers Association, and the California Council for Environmental and Economic Balance (for utilities and oil companies). The California Chamber of Commerce alone boasts 16,000 member companies that employ one-fourth of the private sector workforce in California.

Agribusiness is particularly active, because farming depends on the government on issues such as water availability and the regulation of pesticides. The giant farming operations maintain their own lobbyists, but various producer groups also form associations. Most of the state's winemakers, for example, are represented by the 850-member Wine Institute. The California Cotton Ginners Association has only 87 members, yet produces 750 million bales of cotton annually. Broader organizations, such as the California Farm Bureau Federation, one of the state's most powerful lobby groups, speak for agribusiness in general by representing 85,000 members with crops in excess of $36 billion in value.

Recently, high-tech industries have asserted their interests on issues ranging from Internet taxation and H-1B visas for foreign workers to transportation and public education. Organizations such as TechNet, the Silicon Valley Leadership Group, and the American Electronics Association have lobbied for regulatory changes, tax relief, research and development tax credits, "green" incentives in new areas such as solar energy, and other changes. The tech-heavy Silicon Valley Leadership Group alone represents 305 companies that provide $1.1 trillion worth of services and products in the global economy, exceeding the entire gross domestic product of India.[2]

Professional Associations and Unions

Professional associations such as the California Medical Association (CMA), the California Association of Realtors (CAR), and the Consumer Attorneys of California (CAOC) are among the state's most active groups, and they are regularly among the largest campaign contributors. Other professionals, such as chiropractors, dentists, and general contractors, also maintain active associations. Because all these professionals serve the public, many promote their concerns as broader than self-interest. Their credibility is further enhanced by expertise in their respective fields and by memberships consisting of affluent, respected individuals.

Teachers' associations and other public employee organizations fall somewhere between business associations and labor unions. Their members view themselves as professionals but in recent years have increasingly resorted to traditional labor union tactics, among them collective bargaining, strikes, and political campaign donations. Other public workers, including the highway patrol and state university professors, have their own organizations. The California State Employees Association (CSEA) is the giant among these groups, with more than 141,000 members and the ability to raise large campaign war chests for candidates and election issues.

Unions have done reasonably well in California, which ranks sixth among the fifty states in per capita union membership. Unions here represent 18 percent of the workforce, compared with 12 percent nationwide. Traditional labor unions represent nurses, machinists, carpenters, public utility employees, and dozens of other occupations. In 2002 unions worked to persuade the legislature to enact the nation's first paid family leave program, allowing workers to take leave from their jobs for up to six weeks at 55 percent of their salary or a maximum of $728 per week. In 2004 California became the first state in the nation to provide paid paternity leave. The new laws drew the wrath of the California Chamber of Commerce, which predicted that they would create hardship for businesses. Yet, only a fraction of those eligible to participate actually do so.[3]

Perhaps the most controversial union in state politics is the California Correctional Peace Officers Association (CCPOA), which contributed more than $600,000 to the reelection campaign of Governor Gray Davis in 2002, just before the governor signed a three-year pay increase of 35 percent in the midst of a huge state budget deficit. The agreement drew heated criticism of the union and

Davis, adding fuel to the recall accusation that Davis was little more than a tool of major contributors.[4] In 2004 Governor Arnold Schwarzenegger renegotiated the contract and won a slight modification in the pay raises, achieving only about one-third of the targeted savings. Still, the CCPOA is adept at looking out for its own interests. In 2008 the union funneled $1.8 million into a campaign to derail Proposition 5, which would have provided drug treatment and rehabilitation programs for many nonviolent drug offenders who otherwise would be sent to prison. The proposition failed, with 60 percent of the electorate voting against the measure.

Demographic Groups

Groups that depend more on membership numbers than on money can be described as **demographic groups**. Based on characteristics that distinguish their members from other segments of the population, such as their ethnicity, gender, or age, such groups usually have an interest in overcoming discrimination. Most racial and ethnic organizations fall into this category.

Virtually all of California's minorities have organizations that seek to be their voice. One of the earliest of these was the Colored Convention, which fought for the rights of African Americans in California in the nineteenth century. Today, several such groups advocate for African Americans, Asian Americans, and Native Americans. The United Farm Workers (UFW), GI Forum, Mexican American Legal Defense Fund (MALDEF), and Mexican American Political Association (MAPA) represent Latinos.

The National Organization for Women (NOW), EMILY's List (Early Money Is Like Yeast), and National Women's Political Caucus (NWPC) actively support women candidates and feminist causes. Unlike some of the other statewide organizations, these groups are better organized at the local level than at the state level, however.

Several organizations have become prominent over the definition of sexual equality. Gay rights groups have increased in numbers and voice in recent years, particularly over the issue of gay marriage. Equality California, the largest, has worked to elect gay legislators, obtain passage of equal rights legislation, and pursue gay marriage through both the courts and the legislative process. They have been opposed by groups like Campaign for California Families, which led the way to declare marriage as an act between a man and a woman in 2000 through **Proposition 22, the California in Defense of Marriage Act**. Californians have been battling over the issue ever since.

Age groups play a smaller part in state politics. California has an aging population heavily dependent on public services, however. Organizations such as AARP (formerly the American Association of Retired Persons), with no fewer than 3.3 million members in California, have achieved a higher profile in state politics, particularly on health-care issues.

Single-Issue Groups

The groups discussed so far tend to have broad bases and deal with a wide range of issues. Another type of interest group operates with a broad base of support for the resolution of narrow issues. **Single-issue groups** push for a specific question to be decided on specific terms. They support only candidates who agree with their particular position on an issue. The California Abortion Rights Action League (CARAL), for example, endorses only candidates who support a woman's right to choose (pro-choice), whereas antiabortion (or pro-life) groups such as the ProLife Council work only for candidates on the opposite side. Likewise, the Howard Jarvis Taxpayers Association evaluates candidates and ballot propositions solely in terms of whether they meet the association's objective of no unnecessary taxes and no wasteful government spending. Each of these groups exercises power on occasion, but their reluctance to compromise limits their effectiveness in the give-and-take of state politics.

A single-interest group's potential ability to deliver a solid bloc of voters on a controversial issue can affect the outcome of a close election and thus enhance its clout, at least on a temporary basis. That's what happened in 1982, when National Rifle Association (NRA) opposition to a proposed gun control initiative brought out sympathizers in droves and led to the defeat of antigun Democratic gubernatorial candidate Tom Bradley, who had been expected to win. An exception occurred in 2008, when antigay groups qualified and campaigned heavily for Proposition 8, a proposed constitutional amendment designed to overturn a state supreme court decision that had legalized same-sex marriage.[5] Advocates urged voters to use presidential candidate positions on the proposition as a guide to their votes. Barack Obama opposed the measure, yet he won California handily as the initiative squeaked by.

Public Interest Groups

Although virtually all organized interest groups claim to speak for the broader public interest, some groups clearly seek no private gain and thus more correctly can claim to be **public interest groups**. These groups are distinguished from other organizations by the fact that they pursue goals to benefit society, not just their members.

Some public interest groups, such as California OneCare, have been instrumental in the fight for health-care reform. Part of that organization's decade-long struggle was realized when Congress passed the Patient Protection and Affordable Care Act in 2010. Others, such as The Utility Reform Network (TURN), monitor rate requests by the utilities before the state Public Utilities Commission. In 2010 TURN led a coalition of consumer groups against PG&E–sponsored Proposition 16—a proposal that would have made it very difficult for municipalities to purchase renewable power.

Environmental organizations such as the Sierra Club and Friends of the Earth have been very active in California on issues such as water management, offshore oil drilling, air pollution, transportation, and pesticide use. Another important concern of these groups is land use, both for private development in sensitive areas and for public lands, which make up half the state. Surveys have reported that one in nine Californians claims membership in an environmental group.[6] The Sierra Club alone has more than 1.3 million members.

Other public interest groups, such as California Public Interest Research Group (CALPIRG), Common Cause, and the League of Women Voters, focus on governmental reform and voter participation. These groups have been involved in several efforts to reform campaign finance in California.

A final type of public interest group isn't really a group at all: local governments. Cities, school districts, special districts, and counties all lobby the state government—on whose funds they depend heavily—through the League of California Cities, the California School Boards Association (CSBA), and the California State Association of Counties (CSAC). Dozens of cities and counties employ their own lobbyists in Sacramento, as do other governmental agencies. One study found that local governments collectively spend more on lobbying than organized labor, oil companies, or businesses.[7] They also endorse ballot measures that affect their interests and, on rare occasions, even sponsor initiatives. Unlike other groups, cities and counties cannot make campaign contributions or organize their constituents, but they can make themselves heard. In 2010, local governments banded together to promote **Proposition 22, the Local Taxpayers, Public Safety and Transportation Act**, an initiative to keep the state government from borrowing or raiding funds that voters have dedicated to public safety.

TECHNIQUES AND TARGETS: INTEREST GROUPS AT WORK

Interest groups seek to influence public policy. To do this, they must persuade policymakers. The legislature, the executive branch, the courts, the bureaucracy, and sometimes the people are thus the targets of the various techniques these groups may use. Their primary weapons include lobbying, campaign support, litigation, and direct democracy.

Lobbying

The term **lobbying** refers to the activity that once went on in the lobbies adjacent to the legislative chambers. Advocates for various causes or issues would buttonhole legislators on their way in or out of the legislature and make their cases. This still goes on in the lobbies and hallways of the capitol, as well as in nearby bars and restaurants and wherever else policymakers congregate. Lobbyists are so integral to the legislative process that they are commonly referred to as members of the "third house," alongside the assembly and senate.

Until the 1950s, lobbying was a crude and completely unregulated activity. Lobbyists lavished food, drink, gifts, and money on legislators in exchange for favorable votes. Today's lobbyists, however, are experts on the legislative process. Many have served as legislators or staff for legislators. Often, they focus on legislative committees and leaders, lobbying the full legislature only as a last resort.

Unlike old-time lobbyists, today's advocates must be well informed to be persuasive. When inexperienced legislators are unable to grasp major issues, lobbyists fill the void, often by actually writing proposed legislation and assembling the coalitions of legislators necessary to pass it.[8] One study during the 2007–2008 legislative session found that 60 percent of the bills that became laws had been introduced by legislators on behalf of lobbyists.[9] Today's lobbyists still use money, but less cavalierly than in the past, instead strategically contributing to campaigns. Legislators and lobbyists alike assert that contributions buy access, not votes, but the tie between money and access can be powerful in its own right. "The bottom line," one strategist states, is that "the system favors the moneyed—and there's been no sign of political reform."[10] All of this makes lobbying not only a highly specialized profession but also an expensive activity. In fact, during 2009 lobby firms spent about $151 million just to influence the legislature alone—that averages out to $1.26 million per legislator.[11]

Although most lobbying activity is focused on the legislature, knowledgeable professionals also target the executive branch, from the governor down to the bureaucracy. The governor not only proposes the budget but also must respond to thousands of bills that await his or her approval or rejection. In the process, the governor frequently meets with lobbyists in an effort to come to terms on proposed legislation before it goes to the legislature.[12]

The roles and responsibilities of bureaucrats do not escape the attention of astute interest groups. The bureaucracy must interpret new laws and make future recommendations to the governor and legislature. Moreover, on questions ranging from tax exemptions to coastal access to energy regulations, bureaucrats often have the final say on how laws will work. One study on the implementation of AB 32, the Global Warming Solutions Act of 2006, found energy interests lobbying the California Air Resources Board more than the governor or legislature to gain favorable regulations. In the words of one energy lobbyist, "I'm not going to say we love the thing (AB 32), but if that's the way the state wants to go ... we want to make sure that we write regulations that we can comply with and are feasible to do."[13] Sometimes lobbyists will go so far as to offer "talking points" to help bureaucrats justify their decisions on public matters. "It's called 'spoon feeding,'" a lobbyist recently explained to a California coastal commissioner regarding a matter before the commission, "but we're happy to do it."[14]

Lately, the public has become a target of lobbying, too. In media-addicted California, groups have begun making their cases through newspaper and television advertising between elections. Health care, education, Indian gaming, and other issues have been subjects of costly media campaigns with the intent to motivate voters to communicate with state leaders.

Professional Lobbyists.   Between 1977 and 2007, the number of registered lobbyists in Sacramento nearly doubled, from 582 to 1,074, including about three dozen former legislators. That's about nine lobbyists per legislator. State law prevents former legislators from lobbying for one year after they leave office, but as one legislator has noted, "I would certainly be available to give people political advice."[15]

Most lobbyists represent a particular business, union, organization, or group. Others are **contract lobbyists**, advocates who work for several clients simultaneously. Whether contract or specialized, more and more lobbyists make a career of their professions, accruing vast knowledge and experience. These long-term professionals became even more powerful when term limits eliminated senior legislators with countervailing knowledge, although some lobbyists complain that term limits mean they must constantly reestablish their credibility with new decision makers. One prominent lobbyist, however, explains his lack of concern about term limits or other reforms: "Whatever your rules are, I'm going to win."[16]

Nonprofessional Lobbyists.   Some groups can't afford to hire a lobbyist, so they rely on their members instead. Even groups with professional help use their members on occasion to show elected officials the breadth of their support. Typically, this sort of lobbying is conducted by individuals who live in the districts of targeted legislators, although groups sometimes lobby en masse, busing members to the capitol for demonstrations or concurrent lobbying of many elected officials.

Such grassroots efforts by nonprofessionals have special credibility with legislators, but well-financed groups have learned to mimic grassroots efforts by forming front groups or "Astroturf" organizations that conceal their real interests. In 2008, for example, representatives of pornography filmmakers flooded the capitol for hearings on AB 2914, a bill that would have hiked taxes on the industry from 8 percent to 25 percent, adding $665 million to the beleaguered state coffers. Bill opponents included spokespersons from the Free Speech Coalition (FSC), an adult industry–funded group purportedly concerned with government efforts to limit free speech, regardless of the topic or issue. In this case, the FSC representatives argued that the tax would discriminate against those with different opinions. Through this vehicle, the porn industry appeared less self-serving and provided the logic for legislators to defeat the bill.

Campaign Support

Most groups also try to further their cause by helping sympathetic candidates win election and reelection, commonly through financial contributions to their campaigns. Groups with limited financial resources do so by providing volunteers to go door-to-door or to serve as phone-bank callers for candidates. Labor unions typically fall into this category, along with public education interests.

Groups with greater resources make generous campaign contributions. Sometimes such contributions appear to get the groups what they want. Take

TABLE 4.1 Top Ten Campaign Contributor Groups, 2008

Category	Money
Tribal governments	$163,223,555
Public-sector unions	37,926,398
Electric utilities	33,932,562
Oil and gas	25,491,497
Party committees	24,075,526
Gay/lesbian rights and issues	21,747,420
Candidate committees	18,115,167
General trade unions	17,075,442
Gambling and casinos	16,616,687
Real estate	15,408,393

SOURCE: Institute on Money in State Politics, www.followthemoney.org.

the issue of consumer protection from cell phone companies. Between 2006 and 2007, the legislature considered nine bills concerning billing transparency, contract grace periods, termination fees, and contract dispute rules. The industry opposed the bills as intrusive and unnecessary. Only one bill was signed to the law by the governor, while the rest never emerged from the legislature or were vetoed. Meanwhile, during the same period, the telecommunications industry pumped more than $7.2 million into political campaigns.[17] Table 4.1 illustrates the top ten interest group contributors in 2008.

Sometimes groups fail, no matter how much they contribute. In 2002 banks, insurance companies, and similar interests contributed more than $20 million in campaign contributions to defeat a bill by state senator Jackie Speier aimed at protecting the financial privacy of consumers.[18] Facing a similar outcome in 2003, Speier organized an initiative campaign and quickly collected 600,000 signatures; the moneyed interests retreated, and Speier's bill (SB1) was signed into law by Governor Davis. While they may not always succeed, powerful groups rarely hesitate to use their resources to tilt the outcomes in their favor.

Campaign contributors claim that their money merely buys them access to decision makers. The press and the public often suspect a more conspiratorial process, however, and evidence of money-for-vote trades has emerged in recent years. Federal Bureau of Investigation (FBI) agents posing as businesspeople asked legislators for favors in exchange for campaign contributions, resulting in the 1994 convictions of fourteen people, including five legislators. Their trials revealed the extent to which legislators hustle lobbyists for contributions. In another instance Chuck Quackenbush, California's elected insurance commissioner, was forced to resign in 2000 when it was discovered that he let insurance companies accused of wrongdoing avoid big fines by giving smaller amounts to foundations that subsequently spent the money on polls, ads featuring the commissioner, and other activities. And in 2005 Secretary of State Kevin Shelley resigned from his office after several allegations of illegal activities, including campaign contributions from a company that was awarded a major grant from his office.

As a result of these scandals, politicians and contributors probably exercise greater caution. The high cost of campaigning in California, though, means that candidates continue to ask and lobbyists and interest groups continue to give. Of significance, however, is that the campaign funds come from a variety of interest groups, as well as other sources.

Litigation

Litigation is an option when a group questions the legality of legislation, and in recent years many groups have turned to the courts for a final interpretation of the law. Groups have challenged state laws, regulations, and actions by the executive branch in court. In 2005, for example, the California Nurses Association successfully sued to force Governor Arnold Schwarzenegger to comply with a new state law that reduced the nurse-to-patient ratio. Although the governor lost that battle, he won another when he fended off a court challenge by the powerful California Teachers Association because he rescinded an earlier promise to return $2 billion he had denied the schools the previous year.

Over the years, interest groups have also raised legal challenges to several successful ballot measures—including measures on immigration, affirmative action, campaign finance, bilingual education, and same-sex marriage—hoping that the initiatives would be declared unconstitutional. Even if a group loses its case, it may be able to delay the implementation of a new law or at least establish a principle for debate in the future. In 2001 MALDEF challenged the legislature's redistricting plan, claiming underrepresentation of Latinos. Although the legislature's plan prevailed, MALDEF's tactic kept the issue on the public agenda throughout the decade.

Direct Democracy

In his 1911 inaugural address, Governor Hiram Johnson championed direct democracy to "place in the hands of the people the means by which they may protect themselves." He and his fellow Progressives envisioned the public as the ultimate custodian of the legislative process. A century later, however, only broad-based or well-financed groups have the resources to collect the necessary signatures or to pay for expensive campaigns. **Direct democracy** gives interest groups the opportunity to make policy themselves by promoting their proposals through initiatives and referenda.

Sometimes interest groups mobilize to gain passage of a ballot proposition; other times they work to defeat one. In 1998, for example, tribal supporters of gambling on Indian lands spent $10 million qualifying an initiative for the ballot in just thirty days—the most expensive petition campaign in history. The subsequent campaign on the proposition itself also broke records, with the two sides spending a total of $96 million. The voters ultimately approved the initiative. Since then, the costs have gone up. In 2008 the voters were asked to ratify four agreements allowing for 17,000 more slot machines in Indian casinos in addition to the 62,000 already in place, with projected annual taxes for the state at about $450 million. The pro-gaming interests spent more than $150 million on campaign activities—far exceeding the "no" side, which spent less than $40 million. The ballot propositions sailed through.

Big money was spent against two other initiatives in 2006. In one case the tobacco industry marshaled more than $65 million against Proposition 86, which sought to increase tobacco taxes by $2.60 per cigarette package (which would make California the highest tobacco-taxed state in the nation). Similarly, major oil companies spent more than $100 million in opposition to Proposition 87, an effort to tax oil profits with the proceeds used to pursue alternative-energy programs. The campaigns were successful, and the voters rejected both propositions.

But big money doesn't always win. For example, utility giant PG&E spent more than $3 million in 2010 gathering signatures for Proposition 16, the so-called Taxpayers Right to Vote Act. The proposal was actually a thinly veiled effort to change the state constitution to require any municipal power company to get a two-thirds vote of the people before buying renewable energy. PG&E poured more than $46 million into the effort against about $90,000 spent by the "no" side. The proposal was defeated, even though the opponents were outspent by a margin of 19,565 to 1.

The recall is also sometimes used by interest groups, usually to remove local elected officials. Teachers' unions, conservative Christians, and minority groups have conducted recall campaigns against school trustees, for example. These efforts, however, pale in comparison with the recall effort against Governor Gray Davis. The People's Advocate, a conservative antitax group, was among the leading forces early in that recall effort. During the campaign, groups ranging from the Howard Jarvis Taxpayers Association to the League of Conservation Voters weighed in on the issue.

REGULATING GROUPS

Free spending by interest groups and allegations of corruption led to the Political Reform Act of 1974 (introduced in Chapter 3), an initiative sponsored by Common Cause. Overwhelmingly approved by the voters, the law requires politicians to report their assets, disclose contributions, and declare how they spend campaign funds. Other provisions compel lobbyists to register with the secretary of state, file quarterly reports on their campaign-related activities, and reveal the beneficiaries of their donations. The measure also established the **Fair Political Practices Commission (FPPC)**, an independent regulatory body, to monitor these activities. When the commission finds incomplete or inaccurate reporting, it may fine the violator. Of greater concern than the financial penalty, however, is the bad press for those who incur the commission's reprimand.

The voters approved new constraints in 1996, when they enacted strict limits on interest groups' practice of rewarding supportive legislators with travel and generous fees for speeches. However, this legislation was soon challenged, creating an atmosphere of uncertainty. In 2000 voters approved yet another initiative, **Proposition 34**, which placed new constraints on political action committees and attempted to limit contributions to political campaigns. Yet between self-financed campaigns and the vigorous activities of groups engaged in independent expenditures, any thoughts of reduced spending quickly vanished.

MEASURING GROUP CLOUT: MONEY, NUMBERS, AND CREDIBILITY

Campaign regulations are generally intended to reduce the disproportionate influence of moneyed interests in state politics, but economic groups still have the advantage. Their money makes the full panoply of group tactics available to them and gives them the staying power to outlast the enthusiasm and energy of grassroots groups. The California Chamber of Commerce, for example, contributes lavishly to legislative campaigns and has been a major source of funds for Arnold Schwarzenegger, the first gubernatorial candidate endorsed by the Chamber in its 115-year history. Between 2004 and 2008 the Chamber listed fifty-one "job killer" bills that would be harmful to California business that reached the governor's desk; forty-seven were vetoed by Governor Schwarzenegger. Allan Zaremberg, president of the Chamber, attributes this to the "parallel agendas" of the governor and his organization, but campaign contributions and effective lobbying surely helped.[19] Of course, when Gray Davis was governor, labor unions enjoyed much the same kind of special relationship. Some interest groups are always likely to be more successful than others.

Public interest groups and demographic groups, however, gain strength from numbers, credibility, and motives other than self-interest. Occasionally they prevail, such as in 1998, when children's groups and health groups overcame a financial disadvantage to pass Proposition 10, a cigarette tax dedicated to children's health programs, and in 2010, when financially impotent public interest groups won the Proposition 16 battle against PG&E. More commonly, interest groups affected by potentially harmful new costs rise to the occasion, as was the case in 2006, when the oil and tobacco industries spent nearly $200 million and reversed public opinion—and the votes—on measures to tax oil and increase tobacco taxes.

How powerful are interest groups and their lobbyists? It's hard to tell, but one informal survey of twelve first-time legislators reported that lobbyists wrote 70 percent of the bills they proposed.[20] Whatever the balance among groups, they are central to California politics. In a political environment characterized by weak political parties and direct democracy, California's myriad interests have plenty of opportunity to thrive.

NOTES

1. See Stephanie S. Pincetl, *Transforming California: A Political History of Land Use and Development* (Baltimore, MD: The Johns Hopkins University Press, 1999), pp. 20-22.

2. *CEO Business Climate Survey, 2008* (San Jose, Calif.: Silicon Valley Leadership Group, 2009), p. 2.

3. *California Business Issues, 2004* (Sacramento: California Chamber of Commerce, 2004), p. 77; also see "Few Take State's Family Leave," *San Jose Mercury News*, July 4, 2006, pp. 1C, 9C.

4. See Larry N. Gerston and Terry Christensen, *Recall! California's Political Earthquake* (Armonk, NY: M. E. Sharpe), 2004, p. 22.

5. The ruling was *In re Marriage Cases*, S147999.

6. Public Policy Institute of California, *Statewide Survey*, June 2000, www.ppic.org.

7. "Cities, Counties, Pay Price for Capitol Clout," *Los Angeles Times*, September 10, 2007, pp. B1, B4.

8. See "Bumper Crop of Clout," *Los Angeles Times*, September 22, 2004, pp. A1, A22, A23.

9. "How Our Laws Are Really Made," *San Jose Mercury News*, July 11, 2010, pp. A1, A6, A7.

10. "Special Interests: How They Get around Voter-Approved Limits on Campaign Contributions," *San Francisco Chronicle*, February 11, 2008, pp. A1, A6.

11. "End of Session Money Rains Down on Candidates," press release, California Fair Political Practices Commission, September 16, 2009.

12. See "A Lobbyist by Any Other Name?" *San Jose Mercury News*, May 20, 2005, pp, 1A, 17A.

13. "Lobbyists Heat up over Climate Law," *Sacramento Bee*, July 12, 2010, pp. A1, A10.

14. "E-mails Put California Coastal Commissioner in an Awkward Spot," *Los Angeles Times*, July 10, 2010, p. AA3.

15. "Elective Office Improves a Resume," *Los Angeles Times*, November 24, 2006, pp. B1, B11.

16. Douglas Foster, "The Lame Duck State," *Harper's*, February 1994.

17. See "Cell Phone Lobby Thwarts Reform Efforts," *San Jose Mercury News*, September 18, 2007, pp. 1A, 15A.

18. "$20 Million Tab to Defeat a Privacy Bill," *San Francisco Chronicle*, September 7, 2002, pp. A1, A11.

19. "Business Czar Delivers Major Cash to Governor," *San Jose Mercury News*, February 22, 2005, pp. 1A, 12A; also see "Business Sees an Ally in Governor," *Los Angeles Times*, October 18, 2004, pp. B1, B7.

20. Foster, *op. cit.*

LEARN MORE ON THE WEB

California Association of Realtors (CAR):
  www.car.org

California Chamber of Commerce:
  www.calchamber.com

California Labor Federation:
  www.calaborfed.org

Common Cause:
  www.commoncause.org

Howard Jarvis Taxpayers Association:
  www.hjta.org

Latino Issues Forum:
  www.lif.org

League of Women Voters of California:
  www.ca.lwv.org

Sierra Club:
  www.sierraclub.org/ca

LEARN MORE AT THE LIBRARY

Mark Arax and Rick Wartzman. *The King of California.* New York: Public Affairs Press, 2003.

Derek Cressman. *The Recall's Broken Promise: How Big Money Still Runs California Politics.* Sacramento, CA: The Poplar Institute, 2007.

Frank Norris. *The Octopus.* New York: Doubleday and Company, 1901.

Stephanie S. Pincetl. *Transforming California: A Political History of Land Use and Development.* Baltimore, MD: The Johns Hopkins University Press, 1999.

Arthur H. Samish and Bob Thomas. *The Secret Boss of California.* New York: Crown Books, 1971.

Dan Walters and Jay Michael. *The Third House.* Berkeley: Berkeley Public Policy Press, Institute of Governmental Studies, University of California, 2002.

5

The Legislature: The Perils
of Policymaking

CHAPTER CONTENTS

**The Making and Unmaking of a
Model Legislature**

A Little History

The Shift toward Professionalism

*Redistricting: Keeping and Losing
Control*

Term Limits

New Rules, New Players

Leaders and Staff Members

Staffing the Professional Legislature

How a Bill Becomes a Law

The Formal Process

The Informal Process

Other Factors

Unfinished Business

Thousands of bills are introduced in the California legislature every year. Some are narrow in focus, such as requiring egg-laying chickens to have enough room to walk in their cages (passed in 2010) or a truth-in-advertising law about pomegranate juice (passed in 2009). Others, such as sweeping tele-communications legislation (passed in 2010) or mortgage fraud legislation (passed in 2009) attempt to settle disputes between competing industries that have a great deal of resources at stake. Some of these laws may seem a waste of time to the casual observer, although they usually are critically important to the con-stituencies they affect.

But along with deciding relatively obscure matters removed from the public eye, the legislature is responsible for solving the state's thorniest problems, including underfunded public education, inadequate revenues, the need for environmental protection, a decaying infrastructure, and an ever-fraying social safety net. Each year the members write thousands of laws and, along with the governor, determine the budget and fund services and programs. As a focal point of power, the legislature is a natural target of public scrutiny, and criticism of it is understandable. Less understandable, however, is its inability to resolve big issues in a contentious political environment.

Of course, the legislature does not act in a policymaking vacuum; rather, it must share power with the other branches of government. Nowhere has there been more disdain for that requirement than in the relationship between the legislature and the governor. For the last twenty-five years, California governors and the legislature have tangled on a regular basis. During that period, the legislature has rarely enacted the state budget before the start of the fiscal year on July 1. In addition, the legislature has suffered internally due to political— and philosophical—battles not only between Democrats and Republicans, but also internally between assembly Democrats and senate Democrats and assembly Republicans and senate Republicans. As one beleaguered assembly member said during lengthy budget negotiations, "More times than not, it seems that we have four political parties in the legislature alone!" Partisanship and ideological schisms drape the legislative process in California in ways rarely observed elsewhere, and these stark divisions often leave the body tied in political knots.

Then there's the question of public policy priorities. Some observers have wondered in recent years how the legislature could immerse itself in issues such as tanning salon rules for teenagers and imported kangaroo leather regulations, yet seemingly avoid questions about tax reform, water policy, and universal health insurance. It's no wonder that a 2010 public opinion survey found a whopping 75 percent of likely voters critical of the state legislature—a disapproval rating even higher than that of Governor Arnold Schwarzenegger.[1] Still, the legislature was established as the state institution most directly linking the people with their government. The question is, Does it still do its job in the twenty-first century?

THE MAKING AND UNMAKING OF A MODEL LEGISLATURE

Structurally and numerically, much of today's state legislature parallels its original design and intent. But a series of circumstances in the state's political environment have left the legislative branch considerably different than its national counterpart.

A Little History

California's first constitution, in 1849, provided a **bicameral (two-house) legislature** similar to the U.S. Congress. When the constitution was revised thirty years later, the senate was fixed at forty members serving four-year terms (with half the body elected every two years), and the assembly was set at eighty members serving two-year terms. Those numbers and terms of office continue to this day. Throughout the first hundred years of governance, legislators met on a part-time basis, with budgets crafted in two-year increments—characteristics that would change over time.

Beginning in 1926, the organization of the legislature paralleled that of the U.S. Congress. Assembly members, like their counterparts in the U.S. House of Representatives, were elected on the basis of population, and senators were elected by county in the same way that each state has two U.S. senators.[2] The large number of lightly populated counties north of the Tehachapi Mountains enabled the rural north to dominate the state senate despite Southern California's growth. By 1965, twenty-one of the forty state senators in California represented only 10 percent of the population; Los Angeles County, then home to 35 percent of the state's residents, had but a single state senator.

The Shift toward Professionalism

Then came change. The United States Supreme Court's *Reynolds v. Sims* decision in 1964 ordered all states to organize their upper houses by population rather than by county or territory. In California, the shift increased urban and southern representation dramatically, with rural and northern representation experiencing a corresponding decline. The revised method of organization produced numerous consequences—some intended, some not. The new legislators were younger, better educated, and more ideological, and more of them were members of racial minorities. More women also were elected. The transition to modernity was completed in 1966, when the voters created a full-time legislature with full-time salaries.

These days, the legislature meets an average of more than two hundred days per year, with full-time salaries to match. As of 2011, their base salary is $95,291—down from the $116,208 that legislators collected until the most recent recession, but still the highest among the fifty states. Perks push annual incomes close to $140,000.[3] Only nine other states have full-time legislatures.[4]

Redistricting: Keeping and Losing Control

By law, every ten years after the national census, the state realigns congressional and state legislative districts so that all have the same population. This process is known as **redistricting**. As of January 1, 2010, the California State Demographics Unit (the state equivalent to the U.S. Census Bureau) estimated California's population at 38,600,000. The state's population grows unevenly. So, during 2011, the state's new fourteen-member **Citizens Redistricting Commission** must realign legislative districts to be equal in size once again—482,500 for each assembly district and 965,000 in each senate district. This task is a first of its kind in California.

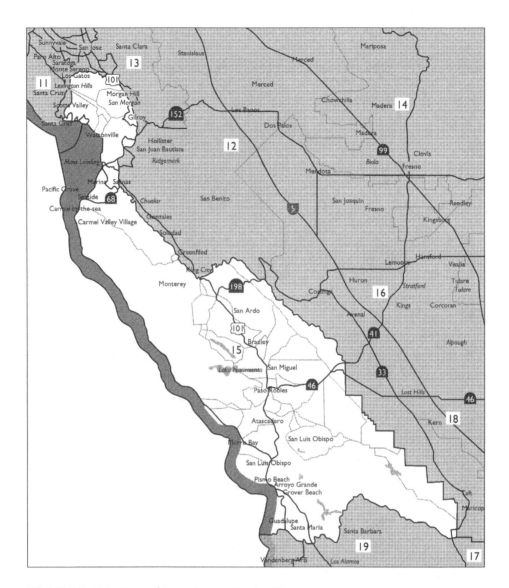

FIGURE 5.1 Map of State Senate District 15

Until 2011, redistricting had been left to the legislature, as is the case in most states. But in recent years, critics charged the legislature with being more intent on self-preservation than on providing compact geographic boundaries. After completion of the 2001 redistricting process, one senate district was two hundred miles in length, while others appeared almost as a Rorschach inkblot personality test. Figures 5.1 and 5.2 show examples of the legislature's work. As a result, the partisan compositions of the legislature remained almost identical throughout the decade. Some observers attacked the 2001 redistricting plan as an "incumbency protection plan" that needlessly split cities and ignored natural communities.[5] They argued that packing districts with disproportionate numbers of Democrats

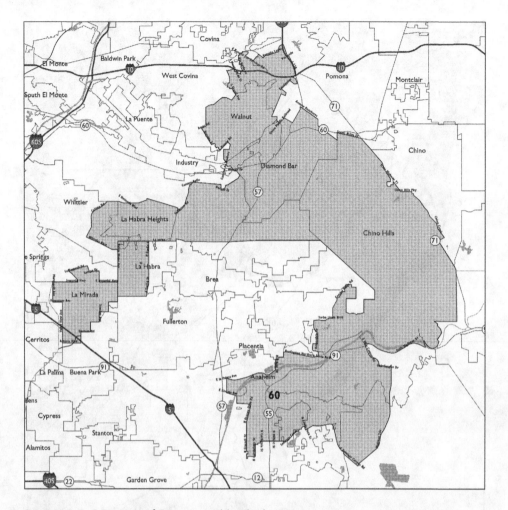

FIGURE 5.2 Map of State Assembly District 60

or Republicans reduced competition. As one legislator complained, "What happened to drawing lines for the people of the state rather than ourselves?"[6]

Governor Arnold Schwarzenegger campaigned to establish a redistricting commission of retired judges in a 2005 special election, but the voters soundly rejected his proposal after legislative leaders promised to come up with a better plan. They never did. In 2008, Schwarzenegger joined with Common Cause, the League of Women Voters, and other reform groups to craft **Proposition 11, the Voters FIRST Initiative**. The ballot proposal placed redistricting in the hands of a fourteen-member independent commission. This time, the voters approved the measure, which takes effect before the 2012 state elections. But the redistricting battle has not gone away. Legislative supporters placed the redistricting issue before the voters again in 2010 with Proposition 27, the Financial Accountability in Redistricting Act. However, the voters were content to try the independent commission concept and rejected the proposal. With a new redistricting system in place, it remains to be seen whether the legislature will

TABLE 5.1 Political Parties in the State Legislature, 1981–2011

Legislative Session	Senate			Assembly	
	Democrats	Republicans	Independents	Democrats	Republicans
1981–1982	23	17		48	32
1983–1984	25	14	1	48	32
1985–1986	25	15		47	33
1987–1988	24	15	1	44	36
1989–1990	24	15	1	47	33
1991–1992	27	12	2	47	33
1993–1994	23	15	2	49	31
1995–1996	21	17	2	39	41
1997–1998	22	17	1	42	38
1999–2000	25	15		48	32
2001–2002	26	14		50	30
2003–2004	25	15		48	32
2005–2006	25	15		48	32
2007–2008	25	15		48	32
2009–2010	25	15		50	30
2011–2012	25	13		52	28

SOURCE: California Secretary of State.

become less partisan and more effective. Table 5.1 displays the partisan breakdown of the legislature since 1981.

Term Limits

Much of the legislature's recent look stems from rising voter antipathy toward incumbents and the near certainty of their perpetual reelection. In 1990 the voters passed **Proposition 140**, an initiative that limited elected executive branch officers and state senators to two 4-year terms and assembly members to three 2-year terms, while reducing the legislature's operating budget (and thus its staff) by 38 percent. Clearly, California voters thought their legislature had become too professional for its own good.

Term-limits advocates envisioned a "turnstile" type of legislature, with members in office for relatively short periods. The system was designed to guarantee new faces, reduce the influence of money, and prevent incumbents from becoming entrenched in excess. Of the fifteen states currently with term-limit legislation in place, California is tied with Arkansas and Michigan for the strictest conditions in the nation. Once legislators complete their terms of service, they may never run for election again.

Some objectives associated with **term limits** have been met, while others show no sign of coming to pass. New faces have certainly appeared—particularly women and minorities in much larger numbers than in the past—but in many cases legislators have simply jumped from one house to the other. And at least one study shows that the most common vocational backgrounds of legislators before term limits—law and business—remain the dominant career patterns in the term-limits era.[7] Those from relatively affluent backgrounds continue be disproportionately elected to the legislature. In this sense, little has changed.

There also have been increasing instances of political cannibalism. In some cases, **termed-out** assembly members have challenged senators from their own political party who are eligible to serve another term. In other cases, senators who have a term left in the assembly have attempted to return to that house. In other instances still, termed-out legislators have returned to their counties to run for county supervisor. The term-limits concept in California has spawned the state's version of "musical chairs."

Although the flow of money into campaign coffers has been slowed, the overall costs of campaigning continue to set new records. Research also reveals that another significant impact of term limits has been a considerable decline in the quality of legislation in the postlimits era.[8]

Another criticism of term limits centers on the loss of legislative knowledge because of the rapid turnover. Because legislators have little opportunity to gain expertise, they tend to rely more on the governor and lobbyists,[9] the former because of the governor's access to the bureaucrats who advise him or her and experts who work as aids in the governor's office, and the latter because of the permanence of the lobbyists in the state capital. Legislators may be termed out, but lobbyists are not.

Meanwhile, leadership positions in the legislature no longer carry the clout that once made that branch an effective counterweight to the executive branch. Karen Bass, for example, who was elected speaker of the assembly in 2008, was termed out of the assembly as of 2010. John Perez, her successor, was elected to the assembly's highest post with only a year of experience under his belt. Both approaches show the problems that can develop with erratic leadership changes.

Nationwide, the term limits movement seems to be abating. Mississippi voters rejected the concept in 1999. In 2002, the Idaho legislature removed term limits, and the Oregon Supreme Court found the state law on term limits unconstitutional. In 2003, the Utah state legislature repealed term limits in that state. But in California, the voters continue to favor term limits. A public opinion poll in 2009 found that a resounding 65 percent of Californians supported the concept.[10]

New Rules, New Players

Redistricting, the change from part-time to full-time legislators, higher salaries, and term limits transformed the legislature, albeit unevenly. To be sure, the new framework attracted better-educated and more professional individuals and also made election to office more feasible for women and minorities. Thus, in 2011,

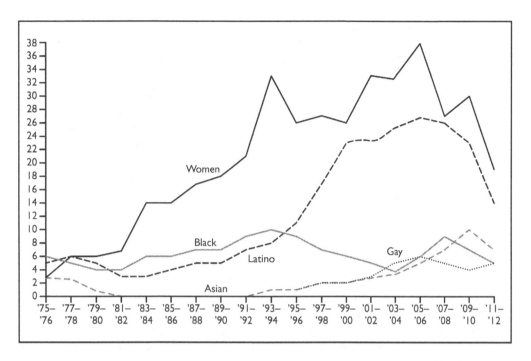

FIGURE 5.3 Women and Minorities in the California Legislature

the assembly included 19 women, 14 Latinos, 5 African Americans, 7 Asian Americans, and 5 openly gay members; the senate included 13 women, 10 Latinos, 2 African Americans, 2 Asian Americans, and 2 openly gay members. (see Figure 5.3).

Despite greater diversity, the legislature has narrowed in terms of vocational backgrounds. During the 1980s, legislative aspirants from the business world were flanked by large numbers of lawyers, local activists, educators, and former legislative aides. But increasingly, the "business candidate" has emerged as the dominant category of self-description. During the 1990s, about half of all legislative candidates on the ballot listed some form of business as their occupation. Beginning in the late 1990s, large numbers of people from city- and county-elected posts also took seats in the legislature.[11] These patterns continue today.[12]

LEADERS AND STAFF MEMBERS

Although the two houses share lawmaking responsibilities, they function differently. Because the assembly is larger, it is more hierarchical in organization. The **speaker of the assembly** is clearly in charge of that body and wields considerable power. The speaker controls the flow of legislation, designation of committee chairs and assignments, and distribution of vast campaign funds to the members of his or her political party. The number of standing, or topical, committees varies each term with the speaker's term in office. For example, there were thirty such committees in the assembly during 2009–2010, one more than in the previous session. Some committees are far more important than others, so the speaker's friendship is of great value to a legislator. The speaker also may carry favor with the governor, especially if the two work well together.

By tradition, the party with a majority in the assembly chooses the speaker in a closed meeting, or caucus. A vote is then taken by the full assembly, with the choice already known to all. The minority party selects its leader in a similar fashion. Majority and minority floor leaders, as well as their whips (assistants), provide further support for the legislative officers. With solid majorities for most of the past half-century, the Democrats have controlled the speakership for all but four years during the period.

Before the term-limits era, speakers often held their posts for ten years or more. However, since 1996—the year when term limits set in—the tenures of speakers have been limited to between one and three years. The current speaker, John Perez, may stretch that life span a bit. He was elected to his post in 2009 and may serve through 2014, assuming he is re-elected.

Prior to the court-ordered redistricting in 1966, the senate emphasized collegiality and cooperation over strong leadership, strict rules, and tight organization. Since the late 1960s, the senate has operated with a level of partisanship closer to that found in the assembly. The most powerful member is the **president pro tem**, who, like the speaker, is elected by the majority party after each general election. The minority party also elects its leader at that time. The key to senate power lies with the five-member **Rules Committee**, or **Senate Rules Committee**, which is chaired by the president pro tem and controls all other committee assignments and the flow of legislation. In 2009–2010 the senate had twenty-three standing committees, the same number as the previous session.

When Democrat John Burton presided as the pro tem, he used the office to raise and dispense large sums of money to grateful fellow Democrats. Burton was president pro tem for six years (1998–2004). More significantly, he had been an assembly member for nearly twenty years, mostly before the term-limits era. Because of his experience, Burton became the legislature's lightning rod against Governor Arnold Schwarzenegger. Many observers viewed him as the legislature's most formidable leader, despite the assembly speaker's traditionally dominant role.

The current president pro tem, Darrell Steinberg, was elected to the position in 2008. He will not be termed out until 2014. Like most others in leadership positions, Steinberg assumed his post with relatively little experience, although he did serve six years in the state assembly.

Although Democrats hold leadership positions in both houses, in recent years they have had as much trouble dealing with one another as they have had with Republican governor Schwarzenegger. Some of this trouble may be due to the differing leadership styles of Senate President Pro Tem Steinberg and Assembly Speaker Perez. Steinberg has a record of crossing party lines to forge necessary, if distasteful, compromises. Perez has a reputation for being unwilling to part with core values.[13] Their internal gridlock has taken considerable pressure off the minority Republicans, who have watched internal struggles within the majority party with some glee. Nowhere has this been more evident than in the struggle to balance annual state budgets facing huge deficits. As the legislature grappled with its responsibilities in 2010, interest groups loyal to both sides actually began letter-writing campaigns and purchased television ads—all of which points to the lack of cohesion within the political parties.[14]

STAFFING THE PROFESSIONAL LEGISLATURE

The evolution of the legislature into a full-time body was accompanied by a major expansion of its support staff. In 1990 the number of legislative assistants totaled 2,400—a far cry from the 485 employed by the last part-time legislature in 1966. Reductions from Proposition 140 pared the number of staffers to about 1,750, although increases in the state's population have led to a slow increase in the number of positions. As of 2010, about 2,500 staffers worked for the legislature. Those in the capital usually concentrate on pending legislation and research, whereas staffers in the legislators' home district offices spend much of their time responding to constituents' problems. The efforts of these staffers help each legislator to remain in good standing with his or her district.

Legislators spend much of their time in committees, the heart of the legislative process. Most committees cover specialized policy areas such as education or natural resources. A few, such as the senate and assembly rules committees, deal with procedures and internal organization. Each committee employs staff consultants who are experts on the committee's subject area and who are politically astute individuals in general—important attributes because they serve at the pleasure of the committee chair. Besides the traditional or standing committees, staffers assist more than sixty select committees that address narrow issues and nine joint committees that coordinate two-house policy efforts.

Another staff group is even more political. Employed by the Democratic and Republican caucuses and answering to the party leaders in the senate and assembly, these assistants are supposed to deal with possible legislation. However, their real activities usually center on advancing the interests of their party.

In addition to personal, committee, and leadership staffers, legislators have created neutral support agencies. With a staff of fifty-two, the **legislative analyst** (a position created in 1941) provides fiscal expertise, reviewing the annual budget and assessing programs that affect the state's coffers. The **legislative counsel** (created in 1913) employs about eighty attorneys to draft bills for legislators and determine their potential impact on existing legislation. The **state auditor** (created in 1955) assists the legislature by periodically reviewing ongoing programs.

Historically, staffing has enhanced the legislature's professionalism. Yet some staffers, especially those who work for the legislative leaders, clearly spend more time on partisan politics than on legislation. Many have used their positions as apprenticeships to gain knowledge, skills, and contacts for their own campaign efforts. All this, critics point out, is funded by the taxpayers. Defenders of the system counter that this staffing system helps compensate for weak party organizations and the information gaps associated with rapid legislative turnover.

HOW A BILL BECOMES A LAW

The legislature passes laws. It also proposes constitutional amendments, which may be submitted for voter approval after they receive absolute two-thirds majority votes in both houses (the votes of two-thirds of the full membership—that is, twenty-seven votes in the senate and fifty-four in the assembly). The same absolute two-thirds majority votes are required for the legislature to offer bond measures—money borrowed for long-term, expensive state projects. Proposed bond measures must then obtain majority votes at the next election before becoming law.

Most of the legislature's energy, however, is spent on lawmaking. Absolute majorities—twenty-one votes in the senate and forty-one votes in the assembly—are required to pass basic laws intended to take effect the following January, but absolute two-thirds votes in both houses are required for appropriations, urgency measures (those that become law immediately upon the governor's signature), and overrides of the governor's veto. The process, however, is far from simple.

The Formal Process

The legislative process begins when the assembly member or senator sponsoring a bill gives the clerk of the chamber a copy, which is recorded and numbered (see Figure 5.4). The process is known as moving the bill "across the desk" (of the receiving clerk), signifying that the proposed measure is now officially under consideration. The bill then undergoes three readings and several hearings before it is sent to the other house, where the process is repeated. The first reading simply acknowledges the bill's submission.

Depending upon the bill's origin, either the senate Rules Committee or the assembly Rules Committee decides on the route of the bill. The chairs of these important committees can affect a bill's fate by sending it to "friendly" or "hostile" committees and by assigning it a favorable or unfavorable route. Typically, a bill is assigned to two or three committees for careful scrutiny by members who are experts in that bill's subject area. More than half of all bills die in committee, either through a formal vote or because the chair decides not to call for a vote.

More than six thousand bills are introduced during each two-year session, with assembly members limited to fifty proposals and senators limited to sixty-five. With such volume, the **legislative committees** are essential to getting laws passed. They hold hearings, debate, and may eventually vote on each bill delegated to them. Most committees deal in narrow areas, but a few—such as the senate Budget and Fiscal Review Committee and the assembly Committee on

Appropriations—focus on the collection and distribution of funds and thus enjoy clout that goes beyond any one policy area.

At the conclusion of its hearings, a committee can kill a bill, release it without recommendation, or approve it with a "do pass" proposal. It may also recommend approval contingent on certain changes or amendments, which can be substantial or minor and technical. Only when a bill receives a positive recommendation from all of the committees to which it was assigned is it likely to get a second reading by the full legislative body. At this stage, the house considers additional amendments. After all proposed revisions have been discussed, the bill is printed in its final form and presented to the full house for a third reading. After further debate on the entire bill, a vote is taken.

Sometimes, the bill changes so dramatically that the original author abandons sponsorship in disgust; the bill then dies unless another legislator assumes sponsorship. On other occasions, a bill is introduced about a topic of little significance or with little more than a number. Then, later in the term, when the deadline for introductions has passed, the author may strip the bill of its original language and offer replacement language to deal with a pressing topic new to the legislative agenda. This strategy, known as **gut-and-amend**, isn't pretty, but gives a legislator flexibility he or she would not have otherwise. It also circumvents the normal legislative process of committee hearings and due deliberation, much to the chagrin of some lobbyists and interest groups.

If a bill is approved by the members of one house, it goes to the other house, where the process starts anew. Again, the bill may die anywhere along the perilous legislative path. If the two houses pass different versions of the same bill, the versions must be reconciled by a **conference committee**. Senate members are appointed by the Rules Committee; assembly members are chosen by the speaker, yet another sign of the power that comes with that position. If the conference committee agrees on a single version and if both houses approve it by the required margins, the bill goes to the governor for his or her approval. Otherwise, the proposed legislation is dead.

Usually, a bill becomes law if the governor signs it or takes no action within twelve days. However, if it is passed immediately before a session's end, the governor has thirty days to act. If the governor vetoes a bill, an absolute two-thirds majority must be attained in both houses for it to become law. Attaining such a lopsided vote is next to impossible, so vetoed bills generally fall by the wayside.

The Informal Process

Politics permeates the formal, "textbook" process by which a bill becomes law. This means that every piece of legislation is considered not only on its merits but also on the basis of a variety of factors, including political support, interest group pressure, public opinion, and personal power.

Members of the majority party chair most, if not all, of the committees in any given year. With Democrats in control for most of the last five decades, they have reaped the benefits of the committee chairs (extra staff, procedural advantages, and so forth), secured the best committee assignments, and been assigned

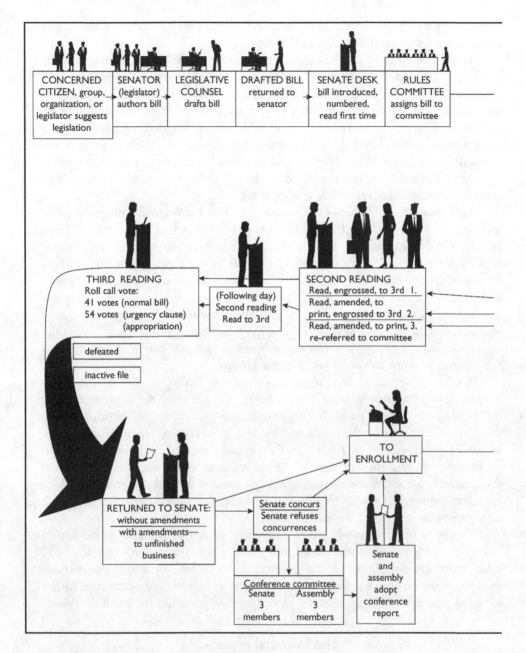

FIGURE 5.4 How a Bill Becomes a Law (Continued)

the best offices. Likewise, when assembly Republicans briefly held a bare major-ity in 1996, they assumed control of twenty-five of the twenty-six committees, and the benefits were reversed.

Political support within the legislature is essential to numerous decisions. So many bills flow through the process that members often vote on measures they haven't even read, relying on staff, committee, or leadership recommendations. Sometimes, a bill's fate rests with key legislative leaders, who can use their

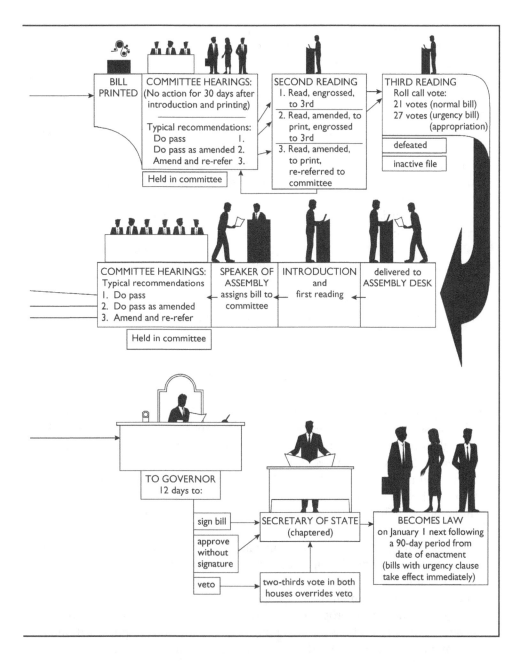

positions to stifle or speed up a proposal at various points in the legislative process. In the assembly, the speaker may actually appoint extra members to a committee temporarily to move a bill along. Outcomes are also affected by **logrolling**, a give-and-take bargaining process in which legislators agree to support each other's bills. More often than not, legislators give away their votes on matters of little concern to them in hopes of mollifying opponents or pleasing powerful leaders. And on occasion, some members of the assembly have been known to cast the votes of other members by clicking their electronic devices.

This illegal activity, called **ghost voting**,[15] can't take place in the senate, where members cast votes by a show of hands.

Public opinion also affects legislation, sometimes dramatically. Recent statutes on excessive drinking, smoke-free restaurants and bars, environmental quality, and longer sentences for repeat felons have been enacted in direct response to public concern.

As noted in Chapter 4, pressure from interest groups permeates the legislative process. With the combined cost of legislative campaigns leaping from $7 million in 1966 to $100 million in 1998, candidates welcomed the contributions of these interest groups. Proposition 34, enacted in 2002, attempted to impose some constraints on such fund-raising. Thus, in 2002 the cost of state legislative campaigns declined to $76.5 million.[16] Nevertheless, by 2008 the cost of state legislative campaigns had grown by more than 60 percent, to $129.75 million.[17] At just under $1.3 million per seat (eighty assembly, twenty state senate), California's legislative elections were the most expensive in the nation. And given the millions of dollars spent by independent expenditure committees that were not tied officially to any candidate, the total spent on legislative campaigns in the state in all likelihood exceeded $150 million.

OTHER FACTORS

Finally, personal power within the legislature remains a component of the political process, especially in cases of conflict. One such example occurred in 2008, when then senate president pro tem Don Perata and the Democratic majority of the senate Rules Committee blocked four Schwarzenegger nominees to the twelve-member California Parole Board. For months, Perata had complained about California's low parole rate, implying that the problem rested with the parole board. This action sent a clear message to both the board and the governor.[18]

Sometimes the mere threat of an initiative spurs the legislature into action that institutional gridlock might otherwise have prevented. In 2003 and 2004, after prodding by governors Davis and Schwarzenegger and the early signature-gathering efforts of an initiative proposal, the legislature reformed the state's workers' compensation program.[19] Conversely, the legislature's work on climate change was nearly undone in November 2010 by a business-sponsored initiative to delay implementation of AB 32. On this occasion, the voters elected to let the controversial law remain in place.

UNFINISHED BUSINESS

Today's legislature faces myriad issues, ranging from a questionable public education system to a deteriorating infrastructure. Faced with revolving participants, the legislature operates with little stability and less tradition. Term limits, restrictions on budget growth (see Chapter 8), and recession for most of the last decade have added to the woes of this policymaking body. Nothing has suffered more than the annual budget, which more times than not emerges well after the start of the next fiscal year. As a result, this outcome can be painful to recipients of services and programs, many of whom are poor, elderly, and sick.

In 2010, the voters attempted to ease budget gridlock by passing a ballot measure which reduced the required budget vote to a simple majority. But with an absolute two-thirds vote still required for raising revenues, it remains to be seen whether the change is anything but symbolic. Earlier, Governor Schwarzenegger tapped into voter anger when he casually suggested that the state would be better off with a part-time legislature, but he dropped the proposal after it garnered little traction in state public opinion polls. His contempt for the legislature seemed rather transparent, although Schwarzenegger isn't the only California to bear such sentiments.

Still, while the voters have blamed the legislature for gridlock, they rejected a ballot measure in 2010 that would have made it easier to pass budgets by reducing the required majority from two-thirds to a majority. Arnold Schwarzenegger tapped into this anger early on in his governorship when he casually suggested one day that perhaps the state would be better off with a part-time legislature, but he dropped the proposal after it garnered little traction in state public opinion polls. Yet his contempt for the legislature seems rather transparent, although he's not the only California governor ever to have borne such sentiments.

With all these pressures, legislators often seem to react to problems rather than to anticipate or solve them. As a consequence, public policies are made increasingly by initiative, the governor, or the courts. Nevertheless, the legislature continues to grapple with the leading issues of the day, and at least sometimes, lawmakers manage to overcome assorted obstacles in a fractured political environment to enact policies of substance.

NOTES

1. *Californians and Their Government*, Public Policy Institute of California Statewide Survey (San Francisco: PPIC, January 2010).

2. In general, the plan provided one senator per county. In a few cases, two low-populated counties shared a senator, and in one case, three low-populated counties—Alpine, Inyo, and Mono—shared a senator.

3. Legislators receive monthly allowances for cars (including gasoline and maintenance); life, health, dental, vision, and disability insurance; and a daily housing allowance when they are in session in Sacramento. On average these benefits amount to about $42,000 annually, almost all of which is nontaxable. For an interesting critique, see Dan Walters, "Legislative Per Diem Boondoggle," *Sacramento Bee*, July 7, 2007, p. A3.

4. The other full-time legislatures are Alaska, Florida, Massachusetts, Michigan, New Jersey, New York, Ohio, Pennsylvania, and Wisconsin.

5. "Plan to Redraw Districts Passes," *Los Angeles Times*, September 14, 2001, p. B8.

6. *Ibid.*

7. Rene Bukovichik Van Vechten, "Taking the Politics Out of Politics? State Legislative Politics and Institutional Reform in Twentieth Century California" (Ph.D. diss., University of California, Irvine 2002), 203–213.

8. *Ibid*, p. 21.

9. "Report Chronicles Downside of Term Limits," Stateline.org, August 16, 2006, www.stateline.org/live/details/story?contentId=134247.

10. Public Policy Institute of California, *Californians and Their Government*," (San Francisco: PPIC, September 10, 2009), p. 7.

11. Kathleen Les, "Mr. Mayor Goes to the Capitol," *California Journal* 30, no. 10 (October 1999): 36–38.

12. See Bruce E. Cain and That Kousser, *Adapting to Term Limits: Recent Experiences and New Directions* (San Francisco: Public Policy Institute of California, 2004), p. 15.

13. "Choosing Sides in State Budget Fiasco," *Los Angeles Times*, June 26, 2010, pp. A1, A14.

14. *Ibid.*

15. See "Ghost Voting: A Long History," *San Francisco Chronicle*, June 10, 2008, pp. A1, A16.

16. "What Limits? New Law Can't Stop Big Money," *Los Angeles Times*, September 3, 2003, pp. A1, A18.

17. Institute on Money and State Politics, "State Elections Overview, 2008," Helena, Mont., April 2010, www.followthemoney.org/database/StateGlance/state_candidates.phtml?s=CA&y=2008&f=0&so=a&p=7#sorttable (accessed April 2010).

18. "Dems Reject Two of Schwarzenegger's Parole Appointees," *Sacramento Bee*, June 26, 2008, p. A3.

19. "State Fund Posts 9.9% Dip in Comp Rates," *Los Angeles Times*, June 5, 2004, pp. C1, C2.

LEARN MORE ON THE WEB

California State Assembly:
www.assembly.ca.gov

California State Senate:
www.senate.ca.gov

Campaign finance:
www.followthemoney.org

Daily politics and policy-related news:
www.rtumble.com

Legislative Analyst's Office:
www.lao.ca.gov

Legislative histories and bill analyses:
www.leginfo.ca.gov/bilinfo.html

National Conference of State Legislatures:
www.ncsl.org

Search for your legislator:
www.legislature.ca.gov/legislators_and_districts/districts/districts.html

Watch or listen to the legislature in session:
www.legislature.ca.gov/the_state_legislature/calendar_and_schedules/
audio_tv.html

LEARN MORE AT THE LIBRARY

Bill Boyarsky. *Big Daddy: Jesse Unruh and the Art of Power Politics*. Berkeley: University of California Press, 2008.

Willie L. Brown, Jr., and P. J. Corkery. *Basic Brown: My Life and Our Times*. New York: Simon & Schuster, 2008.

Gerald C. Lubenow, ed. *Governing California*, 2d ed. Berkeley, Calif.: Institute of Governmental Studies Press, 2006.

Gary F. Moncrief, Peverill Squire, and Malcolm Jewel. *Who Runs for the Legislature?* Upper Saddle River, N.J.: Prentice Hall, 2001.

Peter Schrag. *California: America's High Stakes Experiment*. Berkeley: University of California Press, 2006.

6

California Law: Courts, Judges, and Politics

CHAPTER CONTENTS

Courts are very much a part of the political process. Judges and politicians have always known this, but the public has been slower to understand the political nature of the judiciary. When governors made controversial appointments to the courts during the 1970s and 1980s, however, judicial politics became a very public matter. Later, judicial politics became apparent in court decisions that overturned popular initiatives and, of course, in the appointment and confirmation of justices to the United States Supreme Court.

What makes the courts political? It's not just controversial judicial decisions or even the involvement of party politicians. Courts are political because their judgments are choices between public policy alternatives. When judges consider cases, they evaluate the issues before them both in terms of existing legislation and in the context of the U.S. and California constitutions. Rulings based on differing judicial interpretations of these documents help some people and hurt others. This is why the courts, like members of the executive and legislative branches, are subject to the attentions and pressures of California's competing interests, and this is why the courts are political.

THE CALIFORNIA COURT SYSTEM

The California court system is the largest in the nation, with more than two thousand judicial officers and nineteen thousand court employees. The three levels within the system are linked, but each has its own responsibilities. Most cases begin and end at the lowest level. Only a few move up the state's judicial ladder through the appeals process (see Figure 6.1), and even fewer end up in the United States Supreme Court.

The Judicial Ladder

The vast majority of cases begin and end in trial courts, the bottom rung of the judicial ladder. In California, **superior courts** in each county are the trial courts, handling misdemeanor cases (minor crimes, including most traffic offenses), felonies (serious crimes subject to sentences of one year or more in state prison), civil suits (noncriminal disputes), divorces, and juvenile cases. Superior courts also operate small claims courts, where individuals can take cases with damage claims up to $7,500 before a judge without attorneys—sort of like television's *Judge Judy*.

Losers in trial courts may ask the court on the next rung of the judicial ladder to review the decision. Most cases aren't appealed, but when major crimes and penalties or big money are involved, the losers in the cases sometimes request a review by one of California's six district **courts of appeal**. As appellate bodies, these courts do not hold trials like the ones we see on television. Lawyers make arguments and submit briefs to panels of three justices, who try to determine whether the original trial was conducted fairly. These justices consider only possible legal errors, not the verdict in the case. If they find errors, they can send the case back for another trial or even dismiss the charges.

Ultimately, parties to the cases may petition for review by the seven-member state **supreme court**, the top of California's judicial ladder. Few cases reach this level because most are resolved in the lower courts and the high court declines most of the petitions. When the California Supreme Court hears a case, its decision is final unless issues of federal law or the U.S. Constitution arise; the United States Supreme Court may consider such cases.

If a higher court refuses an appeal, the lower court's decision stands. Even when a case is accepted, the justices of the higher court have agreed only to consider the issues. They may or may not overturn the decision of the lower court.

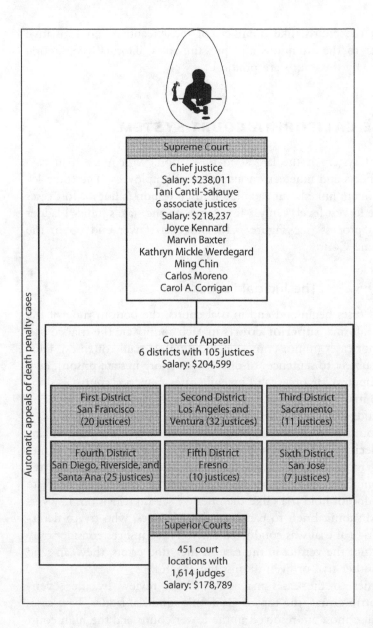

FIGURE 6.1 The California Court System

SOURCE: California Judicial Council

Judicial Election and Selection

Although the tiered structure of the California courts is similar to that of the federal courts, the selection of judges is not. Federal judges and members of the United States Supreme Court are appointed by the president subject to confirmation by the U.S. Senate. Once appointed, they serve for life. California judges and justices, however, gain office through a more complicated process and regularly face the voters. This periodic scrutiny by the public, the media, and interest groups helps keep judges and their decisions in the news.

Formal qualifications to become a judge are few: candidates must have been admitted to practice law in California for at least ten years. Technically, superior court judges are elected, but most actually gain office through appointment by the governor when a sitting judge dies, retires, or is promoted between elections. The governor also appoints people to the bench when the legislature creates new judgeships. A governor who is elected to two terms of office may appoint as many as half of the state's sitting judges, significantly affecting judicial practices. Governors generally appoint judges who are members of their own political parties, although Republican governor Arnold Schwarzenegger was more willing than any of his predecessors to appoint judges who are not members of his own political party.[1] Prior service as a district attorney (prosecutor) is common for successful appointees—a fact leading to complaints that judges in general are biased against defendants and defense attorneys.[2]

Appointed judges must run for office when their terms expire, but running as incumbents, they almost always win. Superior court judges can also gain office simply by declaring their candidacy for a specific judicial office and then running. If no candidate wins a majority in the primary election, the two candidates with the most votes face each other in a **runoff election** in November. Superior court judges serve six-year terms and then may run for reelection, usually without opposition. Judges have no term limits.

Appointments and the Higher Courts

Unlike lower court judges, members of the district courts of appeal and the state supreme court attain office only by gubernatorial appointment. The governor's possible nominees are first screened by the state's legal community through its Commission on Judicial Nominees Evaluation. Then the nominees must be approved by the **Commission on Judicial Appointments**, consisting of the attorney general, the chief justice of the state supreme court, and the senior presiding justice of the courts of appeal. The commission may reject a nominee, but it has done so only twice since its creation in 1934.

Once approved by the Commission on Judicial Appointments, the new justices take office, but they must go before the voters at the next gubernatorial election. No opponents or political party labels appear on the ballot; the voters simply check yes or no on the retention of the justices in question. If approved, they serve the remainder of the twelve-year term of the person they have replaced, at which time they can seek voter confirmation for a standard twelve-year term and additional terms after that.

Eleven other states select their supreme court justices in a similar fashion, but twenty-six rely solely on elections. The governor or legislature appoints justices in the remaining twelve states.

Firing Judges

Almost all judges easily win election and reelection, mostly without opposition. Those who designed the system probably intended it to be this way. They wanted to distance judges somewhat from politics and to ensure their independence by giving them relatively long terms, thus also ensuring relatively consistent interpretation of the law. Avoiding costly election campaigns that depend on financial contributors also promotes independence. The framers of the U.S. Constitution put such a high value on judicial continuity and independence that they provided for selection by appointment rather than by election and allowed judges to serve for life. For most of California's history, these values also seemed well entrenched in the political culture, and the state's judges functioned without much criticism or interference. Nevertheless, California's constitution provides several mechanisms of judicial accountability, all of which have been used recently. Judges can be removed through elections, but they can also be reprimanded or removed by the judicial system itself.

Incumbent justices of the California Supreme Court routinely won reelection without serious challenge until 1966, when a backlash against decisions that supported racial integration led to an unsuccessful campaign to unseat justices who were viewed as too liberal. Over the next two decades, several lower court judges faced challenges because critics viewed them as lenient toward criminals, and some were defeated. Although early efforts to oust liberal members of the state supreme court failed, anticourt elements triumphed in 1986, when Chief Justice Rose Bird and two other liberal justices appointed by former Democratic governor Jerry Brown were swept out of office—the only justices removed by the voters in California history. Since then, the anticourt fervor has subsided. Today, sitting judges are rarely challenged.

Judges also can be removed by the judicial system itself. The **Commission on Judicial Performance** was created in 1960 to investigate charges of misconduct or incompetence. Its members include three judges (appointed by the supreme court), two lawyers (appointed by the governor), and six public members (two each appointed by the governor, the senate Rules Committee, and the speaker of the assembly). Few investigations result in any action, but if the charges are confirmed, the commission may impose censure, removal from office, or forced retirement.

Hundreds of complaints against judges are filed with the commission each year; about one-third are investigated. In the rare cases in which the commission finds a judge to be at fault, it usually issues a warning or reprimand. Even more rarely, the commission may remove a judge from the bench. In recent years, judges have been removed for lying about campaign funds, threatening a district attorney, inappropriate interventions in trials, and in one case, excessive delays and neglect of court orders. Actual removals from the bench are rare, however, because those whose conduct is questionable usually resign before the commission's investigation is completed.

THE COURTS AT WORK

In 2007–2008, 9,552,781 cases were filed in California's trial courts. Traffic infractions made up 68.4 percent of these cases. Felony and misdemeanor (criminal) cases numbered 1,252,556 (13.1 percent), and the balance were civil suits (on contract disputes, for example) or divorce and family law cases.[3]

California's constitution guarantees the right to a jury trial for both criminal and civil cases; if both parties agree, however, a judge alone may hear the case. In jury trials, prospective jurors are drawn from lists of licensed drivers, voters, and property owners, but finding a twelve-member jury is often difficult. Many people avoid jury duty because it takes time away from work and pays only a few dollars a day. Homemakers and retired people are most readily available, but they alone cannot make up a balanced jury. Poor people and minorities tend to be underrepresented because they are less likely to be on the lists from which jurors are drawn and because some avoid participation in a system that they distrust.

The parties in civil cases provide their own lawyers, although legal aid societies sometimes help those who can't afford counsel. In criminal cases, the **district attorney**, an elected county official, carries out the prosecution. Defendants hire their own attorney or are provided with a court-appointed attorney if they cannot afford one. California's larger counties employ a **public defender** to provide such assistance. Well over half of all felony defendants require court-appointed help.

Most cases never go to trial, though. In over 90 percent of all criminal cases, the defendant pleads guilty, often by **plea bargaining**, which results in a pretrial agreement on a plea and a penalty. Plea bargaining reduces the heavy workload of the courts and guarantees some punishment or restitution, but it also allows those charged with a crime to serve shorter sentences than they might have received if convicted of all charges. Most civil suits are also settled without a trial because the parties to the cases reach an agreement to avoid the high costs and long delays of a trial. Only about 0.1 percent of all cases are tried before a jury (11,218 in 2007–2008); a judge alone hears the others that go to trial.[4]

It is important to note that the judicial system as a whole—including judges, prosecutors, public defenders, lawyers, and juries—does not reflect the diversity of California's people. About 83 percent of California's nearly 170,000 active attorneys are non-Hispanic whites, even though minority group members make up 58 percent of the population. About one-third of the state's attorneys are women, however—a number that is quickly rising.[5] Ethnic representation among California's judges is similar: 71 percent are male, and 73 percent are white.[6] These numbers lead critics to express concern about the fact that a predominantly white judicial system metes out justice to defendants who are, in the majority, nonwhite and that punishment is less severe for whites than for minorities convicted of the same crime.[7] African Americans, and to a lesser extent other minorities, perceive this situation and express deep mistrust of the system. Minority participation as attorneys and court officials has increased over time (Table 6.1 shows increasing diversity in judicial appointments), but considerable disparities remain.

Appeals

When a dispute arises over a trial proceeding or its outcome, the losing party may appeal to a higher court to review the case. Most appeals are refused, but the higher courts may agree to hear a case because of previous procedural

T A B L E 6.1 Judicial Appointments by California Governors, 1959–2010

	Male	Female	Non-Hispanic White	Non-Hispanic Black	Hispanic	Asian
Ronald Reagan (R), 1967–1975	97.4% (478)	2.6% (13)	93.1% (457)	2.6% (13)	3.3% (16)	1.0% (5)
Jerry Brown (D), 1975–1983	84.0 (691)	16.0 (132)	75.5 (621)	10.9 (90)	9.4 (77)	4.3 (35)
George Deukmejian (R), 1983–1991	84.8 (821)	15.2 (147)	87.7 (849)	3.6 (35)	5.0 (49)	3.6 (35)
Pete Wilson (R), 1991–1998	74.6 (517)	25.4 (176)	84.4 (585)	5.2 (36)	4.9 (34)	5.5 (38)
Gray Davis (D), 1999–2003	65.8 (237)	34.2 (123)	70.8 (255)	9.25 (33)	12.8 (46)	7.2 (26)
Arnold Schwarzenegger (R), 2003–2010	65.0 (370)	35.0 (199)	73.7 (419)	7.6 (43)	10.7 (61)	8.0 (46)

SOURCE: Governor's Office.

problems (for instance, if the defendant was not read his or her rights) or because it raises untested legal issues. Appellate courts do not retry the case or review the facts in evidence; their job is to determine whether the original trial was fair and the law was applied appropriately. In addition to traditional appellate cases, the state supreme court also automatically reviews all death penalty decisions. Although few in number (17 in 2007–2008), these cases take up a substantial amount of the supreme court's time. A few other cases come to it directly. Known as *original proceedings,* these include cases involving writs of *mandamus* (ordering a government action) and *habeas corpus* (a request for reasons why someone is in custody). Neither the courts of appeal nor the state supreme court can initiate cases. No matter how eager they are to intervene in an issue, they have to wait for someone else to bring the case to them.

Every year, about 10,000 petitions are filed with the California Supreme Court, mostly requesting reviews of cases decided by the courts of appeal. Each year the members of the court, meeting "in conference," choose about two hundred petitions for consideration, a task that consumes an estimated 40 percent of the court's time. By refusing to hear a case, the court allows the preceding decision to stand. When the court grants a hearing, one of the justices (or a staff member) writes a calendar memo analyzing the case. Attorneys representing the two sides present written briefs and then oral arguments, during which they face rigorous questioning by the justices.

After hearing the oral arguments, the justices discuss the case in conference and vote in order of seniority; the chief justice casts the final, and sometimes decisive, vote. If the chief justice agrees with the majority, he or she can assign a justice to write the official court opinion; usually this is the same justice who wrote the initial calendar memo. A draft of the opinion then circulates among the justices, each of whom may concur, suggest changes, or write a dissenting opinion. Finally, after many months, the court's decision is made public. The court issued 116 opinions in 2007–2008—about 1 percent of all the cases filed.

This time-consuming process allows plenty of room for politicking among the justices and depends on a high degree of cooperation and deferential behavior among them—what judges call **collegiality**—as a way of building consensus on issues under consideration. With seven independent minds on the court, ongoing negotiations are needed to reach a majority and a decision.

Running the Courts

In addition to deciding cases, the chief justice acts as the administrative head of the California court system. This entails setting procedures for hearings and deliberations, managing public information for the supreme court, and overseeing its staff. The chief justice also assigns cases to specific appellate courts and appoints temporary justices when there are vacancies on the supreme court due to disqualification, illness, or retirement.

As chair of the **Judicial Council,** the chief justice also takes a hand in managing the entire state court system. The Judicial Council has twenty-one members, including fourteen judges (appointed by the chief justice), four attorneys (appointed by the state bar association), and one member from each house of the state legislature. The Judicial Council makes the rules for court procedures, collects data on the operations and workload of the courts, and oversees the Administrative Office of the Courts with 901 employees and a $220 million budget. During the state budget crisis of 2009, the Judicial Council voted to close the courts one day a month, despite an increasing workload.

THE HIGH COURT AS A POLITICAL BATTLEGROUND

The courts are particularly important and powerful in California because of the nature of California's government and politics. California's constitution has been amended more than five hundred times since it was written in 1879, making it both long and elaborately specific, with components addressing all sorts of matters, both major and mundane. The density of California's constitution is reflected in the structures of government it sets out and is increased through constant revision by initiative. In turn, the length, detail, and continually changing complexity of California's constitution give the courts greater power, because they have the job of determining whether laws and public policy are consistent with the constitution. One scholar called the courts a "shadow government"[8] because of their importance in shaping public policy, but others view this as the courts' appropriate constitutional role.

At the top of California's judicial ladder is the state supreme court, the ultimate interpreter of the state constitution (unless issues arise under the U.S.

Constitution). The court's power makes it a center of political interest: governors strive to appoint justices who share their values and pay close attention to the appointment process. As governors have changed, so have the sorts of justices they appoint. And as its membership has changed, the California Supreme Court has moved across the spectrum from liberal to conservative.

Regardless of its collective political values, the court has not backed away from tackling controversial issues, including occasionally overturning decisions of the legislature or the people (as expressed in initiatives). This willingness is less because of interventionist attitudes on the part of the justices than because of a long, complex, and frequently amended constitution and poorly written laws and initiatives.

Governors, Voters, and the Courts

Long dominated by liberals, California's supreme court took a distinct turn toward the right in 1986, after the voters rejected the reelections of three liberal justices, including Rose Bird, the controversial chief justice at the time. Appointed in 1977 by Governor Jerry Brown, Bird and her colleagues waded into controversy with unpopular rulings on busing for school desegregation and Proposition 13 (the popular property tax reduction initiative), as well as consistently reversing death sentences even as public concern about crime increased. When Bird and two other liberal justices were on the ballot in 1986, conservative Republican governor George Deukmejian led a successful campaign to defeat them. With three new openings, Deukmejian transformed the court with conservative appointees, including a new chief justice.

Subsequent appointees have maintained the court's conservative majority. Today's court includes Marvin Baxter and Joyce Kennard (both Deukmejian appointees) and Kathryn Werdegar and Ming Chin (appointed by Republican governor Pete Wilson). Governor Gray Davis appointed Carlos Moreno, the court's only Democrat, in 2001. The newest justices are Carol A. Corrigan, a 2006 appointment by Governor Schwarzenegger, and Tani Cantil-Sakauye, appointed chief justice by Schwarzenegger in 2010. Minority members of the court include Cantil-Sakauye (who is Filipina), Moreno (who is Latino), Chin (who is Chinese), and Kennard (who is Dutch-Indonesian). Four of the court's seven members are women. All of the current justices have won voter approval, with 65 to 76 percent voting for their retention. Cantil-Sakauye was confirmed for a 12-year term by the voters in 2010 and Justices Chin and Moreno each won an additional 12-year term that year.

With a majority of the justices appointed by Republican governors and solidly confirmed by the voters, California's supreme court today is moderately conservative and less controversial than in the past. The court's conservatism is reflected in its tendency to be pro-prosecution in criminal cases and pro-business in economic cases.[9] The court also disappointed local governments seeking new taxes with rulings that rigidly applied a requirement for two-thirds voter approval, a strict interpretation of 1978's Proposition 13 (see Chapter 8).

Overall, the supreme court avoids **judicial activism** (making policy through court decisions rather than through the legislative or electoral process), but even the current conservative court sometimes asserts its independence, wading into political controversy and significantly affecting state politics. For example, it has followed the Bird court's precedent of approving state-funded abortions, and in 1997 the court ruled against Governor Pete Wilson's plan to privatize the work of the state transportation agency. In 2009, the court rejected a plan by the governor and state legislature to solve their own budget problems by taking transportation and redevelopment funds from local governments.

Most controversially, the courts sometimes overrule decisions of the voters, as they did when they struck down portions of voter-approved initiatives that required tougher sentences of criminals because the proposals shifted discretion from judges to prosecutors. Probably the highest-profile and most controversial action taken by the supreme court, however, was its 2008 ruling on same-sex marriage. When the City and County of San Francisco licensed such marriages in 2004, the supreme court ruled the marriages illegal on the basis of state law, as approved by the voters in 2002. But the constitutionality of that law was challenged in 2008, and on a four-to-three vote, the court ruled that "the California Constitution properly must be interpreted to guarantee this basic civil right to all Californians, whether gay or heterosexual, and to same-sex couples as well as to opposite-sex couples."[10] Opponents quickly qualified **Proposition 8**, an initiative constitutional amendment to restrict marriage to opposite-sex couples. Voters approved the measure, thus overruling the court. That initiative was subsequently challenged in court, but the California Supreme Court accepted it as a legitimate amendment to the state constitution. Then chief justice George wrote that the court's decision was not based on whether Proposition 8 "is wise or sound as a matter of policy," but rather "concerns the right of the people . . . to change or alter the state constitution itself . . . Regardless of our views as individuals on this question of policy, we recognize as judges and as a court our responsibility to confine our consideration to a determination of the constitutional validity and legal effect of the measure in question."[11]

This decision did not put the issue to rest, however. The federal courts are sometimes drawn into battles over California initiatives, too. Since the 1990s, federal courts have overturned initiatives on campaign finance, open primary elections, and limits on public services for immigrants as violations of the U.S. Constitution, which trumps any state law or state constitution. In 2010, proponents of same-sex marriage took their case to a federal district court, arguing that Proposition 8 constituted a denial of equal rights under the U.S. Constitution. The judge in that case ruled in favor of the plaintiffs, thus overriding both the voters of the state of California and the state supreme court. The federal court ruling is being appealed, and the final decision will rest with the United States Supreme Court—or the voters of California when the issue comes back to them in yet another initiative.

Although judicial rulings against voter-approved laws appear undemocratic, the state and federal courts are doing their duty by interpreting these controversial propositions not only for their content but also for their consistency with the California and U.S. constitutions. When the courts find an act of another branch of government or of the voters to be contrary to existing law or to the state or federal constitution, it is their responsibility to overturn that law, even if their decision is unpopular. "When we invalidate one of these initiatives," former chief justice George argued, "what we are doing is not thwarting the public's will. We are adhering to the ultimate expression of the popular will: the Constitution of the United States, or the Constitution of the State of California, which has been adopted by the people and which imposes limits on the initiative process and on lawmaking by legislatures and by the executive."[12]

As controversial as the California Supreme Court's decisions sometimes are, the court's influence goes well beyond this state. A study of court decisions throughout the country found that courts in other states followed precedents set in California more than precedents set in the courts of any other state.[13] This suggests that the California court is well within the mainstream of jurisprudence in the United States. It's also one reason why the court battle over same-sex marriages was so hard fought.

COURTS AND THE POLITICS OF CRIME

Crime topped the list of voter concerns in California and the nation during much of the 1980s and 1990s. Murder, rape, burglary, gang wars, and random violence seemed all too common. Republicans George Deukmejian and Pete Wilson were elected governor at least partly because they were seen as law-and-order candidates.

Capital punishment was a key issue in the 1980s, when a liberal supreme court overturned the vast majority of the death penalty cases it reviewed. Since 1986, when the voters rejected these liberals, the supreme court has affirmed most death sentences. The issue has not gone away, however. Law-and-order advocates still condemn the lengthy delays that plague death penalty appeals—up to ten years for the state courts and another ten years for the federal courts—but experts say that much of the delay is because the courts are unable to either find legal counsel for the condemned or handle the workload. A recent report called the system "broken" and "dysfunctional."[14] Neither the proponents nor the opponents of the death penalty are satisfied with its current administration. Meanwhile, forensic methods such as DNA testing have revealed wrongful convictions in death penalty cases so frequently that a moratorium on executions has been proposed.

In 2006 a federal judge took the issue of capital punishment out of the state courts with a ruling suspending executions in California due to concerns about the drugs used for lethal injections and the conditions of outdated prison facilities for executions. Since then, the state has built a new death chamber, but executions remained suspended as of 2010 because the state failed to satisfy the federal court regarding lethal injections.

Law-and-order proponents also pushed for tougher sentences for other crimes. Beginning in the 1980s, voters passed a series of initiatives that strengthened penalties for many crimes, and in 1994 the electorate approved the "three-strikes" initiative. The new law reflected the view that liberal judges who were "soft on crime" were letting criminals off with light sentences. "**Three strikes**" required anyone convicted of three felonies to serve a sentence of twenty-five years to life: "three strikes and you're out."

The three-strikes law quickly increased the state's prison population, as well as its spending on prisons (see Chapter 8). New prisons were built, and operating the state prison system absorbs an ever-growing share of the state budget. With many of the state's worst criminals incarcerated for life, three-strikes prosecutions declined, and so did California's crime rate. Violent crime in California peaked in 1992 (two years before the three-strikes law) and has declined since then. In 2008 the number of violent crimes was about the same as in 1979, even with 14 million more people living in the state.[15] Conservatives attribute this decline to tougher judges and penalties, but many experts argue that the declining crime rate was due to economic prosperity and demographics, with fewer people in the age group that is most commonly associated with criminal activity. Even in the recent recession, crime rates continue to decline. In any case, crime has resonated far less as an issue in recent statewide elections. In the last few years, education, the economy, and health care have outranked crime as the top concerns of California voters.

Meanwhile, the prison population in California remains huge, which means the cost of incarcerating all these men and women is also huge. But despite a massive investment of tax funds, California's prisons are overcrowded and beset by violence and disease. A system built for 84,271 inmates housed 173,479 in 2006 (a historic high) and 168,830 in 2009.[16] Conditions in the prison health-care system were so bad that a class action suit was brought to a federal court, which intervened on grounds that these conditions constituted "cruel and unusual punishment" under the U.S. Constitution. In 2005 a federal judge put the prison health system in the hands of a court-appointed monitor. In 2009, seeing minimal progress, federal judges gave the state forty-five days to come up with a plan to reduce the prison population—and then rejected the plan submitted by Governor Schwarzenegger, who was unable to persuade the legislature to fund new prisons or approve release of some prisoners (the elderly or low-level offenders, for example). Schwarzenegger appealed the case to the United States Supreme Court, but a ruling was not expected before 2011.

CALIFORNIA LAW

Crime and other issues discussed in this chapter remind us that the courts play a central role in the politics of our state. Controversies about judicial appointments and decisions make the political nature of the courts apparent, especially when the rulings of the court conflict with the will of the electorate as expressed in initiatives. Yet the courts can never be free of politics. They make policy and interpret the law, and their judgments vary with the values of those who make them.

NOTES

1. "Forum Sheds Light on How Judges Are Screened, Chosen," *San Jose Mercury News,* June 4, 2006. As of 2006, 54 percent of Schwarzenegger's appointees were Republican, 34 percent were Democrats, and 12 percent had "unstated" party affiliations.

2. Rodney F. Kingsnorth, "Change How We Appoint Judges," in *Remaking California,* ed. R. Jeffrey Lustig (Berkeley, Calif.: Heyday Books, 2010), pp. 226–227.

3. Judicial Council, *2009 Court Statistics Report,* www.courtinfo.ca.gov (accessed July 7, 2010).

4. *Ibid.*

5. California Bar Association, "The State Bar of California: What Does It Do? How Does It Work?" 2006, www.calbar.org (accessed August 12, 2008).

6. Judicial Council of California, "Demographic Data Provided by Justices and Judges Relative to Gender and Race/Ethnicity," www.courtinfo.ca.gov (accessed July 7, 2010).

7. Elsa Y. Chen, "Cumulative Disadvantage and Racial and Ethnic Disparities in California Federal Sentencing," in *Racial and Ethnic Politics in California*, ed. Sandra Bass and Bruce M. Cain (Berkeley: Public Policy Press, Institute of Governmental Studies, University of California, 2008).

8. Charles Price, "Shadow Government," *California Journal,* October 1997, p. 38.

9. See Preble Stolz, Gerald F. Uelmen, and Susan Rasky, "The California Supreme Court," in *Governing California,* ed. Gerald C. Lubenow, 2d ed. (Berkeley: Public Policy Press, Institute of Governmental Studies, University of California, 2006), p. 103.

10. *In re Marriage Cases*, S147999.

11. *Strauss v. Horton*, S168047; *Tyler v. State of California*, S168066; and *City and County of San Francisco v. Horton*, S168078, www.courtinfo.ca.gov/courts/supreme.

12. Ronald George, "Promoting Judicial Independence," *The Commonwealth*, February 2006, p. 10.

13. Jake Dear and Edward W. Jesson, "Followed Rates and Leading Cases, 1940–2005," *University of California, Davis, Law Review* 41 (April 2007): 683.

14. California Commission on the Fair Administration of Justice, "Fair Administration of the Death Penalty," June 30, 2008, www.ccfaj.org (accessed August 1, 2008).

15. "California Crime Rates, 1960-2008," www.disastercenter.com/crime/cacrime.htm (accessed July 9, 2010).

16. Department of Corrections, "Population Reports," www.cdcr.ca.gov (accessed July 9, 2010).

LEARN MORE ON THE WEB

California's court system:
www.courtinfo.ca.gov

California Court Association:
www.calcourt.org

For more on the courts:
www.judgepedia.org

State Bar of California:
www.calbar.org

Ratings of attorneys:
www.avvo.com

LEARN MORE AT THE LIBRARY

Elsa Y. Chen. " Cumulative Disadvantage and Racial and Ethnic Disparities in California Federal Sentencing." In *Racial and Ethnic Politics in California*, edited by Sandra Bass and Bruce M. Cain. Berkeley: Berkeley Public Policy Press, Institute of Governmental Studies, University of California, 2008.

Preble Stolz, Gerald F. Uelmen, and Susan Rasky. " The California Supreme Court." In *Governing California*, 2d ed., edited by Gerald C. Lubenow. Berkeley: Berkeley Public Policy Press, Institute of Governmental Studies, University of California, 2006.

Franklin E. Zimring, Sam Kamin, and Gordon Hawkins. *Crime and Punishment in California: The Impact of Three Strikes and You're Out*. Berkeley, Calif: Institute of Governmental Studies Press, 1999.

7

The Executive Branch: Coping with Fragmented Authority

CHAPTER CONTENTS

The Governor: First Among Equals

Formal Powers

Informal Powers

Ever-Changing Relationships

The Supporting Cast

The Lieutenant Governor

The Attorney General

The Secretary of State

The Superintendent of Public Instruction

The Money Officers

The Insurance Commissioner

The Supporting Cast—Snow White's Seven Dwarfs?

The Bureaucracy

Making the Pieces Fit

The **governor** is California's most powerful public official. He or she shapes the state budget, appoints key policymakers in the executive and judicial branches, and both responds to and shapes public opinion by taking positions on controversial issues. The governor also is the state's chief administrator; the unofficial leader of his or her political party; and liaison to other states, the U.S. government, and other nations. There are times when the governor's powers extend even beyond their normally broad limits to international issues such as immigration or global warming. At times, the governor's performance can generate intense reactions, as evidenced by the public's rejection of the items put forth in special elections by Governor Arnold Schwarzenegger in 2005 and 2009. No one in state government is in the spotlight as often the governor.

Unlike the president of the United States, the governor of California shares authority with seven other independently elected executive officers. Occasionally, these other executives clash with the governor over the use of power, as do the legislature and the judiciary. Simply put, the executive branch is anything but a unified body. Endless schisms between officeholders contribute to the state's fragmentation.

There has been one change in the drama among elected officials, however. Term limits, although applicable to both the executive and legislative branches, have left the governor in a stronger position relative to the legislature because of the governor's near certainty of two 4-year terms of office. With legislative leaders ascending to power on much shorter time schedules, the governor's experience has worked to his favor.

THE GOVERNOR: FIRST AMONG EQUALS

The current governor of California, Democrat Edmund J. ("Jerry") Brown, Jr., was elected in 2010. Brown succeeded Arnold Schwarzenegger, who had been elected after the recall of Gray Davis from office (see Table 7.1). With an annual salary of $206,500, he is the highest-paid chief executive of the fifty states. The governor of New York, second highest in the nation, receives $179,000. Still, this compensation is well below the salaries earned by many other government employees in California, particularly in large cities and counties. Even among state employees, prison wardens, retirement program coordinators, physicians, and university presidents earn considerably more than the governor.

T A B L E 7.1 California Governors and Their Parties, 1943–2015

Name	Party	Dates in Office
Earl Warren	Republican*	1943–1953
Goodwin J. Knight	Republican	1953–1959
Edmund G. Brown, Sr.	Democrat	1959–1967
Ronald Reagan	Republican	1967–1975
Jerry Brown	Democrat	1975–1983
George Deukmejian	Republican	1983–1991
Pete Wilson	Republican	1991–1999
Gray Davis	Democrat	1999–November 2003
Arnold Schwarzenegger	Republican	2003–2011
Jerry Brown	Democrat	2011–2015

*Warren cross-filed as both a Republican and a Democrat in 1946 and 1950.
SOURCE: California Secretary of State.

Jerry Brown's election to the governor's office is the latest example of California's bizarre politics. A political fixture in the state since his first election to the Los Angeles Community College District Board of Trustees in 1969 (that's not a typo!), Brown served was elected governor in 1974 and 1978 after serving as the Secretary of State. His father, Edmund G. (Pat) Brown also was governor in 1958 and 1962. Because his governorship occurred before California adopted term limits in 1990, Brown was eligible to run again. With his third term Brown is in rare company. Only Earl Warren was elected to three terms in the pre-term limit era.

Brown's election is significant on another way: He was outspent by a margin of more than 6-to-1, courtesy of Meg Whitman's largely self-funded campaign in which the Republican donated $175 million of her own fund to her ill-fated cause. Indeed, a cornerstone of Brown's campaign accused Whitman of trying to buy the governorship. Apparently there was no sale.

Formal Powers

Much of the governor's authority comes from formal powers written into the state's constitution and its laws. These responsibilities guide his or her relationships with the legislative and judicial branches, as well as with the other office-holders in the executive branch.

Submission of an Annual Budget   No formal power is more important than the governor's budgetary responsibilities. The budget outlines the sources of state revenues and the programmatic recipients of state funds. According to the state constitution, the governor must recommend a balanced budget to the legislature within the first ten days of each calendar year. Budget work is virtually a year-round task, and it consumes more of the governor's time than just about any other activity except responding to emergencies such as earthquakes or fires. The governor is assisted in this effort by an appointed **director of finance**, the key person in charge of developing the budget document, who spends months with his or her staff gathering data and budget requests from the dozens of departments and agencies that make up the state's bureaucracy. Initial preparations begin on July 1—the start of the fiscal year—and culminate with the governor's submission of a proposal to the legislature the following January (see Chapter 8). Officially, the annual process ends with the signing of the budget document by the governor before the end of the fiscal on June 30, so that the next year can begin with a budget in place. More often than not, however, budget negotiations linger well into summer.

Vetoes   The state constitution requires the legislature to respond to the governor's budget no later than June 15 so that the budget can go into effect by July 1—a formidable task because the proposed document is several hundred pages in length. Technically, legislators can disregard any or all parts of the budget package and pass their own version, but usually they stay reasonably close to the governor's proposals. They realize that the governor has the final say, albeit with some limitations. The governor cannot add money, but he or she can reduce or eliminate expenditures through use of the **item veto** before signing the budget into law. An absolute two-thirds vote from each house of the legislature—a near impossibility (see Chapter 5)—is necessary to overturn item vetoes. Accordingly, legislators often attempt to head off vetoes by negotiating with the governor in advance.

Of course, bills on topics other than budget matters also reach the governor's desk. Whereas the item veto is restricted to appropriations measures, the **general veto** allows the governor to reject any other bill passed by the legislature. It, too, can be overturned only by an absolute two-thirds vote in each house. Over a period of more than twenty years, George Deukmejian, Pete Wilson, and Gray Davis exercised general and item vetoes without a single one being overturned by the legislature.

Arnold Schwarzenegger used the veto even more than Davis, wielding his veto pen with vigor (see Table 7.2). He vetoed more than one-fourth of the bills that reached his desk. More than any governor in history, Schwarzenegger turned the veto into a potent legislative weapon. And, as with his immediate predecessors, he did not suffer any legislative rejections.

Under most circumstances, the governor has twelve days to act after the legislature passes a bill. On the hundreds of bills enacted by the legislature at a session's end, however, the governor has thirty days to act. Only a veto can keep a bill from becoming law. After the governor's time limit has passed, any unsigned or unvetoed bill becomes law the following January (unless the bill is an urgency measure, in which case it takes effect immediately upon signature).

Special Session.   If the governor believes that the legislature has not addressed an important issue, he or she can take the dramatic step of calling a **special session**. At that time, the lawmakers must discuss only the specific business proposed by the governor. Special sessions often are called to respond to specific crises, as when Governor Schwarzenegger called on the legislature in 2006 to correct a prison system so overcrowded that a federal judge assumed oversight responsibilities.[1] He also called special sessions on health-care reform, water

TABLE 7.2 Vetoes and Overrides, 1967–2010

Governor	Bills Vetoed (%)	Vetoes Overridden
Ronald Reagan (1967–1975)	7.3	1
Jerry Brown (1975–1983)	6.3	13
George Deukmejian (1983–1991)	15.1	0
Pete Wilson (1991–1999)	16.6	0
Gray Davis (1999–November 2003)	17.6	0
Arnold Schwarzenegger (November 2003–2011)	26.4	0

SOURCE: Clerk, California State Senate.

policy, public education, and repeatedly on state budget deficits. Schwarzenegger called sixteen special sessions during his years in office—the most of any governor in state history—leading some to believe that he had diluted the significance of the concept.[2]

Executive Order.   On occasion, the governor can make policy by signing an **executive order**, an action that looks similar to legislation. Governors must exercise this power carefully because such moves often lead to lawsuits over the breadth of their powers. Immediately after taking office in 2003, Arnold Schwarzenegger signed an executive order to repeal the vehicle license fee, a revenue source that had been restored by Governor Gray Davis to reduce the state deficit but that offended many voters. By taking this action, Schwarzenegger honored a crucial campaign promise, although removal of the motor vehicle license fee contributed to a revenue gap almost as large as the one that helped chase Gray Davis from office. Later in his tenure, Schwarzenegger used the executive order to force furloughs on state workers as a means of lessening the state's budget deficit. Here he was only partially successful, as lawsuits overturned the furloughs affecting about one-fourth of the state's workers.[3]

Appointment Powers.   The governor's appointment powers, although substantial, are somewhat more restricted than his or her budgetary authority because others must approve all appointments except personal staff. Moreover, gubernatorial appointees hold only the top policymaking positions in the state system. Before the Progressive reforms, California governors could rely on patronage, or the "spoils" system, to hire friends and political allies. Today, 99 percent of all state employees are not appointed by the governor but rather are selected through a civil service system based on merit. The governor still fills about 2,500 key positions in the executive departments and cabinet agencies, except for the Departments of Justice and Education, whose heads are elected by the public. Together, these appointees direct the state bureaucracy (see Figure 7.1).

The state senate must approve most of the governor's appointees. Generally, senate confirmation is routine, but occasionally the governor's choice for a key post is rejected for reasons other than qualifications. In instances of an opening in the executive branch, both houses must weigh in with positive majorities. In early 2010, the legislature confirmed the selection of Abel Maldonado to fill the lieutenant governor vacancy that resulted from Lieutenant Governor John Garamendi's winning election to a vacated seat in the House of Representatives. After several months of fits and starts, Maldonado was confirmed and ran as the incumbent in the November 2010 general election.

The governor also appoints people to more than three hundred state boards and commissions. Membership on some boards—such as the Arts Council and the Commission on Aging, which have only advisory authority—is largely ceremonial and without pay. Other boards, however, such as the California Energy Commission (CEC), the Public Utilities Commission (PUC), the California Coastal Commission (CCC), and the California Division of Occupational Safety and Health (DOSH; better known as Cal-OSHA), make important policies free from gubernatorial control. Nevertheless, the governor affects key "independent" boards through his or her appointments and manipulation of the budget.

Perhaps the most enduring of all gubernatorial appointments are judgeships. The governor fills both vacancies and new judgeships that are periodically created by the legislature. In his eight years as governor, Pete Wilson filled 693 posts. During his five years in office, Gray Davis appointed 360 judges. Between his election in 2003 and 2010, Arnold Schwarzenegger appointed 545 judges, including two members of the state supreme court. Most judges continue to serve long after those who appointed them have gone. However, the governor's power is checked here to a degree, too, by various judicial commissions and by the voters in future elections. During his tenure as governor, Arnold Schwarzenegger was much less partisan with his judicial appointments than his predecessors (see Chapter 6).

In addition to the major formal authority discussed above, the governor has a wide range of other formal powers. He or she is commander in chief of the California National Guard, which on occasion is sent to help manage local crises in the state on a short-term basis. The governor also has the power to grant pardons, reprieves, or sentence commutations, although such authority is rarely exercised. Finally, the governor is the ceremonial head of state for greeting dignitaries from other countries. Along with the other major functions, these powers keep the governor on a fast track.

Informal Powers

Formal constraints on the governor can be offset to some extent by a power that is not written into the constitution at all: the governor's popularity. As the top state official, the governor is highly visible. The attention focused on the office provides a platform from which the governor can influence the public and overcome political opponents.

Historically, California's governors have used the prestige of their office to push their own agendas. Republican governor Pete Wilson touted **Proposition 187**, an attempt to reduce government benefits to illegal immigrants that was ultimately declared unconstitutional by the federal courts. In 1996 Wilson championed **Proposition 209**, titled the California Civil Rights Initiative, to eliminate affirmative action. And in 1998 he promoted **Proposition 227**, an initiative restricting bilingual education.

Democratic governor Gray Davis used his executive powers to relax the state's air standards during the 2001 state energy crisis, permitting older, dirtier electricity plants to produce more energy. When Davis was reelected in 2002, energy problems were compounded by a lengthy recession and huge budget shortfalls (see Chapter 8). But his inability to rely upon informal power stemmed from Davis's personality. He attacked the other branches of state government, claiming that state legislators were supposed to implement his vision[4] and that judicial appointees should reflect his views.[5] Further, his obsession with constant fund-raising from individuals and organizations in search of state business added

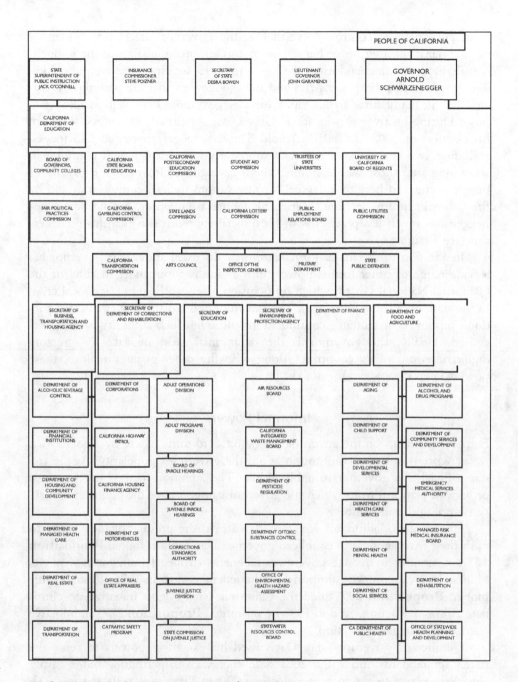

FIGURE 7.1 State Departments and Agencies.

to his image problems. In a July 2003 field poll, 61 percent of the respondents blamed Davis for the state's problems.[6] Thus, as an unprecedented recall effort moved along during 2003, Davis first lost his public support and informal power, and soon after that, his job.[7]

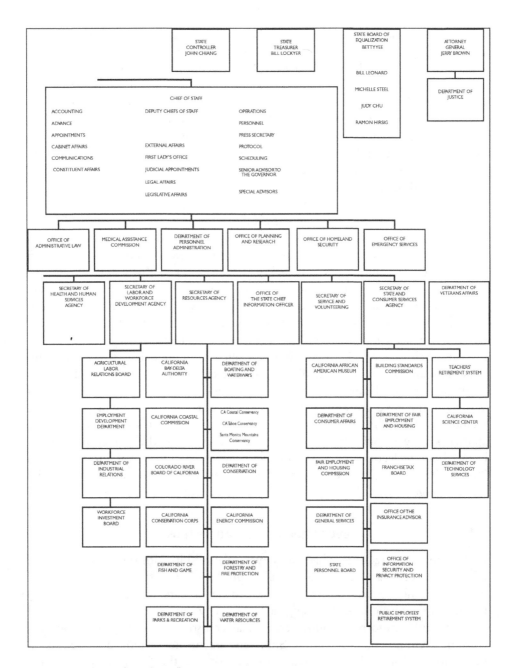

FIGURE 7.1 (Continued)

Arnold Schwarzenegger, in contrast, tried to use his informal powers both by schmoozing with and cajoling legislators and by appealing directly to the public. His record was mixed. He belittled the legislature, calling members "girlie men" for not adopting his budgets.[8] Sending the legislature into special session on sixteen occasions, rarely with any concrete plan, also did not win him friends among Democrats or Republicans. Frustrated, Schwarzenegger often went beyond the legislature to the chagrin of many members, cutting deals directly with organizations and institutions from local governments to universities, prison guards, and Indian gaming interests. Sometimes he prevailed, but other times he did not. Many of his item vetoes of "safety net" programs were overturned by the courts, yet his executive order to furlough state workers because of a budget shortfall was partially successful. And in 2010, Schwarzenegger worked out pension deals with several state employee unions that mandated higher employee contributions—something the legislature had not dared to even tackle.[9] In his own way, although clumsily at times, Schwarzenegger did attempt change.

Like Pete Wilson, Schwarzenegger went directly to the voters, but with mixed results. In March 2004 he barnstormed the state for Proposition 57, described as a $15 billion "recovery" bond, and **Proposition 58**, a measure designed to create more reserves in the future; both measures passed. But in 2005 Schwarzenegger suffered a major defeat, when he asked the voters to approve ballot measures on teacher tenure, union campaign contributions, strict state budget controls, and redistricting. So unpopular was the governor during this time that his standing in the public opinion polls plummeted from 64 percent to 35 percent in ten short months.[10] He never fully recovered.

Still, Schwarzenegger used his personality even in defeat to resurrect his standing with the public. Immediately after the election, he accepted full responsibility for the failed campaign, saying, "The buck stops with me." Using himself as the foil, the governor reflected, "I should have listened to my wife [prominent Democrat Maria Shriver], who said don't do this."[11] That kind of self-effacing approach allowed Schwarzenegger to begin anew with the voters and helped bring about reelection in 2006. But his ballot box success was short-lived. In 2009, Schwarzenegger placed his reputation on the line with support for a series of five budget-related legislative initiatives, all of which failed at the polls.

Ever-Changing Relationships

In the end, Schwarzenegger had an uneven relationship with the public. A blend of fiscal conservatism and social liberalism produced an antitax, antilabor governor who simultaneously was pro-choice, pro-health care, and pro-environment. His values may have lacked ideological consistency, but enough of them seemed to mesh with California's contradictory characteristics—especially his strong record on environmental protection. Still, Schwarzenegger's vision often exceeded his ability to deliver. In successive years, he declared the "year" of political reform, which ended with the defeat of four Schwarzenegger-tailored ballot measures; the "year" of health-care reform, which fizzled in the legislature; and the "year" of education reform, which sputtered out after he cut public funding several years in a row to leave California near the bottom of the fifty states in per capita spending.

Schwarzenegger's biggest political headache came from a poor relationship with members of his own political party. Particularly on social issues, he and the largely conservative Republican legislators had little agreement. Even on fiscal questions, Schwarzenegger and legislative Republicans had great difficulty forging a unified approach against the Democrats, as witnessed by his support for, and their resistance to, a state-funded health-care program, environmental protection legislation, and prison reform. Out of sync with his own party and never in sync with the Democrats, Arnold Schwarzenegger spent much of his governorship isolated from other leaders.

THE SUPPORTING CAST

If California's executive branch were composed solely of the governor, appointed department heads, and the civil service system, it would parallel the federal executive branch. However, the state's executive branch also includes a lieutenant governor, an attorney general, a secretary of state, a controller, a treasurer, an insurance commissioner, a superintendent of public instruction, and a five-member Board of Equalization. All are elected at the same time and serve four-year terms. Unlike the president and vice president, though, who are elected on the same political party ticket, each of these officeholders runs independently.

Most other states provide for the election of a lieutenant governor, a secretary of state, a treasurer, and an attorney general, but few elect an education officer, a controller, a Board of Equalization, and an insurance regulator. Moreover, most states call for the governor and the lieutenant governor (and others, in some cases) to run as a team, thus providing some executive branch cohesion. Not so in California, where each elected member of the executive branch is beholden to no one.

The consequences can be quite serious. For example, when Governor Schwarzenegger unilaterally withheld $3.1 billion for the public schools in 2005 in defiance of what many believed were state guarantees, Superintendent of Public Instruction Jack O'Connell sued. Ultimately, O'Connell dropped the suit after the governor and public school officials found agreement. In 2008 and 2010 Governor Schwarzenegger ordered reductions in the salaries of 200,000 state employees to the federal minimum wage ($6.55 per hour in 2008; $7.25 in 2010) until the legislature provided a budget. State Controller John Chiang, the individual responsible for issuing checks, refused to abide by the order, which he said exceeded Schwarzenegger's authority. Both times the courts found for the governor in principal, but an antiquated payroll system kept the controller from following through before the budget issue was resolved. On another occasion, then state insurance commissioner Steve Poizner sued to stop the sale of the state-run workers' compensation insurance fund, proposed by the governor to help balance the state budget. The issue languished in the courts long after Schwarzenegger and Poizner left office.[12] These examples show the extent to which very public fights can occur between two independently operating officeholders in the executive branch.

The Lieutenant Governor

The **lieutenant governor** is basically an executive-in-waiting with few formal responsibilities. If the governor becomes disabled or is out of the state, the lieutenant governor fills in as acting governor. If the governor leaves office, the lieutenant governor takes over. This has happened seven times in the state's history; the last time was in 1953, when Goodwin Knight replaced Earl Warren, who became chief justice of the United States Supreme Court. The current lieutenant governor, Democrat and former San Francisco Mayor Gavin Newsom, was elected in 2010, displacing Abel Maldonado, who had been appointed to the office earlier in the year.

The lieutenant governor heads some units, such as the State Lands Commission and the Commission on Economic Development, and is an ex officio member of the University of California Board of Regents and California State University Board of Trustees. He or she also serves as president of the state senate, but this job, too, is long on title and short on substance. As senate president, the lieutenant governor may vote to break ties, an event that last occurred in 1976. So minimal are the responsibilities of the lieutenant governor that an occupant of the office once quipped that his biggest daily task was to wake up, check the morning newspaper to see whether the governor had died, and then return to bed![13] That description may stretch the point a bit, but not by much. Still, the officeholder can be a nuisance to the governor, if nothing else. After a contentious budget battle in 2009 in which then Democratic lieutenant governor John Garamendi criticized Governor Schwarzenegger's management of the process, Schwarzenegger slashed Garamendi's office budget by 62 percent.

The Attorney General

Despite the lieutenant governor's higher rank, the **attorney general** is usually considered the second-most powerful member of the executive branch. As head of the Department of Justice, the attorney general oversees law enforcement activities, acts as legal counsel to state agencies, represents the state in important cases, and renders opinions on (interprets) proposed and existing laws. The current attorney general, Republican Steve Cooley, defeated San Francisco District Attorney Kamala Harris for the position in 2010. Previously, Cooley had served as district attorney in Los Angeles County longer than anyone in the county's history. He succeeds Jerry Brown, who served between 2006 and 2010.

Substantial authority and independent election allow the attorney general to chart a course separate from the governor's on important state questions. During his tenure as attorney general, for example, Jerry Brown sued insurance companies for misleading ads, prosecuted companies for not paying at least the minimum wage, and petitioned the federal government to regulate greenhouse gases. This same very public platform will allow Cooley to emphasize themes he mapped out earlier as district attorney. For example, Cooley long has advocated reform for California's "three strikes" law, which imposes long sentences on third-time lawbreakers, even if the third crime is a relatively harmless misdemeanor. No doubt, Cooley will be speaking out this and other issues.

The Secretary of State

Unlike the U.S. cabinet official who bears the same title, the **secretary of state** of California is basically a records keeper and elections supervisor. The job entails certifying the number and validity of signatures obtained for initiatives, referenda, and recall petitions; producing sample ballots and ballot arguments for the voters; publishing official election results; and keeping the records of the legislature and the executive branch. The current secretary of state, Democrat Debra Bowen, was first elected in 2006. She has brought order to an office that was rocked by scandal in 2005, when then secretary of state Kevin Shelley resigned because of a scandal involving illegal campaign contributions.

Recently, the secretary of state has had responsibility for converting California's election system from paper ballots to electronic voting machines. Bowen, a skeptic about electronic voting, has responsibility for modernizing the machines. She has been in no great hurry. In 2007 she announced a ban on almost all electronic voting machines in thirty-nine counties until it could be demonstrated that the machines are not prone to any viruses or manipulation.[14] This policy has required counties to either invest in new state-certified machines that include paper verification or resort to paper ballots.

The Superintendent of Public Instruction

The **superintendent of public instruction** heads the Department of Education. He or she is the only elected official in the executive branch chosen by nonpartisan ballot. Candidates are identified on the primary ballot only by their name and vocation. Unless one candidate wins a majority, the top two candidates face each other in the November general election. The current superintendent of public instruction, for State Senator and Assemblyman Tom Torlakson, was elected in 2010. While in the legislature, Torlakson was a champion of public education. During the fall 2010 campaign, he received strong support from the California Teachers' Association, the most powerful education organization in the state.

In general, the electorate knows little about the candidates for superintendent of public instruction, but teachers' unions, education administrators, and other affected groups take great interest in the choice of superintendent because this official oversees California's massive public education system. The superintendent's powers are severely limited, however—funding is determined largely by the governor's budgetary decisions, and policies are closely watched by the governor-appointed state board of education and the education committees of the legislature.

The Money Officers

Perhaps the most fractured part of the executive branch of California government is the group of elected officials who manage the state's money. Courtesy of the Progressive reformers who feared a concentration of power, the controller, the treasurer, and the Board of Equalization have separate but over-lapping responsibilities in this area. The **controller** supervises all state and local tax collection and writes checks for the state, including those to state employees. The controller is also an *ex officio* (automatic, by virtue of the office) member of several agencies, including the Board of Equalization, the Franchise Tax Board, and the State Lands Commission. Of all the "money officers," the controller is the most powerful, and thus the most prominent. The current controller, Democrat and former Board of Equalization member John Chiang, was elected in 2006 in his first run for statewide office and re-elected in 2010. From time to time, he has been outspoken on California's ongoing budget crisis.

The **treasurer** invests state funds raised through taxes and other means until they are needed for expenditures. The treasurer also borrows money for the state by issuing bonds approved by the voters. Typically amounting to several billion dollars, the bonds are sold in financial markets so that the state can finance long-term projects such as highways, water projects, or other infrastructure needs. The state then "redeems" the bonds over time through interest payments. Democrat Bill Lockyer, former state attorney general, was elected to this office in 2006 and re-elected in 2010. Unlike his predecessors, Lockyer has pushed the limits of his office by presenting periodic reports that reflect on the state's financial status with lending institutions that purchase California bonds.

The **Board of Equalization**, also part of California's fiscal system, oversees the collection of excise taxes on sales, gasoline, and liquor. The board also reviews county property assessment practices to ensure uniform calculation methods and practices. The board has five members—four of whom are elected in districts of equal population plus the controller.

Historically, the Board has attracted little attention. That changed in 2007, when the members voted to tax "alcopops"—sweet alcohol drinks often consumed by underage drinkers—at the same rate as hard liquor instead of beer. The change would have raised the tax from 20 cents per gallon to $3.30 per gallon and would have increased the cost of alcopop drinks by about 25 percent. But manufacturers avoided the tax by lowering the alcohol content below beer percentages. Still, the activism on the part of the Board of Equalization portended a new era for the tax agency.

The Insurance Commissioner

The office of **insurance commissioner** exemplifies the persistent reform mentality of California voters. Until 1988, the office was part of the state's Business, Housing, and Transportation Agency. However, with soaring insurance rates, voters approved an initiative that called for 20 percent across-the-board reductions in insurance premiums and created the elected position of insurance commissioner. ConsumerWatchdog, the public interest group behind the proposition, claims that the law saved California drivers more than $60 billion during its first twenty years of existence.

Democrat Dave Jones, a termed out member of the state assembly, was elected to the office in 2010, succeeding Steve Poizner, who elected to run for governor instead of seeking a second term. Known as a consumer advocate, Jones was named "2008 Consumer Champion" by the California Consumer Federation. He campaigned on the theme to hold health insurance companies accountable for any rate increases.

The Supporting Cast—Snow White's Seven Dwarfs?

Combined, the seven other elected members of the executive branch (plus the Board of Equalization) present an appearance of tremendous political activity. Still, their efforts often center on narrow policy areas and frequently are in opposition to one another, as well as to the much more powerful governor.

THE BUREAUCRACY

Elected officials are just the most observable part of the state's administrative machinery. Backing them up, implementing their programs, and dealing with citizens on a daily basis are about 335,000 state workers—the **bureaucracy**. Only about 5,000 of these workers are appointed by the governor or by other executive officers. Of the rest, 90,000 work at the University of California and California State University. The remainder are hired and fired through the state's **civil service system** on the basis of their examination results, performance, and job qualifications. The Progressives designed this system to insulate government workers from political influences and to make them more professional than those who might be hired out of friendship.

The task of the bureaucracy is to carry out the programs established by the policymaking institutions—the executive branch, the legislature, and the judiciary, along with a handful of regulatory agencies. However, because bureaucrats are permanent, full-time professionals, they sometimes influence the content of programs and policies, chiefly by advising public officials or by exercising the discretion built into the laws that define bureaucratic tasks. The bureaucracy can also influence policy through the lobbying efforts of its employee organizations (see Chapter 4).

State bureaucrats work for various departments and agencies (see Figure 7.1), each run by an administrator who is appointed by the governor and confirmed by the senate. Although civil servants are permanent employees, most administrators serve at the governor's pleasure and must resign at his or her demand. Sometimes, political appointees and civil servants clash over the best ways to carry out state policy. If the bureaucracy becomes too independent, the governor can always use his or her budgetary powers to bring it back into line or, in some cases, dismiss individual employees.

In recent years, California's bureaucrats have been particularly ambitious on climate change. The California Energy Commission has instituted energy efficiency standards for televisions and other electrical appliances. Also, the California Air Resources Board has led the way in regulating greenhouse gas levels.

These efforts have kept California's energy consumption flat during the past three decades, compared with a 40 percent increase in energy consumption nationwide.[15] They have also established California as a trendsetting state on the issues of global warming and energy use.

Some observers have criticized California's bureaucracy as unnecessarily inflated and unresponsive, even though the size of the state's system ranks forty-eighth of the fifty states on a per capita basis.[16] Still, there is no denying that slim or not, the state's bureaucracy has grown in recent years under the Schwarzenegger administration, despite his promise to "blow up the boxes" of the bureaucracy shortly after taking office. Between 2004 and 2008 the number of state employees per resident grew from 8.8 per thousand to 9.5 per thousand. Salary costs during the first five years of Schwarzenegger's governorship increased 37 percent, compared with 5 percent for a similar period under his predecessor, Gray Davis.[17] Clearly, there were differences between the governor's tough talk and reality.

MAKING THE PIECES FIT

The executive branch is a hodgepodge of independently elected authorities who serve in overlapping and conflicting institutional positions. Nobody, not even the governor, is really in charge. Each official simply attempts to carry out his or her mission with the hope that passable policy will result. Occasionally, reformers have suggested streamlining the system by consolidating functions and reducing the number of elective offices, but the only recent change has been the addition of yet another office, that of insurance commissioner.

Despite these obstacles, the officeholders—most notably governors—have been active policymakers. Pete Wilson waged war against illegal immigrants, affirmative action, and welfare while trumpeting the "law and order" theme. Gray Davis responded to the state's power shortage crisis. Arnold Schwarzenegger was instrumental in environmental reform.

Still, the governor does not operate in a vacuum. He or she must contend with other members of the executive branch, a fractured and suspicious legislature, independent courts, a professional bureaucracy, and most of all, an electorate with a highly erratic collective pulse. Whether these conditions are challenges or impediments, they make the executive branch a fascinating element of California government.

NOTES

1. "Gov. Calls for New Spending on Prisons," *Los Angeles Times*, June 27, 2006, pp. A1, A7.

2. "Special Sessions Define Schwarzenegger," Sign on San Diego, October 22, 2009, http://signonsandiego.printthis.clickability.com/pt/cpt?action=cpt&tit.

3. "Judge Halts Many State Furloughs," *San Francisco Chronicle*, March 25, 2010, pp. A1, A12.

4. "Tensions Flare between Davis and His Democrats," *Los Angeles Times*, July 22, 1999, pp. A1, A28.

5. "Davis Comments Draw Fire," *San Jose Mercury News*, March 1, 2000, p. 14A.

6. *The Field Poll*, Release #2074, July 15, 2003.

7. For an account of how Davis fell from power, see Larry N. Gerston and Terry Christensen, *Recall! California's Political Earthquake* (Armonk, N.Y.: M. E. Sharpe, 2004).

8. "Gov. Criticizes Legislators as 'Girlie Men,'" *Los Angeles Times*, July 18, 2004, pp. B1, B18.

9. "Governor Slashes Workers' Pay," *San Francisco Chronicle,* July 2, 2010, pp. C1, C6.

10. "Schwarzenegger's Popularity Slide," *Los Angeles Times*, October 28, 2005, p. B2.

11. "Schwarzenegger Says the Fault Is His," *New York Times*, November 11, 2006, p. A14.

12. "Plan to Sell Portion of State Fund Collapses," *Los Angeles Times*, December 30, 2009, pp. B1, B5.

13. "The Most Invisible Job in Sacramento," *Los Angeles Times*, May 10, 1998, pp. A1, A20.

14. "Touch Vote Machine Ban Hurts Counties, *San Francisco Chronicle*, August 7, 2007, p. B3.

15. "California Imposes Rule for Efficiency on Some TVs," *New York Times*, November 19, 2009, p. A16.

16. "Looking for Waste," *Economist*, May 1, 2010, p. 33.

17. "Soaring Payroll Stymies 'Reform' Governor," *San Francisco Chronicle*, May 28, 2008, pp. A1, A6.

LEARN MORE ON THE WEB

Office of the Attorney General:
www.caag.state.ca.us

Office of the Governor:
www.gov.ca.gov

Office of the Secretary of State:
www.ss.ca.gov

Office of the State Board of Equalization:
www.boe.ca.gov

Office of the State Controller:
www.sco.ca.gov

Office of the State Insurance Commissioner:
www.insurance.ca.gov

Office of the State Treasurer:
   www.treasurer.ca.gov

Office of the State Superintendent of Public Instruction:
   www.cde.ca.gov/eo

Salaries of state employees:
   www.capitolweekly.net/salaries/index.php?_c=yzbexjathf9ge0

LEARN MORE AT THE LIBRARY

John C. Bollens and G. Robert Williams. *Jerry Brown in a Plain Brown Wrapper.*
   Pacific Palisades, Calif.: Palisades Publishers, 1978.

Larry N. Gerston and Terry Christensen. *Recall! California's Political Earthquake.*
   Armonk, N.Y.: M. E. Sharpe, 2004.

Gary G. Hamilton and Nicole Woolsey Biggert. *Governor Reagan, Governor Brown: A
   Sociology of Executive Power.* New York: Columbia University Press, 1984.

Joe Mathews. *The People's Machine.* New York: Public Affairs Press, 2006.

8

Taxing and Spending: Budgetary Politics and Policies

CHAPTER CONTENTS

No issue is more critical to Californians than taxation, and no resource is more important to state policymakers than the revenues generated from taxation. Those dollars become the foundation of the annual state budget, the document that determines where and how state funds will be spent.

The connection between taxing and spending can be difficult. Even though most people may agree on taxes in principle, they often disagree on how much should be collected and from whom, as well as who the recipients of those funds should be. When policymakers seem to stray from general public values on budgetary issues, the voters are not shy about using direct democracy to reorder the state's fiscal priorities—and with so many more policy areas of need than dollars available, much is at stake.

CALIFORNIA'S BUDGET ENVIRONMENT

Unlike the national government, which usually operates with a deficit, states are required to balance their budgets. This has been difficult in California, where a steady flow of immigrants, a burgeoning school-aged population, massive attention to crime, and deteriorating infrastructure make for a challenging budget environment. Since a recession in 2002, the state has struggled with one projected state revenue deficit after another regardless of who has been in power. An astronomical projected deficit in 2003 no doubt contributed to the recall of then governor Gray Davis. The state languished in fiscal crisis.

All of that was supposed to change with the fresh approach of Arnold Schwarzenegger. Relying on federal assistance, deferred expenditures, and income sources not even considered by the legislature, Schwarzenegger promised a "balanced" budget. In fact, his first budget was $8 billion out of balance immediately upon signature, according to the state legislative analyst.[1] A temporary economic upswing in 2006 helped the governor and state legislature reach agreement on a balanced, on-time budget for the first time in years. But the joy was short-lived.

By 2008, the state faced a revenue shortfall in excess of $15 billion, once again forcing state leaders to consider drastic cuts, major tax increases, or a combination of the two. In the end, legislators and the governor agreed to a gimmicky document that was "balanced" in name only. In fact, the budget was the most unbalanced in state history. Twice in 2009, the governor and legislature grappled with the deficit. First, they sutured a massive $42 billion hole in March through a combination of new taxes, program cuts, and transfers. Three months later, state leaders had to overcome a new $24 billion gap—this time in program and services cuts only. These events occurred because of a terribly weak state economy, which led to reduced tax revenues and increased demands for social services. Much of the "fix" centered on deferred maintenance, withholding of local government redevelopment funds, and higher withholding of state income taxes. Budget makers even delayed payment of state employee paychecks from June 30 to July 1 so they could "save" $900 million.[2]

The state's economic malaise continued into the 2010–2011 fiscal year, when the weary governor and legislature faced a new $21 billion hole. Again they cut. As a result, California's state budget has shrunk from about $105 billion in 2005–2006 to $83 billion in 2010–2011, even though the state's population has grown from 36 million to 38.6 million.

The voters haven't helped with this ongoing dilemma. Repeatedly, the public has rejected new taxes while embracing new programs and services—the kind of logic that has California in its present-day bind. When two Field polls in March 2010 asked the best way to balance the state budget, respondents who favored spending cuts outnumbered those who favored tax increases by a margin of nearly 4 to 1.[3] Yet when survey respondents were asked where the cuts should be made, majorities could be found in only two of fourteen major public policy areas—prisons and parks.[4] Moreover, over the past quarter century, voters have passed a series of ballot propositions directing the state to spend money on various programs ranging from longer prison sentences to more comprehensive public education without providing the funds. This is the political environment in which elected officials must make tough decisions.

THE BUDGETARY PROCESS

Budget making is a complicated and lengthy activity in California. Participants include the governor and various executive-branch departments, the legislature and its support agencies, the public (via initiative and referendum), and increasingly, the courts when judges uphold or overturn commitments made by the other policymakers.

The Governor and Other Executive Officers

Preparation of the annual budget is the governor's most important formal power. Other policymakers participate in the budgetary process, but no other individual has as much clout. The governor frames the document before it goes to the legislature and then has additional say afterward through use of the item veto on budget items that he or she opposes. Given this unique power position, legislative leaders often negotiate with the chief executive over what he or she will accept long before the budget lands on the governor's desk.

During the summer and fall, the governor's director of finance works closely with the budget heads of each state agency. Supported by a staff of fiscal experts and researchers, the director of finance gathers and assesses information about the anticipated needs of each department and submits a "first draft" budget to the governor in late fall. The governor presents a refined version of this draft to the legislature the following January. The state constitution gives the legislature until June 15 to respond. The annual budget is supposed to take effect on July 1, but as we learned in Chapter 5, on-time delivery is anything but routine.

Legislative Participants

Upon receiving the budget in January, the legislature's leaders do little more than refer the document to the legislative analyst. Over the next two months, the legislative analyst and his or her staff scrutinize each part of the budget, considering needs, costs, and other factors. Often, the analyst's findings clash with those of the governor, providing the legislature with an independent source of data and evaluation.

Meanwhile, two key legislative units in each house—the appropriations committees and the budget committees—guide the budget proposal through the legislative process. After the staffs of these committees spend about two months going through the entire document, each house assigns portions to various other committees and their staffs. During this time, lobbyists, individual citizens, government officials, and other legislators testify on the proposed budget before committees and subcommittees. By mid-April, the committees conclude their hearings, combine their portions into a single document, and bring the budget bill to their respective full house for a vote.

As June nears and the two houses hone their versions, a select group of leaders enter into informal negotiations over the document. Known as the **Big Five**, the governor, the speaker of the assembly, the president pro tem of the senate, and the minority party leaders of each house become the nucleus of the final budgetary decisions. In recent years, the Big Five have cast long shadows over just about all of the other players. Should the two houses differ on specifics, the bill goes to a two-house conference committee for reconciliation, after which both houses vote again. Because of a voter-passed initiative in 2010, it now takes a simple majority to pass the budget, a change from the previous long-standing two-thirds requirement. However, inasmuch as a two-thirds vote is still required for revenue increases, the significance of this change is questionable.

The Courts

Sometimes, the courts weigh in on key budget issues to address some of the "quick fixes" to complex budget issues enacted by public policymakers or the voters. Governor Schwarzenegger was humbled in 2005 when a state superior court judge ruled that he was obligated to enforce a new law that reduced the ratio of patients to nurses from 6–1 to 5–1. In 2008, a decision by the U.S. District Court forced the state to spend billions of dollars on improved prison conditions, adding still more to a budget already billions in the red. In 2009 a federal court rejected $500 million in social service cuts as incompatible with federal law, a decision that added to the budget crisis of that year. And even as California attempted to comply with a federal court order to reduce the inmate population of its overcrowded state prisons, a court-appointed receiver rejected the state's effort to reduce costs as excessive. Clearly, the courts have found reason to shape state budgets.[5]

Even the will of the voters has been subject to judicial review on matters relating to the state budget. Particularly significant have been the many cases arising from Proposition 13. Also, decisions on the famous "three strikes and you're out" initiative (see Chapter 6) have added greatly to state incarceration costs.

The Public

On occasion, the public shapes the budget through initiatives or referenda. The voters relied on ballot propositions to approve the sales tax (1933) and repeal the inheritance tax (1982).

In 1993 the voters passed a proposition that increased the state sales tax by 0.5 percent, with new revenues exclusively earmarked for public safety provided by local governments. In 2004 the voters enacted an initiative that created an additional 1 percent tax bracket for people with taxable incomes of $1 million or more, with the funds designated for mental health programs. The public doesn't always agree to increases, however. The voters soundly rejected a 2006 initiative that would have added an additional tax bracket of 1.7 percent beyond the highest level for individuals with taxable incomes of $400,000 or more, with the revenues earmarked for a statewide preschool program.

In 2009, the governor and legislature strung together five ballot proposals that would simultaneously cap spending and temporarily increase sales taxes (0.25 percent), income taxes (1 percent) and motor vehicle fees (0.50 percent). The ballot proposals also would have earmarked half of any extra revenues to the public schools. The package also would have given the governor new powers to cut programs midyear. The public said no to all five propositions.

Perhaps the most dramatic tax-altering event came in 1978 with the passage of **Proposition 13**, an initiative that reduced local property taxes by 57 percent. Since then, property owners have saved more than $528 billion in taxes,[6] while local governments have become increasingly dependent on the state for relief. As a result, the state has become the major funder for local services such as public education, although support has varied with the health of the economy. This uncertainty has brought endless criticism from local government officials.

The bottom line is that there are many more players in the budget process than meet the eye. This complexity both slows down the process and requires near unanimity among the various parties before any major decisions are made.

REVENUE SOURCES

Like most states, California relies on several forms of taxation to fund its general fund budget (that is, the budget exclusive of federal funds). The largest sources of revenue are personal income tax, sales tax, and bank and corporation taxes. Smaller revenue supplies come from motor vehicle, fuel, insurance, tobacco, and alcohol taxes. The state's major revenue sources and expenditures for fiscal year 2010–2011 are shown in Figure 8.1.

Other taxes are levied by local governments. Chief among these is the property tax, although its use was reduced considerably by Proposition 13. This tax is collected by counties rather than by the state, but the state allocates it among the different levels of local government, and it still is a part—directly or indirectly—of the tax burden of all Californians.

All too aware of the state's antitax mood, policymakers have refused to add taxes to cope with burgeoning needs. As a result, the state's commitments to most services have decreased considerably over the past three decades. Individual recipients, school districts, and local governments have been thrown into

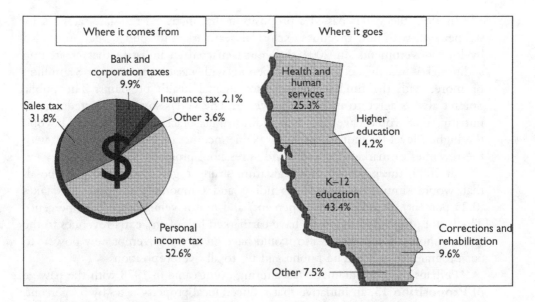

FIGURE 8.1 California's Revenue Sources and Expenditures, 2010–2011

turmoil. Infrastructure work, such as repairs after the 1989 and 1994 earthquakes, and certain highway maintenance programs have been stretched out. Placement of a new earthquake-resistant Oakland–San Francisco Bay bridge will not be complete until 2013, twenty-four years after the earthquake that caused its damage. In fact, a recent study ranks California forty-seventh of the fifty states in per capita highway expenditures.[7]

The Sales Tax

Until the Great Depression of 1929, a relatively small state government garnered funds by relying on minor taxes on businesses and utilities. After the economic crash, however, the state was forced to develop new tax sources to cope with hard times. The first of these, a 2.5 percent **sales tax**, was adopted to provide permanent funding for schools and local governments. Today, the statewide sales tax is 8.25 percent. Of that amount, cities and counties get 2 percent to help meet health and public safety needs. The state keeps the rest. In addition, as much as 1.5 percent is tacked on by counties engaged in state-approved projects, most of which are transportation related.

Occasionally, changes take place in response to economic conditions. In 1991, Governor Pete Wilson and the legislature cut the sales tax by 0.25 percent when the state enjoyed a huge budget surplus. This reduction remained in place until 2002, when the revenue shortfall forced an adjustment upward. In response to the budget crisis in 2004, Governor Schwarzenegger persuaded voters to approve Proposition 57, which provided $15 billion in bonds, or borrowed money, to be repaid over the next decade by diverting 0.25 percent of local governments' share of the sales tax. Today, the sales tax accounts for about 31.8 percent of the state's tax revenues.

The Personal Income Tax

A second major revenue source, the **personal income tax**, was modeled after its federal counterpart to collect greater amounts of money from those residents with greater earnings. Today, the personal income tax varies between 1.0 and 10.3 percent, depending on one's income. The last revision was in 2004, when voters approved a ballot proposition that added a 1 percent tax to those Californians with incomes of $1 million or more. That money is earmarked for mental health programs.

The personal income tax is now the fastest-growing component of state revenue (see Figure 8.2)—a significant fact because Californians ranked tenth among the fifty states in per capita income in 2009. Inasmuch as the tax goes up with increasing incomes, it filled the state coffers in the dramatic economic boom during the later part of the 1990s and slowed just as dramatically in the first few years of the twenty-first century. As of 2010, the personal income tax accounted for 52.6 percent of the state tax bite.

Bank and Corporation Taxes

Financial industry and corporation income taxes contribute much less to California's budget than do sales and personal income taxes. Taxes on bank and

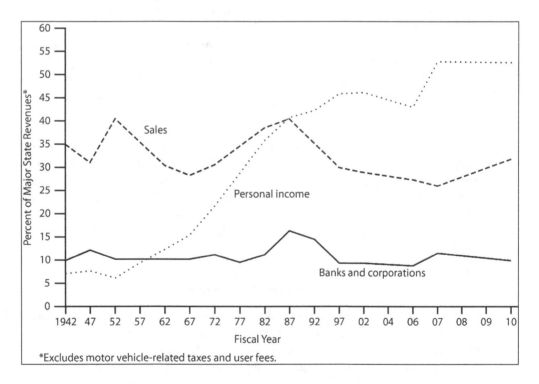

FIGURE 8.2 California's Tax Burden, 1948–2011

corporate incomes did not exceed 5.5 percent until 1959, when the legislature enacted the first of a series of rate hikes. The last increase occurred in 1980, when, responding to local governments' losses from Proposition 13, the legislature boosted the **bank and corporation tax** from 9.6 percent to 11.6 percent. Between 1987 and 1996, however, the legislature reduced the tax to 8.84 percent, where it remains for corporations today. Since 1996 the corporate tax for banks has been fixed at 10.84 percent. Together, bank and corporation taxes now account for about 9.9 percent of state revenues.

Aside from Proposition 13 and the expanded reliance on **user taxes**, such as those levied on gasoline and cigarettes, California's revenue collection system has undergone gradual adjustments over the past sixty years. Figure 8.2 shows the changing weight of the sales, personal income, and bank and corporation taxes from 1942 to the present. Recent data indicate a steady drift toward increased dependence on the personal income tax and decreased dependence on sales and corporation taxes, although the recession of 2008–2010 pushed income tax receipts down somewhat, while sales taxes increased.

Other Sources

From time to time, state leaders have asked voters to approve bonds, thus obligating the electorate to long-term commitments. These projects, sometimes lasting as long as forty years, finance major infrastructure commitments such as school classroom, transportation, and water projects.

The state has turned to bonds with increasing frequency. In 1991, California ranked thirty-second among the fifty states in indebtedness on a per capita basis. By 2009, the state's bond debt increased to more than $140 billion, $70 billion of which had been enacted during the Schwarzenegger administration alone. That represents a per capita indebtedness of $1,805—well above the national average.

California also gets a small but growing portion of its revenue from fees and charges for services. For example, 90 percent of the operating costs of state parks were funded by taxes in 1982–1983, but within a decade, only 40 percent came from tax revenues, while 57 percent came from fees and concessions. Although Governor Davis and the legislature reduced those fees in 2000, new budget pressures led Governor Schwarzenegger and the legislature to increase them again in 2004 and 2008.

Taxes in Perspective

Viewed in a comparative context, the overall tax burden for California ranks ninth in the nation on a per capita basis, remarkably close to its per capita income ranking. Nevertheless, there have been changes in the state tax blend, with the state becoming increasingly dependent on the personal income tax as its primary source of income.

When calculating state and local taxes as a percentage of personal income, California ranks thirteenth. On a per capita basis, the state ranks seventeenth in sales taxes, eighth in personal income taxes, seventh in bank and corporation taxes, and twenty-ninth in property taxes.[8]

In other areas, California taxes are near the bottom, due largely to the influence of powerful interest groups. For example, the state ranks forty-ninth in both fuel taxes and alcoholic beverage taxes. Reformers attempted to establish oil production taxes of $400 million over ten years via initiative in 2006, but the measure was soundly defeated at the polls. As a result, California is the only one of fourteen major oil-producing states that does not tax oil. With respect to tobacco taxes, California ranks thirty-third in the nation.[9] Had the voters approved a ballot proposition in 2006 increasing the tobacco tax by $2.60 per pack, the state would be collecting an additional $2 billion for children's health care—but that measure, too, was defeated. In these and other cases, interest groups have carried great sway with the legislature and public.

SPENDING

The annual state budget addresses thousands of financial commitments, both large and small. Major areas of expenditure include public education (grades K through 12), health and welfare, higher education, and prisons. Outlays in these four areas account for nearly 90 percent of the general fund. The remainder of the budget (the difference between total expenditures and the general fund) goes to designated long-term projects such as transportation, parks, and veterans' programs, many of which have been authorized by public ballot.

Since 1979 state spending has been determined more by the public than by the legislature and the governor. Under Proposition 4 (1979) and Proposition 111 (1990), budgets have been determined largely by formulas rather than by need. In 2004—again at the urging of Governor Schwarzenegger—the voters passed **Proposition 58**, which requires the state to gradually set aside up to 3 percent of all revenues in a "rainy day" fund, beginning in 2006. Some critics have characterized the formula approach as a political "straitjacket" that is unresponsive to changing times and needs; others have viewed it as inconsequential, since the state rarely has enjoyed any surplus. Defenders of "formula government" argue that it is the only way to keep state leaders from operating with a blank check.

Push came to shove in 2008. As Democrats and Republicans battled over whether to increase taxes or cut expenditures, the governor waited in frustration for a budget that eventually reached his desk a record eighty days late. Yet all that paled in comparison to the budget crisis in 2009. Confronted with a $42 billion deficit, the governor and legislature asked the voters to help bridge the gap by passing a series of temporary tax increases and tougher spending rules. The voters declined for a variety of reasons. Some argued that they were overtaxed already; others didn't like the extent to which the governor would have had increased budget-making authority with little legislative oversight; others still rejected more creative borrowing, this time through future revenues from the state lottery.[10] The result was that the legislature and governor made massive spending cuts.

More cuts, though less dramatic, were made in 2010 after the budget came in one hundred days late—yet another dubious record. Some observers noted that the damage to education and social welfare programs was not as bad as in the past, but others were quick to point out that the reductions only compounded the cuts that have occurred over the past several years.

Public Education: Grades K through 12

The state constitution gives public education a "superior right" to state funds; as such, public schools get the largest share of the state budget. Local school districts periodically add relatively small amounts to education through voter-approved bonds and parcel taxes, but the preponderance of support comes from the state legislature through its annual allocations.

Funding for public education in California has an uneven history. The state ranked among the top-funded states throughout the 1950s and 1960s. Then the pattern changed. During the 1970s and 1980s, the state consistently reduced its per capita support for K through 12 public education, shrinking it to 37 percent of the general fund in 1988. That same year, amid growing concerns about weak funding and poor classroom performance, education reformers secured voter approval of **Proposition 98**, a measure that established 40 percent as a minimum funding threshold except in times of fiscal emergency. With this mandate, the state poured money into reducing class sizes in grades K through 3 and lengthened the school year from 180 to 190 days. But the upward direction was short lived.

State aid for public education has dropped precipitously with declining state revenues. Between 2008 and 2010 alone, support fell from $50.3 billion to $44.6 billion, a drop of $470 per student; per capita spending dropped more than another $400 after completion of the 2010-2011 budget. At $8,784 per student (2008–2009 figures), California expenditures remain about $1,900 below the national average. According to former state superintendent of public instruction Jack O'Connell, California now ranks forty-sixth of the fifty states in per capita expenditures—despite having one of the highest per capita incomes in the nation (see Figure 8.3).[11] Meanwhile, the school year minimum has fallen to 175 days—three full weeks less classroom instruction than fifteen years ago.

California continues to be near the bottom (forty-ninth) among the states in its student-teacher ratio (a commonly used criterion for assessing education effectiveness) and in reading achievement. The state also ranks forty-seventh in the number of computers per classroom. All this has produced a sorry, if not unexpected, outcome in terms of high school graduation. As of 2010 the state ranked forty-eighth in high school graduation rates.[12] According to studies by the National Assessment of Educational Progress, a well-known nonprofit group, California hovers near the bottom of almost every assessment category. Table 8.1 shows the most recent data available.

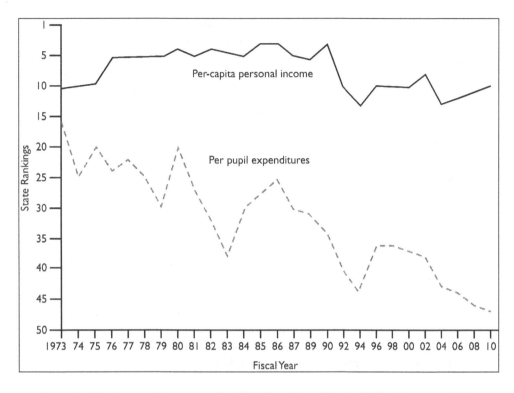

FIGURE 8.3 Personal Income and Public School Spending in California, 1973–2008

TABLE 8.1 California Rankings in Key Education Categories

Category	Rank	Year
Reading, 4th grade	49th	2009
Math, 4th grade	44th	2009
Math, 8th grade	48th	2009
Science, 8th grade	42d	2005*

*Only 44 states participated in the 8th grade science survey.
SOURCE: National Assessment of Education Progress, 2010.

With Latino and Asian American students accounting for 49 percent and 12 percent of the school population, respectively, language-related issues have emerged. In 1998 the passage of **Proposition 227**, a measure limiting bilingual education for non-English–speaking students to one year, added to the debate over how to "mainstream" the diverse California student community. All of this has occurred in a state where one-fourth of all public school students are "English learners" (English is not the first language), compared with 9 percent nationally.

There are chilling consequences from these policies. For starters, California has a high-school dropout rate of 24 percent, or about 125,000 students annually.[13] With few skills, their futures are very limited. At the other end of the spectrum, large numbers of those who do graduate high school are unprepared for college. A recent California State University study found that 55 percent of the incoming freshman class needed remedial instruction in either English or math.[14] Neither of these statistics points to educational excellence.

Nevertheless, the debate goes on. Some reformers have turned to "charter schools"—independent, community-controlled alternatives to what many describe as a broken system. As of 2010 there were about 800 charter schools in California—still a small number compared with the state's 9,700 traditional public schools, although up from 600 in 2008. Other reformers have promoted vouchers—cash payments for parents to use in selecting an educational institution—but the voters have rejected such measures twice in recent years.

The process of fixing California's public education problems will be neither quick nor cheap. In 2007 a 1,700-page report commissioned by Governor Arnold Schwarzenegger declared that it would cost a staggering $1.5 trillion more each year to make all students academically proficient in traditional core knowledge areas such as reading, math, and science.[15] With current state and local expenditures for public education in the neighborhood of $75 billion, even the first step in such a leap would seem highly unlikely.

Higher Education: Colleges and Universities

California's budget woes have cut deeply into support for higher education. Once viewed as the role model for public universities,[16] the higher education system has suffered for a lack of funding and greatly reduced admission slots.

Three components share responsibility for higher education in the state. The state's 110 two-year community colleges enroll about 2.9 million students. Historically, community colleges have been viewed as the entry institutions for students who otherwise did not qualify for, or who could not afford to attend, California's four-year public universities. Funding for these community colleges is connected to the formula for primary and secondary public schools; to that extent, they have benefited from Proposition 98. Still, reduced budget allocations from the state have forced the community colleges to pare back instruction offerings. As a result, during the 2009–2010 academic year, community colleges turned away approximately 140,000 students.[17]

With 222,000 students, the University of California (UC) educates both undergraduate and graduate students at ten campuses throughout the state. Designated as the state's primary research university, UC is the only public institution permitted to award professional degrees (such as medical and law degrees) and doctorates. The California State University (CSU) system, with 433,000 students at twenty-three campuses, concentrates on undergraduate instruction, awarding master's degrees most commonly in such fields as education, engineering, and business.

State support for public universities was fairly constant until the 1990s, holding at about 11 percent of the general-fund budget, and it peaked at 12.7 percent during the 2002–2003 fiscal year. Support eroded considerably during the budget crisis that followed, with the state allocation resting at about 11.7 percent of the general fund in 2008–2009. More significantly, the state's share of the cost of education has decreased dramatically. For example, whereas California provided 90 percent of UC's education costs in 1969–1970, support dropped to 62 percent in 2009–2010. And at CSU, the 90 percent paid by the state in 1969–1970 fell to 69 percent in 2009–2010. Students have been forced to make up much of the shortfall. At both UC and CSU, student fees have more than doubled between 2003–2004 and 2010–2011. Meanwhile, CSU has cut back new enrollments by 40,000; UC has reduced enrollments by 1,500. Between tuition increases and the lack of room, the college participation rate of nineteen-year-olds has fallen precipitously—from 43 percent to 30 percent between 1996 and 2004 alone, dropping California from 17th to 46th place among the 50 states.[18]

Health and Human Services

Health and human services programs receive the second-largest share of the state budget. The programs accounting for the most significant state commitment include California Work Opportunity and Responsibility to Kids (CalWORKS), Medi-Cal, and the Supplemental Security Income (SSI) program. Medi-Cal provides health-care benefits for the poor, and SSI offers state assistance to the elderly and the disabled. But no program is as politically charged as CalWORKS, the primary welfare program.

California has sizable welfare costs. With about 12 percent of the nation's population, the state is home to 25 percent of all welfare recipients. In 1990, in contrast, California had 10.5 percent of the nation's population and 12 percent of all welfare recipients.

As welfare numbers have increased, per capita spending has gone down. Changes in state policy began in 1997 after Congress passed the Welfare Reform Act, limiting welfare payments to no more than five years. Shortly thereafter, the legislature passed its CalWORKS legislation, which provides cash grants and welfare-to-work services for needy families with children ten years of age or younger and requires all adults to work at least thirty-two hours per week. As of 2010, about 1.3 million Californians were CalWORKS recipients, two-thirds of whom were children. For the 2010–2011 budget, Governor Schwarzenegger proposed an end to CalWORKS. Elimination would have saved the state budget $1.6 billion annually, although California would have lost $4 billion in matching federal funds. The legislature rejected Schwarzenegger's proposal, although benefits were trimmed. Every other state has a welfare-to-work program.

As of 2010, health and human services programs accounted for about 25 percent of the general fund. Average monthly welfare payments were less than $500 for the typical family of three, down by one-third from five years earlier. Still, with the state scrambling to close a $21 billion budget hole for the coming fiscal year, Governor Schwarzenegger proposed cutting in-home health care for the elderly and disabled by one-third to save $6.04 billion. As with CalWORKS, the legislature greatly tempered the governor's proposal.

Prisons

Of the major state allocation categories, the budgets for prisons and corrections have grown the most in recent years. As with education, the public has played a role in this policy area. Several initiatives have established mandatory prison terms for various crimes and extended the terms for many other crimes. Even more sweeping changes occurred in 1994, when the legislature (and later the voters, through an initiative) enacted a new **"three strikes"** law. This new law required a sentence of twenty-five years to life for anyone convicted of three felonies and added more than 43,000 long-term prisoners to the corrections system between 1994 and 2004.

As a result of the three-strikes law and other policy changes, California's prison population has swelled beyond belief. In 1994 the total prison population was 125,000; it had jumped to 168,000 by 2009—more than double the official capacity. Currently, the costs for incarceration average $49,000 per convict per year. The demographics are equally interesting: 37 percent Latino, 27 percent African American, and 27 percent white. Phenomenal incarceration growth has forced the construction of new prisons, such as the new prison in Delano in 2005. Still, with a soaring inmate population, in 2006 Governor Schwarzenegger asked the legislature to build at least two more state prisons at a cost of $500 million each.[19]

About 10 percent of the state's general fund was used for corrections and rehabilitation during the 2009–2010 fiscal year—once again reflecting the sharpest increase of any major budget category. Meanwhile, lawsuits have led federal court orders requiring the state to release as many as 40,000 prisoners by 2012. Should that occur, the prison budget may moderate.

Other Budget Obligations

California's budget crisis has many sources, some obvious and others not. Clearly, a prolonged recession has contributed mightily to the state's revenue grief. On the expenditure side of the budget ledger, out-of-control prison spending has been of great concern. Two other less known, yet fast-growing state expenditure categories are payment of bond debt and pension payouts. Together, they now consume more than 10 percent of the state general fund and show little sign of slowing down.

Bonds   While voter-approved borrowing through bonds represents an "easy" way to fund major projects over time, cumulatively these bonds are taking a toll on the state. California now ranks tenth in per capita bond debt, up from thirty-second in 1991. Our propensity to rely upon bonds has generated the lowest credit rating of any state, which adds to the interest costs to retire the bonds. About 6.7 percent of the state budget now goes to paying interest on the debt. Moreover, State Treasurer Bill Lockyer estimated in 2009 that at present rates, 10 percent or more of the state budget will be dedicated to debt payment by the middle of this decade.[20] The state's propensity for financing through bonds has left it with the lowest bond rating of any state, which means the highest interest payments.[21]

Retirement Pensions   California's massive public employee pension program, the California Public Employees' Retirement System (CalPERS), covers more than 1.6 million employees, retirees, and their families, or about 4 percent of the state's population. Just under 500,000 are retirees who have worked for various state government agencies. Employees contribute a small portion of their salary to the program, with the state providing the rest as part of the salary compensation package. For years CalPERS gushed with surpluses, thanks to a robust financial market that contained most of the fund's investments. Since the onslaught of the recession in 2008, CalPERS payments have exceeded revenues. By law, the state must make up for any shortfall, and that money comes out of the state budget. In fiscal year 2009–2010, the state was required pay out 5.6 percent of the general fund into CalPERS—up dramatically from a figure that historically averaged 3.4 percent.

CALIFORNIA'S BUDGET: TOO LITTLE, TOO MUCH, OR JUST RIGHT?

Have you ever met anyone who claims that he or she should pay more taxes? Neither have we. Almost everybody dislikes paying taxes, and almost everybody thinks that the money collected is spent incorrectly or unwisely. That seems to be a perennial dilemma in California. However, although most people oppose increased taxes, they also oppose program cuts. It's a modern-day dilemma for state policymakers and the public alike.

Like their counterparts elsewhere, California policymakers have struggled to find a fair system of taxation to pay for needed programs. Given the involvement of so many public and private interests, however, it's difficult to determine what is fair. Moreover, during the last few decades, taxation and budget decisions have been subject to radical change. Somehow, the state's infrastructure has survived, although critics have been less than thrilled with the fiscal uncertainty that has become commonplace in California government.

NOTES

1. "Debt Remains in Governor's Budget Plan," *San Jose Mercury News,* July 1, 2004, pp. 1A, 17A.
2. "Deal Puts State in Hole for Next Year," *San Francisco Chronicle,* July 26, 2009, pp. A1, A17.

3. Field Poll, Release No. 2329, March 2, 2010.

4. Field Poll, Release No. 2335, March 24, 2010.

5. "California Finding That Prisons Costs Aren't So Easy to Cut," *San Jose Mercury News*, March 24, 2010, pp. B1, B9.

6. Howard Jarvis Taxpayers Association, 2009, www.hjta.org/index.php.

7. "Highway Spending," in *Governing: State and Local Sourcebook* (Washington, D.C.: Congressional Quarterly, 2006), pp. 32–36.

8. "Finance," in *Governing: State and Local Government Sourcebook* (Washington, D.C.: Congressional Quarterly, 2006), pp. 32–36.

9. "State Cigarette Excise Tax Rates and Rankings, 2010," www.tobaccofreekids.org.

10. See "Ballot Battle to Follow Wrangling over Budget," *San Francisco Chronicle*, February 17, 2009, pp. A1, A14; and "Traditional Foes Team Up over Prop. 1A," *San Francisco Chronicle*, April 6, 2009, pp. A1, A7.

11. Testimony before Assembly Budget Subcommittee No. 2, March 11, 2008.

12. See *Just the Facts* (Albany: Public Policy Institute of New York State, 2007).

13. "State Education Rankings: Graduation Rates for High School, College and Grad/Professional School," Associated Content, July 21, 2010, www.associatedcontent.com/article/5562698/state_education_rankings_graduation.html

14. "CSU Freshmen Face Challenges," *Los Angeles Times*, March 15, 2006, p. B9.

15. "No Quick, Cheap Fix for State's Schools," *Los Angeles Times*, March 15, 2007, pp. B1, B10.

16. See James Richardson, "What Price Glory?" *UCLA Magazine*, February 1997, p. 30; also see "A Crown Jewel of Education Struggles with Cuts in California," *New York Times*, November 20, 2009, pp. A1, A25.

17. "Community Colleges Make Concerted Effort to Meet Demand," press release issued by the California Community Colleges Chancellor's Office, Sacramento, June 3, 2010.

18. Christopher Neufeld and Stanton Glantz, "Ending the California Dream," op-ed in *San Francisco Chronicle*, July 14, 2009, p. A11.

19. "Gov. Calls for New Spending on Prisons," *Los Angeles Times*, June 27, 2006, pp. A1, A7.

20. "Rising Debt a Threat to State General Fund," *San Francisco Chronicle*, November 24, 2009, p. C3.

21. "California Bond Rating Now Lowest of Any State," *Los Angeles Times*, February 4, 2009, pp. A1, A11

LEARN MORE ON THE WEB

California Budget Project:
www.cbp.org

California state budget—Department of Finance:
www.dof.ca.gov

California state budget—Legislature:
www.lao.ca.gov

California Tax Reform Association:
www.caltaxreform.org

California Taxpayers' Association:
www.caltax.org

National Center for Education Statistics:
www.nces.ed.gov

National Governors Association:
www.nga.org

LEARN MORE AT THE LIBRARY

Jack Citrin and Isaac William Martin, eds. *After the Revolt: California's Proposition 13.* Berkeley, Calif.: Berkeley Public Policy Press, 2009.

John Decker. *California in the Balance: Why Budgets Matter.* Berkeley, Calif.: Berkeley Public Policy Press, 2009.

Joe Mathews and Mark Paul. *California Crack Up: How Reform Broke the Golden State and How We Can Fix It.* Berkeley: University of California Press, 2010.

Alvin Rabushka and Pauline Ryan. *The Tax Revolt.* Stanford, Calif.: Hoover Institution Press, 1982.

Peter Schrag. *California: America's High-Stakes Experiment.* Berkeley: University of California Press, 2006.

9

California's Local Governments: Politics at the Grassroots

CHAPTER CONTENTS

The public and the media tend to focus on state and national politics, but the activities of local governments often have a greater impact on our daily lives. Our city governments make decisions about traffic on our streets; safety in our neighborhoods; and access to parks, libraries, and affordable housing. Our county governments manage transit systems and provide important social services to those most in need, including people who are homeless, mentally ill, and impoverished. Our school districts make decisions about what sorts of teachers are in our classrooms and what our children are taught.

Yet local governments are created by the state, which assigns them their rights and duties, mandating some functions and activities and prohibiting others. The state also allocates taxing powers and shares revenues with local governments. But the state can change the rights and powers granted to local governments, expanding or reducing their tasks, funding, and independence. Cities and counties are infuriated when the state tells them to do things they don't think they can afford or takes away previously committed funds to balance the state budget. School districts depend on the state for funding but are exasperated by burdensome state rules, regulations, and testing requirements.

But local government is also where we—the residents of California—have the greatest influence over our lives, simply because we are closer to it than to Sacramento or Washington, D.C. We can participate directly in local politics precisely because it's local. We can volunteer for candidates, whom we can actually meet and get to know—or we can run for office ourselves. We can lobby elected officials without relying on paid professionals. We can attend city council meetings and testify in person. We can find allies and form interest groups like those described in Chapter 4 (and all those types exist in communities). Local government is the most democratic of all levels of government, and thousands of people participate constantly—go to your own city hall and see for yourself.

COUNTIES AND CITIES

California's 58 counties and 481 cities were created in slightly different ways and perform distinctly different tasks.

Counties

California is divided into counties (see the map inside the front cover) ranging in size from San Francisco's 49 square miles to San Bernardino County's 20,164, and ranging in population from Alpine County's 1,201 residents to Los Angeles County's 10,393,185. **Counties** function both as local governments and as administrative units of the state. As local governments, counties provide police and fire protection, maintain roads, and perform other services for rural and unincorporated areas (those that are not part of any city). They also run jails, operate transit systems, protect health and sanitation, and keep records on property, marriages, and deaths. As agencies of the state, counties oversee elections, operate the courts, administer the state's welfare system, and collect some taxes.

State law prescribes the organization of county government. A county's central governing body is a five-member **board of supervisors**, whom voters elect by districts to staggered four-year terms. The board sets county policies and oversees the budget, usually hiring a chief administrator, or **county executive**, to carry out its programs. Besides the members of the board of supervisors, voters elect the sheriff, district attorney, tax assessor, and other department heads (see Figure 9.1). Conflicts often occur as the elected board tries to manage the budget and the elected executives attempt to deliver services. Unlike most of their state counterparts, these local officials are chosen in nonpartisan elections, a Progressive legacy that keeps party labels off the ballot; all serve four-year terms. As of 2010, California's 296 elected county supervisors were overwhelmingly white

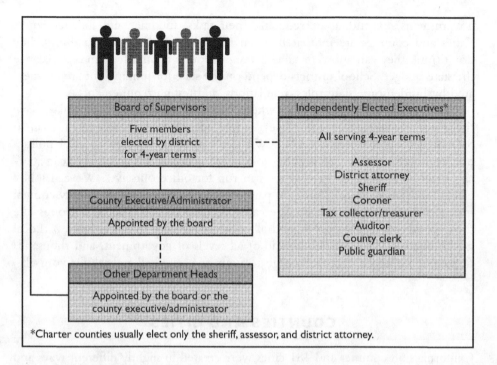

Board of Supervisors

Five members
elected by district
for 4-year terms

County Executive/Administrator

Appointed by the board

Other Department Heads

Appointed by the board or the
county executive/administrator

Independently Elected Executives*

All serving 4-year terms

Assessor
District attorney
Sheriff
Coroner
Tax collector/treasurer
Auditor
County clerk
Public guardian

*Charter counties usually elect only the sheriff, assessor, and district attorney.

FIGURE 9.1 County Government: An Organizational Chart for California's Forty-five General-Law Counties

and male; only 23.5 percent were female, 9.5 percent were Latino, 3.4 percent were Asian, and 1.7 percent were African American. These numbers were roughly the same as in 2002, despite the growth in numbers and political engagement of some of these constituencies.

Although most counties operate under this general-law system, fourteen have used a state-provided option to organize their own governmental structures through documents called **charters**. Most of these charter counties, including Los Angeles, Sacramento, San Diego, and Santa Clara, are highly urbanized. County voters must approve the charter and any proposed amendments. Generally, a "home rule" or **charter county** uses its local option to replace elected executives with appointees of the board of supervisors or to strengthen the powers of the appointed county executive.

San Francisco is unique among California's local governments because it operates as both a city and a county. Most counties have several cities within their boundaries, but the separate city and county governments of San Francisco were consolidated in 1911. San Francisco thus has a board of supervisors with eleven members rather than a city council, but unlike any other county, it has a mayor.

No new county has been formed in California since 1907, although in some large counties such as Los Angeles, San Bernardino, and Santa Barbara, rural areas frustrated by urban domination have tried unsuccessfully to break away and form their own jurisdictions. One city in massive San Bernardino County is so far away from the city where county government is headquartered that some residents say they want to "move" to nearby Arizona.

Cities

Whereas counties are created by the state, **cities** are established at the request of their citizens through the process of **incorporation**. Starting with just 8 cities in 1850, California has 481 today. As unincorporated areas urbanize, residents begin to demand more services than their county government can provide. These may include police and fire protection, street maintenance, water, or other services. Residents may also wish to form a city to preserve the identity of their community or to avoid being annexed by some other city. Wealthy areas sometimes incorporate to protect their tax resources or their ethnic homogeneity from the impact of an adjacent big city and its economic and racial problems. California's newest city, incorporated in 2010 with a population of 47,635, is Eastvale, in Riverside County.

The process of incorporation starts with a petition from citizens who live in the area. Then the county's **local agency formation commission (LAFCO)** determines whether the area has a sufficient tax base to support city services and makes sense as an independent entity. If LAFCO approves, the county's board of supervisors holds a hearing, and then the voters of the proposed city approve or reject the incorporation.

Once formed, cities can grow by annexing unincorporated (county) territory. Sometimes, small cities that can't provide adequate services disband themselves by consolidating with an adjacent city. More rarely, residents of an existing city seek to de-annex, or secede. This was the case in the San Fernando Valley, a 222-square-mile section of Los Angeles that contains one-third of the city's population. Residents who felt isolated and ignored agitated to secede from the City of Los Angeles; their proposal was voted on in November 2002, along with a similar proposal for secession by Hollywood. Secession required approval by the voters of both these areas and the city as a whole, however, and while the San Fernando Valley narrowly supported secession, the voters of Los Angeles and Hollywood rejected the plan.

Like California counties, most California cities operate under the state's general law, which prescribes their governmental structure. **General-law cities** typically have a five-member **city council**, with members elected in nonpartisan elections for four-year terms. The council appoints a **city manager** to supervise daily operations; the manager, in turn, appoints department heads such as the police and fire chiefs (see Figure 9.2).

Cities with populations exceeding 3,500 may choose to write their own charters. A hundred and eighteen California cities have done so. A **charter city** has more discretion in choosing the structure of its government than a general-law city does, as well as somewhat greater fiscal flexibility and the freedom to set policies, provided that no state law supersedes them. All of California's largest cities have their own charters to enable them to deal with their complex problems.

Whether operating under general law or a home-rule charter, once incorporated a city takes on extensive responsibilities for local services, including police and fire protection, sewage treatment, garbage disposal, parks and recreational services, streets and traffic management, library operation, and land-use planning. The county, however, still provides courts, jails, social services, elections, tax collection, public health, and public transit.

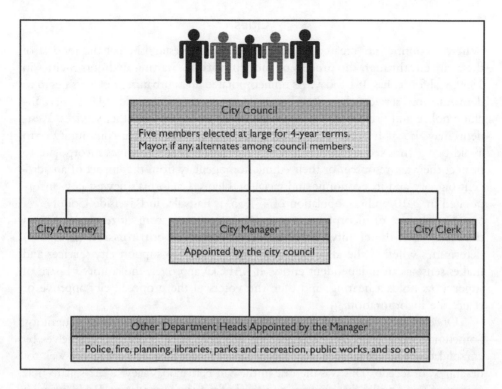

F I G U R E 9.2 City Government: An Organizational Chart for California's 363 General-Law Cities

POWER IN THE CITY: COUNCIL MEMBERS, MANAGERS, AND MAYORS

Most of California's cities have five-member city councils with appointed city managers as executives, as set forth by state law. Some cities, particularly older and larger communities, have developed municipal government structures uniquely suited to their own needs and preferences. City councils, for example, may be chosen in a variety of ways or expanded in size to allow for more representation. Los Angeles has fifteen council members, San Jose ten, and San Diego eight. San Francisco's board of supervisors has eleven members. The executive office also varies among these cities; some opt for a stronger mayor rather than the manager prescribed by the state for general-law cities.

Elections

In most California cities, each council member is chosen by the whole city in **at-large elections**. This system was created by the Progressives to replace **district elections**, in which each council member represents only part of the city. At-large elections were intended to reduce the parochial influence of machine-organized ethnic neighborhoods on the city as a whole. The strategy worked, but as a result, ethnic minority candidates, unable to secure enough votes from the city as a whole to win at large, were rarely elected.

As cities grew, citywide campaigns also became extremely costly. The Progressives added to the difficulties of minority candidates and further raised the costs of campaigns by making local elections nonpartisan. This weakened the old party machines, but voters lost the modest cue provided by the listing of parties on the ballot. Furthermore, minority candidates were denied the legitimization of a party label, and campaigns cost more because candidates had to get their messages out without help from a party organization.

To increase minority representation and cut campaign costs, some cities have returned to district elections. Los Angeles has used district elections since 1924; Sacramento converted in 1971, followed by San Jose, Oakland, and later, San Diego and San Francisco. Thirty-eight California cities use some form of district elections. Most are large cities, and most have reverted to district elections through voter-approved charter amendments.

District elections increased opportunities for minority candidates in some cities, but minorities remain substantially underrepresented among California's local elected officials. Women have done somewhat better but are also underrepresented. Women and minority candidates, as well as gay and lesbian candidates, have been more successful in local elections than in state elections; they are still held back, however, by discrimination, low participation, at-large elections, high campaign costs, and the lack of party support that results from nonpartisan elections.

In most California cities, especially smaller cities that elect their councils at large, candidates who get the most votes win election even if they don't get a majority. In larger cities and cities that elect their council members by district, if no candidate wins a majority in the primary election, the top two compete in a **runoff election**, ensuring that the winner is elected with a majority of the votes. Critics object to the high cost of such elections—both to taxpayers and in campaign spending. In 2004 San Francisco responded to such criticism with **instant runoff voting**, in which voters rank candidates in order of preference. If no candidate wins a majority, the candidate with the fewest votes is eliminated and those votes are assigned to the voters' second choice—and so on until one candidate attains a majority. Oakland, Berkeley, and San Leandro—all in Northern California—have followed San Francisco's example in hopes of saving time and money and simplifying the task of voting. Other cities and counties are now considering adoption of instant runoff voting. Advocates hope that such simplification will enhance voter participation in local elections, which varies considerably from city to city. Turnout is generally higher in cities with elected mayors and district elections, but the key factor related to turnout is when the elections are held.

About one-third of California's cities hold their elections separate from state and national elections. Median turnout in these elections is less than 30 percent.[1] Los Angeles, for example, holds its elections separately, and turnout in that city's 2009 city council and mayoral contests was 18 percent. Lower turnout significantly affects outcomes because the composition of the electorate changes along with the number of voters; older, more affluent voters predominate, which usually gives an advantage to more conservative candidates. Research tells us that in cities with low voter turnout, municipal government spends less money on programs that might aid the poor. Instead, such governments fund downtown development and other projects that aid business. In short, local governments spend their revenues on those who vote.[2]

Turnout in cities that hold their elections concurrently with state and national elections is nearly twice as high.[3] The Silicon Valley city of Santa Clara started holding local elections at the same time as state and national elections in 1988, and voter turnout went from 23–24 percent to 74 percent. Unlike cities, all of California's counties hold their elections at the same time as the state and national elections. Voting for local officials may still be lower, however, due to "drop-off," with some participating voters declining to cast ballots in local races because of lack of interest or information.

As with state-level campaigns, local reformers have been concerned about the costs of city and county races and the influence of money on politics. Spending on local campaigns has risen steadily since the 1980s, when professional campaign consultants and their techniques (see Chapter 3) became common in local races. One hundred and fifty-seven California cities and counties have enacted local campaign-finance laws that require disclosure of contributors and expenditures and sometimes limit the amount of contributions. In most of these cities, the data are available to the public online. Los Angeles also restricts spending and provides limited public financing for campaigns. Long Beach, Sacramento, Oakland, Richmond, and San Francisco are also experimenting with public financing of campaigns.[4] Even in these communities, candidates and interest groups manage to raise and spend substantial sums on campaigns, often through independent expenditures or special campaign committees.[5]

Executive Power

Most people assume that mayors lead cities and have substantial power, but that's not usually the case in California communities. Because mayors were once connected with political machines, the Progressive reformers stripped away their powers, shifting executive authority to council-appointed city managers who were intended to be neutral, professional administrators. Most California cities use this **council–manager system**. While the manager administers the city's programs, appoints department heads, and proposes the budget, the council members alternate as mayor—a ceremonial post that involves chairing meetings and cutting ribbons.

San Francisco, however, uses a strong-mayor form of government, in which the mayor is elected directly by the people to a four-year term and holds powers similar to those of the president in the national system, including the veto, budget control, and appointment of department heads. San Francisco mayor Gavin Newsom exercised his powers to gain a national reputation as a leader on such issues as same-sex marriage and health insurance for all city residents—and as a platform for his successful candidacy for lieutenant governor in 2010. Los Angeles also has an empowered mayor after voters approved a new charter in 1999 giving the mayor enhanced authority, including the power to appoint forty-four department heads. Mayor Antonio Villaraigosa, elected in 2005 and reelected in 2009, thus exercises more authority than any of his predecessors. Fresno (in 1997), Oakland (in 1998), and San Diego (in 2005) have also switched to a strong-mayor form of government. Sacramento mayor Kevin Johnson has pushed for such a change in his city, but he has failed thus far to persuade the city council to put a charter amendment to the voters.

Many California cities have moved away from the pure council–manager system of government, however. While retaining their city managers, 149 California cities have revised the system so that the mayor is directly elected and serves a four-year term. Some have also increased the powers of their mayors, although they continue to sit as council members. Even without much authority, being a directly elected mayor brings visibility and influence. Mayors of San Jose, for example, exercise substantial clout despite their limited official power.

California mayors will probably continue to grow stronger, partly because of media attention but also due to the need for leadership in the tempest of city politics. Elected officials and community groups often complain about the lack of direct accountability inherent in the city manager form, in which the executive is somewhat insulated from the voters. Giving more authority to mayors and council members makes accountability more direct, but it may also decrease the professionalism of local government.

MORE GOVERNMENTS

In addition to cities and counties, California has thousands of other, less visible local governments (see Table 9.1). Created by the state or by citizens, they provide designated services and have taxing powers, mostly collecting their revenues as small portions of the property taxes paid by homeowners and businesses or by charging for their services. Yet except for school districts, most of us are unaware of their existence.

T A B L E 9.1 California's Local Governments, 2010

Type	Number
Counties	58
Cities	481
School districts	1,043
Special districts	4,776
TOTAL	6,358

SOURCE: California State Controller, www.sco.ca.gov, and Ed-Data, www.ed-data.ca.us.

School Districts and Special Districts

In California, 1,043 local governments called **school districts** provide education. They are created and overseen by the state and governed by elected boards, which appoint professional educators as superintendents to oversee day-to-day operations. Except for parents and teachers, whose involvement is intense, voter participation in school elections and politics is low. One challenge for the schools is that while the majority of students are Latino, Asian, or African American, a majority of those who vote in school elections and the majority of school board members are non-Hispanic whites.[6]

Of the $66.7 billion in school spending in 2009–2010, the state supplied 58 percent, the federal government provided 14 percent, and 28 percent came from local property taxes and other local sources.[7] Just two years earlier, local governments provided only 21 percent of school funding, providing a poignant example of where the state's budget crisis has left these governments with more responsibilities. The shift has not been without costs. In 2010, 16 percent of the state's school districts were declared "at risk" because of inadequate funding, and California has ranked low among the states in per-pupil spending for years.[8] These figures refer to funds for salaries and operating expenses. Money for building repairs and construction of new schools comes mostly from **bonds** (borrowed money paid by local taxes), which until recently required approval by a two-thirds majority of the voters. Following the Proposition 13 tax revolt, such approvals became rare; in 2000, however, voters approved lowering the percentage required for approval to 55 percent, and passing bonds became easier.

Special districts are an even more common form of local government, with no fewer than 4,776 in California. Unlike cities and counties, which are "general-purpose" governments, special districts usually provide a single service. California law provides for fifty-three different types of special districts, ranging from water and waste disposal districts to hospital and cemetery districts. They are created when citizens or governments want a particular function performed but either have no appropriate government agency to perform the service or choose not to delegate it to a city or county. Sometimes special districts are formed when small communities share responsibilities for fire protection, sewage treatment, or other services that can be more efficiently provided on a larger scale. Depending on the nature of the special district, funding usually comes from property taxes or charges for the service that it provides. The number of special districts increased when Proposition 13 imposed tax constraints on general-purpose local governments, because some services can be funded more easily in this way. Their impacts in terms of taxes and services have been considerable. Altogether, California's special districts spend $39.6 billion a year, while California's cities spend $57 billion and its counties spend $48.4 billion.

A city council or a county board of supervisors governs some special districts, but most are overseen by a commission or board of directors that may be elected or appointed by other officials. Like a school board, this body usually appoints a professional administrator to manage its business. Accountability to the voters and taxpayers is a problem, however, because most of us aren't even aware of these officials.

Regional Governments

The existence of so many sorts of local governments means that many operate in every urban region of California. The vast urban areas between Los Angeles and San Diego or San Francisco and San Jose, for example, consist of many cities, counties, and special districts, with no single authority in charge of the whole area. Los Angeles County alone hosts eighty-eight cities and two hundred special districts. This fragmentation creates small-scale governments that are accessible to citizens, but that are sometimes too small to provide services efficiently. In addition, problems such as transportation and air pollution go far beyond the boundaries of any one entity.

Many California cities deal with this situation by **contracting for services** from counties, larger cities, or private businesses. Cities in Los Angeles County, for example, may pay the county to provide any of fifty-eight services, from dog catching to tree planting. Small cities commonly contract with the county sheriff for police protection rather than fund their own forces. Contracting allows such communities to provide needed services while retaining local control, although some see the system as unfair because wealthy communities can afford more than poor ones.

Another solution to urban fragmentation is **consolidation**, or the merger of existing governmental entities. With voter approval, small school districts, special districts, or even cities can unite to provide services more efficiently. In the past consolidation has occurred mostly with school districts, but proposals for consolidations have become more common lately due to California's prolonged budget crisis.[9]

Special districts are yet another way to address fragmentation and regional problems—particularly problems, such as air pollution and transportation, that extend beyond the boundaries of existing cities or counties. For example, California has forty-seven transit districts that run bus and rail systems. Most are countywide, but some, including the Bay Area Rapid Transit (BART) system, cover several counties.

Twenty of California's urban areas also have **councils of government (COGs)**, in which all of the cities and counties in the region are represented. The biggest COGs are the six-county Southern California Association of Governments (SCAG) and the nine-county Association of Bay Area Governments (ABAG) in Northern California. These regional bodies focus on land-use planning and development. Because they can't force their plans on cities and counties, though, they serve mainly as forums for communication and coordination among the jurisdictions they encompass.

As regional problems have grown and competition among cities has increased, the need for regional planning has also grown. The state has asserted its authority over local governments to require the implementation of regional plans through agencies such as ABAG and SCAG. Other state-created agencies, such as the Metropolitan Water District and the South Coast Air Quality Management Board in Southern California, exercise great power. Reformers sometimes advocate the creation of multipurpose regional governments, perhaps by merging existing regional special districts, to provide government capable of dealing with area-wide issues including transportation, air quality, and growth; however, existing cities firmly oppose any loss of local control.

DIRECT DEMOCRACY IN LOCAL POLITICS

Direct democracy is used even more locally than statewide. Between 1995 and 2008 an average of 428 local ballot measures were voted on by Californians each year.[10] All charter changes—such as increasing the powers of the mayor or introducing district council elections—are subject to voter approval. Voters must also approve proposals for local governments to introduce or raise taxes or to borrow money by issuing bonds. Charter changes require a simple majority, but a supermajority of two-thirds is required for most taxes. Resulting from a series of statewide initiatives, these requirements have severely restricted the ability of local governments to raise money, because voter approval on funding issues is difficult to win.

Most local measures are placed on the ballot by a city council, county board of supervisors, or school board. They include tax measures and charter amendments, but the most common measures have to do with education (usually seeking additional funding). Citizens also put proposals to the voters through the initiative process, although initiatives constitute only a tiny percentage of local measures. Most often, the initiatives are attempts to control growth or amend charters. Some are frivolous, like the 2008 San Francisco initiative that proposed renaming the city sanitation facility the "George W. Bush Sewage Plant," but most are more serious. District elections, for example, were introduced in some cities by initiative, as were **term limits** (usually restricting elected officials to two 4-year terms). Several California counties and over forty cities now limit the terms of elected officials. As a last resort, voters may express their dissatisfaction with elected officials through recall elections. Recalls of local officials are rare, however, averaging fewer than a dozen a year, even after the dramatic recall of the governor in 2003.[11]

Land Use: Coping with Growth

One of the most frequent uses of direct democracy in California cities and counties is by citizens seeking to control growth. Deciding how land can be used is a major power assigned to local governments by the state. The way they use this power affects us all. If local governments encourage growth in the form of housing, industry, or shopping centers, for example, the economy may boom, but streets may become clogged, schools overcrowded, sewage treatment plants strained, and police and fire protection stretched too thin. When this happens, environmentalists or residents who merely expect adequate services may grow frustrated and demand controls on growth. If the city council or county board of supervisors is unresponsive, discontented groups may take their case to the voters through an initiative.

Since 1971, when development became a major local issue, almost all California communities have enacted some form of growth control. The battle typically pits a grassroots coalition with little money against big-spending developers and builders. The recent recession brought growth to a halt in most communities, decreasing the salience of this issue, but even so the cities of Buellton, Pleasanton, and San Juan Capistrano approved growth limits and protections for open space in 2008.

TAXING AND SPENDING

The way local governments raise and spend money reveals a great deal, not only about what they do but also about the limits they face in doing it.

The biggest single source of money for California's local governments was once the **property tax**, an annual assessment based on the value of land and buildings. Then, in 1978, taxpayers revolted with **Proposition 13**, a statewide initiative that cut property tax revenues by 57 percent. Cities adjusted by cutting jobs and services to save money. Many introduced or increased **charges for services** such as sewage treatment, trash collection, building permits, and the use of recreational facilities. Such charges are now the largest source of income for most cities (see Figure 9.3), followed by the sales tax, which returns 2 percent of the state's basic 8.25 percent sales tax to the city or county where the sale occurs. Some counties add to the base sales tax to fund transportation. Some cities and counties have also added taxes on hotel rooms, utilities, or other things. In 2009 voters in Oakland approved a tax on the sale of medical marijuana, undoubtedly setting a precedent for other cities.

The shift from property taxes to other sources of revenue also affects local land-use decisions. When a new development is proposed, most cities now prefer retail businesses to housing or industry because of the sales taxes that such businesses generate. This trend has been labeled the **fiscalization of land use** because instead of choosing the best use for the land, cities opt for the one that produces the most revenue.

With more legal constraints on their taxing powers, counties had an even rougher time after Proposition 13. State aid to counties increased slightly, but with no alternative local taxes readily available after the passage of Proposition 13, most counties cut spending deeply. Years later, they are still struggling to provide essential services. Like cities, most counties increased charges and fees for services.

Over half of county revenues come from the state and federal governments (32.5 percent and 19.4 percent, respectively), but this money must be spent on required programs such as social services, health care, and the courts. Even so, state and federal aid does not cover the cost of these mandatory services, leaving counties with little money to spend as they choose.

Just as the revenue sources of cities and counties differ, so do their spending patterns, largely because the state assigns them different responsibilities. As you can see in Figure 9.3, public safety is the biggest expenditure for California cities, whereas welfare is the biggest county expenditure.

Although Proposition 13 is much loved by homeowners for reducing property tax bills, the initiative caused serious fiscal problems for local governments by cutting property tax revenues and making approval of new taxes or tax increases more difficult. That combination necessitated severe budget cuts for cities and counties. Beyond that, Proposition 13 gave the state the responsibility to

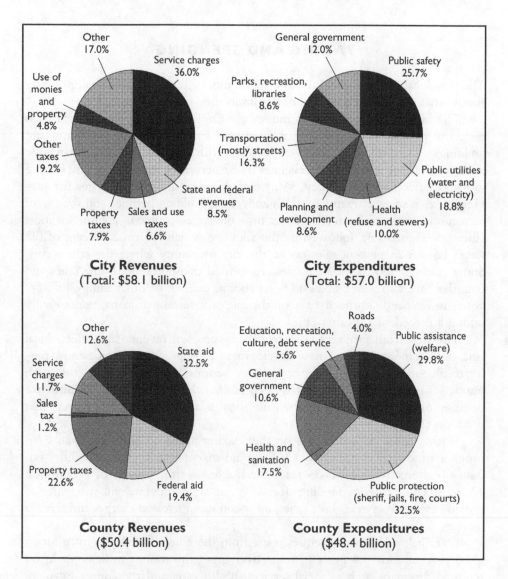

FIGURE 9.3 Expenditures of California Cities and Counties, 2007–2008

SOURCE: California State Controller, 2010, www.sco.ca.gov.

allocate property taxes among local governments even as Proposition 98 (see Chapter 8) mandated allocation of a fixed percentage of the state budget to education. As a consequence, a portion of property taxes that had previously gone to cities and counties was shifted to schools—putting even further pressure on city and county budgets and resulting in further cuts in services. Moreover, cities and counties, which previously had some control of their own revenues, became dependent on the state for property and sales tax revenues, a significant loss of local control.[12]

These problems were compounded when successive recessions hit California in the early 1990s and again in 2001–2003 and 2009–2010. Facing massive deficits, the state balanced its budget by "take-backs" of local property tax revenues totaling billions of dollars. In 2004 Governor Arnold Schwarzenegger exacerbated circumstances for local governments by reducing vehicle license fees, which had previously been a significant source of local revenues.

Cities were so frustrated by all this that they pushed for a way to lock in their revenues through a constitutional amendment to guarantee future revenues and prevent such state take-backs. Voters approved **Proposition 1A** in 2004. Local governments hoped it would give them greater financial security in the future, but in the 2009 fiscal crisis, the state diverted nearly $4 billion in local property taxes from schools, cities, counties, and redevelopment agencies. Under Proposition 1A the state must eventually repay these funds, but in the short term the action only worsened the fiscal problems of local governments. Cities and counties responded in 2010 with **Proposition 22** banning state borrowing from local governments and won voter approval.

Meanwhile, California cities and counties have been pushed to the fiscal brink. Vallejo (near San Francisco) declared bankruptcy in 2008 when tax revenues dropped and the city couldn't meet its commitments to employee salaries and benefits. In 2010 Oakland laid off over 10 percent of its police force, despite its high crime rate. Facing a $529 million deficit, Los Angeles mayor Antonio Villaraigoso, usually an ally of public employees, proposed layoffs and demanded salary concessions from the city's unions. Maywood, in Southern California, laid off all its city employees, including police officers, and contracted with other cities for some services and with Los Angeles County for police protection. "We will become 100 percent a contracted city," said Maywood's interim city manager.[13] Other cities also considered contracting for services. Redding, in Northern California, and Santa Clarita, in Southern California, for example, contracted with a private company to provide library services. Still other cities considered merging police or fire departments with neighboring cities. In some areas, reformers called for consolidation of small school districts, special districts, and cities as a partial solution to budget problems.

Cities from San Diego to San Jose, along with many other local agencies, also faced fiscal strain due to the pensions and other benefits they had offered their employees when their budgets were flush with cash. Now unable to meet these commitments but bound by contracts, local governments, like the state (see Chapter 8), are seeking to renegotiate the contracts to win concessions from current employees or to move to a two-tier pension system, preserving benefits for current workers but reducing them for future hires.

Despite their fiscal trials, local governments remain a major component of the California economy, with nearly 1.3 million employees (half are in education)[14] and combined budgets totaling over $212 billion. Local governments cost a lot, but they also do a lot.

LOCAL GOVERNMENT

The state limits what local governments can do, as demonstrated by Proposition 13 and ongoing budget battles. Some may dispute such interventions, but the state's authority remains supreme. At the same time, local governments can lead the way to innovations in public policy, as illustrated by San Francisco's health insurance policy, Long Beach's public financing for campaigns, and Oakland's tax on medical marijuana. California's political system gives residents many opportunities to decide what sort of communities they want, and many Californians take advantage of these opportunities by engaging in local politics.

NOTES

1. Zoltan L. Hajnal, Paul G. Lewis, and Hugh Louch, "Municipal Elections in California: Turnout, Timing, and Competition," Public Policy Institute of California, March 2002, www.ppic.org.

2. Jessica Trounstine and Zoltan Hajnal, "Low Voter Turnout Does Matter: Spending Priorities in Local Politics" (paper presented at the annual meeting of the Midwest Political Science Association, Chicago, April 2004).

3. Hajnal, Lewis, and Louch, *op. cit.*

4. Jessica Levinson, "Local Public Financing Charts" (Los Angeles: Center for Governmental Studies, May 2009), www.cgs.org (accessed July 13, 2010).

5. See Center for Governmental Studies, *Money and Power in the City of Angels,* July 2010, www.cgs.org (accessed July 16, 2010).

6. Belinda I. Reyes, "Demographic Change and the Politics of Education in California," in *Racial and Ethnic Politics in California,* ed. Sandra Bass and Bruce M. Cain (Berkeley: Berkeley Public Policy Press, Institute of Governmental Studies, University of California, 2008), pp. 236, 241.

7. EdSource, www.edsource.org (accessed July 14, 2010).

8. California Department of Education, www.cde.ca.gov (accessed July 14, 2010). For California's rank among the states on education spending, see Public Policy Institute of California, *California 2025,* www.ppic.org (accessed July 14, 2010), or California Budget Project, "School Finance Facts," June 2010, www.cbp.org (accessed July 14, 2010).

9. For more on regional fragmentation and special districts, see Brian, P. Janiskee, "The Problem of Local Government in California," in *California Republic*, ed. Brian P. Janiskee and Ken Masugi (Lanham, Md.: Rowman and Littlefield, 2004).

10. California Elections Data Archive, Institute for Social Research, California State University, Sacramento, www.csus.edu/isr (accessed July 15, 2010).

11. *Ibid.*

12. For further discussion of these effects of Proposition 13, see John Decker, *California in the Balance* (Berkeley, Calif.: Berkeley Public Policy Press, 2009), pp. xi, 116, 137–138.

13. "Maywood to Lay Off All City Employees, Dismantle Police Department," June 22, 2010, www.latimesblogs.latimes.com/lanow/2010/06.

14. U.S. Census, www.census.gov/govs/apes (accessed July 16, 2010).

LEARN MORE ON THE WEB

ABZY News Links (listing state and local media and online news sources): www.abyznewslinks.com/uniteca.htm

California Elections Data Archive (CEDA) (information on local elections): www.csus.edu/isr/reports/california_elections/index.html

California State Association of Counties: www.csac.counties.org

California State Controller (data on cities, counties, schools, and special districts): www.sco.ca.gov

Councils of Government (COGs):
  Association of Bay Area Governments (ABAG): www.abag.org

  Southern California Association of Governments (SCAG): www.scag.ca.gov

On instant runoff voting (IRV): www.instantrunoff.com

League of California Cities: www.cacities.org

Public Policy Institute of California (studies on local government): www.ppic.org

LEARN MORE AT THE LIBRARY

Terry Christensen and Tom Hogen-Esch. *Local Politics: A Practical Guide to Governing at the Grassroots*. Armonk, N.Y.: M. E. Sharpe, 2006.

Jack Citrin and Isaac William Martin, eds. *After the Tax Revolt: California's Proposition 13 Turns 30*. Berkeley, Calif.: Institute of Government Studies, 2009.

Paul G. Lewis. *Deep Roots: Local Government Structure in California*. San Francisco: Public Policy Institute of California, 1998.

Paul Lewis and Max Neiman. *Cities under Pressure: Local Growth Controls and Residential Development Policy*. Public Policy Institute of California, www.ppic.org, 2002.

10

State-Federal Relations: Conflict, Cooperation, and Chaos

CHAPTER CONTENTS

California's uniqueness stems in part from its position as the nation's most populated state; it also emanates from the state's vast resources, size, diversity, and engagement in thorny issues. We see problems and their outcomes on a scale here that is unequaled elsewhere. And so it is with the state's relationship with the federal government, which can be described as wary, uneven, and often fraught with controversy.

Sometimes state and national leaders differ about how California should be managed. Public education reform is one such controversial policy area, with the federal government and state legislature at odds over the definition of *reform*. On other issues, such as water policy, however, officials from the two governments have worked well together. There are also instances where California has moved forward with its own response to national issues, with the federal government eventually moving into line; nowhere is this more obvious than with environmental protection. Deciding the best responses to problems that affect both the nation and state can be a challenge because, like its forty-nine counterparts, California is both a self-governing entity and a member of the larger national government.

Matters become even more complicated when attempts are made to determine financial responsibility for costly issues such as massive transportation projects, immigration control, or homeland security, to name a few. Because the state is so large and complex, federal assistance almost always seems inadequate. When federal aid or programs are cut, California seems to suffer disproportionately compared with other states.

Nevertheless, when the state confronts a complex issue, its internal battle is often the harbinger of similar concerns likely to affect the rest of the nation. The women's right-to-choose movement, gun control, political reform, the tax revolt, medical marijuana, stem cell research, and same-sex marriage all had early beginnings—and in some cases, origins—in California.

In this chapter we review California's impact on national policymaking and policy actors. We also explore some of the critical policy areas that test California's relationship with the federal government: immigration, greenhouse gas emissions, and the distribution of federal resources to the state of California. Each topic touches on the delicate balance between state autonomy and national objectives—perspectives in federalism that are not always viewed the same ways by state and federal government leaders. These issues are important not only because of their present urgency but also because of their effects on California's Clout with the President, Obama visited California on eleven occasions.

CALIFORNIA'S CLOUT WITH THE PRESIDENT

Despite its size and huge bloc of Electoral College votes, California hasn't figured prominently in presidential elections in recent years, largely because the state has been predictably secure for Democratic candidates in every election since 1992. As a consequence, we don't see as much of the candidates in California as voters do in other states. Republican presidential candidates do not invest significant resources on California because they don't see much return, and Democrats stay away because of their need to pursue electoral votes in more competitive states. But California is important to both national political parties in one major respect—namely, as the top state for campaign contributions. That alone keeps candidates coming, albeit infrequently, to places such as Orange County, Silicon Valley, and Hollywood.

California has had an uneven relationship with the nation's presidents. Democrat Bill Clinton, who benefitted from California's then fifty-four electoral votes in 1992 and 1996, funneled discretionary federal funds to California, particularly in the areas of high-tech research and defense industry projects. Clinton was also pro-choice, pro–gun control, and environmentally sensitive—themes that resonate with most Californians. None of this was lost on the California electorate, which supported Democratic candidates Al Gore in 2000 and John Kerry in 2004 over the winner, Republican George W. Bush.

Republican president George W. Bush approached California with a different point of view than Clinton, largely due to his general hands-off attitude on domestic policy issues. For example, the Bush administration rejected California's claim of illegal electricity price hikes in 2001, although the courts eventually found otherwise. Other areas of disinterest on the president's part included agriculture, border patrol assistance, and terrorism funding. Even the election of fellow Republican Arnold Schwarzenegger in 2003 failed to bond the two Republican leaders except in the most cosmetic fashion. Given the clash of cultural and political values between most Californians and the conservative Republican president, it's easy to see why the distance between the state and the president was more than a matter of miles. Bush visited California fewer than two dozen times during his presidency, compared with seventy visits by Clinton in his eight years in office.

The administration of Democrat Barack Obama falls somewhere between Clinton's "love fest" for and Bush's seeming indifference to California. On the one hand, Obama has been sensitive to the role of technology in California and called for extension of the soon-to-expire $74 billion research and development tax credit immediately upon assuming office. The Obama administration has also embraced California's strict rules on automobile exhaust emissions, a move completely opposite to the approach of George W. Bush. On the other hand, the Obama administration has been willing to compensate California for only a fraction of the hundreds of millions of dollars spent on the incarceration of illegal immigrants awaiting transport to their home countries. And California was unsuccessful in wresting any of the $4.35 billion in Obama's "Race to the Top" education improvement funds at a time when public education has been gasping for support. During the first two years of his administration, Obama visited California on eleven occasions.

CALIFORNIA'S CLOUT WITH CONGRESS

As the nation's most populated state, California has fifty-three members in the House of Representatives, dwarfing the delegations of every other state. Texas and New York are second and third, with thirty-two and twenty-nine members, respectively. The majority party in each house of Congress chooses committee chairs who, in turn, control the flow of national legislation. Republicans possessed a majority of seats between 1995 and 2007, resulting in the accumulation of considerable power. By 2005 Californians held a record six chairmanships of the twenty-one standing committees. Then the political winds shifted.

In 2006 growing discontent with the war in Iraq, an uneven national economy, and political corruption in Congress led the nation's voters to elect a

Democratic majority to the House of Representatives. San Francisco's Nancy Pelosi, elected in 2002 to the post of minority leader of the House, was chosen to be Speaker. With that election, she assumed the highest national leadership ever held in the United States by a woman. As a result of the election outcome, several prominent California Democrats assumed key committee chairmanships by virtue of their years of seniority in the House.

Political party fortunes took a turn in 2010 when the Republicans captured control of the House and increased their minority in the Senate. As of 2011, Republicans were poised to gain at least three chairmanships: Oversight and Governmental Reform (Darrell Issa); Armed Services (Howard "Buck" McKeon; and Appropriations (Jerry Lewis). In addition, Kevin McCarthy was elected majority whip, the third highest party post after speaker and majority leader.

The political winds also have shifted in the U.S. Senate, but not as much as in the House. Although the upper house is a bit less partisan than the lower house, the majority party still controls all committee chairmanships, and therefore the flow of legislation. In 2006 the off-year revolution produced a slim 51-to-49 Democratic majority, thanks to the cooperation of two independents who promised their loyalty to the Democratic side of the aisle. Suddenly, Senators Dianne Feinstein and Barbara Boxer, both first elected in 1992, emerged as key players on issues dealing with the environment, foreign relations, and the judiciary. By 2009 the Democratic majority hit 60, a number larger enough to cut off filibusters. Within a year, however, the supermajority was lost with the death of Massachusetts senator Ted Kennedy.

Democrats in California enjoy a comfortable margin of 34–19 over Republicans in the House of Representatives. In other respects California's congressional makeup is as diverse as the rest of the state. As of 2011, the delegation includes seven Latinos, four African Americans, and three Asians; nineteen women are members of the delegation. Both of California's U.S. senators are women as well.

The Republican ascendancy to power in the House opens the way for a new chapter in governance at the national level. With divided government, Republicans and Democrats find themselves with tough choices: either cooperate on major issues in the name of consensus or hold out with gridlock as the outcome. Consideration of each strategy is important, given the upcoming national election in 2012.

Divisiveness

One other fact must be added to the discussion of Californians in Washington: historically, the state's **congressional delegation** has been notoriously fractured in its responses to key public policy issues affecting California. Much of the conflict stems from the makeup of the districts. North/south, urban/suburban/rural, and coastal/valley/mountain divisions separate the state geographically. Other differences exist, too, in terms of wealth, ethnicity, and basic liberal/conservative distinctions. To be sure, no congressional district is completely homogeneous, yet most members of Congress tend to protect their districts' interests more than those of the state as a whole. Thus, on issues ranging from desert protection to immigration, California's representatives have often canceled each other's votes, leaving states such as Texas far more powerful because of their relatively unified stances. Even on foreign trade, members from California often have worked at cross-purposes, depending on the industries, interest groups, and demographic characteristics of their districts.

Only on the question of offshore oil drilling have most members of the state's delegation voted the same way. In 2008, with gasoline prices hitting record levels, President Bush called for an end to the twenty-seven–year federal moratorium on offshore drilling. Almost the entire California delegation opposed the proposal, and the damaging Gulf of Mexico offshore oil blowout in 2010 silenced any further discussion.

Controversy over the Proposed Auburn Dam—Case in Point

The struggle over the proposed Auburn Dam in Northern California is a current case in point. California hungers for more water, but the real debate has been over the best ways to get it and at what cost. The massive $9.6 billion proposal has been considered in Congress since 1960. Federal agencies have spent $325 million just on feasibility studies. Yet California lawmakers in Washington have remained paralyzed over the issue, due in no small part to the conflicting objectives of environmentalists and farmers. The various sides struck a compromise in 2003 by upgrading another dam downstream. But concerns over California's weakened levee system led House Republican Dan Lungren to pursue the idea yet again in 2007 after the release of a 152-page report by the U.S. Department of the Interior.[1] Meanwhile, Democrats Pete Stark and George Miller have used their clout with the majority to thwart consideration of the project as an environmentally unsound proposal. The issue of whether the project is a boondoggle or a vital flood-control program is not as significant as the fact that it has polarized the California congressional delegation. As a result, while Californians have fussed among themselves over this vexing question, representatives from other states have worked in bipartisan ways to garner federal dollars for their projects.

TERRORISM

September 11, 2001, represented a turning point in American history. Never before had terrorists penetrated onto American soil in such a punishing way. As expected, the federal government took the lead in responding to this unprecedented event. With passage of the USA Patriot Act on October 26, 2001, the national government assumed expanded powers to search out terrorism and terrorist-related activities in the areas of hazardous substances, money laundering, illegal immigration, cyber crime, fraud, and other areas. Acting under these new powers, the U.S. attorney general asked states and local governments to help in detaining and questioning suspicious persons; the new Transportation Security Administration assumed security responsibilities at the nation's airports; and the U.S. Border Patrol increased its vigilance against illegal entry. Statewide, between 2002 and 2010, the Governor's Office of Homeland Security distributed more than $1.3 billion in federal funds for state and local equipment and training.

Although the federal government has picked up much of the tab, the states have been burdened with significant costs, too, and are likely to see those costs continue well into the future. From transportation systems and port security to water pipelines and canals to electricity lines, California's infrastructure now requires additional protection against terrorists. As a result, the state has absorbed major security obligations without federal funding. For example, the Real ID Act, a federal law requiring states to issue universal driver's licenses, has an estimated price tag in California of $500 million to $750 million between 2008 and 2013, yet only a small fraction of the cost was funded by the federal government.[2] Such costs are difficult for governments to swallow in good economic times, and with California plagued by out-of-balance budgets for most of the time between 2002 and 2011, they have made a major dent in available resources.

The state's surge in congressional chairmanships has somewhat helped California's position with the federal government on homeland security allocations. Following the September 11 terrorist attacks on the United States, the federal government made antiterrorism funds available to all fifty states. With $5.03 per capita for the 2004–2005 fiscal year, California ranked last despite its coastal location, huge seaports, nuclear power plants, massive power line grids, and other targets that are ripe for terrorist attacks. Meanwhile, Wyoming ranked first with $37.94 per capita, followed by Vermont ($31.56 per capita), North Dakota ($30.81 per capita), and Alaska ($30.42 per capita). Hard work by Senator Feinstein and California House Republican leaders produced a new method of allocation at the Department of Homeland Security. Thus, for the 2006–2007 fiscal year, California climbed to twenty-first place, with $6.81 per capita. Meanwhile, Vermont took over first place, with $20.03 per capita; Wyoming dropped to second, with $18.06.[3] Since then, the Obama administration has promised to review the funding formula in recognition of high-risk states such as California, but serious economic issues have prevented the development of new legislation.

IMMIGRATION

California has long been a magnet for those in search of opportunity. And they have come—first the Spanish; then Yankee, Irish, and Chinese immigrants during the nineteenth century; followed by Japanese, Eastern European, African American, and Vietnamese immigrants beginning in the 1970s, Asian Indians in

T A B L E 10.1   California's Immigrants: Leading Countries of Origin, 2006

Country	Number
Mexico	4,396,000
Philippines	750,000
China	659,000
Vietnam	446,000
El Salvador	396,000
Korea	323,000
India	303,000
Guatemala	241,000
Iran	182,000
Taiwan	163,000
Canada	134,000
United Kingdom	126,000

SOURCE: U.S. Decennial Census, 2005.

the 1990s, and more Latinos throughout the last half century (see Table 10.1). But over the past two decades, several independent events have converged to influence the moods of the state's residents and would-be residents. Lack of opportunity in other nations has led millions to choose California as an alternative; meanwhile, an overburdened and underfunded infrastructure has led many of those already here to oppose further immigration. Much of the antipathy has been directed at Latinos—particularly those from Mexico—but anger has also been aimed at Asians.

The numbers are substantial. Whereas 15.1 percent of California's population were foreign born in 1980, 27 percent fell within that category in 2010, with projections showing that percentage remaining in place through 2030.[4] During the same period, the percentage of foreign-born residents of the United States as a whole edged up from 6.2 to 12.1 percent (see Figure 10.1). Between 1990 and 2005 California's population grew by between 500,000 and 600,000 annually, and more than 40 percent of that number came from foreign immigration. In 2010 the Pew Hispanic Center estimated that there were between 11.4 million and 12.4 million illegal immigrants nationwide, with between 2.5 million and 2.85 million of them in California.[5] Between 1990 and 2008 the percentage of illegal immigrants living in California dropped from 42 percent to 22 percent, indicating greater movement to other states.[6]

With these dramatic events reshaping California, experts have argued about whether the immigrants help or harm the state's economy. For example, one recent study finds that only about one-third of recent immigrants have health

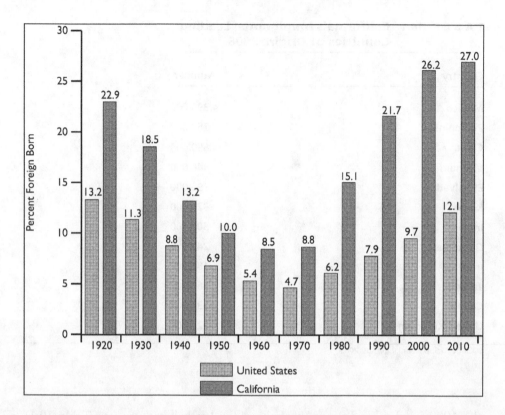

FIGURE 10.1 Population of Foreign-Born Residents, California and United States Comparison

insurance, suggesting a financial burden for public health institutions and services.[7] At the same time, other studies show that immigrants—legal and illegal combined—are very similar in economic makeup to the rest of America.[8] Moreover, in some industries, such as California farming, illegal immigrants are critical to harvests, making up as much as 90 percent of the workforce. To the extent that these workers are prevented from laboring in the fields, California's $36 billion agriculture industry could suffer irreparable damage.[9] All these findings suggest a growing ambivalence toward the illegal immigration issue in California.

None of this has stopped the federal government from moving on immigration, although observers disagree about the appropriate level of federal involvement. In 2008 the Bush administration increased surveillance of U.S. companies with illegal immigrant employees, leading to fines for employers, imprisonment for undocumented workers, and workforce shortages in some industries.[10] At the same time, between a more vigilant border protection system and a declining U.S. economy, the number of attempted border crossings by illegal immigrants declined.[11]

The largest issue related to immigration is determining which level of government should assume responsibility for its costs. While the federal government has long established the criteria for immigration and the conditions for enforcement, it leaves the states responsible for meeting the needs of immigrants. Nowhere does this contradiction ring louder than in California. Among unauthorized immigrants alone, recent estimates cite health-care costs of $1 billion, education costs for 400,000 of their children at $1 billion, and incarceration costs for 18,000 illegal immigrants at $500 million.[12] Few of these costs have been picked up by the federal government, yet their day-to-day impact is a reality.

Controversy continues over how much responsibility California should assume for stemming the tide of illegal immigration. In 2006 President Bush asked Governor Schwarzenegger to send 2,500 members of the National Guard to Arizona and New Mexico to help U.S. Border Patrol agents. The governor dispatched only 1,000 troops, arguing that the rest were needed at home to assist in cases of wildfires, earthquakes, or other unanticipated calamities.[13] Clearly, the role of each government in managing the immigration question remains a tough issue to sort out.

CLIMATE CHANGE

California and the federal government have had a rocky relationship with respect to climate change. At times, the state has fought national objectives; at others, California has taken the lead. No example of state resistance is more obvious than the issue of air quality. According to the U.S. **Environmental Protection Agency (EPA)**, the ten smoggiest counties in the nation are found in California. Metropolitan Los Angeles, an area that extends east to Riverside and south to Long Beach, tops the list as the smoggiest area in the nation. Actually, the number of "unhealthful" days in the L.A. basin has declined from an average of 189.6 during the 1996–1998 period to 141.8 during the period of 2006–2008, according to the American Lung Association, although progress has stopped since 2004.[14] Statewide, the costs have been great. One recent study finds that annual losses in California from unhealthy air amount to $28 billion in the form of premature deaths, illness, and lost productivity in the workplace.[15]

Congress and the EPA have been unhappy with the inability of the state to move forward on clean air. But given the state's dependence on manufacturing, particularly in the vast Los Angeles basin, it has been difficult to meet national standards without choking off the local economy. In 1992 state regulators in Southern California established the Regional Clean Air Incentives Market Program (RECLAIM), a program in which manufacturers buy and sell emissions permits as a means of encouraging emissions reduction. The program has led to substantial reductions in environmental decay,[16] although the region remains far from healthy.

The state has enjoyed more success in the area of auto emissions, although at times the road has been bumpy for other reasons. California has a history of leading the nation in reducing auto emissions, which account for 28 percent of the state's greenhouse gases. Since the passage of the original Clean Air Act of 1970, state environmental regulators have asked for and received forty-four waivers from the EPA to establish standards beyond federal requirements. That's what happened until 2007, when the Bush administration–guided EPA ruled that there was no evidence suggesting that auto emissions contained greenhouse gases,[17] to the amazement of most scientists in the United States and worldwide. Since the agency gave no scientific explanation for its ruling, California and sixteen other states sued the EPA for not carrying out its mandate. The United States Supreme Court agreed, and thus began another chapter in the struggle for control over emissions standards.

The political environment regarding auto emissions changed dramatically with the election of Barack Obama to the presidency in 2008. Early in 2009 he asked his new EPA administrator to review previous decisions on California's waiver petitions. In June 2009 the EPA approved California's proposal and announced a new national policy on higher gasoline mileage and lower emissions by 2017, based on California's standards. On this occasion, at least, California set the trend for the rest of the nation.

WATER

Not all of California's jurisdictional disputes have occurred with the federal government. In several areas, the state has tangled with other states. The storage of nuclear waste and agriculture rules are two such examples of interstate fights, but no argument has as much significance as California's struggle for freshwater. Three-quarters of California's water comes from north of Sacramento. Three-quarters of the water is consumed south of the capital. For this transfer to work, water must move, and it does so thanks to two giant systems. The federal Central Valley Project, which dates from 1937, supplies the farmers of the southern Central Valley. The State Water Project, begun in 1960, largely supplies southern urban areas. Both systems intercept freshwater near the Sacramento–San Joaquin Delta before it can flow out to the ocean through San Francisco's Golden Gate. Given the state's huge population and pivotal role in agriculture, water is a resource that California can ill afford to do without, and that fact has led to ugly entanglements.

The linchpin of the water dispute between California and other states is the Colorado River, the freshwater source that begins in Colorado and winds through six other states. Under a 1922 multistate agreement, California is entitled to 4.4 million acre-feet, or 59 percent, of the lower basin river annually. Yet according to some critics, California exceeded its share by as much as 800,000 acre-feet per year, enough to provide for the annual water needs of 1.6 million households in rapidly growing nearby states such as Arizona and Nevada.[18]

Fearing an all-out water war that would spill into Congress, officials from seven states held talks for eighteen months to resolve the problem. In 2000 they agreed to a formula that would allow California to gradually reduce its consumption of the excess over a fifteen-year period. During the transition, officials from Arizona offered to "bank" surplus water for California, should the state require it. But with Arizona, Nevada, and other western states growing faster than any other parts of the nation, it remains to be seen how long the fragile agreement will remain in play. At least for the time being, the seven western states have solved a troublesome issue without federal participation.

Meanwhile, the federal government's Department of the Interior and the state of California worked to resolve the ongoing three-way battle among agribusiness (which uses 80 percent of the state's water consumption), environmentalists seeking to preserve rivers and deltas, and urban areas in need of water to grow. Under the auspices of CalFed, a joint federal and state water agency, the two governments developed a plan in 2000 to expand existing federal reservoirs in California, improve drinking water quality, and develop a creative water recycling program. Most of the $8.5 billion price tag will be borne by the federal government, with Californians providing $825 million from the passage of Proposition 50 in 2002. In 2004 Congress reauthorized CalFed, with a commitment of $10 billion over thirty years to improve the quality of water flowing into the Sacramento Delta and San Francisco Bay.

Uncertainties remain, however. In 2002 the U.S. Department of the Interior modified a plan previously favored by environmentalists. The new plan sent more water from the Central Valley Project to farmers, rather than using it for ecosystem restoration. Still, water can only be distributed to customers if it is available, and recent droughts in California and the West have left the region thirsty. The issue has become so important that in 2007, responding to a record-low snowpack in the Sierra Nevada Mountains and concern for the welfare of endangered species, a federal court judge reduced deliveries of Northern California water to Southern California by 25 percent. The impact of the order put Southern California governments on notice: until water supplies could be assured, major construction projects in that portion of the state would be put on hold.[19] So the battle over water continues, not only between California and the federal government but also between farmers, environmentalists, and developers.

SHARED RESOURCES

The word **federalism** refers to the multifaceted political relationship that binds the state and national governments. One aspect of that relationship centers on financial assistance that wends its way from federal coffers to state and local treasuries, and that amounted to about $653 billion in fiscal year 2010. The preponderance of this assistance comes in the form of **grants-in-aid**, amounting to about 20 percent of all state and local government revenues. This assistance is the result of more than six hundred federal programs designed to assist states in areas ranging from agricultural development to high-tech research. For decades, California received more than its fair share of grants-in-aid from the federal government. With defense- and space-related research serving as a huge economic magnet, the Golden State obtained more money from the federal government than it sent in.

That has changed. In 1983 California had 10 percent of the national population but received 22 percent of the national government's expenditures. Then came the slide: with a pared defense budget, cutbacks in infrastructure work, and the push for a balanced budget, federal contributions have shrunk considerably over the past two decades. As of 2007 California had 12.1 percent of the nation's population but received 11.8 percent of the nation's federal funds. The state now ranks thirty-seventh in the distribution of federal spending on a per capita basis—down sharply from twentieth in 1990.[20]

There is another way to appreciate the changing relationship between the federal government and California. Because of the state's massive growth and receipt of federal assistance in highway and water projects and environmental protection, California had a long history of getting more dollars from the federal government than it contributed. Beginning in 1986, however, California became a "donor" state. Ever since, California has contributed more money to the national treasury than it has received, and the disparity is increasing every year. In 1992, for every dollar California sent to Washington, D.C., the state received 93 cents in federal goods and services. In 2005, for every dollar California sent to Washington, only 78 cents came back in goods and services, leaving the state in forty-third place in per capita federal spending (see Table 10.2). No matter how you slice it, California is getting less of the federal "pie" today than in the past.

But there is more to the story than just numbers; it's the kind of numbers that make a huge difference. Data compiled in 2006 found that if the cost of living is added to the mix, more than 16 percent of all Californians fall under the poverty line, compared with about 12 percent nationwide.[21] And when we

T A B L E 10.2 Federal Expenditures per Dollar of Taxes, Fiscal Years 1992 and 2005—California and Selected States

	Expenditures per Dollar of Taxes		Ranking	
	FY1992	FY2005	FY1992	FY2005
New Mexico	$2.08	$2.03	11	1
Maryland	$1.27	$1.30	15	18
Kansas	$1.05	$1.12	27	22
Texas	$.93	$.94	37	35
Massachusetts	$1.01	$.82	31	40
California	$.93	$.78	38	43
New Jersey	$.66	$.61	50	50

SOURCE: Tax Foundation.

consider that the state's immigrant population is more than twice the national average on a per capita basis, it becomes clear that the state's needs fare particularly poorly when it comes to federal funding.

The data presented here fly in the face of the political posturing that has emerged from both Congress and the presidency in recent years. Instead, they show a California with unlimited potential, and a California that has been much better for some than others. They reveal a state that in recent years has given much more to the federal government in taxes than it has received in programs and services. They also reflect the fragmentation that has haunted the state's congressional delegation on virtually every issue except offshore oil drilling. As a result, California's "Golden State" nickname has a different meaning in Washington than in California—namely, sizable economic resources that have landed disproportionately in the federal treasury.

CALIFORNIA TODAY: GOLDEN STATE OR FOOL'S GOLD?

Is today's California still the state with unlimited potential or the state with too many burdens to survive? When it comes to relations with the federal government, perhaps the answer is a little of both. California is king when it comes to campaign contributions for national candidates, research and development, the center of agriculture, and auto emissions standards. At the same time, California is a pauper in matters of dealing with a perpetual state budget deficit, a dilapidated infrastructure, and a frayed social safety net. Once upon a time, the state would have looked to the federal government for rescue, and the federal government would have been happy to help. That relationship has been replaced by one in which the state and federal government are often at odds, and occasionally in sync.

Some of the shift has been because of the ebb and flow of national politics. By most accounts, California is a "blue" (Democratic) state when it comes to national elections. Thus, during the Clinton years, the state benefitted from extra federal attention on research and development tax credits, H1-B visas, and even some defense contracts. During the Bush years, California didn't fare so well, as attested by the administration's disregard for the state's immigration issues, antiterrorism concerns, and exorbitant electricity bills.

We're still sifting the relationship with Democratic president Barack Obama, although there are some early hints of an uptick in the relationship. The Obama administration has backed off on prosecuting for marijuana possession, supported continuation of the research and development tax credit, and sent hundreds of millions of federal dollars to help California homeowners deal with foreclosure issues. At the same time, California has not fared well in capturing a chunk of federal dollars in the Race to the Top education reform program. Moreover, the state did not do so well in capturing a large share of the $787 billion in economic stimulus funds provided in the American Recovery and Reinvestment Act passed in 2009. Whereas the state had the fourth highest unemployment rate, it ranked eighteenth in per capita funding.

If nothing else, California operates more independently of the federal government today than in the times of heavy government defense spending. To this extent the state has been weaned of federal dependence. The process may not have been enjoyable, but the state has become more self-reliant as a result. To that end, California's growing autonomy may be the hallmark of the state's direction in the coming years. Whatever the future, it will be an interesting experiment.

NOTES

1. U.S. Department of Interior, "Reclamation: Managing Water in the West, Auburn-Folsom South Unit Special Report," December 2006.

2. For example, for fiscal 2009 the entire federal commitment to all fifty states plus the District of Columbia was $48,575,000, of which California received a small percentage. See Department of Homeland Security, "Driver's License Security Program," www.dhs.gov/files/programs/gc_1214423542432.shtm.

3. Dowell Myers, John Pitkin, and Julie Park, *California Demographic Features* (Los Angeles: School of Policy, Planning, and Development, University of Southern California, February 2005), p. ix.

4. U.S. Census Bureau, *Statistical Abstract of the United States: 2009* (Washington, D.C.: Government Printing Office, 2008), p. 19.

5. "Report: One in 10 Workers in California Is Illegal," *Sacramento Bee*, April 15, 2010, pp. A1, A20.

6. "Illegal Immigrants Become Subject of Coverage Debate," *San Francisco Chronicle*, September 11, 2009, pp. A1, A18.

7. *The Size and Characteristics of the Unauthorized Migrant Population in the U.S.* (Washington, D.C.: Pew Hispanic Center, 2006), p. 9.

8. "Immigrants in the Work Force: Study Belies Image," *New York Times*, April 10, 2010, pp. A1, A3.

9. "Border Policy Is Pinching Farmers," *Los Angeles Times*, September 22, 2005, pp. C1, C2.

10. See "Bush Orders Some Firms to Show Workers' Status," *Wall Street Journal*, June 10, 2008, p. A6; and "Shortage of Skilled Workers Looms in U.S.," *Los Angeles Times*, April 21, 2008, p. A1, A7.

11. "Crossings by Migrants Slow as Job Picture Dims," *Wall Street Journal*, April 9, 2008, pp. A1, A12.

12. "These data are cited in Bernard L. Hyink and David H. Provost, *Politics and Government in California*, 16th ed. (New York: Pearson Longman, 2004), p. 233.

13. "Gov. Refuses Bush Request for Border Troops," *Los Angeles Times*, June 24, 2006, pp. A1, A18.

14. "Smog in L.A. Still Tops in Nation," *Los Angeles Times*, April 28, 2010, pp. AA1, AA6.

15. California Healthline, November 13, 2008, www.californiahealthline.org.

16. See Daniel A. Mazmanian, "Achieving Air Quality: The Los Angeles Experience" (unpublished paper, University of Southern California, March 2006), p. 28.

17. "E.P.A. Says 17 States Can't Set Greenhouse Gas Rules for Cars," *New York Times*, December 20, 2007, pp. A1, A30.

18. "California Water Users Miss Deadline on Pact for Sharing," *New York Times*, January 1, 2003. The six states in addition to California are Arizona, Colorado, Nevada, New Mexico, Utah, and Wyoming.

19. "Enforcing Recent Water Laws May Throttle State's Growth," *Los Angeles Times*, January 14, 2008, pp. B1, B8.

20. U.S. Census Bureau, *op. cit.,* table 467.

21. Deborah Reed, "Poverty In California," *California Counts* 7, no. 4 (May 2006), www.ppic.org.

LEARN MORE ON THE WEB

California and federal taxes:
www.taxfoundation.org

California Institute for Federal Policy Research:
www.calinst.org

Environmental Protection Agency:
www.epa.gov

Immigration:
www.irps.ucsd.edu

Office of Management and Budget:
www.whitehouse.gov/omb

U.S. House of Representatives:
www.house.gov

U.S. Senate:
www.senate.gov

LEARN MORE AT THE LIBRARY

Larry N. Gerston. *American Federalism: A Concise Introduction.* Armonk, N.Y.: M. E. Sharpe, 2007.

Robert F. Nagel. *The Implosion of American Federalism.* New York: Oxford University Press, 2001.

Laurence J. O'Toole. *American Intergovernmental Relations: Foundations, Perspectives, and Issues.* 4th ed. Washington, D.C.: CQ Press, 2007.

G. Ross Stephens and Nelson Wikstrom. *American Intergovernmental Relations: A Fragmented Federal Polity.* New York: Oxford University Press, 2007.

Glossary

at-large elections City council elections in which all candidates are elected by the community as a whole rather than by districts.

attorney general The top law enforcement officer and legal counsel; the second most powerful member of the executive branch.

bank and corporation tax A tax on the profits of lending institutions and businesses; the third most important source of state revenue.

bicameral legislature Organization of the state legislature into two houses: the forty-member senate (elected for four-year terms) and the eighty-member assembly (elected for two-year terms).

Big Five The governor, assembly speaker, assembly minority leader, senate president pro tem, and senate minority leader, who gather together informally to thrash out decisions on the annual budget and other major policy issues.

Board of Equalization The five-member state board that maintains uniform property tax assessments and oversees the collection of sales, gasoline, and liquor taxes; members are elected by district; part of the executive branch.

board of supervisors The five-member governing body of counties; elected by district to four-year terms.

bonds Subject to voter approval, state and local governments can borrow money by issuing bonds, which are repaid (with interest) from the general fund budget or from special taxes or fees.

bureaucracy State or local government workers employed through the civil service system rather than appointed by the governor or other elected officials.

central committees Political party organizations at county and state levels; weakly linked to one another.

charges for services Local government fees for services such as sewage treatment, trash collection, building permits, and the use of recreational facilities; a major source of income for cities and counties since the passage of Proposition 13 in 1978.

charter city or county A local government that drafts its own structures and organization through a document like a local constitution (also known as a "home-rule" charter), subject to voter approval.

charter The equivalent of a constitution for a local government; includes government structures, election systems, powers of officeholders, conditions for employing local government workers, and often much more.

cities Local governments in urban areas, run by city councils and mayors or city managers; principal responsibilities include police and fire protection, land-use planning, street maintenance and construction, sanitation, libraries, and parks.

Citizens Redistricting Commission Enacted by the voters in Proposition 11 (2009), this commission will assume responsibility for determining the boundaries of state legislative districts and Board of Equalization districts.

city council The governing body of a city; members are elected at large or by district to four-year terms.

city manager The top administrative officer in most California cities; appointed by the city council.

civil service system A system for hiring and retaining public employees on the basis of their qualifications or merit; replaced the political machine's patronage, or spoils, system; encompasses 98 percent of state workers.

closed primary An election of party nominees in which only registered party members may participate.

collegiality Deferential behavior among justices as a way of building consensus on issues before the court.

Commission on Judicial Appointments A commission to review and make recommendations on the governor's nominees for appellate and supreme courts; consists of the attorney general, the chief justice of the state supreme court, and the senior presiding judge of the courts of appeal.

Commission on Judicial Performance The state board empowered to investigate charges of judicial misconduct or incompetence.

conference committee A committee of senate and assembly members that meets to reconcile different versions of the same bill.

congressional delegation Members of the House of Representatives and Senate representing a particular state.

consolidation The merger of cities, school districts, or special districts; usually requires voter approval.

Constitution of 1849 California's first constitution, which was copied from constitutions of other states and featured a two-house legislature, a supreme court, and an executive branch including a governor, lieutenant governor, controller, attorney general, and superintendent of public instruction, as well as a bill of rights. Only white males were allowed to vote.

Constitution of 1879 California's second constitution, which retained the basic structures of the Constitution of 1849 but added institutions to regulate railroads and public utilities and to ensure fair tax assessments. Chinese individuals were denied the right to vote, own land, or work for the government.

constitutional amendments May be placed on the ballot by a two-thirds vote of the legislature or through the initiative process; must be approved by a simple majority of the voters.

constitutional convention An occasion for extensive revision or reform of the state constitution. A two-thirds vote of the state legislature is required to put a proposal for a convention on the ballot. If voters approve, delegates are elected by district.

contract lobbyist An individual or company that represents the interests of clients before the legislature and other policymaking entities.

contracting for services Smaller cities contract with counties, special districts, other cities, or private companies to provide services they cannot efficiently provide themselves.

controller An independently elected state executive who oversees taxing and spending.

council–manager system A form of government in which an elected council appoints a professional manager to administer daily operations; used by most California cities.

councils of government (COGs) Regional planning organizations with representation for cities and counties.

counties Local governments and administrative agencies of the state, run by elected boards of supervisors; principal responsibilities include welfare, jails, courts, roads, and elections.

county executive The top administrative officer in most California counties; appointed by the board of supervisors.

courts of appeal Three-justice panels that hear appeals from lower courts.

cross-filing An election system that allowed candidates to win the nomination of more than one political party; eliminated in 1959.

demographic groups Interest groups based on race, ethnicity, gender, or age; usually concerned with overcoming discrimination.

direct democracy Progressive reforms giving citizens the power to make and repeal laws (initiative and referendum) and to remove elected officials from office (recall).

direct mail A campaign technique by which candidates communicate selected messages to selected voters by mail.

director of finance The state officer primarily responsible for preparation of the budget; appointed by the governor.

district attorney The chief prosecuting officer elected in each county; represents the people against the accused in criminal cases.

district elections Elections in which candidates are chosen by only one part of the city, county, or state.

economic groups Interest groups with sizable financial stakes in the political process who seek to influence legislators and other public policymakers.

Environmental Protection Agency (EPA) The federal government body charged with carrying out national environmental policy objectives.

executive order The power of the governor to make rules that have the effect of laws; may be overturned by the legislature.

Fair Political Practices Commission (FPPC) Established by the Political Reform Act of 1974, this independent regulatory commission monitors candidates' campaign finance reports and lobbyists.

federalism The distribution of power, resources, and responsibilities among the national, state, and local governments.

fiscalization of land use Cities and counties, when making land-use decisions, opt for the alternative that produces the most revenue.

general elections Statewide elections held on the first Tuesday after the first Monday of November in even-numbered years. Voter turnout is higher than in primary elections and highest during presidential elections.

general-law city or county A city or county whose organization and structure of government are derived from state law.

general veto The gubernatorial power to reject an entire bill or budget; overruled only by an absolute two-thirds vote of both houses of the state legislature.

ghost voting When legislators cast electronic votes in place of assembly members who are not at their posts; this practice is against the law.

governor California's highest-ranking executive officeholder; elected every four years.

grants-in-aid Payments from the national government to states to assist in fulfilling public policy objectives.

gut-and-amend The process of removing the original provisions from a bill and inserting new, unrelated content.

"hourglass economy" The tendency of the California economy to include many people doing very well at the top, many barely getting by at the bottom, and fewer and fewer in the middle; symptomatic of California's vanishing middle class.

incorporation The process by which residents of an urbanized area form a city.

independent expenditures Campaign spending by interest groups and political action committees on behalf of candidates.

initiative A Progressive device by which people may put laws and constitutional amendments on the ballot after securing the required number of voters' signatures.

instant runoff voting Voters rank candidates in order of preference. If no candidate wins a majority, the candidate with the fewest votes is eliminated, and those votes are assigned to the voters' second choice—and so on until one candidate attains a majority.

insurance commissioner An elected state executive who regulates the insurance industry; created by a 1988 initiative.

interest group An organized group of individuals sharing common political objectives who actively attempt to influence policymakers.

item veto The power of the governor to delete or reduce the budget within a bill without rejecting the entire bill or budget; an absolute two-thirds vote of both houses of the state legislature is required to override.

judicial activism Making policy through court decisions rather than through the legislative or electoral process.

Judicial Council Chaired by the chief justice of the state supreme court and composed of twenty-one judges and attorneys; makes the rules for court procedures, collects data on the courts'

operations and workload, and gives seminars for judges.

legislative analyst An assistant to the legislature who studies the annual budget and proposed programs.

legislative committees Small groups of senators or assembly members who consider and make legislation in specialized areas such as agriculture or education.

legislative counsel Assists the legislature in preparing bills and assessing their impact on existing legislation.

legislative initiatives Propositions placed on the ballot by the legislature rather than by citizen petition.

lieutenant governor The chief executive when the governor is absent from the state or disabled; succeeds the governor in case of death or other departure from office; casts a tiebreaking vote in the senate; is independently elected.

litigation An interest group tactic of challenging a law or policy in the courts to have it overruled, modified, or delayed.

lobbying Interest group efforts to influence political decision makers, often through paid professionals (lobbyists).

local agency formation commission (LAFCO) A county agency set up to oversee the creation and expansion of cities.

logrolling A give-and-take process in which legislators trade support for each other's bills.

mayor The ceremonial leader of a city; usually a position that alternates among council members, but in some large cities the mayor is directly elected and given substantial powers.

nonpartisan elections A Progressive reform that removed party labels from ballots for local and judicial offices.

open primary Voters may cast their ballots for any listed candidate for an office irrespective of the voters' party affiliation; the top two vote winners proceed to a runoff in the general election; instituted by a 2010 ballot measure to take effect in 2012.

personal income tax A graduated tax on individual earnings adopted in 1935; the largest source of state revenues.

plea bargaining An agreement between the prosecution and the accused in which the latter pleads guilty to a reduced charge and lesser penalty.

political action committees (PACs) Mechanisms by which interest groups direct campaign contributions to preferred candidates.

political consultants Expert professionals in political campaigning available for hire; most consultants work exclusively for candidates of one of the major political parties.

Political Reform Act of 1974 An initiative requiring officials to disclose conflicts of interest, campaign contributions, and spending; also requires lobbyists to register with the Fair Political Practices Commission.

preprimary endorsement Political parties' designation of preferred candidates in party primary elections, thus strengthening the role of party organizations in selecting candidates; banned by state law until 1990.

president pro tem The legislative leader of the state senate; chairs the Rules Committee; selected by the majority party.

primary elections Elections to choose nominees for public office; held in June of even-numbered years. Voter turnout is typically low.

Progressives Members of an antimachine reform movement that reshaped the state's political institutions between 1907 and the 1920s.

property tax A tax on land and buildings; until the passage of Proposition 13 in 1978, the primary source of revenues for local governments.

Proposition 1A (2004) A ballot measure designed to prevent the state from taking revenues from local governments in times of fiscal stress.

Proposition 8 (2008) An initiative that amended the state constitution to restrict marriage to opposite-sex couples.

Proposition 11, the Voters FIRST Initiative (2008) An initiative that placed legislative redistricting in the hands of a fourteen-member citizens commission instead of the state legislature.

Proposition 13 (1978) Also known as the Jarvis-Gann initiative; a ballot measure that cut property taxes and significantly reduced revenues for local governments.

Proposition 22, the California Defense of Marriage Act (2000) A ballot initiative that declared marriage an act between a man and a woman.

Proposition 22, the Local Taxpayers, Public Safety and Transportation Act (2010) An initiative that keeps the state government from taking local government funds.

Proposition 34 (2000) A legislative initiative setting contribution limits for individuals and political action committees; commonly circumvented through independent expenditures.

Proposition 58 (2004) A proposition that set broad spending limits on state government and required the state to gradually set aside up to 3 percent of all revenues in a "rainy day" fund.

Proposition 98 (1988) An initiative awarding public education a fixed percentage of the state budget.

Proposition 140 (1990) An initiative limiting assembly members to three 2-year terms and senators and statewide elected officials to two 4-year terms and cutting the legislature's budget.

Proposition 187 (1994) An initiative reducing government benefits for illegal immigrants; parts of Proposition 187 were declared unconstitutional by federal courts in 1995.

Proposition 209 (1996) An initiative that eliminated affirmative action in California.

Proposition 227 (1998) An initiative limiting bilingual education to no more than one year.

public defender A county officer representing defendants who cannot afford an attorney; appointed by the county board of supervisors.

public interest groups Organizations that purport to represent the general good rather than private interests.

reapportionment The adjustment of legislative district boundaries to keep all districts equal in population; done every ten years after the national census; done by a citizens commission beginning in 2011.

recall A Progressive reform allowing voters to remove elected officials by petition and majority vote.

redistricting Another term for *reapportionment*, the adjustment of legislative districts by population every ten years.

referendum A Progressive reform requiring the legislature to place certain measures before the voters, who may also repeal legislation by petitioning for a referendum.

register to vote Citizens who are over eighteen years of age and who are not incarcerated or in a mental institution are eligible to sign up to vote by completion of a registration form. Nearly 30 percent of those eligible to register in California do not do so and thus cannot participate in elections.

Reynolds v. Sims A 1964 United States Supreme Court decision that ordered redistricting of the upper houses of all state legislatures by population instead of land area.

Rules Committee See *Senate Rules Committee*.

runoff election When no candidate receives more than 50 percent of the vote in a nonpartisan primary for trial court judge or local office, the top two candidates face each other in a runoff.

sales tax A statewide tax on most goods and products; adopted in 1933; local governments receive a portion of this tax.

school districts Local governments created by states to provide elementary and secondary education; governed by elected school boards.

secretary of state An elected state executive who keeps election records and supervises elections.

Senate Rules Committee A five-member committee consisting of the senate president pro tem and two other members from each party in the senate; assigns chairs and committee appointments; functions as the gatekeeper of most senate legislation.

Silicon Valley The top area for high-tech industries; located between San Jose and San Francisco.

single-issue groups Organized groups with narrow policy objectives; not oriented toward compromise.

Southern Pacific Railroad A railroad company founded in 1861; developed a political machine that dominated California state politics through the turn of the century.

speaker of the assembly The legislative leader of the assembly; selected by the majority party; controls committee appointments and the legislative process.

special districts Local government agencies providing a single service, such as fire protection or sewage disposal.

special session A legislative session called by the governor; limited to discussion of topics specified by the governor.

state auditor An assistant to the legislature who analyzes ongoing programs.

superintendent of public instruction The elected state executive in charge of public education.

superior courts Lower courts in which criminal and civil cases are first tried.

supreme court California's highest judicial body; hears appeals from lower courts.

term limits Limits on the number of terms that officeholders may serve; elected executive branch officers and state senators are limited to two 4-year terms, and assembly members are limited to three 2-year terms. Some local elected officials are limited to two or three 4-year terms.

termed out An elected official must leave office when he or she has completed all the terms of office allowed under California's term limits law.

third parties Minor political parties that capture a small percentages of the vote in the general election but are viewed as important protest vehicles.

"three strikes" A 1994 law and initiative requiring sentences of twenty-five years to life for anyone convicted of three felonies.

treasurer The elected state executive responsible for managing state funds between collection and spending.

user taxes Taxes on select commodities or services "used" by those who benefit directly from them; examples include gasoline taxes and cigarette taxes.

veto See *general veto* and *item veto*.

vote by mail Voters who prefer not to vote at their polling places or who are unable to vote on Election Day may apply to their county registrar of voters for an absentee ballot and vote by mail; nearly half of those who vote in California elections vote by mail.

voter turnout The proportion of eligible and/or registered voters who actually participate in an election. When turnout is high, the electorate is usually more diverse and liberal; when it is low, the electorate is usually older, more affluent, and more conservative.

Workingmen's Party Denis Kearney's antirailroad, anti-Chinese organization; instrumental in rewriting California's constitution in 1879.

Index

Americans did not invent editorial cartooning. Drawings of political satire—what we might call political cartoons—existed in sixteenth-century Europe. Today this art form flourishes throughout the world. We can see the influence of globalization in editorial cartooning by the tendency for artists in other countries to focus on people and events in the United States. These four examples show cartoons in widely different countries passing judgment on contemporary American politics.

★ The problem of financial reform in the United States, discussed in Chapter 18, "Economic Policy," is known across the world. This cartoon was in the *Khaleej Times* of Dubai, a small nation in the Persian Gulf.

(PARESH / *The Khaleej Times* - Dubai, U.A.E. / CartoonArts International)

★ When terrorists hijacked airlines to attack the United States on September 11, 2001, the United States created the Transportation Security Administration (discussed in Chapter 13, "The Bureaucracy") and increased airport security. Travel around the world was affected. This cartoonist in the London *Independent* portrays the extreme search of airline passengers.

(CHRANK / *The Independent* - London, England / CartoonArts International)